MAYNARD KEYNES

MAYNARD KEYNES

An economist's biography

D. E. Moggridge

London and New York

First published 1992
by Routledge
11 New Fetter Lane, London EC4P 4EE
Simultaneously published in the USA and Canada
by Routledge
a division of Routledge, Chapman and Hall, Inc.
29 West 35th Street, New York, NY 10001

© 1992 D. E. Moggridge

Typeset in Garamond by
Falcon Typographic Art Ltd, Edinburgh
Printed and bound in Great Britain by
Biddles Ltd, Guildford and King's Lynn

British Library Catloguing in Publication Data

Moggridge, D. E. (Donald Edward), 1943–
Maynard Keynes: an economist's biography
I. Title
330.156

Library of Congress Cataloging in Publication Data

Moggridge, D. E. (Donald Edward), 1943–
Maynard Keynes: an economist's biography / by D. E. Moggridge.
p. cm.
Includes bibliographical references and index.
1. Keynes, John Maynard, 1883–1946. 2. Economists – Great Britain –
Biography. 3. Educators – Great Britain – Biography. 4. Bloomsbury
group. I. Title.
HB103.K47M563   1992
330.15′6 — dc20 [B] 91–25882 CIP

ISBN 0–415–05141–X

To
W.R.M., R.F.K.,
E.A.G.R. and S.K.H.

He must undertake that he will not only always pronounce that name rightly himself, but will never allow the slightest mispronunciation on the part of others. Tell him firmly that it rhymes with 'brains' and that there is no harm in that.

(KCKP, JMK to D. von Eisner
on the naming of his son Keynes Don, 26 March 1942)

CONTENTS

CONTENTS

PLATES

PREFACE

Almost any biographer, if he respects fact, can give us more than another fact to add to our collection. He can give us the creative fact; the fertile fact; the fact that suggests and engenders.

(Virginia Woolf, 'The Art of Biography')

I first encountered Keynes in the fall of 1961 when my College ran supplementary tutorials for students in introductory economics. Ian Drummond, who took the class, decided that we would work our way through Keynes's *General Theory* and Alvin Hansen's *A Guide to Keynes* (1953). Both were heavy going for someone with no previous exposure to economics. But by the end of that year I had decided to read economics. I did not read all that much Keynes for undergraduate examinations, but I was sufficiently interested to persuade my mother to give me Roy Harrod's *The Life of John Maynard Keynes* (1951) as a Christmas present in 1963 and to prepare papers on Keynes for undergraduate discussion societies in my final year. But I did not intend to pursue my interest in Keynes at an academic level: I was much more interested in becoming an economic historian.

In the fall of my final undergraduate year, I made the usual applications to graduate schools in the United States. But then, indirectly, Keynes again entered my life – and changed it. After the war, King's College, Cambridge, had decided to use some of the wealth which Keynes as Bursar had created to establish two overseas studentships, one for Canada and one for Australasia. 1965 was the year for the Canadian studentship, which was then in the gift of Derwyn Owen, the Provost of my College at the University of Toronto, Trinity. In December 1964 I was called to the Provost's Office and asked if I would like the studentship. After consulting my father, I accepted. I thus applied to be a research student in economic history in Cambridge.

The autumn of 1965 found me in King's. I had gone to England on the *Queen Mary* and arrived after the beginning of term. On arriving in Cambridge I found an invitation to meet the King's economists that first evening. I met Richard Kahn, Nicholas Kaldor, Robin Marris, Luigi Pasinetti and Richard Stone, as well as Joan Robinson, in those days already an 'honorary Kingsman'. Before taught master's degrees reached Cambridge, overseas graduate students had to take a qualifying examination which consisted of three papers from Part II of the Economics Tripos. Over sherry that evening in King's, I learned that my supervisor for the examination was to be Joan Robinson.

The supervisions were formidable, but not all that relevant. Joan thought I was sitting paper 4, advanced economic theory. I knew I was not. But it was an education and she relented occasionally to let me indulge myself with papers on such things as the collapse of the inter-war gold standard. At the end of the year I qualified, still interested in doing a dissertation in economic history. But, partially as a result of Joan's influence, I had settled on a topic in monetary history: the effects of Britain's return to the gold standard in 1925. Joan had sensibly decided that she would not be a useful supervisor for such a topic. She passed me on to Richard Kahn, whose only qualification for supervising the topic, other than having lived through the period, was a command of the relevant monetary theory.

Thus in 1966 I started on a dissertation. My progress through the secondary literature and the surviving contemporary sources was slow at first. But then Richard suggested that I should look for leads in Keynes's own papers, then in the process of being edited by Elizabeth Johnson. After all, Keynes had opposed the return to the gold standard, been a steadfast critic of official policy, and been involved in various advisory bodies between 1929 and 1931. I was sent off to see Austin Robinson and began an acquaintance with the papers which has lasted ever since.

Keynes's own papers were only marginally useful for the dissertation. It was a grant from the Bank of England enabling me to spend the summer of 1967 in the archives of the Federal Reserve Bank of New York and the shift from a fifty-year to a thirty-year rule from January 1968 for access to the British public records that really got the dissertation off the ground. Richard Kahn thought I was on to something and persuaded Brian Reddaway to publish my early results in a Department of Applied Economics Occasional Paper. Nicky Kaldor helped by getting me access to the Chancellor's decision-making documents which had never been transferred to the Public Record Office. The first part of the dissertation appeared as *The Return to Gold, 1925* in the spring of 1969 and the whole thing went to the examiners in the fall of that year. A revised version of all of it was published as *British Monetary Policy, 1924–1931: The Norman Conquest of $4.86* in 1972.

By 1969 I was settled in Cambridge as a research fellow of Clare College. The fellowship, the almost completed dissertation and Richard Kahn led Austin Robinson to ask me in the spring of 1969 if I would be interested in joining in the editing of *The Collected Writings of John Maynard Keynes*, a job Austin said would only take three or four years. I accepted. Thus in October 1969, after discussions with Elizabeth Johnson, I started editing my part of the papers. It took more than three or four years: increases in the material available and, hence, in the size of the edition, financial problems which delayed printing for several years during the 1970s and the sheer scale of the enterprise meant the final volume did not appear until December 1989.

As work on the edition proceeded, I naturally started publishing on Keynes. One such excursion into print was the Fontana Modern Master, *Keynes*, which appeared in 1976. As it appeared, both Richard Kahn and Geoffrey Keynes suggested I try my hand at a biography. Their encouragement overcame my initial doubts as to whether I should undertake it. The Canada Council, its successor the Social Sciences and Humanities Research Council of Canada and the University of Toronto, where I had moved in 1975, all seemed willing to provide financial support. Thus in the intervals of the edition I started casting my net more widely in archives in Britain and the United States. Two years of leave at Clare between 1979 and 1981 gave me an opportunity to do more research and some initial writing.

But progress was slow. I easily missed the centenary of Keynes's birth in 1983. Then, with a very rough first draft in my bottom drawer, in 1985 I became an academic administrator. University administration is not conducive to large-scale projects that require sustained writing: you cannot do it between the telephone calls from other administrators or in the seemingly endless meetings, although there are sufficient gaps in both for editorial footnotes. I retreated to editing the diaries of James Meade and Lionel Robbins with my colleague Susan Howson. It was not until the autumn of 1988 that I was able to retrieve my Keynes draft from the bottom drawer, this time in a study generously provided as part of the Benians Fellowship by the Master and Fellows of St John's College, Cambridge. I re-read what I had written years earlier, wondering all the time whether it was worth continuing. It was. The absence of distractions in John's allowed me to see the volume as a whole. By the summer of 1989 I had another draft. It was refined and improved under the remorseless criticism of Susan Howson during the ensuing academic year to the point that I could send it out to others. There followed further helpful criticism and advice and more redrafting before the volume went to the publisher.

As the reader will soon see, the core of what follows comes from Keynes's own papers. Not only did Keynes produce a lot of paper, but he also kept it. So too did his correspondents. One might think that the 13,500 pages of the *Collected Writings* were enough, but their concern was merely his professional life as an economist and his contributions to public affairs and, even then, they were selective. Austin Robinson guesses that if we had published all the materials by Keynes and the related correspondence that are in the 'Keynes Papers' in Cambridge and the Public Record Office we would have had an edition of a hundred volumes.

The amount of material that has survived in the Cambridge papers suggests that Keynes did not tamper with his record for posterity. He was too busy creating to read and then to destroy selectively. His not moving college rooms, or, after 1916, house, probably helped preserve the record. Of course, some papers have disappeared: some of them are in the Harrod papers in Japan and the editorial records of the *Economic Journal* in particular have large gaps. But, aided by the fact that he had a secretary and thus kept carbon copies of much of his correspondence, Keynes's own records are remarkably complete and, where they are not, the papers of others, particularly in the Bloomsbury group, provide useful supplements. More papers will almost certainly come to light in the years to come, but I suspect that major finds on the scale of the hoard discovered at Tilton in 1976 after Lady Keynes had gone into a nursing home, which arrived in my Cambridge office in a laundry hamper and necessitated an additional volume of the *Collected Writings*, are unlikely.

But why another biography of Keynes, especially another one by an economist? Penelope Lively remarks in *According to Mark*, the 'obsessive shadowing of another man's life is one of the more bizarre ways to spend one's time'.[1] It is perhaps even more bizarre for an economist.

One of the characteristics of modern economics is that it does not care all that much for its own history – or history in general. 'Economists suffer badly from "Cliophobia" '.[2] Economics' sense of its past has also recently been in decline. Courses in the history of economics (or the history of economic thought as it is called in the trade) do exist, but they are far from universal and rarely near the centre of the curriculum. In many departments, even those with strength in the field, graduate students are actively discouraged from undertaking dissertations on the history of economics lest they impair their chances of success in a job market which puts technical expertise in developing the tools of the trade at a premium. Similar pressures afflict economic history.

This growing emphasis on technical skills in economics has also been accompanied by what one might call a crude 'natural scientific' or Whig attitude to the past. Newest is best and involves all that is worth saving from the past. Why concern oneself with what A. C. Pigou once called 'the wrong opinions of dead men'? If it comes in at all in modern economics, the past has a minor supporting role – one it also played for Keynes: it provides useful justification for positions taken up for other reasons. Rarely do economists reflect on the fact that they are probably less interested in their past than their role models in the natural sciences.

Economists' lack of interest in their past shows up in the biographies of economists. If one excludes obituary notices – and given the traditions once followed (but symptomatically abandoned in the last twenty years) by journals such as the *Economic Journal* and the *American Economic Review* (but still maintained by economist members of the British Academy) this means that one excludes some classic essays[3] – there are very few biographies of economists. There are, of course, still 'biographical' appraisals for special occasions: Keynes on Malthus and Jevons, or Schumpeter on Marshall, to stick to classics.[4] But there are remarkably few monographs. There are some written by family members.[5] There are the 'authorised' biographies such as Leslie Stephen on Henry Fawcett, Roy Harrod on Maynard Keynes and J. H. Jones on Josiah Stamp.[6] But beyond these the field starts to get very thin, although Keynes would still be represented, as would Richard Cantillon, David Ricardo, Thomas Malthus, Knut Wicksell, William Beveridge, Hugh Gaitskell, Hugh Dalton, Walter Layton, Michal Kalecki, Nicholas Kaldor, Joan Robinson and, most recently, Joseph Schumpeter.[7] But this list is padded: many of the biographies I have mentioned are primarily concerned with the careers pursued by their subjects outside of economics and, as their authors often are not economists, they have very little, if anything, to say about their subjects' professional activities. But the fewness of biographies does not in itself justify another one, especially one of Keynes.

Such is the stock of economists' biographies. That small stock has developed a literature. To take the inevitable classification scheme of the economist, this small literature can be divided into two parts: the supply side and the demand side. In other words, there are some contributions from the suppliers of biography and some from those who consume it for their own purposes, sometimes in the history of economics. Leaving to one side the general agreement, if only for the sake of avoiding unnecessary argument, that biography, somehow considered, is worth doing for its own sake, it is useful to look at the various attitudes adopted to the enterprise.

On the supply side, there are a number of rationales. One is 'nobody has ever written a full biography of the man' – the justification used, for example, by Patricia James for her *Population Malthus* – often with a subsidiary task in such a context of setting the record straight.[8] Another, possibly related one, is 'here was an interesting man who lived at an interesting time'.[9] A third possibility which, as in Roy Harrod's case, can be added to the first and second, both of which start with some criterion of achievement, is that in some sense 'an understanding of the background to his thought is indispensable for a correct interpretation of his conclusions'. In Harrod's case, there was also the belief that

> I cannot conceive how a future student, however conscientious and able, who had first-hand knowledge neither of Keynes nor of the intellectual circles which formed his environment could fail to fall into grievous errors of interpretation.[10]

This might be called setting the record straight before some of the evidence disappears, although in Harrod's case some of the evidence also 'disappeared' into Harrod's own papers.[11] As well as setting down the record, there is what Robert Skidelsky, in his review of the reviews of the English edition of his

Keynes biography (which significantly included bewilderment at the 'typical' reactions of one professional economist, Maurice Peston), calls 'the itch to "explain"'.[12] Here might be a belief that one might, as in Charles Hession's case, relate through what is known about Keynes's personality and the inner springs of his creativity to his career as an economist and statesman.[13] Finally, there is what I might call the moral purpose, strongly present in Harrod's biography of Keynes, but perhaps clearest in Leslie Stephen's study of Henry Fawcett, Alfred Marshall's predecessor as Professor of Political Economy in Cambridge.[14]

There is, then, a story to tell, or something to 'explain' or illuminate. There is also often an implicit belief, explicit in Harrod's case, that the creation of the biography will add something to our knowledge not only of the individual, but also of economics. Such a view was strongly expressed by William Jaffé, a distinguished historian of economics who in the course of his studies of Walras strayed into the realms of biography. Decrying the view that some 'historians of our science think it a virtue to overlook it, as if the personal aspects of a theory were a contaminating substance about which the less said the better', he attempted to make a case, with examples from his own work on Walras, 'for the importance of biography for an understanding of analysis'. In essence, his case rested on the argument that for the individual economist, in this case Walras, 'theory must be understood as a work of art, and that, like all works of art, it was marked with the personality of its creator'.[15] Biography was important to an understanding of the meaning of an author's work, its genesis and the process of its acceptance.

Jaffé's propositions met with something of a demand-side reaction. First into the field was George Stigler, who has a reputation as the archetypal critical consumer in economics. Working from the position that 'science consists of the arguments and evidence that lead *other* men to accept or reject scientific views', he argued

> Science is a social enterprise, and those parts of a man's life which do not affect the relationships between that man and his fellow scientists are simply extra-scientific. When we are told that we must understand a man's life to understand what he really meant, we are being invited to abandon science. . . . The recipients of a scientific message are the people who determine what the message is, and no flight of genius which does not reach the recipients will ever reach and affect the science.[16]

He was arguing that in understanding this process 'very little biographical information' was needed, although in the study of the sociology of a particular discipline as such biographical information had a role.

In 1983, Donald Walker attempted to develop a taxonomy of the ways biography, or more specifically different types of biographical information (personal, professional, environmental and bibliographic), could be useful for the history of economics. Walker accepted Stigler's general view of the way economics worked, although to do so he had to fit in re-interpretations of an economist's work using material not available to all – or at least some – contemporaries as in effect separate, later items, from the original texts. He suggested that for modern economics – 'economists who wrote since about 1770' – it was 'ordinarily' not necessary to have biographical information to establish the meaning of their theories.[17] He had been unable to find a valid example of where the sort of environmental information provided by a biography had helped to establish an author's meaning, although he allowed that might possibly happen. Similarly, he argued that such information was unnecessary for an account of the intellectual evolution of economics. Rather, like Stigler, he suggested that the major role of biography lay in its assistance to an understanding of the sociology of the discipline and, to a subsidiary extent, in the study of the genesis of an author's ideas, although here he was inclined to believe that these possibilities were limited owing to the absence of information and to the fact that investigations of the process of creation of new ideas are 'more like psychology than a study of the evolution of economic thought. Their central concern is the creative act rather than the character of scientific ideas'.[18] No chance of an economist's variant on Russell McCormmach's marvellous novel *Night Thoughts of a Classical Physicist* arising from such attitudes.[19]

But looking at more recent writing by Stigler, I wonder whether, even in the restricted area of economic analysis, the case is so cut and dried. In his *Memoirs of an Unregulated Economist*, Stigler accepts that personal knowledge might help in understanding an economist's thought. He accepts that 'One surprising feature taught by intellectual history is the persistence of uncertainty over what a person really meant'.[20] It is this continued uncertainty as to meaning that leads him to suggest, when he is talking of the advantages of the concentration of work at the frontiers of economics in a few departments, that one of the benefits of these arrangements, over and above the stimulation of able colleagues and graduate students and the more likely early discovery of error, is the advantage of easy communication.

> Even though Jones and I have always spoken English and may even have gone to the same graduate school, each of us thinks somewhat differently; we each have a different order in which we think and probably a different pace in expressing ideas. Family members use words which have special meanings for them. . . . So it is with every person, and that is why intimate association makes communication between people efficient and accurate. If I had known David Ricardo, I would be better able to understand his written words. That would be a help, because to this day the meanings of his theories are much debated.[21]

This raises the question of the uses of biography in economics in an important way – one that Donald Walker touched on, even though he suggested, on the basis of his own experience, that it would rarely be useful.

But the Stigler/Walker view casts the role of the economist in the history of the subject narrowly. They are primarily concerned with the history of economics as a 'box of tools'. They do not meet the narrowness of this concern by calling everything else the 'sociology' of economics. The notion of the sociology may be useful in explaining, as Walker puts it 'the history of how he [the writer] secured that place for them [his ideas] and of the circumstances, other than purely intellectual ones,[a] that affected the reception of his ideas'.[22] Walker tries to make that category fairly all-encompassing, covering as it does 'professional activities'; contemporaries' knowledge of the writer's professional biography and track record; and the characteristics and experiences of the recipients of an idea – for all of which biographical data may be useful. I doubt it is as cut and dried as all that.

Part of the problem here is conceptual. Throughout the work of Jaffé, Stigler and Walker, when they are not talking of the sociology of the discipline or the act of creation, the understanding of which two of them put outside economics – as if some other discipline has well-established and agreed accounts of what goes on – they confine their discussions to economic analysis – or formal economic theory – where there are more or less agreed rules of procedure and tests of logical consistency, even though there might be disagreement over the fruitfulness of proceeding along particular lines, as there was, for example, in inter-war macroeconomics. Economics historically has not just been a matter of formal theory, and that theory, although it may proceed in particular directions at specific times for reasons internal to the discipline, has not been created in a vacuum. Many economists have attempted to change their worlds. This has not always been just a simple matter of applying existing analysis. Nor, at a more complex level, has it been just a matter of changing analysis and persuading one's colleagues to adopt it, although collegial persuasion may be an important part of the process.

Moreover, the process does not stop at some convenient point where non-economists or some other specialists take over. There is still the matter of persuading others – politicians, public servants, public opinion. It is always worth remembering that, to some extent, what is politically possible, even in economic matters, is a product of persuasion. As Richard Sayers noted in his discussion of the problems of British Second World War finance:

Financial policy has, in the end, to accept limits dictated by public

---

a Or, more correctly, discipline-related intellectual ones. There are presumably intellectual reasons for the acceptance of ideas, just as there are in Walker's schema for their creation, which lie outside of economics.

opinion. This does not absolve the nation's political leaders, or indeed its administrators, from the effort to stretch those limits. Much can be done to persuade the public to accept and co-operate in extreme or novel measures. But too much cannot be expected in this way, for financial policy is never a strong candidate for the attention of the man-in-the-street, and in time of war it has spectacular rivals for the scanty newspaper space. Moreover, war is apt to throw up political leaders whose tastes run in other directions, and it would be miraculous to find in a national war leader the genius, and in his daily round the time, for the exposition of stern financial measures. In fact Britain in 1939–45 did not have the advantage of such a miracle. She did however have the advantage that a great pamphleteer in political economy was still at the height of his powers, and there were many followers who were quick to grasp and to propagate the war-time lessons of Keynesian economics. Whatever may be said of the direct interventions of Keynes in particular questions of economic policy, there can be no doubt at all that his hold upon the professional economists was from the first a major factor in leading public opinion to the acceptance of a relatively strong financial policy.[23]

There was some sociology of the profession here: note the role of the 'followers'. But more was at stake, as is clear if one examines in Chapter 25 below the ways in which Keynes carefully orchestrated his campaign for the adoption of the approach to war finance outlined in *How to Pay for the War* (1940).[24] I would agree that acceptance of one's analytical ideas by his professional colleagues was an important part of the process, but it was not all of it. The whole process certainly has something to do with the history of economics – and not only its sociology.

In short, I do not think that the categories of Donald Walker's taxonomy are sufficient, even for economist consumers. First, as regards the genesis of ideas in economics, he is too inclined to exclude parts of the process from his subject matter. It may be that there is not, as yet, sufficient material available in many cases, but this does not mean either that the materials may not be available or that the work should not be attempted. Maynard Keynes left such a wealth of material that in his case it is certainly worth the attempt. Second, as regards what Walker calls the 'environmental biography', it would seem that he leaves his subjects too passive. Not only does the environment affect an economist's thought and his work, but that thought and work may be intended to change and may actually succeed in changing that same environment.

It is not completely clear to me from reading most of my economist predecessors, as consumers of biographical information, what form their ideal biography of any economist would take. One could never satisfy everyone, just as in the Keynes edition one could not satisfy all potential users unless the edition was much, much more complete than it is. It is clear that readers want 'facts' in the way that users of editions want documents. But both biographies and non-complete editions involve selections or choices from all that is available. One cannot, even in a multi-volume life on the projected scale of Robert Skidelsky's, provide all the biographical 'facts' which Donald Walker's ideal user might want. One doubts that anyone would read, much less publish a biography which told the reader of everything that was ascertainable – unless, of course, there was so little information as to make the whole exercise pointless. But, as Leon Edel has put it, 'A biography is not an engagement book'.[25] Nor is it a bibliography, or list of books read. One should probably not, as far as I see it, even let the subject 'speak for himself': if that is one's aim perhaps it would be more useful to edit your subject's papers instead – something which in the case of Keynes I have, for better or worse, already done. Thus the biographer must select. But for what purpose?

From the start one must accept that selection is shaped by the achievements of the subject. For it is the achievements that make the subject the possible object of a biography. If he or she were simply an average economist, to stay with my subject, he or she would, it is true, be a possible subject for some aspect of the 'sociology' of the discipline for which one might want biographical information, but hardly for a biography. This exceptional achievement inevitably shapes the biography.

Thus one starts with an achievement or a series of achievements, some of which may, of course, have nothing to do with economics, such as Fawcett's becoming Postmaster-General under Gladstone. The presence of the achievement produces its own problems and risks. To the biographer, as to the historian of economics, it exists, even if its exact shape is the subject of some dispute. We know what happened. But it was not inevitable: there was no pre-ordained fate that determined it should turn out the particular way it did. One cannot explain actions as if they were 'steps towards the fulfilment of a manifest destiny'.[26] There is little room for predestination. Keynes, for example, was self-confident, even arrogant, but the way matters would eventually evolve for him was concealed from him until they did so. All that he could do, for good or ill, was at any particular point make certain choices as to what to do (or not to do) and how to do it, and hope for the best. These choices themselves were constrained and shaped by a whole host of factors – personal, environmental, logical, etc. A good part of a biographer's task is to 'explain' these choices or decisions, as they appeared at the time, with all that this involves in terms of surrounding information.

In making these choices, most of the economists that would interest a historian of economics were creating something – a piece of what would eventually become part of economic analysis. In doing so, they were addressing their fellow professionals. In these circumstances their creations were subject to certain rules of the game, as were many of the strategic choices that underlay them. Good examples appear in the discussion of Keynes's *General Theory* below.

The fact that economists were writing for their fellow professionals and were subject to certain rules of the game does not mean that the products of their pen were anonymous, standard 'economese'. Anyone who successively reads pieces by Ralph Hawtrey, Maynard Keynes, A. C. Pigou and Dennis Robertson, to take examples from inter-war macroeconomics, would certainly know which was whose. In other words there was a distinctive style to the initial product, irrespective of its formal ideas. That style disappeared as 'time, experience and the collaboration of a number of minds' found 'the best way of expressing them' and they became incorporated into the general run-of-the-mill economist's analysis.[27] But it was there initially.

That initial style, as much as the ultimate collaborative result, was important. First, it encapsulated not only the formal elements of the author's theory but also an associated bundle of intuitions. As Keynes repeatedly emphasised, at the centre of the act of creation is an intuition or insight that allows the creator to 'see through the obscurity of the argument or of the apparently unrelated data' as a result of which 'the details will quickly fall into a scheme or arrangement, between each part of which there is a real connection'.[28] Then, of course, came the often lengthy matter of tidying it up. But as the intuition came first, and always ran ahead of the formal analysis, readers of the original text always got a mixture of the two. How that mixture was initially expressed was important, even if the intuitions eventually disappeared in the formalism of professional acceptance. It was important for two reasons:

(1) The factual historical one that it was this particular bundle that was presented to the profession which, often with supplementary supporting papers, persuaded the profession that there was something there to formalise.

(2) The doctrinal, historical one that whenever two or more economists are disputing over what 'x' really meant, they are forced back to dealing with this original text with its mixture of formalism and intuition, fully and far less fully worked out ideas.

In a paper of February 1909, 'Science and Art', Keynes compared the process of scientific creation to the work of an artist. 'He [the scientist] is dealing with facts regarded as facts, very much as the artist is dealing with perceptions regarded as perceptions'. No wonder William Jaffé argued that Walras' general equilibrium theory, in the form he created it, 'must be understood as a work of art, and that like all works of art, it was marked with the personality of its creator'.[29] In the hands of the profession it eventually became something else, but originally it had this particular form.

It is in this area that I think the economist biographer (although he or she is not the only possibility, for the sort of biographical information I am talking about could be produced otherwise) may be of use to the historian of economics. With luck the biographer may provide the historian with Stigler's equivalent of having Ricardo as a colleague. For although the biographer cannot reproduce the inner world of the economist in question, he or she may be able, after watching it operate on occasion after occasion, rather than the more usual historian of thought's much smaller sample, be able to describe or illuminate it more completely. And that may be of some use to the analyst, who, after all, to judge by the material at present available for economists, has not had all that much to work from.

I have concentrated thus far on one aspect of achievement: the creation of a theory or theories, which in some form pass into the standard usage of economists. But with Keynes, and with other economists, theories were not the whole story. Keynes was also an applied economist using the existing body of theory in conjunction with the available facts of the world to try to shape certain outcomes, be they the international monetary system in 1931–2 or 1941–6, or the financial policy of the British Government in 1915, 1929–33 or 1940–6. And shape them he did with some success through various forms of private and public persuasion. How he did so and why he did so are also subjects for historians of economics, not to mention biographers, who may in the process of writing a biography have acquired additional perspectives.

I have concentrated on more 'professional' activities. What of the rest? Inevitably they get covered. In the case of some personal traits, they may even be related to the professional concerns of historians of economics: it may be possible to link certain personal traits to professional success or the desire for professional success. But is that all? Especially in this modern world of 'warts and all' or 'tell it all' biography? What is the point in Keynes's case of telling the story 'boy by boy' – from Dilly to Dan to Lytton to James to Hobby to Duncan to the 'stall boy of Park Lane' to the 'auburn haired of Marble Arch' and the 'lift boy of Vauxhall' – to move from the better known to the less known of the twenty-six, all of whom Keynes carefully recorded and tabulated between 1901 and August 1915? Surely, it is not just to sell books. It may be that there are relationships between homosexuality and creativity, as has been suggested in the case of literary studies by Geoffrey Meyers and is suggested in the case of Keynes by Charles Hession.[30] I must admit that I am not as yet convinced, beyond seeing the parallels in the desire for achievement amongst certain minority groups that have been a staple of economic historians' arguments for decades. But still, boy-by-boy? I certainly do not see any peculiarities that need exercise the historian of economics, even if he does worry himself with acts of creation. This does not mean that such information may not be biographically important in other contexts, which may be relevant to some other aspects of a subject's activities, but if one cannot find a relevance, why select it or relate it in particular degrees of detail?

I am back to the fact that a biography is by its nature selective. As Pirandello put it:

> A fact is like a sock which won't stand up when it is empty. In order that a fact may stand up, one has to put into it the reason and the feeling which have caused it to exist.[31]

I could go on to other matters. For example, a biography, like a large edition, distorts one's subject. In biography, concentrating on one person, no matter how much one adds of 'the times' means that the cast of supporting characters or events, although they may be more important historically, are only relevant in so far as they impinge on the subject. In the case of an edition, the volume of readily available material probably performs a similar distorting function, although probably less significantly, if only because there are always the publications of others.

Thus I should like to emphasise four points. First, although there are outstandingly good examples of biographical treatments of economists, that group is not that well served. To some extent this is the fault of economists themselves. They no longer greatly value biography. As well, although the relevant materials may not exist in some cases, economists have not been that assiduous in using what is available. Second, perhaps because there are so few good studies, economists tend to undervalue and misunderstand the exercise when they think of their subject. They can see the usefulness of certain types of biographical 'facts' as data for other enterprises, but they behave, at least in public, despite continuing disputes concerning meaning, as if, rather than just being one way to look at the subject, the history of technical economic analysis as some sort of scientific process is the only approach to the subject and, hence, that individual peculiarities do not count for much in the end. In the long sweep of history, this may indeed be the case, but the history of a subject even as young as economics suggests that short periods where the opposite is the case may last decades. Third, even in attempting to be 'scientific', historians of economics tend to forget, surprisingly for a group that claim to be historians *as well as* economists, that facts do not speak for themselves. There are 'fertile' facts and 'creative' facts. Selection and arrangement do matter – both for purposes of persuasion and enlightenment – even when some of the arrangements may be constrained by certain rules of the game. When dealing with economists as a group, regularities may be important, but when dealing with individuals and their achievements peculiarities are important. If they were not, why would George Stigler think it useful to have Ricardo as a colleague? Given that he cannot, perhaps the role of biography in the history of economics is more important than many economists have been prepared to allow. Finally, biography, like any other scholarly activity is not only about selection but also then about forming what one selects. As Leslie Stephen, Virginia Woolf's father and one of my economist's biographers put it:

To write a life is to collect the particular heap of rubbish in which is his [the biographer's] material is contained, to sift the relevant from the superincumbent mass and then try to smelt it and cast it into its natural mould.[32]

In the case of Keynes, where there is a large economists' literature on 'what Keynes really meant' or 'what Keynes should have meant', finding this 'mould' is even more of a problem. Generally I have tried to stay clear of discussing much of that literature, largely because it is often not germane to the *biographical* problem at hand. Thus, if this book is to make a contribution to the economists' literature on Keynes it will be because it will provide a better context in which one can carry on such discussions. If I have succeeded in casting Keynes into his 'natural mould' and given the reader a glimpse of what Keynes might have been like as a colleague, to borrow George Stigler's notion, I will have done enough.

I dedicate this book to four people who made it possible. My father was important in my original decision to go to Cambridge. Richard Kahn and Austin Robinson were central to my getting to know Keynes further. Sue Howson, my friend, colleague and occasional co-author and co-editor, has, along with Austin Robinson, provided continual stimulus and support over many years. I thank them all. None of them, and none of those acknowledged elsewhere, is responsible for the defects in what follows.

Toronto, February 1991

NOTES

1 Lively 1988, 60.
2 Blaug 1990, 27.
3 It means, for example, that one loses Keynes on Marshall, Edgeworth and Foxwell; Schumpeter on Keynes; Austin Robinson on Keynes; Henry Phelps Brown on Harrod and Robbins; John Hicks on Robertson; and R. D. C. Black on Hawtrey.
4 See *The Collected Writings of John Maynard Keynes*, hereafter *JMK*, X, and Schumpeter 1952.
5 See Jevons 1886; Sidgwick and Sidgwick 1906; Ashley 1932; Bowley n.d.; Clarks 1935; Cole 1971; Fisher 1956.
6 Stephen 1885; Creighton 1957; Harrod 1951; Jones 1964.
7 Harris 1955; Hession 1983; Skidelsky 1985; Murphy 1986; Weatherall 1976; James 1979; Gardlund 1958; Harris 1977; Williams 1977; Pimlott 1985; Hubback 1985; Feiwel 1975; Thirlwall 1987; Turner 1989; Allen 1991. The Thirlwall volume is the first of a series on 'Grand Masters in Economics' specialising in intellectual biography. There are also discussions of economists' ideas, with varying elements of biography, in series such as the Fontana Modern Masters (Keynes and Marx) and the Oxford Past Masters (Smith, Malthus, Marx and Mill).
8 James 1979, 1.
9 Weatherall 1976, v.

10 Harrod 1951, v.
11 See the sale catalogue for *The Papers of Sir Roy Harrod* prepared by Hamish Riley-Smith, which included such things as letters from JMK to his parents, his description of Roosevelt (quoted in Harrod 1951, 448–50), and notes for a speech for his parents' Diamond Wedding celebrations.
12 Skidelsky 1985, xvii.
13 Hession 1983, xv.
14 Stephen 1885, 468.
15 Jaffé 1965, 224, 226.
16 Stigler 1976/82, 91.
17 Walker 1983, 55.
18 Walker 1983, 52.
19 McCormmach 1983.
20 Ibid., 216.
21 Ibid., 36–7.
22 Walker 1983, 53.
23 Sayers 1956, 2–3.
24 See also *JMK*, XXII, ch. 1; Moggridge 1980, 120–30; Sayers 1956, chs II and III, esp. 31–5, 67–74, 80–5.
25 Edel 1987, 104.
26 Lord Blake in Homberger and Charmley 1987, 89.
27 *JMK*, XIV, 111.
28 KCKP, UA/10/1, 'Science and Art', 20 February 1909, 5.
29 Jaffé 1965, 226.
30 Meyers 1977; Hession 1983.
31 Quoted in Nadel 1984, 10.
32 Ullmann (ed.) 1965, 132.

ACKNOWLEDGEMENTS

In over twenty years of working on Keynes, I have incurred many debts. Some can be documented in specific footnotes. But, especially as the effects are often cumulative, one cannot recall every stimulus arising from innumerable conversations on Keynes or from hundreds of papers on aspects of Keynes that I have heard at conferences and seminars or read as a referee. However my debt to the community of Keynes scholars and others remains.

More specifically, there are a number of people who have provided advice over the years: Sue Howson, Richard Kahn, Austin Robinson and Pat Rosenbaum. Then there are those who have given extravagantly of their time to read earlier drafts of this volume: Brad Bateman, Peter Clarke, Geoff Harcourt, Sue Howson, Don Patinkin, Leslie Pressnell, Austin Robinson and Donald Winch. Their thoughtful advice has made this a different, and I think better, volume from the original. There are also those who have provided useful assistance: my Keynes co-editor, Elizabeth Johnson; my former students – Anna Carabelli and Patrick Deutscher; various members of the extended Keynes clan – Polly Hill, Anne Keynes, the late Sir Geoffrey Keynes, Milo Keynes and Richard Keynes. Finally, there is Beth Morgan, who not only provided the bulk of the index to the *Collected Writings* but then agreed to take on the index to this volume.

Any project carried on over so many years also accumulates debts to those who have provided material support. In this case I am grateful to the Canada Council; the Humanities and Social Sciences Committee of the Research Board, University of Toronto; the Master and Fellows of Clare College, Cambridge; the Master and Fellows of St John's College, Cambridge; the Office of the Dean of the Faculty of Arts and Science, University of Toronto; and the Social Sciences and Humanities Research Council of Canada.

Any book such as this depends heavily on libraries and archives. In this case, I should like to thank the staffs of the following: Cambridge University Library; Marshall Library of Economics, Cambridge; Modern Archives Collection, King's College, Cambridge; Trinity College Library, Cambridge; Pepys Library, Magdalene College, Cambridge; Bodleian Library, Oxford;

Northwestern University Library; Kress Collection, Baker Library, Harvard Graduate School of Business Administration; British Library of Political and Economic Science, London; Franklin Delano Roosevelt Library, Hyde Park, New York; New York Public Library; British Library, London; Arts Council of Great Britain, London; India Office Library, London; Federal Reserve Bank of New York; Bank of England; Public Record Office.

For permission to quote published material beyond the usual limits of fair usage, in the case of *The Collected Writings of John Maynard Keynes* I am grateful to the Royal Economic Society. For unpublished material, I am grateful to the following: the Provost and Fellows of King's College, Cambridge (Keynes, Ramsey and Joan Robinson Papers); Richard Keynes and Polly Hill (Keynes Papers); Sir Edward Ford (Brand Papers); Sir Frederic Harmer (his diary of the 1945 Loan Negotiations); James Meade; the Strachey Trust and the Society of Authors (Lytton and James Strachey); Angelica Garnett (Vanessa Bell); Henrietta Garnett (Duncan Grant); Timothy Moore (G. E. Moore); Magdalene College, Cambridge (A. C. Benson); Trinity College, Cambridge (Edwin Montagu); the Trustees of the Thomas Lamont Papers, Harvard University; the Royal Economic Society; the Arts Council of Great Britain; the Controller of Her Majesty's Stationery Office; the Bank of England; the Federal Reserve Bank of New York; the British Library of Political and Economic Science (Webb, Dalton and Cannan Papers); the Marshall Library of Economics (J. N. Keynes and Foxwell Papers). For photographs, I should like to thank Austin Robinson; Milo Keynes; Henrietta Garnett, (for the Duncan Grant Estate); Craufurd Goodwin; the International Monetary Fund; the Associated Press; the Hulton Picture Company and the late W. H. Haslam.

Finally I should like to thank my various editors at Routledge for their calm patience over the years that this, inevitably very late, volume evolved and in particular Alan Jarvis and Alison Walters for the care with which they saw the text through the press.

ABBREVIATIONS

BERG   Berg Collection, New York Public Library
BL   British Library
BLPES British Library of Political and Economic Science
BoE   Bank of England
CUL   Cambridge University Library
DG   Duncan Grant
DHR   Dennis Holme Robertson
FAK   Florence Ada Keynes
FDRL   Franklin Delano Roosevelt Library, Hyde Park
FRUS   *Foreign Relations of the United States*
GLK   Geoffrey Langdon Keynes
GLS   Giles Lytton Strachey
HBL   Harvard University, Baker Library
IO   India Office Library, London
JMK   John Maynard Keynes
JMK   *The Collected Writings of John Maynard Keynes*
       (eds Johnson and Moggridge)
JNK   John Neville Keynes
KCCP   King's College, Cambridge – Charleston Papers
KCJRP King's College, Cambridge – Joan Robinson Papers
KCKP   King's College, Cambridge – Keynes Papers
KCPH   King's College, Cambridge – Polly Hill Collection
LSE   London School of Economics and Political Science
MCPL   Magdalene College, Cambridge, Pepys Library
MK   Margaret Keynes
MLC   Marshall Library of Economics, Cambridge
NUL   Northwestern University Library
OBL   Oxford Bodleian Library
PRO   Public Record Office
RES   Royal Economic Society
RFK   Richard Ferdinand Kahn
RKP   Richard Keynes Papers

ABBREVIATIONS

SRO   Scottish Record Office
TCL   Trinity College Library, Cambridge
VWD   *The Diary of Virginia Woolf* (ed. Bell)
VWL   *The Letters of Virginia Woolf* (ed. Nicolson and Trautman)

1

FOREBEARS AND CHILDHOOD

I like the name suggested. John Maynard Keynes sounds like the substantial name of the solid hero of a sensible novel.

(KCKP, John Brown to F. A. Keynes, 6 June 1883)

John Maynard Keynes was born at 9.45 a.m. on Tuesday, 5 June 1883 at 6 Harvey Road, Cambridge, a solid, double-fronted, three-storey house of dark yellow brick finished the previous autumn. It had been built by his father, John Neville Keynes, for his bride, Florence Ada Brown, whom he had married in August 1882. Maynard, as he was to be called – although his mother occasionally used, and originally preferred, John – was to be the first of three children.[a] The other two were Margaret Neville, born on 4 February 1885, and Geoffrey Langdon, born on 25 March 1887.

Victorian changes in the University had brought his parents to Cambridge. The further transition from the last Victorian reforms of the 1880s to the modern state-supported institution that emerged after the First World War encompassed both Neville and Maynard Keynes's connections with the administration of the University. For this reason it is necessary to provide some institutional background against which the Keyneses' lives and times can be set.

At the beginning of the nineteenth century, candidates for honours degrees in the University of Cambridge had only one tripos, Mathematics. The next half century saw the addition of three more – Classics (1824), Moral Sciences (1848) and Natural Sciences (1848) – but these were only open to those who had taken a first degree, which in the arts subjects meant the Mathematics Tripos. Not surprisingly, examination results in the Mathematics Tripos remained the dominant criterion for election to College fellowships, the next step in a Cambridge career. Inevitably, this meant that trained mathematicians dominated the early development of the 'newer' subjects. It was only after 1850 that the new triposes came to stand on their own as possible direct routes

---

a In the pages that follow, I will call my subject Maynard during his childhood and youth but revert to the more distanced Keynes once he leaves university.

to an honours degree – Classics in 1854, Moral and Natural Sciences in 1860.

Candidates for honours degrees were not in a majority amongst those who matriculated, or entered, into the Victorian or Edwardian University. There was the alternative of the ordinary degree, now only a consolation prize for students after academic disasters. The standard of this degree was low, in part because the Colleges' standards of admission were low and in part because in the Victorian education system the pool of candidates sufficiently qualified to consider even trying for honours, although growing, was not large.

For both ordinary and honours candidates, the Colleges and the University at mid-century provided little in the way of instruction. The professors, the only teaching officers appointed by the University, lectured, but their lectures were not integrated into the programme of undergraduate studies. Nor did many professorships provide an adequate income for their incumbents, who themselves were not obliged to be resident in Cambridge.[b] Even if the professors took undergraduate teaching seriously, and some did, the University had few places where lectures could take place and laboratory space was even scarcer. Nor were the Colleges an alternative source of education. They did provide some elementary lectures, but these were often inferior to those given to the top form at a good public school. The Colleges did not provide extensive tuition.

The combination of the poor University and College arrangements for undergraduate teaching and the existence of prizes in the form of College fellowships for those coming highest in Tripos examinations resulted in the growth of a set of teaching arrangements outside the system. Private tutors, or coaches, mainly College fellows or lecturers or married graduates whose success was measured by the examination results of their clients, came to dominate the day-to-day teaching in Cambridge. The rewards for success as a coach were high: the best earned far more than College fellows, not to mention most professors.[1] However, the system did not reward originality in teachers or taught.

The Colleges did not offer career prospects likely to attract good teachers or, for that matter, scholars. By mid-century, changes in ecclesiastical standards and practices plus the expansion of secular opportunities for educated men made it less likely that the few available College teaching posts would attract good candidates. Most College fellowships, which often did not require their holders to be resident in Cambridge, were restricted to celibates. If a College fellow took holy orders, he was guaranteed a fellowship for life – or until a lucrative College living turned up. Normally College offices were restricted to those in holy orders. Otherwise, except in certain

b Of the twenty-five professorships that existed in 1850, only 8 had incomes above the £400 per annum the Royal Commission appointed in 1850 to inquire into the affairs of the University regarded as necessary to attract good candidates, while 13 had incomes below £300 (six received £100 or less) (Roach 1959, 248).

specific cases, tenures were limited. In neither case was scholarly attainment a condition of continued tenure.

Mid-Victorian Cambridge was thus an Anglican society. The Act of Uniformity of 1662 required all professors, readers, masters and fellows of Colleges, on pain of losing their posts, to declare their adherence to the doctrine of the Church of England, to disclaim the right of resistance to the King and to declare the Solemn League and Covenant an illegal oath. A further Act of 1714 required all Heads of Houses and all persons supported on the foundation of a College aged 18 or over to declare on oath 'that no foreign Prince, Person, Prelate, State or Potentate hath, or ought to have, any jurisdiction, power, superiority, pre-eminence or authority, ecclesiastical or spiritual, within this realm'.[2] Just after mid-century, the Cambridge University Act of 1856 removed the requirement for an oath under the 1714 Act from holders of scholarships. However, it added that no Cambridge MA or doctor could sit in the Senate of the University, and thus take part in its government, unless he declared himself a *bona fide* member of the Church of England.

Despite this provision, the 1856 Act marked the beginnings of serious reform in Victorian Cambridge. Between 1850 and 1878 the University was the subject of parts of the deliberations of three Royal Commissions and three major Acts of Parliament. The first Royal Commission, the Graham Commission of 1850–2, resulted in the 1856 Act, which produced the first major revision of University and College statutes since the reign of Elizabeth I (or in the case of King's College since 1453). Here, as later, the purpose was to adapt University government to changed circumstances and to face the problem of financing the expansion of University activities that the new age seemed to require. The process of adaptation was far from simple. It involved a delicate interaction between the Statutory Commissioners appointed under the Act and the members of the bodies subject to reform. Initially, the University and the Colleges made proposals to the Commissioners, who would then decide on them. If the process of negotiation failed, or if it proved too lengthy, after 1 January 1858 the Commissioners could make the necessary remaining statutes themselves. The result was a complicated bargaining process in which the dons, or senior members of the Colleges, had considerable influence over the direction of reform. Between such bouts of externally organised reform, the University and the Colleges worked within the established framework. The dons maintained considerable control over the direction and speed of change.

Another constraint on change was the income available to the University. In 1852 the Graham Commission estimated that the University's general income was £8,000, with another £10,000 tied up in appropriations for special subjects.[3] This represented about a tenth of the gross income available to the Colleges. Unless the University received new sources of income, every new professorship, building or activity meant an often lengthy search for funds through fees, voluntary College donations or private benefactions, one of the most visible being the gift of the original Cavendish Laboratory by the Duke of Devonshire.

The 1850s, 1860s and 1870s, despite difficulties, were a period of slow progress.[4] New triposes in Law, History, Theology, Semitic and Indian Languages made their appearance. After the inevitable initial period, when they were considered what we would call 'soft options',[c] these and the triposes started just before mid-century became more popular and even began to attract good students. By the 1870s, some were prepared to argue that the distinction of the Senior Moralists – those who came top of the first class in Moral Sciences – was superior to that of the Senior Wranglers in Mathematics.[5] As well as new triposes, new professorships appeared in archaeology, zoology, Sanskrit, mechanism and applied mechanics and Anglo-Saxon, while many old foundations were reorganised. In an attempt to improve standards in the schools the University created a local examinations scheme. It also started to reach out into the wider community with extra-mural lectures. Following from these examinations and lectures came schemes and facilities for the full-time higher education of women with the founding of what are now Newnham and Girton Colleges, although it would be only after the Second World War that women would become full members of the University.

There were also stirrings of change in collegiate teaching arrangements, particularly in Trinity and St John's. In this period, these made a number of distinguished teaching appointments – for example, Henry Sidgwick, James Ward, J. E. B. Mayor, J. B. Pearson, Alfred Marshall, H. S. Foxwell and Henry Cunningham in the moral sciences. It was these appointees who provided the beginnings of another innovation, an inter-collegiate programme of lectures for tripos candidates.[6] Still later came the modern College provision of supervisions.

In this period, the University also became more open. In 1871, after almost a decade of intermittent debate, Parliament passed an Act abolishing the religious tests for all but Heads of Houses and candidates for divinity degrees. This opened posts at Oxford, Cambridge and Durham to non-Anglicans who had hitherto been allowed posts only in the secular University College, London and the newly formed northern civic colleges – the forerunners of the redbrick universities.

Despite these changes, Cambridge, along with Oxford, was still subject to considerable criticism. There was a widespread belief that in higher education Britain was falling behind other countries, particularly Germany. Much of the emphasis in this criticism fell on scientific and technological education, but there was also criticism of the lack of professionalism in Oxbridge university teaching.[7] Contemporary concerns became manifest in the appointment

c For example, Henry Sidgwick thought it necessary to 'ballast' the new Historical Tripos with political economy and international law (Sidgwick and Sidgwick 1906, 295); see also Winstanley 1947, 186–8.

of a Select Committee on Scientific Instruction in 1868 and subsequently of a Royal Commission on the subject under the Duke of Devonshire. Both bodies heard of the strained financial position of Cambridge. The Devonshire Commission, which devoted a separate report to Oxford and Cambridge, also remarked on the problem of using the existing resources of the Colleges to create genuine careers in teaching, given the celibacy restrictions on most College posts and the fact that few College fellowships (120 out of 350) were held by persons resident in the University engaged in educational or administrative tasks.[8] Before the Devonshire Commission reported, partly in response to continued criticism of the existing situation from within the Universities themselves, the Government set up another Royal Commission to enquire into the finances of the ancient Universities and their Colleges. This revealed that, in contrast to the relative poverty of the universities, many colleges had incomes in excess of what they needed for educational purposes.

Revelations such as these, plus the climate of criticism and concern, brought action from the Government. In 1875 Disraeli promised that university reform would be part of the Government's programme. The next Queen's Speech referred to forthcoming legislation. The proposed legislation was some time in appearing, but in 1877 the Government introduced a Bill appointing Statutory Commissions for Oxford and Cambridge. The resulting Act required that the revised statutes should make provision for College financial contributions for University purposes, that fellowships and other College emoluments should be attached to University or College offices and that the tenure of unattached College fellowships should be reviewed.

The ensuing process of statute-making was lengthy: the Statutory Commissioners for Cambridge did not agree to affix their seal to the University statutes until 15 March 1881. The new University statutes, which took effect in 1882, provided for a scheme of College contributions for University purposes which would rise to £30,000 per annum in 1896, if the contributions were not reduced by the Chancellor on the recommendation of the Financial Board because of continuing agricultural depression. The statutes created new professorships, readerships and University lectureships, a General Board of Studies to organise University teaching and a Financial Board, as well as regularising and raising professorial stipends. The new College statutes would not allow Colleges to require that their heads be in holy orders,[9] eliminated celibacy as a condition for most College fellowships, limited the tenure of College fellowships not associated with College or University offices, limited the size of College fellowship dividends and regularised the maximum value of entrance scholarships. The upshot was that Cambridge became still more secular and the University bulked larger in local affairs. Cambridge was to spend the ensuing 40 years trying to make the new arrangements work before amending them in a manner that further increased the relative power of the University.

The period was one of almost perpetual financial difficulties for the University. At the root of these was the collapse of agricultural prices which, for example, carried the price of corn from an average of 57s. (£2.85) per quarter between 1871 and 1874 to a low of 22s. 10d. (£1.14) in 1894. Thereafter, recovery was slow: even in 1911–13 corn prices averaged only 32s. 8d. (£1.63) per quarter. Falling agricultural prices dramatically affected the incomes of the Colleges, thereby creating the risk that the 1882 scheme for University finance, which was fixed in nominal terms, would harm the Colleges. The extent of the Colleges' difficulties can be seen in the behaviour of fellowship dividends: in King's the dividend fell from £280 in 1875–7 to £80 in 1895 and never rose above £130 in the years to 1914, while in St John's it fell from £300 in 1872–8 to £80 in 1894.[10] As a result, the University postponed the date on which the full operation of the 1882 financial arrangement would begin – eventually until 1906, a decade later than originally envisaged. Its reduced income brought deficits and various expedients were attempted to raise sums from other sources in order that it could continue its ordinary activities and meet new demands.

And new demands there were. There were new triposes – Modern and Medieval Languages (1886), Mechanical Sciences (1894), Economics (1903), Anthropology (1913) – as well as the expansion and elaboration of older ones. Rising numbers of students – matriculations rose from just over 800 in 1880–1 to just under 1,200 before the First World War – the expansion of the University's activities and the experimental demands of the sciences also brought a need for new buildings. There was also the need for new chairs, especially in the sciences. With increased demands yet strained finances, it was often touch and go – a building for anatomy and physiology depended on a gift of £1,500 from Henry Sidgwick, while the chair in mental philosophy projected in 1882 had to wait until 1896 when Sidgwick again came to the rescue by reducing his own salary so that the new professor could have the normal full salary of £750.[11] It was not surprising that in 1896 Sidgwick could write to his sister-in-law, during one of the University's perpetual appeals for money characteristic of those years:

> The only thing we are interested in is our poverty: we are wondering whether the sums dropped into the hat we are holding out at George Darwin's instigation will compensate for the humiliation of holding it out. We haven't yet nearly enough to compensate – only a little over £3,000 – but we still dream of a millionaire waking up to the opportunity of the undying fame that we have offered.[12]

Millionaires seemed relatively thin on the ground: total contributions to the benefactions fund had only reached £126,429 eleven years later.

A more permanent solution to the University's financial problems, extensive funding from government, would come while Neville Keynes was the University's Registrary, or chief administrative officer. Before 1914, individual departments or programmes had made separate approaches to the government for funds – to teach Indian Civil Service (ICS) candidates, to erect buildings for agriculture and forestry, to teach agriculture and forestry. All of these approaches had been for activities outside the University's degree programmes. However, the First World War made the financial problems more acute, as student numbers collapsed from 3,263 in Michaelmas 1913 to 575 in Easter 1916 and the price level more than doubled.[13] The University weathered the storms of war by diverting funds from suspended posts to general purposes, but the post-war position looked bleak. At the end of 1918, in response to an enquiry from the Secretary of the Board of Education, the University estimated its additional needs at £20,000 per annum for salaries, £3,000 per annum for a pension scheme approved before the war but not implemented owing to lack of funds, £30,000 for new posts and £750,000 for capital expenditure. Sums on that scale were not available. Instead, the University received an interim grant of £30,000 while a Royal Commission on Oxford and Cambridge Universities chaired by Asquith did its work. There followed the familiar Act and Statutory Commission and it was only in 1925–6 that Government grants became sizeable, amounting to £85,000.[14] By the end of the decade, the Government grant would represent over half the University's income, a far cry from the initial £500 from the Secretary of State for India for the teaching of ICS candidates in 1892.[15]

The 1919 Royal Commission and the subsequent legislation and Statutory Commission also created the basis of modern University and College structure with its centralised faculties for teaching by individuals paid by the University who could regard such teaching as a career, its centralised administrative structure, its control of the University's government by resident holders of University and College posts, and its progressive taxation of the Colleges for University purposes. The only important matter ducked at the time was the position of women in the University: in 1926 University teaching posts became open to women, but it was another generation before they became full members of the University in 1948.

This sketch of changes in the University of Cambridge in the 75 years after 1851 provides a backcloth against which we can place other strands of our story. It also, appropriately, spans the period between Neville Keynes's birth in 1852 and his retirement as University Registrary at the end of 1925. The end of the period of change also coincides with the end of Maynard Keynes's involvement in the central administration of the University, for he resigned from the Council of the Senate in February 1927 after having served during the whole period of post-1918 reform. The entire process of change had been slower than many had wished, and less radical, for in the end 'the revolution of the dons' (to use Rothblatt's phrase for the era of nineteenth-century reform) succeeded more in staffing the expanding professions and public life and in perpetuating amongst graduates a disdain for money-making, at least outside the City of London, than in providing the business world with graduates able to respond to the challenges faced by industry. Yet, the long process of reform, such as it was, would colour Maynard Keynes's view of the world. It was the product of argument amongst intelligent men who, in most cases, accepted the final result. It put a premium on persuasion and patient argument – tempered as readers of a classic contemporary guide to Cambridge academic politics will remember,[16] by certain skills and debating ploys that are still central to most academic discussions of the same subjects the world over. Patient argument and skilful persuasion, if not always the appropriate tactics, were to be an important part of Maynard Keynes's success.

Maynard was a child of reforming Cambridge. Neville and Florence Keynes, aged 31 and 22 respectively in 1883, had both been beneficiaries of the early reforms. Neville Keynes would never have been a fellow of Pembroke between 1876 and 1882 without the 1871 removal of the religious tests. Florence Keynes, an early student at Newnham, had been one of the first beneficiaries of the movement to increase the educational opportunities available to women.

Neville Keynes was one of the earliest fellows of the Cambridge Colleges to put himself under the 1882 statutes which allowed fellows to marry. Ironically, by putting himself under these statutes Neville Keynes ceased to be a Fellow of Pembroke as surely as he would have under the old régime, for the statutes, unlike those made under the Act of 1856, limited the tenure of a fellowship to six years with no possibility of re-election. Of course, there were exceptions to the six-year limit of tenure at Pembroke. Fellows whose work two-thirds of the total fellowship agreed was 'College work of importance' could count each year of such work as only one-half year for the purposes of the limit on tenure. Periods spent in certain College offices in Pembroke – Principal Tutor, Principal Mathematical or Classical Lecturer, Dean, or Treasurer – also did not count as parts of the six years. Neville Keynes had been both Bursar and Steward of Pembroke, but as these offices were not specified in statutes and as he was told in May 1882 that the College was unable to declare him a 'half-timer' for his work, his fellowship lapsed on his declaration of intent to be under the 1882 statutes, six years and a day after his admission as a Fellow.[17]

The lapsing of his Pembroke fellowship did not end Neville Keynes's association with Cambridge. Although he had applied for the Chair of Political Economy at University College, London, which had become vacant on the resignation of William Stanley Jevons, he withdrew from the competition on being appointed Assistant Secretary to the Cambridge Local Examinations Syndicate, yet another product of earlier Cambridge reform. To his successors such a decision may seem odd. The London post only involved giving two lectures a week and the incumbent could hold other posts concurrently: the successful candidate after Neville's withdrawal, Herbert Somerton Foxwell, was to hold it concurrently with a fellowship at St John's College, Cambridge throughout almost all of his tenure of the chair, which ran to 1927.[d] However, Neville Keynes believed that the demands of his new Cambridge job would be too great for such pluralism and he was already engaged to be married. Moreover, the London chair did not pay well: Jevons regarded it as 'almost an honorary one, the Professor receiving only the fees of about £2.2s. from each student'. The number of students was so small that, even building up the numbers from the four of 1875–6, he reckoned that the post yielded only £70 per annum.[18] The post with the Examination Syndicate was much more remunerative. Moreover, in 1883, using the new powers available under its 1882 statutes, the University created a University Lectureship in Moral Sciences for Neville Keynes. He was to hold it until 1911.[e] With its stipend of £50 plus students' fees, the Cambridge lectureship yielded more than Jevons's chair! With his assistant secretaryship, his lectureship and fees from examining, he could count on an income of at least £500 per annum. Neville Keynes remained in Cambridge.

Bertrand Russell remembered Neville Keynes as 'an earnest Nonconformist who put morality first and logic second'.[19] Maynard Keynes portrayed his father at a lunch in King's in 1942 celebrating his ninetieth birthday and his diamond wedding anniversary as follows:

> I should like to imagine him as he was *before* I knew him. For this is the only way I can really see him really different from what he is now – and even so perhaps it is not really different, one never changes – elegant, mid-Victorian highbrow, reading Swinburne, Meredith, Ibsen, buying William Morris wall-paper, whiskered, modest and industrious, but rather rich, rather pleasure-loving, rather extravagant within carefully set limits, most generous, very sociable; loved entertaining, wine, games, novels, theatre, travel; but the shadows of work gradually growing, as migraine headaches set in a readiness to look on the more gloomy or depressing side of any prospect. And then his withdrawal, gradual, very gradual, to his dear wife and the bosom of his family, but just the same as before in his firm habits and buttoned shoes.[20]

Although as a schoolboy at Eton, Maynard Keynes would proudly construct a family tree that stretched back to the Keynes ancestor who had come over with William the Conqueror, by the time we get to Neville Keynes's immediate ancestors we find a Wiltshire Baptist family of brushmakers and ornamental plasterers. Neville Keynes was the only son of John Keynes of Salisbury and his second wife Anna Maynard Neville. John Keynes

d Foxwell did not hold both posts during the years 1899–1905 (*JMK*, X, 268, 276–7). As well, Foxwell was Newmarch Lecturer in Statistics in the University of London.
e His successor in the lectureship would be G. E. Moore.

had started work as an apprentice in his father's brush factory, which he eventually took over. He was a capable and successful businessman, but, after the death from cholera of his first wife, who bore him a daughter, he gave the business over to his brother and took up his long-standing hobby, horticulture, on a commercial scale. He was enormously successful with roses and dahlias and, with a keen eye for profit, developed a large trade in pot vines to keep his glasshouses fully utilised. John Keynes was substantially involved in the life of Salisbury in banking (his son was later to be a typically anxious sleeping partner in a syndicate at Lloyds of London), in Sunday school education and in local government. His election as mayor in 1876 was seconded by William Fawcett, the father of Alfred Marshall's immediate predecessor as Professor of Political Economy in Cambridge and Postmaster-General under Gladstone (1880–4). When John Keynes died in 1878 he left assets valued at over £40,000.

Neville Keynes was educated to rise beyond his father's commercial origins, first at a local dame school, then at a prep school at Poole, managed by relatives, and at Salisbury Cathedral School. In 1864, he went to Amersham Hall near Reading, where Ebenezer West, the headmaster, kept extremely high standards in part to offset the academic disabilities of non-conformity.[f] In 1869, aged 17, Neville Keynes entered University College, London with the Gilchrist Scholarship to University Hall, a residential hostel in Gordon Square. The purpose of his period at University College was straightforward: he was to do well enough in the relevant examinations to move on to Cambridge, a goal suggested by Henry Fawcett, whom he knew from Salisbury. Neville Keynes worked extremely hard, taking breaks only for Saturday evening visits to the theatre, a passion for which he had developed during visits to London with his father, tournament chess, where again his father had provided the initial stimulus, and occasional games of fives. In 1870 and 1871 he took both parts of his BA with first class honours, specialising in his Part II in logic and moral philosophy. He then started work for a London BSc, which he completed later while he was in Cambridge, where he had gained a place and a minor scholarship in mathematics at Pembroke after failing to get a place at Trinity Hall, Henry Fawcett's College.

Once in Cambridge, Neville Keynes almost immediately decided that the Mathematics Tripos was not for him. Perhaps it was the competition, for the Tripos still tended to attract the most able candidates, who were trained in daily sessions with coaches whose own incomes and reputations were dependent on Tripos results. Certainly Neville Keynes's own coach, Edward John Routh, the 'Wrangler maker' of the day and the best of his generation,

---

f West was succeeded as headmaster in 1876 by his son Alfred, who had been educated at University College, London and Trinity College, Cambridge. Alfred West, who was an examiner with Jevons and Foxwell for the Moral Sciences Tripos in 1875 when Neville Keynes was Senior Moralist, ran the school until it closed in 1892. While a schoolboy at Eton, Maynard would see Alfred West frequently, as well as visit his daughter at Slough.

would have made clear what success in the Tripos involved. Perhaps Neville Keynes reacted as he did because of the heavy work he had done at University College just to get into Cambridge. Whatever factors were at work, he felt out of his depth and by 19 October 1872, soon after the beginning of his first term, he was suggesting to his parents that it would be best if he left Cambridge at Christmas and finished his London BSc. After discussions with his parents, he agreed to stay the year, even though he did not think that he would do well enough in mathematics to reach fellowship standard. But he remained unhappy with mathematics, informing his tutor after his first term that he intended to switch to Moral Sciences, and only agreeing to stick with mathematics when he returned for his second term in January 1873 on the advice of his father, his tutor and Professor Fawcett. At the end of his first year, despite his continuing unhappiness and his work for his London BSc, he did well enough to win a foundation scholarship in mathematics at Pembroke. Yet, he had enough, and, despite further advice from Fawcett to persevere with mathematics, he switched to the Moral Sciences Tripos.[21]

The change in tripos was successful. He went to Henry Sidgwick for moral and political philosophy, Alfred Marshall for economics, H. S. Foxwell for psychology and John Venn for logic. Despite continuing his London BSc, playing chess for the University and 'spending an inordinate amount of time making up and solving chess problems',[22] when it came to his finals for the Tripos he 'was a very good first as expected', writing 'powerful' answers which Jevons several years later remembered reading with 'pleasure'.[23] All his examiners agreed that Pembroke should offer him a fellowship; some colleges immediately began sending him pupils. Earlier in the year, Fawcett had made enquiries at Pembroke which had led to the suggestion that if he were Senior Moralist there would be considerable support in College for his election to a fellowship, but that the gold medal in the University of London's MA examinations in moral sciences would 'materially assist' his election.[24] In fact, it was only after he had become Gold Medallist that the Pembroke fellowship offer materialised. He was also elected a fellow of University College, London.

The years following Neville Keynes's election to Pembroke saw him involved in the normal routines of college teaching and odd jobs. Although he was interested in both logic and political economy, the main demands on his teaching were for logic, his best paper in the Tripos and the one in which he had most impressed Jevons.[25] Alfred Marshall's departure to be Principal of University College, Bristol in 1877 did not change the situation, for Foxwell shifted his teaching to replace Marshall's, leaving Keynes to cover the lectures in formal logic. He did manage to do a little teaching in political economy in Pembroke and, between 1882 and Mary Marshall's return in 1885, he found a temporary niche teaching political economy in Newnham, but these were minor diversions. None the less, he maintained an interest in political economy. He was in demand by both Marshall and Sidgwick as an adviser. With Marshall's encouragement and assistance he tried unsuccessfully for the University's Cobden Prize (the successful essay by J. S. Nicholson was published as *The Effects of Machinery on Wages* (1878)). He even thought of publishing an elementary textbook on political economy, but, given Marshall's always obsessive concern over private property in ideas (especially his own), Neville Keynes got no further than to sign a contract.g In the end, his only publication from the period of his fellowship was 'On the Position of Formal Logic' which appeared in *Mind* in July 1879.h

Amongst Neville Keynes's Cambridge friends was Henry Bond with whom he had been at Amersham Hall and University College. Bond's father, William, was a successful Cambridge grocer, a keen Liberal politician and a local alderman. Amongst William's friends was John Brown, minister of Bunyan's Meeting, Bedford. When John Brown's daughter Florence came up to Newnham in October 1878, William Bond took a friendly interest in her and invited her to join the group of young people who regularly came to his house in Brookside. On her first visit to the house Florence Brown met Neville Keynes. Before she left Newnham in 1880 they were engaged.

Florence Brown's presence in Cambridge was also a result of the nineteenth-century educational reforms in Cambridge. Here the force at work was not the repeal of the religious tests, for women did not become full members of the University until 1948, but rather the University's attempt to raise standards in the schools – Neville Keynes's University concern after 1882 – and the movement for the higher education of women. The University established local examinations in 1858. In 1865, largely as a result of the efforts organised by Emily Davies, girls succeeded in gaining access to the Cambridge local examinations. Subsequently Emily Davies pressed for the opening of a women's college offering programmes of study along traditional Cambridge lines. The resulting foundation opened at Hitchin in 1869.

Concurrently a North of England Council for promoting the Higher Education of Women, which grew out of the extension lecture movement, pressed for a more substantial programme of lectures and a more sophisticated standard of examination for women than then available in local examinations, largely to supply the need for school teachers.

g See below p. 84. The classic case here is Marshall's testy reaction to a report that Keynes was helping Sidgwick with what would become his *Principles of Political Economy* (1883) and the possibility that Keynes might show Sidgwick his notes of Marshall's lectures. MLC, JNK Papers, I, 75, Marshall to JNK, undated, but as the letter also concerns Neville's standing for Jevons's chair at University College, it must date from the autumn of 1880, after Jevons had resigned the chair but before he had asked Jevons for a testimonial. See also Black (ed.) 1972–81, V, 116–17.

h This one publication, overlooked by Professor Skidelsky (1985), makes Neville Keynes seem prolific by the standard of the early Marshall (below p. 85) and the early Foxwell, whose first publication came at the end of his first decade as a Fellow of St John's.

Henry Sidgwick became involved. A Cambridge scheme for such higher examinations was approved in 1869, with men being admitted in 1875. The next stage was to organise lectures for these examinations in Cambridge in 1870. Provision of accommodation for those attending the lectures came a year later, when Sidgwick took and furnished a house in Cambridge for the purpose and persuaded Anne Clough, the focus of the North of England Council's efforts, to come and manage it. Amongst the first five students in Miss Clough's household was Mary Paley. She was at the forefront of the next stage in 1874 when, on Alfred Marshall's persuasion, she and another student as the result of an informal arrangement sat the papers for the Moral Sciences Tripos. Two of her examiners put her in the first class; two in the second. In 1875 she became the first resident lecturer under the Clough/Sidgwick scheme.

In the interim, Miss Davies' establishment had moved from Hitchin to Girton, a village near, yet suitably remote from the distractions of, Cambridge. The Clough/Sidgwick scheme also outgrew its original premises and moved twice before settling in Newnham, a western suburb of Cambridge in 1875. By the time that Florence Brown came to Cambridge, there were two institutions of higher education for women in Cambridge – Girton, which offered the normal tripos programme, and Newnham Hall, which offered instruction for the higher local examinations as well as the final tripos papers.

Like Neville Keynes, Florence Brown was the product of a dissenting Liberal background.[26] Her father, John Brown, was a minister, first in Manchester and then, from 1864 to 1903, in Bedford. He was chairman of the Congregational Union in 1891. John Brown was also a considerable scholar with several works of church history and the standard biography of Bunyan to his credit, as well as editor of the Cambridge University Press edition of Bunyan's works. In 1887 he received an honorary Doctorate of Divinity from Yale University. Florence's mother, Ada Haydon Ford, a child of the manse, whose father, grandfather and uncle had all been clerics, also inherited from her grandmother and aunt a tradition of work in education. Bedford was noted for its educational provisions for boys but was deficient in those for girls. Ada Brown found herself running a school for her own six children and others in the manse in Dame Alice Street, using masters from the local boys' schools to supplement her teaching in special subjects. The teaching she provided seems to have been good: the school was profitable and expanded, and Florence Brown's own results in the Cambridge local examinations won her an exhibition, or minor scholarship to Newnham. There she prepared for the Cambridge higher local examinations rather than the tripos, largely it seems because there were not the means to give her the time in Cambridge necessary for the latter. However, there were sufficient means available to send her off to Germany for the gap between her locals and her coming up to Cambridge, in order that she could improve her languages.

This experience was successful: not only did it give her sufficient skills to assist her father when he needed to know German theologians' views on particular points and her future husband when he too needed to know of recent German scholarship in preparing his own publications, but it also gave her sufficient appreciation of things German to want to expose her children to the same influences through the employment of a German governess at Harvey Road and, in the cases of Maynard's sister and brother, similar extended stays in Germany.

Dame Alice Street, Bedford, was certainly more austere and probably more earnest than Castle Street, Salisbury. There were more mouths to be fed on much less, with inevitable sacrifices in other areas, save education. Here was a world where one coped with the cold with minimal heating and no eiderdowns or hot water bottles. Activities were more purposive: even 'recreation was kept in its place as a preparation for further efforts' – scholarly, spiritual or social.[27] There was the aura of community service that went with the house and the job. Yet, despite the austerity and purposiveness of the manse, in many respects life was probably more easygoing. There were more children. Certainly Florence Brown was not subject to many of the pressures which afflicted Neville Keynes. There was not the pressure to excel academically, almost irrespective of cost. Nor were there the related anxieties.

Anxieties clouded Florence's and Neville's engagement. There was the question of Neville Keynes's career as Assistant Secretary of the Local Examinations Syndicate after the end of his Pembroke fellowship, a safe but unexciting decision, although it is far from clear that if he had not withdrawn his application for Jevons's chair at University College he would have got the post that went to Foxwell.[i] Then there was the question of his and Florence's relationship with his recently widowed mother, also an only child, who seems to have had no serious outside interests other than her son. There was also the adjustment to the world of Dame Alice Street. Neville Keynes's diaries suggest that it was all very difficult. However, the couple survived and were married in Bedford by John Brown on 15 August 1882. A month's holiday in Switzerland followed. When the couple returned to Cambridge, they stayed with the Bonds in Brookside while waiting for the completion of 6 Harvey Road. It was 11 November before they slept there for the first time. By then Florence knew she was pregnant and she had informed her family of the prospect.

In the background to Maynard's early childhood was the recurring question of Neville Keynes's ultimate career. Thus far he had opted for administration with a modicum of teaching, eventually as University Lecturer in Moral

i It is true that Marshall gave Neville Keynes's application glowing support, but Jevons himself later suggested that Foxwell dominated the list of candidates from the beginning (Black (ed.) 1972–81, V, 136–7).

Sciences. He also retained contact with University College, London as an examiner, first for scholarships and then in political economy where Jevons supported his appointment.[28] Yet there was always the lurking question of whether he was doing the right thing. Alfred Marshall had his doubts. As he put it in 1891 when Neville Keynes became Secretary to the Local Examinations Syndicate: 'I never felt quite sure that the work [at the Syndicate] was the right thing for you; but I was always certain that you were the right man for the work'.[29]

Throughout the 1880s Marshall kept pressing Neville Keynes to take a more active role in the wider world of economics, even though it was his own return to Cambridge that had effectively eliminated whatever interesting teaching opportunities Neville Keynes might have had in this area. In part this was a reflection of his respect for Neville Keynes's abilities: it was Keynes whom Marshall regarded as one of the attractions of Cambridge and Neville Keynes whom he used most intensively as a critic for his *Principles of Economics*.[30] Yet Marshall, and his normal supporters such as Foxwell, had an agenda for economics in Britain and it was not surprising that he tried to fit Neville Keynes into it. When taking the Cambridge chair left his fellowship open at Balliol College, Oxford, Marshall, with visits, letters and telegrams, pressed Neville Keynes to take it, using persuasive flattery, appeals in the name of science and the prospect of eventually becoming Drummond Professor of Political Economy. Neville Keynes did not rise to the bait, much to Sidgwick's relief,[j] although he agreed to go over one day a week for a term to lecture on 'The Methods of Political Economy', the intended subject for his next book. Initially he did not believe that his chances of success at Oxford warranted his giving up his Cambridge job. The experience of Oxford did not make him any more enthusiastic. Marshall tried again in 1888 when Bonamy Price, the Drummond Professor, died. He realised that Neville Keynes's chances were uncertain – so uncertain that one recent scholar has read one of his letters as an attempt to *dissuade* Neville Keynes from standing – largely because he had published nothing in the field, although his book on method was in part in proof, but his support for Neville's application was echoed by Florence Keynes's father, Henry Sidgwick and James Ward.[31] Yet Cambridge opinion was not unanimous in its support for the application. Foxwell, while accepting that the appointment would be good for Oxford, urged otherwise.

> Pray don't go. It is much better that a study should be concentrated in a particular place. There are many of the same advantages as in the localisation of industry. Your departure would leave a nasty ragged wound in our Moral Sciences organisation.

j The best Sidgwick could say about Oxford was that the post 'seemed to offer great opportunities, though of a rather indefinite kind' (CUL, Add.7562/25, Sidgwick to JNK, 13 January 1885).

What is the use of your being a settled family man if you are to drift from your moorings in this fashion! Think of the effect your move may have on your son. He may grow up flippantly epigrammatical, tend to becoming the proprietor of a Gutter Gazette or the hero of a popular party: instead of emulating his father's noble example, becoming a clear-headed Cambridge man, spending his life in valuable and unpretentious service to his kind, dying beloved of his friends, venerated of the wise and as unknown to the masses as true merit and worth mostly are. Let me as earnestly as a bachelor can, appeal to your feelings as a father. Can you hesitate?[32]

In the end, Neville Keynes put in for the job, but as Marshall had predicted, Thorold Rogers was the successful candidate. When Rogers died in October 1890, Neville Keynes was not a candidate. Nor was he pressed to be one. Then Marshall's support went to F. Y. Edgeworth, who was successful.

Nor was the pressure on Neville Keynes only to take posts in Oxford. In 1883 Foxwell tried with success to get him to be secretary to Section F of the British Association for the Advancement of Science.[33] Two years later Foxwell was trying to get him to read a paper to the Association – this time without success.[34] In both cases his grounds were that Neville Keynes's contribution would raise the quality of economics in the Association, where as late as 1878 there had been the suggestion that economics be abandoned as a subject for discussion because it was not a 'science'. Then in 1888, in the same letter in which he reported Thorold Rogers' election to the Oxford chair, Marshall tried to persuade Neville Keynes to act as editor of the projected professional journal of the British Economic Association with the plea, 'you are the right man for the work, and it is very important work'.[35] Foxwell had already raised the matter two months earlier in his letter which attempted to dissuade Neville Keynes from applying for the Oxford chair. Both men failed in their attempt. Marshall tried again a year later with the plea *'Everyone* would *very much* prefer you' over the other candidates, F. Y. Edgeworth and L. L. Price, but to no avail.[36] Instead the editorship of what became the *Economic Journal* went to Edgeworth in Oxford. Edgeworth retained the job until the end of 1911, when it passed to Maynard Keynes.

The *Economic Journal* episode marked the end of Marshall's attempts to push Neville Keynes towards jobs related to his efforts to establish the hegemony of his vision of economics. Others still tried. As late as 1894 the University of Chicago offered him a chair, but he was 'far too rooted in Cambridge' to move, noting in a sentence crossed out on his copy 'I feel I am settled here for life'.[37] And so he was.

Before he finally settled into administration in Cambridge, a move symbolised by his election to the University's Council of the Senate in November 1892 and his becoming Secretary to the Council in April

1893, Neville Keynes would produce two books and several contributions to Palgrave's *Dictionary of Political Economy* (1894–9). The first book *Studies and Exercises in Formal Logic* (1884, 4th edn 1906) grew out of his Cambridge teaching. It was, according to C. D. Broad, 'an extremely good book, far and away the best which exists in English on the old fashioned formal logic and its development in the nineteenth century'.[38] Wittgenstein's recent biographer has noted that it is 'still one of the best and most technical expositions of syllogistic logic'.[39] John Passmore notes that 'It is easy to underestimate Keynes's originality and ingenuity'.[40] Despite the fact that it soon became a standard textbook, and remained in print until after 1945, unlike most texts it became the starting point for further work, notably by W. E. Johnson, a Harvey Road neighbour who was later a fellow of King's. Johnson's work led on to that of G. E. Moore, Bertrand Russell and Maynard Keynes.

Neville Keynes's second book, *The Scope and Method of Political Economy* (1891, 4th edn 1917) was an outgrowth of his Oxford lectures. In fact he had picked the topic for his lectures with the 'idea of writing a small book on the subject. This will be my work during the long vacation'.[41] It took more than one long vacation: he was not through with the manuscript until late in 1890. Part of the reason for the delay came from his other commitments, including his agreeing to read the full proofs of Marshall's *Principles of Economics*.[42] Yet the major reason was that Marshall was himself less than happy with the results of Keynes's efforts. The problem was not that Marshall did not think the book good: even when criticising an early draft and suggesting the complete re-writing that sent Florence to brush up her German so that Neville Keynes could be better informed of the details of the *Methodenstreit*, he remarked, 'I have no doubt that the book will be the best on the subject, and will have a large circulation even if you bring it out as it is'.[43] Rather he thought that the book could be better. But 'making things better' for Marshall, the tireless tinkerer with his own *Principles of Economics*, was a very trying business. The position was complicated by the fact that Marshall was basically uninterested in what he called 'philosophical economics'.[44] He was unhappy, as he said repeatedly, with Neville Keynes's sharp distinctions and attempts at classification, and tried to blur them wherever possible. Neville's volume, despite its apparent even-handedness, was 'a subtly disguised attempt to vindicate the abstract-deductive view of economics',[45] a fact picked up by supporters such as Edgeworth and critics such as L. H. Phelps of the rival Oxford school. Marshall, on the other hand, if ultimately pressed, would put himself much closer to the inductivists. As he told Foxwell, '[A]s regards method I regard myself mid-way between Keynes + Sidgwick + Cairnes and Schmoller + Ashley'.[46] No wonder Neville Keynes had so much difficulty satisfying Marshall!

Yet Keynes's *Scope and Method* became a classic. As Joseph Schumpeter put it:

> Keynes settled most of these methodological issues in a spirit of judicial reasonableness and to the satisfaction of the profession. For two decades this book held a well-earned position of authority. Its perusal may be recommended even at this distance of time because of its merits as well as of its success.[47]

Yet success had its price: soon the book was not read, even in Cambridge. Dennis Robertson, speaking of methodology, later remembered:

> This is a topic which, when I started to read economics at Cambridge in 1910, was not, I think, fashionable among us to think much about – less fashionable, I dare say, than it may have been a few years previously, when the separate courses in economics had not yet been extracted like Eve from the ribs of the Moral Science[s] Tripos. To us, I think, it seemed a topic more suitable for discussions by Germans than by Englishmen. There was on our reading list what I have since come to regard as a good, if dry, book on it, J. N. Keynes's *Scope and Method of Political Economy*, but to be quite honest I doubt if many of us read it. We thought we knew pretty well what sort of things we wanted to know about.[48]

Neville Keynes then withdrew from active research. He did so with something of a reputation, as shown by the ScD he received from his own University in 1891, the invitation, declined as usual, to became President of Section F of the British Association in 1895 and the offer, also declined, of an honorary degree by Princeton in 1896.[49] Now, except for the occasional pieces such as the article on Jevons in the *Encyclopaedia Britannica* of 1911, he was caught up in the web of committees, boards and syndicates that were, and are, along with teaching and research, a part of Cambridge life.

As Neville Keynes was moving into his administrative career and becoming more and more indifferent to 'strenuous intellectual activity in general, to economics, to the future of Cambridge economics, to economics students and above all to the professor of economics',[50] he took more refuge from the world in the activities of his growing family. At the same time, Florence Keynes was moving out of the home and into the world of voluntary work and social services. This movement was at first a case of taking classes and addressing mothers' meetings, but she soon became heavily involved in more organised affairs. By 1890 she had joined the Cambridge Association for the Care of Girls, the local branch of the National Association for Physical Education and Improvement and the local Charity Organisation Society which, under Sidgwick's leadership, had evolved from a much older Mendicity Society in 1879. In the years after 1890 she became more involved in these sorts of organisations and began to assume positions of responsibility, first in 1895 as secretary of the Charity Organisation Society and, later, more generally, as a member of the Board of Guardians and, after she had helped change the legislation in 1914 to allow non-householders to stand, a town councillor. She became an alderman and in 1932–3 Cambridge's first woman mayor. Nationally she was President of the National Council of Women in 1930–1.

This was the pattern of his parents' lives outside 6 Harvey Road during Maynard's early years. Inside that three-storied structure of dull, yellowish brick, or 'corpse brick' as the children called it, life was comfortable but, despite Neville Keynes's upper-middle-class income of well over £1,000 per annum from his various posts plus his inheritance, hardly grand. For one thing, with three living-in servants and, later, a governess for the children, plus extra help during Florence Keynes's confinements, it was rather crowded. The house was solidly furnished: many of the original items, including the blue and crimson William Morris wallpaper in the dining room, were still in good condition when Florence Keynes died in 1958. Amidst the solidity, there were some family photographs and prints, but the latter were the conventional ones common to Victorians of their class. There were also some oils that had come to Neville Keynes from his family home in Salisbury, but apart from one modest Moreland these did not alter the overall aesthetic tone of uninteresting conventionality. This was not surprising, given Neville's tastes. In May 1893, after a visit to an exhibition of the British Art Club which, according to his account, included works by Sickert, Claude, Monet and Dégas, he remarked that it was 'Quite the funniest thing I have seen for many a long day'.[51]

If 6 Harvey Road was to offer little aesthetic stimulus to its younger inhabitants, it was to compensate in other ways. Most important were books. Neville and Florence Keynes were avid readers, a habit they passed to their children. The adults' reading ranged widely through the classics of Victorian literature to contemporary potboilers and on to such moderns as Ibsen and Olive Schreiner. Neville Keynes's reactions to the moderns were in some ways predictable: *A Doll's House* – 'impossible to justify Nora's desertion'; *The Wild Duck* – 'annoys me';[52] *Rosmersholm* – a very unpleasant story but . . . the most powerful of Ibsen's plays I have yet read';[53] *The Story of an African Farm* – 'repellant as well as extremely crude'.[54] Yet he kept reading such material: he read four plays of Ibsen in a two-month period in 1890 and another in 1891. Although problem plays such as Ibsen's enjoyed some vogue in London, with George Bernard Shaw as their principal publicist, after the success of *A Doll's House* in 1889, many of the plays had not been performed in England. *Ghosts*, which Neville Keynes read in 1890, did not receive a licence from the Lord Chamberlain until July 1914.[55] Probably he persevered because of his love for the theatre. He passed his enthusiasm on to Maynard, who saw his first live performance in November

1891 and went regularly soon afterwards.[k] One of Maynard's favourite toys was a model theatre which provided hours of enjoyment. Finally there was the stimulus of conversation. Amongst the regular visitors to Harvey Road was W. E. Johnson, Neville Keynes's younger logician colleague of whom Maynard would later write:

> Indeed, conversation discussion was his greatest gift; the sweetness of his disposition joined to the subtlety of his mind to make possible the half-social, half-argumentative intercourse which must always be the best means of promoting philosophy.[56]

Other regular Cambridge callers included James Ward, the philosopher and psychologist, Foxwell, who became a neighbour in Harvey Road when he married in 1898, and Sidgwick. Marshall made business calls, but he was not on the Keynes's guest list for entertaining in the period of more than 30 years covered by Neville Keynes's diaries. There were visitors who came often to Cambridge for examinations or meetings – Phillip Wicksteed, Robert Giffen, Inglis Palgrave, and J. S. Nicholson – not to mention the neighbours, for as one might expect Harvey Road was largely populated by youngish dons and their growing families.

Inevitably, the Keyneses were serious about their hobbies. We need only remember that John Keynes had made a spectacular commercial success of his love of gardening. In Neville Keynes's case, he had been a very serious chess player before marriage and, although not good at games, enjoyed his tennis. After 1882 there were the activities of Harvey Road, whose residents shared tennis courts and quickly formed book and whist clubs. Neville Keynes's growing family brought more hobbies which also served as a source of companionship between him and his sons.

In February 1887 Neville Keynes noticed that Maynard was quite interested in his old childhood stamp collection. A month later Neville Keynes started to take up the hobby again – and did so with a passion that grew over the years and would cause his sons to worry in the 1940s whether their father's enthusiasm for stamps would impair his finances.[57] In the 1880s and 1890s this enthusiasm had not reached such a pitch and collecting was a family affair. As each child grew old enough, he or she would receive a stamp album which became a refuge for Neville's duplicates. As Florence Keynes later recalled:

> It was his custom every Sunday morning to lay on the study table a pile of stamps, castouts from his own [collection], and each child in turn would choose one until the stamps were exhausted. Armed with a catalogue they studied the values carefully and chose accordingly. In this way they learnt how to use a catalogue and acquired a considerable knowledge of other countries.[58]

k Maynard's list of theatres and plays seen between 14 January 1894 and 13 July 1898 runs to 37 productions.

Maynard also found the job of counting his father's stamps a source of pocket money and found in stamps a point of contact with boys his own age.[59] With his second son, Neville Keynes found himself with another hobby, entomology. The result was a vast joint collection, housed in cases specially constructed to Neville Keynes's specifications, which now rests in the Museum of Zoology in Cambridge. Neville and Geoffrey initially confined themselves to England and Wales, but in the seven years after 1905 butterflies became an excuse for regular expeditions to Switzerland, the Pyrenees, Hungary and the Austrian Tyrol, with the results recorded in *The Entomologists Record and Journal of Variations* for the benefit of others.[60] In the 1890s Neville Keynes also discovered golf, which he took to with his customary thoroughness. He succeeded in introducing Maynard to the game, which the latter played for over a decade, despite the fact that, according to C. R. Fay, he was one of the world's worst players.[61] Neville Keynes's diaries became full of games on the courses at Royston and the Gog Magog Hills and golf holidays with Maynard at Sheringham on the Norfolk coast, as well as careful statistical records of his and Maynard's scores, suitably smoothed with the use of moving averages to catch any indications of emerging trends. Both Maynard and Geoffrey were to take over their father's tendency to take their hobbies seriously: one need only think of their book collecting. Others will emerge.

Almost all of what we know of Maynard's development before he went to Eton in September 1897 comes from Neville Keynes's records, particularly his diaries. Neville was a compulsive record-keeper, recording not only day-to-day events but also letters received, hours worked (both at academic and administrative tasks), golf scores, his children's heights and weights, his annual income, savings and securities valuations. He was to pass this habit on to Maynard, who, although he only kept diaries briefly during 1894–6 and during his last seven terms at Eton – and a very patchy one towards the end – provided his potential biographers with a wealth of lists and accounts, at least one of which would have shocked his father. Neville Keynes's diaries and other records, as well as providing information, also present problems which the reader should keep in the back of the mind in the pages which follow. They are, after all, Neville Keynes's own record of his world, his thoughts, his hopes and his anxieties, not his elder son's. When they present, as they do, a much more complete chronicle of Maynard's development than of Geoffrey's, we may be getting a reflection of the relative strength of his feelings for his sons or a reflection of the process by which parents learn the ropes of their new role through their first child, especially when, as in Neville Keynes's case, they had no experience of younger siblings. Similarly, when we see that Neville Keynes records in his diary Maynard's greater attachment to his mother over a period of years, we may, while taking the remarks at

21

face value, at least allow for his own hopes for his relationship with his son, perhaps in the light of his own relationship with his parents. We must also allow for the fact that, over time, the nature of Neville Keynes's diaries may have changed. Certainly by the late 1890s the diaries had become, to some extent, 'public' documents, for at least once during the period when Maynard kept his own diary he used his father's as an aid to writing up his own. Thus on 29 August 1900 he remarked, 'I have spent the evening writing up this diary with the help of father's. I had got an unheard amount behindhand'. All that Maynard may have seen was his father's small, separate holiday diary for that year, but it does raise the question of the diaries' consistent reflection of events and reactions. The question is also raised by the fact that, although the diaries run to the end of 1917, when they stop for some unaccountable reason, Neville Keynes's entries become much more laconic as he got older. All of this suggests that authors or readers should not read too much about Maynard into any entry or series of entries.

Although Neville Keynes had hoped for a daughter, he soon got over his disappointment and was besotted with his son.[62] The child was named John Maynard – John following his father, grandfather and great grandfather on the Keynes side, as well as his grandfather Brown, Maynard after his grandmother and great aunt – and Neville quickly decided to call him Maynard, although Florence maintained a preference for John which lingered in her correspondence until the turn of the century. Soon after birth, he was found to be tongue-tied, something easily corrected. Traces of a lisp remained, despite his parents' best efforts to correct it, as did traces of a childhood tendency to stammer, especially when excited.

As a child, and well into his youth, if we can judge by the evidence available, – and this was still an age when each illness was potentially more serious than is now the case – Maynard was rather sickly and prone to illnesses. Some of this reflected the relatively common diseases of childhood – measles, chicken pox, whooping cough and the like. But Maynard seems to have been excessively prone to colds and attacks of liverishness, so much so that he seemed to Neville Keynes to be sufficiently underweight for his age to merit the nickname 'the little shrimp'. Part of this tendency to be 'below par' so often may, at times, have had psychological causes, for he always seemed to be so at the time of events that might be important for his future such as a set of examinations or first going to Eton. These problems may, of course, simply reflect the exhaustion from overwork before such occasions, but Florence Keynes believed that Maynard's illnesses on occasion reflected Neville Keynes's own anxieties in such circumstances.[63] Neville Keynes was always inclined to fear for the worst on every possible occasion and accordingly to discuss contingency plans. Beyond such runs of illness, whatever their origins, during his childhood Maynard at least avoided serious accidents – with one exception. This occurred a week after his thirteenth birthday when he had received his first bicycle from his grandmother Keynes. As he rushed out of the bottom of the then tranquil Harvey Road into the much busier Hills Road, he collided with a hansom cab. The collision threw him against the wheel of the cab, cutting his forehead badly, and the wheel went over the end of the little finger of his right hand. The bone was not crushed, but the finger was permanently deformed. This deformity, perhaps, lay behind his fascination with other people's hands, first recorded two years later when he reported to his father after meeting George Darwin on his way back to Eton: 'I had a short conversation with Prof. Darwin at the end of the journey. His hands certainly look as if he might be descended from an ape'.[64] This fascination continued through his descriptions of Clemenceau and Wilson at the meetings of the Council of Three in Paris in 1919 to the 1930s, when he would report to Lydia that he was impressed by W. H. Auden despite his fingernails.[65] Characteristically, later in life Maynard in meetings would keep his own hands hidden in the opposite sleeves of his jackets, which were specially designed for the purpose.[66]

During his childhood, Maynard's relations with both his parents seem to have been close, even if for a long period it seemed to Neville Keynes that he was closer to his mother. References to this in Neville Keynes's diaries begin as early as March 1884, when he noted, 'Now he treats his mother with special affection'.[67] They continued through the period when Maynard posed a disciplinary problem for Neville, the somewhat unwilling family disciplinarian.[68] Amidst reports of Maynard being 'often self-willed and not ready to obey' and so 'lacking in self-control' and his being smacked, slapped, or even whipped as a consequence, came reports such as 'Mummy asked to kiss the place where Papa hit him' and 'Mummy spoils me. 'Oo don't do 'oo?', as well as a note from Florence, then visiting in Hastings, 'I do not think I should have let you whip him husb., if I had been at home'.[69] Even when Maynard began to succumb to reason and punishments became less frequent, Neville Keynes found that 'an appeal to Maynard's love for his Mother will sometimes avail when other appeals fail'.[70] Apart from instances of disciplinary problems, Neville Keynes's diaries contain Maynard's repeated comparisons of his two parents to his father's disadvantage.[71] Yet as the diaries moved into the 1890s, such references became less frequent and eventually disappeared. By then, Neville Keynes and Maynard were coming to have more and more in common – interests in stamps, in backgammon and chess (and later kriegspiel and golf), in the theatre and reading. They seem to have enjoyed being together. After a whole day indoors in his study Neville reported, 'Maynard and I confided to each other how much we enjoy a day of this kind'.[72] Maynard's impending departure for Eton brought Neville Keynes's feelings out more strongly:

I miss Maynard very much, It is not merely the stamping but altogether. I suppose after this summer I shall never again have the dear boy so much with me as in the past.[73]

Like almost all children, Maynard was imitative, thus giving Neville Keynes chances to report in 1886.

Maynard is fond of coming down while I am having tea to 'tidy' my study. It is tidying with a vengeance.

I think I am fonder than ever of our darling little son. He has appropriated one of the cupboards in the breakfast room for his own collection of circulars, old envelopes, etc. To that cupboard he frequently betakes himself to 'ork (that is work).[74]

A year later he was copying his father's habit of writing notes to himself on scraps of paper, and, soon afterwards, attired in Neville's gown he began giving lectures which discussed, among other things, his mother's morning, the servants and pin-making.[75] Doubtless imitation played its part in the following 1888 incident as well:

This morning after breakfast Wicksteed and I were talking together. Presently Maynard breaks in with – 'I *cannot* do my lessons with all this talking going on.'[76]

It is clear from Neville's diary that as a child Maynard was quite quick on his feet. Harrod's biography provides a few examples, but others abound in Neville Keynes's diaries, suggesting that the phenomenon was not merely random.

Maynard is very anxious to see a hen lay an egg. I told him I have never seen that operation performed. 'Then how', said he, 'do you know that they lay eggs at all?'

One day last week when Florence and Maynard were leaving Geoffer boy [Geoffrey] in the nursery and he began to cry, Maynard said cheerfully – 'Never mind, he'll forget it in a minute. He doesn't keep things long': and then he added reflectively, 'I don't either.'

Maynard has a little cold, and I tell him he must put on his overcoat when he goes out. He doesn't want to, and of course has a reason ready: 'My cold is in my nose and of course my coat doesn't go over my nose.[77]

I can conclude with Maynard's first recorded conversation with W.E. Johnson.

In the nursery a day or two ago Alice heard Maynard arguing with Margaret and reducing her to tears by proving that she was a *thing*.

She wouldn't like to be nothing, he said, and if she weren't nothing she must be something, and if she was something she must be a thing.

We were telling this story in Maynard's presence to W. E. Johnson, who tried to puzzle him – 'You call Margaret a thing. But can things talk? Is a table a thing?'

'Yes.'

'Well it can't talk and Margaret can talk.'

The answer was ready in a moment.

'*Some* things can't talk, but *some* things *can* talk.'

– with emphasis on the words I have underlined.[78]

In January 1889 Maynard began his formal education. At home he had already been taught his letters and some arithmetic. Indeed, so much had gone on at home that in May 1888 he was complaining to his father that he didn't have time to play.[79] His first school was the kindergarten of the Perse School for Girls. He seems to have enjoyed it and adapted well, despite frequent absences for illness – he missed 21 days in his first term. His first report noted that he showed 'promise in mental work', but was 'somewhat slow in manual occupations'.[80] Joined by his sister in June 1889, he remained in the kindergarten until January 1891, when his mother brought him home for lessons, at first from herself and subsequently from a governess, Beatrice Mackintosh. Neville Keynes reported him delighted with the new arrangements, perhaps because, although he had made good progress in his reading and arithmetic at the Perse, the new arrangements were more stimulating and demanding.[81] By the end of the year, his reading had developed considerably; he had discovered the pleasures of reading poetry aloud and was even composing his own verses for the family's Christmas games.

In January 1892 he began preparatory school as a day boy at St Faith's in Cambridge where Ralph Goodchild was headmaster. Although he was far younger than the rest of the class, he seems to have adapted well, although, perhaps naturally, he preferred to watch rather than take part in games. By 14 March he was 'greatly rejoiced because he is no longer bottom in his class' and he didn't seem to mind being 'douse[d] . . . well with Latin'. He did not seem to find the work difficult and on seeing some of his examination papers (he was, again, ill at home) Neville Keynes thought it 'clear that he is very much more advanced than I was at his age'.[82] His first school report in April 1892 commented:

> [H]e has done fairly well for his first term; he is careless with his writing and spelling, and candidly assured me one day, when I pulled him up for an untidy lapse, that he had not been trying that morning.[83]

In his second term, as well as beginning cricket, for which, as is perhaps inevitable for a small boy with the University Cricket Ground at the end

25

VISTA

of his street, he would develop a fascination, he went to the top of his class for the first time and, despite his comparative youth ended up second in the class for term work and third in the examinations. Characteristically, Neville Keynes insisted that he got questions on something other than the Church of England catechism for his divinity examination.[84]

Although there are no reports of Maynard's particular friends at St Faith's, it is probable that he had some. F. H. Smith, whose father had come to live at 8 Harvey Road when he became vicar of St Andrew's, recalled becoming friendly with Maynard while walking to school and often calling in on Grandma Keynes in Bateman Street on the way home. Maynard mentioned Smith several times in the fragmentary diary he kept between November 1894 and April 1896. There are reports of the boys trading stamps at school, of Maynard having 'a slave' who walked behind him carrying his books in return for help and protection, and of a 'commercial treaty' with another boy, who in return for books from a local lending library placed on a convenient letterbox, agreed never to approach within 15 yards of Maynard. Later, after walking home to Harvey Road in the snow, he would remember in similar conditions in his childhood 'how I feared someone would start a snowball fight, oh I hated the idea of snowballing, never being robustious enough for that'. There were also the children living in Harvey Road – about thirty according to Margaret Keynes – as contemporaries for the three Keynes children. Life was not dull or lonely, although Maynard, as one of the eldest in the road, must have had fewer contemporaries than Geoffrey and Margaret. In all probability his closest friend at this period was his uncle, Kenneth Brown, who was four years his senior.[85]

Maynard's second year with Mr Goodchild was a continuation of the first. In the autumn term of 1892 he went into school for evening preparation and, perhaps as a result, came second in his class and first in his term work. However, the next term Neville Keynes started to worry:

> Maynard is being pushed on rather too rapidly. He has work that he does not really understand, and without Florence's assistance would hardly be able to do anything with his homework.
>
> Quadratic Equations and a fairly long piece of Latin Prose for a boy of nine.[86]

Yet only a fortnight earlier the family had started French lessons for the children! Later in February, after Maynard had been away from school with a rash, his parents arranged that he should have no homework or evening preparation at all. Without this he fell to seventh in the class, but Goodchild noted that although he was 'far too untidy on paper' he 'promises to excel'. The worries about Maynard's being overworked continued the next term. By the end of April, he had finished Book I of Euclid, was continuing quadratics, doing Ovid and continuous prose in Latin and 'Samson Agonistes' in English, and about to start Greek. As a result of the worries, Florence Keynes had Maynard medically examined for signs of overwork, with no result, and considered taking him out of school for a term, but nothing happened for the moment beyond postponing his starting Greek. Yet the term was so broken by illness that Maynard was unable 'to appear in his true colours' in the final results and his parents agreed to remove him from St Faith's for the next term and instead try his Grandmother Brown's school in Bedford.[87]

Although Neville Keynes may have had occasional doubts, the term at Bedford seems to have been a success, for on his return to St Faith's in January 1894 Maynard surged to the top of his class 'with so little effort'. He remained there for the rest of his time at the school. From this time onwards, his flair for mathematics, which Goodchild had spotted earlier, began to show itself. He began to get special teaching in mathematics from a former Wrangler for two hours a day, four days a week, and, despite the usual reports of carelessness and lack of thoroughness, his school reports became more encouraging. Even the family's addition of Hedwig Rotmann, the first of two German governesses, with the ensuing extra language lessons made no difference. By the end of 1895, Mr Goodchild was beginning to speak of Maynard as one of the cleverest boys he had ever taught. Later his praises would become even more fulsome.[88]

With Maynard's successes at St Faith's and his approaching his teens, his parents began to consider the next step in his educational career. Initially Mr Goodchild favoured Tonbridge, but Maynard's parents favoured a larger school. Eton was the one most frequently mentioned in Neville's diaries, along with Mr Goodchild's rearguard attempts to dampen their enthusiasm by questioning its suitability for someone with Maynard's apparent talents in mathematics. As the time for a final decision approached, Neville Keynes began to worry. In the end, as the Eton entrance examinations occurred at the same time as those for Winchester, the other large-school alternative, the decision proved easier than expected and Neville Keynes entered Maynard for the Eton examinations.[89]

The preparations began in earnest. Neville Keynes engaged special tutors, including Robert Walter Shackle, a leading coach for the Mathematics Tripos who was later the father of the economist G. L. S. Shackle and the civil servant R. J. Shackle. On 2 June, Neville reported:

Maynard and I are now getting up at 7 o/c every morning and doing some work before breakfast in order to accustom him to what he will have to do in the Eton Scholarship Exam.

The régime of tutors and early rising continued for a month until Maynard was allowed to take it easy in the final week before the examinations started on 6 July. By then Neville Keynes was becoming nostalgic:

It is a grief to me to think that the dear boy will not in any case do his work very much longer with me in the study. I like to see his books arranged opposite me; and I like all his little ways.

By then Neville Keynes's usual anxieties had taken over and he was 'in a fearful state of worry'. Florence Keynes, who was 'more philosophical', was concerned lest Neville's worries made Maynard too nervous. The three left for Eton on 5 July.[90]

The examinations themselves took place over three days, starting on 6 July, with papers from 7 to 9, 10.30 to 12.30 and 3 to 5 on the first two days and from 7 to 9 and 10.30 to 1 on the third. The subjects covered were (in order) Latin composition, Latin translation, easy mathematics, Greek grammar, harder mathematics, Greek translation, Latin verse and a general paper. At the time, things seemed to go reasonably well, probably better than Neville expected, but then came the inevitable waiting for and worrying about the results. Neville Keynes's anxieties were fuelled by a conversation with Mr Goodchild, who had seen all the papers and reported 'Maynard has not done himself justice on any paper, but there is hope' and by his failure to get any indication of the situation, other than the fact that the examiners had held their meeting, from the Vice Chancellor of the University who was one of Maynard's examiners. Then came the day, 12 July, when a telegram with the results was expected between 2 and 3 p.m. It did not come and there was 'despair' at 6 Harvey Road. When it did arrive at 5.30 p.m., Neville Keynes was deep in *The Public Schools Yearbook* and wondering whether Maynard should next try for Rugby or Tonbridge. In the event, the worry was unnecessary, for Maynard had been elected 10th King's Scholar. His mathematics, where he had been bracketed first, had been the key to his selection, according to the Provost of King's, another examiner. In celebration he was allowed to join the guests for dessert at his parents' next dinner party on 15 July.[91]

In the three weeks that followed before the family went off for its summer holiday at Leigh near Bude in Devon, the family made preparations for Eton. After failing to get Lionel Ford or H. J. Bowlby to act as Maynard's classical tutor or 'master responsible for his general intellectual culture and academic progress', Neville Keynes took advice in King's and persuaded Samuel Gurney Lubbock, who had taken a first in Part II of the Classical Tripos in 1896 and was just beginning his career as an Eton master, to act.[92] There were arrangements for clothing to be made. Late in July Maynard was again getting up early, this time to learn from the family's cook how to prepare eggs for his fag master. But, at last, there was the holiday. During it, Neville Keynes noted of his son, who at 14 had recently shot up and was now taller than he was and whose voice had recently broken:

Maynard is just now a curious combination – quite childish in some things, thoroughly entering into the simplest enjoyments such as Geoffrey or even younger children can share with him, while in other things he is thoroughly grown up, entering most sensibly into what are quite men's ideas.[93]

NOTES

1 Rothblatt 1968, 200–1.
2 Winstanley 1947, 39.
3 Roach 1959, 255.
4 Winstanley 1947, 193–5.
5 *JMK*, X, 267.
6 Rothblatt 1968, 230.
7 Roach 1959, 262; Ashby 1958, ch. 2.
8 Roach 1959, 263.
9 There was an exception for St Catharine's College, whose Master was also a canon of Norwich Cathedral.
10 Roach 1959, 404, 446.
11 Ibid., 266.
12 Sidgwick and Sidgwick 1906, 554–5.
13 Roach 1959, 287.
14 Ibid., 293, 295.
15 Ibid., 267.
16 Cornford 1908.
17 *Statutes of Pembroke College, Cambridge, 1882*, ch. III(18–21), ch. XII(2); CUL, Add.7832, entries for 29 May and 12 August 1882.
18 Black (ed.) 1972–81, IV, 142, 156 n. 1; V, 117.
19 Russell 1978, 68.
20 KCKP, Box 37.
21 CUL, Add.7829, entries for 19, 20 and 22 October 1872, and 12 and 22 January and 30 June 1873.
22 F. Keynes 1950, 45.
23 Black (ed.) 1972–81, IV, 149; V, 105.
24 CUL, Add.7562/2, H. Fawcett to JNK, 23 January 1875.
25 Although perhaps now best remembered as an economist, Jevons published extensively in logic with his *Pure Logic* (1863), *Elementary Lessons in Logic* (1870), *The Principles of Science: A Treatise on Logic and Scientific Method* (1874), *Primer of Logic* (1876) and *Studies in Deductive Logic, A Manual for Students* (1880).
26 For sketches of the Brown side of the family, see Brown 1988.
27 F. Keynes 1950, 31.
28 Black (ed.) 1972–81, V, 177.
29 MLC, JNK Papers 1(101), Marshall to JNK, 13 March 1891.
30 MLC, JNK Papers 1(74), Marshall to JNK, 30 April 1883.
31 CUL, Add.7837, entries for 13 January 1888 and days following. MLC, JMK Papers 1(71), Marshall to JMK, 7 February 1888; see also his undated letters 1(55) and 1(56). Kadish 1982, 178 reads the letter of 7 February as an attempt to dissuade Neville from standing.
32 MLC, JNK Papers 1(27), Foxwell to JNK, 15 January 1888.
33 MLC, JNK Papers 1(23), Foxwell to JNK, 22 March 1883.
34 MLC, JNK Papers 1(25), Foxwell to JNK, 2 April 1885.
35 MLC, JNK Papers 1(80), Marshall to JNK, 17 March 1888.
36 MLC, JNK Papers 1(89), Marshall to JNK, 7 February 1889.
37 CUL, Add.7834, JMK to J. L. Laughlin, 8 January 1895.

38 Broad 1950, 405.
39 McGuinness 1988, 97.
40 Passmore 1968, 135.
41 CUL, Add.7834, 16 February 1885.
42 For the scale of this enterprise, see Whitaker 1975, I, 91–2.
43 MLC, JNK Papers 1(67), Marshall to JNK, 26 April [1888].
44 For Marshall's views see Coase 1975.
45 Blaug 1980, 82.
46 *JMK*, X, 271–2 n. 5, quoting a letter of 30 January 1897.
47 Schumpeter 1954, 824.
48 Robertson 1951, 14.
49 CUL, Add.7846, 9 March 1896.
50 Maloney 1985, 63.
51 CUL, Add.7843, 13 May 1893. For Geoffrey Keynes's views see G. Keynes, 1981, 17–19.
52 CUL, Add.7840, February to April 1890.
53 CUL, Add.7841, 9 March 1891.
54 CUL, Add.7840, 2 April 1890.
55 Hynes 1968, 74, 252.
56 *JMK*, X, 349.
57 CUL, Add.7836, 12 February and 20 March 1887; KCKP, FAK to JMK, 18 December 1941.
58 F. Keynes 1950, 65. Neville continued this practice with his grandchildren (information from Richard Keynes).
59 CUL, Add.7841, 1 and 22 March 1891; Add.7842, 10 February 1892.
60 G. Keynes 1981, 28–31, 34, 44–7.
61 King's College 1949, 14. His scores, as recorded by Neville confirm this point.
62 CUL, Add.7833, 5 June 1883.
63 CUL, Add.7847, 3 July 1897.
64 KCKP, JMK to JNK, 30 March 1899.
65 *JMK*, II, 18, 25; KCKP, JMK to Lydia, 15 November 1936.
66 Durnford in King's College 1949, 20; LePan 1979, 78–9.
67 CUL, Add.7833, 25 March 1884.
68 CUL, Add.7834, 17 November 1885; 7835, 3 June 1886; 7836, 7 September 1887.
69 CUL, Add.7834, 25 November 1885; 7839, 6 January 1890; 7834, 17 November 1885; 7835, 15 February and 3 June 1886.
70 CUL, Add.7839, 15 August 1890.
71 CUL, Add.7837, 29 January 1888; 7838, 31 August and 10 October 1889; 7839, 18 April 1890; 7840, 17 November 1891.
72 CUL, Add.7846, 9 November 1896.
73 CUL, Add.7847, 17 April and 28 June 1897.
74 CUL, Add.7835, 28 January and 18 November 1886.
75 CUL, Add.7836, 27 November 1887; 7837, 1 March 1888.
76 CUL, Add.7837, 12 May 1888.
77 Harrod 1951, 8–9; CUL, Add.7836, 10 September 1887; 7837, 5 January and 13 September 1888.
78 CUL, Add.7838, 5/6 June 1889.
79 CUL, Add.7837, 8 May 1888.
80 CUL, Add.7838, 15 April 1889.
81 CUL, Add.7840, 29 January 1891; 7841, 6 and 13 March 1891.

82 CUL, Add.7842, 22 January, 14 and 29 March and 20 April 1882.
83 KCKP, R. Goodchild to JNK, 14 April 1892.
84 CUL, Add.7842, 28 May, 5 June, 22 July and 7 August 1892.
85 KCKP, Memoirs by F. H. Smith and Margaret Hill; JMK Diary, November 1894–February 1896, entries for 10 and 14 November 1894 (the diary ran from 4–26 November 1894 and 16 February–18 April 1896); JMK to Lydia, 17 December 1925; M. Keynes (ed.) 1975, 29.
86 CUL, Add.7843, 14 February 1893. See also the entry for 19 February.
87 CUL, Add.7843, 30 January, 21 February, 26 March, 2, 4, 6 and 8 May, and 31 July 1893.
88 CUL, Add.7844, 31 July, 8 October and 21 December 1894; 7845, 5 April, 30 July and 19 December 1895.
89 CUL, Add.7846, 22 September, and 17, 21 and 31 December 1896; 7847, 12 January, 15, 17 and 27 April 1897.
90 CUL, Add.7847, 2, 4, 26 and 28 June, and 1, 2 and 4 July 1897.
91 CUL, Add.7847, 6, 7, 8, 9, 12, 13 and 15 July 1897.
92 Ollard 1982, 156.
93 CUL, Add.7847, 24 July and 2 August 1897; KCKP, JMK's Holiday Diary of 1897, entry for 23 August.

2

ETON

One seems to have, in a way, two entirely different lives, one at home and the other at school, and when you are living one of them, the other doesn't seem more than a dream, a trifle more realistic than usual.
(KCPH, JMK to Margaret Keynes, 2 February 1900)[1]

Maynard's first Eton half, as each of the three terms are called, began on 22 September 1897. Almost to cue, he caught a chill and a fever three days earlier. He did not arrive until the third day of term. When he arrived, he found that he would be living with the other members of his Election (those elected to scholarships at the same time) in Chamber, a long room divided into small cubicles, each with a bed, a burry (a combination desk, bookcase and chest of drawers) and a wash basin with cold water. Chamber was heated by a large fireplace, which Maynard's cubicle was fortunately opposite. In Chamber lived the fifteen most junior of the seventy Collegers or King's Scholars at Eton. At the time Maynard entered, it contained the members of his Election and a few boys from the previous Election who moved out as rooms became available elsewhere in College.[a] The members of his Election were initially just names on an Eton scholarship list. Soon, especially since Eton conventions firmly discouraged friendships with boys outside one's Election, they were contemporaries. Some became life-long friends.

With Maynard's arrival at Eton, our main sources of evidence widen, for from his first day there were regular letters to his parents and, from his sixteenth birthday to his departure from Eton in 1902, Maynard's diary, which, although often written up in arrears, provides some indication of the range of his activities until its deterioration in his final year. Then, there

---

a Among his Election, taking them in order of their examination merit, were Dillwyn Knox, later a Fellow of King's with Maynard; Thomas Balston, later a writer and publisher; Grenville Hamilton (subsequently Proby), later Clerk to the House of Lords and an antiquary; Gerard Young, later an Indian civil servant and subsequently Director of the British School at Athens; W. Hope-Jones, later a mathematics master at Eton; Robin Dundas, later a tutor in Greek history at Christ Church, Oxford; and Bernard Swithinbank, later a distinguished civil servant in Burma.

were occasional warm, brotherly letters to Margaret and Geoffrey. Finally, there were memories.

Maynard's letters to his parents, most frequently to Neville Keynes, began as straightforward accounts of his activities. As he (and they) matured, they also became commentaries upon events at Eton and elsewhere and attempts to keep in touch with his father's world. They indicate the range of contact between father and son, and Maynard's developing independence.

On reaching Eton, Maynard entered a different world from the small, comfortable, non-conformist circles of Cambridge, Bedford or Salisbury. Eton was a worldly, long-established foundation, renowned for its aristocratic, scholarly and establishment connections. It was also a larger world. Maynard was one of seventy Collegers whose numbers, since the reforms of the 1840s, were topped up from the results of an annual competitive examination. The school also contained almost a thousand Oppidans (or non-Collegers) lodged in houses around the College, plus masters and supporting staff. In this larger world, Maynard was out of contact with former friends, siblings, parents or relatives. He was on his own as never before.

The separateness from ordinary life at Eton was a product of many features. At a formal level the routines differed from the outside world's, from early school before breakfast and chapel onwards. There were distinctive uniforms: for those like Maynard who were above five feet four inches tall the uniform ran to a gown, black silk top hat, black suit of morning tails, and a white shirt with stiff turned-down collars and a white tie tucked into them. There were gradations for those who were shorter or were members of the sixth form (the ten senior Collegers in order of academic merit – the Library being the Oppidans' equivalent) or were members of the Eton Society also known as Pop. Games, which had swept Eton in the decade before Maynard arrived,[2] had their own range of uniforms, carefully distinguished to indicate the wearer's origins and his level of skill. There were regulations as to details of behaviour – where one could go and with whom – as well as conventions enforced by the older boys and the sixth form. The private language of the school also emphasised separateness: 'sap' for diligent study and those who overdid it, 'beaks' for masters, 'swipe' for birch, 'absence' for roll call, 'staying out' for absence due to illness, 'sock' for food and drink bought for oneself. There were peculiar games each with its own technical language: the Wall Game, 'the nation's most famous character-building brawl over a ball', which defies description to the uninitiated 'but to the detached observer . . . appears to consist of aimless pushing in the mud interspersed by occasional wild kicks';[3] the Field Game, a primitive variant of football played with a smaller ball and narrower goals to peculiar rules; and aquatics, a variant of cricket played by wet bobs, or those who rowed. In practice, Eton was a total society which exercised extensive control over its inhabitants' behaviour and values through its provision of so many aspects of life within its confines.

Maynard seems to have adapted to this new world relatively easily. Fagging for his fag master Macnaughton seems not to have involved much more than making toast. However, as he was often the only one in Chamber when others were out playing games, Maynard was more frequently required to do downtown fagging – fetching things from the Eton shops. On one occasion, he reported, he had been 'downtown' five times the previous day.[4] This aloofness over games, which had been evident at St Faith's, was to remain. Yet, as everyone in the school was expected to take part in some form of physical exercise every day except Sunday, he soon adapted, reporting playing and buying equipment for the Wall Game,[5] and learning such ball games as fives, racquets and squash. At the end of his first half he was sufficiently integrated to be elected at the top of the list as a member of Chamber Pop, the Chamber debating society.

At the end of his second half, Lubbock reported to Neville Keynes:

He has worked into the ways of the place thoroughly well by now and seems, if I may say so, to have become a little more boyish in his attitude towards things in general.[6]

This boyishness must have been there the previous term: witness his election to Chamber Pop. Traces of it appeared in his letters:

Last night we had Chamber Singing which was a glorious rag lasting an hour and a half. All fags are required to sing but any amounts of older ones are present and after the fags are finished several are called on and the night is made hideous with the row.

I will leave you to guess what I sang, but it was the success of the evening (as far as the fags go) and was the only one to be encored later in the evening.[7]

Reports of his singing this song 'Three Blue Bottles' were to recur:

Last night College Pop supper took place and I and three other fags were deputed to wait. They had a glorious feed, turkey, champagne, etc. When they got to the dessert stage we fags retired to Lower Tea Room and made a supper on the remnants and a bottle of champagne. As one of the fags did not take any, the other three had to do their duty and finish it.

When we had finished we went in again and songs, etc. proceeded for about an hour. I was called on to sing 'T.B.B.'. Afterwards we handed coffee round. In fact we had a very fine time.

I was not the fag who abstained from champagne.[8]

Nor did Maynard abstain from work. By the time Neville Keynes visited him on 9 October, Maynard had been moved up three divisions in mathematics. By the end of the first half, he was first in classics, second in mathematics and third overall. It was the beginning of an Eton academic career that would be distinguished by any criterion. The following years saw him win a succession of prizes, not only in particular subjects amongst his own peers, but also in wider competitions. Naturally he took the major mathematical prizes – the Junior Mathematical, 1898; the Senior Mathematical, 1900; and the Tomline, 1901. But he also managed the Richard's English Essay, 1900; the Chamberlayne Scholarship, 1901; and to be in the select for the Newcastle, the major prize in classics and divinity which required familiarity with the New Testament in Greek. He was in 1902 the first Tomline prizeman to get into the Newcastle select since 1888. His academic success inevitably made his termly reports a record of praise – except in French and in one case where he did not hit it off with the master in a division where the class was much slower than he was:

Mike is dull and soporiferous beyond words.

I could hardly have imagined that a man could be so dull; anyhow I shall not suffer from want of sleep this half.[9]

The feeling was reciprocated by the master, R. A. H. Mitchell:

Rather a provoking boy in school. Reads notes when he should be attending to the lesson. Apt to talk to his neighbours unless severely repressed. He gives one the idea of regarding himself a privileged boy with perhaps a little intellectual conceit.[10]

But this was a minority view, partially echoed only in Gurney Lubbock's first term report: 'I should like in certain things to see him a little more dissatisfied, a little more ready to note the points in which he fails'. Normally Neville Keynes received reports of how he took a broad view of his work, how he had 'absolutely nothing of the mercenary, mark-getting feeling which so often spoils excellent scholars'; how there was 'nothing priggish about him; he is just what one would wish a boy to be'. And they went on: 'Certainly he has a remarkable mind: full of taste and perception with all its precision and accuracy.' Ultimately Lubbock would be 'fairly dazzled' by Maynard's results on the School Certificate examinations. He even managed to find praise for his football by the time he left Eton.[11]

Although, with his father's training and constant concern about his academic work and his standing, one might expect Maynard to be academically competitive, these academic results were not the result of skimping on other activities. He had a modicum of athletic success. He persevered at the Wall Game and won his colours as twelfth man in 1900 and played for College in the highlight of the Eton season, the St Andrew's Day match against the Oppidans in 1901. The Wall Game became his major autumn athletic preoccupation, although he would occasionally play a field game and win his colours there in 1901. In the Lent half he normally switched to ball games, particularly fives, until the beginning of rowing in March. Although not very good, he still managed to get his colour for Lower Boats in 1901, but he soon transferred to *Monarch* 'nominally the first boat on the river, – but . . . generally recognised as the home of bad oars'. 'Apart', he continued, 'from the slight opprobrium, it is all bliss. One has all the advantages of wet bobbing without any of its disadvantages'.[12] Moreover, he kept up all of these activities after he went up to Cambridge, although rowing only survived for slightly more than a term. Only cricket seems to have been a complete disaster: his first scores were 5, 3, and 2 and they did not improve.[13] Yet he maintained a spectator's interest in the game, accumulating vast stores of knowledge. As Neville Keynes remarked after attending a Varsity match with his son:

> If the theory and history (*not* the practice) of cricket were included in Trials he would do well in the subject. Under his able tuition I am myself beginning to take quite an intelligent interest in the game.[14]

Cricket, of course, is the ideal spectator sport for those with a statistical bent.

Maynard also developed a taste for debating, first in Chamber Pop and then in College Pop. His letters to his father and his diaries are full of the topics discussed. In January 1898, reporting that the next topic for Chamber Pop was to be university degrees for women, he asked 'Please send me some pamphlet or report for me to get some facts on this piece of ancient history'.[15] On 9 March 1901 he recorded in his diary:

> College Pop was proposed by Pallis – that a more general education than that at present current at Eton is to be desired. I spoke on Pallis's side but he had no other supporters – the house is very prejudiced with regard to its own customs. The debate was continued for 2 hours until 11.45 – chiefly to rag the man [A. M. Goodhart, the master in Greek] – and he eventually came in and said that closure must be applied.

Similarly in May 1901:

> In College Pop Hamilton proposed and Pallis opposed (in an excellent speech) 'that Mr Gladstone as a statesman is unworthy of your admiration'. I spoke immediately after Pallis and made the longest speech I have yet attempted – about a quarter of an hour.
>
> The debate was very good, but we had to stop abnormally early because of P.B. [private business]. We condemned Mr Gladstone by a small majority.

To this, in his weekly letter to his father, he added what would become a characteristic attitude, 'I knew more of the facts of the case than most people'.[16]

Private business in College Pop was not always an intrusion. In February 1901 Maynard had his own axe to grind. He told his father a week later:

> Last night I put up a motion at Private Business in College Pop but was defeated by one vote. The facts were these: a fine of 6*d.* is extracted for every article left in the reading room after 9.30. I left a pair of fives gloves and a double fine of 1*s.* was demanded of me. I held that a pair of fives gloves only constituted one article within the meaning of the Law. I was surprised at so nearly winning as it is almost impossible to make the House pass anything that will diminish its revenue from fines. Personally I don't think it good policy to make fines a source of revenue; it is an extremely vexatious form of indirect taxation and one which involves considerable trouble in collection. Quite a large amount of money is obtained in this way, but I should prefer a fixed subscription in lieu of fines.[17]

As well as debating and games, Maynard made the most of the opportunities Eton offered – outside lecturers, expeditions with masters and societies, including the Shakespeare Society and an essay-reading Literary Society that he revived in collaboration with Harold Butler, later a distinguished public servant and the first Master of Nuffield College, Oxford. He also seemed to accumulate various committee assignments, not surprisingly, perhaps, given his parents' experiences. As he ruefully remarked to his father after being elected 'as a person competent to check the financial affairs' to the Committee of Management of the School Stores, 'I am finding that like you when I am elected to a committee I am invariably made to do all the work'.[18]

With his range of activities and accomplishments, even at games, it is perhaps not surprising that Maynard was elected to the Eton Society, or Pop, in December 1901. Founded in 1811 by Charles Fox Townshend as a social club and debating society, it had by the end of the century become a social and athletic club whose membership was 'almost wholly athletic'. In 1898 Warre, the Headmaster, attempted 'with only moderate success' to reform the body by insisting that the Captain of School, Captain of Oppidans and at least five other members of the sixth form be included as members and that nobody below the upper division of the fifth form be eligible.[19] Maynard may have got in as a result of that attempt at leavening, but it is impossible to tell. Members of Pop had no prefectorial duties by virtue of membership except to act as constables at outdoor events: prefectorial duties were the province of the sixth form. Rather its members ruled 'supreme throughout the school in all matters of dress and etiquette'. Members of Pop had privileges denied others – wearing coloured waistcoats, braid edges on their tailcoats, flowers in their buttonholes and sealing wax on the brims of their top hats and having the exclusive right to carry rolled umbrellas and walk arm-in-arm with whomever they chose. Membership in this self-perpetuating society was prized by many as the coping stone to an Eton career and some, notably

Cyril Connolly, worked extremely hard to get elected.[20] Maynard seems to have had fewer problems.

As well as being academically stimulating and giving him room to spread himself, Maynard's Eton does not seem to have been the relatively brutal Eton of, say, George Orwell, but more akin to the milder world of A. J. Ayer.[21] True, the place had swung towards the extreme of Victorian athleticism and the Headmaster's other enthusiasm, the Corps, 'became a sacred duty', but at least amongst Collegers there seems to have been a fair degree of tolerance. Nor was the discipline all that severe. Maynard recounted two of his encounters with the sixth form in his diary:

> Herringham and I were worked off by Tomkinsom tonight, absolutely unjustly; he told hopeless lies. But what can you expect with six – [word missing in original] in sixth form. I was never worked off in my first five halfs but this my sixth I have already been escopered 3 times.

> I was worked off very gently by Chute for throwing one pellet in hall last Thursday. He said I was going to throw more he could see it in my eye. It gives him a great deal of pleasure and does not do me much harm.[22]

Nor did he observe many beatings in his two one-week terms as a sixth-form praeposter, going around the school at 11.15 with 'the bills' summoning offenders to the Headmaster for punishment. (The two praeposters witnessed any beatings administered.) On the first occasion in November 1901 he reported no beating; on the second in March 1902 he noted two.[23] Nor did he report much more as a member of sixth form: his diary only carries one such entry, on 8 October 1901 – 'All Lower Tea Room was worked off in evening for failing to observe strict order'.[24] But then the tenure of Warre as Headmaster was noted for its disciplinary reforms and a reduction of corporal punishment.[25]

> The Head preached this morning and gave us one of his impressive reminders. Perhaps he ought hardly to do it before visitors.

Thus ran an entry in Maynard's diary for 30 July 1899. As Headmaster, Warre took a strong line on adolescent immorality. However, he made it a point of honour to assume that all boys adopted his moral code and obeyed it. Only if he obtained irrefutable evidence of a breach of the code would he act, and instantly expel the guilty parties.[26] Such was the formal position, which differed little from that elsewhere at the time – although there may have been less prying at Eton. What was the reality?

It is impossible to be precise as to the incidence of particular sexual practices in any public school at any time. There is no need, however, to go to the extreme of some authors and suggest that public schools 'seethed' with sexual passions or 'that they were, and are, the most sexual places in the world'.[27] All that one needs to note is that males mature, albeit earlier now than then, and, if we are to believe the literature, some reach the peak of their sexual drive during the years in which they might attend a boarding school. In these circumstances, 'the development, control and fulfilment of their sexual energies' could be 'a matter of overriding importance'.[28] Moreover, in the world of Maynard's youth, where males were isolated from the opposite sex not only during term but also during vacations, school experiences may have proved more important than they would to a subsequent generation. It is possible, on the other hand, that his generation may have been less aware of – and probably less open about – their schoolboy sexual drives than, say, the students of the 1960s whose attitudes and experiences were the subject of Royston Lambert's and his associates' studies of boarding education.[29] Even Lambert's study, although it agrees that boarding 'stimulates pupils' homosexual instincts and their perception of it as a sexual response and an ethos', admits that 'increased homosexual awareness does not mean that . . . schools are hotbeds of homosexual activity'.[30] Even when such activity does occur, it is not uniform across schools. As Lambert puts it:

> It is subtle components of social structure, tradition and even the alchemy of individual personalities which work on the conditioning single sex situation of some schools and activate the homosexuality latent in them.[31]

It is largely the pupil society which activates these latent tendencies rather than influences coming from the staff. The overall conclusion of Lambert's research is also of some interest.

> All this is not to say that homosexual activity is widespread in boarding schools; on the contrary, except for the experimental kind, it seems remarkably restricted as a social as distinct from a private phenomenon.[32]

This is from a modern study. What of Keynes's Eton? There the single sex character of the institution, the age of its inhabitants, the cult of games and the emphasis on the classics, especially on Greek, may all have played a role in creating an ethos, as would the often repressed longings of some masters – one need only think of A. C. Benson.[33] But what of practice? I think it is clear from the diary entry above, if not from the sheer size of the school, that 'immorality' existed. During the same period some of Maynard's diary entries suggest something of an atmosphere.

> Young and I spoke to R.M.
> Nothing eventful happened that I can write here. R.M. is behaving magnificently. I think he is safe now. We have to cheer up H.W.Y. I must leave the rest to memory.
> I spoke to Herringham this morning and I am glad that I did so. This

last week has seemed an eternity and I can scarcely believe a week ago
—— [line in the original]
We had another fear about the old thing this evening.b

As this was the term in which Keynes was beaten several times, 'the old thing' may refer to that, but the entries raise other possibilities.

There is other evidence to consider, however. In March 1905, after sorting through some old correspondence, Maynard reported to Lytton Strachey:

> But the thing that interested me most was the outstanding apostalicity of the goings on of my circle during the last year at school – especially with Swithinbank. I had no idea of it – the thing was complete.
>
> The amours – Swithin and I in agreement and corresponding about the object.
>
> The solid indecency – laughingly quelled by Dundas.
>
> . . . A little box of letters brought the whole thing back – I had quite forgotten it.34

Taken at face value, especially, as we shall see below, given the intellectual nature of the homosexuality of the younger Apostles of 1905, this letter suggests an atmosphere of feelings and discussion rather than of performance. The same atmosphere is confirmed in R. H. Dundas's last letter from Eton to Maynard, cited in part by Harrod, which went on to note that Somerville, Maynard's fag 'had an "immoral proposition" made to him straight in his first week' and that 'it settles any doubts there may have been in Somerville's future'.35

We can take the matter further, for from May 1906 to August 1915, as well as recording meetings and engagements in his 'Cambridge University Diary', Maynard also entered a code: 'a', 'w', 'c'. At the end of that period, he also tabulated the results, as shown in Plates 9 and 10, with a list of individuals involved in 'c' in each year. From this list, it would seem that 'a', 'w' and 'c' were shorthand for masturbation (or abuse), wet dream and copulation respectively. In the list just mentioned, Maynard carried his record of those involved back before 1906 – to his last two years at Eton. There he recorded Dillwyn Knox under 1901 and 1902 and Dan Macmillan under 1902. There were no entries for 1903, 1904 and 1905. Knox's biographer, Penelope Fitzgerald, mentions that during Dillwyn's last half:

> Dilly and Maynard Keynes had calmly undertaken experiments, intellectual and sexual, to resolve the questions of what things are necessary to life.36

Maynard reminded Knox of the affair in 1905, when he remarked that since

b KCKP, JMK diary, 18, 20, 25 June and 23 July 1899. R.M. was Ralph Micklin; Young was Gerald Mackworth Young; H.W.Y. was Hubert Winthrop Young, brother of Gerald Young; and Herringham was Geoffrey Wilmont Herringham.

'the curious incidents that marked our last two years at Eton, there has been a kind of affection between us'.[37] Yet it seems that these 'incidents' were not known to Maynard's closest friends, for years later he reported a heart-to-heart conversation to Swithinbank:

> In return I told him about Dil and me long ago at Eton. I've never seen anyone so much surprised – and so jealous. I thought he would never get over it.[38]

Such is the available evidence. From it, it is clear that Maynard had some homosexual experience at Eton. We do not know the frequency or intensity of such experiences. However, the gap in such activity after Maynard left Eton, especially as one can hardly argue that the King's College, Cambridge of his undergraduate years was devoid of the appropriate ethos or of opportunities, suggest that the initial experiences were just 'experiments'. We can only guess at their emotional content.

Maynard was growing up. He was also coming to form his own views and to stick to them even at the risk of some unpopularity. The most notable case was over the Boer War. Here Maynard's views and attitudes were somewhat at variance with his parents' and the dominant strain of opinion at Eton. From his correspondence with his son and his diary, it is clear that Neville Keynes was anti-Boer, although he couldn't quite 'convince' himself 'that Great Britain is going to wage a righteous war'.[39] At the same time, war would raise the question of joining the Corps at Eton. This, along with games, was the Headmaster's great enthusiasm. Maynard had been approached about joining the Corps the previous year, but had, with Neville's support, declined. Now the issue would come up again.[40]

As Britain and the Boers drifted towards war in October 1899, Maynard recorded in his diary that he couldn't 'get clear about the rights of the case'. Three days later, he reported to his father, 'I don't know what to think about this Transvaal business, but I think I am getting more and more anti-war'. When war actually broke out, he and Gerard Young prepared 'a special War Number of the Acorn', one of the series of family newspapers produced by the children at 6 Harvey Road and their friends, for Geoffrey Keynes. When sending it off, Maynard remarked:

> I am no more jingo than I was previously, but now that the war has begun one must perforce be reconciled to it. Besides, when writing for journals such as the Acorn, it is necessary to be a little rampant to keep up its circulation.[41]

There matters rested until the new year, except for a comment on early British reverses which reveals considerable maturity and understanding:

> I agree with you that the news from South Africa is bad ... But

we must console ourselves with history which makes our losses and reverses seem puny. In the battle of Albuera, nearly one hundred years ago in the Peninsular War, our losses were seven times as heavy per cent as at the Modder River. Yet we won. . . .

It is hard luck on generals that news should be transmitted so quickly. The people don't see the result of the campaign but seem to gloat over every little loss. Seventy men killed in a battle is terrible for their families but it is a tiny loss for a nation of thirty million.[42]

During the vacation, except for the mention of various engagements in his diary, there was little comment on the war, but soon after the start of the new Eton half, Maynard reported to his father that the Headmaster

gave us a stirring oration on the volunteer movement. He declared it to be, in the present circumstances, the duty of all to get what military training they could, and he said that he expected all boys of the right age to join our corps.

For once in a way his words have had an effect and people are joining and being coerced into joining in throngs, including all the sixth form and the greater part of the College.

Am I to join?

I am not keen and the drill would be a nuisance, but I am perfectly willing to do so if I ought. It would be unpleasant to be almost the only non-shooter.[43]

The Headmaster's appeal produced over 100 recruits, including almost half of Maynard's election and 'most of the people I see much of'; so there was certainly social pressure to join.[44]

Maynard's parents, who had discussed the question of the corps in 1898, replied that, on balance, they would prefer that he didn't join, but that they would not pronounce a veto if he thought it was the right thing to do and if he would be uncomfortable in not joining. Thus, to some extent at least, Maynard could do as he wished.[45] On 4 February he reported to his father:

About the volunteers – I have not joined.

Taking into regard my feelings and the terms of your letter, I consulted people and they agreed I should be justified in not joining.

I wavered a little and hey presto! it was done – or rather it was not done.

I think that without your letter which amounted to a refusal, I should have been compelled to be engulfed in this marvellous martial ardour that has seized the school.

Some say that patriotism requires one to join the useless Eton shooters but it seems to me to be the sort of patriotism that requires one to wave the Union Jack.

That settled the question of the volunteers. But it did not settle Maynard's attitude to the war and the occasional bursts of patriotism around him. In some respects he came to be more critical. The Headmaster, he reported, was 'quite dotty with war enthusiasm'. Other comments followed:

The sermon was by the Rev. H. E. Fox and was one of the most revolting performances that I have heard for a long time.

I find the war news in *The Times* more accurate if less copious than that which is in sermons.

Roberts's triumphal procession through the Orange Free [State] is grand, but I think that too much has been made of the joy with which the inhabitants of Bloemfontein received him; for, after all, the majority of those who are left are of British descent.

. . . It is evident that the whole nation has gone in for what we call at Eton an organised rag. The papers call it a 'fervent thanksgiving from the heart'.

I do not think we are quite such hypocrites here. Most of us know that Mafeking is a glorious pretext for a whole holiday and for throwing off all discipline. We do not break windows because we are mad with joy, but because we think that under the circumstances we can do so with impunity.[46]

A similar spirit made him pro-Boxer during the rebellion in China. As he drew the parallel for his father on 8 July 1900, 'I am a confirmed pro-Boxer. By the way, take away x, the unknown quantity, and what does Boxer become?'

It was during his period at Eton that Maynard naturally began to develop his capacities for independent judgement. These appeared not only in his comments on foreign affairs but also in his comments on his reading and other matters.

I have enjoyed *Richard Peverel* immensely. It is my first Meredith and I find it quite different from anything I have ever read. When I am reading it I get quite absorbed in a way that is not very usual with me. Is Meredith one of those dreadful people who think that a happy ending is inartistic?

At 8.30 began the Greek Play – The Agamemnon – the *raison d'être* of my leave, and we unexpectedly found ourselves in the front row of the stalls.

The performance was good and extremely interesting but not quite what I had expected reading the play. I did not experience the feeling of doom that the play had given me, and so like I fancy most other people I was disappointed. Crace as Cassandra was splendid, and Lucas as Clytemnestra did a long and difficult part well. The chorus was good and I like the music. Agamemnon and Aegisthus not so good.

Ken, Margaret and I finished the evening by seeing 'The Life We Live', a howling melodrama at the theatre.

It was the genuine article, a thing which I had never seen before, and therefore found entertaining as well as interesting.

We hissed the villains.

Father and I travelled to London this morning to see a matinée of 'Mrs Dane's Defence' at Wyndham's Theatre. It is a problem play, a type I have not seen before, but I enjoyed it immensely.

Miss Lena Ashwell as Mrs Dane was extremely good, and Wyndham's acting was extraordinarily natural. The theatre is new, and although we were far back in the dress circle we could see perfectly.[47]

Throughout Maynard's period at Eton, his programme of studies was the subject of almost continuous discussion between father and son. Neville Keynes was determined that his son should excel and urged him on to greater efforts, warned him of the threats from potential rivals, and worried over the details of his programme.[48] This emphasis on Maynard's doing well, plus Maynard's own developing academic interests, almost inevitably led to disagreements about the Eton curriculum.

The heart of the curriculum was classics. Victorian reforms had resulted in marked improvements in the teaching arrangements for mathematics and French, and other subjects began to enter the curriculum in a tentative way – for example, Henry Marten arrived in 1895 as the first master specialising in history – but classics still took most of students' time.

Maynard with his strong mathematical bent was not always happy with this emphasis. After his first half, he asked for permission to replace 'extra books', the reading of a book of Homer's *Odyssey* each half, with more mathematics. Neville Keynes, after characteristically consulting someone in Cambridge (on this occasion Mr Goodchild), demurred, as he thought the move would adversely affect Maynard's examination results. Maynard persisted in his proposed course and Neville grudgingly acquiesced with the comment, 'It will be an interesting experiment'.[49] Perhaps because it did not seem to lead to adverse results, Maynard continued the practice, enlarging his mathematics extras to three in the autumn of 1898, thus causing Neville Keynes to worry whether he was working too hard.[50] For the moment, this seemed sufficient, for when there was further pressure to do more mathematics, Maynard reported:

He [the mathematics master] asked me to ask Lubbock to let me off private [business]c so that I could go more often, but my tutor stuck at this, I think quite rightly. He says that he does not want me to specialise too much yet.[51]

c The Eton term for non-classroom tutorial teaching.

There matters rested for the moment. In fact, the next half Lubbock successfully persuaded him to take history as an extra. Henry Marten and Maynard seem to have clicked, for he continued with history for the rest of his Eton career. In part, perhaps, it was Marten's influence that led him to the extensive ancestor studies which occupied his last years at Eton – not to mention a subsequent lifelong interest in history in general.

Yet the tension between his interests and the demands of examinations continued. In the autumn of 1900, he reported:

> I am enjoying all my work now, and Lubbock says that my verses have greatly improved, but to really get on in classics I ought now to do a lot of private reading.
>
> It would [be] very pleasant getting though one's favourite classical authors in that way, but it is absolutely impossible as well as Mathematical Extras.
>
> Like you I should not mind 36 hours a day and 14 days a week, etc., etc.[52]

The next half saw his classics suffer further – at least by Eton standards – as he prepared for the Tomline Prize examinations. Yet he was determined not to spend more than half his time on mathematics, although for a brief period before the examinations, and against his father's advice, he let his classics go almost completely by the board.[53] Once the examinations were over, he returned to his classics, but never enough to keep Neville Keynes happy. His father tried to persuade him to give up history, but Maynard persevered, 'chiefly because it does not really take up too much time and it is a pleasant change from a flood of mathematics'.[54]

He was still able to keep a sense of perspective, noting of the mathematics master, 'His jealousy of Classics is most curious and interesting'. The whole thing came out more clearly when the Cambridge results appeared of another Etonian mathematician who, like Maynard, would become an economist, R. G. Hawtrey:

> Hawtrey, as perhaps you saw, was eighteenth in the Mathematical Tripos. Dyer – whose pupil he was – is very disappointed and thinks he ought to have taken a very high place, and Hurst holds him up to me as a dreadful example of a person who has tried to do too many things. I think they are both wrong – Dyer in thinking him a person of surpassing mathematical ability – Hurst in thinking he has lost his soul knowing something besides mathematics.[55]

Neville Keynes, recently worried about the quality of Eton's teaching in mathematics, replied, 'I fancy that at Eton his mathematical ability was overrated'.[56]

By this stage, the issues surrounding the balance of Maynard's programme at Eton had become intertwined with the question of his further education. There is no indication that he or his father ever thought of his going anywhere other than Cambridge, which is hardly surprising given its reputation in mathematics. But within Cambridge, there was still the question of which College. It was not a matter of Pembroke, his father's old College *versus* somewhere else: Pembroke never came up except when Neville Keynes reported that one fellow of the College was put out because Maynard was not considering it.[57] King's with its Eton connection and its large number of closed scholarships reserved for Etonians (half the total) was less risky, especially given Maynard's performance at Eton. However, at King's mathematics had only come to be taken seriously since the 1870s[58] and its two mathematics dons, Arthur Berry and H. W. Richmond, although distinguished, were not of the distinction of those in St John's or, of course, Trinity, that hothouse of Cambridge mathematics. Of course King's could, and did, supplement its teaching resources with outside coaching, but there was still the likely absence of very good peers.[d] Against this, although Trinity and St John's were larger than King's, the competition for scholarships would be more intense. Maynard's going to Cambridge did not, of course, depend on a scholarship, or even an exhibition, for Neville Keynes could easily afford it, but financial considerations do not seem to have entered into the family's calculations. Rather, from an early stage in the discussions, King's seems to have dominated, partly because, in addition to the closed scholarships, Maynard's classics would count for more in its scholarship examinations.

The discussions began in earnest late in 1900 when Lubbock suggested that Maynard was sufficiently good in classics that he would get a first class degree in the Classical Tripos, and Hurst presciently predicted that he would end up among the first twelve Wranglers if he pursued mathematics.[59] The matter remained in the background as Maynard prepared for the Tomline Prize examinations in June 1901, but it still figured in decisions made about the balance of Maynard's studies; Neville felt happier about his cutting back on classics after Lubbock reported that this would not be inconsistent with a scholarship at King's. Not that this stopped him worrying.[60]

With the Easter holidays, work began in earnest for the triple challenge ahead – the Tomline, the Schools Certificate and the King's scholarship examinations. Maynard was to spend at least two to three hours a day working on his mathematics over and above his other activities such as golf and genealogical history. He could only take time off if he had 'some extraordinarily sound excuse'.[61] By 11 April Neville Keynes reported in his diary: 'Maynard is working steadily about three hours a day under my direction. I feel quite like a trainer, as if I were training him for a race or a

d Between 1885 and 1901 only four Kingsmen (including Berry, Richmond and Hurst, Maynard's Eton master) were placed 10th Wrangler or above. For Trinity and St John's the figures were 69 and 46 respectively.

prize fight'. Once he started working with his son, Neville Keynes began worrying that Maynard's mathematical preparation at Eton was inadequate for the tasks ahead, as it was deficient in bookwork and as he was not devoting himself to it with the necessary enthusiasm. His worries were not assuaged by his characteristic consultations in Cambridge, for both Charles Smith, the Master of Sidney Sussex (3rd Wrangler in 1868) and Arthur Berry of King's (a former Senior Wrangler) agreed with him.[62] Maynard did go to see Smith on 26 April, but all he recorded was seeing the proofs of 'a new Euclid he is bringing out'.[63] Worries now reached such a pitch that even the normally unflappable Florence Keynes suggested giving up the family's projected August holiday in Switzerland in favour of a crammer. This proved unnecessary. Neville's consultations, which included two with Walter Durnford of King's, strengthened his view that Maynard should keep up his classics and that he should apply to King's, as the fellows had more discretion in awarding closed than open scholarships. Once Maynard won the Tomline it seemed agreed that he would prepare for King's.[64]

After his Tomline, Maynard increased his classics and cut back on his mathematics during the remainder of the half, which also brought him the Chamberlayne Scholarship of £60 per year for four years on the basis of his Schools Certificate performance. After the family's month-long Swiss holiday, he resumed the routine of three hours of mathematics a day until he went back to school. At this stage, the question of which Cambridge College was re-opened. First Dickson, the examiner in mathematics for the Schools Certificate reported to Neville that his son should get a scholarship at Kings 'or even Trinity'.[65] Then, soon after Maynard returned to Eton, the matter came up again.

> Mr Marten and Hurst have within the last two days been urging me to go up to Trinity instead of King's. The latter wanted to know if you would be coming to Eton any time soon as he would like to see you about my work. I promised I would write and forward his remarks.
>
> Hurst's case is briefly this:
>
> He says that my having won the Chamberlayne puts a different complexion on matters; now that I have that, it would not so much matter if I only got a minor [scholarship] or an exhibition at Trinity.[e] His reason for wishing me to go to Trinity is that he thinks that Mathematics are at a rather low ebb at King's. They do chiefly Classics and Science there. There are not many doing Mathematics; Berry is entirely pure and I should have to go elsewhere for my applied. I should not get a mathematical atmosphere.
>
> It is my very strong impression that he thinks that if I go to King's I

e Trinity minor scholarships ran to £50–75, exhibitions to £40 per annum. A King's scholarship was worth £80.

47

shall be drawn from Mathematics altogether. Marten's reason was but a small one; he thinks my History might count for something in the Trinity general paper.

For myself I still think that I would rather go to King's. I have been imagining myself going there for some time and it is difficult to dispel 'a fixed idea'. Besides, Trinity is all too risky.[66]

When Neville Keynes replied on 6 October that he agreed with Maynard's preference for King's and that the greatest advantage of Trinity would be competition, and when Lubbock reported that a Chamberlayne Scholarship was tenable at King's with an Eton Scholarship, Maynard brought matters to a head:

Hurst has said no more about Trinity; Lubbock would very much prefer me to go to King's and I would rather go there myself; so don't you think we had better decide on the latter.[67]

After this, and as Montagu Rhodes James, the Tutor of King's was willing to change the examination timetable so that Maynard could sit a paper in Latin verse with his mathematics, he was entered for King's.[68] The examination started on 3 December 1901. As usual, Neville Keynes worried over the outcome and convinced himself that Maynard would only get a £60 exhibition. His worries were again unfounded. Maynard's mathematics got him an Eton scholarship, while his classics transformed that into an open scholarship in mathematics *and* classics. The open scholarship brought him not only £80 per annum but also free tuition and rooms until he took his BA.

With this hurdle over, Neville Keynes began to look to the future and add new steps to Maynard's future career:

I have been looking up the King's Statutes & find that Maynard will probably be superannuated for a Fellowship after Mich. T. 1908. I suppose he will take his Tripos in 1905, & his C[ivil]. S[ervice]. exam*n* in 1906; so this leaves a good margin for a Fellowship Dissertation.[69]

Maynard still had two more halves left at Eton. Academically he did not let up, gaining his place in the Select for the Newcastle Prize in March and giving a sparkling performance in his second go at the Schools Certificate which again saw him at the top of the order. During the previous summer half in private business with Lubbock, he had been introduced to the poetry of St Bernard of Cluny in the translation by J. M. Neale. This had stirred an interest which, after more research, resulted in a paper to his Literary Society in May 1902, good reports of which filtered back to Cambridge.[70] There were various plays to do for the Shakespeare Society, scenes from *The Rivals* and *Much Ado About Nothing* for the celebrations of the fourth of June and the usual responsibilities of a member of the sixth form and Pop, the latter enabling him to indulge in 'a perfect dove of a waistcoat, lavender with pale pink spots'.[71] Certainly Eton came to an end in a rush of activity, emotion and nostalgia:

> There is great buying and selling of goods going on. I have raised quite a respectable sum by the sale of worthless and useless effects.
> ... College Pop P.B.
> Pallis did not get a vote of thanks; Williams, Butler and I did – to my great joy.
> I took leave of the Head after 12 ... Pallis gave tea to the Sixth Form.
> ... Dining with Goodhart and many farewells, but no sentiment is allowed in this diary.[72]

And so it was back to Cambridge. On 3 August he noted 'Another long lie and little else ... Margaret puts her hair up, and I begin smoking.[73] Two days later the family went off to Tintagel for a month's holiday. On their return to Cambridge, as well as playing golf as often as possible, Maynard made his final preparations for King's.

NOTES

1 See also Maynard's similar comment to his brother soon after the latter went to Rugby (RKP, JMK to GLK, 14 October 1901).
2 Ollard 1982, 85; Newsome 1980, 69.
3 John Roberts in a humorous attempt (complete with a photograph) to report the 1988 Collegers and Oppidans game in *The Independent*, 28 November 1988; Austen-Leigh 1981, 99.
4 KCKP, JMK to JNK, 29 September 1897.
5 CUL, Add.7847, 5 October, 2 and 21 November 1897.
6 KCKP, S. G. Lubbock to JNK, 31 March 1898.
7 KCKP, JMK to JNK, 17 October, 6 and 12 December 1897.
8 See also JMK's letter to JNK for 15 October 1899, his diary entry for 13 October 1900 and RKP, JMK to GLK, 14 October 1901.
9 KCKP, JMK Diary, 5 May 1900; JMK to JNK, 6 May 1900.
10 KCKP, Report by R. A. H. Mitchell, July 1900.
11 KCKP, S. G. Lubbock to JNK, 17 December 1897, 28 July 1898, 31 March 1899, 21 December 1900, 2 April and 2 July 1901.
12 KCKP, JMK to JMK, 12 May 1901.
13 KCKP, JMK to JNK, 22 May 1898. His 1899 diary reported his average for four innings as 1 (27 June 1899).
14 CUL, Add.7849, 5 July 1899.
15 KCKP, JMK to JNK, 30 January 1898. As in Cambridge, the vote went against women's degrees. Maynard seems to have approved of degrees for women, an opinion he continued to hold (KCKP, JMK to JNK, 6 February 1898).
16 KCKP, JMK to JNK, 15 May 1901.
17 The incident appears in his diary for 23 February 1901, yet the letter to JNK, dated 3 March, opens as it does.
18 KCKP, JMK to JNK, 9 February 1902.
19 Hollis 1960, 209.
20 Connolly 1961, 249–50; Price-Jones 1983, 43–4.
21 Crick 1980, ch. 4; Ayer 1977, ch. 2.

22 KCKP, 3 July 1899, 3 March 1900.
23 KCKP, JMK to JNK, 3 and 10 November 1901, 9 March 1902.
24 See also RKP, JMK to GLK, 14 October 1901.
25 Hollis 1960, 205.
26 Ibid., 288.
27 Gathorne-Hardy 1979, 177.
28 Lambert 1975, 301.
29 Ibid., and Lambert 1968, 270–3 and ch. 11.
30 Ibid., 317–18.
31 Ibid., 320.
32 Ibid., 322; Lambert 1975, 249–50.
33 See Newsome 1980.
34 KCKP, JMK to L. Strachey, 27 March 1905.
35 KCKP, R. H. Dundas to JMK, 3 August 1902. Parts of the letter are quoted in Harrod 1951, 34.
36 Fitzgerald 1977, 67. As Knox remained at Eton a year longer than Maynard, her dating is incorrect.
37 KCKP, JMK to D. Knox, 25 December 1905.
38 BL, ADD.57931, JMK to D. Grant, 22 December 1908.
39 KCKP, JNK to JMK, 1 October 1899; see also his letter to JMK of 24 October.
40 KCKP, JMK to JNK, 27 November 1898; JNK to JMK, 23 November and 2 December 1898.
41 KCKP, JMK Diary, 5 October 1899, JMK to JNK, 8 and 27 October 1899.
42 KCKP, JMK to JNK, 17 December 1899.
43 KCKP, JMK to JNK, 29 January 1900. In his diary for that date, Maynard noted that the Headmaster spoke of a 'national crisis'.
44 KCKP, JMK to JNK, 11 February 1900.
45 CUL,Add.7850, 31 January 1900; KCKP, FAK to JMK, 30 January 1900.
46 KCKP, JMK to JNK, 18 February, 18 March and 20 May 1900. See also JMK's diary for 22 July 1900.
47 KCKP, JMK to JNK, 20 May 1900; JMK Diary, 17 November and 29 December 1900, 9 January 1901.
48 See, for example, KCKP, JNK to JMK, 14 and 22 October 1897; 12 May and 2 July 1898; 5 March, 21 May and 17 June 1900.
49 KCKP, JMK to JNK, 6 and 8 February 1898; JNK to JMK, 7 and 9 February 1898.
50 CUL, Add.7848, 29 October 1898.
51 KCKP, JMK to JNK, 14 May 1899.
52 KCKP, JMK to JNK, 21 October 1900.
53 KCKP, JMK to JNK, 24 February and 17 March 1901; CUL, Add.7851, 12 and 19 March, 8 and 13 May 1901.
54 KCKP, JMK to JNK, 13 October 1901; CUL, Add.7851, 10 and 16 October 1901.
55 KCKP, JMK to JNK, 10 October and 16 June 1901.
56 KCKP, JNK to JMK, 17 June 1901; on the consultations, see p. 47.
57 CUL, Add.7851, 15 October 1901.
58 Wilkinson 1980b, 173.
59 CUL, Add.7850 18 and 21 November 1900.
60 CUL, Add.7851, 29 January and 12 March 1901.
61 CUL, Add.7851, 5 April 1901; KCKP, JMK Diary, 5 April 1901.
62 CUL, Add.7851, 14, 19 and 25 April and 2 May 1901.

63 KCKP, JMK Diary, 26 April 1901.
64 CUL, Add.7851, 26 and 30 April, 2 and 8 May and 23 June 1901.
65 Ibid., 12 September 1901.
66 KCKP, JMK to JNK, 4 October 1901.
67 KCKP, JMK to JNK, 13 October 1901.
68 CUL, Add.7851, 24 and 28 October 1901.
69 CUL, Add.7852, 14 January 1902.
70 Ibid., 11 June 1902.
71 KCKP, JMK to FAK, 2 May 1902.
72 KCKP, JMK Diary, 25, 26, 27 and 30 July 1902.
73 Ibid., 3 August 1902.

3

KING'S UNDERGRADUATE

I don't think one realises how very discrete (in the mathematical sense)
one's existence is. My days at school don't seem to have the remotest
connexion with my doings up here: nor my life in one term with my life
in any other.

(KCKP, JMK to A. L. Hobhouse, 27 March 1905)

The College that Maynard entered in October 1902 in many outward
appearances differed little from the one visited by hundreds of thousands
of tourists annually nine decades later. The iron railings along the King's
Parade front disappeared in 1932, replaced by the current low, stone wall.
However, the front court with the Chapel, begun in 1446 by Henry VI and
completed by Henry VIII, dominating the north side of the large lawn;
the classical early eighteenth-century Gibbs building on the west; Wilkins's
fantastic 1824–8 Gothic screen, gatehouse and cupola on the east; and the
same architect's Hall range on the south which continues westwards to form
the spur of buildings running down to the river all remain unchanged in
most of their externals from Maynard's time as an undergraduate. Only
at the extremities of the College would one notice a difference: near the
river, where Bodley's buildings (1893) were extended and linked to the
Old Provost's Lodge between the wars; south of Wilkins's raised library,
where Webb's Court (1907) was completed with a new Provost's Lodge
(1927–9); and behind the Hall, where the Keynes Building of the 1960s
covers the old kitchens and the old tenement range in King's Lane,
known as the Drain, Maynard's first home in King's. There King's put
its new scholars and other freshmen who had managed to obtain rooms
in College.

At the turn of the century, with just over 150 undergraduates, King's was
a smaller, more intimate place than it is now. Then, as now, it was towards
the smallish end of the middle-sized Cambridge Colleges, but its fellowship
was large by Cambridge standards, 46 being the statutory limit during this
period. Although fellows could, and did, marry after 1882, there was a large
enough body of resident dons (30 in 1900) to sustain the intimate contact
between don and undergraduate that remained part of the King's 'style'

until the expansion of undergraduate numbers, the explosion of graduate students and the accompanying increased academic professionalism of the post-1945 world put paid to much of the old order.

The King's 'style' had several roots. There were the traditions carried over from the Eton connection, for until 1873 only Etonians were scholars or fellows – and most of those had been Collegers. Shared past experiences and the Eton tradition of close contact between masters and scholars provided fertile ground. Perhaps more important by Maynard's period were several individual dons who established a habit of being accessible to undergraduates, prepared, moreover, to talk with them on any subject and to listen to them sympathetically. Most notable among these were Henry Bradshaw, Oscar Browning (or O.B.), Nathaniel Wedd and Goldsworthy Lowes Dickinson, but all the Provosts of the period also played a part. The resulting atmosphere of easy informality, mutual interest, shared experiences and, in many cases, lifelong friendships made the King's of Maynard's undergraduate years a relatively small but exciting place, even if it was sometimes rather inward-looking and precious.

The Mathematical Tripos for which Maynard was entered was not only the oldest of the Cambridge triposes but also the most conservative in its practices. While other disciplines had ceased to rank honours candidates in order of merit within classes and subdivisions of classes in the 1880s and 1890s, the mathematicians continued the practice until 1908. Similarly, while in most other subjects the College-based supervision system had come to the fore by 1900, in mathematics the practice of using outside coaches whose renown – and incomes – depended on their ability to produce Wranglers remained widespread. Neville Keynes was quite pleased that Maynard's coach would be Ernest William Hobson, a fellow of Christ's, University Lecturer in Mathematics (1883–1910) and Sadlerian Professor of Mathematics from 1910. Hobson had been first Wrangler in 1878. In 1902 he had coached the top three Wranglers, plus those placed ninth and sixteenth. Under such a régime, intensive teaching, cramming and drill were the norm and all eyes rested on the result at the end of the day, the candidate's place in Part I of the Tripos.

By 9 October 1902 Maynard had settled into his first floor rooms in King's Lane. Above him on the same staircase were C. R. Fay, later an economic historian, who was about to play rugby for the University, and Robin Furness, a classicist who was to become Maynard's closest undergraduate friend in Cambridge. Opposite Maynard was W. M. Page, a mathematics scholar who was to go with him to Hobson, to be above him in the list of Wranglers in 1905 and to win a fellowship at King's in 1908 – the year Maynard was unsuccessful. Below him was John Capron, whom he had known at Eton and who would later set up an altar in his bedroom with the permission of the Bishop of London and claim to have exorcised an evil spirit in Maynard. Fay remembered the impression Maynard made:

> When I arrived in the Lane for Little-go[a] on 1 October 1902, there was only one other person on the staircase; and as I descended from my about-to-be-furnished rooms, he asked me to come in and have some tea. 'My name is Keynes. What's yours?' He had a moustache and fancy waistcoat, a beautifully carved desk and a wicker basket with a pair of gloves in it. He asked me if I liked the place, and I said 'Rather', and to keep the ball rolling I lugged in O.B. whereupon he said 'I was at Eton too'.
>
> . . . A Puritan in soul and bodily habit, he yet was fond of sumptuous things, of old books, of social breakfasts, *de luxe* travel and *petits cheveux* . . . and fond above all of being in the swim . . .
>
> As an undergraduate he did many things, and once out of bed worked really hard trying to keep up with Page in Mathematics and always finding time for his other interests, literary, social and political. . . . Neither Page nor I was his bosom friend. This was our Classic, R. A. Furness, whose familiarity with Rabelais and Sterne *et hoc genus omne* caused Page to blush, me to feel [an] inferiority complex and Keynes to be enviously competitive. . . . But what I remember now are the pronouncements of his Freshman year, such as (and this is literally true) 'I've had a good look round the place and come to the conclusion that it's pretty inefficient.'[1]

Maynard did not take long to get settled into King's and undergraduate life. He got used to his College supervisor, H. W. Richmond, and the 9 a.m. class he held for him and Page three times a week.[b] At the outset, as Neville Keynes reported, he made a firm decision that 'he would not, even if he could thereby be Senior Wrangler, devote himself exclusively to mathematics'.[2] Yet he did settle down with Hobson, who commented on his good logical grasp and his need to develop a quick mathematical perception, and, with difficulty, he managed to put in six hours a day at the subject. This enabled him to keep up, but it meant that there were soon reports in his father's diary that Maynard would have to work harder and devote less time to outside activities.[3] He seems to have enjoyed working with Hobson, for in February 1903, when the Lucasian Professorship fell vacant, he reported that he would give up mathematics if his coach got the chair. And, despite a brief period of doubt when he believed mathematics his worst subject, he

a The Little-go, or Previous Examination, was required of all Cambridge candidates for degrees unless they had obtained exemption by passing similar examinations for the Schools Certificate. It consisted of Latin, Greek and mathematics.
b Harrod (1951, 37) is incorrect in stating that he went to Hobson at that time. According to Maynard's appointments diary for 1902–3 he went to Richmond at 9 and Hobson between 11 and 12.

continued to satisfy Hobson, who believed that he was capable of finishing in the lower half of the first ten Wranglers.[4]

Outside his academic concerns, Maynard quickly spread his wings. 'I have never enjoyed myself so much before', he reported to Swithinbank on 13 November. At the outset, he had, as expected, joined the Union, which he was to use extensively, and the Pitt Club, which he used relatively little despite (or because of) its dominance by Etonians.[c] He was soon trying the myriad of small societies in King's and Cambridge. On 19 October he was elected to the Apennine Society, the oldest literary club in King's. Within the next month there were reports of his taking part as a visitor in Oscar Browning's Political Society, but O.B. did 'not find favour in Maynard's eyes' and the feeling seems to have been mutual.[d] However, he did take part in the Walpole Society, Richmond's Shakespeare Society and Dickinson's Philosophical Essay Society. By the end of November he could, through his various societies, manage five debates a week, if he chose to. In November too, he made his maiden speech at the Union in favour of the motion 'that the British system of government by party is becoming a hindrance to useful legislation'. Although he nervously spoke too quickly, the 'quiet manner . . . so rare in the Union' and 'interesting opinions' meant his late evening contribution was well received.[5] Edwin Montagu, then President of the Union, approached him to speak fourth two weeks later, opposing the motion 'that this House welcomes the proposal that Mr. Chamberlain should visit South Africa'. From then onwards he was a regular contributor to Union debates and developed a reputation for being clear, fluent and logical, if initially tending towards undemonstrativeness and flatness, the latter characteristic diminishing with time.[6] If all this was not enough, he kept up his sporting interests, rowing almost every day in a crew that won the College cup in Michaelmas of 1902 (although abandoning rowing early in the next term) and going to Eton to play for King's in the annual Wall Game between the two sister foundations. Then there was the by now usual round of book buying (another 50 by November bringing his total by year end up to 330), lunches, dinners, teas, and evenings visiting dons, including two Thursday 'evenings' with J. E. McTaggart, the Trinity philosopher, and visits with friends new and old.[7] The new year was to see him initiated into an institution and concerns that had their strongest roots in Victorian Cambridge.

Victorian England had been a period of transformation.[8] Rapid economic

c However, he did use its letterhead for one letter to each of his siblings in February 1903 (KCPH, JMK to MK, 19 February 1903; RKP, JMK to GLK, 19 February 1903).
d CUL Add.7852, 20 and 22 October, 16 November and 3 December 1902; Wortham 1927, 285. Wortham's biography (322–4) does not include Maynard amongst the members of the Society.

development was changing her from an agrarian-commercial society to the highly urbanised workshop of the world. Then, from as early as the 1850s, her leadership was threatened as the process produced new overseas competitors, notably the United States and Germany. It was also a period of intellectual ferment. Old certainties looked less certain and the reconstruction of many areas of thought came to seem a necessity. Yet Victorians, especially of the earlier period, never doubted that it was possible to arrive at the truth – or at least an interim version of the truth. Their successors would be less optimistic. Meanwhile, there was the prospect of progress, both material and intellectual. Vestiges of this optimistic prospect remained down to 1914.

Progress, or appearance of progress, came at a price. The challenging of old forms and old ideas produced considerable anxiety. At least until the 1860s there were fears of political and social revolution. The challenges to established religion resulted in fears that the collapse of faith would remove the supports to traditional morality and produce social disintegration. Fears and doubts in the context of rapid change afflicted many with worry and fatigue – so much so that the shattering mid-career breakdown was a familiar feature of Victorian life. The new industrialism produced the Victorian city – anonymous, psychically and socially isolating, unhealthy and often ugly. It might also be argued that the difficulties and fears of urban life played a significant role in developing the nostalgia for a supposedly simple rural existence which still plays an important role in English thought.

The contradictory pressures of the Victorian age helped to shape the peculiarities of the Victorian mind. Doubts, uncertainties and anxieties often resulted in intense activity, partly to deal with them, partly to escape from them. Insecurity often meant that conventions and proprieties came to have even larger force than normally. Perhaps, because individuals frequently expected that subversive thoughts or facts might, on further inspection, turn out to be true, insecurity often led to evasiveness. Doubt, plus the desire to believe, frequently led to what strikes the modern observer as credulity. It is easy to debunk 'eminent Victorians', as well as those who were not so eminent.

One Victorian figure, Henry Sidgwick (1838–1900), is particularly important for what follows. Another, Alfred Marshall (1842–1924), will appear later. Sidgwick was certainly plagued by doubts, yet he was candid about them. Marshall gave fewer outward signs of inner doubt, but he was much more insecure. He was certainly evasive. The work of both men was to play an important role in the life of Maynard Keynes.

Keynes was later, in his obituary notices of C. P. Sanger and Frank Ramsey, to borrow a paragraph from Goldsworthy Lowes Dickinson's obituary of the two which aptly sums up the influence and achievement of Sidgwick's type.

It does not become a Cambridge man to claim too much for his university, nor am I much tempted to do so. But there is, I think, a certain type, rare, like all good things, which seems to be associated in some peculiar way with my *alma mater*. I am thinking of Leslie Stephen (the original of Meredith's Vernon Whitford), like Henry Sidgwick, like Maitland ... It is a type unworldly without being saintly, unambitious without being inactive, warm-hearted without being sentimental. Through good report and ill such men work on, following the light of truth as they see it; able to be skeptical without being paralysed; content to know what is knowable and reserve judgement on what is not. The world could never be driven by such men, for the springs of action lie deep in ignorance and madness. But it is they who are the beacon in the tempest, and they are more, not less, needed now than ever before. May their succession never fail![9]

Sidgwick is important on more than one level. There is the matter of his intellectual achievements – although some are frankly dismissive of these, be they in ethics or economics.[10] More important in some respects was his impact on Cambridge, not only as one of the leaders from the 1860s of the reform movement of which I have already spoken, where 'his hand, sometimes his inspiration, was in every major administrative and teaching reform',[11] but also more generally. J. P. C. Roach called him

one of the most important academic figures of the century because he is the first modern Cambridge don. His ideals, his character, his interests, even his uncertainties are of a type which is recognisable today.[12]

Joseph Schumpeter, one of Sidgwick's intellectual critics, noticed this, while dismissing the long-term impact of his academic work.

But he was one of the greatest English University men all the same: milieu-creating, milieu-leading, soul-shaping to an extraordinary degree. Perhaps lack of originality is one of the conditions for this peculiar kind of academic achievement.[13]

He went on to describe Sidgwick's mind as 'so lucid and so wingless'.

Henry Sidgwick, the son of a clerical headmaster who had been at Trinity and last Wrangler in 1829 and the grandson of a self-made cotton spinner, was born at Skipton in the West Riding of Yorkshire on 31 May 1838. His father died in 1841 leaving his mother with five surviving children, one of whom died soon afterwards. The remaining three boys and a girl all made their mark in the world.

Sidgwick was educated at a day school in Bristol and a boarding school at Blackheath before he went to Rugby in 1852. He was a boarder for only one year, for his mother moved the family there in 1853. At Rugby,

Henry came under the influence of his cousin E. W. Benson. Benson, a moderate, moralistic, high churchman, after being a master at Rugby and headmaster of Wellington College, went on to a career of rapid ecclesiastical preferment, moving from being Chancellor of Lincoln to Bishop of Truro to Archbishop of Canterbury within a decade. He married Sidgwick's sister Mary in 1859.

In 1855 Sidgwick went up to Trinity College, Cambridge determined to win himself a fellowship. Despite the risks involved, and despite a period of illness, he read for the Classical and Mathematical Triposes simultaneously. He was successful – 33rd Wrangler, Senior Classicist and Chancellor's Medallist in 1859. He became a Fellow of Trinity and College Lecturer in Classics in October 1859.

During his second undergraduate year, Sidgwick was elected a member of the Cambridge Conversazione Society or the Apostles, a semi-secret discussion society founded in 1820. Initially he was reluctant to join the Society because he thought membership might interfere with his scholarly ambitions, but he relented and found the attachment 'the strongest corporate bond which I have known in life'.[14] He later credited the Society with making him realise 'that the deepest bent of my nature was towards the life of thought – thought exercised on the central problems of human life'.[15] Many of his closest, life-long friends were members of the Society, although some remained from his schooldays at Bristol and Rugby.

One of the characteristics of the discussions of the Apostles, according to Sidgwick, was their

> spirit of the pursuit of truth with absolute devotion and unreserve . . . . Absolute candour was the only duty that the tradition of the Society enforced. . . . [T]here were no propositions so well established that an Apostle had not the right to deny or question if he did so sincerely.[16]

It was in this setting – he was to give thirty-two papers to the Society in his nine years of active membership – that most of Sidgwick's characteristic intellectual attitudes and philosophical ideas were to develop.

The foci of Sidgwick's early concerns were morality and religion. He had grown up in the firm, orthodox, Christian certainties of the age. During the period of his active membership of the Society these certainties were challenged from several quarters, even though elsewhere these were years of spiritual revival. The challenges came in science from the work of Darwin, Huxley and Lyell; in anthropology from E. B. Taylor and others; and in moral science from Comte and John Stuart Mill. These challenges were significant not only for their effects on the bases for religious belief but also for their effects on the bases for morality in an age when many believed that beliefs about personal immortality, divine judgement, and eternal penalties and rewards served as the foundation for the decencies of civilisation.

Initially the questionings of Sidgwick and his Apostolic contemporaries were directed by the new scientific attitudes to human institutions and behaviour associated with Mill and Comte. With regard to religion:

> What was fixed and unalterable was the necessity and duty of examining the evidence for historical Christianity with strict scientific impartiality; placing ourselves outside traditional sentiments and opinions, and endeavouring to weigh the *pros* and *cons* on all theological questions as a duly instructed rational being from another planet – or let us say China – would weigh them.[17]

More generally:

> What we aimed at from a social point of view was a complete revision of human relations, political, moral and economic, in the light of science directed by comprehensive and impartial sympathy; and an unsparing reform of whatever, in the judgement of science, was pronounced to be not conducive to general happiness. This social science must of course have historical knowledge as a basis . . . .History, in short, was conceived as supplying the material on which we had to work but not the ideal which we aimed at realising; except so far as history properly understood showed us that the time had come for the scientific treatment of political and moral matters.[18]

With these broad ends in view, it is perhaps not surprising that Sidgwick not only lost his faith but also wrote a series of treatises – *The Methods of Ethics, The Principles of Political Economy* and *The Elements of Politics*. By the time he had lost his faith Sidgwick had prepared the ground for all of these enterprises.[19]

The process by which Sidgwick lost his faith and then came to the conclusion that he must resign his Trinity fellowship, which required subscription to the 39 Articles of the Church of England, was long and involved – and need not detain us in its details. But I should note the systematic thoroughness with which he approached his problem in ways that his successors, including the young Maynard Keynes, often find odd.[20] Under the influence of Renan's *Etudes d'Histoire Religieuse*, he came to believe that in examining the evidence for historical Christianity it was necessary to try to get inside the Middle Eastern mind from which the religion came, with the result that he spent several years learning Arabic and Hebrew in his spare time. Similarly, a concern with the existence of miracles and the question of continued individual existence after death saw him engage in his 'ghostological enquiries' which eventuated in the founding of the Society for Psychical Research in 1882.[21] Maynard Keynes would get involved in the activities of the Society in the years before 1914.

Having lost his faith, and after making careful provision for the decrease in income by increasing the amount of coaching he did, Sidgwick resigned his Trinity fellowship in 1869. His grounds for resignation were essentially utilitarian. As he told Anne Clough, with whom he was involved in the founding of what became Newnham College,

> It is my painful conviction that the prevailing lax subscription is not perfectly conscientious in the case of many subscribers: and that those who subscribe laxly from the highest motives are responsible for the degradation of moral and religious feeling that others suffer. It would require very clear and evident gain of some other kind to induce me to undergo this responsibility. And this gain I do not see.[22]

Sidgwick was not the first Cambridge utilitarian. When he fell under the spell of Mill, the latter's influence in Cambridge was actually on the wane from the peak of the 1840s and early 1850s when it had affected Henry Fawcett, Henry Maine and Leslie Stephen.[23] Yet Sidgwick attempted to give the position new life and to combine social and moral philosophy within one over-arching principle.

At the time Sidgwick began his attempt, the two dominant schools of moral philosophy, which had their echoes in other fields, were utilitarianism and intuitionism. The utilitarians argued that conduct should be judged by its consequences; the intuitionists started from the position that there were certain self-evident general truths or supreme moral principles which formed the basis of ethics and which could be grasped by intuition. Both doctrines had religious roots – utilitarianism in the work of William Paley (incidentally the great grandfather of Alfred Marshall's wife Mary), intuitionism in that of Bishop Butler. In the hands of William Godwin and Jeremy Bentham, utilitarianism came to be associated with reform and hostility to the teachings of Christianity. Intuitionism as a position critical of utilitarianism remained associated with the church, but increasingly it had to take on a purely reasonable or secular basis.

The major battleground between the two schools came to lie over the exact status of commonsense morality. The utilitarians, with their own fundamental principle which judged actions by their consequences, argued that one could not presume that commonsense morality was rational. They provided a rational method for the reform of that morality. Their intuitionist critics on their part had to show how practical commonsense morality might be rational even if it stemmed from a plurality of principles which might give inconsistent guidance in particular cases.

When Sidgwick became involved, the leading proponent of utilitarianism was John Stuart Mill, while the dominant intuitionist was William Whewell, Master of Trinity College, Cambridge (1841–66) and Knightbridge Professor of Philosophy (1838–55). Mill's *Utilitarianism*, which appeared in *Fraser's Magazine* in 1861 and in book form in 1863, was an attempt to remove popular antipathy to and suspicion of the position and to convince intellectuals of its soundness. But in his attempt to appear open-minded and reasonable, Mill left utilitarianism in some disarray, for he threw over the simple egotistical calculus of pleasures and pains that had been the strength of Benthamism. His new distinction between higher and lower pleasures raised, as Mill recognised, problems of calculability in any simple sense. The suggestion 'It is better to be a human being dissatisfied than a pig satisfied: better to be a Socrates dissatisfied than a fool satisfied.'[24] raised the suggestion that there might be objects of desire valuable in themselves and that a knowledge of the individual involved might affect the morality of the outcome. Again, the suggestion that utilitarianism recognised 'in human beings the power of sacrificing their own greatest good for the good of others'[25] raised the possibility of a conflict between the claims of private and public happiness, thus also weakening the simplicity of the doctrine. Finally, Mill's acceptance of the rules of commonsense morality as the secondary rules to be applied in day-to-day practice as a utilitarian opened the way for extensive debate with the intuitionists, as well as raising the question of whether society was an aggregate of individuals motivated by self-seeking or something more. Thus he left utilitarianism as a moral philosophy with several problems.

In the course of sorting out his religious views, Sidgwick also attempted to sort through his views of ethics. The exercises were, in part, related, as Sidgwick noted:

> I had been led back to philosophy by quite a different line of thought [than teaching or examining] from a practical point of view – that is, by the question that seemed to me continually to press with more urgency for a definite answer – whether I had a right to keep my Fellowship. I did my best to decide the question methodically on general principles but found it very difficult, and I may say that while struggling with the difficulty thence arising, I went through a great deal of the thought that was ultimately systematised in the *Methods of Ethics*.[26]

The title of Sidgwick's book is important. He was not trying to produce a final or complete solution, or even primarily to defend utilitarianism as the best available method. In the end he argued that any complete system of ethics would require the acceptance of the truth of a theological or metaphysical proposition asserting a moral order in the universe which would also solve systematic differences of opinion on moral issues resulting from the exercise of free will. And his belief that commonsense morality was improving left open the question whether any synthesis could be final. Rather, what Sidgwick was attempting was to see the extent to which commonsense morality, which both sides of the ethical debate in the previous decade had recognised as important, could be systematised on a self-evident basis. To this end, he investigated three methods – egoistic humanism, universalistic hedonism (or utilitarianism) and intuitionism. Or, more correctly, he investigated two methods in detail, for he could not decide by reason alone between the claims of egoism and morality.

In adjudicating between utilitarianism and intuitionism, Sidgwick engaged in an extensive survey of commonsense morality, or those conclusions and arguments which might find favour with educated, cultivated or morally sensitive persons. He did so with the aim of seeing whether it was possible to derive many of its conclusions from a clear, limited set of principles and, where parts of received opinion did not make sense, to use the general principles to criticise them. Eventually he came to the conclusion that dogmatic intuitionism would not suffice and that any more satisfying exercise required the principles of utilitarianism. Thus, at one level he suggested that the sharp distinction between intuitionism and utilitarianism was wrongly drawn. In fact, as he had himself discovered over a decade earlier, intuitionism was necessary to complete utilitarianism.[27] The intuitions required were very abstract and general propositions about justice, prudence and benevolence. With these he proceeded to demonstrate that he could make utilitarianism an ethical theory capable of systematising moral intuitions. He could offer a utilitarian account of values commonly thought as not being inspired by utilitarianism and often considered as good counter examples to the utilitarian outlook – truth-telling, spontaneous affection.

As Sidgwick noticed, there were problems with the system he had created.[28] Perhaps the most notable concerned exceptions to rules where 'the general observance is necessary to the well-being of the community, while a certain amount of non-observance is rather advantageous than otherwise'.[29] Schneewind puts one example most concisely:

> Suppose one has in mind a class of exceptions to a rule, on the grounds that allowing this class of exceptions would be hedonistically better than prohibiting it; but also that the use of the rule with this exception-clause in it would require more subtlety or sophistication than one can rightly expect from most people. Then, Sidgwick thinks, if one is known to advocate or act on that particular moral belief, one runs the risk of weakening public morality. It seems to him to follow that it may be right to do secretly what one could not openly advocate. This, as he points out, is paradoxical in the eyes of common sense, and a good utilitarian will generally want to support the common belief that it cannot be right to do secretly what it would be wrong to do openly . . . He will therefore want to keep secret what it is not right to do openly. In fact, the utilitarian will be led, more generally, to the conclusion that it is undesirable to have everyone calculating everything on a utilitarian basis, since the unavoidable indefiniteness of such calculations leaves scope for the wicked and the weak to construct specious excuses for their misbehaviour.[30]

As Bernard Williams puts it, utilitarianism thus emerges as the morality of an élite – hardly a satisfactory solution.[31] Yet in explicitly facing such difficulties Sidgwick was being characteristically himself, and his openness made his book more influential, if less satisfactory for those in search of a system.

Sidgwick's attempt to reconcile previously radical utilitarian views with the existing state of society appeared again in his *Principles of Political Economy*, noted for its careful, correct distinction between reasoning about 'what is' and 'what ought to be' and its path-breaking discussion of the principles of state intervention to remedy the defects of competition.[32] It also appeared in *The Elements of Politics*, where, according to one observer, 'he uses the method of Bentham to arrive at the conclusion of Burke'.[33] Throughout all his work there was a remarkable unity in the principles proposed – and in the rather conciliatory results – which is not all that surprising since the origins of all his major projects lay in his own intellectual difficulties of the 1860s.

There was also a streak of melancholy in Sidgwick. From the time of his undergraduate illness, he was subject to recurrent periods of depression accompanied (or caused) by insomnia. These often coincided with the later stages of a major piece of work. This happened with *The Methods of Ethics*. As he told George Eliot:

> I feel rather dull from the task of weaving a sieve to hold the water of life in – for a book on Morals often seems like that; however tight one tries to draw the meshes, everything of the nature of wisdom seems to have run through when one examines the result – that is, if it was ever there.[34]

It also happened with *The Elements of Politics*.[35] Yet at an earlier stage of writing *The Elements* another, reassuringly familiar, attitude appeared.

> Personally, I am trying to absorb myself in my Opus Magnum on *Politics*. My position is that I seem to myself now to have grasped adequately the only possible method of dealing systematically with political problems; but my deep conviction is that it can yield as yet little fruit of practical utility – so doubt whether it is worth while to work it out in a book. Still man must work – and a Professor must write books.[36]

This sense of duty, of role, keeps cropping up in Sidgwick. His larger speculations invariably ended up with the practical question, 'What is to be done here and now?'[37]

Sidgwick had a particularly bad bout of speculative doubts, with their related worries as to their consequences for him, in the late 1860s when he lost his faith. They reappeared on an extensive scale – or at least the records are better, given the diaries he kept for John Addington Symonds – in the late 1880s.[38] By that stage his vision of a Moral Science Tripos was running into opposition from Alfred Marshall, John Seeley and Brooke Westcott, and the movement for University reform of the 1860s and 1870s was beginning to be stranded on the sandbars of the agricultural depression. Many of his mentors had died. Over twenty years of ghostological enquiries had done little more than disclose frauds and the extent of human credulity. Thus, for an extended period, Sidgwick, who in *The Methods of Ethics* had stated that practical reason ultimately made contradictory demands upon action unless one could draw on some datum beyond experience such as the existence of a god or some moral order in the universe, found himself worried about the consequences. As he put it, 'the question is whether to profess Ethics without a basis' or 'what course can the sage recommend to a philosopher who has philosophised himself into a conviction of the unprofitableness of philosophy'?[39] He resolved the problem by working harder – at *The Elements of Politics* and his posthumous *The Development of European Polity*. But his exercise in ethical system-building lay in ruins.

That period of philosophical depression had been preceded by one of political depression. Sidgwick was very well connected politically. In 1876 he had married Eleanor, the sister of his former pupil Arthur James Balfour, who in the mid-1880s began his rise in the Conservative Party that would make him Prime Minister in 1902. He was part of a circle which included, from the other side of the House, George Trevelyan and James Bryce. The 1880s were a period of political change in Britain as the Liberal Party split over Home Rule for Ireland. Sidgwick had become progressively disillusioned with Gladstone. He would eventually use the Liberal split as an opportunity to move with the Liberal Unionists into the Conservative Party, cutting short a holiday to come home and vote Tory in the election of 1886, even though the Cambridge Conservative seat was a safe one.[40] Yet his alienation from Liberalism worried him, especially given his work on his *Elements*.[41] He had also come to the conclusion that England's economic greatness was in decline and that 'individualism of the extreme kind has had its day'.[42] In these circumstances, with worries about the Poor Law – he was active in the local Mendicity Society and instrumental in its reform along Charity-Organisation-Society lines – he ruefully mused:

> I have a certain alarm in respect of the movement of modern society towards Socialism, *i.e.*, the more and more extensive intervention of Government with a view to palliate the inequities in the distribution of wealth. At the same time I regard this movement as *on the whole* desirable and beneficent – the expectation of it belongs to the cheerful side of my forecast of the future; if duly moderated it *might*, I conceive, be purely beneficent, and bring improvement at every stage. But – judging from past experience – one must expect that so vast a change will not be realised without violent shocks and oscillations, great blunders followed by great disasters and consequent reactions; that the march of progress, perturbed by the selfish ambitions of the leaders and the blind appetites of the followers will suffer many spasmodic deviations into

paths which it will have to painfully retrace. Perhaps . . . one country will have to suffer the pains of experiments for the benefit of the whole system of states; and, if so, it is on various grounds likely that this country may be England.

In this way I sometimes feel alarmed – even for my own 'much goods laid up for many years' – but not, on the whole, seriously. Considering all the chances of misfortune that life offers, the chance of having one's railway shares confiscated is not prominent, though I should not be surprised at being mulcted of a part of my dividends.[43]

This is quintessential Sidgwick – thoughtful, open-minded, tentative, slightly pessimistic (although tinged with optimism), self-deprecating. It would have been impossible for such a person to teach a system dogmatically, much less to found a school. He was too uncertain of his own results for that.[44] In consequence, Cambridge moral sciences, unlike Cambridge economics, remained diverse in his lifetime – and after.

Some student societies in King's overlapped in membership with another Cambridge royal foundation, Trinity. Among these was the Decemviri, to which Maynard was elected in November 1902. Its members included John Sheppard and Lytton Strachey. Perhaps through this connection, but probably also through other members in King's – Lowes Dickinson, H. O. Meredith, L. H. Greenwood – towards the end of the Michaelmas term of 1902 he was visited by Lytton Strachey and Leonard Woolf with the purpose of vetting him for membership in yet another society.[45] The vetting continued early in the next term: John Sheppard took him to tea with G. E. Moore,[46] and his appointments diary includes the following entries in February: 4th, dinner with A. W. Verrall (the other guests were Sheppard and Strachey); 5th, tea with Strachey; 11th, tea with Sheppard; 22nd, tea with Woolf; 22nd and 25th, meetings with Sheppard. He also attended the lectures of two senior members of this society in the Lent term, J. E. McTaggart's on metaphysics and G. E. Moore's on modern ethics. Moore's lectures, for which Keynes's notes survive, overlapped with the final stages of the preparation of *Principia Ethica* which Moore delivered to Cambridge University Press on 18 March 1903, two days after the end of full term.

The society for which Maynard was being so carefully vetted and to which he was elected on 28 February 1903 was the Cambridge Conversazione Society, or the Apostles. The Society and its members were to play an important role in Maynard's life, for he was to remain involved in and concerned about its activities until 1937 and close to many members until his death.

According to Paul Levy, Maynard's was the 243rd election to the society.[47] It had begun life in 1820 when George Tomlinson, later Bishop of Gibraltar, founded a discussion group with eleven other friends in St John's. In its early years, its existence and membership were not secret (to this day its existence never seems to have been secret), for it was just one of many small undergraduate discussion societies whose existence, although of some importance to its members, is of no importance to the larger world – beyond indicating the vitality of undergraduate life. What was to make the Society important in Cambridge's intellectual life was its longevity and, after its obscure early years, the intellectual importance of many, although far from all, of its members. A significant proportion of the reformers of Victorian Cambridge were members: we have already met Sidgwick, but we could also add Frederick Maurice, Oscar Browning, Henry Jackson, James Stuart, Richard Jebb and F. W. Maitland. The dominance of its members in more than a century of Cambridge philosophy is also remarkable – Frederick Maurice, Sidgwick, James Ward, Alfred North Whitehead, J. E. McTaggart, Bertrand Russell, G. E. Moore, Ludwig Wittgenstein, Richard Braithwaite and Frank Ramsey.

The change in the Society from the early Johnian group to one so eminent that its current membership and activities became secret in the 1850s was largely the result of Frederick Maurice, who, with John Sterling, toughened its intellectual discipline while leaving its range of concerns wider than before. The Society's business became 'to make its members study and think on all matters except Mathematics and Classics *professionally* considered' and yet to impose no restrictions on such thought other than rationality and sincerity.[48] As Sidgwick put it in a passage partially quoted earlier:

> I can only describe it as the spirit of the pursuit of truth with absolute devotion and unreserve by a group of intimate friends, who were perfectly frank with each other, and indulged in any amount of humorous sarcasm and playful banter, and yet each respected the other, and when he discourses tries to learn from him and see what he sees. Absolute candour was the only duty that the tradition of the society enforced. No consistency was demanded with opinions previously held – truth as we saw it then and there was what we had to embrace and maintain, and there were no propositions so well established that an Apostle had not the right to deny or question, if he did so sincerely and not from mere love of paradox. The gravest subjects were continually debated, but gravity of treatment, as I have said, was not imposed, though sincerity was. In fact it was rather a point of the apostolic mind to understand how much suggestion and instruction may be derived from what is in form a jest – even in dealing with the gravest matters.[49]

Inevitably not every meeting nor every paper of the Society reached this ideal, but its existence, plus the emphasis on self-examination and spiritual development, proved an important supplement and counterweight to the norms of University life.

With the ideals came a formalisation of routine. Members of the Society were the 'brethren' – there were no special privileges dependent on outside status. Members were expected to attend every meeting when in Cambridge in term. Members who could not meet these requirements – and 'membership' was for life – 'took wings' and became 'angels'. They could still attend any meeting they wished and take part in the discussions. Members and angels met in London annually for the Dinner. Angels often played an important role as advisers, especially over the election of new members. The world outside the Society was 'phenomenal'. Prospective members or 'embryos' were subject to the scrutiny of the active members and such angels whose opinions were important, normally without the embryo's knowing it. If elected – and election required unanimity among the members – the new member was subjected to an induction ceremony called 'birth' and his sponsor was sometimes referred to as his 'father'. The records of the Society – membership, topics discussed and voted on and some papers – were held in the Ark, in Maynard's time a cedar chest donated by Oscar Browning.

The routine for meetings was straightforward. Members met on Saturday evenings in the rooms of the paper-giver or moderator. He[e] read his paper from the hearthrug on a topic agreed at the previous meeting. The others present drew lots to determine their order of speaking and proceeded in turn to discuss from the hearthrug matters the moderator had raised – or anything else. At the end of the discussion a question would be put to the vote. From the mid-nineteenth century the question could not bear an obvious relationship to the topic under discussion, although it normally arose from some aspect of the evening's conversations. Once the question was formulated and written down in a book, votes took the form of members signing in agreement, disagreement or abstention. Sardines on toast, or 'whales', and coffee followed before those present proceeded to decide the topic for the next Saturday and to draw lots for the next week's moderator. Of course, papers went unprepared on occasion, but then the defaulting member often paid the price of entertaining those in attendance to dinner and the basis for the evening's discussion might become an old paper from the Ark. These rituals and slang remained remarkably constant for over a century.

At the time of Maynard's election, the active members appear to have been as follows:[50] Austin Smyth, a Trinity classicist and Prize Fellow, then a clerk of the House of Commons; A. R. Ainsworth, a King's classicist and moral scientist, then a lecturer in classics at Manchester; Ralph Hawtrey, a Trinity mathematician, then a civil servant in the Admiralty prior to a long Treasury career; Hugh Owen Meredith (HOM), a King's historian with a studentship at the London School of Economics about to become a fellow of King's; E. M. (Morgan) Forster, a King's classicist who was living in London after a year in Italy; John Sheppard, another King's classicist working for Part II

e Women did not become members until 1971 (Deacon 1985, 174).

of the Tripos; Lytton Strachey, a final-year Trinity historian; Saxon Sydney Turner, a Trinity classicist about to take Part II of the Tripos in his third year; Leonard Woolf, another Trinity classicist reading for Part II of the Tripos in his fourth year and hoping for a fellowship; and L. H. Greenwood, yet another classicist, this time from King's, reading for Part II. Among the more active angels were a number of King's and Trinity dons – Lowes Dickinson, J. E. McTaggart, G. H. Hardy and G. E. Moore – and a few who had left Cambridge – Desmond MacCarthy, R. C. Trevelyan and Roger Fry. Of these Moore would turn out to be the most important.

G. E. Moore had come up to Trinity from Dulwich in 1892. He had a successful academic career, a First in Part I of the Classical Tripos and a First, with distinction, in Part II of the Moral Sciences Tripos, which he had taken at the urging of Bertrand Russell. He then spent two years working on a fellowship dissertation which was successful on his second attempt in 1898. The Prize Fellowship enabled him to remain in Cambridge until 1904, when he left for a period in Edinburgh and Richmond before returning in 1911 to succeed Neville Keynes as University Lecturer in Moral Sciences. Moore then remained in Cambridge until the Second World War, becoming Professor of Moral Philosophy and Logic in 1925. His successor in the chair would be Ludwig Wittgenstein.

Although his own conversation was not witty or scintillating, Moore enjoyed the humour of others immensely, and his love of music, singing, walking and even games such as fives made him an enjoyable companion for the young – and not so young, for he remained a life-long friend of many of the younger brethren. I will discuss his effects on Maynard's early beliefs and subsequent thought in Chapter 5.

Just before his election to the Society, Maynard made his mark in King's as a leader of the secular wing in College affairs. In the recent past most Cambridge Colleges, as those in Oxford, maintained some type of mission or settlement in the poorer parts of London, but King's had remained aloof from this movement. In Maynard's first term, however, the idea of an association with a parish in South London was raised. As it evolved the idea became a proposal to associate with Holy Trinity, Southwark, whose incumbent, G. H. Martin, was High Church. A meeting to discuss the proposal was held in King's Hall on 25 January 1903. It revealed considerable opposition to the scheme, not all of it from agnostics, and the meeting was eventually adjourned for one week. The leaders of the High Church party were two Etonians, E. A. Edghill and Stephen Gaselee. A Low Church supporter of a religious link, but not with the vicar of Holy Trinity, was Alister Grant, who produced two emotional tracts on the controversy which have led some, notably P. N. Furbank,[51] to believe that he was instrumental in the scheme. The opposition from the College's agnostics included John Sheppard and L. H. Greenwood, both Apostles.

The meeting on 1 February took place in Hall. It was attended by most of the junior members of College and several dons, including the Provost. To increase their strength, the opposition brought several Kingsmen up from London including Hugh Meredith, George Barger, and Morgan Forster. When those favouring the Southwark mission moved a supporting motion, they met an amendment from Sheppard that the scheme be on a secular basis. Maynard seconded the motion. Although he was not the experienced Union debater Sheppard was, his notes suggest that Maynard took a cool, sober approach to the issue. He suggested that the scheme as originally raised might be a good one, but that the proposal before the meeting seemed to emphasise conformity and communication over good citizenship and it contained no commitment to avoid religious tests in the future. He made it clear that to him secular did not mean irreligious: it meant non-sectarian. This tolerance of all views, he argued, would accurately reflect the diversity of views in College, allow freedom of conscience, and reflect more accurately the intentions of the original proponents of a London settlement. After further discussion and speeches from Barger and Meredith, the amendment was carried by a three-to-one margin.

At a further meeting the next week a Social Work Committee of twelve was formed. It included Maynard, Greenwood, Sheppard, Lowes Dickinson, H. M. V. Temperley and W. F. Reddaway. The Committee worked until May 1903 before recommending an association with Cambridge House in South London through a scholarship for the school there. Although approved by the College, the proposal came to grief when the Head of Cambridge House objected to the wording of one clause in the scheme concerning religious teaching, which he claimed the Committee had altered after showing him a draft. As neither side would budge from its position, the Committee tried again and reported in November 1903 that the College should not associate itself with any scheme in South London but consider proposals for similar work on the College's estates. Yet another College meeting accepted this report and appointed another committee. Reddaway and Temperley were the only carryovers on the new committee. The outcome was a boys club in Barnwell, an eastern district of Cambridge. As a compromise it had both a Sunday school and secular activities on weekdays. Run by the College chaplain after 1918, the scheme continued until a slum clearance scheme changed the area in the 1930s.

Maynard's activities outside the Society remained varied. He was reported as using the University Library, thus raising worries in Neville Keynes that if he spent too much time there he would impair the quality of his degree![52] He continued to take an active part in the Union. At the end of the Lent term 1903, he tried unsuccessfully for election to the Union Committee; the next term he was successful, coming top of the poll. He continued to debate in smaller societies – the Decemviri, the Walpole and the Knave of Clubs. With a paper on Peter Abelard to the Apennine Society in February he continued his interest in matters medieval cultivated at Eton, while with his May paper on Time to the Parhesiasts he was showing the influence of his recent exposure to philosophical issues, especially McTaggart's lectures. As he introduced the latter paper, he reflected on these:

> When I have attended Dr McTaggart's lectures, I have felt the plunge from ordinary life into metaphysics a very violent one; it usually takes me an appreciable time to gather my wits for a sustained dialectical outlook upon the Universe, despite the lecturer's efforts to relieve the tension by the introduction of so unmetaphysical a thing as laughter, – I mean therefore to approach the subject gently.

His new philosophical interests were also reflected in his joining the Moral Science Club, while his political interests and commitments came out in his Union speeches, where he took a strong Liberal line on such matters as temperance and fiscal reform, and in his membership of the University Liberal Club. With the Club he first heard David Lloyd George in May 1903 and with the Liberal League in Oxford – 'all very mysterious but rather pleasant' and 'a better looking place than Cambridge'[53] he heard Sir Edward Grey a few weeks later.[f]

He continued to take regular physical exercise. He played golf regularly at Royston with C. R. Fay, who regarded him as 'the worst player I have know with the exception of [Nathaniel] Wedd whose method was: first to miss the ball, then to talk to it, then to refill his pipe, and finally to wave through the players behind'.[54] He managed to play fives regularly, first with Wedd, but later with Moore and A. C. Pigou, the recently elected economics don in King's. All of this activity was made possible by 'practically refusing to go to lectures', something that worried Neville Keynes, who occasionally wondered whether Maynard had taken the wrong subject, and his teachers, who thought it unwise.[55]

Nevertheless, when it came to the Mays, the Cambridge progress exams usually held in June which, unlike the tripos examinations, do not count for a degree, Maynard did respectably, coming fifth overall despite feeling unwell during two papers. (Neville Keynes believed that if he had kept up the standard of the papers he had written when well he could have come second.)[56] Thus, despite his father's almost chronic worries and his own wide range of outside activities, Maynard had made a good start to his career in Cambridge. After the examinations Maynard and his parents went off for almost a month's holiday in Switzerland.

Despite his election to the Society, during his first year Maynard's friendships seen to have remained largely outside that group. He still kept

---

f From Oxford, he reported to his brother that he found politics 'in moderation, a very amusing game – quite an adequate substitute for Bridge' (RKP, JMK to GLK, 30 May 1903).

up with his Eton contemporaries – Swithinbank, Butler, Williams, Dundas, Humphrey Paul and Dan Macmillan. The new Cambridge friends with whom he undertook expeditions and theatre visits tended not to be brethren. He went with C. R. Fay to Manchester during the Christmas vacation and visited Dan Macmillan in the summer. Robin Furness loomed large. True, Strachey and Woolf came to lunch or tea at Harvey Road, but so did others. He did not take part in reading parties with other brethren, nor did he visit them during the vacations. The same pattern continued into his second year. The only sustained non-Cambridge contact with an Apostle did not come until the end of August 1904, when he went on a walking tour of North Wales with Leonard Woolf. The tour included a visit to C. P. Sanger, a brother of the mid-1890s. This does not mean that he did not meet members of the Society – far from it. But members of the Society did not yet play a central role among his friends.

Maynard's second year opened with the publication of Moore's *Principia Ethica*, 'a stupendous and entrancing work, *the greatest* on the subject'.[57] He had a new coach, J. G. Leatham of St John's, as Hobson had retired from the trade. Although more active in giving papers to the Society, Maynard continued the same hectic pattern of diverse activities established during his first year. In late November 1903 he managed only one free evening in a fortnight.[58] He was even more active in the Union, on the Committee for the first two terms of the year and speaking on average once a fortnight throughout the year. Such activity had its rewards: at the end of May 1904 he was elected Secretary of the Union. With the conventions of that society, he could expect to be successively Vice-President and President in his last two terms as an undergraduate. His debating did not stop with the Union. He maintained close links with the King's debating societies and took an active part in debates in other colleges – Queens', St John's, Downing and Pembroke – as well as the Majleis, a debating society for Indian students at Cambridge.

Nor were his activities restricted to debating or discussion societies. He got 'dead drunk' for the first time in his life.[59] He was also reporting Union debates for the *Cambridge Review*, to which he also contributed a review of one volume of *The Cambridge Modern History* – oddly enough the volume dealing with North America, where he regarded the contribution on 'States Rights' by Woodrow Wilson, then President of Princeton, as 'the best . . . in the volume'.[60] He was an active member of the Liberal Club, a member of a bridge club and, not surprisingly with his book collecting habits, a Baskerville club. He remained an active theatre-goer. He maintained his ties with Eton, going down again to play in the annual Eton–King's wall game and exchanging visits with Humphrey Paul, Young, Hamilton, Swithinbank, Dundas, Herringham and Dan Macmillan. He even kept up a pretence of physical activity with regular games of fives – his partners being Moore and

A. C. Pigou – and, weather permitting, golf with his father or friends.

Nor, despite his inattention to the subject for examination purposes, did he completely ignore mathematics, although Neville Keynes worried to his diary as usual. In the Easter term he went three times a week to A. N. Whitehead's lectures on 'Non-Euclidian Geometry'. He was the only member of the audience. According to his father, Maynard said 'the lectures are interesting, but they will pay little if at all for the Tripos'.[61] Later Whitehead would mention Maynard and Bertrand Russell as being among his best pupils.[62]

At Easter he went to Germany with his mother to collect his sister who had gone to the family of Baroness von Büsing in Wittenberg for three months to improve her German. For the first part of the journey, Maynard kept a diary, which is full of his reactions to the passing scene. A few entries are of interest:

17.3.04. – In the evening to the Schiller Theatre to see Ibsen's Wildente; ... half I had succeeded in reading beforehand and that I could follow excellently – the rest I could eke out. The acting was quite supreme – completely natural and never unreal; the players seemed to have as much regard for Walarbeit as the playwrite [*sic*]. The more I contemplate the play the greater does it appear;[63] but the whole setting and the whole dialogue is so intensely German, that it is obvious that it is in Germany that one ought to see the man performed; there are bound to be absurdities in an English rendering. Nevertheless, it is a little astonishing to see such a piece completely fill a large theatre.

17.3.04. – Berlin does not oppress one with the hugeness of London, nor, on first sight at least, even with the hugeness which it really professes.

The streets are broad and very clean, and in the parts we have frequented very regularly laid out ... The architecture is huge and pompous with a great deal of statuary not ineffective in the mass; indeed the public places possess considerable magnificence. There seem to be no slums mixed up with fashion Londonwise; their poverty is more hushed up than ours, perhaps concealed by the system of workmen's flats, which are at least new and imposing to look at.

19.3.04 – Almost Egyptian in massiveness, but essentially Teutonic in its ponderous pomposity, the public architecture of Berlin is not a bad attempt to create in a brief period an atmosphere of national greatness and solidity. But Bismarck was right – it would all have fallen rather flat without the Franco-German war.

17.3.04. – The display in the booksellers' windows is interestingly different from ours: – immense translations from French and English (Bernard Shaw and Maeterlinck everywhere), very little native modern literature but the classical writers of all languages translated and fabulously cheap (we bought very tolerable copies of Ibsen's Wildente for .2'); a good deal of medicine especially quasi sexual. In what booksellers call format they are leagues behind us, but precious printing is beginning; partly, perhaps from their system of paperbinding, they are before us in cheapness.

In Berlin and later in Dresden, Maynard also enjoyed the galleries and was impressed by Raphael and the early sixteenth-century Germans – Dürer, Cranach and Holbein – as well as the classical statuary. After Berlin, the trio (for they had met Margaret there) went on to Dresden, where they saw a production of *Götterdämmerung* – 'exciting in a different way than anything else I have ever heard'[64] – Leipzig, where Gorki's *Nacht Asile* (Doss House) was the theatre treat, Weimar and Lehrte, the last to visit a former governess. It was not Maynard's last visit to Germany.

The summer, with journeys to the north to stay with Fay in Liverpool, to the Macmillans at North Foreland and the week's walking tour with Woolf, also included a visit to Bertrand Russell at Ivy Lodge in Surrey on 16 and 17 July. Russell later recalled it:

> Once in the year 1904 when I was living in an isolated cottage in a vast moor without roads, he wrote and asked if I could promise him a restful weekend. I replied confidently in the affirmative and he came. Within five minutes of his arrival the Vice Chancellor turned up full of University business. Other people came unexpectedly to every meal, including six to Sunday breakfast. By Monday morning we had twenty-six unexpected guests, and Keynes, I fear, went away more tired than he came.[65]

This is improbable. The invitation went out from Russell to Maynard on 5 June; so it was hardly a 'spur of the moment' visit. Maynard had just been visiting with Fay, seeing his relatives at Disley and visiting his brother Geoffrey at school at Rugby. He had travelled quite a bit, but would hardly 'need' a restful weekend. It would be most unlikely that the Vice Chancellor would come to Surrey to consult Maynard, an undergraduate who had just finished his second year, on University business. One also doubts the run of visitors. The whole story might be plausible only some years later. Could Russell have confused his dates?

Maynard's only comment on the weekend came in a letter to Lytton Strachey on 20 July:

> Last Sunday I stayed with Russell; everybody was there or near. For hours on Saturday night Russell wiped the floor with a man – Leonard Hobhouse – a most superb display.

True, there is a suggestion of visitors, but no more.

The summer also brought the meetings of the British Association for the

Advancement of Science to Cambridge. Both Geoffrey and Maynard became associates of the British Ass., as it is known. The meetings inevitably brought many visitors to Cambridge, including the Keynes's house guests at 6 Harvey Road, Professor John Cox and his wife from Montreal along with their niece Katherine, or Ka as she was better known after she went up to Newnham in 1906. Later she would be part of both Maynard's and Geoffrey's lives.

With the autumn of 1904 came Maynard's final year as an undergraduate. Before term, using a standard edition of Burke he had purchased the previous year, Maynard prepared an essay on Burke's political principles. He had it ready for his parents' comments by the beginning of October and, after revision submitted it for the Members' Prize for an English Essay.[g] He was successful, much to the chagrin of C. R. Fay,[66] and later won a £5 Declamation Prize for the same essay.[h] Soon after the beginning of term, he became President of the University Liberal Club. With this, the Union (where he became Vice President at the end of term), the *Cambridge Review*, College societies, visits to Eton and Oxford and the Society, it was not surprising that Neville Keynes would worriedly report:

> Berry says he believes Maynard is honestly giving his 'spare time' to Mathematics. In the circumstances he is surprised at how much he gets done.[67]

From the entries in Maynard's appointments diary, it would seem that his 'spare time' amounted to four to six hours a day, so it was not all that surprising that in the practice examinations in December he came out fifth among the firsts.

In the Lent Term, after a Christmas vacation that included a visit to Butler, Dundas and Williams at Forest Row and 20 to 30 hours a week of mathematics, Maynard had a stroke of luck. The President of the Union, H. G. Ward, had to retire and so, as Vice-President, Maynard succeeded to the presidency a term early. Nor did his usual round of activities keep him from his mathematics, for he continued to average in most weeks between 25 and 30 hours at his studies. This rate of work continued during the Easter vacation before he pushed himself regularly above 35 hours a week in an attempt to keep to the schedule he had set himself for his Tripos revision. As the examinations approached, Neville Keynes began his worrying and fearing for the worst; whereas Maynard, although finding a life dominated by revision 'rather a burden', was more sanguine.[68] The day after the Tripos examinations, he estimated that he might be as high as Twelfth Wrangler –

g So called because it and a similar prize for a Latin essay were gifts of the Members of Parliament for the University.

h The essay itself, along with other Burke-influenced undergraduate papers from the same period, is discussed in Chapter 5.

the position he actually attained when the results came out on 13 June.[69] Neville Keynes was resignedly satisfied:

> On the whole we are satisfied, though the boy might have done better had he devoted himself more exclusively to his mathematics.

> I fancy Maynard was not very well or wisely taught for Tripos purposes. He maintains that he is glad he gave no more time to Mathematics, even though it would have meant a much better place in the Tripos list.[70]

In the course of his final year, Maynard had became much more involved in the affairs of the Society and much more closely acquainted with Lytton Strachey. Lytton had come up to Trinity in 1899 after an unconventional education to read history, at which he proved an uninspired examinee with seconds in both parts of the Historical Tripos. After his Part II examinations in 1903, he stayed on in Cambridge to try unsuccessfully for a Trinity Fellowship with a dissertation on Warren Hastings. Initially, Strachey's closest friend among the brethren was Leonard Woolf. In his fourth and fifth years, however, he moved away from Woolf, as the latter prepared for the Civil Service examinations that would take him to Ceylon in October 1904, and more and more into a circle of friends in King's. His first close King's companion was John Sheppard, a diminutive, cherubic, white-haired, young man who always struck his contemporaries as prematurely aged. Sheppard's passion for the theatre, his light-heartedness, zest and whimsy made him a charming companion for some, although others saw in him an underlying intellectual soft-headedness. Strachey's attachment to Sheppard lasted for more than a year before they drew apart, almost entirely on the same initiative that had started the relationship – Lytton's. By the autumn of 1904 Lytton was looking to fill a gap in his emotional life.

By the summer of 1904, when Maynard and Lytton passed the opening letters in a correspondence that would grow to massive proportions in the years to come, Lytton had successfully managed to cultivate a distinctive public persona. Although physically frail, unusual in appearance, plagued by perpetual ill-health and emanating a general air of unfitness, he used his wit and cultivated capacity to shock to establish an ascendancy among a circle of Cambridge undergraduates. In dress he tended towards an unconventional anti-dandyism, while he used his voice, which had broken late and could still cover a wider than normal range, to provide unconventional emphasis when he spoke. Resolutely irreligious, he used awkward silences, brutal retorts and putdowns, and barbed remarks to show his contempt for most of mankind's activities, views and morality and to shock others into rethinking their own views. More widely read than most of his contemporaries, not only in the classics but also in more recent or less known European literature, he was to play an important role in filling out Maynard's education.

In the autumn of 1904, when G. E. Moore's Trinity Fellowship lapsed and he left Cambridge for Edinburgh, the Society entered a potentially difficult period. It had only one undergraduate member – Maynard. Most of the other active brethren, such as Ralph Hawtrey, Morgan Forster, Saxon Sydney Turner, Leonard Greenwood, and even Strachey himself were less likely to be in Cambridge to provide continuity. However, taking over Moore's position of secretary, Strachey decided to give the Society's welfare much of his time. In the circumstances, it was inevitable that he and Maynard would be thrown together.

Before Lytton and Maynard had become members, the Society had frequently discussed sexual mores and had developed a decidedly 'camp' set of conventions. Thus,

> it was obligatory to make the humorous assumption that all sexual relations were homosexual ones, so that even heterosexual love had to be treated as only a special case of the higher sodomy.[71]

Members maintained a legacy of homosexual jargon that passed from generation to generation. As a result of Lytton's stewardship as secretary with its access to the Society's records, this tradition was brought to the fore and refurbished. Although at the time it was not likely that Lytton, unlike Maynard, was sexually experienced, his unattractiveness to members of the opposite sex, his emotional reaction to the female-dominated Strachey household and his emotional dependence on a series of more vigorous male contemporaries, allied to his desire to shock, led him to create the impression that the Society had been more homosexual than, in fact, it had been. He also suggested it would be advantageous both to the Society and the community at large if members were more open to and more accepting of their true natures – and of the advantages of homosexual love. Added to these forces for change was another facet of Strachey's character – his dislike of the more serious realms of formal argument – and this brought a more frivolous, more lighthearted, tone to the meetings and the topics under discussion.

The Strachey–Keynes attempt to manage the Society did not go smoothly at first. Indeed, their own developing relationship came under severe strain with the election of the new régime's first embryo, Arthur Hobhouse, a Trinity undergraduate who had come from Eton and St Andrew's University.[i] He seems to have come into Strachey's ken in the course of November 1904 and soon became an embryo. Maynard lunched with him on 30 November and 7 December and seemed to approve; so Strachey set about organising his election. There seems to have been some difficulty in this because he was a freshman, which is surprising in that there were no reports of difficulties

---

i Hobhouse was disguised as Edgar Duckworth in Holroyd's biography of Strachey and misnamed Arthur Lee Hobhouse in Levy's biography of Moore and in the text (but not the dramatis personae) of both the English and American editions of Skidelsky's biography of Keynes. His actual middle name was Lawrence.

over the previous election in the same circumstances – Maynard's.[72] By the end of the Christmas vacation, however, it seemed that Hobhouse's election was secure. Strachey's growing attachment to the young man – an attachment he confided to Maynard[73] – was also apparent. But although the election went ahead as planned on 18 February, Strachey found himself in competition with Maynard for Hobhouse's affections. Maynard was victorious and sponsored his election, much to Strachey's despair. The upshot was a break in the developing Keynes–Strachey relationship, highlighted by Strachey's public attack on Maynard at the next meeting of the Society.

> For it is one of his queer characteristics that one often wants, one cannot tell why, to make a malicious attack on him, and that, when the time comes, one refrains, one cannot tell why. His sense of values, and indeed all his feelings, offer a spectacle of complete paradox. He is a hedonist and a follower of Moore; he is lascivious without lust; he is an Apostle without tears.[74]

As he later told Maynard, '[F]or a week or two, I hated you like hell'.[75]

There was thus some cooling of relations between the two, although letters continued from Maynard's side. They met on 29 March as Maynard was preparing to visit Hobhouse for three weeks. Just before Maynard left for Truro, where he would be staying, he also wrote to Hobhouse, beginning his letter 'My dear?' and concluding it with the words 'You know my feelings – I shall know yours in time'.[76] In the letter, he provided another snapshot of his reactions going through old letters.

> And then the letters – the periodic, sermonic, typical scrives from Trevy – I feel rather shy reading them. Strachey's – always indecent and always exactly recalling the precise situation at the moment. And the correspondence with school friends – growing very steadily thinner.
>
> The whole thing made me feel that one ought to keep a diary – even though it merely records events: for these letters recalled the most supreme things, but there were many gaps.
>
> Wouldn't you like to know exactly what happened to you on every day of the last two terms? I swear you don't remember much of it. I don't think one realises how very discrete (in the mathematical sense) one's existence is. My days at school don't seem to have the remotest connexions with my doings up here: nor my life in one term with my life in any other.
>
> One's always first cousin to oneself, but the relationship is not often much nearer.[77]

The visit appears to have been successful, although Hobhouse was ill for most of the time. Maynard profitably used what time he had on his own, averaging five to six hours a day on his mathematics. The visit was not so successful, however, as to prevent him from writing to Lytton on his return to Cambridge:

> The episode is over; I wonder if you will know exactly what happened – you will probably gather a great deal in the course of time. My memory will never be accurate enough to make the sequence of events seem plausible – and I am not sure that I would tell you everything anyhow. As it is, because I can't tell you everything, I may for fear of misunderstanding tell you nothing.
>
> I swear I had no idea I was in for anything that would so utterly upset me. It is absurd to suppose that you would believe the violence of the various feelings I have been through.
>
> However – perhaps you will gather a little when we meet. All I will say is that at the moment I am more madly in love with him, than ever and that we have sailed into smooth waters – for how long I know not.[78]

The letter appears to have resulted in a reconciliation with Lytton and ended his first major attack of what later became known as 'Pozzophobia' – Pozzo being Strachey's later nickname for Maynard[j] – for their correspondence and exchanges resumed.

Maynard continued his pursuit of Hobhouse, or Hobby as he came to be known, signing his letter of the same date 'Your most constant true lover'. Four days later he wrote to him again confiding: 'Yes, I have a clear head, a weak character, an affectionate disposition and a repulsive appearance'.[79] Yet the pursuit was not initially successful. As he told Lytton on 31 July:

> For months I courted him and he turned a cold cheek.
>
> For 3 weeks I have cultivated the demeanour of the utmost apparent coldness; I have rated him and jeered at him; I have appeared as white-hearted as a man could be. And tonight he comes round and declared he is in love with me.
>
> What do you think?
> Is he to be trusted?
> Won't he veer off again as soon as I show my feelings?
> Heavens!

Maynard then spent 'two glorious days' with Hobby before going off to Switzerland for a holiday. He visited him at home at Castle Cary, Somerset,

---

j The nickname does not seem to be related, as often thought, to Count Carlo Pozzo di Borga, the Tsar's ambassador to Paris after 1815, for as Lytton told his brother James on 26 November 1908, 'I don't know who or what that is but it sounds like a suitable name for a certain person.' (BL, ADD.60707) It is more likely related to the Italian word for well or fount: *Un pozzo di dottrina* or *Un pozzo di sapienza* are phrases meaning 'a mine of learning'. Strachey does not seem to have spoken Italian (Holroyd 1971, 532), but he had visited Italy and could have picked up the usage and bestowed it on Keynes. I am grateful to Leslie Pressnell for drawing my attention to this.

for a week at the end of September 1905. After that the affair cooled, as Hobby moved into other circles and took up with Lytton's cousin Duncan Grant.[k]

The highlight of the summer was a climbing holiday in Switzerland with Geoffrey Young (the brother of Gerard), a former Eton master and noted alpinist, Robin Mayor, and Will Slingsby.

Maynard left Cambridge for Lausanne on 2 August and arrived there a day later. Initially the weather was bad, but on 6 August they determined to make their way to a hut above Fionay. The next day Maynard made his first climb over the Col des Maisons Blanches to Bourg St-Pierre. Fresh snow made the going heavy, but Maynard reported enjoying it enormously even though he was out for 9½ hours. The next day the party prepared for a more ambitious passage over the passes from Orsières to Chamonix. They climbed to a hut at Saleinar to sleep before setting out at 3 a.m. They crossed the Col du Chardonnet, climbed the Aiguille d'Argentière and traversed the Chardonnet and Argentière glaciers before they reached Montenvers almost 19 hours later. There were moments of danger in the dark and on the glaciers, and one of the guides caused problems, but Young, always the most careful of climbers, took care of Maynard, who found that 'The beauty of the view was beyond words'.[80] True, the pleasures of nature, as he told both Hobby and Lytton, were second to those of friendship and intellect, but he had enjoyed himself enough to want to try it again later – even if he didn't in the end.[81]

After a few days of more leisurely walking around Chamonix with Mayor and his sister Fiona (the novelist F. M. Mayor), Katherine Leaf and Mary Sheepshanks, Maynard went on 14 August on to join his family at Simplon Kulm. The family remained in Switzerland until the 26th when they started back via Paris, where Maynard remained with his mother for a week. Paris meant art galleries, with Maynard making five visits to the Louvre, as well as seeing the modern collections at the Luxembourg Palace. He reported to Lytton on the latter:

> The Impressionist room was more interesting than the entire Louvre. I liked Monet best. I enclose some post cards of those they had in that shape. I remember one or two of them reproduced in your little book.[82,l]

To Hobby he also reported:

> I like Paris very well, but it altogether lacks the subtlety of London – all of its effects are obvious and intended. And as in Berlin, I was without that intense sense of infinite multitudes and endless whirl of traffic that alike oppresses and excites me in London – yes, London is the more

---

k Maynard visited Hobby briefly at Hadspen in August 1906 and listed him in his 1915 record as one with whom he had copulated in 1906.
l The book is unknown.

absorbing though so far as deliberate arrangement can achieve success Paris is complete.[83]

In Paris, he also ran across Dan Macmillan, who crossed the Channel with Maynard and his mother on 1 September.

NOTES

1 Fay in King's College 1949, 13–15.
2 CUL, Add. 7852, 15 October 1902.
3 Ibid., 5 and 21 November, 4 and 8 December 1902.
4 CUL, Add. 7853, 12, 18 and 20 February 1903. Hobson believed that Page was capable of being Senior Wrangler.
5 *Granta*, 8 November 1902.
6 CUL, Add.7852, 9 November 1902. See also the reports in *Granta* for 22 November 1902 and those in *The Cambridge Review* for 24 January, 12 March and 14 May 1903.
7 For McTaggart's Thursday evenings see Woolf 1960, 132–3. JMK's appearances there are recorded in his appointments diary.
8 Much of what follows has been influenced by Houghton 1957.
9 *JMK*, X, 325, 340.
10 Schumpeter 1954, 408, n. 5.
11 Rothblatt 1968, 133.
12 Roach 1959, 257.
13 Schumpeter 1954, 408, n. 5.
14 Sidgwick and Sidgwick 1906, 35.
15 Ibid., 35.
16 Ibid., 34.
17 Ibid., 40.
18 Ibid., 39–40.
19 See Sidgwick 1874, ch. 1; Collini, Winch and Burrow 1983, 287.
20 Below, p. 101–2.
21 Sidgwick and Sidgwick 1906, 143.
22 Sidgwick and Sidgwick 1906, 200–1.
23 Rothblatt 1968, 136.
24 Mill 1863 (Everyman edition), 9.
25 Ibid., 15.
26 Sidgwick and Sidgwick 1906, 38.
27 Schneewind 1977, 41–3.
28 Sidgwick and Sidgwick 1906, 277.
29 Sidgwick 1874, 486, quoted by Schneewind 1977, 345.
30 Ibid., 346–7.
31 Williams 1982, 189.
32 Schumpeter 1954, 805–6; Myint 1948.
33 Collini, Winch and Burrow 1983, 294. The observer is Stefan Collini (ibid., ix).
34 Sidgwick and Sidgwick 1906, 277, 282.
35 Ibid., 277, 282.
36 Ibid., 283–4.
37 Ibid., 481.
38 Ibid., 473, 475; see also 466–7, 484–5, 488.
39 Ibid., 449.

40 Ibid., 439.
41 Ibid., 399.
42 Ibid., 342, 417–19.
43 Ibid., 441–2.
44 See the comments by Maitland, J. N. Keynes, Sorley and Balfour quoted in ibid., 304–11.
45 Harrod 1951, 69.
46 Levy 1979, 236.
47 Ibid., 311.
48 Allen 1978, 13.
49 Sidgwick and Sidgwick 1906, 34–5.
50 Levy 1979, 310–11.
51 Furbank 1977, I, 99–101. For more information see also Harrod 1951, 93–4; Wilkinson, 1980a, 46–7; KCKP, Box 2, 'The Social Service Scheme'; KCKP, JMK to B. W. Swithinbank, 5 February 1903.
52 CUL, Add. 7853, 21 January 1903.
53 KCKP, JMK to B. W. Swithinbank, 30 May 1903; RKP, JMK to GLK, 30 May 1903.
54 Fay in King's College 1949, 14.
55 CUL, Add.7853, 16 June 1903; see also 10 May 1903.
56 Ibid., 13 June 1903.
57 KCKP, JMK to B. W. Swithinbank, 7 October 1903.
58 CUL, Add.7853, 2 December 1903.
59 KCKP, JMK to B. W. Swithinbank, 15 December 1903.
60 *JMK*, XI, 504.
61 CUL, Add.7854, 28 April 1904.
62 Harrod 1951, 97.
63 He used the same phrase in a letter to Swithinbank on 22 March.
64 KCKP, JMK to B. W. Swithinbank, 22 March 1904.
65 Russell 1978, 68.
66 Fay in King's College 1949, 14.
67 CUL, Add.7854, 6 December 1904.
68 CUL, Add.7855, 25 May 1905.
69 Ibid., 4 June 1905.
70 Ibid., 13 and 20 June 1906.
71 Levy 1979, 140.
72 Holroyd 1971, 246; Levy 1979, 239; CUL, Add.7855, Strachey to Moore, 13 December 1904. However, after a run of freshman embryos, McTaggart would complain in 1906, '[I]t's a pity to always elect freshmen'. KCKP, JMK to GLS, 1 February 1906.
73 KCKP, GLS to JMK, 13 December 1904.
74 Holroyd 1973, 252.
75 KCKP, GLS to JMK, 10 April 1906.
76 KCKP, JMK to Hobhouse, 27 March 1905.
77 The letter he wrote to Strachey the same day is cited on p. 102.
78 KCKP, JMK to GLS, 23 April 1905.
79 KCKP, JMK to Hobhouse, 27 April 1905.
80 KCKP, JMK to JNK, 11 August 1905.
81 KCKP, JMK to GLS, 11 August 1905; to A. L. Hobhouse, 11 August 1905.
82 KCKP, JMK to GLS, 8 September 1905.
83 KCKP, JMK to Hobhouse, 3 September 1905.

4

POST-GRADUATE

By nature I simply ooze letters.
(KCKP, JMK to B. W. Swithinbank, 7 January 1906)

At 22, with his Tripos behind him, the question for Maynard was what to do next. His King's scholarship entitled him to a fourth year, so another year in Cambridge was inevitable no matter what he ultimately chose to do. But it remained unclear whether he would read for another tripos – Moral Sciences and Economics were the candidates – or prepare for the 1906 Civil Service examinations, as Neville had forecast in 1902, or a career at the bar (with politics as a possible ultimate goal), as suggested by G. M. Trevelyan. Initially, he seems to have kept his options open – eating dinners at the Inner Temple and reading economics. The summer's economics programme for 1905 began on 27 June with Marshall's *Principles*. On 3 July A. C. Benson saw him travelling to Royston to play golf with a copy of Jevons's *Theory of Political Economy* in his pocket. Benson described him as 'the odd, shy, clever, influential Keynes . . . a very advanced young man' who spoke so quietly 'that the train, not I, had the benefit'.[1] Almost immediately Maynard took to Jevons, reporting to Strachey on 8 July

> I have discovered someone whom I had not realised to be very good
> – namely Jevons.
>   I am convinced that he was one of *the* minds of the century. . . .
> 'Investigations into [sic] Currency and Finance', a most thrilling
> volume.

He even thought Jevons Apostolic. The same day he reported a supplementary summer programme involving 'a long criticism of *P[rincipia] E[thica]*', fragments of which he sent to Strachey later in the month.[2] On 8 July he went into residence in King's for three weeks of more reading. Hobby was up, and he also mentioned spending time with Greenwood and Sheppard. He seems to have spent more time with the young King's economics don, now Girdlers' lecturer, Arthur Cecil Pigou. Maynard reported him as being 'very nice but a little depressed and lovelorn'. Pigou's taste for male undergraduates was 'becoming a scandal',[3] but the two got on well enough together and Maynard provided assistance in checking the proofs of Pigou's *Principles and Methods of Industrial Peace* (1905), for which he had also provided 'valuable help' in connection with the formal, mathematical Appendix A.[a] He was entering the world of Alfred Marshall.

Alfred Marshall was a master at concealment. He even left posterity with an inaccurate account of his origins! Maynard Keynes would be one who was taken in.[4] Marshall was born in Bermondsey on 26 July 1842. His father, an evangelical and, from modern accounts, a 'wicked old tyrant', was a clerk at the Bank of England; his mother the daughter of a butcher.[b] On the nomination of a Bank director, Marshall was educated at Merchant Taylors' School, where in 1861 he was entitled to a scholarship to St John's College, Oxford, with the prospect of a career in holy orders. But he did not have the taste for classics this entailed, for he had discovered the joys of mathematics, partly because his father did not understand it. Fortunately, an uncle who had made his fortune as a pastoralist in Australia was prepared to lend him enough to supplement the exhibition he won at St John's College, Cambridge, then ranked second in reputation to Trinity.[5] He thus, despite his father's wishes for classics, Oxford and a career as a cleric, went to Cambridge. He was Second Wrangler after the future Lord Rayleigh in 1865. A fellowship at St John's followed.

Before taking up residence in Cambridge as a Fellow of John's, to help repay his uncle Marshall worked briefly as a mathematics master at Clifton. His work at Clifton brought him into contact with H. B. Dakyns who opened the door for him into Sidgwick's circle and, in 1866 or 1867 into the Grote Club, the name given after his death in 1866 to the after-dinner discussions that took place in the Trumpington vicarage of the Revd John Grote, Knightbridge Professor of Philosophy 1855–66. At the time Marshall joined the Club – certainly before 5 February 1867 when notes exist in his hand of a discussion opened by Sidgwick on systems of morality[6] – its other members included F. D. Maurice, John Venn, J. R. Mozley and J. B. Pearson. The Club devoted itself to 'keen and perfectly free discussion of fundamental principles',[7] this at the 'moment at which Christian dogma fell away from the serious philosophical world of England, or at any rate of Cambridge',[8] and Sidgwick was considering resigning his Trinity fellowship. At this stage, Marshall still looked forward to taking holy orders, but under the influence of the contemporary metaphysical speculation he, too, soon lost his faith. But Marshall could lose his faith and not feel obliged to resign his fellowship.

---

a 'On the extent to which wage bargains between industrial combinations are indeterminate'.

b Marshall suppressed his birthplace (so that Keynes put it as Clapham); improved his father's position at the Bank to that of cashier (one he reached 20 years later) and changed his maternal father's occupation to that of a druggist.

Instead he put the metaphysical speculations to good use and in 1868 became a lecturer in moral sciences at St John's.

In 1868 Marshall did not commit himself to economics. He slowly drifted towards it, in part because J. B. Pearson, the other College lecturer in moral sciences, did not wish to teach it. For Marshall, also lecturing on logic and ethics, merely regarded himself as 'a philosopher straying in a foreign land'.[9] Still he persisted 'in the land of dry facts; looking forward to a speedy return to the luxuriance of pure thought'[10] and began lecturing in the subject to members of his own College and auditors from elsewhere. Amongst his listeners in these early years were H. H. Cunynghame, H. S. Foxwell, J. S. Nicholson and J. N. Keynes. He was also enlisted as a lecturer in political economy in Sidgwick's scheme to provide lectures for women. One of his earliest students was Mary Paley, who became Newnham Hall's first resident lecturer.

During this early period before Marshall fully committed himself to economics (this only happened during 1872–3) the subject began to undergo at the hands of W. Stanley Jevons, Carl Menger and Leon Walras what has subsequently become known as the 'marginal revolution' which was to alter the methods and agenda of the subject. All three of the economists mentioned came to their views independently: Jevons, the bibliophile, never knew of Menger's contribution, the *Gründsatze* of 1871, before his death in 1882. On several occasions later in life Marshall was to claim that he, too, had come to many of the central ideas of the 'revolution' independently of the three pioneers. For example, he wrote to Walras in November 1883:

> I cannot be said to have accepted Mr. Jevons' doctrine of 'final utility'. For I had taught it publicly in lectures at Cambridge before his book appeared [in 1871]. I had indeed used another name, *viz*: 'terminal value in use'. But following the lead of Cournot I had anticipated all the central points of Jevons' book, and had in many respects gone beyond him. I was in no hurry to publish . . .[11]

Marshall also made claims to the independent discovery of the concepts of consumer surplus, quasi-rent, the marginal productivity theory of distribution and parts of the theory of wages.[12] He seems to have convinced Foxwell, who echoed Marshall's claims.[13] Recent research has suggested that most of Marshall's private claims were exaggerated.[c] Indeed Marshall's continued inadequate acknowledgement of the published priority of Jevons, Menger and Walras was remarkable.[14]

One of the problems in evaluating Marshall's own claims is that he

---

c Whitaker (ed.) 1975, esp. I, 2; Stigler in Whitaker (ed.) 1990. This same would be true of Marshall's later claim (*JMK*, X, 182) that he was urged by Walras 'about 1873' to publish his diagramatic illustrations of economic problems. The first surviving letter between the two was dated 1883 (Jaffé (ed.) 1965, I, 744) and the first reference to Marshall in Walras' correspondence came in 1882 (ibid., I, 738).

published so little during the relevant period. Except for a rather grudging review of Jevons's *Principles of Political Economy* in *The Academy* for 1 April 1872, five months after the book's appearance, Marshall published nothing between his election to his fellowship in 1865 and 1874 when he published two articles on political economy, based on lectures he had given in Halifax. They appeared in *The Beehive*, a trade union paper, and as a paper on 'The Future of the Working Classes' in a St John's College magazine, *The Eagle*. Another, more substantial article on J. S. Mill followed two years later. Yet less on the basis of this or other articles than on his teaching experience and promise, Jevons and Sidgwick warmly supported Marshall when he applied for the posts of Principal and Professor of Political Economy at University College, Bristol in 1877.[15]

The reason for this application was his impending marriage to Mary Paley, which would mean the end of his fellowship at St John's. The couple were married in August 1877 after the Bristol appointments came through. For the next 47 years Mary Marshall's life was merged with Alfred's. In 1876 she had been asked by James Stuart, the founder of the university extension movement in Cambridge, to write a textbook on political economy for extension audiences. After their engagement, Alfred became involved and eventually took charge – so much so that 'it seems improbable that Mrs. Marshall contributed much, outside the opening and closing chapters, apart from literary advice and assistance in drafting'.[16] Indeed she became increasingly subordinate to him, despite the pain it must have cost her. In 1944 Maynard Keynes could never remember her talking economics at home amongst company. Nor did she do so abroad: he may have talked with the leading Austrian economists of the day during holidays in South Tyrol, but she painted.[17] It must also have hurt her when he came to the conclusion that women were incapable of constructive intellectual work and came out as the strongest opponent of the advancement of women in Cambridge, either as students or lecturers: a complete reversal of his views of a decade earlier.[18] But in 1877 the full implications of the marriage for her lay in the future.

At first Bristol went swimmingly: he got on with *The Economics of Industry*, the extension textbook, and proved to be a popular and successful lecturer and a reasonably competent administrator. Mary Marshall was also a successful lecturer. True, he had abandoned work on a volume on foreign trade on which he had been working since 1875 because he did not have the time to re-cast it on the lines he thought necessary.[d] However, Marshall's health collapsed in the spring of 1879. The diagnosis was a kidney stone.

---

d At Sidgwick's instigation, two parts of this volume were privately printed for circulation in Cambridge under the titles *The Pure Theory of Foreign Trade* and *The Pure Theory of Domestic Values*. Through Jevons and F. Y. Edgeworth they soon became part of the professional literature, but their ambiguous, unpublished status was to complicate Marshall's relations with Walras with unfortunate results (Whitaker (ed.) 1975, I, 105–7).

The prescription was a complete rest and he tried to resign his post, but was persuaded that he could not cease to be Principal until a successor was available. It was not until September 1881 that he was free – and then only briefly, for he was back in Bristol the next autumn because Balliol College, Oxford had arranged to finance a professor of political economy. The next year he moved to Balliol as successor to Arnold Toynbee, lecturing to selected candidates for the Indian Civil Service, but after four terms there Henry Fawcett's death opened up the Cambridge chair. By that time, the little-published man of promise who had left Cambridge in 1877 was being described as 'the ablest of our living Economists'.[e]

The Bristol illness left its mark. According to Maynard Keynes, Marshall 'remained for the rest of his life somewhat hypochondriacal and inclined to consider himself on the verge of invalidism'.[19] His powers of intense intellectual concentration, never great, were diminished. Henceforward his nerves were easily upset by heavy activity or excitement or controversy. 'He became dependent on a routine of life adapted even to his whims and fancies'.[20] He was even more dependent on, and demanding of, his wife. Yet, frail as he might seem, he had a mission – one about which he had few doubts.

Marshall's mission was to establish economics as a respectable, recognised science – a status that the old political economy had lost in the face of attacks from Comtists and historical economists, disciplinary disunity and low public esteem. This process had two important strands: institutional and theoretical. At the institutional level Marshall's efforts in Cambridge would be directed towards the recognition of economics as an independent, respectable field of study with, if necessary, its own tripos. Nationally the institutional change would come in the founding of the British Economic Association, later the Royal Economic Society, with its associated professional *Economic Journal*. At an intellectual or theoretical level, Marshall's efforts would be directed in two directions: in developing a rationale for the subject and defining its place on the map of learning which would provide the underlying consensus for day-to-day work in the field; and at providing the discipline with an authoritative statement of theoretical principles – his projected multi-volume *Principles of Economics* (the first English work to use the word, suggested by Jevons, rather than the older political economy) on which he had already started work.[21]

Marshall made his views known very early on. Four days after his election as Professor of Political Economy he called on Henry Sidgwick in Cambridge. Sidgwick recorded that he

heard my views of the lectures required, then suddenly broke out. I had produced on him the impression of a petty tyrant 'dressed in a

e Foxwell to Walras, 30 December 1882 in Jaffé (ed.) 1965. Jevons had died while swimming in the English Channel on 13 August 1882.

little brief authority' (Chairman of the Board of Moral Science) who wished to regulate, trammel, hamper a man who knew more about the subject than I did.

Correspondence followed in which Marshall analysed Sidgwick's academic career and its failures.[22] Others also felt the new broom.[f] Then on 24 February 1885 Marshall gave his inaugural lecture, 'The Present Position of Economics', which to Sidgwick contained 'the threatened declaration of war against me and my efforts at University organisation'.[23]

Marshall's lecture gave him an opportunity to stake out a positive position for economics against its professional critics, either Comtist or historicist. Linking himself with the giants of the past, he argued that his predecessors' main contribution had been the development of a method of enquiry, an 'organon' of universal applicability. Economics was 'not a body of concrete truth, but an engine for the discovery of concrete truth, similar to, say, the theory of mechanics'.[24] This engine, which was an aid to reasoning about human motives which were measurable, could, if improved and developed, prove a powerful tool in the analysis of changing economic reality and in achieving a vast improvement in working-class life. It could not be subsumed within the methods of some higher social science as some Comtists believed.

No doubt if that existed Economics would gladly find shelter under its wing. But it does not exist; it shows no signs of coming into existence. There is no use in waiting idly for it; we must do what we can with our present resources.[25]

One of these resources was the economic organon which introduced 'systematic and organised methods of reasoning' into one aspect of important social problems. For the historical school's emphasis on induction from the facts of history Marshall had little use. Facts by themselves were silent. At best they could provide guidance in circumstances where history repeated itself. They were hardly likely to be of much use when history did not repeat itself. Normally facts needed to be selected, organised and grouped. This was where economics as a science came in.

Although in his inaugural Marshall moved closer to Sidgwick's position in arguing that the economist *qua* economist should not become involved in debates over practical measures, when he turned to Cambridge he staked out economics' claim for its place in the sun, if necessary, outside the umbrella of the Moral Sciences. Many of those best suited for economics were not attracted to 'the metaphysical studies lying at the threshold of the [Moral

f Archdeacon Cunningham, an unsuccessful candidate for the chair was told by Marshall, a ruling confirmed by the Faculty Board, that he must lecture on formal political economy for at least a term a year (Maloney 1985, 99.)

Sciences] Tripos'.[26] Yet given the economic evils of the world was it sensible to exclude them? No, he argued, for the material improvement to which the study of economics could contribute was important, in that it would allow 'the great mass of our people . . . a life far higher and far more noble' than that available at present. Surely, in these circumstances, 'an attitude of philosophic indifference to wealth and all its concerns' would be 'a great and disastrous mistake'.[27]

Although Marshall's inaugural lecture placed its emphasis on the power of economic analysis to effect human improvement, it would be a mistake to underplay his concern for the facts of economic life. In many ways, his concern for the facts and details of experience delayed the publication of the *Principles*. Throughout his work, Marshall was concerned that his logical analysis should appear together with its applications to the contemporary world. Thus he took an immense amount of time and trouble to study the details of economic life. Summer after summer, vacation after vacation were spent seeing factories and workshops, finding out about machines and tools, conditions of work and leisure.[28] Along with his wide historical reading, largely a product of his evolutionary conception of progress, his studies also made him a well-informed economic historian, even if he disclaimed the role to avoid further brushes with Archdeacon Cunningham, who took exception to the use of history in the first chapters of the first edition of the *Principles*. These investigations delayed the appearance of his analytical ideas outside the lecture notes of his pupils. Nevertheless, Marshall's clothing of his formal economic analysis in a web of closely investigated fact, along with his moralism and evolutionism, meant that he probably reached a wider public than he otherwise would have.

Despite his attempts to minimise them, Marshall's growing public responsibilities also delayed the publication of the *Principles*. To a considerable extent, these came with his position. It was only natural that he should be asked for evidence by the Royal Commission on the Depression of Trade and Industry (1886) and the Royal Commission on the Values of Gold and Silver (1887–8). He really overdid himself for the latter with three memoranda and three days of oral evidence involving answers to over 500 questions (one of which, incidentally, introduced the word unemployment into English).[29] There were also invitations to give papers and act as president of bodies such as the Co-operative Congress and Section F of the British Association for the Advancement of Science. As a result, it was July 1890 before the *Principles* appeared. Four months later the British Economic Association, an outgrowth of Marshall's 1890 presidency of Section F, was founded at a meeting at University College, London.[30]

Marshall's *Principles of Economics* enjoyed a remarkable success. It is, for example, probably the only major nineteenth-century treatise in economics to have remained *continuously* in print since first publication. Below the closely investigated facts and evolutionary moralising, and despite Marshall's deliberate attempts to appear as unrevolutionary as possible, lay an extremely powerful set of analytical tools which modern economists treat as part of their stock in trade, even if they do not necessarily know their origins. At the core of the book was a full exploration of the interactions of supply and demand which took account of the frictions that impede rapid adjustment, the fact that the demand for factors of production was derived from the products they co-operated to produce and the fact that many goods are jointly demanded (tea and milk) or supplied (heating oil and gasoline). Although Marshall was aware of the *general* equilibrium interactions of everything on everything else in the economic system, the subject explored by Walras, his distinctive analytical contribution in the *Principles* was the method of *partial* equilibrium, where, using certain *ceteris paribus* assumptions to impound more remote consequences of change, he was able to focus his attention on particular markets, particular firms and particular industries and to couch his analysis in a wealth of contemporary detail.

Marshall had envisaged his *Principles* occupying several volumes – the book carried the words 'volume 1' on the title page down to the sixth edition of 1910. His plans for the later volumes changed as he gathered more and more material.[31] When he originally offered the book to Macmillan, he thought that one additional volume would be sufficient.[32] By 1895 he had expanded his programme to three additional volumes.[33] A decade later he thought that four additional volumes would be necessary. In the end he published only *Industry and Trade* (1919), which was to have been the second volume in both the 1885 and 1895 schemes, and *Money, Credit and Commerce* (1923), a desperate attempt to complete the scheme and rescue some material written as much as 50 years previously.

This delay in even partially completing the original scheme of the 1880s had several causes. Of these, perhaps the most important was Marshall's obsessive preoccupation with the revision of the published portion of the *Principles* which went through eight editions between 1890 and 1920. Although the important revisions came in the third and fifth editions of 1895 and 1907, the remaining editions also saw significant changes, all of which took time and effort. Then there were the limited, but significant, other calls on his time, most notably membership of the Royal Commission on Labour of 1891–4 and the continuously interrupting job of lecturing and teaching – all very important to one who lacked rapid powers of execution, continuous concentration or continuous sensitivity to the enterprise as a whole, and who spent so much of his vacation time in the search for illustrative facts.

Despite Marshall's devotion to teaching, it bore little fruit in students committed to economics in the years after his return to Cambridge. Before he had gone to Bristol he had taught Mary Paley, Henry Cunynghame, H. S. Foxwell, Neville Keynes, William Cunningham and, to a lesser extent,

J. S. Nicholson. The years after 1885 were so barren that he could complain to Neville Keynes that

> *The curriculum to which I am officially attached has not provided me with one single first class man devoting himself to economics during the sixteen years of my Professorship.* (emphasis in the original)[34]

True, he had made catches with graduates from other subjects such as mathematics in A. W. Flux, later statistical adviser to the Board of Trade, and A. L. Bowley, later Professor of Statistics in the University of London. But it was only with the turn of the century that the more familiar names began to appear regularly in any number – A. C. Pigou, D. H. Macgregor and C. R. Fay.

The absence of good students was one factor lying behind Marshall's desire for greater independence for economics. As we have seen, in his 1885 inaugural lecture he had 'declared war' on the existing arrangements where economics was part of the Moral Sciences and Historical Triposes. For the rest of Sidgwick's life, Marshall, with H. S. Foxwell as his second-in-command, continued almost constant guerrilla warfare against Sidgwick's attempts to hold the Moral Sciences Tripos together and to ensure that prospective economists had a basic philosophical training before specialising.[35] Signs of this warfare began to appear in Neville Keynes's diaries soon after Marshall returned to Cambridge.[36] The ensuing strains told not only on Neville Keynes, for whom Marshall had plans in his larger campaign for economics, but also on Sidgwick who, in a moment of depression in 1888, even thought of leaving Cambridge altogether.[37] Such strains were inevitable in dealing with Marshall, for he was 'tiresome and obstinate' in his dealings with colleagues,[38] but his passion for the academic independence of economics probably made matters worse. He gradually wore down the opposition and gained support. The possibilities for specialising in economics within both the Moral Sciences and Historical Triposes increased, although the changes seemed to have little effect in increasing the number of distinguished graduates, much less those who remained economists. By 1900 Sidgwick had become converted to the idea of a separate tripos for economics, but this made little immediate difference as he died soon afterwards.[39]

Marshall continued to push his project, not only on the Moral Sciences Board but also on the History Board. The latter Board had the advantage for him in that there he was the only economist, whereas with the Moral Sciences Board there were also Foxwell and Neville Keynes with claims to expertise. It was, for example, on the History Board in 1901 that he succeeded in getting a committee to report on the extension of the teaching of modern economics and politics in the University, thus, possibly for tactical reasons, tying himself into another perennial Cambridge worry, the proper teaching of politics. Matters now seemed more urgent because economics was becoming established elsewhere and, in many cases, making appeals for business support: there was, for example, the London School of Economics with some support from the London Chamber of Commerce, and W. J. Ashley's move to Birmingham from Harvard as the first professor of commerce, again with strong business support. Marshall certainly played on these developments in his campaign.[40] In 1902, after extensive consultations on earlier drafts to secure widespread support, he circulated to members of the Senate of the University 'A Plea for the Creation of a Curriculum in Economics and Associated Branches of Political Science'.[41] Marshall's 'plea' highlighted the problems of the existing arrangements by noting

> that of those who have passed through Cambridge in the last fifteen years and are now engaged in constructive work in economics, only one has followed the Moral Sciences curriculum; and he [S. J. Chapman] having taken his MA degree in London in mental and moral sciences and economics before he entered here as an undergraduate had plenty of time at his disposal.[42]

Marshall's grounds for the new tripos were that it would be in the national interest to increase the limited supply of trained economists for government, especially given Britain's recent relative economic decline as compared with Germany, and as a preparation for business and public responsibilities, especially when supplemented by the character-building environment of a residential university.

Marshall's 'plea' fell on receptive ears. On 26 April 1902 the Council of the Senate received a memorial from 126 members of the Senate asking for the appointment of a syndicate 'to enquire into and report upon the best means of enlarging the opportunities for the study in Cambridge of Economics and associated branches of Political Science'.[g] The Memorial achieved its purpose. A Syndicate, including Marshall, Foxwell, Neville Keynes and G. Lowes Dickinson, was appointed. It reported in favour of a new tripos on 4 March 1903, two members dissenting.[43] There followed the usual discussion[44] and a successful grace or legislative act. Marshall had finally got his way.

To staff the new Tripos, Marshall set about increasing the teaching resources. In 1899, when St John's had raised its fellowship dividend for professors to £200, he had set aside that sum to pay for additional teaching. His first candidate was A. C. Pigou who was just finishing Part II of the Moral Sciences Tripos after taking a first in Part I History. He also negotiated with the Girdlers' Company for an endowed University lectureship. Again

g *Cambridge University Reporter*, 29 April 1902, 702–3. Neville Keynes did not sign the Memorial. Amongst the 'economists' who did were Arthur Berry, A. L. Bowley, J. H. Clapham, Henry Cunynghame, A. W. Flux, H. S. Foxwell, J. S. Nicholson and C. P. Sanger. Other signatories included W. W. Rouse Ball, G. Lowes Dickinson, Walter Leaf, F. W. Maitland, J. R. Mayor, G. W. Prothero, Bertrand Russell, W. R. Sorley, Leslie Stephen, G. M. Trevelyan, John Venn and James Ward.

Pigou was the first incumbent. It is clear by this stage that Pigou had become Marshall's favourite. When Marshall resigned in 1908 it would be for Pigou's election as his successor that he lobbied intensively – and successfully, much to the chagrin of Foxwell, who had already started writing his inaugural lecture.[45]

The organisation of the new tripos in a University short of cash and the assurance of Pigou's succession marked the successful conclusion of Marshall's campaign. With his retirement, he withdrew from the affairs of the University. He also became less active professionally,[h] as he concentrated on completing his multi-volumed treatise, publishing nothing else other than an article on post-war taxation and a few letters to the press. But, before I return to Keynes, there is one part of Marshall's thought relevant to later discussions that is best dealt with here. I leave Marshall's monetary economics until Chapter 8.

This aspect of Marshall's thought – one his successors did not follow in detail, although echoes of his notions did appear in the work of Maynard Keynes – was his view of progress. As with most things with Marshall, the bare bones of his ideas were present in the 1870s, although his detailed expression of them and their implications varied over the next fifty years, moving generally in a conservative direction.

At the base of the views I am considering was a rejection of narrow utilitarianism, not uncommon in his generation. He rejected the notion of basing economics on the concept of economic man 'mechanically and selfishly' pursuing pecuniary gain and was prepared to argue that the love of money was but one of the many motives for action. In particular he was prepared to argue that desires for public esteem, the pleasure of activity for its own sake, one's feeling of duty towards others and even the longer-term development of one's latent potential were also important. This widening of motives did not involve Marshall in any sacrifice of his analytical structure, for they could either be captured in a suitable way under the rubric of utility maximisation or be relegated to longer-term changes that stretched beyond his analytical long run and were caught up in his biological, evolutionist analogies. Yet his consideration of a wider range of motives did distance him from his predecessors, especially when it came to evaluating changes in policies.

In the 1930s, Talcott Parsons noted that Marshall distinguished between 'wants' – the subject matter of a 'science of wealth' – and 'activities', where economics became 'part of the Social Science of man's action in Society'.[46] It was this distinction that enabled Marshall to move beyond the limited concerns of utilitarian economics, the study of the satisfaction of given wants, and encompass the grand theme of economic progress. For

h However, he did emerge occasionally, for example, to chair the special meeting of the Council of the Royal Economic Society that elected Maynard Keynes as editor of the *Economic Journal* on 17 October 1911 (RES Minute Book, I).

if, as Marshall believed, character was mutable and conditioned by the economic environment, he could, and did, view the economic problem more broadly as 'contriving the emergence of suitable characteristics with suitable accompanying wants'.[47] Moreover, if material and moral progress were mutually reinforcing, the role of economics as a branch of enquiry would be enhanced, as would be the role of the economist. As Maynard Keynes remarked,

> The solution of the economic problem was for Marshall, not an application of the hedonistic calculus, but a prior condition of the exercise of man's higher faculties, irrespective, almost, of what we mean by higher.[48]

For Marshall, this line of thinking that the standard of life, defined in a broad sense,[49] and its improvement took precedence over the short-term maximisation of satisfactions, affected the way in which he viewed contemporary events and institutions. For it meant that he could accept interferences with or imperfections in any existing set of economic arrangements on the grounds that they would allow the attainment of a higher standard of living. Inevitably, over time his detailed views in this area underwent change.

As Rita McWilliams-Tullberg has pointed out, the Marshall of the 1870s had, as he later described it in his preface to *Industry and Trade*, 'a tendency to socialism'.[50] At that time he was prepared to support East Anglian agricultural workers in their attempts to unionise and was generally sympathetic, at least in his initial presumptions, to the advantages of workers combining in unions and co-operative societies to improve their bargaining positions against employers or producers. During this period as well, his unfavourable references to schemes of state control were limited. From the early 1880s onwards he distanced himself from these earlier views – as he did in the matter of the education of women. He became more sceptical of the benefits of trade unions, even though he claimed to think that their educational activities could 'make the working classes more intelligent and more capable of governing themselves'.[51] With his declining faith in the overall benefits of trade unionism, he came more and more to look to the co-operative movement as being the better vehicle to achieve the aim of education and an altruistic consideration of broader social interests. This probably explains his 1889 willingness to be President of the Co-operative Congress. By the 1890s his attitude to unions bordered on hostility, as he became convinced that the 'new unionism' of the period with its aggressive pursuit of sectional interests was contributing significantly to Britain's relative decline and threatening the improvement in the standard of life.

As he became more sceptical about the benefits of combinations by workers, Marshall became more and more infatuated with the role of the pioneering entrepreneur as an agent of moral and material progress. With this shift in emphasis came a greater concern about the possible damage that could result from state intervention and the inhibiting effects of combinations on the part of business or labour. Yet his distrust of government intervention came from another source as well. Governments were composed of individuals who were subject to the same limitations as the members of society at large. Policies which might be effective if all of those involved acted from high-minded or altruistic motives might be counterproductive in the present world of less than perfect or universal high-mindedness or altruism. Yet, even allowing for the imperfections of the present world, he was prepared on occasion to advocate intervention such as providing subsidies to industries subject to increasing returns to scale.[52] He was, despite his distrust of intervention, to allow that public authorities were becoming more competent, thus enlarging the scope for potentially beneficial state intervention.[53] Indeed, as economic chivalry and altruism became more widespread, intervention and control would become more flexible, if less necessary, as the same process would reduce the deleterious side effects of the system of competition and private property. In the interim, state intervention could assure minimum standards while voluntary private action, more attuned to the needs of particular individual circumstances, could act as a useful supplement.

In this general scheme of thought economists played an important role, which was primarily educational. He did not see the economist as preacher:[54] indeed in the first decade of his professorship in Cambridge, he successfully conducted a campaign (with occasional mopping-up operations afterwards) against a group of younger economists associated with the University of Oxford who held to a broader social historical and ethical conception of political economy, eventually shunting them off into the new sub-discipline of economic history.[i] Rather, the role of the economist was to provide individuals with information in order that the range of human motives broader than self-interest might come to the fore. As he put it in 1874, while still using the old-fashioned name for the subject:

> Political Economy will have wider opportunities of aiding each man to judge his own conduct by analysing it, and by putting it before him, as Nathan did before David, the likeness between it and other conduct on which he is able to give an unbiased judgement. In this indirect mode will she contribute to the clearness of men's notions about duty; direct decisions on questions of moral principle she must leave to her sister, the Science of Ethics.[55]

Thus economics could affect individual behaviour and further social improvement. No wonder Marshall concluded his Cambridge inaugural:

i A part of this process involved the founding of the British Economic Association and the *Economic Journal*. For discussions of this matter see Kadish 1982, Maloney 1985, Koot 1987 and Riesman 1990. Similar motives lay behind his attempt to demarcate the boundaries of his subject by calling it economics rather than political economy.

It will be my most cherished ambition, my highest endeavour . . . to increase the number of those, whom Cambridge, the great mother of strong men, sends out into the world with cool heads but warm hearts, willing to give some at least of their best powers to grappling with the social suffering around them; resolved not to rest content till they have done what in them lies to discover how far it is possible to open up to all the material means of a refined and noble life.[56]

During September 1905 Maynard devoted some of his time to economics, working through the Victorian classics of the subject: Marshall, Edgeworth, Cournot, Bastable and Jevons. He continued working at economics into the Michaelmas term. Then he formally declared his interest in the subject. On 12 October he filled out an entry for Marshall's lectures,[57] in which he stated that he was interested in 'Advanced Economics mainly *analytic*' and noted 'I am inclined to specialise on C. Money, Credit and Prices D. International Trade'. At this stage his purposes were clear. As he told Marshall:

I shall not be able to devote the whole of my time to Economics as I intend to enter for the Civil Service Examination in Aug. 1906. It will be necessary for me to complete my work for the papers on philosophy (Logic, Metaphysics, Psychology and Ethics) *before* my tripos.

It is my intention to devote only the latter half of June and July to cram pure and simple.

Such statements seem rather strong from a dabbler in the subject merely reading up his economics for the Civil Service examinations. So too is the list of books he told Marshall he had *already* read.j Together they cast some doubt on the view that Maynard's formal study of economics was undertaken 'out of indecision' or that his exposure to economic theory was limited.[58] If he was, as some argue, so interested in philosophy, why did he not proceed with the Moral Sciences tripos in 1905? It, too, would have been useful for the Civil Service examinations.

Maynard proceeded to spend the autumn on economics: reading, going to Marshall's lectures and writing essays for the Professor. Several of these essays survive in his papers, covered with Marshall's extensive comments

---

j Marshall's lecture entry asked for a 'List of Books on Economics which you have read, inclosing in brackets the names of any that you have only read hastily'. Keynes's list ran as follows: Marshall – *Principles of Economics, Pure Theory of Foreign Trade, Pure Theory of Domestic Values*, Miscellanea; Jevons – *Principles of Political Economy, Investigations in Currency and Finance, Money*; Bowley – *Elements of Statistics*; Cassel – *Nature and Necessity of Interest*; Bagehot – *Lombard Street*; Toynbee – *Industrial Revolution*; Cournot – *Principles Math. des Richesses*; sundry articles on Cournot; Bastable – *International Trade*; *Public Finance*; Ricardo – *Principles of Political Economy*; Nicolson – *Principles of Political Economy*, vol. I; Goschen – *The Foreign Exchanges*; Clare – *A.B.C. of Foreign Exchanges*; Keynes – *Scope and Method*; Edgeworth – articles in the incidence of urban taxation, the theory of international values, the pure theory of taxation and index numbers; Pierson – articles on index numbers; Darwin – *Bimetallism*.

and queries in red ink. His first essay was on the construction of index numbers to represent general purchasing power, a not surprising topic given Marshall's concern for a stable standard of value. It was a topic to which Maynard would return several times in the years to come.[k] As became usual in cases where disagreements remained, Maynard prepared a supplementary answer for 31 October on the same subject. Marshall's concluding comment on that essay ran:

> This is a very powerful answer.
> I trust that your future career may be one in wh. you will not cease to be an economist.
> I should be glad if it could be that of economist.
> I shall be compelled in lecture to say a good many things wh. you know already.

The essays continued on topics such as the application of the theory of consumer surplus, the definition of capital, railway freight rates, and price discrimination by trusts. By mid-November, Maynard was reporting to Lytton:

> I find Economics increasingly satisfactory, and I think I am rather good at it. I want to manage a railway or organise a Trust or at least swindle the investing public. It is so easy and fascinating to master the principles of these things.

And eight days later:

> Marshall is continually pestering me to turn professional economist and writes flattering remarks on my papers to help on the good cause. Do you think there is anything in it? I doubt it.
> I could probably get employment here if I wanted to. But prolonging my existence in this place would be, I feel sure, death. The only question is whether a Government Office in London is not death equally.
> I suppose I shall drift.
> I expect Hitchin[l] is really the only place to live in.

Marshall's efforts were sufficiently successful to worry Neville Keynes, perhaps because they did not fit his plans:

> He [Maynard] does a great deal of work for Marshall who described some of his answers as brilliant. I am afraid Marshall is endeavouring to persuade him to give up everything for Economics.

k The essay was preserved with his successful 1909 Adam Smith Prize essay 'The Method of Index Numbers with Special Reference to the Measurement of General Exchange Value' (*JMK*, XI, 49–156). He returned to the subject again in *A Treatise on Money* (1930).
l A railway town half-way between Cambridge and London King's Cross station.

Maynard himself has this afternoon broached the idea that he should give up reading for the Civil Service![59]

On 3 December he made another entry:

Marshall writes 'Your son is doing excellent work in Economics. I have told him that I should be greatly delighted if he should decide on the career of a professional economist. But of course I shall not press him.'

There matters rested for the moment. At the end of term Maynard's reading moved away from economics. On 18 December, Neville Keynes reported that Maynard's latest idea was 'to give up the Economics Tripos so as to concentrate on preparation for the c.s. exam*n*.'. Certainly his reading reflected a change, for between 11 December 1905 and May 1906 he recorded reading only one economics book. Marshall tried once more. Maynard turned him down, but the Professor persisted with one last letter on 2 May:

My dear Keynes,
I was very sorry to get your letter this morning. But I must not push you further. I think that if you went in for the Tripos, merely re-reading Economics in the ten days before it, you would *probably* get a first class: & that if you did not, you wd. not injure your position, since it wd. be known that you had little time for economics. But I must say no more.
The list of Cobden Prize[m] subjects is reprinted . . . in the current *Reporter*.
After you have taken your well earned holiday in August and September, I hope you will see your way to working at one of these, for your own good, for the glory of Cambridge and to the great satisfaction of

> Yours vy sincerely
> Alfred Marshall[60]

Although after his return from Switzerland in September Maynard had settled back into reading economics, he took some time off for golf, as well as to work on two essays, 'Miscellanea Ethica' and 'A Theory of Beauty' (below, pp. 127, 130), the latter delivered to Dickinson's Discussion Society on 6 November, and to read 'the superb Hume' who 'very nearly discovered Ethics, and was a sodomite'.[61] Then at the end of the month he went off for ten days of

---

m The Cobden Prize was a triennial prize in political economy worth £20. The topics for the next competition, with a deadline of October 1907, included causes of variations in the rate of interest, changes in the character of commercial fluctuations over the previous 80 years, the causes of changes in relative wage rates in five occupations over the previous 50 years, and the relationship between the physiocrats and British economic theory. Maynard did not submit an essay. The prize was won by Walter Layton.

visiting – Lytton at Kettering and Hobby at Castle Cary before returning to Cambridge for the beginning of term.

With the Michaelmas term came a visit from Swithinbank, plus 'unrestrained fresher excitement'[62] as, with Lytton down from Cambridge after his unsuccessful fellowship dissertation, Maynard and Hobby started looking over possible embryos. During the weeks and months that followed, as their correspondence moved from Dear Keynes to Dear Maynard at his initiative,[63] he reported the possibilities to Lytton – Lytton's brother James Strachey, H. T. J. Norton, Ernst Goldschmidt, Dillwyn Knox. In all of this he appeared to take immense trouble to see how they got on with each other and the other brethren and angels whose opinions mattered. It could be wearing. He reported to Lytton on 6 November:

> Was there ever anything more complete than the present lack of civilisation in Cambridge? What's to be done? I can't believe it's the fault of the Society.
>
> There is *nothing* except the occasional wearing embryonic meetings. No salon: no place where one can rest and be amused. . . . Unless something happens in the interval it will not be with the complete sorrow I once foresaw that I shall leave this place.
>
> The great days are gone – for there were comparatively great days once.

As he looked back at the end of term to the previous year: 'Still it was a glorious civilisation in its day'.[64]

During most of the Christmas vacation, apart from journeys to eat more dinners at the Middle Temple or to visit Lytton – on one visit they went to Windsor Castle to look at Holbeins – Maynard kept his nose to the grindstone, initially with psychology and English literature but at the turn of the year with logic and philosophy. As ever there were occasional rounds of golf at Royston, but Maynard seems to have decided that, with an invitation to visit Mary Berenson in Italy during the Easter vacation, it was better to get on with his work.

Yet there were Moorean diversions. On 18 December 1905 Moore read a paper, 'The Nature and Reality of Objects of Perception',[65] to the Aristotelian Society in London. It is not clear from his own or his father's diaries whether Maynard attended the paper, but he was in London the day before and did not return to Cambridge until some time on the 18th itself, and, perhaps more important, he did not get hold of a copy of the paper until McTaggart gave him a copy of the proofs in March 1906.[66] On 20 December he remarked to Lytton:

> I shall never meet Moore again without the protection of Sanger or the like. He is too remote for ease or intimacy, but one could hardly treat him as a stranger.

Certainly his subsequent letters suggest that he had heard the paper. On 2 January Lytton had written:

> Who d'you think – talking of intellects – has been here half to-day? Moore. He was really splendid. We talked about the Society and his Aristotelian paper from 2.30 to 4.30. Then he sang. . . . On the question of secondary qualities, etc. he was quite superb. He had used an argument in his paper about hens and eggs[n] which Hawtrey said was 'too simple'. It was, that in order to know that hens laid eggs, *someone* must have seen both a hen and an egg. Hawtrey denied this – because the fact that hens laid eggs determined your mental state, and therefore you could infer it from your mental state. Moore said he could only say such things because his head was full of philosophical notions. Quite magnificent! I was with him heart and soul. But I wish I could tell you more of what he said.

Maynard's reaction the next day was tinged with scepticism.

> Even still the old faith is strong upon me: I am prepared to throw over all philosophy and believe every word he tells me, even the most monstrously absurd.
>
> Besides, if you believe one single article, you're probably involved in all the others too.
>
> And one hardly feels prepared to disagree with Moore on everything.

After another weekend in London, there was a further reaction on 17 January.

> Oh! I have undergone conversion. I am with Moore absolutely and on all things even secondary qualities. . . . Something gave in my brain and I saw everything clearly in a flash. But the whole thing depends upon intuiting the Universe in a particular way – I see that now – there is no hope of converting the world except by Conversion, and that is pretty hopeless. It is not a question of argument; all depends upon a particular twist of the mind.

But he wavered after a discussion on 20 January:

> I have just come back from tea with the Russells and Whiteheads. There was an argument about Moore's paper and I was a little shaken in my new found Moorism, but Russell [who had been a discussant of the paper on 18 December] seemed quite frankly to admit Moore's charge that he had asked M. difficult questions rather than fairly grappled with M.'s special arguments.

n Moore 1922, 64–7. The problem of hens and eggs had fascinated Maynard as a child.

Finally, in March 1906 Maynard read the paper and reported to Lytton on the 16th:

> I have read Moore's paper and agree with every word without exception. I think the *style* is more marked than ever. But it seems to me that only a passionate sense of duty could persuade him to do it. When one reads some philosophy, the pleasure of the spinning is obvious. But this is not spinning. It is wrung out, squeezed with pain and contortion through a constipated reaction. I almost see him sweating.
>
> The whole thing has simply been produced by mental muscles and by keeping his nose to the stone when anyone else would have given way. And I'm terrified lest he should some day soon. If he doesn't and if he lives forever, I think that there is no doubt the riddle of the universe will be printed. Lord! the distinctions.

Later Maynard was to use arguments similar to Moore's in his *Treatise on Probability*,[67] for which he had already started accumulating books.

After the excitement of electioneering for the Liberals before their victory on 12 January 1906 – specifically for Edwin Montagu in West Cambridgeshire and Frederick Guest in Staffordshire – the Lent term saw Maynard deep in philosophy and ethics for his Civil Service examination preparations. After reading Mill's *Utilitarianism* and Sidgwick's *The Methods of Ethics*, he reported to Lytton on 21 February:

> It is *impossible* to exaggerate the wonder *and originality* of Moore: people are already beginning to talk as if he were a kind of logic chopping eclectic.
>
> Oh why can't they see!
>
> How amazing to think that we and only we know the rudiments of the true theory of Ethic[s]; for nothing else can be more certain than that the broad outline is true. What is the world doing?
>
> It does damned well to bring it home to read books written before *P.E.* I even begin to agree with Moore about Sidgwick – that he was a wicked and edifictious person.

Six days later Sidgwick's *Life*, edited by his widow and his brother Arthur, was published.[68] Maynard's parents had been close to Sidgwick. Maynard had played golf with him soon before his death in 1900 and had helped with his father's *Economic Journal* obituary notice and with his posthumous edition of Sidgwick's *Principles of Political Economy* (1901).°

° Neville Keynes had been thanked by Sidgwick for his reading and criticising the proof sheets of the first edition of the book which appeared in 1883 and for useful suggestions for the second edition of 1887. The third edition was probably the first book on economics that Maynard read.

Maynard read the memoir almost immediately and reported to Lytton on 8 March:

> . . . Have you seen Sidgwick's life? The Society employed its time* [on 3 March] reading the passages about itself, and wrote in the book that it had read with displeasure pages so and so.[69]
>
> There is a good deal about the Society. What Sidgwick wrote himself in the autobiographical fragments is all right. But Arthur's supplementary description merely panders to vulgar curiosity and really increases the likelihood of the Society's being identified. An embryo who had just read the life could hardly fail to see what was happening to him.
>
> I find the book itself absorbingly interesting – by way of contrast. Sidgwick was certainly very apostolic but with what a difference. God! his letters. Dakyns was his most intimate friend, and when D. went away he arranged that his father should open his letters – without informing S. of the arrangement. As a matter of fact there were ructions because of unguarded allusions to Christianity; but I think it proves that Arthur and Mrs haven't edited away anything very important.
>
> There is very little about people and what there is very superficial. And all the chief worries are about Christianity and Careers.
>
> . . .
>
> It all seems dreadfully remote, but Sidgwick does seem to me very charming.
>
> What were they all doing fussing themselves to death about God, when it's perfectly obvious that they knew quite well all the time that there was no such person?
>
> Sidgwick was very *good*; but I don't see why goodness shouldn't be added to the more modern accomplishments, if only we happened to be good.
>
> *Sheppard failed to give a paper again.

Strachey himself had not read the book and would not get it until Maynard lent it to him in Genoa,[70] but he reacted in such a way that, along with subsequent conversation, may have influenced Maynard's comments on the book to Swithinbank at the end of March. Lytton wrote:

> What an appalling time to have lived! It was the Glass House Age. Themselves, as well as their ornaments, were left under glass cases. Their refusal to face any questions fairly – either about people or God – looks at first sight like cowardice; but I believe it was simply the result of an innate incapacity for penetration – for getting either out of themselves or into anything or anybody else. They were enclosed in glass. How intolerable! Have you noticed, too, that they were nearly all physically impotent? – Sidgwick himself, Matthew Arnold, Jowett,

Lighton, Ruskin, Watts. It's damned difficult to copulate through a glass case.[71]

Harrod disputed the Strachey influence: he merely referred to the existence of Maynard's letter to Lytton. However, he ignored Lytton's reply and did not mention the fact that Lytton was with Maynard when the letter to Swithinbank was written, before he printed the relevant part of the letter sent to Swithinbank on 27 March:

Have you read Sidgwick's life? It seems to be the subject of conversation now. Very interesting and depressing and, the first part particularly, very important as an historical document dealing with the mind of the period. Really – but you must read it yourself. He never did anything but wonder whether Christianity was true and prove it wasn't and hope that it was. He even learnt Arabic in order to read Genesis in the original, not trusting the authorised translations, which does seem a little sceptical. And he went to Germany to see what Ewald had to say and fell in love with a professor's daughter, and wrote to his dearest friends about the American Civil War.

I wonder what he would have thought of us; and I wonder what we think of him. And then his conscience – incredible. there is no doubt about his moral goodness. And yet it is all so dreadfully depressing – no intimacy,[p] no clear-cut crisp boldness. Oh, I suppose he was intimate but he didn't seem to have anything to be intimate about except his religious doubts. And he really ought to have got over that a little sooner; because he knew that the thing wasn't true perfectly well from the beginning. The last part is all about ghosts and Mr Balfour. I have never found so dull a book so absorbing.[72]

The Lent term also saw Maynard busy with the Society and its affairs. He attended every meeting of the term, except on 3 March when he was in Oxford seeing Swithinbank and Dan Macmillan, opening a discussion at the Jowett Society after a paper on 'Time and the Absolute' and enjoying 'the pomp' and 'series of heavens' of a dinner in All Souls.[73] He was carefully arranging the final stages of the elections of James Strachey and H. T. J. Norton. Just before that he had taken great pains to make certain that other embryos such as Dilly Knox, who was supported by Sheppard, wouldn't do.[74] The affairs of the Society got him down on occasion:

I wish the Society didn't exist – at least just now. It is a mere lump of oppression. . . . Ugh! I feel as if I can't be bothered about this damned Society. I really believe that I would leave Cambridge and come to

p Maynard's autumn 1905 paper to the Society, 'Modern Civilisation' had discussed changes in degrees of intimacy between members of his generation and their predecessors. See below p. 128.

London at once – but for one reason. I suppose the Society must be put on its legs again – or at any rate one has to try.

I labour for myself most of the time, but I am certainly labouring for future generations in this.[75]

He was nonetheless pleased with the results of the elections. But the endless exchanges with Lytton on relationships, mostly in the sodomitical camp they both used, eventually revealed that it was at this stage at least largely talk on Maynard's side. Lytton came out point blank:

Dear me, it does strike me as a little bit odd that you should be so averse from buggering. I quite agree that being in love's much better, but surely there are charms & splendours in the more animalistic act? . . . I can't profess to understand your queer sort of prudery.[76]

A week later Maynard replied, after admitting a failure of nerve with Dan in Oxford:

My dear. I have always suffered and I suppose always will from a most unalterable obsession that I am so physically repulsive that I've no business to hurl my body on anyone else's. The idee is so fixed and constant that I don't think anything – certainly no argument – could ever shake it.

Well it may be lunacy but I can't help it.

For a time, nothing was to happen to change the situation.

In the Easter vacation Maynard set off to Italy where, on the advice of Alys, Bertrand Russell's wife, he had been invited by her sister Mary Berenson. A tall, imposing woman, direct in conversation and extremely enjoyable company, Mary had left her husband, Frank Costelloe, and her two children, Rachel and Karin, in 1892 for Bernard Berenson, the connoisseur, collector and intimate of dealers. After Costelloe's death she married him, in 1900. At the time of their marriage they had taken Villa I Tatti in the hills above Florence. Maynard's invitation was for a week touring by car and then for a visit to I Tatti on his way back to London. Geoffrey Scott, then an undergraduate at New College, Oxford, and a nephew of C. P. Scott, editor and owner of the *Manchester Guardian*, was also invited. It also appears that Mary may have asked Lytton, but he evaded the invitation. The automobile tour was to begin on 25 March.

Lytton had been wintering at Menton in another attempt to improve his health. He attempted to get Maynard to stop with him on the way out to Florence, but, as Maynard seemed unhappy with the extra travel involved and as Menton was rather crowded, they agreed to meet in Genoa on 20 March, before Maynard met up with Mrs Berenson on 24 March and started the automobile journey outside the Uffizi on 25 March.

The motoring holiday lasted until 31 March. As well as Scott, Mary and Maynard, the party included Mary's two daughters. Among the places they visited were Siena, Orvieto, Spoleto and Assisi before Mary, who paid all their expenses,[77] dropped Scott and Maynard at Poggibonsi so that they could return to Siena, which had attracted them, via San Gimignano for a period of reading. Maynard thoroughly enjoyed the journey, although it was very wet and cold with occasional snow, and the company, although the tone of his letters to Lytton was rather critical of the 'dreadfully Oxford' aesthete Scott.[78] He thought 'Mary Berenson . . . grossly slandered. She's simply Alys [Russell] turned competent and hedonist'.[79] He reported home that he didn't think 'I ever spent a pleasanter week'.[80] The countryside was 'incredibly beautiful'; the food was so good that 'I've seldom taken so constant and open interest in my meals'.[81] Maynard, according to his brother Geoffrey 'the antimotorist motorphobe, the giber of all forms of motoring', even took to the automobile.

> I must confess rather a conversion to the engine. The pleasure of the motion is exquisite, and you visit so many places and so many different hotels in a week that it really seems weeks and months since we started. One symptom which overcame all of us (except Mrs B.) was motor stickiness – an intense disinclination to get out of the car to look at wayside frescoes and a mere desire to go on and on forever in a kind of trance.[82]

Maynard also enjoyed his longer stay in Siena, in the Stracheyesque 'pension with eleven spinsters'.[83] He spent six hours a day reading history, 'a subject that is so easy and cloys so quickly',[84] for his Civil Service examinations. By the end of his visit he had finished everything that he had brought out with him to read and was reduced 'to a lump of Italian idleness'.[85]

Maynard and Scott returned to Florence and I Tatti on 10 April. Maynard spent a further five days there before he went off to to London via Germany to collect his brother who had been spending a term in the Black Forest improving his German before going up to Pembroke College, Cambridge, to read natural sciences. By the time he left, he felt quite at home and had become 'quite a clown in his way'. The young people thoroughly enjoyed themselves dressing up in drag: 'Maynard in a gown of chiffon with a headdress of pink ribbons', Scott in Mary's black dress and Ray in Maynard's dress suit. He 'was almost converted to food'. There even seemed the risk of another conversion.

> I seem to have fallen in love with Ray a little bit, but as she isn't male I haven't [been] able to think of any suitable steps to take.
>
> Of course she practically is male – for she obviously practices sapphistries and its attendant train. But you would really be surprised how nice she is. I would even be prepared to elect her at once – without a qualm of any kind.

Oh Ray looks like a very charming boy in her pyjamas with her hair down. I did get a little time alone when she was thus, lying on the banks of a lake.[86]

He left for the north convinced that Mary was 'really the most amazing person in Europe'.[87] She was 'much taken' by the young men, even if, unlike her daughter, she preferred Scott.[88]

'Alas, my last term . . .'.[89] Now Maynard was in the later stages of preparation for his Civil Service examinations. He was to spend a month on history and political science before beginning his final revisions for the examinations that started on 2 August. From his appointments diary, it seems he set himself a target of six hours work a day, six days a week, for he kept regular track of his surplus or deficit hours from that average. At first, progress was regular: in the period 24 April to 26 May the deficit rarely rose above ten hours. Nor during that period did he do much else. True, there were two trips to London – one to comfort Lytton who had been rather shattered by Hobby's falling in love in May with his cousin, Duncan Grant – rounds of golf at Royston with C. R. Fay, several dinner or lunch parties, including one on 6 May that brought Ray Costelloe to 6 Harvey Road, and the usual meetings of the Society. Contacts with others were limited.

I'm rather depressed by work – I am doing nothing else whatever seriously. Indeed one can't – that's the devilish disease of work.

I have all my meals in my own room and really never speak to a phenomenon except Furness and Lamb.[90]

Inevitably there came a reaction. It started in the course of Lytton's visit to Cambridge between 23 and 30 May, which was followed by an unexpected one from Swithinbank the next day. He reported to Lytton that his 'brain power seems to have given up for the time being' and in the weeks that followed there were several days with no work whatever recorded as he took part in May Week festivities, including the eights bumping races on the river, and renewed acquaintance with cricket at Fenners. He even went to Chapel in King's for the first time in two years. Then there was a special meeting of the Society on 9 June, at which A. W. Verrall, an angel from the 1870s who had been Moore's tutor and would later be the first professor of English literature at Cambridge, had invited nine members – Dickinson, McTaggart, Sanger, Maynard, James Strachey, Norton, Hobhouse, Sheppard and Lytton – to dinner before reading a paper on Tragedy. There followed a visit to Oxford to see Swithin and the outing to the Society's annual dinner, after which, if we are to believe his appointments diary, he probably ended his record of celibacy since Eton with Lytton. By the third week in June he was over twelve working days behind his revision schedule. He had to knuckle down.

He took advantage of his family's summer holiday in Switzerland and moved into 6 Harvey Road. He was alone – and enjoying it. The cook was co-operative, for he managed a hot breakfast at 10.30. Moreover, the sense of well-being continued. As he told Lytton on 1 July:

> I want to live alone for ever and ever. It is too superb. I doubt whether the nervous wear and tear of living with other people is really worth it. One's health and spirits and energy of mind – incredible. My mind is a different instrument altogether than it was last term.
>
> But alas! I see my doom clearly before me. I am *bound* to become a work machine. It is no good. It is in the blood. I may ward it off for a few months or a year – but it will come. Swear to help me – for you are safe. Your doom is quite different.[91]

In his solitude, as well as revising logic and mathematics, Maynard was commenting on the proofs of the fourth edition of his father's *Formal Logic*. In the course of his revisions he read H. W. B. Joseph's *An Introduction to Formal Logic* (1906):

> It appears rather Bosanquetian at a distance – anyhow Oxford beyond belief. What a home of diseased thought the place is. But I believe that posterity will see it in its true light.

> I have now read Joseph's book and must withdraw my prophecy. I thought he was going to be Bosanquetian. But Bosanquet at least belongs to the early part of the nineteenth century. Joseph is mediaeval.
>
> It is indeed a very bad book – if one is searching for the truth. But it has its merits . . . In fact a book for Greats Men by a Greats Man. . . . As history then it has merits, but as an exposition of truth it seems to me *awful* that such things should be . . . Even his account of Induction is entirely based on Aristotle with just a dash of Bacon – so of course he misses the whole point. Even in the formal part his equivocations with the word *meaning* are terrible. He never makes distinctions and at least half his arguments depend on using the same word twice with different meanings. Also he is very fond of mathematical illustrations – and of course nearly always comes to grief.
>
> It would have gained incredibly – but then it would never have been written – if only he had mastered yours. The worst of your book is that when one is reading it everything seems so hopelessly obvious and uncontroversial. It needs a Joseph to open one's eyes.[92]

By the end of the first week of July, Maynard decided he needed a holiday:

he took two days off in London to attend the Varsity cricket match at Lord's with James Strachey, see La Genée in *Coppélia* at the Empire, and dine with Fay and Furness. He then went back into King's to continue revising – now psychology, metaphysics and ethics. He hoped to finish these and political science by 21 July, which would leave him a final week for history and economics. Otherwise, he kept himself occupied with games of golf, talks with James Strachey and visits to David, his favourite Cambridge bookseller, as well as selling off various fixtures and furniture from the rooms he would be vacating in King's.q

> With the advent of history revision, I have lost my last vestige of interest in this dismal examination. I brood over my documents for nearly six hours a day but I doubt if my thoughts are inspired by Bishop Stubbs for more than two of them.[93]

On 29 July he said farewell to Furness, who was going to Egypt as a civil servant, and on 1 August moved to London, where his mother and sister had taken a flat in South Kensington to minister to his needs during the examination. The next day he entered 'the valley of death and sweat': the Civil Service examinations.[94]

The examinations lasted until 24 August. In the intervals between examinations, reading and studying, Maynard made various visits and side trips. He went to Lord's with James Strachey to see Middlesex play Surrey, to Greenwich by river with his mother, and to the theatre. The examinations went well at first, but at the end of the second week, he was unable to sleep on Friday night and that, plus two papers the next day, rather took it out of him. The actual Saturday examinations in English history did not suffer as badly as might be expected, for on one he was asked to write on chronicles and records, where he could use his researches into the history of the Keynes family to good effect. But he was 'reduced to a state of excessive weakness and dependence on brandy' afterwards.[95] He was certainly well enough to use a clear day and a half after his second English history examination on the Monday to go to see Lytton at Betchworth House in Surrey. What they discussed is unknown, but one doubts that they discussed Maynard's two instances of actual as opposed to theoretical sodomy with James Strachey the previous Thursday and Friday.[96] Perhaps these caused the insomnia. Then it was back to the examinations, where he found the moral and metaphysical papers unhelpful; his father found 'the almost entire exclusion of formal and symbolic logic' on the logic paper 'indefensible: but the examiners probably didn't know any'.[97] He was happier with his last few papers, after he had got clear of three rather difficult mathematics papers where he expected his

q Until after 1945, it was normal for Cambridge undergraduates to provide their own furniture for their College rooms. Hence the sales. A residue of this older practice survives in the separate furniture rent that appears in addition to room rents on Cambridge College bills.

worst marks, perhaps because the weather had turned cooler and an attack of indigestion had ceased.

After the examinations he went to Forest Row for a weekend to stay with Humphrey Paul and visit Dan Macmillan, where he found his 'little brother Harold . . . growing up in the Dan style but much more exquisite than Dan ever was – indeed very',[98] before returning to Cambridge. At the end of the month, the list of Civil Service vacancies appeared. There were only two that interested him: in the Treasury and the India Office. Although he expected to be in the top ten, the fewness of the vacancies which candidates would choose from in the order of merit on the examinations led Neville – and Maynard – to doubt that the autumn would find him in the Service.[99]

But there was still a month to wait for the results. On 1 September he and his sister visited Mary Berenson and her family at Fernhurst near Haslemere, where Mary reported to her husband that he was 'a perfect dear', even though Ray reported from his talk

> which is sometimes wild and mystical, the whole doctrine of the peculiar *culte* to which he and Scott belong – I mean the more spiritual sides of it – and I very much doubt whether, in their cases, it has gone much further.[100]

She was just a bit late in that guess. He went on to Hobby at Hadspen and then for a holiday with Lytton and James and Harry Norton in a cottage at Feshie Bridge near Inverness. There they walked and talked and Maynard finished the proofs of *Formal Logic*. He also began seriously to think about his fellowship dissertation, reporting to his father on 21 September, 'My method is quite new, and I think amongst other things that I have a formal proof of the principle of inverse probability'.

He returned to Cambridge on 29 September to face the examination results. He was second, with 3,498 marks out of 6,000 – 417 behind O. E. Niemeyer, who had graduated from Oxford with a first in Greats in 1905. Neville Keynes made his by now usual note – 'a wonderful achievement considering the amount of work he has done in preparation'.[101] Maynard had come first in logic, psychology, English essay, and political science; second in moral and metaphysical philosophy; and 'unaccountably low' in political economy, as well as not doing well in mathematics, according to his father.[102] To Lytton, Maynard remarked on 4 October:

> My marks have arrived and left me enraged. Really knowledge seems an absolute bar to success. I have done worst in the only two subjects of which I possessed a solid knowledge – Mathematics and Economics.[r]
> My dear. I scored more marks for English History than for mathematics

---

r Later he would remark that he knew more economics than his examiners, which, as Austin Robinson remarked, was unlikely, even though Roy Harrod tried to make the opposing case (Robinson 1947, 12; Harrod 1951, 121–2).

– is it credible? For economics I got a relatively low percentage and was 8th or 9th in order of merit – whereas I knew the *whole* of both papers in a really elaborate way. On the other hand in Political Science, to which I devoted less than a fortnight in all, I was easily first of everybody. I was also first in Logic and Psychology and in Essay.

However, by that stage 'the last tack' was 'nailed in my coffin'.[103] Lytton 'imagine[d] a temporary India Office with a vista of Treasuries and K.C.Bs. Dear, dear!'[104] Niemeyer had taken the Treasury vacancy and Maynard, having passed the medical on 1 October, was a member of the India Office. After some work on his dissertation, organising a service flat at 125B St James Court in the Buckingham Palace Road, and a weekend with the Russells in Oxford, Maynard started work in the Office on 16 October 1906.

NOTES

1 MCPL, A. C. Benson Diaries, vol. 71, 52.
2 KCKP, JMK to GLS, 31 July 1905.
3 KCKP, JMK to GLS, 20 July 1905.
4 See Coase 1984; *JMK*, X, 161.
5 Roach 1959, 242.
6 Schneewind 1977, 47.
7 Venn quoted in Sidgwick and Sidgwick 1906, 135.
8 *JMK*, X, 168.
9 Whitaker (ed.) 1975, I, 7.
10 *JMK*, X, 171.
11 Jaffé (ed.) 1965, I, 794; see also II, 162.
12 Pigou (ed.) 1925, 404–6, 412–14; Whitaker (ed.) 1975, I, 37–9.
13 Black (ed.) 1972–81, V, 78; Foxwell 1887, 88; Cunynghame 1904, 9.
14 Schumpeter 1954, 839–40.
15 Black (ed.) 1972–81, IV, 204–5; Riesman 1990, 29.
16 Whitaker (ed.) 1975, I, 67.
17 *JMK*, X, 242.
18 McWilliams-Tullberg 1975a, 105–6, 112–13, 124–5, 236 n. 8; Pigou (ed.) 1925, 100.
19 *JMK*, X, 178.
20 Ibid.
21 On the whole process, see Maloney 1985; Riesman 1990.
22 Sidgwick and Sidgwick 1906, 394–5.
23 Sidgwick and Sidgwick 1906, 402. The lecture appears in Pigou (ed.) 1925, 152–74.
24 Ibid., 159.
25 Ibid., 164.
26 Ibid., 172.
27 Ibid., 172.
28 For details see Whitaker (ed.) 1975, I, 52–7.
29 The memoranda and evidence are in Keynes 1926, 19–193. The use of the term unemployment appears on page 93. On the use of the term see Harris 1972, 4 n.3, which mistakenly puts Marshall's first use of the term on page 92.
30 *JMK*, XII, 846–55.
31 See Whitaker in Whitaker (ed.) 1990 for the full details.
32 Whitaker (ed.) 1975, I, 88.

33 Marshall 1961, II, 45–6.
34 MLC, JNK Papers 1(125), Marshall to Keynes, 30 January 1902, emphasis in the original.
35 For a detailed discussion of that campaign, see Kadish 1989, chs 5 and 6.
36 CUL, Add.7834, entries for 4 March and 19 April 1885.
37 Sidgwick and Sidgwick 1906, 488.
38 *JMK*, X, 223.
39 Ibid., 222 n. 2; Marshall 1961, II, 163; *Cambridge University Reporter*, 14 May 1903, 763.
40 Ibid., 774; Marshall 1961, II, 164.
41 This appears in ibid., 160–81. Among those whom Marshall consulted was Neville Keynes, who could not support the scheme.
42 Ibid., 162–3.
43 For the report, see *Cambridge University Reporter*, 10 March 1903, 528–38. For the existence of dissent see ibid., 14 May 1903, 763.
44 Which, uncharacteristically, Neville Keynes cut after an hour and forty-five minutes (CUL, Add.7853, 7 May 1903).
45 On the election see Coats 1968 and 1972, Coase 1972 and Jones 1978.
46 Parsons 1931 and 1932.
47 Whitaker 1977, 175.
48 *JMK*, X, 104.
49 For a discussion of Marshall's concept see Chasse 1984, 393–4.
50 McWilliams-Tullberg 1975b.
51 Whitaker (ed.) 1975, II, 351. Marshall's published views on unions remained more restrained than those he expressed in private. See Petrides 1973.
52 Pigou (ed.) 1925, 385, 398–403.
53 Marshall 1961, I, 473.
54 Pigou (ed.) 1925, 334–6.
55 Harrison 1963, 429.
56 Pigou (ed.) 1925, 174.
57 I am indebted to Professor Beccatini for this document, which he discovered while working on Marshall.
58 Skidelsky 1985, 166, 206; O'Donnell 1989, 14.
59 CUL, Add.7855, 26 November 1905.
60 MLC, Marshall Papers, Marshall to JMK, 2 May 1906.
61 KCKP, JMK to GLS, 17 September 1905.
62 KCKP, JMK to GLS, 15 October 1905.
63 KCKP, JMK to GLS, 24 October 1905.
64 KCKP, JMK to GLS, 7 December 1905.
65 *Proceedings of the Aristotelian Society*, 1905–6; reprinted in Moore 1922.
66 KCKP, JMK to GLS, 15 March 1906. Lytton relied throughout, even after Maynard received a copy of the paper, on others' accounts of its contents. CUL, Add.8330, GLS to Moore, 28 March 1906.
67 *JMK*, VIII, 266.
68 Sidgwick and Sidgwick 1906.
69 The pages in question were probably 29–32 and 34–5. See also pages 63, 133, 297, 403, 492 and 591.
70 KCKP, GLS to JMK, 3 March 1906; BL, ADD.57932, GLS to D. Grant, 24 March 1906.
71 KCKP, GLS to JMK, 11 March 1906.
72 Harrod 1951, 115. The letter itself is odd, because Maynard had seen Swithinbank in Oxford at the beginning of the month.

73 KCKP, JMK to GLS, 7 March 1906.
74 Maynard seems to have also proposed Furness. CUL, Add.8330, GLS to G. E. Moore, 28 March 1906.
75 KCKP, JMK to GLS, 19 and 20 January, 1906.
76 KCKP, GLS to JMK, 4 March 1906.
77 Maynard's total expenses between 18 March and 22 April for Italy and Germany came to £11 9s. plus an additional £9 16s. for tickets.
78 KCKP, JMK to GLS, 2 April 1906.
79 KCKP, JMK to GLS, 2 April 1906.
80 KCKP, JMK to JNK, 31 March 1906.
81 KCKP, JMK to A. L. Hobhouse, 31 March 1906.
82 KCKP, GLK to JMK, 9 March 1906; JMK to FAK, 31 March 1906.
83 KCKP, JMK to GLS, 2 April 1906.
84 KCKP, JMK to GLS, 6 April 1906.
85 KCKP, JMK to GLS, 15 April 1906.
86 Strachey and Samuels 1983, 129; Strachey 1981, 231; KCKP, JMK to JNK, 11 April 1906, to GLS, 15 April 1906.
87 KCKP, JMK to GLS, 18 April 1906.
88 Strachey and Samuels 1983, 133.
89 KCKP, JMK to GLS, 6 April 1904.
90 BERG, JMK to GLS, 16 and 21 May 1906.
91 BERG, JMK to GLS, 1 July 1905.
92 KCKP, JMK to JNK, 29 June and 2 July 1906.
93 BERG, JMK to GLS, 27 July 1906.
94 BERG, JMK to GLS, 6 August 1906.
95 BERG, JMK to GLS, 11 August 1906.
96 BL, ADD.60682, H. T. J. Norton to GLS, 4 and 11 August 1906.
97 KCKP, JNK to JMK, 21 August 1906.
98 BERG, JMK to GLS, 28 August 1906.
99 BERG, JMK to GLS, 28 August 1906; CUL, Add.7856, 31 August 1906.
100 Strachey and Samuels 1983, 134.
101 CUL, Add.7856, 28 November 1906.
102 Ibid., 3 October 1906.
103 BERG, JMK to GLS, 30 September 1906.
104 BL, ADD.60720, GLS to JMK, 2 October 1906.

5

MOORE AND KEYNES'S EARLY BELIEFS

We were at an age when our beliefs influenced our behaviour, a characteristic of the young which it is easy for the middle-aged to forget.

(*JMK*, X, 435)

The beginning of Keynes's second year in Cambridge coincided with the publication of Moore's *Principia Ethica*. Like most of his generation of Apostles, Keynes read it with enthusiasm although, unlike some of them, he did not send Moore his praises. He did tell Swithinbank that it was 'a stupendous and entrancing work, *the greatest* on the subject'.[1] As the ideas in the book were to play a significant role in his thinking, they – and his reactions to them – deserve attention.

The book opened with the typically Moorian statement:

It appears to me that in Ethics, as in all other philosophical studies, the difficulties and disagreements, of which its history is full, are mostly due to a very simple cause: namely to the attempt to answer questions, without first discussing what question it is you are trying to answer.[2]

He proceeded to argue that the primary business of ethics was the discussion of the question (or questions) 'What is good?' and 'What is bad?'.[3] He suggested that 'good' was a simple notion such as 'yellow'. It could not be broken down into simpler ideas. As he put it 'good is good and that is the end of the matter'.[4] In other words:

'Good' then is indefinable; and yet, so far as I know, there is only one ethical writer, Prof. Henry Sidgwick, who has clearly pointed this out.[5]

Moore then turned to previous writers who had identified good with pleasure, or progress in the form of, for example, evolution or some other natural property, and claimed that they had committed what he called the naturalistic fallacy – naming some 'natural' property and thinking it defined good. Those who had used some metaphysical property as the ground for ethics had committed a similar fallacy. He also argued that egoism – in the sense that each person's interests were the sole good – was self-contradictory and that, if this were the case, Sidgwick's problem of the resolution of the conflict between rational egoism and rational benevolence which had required him to bring divine omnipotence, or something similar, into play had resulted from a false antithesis.

With the ground cleared of the confusions of previous approaches, Moore turned in his last two chapters to answering the two central questions of ethics: 'What ought we to do?' and 'What things are goods or ends in themselves?'. The answer to the first was that individuals should undertake actions which would on the whole have good effects or 'cause more good to exist in the Universe than any possible alternative'.[6] In other words, the value of actions lay in their consequences, a characteristically utilitarian view. Yet, for Moore, such a doctrine had its own problems. It meant, for example, that ethics was unable to provide a list of duties or statements that certain actions would always produce the greatest sum of good. For to provide such lists or statements one needed to know what other conditions would, conjointly with the actions, determine their effects and to know all the events affected by the action through an indefinite future. At best, therefore, ethics could in any given instance provide an indication over a limited future that a few alternatives might prove to be generally better than others. Anything more produced enormous computational difficulties given the many probabilities involved. In the end Moore came to the conclusion that individuals would probably act rightly if they conformed to generally accepted rules of commonsense morality. As in Sidgwick's case, this conclusion raised the possibility of exceptional cases where one might produce a better or more desirable result by ignoring commonsense morality, but here Moore's answer was straightforward:

> Can the individual ever be justified in assuming that he is one of these exceptional cases? And it seems that this question may be definitely answered in the negative. For if it is certain that in a large majority of cases the observance of a certain rule is useful, it follows that there is a large probability that it would be wrong to break the rule in any particular case; and the uncertainty of our knowledge both of effects and their value, in particular cases, is so great, that it seems doubtful whether the individual's judgement that the effects will probably be good in his case can ever be set against the general probability that that kind of action is wrong. . . . It seems, then, that with regard to any rule which is *generally* useful, we may assert that it ought *always* to be observed. . . . In short, though we may be sure that there are cases where the rule should be broken, we can never know which those cases are, and ought therefore never to break it. It is this fact which seems to justify the stringency with which moral rules are usually enforced and sanctioned.[7]

Having thus dealt with his first question in a fairly conservative Sidgwickian manner, with his second question he argued that it was humanly impossible to describe absolutely the best of all states of things. All one could do, taking into account that the value of the whole was not simply the sum of the values of its parts, was to make suggestions as to intrinsic goods, intrinsic evils, and intermediate or mixed situations. In this context he was prepared to argue that

> By far the most valuable things, which we know or can imagine, are certain states of consciousness, which may be roughly described as the pleasures of human intercourse and the enjoyment of beautiful objects. No one, probably, who has ever asked himself the question has ever doubted that personal affection and the appreciation of what is beautiful in Art or Nature are good in themselves; nor, if we consider strictly what things are worth having *purely for their own sakes*, does it appear probable that anyone will think that anything else has *nearly* so great a value as the things which are included under these two heads. . . . [I]t is only for the sake of these things – in order that as much of them as possible may at some time exist – that anyone can be justified in performing any public or private duty; that they are the *raison d'être* of virtue, that it is they . . . that form the rational ultimate end of human action and the sole criterion of social progress.[8]

This doctrine provided potentially endless grounds for discussion and argument, as well as possible links towards activities in the real world.

It is clear from the available biographies, memoirs and papers of Keynes's contemporaries that *Principia Ethica* affected them in a variety of ways. The book's impact on Keynes can be judged from a number of sources. First, there is his own 1938 memoir 'My Early Beliefs'.[9] Second, there are his papers, in particular a number of essays, many intended for the Society. Although these do not all carry dates, it would appear that none date from his first two terms as an Apostle. From 1904 onwards there is a good selection.[a] Of those papers and fragments which we can date, the titles (or subject matter if untitled) are as follows:

Beauty, 30 April 1904
The Political Doctrines of Edmund Burke, finished 2 October 1904[10]
Truth, October 1904 (12 November 1904)
Toleration, November 1904
Virtue and Happiness (6 May 1905)
Miscellanea Ethica, July–September 1905

---

a Before the amalgamation of the Keynes Papers, these papers were in KCKP, Box 23 or in MLC, JMK Papers, Files UA/1 and UA/2. Where a date (or dates) appear on the documents themselves, they are listed immediately after the title. Dates which appear in brackets have been ascertained from Keynes's correspondence or in consultation with Professor G. E. R. Lloyd and refer to the date of their discussion – normally at a meeting of the Society.

A Theory of Beauty, August–October 1905 – read in part to the Society on 25 May 1912 (read to Dickinson's Philosophical Society on 1 November 1905)

Modern Civilisation (28 October 1905)

Paradise (1905)

Shall We Write Melodramas? (3 February 1906)

Egoism, 24 February 1906

Obligation, 21 April 1906

Posterior Analytics (19 May 1906)

Appearances, 8 February 1908 (re-read 19 November 1910)

Prince Henry or Prince Rupert, 28 November 1908

Science and Art, 20 February 1909

The Present Position of Metaphysics in the Society, 29 May 1909

Can We Consume our Surplus? or The Influence of Furniture on Love (13 November 1909)

The as yet undated papers are as follows:

Shall We Write Filth Packets?

Proposition 93 of *Principia Ethica*, 'Ethics in Relation to Conduct'[b]

Have We a Panacea?

On Art Criticism

The Principle of Organic Unity, read again 22 January 1921

Finally there are the early drafts of what eventually became *A Treatise on Probability* (1921).

The first thing to note about the titles and dates is that a large number are addressed to issues raised by Moore. Of these, there would seem to be three groups: early papers written before graduation in June 1905; those written during the year after graduation in Cambridge; and a mixed series of papers written after his return to Cambridge to teach in 1908. The papers most critical of *Principia Ethica*, leaving for the moment the one concerning Proposition 93, are those in the second group. These were probably the outcome of his re-reading *Principia Ethica* in early July 1905, for he told Lytton Strachey on 8 July that after re-reading he wanted 'to write a long criticism of it'. He sent Strachey the first few pages of the resulting manuscript 'Miscellanea Ethica' on 31 July. This stream of more

b Professor Skidelsky (1985, 152) states that this paper was presented to the Society on 23 January 1904. However, he provides no evidence as to how he arrived at that date. Dr O'Donnell (1982, 10) dated it as 'sometime around early 1904, probably before April', but provided no evidence for this dating beyond, perhaps, its position in the King's College collection box where, of course, it had been used by others before him and where no order was set. More recently, he has accepted Professor Skidelsky's dating but provides no justification for doing so (1989, 12). As this paper is of importance to Skidelsky's (and O'Donnell's) accounts of the development of Keynes's beliefs, I shall discuss its more probable dating in detail in Appendix 1 below.

critical papers lasted less than a year during which he decided to write his fellowship dissertation for King's on probability. He drew up 'A Scheme for an Essay on the Principles of Probability' on 5 September 1905.[11]

By the time Keynes had finished his dissertation for the second time in December 1908 and had become a Fellow of King's in March 1909, the Society had temporarily lost interest in metaphysical questions, because, as he suggested, the subject had ceased to be 'literary' and had become 'scientific'.

> [T]he subject has become professionalised – like mathematics or Political Economy. There is a certain number of things which most of us think we know, but it would be a bore to repeat; and, beyond those, technically rigorous. The amateur is out of it and even amongst experts conversation is becoming an awkward medium of discussion. If metaphysics is not all p's and q's, it's something of the kind – something with which the hearthrug has, plainly, nothing to do.[12]

It was only some time after these remarks that Keynes returned to these subjects in a paper for the Society. By then, having been grappling with Moore's ideas for the better part of a decade, he had reversed some of his earlier opinions. I shall return to these papers in more detail, but first I consider his own connected account of his ideas during that period.

On Sunday, 11 September 1938 a group of friends met at Tilton, Keynes's Sussex farmhouse. They were members of the Memoir Club, founded in 1920 to read memoirs of an earlier age. Amongst those present were four former Apostles – Keynes, Morgan Forster, Desmond MacCarthy and Leonard Woolf – as well as Lydia Keynes, Clive and Vanessa Bell, Molly MacCarthy, Duncan Grant, David Garnett, Quentin and Angelica Bell (Vanessa's children by Clive Bell and Duncan Grant) and Janie Bussy (Lytton Strachey's niece). The stimulus for Keynes that afternoon was a paper read by David Garnett at the previous meeting which had described his introduction of his friends to D. H. Lawrence, Lawrence's bitter dislike of them (most particularly of Keynes), and Garnett's subsequent disappointment, which had led him to cease seeing Lawrence. Keynes also took memories back to before 1914 when he thought he had met Lawrence in Russell's rooms in Trinity – and to what he called 'My Early Beliefs'. This essay, one of two unpublished works for which he explicitly sanctioned publication in his will, has caused no little confusion, and it is best to examine it here in the context of Moore's work and Keynes's contemporaneous writings.

In his memoir, after a brief, inaccurate[13] reference to his meeting Lawrence, Keynes recollected the effects of *Principia Ethica*.

But, of course, its effect on *us*, and the talk that preceded and followed it, dominated, and perhaps still dominates everything else. We were at an age when our beliefs influenced our behaviour . . . and habits of feeling formed then still persist to a recognisable degree. . . . The influence was not only overwhelming; . . . it was exciting, exhilarating, the beginning of a renaissance, the opening of a new heaven on a new earth, we were the forerunners of a new dispensation, we were not afraid of anything. . . .

Now what we got from Moore was by no means entirely what he offered us. He had one foot on the threshold of the new heaven, but the other foot in Sidgwick and the Benthamite calculus and the general rules of correct behaviour. There was one chapter in the *Principia* of which we took not the slightest notice. We accepted Moore's religion, so to speak, and discarded his morals. Indeed, in our opinion, one of the greatest advantages of his religion, was that it made morals unnecessary – meaning by 'religion' one's attitude towards oneself and the ultimate and by morals one's attitude towards the outside world and the intermediate.

. . . Nothing mattered except states of mind, our own and other people's of course, but chiefly our own. These states of mind were not associated with action or achievement or consequences. They consisted of timeless, passionate states of contemplation and communion, largely unattached to 'before' and 'after'. Their value depended, in accordance with the principle of organic unity, on the state of affairs as a whole which could not be usefully analysed into parts. For example, the value of the state of mind of being in love did not depend merely on the nature of one's own emotions, but also on the nature of the object and also on the reciprocity and nature of the object's emotions; but it did not depend, if I remember rightly, or did not depend much, on what happened, or on how one felt about it, a year later, though I myself was always an advocate of a principle of organic unity through time, which seems to me only sensible. The appropriate subjects of passionate contemplation and communion were a beloved person, beauty and truth, and one's prime objects in life were love, the creation and enjoyment of aesthetic experience and the pursuit of knowledge. Of these love came a long way first. . . .

Our religion closely followed the English puritan tradition of being chiefly concerned with the salvation of our own souls. The divine resided within a closed circle. There was not a very intimate connection between 'being good' and 'doing good'; and we had a feeling that there was some risk that in practice the latter might interfere with the former . . . [O]ur religion was altogether unworldly – with wealth, power, popularity or success it had no concern whatever, they were thoroughly despised.[14]

After a brief discussion of how they 'knew' what states of mind were good, how they used Moore's method to settle disputes, and how they combined 'a dogmatic treatment of the nature of experience with a method of handling it which was extravagantly scholastic',[15] Keynes returned to the 'morals' in Moore. He admitted that the 'large part played by considerations of probability in his [Moore's] theory of right conduct' was an important influence in his undertaking a study of probability which refuted Moore on an analytical level.[16] But he also held that Moore's admonitions to follow rules were considered, and rejected, by his Apostolic contemporaries.

> But we set on one side, not only that part of Moore's fifth chapter on 'Ethics in Relation to Conduct' which dealt with the obligation to act so as to produce by causal connection the most probable maximum of eventual good through the whole procession of future ages (a discussion that was riddled with fallacies), but also the part which discussed the duty of the individual to obey general rules. We entirely repudiated a personal liability on us to obey general rules. We claimed the right to judge every individual case on its merits, and the wisdom, experience and self-control to do so successfully. This was a very important part of our faith, violently and aggressively held, and for the outer world it was our most obvious and dangerous characteristic. We repudiated entirely customary morals, conventions and traditional wisdom. We were, that is to say, in the strict sense of the term immoralists. The consequences of being found out had, of course, to be considered for what they were worth. But we recognised no moral obligation upon us, no inner sanction to conform or obey. Before heaven we claimed to be our own judge in our own case.
>
> . . . We were among the last of the Utopians, or meliorists as they are sometimes called, who believe in a continuing moral progress by virtue of which the human race already consists of reliable, rational, decent people, influenced by truth and objective standards, who can safely be released from the outward restraints of convention and traditional standards and inflexible rules of conduct, and left, from now onwards, to their own sensible devices, pure motives and reliable intuitions of the good. . . .
>
> In short, we repudiated all versions of the doctrine of original sin, of there being insane and irrational springs of wickedness in most men. . . . We had no respect for traditional wisdom or the restraints of custom.[17]

We do not know the content of the subsequent discussion that Sunday afternoon, although we know from recollections that part of the paper succeeded – perhaps intentionally – in irritating the two young, 'left wing' members of the party, Janie Bussy and Quentin Bell.[c] Leonard Woolf subsequently complained, with chronological precision, that Keynes's paper gave 'a distorted picture of Moore's beliefs and doctrine at the time of the publication of *Principia Ethica* and of the influence of his philosophy and character when we were young men in Cambridge between 1901 and 1904'.[18] He categorically rejected Keynes's characterisation of the group as 'immoralists' and of its being unconcerned with ordinary life and practical affairs.[19]

Some of this apparent disagreement may arise from Woolf's careful choice of dates. He left for Ceylon in October 1904 and the beliefs that Keynes attributed to himself and his Apostolic friends may have reflected a slightly later stage of practice than Woolf had experienced. Bertrand Russell recorded in his memoirs:

> The tone of the generation [of Apostles] some ten years junior to my own was set by Lytton Strachey and Keynes.... They aimed ... at a life of retirement among fine shades and nice feelings, and conceived of the good as consisting in the passionate mutual admiration of a clique of the elite. This doctrine, quite unfairly, they fathered upon G. E. Moore, whose disciples they professed to be. Keynes, in his memoir 'Early Beliefs' has told of their admiration for Moore and, also, of their ignoring large parts of Moore's doctrine. Moore gave due weight to morals and by his doctrine of organic unities avoided the view that good consisted of a series of isolated passionate moments, but those who considered themselves his disciples ignored this aspect of his teaching and degraded his ethics into advocacy of a stuffy school-girl sentimentalising.
>
> From this atmosphere Keynes escaped into the great world.[d]

Note that for Russell, Keynes at some later date appears to have changed his mind – or his priorities.

Leonard Woolf's comments raise the question of how accurate Keynes's statement was for those other than himself for the period up to 1904, a period for which we have limited evidence for Keynes. 'My Early Beliefs' itself raises a number of other problems. Most important is the question of whether, assuming that the memoir provides an accurate reflection of Keynes's beliefs at sometime soon after 1903, he held these views for very long. For in the 1938 memoir he also evaluated the

c Q. Bell 1974, 50; Q. Bell in Crabtree and Thirlwall 1980, 85–6. Virginia Woolf's Diary spoke of the paper being 'packed, profound & impressive' and of her being 'impressed by M.' and feeling 'a little flittery & stupid', but she tells nothing of others' reactions or of any discussion (VWD, V, 168–9).

d Russell 1978, 67–8. Russell's account, first broadcast in 1952 and subsequently included in his *Autobiography*, was subsequent to and not independent of 'My Early Beliefs'.

beliefs. He argued that their 'pseudo-rational' view of human nature 'completely misunderstood' it and resulted in 'a superficiality, not only of judgement, but also of feeling'. They had ignored 'whole categories of valuable emotion', including irrationality and wickedness, and 'the ways in which states of mind can be valuable, and the objects of them ... more various, and also much richer than we allowed for'.[20] It was not, he argued, that the beliefs were pre-Freudian: it was also that they were superficial even in their own historical terms. He saw himself and his friends as 'water-spiders, gracefully skimming, as light and reasonable as air, the surface of the stream without any contact at all with the eddies and currents underneath'. It may have been a 'good dispensation' for an Edwardian undergraduate, but he agreed that Lawrence had a point when he said that they were 'done for'.[21] Thus there is a natural further question: When did Keynes's beliefs change? This question of dating plays an important part in the literature interpreting Keynes's work.

The existing literature of Moore's influence on Keynes and his contemporaries takes a variety of tacks. Paul Levy, Moore's recent biographer, argues that his influence 'was not importantly doctrinal at all, but *personal*': it was not even the result of reading *Principia Ethica*, but was based 'upon love and admiration for his character . . . integrity, incorruptibility, thoroughness and shining innocence'.[22] It was because of their admiration that Keynes and his contemporaries showed their allegiance by proclaiming that they believed his philosophical arguments.

Roy Harrod, Keynes's official biographer, took another tack. He accepted that 'the veneration which his young admirers accorded him almost matched that due to a saint' partly because of the impact of his personality.[23] Yet, he argued, their treatment of Moore as recounted in Keynes's memoir was a reflection of his high spirits of youth. It was something that Keynes grew out of, partially because he came to realise the defects of Moore's book – his 'cloistered and anaemic' list of goods and his inadequate treatment of duty.[24] But Harrod did little to explain or date the process.

Now there is no denying that personality had some role in Moore's influence, as Levy and Harrod suggest, but this was not the whole story. In the earlier generation of brethren, both Bertrand Russell and Ralph Hawtrey admitted Moore's influence on their philosophy.[25] But the intellectual influence was more general. Leonard Woolf, looking back from old age, called him 'the only great man whom I have ever known or met in the world of ordinary, real life'.[26] Even Russell admitted that 'for some years he fulfilled my ideal of genius'.[27] What seems to have attracted them and others were the clarity of his thought, his passion for truth and his emphasis on pursuing seemingly important matters for their own sakes. Woolf continued:

On the surface and until you got to know him intimately he appeared to be a very shy, reserved man, and on all occasions and in any company he might fall into protracted and profound silence. When I first got to know him, the immensely high standards of thought and conduct which he seemed silently to demand of an intimate, the feeling that one shouldn't say anything unless the thing was both true and worth saying, the silences that would envelop both him and you, tinged one's wish to see him with some anxiety. . . . For a young man it was a formidable, and alarming experience . . . but once one had nerved oneself to take it, extraordinarily exhilarating. This kind of tension relaxed under the influence of time, intimacy, and affection, but I do not think it ever disappeared. . . .

His reserve and silences covered deep feeling. When Moore said: 'I *simply* don't understand *what* he means,' the emphasis on the 'simply' and the 'what' and the shake of his head over each word gave one a glimpse of the passionate distress which muddled thinking aroused in him.[28]

As Richard Braithwaite recalled:

Moore's mere presence raised the tone of a philosophical discussion: it made flippancy or sarcasm or bombast impossible. We were compelled, sometimes against our wills, to be as serious, and to try and be as sincere, as Moore so obviously was himself.[29]

Along with this emphasis on certain habits of thought came a freshness of approach which was very appealing to the young. As Moore was to say in 1925:

I am one of those philosophers who have held that 'the Common Sense view of the world' is, in certain fundamental features, *wholly* true. . . . According to me, *all* philosophers, without exception, have agreed with me in holding this: . . . the real difference . . . is only between philosophers, who have *also* held views inconsistent with these features in 'the Common Sense view of the world', and those who have not.[30]

Let us move beyond Moore's personality and his style of thought to the influence of his ideas. A view of Moore's influence on Keynes in particular comes from the philosopher Richard Braithwaite, who had known Keynes since 1919. Braithwaite had stated in an obituary in *Mind* that Keynes's 'ethic was essentially that of *Principia Ethica*' and called him 'a most "humane utilitarian"'.[31] When 'My Early Beliefs' appeared in 1949, Braithwaite was surprised and puzzled. He decided that he could only make sense of it, given that Keynes had, after all, expressly requested its publication in his will, by working back to 'what might have been Keynes's reasons for saying some of the things in the memoir which seemed particularly perverse' from Braithwaite's previous point of view.[32] He summarised his conclusions as follows:

> On my reading . . . of 'My Early Beliefs' Keynes was brought up and never departed from a consequentialist moral philosophy; he learned from Moore the 'religion' of 'passionate contemplation and communion', but later realised that there were more and richer ways in which states of mind could be valuable than those mentioned in *Principia Ethica*. . . . The genuine volte-face reported in the memoir is the abandonment of the belief that 'human nature is reasonable'. It was Keynes's psychological beliefs that changed in the course of time, not his fundamental ethical ones.[33]

Braithwaite leaves the dating of the change in Keynes's psychological beliefs to the reader, but the general tendency in the literature has been to put it quite late – in the years surrounding the composition of the *General Theory* – and to point to external events – Stalin, Hitler, Mussolini – as possible reasons for this concession.[34]

More recently, Robert Skidelsky has argued

> Keynes took his moral philosophy seriously; that he felt a need for 'true beliefs'; that he needed to justify his actions with reference to his beliefs; that his actions were influenced by his beliefs.[35]

As Moore had not provided Keynes with the necessary logical link between ethical goodness and socially concerned conduct – political, social or economic welfare – a full set of beliefs required 'something else' to link public conduct to Moore's system. With this approach, Skidelsky is then prepared to suggest that Keynes 'always remained a Moorite' in that he regarded his 'duty as an individual to achieve good states of mind for himself and those he was directly concerned with'. Yet he had a separable duty as a citizen 'to help achieve a happy state of affairs for society'.[36] This latter duty came from his being the son of Florence and Neville Keynes. In constructing this argument, Skidelsky considers several of Keynes's early philosophical papers, as well as his 1904 prize essay on Burke. However, he also argues that the First World War had an important effect on Keynes's view of the world, for with the war, 'The prospect of civilisation briefly opened up by *Principia Ethica* had receded over the horizon. The rest of Keynes's life was spent in trying to bring it back into sight'.[37]

S. P. Rosenbaum, although predominantly concerned with the literary history of Bloomsbury which forces him to cast his net much more widely, has also tackled Keynes's 'Early Beliefs' and the impact of Moore. In 1982, when discussing the circumstances surrounding Lawrence's 1915 visit to Cambridge (not 1914 as Keynes had suggested), he attempted to give

Keynes's 'beliefs' some context.[38] More recently, in a more general study of the literary history of Bloomsbury he has made a convincing case for Moore's general intellectual influence on the group as a whole and, in passing, on Keynes.[39] This case, Rosenbaum argues, goes well beyond the influence of *Principia Ethica*, although he admits that the effect of that was 'quite extraordinary', a theme he establishes with reference not only to the later, literary writings of the group but also their undergraduate and early post-graduate writings, such as papers to the Society, including most of the surviving ones of Keynes.[40]

These undergraduate and early post-graduate writings of Keynes and their relationship to Moore are also the subject of scrutiny in recent writings on Keynes's methodology.[41] O'Donnell's 1982 dissertation played an important role in shaping Skidelsky's views mentioned above, even though in his recent book O'Donnell argues that he was misunderstood, while both Carabelli and Fitzgibbons deal with Skidelsky's views[42] and, in the case of Carabelli, O'Donnell's views of 1982. These four works are predominantly concerned with the *Treatise on Probability*, but make use of the unpublished papers. Then there is Bateman's 1988 piece on Moore and Keynes which relates the influence of the young Keynes to the evolution of Moore's thought between *Principia Ethica* and *Ethics* (1912). All of them also deal with all or part of 'My Early Beliefs'. In this respect, however, they differ substantially: Bateman deals only with those aspects of the paper relevant to his theme, the influence of Keynes on Moore's use of probability in relation to conduct; Fitzgibbons's approach takes the 1938 paper at face value and is fairly conventional in attributing any change in his views either to the First World War or the inter-war era of the dictators; Carabelli's, on the other hand, concludes:

> [T]he picture sketched in 'My Early Beliefs' may describe the beliefs of the Bloomsbury group, Keynes included, around 1903 (when Keynes was 20) and for a certain period after; but it does not apply to Keynes's cultural attitude from 1907 onwards, i.e. well before his meeting with Lawrence. . . . 'My Early Beliefs' should be titled 'My Very Early (around 1903–6) Beliefs'.[43]

O'Donnell accepts that the paper shows that Keynes 'still adhered to his original philosophy in essential respects, wishing only to effect those changes that issued from a broadened, more realistic view of human nature and its rationality'.[44]

With these differing views, it would seem worthwhile re-sorting through Keynes's early beliefs and their development. In doing so, I must, at the outset, face one problem. Some of the coherence of Professor Skidelsky's and Dr O'Donnell's accounts hangs on the dating of 'Ethics in Relation to Conduct' as delivered to the Society on 23 January 1904, i.e. at the beginning of the second term of Keynes's second year. Leaving aside the possibility that the argument of the paper may be too sophisticated for a student, even of

Keynes's ability, at the end of his fourth or the beginning of his fifth term in Cambridge, there are problems with this dating of the paper for which, as I have mentioned, neither Professor Skidelsky nor Dr O'Donnell offer any evidence. I discuss these problems in detail in Appendix 1 to this chapter. If the general line of argument in that Appendix is correct: if 'Ethics in Relation to Conduct' comes into the story at a much later time and dates from the period well *after* Keynes had decided to begin to investigate in detail 'the principles of probability', it would seem appropriate to reconsider how he got to that point and to re-examine the early papers referred to above. In this way we shall get a better picture of Keynes's 'early beliefs' and their evolution.

I should take the papers in chronological order. As I have noted above, they fall into three groups (only two of which need concern us at this initial stage): undergraduate papers (i.e. those before the summer of 1905); postgraduate papers (1905–6) and post-India Office papers (1908 and after), including in the last the February 1908 paper on 'Appearances'.e

The first group of five papers includes what we may call three 'Burke' papers: 'The Political Doctrines of Edmund Burke' and the two papers, 'Truth' and 'Toleration', which explicitly treat issues that were originally raised in the Burke paper; and two papers on 'Beauty' and 'Virtue and Happiness'. Let me take the last two first. The operative question in 'Beauty' comes at the end of the second page:

> Moore tells us that beauty is that of which the admiring contemplation is good; and it seems to me that the admiring contemplation of beauty *is* good; but I am not so clear that there is one specific thing *beauty* attaching to everything of which the admiring contemplation is good.

The paper explored this problem in several dimensions, playing particular attention to the question of beauty in pictures, and coming to the conclusion that such a 'class, possessing a specific quality, much narrower than that hotchpotch of entities commonly called beautiful . . . appear[ed] to posses the simple, unalloyed essence of the thing'.

'Virtue and Happiness' asked:

> What precisely was it that Plato and Mr Aristotle had in their minds when they spoke of happiness? Was it a state which tends to accompany good rather than bad wholes, a state essentially distinct from pleasure, but as naturally and as fundamentally an object of desire?
>
> Can we ourselves detect and distinguish such a state by introspection? Or might we come to the conclusion that Plato escaped his own notice being a hedonist and that the belief that the good are the happy was the faith of philosophers who either lived in a very

---

e This leaves all the undated papers to one side, but I do not believe that this materially affects the result.

different universe from ours, or were strangely oblivious of the most patent phenomena of human life?

In answering he suggested that happiness was a class midway between, but distinct from, goodness and pleasure and bearing a family relationship to both. He began to explore the implications of such a notion but did not reach a conclusion.

'The Political Doctrines of Edmund Burke', by contrast, is a more substantial paper – so substantial that Skidelsky, Fitzgibbons and O'Donnell make much it in their discussion of his political beliefs. Keynes, unusually for the period, did not consider Burke an ethical utilitarian (pp. 7, 81). However, he accepted and found interesting the political beliefs that underlay his ethics: his 'political utilitarianism', as Keynes somewhat misleadingly called it, which saw 'the happiness of the community as the sole and ultimate end of government' (ibid.). This produced three distinctive views that coloured his political practice: a 'preference for peace over truth', a 'timidity in introducing present evil for the sake of future benefits' and a 'disbelief in men's [normally] acting rightly . . . because they have *judged* it right to so act' (p. 10). Keynes was uncertain about the balance of the first, for 'it led him to undervalue the importance of truth in general' (p. 11), but he found the second more attractive:

> [H]e is emphasising a principle that is often in need of such emphasis. Our power of Prediction is so slight, our knowledge of remote consequences so uncertain that it is seldom wise to sacrifice a present benefit for a doubtful advantage in the future. Burke held, and held rightly, that it can seldom be right to sacrifice the well-being of a nation for a generation, to plunge whole communities into distress, or to destroy a beneficent institution for the sake of a supposed millennium in the comparatively remote future. We can never know enough to make the chance worth taking, and the fact that cataclysms in the past have sometimes inaugurated lasting benefits is no argument for cataclysms in general. (pp. 14–15)

Keynes was also sceptical of the third principle. He could see the advantages of habitual action rather than constantly inquiring into the grounds of conventional morality but he added, '*If* it were certain that a set of rules of action, suitable to all occasions, exists and is perfectly well known, this would be a very difficult position to refute.' (p. 13, emphasis added).

When it came to the details of Burke's arguments, Keynes was even more sceptical. Thus on the doctrine on the non-interference with property and the inevitability and desirability of inequality in its distribution, Keynes in his discussion regularly used such words as 'over fond', 'worst argument ever used', 'wholly inadequate' and 'exaggeration' and 'certainly ought to convince nobody else'. When he dealt with Burke's argument that the poor so vastly outnumber the rich that any steps towards greater equalisation would not make significant differences to the lower classes while having a dramatic effect on the rich and the advantages they bring to the state, he continued:

> This argument undoubtedly carries very great weight. . . . But its validity is very much less when it is directed against any attempt whatever to influence the channels in which wealth flows or to regulate either its management or its distribution (p. 25).

What most impressed Keynes were Burke's maxims of government (paying close attention to the feelings and prejudices of the governed – 'Public opinion can never make wrong right, but, if it is a lasting nature, it can often convert expedience into inexpedience' (p. 38)); clemency; and reform in the context of past developments. He also accepted Burke's argument that self-government was a means to an end rather than an end in itself, but he was much more prepared to tolerate a wide measure of democracy:

> [I]t is to be doubted whether any rational and unprejudiced body of men, who were not, to some extent, under the influence of a fallacious notion concerning natural political rights, would ever have dared the experiment of a suffrage a little short of universal. There is no very great *a priori* probability of arriving at desirable results by submitting to the decision of a vast body of persons, who are individually wholly incompetent to deliver a rational judgement on the affair at issue. But whatever may be our conclusions concerning the eventual benefits that are likely to be derived from an ultrademocratic form of government, it must be admitted that the disasters foretold by its opponents have not come to pass. Democracy is still on its trial, but so far it has not disgraced itself; it is true that its full force has not yet come into operation.
>
> . . . It is difficult to know how much truth there is in the common talk of the educational powers of democracy, but it is an aspect that cannot be overlooked in weighing the advantages of the system. (pp. 57–9)

Where Keynes found difficulties in Burke were in his discussions of the role of truth and toleration, subjects to which he devoted two separate papers in the autumn of 1904. With regard to truth, Keynes believed that 'there is no a priori ground for supposing that knowledge of the truth must necessarily be of ethical utility'. He accepted, in other words, that only 'by an act of faith could we unreservedly and without qualification follow the pursuit of truth' and he argued that the 'act of faith . . . [was] right and necessary' for qualifications to the love of truth led to 'chaos'. As he put it, 'It is impossible to know what ought to be omitted, unless nothing is omitted'. He was prepared to reverse Burke's tendency to value peace over truth, but it was a reversal of tendency made on pragmatic grounds. As he would put it in September 1905 in 'Beauty' and in 'Miscellanea Ethica' – 'The advantage of truth lies in the greater stability that it gives'.

As for toleration *in action*, rather than as a sentiment or opinion, as in the Burke paper, he was prepared to agree that it was difficult to make out a case for it in the abstract. Yet he was prepared, as a doctrine of expediency, to argue that it would be a good thing if individuals were to act as if it were true in the abstract. It was a useful rule of thumb, if only because exceptions allowing the opposite as a guide to action more often than not would lead to difficulties. Again, he was unwilling to allow the exceptions, for, as he put it, in Burke 'too great a tendency to search out exceptions is equally dangerous to the causes of truth and peace' (p. 74).

Thus, what we might call the Burke papers left Keynes with certain predilections in considering political action. As with Burke, there was a doubt about basing action on absolute principles, although Keynes was more prepared than Burke to weigh his particular presumptions on the other side of the balance. As with Burke there was an emphasis on expediency in practice, with a presumption favouring the general well-being and the immediate benefit over the less certain and perhaps immediately costly future gains, with statesmen paying close attention to contemporary opinion. Yet, as he was to emphasise just over a year later in 'Modern Civilisation', the old Burkean certainties were becoming less relevant in the face of economic changes which affected the scale of the social organism. Expediency might still be a desirable principle of day-to-day action, but its bases needed constant rethinking and readjusting in the light of changing circumstances. This was hardly consistent with the rhetoric of 'unworldliness' of 'My Early Beliefs', even if Keynes had not as yet developed an analytical understanding appropriate to that world.

Mention of 'Modern Civilisation' takes us to the second group of papers, those of 1905–6. Of these papers, three – 'Modern Civilisation', 'Egoism' and 'Obligation' (and to a lesser extent, perhaps, parts of 'Miscellanea Ethica') – concern themselves not only with issues raised by Moore, but with issues that extend beyond Moore to the world of action. Two – 'A Theory of Beauty' and 'Miscellanea Ethica' – (and to a lesser extent 'Paradise') – concern themselves almost solely with non-action-oriented issues raised by Moore. The remainder, although Moorite in their influences, are more lighthearted performances suitable for the Society on a less serious night.

Perhaps the most wide-ranging was 'Modern Civilisation'. Here Keynes turned to 'the borderland between Ethics and the phenomenal world' even though he was concerned with the 'real' rather than the 'phenomenal' meaning of modern civilisation. At the basis of his argument was the notion that human progress had in the very recent past resulted in more rapid social change than society had been accustomed to and that this change was, in particular, changing the notion of duty.

Since the time of Moore we have known that our ultimate goods are eternal and unchanged, sitting at the right hand of and at the left hand of God before and behind throughout all times, founded in the nature of things and of goodness, made for man but not by him, the unalterable beacons and rewards of all his efforts. But we have also known that it is not by reference to these alone that our duty is determined. What we ought to do is a matter of circumstance; metaphysically we can give no rules. But where metaphysics is unavailing, the guidance of practice does not altogether fail us. There are rules, which though not immutable have nevertheless so wide and general validity that they ought to be obeyed as if they were themselves universal. One may accept the experience of the race in certain matters – in fact we *ought* so to accept it – and not all cases of action ought to be decided by us individually. We shall do well, as Burke says, to avail ourselves of the general bank and capital of nations and of ages.

It is out of this that arises that class of actions commonly known as duties.

. . . What I wish to suggest is . . . that there is and is coming a Revolution in duty. We may have reached a critical point in some matters where the general bank and capital of nations and ages is no longer useful to us.

So great a change may have hold of the social organism that in a hundred years there may be a revolution in duty greater than in the previous thousand.

The change he referred to was primarily a change in the scale of the social organism caused by changes in the economic organisation of society. These changes, largely changes of scale, had made duties based on small communities and units of organisation far less relevant. 'The field that is relevant for any individual has grown; but the individual has not grown in proportion'. There had also been an intellectual change – a greater contrast between public and private life. Whereas there seemed 'a kind of semi-publicity about all our forefathers thought and did', individuals now sought a greater intimacy in an age when the circle of publicity had become wider.

Their inner unit was larger and their outer unit smaller than ours. The increasing publicity of publicity drives us by contrast and reaction into an increasing intimacy of intimacy.[f] We have more secrets from the world and fewer from our friends. We have less timidity and greater

---

f This sentence caused some problems when it was read to the Society. As Keynes put it to Lytton Strachey (KCKP, 29 October 1905): 'I dragged some foolish remark into my paper last night – about our wanting a greater intimacy of intimacy than our great grandfathers did. And one after another the others denounced the suggestion as preposterous. Hawtrey in particular was most emphatic'.

shamelessness of mind in the range of our inquiries, of our feelings, of our search for beauty.

All of that was by way of description. He stated the problem of those like himself:

> We, moving for the most part in a narrow circle and an academic atmosphere, tend to turn introspectively to the permanent feelings and emotions, or outwardly to the changelessness of beauty, or casually to the amenities of our immediate surroundings, or retrospectively to the past, or scientifically to permanent truths.
>
> We prefer to analyse and to discuss ends; and have not very much to say about means or duties. We know that our elders and the outside world are used to fuss about those matters; and we are inclined to think their conclusions and their methods alike irrelevant; they seem to worry about absurdities. And we are, I still maintain, most often right. But we cannot, for that reason, ignore the outside world, real life – London and New York and Paris and Vienna, where fortunes are made and tragedies enacted, where men really bugger one another and go to prison for it, where some are hungry and where others are cruel and rapacious, not because they are wicked, but because they are in the grip of the machine. We are *not* in the grip of the machine, but we consume its products; we have hardly any duties, as I understand the word. We can see far enough that many of the old moralities may be unfounded.

'Modern Civilisation' was an unsatisfactory paper. It was better at description than prescription. It could be read as repudiating 'the liability to obey general rules', for 'while the good is changeless and apart, the ought shifts and fades and grows new shapes and forms'. But its concern with the 'phenomenal' world sits oddly with the unworldly picture painted in 'My Early Beliefs'.

'Egoism' and 'Obligation' were more directly concerned with Moore and his doctrines; yet they still concerned the world of action rather than contemplation. In 'Egoism' Keynes argued that Moore had assumed rather than proved 'the invariable and necessary connexion between *universal* good and ought'.

> I grant with Moore that good is a simple indefinable quality which I can only identify by direct inspection – analogous to blue or beautiful; I also grant that the perception of this quality is normally accompanied by a certain specific emotion, and this emotion may, that is if it is appropriate, be in its turn good. But why on earth should I sacrifice my peace and comfort in order to produce this quality in remote parts of the globe or in future time, where and when I shall have no opportunity of perceiving or appreciating it? Where is the motive? Where is the obligation? . . .

Is it intuitively rational, is it intuitively obvious to the intelligence, that the pursuit of the general good justifies itself as paramount because general good is general good?

As Keynes saw it, there was a conflict between 'being good' and 'doing good' in the sense that it was possible, especially given the principle of organic unities, that the good of the universe had no necessary connection with individual goodness, that 'it *may* sometimes occur that we *ought* to choose personal badness' to achieve the good of the universe. In these circumstances, after examining the alternatives, he concluded,

> Fortunately we can do quite well if we are good enough to pursue our own good; if by some mysterious arrangement we are at the same time helping universal good, so much the better.

In 'Obligation' Keynes returned to the same range of questions. As he put it,

> I think I know now – at any rate in some cases – what states of mind are good, but I still waver as to what ought to exist. And my attempt to identify the two has constantly led to difficulties.

He then raised examples of his difficulties that he had encountered and tried to find a way around them – without success. The conflict between being good and doing good remained.

As I have noted, Keynes's other serious papers from 1905–6 also dealt with issues raised by Moore and their implications, but the emphasis was less on action. In many substantial areas the papers are the same as can be seen if one looks carefully at the dated pages in each. Although 'Miscellanea Ethica' alone has the programmatic 'scheme of a complete ethical treatise' (quoted in full on pp. 133–4 below), as well as a taxonomy of qualities and their relationship to organic unities, and 'A Theory of Beauty' has a more extensive discussion of aesthetics, both are dealing with much the same broad range of subjects. There are discussions of the relationship of ethics to one's theory of the nature of the external world, where it is agreed that as 'mental objects are the sole field of ethics' the issue can be left to metaphysicians. Both also contain discussions of 'fitness', of 'goodness', of 'feelings', of 'objects' and of Moore's use of 'organic unities' to draw them together, with all the pieces on the board assembled and reassembled to suit the purposes at hand. No one could describe the exercises as other than Moorite, nor doubt the seriousness of their attempts to clarify concepts and relationships. Perhaps, as Professor Skidelsky and Dr O'Donnell suggest,[45] the distinction between objects and feelings was an important one, not only as a basis for criticising Moore's use of organic unities to link the two but also for practical ethics. Certainly, Keynes held on to, or at least didn't cross out, the basic notions of 'A Theory of Beauty' when he read it to the Society on 25 May 1912.

These papers are also different from but not unrelated to the major work which Keynes began to consider at the same time – the fellowship dissertation that eventually became *A Treatise on Probability*. It has been suggested that an understanding of *Probability* is necessary for a full understanding of Keynes's 'early beliefs', even if only because they began to change as he wrote his treatise.

APPENDIX 1
THE DATING OF 'PROBABILITY
IN RELATION TO CONDUCT'

Before accepting the Skidelsky/O'Donnell dating of this paper there are, I believe, several loose ends ends in the evidence to address.

The first arises from the internal references in the paper. There are references to two books: De Morgan's *Formal Logic* and Pearson's *The Chances of Death and Other Essays*. One of the characteristics of the younger Keynes is that he kept lists of books bought, books read, expenses, etc. This list of books on probability records him reading De Morgan in December 1906 and Pearson in October/November 1907 – although it does not also rule out his having read the books earlier as well and not recording it.[46]

The second is also internal. If Keynes had developed his approach to probability by January 1904, surely it should appear at appropriate points in other papers that he wrote after that date? As there are several places where he could have done so over the next year or so, particularly the papers 'Truth', 'Toleration' and 'Miscellanea Ethica', the last of which has a whole outline programme of 'practical ethics', it is worth comparing the treatment of notions of probability in these with that in 'Ethics in Relation to Conduct'.

'Ethics in Relation to Conduct' begins with a quotation from Chapter 5 of the *Principia*:

> We can certainly only pretend to calculate the effects of actions within what may be called an 'immediate' future. . . . in general, we consider that we have acted rationally, if we have secured a balance of good within a few years or months or days. Yet if a choice guided by such considerations is to be rational, we must certainly have some reason to believe that no consequences of our action in a further future will generally be such as to reverse the balance of good that is probable in the future which we can foresee. This large postulate must be made, if we are ever to assert that the results of our action will be even probably better than those of another. Our utter ignorance of the far future gives us no justification for saying that it is even probably right to choose the greater good within the region over which a probable forecast may extend.[47]

After pointing out that Moore then discussed certain reasons favouring the truth of the postulate and that it might be capable of proof, Keynes gave Moore's conclusion:

> Failing such a proof, we can certainly have no rational ground for asserting that one of the two alternatives is even probably right and another wrong.

Keynes argued that the crux of the matter lay in the meaning of probability and that there were meanings of the term that did not necessitate the proof that Moore seemed to require. He suggested that Moore's view of the meaning of probability and its related emphasis on the need for certainty was related to discussions of probability in connection with problems concerning dice or cards where there was a certain plausibility attaching to such a view. However, such questions were 'not typical of all questions on probability' and formed only a limited class of questions: those capable of numerical treatment which depend on equiprobabilities. He then gave a critical account, with examples, of this use of the term, using material from Pearson's collection dealing with sequences of Monte Carlo results and sequences of coin tossings which had caused problems with that frequentist approach. He concluded that 'this view of basing probability upon series is certainly false':

> my point is . . . that the evidence need not always be of this nature and that in any case to base a statement of probability on a past frequency is not the same thing as to make a certainly true statement with regard to future frequency.

He then proceeded to give a counterexample:

> [F]or the existence of A there are five necessary and sufficient conditions, and for B a similar number of independent conditions; my sole evidence consists of the premiss I have stated and of the knowledge that three of the necessary and sufficient conditions for A actually exist. I assert that A is more probable than B.
>
> I believe that probable moral judgements are another such instance.

After trying to reformulate Moore's argument again, he remarked:

> Ignorance can be no bar to the making of a statement with regard to probability. Probability implies ignorance; it is because we do not know for certain that we use the word at all; and the fact that it is possible (in the sense that is not self contradictory) that every action providing a balance of good in the immediate future may produce a vast balance of evil on the whole is no bar to our assertion, until we have further evidence that such an action is probably right. There is no necessity first of all to convert this probability into an impossibility.

This line of argument presages much of the argument of Keynes's *Treatise on Probability*. Yet, if he had reached this level of sophistication in January 1904, would he have put things in the following manner in October?

> Is it really a benefit to gain an accurate knowledge of the laws and tendencies that govern the phenomenal world? Does reality gain when man has enslaved phenomenalism? Perhaps some kind of vague answer may be made to questions such as these; but I am doubtful whether any final rejoinder can be offered. And in any case, granting that we can just weigh down the balance on the side of truth, is that our real and genuine reason for the pursuit of it? I fancy we follow truth because it is truth, and not because we have justified our course by the calculus of probabilities. We do somehow believe that the truth must turn out better in the end, and yet I find it difficult to ascertain that the probabilities are strongly in its favour, before the end, whenever it is, is reached.[48]

Or, alternatively, in November 1904?

> We can never say – The performance of X will, on no occasion whatever, produce less good than its non-performance. But perhaps we can say: – There is on all occasions *a probability* that the performance of X will produce less good than its non-performance: and it is probabilities that must guide our actions. This last position may or may not be true: *I am not sufficiently clear about the meaning and the method of determining probability.* But this is an involved question, not peculiar to the principle of toleration. [Italics added][49]

Between July and September 1905, Keynes wrote a series of reflections, entitled 'Miscellanea Ethica'. Iis last pages are dated 19 September, fourteen days after he sketched out the first surviving draft 'Scheme for an Essay on the Principles of Probability'. On 31 July he had been writing as follows:

> My scheme of a complete ethical treatise would be somewhat thus: the first division would be twofold – into Speculative and Practical Ethics.
> Speculative Ethics would concern itself, in the first instance, with certain quasi-metaphysical or logical questions; it could establish the usage and significance of the more fundamental terms. Out of this would follow such an analysis, as I believe to be possible and whose outlines may be suggested at the conclusion of this paper, of the notion of 'good' itself. It would, in fact, include (in Moore's words) 'Prolegomena to any future Ethics that can possibly pretend to be scientific'. Moore himself might be employed (at a small but sufficient salary) to write it under direction.
> Upon this basis would be raised a Catalogue Raisonée of fit objects

and good feelings. Bad feelings would come in for their share of attention; and there would be very little in the field of experience or of passion, which the writer could not introduce if they had the mind for it.

The nature of beauty and tragedy and love and the attitude a man should have toward truth would prove of interest in the discussion, though the conclusion appear in the end no wiser than Aristotle's.

The second division – of Practical Ethics – would concern itself with Conduct; it would investigate the difficult question of the probable grounds of actions, and the curious connection between 'probable' and 'ought'; and it would endeavour to formulate or rather to investigate existing general maxims, bearing in mind their strict relativity to particular circumstances. It would also concern itself with the means of producing (a) good feelings (b) fit objects.

Perhaps this discussion would be less interesting than that of Speculative Ethics, but it ought to attempt the answer to such questions as the following: –

(i) The nature and value of virtue
(ii) The theory and methods of Education
(iii) The theory and methods of Politics
(iv) The practical expediency and proper limits of Egoism – i.e. the extent to which we ought to regard ourselves as ends and means respectively.
(v) The exceptions to the rule that truth stands first.

The whole would be printed in Baskerville type and published in 150 volumes.

In the remaining pages of 'Miscellanea Ethica' there is only one reference to probability. This comes at the end of the discussion of organic unities and of aiming at the goodness of the largest possible whole, the universe, where he remarks in passing:

Although there is no direct relation between the goodness of parts of the Universe and of the whole, he [Moore] supposes nevertheless that an improvement of a part gives a rational probability of an improvement of the whole. The proof or disproof of such a proposition would require an investigation of what in such a case as this the precise meaning of probability would be.

I wish to propose another way out of the difficulty.

Again, this sort of statement would seem to be *prior* to those in 'Ethics in Relation to Conduct'.

There are two additional pieces of evidence from the period of composition of *Probability* itself. The first comes from the draft tables of contents Keynes kept for this and most of his other works.[50] As noted above, the first of these dates from September 1905. In that draft, the 'applications' of probability in the relevant area would have come in as Chapter 13, 'The application of Probability to certain ethical questions', a title that shows, naturally, that there were problems in the area but hardly shows great precision. By 30 December 1906, that section of the proposed dissertation had become even more general as Chapter 8 of Part I, 'Relation of Probability to Practice'. It was probably only in the summer of 1907 or later that the chapter title took on the precision of the paper, first as Chapter 8, 'Mathematical Expectation – Relation of Probability to Practice and Ethics – The Petersburg Problem', in an undated table of contents of 1907 and then as Chapter 16, 'Mathematical Expectation – Relation of Proby to Ethics', on 18 October[g]. In the final version submitted in December 1907 this last chapter bore the title 'The Relation of Probability to Ethics, and the Doctrine of Mathematical Expectation'. It bore a close resemblance not only to the paper under discussion but also to the Chapter 26 of his published *Treatise on Probability*.

The final piece of evidence occurs in the book itself. In the introduction to Part II, 'Fundamental Theorems', Keynes remarked:

> In the development of my own thought the following chapters have been of great importance. For it was through trying to prove the fundamental theories of the subject on the hypothesis that probability was a *relation* that I first worked my way into the subject; and the rest of this treatise has arisen out of attempts to solve the successive questions to which the ambition to treat probability as a branch of formal logic first gave rise.[51]

g It may be for one of these drafts, probably the latter, given the dates of his reading, that the undated outline 'Prob. and Ethics' exists. This outline runs as follows:
  Locke 337 Tell a man passionately
  Port Royal 369 Eternity and salvation
  Butler 272 doubt fitness of our salvation
  refutation of Moore Butler 272
  organic difficulty
  non-numerical prob. difficulty
  lack of Evidence
  B's second maxim
  Mathematical expectation
  Petersburg problem D'Alembert Bertrand
  Bernoulli's formula Bertrand
  Risks Cuzber 183
  Justice and Common good really follows from first Galton D'Alembert
  Infinite stakes Port Royal Locke
  Induction
All the authors referred to Keynes read between November 1906 (Bertrand) and August 1907 (D'Alembert). The note, 'Ethics in relation to Conduct' would certainly fit within this scheme of things. Moreover, it is consistent with the dating of Keynes's reading in the area. (All the material referred to, except 'Ethics in Relation to Conduct' is in KCKP, TP7.) Moreover, the outline bears a recognisable version to the form the chapter took in the 1907 dissertation – and later.

If this ordering is correct – and we know that Keynes had only started working on his fundamental theories *after* his 1906 Civil Service examinations[h] – if Keynes started with the notion of probability as a relation, then proceeded to the fundamental theories and then worked through his other ideas, it would seem extremely unlikely that 'Ethics in Relation to Conduct' would come at the beginning of the story, much less in 1904.

APPENDIX 2
KEYNES'S 1915 MEETING WITH D. H. LAWRENCE

During Keynes's early months in the First World War Treasury, he had one meeting which, as noted above, has produced confusion in the literature – some of it of his own making.[52] In March 1915 Bertrand Russell invited D. H. Lawrence to Cambridge. They dined in Hall in Trinity on 6 March. Lawrence sat next to G. E. Moore and then afterwards met several Trinity dons, including G. H. Hardy. The next morning, having heard from Ottoline Morrell, with whom he was having an affair, that Keynes would be in Cambridge, Russell took Lawrence round to King's to see him at about 11. He didn't appear to be in, but as Russell was writing him a note, Keynes appeared in his pyjamas, full of sleep. Keynes joined Russell and Lawrence for dinner that evening.

Over twenty years later, in 1938, David Garnett, who had also known Lawrence, read a paper to the Memoir Club discussing his relationship with Lawrence and quoting from a letter that Lawrence had written him the month following the Cambridge visit. Keynes, who was too ill to attend the meeting, borrowed Garnett's paper and incorporated the incident into his own paper 'My Early Beliefs', which he read to the Club at Tilton on 9 September 1938. After Keynes's death, Garnett published an introductory note to Keynes's memoir, as well as two later accounts of his relations with Lawrence, while other aspects of the story have come out in the autobiographies and biographies of Ottoline Morrell and Bertrand Russell.[53] More recently, Professor S. P. Rosenbaum, using additional evidence from the Moore and Garnett papers, has tied the various accounts together.[54]

Keynes's version of the visit, and here he was relying entirely on memory ran as follows:

> It was at a breakfast party given by Bertie Russell in his rooms in Neville's Court. There were only the three of us there. I fancy that Lawrence had been staying with Bertie and that there had been some meeting or party the night before, at which Lawrence had been facing

h See his letter of 21 September 1906 to Neville Keynes quoted above (p. 108).

Cambridge. Probably he had not enjoyed it.[i] My memory is that he was morose from the outset and said very little, apart from indefinite expressions of irritable dissent, all morning. Most of the talk was between Bertie and me, and I haven't the faintest recollection of what it was about. But it was not the sort of conversation we should have had if we were alone. It was *at* Lawrence and with the intention largely unsuccessful, of getting him to participate. We sat round the fireplace with the sofa drawn across. Lawrence sat on the right-hand side in rather a crouching position with his head down. Bertie stood up by the fireplace, as I think I did, too, from time to time. I came away feeling that the party had been a failure and that we had failed to establish contact, but with no other particular impression. You know the sort of situation where two familiar friends talk *at* a visitor. I had never seen him before, and I never saw him again. Many years later he recorded in a letter, which is printed in his published correspondence, that I was the only member of Bloomsbury who had supported him by subscribing for *Lady Chatterley*.

That is all I *remember*.[55]

Keynes used his version of the events as a vehicle for discussing and criticising his own early beliefs and the influence of Moore on his contemporaries. In this chapter I have discussed these beliefs and the disagreements over them in so far as they applied to the Cambridge members of Bloomsbury. What is of interest at this point is that Keynes's own memoir of the events and his speculation as to Lawrence's reaction are misleading.

Keynes's account suggested that Lawrence's reaction was a product of jealousy of Garnett's Cambridge friends and repulsion from and attraction to Cambridge civilisation.[56] It is clear that Lawrence enjoyed meeting some people in Cambridge, as Moore pointed out to Garnett after the publication of *Two Memoirs* when he explicitly corrected Garnett's footnote cited above.

> Lawrence talked that night in Russell's rooms, not specially to Hardy, but to the whole group of people who were there in a general conversation, i.e. certainly to Russell as well as Hardy, & probably to a few others as well (Hardy did not tell me whether any others were there, or who they were, but I think it is likely that there were one or two more). I remember Hardy told me that what he talked about was Socialism & I find from my Diary (which I have now looked up) that what Hardy was specially struck by was Lawrence's eloquence. . . .

i Garnett added a footnote here: 'Professor G. E. Moore tells me that he sat next to Lawrence in Hall that night and found nothing to say to him, but afterwards Lawrence was introduced to Professor Hardy, the mathematician, with whom he had a long and friendly discussion. From the moment of Lawrence's introduction to Hardy the evening was a success'.

[I]t also shows (what surprises me) that when I sat next to him in Hall I did not know who he was! Apparently at that time I had never heard of D. H. Lawrence. I noted he gave me the impression of being very shy; and of course I felt shy too. But I think that there is no doubt that, since afterwards, in Russell's rooms, he talked a great deal & very eloquently, he must have enjoyed that part of the evening . . . . I think he must have taken a dislike to Keynes almost at first sight, and that was why he was morose, not as Keynes supposes, because he had been facing Cambridge the night before and had not enjoyed it.[57]

We can get an idea of what happened the next day from Russell's letters to Ottoline Morrell. On Sunday, 7 March he wrote to her:

I was grateful to you for telling me Keynes was up – I am having him for dinner tonight. Lawrence rather liked him before – but seeing him this morning at 11, in pyjamas, just awake, he felt him corrupt and unclean. Lawrence has quick sensitive impressions which I don't understand . . . . He can't stand the lack of vitality and force in the dons.[58]

The next morning he continued:

Lawrence is gone, disgusted with Cambridge, but not with me I think. . . .
  Keynes came to dinner, and we had an interesting but rather dreadful evening. Keynes was hard, intellectual, insincere – using intellect to hide the torment and discord in his soul. We pressed him hard about his purpose in life – he spoke as tho' he only wanted a succession of agreeable moments, which of course is not really true. Lawrence likes him but cannot get on with him; I get on with him, but dislike him. Lawrence has the same feeling against sodomy as I have; you had nearly made me believe there is no great harm in it, but I have reverted; and all the examples I know confirm me in thinking it is sterilising.

This second letter to Ottoline gets us closer to the basis of Lawrence's antipathy to Keynes – his homosexuality. This becomes even clearer when one reads in full the letter that Garnett had quoted from in his introduction to 'My Early Beliefs'. Written after Garnett and Francis Birrell had come to visit him at Greatham, near Pulborough in Sussex in April this ran:

My dear David,
  I can't bear to think of you, David, so wretched as you are and your hand shaky – and everything wrong. It is foolish of you to say it doesn't matter either way – the men loving men. It doesn't matter in a public way. But it matters so much, David, to the man himself – at any rate to us northern nations – that it is like a blow of triumphant

decay, when I meet Birrell and the others. I simply can't bear it. It is so wrong, it is unbearable. It makes a form of inward corruption which truly makes me scarce able to live. Why is there this horrible sense of frowstiness, so repulsive as if it came from a deep inward dirt – a sort of sewer – deep in men like K. and B. & D[uncan] G[rant]. It is something almost unbearable to me. And not from any moral disapprobation. I myself never considered Plato very wrong, or Oscar Wilde. I never knew what it meant until I saw K., till I saw him at Cambridge. We went into his rooms at midday, and it was very sunny. He was not there, so Russell was writing a note. Then suddenly a door opened and K. was there, blinking from sleep, standing in his pyjamas. And as he stood there gradually a knowledge passed into me, which has been like a little madness to me ever since. And it was carried along with the most dreadful sense of repulsiveness – something like carrion – a vulture gives me the same feeling. I begin to feel mad as I think of it – insane.

Never bring B. to see me any more. There is something nasty about him, like black-beetles. He is horrible and unclean. I feel as if I should go mad, if I think of your set, D.G. and K. and B. It makes me dream of beetles. In Cambridge I had a similar dream. Somehow I can't bear it. It is wrong beyond all bounds of wrongness. I had felt it slightly before in the Stracheys. But it came full upon me in K., and in D.G. And yesterday I knew it again in B.

David, my dear, I love your father and I love your mother. I think your father has been shamefully treated at the hands of life. Though I don't see him, I do love him in my soul – more even than I love your mother. And I feel, because he is your father, that you must leave these 'friends', these beetles. You must wrench away and start a new life. B. and D.G. are done for, I think – done forever. K. I am not sure. But you, my dear, you can be all right. You can come away, and grow whole, and love a woman and marry her, and make life good, and be happy. Now David, in the name of everything that is called love, leave this set and stop this blasphemy against love. It isn't that I speak from a moral code. Truly I didn't know it was wrong until I saw K. that morning in Cambridge. It was one of those crises in my life. It sent me mad with misery and hostility and rage. Go away, David, and try to love a woman. My God, I could kiss Eleanor Farjeon with my body and soul, when I think how good she is, in comparison. But the Oliviers, and such girls, are wrong.

I could sit and howl in a corner like a child, I feel so bad about it all.

D. H. Lawrence[59]

The only other puzzles lying behind this episode are very small ones. Had Keynes met Lawrence before, as Russell suggested? And exactly how much did Keynes know of Lawrence's letter to Garnett when he prepared his memoir?

As for the former, it seems probable that they may have met at Ottoline's on 21 January 1915. Keynes's appointments diary has an entry 'Ott' for that date and Garnett's memoirs are consistent with his being there with Lawrence on that date, while Morgan Forster's biography makes it clear that Forster met Lawrence at Ottoline's that evening.[60]

As to the second question, we lack Garnett's original memoir, and his published 1955 version was as reticent as his introduction to 'My Early Beliefs'. In *Great Friends* he was less reticent, even concerning his sexual preferences, although he does not admit that he and Keynes were lovers. But it would seem to me that if Keynes had seen the full text of the letter, there might have been more reference to homosexuality in his 1938 paper (the original of which does not seem to exist) which only makes passing reference to the discussion of love affairs and to X not having taken up women.[61] Given Keynes's later express wish in his will that the paper be published, one would hardly expect it to be as open as is the present fashion, but if he had seen the letter, I doubt he would have made the mistake about the breakfast party.

NOTES

1 KCKP, JMK to B. W. Swithinbank, 7 October 1903 (emphasis in the original).
2 Moore 1903, vii.
3 Ibid., 3.
4 Ibid., 6.
5 Ibid., 17.
6 Ibid., 148.
7 Ibid., 162–3 (emphasis in the original). For an argument that runs counter to this and suggests that Moore left much more to individual decisions, see Regan 1986, ch. 8.
8 Ibid., 188–9 (emphasis in the original).
9 *JMK*, X, 433–50.
10 CUL, Add.7854, entry for 2 October 1904. Maynard had started writing the essay on 21 September (ibid.).
11 KCKP, TP7, fly-sheet.
12 'The Present Position of Metaphysics in the Society', p. 2.
13 Rosenbaum 1982, using subsequently published correspondence and Moore's own papers, clearly establishes the date of the meeting as 7 March 1915, and also makes clear that there were two meetings on that day, one in Keynes's rooms at 11, where Maynard having just awakened was still in pyjamas, and another at dinner in Trinity that evening. See Appendix 2 to this chapter (p. 136) for further discussion of this incident.
14 *JMK*, X, 435–7 (emphasis in the original).
15 Ibid., 438.

16 Ibid., 445.
17 Ibid., 446–8.
18 Woolf 1960, 147.
19 Ibid, 148–9.
20 *JMK*, X, 448–50.
21 Ibid., 450.
22 Levy 1979, 7–8.
23 Harrod 1951, 76.
24 Ibid., 79.
25 Russell 1978, 61, 136–7; Black 1977, 365, 391–3. For his influence on Keynes see below, especially Chapter 6.
26 Woolf 1960, 131.
27 Russell 1978, 61.
28 Woolf 1960, 135–6.
29 Braithwaite 1961, 305.
30 'A Defence of Common Sense' in Moore 1959, 44.
31 Braithwaite in M. Keynes (ed.) 1975, 242.
32 Ibid., 245.
33 Ibid., 245.
34 Levy 1979, 246 provides an example. Fitzgibbons 1988 swings between the effects of the First World War and the more conventional view expressed by Levy.
35 Skidelsky 1985, 147.
36 Ibid., 157.
37 Ibid., 402.
38 Rosenbaum 1982.
39 Rosenbaum 1987, esp. chs 10 and 11.
40 Ibid., 226. The discussion of Keynes's papers, largely those to the Society, occupies pages 260–3.
41 Particularly O'Donnell 1982 and 1989, Bateman 1988, Carabelli 1988 and Fitzgibbons 1988.
42 Fitzgibbons, although he did not have access to O'Donnell's work, also discussed Carabelli's views.
43 Carabelli 1988, 100.
44 O'Donnell 1989, 154. See also his 1990, 57–8.
45 Skidelsky 1985, 148–9; O'Donnell 1989, 114–17.
46 KCKP, TP7. In a paper delivered to the History of Economics Society in June 1988, Professor J. R. Winter, who also pursues this line of thought in part, says that Keynes's notes on De Morgan's *Formal Logic* were written on India Office notepaper. This is not the case, although it is the case for De Morgan's *Essay on Probabilities* and *Theory of Probabilities* read in February and April 1907 respectively. See J. R. Winter 'Keynes *versus* Friedman: A Question of Methodologies', mimeo. Bateman 1988 also makes the point about Pearson.
47 The quotation comes from p. 152. Keynes was to use the same quotation in his *Treatise on Probability* in the chapter 'The Application of Probability to Conduct' (*JMK*, VIII, 341).
48 In the paper 'Truth'.
49 In the paper 'Toleration'.
50 KCKP, TP7.
51 *JMK*, VIII, 125–6.
52 The commonest sources of the confusion are in two papers by F. R. Leavis, 'Keynes, Lawrence and Cambridge' reprinted in Leavis 1953, 215–60 and

'Keynes, Spender and Currency Values' originally in *Scrutiny* in 1951 and reprinted in F. R. Leavis 1968, I, 185–96.

53 *JMK*, X, 430–2; Garnett 1955, 34–8, 50–5; 1979, 74–93; Gathorne-Hardy 1974, ch. VI.
54 Rosenbaum 1982.
55 No record of his meeting with Lawrence appears in his appointments diaries or other papers. *JMK*, X, 433–4.
56 I leave aside the matter of the date, which is of importance for his memoir where he discussed events and ideas from almost a decade earlier.
57 Moore to Garnett, 17 May 1949 as printed in Rosenbaum 1982, 256–7.
58 Gathorne-Hardy 1974, 56.
59 Finally published in Garnett 1979, 88–9. The letter also appears in Zytaruk and Boulton (eds) 1981, 320–1. See also Lawrence's comments in surrounding letters, especially on pages 311, 319 and 323.
60 Garnett 1979, 85; Garnett 1955, 33; Furbank 1977, II, 5. See also Delany 1978, 49. However, Darroch 1976, 148 says the meeting took place on 25 January, which wasn't a Thursday, while Ottoline herself gives a variety of dates (Gathorne-Hardy 1963, 272).
61 *JMK*, X, 440, 441.

6

PROBABILITY

I foresee that 1000 years hence the manuals on English literature will point out that it is important to distinguish between the two entirely distinct authors of the same name, one of whom wrote the Economic Consequences of the Peace, and the other a Treatise on Probability.

(KCKP, GLS to JMK, 25 August 1921)

Between the date of the first draft table of contents and the ultimate appearance of *A Treatise on Probability* almost fifteen years elapsed. Those fifteen years included the years of the First World War, to which some scholars attach considerable importance in connection with Keynes's developing 'vision', so that if I am to relate the *Treatise* to his 'early beliefs' I must pay some attention to the dating of the evolution of his ideas. Fortunately, Keynes's papers are rich in source material. Not only are there two fellowship dissertations (the unsuccessful one of December 1907 and the successful one of a year later), but there are draft tables of contents, drafts, reading notes and correspondence. Along with the *General Theory*, the *Treatise on Probability* is the most thoroughly documented of Keynes's 'acts of creation'.

This does not mean that it has received the same attention as the later book. For decades it was regarded as a piece of technical philosophy standing apart from the other areas of Keynes's life. This was Roy Harrod's treatment in his biography. In *The Collected Writings of John Maynard Keynes*, the editors were committed to republishing all of Keynes's previously published work, as well as selected unpublished materials relating to his professional life *as an economist*.[1] To emphasise its separateness in this enterprise, they published *A Treatise on Probability* out of chronological order, *after* all his books in economics, as volume VIII rather than volume III, and, in contrast to, say, *A Treatise on Money* and the *General Theory* published none of the surrounding correspondence. Moreover, *A Treatise on Probability* is the only volume in the *Collected Writings* where they provided an introduction, by the philosopher Richard Braithwaite, presumably to set the book in context for economists. But recent years have seen the development of serious interest in the book by economists. This interest, as compared with even a decade ago, is clear not only in the journals but also in publishers' lists, with 1988–9 alone seeing three monographs on the book.[2] More, including an edition of Keynes's early, unpublished papers by Dr O'Donnell will come.

For the purposes of this biography, I am interested in three questions relating to *Probability*, as I shall henceforth, following the convention of economists, call it to distinguish it from *A Treatise on Money*: What were the main ideas of the work? What relation did these ideas have to Moore and Keynes's early beliefs? and What is the relationship between *Probability* and Keynes's contemporaneous and later work as an economist? I shall consider the first two in this chapter, leaving the third to my discussions of relevant aspects of his economics. The answers to none of these three questions are agreed in the literature – partly because the literature is still in a formative stage.

There is also the different question of whether Keynes remained wedded to all of his 1908–21 doctrines concerning the theory of probability. I shall consider this when I come to consider the reception of his book among philosophers after publication and Keynes's subsequent work.

When it appeared, *Probability* was the first systematic work on the logical foundations of probability in English for 55 years. Although they had seen few fundamental advances in the theory of probability, the seventy years after 1830 saw the beginnings of two important movements: the shift from a deterministic world view to one pervaded by law-like chance and the development of statistical methods, particularly in the social sciences. By the end of the century, particularly in the hands of Francis Galton, F. Y. Edgeworth, Karl Pearson and G. U. Yule, statistical techniques had been developed that would lead to much twentieth-century social science as well as the modern discipline of statistics.[3] At the same time, through the work of A. De Morgan, George Boole, William Stanley Jevons and John Venn, traditional formal logic began to incorporate the innovations which mathematicians such as Laplace had introduced into the theory of probability before 1830 and in the process began the mathematisation of formal logic. In Cambridge such work continued with W. E. Johnson and, of course, Bertrand Russell and Alfred North Whitehead.[4] The concerns of Keynes's *Probability* would reflect both streams of development.

The scope of the book is best exemplified in Keynes's quotation from Bishop Butler: 'To us probability is the very guide of life'.[5] Probability was not, as it was for the statisticians, concerned with the frequency or recurrence of events. It was concerned with the cognitive and mental processes involved in the formulation of probability judgements in the broadest sense, with arguments and processes of reasoning. In this concern with logic rather than frequencies, Keynes was returning to the classical traditions of the theory, but with a difference. Whereas classical theorists thought that perfect knowledge based on truth was the only knowledge valid for science and banished probability to the outer fringes, Keynes's approach to the subject, although centrally concerned with knowledge rather than ignorance centred on *limited knowledge*.[a] From the outset, he abandoned the view that science was based only on certain knowledge: rather, certain knowledge was the maximum possible limit of imperfect knowledge.

Probability was concerned with that part of knowledge obtained by argument, but it was not subjective. As he put it,

> A proposition is not probable because we think it so. . . . The theory of probability is logical . . . because it is concerned with the degree of belief it is *rational* to entertain in given conditions, and not merely with the actual beliefs of particular individuals, which may or may not be rational.
>
> (p. 4)

The logic of probability was not that of demonstrative knowledge or relations of truth, rather it concerned non-conclusive, non-demonstrative arguments:

> In most branches of academic logic, such as the theory of the syllogism or the geometry of ideal space, all arguments aim at demonstrative certainty. They claim to be *conclusive*. But many other arguments are rational and claim some weight without being certain. . . . If logic investigates the general principles of valid thought, the study of arguments, to which it is rational to attach *some* weight, is as much a part of it as the study of those which are demonstrative.
>
> (p. 1)

Thus he was attempting to extend the theory of logic to branches of knowledge that traditional logic had excluded from its domain – to the categories of belief, opinion, limited knowledge, and uncertainty.

> As soon as we have passed from the logic of implication and the categories of truth and falsehood to the logic of probability and the categories of knowledge, ignorance and rational belief, we are paying attention to a new logical relation in which, although it is logical, we were not previously interested, and which cannot be explained or defined in terms of our previous notions.
>
> (p. 8)

The next important feature of Keynes's approach to probability was his claim that only propositions could be probable or improbable and that propositions were probable only in relation to others which were taken as premisses. The same proposition could have different probabilities on different premisses.

The terms *certain* and *probable* describe the various degrees of rational

a Some commentators, most notably G. L. S. Shackle (e.g. 1972, 1974), take a contrary view and emphasise ignorance, but this minority view is not supported by the text.

belief about a proposition which different amounts of knowledge authorise us to entertain. All propositions are true or false, but the knowledge we have of them depends on our circumstances; and while it is often convenient to speak of propositions as certain or probable, this expresses strictly a relationship in which they stand to a *corpus* of knowledge, actual or hypothetical, and not a characteristic of the propositions themselves. A proposition is capable at the same time of varying degrees of this relationship, depending upon the knowledge to which it is related, so that it is without significance to call a proposition probable unless we specify the knowledge to which we are relating it.

(pp. 3–4)

Probability was relative to evidence and would vary with the amount of knowledge available at a given time in given cognitive conditions. If this knowledge changed, probability changed also.

The third characteristic feature of Keynes's approach to probability was its relation to uncertainty or, as he put it, 'degrees of certainty', rather than truth. The notion that probability was concerned with 'degrees of truth' was the result of 'a confusion between certainty and truth' (p. 16). As he emphasised in a later chapter 'The Application of Probability to Conduct':

[N]o knowledge of probabilities, less in degree to certainty, helps us to know what conclusions are true, and . . . there is no direct relation between the truth of a proposition and its probability. Probability begins and ends with probability. That a scientific investigation pursued on account of its probability will generally lead to truth, rather than falsehood, is at best only probable. The proposition that a course of action guided by the most probable considerations will generally lead to success, is certainly not true and has nothing to recommend it but its probability.

(p. 356)

The distinction between degrees of certainty and truth implied an analogous distinction between degrees of rationality and of truth. One could rationally believe something that was false, or alternatively hold an irrational belief in something that was true. 'The distinction between rational belief and mere belief . . . is not the same as the distinction between true beliefs and false beliefs.' (p. 10). The whole logic of *Probability* was the logic of rational beliefs rather than of truth. But rationality itself was also relative; it too depended on circumstances.

Such was Keynes's basic view of probability. What were his central doctrines? Here, following his own Book I, I identify five: (1) his concept of knowledge; (2) his notion of probability as indefinable; (3) his emphasis on the usually non-numerical and non-comparable nature of probabilities; (4)

the role of judgements of preference or indifference, relevance or irrelevance in comparing probabilities and determining the preferability of one of them as a basis for belief; and (5) the notion of the weight of argument.

The theory of probability as a theory of knowledge belonged to the realm of argument, or 'derived knowledge'. With respect to the relationship between such knowledge and so-called 'direct knowledge', Keynes first followed Russell, and made a distinction between 'acquaintance' and 'knowledge'. The latter was formulated in propositions. Acquaintance came through three possible means:

> our sensations which we may be said to *experience*, the ideas or meanings, about which we have thoughts and which we may be said to *understand*, and the facts or characteristics or relations of sense-data or meanings which we may be said to *perceive*.
>
> (p. 12)

Acquaintance with things in this schema meant not only external things but also internal things such as logical relations.

When acquaintance had been formulated into propositions and had become knowledge, this knowledge could take three forms. It could arise directly through the contemplation of the objects of acquaintance (experience, understanding or perception). Alternatively, it could arise indirectly through argument, through the perception of the relation of a proposition to other propositions. This indirect knowledge was what was normally called probable knowledge. Finally there was a third type of knowledge, which was less clear cut, but which is important, known neither directly nor by argument. As Keynes put it, 'We may remember it as knowledge, but forget how we originally knew it.' (p. 14). Into this class he put such things as conscious memory, unconscious memory and habit, fully aware that it was hard to draw a clear line between these and pure instinct or the irrational association of ideas which could not fairly be called knowledge.

Keynes was unable to give an account of the 'mental process [by which] we are able to pass from direct acquaintance with things to a knowledge of propositions about the things of which we have sensations or understand the meaning' (p. 13). He thought that it was possible to know directly such things as 'our own existence, our own sense-data, some logical ideas, some logical relations', but that it was not possible to have direct knowledge of the law of gravity or the contents of Bradshaw's railway timetables. He admitted there was dispute or doubt within the theory of knowledge as to which logical ideas or relations we had direct acquaintance of, or whether we could directly know the existence of other people, or whether we knew propositions about sense-data or merely interpreted them. What was important was that the role of direct knowledge should not be overlooked, for knowing something by argument meant some direct acquaintance with some logical relation between

147

a conclusion and a premiss. 'In *all* knowledge', he wrote, 'there is some direct element; and logic can never be made purely mechanical.' (p. 15).

Indirect, or probable, knowledge was acquired through perceiving a probability relation between the proposition about which we seek knowledge and another, secondary, proposition. The secondary proposition, Keynes argued, had to be known both in a direct and in a certain way. This condition of certainty was important, for he did not see how one could ground probable knowledge on probable knowledge. As he put it, he could not analyse the meaning of cases where we have a probable belief relative to another probable belief or 'vague' knowledge. 'It is certainly not the same thing as knowledge proper, whether certain or probable, and it does not seem likely that it is susceptible of strict logical treatment.' (p. 17).

> That part of our knowledge which we obtain directly, supplies the premisses of that part which we obtain by argument. From these premisses we seek to justify some degree of rational belief about all sorts of conclusions. We do this by perceiving certain logical relations between premisses and conclusions. The kind of rational belief which we *infer* in this manner is termed *probable* (or in the limit *certain*), and the logical relations, by the perception of which it is obtained, we term *relations of probability*.
>
> (p. 121)

In discussing probability relationships Keynes often used the terms 'logical intuition' or 'intuition'.[6] Keynes's emphasis on intuition, or what he elsewhere called 'a particular twist of the mind',[7] and on the fact that knowledge was not connected to the condition that the process by which we arrive at it was completely analysable had a connection to his thesis that probability, like Moore's 'good', was indefinable. As he put it at the outset:

> A *definition* of probability is not possible . . . . We cannot analyse the probability relation in terms of simpler ideas. As soon as we have passed from the logic of implication and the categories of truth and falsehood to the logic of probability and the categories of knowledge, ignorance and rational belief, we are paying attention to a new logical relation in which, although it is logical, we were not previously interested, and which cannot be explained or defined in terms of our previous notions.
>
> (p. 8)

He did not see this as a problem:

> In the great majority of cases the term 'probable' seems to be used consistently by different persons to describe the same concept. Differences of opinion have not been due, I think, to a radical ambiguity of language. In any case a desire to reduce the indefinables of logic can

easily be carried too far. . . . In the case of 'probability' the object before the mind is so familiar that the danger of misdescribing its qualities through lack of definition is less than if it were a highly abstract entity far removed from the normal channels of thought.

(p. 9)

Anna Carabelli has drawn the parallel with Moore:

Keynes's probability shared all the attributes of Moore's goodness: it was a simple notion, unanalysable, indefinable, non-natural, directly perceived or intuited and objective. Recalling Joseph Butler's motto which Moore put on the title page of *Principia Ethica* ('Everything is what it is, and not another thing') we could say that Keynes thought that 'Probability is what it is, and not another thing'.[8]

Paralleling Keynes's view that probability was indefinable were his views about its measurability set out in his Chapter 3. As he was to summarise them:

Whether or not such a thing is theoretically conceivable, no exercise of practical judgement is possible, by which a numerical value can be given to the probability of every argument. So far from our being able to measure them, it is not always clear that we are always able to place them in an order of magnitude.

(p. 29)

This, as he recognised, ran against much contemporary thinking about probability, of which he gave examples, and the view that, even if not practicable, numerical degrees of comparison between degrees of probability were conceivable and within men's powers. But he would have none of this, arguing that the relevant definitions of probability were too narrow.

Uncharacteristically, for he was to use diagrammatic examples rarely in his published work, he summarised his view with the aid of a diagram,[9] where 0 represented impossibility, 1 certainty; A is a numerically measurable probability relation; and U, V, W, X, Y and Z are non-numerically measurable probability relations, some of which (those along any path)

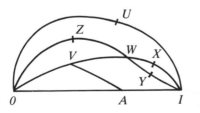

Figure 1 Keynes's view of the measurability and comparability of probabilities.

are non-numerically comparable but not necessarily comparable with those on other paths.

In his fourth chapter Keynes turned to cases where we might allow probabilities to be measurable, to one of the centrepieces of the classical theory of probability – the principle of non-sufficient reason. This provided a tool for assigning the condition of equiprobabilities amongst various alternatives and allowed the definition of a numerical measure of probability of the ratio of favourable alternatives to the total number of alternatives, thus opening the way for a mathematical theory of probability. As he described the principle, renaming it 'the principle of indifference':

> The principle of indifference asserts that if there is no *known* reason for predicting of our subject one rather than another of several alternatives, then relatively to such knowledge the assertions of each of these alternatives have an *equal* probability. Thus *equal* probabilities must be assigned to each of several arguments, if there is an absence of positive ground for assigning *unequal* ones.
>
> (p. 45)

His assessment of the principle was shaped by his own approach to probability, which emphasised knowledge rather than ignorance. He pointed out a series of cases where the principle led to contradictions and paradoxes: situations involving colours, qualities of a substance, continuous magnitudes, geometrical probabilities and non-enumerable magnitudes where the number of alternatives was infinite or indefinite. These cases had common characteristics: they were not ultimate, indivisible, elementary and finite in number.

> In short, the principle of indifference is not applicable to a pair of alternatives, if we know either of them is capable of being split up into a pair of possible but incompatible alternatives of the same form as the original pair.
>
> (p. 66)

The chapter also contained some positive doctrine. In comparing the probabilities of different arguments to assess the preferability or rationality of one of them as a basis for belief, one worked through what Keynes called judgements of 'preference' or 'indifference' and of 'relevance' or 'irrelevance'. The former, judgements of preference or indifference, are necessary when one is comparing the probabilities of arguments with different conclusions but the same evidence – using his notation, whether we are comparing x/h and y/h where x and y are the conclusions and h the evidence. Where there is an equality between x/h and y/h we have a judgement of indifference; with an inequality a judgement of preference. With judgements of relevance or irrelevance, we consider what difference a change in the evidence makes to the conclusions. Using his notation, we compare x/h with $x/h1\ h$ to see whether the addition of $h1$ to evidence h is relevant or irrelevant to x.

The final building block of Keynes's doctrine came in his Chapter 6, 'The Weight of Arguments'. Although he was tentative in introducing the notion of weight, and somewhat doubtful about its importance,[10] it was the only doctrine from *Probability* that he would later explicitly introduce into his *General Theory*, an introduction later expanded in correspondence with Hugh Townshend.[11] To Keynes, probability turned on the balance of favourable and unfavourable evidence, while weight turned on the absolute amount of evidence available. Increased evidence might increase or decrease the probability of an argument, but it would always increase its weight.

Weight was similar to probability in that it could not normally be measured. Only in cases where the conclusions of two arguments were the same and the evidence for one included and exceeded the other would this be possible. If the new evidence was 'relevant', in the sense used above, the weight would be increased; if it was 'irrelevant' the weight would be unchanged. In other words, 'relevant' evidence in this sense increased the weight of an argument. However, where the conclusions of arguments differed or the evidence did not overlap it was impossible to compare weights, just as it might be impossible to compare probabilities.

In Part II of *Probability*, Keynes concerned himself with the formal logic of probability and attempted following the example of Russell and Whitehead's *Principia Mathematica* to deduce the usual theorems from simple and precise definitions. In Parts III, IV and V, he returned to more complex arguments of a probable kind. Before turning to these, it is worth noting the traces of Moore's influence revealed thus far in Part I.

The first and clearest influence has already been noted – the parallel between Keynes's indefinable probability and Moore's indefinable good.[12] However, there are others. Moore's notion of good was, in the end, an intuitive judgement, beyond the realm of proof. As he put it in his preface when discussing the answers to the question 'What sorts of things ought to exist for their own sakes?':

> It becomes plain that . . . no relevant evidence whatever can be adduced: from no other truth except themselves alone can it be inferred that they are true or false.[13]

Or later:

> You can give a definition of a horse, because a horse has many different properties and qualities, all of which you can enumerate. But when you have enumerated them all, when you have reduced a horse to his simplest terms, then you can no longer define those terms. They are something which you think of or perceive, and to any one who cannot think of or perceive them, you can never, by any definition, make their nature known.[14]

For Moore, as for Keynes, such intuitions were objective.

The expression 'self-evident' means properly that the proposition so called is evident or true, by *itself* alone. . . . The expression does *not* mean that the proposition is true, because it is evident to you or me or all mankind, because in other words it appears to be true. . . . We must not therefore look on Intuition, as if it were an alternative to reasoning. Nothing whatever can take the place of *reasons* for the truth of any proposition: intuition can only furnish a reason for *holding* any proposition to be true: this however it must do when any proposition is self-evident, when, in fact, there are no reasons which prove its truth.[15]

This emphasis on the incompletely analysable nature of knowledge would also appear in Keynes's discussion of induction later in *Probability*.

Keynes may have taken other notions over from Moore. His notion that knowledge referred to propositions rather than objects or events may have come from Moore's 'Experience and Empiricism' (1902–3). He may also have been comforted by Moore's 'The Nature and Reality of Objects of Perception' (1905), to which he referred in *Probability* and in his own correspondence,[16] and its stress on the reality of non-empirical entities. Finally, Keynes's attitudes to common sense and to pragmatism were also very Moorite. Indeed, as Anna Carabelli has argued, Moore may have been an important source of Keynes's anti-empiricism in the *Treatise on Probability*.[17]

Let us return to the arguments of *Probability*. In Book III, Keynes turned to the matter of induction – the inference of general statements from statements referring to particulars. He saw it as playing a much wider role than that normally granted to it in the contemporary literature. Not only did it belong to natural philosophy and the empirical sciences, but it also had a role in the social sciences, logical and mathematical arguments, metaphysical arguments and everyday life. To reach this position, he had to dispose of doctrines associated with the traditional view, such as the uniformity of nature and the conception of causation as physical causation. Then he had to emphasise that induction belonged to logic, that is to processes of reasoning – for 'inductive processes . . . formed . . . a vital, habitual part of the mind's machinery' (p. 241). Traditional views, he argued, had limited the notion of induction to what he called 'pure induction', or quantitative, empirical induction based on repetition of instances, and ignored the role of analogy, reasoning that took into account the likeness and unlikeness of events.

For Keynes, the strength or force of inductive arguments depended on logical elements prior to any mere counting. He outlined the first step as follows:

In an inductive argument, . . . we start with a number of instances similar in some respects *AB*, dissimilar in others *C*. We pick out one or more respects *A* in which the instances are similar, and argue that in some of the other respects *B* in which they are also similar are likely to be associated with the characteristics *A* in other unexamined cases.

(p. 244)

He thought that this approach could overcome the problem raised by Hume with which he opened the analysis. Hume had remarked that although we expect eggs to be all alike we do not expect the same taste and relish in all of them and had asked

[W]here is the process of reasoning, which from one instance draws a conclusion, so different from that which it infers from a hundred instances, that are in no way different from the single instance?

(p. 241)

Keynes suggested that Hume had neglected a fundamental condition that should be present in inductive reasoning: that the instances should not be exactly the same but rather show differences in every respect except the likeness considered. As he put it:

He [Hume] should have tried eggs in the town and in the country, in January and in June. He might then have discovered that eggs could be good or bad, however alike they looked.

(p. 243)

He also suggested that a further condition was required – a judgement as to the characteristics that were required for the generalisation and those which were not. Such a judgement was necessary to distinguish between the positive and negative qualities of likeness of the instances, in other words a judgement of relevance.

In fact it was the variety amongst the non-essential characteristics of instances that increased the negative analogy. As he was to put it later in discussing the role of the Nautical Almanack in increasing one's faith in Newton's generalisations: 'The *variety* of the circumstances, in which the Newtonian generalisation is fulfilled, rather than the number of them, is what seems to impress our reasonable faculties.' (p. 260). The increase in the negative analogy could come either by increasing knowledge of previous instances or by taking account of additional instances.

Keynes emphasised that 'pure induction', the multiplication of instances, followed later in the process. One first obtained through reasoning from analogy a prior or initial probability. As he put it:

The prior probability, which must always be found before the method of pure induction can be usefully employed to support a substantial argument is derived . . . in most ordinary cases . . . from considerations of analogy.

(p. 265)

In fact, he was prepared to argue that most so-called scientific methods depended primarily on analogy rather than pure induction. For if previous knowledge was considerable and the analogy good, pure induction played a subsidiary role. Thus, he noted

> when our knowledge of instances is slight we may have to depend upon pure induction a good deal. In an advanced science it is a last resort, – the least satisfactory of the methods. But sometimes it must be our first resort, the method upon which we must depend in the dawn of knowledge and in fundamental enquiries where we must presuppose nothing.
>
> (pp. 267–8)

In advancing this line of argument he was, of course, being extremely critical of the *a posteriori* criterion of the value of induction in the empirical sciences, where the validity of the inductive generalisation was thought to be determined by confirmation by subsequent facts. Rather, the validity of an induction rested not on facts but on relations of probability. As he summarised his argument:

> The validity of the inductive methods does *not* depend on the success of its predictions. Its repeated failure in the past may, of course, supply us with new evidence, the inclusion of which will modify the force of subsequent inductions. But the force of the old induction *relative to the old evidence* is untouched. The evidence with which our experience has supplied us in the past may have proved misleading, but this is entirely irrelevant to the question of what we ought reasonably to have drawn from the evidence then before us. The validity and reasonable nature of inductive generalisation is, therefore, a question of logic and not of experience, of formal and not of material laws. The actual constitution of the phenomenal universe determines the character of our evidence; but it cannot determine what conclusions *given* evidence *rationally* supports.
>
> (pp. 245–6)

With these considerations in mind Keynes turned to the conditions in which inductive arguments could be applied. He was concerned with the 'logical foundation for analogy' or the issues: 'what sort of assumptions, *if* we could adopt them, lie behind and are required by' inductive reasoning; 'the nature of these assumptions'; and 'their possible justification' (p. 242). Let us take them in order.

In answer to the question 'what sort of assumptions, *if* we could adopt them, lie behind and are required by' inductive reasoning, Keynes began with pure induction arising out of the empirical frequency of experiments or the repetition of instances. He argued that this implied that the initial probability 'approaches certainty as a limit when the number of independent instances are indefinitely increased' (p. 263). For this to be the case, *a priori* the probability must be finite. If this were the case, he argued from an example:

> [P]ure induction can be used to support the generalisation that the sun will rise every morning for the next million years, provided that with the experience we have had there are finite probabilities, however small, *derived from some other source*, first in favour of the generalisation, and second, in favour of the sun's not rising tomorrow assuming the generalisation to be false. Given these finite probabilities, obtained otherwise, however small, then the probability can be strengthened and can tend to increase towards certainty by the mere multiplication of instances provided the instances are so far distinct that they are not inferrible one from another.
>
> (p. 265)

The prior probability normally came by analogy, although he could think of conditions of valid induction independent of analogy, and in these normal cases the analogy must obey the same conditions of an *a priori* finite probability. To put it another way, the amount of independent variety of the system under consideration, the number of constituents, and the laws of necessary connection between them must be finite before probable knowledge could be obtained by pure induction (pp. 279–80). The principle of limited independent variety must hold. There could not be a plurality of generators. If there were a plurality, 'a given character can arise in more than one way, can belong to more than one distinct group' or arise from more than one cause. It was the need to establish a finite probability that a plurality of generators did not exist that made inductive correlations preferable to inductive or universal generalisations, for the former in general would not be upset by one contrary observation, whereas the latter would be, and had the advantage of less stringent logical conditions (pp. 287–8).

He then turned to the second question: 'the nature of these assumptions'. The fundamental assumption that seemed to be implied by these conditions was what he called 'the *atomic* character of natural law' (p. 276). In other words, the material universe must consist of '*legal* atoms' each of which 'exercises its own separate, independent, and invariable effect'. In other words, the wholes could not be organic. As he continued:

> The scientist wishes, in fact, to assume that the occurrence of a phenomenon which has appeared as a part of a more complex phenomenon, may be some reason for expecting it to be associated on another occasion with part of the same complex. Yet if different wholes were subject to different laws *qua* wholes and not simply on account of and in proportion to the differences of their parts, knowledge of a part could not lead, it would seem, even to presumptive or probable

knowledge as to its association with other parts. Given, on the other hand, a number of legally atomic units and the laws connecting them, it would be possible to deduce their effects *pro tanto* without an exhaustive knowledge of all their coexisting effects.

(pp. 277–8)

This brought Keynes to the final stage of the discussion, that of 'their possible justification'. He rightly regarded this stage the most difficult. For 'so long as our knowledge of the subject of epistemology is in so disordered and undeveloped a condition as it is at present', one could not expect 'any conclusive or satisfactory answer to this question' (p. 291). He turned back to his earlier discussions of direct and indirect knowledge and direct acquaintance and direct knowledge.[18] He characterised the current view (although he did not name particular authors and only stated 'It seems generally to be agreed') (p. 292) on direct knowledge as suggesting that individuals could, if they understood their meaning, know propositions about logical propositions that went beyond mere expressions of their meaning, *i.e.* they could know synthetic propositions. As for empirical entities, he suggested that the current view was that individuals could have direct knowledge, but not in a synthetic way. In that case, one could not have direct knowledge of the inductive hypothesis as a result of direct acquaintance with objects.

Keynes held that this view was incorrect. He suggested that individuals could have direct knowledge of empirical entities that went beyond sensation of them or an expression of understanding of them. In other words, one could have synthetic knowledge of empirical entities. This, however, raised a further problem, for he had argued that the probability of the inductive hypothesis itself had to be known in some *a priori* way. For this to be true would be equivalent to an assumption that all systems of fact or objects are finite. But the inductive hypothesis was not a self-evident logical axiom and did 'not appeal to the mind in the same way'. Thus the best one could presume was that 'this assumption is true of *some* systems of fact, and, further, there are some objects about which, as soon as we understand their nature, the mind is able to apprehend directly that the assumption in question *is* true' (pp. 291–2). He concluded his discussion:

> I do not pretend that I have given any perfectly adequate reason for accepting the theory I have expounded, or any such theory. The inductive hypothesis stands in a peculiar position that it seems to be neither a self-evident logical axiom nor an object of direct acquaintance; and yet it is just as difficult, as though the inductive hypothesis were either of these, to remove from the organon of thought the inductive method which can only be based on it or on something like it.
>
> As long as the theory of knowledge is so imperfectly understood as now, and leaves us so uncertain about the grounds of so many

of our firmest convictions, it would be absurd to confess a special scepticism about this one. I do not believe that the foregoing argument has disclosed a reason for such scepticism. We need not lay aside the belief that this conviction gets its invincible certainty from some valid principle darkly present to our minds, even if it still eludes the peering eyes of philosophy.

(pp. 293–4)

Thus Keynes thought that he had justified induction without falling into Hume's trap of scepticism. But had he? Here we must remember the way Hume had set up the problem. Keynes put it thus:

Hume's sceptical criticisms are usually associated with causality; but argument by induction – inference from past particulars to future generalisations – was the real object of the attack. Hume showed, not that inductive methods were false, but that their validity had never been established and that all possible lines of proof seemed equally unpromising. The *full* force of Hume's attack and the nature of the difficulties which brought it to light were never appreciated by Mill, and he makes no adequate attempt to deal with them. Hume's statement of the case against induction has never been improved upon; and the successive attempts of philosophers, led by Kant, to discover a transcendental solution have prevented them from meeting hostile arguments on their own ground and from finding solutions which might, conceivably, have satisfied Hume himself.

(pp. 302–3)

From this statement, it would appear that, as was the case with Sidgwick's treatment of ethics, Keynes thought that one could distinguish between the justification for induction and the practice of induction, and that Hume's attack on the absence of empirical or rational justification for induction did not extend to the practice of it. Here he was mistaken, for Hume considered inductive practice as irrational, illogical and subjective.

So why did Keynes believe that Hume 'might have read what I have written with sympathy' (p. 468)? Partially, perhaps, because the elements of reasonableness that he found in inductive practice were commonsensical – analogy and practical intuition. Partially as well, because he had rejected both purely empirical and purely transcendental means of justification. And, perhaps most importantly because he had recognised that

Much of the cogency of Hume's criticism arises out of the assumption of methods of certainty on the part of those systems against which it was directed. The earlier realists were hampered by their not perceiving that lesser claims in the beginning might yield them what they wanted in the end.

When we allow that probable knowledge is, nevertheless, real, a new method of argument can be introduced into metaphysical discussions. The demonstrative method can be laid on one side, and we may attempt to advance the argument by taking into account circumstances which give *some* reason for preferring one alternative to another.

(p. 266)

Before he proceeded to applications of his approach in philosophy and statistical inference, Keynes had to deal with one matter that he had avoided, at least formally, thus far. This was the 'use of the term *cause*', for which he reserved a note to his Part III. There he admitted that he had been using the term more widely than in the usual technical sense of 'necessary' or 'sufficient cause'. In this he had not departed from the previous practice of writers on probability 'who constantly use the term *cause*, where *hypothesis* might seem more appropriate' (p. 306). His justification for doing so was one which he had used again and again throughout the book, his emphasis on the ordinary use of language rather than the more, formal restricted uses that terms had acquired in the hands of logicians. He had done so 'because, the necessary causation of particulars by particulars rarely being apparent to us, the strict sense of the term has little utility' (p. 306).

His use of cause implied 'some reference implied or expressed to a limited body of knowledge' and it was in this 'wider sense' that he proceeded to discuss the issue with reference to the actual cognitive conditions involved. In doing so, he maintained the traditional distinction between *causa essendi* and *causa cognescendi* – or between 'the cause why a thing is what it is' and 'the cause of our knowledge of an event'.[19] The distinction he made analogous to 'causally independent' and 'independent for probability' and then continued:

> [A]fter all, the essential relation is that of 'independence for probability'. We wish to know whether knowledge of one fact throws light *of any kind* upon the likelihood of another. The theory of causality is only important because it is thought that by means of its assumptions light *can* be thrown by the experience of one phenomenon upon the expectation of another.

This emphasis on knowledge highlights again his emphasis throughout *Probability* on the cognitive conditions involved. And this cognitive, rather than physical, approach to cause was to be important to Keynes's explanations of action.

Closely related to 'cause' was his view of chance, the first 'philosophical application of probability' that he discussed immediately after the note on cause. As he opened the chapter:

> Many important differences of opinion in the treatment of probability have been due to confusion or vagueness as to what is meant by randomness and by objective chance, as distinguished from what,

for purposes of this chapter, may be termed subjective probability. It is agreed that there is a sort of probability that depends upon knowledge and ignorance, and is relative, in some manner, to the mind of the subject; but it is also supposed that there is also a more objective probability which is not thus dependent, or less completely so. The relation of randomness to the other concepts is also obscure.

(p. 311, emphasis added)

He highlighted this sense of opposites by distinguishing between:

(a) 'knowledge and ignorance' or 'events . . . which we have some reason to expect and events which we have no reason to expect, which gives rise to the theory of subjective probability and subjective chance';
(b) 'objective probability and objective chance . . . which are commonly held to arise out of the antithesis between "cause" and "chance", between events, that is to say, which are causally connected and events which are not causally connected'; and
(c) 'chance and design' or 'between "blind causes" and "final causes", where we oppose a "chance" event to one, part of whose cause is a volition following on a conscious desire for an event'.

(pp. 311–12)

He noted that his method had been to regard as fundamental what *only for the purposes of this chapter* he called subjective probability (elsewhere it was objective) and treat other conceptions of probability as derivative. He took examples from other writers who had seen the operation of objective chance – the drawing of balls from an urn, the distribution of drops of rain, the birth of a great man, the motions of molecules of gas, the death of a man in the street as the result of a falling tile. These he suggested confirmed the view that 'subjective chance' concerned with knowledge and ignorance was fundamental and that 'objective' chance was merely a special and derivative case of subjective chance which seemed to depend on a certain type of knowledge being available or potentially available.

[A]n event is due to objective chance if in order to predict it, or to prefer it to alternatives, at present equi-probable, with any high degree of probability, it would be necessary to know a great many more facts of existence about it than we actually do know, and if the addition of a wide knowledge of general principles would be of little use.

(p. 319)

In other words, a situation due to objective chance from Keynes's cognitive perspective of probability was one of irredeemable ignorance: 'we mean not only that we know no principle by which to choose between the alternatives, but also that no such principle is knowable' (p. 318). This was the situation characteristic of games of chance, but not typical of human practice. Knowledge, even if limited, was much more characteristic than ignorance.

Before he turned to statistical inference, Keynes had one more 'philosophical application' of probability – the application of probability to conduct – to discuss. Here he was soon back to the quotation from *Principia Ethica* which he had used in the undated paper, 'Ethics in Relation to Conduct', discussed previously.[20] However, although he took notions from his early papers,[b] the discussion was now expanded to take in such extensions of the utilitarian calculus as 'mathematical expectation'. The results were those one would expect from the discussions thus far: the assumptions necessary for the conclusions were so restrictive as to be almost useless. In general,

> The importance of probability can only be derived from the judgement that it is *rational* to be guided by it in action; and a practical dependence on it can only be justified that in action we *ought* to take some account of it. It is for this reason that probability is to us the 'guide of life', since to us, as Locke says 'in the greatest part of our concernment, God has afforded only the twilight, as I may say, of Probability, suitable, I presume, to that state of Mediocrity and Probationership He has been pleased to place us in here'.
>
> (p. 356)

The last seven chapters of *Probability* were devoted to statistical inference. The argument of these chapters was almost completely developed after the 1907 and 1908 submissions of his fellowship dissertations. At that time, Keynes had clear hunches as to where the arguments of his dissertation would lead him in this area, but he had not had time to develop them.[21] Many of the arguments in these chapters would reappear in his discussions of statistical arguments between 1910 and 1940.

He opened by distinguishing between two parts of the theory of statistics: the *descriptive* part concerned with presenting, describing and summarising series of events or instances; and the *inductive* or inferential part concerned with extending the description of certain characteristics of observed events to those not observed. He noted that in practice this distinction was not always observed as statisticians too often slipped from description to generalisation. In this they had not been helped by the terminology of the subject, for the same terms often found use for both descriptive and inductive purposes:

> The term 'probable error' ... is used *both* for the purpose of supplementing and improving a statistical description, *and* for the purpose of indicating the precision of some generalisation. The term 'correlation'

b And not only 'Ethics in Relation to Conduct': the discussion of organic unities on p. 343 bears a strong family resemblance to the discussion of 'Miscellanea Ethica' and 'A Theory of Beauty'.

itself is used *both* to describe an observed characteristic of a particular phenomenon *and* in the enunciation of an inductive law which relates to phenomena in general.

(pp. 361–2)

Keynes emphasised that he would be concerned with 'the logical basis of statistical modes of argument', with statistical inference or induction. He worked in two stages: first by looking at particular statistical techniques in common use and stating the assumptions on which they were based so as to determine where they might be applied; and second, more generally, taking these earlier conclusions and seeing how they related to the logical conditions for universal induction he had already developed in Book III. In both exercises, although he spent considerable time on the historical origins of the doctrines, again and again he returned to his main targets, the work of contemporary, empirically based English mathematical statisticians: Karl Pearson, F. Y. Edgeworth,[c] A. L. Bowley and G. U. Yule.

The discussion centred around Bernoulli's law of large numbers, his theorem, its inversion and Laplace's law of succession. The law of large numbers states that if the *a priori* probability is known throughout, in the long run a certain determinate frequency of occurrence will be expected. Bernoulli's theorem allows the deduction of statistical frequencies from measures of initial frequencies. Its inversion makes it possible to derive numerical measures of probability from previously observed statistical frequencies. The rule of succession states that if we know that an event has occurred m times and failed n times in given conditions, then the probability of its occurring when the conditions are next fulfilled is $(m+n)/(m+n+2)$.

With regard to Bernoulli's theorem, Keynes pointed out that it 'is only valid, subject to stricter qualifications, than have always been remembered, and in conditions which are the exception, not the rule' (p. 369). The qualifications were:

(1) '[T]he initial *data* are of such a character that additional knowledge, as to the proportion of failures or successes in one part of a series of cases is altogether irrelevant to our expectation as to the proportion in another part'

c His views of Pearson and Edgeworth at the time of writing his 1907 dissertation are of interest:

Pearson's work falls outside the ground I am attempting to cover: his general viewpoint I disagree with .... I regard Pearson as primarily a statistician and in that he is eminent; but his kind of statistics has to rest on some basis of probability, and my complaint against him is that he can give no clear account of this *logical* part and indeed knows very little about it. His mathematics is excellent and doubtless proves something, but whether it proves quite what he thinks it proves I rather doubt ....

Edgeworth's work does not seem to me to come to much: he is very ingenious but often a little perverse and very old fashioned.

(KCKP, TP7, JMK to W. H. Macaulay, 30 August 1907).

(2) '[T]he series should be *long*'.

(pp. 374–5)

He believed that these conditions were generally not characteristic of natural events. The only cases where one could get long series where the experience of the series creation would not lead one to alter one's expectation of the next event were artificial series resulting from coin-tossing, throws of dice, roulette and lotteries – hardly the normal cases where human knowledge was concerned. The rest of the discussion of the chapter concerned attempts to extend Bernoulli's theorem without taking these conditions, especially the first, into consideration.

When he turned from the theorem itself, to its inversion, or inference from an observed statistical frequency to a measure of probability, particularly in the form of Laplace's law of succession, Keynes again was concerned with the limiting assumptions on which the methods might be valid. He found difficulties in giving 'a lucid account of so confused a doctrine' (p. 408). His criticism, other than its internal inconsistency, was that it put too much of a premium on ignorance.

[I]t does not seem reasonable on general grounds that we should be able on so little evidence to reach so certain a conclusion. The argument does not require, for example, that we have any knowledge of how the samples are chosen, of the positive and negative analogies between the individuals, or indeed anything at all beyond what is given in the above statement. The method is, in fact, much too powerful. It invests any positive conclusion, which it is employed to *support*, with far too high a degree of probability. Indeed this is so foolish a theorem to entertain it is discreditable.

(pp. 416–17)

Although Keynes devoted another two chapters to demolishing most of his predecessors before he came to his 'outline of a constructive theory', it is more interesting to turn to that theory. By that stage, he had relegated mathematical statistics to the role of statistical description rather than statistical inference:

I think that the business of statistical technique ought to be regarded as strictly limited to preparing the numerical aspects of our material in an intelligible form, so as to be ready for the application of the usual inductive methods. Statistical technique tells us how to 'count the cases' when we are presented with complex material. It must not proceed, except in the exceptional case where our evidence furnishes us from the outset with data of a particular kind, to turn its results into probabilities; not, at any rate, if we mean by probability a measure of rational belief.

(p. 428)

The central need in statistical practice was to take account of the analogy, or attendant circumstances surrounding the statistical event under consideration. One had to ensure that the observed or probable frequencies of the series that were to form the basis of the induction were stable.

> This method consists in breaking up a statistical series, according to appropriate principles, into a number of sub-series, with a view to analysing and measuring, not merely the frequency of a given character over the aggregate series, but the *stability* of this frequency among the sub-series; that is to say, the series as a whole is divided up by some principle of classification into a set of sub-series, and the *fluctuation* of the statistical frequency under examination between the various sub-series is examined. It is . . . a technical method of increasing the analogy between the instances.
>
> (p. 428)

This method, developed by Wilhelm Lexis, represented the safe way to begin statistical inference. Keynes argued that the same method should be used with correlation coefficients. His reasons for this procedure rested on the reservations he had concerning the empiricist view of nature which lay at the basis of most statistical analysis. He did not see nature as regular. It was because he did not see such order and regularity that he advised examining series for recurrence and stability: social and physical statistics were not so fixed nor the selection so random as those derived from games of chance on which mathematical statistics was based. Indeed, in social and physical statistics 'our so-called "permanent causes" are always changing a little and are liable at any moment to radical alteration' (p. 458). It was only when conditions in scientific examples could be assimilated to games of chance that one could use traditional methods, but this had to be argued for and tested, not presumed.

This brings me to the conclusion of my discussion of *Probability*. It began a long way back in the context of Keynes's 'early beliefs' and I must return to the question of these beliefs. Before doing so, however, I have one more task to perform with *Probability*. We know that he worked on the book at various times between 1905 and its completion 15 years later. Over this time is it possible to date various notions unambiguously?

The answer is yes. It is clear that many of the characteristic doctrines and attitudes of *Probability* were present before the 1907 submission and thus make it possible to argue that Keynes had discarded most of what he regarded as distinctive in his 'early beliefs' by that date. He had, for example already made the distinction between the rational and the true[22] – a distinction that inclines one to question the claim of Professor Skidelsky that 'he felt a need for "true beliefs"'.[23] In *Probability* rationality or reasonableness or practical rationality were not based on 'truth' or 'objective' standards but on modes of reasoning. Moreover, by the 1907 version of his dissertation, he had already taken up the firmly anti-empiricist views that led him to write

> If our experience and our knowledge were complete, we should be beyond the need of the calculus of probability. And where our experience is incomplete, we cannot hope to derive it from judgements of probability without the aid either of intuition or of some further *a priori* principle. Experience, as opposed to intuition, cannot possibly afford us a criterion by which to judge whether on given evidence the probabilities of two propositions are or are not equal.
>
> (p. 94)[24]

Similarly, as early as 1907 he also attacked eighteenth-century utopians and meliorists and emphasised the importance of states of mind and beliefs for action. Thus, it is not without very strong reasons that Anna Carabelli suggested that Keynes's 1938 paper should be retitled 'My Very Early (around 1903–6) Beliefs'.[25]

I should also note one other characteristic of *Probability*, even in its early versions, which runs contrary to 'My Early Beliefs'. Throughout the argument, the reasons or grounds for holding hypotheses were intimately connected with *action* not just contemplation. It was for that reason that probability was the 'guide of life'. As he put it at the beginning of 'The Application of Probability to Conduct':

> To believe one thing *in preference* to another, . . . must have reference to action and must be a loose way of expressing the propriety of *acting* on one hypothesis rather than on another. We may put it, therefore, that the probable is the hypothesis on which it is rational for us to act.
>
> (p. 339)

This view of probability and its relation to action carried with it certain implications. For probable beliefs were based on several sources – knowledge, conscious memory, unconscious memory or habit. He also spoke of '"tendency, impulse or instinct" refined by reason and enlarged by experience' as shaping intuitive probability judgements (p. 275). In these circumstances, beliefs and therefore probabilities for individuals could be affected by persuasion – by providing those involved through ordinary language in given cognitive circumstances with grounds for changing their perceptions of the future. In this way, one might argue, the doctrines of *Probability* tie into the doctrines of Burke, for in Keynes's discussion of Burke the possibilities of expedient action by government depended on the feelings and prejudices of the governed. Also, of course, persuasion might influence individual perceptions of the future risks associated with various courses of action and thus the possibilities of change.

Connected with the doctrines of *Probability*, even in its early 1907 and 1908 versions, was a role for the professional moral scientist/economist that

Keynes was about to become. From 'Miscellanea Ethica', through the first draft table of contents of his dissertation, to the version submitted in 1908 with its additional material on psychical research (which was carried over into the published version of 1921),[26] he had maintained an active interest in the relationship between probability and the moral sciences. This, he suggested, was an area where 'we should be very chary of applying . . . the *calculus* of probabilities'(p. 334). 'The hope . . . of gradually bringing the moral sciences under the sway of mathematical reasoning steadily recedes' (p. 349), yet this does not make the moral scientist less useful. It merely means that the forms of knowledge and criteria of evaluation and usefulness for the resulting models involved might be different from those of the natural sciences.[27] It was not that surprising that Keynes the economist would later use the term 'art' to describe his subject (pp. 553–4). Nor, as he remarked in some of his early papers, in *Probability* and in some of his later *Essays in Biography*, were the procedures very different from those of the artist, even though one might value the outcomes differently and rate the act of artistic creation more highly.[28]

This brings us back to the question of Keynes's 'early beliefs'. The initial impact of Moore was indeed 'overwhelming'. It may also, despite Keynes's worldly continuing concerns in what I have called the Burke papers – 'Miscellanea Ethica' and 'Modern Civilisation' – not to mention in action, have led to an unworldliness and a privateness of concern with fit feelings, objects and emotions – not to mention truth. But I believe that a case can be made for the important role of the period of the creation of *Probability* in bringing Keynes out from the inwardness and ultra-rationality of his 'early beliefs' towards a view of the world that could link 'science and art', his duty to his friends and an active role in the wider phenomenal world. In this process Moore, as I have suggested, remained philosophically important to Keynes, yet in the same process Keynes found an un-Moorian role that would be consistent with what Harrod referred to as the 'presuppositions of Harvey Road' – of ordered progress, moral purposiveness, and open-minded worldly improvement furthered through rational persuasion.[29] As Peter Clarke has suggested, Keynes may not have accepted this heritage 'without putting up a fight', but 'it bears marks of being a put-up fight'.[30] The results of the contest would show themselves in the years that followed.

NOTES

1 See the second page of the editorial introduction to each of the first twenty-nine volumes of *The Collected Writings*.
2 Fitzgibbons 1988; Carabelli 1988; O'Donnell 1989. Both Carabelli's and O'Donnell's books have their origins in Cambridge Ph.D. dissertations dating from 1985 and 1982 respectively.
3 Stigler 1986; Hacking 1987.
4 For a good summary see Passmore 1968, chs 6 and 9.

5 *JMK*, VIII, 341. This quotation appears consistently from the 1907 version onwards. Hereafter all page references in the text are to *Probability*.
6 See, for example, *JMK*, VIII, 18–19, 56, 69, 76.
7 Above p. 99.
8 Carabelli 1988, 31–2. For similar linking see Bateman 1988.
9 *JMK*, VIII, 42. This diagram occurred in all versions of *Probability* after the one submitted in December 1907. That, earlier, version also had a diagram, but it was less persuasive.
10 *JMK*, VIII, 77, 83.
11 *JMK*, VII, 148; XXIX, 293.
12 Above p. 149.
13 Moore 1903, viii.
14 Ibid., 6.
15 Ibid., 143–4.
16 *JMK*, VIII, 266–7; above pp. 98–100.
17 Carabelli 1988, 34–7.
18 Above p. 147.
19 Carabelli 1988, 92, quoting Keynes's notes from 'Induction, Causation and Hypothesis' entitled 'Ground and Cause'.
20 See Appendix 1 to Chapter 5, p. 131.
21 KCKP, TP7, JMK to W. H. Macaulay, 30 August 1907.
22 This issue was discussed in Chapter 2 of the 1907 version of the dissertation.
23 Skidelsky 1985, 147.
24 See also the 1907 draft of his dissertation, p. 18, for an even stronger statement.
25 Carabelli 1988, 100.
26 Ibid., 330–4.
27 See the illuminating discussion in Carabelli 1988, esp. ch. 9.
28 The early papers that come to mind here are the undated one on art criticism and the 1909 paper on 'the real or alleged opposition between Science and Art'.
29 Harrod 1951, 2–3, 183, 193.
30 Clarke 1988, 10–11.

7

CIVIL SERVANT TO YOUNG DON

The India Office that Keynes joined at the age of 23 in 1906 was more leisurely than a modern civil service establishment. Hours, which had recently been increased to align them with the rest of Whitehall, were 11 to 5 Monday to Friday and 11 to 1 on Saturdays, with eight weeks' holiday a year, plus Bank holidays, Derby Day and two or three days around Christmas.

The responsibilities and hence the activities of the Office were varied. Running the London affairs of the British Empire in India meant that it was a miniature government in itself, performing functions comparable with those of the Treasury, Board of Trade, Home Office, Foreign Office and War Office. Yet performing these functions for an empire several thousand miles away meant pushing a lot of paper – over 150,000 pieces a year – and 'mindnumbingly routine work' for many junior clerks whose main function was to provide information for their departmental superiors, who would in their turn draft documents for the Permanent Under-Secretary of State, the Council of India and its functional committees.[1] As Chandavarkar characterises it, the India Office was 'the very embodiment of routine and paperwork reduced to almost an art form'.[2] Financed by its own revenues, part of the so-called 'Home Charges', the Office was largely free of Treasury control and did its best to minimise Parliamentary interference in its affairs. It was also self-contained: promotion was *inside* the Office. As Sir Arthur Godley, Permanent Under-Secretary of State from 1883 until 1909, put it to the Civil Service Commission in 1891: '[T]he man who takes it [an India Office position] will thenceforward become an India Office man [and] must live [and] die here.'[3] Moreover, the office was still small enough and the control of the senior officials so pervasive that Keynes quickly came into contact with his superiors, including Sir Arthur Godley.

Keynes's first posting was in the Military Department. Although he found the work interesting at first, he also soon found that, especially given his quickness, there was not enough to do and he began 'to get into the habit of doing my own work in office hours'.[4] Traces of this survive in notes on various authors on probability made on Office stationery. He also conducted much of his correspondence from the office. His first major job, lasting for several months, was ordering and arranging for the shipment to Bombay of ten young Ayrshire bulls. An indication of the extent of routine in the job comes from a contemporary Department allocation of duties:[5]

Leave and Leave pay.
Assisting Mr Stewart and keeping book.
Medals and Decorations.
Medical Board.
Medical Service, Indian; examination and appointments.
Order of Merit, List of Admissions for King.
Pensions:
  Natives.
  Regimental Warrant Officers, N.C.O.[s] and Soldiers [of the Indian Army].
  Widows of ditto.
  Special campaign.
Prize Money, Donation Batta, and Gratuities.

No wonder he found refuge in probability! However, he was sufficiently successful to be offered a resident clerkship after only four months. This position involved the receipt and processing of despatches, telegrams and incoming material for the Departments, Under-Secretaries and the Secretary of State.[6] He declined it because it would interfere with work on his dissertation and with his private life.

March 1907 brought a change. He was transferred to the Revenue, Statistics and Commerce Department under T. W. Holderness and, as a result, his work became much more interesting. He described his new position to Lytton:

I like my new Department. I haven't much to write at present, but there is an excellent system by which everything comes to me to read, and I read it. In fact there is so much to read, that it takes all my time. Some of it is quite absorbing – Foreign Office commercial negotiations with Germany, quarrels with Russia in the Persian Gulf, the regulation of opium in Central India, the Chinese opium proposals – I have had great files to read on all these in the last two days.[7]

The new job also took him to his first meeting of the Revenue Committee of the Council of India: 'The thing is simply Government by dotardy; at least half those present showed manifest signs of senile decay, and the rest didn't speak'. It also brought him a room of his own overlooking St James's Park. He had been asked to edit 'The Moral and Material Progress of India' which he promised Lytton would have 'an illustrated appendix on Sodomy'. He warned Lytton that 'this is the last *you* will hear of it: for the Appendix is to be marked *secret* and kept in the Office'.[8] Soon, although bored with probability, he found that he hardly had time to touch it.[9] A month later he reported again to Lytton:

> I have really been almost overwhelmed in this office. I really believe that I have written almost every dispatch in the department this week, but I am sometimes to ask with a writer in last week's *Hibavedi* [a Calcutta newspaper] – 'for what purpose there are a few white elephants fattening themselves at our cost in the India Office'.[10]

The move to the India Office and London at first made little other difference to Keynes's way of life. He continued to move in a circle of old Cambridge and Eton friends – Lytton, Hobby, Swithinbank, C. R. Fay, Ralph Hawtrey, Harry Norton, Robin Mayor, C. P. Sanger and the Trevelyans. He also kept in close touch with Cambridge, going up on Saturday afternoons for meetings of the Society and staying over for Sunday lunch at Harvey Road. As yet, he had not made regular contact with the non-Apostle friends of Lytton's earlier years in Cambridge, such as Clive Bell, who would form part of Bloomsbury. He was still sufficiently remote from them that Thoby Stephen's death from typhoid in November 1906 did not enter his correspondence until Lytton mentioned it. However, he did strike out in some new directions, attending the Economic Club at University College to hear C. S. Loch of the Charity Organisation Society talk on the unemployed and taking part as a steward, or 'hired rough' as he described himself to Pippa Strachey,[11] in the 'Mud March' Suffragette demonstration in London on 9 February 1907 – an event to which he also took his sister.[12] And, of course, London meant more theatre.

With his move to London and his Civil Service position, his practising homosexuality brought the possibility of public disclosure of his private life. Under the Labouchère Amendment in the Criminal Law Amendment Act of 1885, any act of 'gross indecency' between males in private or public was a misdemeanour punishable by up to two years' hard labour, while connection *per anum* was a felony punishable by a term of penal servitude of up to life. The existence of such a law left open considerable possibilities for blackmail and slander. In Cambridge, especially in King's, although there was still some need for discretion, there had been a significant adult, gay underworld and the atmosphere was more tolerant. For example, in reviewing Oscar Wilde's *De Profundis* for the *Independent Review* in 1905, Lowes Dickinson could write:

> Every society has a duty, and one more extensive than any society has yet admitted, to control sexual relations in the interest of the children to be born of them. But everything beyond that is a question of private morals and taste. Now the private morals and taste of our society are not such that it has the right to throw the first stone at any man.

And our law on that matter in question [homosexual practices] is a mere survival of barbarism, supported not by reason but by sheer prejudice.[13]

This wider world was less inclined to turn a blind eye.

Thus it is not surprising that a concern for being 'found out' began to appear in Keynes's correspondence from the summer of 1906 onwards. There had been hints before of the worry as in the comments on the Sidgwick memoir (above p. 101) but these had been non-specific. Keynes's first comment came in a letter to Lytton in June, just before he resumed practical, as opposed to theoretical, sodomy:

> We don't live in Russia and the police don't raid our drawers even if we've raided other people's . . .
>
> The drawers of the dead are not sacred – *that* is true.
>
> So long as no one has anything to do with the lower classes or people off the streets, and there is some discretion in letters to neutrals, there's not a scrap of risk – or hardly a scrap.
>
> When lust is triumphant over good taste – then comes Inspector Piles.[14]

All of this was in reaction to an inquest in which a contemporary of James Strachey was involved. As yet, neither Keynes nor Lytton felt directly threatened. A few months later the situation had changed, for Mary Berenson had received an anonymous[a] warning against Geoffrey Scott's associating with her daughters as he was a 'disciple of the deplorable practices of Oscar Wilde. It just shows how damned careful one has to be'.[15] Soon it went further:

> Worse and worse – at least it seems to me. I have never felt more nervous.
>
> Scott has forwarded to me a letter from La B. to himself on the subject. From this it appears (i) that she has always known all about him (that indeed I know: he admitted that he had told *her*) (ii) that she also knows about me. This is news: I have always been a model of discretion – neither word nor hint; and Scott has sworn (for of course I suspected him) that he kept my secrets – but of course, as is *a priori*, he told her. (iii) that La B. has told Ray and goodness knows who else besides.
>
> So I have no doubt now, that, although they are too polite to mention it, everybody in England is perfectly aware of everything.
>
> Well, I suppose it is a fair penalty for going about with such people.

a It later emerged that the letter had been written by the housekeeper at Court House, Iffley. KCKP, JMK to GLS, 9 August 1908.

But – in the present state of public opinion – damn and damn and damn.[16]

This time Lytton was consoling and the whole matter blew over with the participants thinking it a practical joke. Nevertheless, anxiety continued:

Such a shock! about 2 months ago I wrote a most compromising letter to Furness. It was returned through the dead letter office yesterday, addressed *not* to me but simply to the India Office. When I opened it, it was, thank God, not that one, but another quite innocent one I wrote 6 months ago.[b]

Over time, perhaps because nothing happened and because Keynes's liaisons remained relatively restricted, the alarms diminished, but during the years that followed the threat of exposure always lurked, often acknowledged,[17] in the background. This threat and the consequent need to lead a bifurcated existence, meant that 'wise friends'[18] from the 'normal' community who accepted him as he was came to play an important role in his life. The most important of these would be Vanessa Bell.

Keynes's first year at the India Office also saw the beginnings of another friendship that was to last all his life – that with Duncan Grant. Born in 1885, the son of a major in an Indian regiment and a cousin of Lytton and James Strachey, Duncan grew up in India with long leaves in Britain where he spent his holidays with the cousins, to whom he was closest to James. When old enough he came to England for his education, first at Hilbrow Preparatory School, Rugby with James, as well as Rupert Brooke, and then at St Paul's, where he spent all but two terms as a day-boy, living with the Stracheys when his parents were not on home leave. After leaving St Paul's in 1902, he fell under the influence of Simon Bussy, a French painter who was to marry Lytton's sister, Dorothy, in April 1903. He went to the Westminster School of Art until 1905 and then studied in Paris under Jacques Emile Blanche. An attractive person of charming personality, Duncan had been the object of Lytton's real or imagined attentions and his preference for Hobby had been one of the subjects of Lytton's extensive 1906 correspondence with Keynes. When Duncan was in England, Keynes had occasionally met him at the Stracheys or in Cambridge. When Keynes, James Strachey and Harry Norton considered going to Paris for a holiday in March 1907, Keynes suggested they stay with Duncan. The first extended period together from

b KCKP, JMK to GLS, 6 June 1907. Furness reassured him on 5 July that all Keynes's letters had reached their destination, but remarked (KCKP):

Of course if you will address your letters to me to the Minister of the Interior you can hardly expect him to fail to re-export them as indecent matter: and if you only put your initials at the end it is hardly possible for him to re-address them to anyone but Mr John Morley.

24 to 28 March proved quite successful before Keynes, Norton and James returned to England to take part in one of Moore's Easter reading parties, this time at North Moulton, Devon. With his Office commitments, Keynes could only manage the long Easter weekend and he returned to London on 2 April. The other members of the party were Ralph Hawtrey, C. P. Sanger, Bob Trevelyan and A. R. Ainsworth.[c]

The break from the office seems to have done some good. Keynes had been suffering from mild appendicitis early in March which, along with the burdens of the new job had left him rather worn out. He had become rather bored with his dissertation. He had been beginning to work his way through 3–4,000 pages of German and with his reading speeds for English, French and German bearing the ratio of 1:2:3 this was a severe trial.[19] Moreover, after his return the pace of work in the Office rose to an unprecedented level. This, plus two to four hours a day on probability, meant that he was almost hard-pressed – but not hard-pressed enough to pass up an invitation to be Pigou's guest at the London Political Economy Club on 1 May for a discussion on a corn tax and colonial preference.[20] The régime of harder work did not last. In the first full week of May he suffered a severe attack of influenza, which sent him home to Cambridge for a week and slowed him down for a further two. There was then almost a month of work in the Office before he left for another holiday in the Pyrenees with C. R. Fay, just after the Society Dinner at the Star and Garter in Richmond. For part of the time, they joined Neville and Geoffrey, who had gone out a week earlier for a session of butterflying.

The holiday with Fay was 'only a qualified success'.[21] Keynes enjoyed the walking and got on with novels (Jane Austen) and with probability. '[I]t's a very long time since lust has been at so low an ebb (I suppose it is the result of so much walking) and confess it's rather a relief'. At the end of the second week of July, he and Fay descended to Biarritz. Keynes described his existence:

> I have breakfast in bed and read a novel for an hour or so; then I get up and work for two hours; and food and sun and laziness for the rest of the day. I assure you I am as swell as any here with my new clothes, my white shoes, and my tie arranged in folds with an opal pin.[22]

At Biarritz he also tried the tables:

c Moore had not been enthusiastic about the idea of Keynes being on the reading party, saying

> As for Keynes and Hawtrey, I don't *want* to ask them, though I don't care, whether they come or not, for the short time: and very likely there won't be room for them.

(BL, ADD.60680, G. E. Moore to GLS, 5 March 1907).

I lost the most appalling sums at Petits Cheveux, and it is doubtful whether I shall have enough money to provide any meals on the journey home. My dear! last night, I finished up by losing forty times running; and I have had other spells almost as bad.[23]

Only Fay's willingness to play piquet for Keynes's hotel coupons against his French francs kept things going until his return on 17 July. According to his cash book, his losses had amounted to £4.

Then it was back to the round of official duties and probability. The office was so busy that he had to give up writing letters in office time and invest in stationery for St James's Court. His life of officialdom and logic was broken only by long weekends out of London – Burley Hill in the New Forest to visit Lytton, Twyford to visit Norton and Hadspen to visit Hobby, with breaks in Cambridge in between. With the death of Neville's mother on 18 August there were new demands of family life, for Neville was badly affected. Indeed, by the end of the month, Keynes was feeling 'rather careworn': 'The work at this beastly office takes all my time going as fast as I can and then I write probability like the devil in the evening'.[24] There was only the relief of the weekends out of London.

September was not any better. He was chained to the Office and could not get leave for a holiday with the Berensons. Nor was there the prospect of anything but weekends until October. He was 'thoroughly sick' of the place and 'would like to resign. Now the novelty has worn off'. He was 'bored nine-tenths of the time and rather unreasonably irritated the other tenth whenever I can't have my own way'. The manuscript of probability progressed 'steadily but not fast enough'. At least it had the compensation that 'There at any rate I can put down what I like however wild'.[25] In this mood, he rejected a second offer of a resident clerkship from Godley. Nevertheless, it was not all work:

> I am going to spend this weekend on *Exercise*. This afternoon to lunch with the Stracheys and walk on Hampstead Heath – tomorrow with the Sunday Tramps in Surrey.[d]
>
> A pleasant party at the Sangers last night. Tonight I dine with the Macmillans.[26]

Finally on 5 October Godley released him from the Office. He was to have three weeks' leave from 12 October. He spent the first week at Harvey Road before moving into King's 'to have another taste of College life' as he told his father or 'to pretend with more success that I am an undergraduate'

---

d The Sunday Tramps were regular walks organised by G.M. Trevelyan and his friends. They would take a train out from London to Dorking, Haslemere or a country station and then walk a prearranged route for the day before returning to London in the evening.

as he told Lytton.[27] In Cambridge, he played golf almost daily with Fay or Knox and threw himself into the affairs of the Society, including the preliminary stages of Rupert Brooke's election. He also seems to have come across Clive and Vanessa Bell and Virginia Stephen, who were visiting Cambridge.[28] There were visits from Lytton, Hawtrey and Sanger for the Society and on 24 October 'Mr Bernard Shaw converted us all to Socialism'. Here were signs of change in Cambridge and in Keynes's circle of friends, for the Shaw meeting was a reflection of Fabianism moving into King's under the influence of Rupert Brooke and Hugh Dalton, both of whom had come up in 1906, and the Bell/Stephen visit a precursor of Keynes's move into what would come to be known as Bloomsbury.

One result of Keynes's visit to Cambridge was a series of rumours that he had resigned the India Office. He had told Lytton and James of his intention to resign if he obtained a fellowship.[29] However, these rumours came from other sources, Desmond MacCarthy and George Trevelyan, who two years previously had 'conducted a correspondence with me to dissuade me from entering the C.S. on the ground that such a course was cowardly and poor spirited'. Early in November, when Geoffrey Scott stayed with him at St James's Court, he heard that Scott had found out from Thomas Balston, who had picked up a rumour from Humphrey Paul and Geoffrey Young in Oxford 'that Mrs Berenson had persuaded me to resign the India Office and become an Art Critic and that I had done so'.[30] Keynes also heard the same story from Robin Mayor when he dined with the Bells at 46 Gordon Square on 5 November. But resignation could not come yet: he still had to finish his dissertation.

After his leave in Cambridge, Keynes kept on with his dissertation. Occasionally he felt frustrated by the 'trivialities' of the Office which meant 'I can do nothing else here and I depart at the end dazed and sleepy', but fortunately much of November was quiet and he could spend office time on the dissertation.[31] By 29 November he was on his last chapter and the whole thing was ready for submission on 12 December. With that out of the way, he could resume a more active social life, seeing old friends – Hawtrey, Geoffrey Young, Norton, Sanger, Scott, Hobby – as well as some new acquaintances of his brother's vintage – Justin Brooke (of the tea firm Brooke Bond and Co. and no relation to Rupert) and George Mallory – as well as Lytton whom he saw several times in London and once in Brighton, where Lytton was recovering from a bout of illness. Christmas was a family affair at Harvey Road, broken by rounds of golf at Royston.

The New Year was a time of waiting for King's decision on his fate. The India Office, where he was again editing 'The Moral and Material Progress of India' kept him busy, but, as he had already decided to leave if his dissertation was successful, his heart was not in his job. His social life outside the Office retained its old pattern. He indulged his love of the theatre, seeing over twenty productions in the three months after 2 January. He took part in another suffragette meeting and escorted his sister to a suffragette ball, whence came reports of him 'sitting out the dances with various young ladies whom your discourse entranced'.[32] However, he was seeing more of the Bells and the Stephens. He dined at the Bells on 8 January and 12 February before being invited again on 12 March both for dinner and one of Virginia Stephen's Thursday evenings at 29 Fitzroy Square. On Thursday 26 March he went to Fitzroy Square alone. These evenings, plus Vanessa Bell's Friday Club, which he had already attended, provided the link between a group of Cambridge friends who had gone up to Trinity in 1899, Vanessa and Virginia Stephen and a few others that was to become known as 'Bloomsbury'. Later this original nucleus became known as 'Old Bloomsbury' and, with one addition, after the war it would become the Memoir Club of which I have already spoken.

Intellectually, he also began to move in new directions. He had joined the Royal Economic Society in 1907. He was now going regularly to meetings of the Economic Club at University College. On 1 March he told his father of his decision to resign from the Office if his dissertation was successful. Neville Keynes 'argued with him in vain' taking the line that he was giving up a certainty in exchange for risks, but concluding: 'That fits in with his scheme of things and not mine'. Maynard Keynes told Pigou of his intentions two days later.[33] But everything depended on the dissertation.

Keynes had known since October that his dissertation would be subject to reports from W. E. Johnson, a fellow of King's, and Alfred North Whitehead of Trinity. Early in February, his father heard from Johnson that his view of the dissertation was more favourable than Whitehead's.[34] There was still the decision of the electors to come. The news came on 17 March: he was not elected. Page, the mathematician from his year, and A. E. Dobbs, a classicist from 1901, had been successful. The election had been hotly contested. Keynes was far from happy.

> I am very disappointed – for the decision affects not honour and reward, as these things usually go, but one's whole manner of life. And I am enraged that they should give as a reason the possession of another chance another year.[35]

He had heard from Pigou, a view that was later to be echoed from several other quarters in King's, that the fact that he had another chance and Dobbs did not had been the deciding consideration.[36] The same sources told him that he was practically certain to be elected the next year. On 21 March he dined with Pigou, who had made a strong effort to counter the impact of Whitehead's adverse report to the electors, to see the reports.

Afterwards, he reported in what was only his second letter of the year to Lytton:

> I had a very interesting time in Cambridge and heard about everything from Pigou. I really think it was sheer bad luck – a hair would have turned the balance; also a little wickedness on their part, for P. says that there was a solid block who voted against me from the beginning *on the express grounds of seniority*, while admitting that on merits I was better than Dobbs. I was also damaged, I think, by Whitehead's report. He is a follower (an ardent follower) of Venn! and it seems to me from his criticisms, which are futile, that he can have understood very little of the philosophy. He praised the formal logic and the mathematics. Johnson's report is about as favourable as it could possibly be. I spent most of Sunday talking to him and he made a great number of very important criticisms, which with the exception of one fundamental point are probably right, and practically presented me with the fruits of his own work on the subject which have extended over years. On the pure logic of it he is, I think, quite superb and immensely beyond anyone else . . .
>
> Really Whitehead's report was not competent. Of my two most important and original chapters, which whatever their truth are entirely novel, he says, 'are really excellent discussions and expositions, but – as I suspect – contain little that is new to a fairly well instructed philosopher'. While Johnson says 'it is highly original, very neatly executed, and meets an urgent need in logical science'. Whitehead ought not to have said it was old, unless he knew of some passages where it has been said before. It is no good 'suspecting' that it must have been said before because it seems reasonable.[37]

With the spring came two other changes. During late 1907 and the early months of 1908, Keynes's once voluminous correspondence with Lytton had slowed to a trickle – there were only two letters from Keynes's pen between January 1908 and the end of March[38] and Lytton was not much more prolific. This drying up of the correspondence may have reflected their both being in London, but it is more likely that they were drifting apart. A year earlier, Lytton had told Duncan: 'I used to tell Keynes nearly everything, but his commonsense was enough to freeze a volcano, so I've stopped'.[39] By May 1908 he was reporting him 'boring', a phrase he would repeat two months later, noting as well that 'we can hardly speak'.[40] They were certainly meeting less frequently. Moreover, in May Keynes started seeing more of Duncan Grant – he went with him to Cambridge on 2 May and to La Maison de Paupee on 9 May – and the next week he added Duncan to his account-book list of those to whom he lent money – the first of many loans or gifts to come. When he formally resigned from the India Office on 5 June it was Duncan, not Lytton, that he told first. Gradually in the course of May and more completely after mid-June when Lytton was in Cambridge, Duncan and Maynard became lovers.

Duncan provided Keynes with the closest male friendship of the rest of his life. The character of his new friend was markedly different from Lytton's. Dogged by ill-health and lack of worldly success, yet determined to make his mark on the world and force it to reconsider its attitudes, Lytton had developed a black view of the world and its inhabitants. An extremely complex person, emotionally dependent on a sequence of men such as Keynes and Grant, yet ultimately resentful of others' independence and worldly success, his relationship with Keynes had always had an undertone of jealousy at the latter's relative success and the freedom of choice it allowed. This resentment, normally held in check, had come to the fore when Keynes had come second in his Civil Service examinations in 1906.[41] With Duncan it was different. Duncan was basically unworldly – so much so that his indifference to worldly matters was a joke. Although concerned with the success of his art, he did not feel in competition with Keynes. Although unacademic, he was intelligent and original, a delightful companion who could accept and be accepted on his own terms without the frenzies of Lytton. Duncan was to give Keynes relief from his own world and entry into another – just as Lydia was to do thirteen years later.

At the same time as Duncan was taking a central place in Keynes's emotional and sexual life another change was in the offing. In order to increase the teaching resources for the new Economics Tripos, Marshall while Professor of Political Economy had provided for two lecturers from his fellowship dividend from St John's. In 1908, with D. H. Macgregor about to leave to become Professor in Leeds, there was a vacancy and there might be another as a result of Marshall's retirement. However, the position was complicated. Marshall was after all retiring and could hardly commit his successor, whom he hoped would be Pigou but might be H. S. Foxwell. Another complication was added by the fact that one of the electors who would decide between Pigou and Foxwell was Neville Keynes. Nevertheless, inspired by Pigou, who knew the facts of Maynard Keynes's situation, Marshall took advantage of Neville's absence on holiday in the south of France to approach Maynard on 3 April.

> My dear Keynes,
>   Quite recently, since your father left E[ng]land, I have heard in a round-about way, that it is just possible that you might return to Cambridge if you have work to do here. I have also heard that your chance of election to a fellowship in King's next year is good.
>   Under these circumstances, and taking account of the fact that Macgregor is going to Leeds, my course would have been clear if I had not been about to vacate the professorship. I should then have

asked you to allow me to propose you to the Economics Board as a lecturer on general economics probably for the first year, but possibly for the second; and I should have said I would gladly pay you the £100 which I have paid in similar cases.

But I shall cease to be a member of the Economics Board on April 21st; and at its last meeting I said that I would do nothing to hamper the freedom of the reconstituted Board which will meet (probably on June 3rd) to make up its lecture list.

It has however been suggested to me by the same person, to whom the notion of your coming to Cambridge to teach economics is due, that there may be an advantage in calling your attention to the situation. I am in a position to state two things. First (subject to some reserve in the case of one possible election to the Professorship in May) if you approve, a suggestion will be made by a member of the Board on (probably) June 3, that you be asked to lecture. Secondly, if the Board concur – and I have no doubt that (subject to the above mentioned reserve) they will concur gladly – the sum of £100 will be forthcoming for you, just to make you feel that you really are a lecturer. I do not think that the £100 will be paid by me: but I can guarantee that it will be paid either from some other source or by me.[e]

There is a certain air of mystery in this letter, and I dislike mystery. But later on you will understand that it was inevitable.

Answer at your convenience. There is no hurry.

Yours very sincerely,
Alfred Marshall[42]

Keynes left the matter until his father's return to England, but then raised the issue squarely:

But can't I accept? If I get a fellowship next year and resign this office, I am wasting my time now. This job would give me a *raison d'être* at Cambridge: if I refuse I suppose someone else will accept and it will not be open to me next year. I am still quite as decided as before to leave the India Office. Nothing would suit me better than this, and even taking into account the fact that I should have at once to learn a little economics, I should have more time for rewriting my dissertation, with which my mind is much absorbed though not my time.[43]

Neville Keynes was badly caught both as a father and a professorial elector. As a father, it was all caution. He worried that preparing lectures might reduce the time his son had available for revising his dissertation and

e It was paid by Marshall.

noted that, as the 'lectureship' would be a matter of private agreement, taking it would give him no status in the University that he could not gain in his present position or as a Fellow of King's.[44] But his son was bent on leaving the India Office. Further enquiries in King's were initially discouraging:

> My father saw Dickinson the other day and mentioned the Marshall scheme. '"That is assuming a great deal" said GLD in a way which showed he did not like it.'[f] Oh dear, what shall I do. Treasury being choked off, here I am forever I suppose. At the present moment there is no imaginable way of life which does not seem as filthy as any other.[45]

Further enquiries by Maynard Keynes himself were more promising: Dickinson consulted Macaulay, the Senior Tutor of King's, and it seemed that the fellowship was 'the "safest" thing ever known, and that your coming up now would make it about certain'.[46] Thus Keynes was determined to accept, if Pigou was elected on 30 May. He was. On 3 June, the Board met. It elected Neville Keynes chairman and decided on lecturing arrangements. Pigou offered Maynard Keynes the lectureship the same day. He also offered one to Walter Layton, who had gained a first in both parts of the Tripos in 1906 and 1907, as well as winning the Cobden Prize. Keynes resigned from the India Office on 5 June, his twenty-fifth birthday.[47] 'It has been a horrid business – the interviews and conversations and hesitations of mind'.[48] Neville Keynes still worried about his son's future in Cambridge.[49] So too, in a way did Maynard Keynes, as he wrote to Swithinbank.

> I hope it isn't madness and that I shall like being up here as much as I think I shall. There will be a dreadful outcry amongst the middle aged. It is heroic of my people to agree.

> Yes, I've done it, by God; having at last summoned up the spirit to brush aside many head shakings. Those under thirty approve I find; those over thirty think it, for the most part, an immoral action – for, they allege, you will never have the cash to afford legitimised copulation. You may not want to now, these elders say, but by the time you're thirty you will want to copulate most dreadfully, and then you will wish for the assured shekels of the I.O. I reply, of course, that there is no one in the world more ready than me to sell myself for good hard cash; but really the I.O. offer so damned little.
> What I really dread are the horrors of Cambridge, the risk of falling

f Dickinson was also an elector to the Professorship of Political Economy.

in love with some [?] creature and the rest of it. But I suppose one must risk that. All the same heaven ward it off![50]

The reference to his parents reflects not only their agreement, despite his father's worries, but also Neville Keynes's attempt to make him more financially secure by promising him an allowance of £100 per year as long as he needed it. Thus instead of his £200 from the India Office, he would have his £100 a year from Marshall, the £100 from his father, any fees he earned from students who actually attended his lectures (and these could be quite large), and fees from supervision or coaching. Thus the deed was done. Nobody in the India Office seemed surprised at his decision and the senior officials were inclined to the view that he had done the right thing.[51]

He was philosophical in the last stages as the work diminished to 'not more than a quarter of an hour . . . a day':

It seems quite like dying – initiating stages in pieces of work which will move heavily on, knowing that one will never see the outcome. I spent the morning mastering the arrangements of the Customs Dept. – the knowledge dies with me. But I have no regrets – not even now that it has come to it – not one.[52]

On 20 July he spent his last day at the Office. Four days later he came up to Cambridge and moved into King's. He had been in the India Office just over 21 months.

Keynes's departure from the India Office coincided with the revelation of his affair with Duncan to Lytton:

Lytton has been [to St James's Court]. He begins 'I hear that you and Duncan are carrying on together.' I feel quite shattered by the interview, but I suppose it wasn't very dreadful really. He takes the cynical line – much interested as a student of human life. But it gave him, as he said, a turn.[53]

Lytton asked Keynes not to come and see him for the present, although they continued a civilised correspondence.[54] Privately, both Stracheys were more upset. James reported to Lytton after seeing Keynes at 6 Harvey Road:

I confess that I had rather a fit of horror when I saw Maynard so happy – sitting in a chair with a basket of raspberries and the *Statistical Journal*. Why should everything be given to him? But then of course I remembered at once that everything wasn't.[55]

Lytton was philosophical:

I try to imagine – to realise – something. I have been three years at it now, and where have I landed? Oh how dark, how strange, how dreadful, are these things? Yet there are glories too.[56]

The ensuing months saw a sustained outbreak of Pozzophobia among the Strachey brothers.

Between his return to Cambridge and his departure for a holiday in the Orkneys on 17 August, Keynes settled back into Cambridge life. There were old friendships to take up – Fay, Norton, Knox – and company to enjoy. There were new friends from his brother's generation – Rupert Brooke, Hugh (Daddy)[g1] Dalton, and George Mallory – and acquaintances even younger such as Gerald Shove and Arthur Schloss (later Waley), all Fabians, 'very decent fellows, though not too clever perhaps'.[57] His letters to Duncan, first still in London and then in Scotland, with their air of two recently parted lovers which suggest that Keynes had been swept off his feet in a manner that only Lydia would do again in 1921–2, are full of discussions, papers, parties, picnics on the river (with Ka Cox and her sister Rachel), and walks. Cambridge had changed:

> The thing has grown with leaps and bounds in my two years of absence and practically everybody in Cambridge, except me, is an open and avowed sodomite.

There was also a trip with his sister to visit the Costelloe sisters. Present were Marjorie Strachey, Geoffrey Scott and, of course, Mrs Berenson. As usual, the life, with its bathing, punting, sunning and trips to Oxford by launch, was one of 'physical contentment . . . so great that one can't but be contented'.[58]

In all of this Keynes managed to get back to probability, although with some difficulty, for, as he told Duncan,' it will not drive you out of my mind and does not occupy it very well'.

> I wonder that so many books are written – nothing in the world is such hard work. I hope you don't find it as exhausting to paint a picture, as I do to write a chapter. It seems to be so much more tiring to do part of a big thing than a little thing equal in size to the part. When one is writing a chapter, one's mind seems vaguely involved in the whole of the rest of the book.[59]

These views would be echoed in his February 1909 paper to the Society, 'Science and Art'.

Between 17 August and 23 October 1908 Keynes was away from Cambridge. He met Duncan at Stromness in the Orkneys and the pair proceeded across to Hoy, where they alternated between Orgill Farm and

---

[g] The nickname was Keynes's. Although the two would see a lot of each other while Dalton was up, there was an element of scorn on Keynes's side for Dalton's abilities. Dalton felt this and it was to produce a coolness in their relationship in future years (Pimlott 1985, 56).

friends of Duncan's aunt at Melsetter on the Pentland Firth. Despite a brief bout of fever, from which he recovered at Melsetter, it was a period of 'hours of painting and probability',[60] both of which seem to have gone well, in spite of an accident at Stromness when a herd of cows investigated one of Keynes's latest drafts while he and Duncan had gone off for a walk. By mid-September, he had broken the back of the revised dissertation and by the end of the month he was reporting that, if he worked exclusively at it, he could have it finished before he left the island.[61] Instead, however, he began to think about his lectures on money and to begin an article for the *Economic Journal*. 'Recent Economic Events in India'.[62] For his part, Duncan, after several sketches, started a portrait of Keynes in oils that now hangs in the Combination Room at King's after almost 50 years at 6 Harvey Road, as well as several landscapes. With no fixed duties in Cambridge in the Michaelmas term and an invitation to stay and hunt at Rysa Lodge, Keynes remained in the North until well after the beginning of term, then only leaving with reluctance. Duncan, meanwhile, proceeded to Rothiemurchus, the Grant family seat in Invernesshire.

Then it was time for the whirl of a Cambridge term. Within 48 hours he was reporting:

> I live in a breathless condition with work pressing on me from every side and all kinds of social excitement . . . . But Cambridge life is so intricate and so trivial that there's no explaining it in a letter . . . . There seems to be an air of excitement and high spirits everywhere.[63]

Lytton was up for a visit. Keynes found 'his mind and manners are now purely plutocratic'. Lytton's feelings seemed equally cool, although they resumed their correspondence.[64]

On 1 November, Duncan came down from the North ill with influenza and stayed for a week. On 5 November Keynes read a paper based on his dissertation, 'The Nature of Induction', to the Moral Sciences Club. Duncan may have been infectious, for when he went to London to clear up his affairs at St James's Court Keynes collapsed on 9 November with influenza. The case was sufficiently serious for him to go into hospital in Hampstead for a few days before further recuperation at the Stracheys' home at 67 Belsize Park Gardens, where Lytton gave him his bed-sitting room. He was not fit to travel to Cambridge until 16 November, and even then he was so weak that he spent another four days at Harvey Road before going back into King's. He plugged on at probability, which would go to the same examiners again early in December. Once back in King's, he went back to his normal routine. He read a paper to the Society, 'Prince Henry or Prince Rupert' on 28 November. Amongst the possible embryos he examined for the Society was a future economist who would play a central role in his professional life. He had been supposed to look him out earlier in the month, but his illness had intervened.

Mr Robertson of Eton and Trinity came to lunch and for a walk with me yesterday. There is a good deal in his favour, but a little pudding headed perhaps . . .[65]

Dennis Robertson eventually did become an Apostle, a very unusual one, as he was elected when he was over 30 when Keynes was reconstructing the Society after the First World War. There was also a visit from Duncan from 26 November to 16 December to finish Maynard's portrait and to do a drawing of Margaret Keynes. And as soon as Duncan left, Swithinbank came up. He had come third in the Indian Civil Service Examinations at the end of the summer, and, despite Keynes's entreaties, had settled on a career in Burma. He was now preparing his languages in London rather than Cambridge.

With the dissertation revised and submitted, Keynes returned to 'Recent Economic Events in India'. He worked at it 'seven hours a day . . . read nothing but blue books'[66] and finished it before the holidays, when he and his father spent Christmas Day and Boxing Day going over it. He spent a fortnight in London with Duncan – which included some time in the British Museum working on his lectures for the new term and at the India Office checking statistics for his article. After requesting shortening, F. Y. Edgeworth agreed to publish the article in the March 1909 issue of the *Economic Journal*.

Keynes's first lecture on 'Money, Credit and Prices', a series that would run twice weekly over two terms, was on 19 January 1909. His audience numbered about fifteen. From the beginning, Neville Keynes received reports from various sources that the lectures were 'a great success' and popular.[67] Certainly his audiences held up extremely well by modern Cambridge standards, despite his declared intention to keep numbers down, even though students then paid for lectures on a piece-rate basis.[68] From his surviving lecture notes, examples of which appear in Volume XII of his *Collected Writings*, it is clear that they were similar to his other early work: they showed a good grasp of contemporary Cambridge monetary theory combined with a willingness, and an ability, to provide apt illustrations from and applications to contemporary events, as well as particular care in making inductive generalisations.[69] His notes were full of clippings from periodicals that might serve as illustrations, particularly of gold production.

Moreover, his lectures were successful in bringing him requests for further teaching, coaching and supervision, not only for the Economics Tripos but also for Indian Civil Service candidates. His fees from teaching soon outstripped his lecturer's fees. At first, though, he found teaching women a problem:

I think I shall have to give up teaching females after this year. The nervous irritation caused by two hours' contact with them is *intense*. I seem to hate every movement of their minds. The minds of the men, even when they are stupid and ugly, never appear to me so repellent.[70]

He did not do as he proposed.

His first teaching term was not only notable for the jobs he took on. It also saw him refuse an offer to be the British representative on the Permanent International Commission for Agriculture in Rome with almost no duties at a starting salary of £500 per annum. On 3 February he went as Pigou's guest to a second meeting of the London Political Economy Club, where the Professor opened a discussion on 'How far is it practicable for England to tax the foreigner?'.[71] He was also heavily involved in the events of the Cambridge term.

> The excitement of this place when combined with a good deal of work is enough to unhinge anyone, and I really don't know how any of us last through the 8 weeks of it.[72]

At first it would seem that he found it hard to adjust to being a don. He attempted to continue to dine with the BAs but the dons protested that he must dine with them. Partly on grounds of expense, he refused to for over a month and dined at the Union with James Strachey. He then tried high table once and did not dine there again until after the end of term.

> Today I dined for the second time at their High Table. The food is excellent, but, by God, one feels a don. I play the part admirably, perhaps it belongs to me.[73]

He maintained his close links with the Society, reading an interesting and, for the author of a recent fellowship dissertation on probability, introspective paper on 'the real or alleged opposition between Science and Art' on 20 February. While accepting that the artistic career might be the more worthy, he was concerned to argue that the processes of creation of the scientist and artist were similar, and described 'the activity of the scientist' as follows:

> He is presented with a mass of facts, possessing similarities and differences, arranged in no kind of scheme or order. His first need is to perceive very clearly the precise nature of the different details. After concerning himself with this precise and alternative perception, he holds the details clearly before his mind and it will probably be necessary that he should keep them more or less before his mind for a considerable time. Finally he will with a kind of sudden insight see through the obscurity of the argument or of the apparently unrelated data, and the details will quickly fall into a scheme or arrangement, between each part of which there is a real connection.[h]

---

h 'Science and Art', 5. Similar introspective discussions of the 'act of creation' would occur later in his biographical studies of Malthus and Newton. See below pp. 551–2.

He took an active part in the election to the Society of the King's economist and post-war colleague Gerald Shove, and the visits of various angels – Ralph Hawtrey, Bob Trevelyan, C. P. Sanger and, for the first time since 1906, Moore. As so often before, Keynes was impressed by him, reporting to Duncan that 'one cannot doubt that he is the greatest person living'.[74] There were other visitors: L. T. Hobhouse, the leading liberal political theorist of the day stayed with him on 17 February; Desmond MacCarthy came up with Hilaire Belloc for a supper at Rupert Brooke's; Eli Heckscher, the Swedish economist and economic historian, appeared; Clive and Vanessa Bell were up for a weekend.

> Vanessa explained how interesting it was to come up and have a look at us, Lytton having explained every one of our secrets. She was perfectly lovely – I've never seen her more beautiful – and very conversational.[75]

Moreover, there were signs that his hopes for his revised fellowship dissertation would not be disappointed. On 5 February he saw Whitehead in the street and

> [H]e stopped me to speak about the Dissertation. He says that the new version has now convinced and converted him on the fundamental point on which he formerly disagreed with me.[i] His conversion was due to the chapter I wrote chiefly in the field above Stromness, and a reference to the argument brought back to me quite clearly the view of the harbour. He thinks I had better publish at once with a few minor alterations, without waiting to get the argument completely fitted in regarding certain points which I have left so far in an unsatisfactory condition.[76]

Whitehead was as generous in his report on the dissertation, which began

> Mr Keynes' dissertation is a contribution to knowledge of great importance. It is not a mere academic exercise and, when published, will seriously affect all future investigation in the subjects with which it deals. If Mr Keynes publishes much other work of this character, he will attain considerable eminence as a man of science.

On 16 March 1909 Keynes was elected a Fellow of King's. He was to remain one for the rest of his life.

With term over, he was off for a brief family holiday at Whitechurch, near Tavistock, in Devon. While there, as well as playing golf and finding the caddie he and his father had hired attractive, on 21 March he began preparing

i That, as Whitehead put it in his 1909 report, 'probability cannot be solely derived from ideas of "frequency", more or less obscurely present in the mind'.

an essay on the construction of index numbers of general exchange value or the price level, the subject he had treated in his first essay for Marshall in October 1905. Working quickly, with few of his sources readily available,[77] he finished the essay in Versailles, on holiday with Duncan from 7 to 21 April, and submitted it on 23 April for the Adam Smith Prize. He won the prize of £60 which more than paid for the holiday. Parts of the work for the essay found their way into several subsequent publications, including *A Treatise on Probability* and *A Treatise on Money*.

With the beginning of the Easter Term 1909 Keynes began settling into King's and into a way of life that would not greatly change until the outbreak of war in 1914. He soon moved into a set of rooms on the top floor over the archway in the recently completed building on the south side of what is now Webb's Court, the 'back court' of King's. Just before the war he took over the adjacent set to give him more space and later made it, by King's standards, extremely comfortable – adding a bath and a w.c.,[j] built-in shelving and a series of painted panels, first by Duncan and later by Duncan and Vanessa Bell, on the east wall of the sitting room. Although this comfortable set remained his base of operations, he maintained a *pied à terre* in London, first in September–October 1909 at 10 Belgrave Road, St John's Wood, then from November 1909 until the end of 1911 at 21 Fitzroy Square and finally until the outbreak of war at 38 Brunswick Square, where he shared the house with Virginia and Adrian Stephen, Leonard Woolf and, for a time, his brother Geoffrey Keynes. After the outbreak of war, he moved to 10 Great Ormond Street and, then, with his Treasury post and the need for more space to 3 Gower Street, before making his final move in September 1916 to 46 Gordon Square. Except for the first, all his addresses were in that part of London known as Bloomsbury.

Initially, during term time Keynes spent most of his time in Cambridge, and made only fleeting visits to London for meetings, the theatre and friends. After the beginning of 1912, however, with the *Economic Journal* in his charge, he would often spend the middle part of each week in London. Out of term, he led a more peripatetic existence. He made frequent trips abroad, visited friends in the country, joined reading or camping parties of friends, or set himself up in the country for an extended period and invited friends down. Each year between 1909 and 1914 he made at least one trip abroad: to the Pyrenees with his family in June–July 1909; to Greece and Turkey with Duncan between March and May 1910; to Tunisia, Sicily and Italy with Duncan in March and April 1911; to the French Riviera in March–April 1912 and at Christmas 1913 with Gerald Shove and Duncan Grant respectively; to

j Keynes used to joke that it cost him two shillings and sixpence a flush (story from Richard Braithwaite, 25 November 1980). The practice of fellows making extensive structural alterations to their rooms at their own expense was common in Cambridge before the Second World War. See Boys Smith 1983, 35, 39, 256.

Hungary in September 1912 and Egypt in March 1913 by himself. In three of the six summers he took a place in the country to work and entertain friends: in 1909 and 1910 the Little House at Burford in Oxfordshire; in 1912 the Crown Inn at Everleigh near Marlborough. Generally his house parties proved quite successful, but in July 1912 his landlady at Everleigh was so shocked by the behaviour of his guests, which Keynes admitted involved 'reckless disregard of her feelings' that he had to pay an extra £40 in 'blood money' over what he had bargained for.[78] In the summers in which he did not organise a house in the country camping holidays took him to Clifford's Bridge, Devon (1911), Brandon, Suffolk (1913) and Coverack, Devon (1914).

Yet Cambridge was his base in the years before the War. It was also the source of his livelihood. In addition to his allowance from his father, his fellowship dividend and his lecturer's stipend (at first from Marshall and from 1911 as the University's Girdlers' Lecturer in Economics) there were the fees from lectures, coaching and supervision, directing studies for other colleges, and examining in Cambridge and elsewhere, and the beginnings of what would later be a large income from investments and publications. The amounts were not small by the standards of the day. In his first year in King's his earnings came to £595 and by 1914 this had risen to £900, leaving aside his allowance from Neville and the usual perks of College rooms and commons. This certainly compared well with the £700 to £1,000 per annum normally paid to Cambridge professors (subject then as now to a deduction if resident in a College), the £700 paid to his father as University Registrary after 1911, or the then average annual income of those in employment of £53 or the average salary income of £130 per annum. It certainly provided the basis for a comfortable way of life.

It is also true, however, that by modern Cambridge academic standards he was working hard for his income, especially as much of his income came effectively from piece rates. In the 1912–13 academic year he gave 84 lectures, over twice the 'normal' modern Cambridge stint of 40, as well as marking papers for students taking his lectures and supervisions. Outside term, he would supplement his income by taking on examining for the Local Examination Syndicate at various centres. No wonder he would complain to Duncan:

> The work of a don is the hardest work in the world . . . . I am becoming little more than a machine for selling economics by the hour.[79]

Indeed, it is probable that in these years, as later, Keynes tended towards overworking himself – especially since the routines of academic life were not his only activities.

Table 1 Keynes's Lectures 1909–14

Subject	Years taught	No. of terms	No. of hours per week
Money, Credit and Prices	1908/9–1909/10	2	2
The Stock Exchange and the Money Market	1909/10–1913/14	1	1
The Theory of Money	1909/10–1914/14	1	2
Company Finance and the Stock Exchange	1910/11–1913/14	1	1
Currency and Banking	1910/11–1913/14	1	2
The Currency and Finances of India	1910/11	1	1
Money Markets and Foreign Exchanges	1910/11–1913/14	1	1
Principles of Economics	1910/11–1913/14	3	2
The Monetary Affairs of India	1912/13	1	1

With his undergraduate experience of the Society and the various discussion societies that centred around dons in King's, it was not surprising that Keynes in his first year as a Fellow of King's would found yet another one, this time for economists. It was to last until the late 1970s, when it was dissolved in a wave of anti-elitism by his successors in the Faculty.k

This society was the Political Economy Club, which first met in Keynes's rooms in King's on 22 October 1909. Membership, then as later, was by invitation – normally on the basis of tripos performance and recommendations by Directors of Studies for undergraduates – in later years as post-graduate students became more common, graduates also attended. It became a convention for other dons to join in the discussion. The Club's selectivity was one of the many characteristics that Keynes carried over from the Society, such as the practice of giving papers and making comments from the hearthrug and the determination of the order of comments by the undergraduate members by drawing lots. The usual practice was for an undergraduate member to provide the paper for discussion, but contributions could come from the senior members, especially himself. Outsiders visiting him often attended and contributed. After the paper and the undergraduate comments, the dons present might make further points before Keynes summed up, as A. F. W. Plumptre remembered,

> stressing the essentials, taking sides in any disputes, introducing new
> points of view, pursuing some arguments to their logical conclusions

k The Club was re-started in the 1980s, but it did not see the decade out.

and others to their ultimate absurdities, laughing at lapses and mocking at muddles, with epigrams and paradoxes toppling over each other.[80]

Several accounts of the Club, recollected in tranquillity, have come down to us,[81] but one has survived from the heat of the moment in a student's letter home. The correspondent was Michael Straight.

> Then, Heaven help me, I had to go to his Political Economy Club, full of clever dons, third year students who had gotten firsts and we four. Some man called Zambart Lambardi (or with some such name)[l] read a paper on 'The Price Level and Stabilisation'. But beforehand slips were taken around, half with numbers, half with blanks, and any poor devil who drew a number had to get up in front of the fireplace and make a speech saying what he thought of Mr Z. L. Needless to say I got one! So I gritted my teeth and listened, determined to tell Mr Z. L. where he got off.
>
> I felt my stomach contracting continually, in fact almost shrinking through my back. I couldn't understand one word of his wretched paper! It was all about differential movements inside the price level. The way in which commodity A reacted on commodity B, given that commodity's A supply curve regarded in an inverted manner and considering of course the differential movement only was no more than the function of the demand curve of commodity B provided that the elasticity of substitution for one another was no more than $(e-1)/e$ etc . . . .
>
> I was to speak just before Keynes, – 9th; and three others like me spoke before me. Bauer,[m] the Austrian, spoke so fast that no one could understand what he said, so that he got away with it. Stamp,[n] the son of Josiah Stamp, made a long and intricate analogy about a traveller and a map in which he never once mentioned economics – so he get away with it; and Henderson[o] trotted out some phrase from Joan Robinson which he'd obviously just learnt beforehand and sat down before anyone could ask him what he meant – so he got away with it.
>
> I tried to say something about the price level and stabilisation and didn't get away with it! After I had finished a halting pointless speech I turned to Lambardi and put it in a form of a question. But he looked up with a perplexed face and said quite justifiably that he couldn't see the point of what I had just said.
>
> I turned round and asked in a despairing strangled voice if *anybody* could see the point in what I had just said.

l It was Mario Zanardi-Lamberti.
m P. T. Bauer, now Lord Bauer, who was actually Hungarian by birth.
n A. Maxwell Stamp.
o Probably A. Henderson of King's.

But needless to say none of them could and Keynes nobly rescued me by saying 'I think I know what you mean . . . .' and then explaining a long and difficult theory which of course had never entered my head but with which I fervently agreed.

Then he wound up brilliantly and I sneaked out before anyone had a chance to pin me down with any awkward questions as to what I actually had meant.[82]

It was through the Political Economy Club that Keynes came to know the best of each generation of Cambridge economists irrespective of College right down to his illness in 1937 – and to influence them. It was to the Club that he would give one of his last talks on 2 February 1946.

He also maintained links with other undergraduate societies. He frequented those he had attended as an undergraduate in King's: Lowes Dickinson's Discussion Society, the Walpole Society and Dickinson's Sunday evenings At Home. He spoke occasionally at the Union: on the 1909 Budget, in favour of free trade in November 1910, and in support of Sidney Webb in favour of the motion 'That the progressive reorganisation of Society on the lines of collectivist socialism is both inevitable and desirable' in February 1911. He was also on the fringes of Fabian activity in Cambridge, where the leading spirits – Ben Keeling of Trinity, Hugh Dalton, Gerald Shove and Rupert Brooke of King's, Justin Brooke of Emmanuel and Ka Cox of Newnham – moved in his circle. He spoke to the Fabians in December 1909 on foreign investment, probably using material prepared for his paper in Desmond MacCarthy's *New Quarterly* for February 1910. However, despite his links with the left of his day and his father's agitated diary entry of 6 September 1911 – 'Maynard avows himself a Socialist and is in favour of confiscation of wealth.'[83] – his political loyalties of these years were firmly free trade and Liberal.

Once clear of the constraints of the Civil Service, Keynes returned to active Liberal politics. He became secretary of the Cambridge University Free Trade Committee, nominally a non-partisan organisation, spoke to the Majlis, the Indian student debating society, on 'India and Protection' and joined the Eighty Club, one of the more progressive Liberal organisations. The two elections that began and ended 1910 saw him firmly on the Liberal side. He wrote letters supporting the party's position to the local press,[84] and supported Edwin Montagu for a local seat. Between 7 and 15 January he spoke for his friend Hilton Young, running against Austen Chamberlain in East Worcestershire, at a series of meetings around Birmingham. Crowds were large, up to 1,200 on one occasion. As he told Lytton Strachey, 'I've been enjoying myself here enormously, but am leaving here tomorrow. Life without a howling audience to address every evening will seem very dull'.[85] At the end of the year, although he had been asked to work for Hilton Young in Lancashire, as it was still term time he limited his speaking to local candidates such as Edwin Montagu, now the M.P for West Cambridgeshire. This hardly seems the 'weak' commitment to active politics suggested by Professor Skidelsky.[86]

He participated again in Liberal politics at the end of the summer of 1911 when he and Gerald Shove joined an Eighty Club party on a visit to Ireland. The party left Euston for Dublin on 15 September. They stayed in Dublin until the 18th and then proceeded to Belfast for three days before moving westwards through County Armagh to Galway. In the course of his travels Keynes became 'a much more convinced home-ruler than . . . before I started', but he found the party trying:

> I am frequently ashamed of them. With a few exceptions I've seldom met a more stupid and insignificant group of individuals. The want of intelligence is beyond belief, and they will say things one could not have thought possible.[87]

Eventually, tired of 'crowd life' he abandoned the party at Killaloe and spent a week on his own. The journey had been interesting, but it had not raised his opinion of politicians:

> You haven't, I suppose, ever mixed with politicians at close quarters. They're *awful*. I think some of these must have been the dregs anyhow, but I've discovered what previously I didn't believe possible, that politicians behave in private life and say exactly the same things as they do in public. Their stupidity is inhuman.[88]

This was not his last contact with politicians.

As a young don, Keynes also started to be involved in the more practical affairs of his College and the University. In 1909 he became an Inspector of Accounts for King's – one of the three fellows appointed by the Governing Body to examine with the Provost and Vice Provost the Bursars' stewardship for the annual Congregation. In the three Inspectors' reports with which he was associated, there were requests that the Bursars consider the more profitable employment of the sums they held on current account. In 1909 the request was muted; in 1910 the Inspectors presented an argued case for better management by pointing out that for only two weeks in the year did the College's cash balances fall below £3,000, while for all but eight weeks they stood above £4,500 and for nearly a third of the year above £8,000 – this in the face of a predictable stream of outgoings. With no action, there were even sharper comments from the Inspectors in 1911 when they also suggested investigating the possibility of improvements and economies in the administration of the kitchens. Still there was no action, although the administration of the College had made one move: in November 1910 the Provost, M. R. James, had enquired whether Keynes would be prepared to act as one of the Bursars. Nothing came of this for the moment, although in 1911 he was elected to the Estates, or College finance, Committee. In the face of sustained bursarial inactivity it was not surprising that Keynes, with the assistance of Dillwyn Knox and John Clapham, organised the younger fellows into a junior caucus and moved three motions at the next Congregation. The first renewed the attack on the Bursar's large cash balances. It was carried. The second asked for a committee to consider the integration of prices and contracts in the kitchen, buttery and combination room departments and to enquire into the terms and conditions of employment of the College's staff. It too was carried and Keynes was elected to the Committee as one of the junior caucus's candidates.[89] The third was a motion of non-confidence in the senior Bursar in which Keynes proposed to increase the fellowship dividend to £130 from the £120 recommended by the Bursar. It was heavily defeated. However, at the same meeting, Keynes was elected to the College Council. There matters rested for the moment, although in 1913 Keynes was a member of a committee to consider the First Bursar's resignation. (The First Bursar, C. E. Grant, remained in office until 1919.)

Some indication of the attitudes that Keynes and the other younger fellows were up against would be revealed in 1915 when he suggested to Grant that the College invest its spare cash in Treasury bills, by then a regularly available financial instrument in London, and also switch some longer-dated Trustee securities into such bills. At the time, Keynes as a Treasury civil servant was involved in preparing the terms of issue of the second War Loan.[90] The Bursar replied on 4 May that he would probably act on Keynes's first suggestion, but that he would not act on the second. He continued:

> It would seem that this would clearly be to speculate on the value of gilt edged securities nine months hence. And it is a not a matter of great importance to the College. Our mobile capital bears only a small proportion to our total assets, and the occasions on which we realise any part of it extremely rare. We are under no obligation to allow for depreciation of capital.[91]

In University circles, Keynes was also starting to make his mark. In November 1909 he was elected to the Special Boards of Studies for Economics and Politics and for the Indian Civil Service Courses. The next year he became secretary of the Economics Board. Neville Keynes was chairman.

He also became involved in University affairs outside his subject, in particular with the question of University reform. The years after 1905 had seen a renewal of attempts at reform in Cambridge. These attempts reflected several factors: the financial difficulties of the University under the 1882 statutes which had made no provision for falling agricultural prices and rents after the 1870s; the inefficiency of the existing General Board of the Faculties; the unresolved position of the women's Colleges and their members in the

University; and pressures for curricular changes. Most important in many minds was the role of non-resident MAs in the current scheme of things, for through their votes in the Senate they could prevent even small changes in the University's day-to-day operations favoured by those residents actively involved in the University's teaching, research and administration. Similar discontent existed at Oxford. In 1907 Bishop Gore moved unsuccessfully in the House of Lords for a Royal Commission to inquire into Oxford and Cambridge Universities. In 1909 Lord Curzon, the Chancellor of Oxford, published his *Principles and Methods of University Reform*. In the same year, in Cambridge the Council of the Senate was asked to consider reports on the constitution and government of the University and on the relations between the University and the Colleges. Rather than appointing a special syndicate to do so, which was the normal procedure, the Council dealt with the matters itself and produced a report in February 1910 which, among other things, recommended a House of Residents to replace the Senate for matters of current University administration, and a strengthening of the central University bodies. The report met a hostile reception, was revised, but went nowhere: in February 1911 the Council of the Senate stated that it intended to proceed no further with the matters.

As a result, on 7 February 1911, a number of members of the University, including Maynard Keynes, attended a meeting that created a University Reforms Committee. Other Kingsmen actively involved were John Clapham, Walter Durnford and Lowes Dickinson. The Committee's object was to formulate proposals for a possible future commission of inquiry and to do so it set up sub-committees to deal with the constitution of the University and the relation of the University to women students, the finances of the University and the Colleges, and the organisation of teaching and research in the University. Keynes took an active part, producing a series of 'Proposals for College Contributions to a Common University Fund' (April 1911) and a paper on the 'Organisation of Teaching and Research in the University and Colleges' (October 1912), as well as serving on the finance sub-committee and keeping in touch with a similar group at Oxford. The labours of the Committee came to nought, but Keynes gained experience that would stand him in good stead after 1919. Moreover, both his papers display attitudes to certain issues of academic policy that he would retain until his death: an emphasis on strengthening the role of the University rather than the Colleges in facilitating advanced work and research, symbolised by the appointment of 'at least 30 new University posts of the standing of Reader';[92] an emphasis on the important role of University bodies such as Boards of Studies in the co-ordination and encouragement of good lecturing, particularly through schemes involving payment by results; and an emphasis on the need, in a world where central government finance for universities had yet to emerge, of a system of progressive taxation of Colleges to finance the changes.

Keynes's interests in finance in his teaching and in College administration was in part a reflection of his own activities. By 1914 he had become a significant investor on his own account with net investment assets of £4,500. His career as an investor began with what he called in his own records a 'special fund' or 'special account' – the repository for his birthday money, academic prizes and the like, which Neville Keynes had accumulated for his son and which he transferred to him on his majority. Maynard Keynes used the proceeds for loans to his friends (Swithinbank, Lytton, James Strachey, Duncan, John Sheppard, H. T. J. Norton and George Mallory), for furniture and for books on probability, but from July 1905 the 'fund' found its major use as the basis for Stock Exchange investments. His first purchase occurred on 6 July 1905 when he bought four shares in the Marine Insurance Company for £160. Just under six months later he purchased four shares in the engineering firm Mather and Platt. He then made no further investments until 1910. From the extensive records that survive in his own papers, it would seem that this reflected the fact that he was living well up to his income and saving only a few pounds a year. Once his income rose to a level that permitted larger savings, Keynes expanded his portfolio. By 1911 he was not only buying additional shares but also making switches and helping his father manage certain family trust funds. Two years later he indulged in his first outright speculation in the shares of US Steel using money of his own plus some from John Sheppard. It was not wildly successful: it netted him £5 15s.0d. However, he was gaining confidence and on 3 April 1914 he came to an arrangement with Roger Fry, whereby Fry loaned Keynes £1,000, repayable at six months' notice on either side, at 4½ per cent per annum. With the money Keynes set up an investment fund on which any profits or losses after the payment of the 4½ per cent were shared equally. (This arrangement lasted until January 1920 when Fry loaned the money to Duncan Grant for investment in another Keynes speculative venture, The Syndicate. The sum was later used in other speculative vehicles and after many vicissitudes returned to Fry's heirs in 1935.) Such speculation was not yet the norm, however. Keynes's dealing activities were limited and purchases of additional new securities were the order of the day. As in many other areas, a change of scale was to come after 1918.

NOTES

1 For a marvellous discussion of the Office and its world, see Kaminsky 1986. The quotation is from Robin Winks's Foreword, p. xii.
2 Chandarvarkar 1990, 11.
3 Ibid., 26.
4 KCKP, JMK to JNK, 7 November 1906.
5 KCKP, 'Military Department. Distribution of Work', 12 November 1906.
6 Kaminsky 1986, 22.
7 KCKP, JMK to GLS, 7 March 1907.

8 KCKP, JMK to GLS, 1 March 1907.
9 For more detail on Keynes's India Office activities and an assessment of his skills, see Chandavarkar 1990, 10–19.
10 KCKP, JMK to GLS, 18 April 1907.
11 Fawcett Library, JMK to P. Strachey, 5 February 1907. I am grateful to Virginia Clark for providing this letter.
12 KCKP, JMK to Margaret Keynes, 6 February 1907.
13 Quoted in Wilkinson 1980a, 51.
14 BERG, JMK to GLS, 20 June 1906.
15 KCKP, JMK to GLS, 10 April 1907.
16 KCKP, JMK to GLS, 12 April 1907. Of course, Keynes did not know what Mary Berenson had heard from Ray a year before. See above p. 104–5.
17 See, for example, KCKP, JMK to GLS, 6 and 8 November 1907.
18 The phrase is Irving Goffman's 1968, 41–5.
19 KCKP, JMK to JNK, 20 March 1907.
20 KCKP, A. C. Pigou to JMK, undated, but mention of the topic and the date are consistent with this meeting; Political Economy Club 1921, 152.
21 KCKP, JMK to GLS, 5 July 1907.
22 KCKP, JMK to FAK, 13 July 1907.
23 This was the basis for Fay's remark above (p. 54). KCKP, JMK to GLS, 13 July 1907.
24 KCKP, JMK to GLS, 30 August 1907.
25 KCKP, JMK to GLS, 13 September 1907.
26 KCKP, JMK to JNK, 5 October 1907.
27 CUL, Add.7857, 19 October 1907; KCKP, JMK to GLS, 16 October 1907.
28 KCKP, JMK to GLS, 18 October 1907.
29 KCKP, JMK to GLS, 30 October 1907.
30 KCKP, JMK to GLS, 6 November 1907.
31 KCKP, JMK to FAK, 11, 15 and 29 November and 6 December 1906.
32 KCKP, M. Berenson to JMK, 20 January 1908.
33 CUL, Add.7858, 1 and 3 March 1908.
34 CUL, Add.7858, 2 February 1908.
35 KCKP, JMK to JNK, 18 March 1908.
36 See also, for example, CUL, Add.7562, W. R. Sorley to JNK, 17 March 1908.
37 KCKP, JMK to GLS, 23 March 1908.
38 One on 24 February and the one of 13 March quoted above.
39 BL, ADD.53792, GLS to D. Grant, 20 January 1906.
40 BL, ADD.60706, GLS to James Strachey, 1 May 1908; ADD.60707, GLS to James Strachey, 7 July 1908.
41 Holroyd 1973, 290–1.
42 *JMK*, XV, 13.
43 KCKP, JMK to JNK, 21 April 1908.
44 KCKP, JNK to JMK, 23 April 1908.
45 KCKP, JMK to GLS, 9 May 1908.
46 KCKP, JMK to JNK, 22 May 1908. See also ibid., JMK to GLS, 22 May 1908 for more of Dickinson's letter.
47 *JMK*, XV, 15.
48 BL, ADD.57930, JMK to DG, 5 June 1908.
49 CUL, Add.7858, 12 June and 17 July 1908.
50 KCKP, JMK to B. W. Swithinbank, 5 and 10 June 1908.
51 *JMK*, XV, 16; KCKP, JMK to FAK, 16 June and 2 July 1908.
52 KCKP, JMK to FAK, 16 June and 17 July 1908.

53 BL, ADD.57930, JMK to DG, 15 July 1908.
54 KCKP, GLS to JMK, 16, 21, 23 and 26 July 1908; JMK to GLS, 20, 22, 24 and 27 July 1908.
55 BL, ADD.60707, James Strachey to GLS, 26 July 1908.
56 BL, ADD.60707, GLS to James Strachey, 27 July 1908.
57 KCKP, JMK to GLS, 4 August 1908.
58 KCKP, JMK to GLS, 9 August 1908.
59 BL, ADD.57930, JMK to DG, 12 August 1908; 29 July 1908.
60 KCKP, JMK to JNK, 4 September 1908.
61 KCKP, JMK to JNK, 13 and 27 September 1908.
62 *JMK*, XI, 1–22.
63 BL, ADD.57930, JMK to DG, 25 October 1908.
64 BL, ADD.60707, GLS to James Strachey, 17 and 26 November 1908.
65 KCKP, JMK to GLS, 5 November 1908; BL, ADD.57930, JMK to DG, 24 November 1908.
66 KCKP, JMK to B. W. Swithinbank, 17 December 1908.
67 CUL, Add.7859, 31 January 1909.
68 BL, ADD.57930, JMK to DG, 19 January 1909.
69 *JMK*, XII, 701–8, 765–7, 769–72.
70 BL, ADD.57930, JMK to DG, 16 February 1909.
71 Political Economy Club 1921, 157.
72 BL, ADD.57930, JMK to DG, 10 February 1909.
73 BL, ADD.57930, JMK to DG, 19 January and 17 February 1909; KCKP, JMK to GLS, 21 March 1909.
74 BL, ADD.57930, JMK to DG, 31 January 1909.
75 BL, ADD.57930, JMK to DG, 14 February 1909.
76 BL, ADD.57930, JMK to DG, 5 February 1909.
77 *JMK*, XI, 50. The whole essay covers pages 49–156 of the same volume.
78 BL, ADD.57930, JMK to DG, 26 July 1912.
79 BL, ADD.57930, JMK to DG, 20 October 1909.
80 Plumptre 1947, 363.
81 See Robinson 1947; Plumptre 1947; Harrod 1951; Johnson and Johnson 1978; Bryce and Salant in Patinkin and Leith 1977.
82 KCKP, D. Elmhirst to JMK, 19 October 1935 reporting Michael Straight's letter to her. An account of the meeting also appears in Straight 1983, 66.
83 CUL, Add.7861.
84 *JMK*, XV, 39–42, 43. Professor Skidelsky mistakenly refers to one of these, that of 29 December 1909, as an article.
85 KCKP, JMK to GLS, 14 January 1910.
86 Skidelsky 1985, 241.
87 KCKP, JMK to FAK, 24 September 1911.
88 BL, ADD.57930, JMK to DG, 3 October 1911.
89 KCKP, Box 5, A. D. Knox to JMK, 20 November 1912.
90 Below p. 246; *JMK*, XVI, 95–107.
91 KCKP, Box 3, C. E. Grant to JMK, 4 May 1915.
92 KCKP, J.M.K., 'Organisation of Teaching and Research in the University and Colleges', 25 October 1912, p. 2.

8

THE YOUNG ECONOMIST

With 1909 we can really begin to consider Keynes's career as an economist. Prior to that, although he had read considerably, gone to Marshall's lectures and written papers for him, as well as attended one meeting of the Political Economy Club and joined the Economic Club at University College and the Royal Economic Society, he could still be said to be 'toying' with the subject. He had published a review in the *Statistical Journal* of a study of social and industrial problems in West Ham. As a by-product of his dissertation he had entered into a brief controversy in the *Economic Journal* with G. Udny Yule on the construction of the Board of Trade's index numbers of real wages,[1] but he had yet to publish anything substantial. Yet, from this time onwards, even though he would naturally maintain a professional interest in index numbers and would spend an immense amount of time revising his fellowship dissertation for publication, it was as an economist that he would earn his keep as a teacher. As such he would appear most frequently in print. Moreover, it was as an economist that he saw himself. On 30 January 1909, he drew up the following list:

Papers to be written

The 'Long Run' in Economics (The element of doubt in the determination of value)

The Indian Gold Standard Reserve

Proposals for an International Currency

Mathematical Notes on the Median

English Gold Reserves

The Logical Basis of the Theory of Correlation

A Plea for a new official index number of prices

The Riskless Rate of Interest

Monographs

The Method of Index Numbers

The Theory of Crises and Commercial Fluctuations

Treatises

The Principles of Probability

Methods of Statistics

Textbooks

The Principles of Money

The Mathematical Organon of Economics

The list is of interest not only because Keynes actually completed a significant number of these projects, but also because it shows that, from the outset, he had a clear view of where his main interests in economics lay. With the exception of the first and last items in the list, all the more strictly economic projects fall within the area of what one might call monetary economics. It is thus worth considering how and why Keynes may have made these choices at a time when he had only given *four* University lectures on 'Money Credit and Prices'.

Although Keynes had listed 'Money, Credit and Prices' as one of the specialities in the Tripos towards which he was 'inclined' in October 1905, it is not clear from his reading over the previous few years that he would have chosen money rather than anything else. Marshall certainly had not expected it when he made his 'tentative' job offer, for he only mentioned 'general economics'. True, as a part of his 1905–6 reading programme Keynes had read Bagehot's *Lombard Street*, Jevons' *Investigations in Currency and Finance*, Cassel's *The Nature and Necessity of Interest*, Goschen's *The Foreign Exchanges*, Clare's *ABC of the Foreign Exchanges*, Jevons's *Money*, Leonard Darwin's *Bimetallism*, and Böhm-Bawerk's *Recent Literature on Interest*, as well as a couple of lesser-known books on corporate finance and stock exchanges. He had also read some of the standard sets of 'Principles' (Ricardo, Jevons, Marshall, Nicholson, Sidgwick and Pierson). He had, however, also read in other specialist areas, such as taxation or industrial organisation, without becoming attracted to them. Thus I do not think we can put his choice down solely to his reading – or for that matter the essays he wrote for Marshall – even if one places significant weight on his early enthusiasm for Jevons.[2] His India Office experience, even after he moved departments in March 1907, had not been in the monetary area. However, his sixteen months in the Revenue, Statistics and Commerce Department, with its access to a wide range of papers, had coincided with an international financial crisis. The impact of that financial crisis on India was the subject of his first full-length article.

There were, however, strong internal Cambridge reasons for Keynes's specialising in money. Monetary economics had been Marshall's most frequent subjects for lectures, if not for publication. On his retirement, this work could have been taken over by the Keynes's Harvey Road neighbour H. S. Foxwell, who had a long record of teaching and publication in the area. But Foxwell had been the unsuccessful candidate for the Chair in 1908. He believed he deserved it more than Pigou. He was piqued with the result and withdrew from the teaching programme of the Faculty, never to return, even when its resources were sorely stretched by the demands of the First World War.[a] The resulting gap in the teaching could hardly be filled by Walter Layton, whose interests were in labour and industrial organisation. Nor did it fit anyone else's interests. Maynard Keynes could, and did, fill that gap, when Pigou asked him on 6 July 1908 to lecture on 'Money credit and prices' treated 'as realistically as possible'.[3]

During the last decade of his teaching career, Marshall came more and more to the view that the intellectual activities of his generation and its predecessors had fairly firmly established a body of what he called qualitative analysis, or basic economic theory, but that it had not made similar strides with quantitative analysis, or the actual determination of the relative strengths of the various tendencies suggested by theory.[4] As Maynard Keynes's concern in this scheme of things was to be monetary economics, we should look briefly at Marshall's own contribution.

Marshall published relatively little on monetary theory – the economist's shorthand for theories concerning the role of money in the economy. He had unpublished manuscripts dating from as early as 1871 and, as I have said, he found it a favourite topic for lectures, yet, apart from one article 'Remedies for Fluctuations of General Prices' in the *Contemporary Review* for March 1887, he confined expressions of his views to evidence before official enquiries and occasional passages in *The Economics of Industry* and *Principles of Economics* until the publication of *Money, Credit and Commerce* in his eighty-first year.[5] His monetary theory thus became, as Keynes put it, 'a matter of oral tradition' to which his successors added articles before Marshall's own antiquated version appeared in print.[6]

As one would expect, at the centre of Marshall's treatment of monetary theory was an attempt to apply the same procedure or principle that proved so successful in the *Principles* – the careful analysis of supply and demand – to money. As a result of this attempt, he and his successors developed a distinctive approach to the determination of the value of money (or the level of prices) – the Cambridge cash balances version of the quantity theory of money. Here the primary focus was on the factors determining the demand for money, first by individuals and then by the community as a whole. In Marshall's theory, individuals held cash balances for the purposes of convenience in effecting transactions or of speculation (or taking advantage

---

a In 1916, when Pigou successfully appealed against his conscription to a military tribunal on the grounds that there was nobody in Cambridge capable of doing his job, Foxwell wrote an angry letter which led the military member of the tribunal to appeal the decision on the grounds that Foxwell could replace Pigou. The appeal failed on the grounds, proposed by Clapham, that Foxwell, even though he offered to do 'not less than the average work for a Professor', with his chair at University College, London would not be able to bear the heavier than normal load that Pigou had carried while every other member of the Faculty bar himself was engaged on war service of some kind (Maloney 1985, 224–5). Pigou himself drove a voluntary ambulance on his vacations.

of favourable turns in prices). They weighed the advantages from holding such balances with the results of the alternative employment of the same resources in acquiring commodities or financial assets. The total sum of such balances held, determined by the marginal balancing of advantages and disadvantages, would equal the stock of cash in existence. From such a conception, the quantity theory followed straightforwardly. If, given the payments arrangements and institutions of the community in question, individuals had decided to hold a certain proportion of their real resources in cash form, then, assuming *ceteris paribus* (or other things remaining equal), a change in the quantity of cash would result in a proportional change in prices.

Marshall's approach to the demand for money implicitly provided a mechanism through which this change in the quantity of money would affect prices. It was this mechanism which in some eyes made his approach potentially more fruitful than the competing transactions approach to the quantity theory normally associated in the literature with the American economist Irving Fisher. For in Marshall's scheme of things an increase in the quantity of money would, in the first instance, induce individuals to attempt to alter the composition of their portfolios – which, the reader will remember, contained cash, real assets and securities. These attempts to alter portfolios would themselves affect the prices of the components involved and hence rates of return, such as the rates of interest on bills and bonds, with consequent effects on prices or levels of activity. It was this emphasis on the indirect effects of changes in the quantity of money working through relative rates of return to affect prices that lay at the heart of Marshall's theories of balance-of-payments adjustment under fixed (or gold standard) exchange rates and the credit (or trade) cycle. However, Marshall adumbrated only the broadest of outlines of the approach.

The same was true of his examination of its implications for policy. Although Marshall had only a brief fling as a monetary reformer, most notably before the Gold and Silver Commission and in his 'Remedies for Fluctuations of General Prices' (1887),[7] he was prepared to see the gold standard replaced by a symmetallic standard where sterling would be linked to the joint value of the two precious metals (gold and silver) or, ideally if one were interested in domestic price stability, by a tabular standard where the value of money would be indexed to a basket of commodities. This version of what would become later known as 'managed money', even though the ever-cautious Marshall dropped his public support after 1887, had several supporters in the years before 1914.[8] Here as elsewhere in Marshall's monetary economics, filling in the details and tracing further implications was left to his successors.

At the time Maynard Keynes began his career as an economist in Cambridge, the University's provision for teaching for the Economics Tripos consisted of the new Professor of Political Economy, Pigou, and the Girdlers' Lecturer, H. O. Meredith, who had just succeeded Pigou and opened the way for Layton's appointment as lecturer. In addition, there were the two 'lecturers' paid for by Marshall, Keynes and Layton. Additional teaching in theory came from W. E. Johnson and additional teaching in economic history from John Clapham, newly returned from Leeds as a fellow of King's in history in succession to Oscar Browning, and C. R. Fay, now a fellow of Christ's. Lowes Dickinson covered political science. The class lists before 1914 show that this small group managed to attract and train a distinguished collection of students, for among those with first class honours were the subsequently significant economists Frederick Lavington, Gerald Shove, Hubert Henderson, Dennis Robertson, Claude Guillebaud and Philip Sargent Florence. Other Tripos candidates who went on to notable careers were the future financial journalist Oscar Hobson, the future Nobel Peace Prize winner Philip Noel-Baker and a future Chancellor of the Exchequer, Hugh Dalton. Keynes would die while serving the last. Then there were those with whom Keynes would work in other capacities: Dudley Ward, Harold Wright, Frank Nixon and Lawrence Cadbury. Student numbers may have been small, but quality was high.

I have briefly discussed the state in which Marshall left monetary theory. As for practice, the problems on which Keynes could cut his teeth were, fortunately, Indian. Although it may seem odd in the last decade of the twentieth century, before 1914 the matter of appropriate monetary arrangements for India was one of the most discussed issues among British monetary economists.[b] The discussions had their origins in the events of the 1870s, when an increasing number of countries at the centre of the international monetary system, led by Germany, had formally or informally abandoned bimetallism (the system under which gold and silver were both convertible into national currencies at fixed prices) and adopted a gold standard under which currencies were convertible only into gold. The result was a decline in the demand for silver for official monetary reserves and also for coinage as countries shifted from full-weight to token silver coins. At the same time, there was an expansion in new supplies of silver, largely from new mines in the American west.

The combination of decreased demand and increased supply led to a fall in the world (and the gold) price of silver with important effects for countries still remaining on a silver standard. One of these was India.[9] She remained on a silver standard until 1893, when after the breakdown of international negotiations for the restoration of bimetallism at the Brussels Conference of

---

b So well discussed that it passed into the popular consciousness to a sufficient extent that in Oscar Wilde's *The Importance of Being Earnest* Miss Prism could send Cecily, the play's heroine, to her books with the words 'Cecily, you will read your political economy in my absence. The chapter on the Fall of the Rupee you may omit. It is somewhat too sensational. Even these metallic problems have their melodramatic side'.

1892, she closed her mints to the free coinage of silver. The depreciation of (and fluctuations in) the gold value of the rupee had inconvenienced foreign traders and disturbed public finance, always a potentially explosive issue in India, especially as the Government of India had large, fixed annual commitments denominated in sterling, the so-called Home Charges, part of which which financed the India Office establishment.

The closure of the Indian mints raised the question of what to do next. In the course of the 1890s, while the subject was discussed by two official committees, the Government pegged the rupee to gold and left a token silver and paper currency in circulation. Although it retained a gold reserve, the main method used by the Government of India to peg the exchanges was the maintenance of sterling balances in London, which rose or fell as the authorities sold or purchased rupees for sterling to keep the rupee exchange rate within the gold points. Such an interim arrangement did not satisfy financial purists who believed that a proper gold standard on the model of arrangements in advanced countries such as Britain necessitated the internal circulation of gold coin. As a result, the India Currency Committee of 1898 reported in 1899 in favour of such a solution and in 1900 an attempt was made to put sovereigns into circulation at currency offices, District Treasuries, banks and post offices. The experiment was not a success as few sovereigns remained in circulation. They were exported, returned to the Government, or melted down by bullion dealers. The authorities abandoned the experiment, shipped a large part of the gold reserve to London and continued the gold-exchange-standard system which had come into being in the 1890s. The evolving regime came under severe strain during the international financial crisis of 1907–8 – but survived.

Keynes's first article, 'Recent Economic Events in India', was an attempt to link the high Indian price level of 1907, India's unfavourable balance of trade in 1908 and the effects of the resulting support of the Indian exchange rate on the London money market with the behaviour of the evolving currency system we have described. As such, it was an exercise in institutional description and the analysis of economic behaviour. He argued that with existing currency arrangements, a favourable balance of trade plus high levels of new overseas investment in India had led to an increase in her money supply and a rise in prices. The rise in prices, which had been greater than that of her overseas competitors, had then produced some reduction in exports and a rise in imports. The consequent deterioration in the balance of trade might, he argued, have resulted in some check to activity, but famine in 1907–8 and a sharp fall in the inflow of new foreign investment, a result of the effects of the 1907 American financial crisis on European markets, combined with the weakening trade balance to produce severe balance-of-payments difficulties, pressure on the official reserves and the need for official borrowing in London to meet the Government of India's commitments in Britain. He concluded from the experience of 1907–8 that it was clear that the Government of India had not yet hit on the ideal currency system, but at this stage he did not attempt to propose improvements. These were to come later.

The article demonstrated his grasp of institutional detail and his ability to marshal the appropriate descriptive economic statistics, while keeping his eye firmly on the underlying processes at work. His attempts to estimate the various components of India's balance of payments, particularly foreign investment in India, also led him into other discussions. During these it became clear that he would have the support of his former India Office superiors. Always interested in minimising and, if possible, controlling the direction of discussion on such matters, if only to keep them out of Parliament, his former superiors found in Keynes a successor to Marshall, whose retirement meant that he was less likely to be as available as in the past.[10] As Sir Thomas Holderness put it to Keynes after he had published two letters in *The Economist* on the amount of foreign capital in India:

> In your economic studies don't forget the field of observations India offers. We here have not the time (and possibly not the technical training) for a close examination of the economic phenomena of India. You will help us if you will do what we fail to do.[11]

It was not surprising if in these circumstances his writings on India reflected what might be called the India Office view of the world.[12]

Keynes would establish himself as an economist. But in looking at this process, we should realise that professional economists early in this century probably did not have the range of outlets for publication they have now. True there were many fewer economists.[c] There were only three internationally established, English language journals – the *Economic Journal, Journal of Political Economy* and *Quarterly Journal of Economics*.[d] The *Statistical Journal* of the Royal Statistical Society carried a substantial number of more applied articles and publishers, then as now, were always looking for new material in book form. But for less than book-length pieces individuals were perforce committed to places their successors would probably not consider 'professional'. On the other hand, as we have seen from the discussions of Marshall's and Foxwell's careers, the volume of output necessary to 'get on' was smaller: 'publish or perish' had not yet reached academia.

Keynes's first substantial publication after his 'Recent Economic Events in India' grew out of the controversies surrounding the 1909 Budget. This

c In 1915 there were 85 academic appointments in economics and related subjects in British universities, as compared with 20 in 1891 and 286 in 1939. Individual memberships in the Royal Economic Society with British addresses (British plus overseas in brackets) for the same years were: 1891 – 594 (706); 1915 – 502 (697); 1939 – 2,409 (3,989) (Coats and Coats 1973, Tables I and II).

d The *American Economic Review* did not begin to appear until 1911.

had provided for increased income tax, a super-tax on incomes over £5,000, increased death duties, and imposed taxes on unearned increments in land values and heavy taxes on the drink trade. The Budget had led to charges from tariff reformers that the new Liberal policies would drive British investment out of the country. It was to analyse these charges that Keynes prepared 'Great Britain's Foreign Investments'. He started the piece at Burford in August, had a draft ready for Desmond MacCarthy, the editor of the *New Quarterly* by the end of September, and revised it over the autumn.[13]

The article opened with an examination of the considerations that influenced investors: the rate of interest, the kind and degree of risk, the ease of sale and the non-economic 'desire to further some cause or enterprise for other reasons than those of economic profit'. In examining these in more detail, traces of lines of thought characteristic of the author of a recent dissertation on probability showed themselves. Thus, as regards the rate of interest:

> The investor will naturally be determined by the *net* rate . . . . More-over, he will be affected . . . not by the net income which he will receive from his investment in the long run but by his expectations. These will often depend on fashion, upon advertisement, or upon purely irrational waves of optimism and depression. Similarly by risk we must mean, not the real risk as measured by the actual average yield of the class of investment over a period of years to which the expectation refers, but the risk as estimated, wisely or foolishly, by the investor . . . .
>
> Since the risk of which we must take account is the subjective risk, the feeling, that is to say in the mind of the investor, its magnitude very largely depends upon the amount of relevant information that is easily accessible to him. What would be a risky investment for the ignorant speculator may be exceptionally safe for the well-informed expert. The amount of the risk to any investor principally depends, in fact, upon the degree of ignorance respecting the circumstances and prospects of the investment he is considering . . . .

He argued that in an old country such as Britain the longer-term tendency should be for a rising level of overseas investment, because high levels of past investment had increased the number of securities that could be bought and sold with ease, thus diminishing capital uncertainty, and because the world overseas was becoming more stable and less risky. If, for reasons of policy, the authorities thought that the level of such investment was too high they could reduce it through such devices as taxes on the transfer or quotation of foreign securities in London.

He then turned directly to the charges of the tariff reformers. He noted in passing that one of the initial effects of tariff reform would be an increase in overseas investment as protection improved the balance of trade. More seriously, he argued that there was no evidence that higher taxes or death duties had encouraged individuals to invest more abroad as a preliminary step towards emigration or that tax evasion was becoming more prevalent, given the difficulties of doing so and the small sums involved. As he concluded:

> It is within human nature that a strong party man would be willing at first to go to the necessary trouble and expense and to the risks attendant on perjury, in order to satisfy the prejudices of his political leaders, but it is questionable whether he would long continue so unbusinesslike and emotional a practice.

But he emphasised the role of popular opinion:

> We must remember, however, at this point that the relative amount of foreign investment is determined, not by what is actually reasonable, but by what the average investor believes to be reasonable. Politicians, therefore, who persuade their hearers that the probable course of future legislation makes it reasonable to invest abroad, may have some influence, whether what they say is or is not true, in sending away capital.

He ended the article with a more detailed examination of the relative yields of home and overseas securities, the areas into which British overseas investment had been flowing and the recent levels of such investment. All of these suggested to him that there was no evidence that the balance of advantage between home and foreign investment had recently shifted, that there was a recent undue want of enterprise in Britain, or that investment was tending to flow to the competitive industries of major foreign rivals. All in all, he concluded, the case of the tariff reformers was not sustained by the existing evidence.

Keynes's next sustained contribution to the journals also reflected his contemporaneous work on probability. In May 1910 the Francis Galton Laboratory for National Eugenics published a report by Ethel M. Elderton (with the assistance of Karl Pearson) entitled *A First Study of the Influence of Parental Alcoholism on the Physique and Ability of the Offspring*. On the basis of two samples of children taken for other purposes in Manchester and Edinburgh, it attempted to come to some conclusions on the issue by comparing many characteristics of the samples from temperate and intemperate households. The report was written in an academic style and pleaded for a dispassionate study of such social questions. However, the report's finding that there was no marked relationship between parental alcoholism and the intelligence, physique and disease experience of the children in the sample was intuitively somewhat surprising – and inevitably became the subject of newspaper comment in the context of contemporary concerns with temperance reform. Pearson, a vigorous controversialist, played a significant role in subsequent discussions in the letter columns of the press.

Keynes made two unsuccessful attempts to take part in the correspondence in *The Times*.[14] In consequence, he was limited to the *Statistical Journal*, where he reviewed the work in July,[15] and submitted a letter in December replying to Pearson's September 1910 pamphlet, issued in a new series 'Questions of the Day and of the Fray' by the Department of Applied Mathematics at University College, London, *Supplement to the Memoir Entitled: The Influence of Parental Alcoholism on the Physique and Ability of the Offspring: A Reply to the Cambridge Economists*[16] and a letter in February 1911 replying to Pearson's letter of January 1911.[17] At every stage of the controversy, he had the advice and support of Pigou to whom he showed the original review, and of Marshall, who mentioned the initial review favourably in *The Times* of 4 August and whom Keynes consulted over his two published letters.

The controversy, once it is stripped of its rhetoric, saw Keynes trying to establish a number of basic statistical points:

(1) 'In the first place no adequate attempt is made to display to the reader the real character of the evidence upon which it is based. As in an investigation of this kind the value of the conclusion mainly turns upon the trustworthiness of the original material to which the mathematical machinery is applied, everything ought to be said, that can be, to enable the reader to form some sort of independent judgement respecting it.'

(2) 'In the second place, it may be doubted whether, in several instances, anything has been gained by the calculation of coefficients of correlation. . . . Trouble which might have been spent on improving the original material has been needlessly expended on computations which add little to our knowledge, and which confuse, though they may also impress, all readers outside a very restricted class.'[18]

The main burden of his discussion turned on (1), for it was here that the basis for the contrary conclusion lay. Here, Keynes looked for satisfaction on three points:

(1) that the experiment is on a considerable scale;
(2) that the classification – in this case into alcoholic and non-alcoholic – has been skilfully and uniformly carried out;
(3) that its field is truly representative of the population at large.[19]

The nature of the sample and its classification were to Keynes the principal problems. Going back to the original material from which Elderton and Pearson worked, he argued that the sample was far from representative of the population as a whole – a position on which he expanded in both his January and February replies, taking the opportunity to suggest as well that the handling of the wage statistics for the two defectively classified sub-groups of the already non-representative sample had not been reported correctly. He concluded:

> As a contribution to the solution of the general problem the memoir is almost valueless, and, from its failure to direct the reader's attention to essential facts, actually misleading. As a study in statistical method it is a salient example of the application of needlessly complex mathematical apparatus to initial data, of which the true character is insufficiently explained, and which are in fact unsuited to the problem at hand.[20]

All in all, he had given as well as he got – and that was quite a lot of abuse from Pearson.[21]

While he was continuing his controversy with Pearson, Keynes was keeping up his interest in Indian monetary affairs. In May 1910 he was asked to give a series of lectures on Indian finance at the London School of Economics early in 1911. He gave the same set in Cambridge in the Lent term of 1911, and he followed them up with a paper, 'Recent Developments in the Indian Currency Question', for a meeting of the Royal Economic Society on 9 May. The text of his remarks, plus an appendix dealing with contemporary proposals to introduce more gold into the circulating currency of India, was printed and circulated by the India Office and the Government of India.[22] Keynes described its purpose as follows:

> I endeavour to give reasons for thinking that this existing system, to which the name of gold-exchange standard has been given, is something much more civilised, much more economical and much more satisfactory as a gold currency. I should like to see it openly established in India on a permanent basis and all talk of an eventual gold currency definitely abandoned.[23]

To this end, he provided a concise overview of the evolution of Indian monetary arrangements since the 1870s, from a silver standard to the present position where the authorities guaranteed the conversion of international currencies into rupees at a fixed rate and stabilised the exchange rate by being prepared to buy and sell sterling at fixed rates. He argued that this system, proposed for Britain after the Napoleonic Wars by David Ricardo, was the norm throughout Asia, that it was becoming more common in Western Europe and that it was consonant with recent European developments. It had the advantages of economy to the Government of India, which earned seigniorage on the issue of token rupee notes or coins in exchange for foreign currency and gained an investment income from its sterling balances in London. However, he argued, the Government of India could earn more by refusing to sell sovereigns in India at a fixed rate, for in effect all that it did by selling them at present was provide a cheap source of gold to the bullion dealers catering to the demand for gold for hoarding at certain times of the year, and it involved the Government of India's paying to ship sovereigns to India and, on occasion, back to London.

At the time that he prepared the lecture, he intended to expand it into a book, which he had offered to Macmillan as far back as August 1910.e However, before he could get down to the book and before he added to his list of substantial publications anything other than 'The Principal Averages and the Laws of Error which Lead to Them' – a re-working of material from his Adam Smith Prize essay which appeared in the *Statistical Journal* for February 1911[24] – a signally important opportunity to serve his chosen profession came his way. At that stage, he had published three articles, two of which had appeared in respected professional journals, one substantive note and eight book reviews (including all the Pearson pieces as one review), and had signed a contract with Cambridge University Press for the publication of his fellowship dissertation. By modern standards, it was hardly a dazzling performance, but by the standards of the previous generation it was prolific.

In October 1911, F. Y. Edgeworth, who had become editor of the *Economic Journal* after Neville Keynes had declined the post[25] and had been in charge from its first issue in 1891, resigned. On 17 October, the Council of the Royal Economic Society held a special meeting with Marshall in the chair to consider a successor. There were two names carried over from the discussion of the previous meeting: Professor W. J. Ashley of the University of Birmingham, previously a professor at Harvard and Toronto, and Keynes. As Ashley was 'quite unable to find time to undertake the work', Keynes was unanimously elected editor of the *Economic Journal*, from 1 January 1912 or an earlier date to be agreed with Edgeworth. Probably because of Keynes's youth – he was, after all, only 28 – the Council then voted by a margin of 8 to 2 to provide the new editor with a Consultative Editorial Board to:

> advise the Editor, so far as they conveniently can, on matters which he refers to them, and to make to him from time to time any suggestions which they think might be helpful to him.[26]

The Editorial Board disappeared in 1919. Keynes was to remain editor until the April 1945 issue had gone to press, when he was succeeded by Roy Harrod and Austin Robinson as Joint Editors. At the same time, Austin Robinson succeeded him as secretary to the society, a job Keynes had taken on in 1913. Keynes had also become a member of the Council of the Society in January 1912 and was, as President, still a member at his death.

For Keynes, the editorship of the *Journal* solved the problem of where he would place his own professional articles. Unlike modern editors he had no inhibitions about publishing his own articles in his journal. While he was

e BL, ADD.55201, JMK to W. E. F. Macmillan. In the same letter, he turned down Macmillan's suggestion that he do a textbook for them because he had not enough teaching experience yet to know the best method of exposition.

editor, his only publications in other English language professional journals, other than seven replies to critics who had published in them,[f] number two: his invited contribution to the *Quarterly Journal of Economics* in November 1914, 'The City of London and the Bank of England, August 1914' and his Jevons centenary allocution of 1936 to the Royal Statistical Society which appeared in the Society's *Journal*. In fact, he was not to be inhibited from taking advantage of his editorial position to reply to articles by others in the same issue in which they originally appeared, going so far as to place his own comments immediately after the piece that had goaded him into print.[g] As far as one can tell from his papers, he submitted none of these contributions to an external referee, although one should note that external refereeing of articles in the *Journal* was far less common than it is today.[h]

From the beginning, as we might expect, Keynes was sure of his own judgement. Initially he did not use referees at all. Even later, when he felt the need to use external referees, he often sent the contribution to the referee with his own draft letter of rejection or a strong statement of his own views. Thus, for example, he wrote to J. R. N. Stone on 4 April 1944 on a submission on the theory of national accounting:[i]

> May I have your comment on the enclosed? It seems to me to be a very difficult and complicated discussion of a controversy which ought not to exist. The only reason for printing anything is that it has a distinguished history of balminess. But this particular article does not seem to bring all that out with the necessary clarity.
>
> Bowley's treatment of the subject is obviously balmy, as I think he himself now admits. Colin Clark's not less, though whether he admits it I am not so sure. If I really said in 1940 what is attributed to me, I was also balmy.

f Five of these were less than a page long. Only one, the 1937 *Quarterly Journal of Economics* reply to critics of the *General Theory*, is of any significance.

g The outstanding examples here are his 'A Reply to Sir William Beveridge' which followed on that author's 'Population Policy and Unemployment' (December 1923); his 'A Comment on Professor Cannan's Article' replying to that author's 'Limitation of Currency or Limitation of Credit' (March 1924), 'A Rejoinder' to D. H. Robertson's 'Mr Keynes' Theory of Money' (September 1931), and his 'Alternative Theories of the rate of Interest' which appeared immediately after Bertil Ohlin's 'Some Notes on the Stockholm Theory of Savings and Investments, II' (June 1937).

h According to Sir Austin Robinson, Assistant Editor of the *Journal* from 1934 and Joint Editor from 1945 to 1970, refereeing did not become normal practice for the *Journal* until after Charles Carter became Joint Editor in 1961. Sir Austin believes that the *Journal's* refereeing practice under Keynes was typical of most journals of the period (Robinson in Hey and Winch (eds) 1990, 181).

i KCKP. See also JMK to A. L. Bowley, 25 March 1938 concerning Milton Friedman's submission 'The Assumptions of Linearity and Normality in the Analysis of Family Expenditure Data'; and JMK to Joan Robinson, 4 February 1941 (*JMK*, XII, 829–30) on Kalecki's 'A Theorem on Technical Progress'. In the latter case, when Robinson did not fall in with his views, he sent the submission on to Nicholas Kaldor, again with an expression of his views (*JMK*, XII, 834). Kaldor agreed with Keynes and the article never appeared in the *Journal*, but in the *Review of Economic Studies* for May 1941.

For 33 years and one issue Keynes would play a central role in the development of the *Journal*'s character and reputation, and, therefore, in the developing profession of economics.

Throughout he was responsible for the 'front' part of each issue – for the articles, notes and memoranda – as well as for its make up and seeing it through the press. After 1915, editorial colleagues – Edgeworth informally from late in the year and later formally (1919–26), D. H. Macgregor (1926–35), and Austin Robinson (1934–45) – were responsible for reviews, reports of official publications, the noting and listing of books and sharing the responsibility of proof-reading. After 1915 the editors consulted over individual articles and the 'Current Topics' section, but the main responsibility would be Keynes's.

Of course he made errors of judgement. In 1923, he rejected with the words 'This amounts to nothing and should be refused' a paper by Bertil Ohlin which contained the factor proportions theorem which later won Ohlin a Nobel Prize.[27] In 1924 he rejected a less important piece by Wicksell, 'Ricardo on Machinery' which appeared in the *Journal* in 1981.[28] In 1928, on the advice of Frank Ramsey, he rejected Roy Harrod's invention of the marginal revenue curve.[29] Doubtless, there were other editorial mistakes, but one wonders whether other editors were less accident prone.

When Keynes took over the *Journal* in the week before Christmas 1911 and undertook his first editorial act – 'the rejection of an article from the Archdeacon [Cunningham of Trinity] . . . complete wash and . . . nothing whatever to do with economics'[30] – it was running to about 650 pages and about 20 articles a year. At its peak in the 1930s, it would run to 750 pages and publish 27 to 28 articles a year, as well as issue an *Economic History* supplement of about 175 pages containing some 10 articles, as well as reviews.[j] Keynes thus published 143 issues of the *Journal* and its supplements which contained over 1,100 articles, plus several thousand more notes, memoranda, review articles and reviews.

Initially Keynes acted without assistance. It was only in February 1915 that he was even allowed to charge the costs of secretarial assistance to the Society.[31] Taking on the *Journal* was therefore a considerable drain on his time. But he seems to have fitted it in with everything else and, except in exceptional circumstances (such as the outbreak of war in 1914),[32] each quarterly issue appeared on the 15th of March, June, September and December.[33] By the 1920s, he was so accustomed to the editorial burden that he made light of it. As he told Edwin Cannan, who had refused to be Edgeworth's successor in 1926:

j There are suggestions in the literature that the *Economic History* supplement was a Cambridge-inspired attempt to compete with – and hopefully forestall publication of – the *Economic History Review* (Barker 1977, 12). There is, as Barker correctly reports, no evidence in the Keynes Papers or the Minute Books of the Royal Economic Society to support these suggestions.

I sympathise with your reasons. I am sure that I should make the same answer in your place. Indeed, I should make the same answer now, if I hadn't formed a habit, strong enough to defeat reason, of editing the *E.J.*[34]

By the 1930s it was one of the activities that he classed as 'non-work' and did after dinner.[35] He was always prompt in dealing with articles, a month being the maximum time between the submission of an article and its acceptance, and this was exceptional, unless, often as a result of his extensive suggestions for revisions, authors took longer.[36] He never kept a backlog of accepted articles in reserve: the longest an author would normally have to wait for his article to appear was one issue.

Further recognition of Keynes's position amongst English economists came a year later when, on 4 December 1912, he was unanimously elected a member of the Political Economy Club, the first of his generation of economists to be so honoured. At the time, the only active academic economist who was also a member of the Club was Pigou.[37]

Thus in a little over four and a half years from his acceptance of the Marshall/Pigou offer to return to Cambridge, Keynes was well-established in his College, his University and the economics profession. By the First World War his position as an economist was such that, when Knut Wicksell visited England in February 1916, 'the longed-for climax of the visit', which had included discussions with Marshall, was, according to his biographer, lunch with Keynes, whom Wicksell described as 'their keenest theorist'.[38] What he was to make of this professional position will be further discussed in later chapters.

NOTES

1 *JMK*, XI, 174–82.
2 See above p. 82.
3 KCKP, A. C. Pigou to JMK, undated but marked 6.7.08. in pencil.
4 See, in particular, 'The Old Generation of Economists and the New' (1897) and 'Social Possibilities of Economic Chivalry' (1907) in Pigou (ed.) 1925, 295–311, 323–44.
5 The manuscripts are in Whitaker (ed.) 1975, I, 164–77; the 1887 paper is in Pigou (ed.) 1925, 188–211. All the official evidence is collected together in Keynes (ed.) 1926.
6 *JMK*, XI, 375.
7 Reprinted in Pigou (ed.) 1925, 188–211.
8 See Laidler in Whitaker (ed.) 1990 and Laidler 1991, ch. 6 for a fuller discussion of this point.
9 For a discussion of the transition from silver in India see Bagchi 1989, 63–91.
10 Kaminsky 1986, 197–9.
11 The letters appear in *JMK*, XV, 20–8; the letter in ibid., 28. See also Sir Arthur Godley's encouraging letter of a week later printed in ibid., 17.
12 For an elaboration of this view, see Bagchi 1989, esp. 102–8.

13 *JMK*, XV, 44–59.
14 In letters dated 6 June 1910 (*JMK*, XI, 186–8) and 16 January 1911 (ibid., 206–7). The second letter got as far as being set up in type.
15 Ibid., 189–95.
16 Ibid., 196–205.
17 Ibid., 207–16.
18 Ibid., 191–2.
19 Ibid., 192.
20 Ibid., 195.
21 See, for example, KCKP, K. Pearson to JMK, 24 December 1910.
22 For Keynes's close connections with the India Office see above p. 203.
23 *JMK*, XV, 69.
24 *JMK*, XI, 159–73.
25 See above p. 16.
26 RES Minute Book, vol. II, 17 October 1911. The terms of reference of the Board were reprinted on page 665 of the *Economic Journal* for December 1911.
27 Patinkin and Leith (eds) 1977, 161–2.
28 Jonung 1981.
29 Harrod 1951, 159n; see KCKP, EJ1/2, Harrod to JMK, 7, 23 and 27 July 1928; JMK to Harrod, 17 July and 1 August 1928.
30 KCKP, JMK to FAK, 23 December 1911.
31 RES Minute Book, vol. II, 17 February 1915.
32 The September 1914 issue contained in 'Current Topics' (p. 500) financial data that had appeared as late as 10 September. For his part, Keynes had not finished his own contribution to that issue, 'War and the Financial System, August 1914' until 3 September (KCKP, JMK to JNK, 3 September 1914). But printers were more accommodating in those days. They still were in the 1920s and 1930s. See below pp. 424, 440 and 621.
33 During the Second World War, the number of issues dropped to three and the June and September issues were amalgamated.
34 BLPES, Cannan Papers, vol. 1029, JMK to E. Cannan, 18 March 1926.
35 Kahn 1984, 176.
36 The longest discussion appears as pages 321–50 of *JMK*, XIV. However, such long discussions seem to have been characteristic of Keynes from the beginning, the first surviving one being a 5½ page letter to Josiah Wedgwood on his 'The Principles of Land Value Taxation', which appeared in the *Journal* for September 1912 (KCKP, JMK to J. C. Wedgwood, 1 July 1912).
37 At this point, Keynes had, in addition to the meetings mentioned above (pp. 172, 184), attended a meeting that discussed protection and Indian industrial development. Marshall had resigned his membership on his retirement from the Cambridge chair.
38 Gardlund 1958, 294–5.

9

BLOOMSBURY

I should no more regard Maynard Keynes as a typical Bloomsbury than I should regard J. B. Hobbs as a typical member of the Surrey County Cricket Club.

(G. H. Hardy as reported in Robbins 1983, 531)

The years before 1914 were years not only of professional development. Between 1909 and the outbreak of war, Keynes's circle of friends widened and his relationships with individuals changed. When he first returned to Cambridge from the India Office, most of his friends, except Duncan, were of his own generation or the one before at Cambridge or from his schooldays. A good example of this comes from his first summer at Burford in 1909, when his guests, other than his mother and sister and Duncan, were Swithinbank, J. T. Sheppard and his companion Cecil Taylor, James Strachey, Humphrey Paul, and Granville Proby. In contrast, three years later at Everleigh his circle included Ferenc Bekassy, Justin Brooke, Rupert Brooke, Ka Cox, Frederick Etchells, Gordon Luce, Noel, Daphne and Bryn Olivier, Chester Purvis, Archie Rose, and his brother Geoffrey, as well as some holdovers from previous gatherings. If one were to expand this pre-war list of new acquaintances and friends one would add Faith Bagenal, Francis Birrell, Frances Cornford, Elliott Felkin, Freddie Hardman, George Mallory, David Pinsent, Sidney Russell Cooke, Jacques Raverat and a run of the first generation of Cambridge-trained economists – Hubert Henderson, Frederick Lavington, Dennis Robertson, Gerald Shove and Dudley Ward. Finally, one would add his growing intimacy with several members of Bloomsbury – most notably Clive and Vanessa Bell and Virginia Stephen.

The sources and roots of these friendships were various. Many were contemporaries of his brother[a] and Rupert Brooke. Indeed, the group of friends including Rupert and Justin Brooke, Frances Cornford, Ka

a Although the two saw quite a bit of each other, they were not all that close at this time. As Keynes put it after a family holiday in the Pyrenees in 1909 'Geoffrey is *hopeless*, more irredeemably hopeless than anyone I have ever met'. (BL, ADD.57930, JMK to DG, 28 June 1909. See also ibid., JMK to DG, 14 May 1909).

Cox, Gwen Darwin (later Raverat), Geoffrey Keynes, the Olivier sisters, Jacques Raverat, Gerald Shove and Dudley Ward were collectively known by Bloomsbury as the Neo-Pagans. They were a group of friends with Cambridge roots, but they were heterosexual in their tastes, made almost a cult of outdoor pursuits and camping, were much less philosophically oriented and much more inclined to be socialists than his earlier friends. Shove and Rupert Brooke, the two Kingsmen in the group, were also Apostles, which provided a further link of friendship. The Society also provided other friends: Luce, Bekassy and Wittgenstein were all members. Others in Keynes's circle had been considered as possible brethren but in the end had not been chosen: Dennis Robertson, Chester Purvis, E. A. Kann and David Pinsent. Another of the shared contexts was King's itself. In addition to Rupert Brooke, Shove and Bekassy, Birrell, Hardman, Rose, Russell Cooke, Felkin and Purvis were all from that College.

Some of the friendships were homosexual in outcome for Keynes – and the contemporary gossip suggests that the intent may have been present in other cases. Throughout the period, although Duncan Grant remained Keynes's closest friend and lover, it would appear that their relationship became less intense and less exclusive. The Strachey brothers were reporting as much to each other from the middle of 1909,[1] and Duncan seems to have said to Keynes that he no longer loved him late in April after their visit to Versailles.[2] Later in 1909 Keynes took up with St George Nelson, an actor who appears to have been casually involved with Duncan, and Duncan himself took up with Adrian Stephen. However, it is also clear that it was not until 1911 that Keynes became so active in seeking substitutes that he had a run of casual, 'rough' encounters, largely in London. Some of these were reported to Duncan, who, for all the trials and tribulations of the relationship remained his closest friend. One occasion was that of 'the lift boy of Vauxhall':

> I did in the end stroll out on Tuesday night and bring a boy back. He told me that there are many fewer this week because last week the police were active and locked two up.[3]

Some of it may have been sheer daring, as Gerald Shove's comments from the end of 1910 and 1911 suggest:

> I'm not sure your passion for low life isn't vicious: but perhaps you keep it within bounds. If not you'll let me have the brief when it ends as it inevitably must, won't you.

> I'm dying to know what your adventure was and whether you're safe again now. Of course you can't describe it on paper, but do let me hear when you've escaped, or are arrested.[4]

But to judge from his behaviour, Keynes was normally circumspect – in 1913 he was still worrying whether his brother would find out.[5] On occasion, however, it is clear that he let lust take the place of his better judgement.

The most notable instance of this lack of judgement, leaving to one side his casual encounters recorded in detail in plate 10, occurred in Cambridge. The other person involved was B. K. Sarkar, whom Keynes met towards the end of the Michaelmas term 1910, probably as a result of his earlier connections with the Majlis in Cambridge, his India Office experience, his teaching for the Indian Civil Service and his forthright defence of Indian students in Cambridge against a sneering article in the *Cambridge Review* in his published letter in the *Review* of 20 May 1909.[6] As far as we can tell from the available records,[7] Sarkar arrived in England at the end of August 1910. He remained in London until October, for although on the advice of the educational adviser to Indian students at the India Office he obtained a place at Jesus College, Oxford, he fell ill and was unable to take the place. He appeared in Cambridge in the second or third week of November before he fell ill again, this time with pneumonia. He recovered with friends in London and re-appeared in Cambridge at the end of December. At this stage, he ran into difficulties over money with his adviser, W. T. Mitchell. There may have been more than money involved, for Mitchell, referring to his falling under 'dangerous influences in Cambridge', had already denounced him to the Tutor of Trinity and threatened to denounce him to any College in Cambridge which considered his admission. The financial problem dragged on through much of 1910–11, eventually being settled heavily in Sarkar's favour by Keynes, but there still remained the need to find him a place in Cambridge.

Keynes had hoped to persuade W. H. Macaulay at King's to admit Sarkar, even though the College's quota of Indian students was full. He was unsuccessful, for although Macaulay doubted some of Mitchell's tales, those plus what he had learned through other enquiries made it impossible, even with allowances for the young man's inexperience, for him to recommend that the College Council waive the quota in Sarkar's case. However, Sarkar was eventually successful in obtaining a place in Clare, where he matriculated in October 1911. His success in getting into Clare was due to Keynes's recommendation, which seems to have outweighed other advice that Mollison, the Tutor at Clare, had received on this case.

Keynes's mixed motives are clear from a letter he wrote to Duncan after Sarkar had been unsuccessful in obtaining a place at King's. He remarked of Sarkar:

> He is a strange and charming creature. I don't know how our relationship is going to end. I have had all to-day the most violent sexual feelings towards him.[8]

Matters might have ended there but for the fact that Sarkar's people did not provide him with the funds to support his Cambridge career. P. C. T.

Crick, a Clare man who had agreed to act as Sarkar's guardian, was after his first term finding himself liable for his College bill, his landlady's rent and booksellers' bills, plus debts that he had incurred with another landlady before he had come up to Cambridge. Keynes and Crick attempted to get Sarkar's parents to meet these growing debts, and Keynes agreed to cover half Sarkar's eventual deficit. He also threatened to have him sent back to India unless he repaid Crick, who was by now liable for £100. This threat proved empty because the India Office would not repatriate students, and Sarkar was unwilling to go. Sarkar remained in England until 1920, sending letters to Keynes and occasionally asking for references or financial assistance. He seems to have eventually cleared his debts: at least Keynes's financial records indicate no call of the order of magnitude suggested in the correspondence with Crick. Keynes continued to see Sarkar sometimes (he was invited to a reading party at Asheham at Easter 1914). Moreover, if we are to believe the tabulation in plate 10 and his appointments diary, Keynes had sexual relations with him. These appear to have first occurred in January 1912 – at the height of Sarkar's financial problems and immediately before Keynes threatened to have him repatriated to India. It is a rather sordid tale – one that does not reflect well on Keynes.

In the years before 1914, one set of friends came to play a particularly important role in Keynes's life. They are now so well known as the Bloomsbury Group, or just simply as Bloomsbury, that it would seem unnecessary to say much more. Yet the words Bloomsbury and Bloomsbury Group have found so many different, and often extremely loose usages, that any author dealing with the group or its members has to start from the beginning, at the risk of re-covering what is familiar ground for some readers.

With the exception of Roger Fry, Bloomsbury as a group antedates the fame of its members. It was initially – and always remained – 'primarily and fundamentally a group of friends'.[9] That this group of friends believed that they had shared an important common experience is clear from 1920, when thirteen people joined together to form a Memoir Club. The members of the Club met from time to time to dine and to read memoirs to each other.[10] The thirteen people were Virginia and Leonard Woolf, Vanessa and Clive Bell, Molly and Desmond MacCarthy, Adrian Stephen, Lytton Strachey, Duncan Grant, Morgan Forster, Saxon Sydney-Turner, Roger Fry and Keynes. They coincide with Leonard Woolf's membership of 'Old Bloomsbury', whose existence as a group he attributes to 1912–14.[11] Virginia Woolf put it more bluntly in a memoir entitled 'Old Bloomsbury' which she read to the Club in 1921 or 1922: 'Old Bloomsbury still survives. If you seek proof – Look around'.[12] As one might expect, there is disagreement over membership of the Memoir Club. Quentin Bell states that Adrian Stephen was not a member of the Club; while Vanessa Bell's 1942 portrait also leaves him out, but includes three additions: David Garnett, who seems to have been a member from the late 1920s, Quentin Bell, and Lydia Keynes, who was not a part of the Club until at least a decade after her marriage in 1925.[13] When Clive Bell came to list the pre-1914 members of Bloomsbury, he left out the MacCarthys, Morgan Forster and Adrian Stephen, but added H. T. J. Norton 'and perhaps Gerald Shove'.[14] His wife included the MacCarthys and James and Marjorie Strachey.[15] To add further confusion, an organising letter from Molly MacCarthy to Keynes prior to the first meeting also mentions Sydney Waterlow and Granville Proby as possible members and does not mention Lytton Strachey, Adrian Stephen or Saxon Sydney-Turner![16] However, from that letter, it is clear that the membership of the Club was far from firm, but she was aiming at a membership of a dozen.

Despite their disagreements, these various accounts tend to contain a common core of individuals. Moreover, this 'core' had plausible links of friendship. It includes the surviving members of the Midnight Society of 1899, a freshman, undergraduate reading society in Trinity College, Cambridge, whose members were Clive Bell, Lytton Strachey, Thoby Stephen, and Leonard Woolf. It then broadens to include Thoby's two sisters, Vanessa and Virginia, who after the death of their father, Sir Leslie Stephen, moved with him and their brother Adrian to 46 Gordon Square in 1904. There they began to hold regular At Homes for Thoby's Cambridge friends in February 1905. They continued to do so through Adrian's coming down from Cambridge, Thoby Stephen's death from typhoid in November 1906 and Vanessa's marriage to Clive Bell in February 1907, when Virginia and Adrian moved to 29 Fitzroy Square. Vanessa's marriage meant that there were now two foci for entertaining, but they managed it on successive evenings. Even by this stage certain links of friendship were clear, and when, in December 1907 the Play Reading Society met for the first time at 46 Gordon Square, its founder members were Virginia and Adrian Stephen, Clive and Vanessa Bell, Lytton Strachey and Saxon Sydney-Turner.

The circle of friends emerging from these evenings of cocoa, biscuits and whisky at Fitzroy and Gordon Squares was inevitably wider than Thoby's Cambridge contemporaries. Desmond MacCarthy, who was beginning his career as a literary critic; H. T. J. Norton; Charles Sanger; Sydney Waterlow; Ralph Hawtrey; Hilton Young; Robin Mayor; and Theodore Llewellyn Davies were also early visitors. Later visitors, who soon became regulars, included Duncan Grant from 1907 and Keynes from 1907/8 while Leonard Woolf's inclusion had to await his return from Ceylon in 1911. Roger Fry's accession was also later, stemming from a meeting with the Bells on Cambridge railway station in 1910.

By 1911, when Virginia and Adrian took 38 Brunswick Square with Keynes, Duncan and Leonard as lodgers, the core of the group was in place. By that time, they had known each other – or of each other – for over a decade in some cases. By 1911, some of the friendships amongst the 'core' had come under severe strain – and strains on friendships would occur in future years: one needs only to think of the Maynard/Lytton/Duncan problems of 1908, and there would others such as the Duncan/David Garnett/Vanessa triangle of 1916–19, later complicated by David's affair with and eventual marriage to Angelica, Vanessa's daughter by Duncan, in 1942. In 1911 the group was sufficiently coherent to have been dubbed 'Bloomsbury' by Molly MacCarthy amongst others.[17]

If we take Leonard Woolf's membership list of Old Bloomsbury for 1911, we have a group of friends who had reached their late twenties or early thirties – the full range of ages ran from Duncan's 26 to Roger Fry's 45. Among the men there were several common bonds: all but one (Duncan) had been to Cambridge; all but three had been Apostles; almost all had been regulars at Virginia and Vanessa's At Homes; most were beginning to make careers for themselves. Roger Fry was well established: he was a founder and, from 1909, joint editor of *The Burlington Magazine*, had been curator of paintings and later European adviser to the Metropolitan Museum in New York and had already declined the Directorship of the Tate Gallery in London. Morgan Forster had published four novels and a collection of short stories, and Desmond MacCarthy was developing as a critic and edited *The New Quarterly*. But of the younger men only Saxon Sydney-Turner, with his position in the Estate Duty Office of the Inland Revenue, and Keynes, with his King's fellowship and his Girdlers' Lectureship, had even 'established' positions. The others – Lytton, Leonard, Clive, Vanessa, Virginia, Adrian and Duncan – were still trying to establish themselves and in the interim were making do with a mixture of family wealth and such money as they could pick up on the edges of literary and artistic London.

For Keynes, Bloomsbury contained the three greatest friends of his twenties and thirties – Lytton, Duncan and Vanessa. True, his relations with Lytton had cooled by 1910, but he was to remain close to the other two until 1921 when the entry of Lydia Lopokova into his life brought new stresses to old ties. Other members of the group provided less intense friendships, which, with the possible exception of Clive Bell's were never sufficiently strong to allow for successful holidays together. Bloomsbury was to provide a focus for his London life in the years after his return to Cambridge, offering evenings of serious, uninhibited conversation; excursions to the ballet, the theatre or galleries; parties and country visits. It was to become for Keynes a means of relaxation and of greater education *outside* his main area of activity. Bloomsbury and the friendships it offered were *not* to provide him with a means of advancing his career; there was not the possibility of fruitful interaction that proved important for Roger Fry, Duncan Grant and Vanessa Bell. Nor, with the exception of the composition of *The Economic Consequences of the Peace*, were members of Bloomsbury to provide him with support during a period of creation.[18] For Keynes, Bloomsbury and its members were part of a way of life, and a rich one at that, but they were only a part.

In those pre-war years Keynes's relationships with the various members of Bloomsbury changed. I have already touched on his relations with Duncan, who remained his closest friend. With Lytton, the relationship shattered by Keynes's 'conquest' of Duncan never regained its former intimacy. On Lytton's side there were regular outbursts of mild-to-violent Pozzophobia for years to come. Thus during a visit to Asheham, where the company included Vanessa, Duncan, Saxon, Roger and his family:

> Pozzo is the principal figure, I suppose. Very alert & also very soft on Roger's son (aged 1). I read his book on Indian finance. You should see him, with his board & the papers, cheques, notebooks and all the rest spread out before him, re-adjust his accounts and picking up compound interest. The man's a born financier. Terrible, quite: and I should say even dangerous. As for administration, or anything of that sort, it's more than indifferent to him – he hates it. His book is 'able' to a degree –. And then . . . Duncan? Who knows what the state of *that* affair may be?[19]

Again, after Keynes visited Lytton in 1913 at the Lacket, his cottage at Lockeridge near Marlborough:

> That man left this morning. After he'd been gone a few hours, I realised that I never wished to see him again. He has a crapulous egotism and smug impermeability *qui font fremur*. He wallows in secret cynicism, I really do believe. The only subjects in which he takes any interest are what he calls 'fie-nance' and lechery – and they certainly don't seem to make a nice combination. He throws a cloak of itching satisfaction over both – oh terrible! terrible! He brings off his copulations and speculations with the same calculating odiousness, he has a boy with the same mean pleasure with which he sells at the top of the market, and he can hardly tell the difference between pocketing fifteen per cent and kissing Duncan. Do you think that anyone has ever had any effect on him? I don't believe so. He's as scaly as a crab, and walks sideways like one with the same hideous persistency. He even manages to be good-natured through it all – he smiles blandly as one claw follows the other – oh mon dieu![20]

Lytton's aspersions were occasionally tempered by concern and affection, but the tone was more often than not tinged with scorn and jealousy at Keynes's successes.

With most of the other members of Bloomsbury, little record of his relations survives for this period beyond a report by Virginia Woolf of 'desperate work' involved in entertaining Keynes, Duncan, Lytton, James

Strachey, Frankie Birrell, H. T. J. Norton and Horace Cole at Fitzroy Square on 23 December 1909.[21] There is, however, Virginia's memoir, with

> Maynard – very truculent, I felt, very formidable, like a portrait of Tolstoy as a young man to look at, able to rend any argument that came his way with a blow of his paw, yet concealing, as the novelists say, a kind and even simple heart under that immensely impressive armour of intellect.[22]

From his appointments diaries and his letters, it appears that, at least until he moved into Brunswick Square, his most frequent contacts were with the Bells, particularly with Vanessa. This is not surprising, given Vanessa's and Duncan's shared interests. From the outset, he seems to have found her attractive: 'She was perfectly lovely – I've never seen her more beautiful – and very conversational'.[23] On her side, as she told Roger Fry: 'He's very nice & easy and bawdy'.[24] They could holiday together successfully. Accepting Keynes's sexual preferences, Vanessa could act as a confidante. After a visit to Keynes's reading party at Asheham in April 1914 she would write:

> It is plainly quite superfluous for me to write & tell you how much we enjoyed ourselves at Asheham & so the only thing I can do, since you insist upon my writing, is to make my letter so bawdy that you'll have to destroy it at once for fear of Lily's seeing it. Did you have a pleasant afternoon buggering one or more of the young men we left for you? It must have been delicious out on the downs in the afternoon sun – a thing I have often wanted to do. But one never gets the opportunity & the desire at the right moment. I imagine you, however, with your bare limbs intertwined with his and all the ecstatic preliminaries of Sucking Sodomy – it sounds like the name of a station. . . . How divine it must have been. I hope you did not make your throat worse in that delicious drowsy state afterwards on the turf. Perhaps this is all imaginary however & it really took place in a bedroom.

Moreover, she continued:

> Yes it was a very nice interlude & I felt singularly happy & free tongued. You are rather like a Chinese Buddha as host. You sit silent but not so silent as Saxon & manage to create an atmosphere in which all is possible. Perhaps you talk more than a Buddha would though. Anyhow the result is what it would be with a Buddha – one can talk of fucking & sodomy & sucking & bushes & all without turning a hair.[25]

When war came and Duncan moved with Vanessa to Wissett in Suffolk and then to Charleston in Sussex, contacts became more frequent and intimate.

It was through Duncan and Vanessa that Keynes came to a more intense appreciation of the visual arts. He had an introduction to these through

Lytton, but he now began to acquire works of art on a significant scale and he asked Vanessa and Duncan to decorate his rooms both in King's and in Brunswick Square. Perhaps, as Clive Bell, agreeing with Lytton Strachey, suggested, Keynes had little innate feeling of the visual arts.[26] This view is partially echoed by Vanessa's biographer Frances Spalding, who remarks of his collection of paintings by contemporary artists that 'either he did not have a very good eye or he acted on principles of kindness rather than taste'.[27] But Keynes believed in art education and he certainly enjoyed his own pictures, accumulating a large collection with some items of outstanding quality. He also would apply his organisational powers to the promotion and nurture of contemporary artists.[28] The items he would leave in 1946 were a long way from his earliest purchases of an Augustus John drawing in 1908, an Eric Gill sculpture in 1911, Etchells' 'The Dead Mole' the same year and the murals in Cambridge and London. However, he had made a start.

For Keynes, as well as other members of Bloomsbury, one new acquaintance in the years immediately before 1914 was Lady Ottoline Morrell. Ottoline was married to Philip Morrell, who had become Liberal MP for North Oxfordshire in 1906. His election coincided with their move to 44 Bedford Square in the heart of Bloomsbury. Once they had got the house in order, with main rooms in pale grey with yellow taffeta curtains, she began to entertain on a large scale, especially on Thursday evenings. These evenings, a small dinner party followed by a larger At Home threw together writers, politicians and artists, the famous and the not so famous. They soon came to include much of Bloomsbury – the Bells from 1908, Roger Fry and Virginia Stephen from 1909 and Lytton from 1910. Keynes, perhaps because of his Cambridge residence, came later, although he had doubtless heard of the gatherings from his friends and had seen Ottoline's striking figure in the neighbourhood. He had probably heard of her in 1909, because in June he subscribed to the scheme she had launched with Roger Fry, D. S. McColl and C. J. Holmes two months earlier to buy the works of contemporary British artists – a fund which later became the Contemporary Arts Society. But, to judge from his appointments diary, he did not cross the threshold of 44 Bedford Square before 15 June 1911. His visits thereafter were frequent, but he was not as much of an *habitué* as many of his Bloomsbury friends.

June 1911 brought another link between Ottoline and Bloomsbury – the ballet. At the turn of the century – and later – the conventional way to produce ballet in London had been as part of a music hall programme. It was as a segment of such programmes that Karsavina and Pavlova appeared in London in 1910, during the gap in the season of the Mariinsky Theatre in St Petersburg. However, in June 1911, Serge Diaghilev, after seasons on the Continent with a Russian company composed of dancers on leave from the official companies, came to London with his own full-time company for a season. Keynes does not seem to have attended the first season, although his parents did so once, on 25 July, but when Diaghilev's second season opened on 16 October he went twice, in November and early in December. Subsequently, whenever the company returned to London Keynes went to its performances. In 1912, for example, he went on 22 June and came up specially from Everleigh for a party that Ottoline was giving for Nijinski and Bakst. It may have been that evening, although some sources suggest it was earlier, that Nijinski and Bakst saw Duncan Grant and others playing tennis in the Bedford Square gardens and 'they were so entranced by the tall trees against the houses and the figures flitting about playing tennis that they exclaimed with delight: "*Quel décor!*"'.[b] The scene was the inspiration for *Jeux*.

Keynes's attendances continued throughout the next two seasons, when he saw the premières of *Petrushka* and *Jeux*. He also saw Nijinski at least once again while travelling through France on his way to Egypt in March 1913,[29] and he was asked to tea at Ottoline's to meet Nijinski and his wife during the 1914 season. There is no record in his diary that he went on a Sunday, but he did go to Ottoline's on two occasions in the summer of 1914 – on 30 June and 2 July.

On this last occasion, Ottoline was casting the net for Bloomsbury more widely.

> To-night I am to go to a small dinner party at Lady Ottoline Morrell's to meet the Prime Minister [Asquith]. She thinks it's time that he broke out in a new direction and is asking no one but a few of my so-called 'Bloomsbury set'. Duncan was at a party at 10 Downing St. last night! But I am afraid he won't like us much.[30]

Keynes was to see much more of the ballet and of the Asquiths in the years that followed.

As noted above, by the end of 1911, Keynes, despite, by modern standards, relatively few publications, had started to make his mark as an economist. In the remaining years before the war, he would move somewhat further. However, he still had another burden to get out from under – *Probability*. He had signed a contract for 'Principles of Probability' with Cambridge University Press on 10 November 1910. The book, estimated at 320 pages, was to be published on a half profits basis. After the summer's work in 1912, when he had by far the greater part of the book ready for the press, it had grown to 400–420 pages and the Press had revised its estimated costs and asked Keynes to pay £30 for publication. Moreover, it had imposed several

b The quotation is from Gathorne-Hardy 1963, 228. Gathorne-Hardy puts it in the afternoon, as does Richard Buckle (1979, 233–4) who gives it the date of 12 July, Ottoline's biographer Sandra Jobson Darroch (1980, 126) gives the occasion as the evening. Maynard's letter to Duncan concerning the party is dated 26 July and he refers to coming up to London tomorrow for Ottoline's party for Nijinski (BL, ADD.57930). In his King's College papers, there is an invitation dated Wednesday to come to tea on Saturday to meet Nijinski and Bakst. By the way, 12 July was a Friday.

additional conditions: it would not start to print the book until it had received the whole manuscript and it would not provide galley proofs. Keynes was unhappy at the change in the terms, unaccompanied by any explanations, and the disruption that the postponement of printing would involve, for at this stage he hoped to be rid of the book by the end of the 1912–13 academic year.[31] He therefore asked to be released from his contract and, when this was agreed, took the book to Macmillan, who agreed to publish it and his projected book on Indian finance on a half profits basis. Macmillan also agreed to start printing *Probability* as soon as he wished.[32] But by then it was December 1912 and Keynes had other fish to fry. He would not seriously get back to the book until 1914, although he did send Dan Macmillan the first three chapters in July and told him that 'I have at least 20 ready for the press, and will feed the printer up to his appetite'.[33]

One of his other fish was his India book, then called 'The Monetary Affairs of India' but renamed in January 1913 and published as *Indian Currency and Finance*.[34] Keynes had started working seriously on the book after his return from his visit to the Bekassy family seat in Hungary in October 1912. Almost simultaneously, Indian currency policy became a matter of significant public discussion in England, when in a paper before the Manchester Statistical Society Sir Edward Holden, chairman of the London City and Midland Bank, as a part of his campaign to get Britain to hold larger gold reserves criticised existing Indian reserve policy and called for a commission to investigate. In *The Times* of 26 October, Keynes defended the existing policy and suggested that any attempt to establish an effective gold currency in India would thwart the ends Sir Edward had in view. Within the week, the Indian issue arose again.[35] Earlier in the year, the Council of India had arranged through Samuel Montagu & Co., London bullion brokers, for the secret purchase of large quantities of silver for coinage. Although the firm was the customary agent of the India Office and the procedure was a normal one designed to prevent speculation, when the purchases became known Parliamentary critics of the Government made much of the fact that Edwin Montagu, a brother of the firm's senior partner, was Under-Secretary of State for India and that another partner, Sir Stuart Samuel, was the elder brother of Herbert Samuel, the Postmaster-General. At the time of the Marconi scandal this was grist for the mills of rumour. There was also another round of agitation in *The Times* for the implementation of the Fowler Committee's 1898 recommendations for a full gold standard for India. Amid the resulting rash of questions in the House of Commons, at the instigation of Lionel Abrahams of the Finance Department of the India Office Keynes wrote another letter to *The Times* on 9 November defending the existing currency system. The letter pleased the India Office as 'the best statement on our side that has yet appeared' and their 'only regret was that *The Times* did not print it in letters of gold and silver and issue it as a special supplement'.[36] However, although *The Times* acknowledged partial defeat on matters of fact, it continued its campaign for the appointment of a Royal Commission to inquire into the India Office's financial management, as did critics in the House of Commons, who succeeded in promoting a debate on a motion for a Select Committee 'to inquire into the administration of Indian Finance and Currency by the Secretary of State for India and the Council for India' on 13 February 1914.

By the end of January 1913 Keynes's book had started to appear in proof and within a month full sets were available for circulation to Hartley Withers, Lionel Abrahams and Neville Keynes. Discussions of them continued over the next two months. Those with Abrahams concerning both matters of fact and opinion were particularly intense and Keynes made numerous alterations to meet his official critic. However, from an early stage the discussions took on an even more serious aspect, for, while Keynes was in Egypt visiting Robin Furness and, if we are to believe a letter to Duncan, having a 'w–m–n' in Cairo during the Easter vacation – he left Cambridge on 8 March and did not return until 14 April – he was offered first the secretaryship of and then, on the basis of his proofs, a seat on the government's projected Royal Commission to enquire into the Indian currency system and its management.[37] The chairman of the Commission was Austen Chamberlain, the tariff reformer and former Chancellor of the Exchequer, against whom Keynes had campaigned unsuccessfully on behalf of Hilton Young in 1910 and under whom he would work in 1919. After ascertaining from Chamberlain that his membership of the Commission would not compromise his freedom to publish his book, Keynes rushed to put the finishing touches to it before the Commission met for the first time on 5 May. The book appeared on 9 June 1913. Rarely does the unpublished work of an economist receive such recognition.[38]

At 29 Keynes was an extremely young appointee to a Royal Commission. He was also very lucky in his colleagues. In addition to Chamberlain as chairman, his fellow commissioners included his old India Office chief Sir Arthur Godley, now Lord Kilbracken, and Sir Robert Chalmers, who would later be his Permanent Secretary in the Treasury. The Secretary to the Commission, filling the post originally offered to Keynes, was Basil Blackett, a former India Office official now on the finance side of the Treasury and hence another future colleague.

Indian Currency and Finance was an elaboration and extension of the arguments that Keynes had developed in his 1911 lectures, as well as the ground from which he would approach the Royal Commission with positive suggestions for future changes. The elaboration and extension involved greater description of existing Indian institutions and arrangements, and more extensive justification of the gold exchange standard. This last was necessary if he was to defend effectively the arrangements that had evolved and forestall the arguments of those who argued that the Indian system should be assimilated to contemporary British practice, where gold was still in circulation and the smallest Bank of England note was for £5. Such an approach had been recommended by the Fowler Commission in 1899 and was still the stated object of the Government of India. He spent a considerable amount of space arguing that the gold exchange standard was more common than usually supposed amongst 'advanced' countries and that further evolutionary movements in that direction by India were desirable. Thus, after showing the extent to which European central banks held foreign balances and used them for exchange stabilisation, he continued:

> The new method combines safety with economy. Just as individuals have learnt that it is cheaper and not less safe to keep their ultimate reserves on deposit with their bankers, so the second stage of monetary evolution is now entered on, and nations are learning that *some part* of the cash reserves of their banks (we cannot go further than this at present) may be properly be kept on deposit in the international money market. This is not the expedient of second-rate or impoverished countries; it is the expedient of all those who have not attained a high degree of financial supremacy – all of those, in fact, who are not themselves international bankers.[39]

Similarly he emphasised the extent to which the practices underlying existing Indian arrangements had served as a model for recent changes in Latin America and elsewhere in Asia.

In arguing his case, Keynes went further and suggested that any departure from the existing arrangements in the direction of increasing the internal circulation of gold coin would be even more socially wasteful in India than elsewhere. The reason lay in the age-old propensity of the Indian public to hoard precious metals in the form of either currency or jewellery. From the available evidence, he suggested that such hoarding had recently increased perhaps because of the greater willingness of the Government of India to make sovereigns available in India. If they persevered in their attempt to make gold coins more popular, not only would they reduce their income from that generated by the existing policy of using token silver coins and paper currency in the active circulation, but they would have to provide for a larger circulation of currency as a proportion of the gold currency would go into hoards and they would have to hold larger gold reserves. Moreover, a gold circulation would prove more unstable in times of crisis as it would probably be gold coins rather than silver coins or paper currency that would then be hoarded on such occasions. In fact, Keynes thought that it would be wise to discourage even the present level of use of sovereigns in India.

In *Indian Currency and Finance* not only did Keynes advocate a gold exchange standard with a token local currency, but he also suggested measures that would improve the operation of the existing system. He thought the existing system was inelastic in meeting the needs of trade, a problem which the authorities could address either by relaxing the rules governing the securities held by the paper currency reserve or by the creation of a state (or central) bank. Added to this proposal, which he advanced towards the end of the book, was a proposal for the rationalisation of India's reserve-holding policy and the cash-balance management policy of the state. The upshot was that the book contained a first-class discussion of the intricacies of the Indian financial system and a programme of limited reform.

Keynes took an active and conspicuous part in the deliberations of the Royal Commission. One of ten commissioners, he asked one-sixth of the questions when the Commission heard witnesses between 27 May and 6 August and between 23 October and 14 November 1913. With Lionel Abrahams, the Assistant Under-Secretary of State whose preserve was under scrutiny, he was able to draw out and expand the subtleties of official thinking for his fellow commissioners; with Montagu de P. Webb, President of the Karachi Chamber of Commerce and the ardent propagandist of the 'back-to-Fowler' position, whose speeches and articles (including the anonymous set in *The Times* in November 1912) had inspired the inquiry, he was a severe questioner, relentlessly pressing him on the weaknesses and inconsistencies of the arguments he had presented; with most other witnesses he was a critical, detached inquirer. He found the process intriguing, as he told Foxwell on 3 November:

> It has been very astonishing at the Commission how many of our best and (on other points) most intelligent witnesses have stuck up for a gold *currency*. But they can never stand up to cross examination with any sort of success; and their position is usually due, I think, to sheer ignorance of the facts and the arguments on the other side.[40]

Given the Chamberlain Commission's terms of reference – to inquire into the management of the balances of the Government of India in India and the India Office in London; the sale of Council drafts by the Secretary of State in London; the gold standard reserve, the paper currency reserve and the system by which the external value of the rupee was maintained, as well as the financial organisation and procedures of the India Office – it was almost inevitable that it would turn to the question of a state bank for India. Yet when the Commission turned to that question, the members found that there was no general agreement as to what was meant by the term and that it was difficult for them to examine witnesses on it or related matters. To assist them in June 1913 Lionel Abrahams prepared a 'Memorandum on Proposals for a State Bank for India'. Keynes provided comments on Abrahams's draft on 1 July, but soon found himself with an opportunity to take matters further. Before the Commission adjourned in August for its summer recess, he and Sir Ernest Cable, a jute merchant and former President of the Bengal Chamber of Commerce, were asked by the Commission to prepare a detailed scheme for a state bank for consideration in the autumn. Cable produced a skeleton memorandum dealing largely with the bank's capitalisation and left Keynes to fill in the operational details. After staying with Cable in Devon from 27 August to 3 September, and consulting during the visit with William Hunter, the Secretary and Treasurer of the Bank of Madras who had favoured a state bank in his evidence to the Commission, Keynes set out to prepare a final version of the memorandum, dated 8 October 1913. The memorandum, over his signature alone, with a covering note preparing the other members of the Commission for a very detailed scheme, was circulated in the middle of October. It appeared in full as an appendix to the Commissioners' *Report*.[41]

In the end, although the Commission did not see its way clear to endorsing Keynes's proposals in the *Report*, it did, in a section drafted by him, explain the grounds for its decision and direct attention to the memorandum, thus giving it considerable prominence. The Commission's reasons for not endorsing the memorandum – its inability to examine witnesses on its specific proposals and the possible delays that fuller consideration would involve – led it to recommend a further inquiry into Keynes's proposals. The First World War put paid to that: India did not get a central bank until 1935, after another currency committee, another Royal Commission and a White Paper. Keynes was to give evidence to both the Committee and Royal Commission.[42]

Keynes's memorandum went well beyond the brief discussion of the pros and cons of a state bank in *Indian Currency and Finance*. As he told Foxwell:

> With regard to the State Bank, when writing my book I didn't think it was practical politics and so, while always believing in it, dealt cursorily with the topic and tried to devise palliatives. I may say (in confidence) that I have brought the R. Commission round in the course of the last few months to practically everything in the book. But in the meantime, through thinking about the thing more thoroughly, I have come to distrust my own palliatives, and lay more and more emphasis on the State Bank. The fruit of this change of mind is to be found in the enclosed memorandum. I should like you to see this, but it is to be regarded for the present as a strictly private document.[43]

Buttressing his arguments with examples from experience elsewhere (including in the version published in the Commission's *Report* the Federal Reserve Act passed in the United States on 23 December 1913), he deployed the case for an institution located in Delhi whose senior officials would be Government appointees and which would be organised from the three existing Presidency Banks of Bengal, Bombay, and Madras. The new institution would act as banker to the Government, manage the note issue in a manner set out in some detail by Keynes, manage the Government's debt in India and carry out the Secretary of State's remittances to London to meet India's Home Charges. Although it would not hold the gold standard reserve for India, it would act as the Government's agent in any operations involving that reserve. In general, the details of Keynes's proposals were conservative: he carefully preserved the international business of the existing exchange banks; he modelled his proposed bank's note issuing and banking functions on the British Bank Charter Act of 1844 which in dividing the Bank of England into an Issue Department and a Banking Department had confused rather than simplified subsequent monetary analysis; and, much to the dismay of Lionel Abrahams,[44] limited the profits from the note issue transferred to the Government of India. Nevertheless, with its grasp of both institutional detail and economic principles, it was a first-rate intellectual achievement, even if its author had the initial advantage of finishing *Indian Currency and Finance* only five months before. As Marshall told Keynes on 9 March 1914, it was 'a prodigy of constructive work'.[45]

Unable to get the Commission to recommend his proposals for a state bank, Keynes was then faced with the need to obtain the Commission's agreement to proposals that would meet his aims in other ways. Here, he and his colleagues were working with a draft prepared by Austen Chamberlain and Basil Blackett which the chairman, heavily involved at the time in an attempt to obtain a compromise between his Unionist party and the Asquith Government over the question of Home Rule for Ireland, hoped would go through quickly. There was too much opposition, however, and after three days' meetings in December 1913 the Commission adjourned for Christmas. The three days were hectic. As Keynes told his mother on 20 December:

> The last three days have been about the most exacting to character and intellect that I have ever been through and I feel rather a wreck – wishing that I was off to the S. of France for an immediate holiday. We sat for seven hours a day, and one had to be drafting amendments at top speed and perpetually deciding within 30 seconds whether other people's amendments were verbal and innocent or substantial and to be rejected. I must say that Austen came out of the ordeal very well, and I believe he may yet be Prime Minister . . .[46]

After Christmas in Cambridge he went to the South of France with Duncan. (He had originally planned to go with Gerald Shove, an arrangement that unexpectedly broke down at the last moment.) During the holiday he did some drafting for the next meetings of the Commission scheduled for 12 and 13 January. However, he fell ill at Menton on 4 January and the dates of the Commission meetings found him still in Menton suffering from what had proved to be diphtheria. Despite his serious illness – so serious that Florence Keynes went out from Cambridge to be near her son – he tried to keep Chamberlain on the lines he desired, especially as regards the management of the paper currency reserve where, with the failure of his state bank scheme, there was a need to make provision for elasticity in the issuing of currency. He was so busy that he could write Duncan: 'The great disillusionment about an invalid's life that I've discovered is the complete lack of leisure. There seems something to be done every minute'.[47] His persuasion from a distance was partially successful, but over the matter of elasticity he returned to England on 30 January to find that he had not succeeded and that the Commission had held its last meeting and would probably meet him only on small points of drafting. With one last effort, Keynes attempted on paper to convince the Commission that its draft on the paper currency reserve was inconsistent and, more important, to give him his way by allowing him to delete eight words and add twenty-three words – a procedure that succeeded.[48] He managed several other addenda and amendments but none so skilful as the first. He also left his mark on other aspects of the *Report* – the proposals on gold in internal circulation and the organisation of the India Office. The *Report*, signed on 24 February 1914 and published on 2 March, vindicated the gold exchange standard system even if it did not go as far as Keynes wished in discouraging further official attempts to popularise the sovereign or in allowing for the use of excess international reserves for Indian development. Nevertheless, through *Indian Currency and Finance* and his own efforts on the Royal Commission, he had been remarkably successful in shaping opinion and policy recommendations.

Moreover, Keynes's India Office experience also found its way into the body of the Commission's *Report*. His suggestion that the Financial Secretary had become overburdened with matters of routine to the recommendation of the reorganisation of the financial side of the Office – the replacement of the Financial Secretary by two secretaries to the Financial Department: one for routine 'Treasury control' and another for more specialised and technical financial affairs – met with approval. He was also successful in his opposition to a proposal from the Secretary of State to replace the Finance Committee of five members of the India Council attached to the Financial Department with a single member of the Council. Here his successful argument was that a single member would not have such a varied business experience. He could not, of course, resist noting that if his state bank had a London office and board the rationale for the Finance Committee would disappear.[49] For someone who was just thirty, Keynes's accomplishments on the Commission were remarkable.

With the Royal Commission out of the way, Keynes returned to his more mundane, normal pursuits. His major task was *Probability*, proofs of which had started to arrive. Moore had started reading them by 2 March and would report reading and discussing them with W. E. Johnson until May.[50] Neville Keynes was reading them on 7 March and by 19 March was finding them 'very difficult'. W. E. Johnson was also deep in them in March. Meanwhile, Maynard Keynes had to clear up the backlog of work that had built up during his illness and the final stages of the Royal Commission. It was not until 6 April that he could report to his mother that he was clear of everything except *Probability*. He was finding it very hard to get down to that.[51] After the reading party at Asheham he did. On 21 May he discussed them with Moore until midnight. But it was in the long vacation that he really began to make progress. On 19 July he reported to his father that he was

> very deep in Probability and enjoying myself. I had 5½ hours with Johnson on Friday and got some most useful criticisms and suggestions. From conversations with Russell and Broad I have got less. I have been very much encouraged by Johnson's and Russell's reception of my Theory of Induction. They are both exceedingly complimentary.[52]

Work continued during a weekend's reading party at Clark's End near Pangbourne. Moore was there and the two men went through a great deal of the proofs. As well Keynes won 16s. 6d. from Moore at bridge. Presumably it was this rather than *Probability* that led Moore to remark in his diary that 'Keynes somehow leaves a bad taste in my mouth'.[53]

By this stage, however, international events were taking over. Archduke Francis Ferdinand of Austria was assassinated at Sarejevo on 28 June. Over the next month, the world drifted to war. It does not seem to have impinged directly on Keynes until late July, when he reported to his mother that he was 'trying to work but find myself dreadfully distracted about the war news, which makes it hard to think about anything else'. However, he turned down an offer on 30 July from the editor of *The Daily News* for a signed leader on the financial situation 'in order to get in at any rate some Probability'.[54] The next day in a long, rambling letter to his father, then in France on holiday, he speculated further on the possibilities of war and noted that 'this state of affairs interferes dreadfully with work, – I cannot keep my mind quiet enough'. Four days later Britain was at war with Germany. Keynes would return from time to time to *Probability* in August to try and incorporate his father's suggestions on Part III, Analogy and Induction, which Neville Keynes thought 'most original and I think extremely able' if still 'very difficult', and to which he compared his own treatment as being 'hollow & essentially incomplete', and to send half of the new Part V to the printers.[55] He was reasonably happy with the comments. Most of the criticism had concentrated on Part I.

> Part III on induction has now passed all the critics without receiving any substantial criticism; – so I feel much encouraged in regard to it. Most of the critics seem to think it is the best part of the book, though I'm not sure that I quite agree with that view myself. It is probably the most complete in itself and the least open to criticism. But that is largely because it is an old subject. There is much more pioneer work in other parts of the book.[56]

Serious further work on the book, which would soon be almost completely set in type,[57] would have to await the coming of peace.

NOTES

1 BL, ADD.60707, GLS to James Strachey, 5 May 1909; Lytton to James Strachey, 10 July 1909.
2 BL, ADD.60668, DG to GLS, 22 April 1909; see also BL, ADD.57930, JMK to DG, 4 May 1909.
3 BL, ADD.57930, JMK to DG, 7 September 1911.
4 KCKP, G. Shove to JMK, 29 December 1910 and 26 December 1911.
5 BL, ADD.57930, JMK to DG, 29 October 1913.
6 *JMK*, XV, 31–3.
7 The papers for the whole affair are in KCKP, Box 19.
8 BL, ADD.57930, JMK to DG, 7 September 1911.
9 Woolf 1964, 23.
10 For a discussion of one of Keynes's 'memoirs' see above pp. 116–19. See also below pp. 300–3.
11 Woolf 1964, 22.
12 Schulkind 1985, 201.
13 Q. Bell 1974, 14; the 1942 portrait appears in Rosenbaum (ed.) 1975.
14 C. Bell 1956, 130.
15 Rosenbaum (ed.) 1975, 78.
16 KCKP, Molly MacCarthy to JMK, undated but clearly 1920. It refers to the first meeting as being planned for Friday the 27th, which could be either February or August, probably the former.
17 In April 1910, Lytton was referring to 'the Bloomsbury set' having gone off with Virginia to Studland. (BL, ADD.57932, GLS to DG, 4 April 1910.)
18 A possible exception might be Duncan's presence during the final creative revision of *Probability* in 1908 in Scotland.
19 BL, ADD.60709, GLS to James Strachey, 8 September 1913.
20 BL, ADD.60709, GLS to James Strachey, 16 December 1913.
21 VWL, I, 415.
22 Schulkind 1985, 198.
23 BL, ADD.57930, JMK to DG, 14 February 1909.
24 KCCP, Vanessa Bell to Roger Fry, 9 August 1911.
25 KCCP, VBMK10, 16 April 1914.
26 C. Bell 1956, 53–5.
27 Spalding 1983, 227.
28 For the scale of his eventual collection see Scrase and Croft 1983.
29 BL, ADD.579830, JMK to D. Grant, 17 April 1913.
30 KCKP, JMK to FAK, 2 July 1914.
31 KCKP, JMK to JNK, 29 September 1912.
32 KCKP, JMK to JNK, 7 December 1913; JMK to Provost James, 22 October 1912; BL, ADD.55201, JMK to Dan Macmillan, 7 December 1912.
33 BL, ADD.55201, JMK to Dan Macmillan, 9 July 1913.
34 BL, ADD.55701, JMK to W. E. F. Macmillan, 21 January 1913.
35 For a full set of papers on the subsequent controversy see IO, L/F/5/144 and 145.
36 *JMK*, XV, 94.
37 For the various stages of the negotiations see *JMK*, XV, 97–8.
38 Chandavarkar 1990, 66.

39 *JMK*, I, 17–18.
40 MLC, JNK Papers, JMK to Foxwell, 3 November 1913.
41 It also appears in full in *JMK*, XV, 115–211.
42 See *JMK*, XV, 273–98 for his evidence to the 1919 Babington Smith Committee on Indian Exchange and Currency and *JMK*, XIX, 477–525 for his evidence to the 1926 Royal Commission on Indian Currency and Finance.
43 MLC, JNK Papers, JMK to Foxwell, 3 November 1913.
44 *JMK*, XV, 215.
45 *JMK*, XV, 268.
46 *JMK*, XV, 222.
47 BL, ADD.57931, JMK to DG, n.d. [but after 16 Januaury 1914].
48 The memorandum with the suggested changes appears in *JMK*, XV, 258–63. For the surrounding correspondence see ibid., 251–8.
49 *JMK*, XV, 265.
50 CUL, Add.8330, entries for 2 and 13 March, 26 April, 15, 19 and 21 May 1914.
51 KCKP, JMK to FAK, 6 April 1914.
52 KCKP, JMK to JNK, 19 July 1914.
53 CUL, Add.8330, 24–7 July 1914.
54 KCKP, JMK to FAK, 30 July 1914.
55 KCKP, JNK to JMK 11 and 13 August 1914; JMK to JMK, 18 August 1914; CUL, Add.7863, 13 and 25 August 1914.
56 KCKP, JMK to JNK, 14 and 18 August 1914.
57 BL, ADD.55201, JMK to Maurice Macmillan, 25 October 1915.

10

WAR

[A]s one of the few people who combine some special knowledge of these things with *not* having their personal fortune at stake, I chafe at being a purely passive observer.

(TCL, Montagu Papers, AS-IV-9, 2072,
JMK to Edwin Montagu, 4 September, 1914)

The drift of Europe towards war in July and August 1914 was in slow motion. Although the Archduke Franz Ferdinand had been assassinated on 28 June, it was not until 24 July that Austria delivered the ultimatum to Serbia which accelerated matters. That ultimatum was followed by other ultimata, counter ultimata, mobilisations and counter mobilisations until by early August Europe and its overseas allies were at war.

The Austrian ultimatum caused turmoil on Europe's financial markets – and incidentally saw Keynes buying overseas shares as prices fell. As the turmoil swept across the continent, threatening to close, and eventually closing, one stock exchange after another, it placed severe strains on short-term capital and foreign exchange markets, themselves already disrupted by fears of war. Within a few days the whole structure developed for international remittances was in chaos, as the closure of stock exchanges prevented sales of securities or the raising of new funds and the drying up of short-term bill finance prevented short-term accommodation as well. Moreover, the closure of stock exchanges and the end of new short-term finance, coupled with the inevitable moratoria on international payments on the Continent, meant that foreigners could not meet their liabilities in the London financial markets, thus calling into question the solvency of a large part of the London financial community. If foreigners could not make payments, then London accepting houses stood liable for their debts; if these liabilities caused them to fail, then the bill brokers who had discounted their bills (or acceptances) would be liable. The banks also had a substantial acceptance business and, in addition to any losses that they incurred here, faced the possibility of losses on their call loans to the discount market at a time when their other important liquid asset, loans to the Stock Exchange might also be frozen. Over and above this remained the question:

How would their customers react to the first general European war since Waterloo?

A further complication arose from the fact that relations between the clearing banks and the authorities (the Treasury and the Bank of England) were far from cordial. Since the Baring crisis of 1890, there had been intermittent agitation in favour of an increase in the country's comparatively small gold reserves. Although the Bank of England had raised its reserves slightly since the 1890s, it could only do so at the expense of its profits, for it would be replacing earning assets with non-earning gold. Moreover, its profit position had been sufficiently tight in the 1890s that the Bank had become more competitive with the clearing banks for certain classes of business, and, although by 1910 this competitive behaviour had ceased, old grievances remained. The clearing banks had become reluctant to increase their balances at the Bank of England, a step which would allow the Bank to increase its gold reserve without reducing its profits, and had developed the view that they should hold any increased gold reserves themselves and thus gain a say in the conduct of monetary policy. Some had already increased their gold reserves. In January 1914, seven months after the clearing bankers had appointed a 'secret' committee to consider the management of the country's gold reserves in an emergency, Sir Edward Holden, the chairman of the London City and Midland Bank and the most vigorous campaigner for larger reserves, had called for a Royal Commission on the subject. The Bank of England had deprecated Holden's proposal to the Treasury and had clearly told the clearers what it thought. However, partly in anticipation of a possible enquiry, the Treasury had prepared a memorandum, dated 22 May 1914, on the issue. Its author was Basil Blackett, who had taken Keynes's place as Secretary to the Chamberlain Royal Commission on Indian Finance and Currency, itself partly the product of Holden's campaign,[1] a year before. Blackett had also discussed the subject of the memorandum informally with Keynes. On 4 June 1914 Blackett sent him a copy for comment.

Keynes, caught up in tripos examining, did not reply until 24 June. He also discussed the issue with Blackett over lunch on 1 July. In his reply, Keynes had raised a number of points that became relevant at the end of the next month.

> I do not agree that the bankers are the only interested parties in avoiding a panic. In a modern panic it is improbable that the big banks will come to grief, and the main loss which the community suffers arises in rather a different way. This main loss, I should say, is due to forced realisations on the Stock Exchange of international securities. The first effect of a panic is that the banks withdraw their accommodation from their weaker clients and these weaker clients are forced to realise securities for what they can get. . . . It may not be good policy to save the weaker clients of the banks from their own

imprudence . . . . There is I think arising out of this some slight reason why the Government as representative of the general public should interest itself in the gold reserve question. It would not be primarily the bankers who would suffer from a bank rate of 10%.[a]

The main questions really at issue appear to me to be three [:]
(a) the question is not so much are our gold reserves sufficient, as what parties in the changed circumstances of the present day shall bear the responsibility and burden of the normal increase of the reserve which is from time to time necessary. . . . The present controversy, while it appears to be about the magnitude of the reserves, is really about a much more important question – namely, as to where in the future the centre of power and responsibility in the London money market is to lie. . . . [T]his question of distribution of power is a question of first-rate importance, which does deserve very careful consideration on the part of the Government as well as on the part of the bankers.
(b) Is it worth the Government's while to attempt to influence the nature of the settlement by putting pressure on the bankers, or by striking a bargain with them? I think it may be. If I were Chancellor of the Exchequer, I should be inclined to bear part of the burden of the increased gold reserves, not because there is any justice in the demand of the bankers that this should be done on account of the [Post Office] Savings Bank, but in order to give me bargaining power with the banking community. . . .
(c) There remains the question of some legislative change introducing a measure of elasticity into the Bank of England note issue. I regard this as very important, largely for the reasons which I explained to you in conversation. The number of bank branches is now so very great that nervousness on the part of the bankers, leading them to increase the amount of their till money, might very substantially reduce the Bank of England's reserve. It is important that all the gold should be kept either for export or for show, and that extra notes should be available for making the bankers feel quite easy as regards the possibility of a run on them.[2]

With this discussion behind them, it was hardly surprising that, after trying to reach him by telephone on 31 July, Blackett wrote to Keynes on 1 August:

I want . . . to pick your brains for your country's benefit & I thought you might enjoy the process. If by any chance you could spare time to see me on Monday I should be grateful, but I fear the decisions will all

---

a 10 per cent was the traditional level to which Bank rate had risen in previous periods of crisis, when there had been severe pressure on the Bank's free gold reserves and the Bank had asked the Chancellor for a letter promising it retrospective Parliamentary absolution if it violated the provisions of the Bank Act of 1844.

have been taken by then. The Joint Stock Banks have made absolute fools of themselves & behaved very badly.

Keynes received the letter on Sunday, 2 August. He did not wait until Monday. He did not even wait for the next train. He asked A. V. Hill, who had married his sister Margaret in 1913, to take him to London in the sidecar of his motor cycle. Leaving Cambridge, the pair almost ran down Walter Layton at the corner of Silver Street and Trumpington Street, although they did stop to tell him the reason for their reckless haste.[3] On reaching London, Keynes got out at the end of Whitehall, presumably to preserve an element of dignity. Immediately he was in the thick of things.

By the time Keynes arrived, little had been decided. The accepting houses had ceased to take business the previous Monday. Some clearing banks had called funds from the Stock Exchange and all had recalled funds from the discount market, forcing the former to close the previous Friday and the latter to seek additional accommodation from the Bank of England. Although 3 August was a Bank Holiday, the clearing banks had also refused to provide customers with sovereigns and gave them £5 notes instead. As these were hardly useful for holiday expenses, over 5,000 people appeared at the Bank in Threadneedle Street to obtain coin on 31 July and 1 August.[4] Faced with a fall in its reserves and a rise in the demand for accommodation, the Bank applied to the Chancellor for a suspension of the Bank Act of 1844, asked the clearers to provide accommodation to the discount market and raised Bank rate to 10 per cent (it had been at 3 per cent on 29 July).

The clearing banks had a 'plan' to meet the emergency, for their 'secret committee' had completed its work on 22 July. The plan involved paying over to the Bank £12–15 million in gold simultaneously with the issue of a letter of indemnity from the Chancellor to the Bank, plus further deposits of securities to complete the backing (one-third gold, two-thirds securities) of an emergency note issue of up to £45 million. They submitted their proposal to the Chancellor on 31 July, which may partially explain why they were so unwilling to let gold go to their customers. However, as they were also going to suggest to the Chancellor that Britain suspend gold convertibility, they may have sensibly decided not to supply gold for hoarding and left the Bank of England to make its own decisions.

Lloyd George, the Chancellor of the Exchequer, had some sympathy for the bankers' proposals. Keynes's first, and major, task was to write a memorandum for the Chancellor setting out the grounds against a suspension of gold payments. The memorandum, dated 3 August, set out the case against suspension in three stages: (1) that external losses of gold were likely to be sufficiently small to be manageable with existing stocks; (2) that suspension at the first sign of a crisis would impair London's future position as a centre for the deposit of foreign balances; and (3) that any potential internal gold drain could be met by extending the Bank Holiday for two or three days to provide time to prepare £1 and 10s. notes for internal circulation, thus economising gold for internal purposes.[5] This memorandum, along with the verbal advice of Treasury officials and the Governor of the Bank, stayed the Chancellor's hand in his discussions with the bankers. As Blackett later told Keynes:

> You must rest content with the knowledge that you have done a great deal & above all have written a memo[orandu]m which converted Lloyd George from a Holdenite into a Currency Expert.[6,b]

In letters to his father and his brother-in-law, Keynes also mentioned his roles in providing guidance for the press and in the preparation of a scheme for saving the accepting houses.[7] In the latter case, the position had been held by a one month moratorium on bills of exchange. Keynes's memorandum of 5 August provided a discussion of possible schemes that would reopen the market for new business, but his proposed scheme did not foreshadow the one eventually adopted in two stages on 7 August and 4 September. Two days after this memorandum, after a day of conversations at the India Office and in the City, he was finished at the Treasury. He had hoped for a wartime Treasury job, but one had not materialised, for Lloyd George had appointed Sir George Paish to whom he had turned informally for advice in the past.

Keynes thought of returning to *Probability* and clearing off a backlog of *Economic Journal* work, but the war news seemed too distracting to continue with his book, and he turned to writing a history of the financial crisis in which he had just participated. He thought he might put part of it in the September *Journal*, but he also had plans for 'a small book' on the subject in September. It would give him something to do 'without forcing one to divert one's mind altogether from the war'.[8] By this time he had decided to go on a camping holiday near Helston in Cornwall on 18 August. From there, stopping in London to pick up gossip from Blackett in the Treasury and in the offices of *The Economist*, whose editor offered to print anything he cared to write, he went on to Virginia and Leonard Woolf's at Asheham on 26 August. Most of Bloomsbury turned up – the Bells with their children, the MacCarthys, Lytton, Gerald Shove, Harry Norton, and, in the end, even Virginia. It was at Asheham that he reported to his father on 3 September that he had finished the article, 'War and the Financial System, August 1914'.

> I've seldom written so industriously as I have since I came here, and there's a vast length of it – more than 12,000 words. . . . My chief quarrel with the banks is that they are not really in danger themselves and are simply putting other people into danger. If their

b Lloyd George, however, also protested to Blackett at his calling in an outsider for advice on his own responsibility (Harrod 1951, 197).

own position was thoroughly insecure, one could not expect them to risk it further.

He returned to London on 7 September to see the *Journal* through its final stages, adding material as recent as financial statistics for 10 September.[9]

Keynes's proposed book did not materialise. Instead, he published two further articles on the crisis 'The City of London and the Bank of England, August 1914' in the *Quarterly Journal of Economics* for November 1914 and 'The Prospects of Money, November 1914' in the *Economic Journal* for December.[10] In these, as well as in letters to *The Economist* and in his private correspondence, Keynes was sharply critical of the behaviour of the clearing bankers. They had 'completely lost their heads and have been simply dazed and unable to think two consecutive thoughts', had 'signally failed, in courage and public spirit', and 'took every precaution on their own behalf of which they were capable, and abstained from every form of bold or definitely public-spirited action'.[11] To Alfred Marshall on 10 October, he went even further:

> It was impossible [in the September article] to do justice to the question of the behaviour of the banks in the early days of the war without going into personalities, which was not possible in the *Journal*. Schuster and Holden were the spokesmen of the bankers and the men the Treasury looked to as their leaders. The one was cowardly and the other selfish. They unquestionably behaved badly, and it is not disputed that they pressed strongly for suspension of cash payments by the Bank of England. By no means all of the other bankers trusted Schuster or Holden or agreed with their immediate proposals; but they were timid, voiceless and leaderless and in the hurry of the times did not make themselves heard.[12]

In the September article, Keynes had argued that the bankers had played an important role in precipitating several events. First, they were largely responsible for the closing of the Stock Exchange on 31 July.

> They might have come forward at the beginning and assured the Stock Exchange that they would stand by them to the utmost of their power and that, in the matter of calling for additional cover, they would treat old borrowers with as much consideration as they were able. . . . Unfortunately, however, the early action of the banks was such as to give the Stock Exchange no confidence that the banks would stand by them, but rather encouraged the feeling, however, ill-founded, that the bankers, or some of them, had little intention of considering anything other than their own skins.

Second, by calling in considerable amounts of funds from the discount houses on 30 and 31 July and on 1 August, the banks had forced the discount market to borrow from the Bank of England as Bank rate rose from 3 to 10 per cent.

> By Saturday morning the action of the Joint Stock Banks had brought the discount houses near to demoralisation, and those houses began to be afraid that the Bank of England would no longer take their bills – a fear, however, which the Bank of England's action quickly dispelled.

Third, the clearers, despite their own large gold reserves, precipitated a drain of gold into internal circulation from the Bank of England. As Keynes bitingly put it, 'Our system was endangered, not by the public running on the banks, but by the banks running on the Bank of England'. They did this both directly by asking for gold themselves and indirectly by 'making difficulties all over the country in paying out gold coin even . . . for petty cash'.

Finally,

> Some amongst their leaders were ready, it seems to force suspension of specie payment on the Bank of England, while its resources were still intact, without one blow struck for the honour of our old traditions or future good name.[13]

When 'War and the Financial System, August 1914' appeared, at least one of the participants in the crisis, Sir Felix Schuster, was 'very angry'. Schuster told Lionel Abrahams, who told Keynes, and some correspondence ensued.[14] A member of the Council of the Royal Economic Society, Schuster stated that the article had led him to think of resigning in protest, for he did not believe that Keynes had complete information on what had happened. As a preliminary to a meeting, which did not take place, he set out his version of the story in a letter. From its contents, it is far from clear that he knew that Keynes had been in the Treasury during the early days of August, for if he had, he would not, for example, have suggested that it was the Governor of the Bank of England rather than the bankers themselves who had argued for suspension of convertibility.[c] Yet, Keynes gave very little away, either in the exchange of correspondence or in his postscript to 'The Prospects of Money, November 1914', where he mentioned some criticism, but was only prepared to allow that 'perhaps . . . my judgement of what the banks did was harsh and not in all respects just' in one or two respects. But he concluded

---

c The bankers' proposals exist in writing in the Treasury's records (PRO, T170/14, Holland-Martin to Lloyd George, 3 August 1914). Although there is no suggestion of Cunliffe's proposing suspension in Lloyd George's memoirs or in the academic literature on the crisis, including the official history of the Bank of England, there is one hint that he might have taken that line at an early stage. On 31 July, Asquith, the Prime Minister, wrote to his confidante of the period Venetia Stanley:

> They [the bankers] have been having a black day there, and the Governor of the Bank is now waiting here to get our consent to the suspension of gold payments! – a thing that has not happened for nearly 100 years

> (Brock and Brock (eds) 1982, 138).

It was reason for some dismay to see bankers inclined to haggle when they should be constructing, and speaking feebly of 'their duty to their shareholders' – though, of course, no one would have wished or countenanced anything dangerous to the banks or opposed to the permanent interest of their proprietors – when all should have been thinking of the state.[15]

During the crisis, Keynes may also have become involved in the dilemmas of war on a more personal level. David Garnett related the story:

> Maynard told me that he had succeeded in raising enough money for Ferenc Bekassy to leave England the night before. The banks were shut owing to the moratorium and Bekassy was anxious to return to Hungary to fight against Russia. War had not been declared between Britain and Austria-Hungary until the morning after Bekassy left.
>
> I said I thought that Maynard should have refused to find the money on the double grounds that he was sending a friend to his death and strengthening the enemy forces.
>
> Maynard disagreed violently. He said he had used every argument to persuade Bekassy not to go – but having failed to persuade him, it was not the part of a friend to impose his views by force, or by refusing to help. He respected Bekassy's freedom to choose, though he regretted his choice. My second argument was ridiculous: what was one man in a score of millions? I agreed that friendship was more than patriotism, but asked him if he would restrain the friend who contemplated suicide, or would he lend him money to buy poison? Maynard replied that in certain circumstances he would lend him the money – if it was a free choice, made by a sane man after due reflection, for compelling causes.[16]

Garnett's story is plausible: Keynes's arguments certainly ring true. But there are problems with the surrounding details. From the text Bekassy appears to have left England on Sunday, 9 August, for Britain declared war on Austria the next day. But if this were the case, there should have been no problem in getting cash. The Bank Holiday ended on 6 August. Yet, why did Bekassy wait so long to leave? Austria-Hungary had been at war with Russia for over a week and the war had started before the Bank Holiday. Moreover, war looked likely even earlier.

There are other peculiarities. At that time Keynes kept very detailed financial records, including notes of loans or gifts of small sums. Yet his books contain no record of his making any contribution to what, with the disruption of European communications by war or threats of war, would have been a very expensive journey.

Garnett's dating is peculiar: he reports he was not in London when war broke out and he remained in the camp at Helston until the day before

Keynes arrived, which was 18 August 1914. Thus he could not have been present at the time the incident took place.[17]

To confuse the story further, there is a letter from Keynes to Duncan Grant, written after Bekassy's death. The relevant section runs as follows:

> I have heard from Noel [Olivier] that she has just got a letter from him [Bekassy] written five days before starting for the front. It seems now an extraordinarily short time ago that he came rushing back for his sister, and how walking through Leicester Square after going to the Picture Palace near there on the night when war was certain, I very depressed but he excited and not very depressed, he said, – 'It will be a very wonderful experience for those of us who live through it.' He was certain to be killed. When one thinks of him, it is his *goodness*, I think, one seems to remember. But it is no use talking about him. I think it's better to forget these things as quickly as one possibly can.[18]

All in all, one doesn't know how to take Garnett's report. He and Keynes may have discussed Bekassy's return home. Keynes, given his memory of the conversation with Bekassy on 1 or 8 August, 'the night when war was certain', may have expressed the sentiments that Garnett later attributed to him, even going so far as to say that he would have provided the funds. But on the existing evidence, given that Garnett is not always a reliable witness,[19] I think we should discount the story, much as one would like to believe it.[d]

Although Keynes had failed to gain an official Treasury post, he still managed to keep involved in Treasury affairs. On 4 September, while still at Asheham, after hearing of the Treasury's latest moves (which he characterised as 'well on the way to disaster' and 'altogether too clever'[20]) from Basil Blackett, Keynes wrote to Edwin Montagu, now Financial Secretary to the Treasury, expressing his 'great anxiety over Lloyd George's future course of action'.

> As regards currency and the fear of inflation:–
> I have no anxieties on this score at present. I see no objection to the use of the Currency Note Redemption Fund in aid of the Exchequer Balances. The *only* point of holding this fund in gold at present would be in the possible influence this course of action might exert on the Bank Rate, and if it is desirable to increase the Bank Rate, this could be done *directly* better than indirectly. I believe myself that 5 per cent

d After this book went to press, I found a further suggestion that the story is indeed false. Richard Garnett, who reports that his father could never resist improving a good story and that, as a result, his autobiography is sometimes very inaccurate, reports that Bekassy wrote to his grandmother, Constance Garnett about a possible translation on 29 July 1914. The letter was written from Hungary. For details see R. Garnett 1991, 288 and n. 22.

is too low (just as 10 per cent was preposterously too high), and that in the long run this *must* be raised (there may be psychological arguments against raising it immediately) if evils of various kinds are to be avoided. What we want is good facility for accommodation at not too low a price. At present we have the opposite – facilities greatly restricted, and those, that are granted, granted too cheap. . . .
As regards the Stock Exchange and the rest:–

I distrust Lloyd George's temperament in dealing with this. Ever since you guaranteed the pre-moratorium bills, all the other interests have been out for blood money, and inclined to strike work until they get it. There is considerable danger of the Treasury's being blackmailed. The easy thing to do is to proclaim more guarantees and pour out more public money, and thus make all the financiers happy by taking over more of their possible debts. A certain amount of this sort of thing may be necessary and desirable in the public interest; but I do not think that the financiers by themselves are good judges or good advisers as to how much of it is desirable.[21]

Similarly, after lunching with Arthur Dickinson, Goldie's brother and a partner in the accountants Price Waterhouse, on 24 September, and receiving a suggestion for the treatment of German debts, Keynes tried the idea on Lionel Abrahams the next day. When Abrahams reacted favourably, he wrote the scheme up for Sir John Bradbury in the Treasury, who acknowledged it on 30 September.[22] He also saw Edwin Montagu and Bradbury for lunch on 12 October.[23] Two days later he sent Montagu a note on the Reichsbank's latest return and on 24 October he sent Bradbury and Montagu a note of his thoughts on the war loan question as they had evolved since their conversation. He was far from an idle bystander. These activities, plus his term-time teaching commitments, including a course of lectures on the economic problems created by the war, meant that *Probability* stayed in the background where it was to remain for almost six years.

The autumn found Keynes very lonely. Adrian Stephen's engagement and marriage to Karin Costelloe brought an end to living in Brunswick Square. It also ended Keynes's sharing a house with Duncan Grant, for, despite Keynes's suggestion, Duncan did not follow him to Great Ormond Street but took a room with the Bells at 46 Gordon Square. Thus ended an easy intimacy of six years' standing.[24]

Cambridge was hardly more cheerful. It provided constant reminders of the war. In King's, ninety-one nurses moved into Bodley's buildings by the river, while a hospital for 500 went up on the King's/Clare sports ground across Queens' Road beyond the King's Fellows' Garden. Officer trainees filled the Colleges which were denuded of students and young dons. At the division of the Michaelmas term, King's had only sixty-four students in residence as compared to the 170 previously expected. (By the same time in Lent 1916, there were to be only sixteen in residence.)[25] As Keynes put it, with some exaggeration, to Freddie Hardman, who had gone to France in mid-August, 'I lecture to blacks and women'.[26]

Soon there came reports of deaths. When Peter Lucas went off to war, Keynes wrote to Grant:

> It is dreadful that he should go. All my sub-conscious feelings about things are now deeply depressed which they weren't before. It seems to make it hardly any better that we should be winning. There is a very gloomy letter from Geoffrey [Keynes, then working in a military hospital in Versailles] today about the appalling losses of the last week or two.[27]

Slightly later, he wrote to Lytton:

> For myself I am absolutely and completely desolated. It is utterly unbearable to see day by day the youths going away, first to boredom and discomfort and then to slaughter. Five of the College, who are undergraduates or have just gone down, are already killed, including, to my great grief, Freddie Hardman,[e] as you may have seen in the papers.
>
> If the new army ever gets to the front it will be too awful.[28]

In December, Keynes got closer to the war when he spent a week in France visiting his brother at Versailles and, incidentally, accumulating information on French finance that was to serve him well.

After Christmas at Harvey Road, Keynes went to London on 1 January. Two days later Keynes saw Blackett and the next day he returned to the Treasury at the end of the day. He was offered the position of assistant to Sir George Paish, Lloyd George's special adviser, and put to work immediately on a memorandum on French finance for Lloyd George who was off to Paris on the Friday. He finished the memorandum on 6 January, when he reported to his father: 'The Governor of the B of E has been reading my works and has asked me to visit him at the Bank'.[29] However, it took some days to sort out the details of his Treasury arrangements: the offer was not firm until 15 January. By then he had disembarrassed himself of his Cambridge teaching and administrative duties. His employment was for the duration at £600 per annum. It was understood that he could have one day off a week and could continue to edit the *Economic Journal* and write in his spare time, subject to Treasury consent when using official material. He officially started work on 17 January 1915. Years later, he remembered his initial position – and Paish's:

> On the outbreak of the war he [Paish] was sent for by Mr. Lloyd

e The letter to Hardman cited above was returned to Keynes as it arrived after his death.

George to go to the Treasury as his leading financial expert . . . and for about a day and a half in August 1914 he was very important in the Treasury. As usual, however, Mr. Lloyd George soon got bored with him and stopped reading his lengthy memoranda. . . .

But before the end of 1914 the Treasury discovered that there was no very convenient room for him in their building, and he was given a room at a considerable distance, over at the Road Board in Caxton House.

When I first came to the Treasury in January 1915 I was nominally appointed as Paish's assistant. But I was given a seat in Blackett's room, as well as with Paish over at the Road Board. After a few days I came to the conclusion that Paish was barely in his right mind, and before long I almost ceased going over at all to the rooms at the Road Board. Not very much later he had a complete breakdown and retired[30]

Responsibility for Keynes's appointment seems to have rested with Edwin Montagu. When Montagu died in 1924, Keynes, as well as writing a memoir for *The Nation and Athenaeum*, wrote in a letter to Lydia Lopokova:

I am a little sad at the death of Edwin Montagu. I owed – rather surprisingly – nearly all my steps up in life to him. When I was a freshman in Cambridge in 1902, he was President of the Union (the chief undergraduate society) and picked me out in my first term and gave me what is called 'a place on the paper'. The first electioneering I ever did (in 1906) was for him. In 1913 when he was at the India Office, it was he who got me put on the Royal Commission on Indian Currency, which was my first step into publicity (my name was known to no one outside Cambridge before then). It was he who got me called to the Treasury in 1915 during the war. It was he who got me taken to Paris in February of that year for the first inter-Ally Financial Conference and so established me in my war work. It was he who introduced me to the great ones. (I first met Lloyd George in a famous dinner party of 4 at his house; I first met [Reginald] McKenna through him; I first met Margot [Asquith] sitting next to her at dinner at his house.) It was he who got me invited to the dinners of the under-secretaries during the early part of the war (private gatherings of the secretaries of the Cabinet and of the chief ministers who exchanged secret news and discussed after dinner the big problems of the war). . . . Thus for more than 20 years I had reason to be grateful to him; there was a certain affectionate relation between us[31]

Once Keynes's Treasury appointment was cleared, he received his first job, secretary to a Cabinet Committee on food prices presided over by the Prime Minister. Within a week of joining the Committee, he had produced his first Cabinet Paper on wheat prices.[32] A week later, he was off to France in a party consisting of Lloyd George, Edwin Montagu, Lord Cunliffe,[f] the Governor of the Bank, and a private secretary for the first inter-allied financial conference of the war. The night before he left, he dined at Montagu's 'famous dinner party of 4' to meet Lloyd George. At the conference Britain and France agreed to share equally in supporting Russia, while the three allies agreed to pool their resources to support other allies. Russia and France also agreed to lend gold to the Bank of England, while Britain and France agreed to provide facilities for a Russian loan in their markets.

The Treasury Keynes entered in 1915 was a small institution. In 1914 its total strength, including 23 charladies and 41 messengers, was 144. It would rise by two by 1918. At its heart was a small cadre – 37 in 1914, 40 in 1918 – of administrative class civil servants. Many of those present when Keynes joined have already appeared or will appear later in this biography. The Joint Permanent Secretaries were Sir Thomas Heath and Sir John Bradbury. Among the first class clerks were Ralph Hawtrey, Basil Blackett, Otto Niemeyer, Frederick Phillips and Frederick Leith-Ross. Second class clerks included S. D. Schloss (later Waley), Andrew McFadyean, Harry Siepmann, Frank Nixon, and P. J. Grigg, as well as Saxon Sydney-Turner. Leaving aside Paish's small operation, the Treasury was divided into six divisions, each headed by a Principal Clerk. One division was concerned with purely financial questions, four of the remaining five with the control of public expenditure. The small numbers involved and their wide-ranging responsibilities for the domestic and overseas financial affairs of the British Government meant that, in spite of the weakening of Treasury control of expenditure during the war, individual members quickly gained substantial responsibilities at the highest levels of government. Grigg remembers very early in his Treasury career being sent 'on missions to other offices, invariably to see officials very much senior to myself and lay down the law to them'.[33]

To exercise its control, with its very small staff, the Treasury had developed between the reforms of the 1870s and the outbreak of war the characteristics of 'a rather select club', with close contacts between seniors and juniors.[34] As numbers were relatively few in comparison to responsibilities, Treasury officials could not be expert on the details of their spending departments' affairs. Yet they had to be good at clever cross-examination to uncover the implications of proposals. Treasury officials, according to Keynes, 'tended to develop a certain cynical attitude, for the Treasury is not a place where one could attain an unduly exalted idea of human nature'. To deal with departmental enthusiasms it developed weapons characteristic of institutions dependent to a great extent on their prestige: 'precedent,

f Cunliffe's appointment, the first peerage of the war for his services during the financial crisis, was dramatically announced by Asquith during the Lord Mayor's Banquet at the Guildhall on 10 November 1914.

formalism, aloofness, and even sometimes obstruction by the process of delay, and sometimes indefinite replies'. As Keynes was to put it after the war:

> In some ways I think Treasury control might be compared to conventional morality. There is a great deal of it rather tiresome and absurd once you look into it, yet it is an essential bulwark against overwhelming wickedness. It is because in a way the Treasury is always fighting against odds that it is always necessary that it should have all the weapons proper to its prestige. . . . And supported by these various elements, it became an institution which came to possess the attributes of institutions like a college or City company, or the Church of England. Indeed, I think it might have been defended on the same grounds which the eighteenth-century sceptics were accustomed to make: 'A defence that would be as a bulwark against too much enthusiasm.'[35]

Keynes was writing about the pre-war civil service at its peak. War – or perhaps as Keynes suggested even the pre-war years under Lloyd George, who had little institutional sense and 'never the faintest idea of the meaning of money' – weakened the Treasury's powers of control, but the attitudes lingered. 'Spending money, like eating people is wrong'.[36] It is not surprising that Keynes, reared in another small institution designed for control, the India Office, fitted in well and would become as 'Treasury-minded' – 'the highest possible praise', according to him – as the best of them.[37]

During the early part of his service in the Treasury, Keynes's duties were varied. He continued working for the Cabinet Committee on Food Prices until it reported and then, according to his father's diary, prepared the speech that Asquith made to the House of Commons on the report.[38] Subsequently he served on an interdepartmental committee on wheat and flour supplies. Many of his early memoranda, including at least one other Cabinet Paper related to these subjects. He was, however, taking some interest in domestic financial policy, in particular the Government's domestic borrowing arrangements. He spent the weekend of 15 May 1915 with the Governor of the Bank at his country house, Headley Wood near Leatherhead, discussing the terms of the second War Loan.[39] At this stage in the war, he seems to have got on well with the Governor, 'an aggressive character, who enjoyed a game of bluff, even when he lost it', and who 'evidently had the advantage of knowing his own mind, perhaps not a difficult mind to know'.[40] A surviving letter from late March 1915 suggests considerable warmth from Cunliffe's side.[41] His interest in finance meant that with the formation of the first coalition Government in late May 1915, Keynes was transferred to the Finance Division of the Treasury. He was soon 'overwhelmed with work' in his new job. On 3 June he went to Nice with the new Chancellor, Reginald McKenna, to meet the Italian Minister of Finance and to cement the financial arrangements surrounding Italy's entry into the war against Germany on the allied side. Four days later, lacking three nights' sleep, he was back in London having crossed the Channel both ways on a destroyer. Keynes reported it 'a most enjoyable trip'.[42]

The new workload – and, one suspects, the exhaustion after the Italian journey – had its costs, for no sooner was he back in London than his old problem of appendicitis flared up again, this time acutely. Fortunately the day he collapsed his mother was in London and called on him in his new house at 3 Gower Street where he had moved in March. As private ward beds in hospitals or nursing homes were unobtainable, the operation was performed on the kitchen table the next morning. At first he seemed to make a good recovery, for he resumed correspondence, using his mother as secretary on 15 June, but ten days after the operation there was a relapse and pneumonia. Neville Keynes rushed to London to be with his son. There were enquiries from the Governor about his condition. He was not strong enough to be moved to Cambridge by car until 9 July and it was 29 July before he appeared again at the Treasury. He spent part of his recovery in the country – with the Morrells at Garsington Manor near Oxford (16–20 July), with Sidney Russell Cooke at Bellercroft on the Isle of Wight 22–25 July), and then with the Governor at Headley Wood (26–28 and 29 July). After two days in the office, where McKenna was 'most kind', he went back to Garsington for the Bank Holiday weekend as one of a party that included Frankie Birrell's father Augustine, then Chief Secretary for Ireland.

Once back at the Treasury, Keynes was drawn into affairs in a number of new ways. Edwin Montagu had returned to the Treasury as Financial Secretary with the first Coalition Government after a brief period as Chancellor of the Duchy of Lancaster, and Maurice Hankey, who had been Secretary of the Committee of Imperial Defence, was now managing the War Council's secretarial arrangements.[43] In July 1915 they started meeting informally with a group of senior civil servants, normally on Fridays at Montagu's house, 24 Queen Anne's Gate.[44] Dubbed 'the Shadow cabinet' by Asquith, this group provided Keynes with links outside the Treasury and a wider view of affairs. He would need them, for with Basil Blackett's departure on a mission to America to raise an Anglo-French loan Keynes became the second in command of his division, under the Assistant Secretary M. G. Ramsay, responsible for banking, currency, the exchanges and inter-allied finance. His new position was recognised in November, when he was appointed an acting First Class Clerk at a salary of £700 per annum.

With his Treasury post, Keynes began to move in wider circles. I have already mentioned his visits to Lord Cunliffe's country house. These did not last beyond 1915. He also began long-standing friendships with the Asquiths and the McKennas. He had already met the Prime Minister before the war at one of Ottoline Morrell's evenings at Bedford Square. With the second year of the war, Keynes might meet him at Garsington, when Asquith came over from his nearby country house, The Wharf at Sutton Courtney. From autumn 1915, he became a regular visitor to The Wharf – and to social occasions at 10 Downing Street. Margot Asquith, for whom he was 'the best company in the world', recorded that 'I do not think I have ever known a more modest, lovable and perfect companion than Maynard Keynes.'[45] When Edwin Montagu had married Asquith's intimate companion and correspondent Venetia Stanley on 26 July 1915, this reduced the social contact between Asquith and the Montagus, although Montagu remained close to his chief until he accepted the India Office in Lloyd George's second Coalition Government in June 1917. Then there was a break between the two until a rapprochement occurred after Montagu left the Cabinet in 1922. Thus Keynes's social link with the Asquiths was, for much of the period, independent of Montagu. He became quite friendly with the middle Asquith children, Violet, Cyril and Elizabeth whom, although they did not provide the easy pickings guests did at the bridge table,[g] he found good company. On the weekend of 18–19 November 1916, as the crisis that would destroy the first Coalition Government began to bubble in the background, Keynes would report to his mother: 'I spent most of the weekend [at the Wharf] in the romantic pursuit of playing bridge with Mr Bonar Law as my partner!'.[46,h] Little did he expect that the partnership would become much closer in a matter of weeks, for Bonar Law was to become Chancellor of the Exchequer on 7 December. Keynes would later speak of these weekends:

> Those who knew Lord Oxford [as Asquith became in 1925] intimately cannot think of him except in the environment of a unique family. He was the solid core around which that brilliant circle revolved – the centre of the gayest, brightest world, the widest-flung yet the simplest hospitality of modern England. With an incomparable hostess opposite him, with wit and abundance and indiscretion and all that was most rash and bold flying round him, Lord Oxford would love to appear the dullest amid so much light, to rest himself, and to enjoy the flow

g As well as mentioning his winnings occasionally in his letters or his Bloomsbury conversation, Keynes kept detailed records for at least part of this period. Running from the beginning of January 1917 to the end of January 1919, they list the dates and places or individuals involved. He did not always win: he recorded losses of £18/10/0, £14/8/0, £19/17/0 with various Asquiths and their guests on 12 May, 4 and 30 June 1918. However, these losses were offset by some large winnings (£30/3/0 on 17 August 1918) and overall he came out ahead by over £36 in 1917 and £23 in 1918. The most frequently named partners and places are the McKennas, and the Asquith homes at The Wharf and Cavendish Square. These appear 43 times during 1917 and 1918.

h This provides an interesting offset to Bonar Law's strenuous objection to Asquith's playing bridge at a time of crisis (Jenkins 1964, 289).

of reason and of unreason, stroking his chin, shrugging his shoulders, a wise and tolerant umpire.[47]

Next to the Asquiths, Keynes's most frequent source of 'high life' was the McKennas. From early 1916 there were regular reports of weekends with the McKennas at Munstead near Godalming or, occasionally with Lady Jekyll, Pamela McKenna's mother. By the late summer of 1916, after a year of working with McKenna and the trials and tribulations of the conscription crisis, he would report to his mother that he was 'on very intimate terms now and I have got extremely fond of him'.[48] Of these weekends he would later remember that Pamela McKenna's

> personal attention to the happiness of her guests raised bodily comfort above itself to become the gentlest of muses. In leisurely talk, in the setting of music and of country sights and smells, one at least kept the Sabbath, even in time of war, by abstaining from work.[49]

This fondness survived the war and carried over into the inter-war period. McKenna would eventually join Edwin Montagu, Asquith and Bonar Law as the politicians he had served in wartime for whom he wrote obituary notices.

Keynes's 'high life' did not mean that he lost touch with Bloomsbury. However, the fact that as the war progressed, more and more of the group were out of London – Vanessa and Duncan in Suffolk and then Sussex; Virginia and Leonard at Richmond or in Sussex; Clive at Garsington – meant that the easy pre-war informality disappeared, although Keynes's taking over of 46 Gordon Square from the Bells in August 1916 meant that the various bits of suburban or exurban Bloomsbury had a London base where they often met either by chance or design. With his move into Gordon Square from 3 Gower Street (which he managed to pass on to Dora Carrington, Dorothy Brett, Katherine Mansfield and Middleton Murry), he now had the London home he would use for the rest of his life. When he took it over, the Bells' lease had just over two years to run and they were going to leave in order to save on the rates. Initially Keynes had it rent free on the condition that the Bells could have up to four rooms when they were in London, but he took over the lease in his own name in 1918. He shared the house with John Sheppard and Harry Norton.

With Vanessa's move to the country, first to Wissett Lodge outside the Suffolk village of the same name, and then to Charleston, a substantial two-storey farmhouse nestled at the foot of Firle Beacon, the highest point of the Downs stretching from Cuckmere to Newhaven, Keynes's links with the country changed. He still moved in the 'high life' circles, to the amusement of his friends, but Charleston became his refuge from London – and the war. When he went down for the first time in October 1916, he noted to his mother:

It's a most lovely place, a farmhouse of very considerable size with a walled garden and a large pond on the edge of the downs which rise straight up to Firle Beacon.[50]

His visits took on a routine. After arriving, he would tell the inhabitants his news and then retire to his room until lunch the next day. By then, somewhat rested and having spent the morning on his official papers, he would get involved in the house and its problems, weed the gravel path in the garden (the length of the meticulously weeded section of the path proving a good index of the length of his visit), gossip and walk on the South Downs.

Keynes's new responsibilities in the Treasury brought him face to face with the competing demands of the allies and the problems of resource allocation in a fully stretched economy. The two problems were not unrelated, as Keynes would point out frequently in the coming months, for the diversion of more resources to the armed services and the war effort meant less was available for other purposes and, almost inevitably, affected exports and imports and hence the balance of payments position. Any weakening of Britain's balance of payments caused strains on the alliance, for Britain was making large loans for overseas purchases, particularly in the United States, to France, Russia and the lesser allies. Despite the logical interconnections between the two problems, it is probably clearer to treat them separately.

At the outbreak of the war, Britain's balance of payments position was immensely strong – so strong that the international financial crisis in late July and early August 1914 had, as we have seen, its origins in the difficulties foreigners had in purchasing sterling for remittance *to* London. The dollar fell as low as $7 to the pound in thin trading as compared to the normal gold standard par of $4.86. There was a mission to the United States and some talk in the autumn of 1914 of a loan to ease the situation![51] During the last quarter of 1914 exchange markets returned to normal. From the beginning of 1915 exchange rates on London began to take on the appearance that they would have for the rest of the war: sterling tended to appreciate against the currencies of the major European allies – the franc, the rouble and, later, the lira – and to depreciate against the dollar and the currencies of the other major neutrals. By mid-February 1915 sterling had fallen against the dollar to $4.79½. One of the major financial problems of the war – the financing of the allies' large wartime orders outside of Europe, which largely fell on Britain – had arrived. This involved the co-ordination of purchases so as to avoid bidding up the prices of scarce supplies; devising of control systems to avoid waste; allocation of the supplies obtained among competing claimants; and, finally, obtaining the means of paying for the supplies. These issues had provided the bread and butter of the three foreign missions which Keynes had been on before autumn 1915 – Paris in February, Nice in June and Boulogne in August. In these and other negotiations the concerns included allied provision of gold for Britain to cover her foreign deficit, the co-ordination of purchasing and, in the late summer and early autumn of 1915, the terms of a joint Anglo-French loan to be issued in the United States, which was moving away from the position that public loans issued on its markets were inconsistent with its neutrality.

The loan was required to meet the weakness of sterling. As noted above, sterling had fallen well below the pre-war gold export point by mid-February 1915; from 20 February, the firm of J. P. Morgan, the British Government's agent in the United States, in association with the National City Bank of New York, began supporting the exchange rate. Supplemented by shipments of gold from Ottawa, which had become a British depository at the outbreak of war in order to avoid submarine risks, this worked reasonably well until the summer, when the Governor of the Bank, whose gold was being shipped and in whose name the Morgan credits stood, ordered further gold shipments from Ottawa to pay off the credits and refused to support the exchange – in the hope of forcing the Government to make a public issue in New York. In the absence of intervention, sterling fell as low as $4.56 in August in an erratic market. After Montagu and the Prime Minister, without previously consulting McKenna, supported the Governor's actions,[52] the Treasury stepped in to support the exchange with a credit of $500 million, secured on $300 million British-owned dollar securities purchased by the Treasury from British residents, while the mission, headed by Lord Reading, on which Blackett was serving went to New York and successfully negotiated the 1915 Anglo-French Loan of $500 million. Finally, in November 1915, the Chancellor set up an Exchange Committee under the chairmanship of Lord Cunliffe to manage the exchanges. Its detailed operations were conducted by Treasury officials, particularly Keynes and Sir Robert Chalmers, who was intermittently one of the Joint Permanent Secretaries.[i]

Just before the Exchange Committee was set up, the question of Britain's remaining on the gold standard was raised again. As in August 1914, Keynes prepared a memorandum against the suspension of gold convertibility.[53] His grounds this time for the *status quo* were that suspension would impair London's position as an international banker after the war and almost totally destroy Britain's ability to attract short-term foreign balances, and hence command over resources, to London during the war and probably even produce an outflow of such funds, thus complicating Britain's international financial and resource position rather than easing it. A suspension of gold convertibility might have to come eventually, but there was nothing to be said for courting or adopting such a policy until it was inevitable.

The issue of resource allocation, although it also arose in the context of

---

i I say intermittently because he spent part of the war as Governor of Ceylon and as Under-Secretary to the Chief Secretary for Ireland.

loans to allies, came to the fore in the recurrent discussions of military manpower. Soon after the outbreak of war, Kitchener had planned to raise a New Army of seventy divisions[54] and had agreed to do so through voluntary recruiting. From June 1915 the spectre of conscription began to haunt and divide the Coalition Government. Losses on the Western Front were heavy. In July the flow of volunteers began to slacken. In August, in connection with the American exchange problem discussed above, the Chancellor told the Cabinet that Britain could not afford both to maintain an army of seventy divisions and to support her allies financially. McKenna's arguments in favour of a much smaller force of fifty-four divisions were Keynes's.[55] Working from the existing figures for military manpower and expenditure and allied subsidies, he derided a Board of Trade estimate that 840,000 men could be 'spared' for the forces (that figure itself a far cry from the numbers actually demanded). Any reduction in output from these, plus the additional output required to support them under arms, would, unless accompanied by a reduction in consumers' expenditure, result in a spilling over of demands for labour from the more essential industries or in an increase in imports. Rather, he argued, as unemployment was negligible, as the possibilities of borrowing in the United States had already been exploited to the full and as domestic consumption had probably been cut as far as possible, 'without a policy for the confiscation of private incomes, a considerably increased army and a continuance of subsidies to allies are *alternatives*'.[56]

In September there followed another alarmist Cabinet paper from Keynes's pen.[57] The War Policy Committee of the Cabinet did not accept these arguments, perhaps because they were 'presented . . . in too intelligent a way' to those involved – and the problems of war finance were much less understood in 1915 than they would be a generation later.[58] Instead, it agreed to continue to attempt to raise an army of seventy divisions by voluntary means if possible or some sort of conscription if necessary. Yet the battles continued. As Keynes told Foxwell in confidence in mid-October after admitting his authorship of a speech by Montagu:

> The battle of finance is being fiercely fought behind the scenes and the Treasury at least are not behindhand with their warnings. The difficulty is that the consumptionist party,[j] which is beyond measure stupid, regards any counsels for moderation in expenditure as little better than bluff and a sophistry aimed at their particular schemes.[59]

Over the ensuing two months, the offensive at Loos cost 60,000 casualties and heavy losses continued at the Dardanelles. The Chancellor introduced a supplementary Budget containing sharp rises in rates of income tax and surtax, higher indirect taxes, and – surprisingly for a free-trade, Liberal Chancellor, who by doing so lost the Government some liberal support

j Lloyd George, his supporters and the Conservatives.

it could have used later – a measure of protection on cars, motor cycles, cinema films, clocks and watches and musical instruments. These 'McKenna duties' of 33⅓ per cent on imports of these goods, ostensibly intended to conserve shipping space and foreign exchange, were portents of later changes in Britain's free trade policy. Keynes was heavily involved in the Budget preparations, as well as helping seeing various Treasury measures through the House. This was in addition to his continued dealings with overseas financial affairs which in September involved negotiations with the Russians, who, in exchange for their agreeing at the Boulogne conference to ship gold to the United States wanted additional credits in London.

Successive letters to his parents during this period record an increasing burden of Treasury work and such other calls on his time and energy as the *Economic Journal*. The demands of the Treasury post were so 'overwhelming' during the week that in October 1915 he found the *Journal* occupied his weekends.[60] He reduced that burden by bringing Edgeworth back as effective joint editor to manage the time-consuming 'back' of the *Journal*.[61] He could do nothing to prevent the disruption of his nights by Zeppelin bombing raids on London, although by mid-October he claimed that he was sufficiently busy and tired as not to be seriously terrified by these. By this stage, Neville Keynes was noting in his diary:

> Maynard rather oppressed with his work at the Treasury. He seems to think now in millions. He feels very doubtful as to how we can get through financially.[62]

On top of all of this he had to prepare and deliver the six Newmarch Lectures on 'The War Finance of the Continental Powers' at University College London in November and December. As a civil servant, he was allowed to give the lectures only because the Chancellor took 'a more lenient view' than his permanent officials.[63] Not surprisingly, the lectures did not break new ground: they told Sir Charles Addis 'little we did not know – so little is known'.[64]

The autumn's rows over finance accompanied a drift towards the conscription many believed necessary to maintain the army at the desired levels. It was an emotive issue for many Liberals and Labour supporters, for it ran counter to past practice and represented a formidable extension of the power of the state, which many saw as becoming more conservative and authoritarian, over the individual. In July the National Registration Act compelled all citizens between 16 and 65 to supply details of age, sex and occupation, and to state whether they could and would perform work of national importance. It would, as some of its supporters acknowledged, provide the information necessary for conscription. In early October, in a last-ditch effort to avoid conscription, the Government introduced the Derby scheme, named after Lord Derby, the Director-General of Recruiting. On the basis of the National Register of numbers and skills of persons available for the services and industry, all males between 18 and 41 not in essential work were approached by letter and in person asked to attest their willingness to enlist. A statement from the Prime Minister in November that men who failed to come forward would be compelled to serve and that no married men attesting under the scheme would be called up until all available unmarried men had entered the services, either voluntarily or against their will, probably hastened conscription, for, despite extensions, the scheme ended on 15 December 1915 with 650,000 unmarried men outside the forces or essential occupations 'available' but not attesting.[65] With Lloyd George and his supporters threatening to force a dissolution of Parliament, on 28 December the Cabinet met to come to grips with the issue of compulsion.[k] By the next day, four ministers – Sir John Simon, Reginald McKenna, Walter Runciman and Sir Edward Grey – had submitted their resignations. By setting up a committee to consider the long-standing issue of the autumn, the competing military and economic claims over resources, Asquith managed to reduce the number of resignations to one – Sir John Simon's – and yet to introduce a Military Service Bill on 5 January 1916 by which all single men between 18 and 41 would be deemed to have attested. Those with a conscientious objection to military service would be allowed to state their case before a local tribunal which could grant absolute or conditional exemptions.

Keynes was caught up on two levels. He was a temporary Treasury civil servant who would be involved in the work of Asquith's committee of which his chief, McKenna, was a member. And there was Bloomsbury – and Cambridge. Many of his friends had by late 1915, if not at the outbreak of war, a conscientious objection to military service. This objection took a variety of forms from the view that all wars are wrong and should never be resorted to, through the view that although war is an irrational way to settle international disputes it may be necessary in some circumstances but that the state did not have the right to deprive individuals of their right to decide on these circumstances, to more esoteric, individual reasons. Among those involved or at risk were Duncan Grant, David Garnett, Gerald Shove, James Strachey, Francis Birrell and A. C. Pigou. Lytton Strachey, although certainly a conscientious objector, was probably effectively safe on medical grounds, although gaining such an exemption might prove more demeaning and uncomfortable than successfully convincing a tribunal of his moral position. Keynes's views, as we shall see, were probably closest to the view that, although war might sometimes be justified, the state did not have the right to take away the right of individuals to make their own decisions.

k The term of the existing Parliament was due to expire in January 1916, unless there was legislation extending its life. Lloyd George and his associates had taken steps to ensure that such legislation would not receive House of Lords' approval without moves towards conscription.

At first, according to his father's diary, Keynes talked of resigning his Treasury post in protest, a position that worried Neville.[66] Instead, however, he took another tack. He wrote to the *Daily Chronicle* under the pseudonym 'Politicus' putting the argument that the question of expanding the army by conscription, taken simply as one of 'expedience and practical good sense', was unwise given existing pressure on resources.[67] He also worked through Philip Morrell, with whom he had spent Christmas at Garsington, and sympathetic ministers such as McKenna to attempt to ensure that the Military Service Bill would be amended to protect the rights of conscientious objectors. Finally, he drafted the Treasury's contribution to the Report of the Cabinet Committee on the Co-ordination of the Military and Financial Effort.[68] This repeated the argument that a seventy-division scheme was impossible and that, at best, a sixty-seven division scheme (54 divisions in the field and 13 weakened divisions at home) was barely possible in the short term with economies in expenditure and a 30 per cent rise in tax revenues, although by June 1916 the authorities might briefly get as many as sixty-two divisions into the field. A larger programme would court financial disaster, especially as regards overseas payments and the maintenance of the gold standard.

Although Keynes had thought of resigning, by mid-January, perhaps as his behind-the-scenes activities seemed to be going well, he decided 'to stay now until they actually begin to torture my friends'. He thought 'a real split now and a taste of trouble would bring peace nearer, and not postpone it, otherwise I'd swallow a great deal'.[69] As was to become legendary amongst his Bloomsbury friends, especially Virginia Woolf, Keynes's expectations, based on what he would later call 'inner opinion' and his own tendency towards optimism, were more often than not inaccurate:[70] although the authorities did not 'torture' his friends, the war dragged on.

Conscription and Keynes's continuing presence at the Treasury, placed considerable strain on his relationships with other members of Bloomsbury. After a speech in Cambridge by Edwin Montagu, Lytton wrote to James Strachey:

> I cut out the *Observer* report of Montague's [sic] speech (it had *every horror* – not only protection but the necessity of smashing Germany etc.) and wrote on a piece of notepaper the following – 'Dear Maynard. Why are you still in the Treasury? Yours, Lytton.' I was going to post it to him, but he happened to be dining at Gordon Square where I also was. So I put the letter on his plate. He really *was* rather put out when he read the extract. He said that 2 days ago he had a long conversation with Montague in which that personage had talked violently in the opposite way. He said that the explanation was cowardice. I said that if cowardice went as far as that there was no hope. And what was the use of him going on imagining that he was doing any good with

such people? I went on a very long time with considerable influence, Nessa, Duncan, & Bunny sitting round in approving silence. (Luckily Clive wasn't there.) The poor fellow seemed very decent about it, and admitted that *part* of his reason for staying on was the pleasure he got from his being able to do his work so well. He also seemed to think that he was doing a great service to the country by saving some millions per week. I maintained that sort of thing was mere piddle-paddle, and that the really important things were the main principles – such as Free Trade – over which he had no control whatever. He at last admitted that there *was* a point at which he *would* think it necessary to leave – but what that point might be he couldn't say.[71]

Keynes was certainly pulled both ways. He was attempting to get the bill drafted with an appropriate clause for conscientious objectors other than Quakers – itself, regarded historically, a remarkably progressive concession – and with success.[72] He was also one of the early contributors to the National Council Against Conscription (later the National Council for Civil Liberties) giving them £50 as donor No. 130. He even tried the No Conscription Fellowship in April 1916:

> On Saturday morning I went for a short time to the secret convention of the No Conscription Fellowship, – to see what they were like, and was absolutely ravished by a long-haired, dark-eyed C.O. who sat just in front of me. It was rather an impressive gathering, I thought, and Clifford Allen seemed to be very good. In the evening, Sheppard and I gave an all-male party in honour of the Convention.[73]

His most important contribution was testifying on behalf of his friends. On 26 March he reported to his mother: 'I have testified before the wicked leering faces of the Hampstead Tribunal to the genuineness of James's conscientious objection'. Lytton reported the incident in more detail. Both Keynes and Philip Morrell arrived late for the case, Keynes remarking 'I have just arrived from the Treasury on purpose to appear as a witness in this case'. Lytton continued:

> Then *he* took Philip's place – and really it was a startling performance. When James had told me he had asked Maynard to come as a witness I had doubted the advisability of it. I feared he would not be an impressive enough figure. But on the contrary – he was supreme. He stated James's point of view with great incisiveness & vigour: they were very angry – but he persisted and beat them down. His rapidity and dexterity in answering them & making his meaning clear were extraordinary. At last they were reduced to silence – at last they found themselves obliged to listen – as he spoke, one could see them getting visibly uneasy & shifting in their seats. At last it was over and we filed out.[74]

James was awarded non-combatant service and, on appeal, complete exemption. The same pair appeared for Duncan Grant and Bunny Garnett. At first, at Blything, both applications were refused, although Keynes 'was the only person who made any impression on them & he could not say much as they wanted to get through to the next case'.[75] On appeal in July they were both given non-combatant service status to do work of 'national importance'. At the appeal at Ipswich, as at Hampstead, Keynes was aggressive. On arrival he placed his Treasury bag on the table and announced that he hoped for an expeditious hearing as he had important Treasury business to attend to. It worked. The only problem was that Bunny and Duncan, who had settled on a farm outside Wissett in Suffolk owned by an aunt of Duncan's, were not allowed to be their own employers; so Vanessa, Duncan and Bunny had to search for a new base of operations. This turned out to be Charleston. This new base was to prove important to Keynes, as well as the rest who settled down in a *ménage à trois* for the remainder of the war. Keynes also acted before tribunals for others of his friends, including Gerald Shove, and got others, such as Reginald McKenna, to act on behalf of others such as the novelist Gilbert Cannan.[76]

What of his own position? Keynes had not attested under the Derby scheme. However, as an employee of the Treasury, he was given exemption by his superiors until August 1916 on 23 February 1916, but formally told, as required by law, that he could, of course, make representation to his local Tribunal for exemption on the other grounds allowed for under the Act. In spite of his Treasury exemption, on 28 February 1916, three days before the date the Act came into force and the deadline for applications, he applied to the Holborn Tribunal for exemption on the following grounds:

> I claim complete exemption because I have a conscientious objection to surrendering my liberty of judgement on so vital a question as undertaking military service. I do not say that there are not conceivable grounds on which I should voluntarily offer myself for military service. But having regard to the actually existing circumstances, I am certain that it is not my duty to so offer myself, and I solemnly assert to the Tribunal that my objection to submit to authority in this matter is truly conscientious. I am not prepared on such an issue as this to surrender my right of decision, as to what is or is not my duty, to any other person, and I should think it morally wrong to do so.

The hearing for Keynes's case was set for 28 March at 5 p.m. On 27 March, he sent a note to the Tribunal that he was too busy to attend. On 29 March, the Tribunal notified him that they had rejected his appeal on the sensible grounds that he had a Treasury exemption. Of course, he could reapply when the Treasury exemption expired in August 1916. He did not do so, if only because his Treasury exemption was renewed for the duration on 18 August.

The existence of the note to the Holborn Tribunal has presented problems for Keynes's previous biographers. Sir Roy Harrod simply did not record its existence, although he did misleadingly remark that Keynes had sent a note in response to his calling-up notice that he was too busy to attend to the summons.[77] He was concerned to produce the impression that Keynes did not share his friends' views on conscription. In 1956 his view was challenged by Clive Bell's remark in *Old Friends* that he was a conscientious objector 'of a peculiar and, as I think, most reasonable kind. He was not a pacifist . . . he objected to being made to fight. Good liberal that he was, he objected to conscription'.[78] This made Harrod rather unhappy, an unhappiness that showed in his review article for Bell's book in the *Economic Journal* in December 1957, itself unusual except for an editor of the *Journal*, where he defended his previous statements on this and other matters. After something of a struggle within the committee then responsible for the *Collected Writings of John Maynard Keynes* and among the editors of the *Journal*, Elizabeth Johnson published the relevant evidence in the *Journal* for March 1960. The evidence now appears in the *Collected Writings*.[79] In a dismissive comment, Harrod replied that he still believed that Keynes could not be considered a conscientious objector to conscription, a position made clear by his failure to appear before the Tribunal.

In his more recent biography Robert Skidelsky not surprisingly rakes Harrod over the coals on this matter. But he admits that the question remains: Why did Keynes, having lodged his objection which was unnecessary given his Treasury exemption, fail to appear at the hearing? An important Treasury meeting was no excuse: that was probably enough to get the date of the hearing changed. Skidelsky suggests instead that when he had applied for the exemption in February Keynes 'was thinking of *resigning* from the Treasury' but by the end of March he did not intend to do so. The question then would be why did he change his mind?

Harrod in his reply to Elizabeth Johnson supplied one possible ground. By the end of March at least one of his friends, James Strachey, had been granted exemption, as noted above; so perhaps Keynes's friends would not be 'tortured'. On the other hand, Lytton Strachey's application to his Local Advisory Committee for an exemption on conscientious grounds had been rejected on 7 March, the same day as James's. His actual application to the Hampstead Tribunal, with its macabre hearing, less than a fortnight later, had been adjourned pending a medical examination, which Lytton failed, a few days later. However, this ground seems at best weak. It would hardly be rational to make an induction about the authorities' future course of behaviour on the basis of two cases, only one of which (James's) was successful *on its own grounds*. Yet Professor Skidelsky uses the inverse of this argument: 'Keynes had come to realise that he might use his official position to *save* his friends from imprisonment'.[80] On a sample of two? Of course, after the event, Keynes might have justified his behaviour on such grounds. In May 1916 Duncan could report to Vanessa

> I had lunch with Maynard. . . . There was Austen [Chamberlain] there & Bradbury (not with us). Everything was sumptuous & civilised & I saw one must either have that sort of thing & War or Wissett & Peace. There seem to have been several movements for the Conscientious O[bjector]s. There was a deputation to Asquith who put the whole business of making arrangements into McKenna's hands. So it really is entirely up to Maynard to keep him up to the scratch. Maynard thinks we are perfectly safe.[81]

In June 1916 Keynes could say with some truth to Dennis Robertson, then on active duty,

> The Tribunal crisis is getting over now, as concessions to the C.O.s are impending. But it has been a foul business and I spend half my time on the boring business of testifying to the sincerity, virtue and truthfulness of my friends.[82]

He could help his friends in other ways as well. One was financial. It was perhaps not unrelated that in 1916 Keynes helped Vanessa to move to Charleston by beginning his large financial contributions to the running of the house, as well as relieving the Bells of the responsibility for 46 Gordon Square, and agreed to be part of a scheme to finance a cottage in the country for Lytton which only came to fruition over a year later. He could not have helped financially without his Treasury salary – and Harrod was surely correct to suggest that his appearance before the Holborn Tribunal would probably have made continuation of that employment impossible.

There were probably other reasons. He had to some extent helped his friends through his official connections: one need only think of his influence in drafting the original legislation noted above – and it was not the only one as conscription became general in June. He had also to think of his parents, who appear to have been genuinely distressed at the thought he might resign. There was also the fact that Keynes thought he was doing some good at the Treasury by restraining the excesses of those in power, even if he was not always successful. Such restraint would, if he really believed what he was arguing, make civilian life in Britain more tolerable than it would otherwise have been. Of course, as the prospective author of *Probability* this might not amount to much, but present good made it more probable that the ultimate outcome would also be appropriate. None of these arguments individually would have tipped the balance, but together they could have done so in 1916. They may also have left Keynes somewhat uneasy in the face of his friends' criticisms and the fact that at least some of them, unlike Keynes, were actually worse off because of their principles. Such uneasiness may have been an important contributory factor to his behaviour later in the war and in the first months of peace, although there would be other, more proximate, contributory causes at work.

Before we leave the matter, however, there is one other point to discuss. If, as is certain, Keynes held a 'conscientious objection' to conscription, what was its form? In her 1916 paper, as well in the *Collected Writings*, Elizabeth Johnson suggested that Keynes's letter showed the classical liberal view that the state did not have the right to compulsion in this matter. Professor Skidelsky doubts this:

> It was quite out of character for Keynes to take such a stand on abstract right. He was too much of a political utilitarian to deny that the government had the right to do anything that would increase the social advantage. His objection to being conscripted was more concrete and more personal. He did not consider that he should volunteer for military service in the existing circumstances; it was his right to resist the state's attempt to make him do something contrary to his convictions. Although Keynes's language is not ideally clear, the letter sought to draw attention to a conflict of rights rather than to deny the state any rights in the matter. Otherwise, what was the point of dragging in his own attitude to volunteering, which was, strictly speaking, irrelevant to the question of the state's right to conscript?[83]

There is something in this claim. But Keynes would have to bring in the issue of volunteering to distinguish his point of view on conscription from one which took the view that all war is wrong and hence conscription immoral. The language is about more than a 'conflict of rights'. His last sentence, after all, ran 'I am not prepared on such an issue as this to surrender my right of decision, as to what is or is not my duty, to any other person, and *I should think it morally wrong to do so*' (emphasis added). If it was merely a 'conflict of rights', why include the emphasised words? We are, I think, back to the parts of 'My Early Beliefs' that were not repudiated in the process of writing *Probability* – where he stated 'I remain and always will remain an immoralist'.[84] For although the author of the undergraduate papers on Burke might in most circumstances accept that the principles of statecraft should be based on expedience and that against this doctrine there were very few, if any, absolute rights, it was still the case that Keynes claimed to retain the 'right to judge each individual case on its merits' – 'a very important part of our faith, violently and aggressively held'. This was his view in 1938, a year after writing

War resembles matters of faith and belief and differs from most other objects of public policy in that one may reasonably doubt whether even a large majority has a right to enforce it on a minority.[85]

Why should it not have been his view in 1916?

NOTES

1 See above p. 223.
2 KCKP, CO3, JMK to Blackett, 24 June 1914.
3 Layton 1961, 58.
4 Sayers 1976, III, 33 (Sir John Clapham's account of the crisis).
5 *JMK*, XVI, 7–15.
6 KCKP, Blackett to JMK, 13 August 1914.
7 *JMK*, XVI, 15–16.
8 KCKP, JMK to JNK, 14 August 1914.
9 *Economic Journal*, September 1914, 508.
10 The three articles appear in *JMK*, XI, 238–71, 278–98 and 299–328. In September 1915, he would also summarise German developments (ibid., 332–44).
11 *JMK*, XVI, 15, 26 and 29.
12 MLC, JNK Papers, JMK to Marshall, 10 October 1914.
13 The quotations from the article appear in *JMK*, XI, 244, 254, 253, 254, and 255.
14 KCKP, EJ/3, L. Abrahams to JMK, 24 September 1914. The subsequent exchange of letters with Schuster appears in full in Moggridge 1991.
15 *JMK*, XI, 328.
16 Garnett 1953, 271.
17 Garnett 1953, 267, 270–1; KCKP, JMK to JNK, 18 August 1914.
18 BL, ADD.57931, JMK to DG, 24 July 1915.
19 Above, Appendix 2; below, p. 301.
20 KCKP, Blackett to Keynes, 3 September 1914.
21 TCL, Montagu Papers, AS-IV-9, 2072, JMK to Montagu, 4 September 1914.
22 KCKP, S. D. Schloss to JMK, 30 September 1914.
23 Keynes made an eight-page note of the matters discussed: KCKP, JMK, 'Note of a Conversations with Bradbury and Montagu at 24 Queen Anne's Gate, Monday October 12, 1914'.
24 KCCP, VBCBII114, 2 October [1914].
25 Wilkinson 1980a, 352.
26 KCKP, JMK to F. Hardman, 25 October 1914.
27 BL, ADD.57931, JMK to DG, 9 November 1914.
28 KCKP, JMK to GLS, 27 November 1914.
29 The memorandum appears in *JMK*, XVI, 42–57; KCKP, JMK to JNK, 6 January 1915.
30 KCKP, JMK to Andrew Bonar Law, 10 October 1922.
31 *JMK*, X, 42–3; KCKP, JMK to Lydia, 16 November 1924.
32 *JMK*, XVI, 57–66.
33 Grigg 1948, 36.
34 On the pre-war and wartime Treasury, see McFadyean 1964, 44–67; Grigg 1948; and Keynes's own comments in *JMK*, XVI, 293–307. On Treasury society in general, see Heclo and Wildavsky 1974.

35 *JMK*, XVI, 299.

36 Trend 1982, 755.

37 *JMK*, XVI, 306.

38 CUL, Add.7865, 11 February 1915. In one of his letters to Venetia Stanley on 10 February 1915, Asquith noted of the Committee, '[W]e have a clever young Cambridge don called Keynes as Secretary, upon whom I rely for my brief tomorrow' (Brock and Brock 1982, 425).

39 He also provided the Treasury with papers on the subject: *JMK*, XVI, 96–107.

40 Sayers 1976, I, 66.

41 KCKP, Cunliffe to JMK, 27 March 1915.

42 KCKP, JMK to JNK, 1 and 7 June 1915.

43 It was established in November 1914. For a time after the formation of the first coalition, it was known as the Dardanelles Committee. Then in November 1915 it became the War Committee.

44 Waley 1964, 72.

45 Asquith 1943, 156, 59.

46 KCKP, JMK to FAK, 21 November 1916. Law had come to the Wharf to inform Asquith of Lloyd George's plan for a smaller War Committee with himself as chairman.

47 *JMK*, X, 40.

48 KCKP, JMK to FAK, 10 September 1916.

49 *JMK*, X, 59.

50 KCKP, JMK to FAK, 29 October 1916.

51 Sayers 1976, I, 87; Burk 1985, 57–9.

52 Beaverbrook 1956, 94–5.

53 *JMK*, XVI, 143–9.

54 Grieves 1988, 8.

55 *JMK*, XVI, 110–15.

56 Ibid., 115.

57 Ibid., 117–25.

58 The phrase is Roy Jenkins's (1964, 389n). Lloyd George called them 'more alarming and much more jargonish' and suggested that Keynes's 'vaticinations' shook McKenna's nerve, before launching into a paragraph of personal abuse to which Keynes protested in a letter to *The Times* (1938, 409; *JMK*, XXX, 118–19). For a concise discussion of the problems and principles involved in war finance see Sayers 1956, ch. 1.

59 MLC, JNK Papers, JMK to Foxwell, 19 October 1915.

60 BL, ADD.55201, JMK to Maurice Macmillan, 18 October 1915.

61 RES, Minute Books, vol. II, 1 October 1915, Minute 8.

62 CUL, Add.7865, 3 October 1915.

63 MLC, JNK Papers, JMK to Foxwell, 11 October 1915.

64 Dayer 1988, 81.

65 Grieves 1988, 22.

66 CUL, Add.7866, 6 January 1916.

67 *JMK*, XVI, 157–61.

68 *JMK*, XVI, 162–76.

69 KCKP, JMK to FAK, 13 January 1916.

70 For Virginia Woolf's scepticism see VWL, II, 133, 208, 313.

71 BL, ADD.60711, GLS to James Strachey, 22 February 1916. The letter from Lytton of 20 February quoted in the text survives in the Keynes Papers along with the clipping from *The Observer* for 20 February concerning Montagu's

speech in Cambridge which covered Germany and civilisation, conscription, and economy in British museums.

72 KCCP, VBRF189, 4 January 1916; Ceadel 1980, 39.
73 NUL, JMK to Vanessa Bell, 11 April 1916.
74 BL, ADD.60720, GLS to Pippa Strachey, 25 March 1916. The letter to his mother is in KCKP.
75 KCCP, VBRF195, 5 May 1916.
76 BL, ADD.57931, JMK to DG, 10 September 1916.
77 Harrod 1951, 214. Harrod's discussion of the issues covers pages 213–16.
78 Bell 1956, 46–7.
79 The relevant articles are Harrod 1957; Johnson 1960; Harrod 1960 and *JMK*, XVI, 177–9.
80 Skidelsky 1985, 326.
81 KCCP, DGVB 20, May [1916]. The evidence for 1916 is strengthened by the sentence after the last one quoted in the text. He thinks that his Russian journey will come off in a week or so but is not certain.
82 KCKP, JMK to D. H. Robertson, 18 June 1916.
83 Skidelsky 1985, 318.
84 *JMK*, X, 447.
85 *JMK*, XXVIII, 77.

11

EXTERNAL FINANCE
IN TOTAL WAR

> I pray for the most absolute financial crash (and yet strive to prevent it – so that all I do is a contradiction with all I feel)
>   (BL, ADD.57931, JMK to D. Grant, 14 January 1917).

In 1915, Keynes's Treasury work had involved both internal and external finance. In 1916, despite his activities during the conscription crisis, the balance changed. As early as 27 February, he was telling Foxwell:

> I am now almost entirely occupied with our financial relations with the Allies and the European Neutrals. And this is steadily becoming more than one man can really do, Russia alone occupying more than half my time.[1]

His concern with Russian finance almost cost him his life on his 33rd birthday, as he was selected to accompany Lord Kitchener to Russia to take part in discussions on the military and supply situations, starting on 4 June. The previous morning, Keynes had spent his time receiving

> a delegation from the Holy Synod of Russia . . . and doled out presents I should have liked myself. The high priests were so splendidly dressed and so exquisitely beautiful that I could not resist letting them have a little something.[2]

When he wrote this letter, he should have been at sea with Kitchener, but at the last moment was told to stay in London. On the evening of 5 June, the cruiser HMS *Hampshire* carrying Kitchener and his party struck a mine and sank off the Orkneys. The Field Marshal and most of the crew perished.

As in 1915, the international and domestic financial problems came together in the task of finding enough dollars to meet allied import needs. The Treasury urged economy, with some success. On 15 March, at Balfour's request, Keynes took the Treasury view on the issue to the Board of the Admiralty. There he admitted almost what Lloyd George later charged him with – a 'tendency to swing from one extreme to another' in anxiety.

> I used, four months ago, to think that a crucial point would be reached

in May or June. I now think that we shall get through the summer all right.

But anyhow, I at any rate believe we are gambling on a fairly early peace – a gamble which the condition of Germany . . . seems to favour. We may be able to stand the racket 9 mos. We cannot stand it for 18. The worst of it is that different Govt depts are gambling both ways – on a late peace and an early peace.[3]

He tried to point out the consequences of financial exhaustion – a weakening of allies (he referred to all of them bar France as 'mercenaries'); more unpopularity at home; and increasing inefficiency – and that planned economies now would be preferable to forced economies later.

Russia produced particular difficulties, of which he would recollect:

I remember how the day after I had established the principle that the Russian credits should be for munitions only, M. Routkowsky came round for my initials to a Bond Street bill for a Grand Duchess's underclothing; and there was the case of the beeswax for the Little Fathers.[4]

After a decision of the Cabinet's Finance Committee in May 1916 that only unavoidable purchases should be made in the United States and that Russian purchases should come in for more stringent scrutiny, Lloyd George suggested that Russia was being starved of necessary material and American contractors should provide credit for Russian orders. The Treasury reply over the Chancellor's signature, dated 5 July, was primarily Keynes's work.[5] Point by point he went through Lloyd George's suggestions, questioning his knowledge of the facts of the American economic position, his understanding of the intricacies of finance and of Russia's financial position, as well as almost derisively pointing out that *if* the Russians were being stinted of heavy guns, heavy shells and railway material, it might be related to the fact that at the time Lloyd George left the Treasury for the Ministry of Munitions in May 1915 *no* orders for such goods had been placed in America either by or on behalf of the Russians. Although munitions had been ordered in the first three months of McKenna's tenure, they had yet to be delivered and could not have affected the current position of the Russian army. As for railway materials, orders had been placed in July 1915 and deliveries had been in progress since January 1916, taxing the available freight facilities. He noted that in co-operation with the War Office, and more recently with Lloyd George's Ministry of Munitions, the system of supplying Russia had been improved and as a result Russia was likely to be liberally supplied for many months to come. Lloyd George was fended off for the moment – not that it mattered, for he changed departments, succeeding Kitchener at the War Office the next day. However, the memory, and knowledge of the memorandum's authorship, rankled and rebounded later in Lloyd George's *War Memoirs*.[6]

In the autumn of 1916, the external financial situation became still more serious. Relations between Britain and the United States deteriorated as a result of the effects of Britain's more intensive blockade measures against Germany on neutral shipping and of the US Government's Direct Profits Tax on American firms' war contracts. Britain struggled to meet her dollar commitments through issuing bonds, selling dollar securities turned over to the authorities in exchange for sterling, and borrowing at short term from J. P. Morgan and other American banks. The sums raised were large, but not enough, for, as Keynes pointed out on 10 October, the Treasury were having to find £2 million per day to meet American commitments.[7] He set the position out in more detail in a Cabinet paper, 'Our Financial Position in America', dated 24 October, covering an extract of a report from an Anglo-French financial committee.[8] He emphasised that Britain was rapidly approaching the position where the need for an American loan within a week or two would be all that stood between her and insolvency, especially as it looked as though five-sixths of her American expenditure in the next few months would be loan-financed and she had already pledged her most readily available external assets. In these circumstances the paper warned that 'the President of the American Republic will be in a position, if he wishes, to dictate his own terms to us'. The balance of international power was shifting.

Fears of an external financial crisis were not groundless. A public loan of $300 million on 1 November was quite inadequate to meet current commitments and the Government resumed borrowing on overdraft from J. P. Morgan & Co. A plan to keep the overdraft within limits by issuing dollar-denominated Treasury bills went forward, only to be frustrated by a Federal Reserve Board directive to American banks warning them against purchasing foreign short-term securities. The Treasury and the Bank of England did the best they could in the circumstances, borrowing from Morgans, shipping gold, requisitioning English-held dollar securities, and hoping against hope that the strain would ease. There were renewed worries about the possibility of leaving the gold standard: in January 1917, Keynes provided another justification for staying on gold if at all possible.[9] Twenty-two years later, as the authorities contemplated the external financial problems of another war, Keynes remembered:

> The procedure adopted was . . . [that] there were free dealings over the exchange at a rate which was 'pegged' by the Treasury, unlimited dollars being supplied at this rate. . . . [T]he pegging was done in New York and not in London, the dollars being supplied by Morgans as our agents. E. C. Grenfell would come round to the Treasury each morning with a pink cable in his hand, showing what had been paid out on the previous day.
>
> Complete [exchange] control was so much against the spirit of the

age that I doubt if it ever occurred to any of us that it was possible. But the absence of it made my task of preparing a monthly budget of the dollar position very precarious. I used to obtain each month an estimate from the various departments and from the allies both of their total outstanding dollar commitments and of the amounts they expected to mature each month. To this, if I remember rightly, I added my own estimate of the requirements of the 'free exchange'. On the other side, our dollar assets, actual and prospective, were set out in the shape of gold and securities and the proceeds of loans. But the requirements of the 'free exchange' would come in irregularly in great rushes, ... largely depending on the nature of the war and political news. I remember in particular a terrific run at the end of 1916, when the daily requirement (if my memory is correct) ran in excess of $5 million, which in those days we considered simply terrific. Chalmers and Bradbury never fully confessed to ministers the extent of our extremity when it was actually upon us, though of course they had warned them, fully but unavailingly, months beforehand of what was coming. This was because they feared that, if they emphasised the real position, the policy of the peg might be abandoned, which, they thought, would be disastrous. They had been brought up in the doctrine that in a run one must pay out one's gold reserve to the last bean. I thought then, and still think, that in the circumstances they were right. . . . I recall an historic occasion a day or two after the formation of the second coalition government at the end of 1916. The position was very bad. We in the Treasury were all convinced that the only hope was to pay out and trust that the drain would suddenly dry up as it had on previous occasions. But we had no confidence in the understanding of ministers. Chalmers went over to [Sir Edward] Carson's room (my memory tells me that it was in the War Office; but was it?)[a] to report to the newly formed War Cabinet. 'Well, Chalmers, what is the news?' said the Goat.[b] 'Splendid', Chalmers replied in his high quavering voice, 'two days ago we had to pay out $20 million; the next day it was $10 million; and yesterday it was $5 million.' He did not add that the continuance at this rate for a week would clean us out completely, and that we considered an average of $2 million a day very heavy. I waited nervously in his room until the old fox returned. In fact the drain did dry up almost immediately and we dragged along with a week or two's cash in hand until the U.S.A. came in.[10]

a Carson was actually First Lord of the Admiralty.
b The contemporary nickname for Lloyd George. Sir Andrew McFadyean (1964, 54) suggests that the commonest explanation for the nickname was implicit in Chalmers' reply to a question about Lloyd George's doings: 'Much as usual, leaping from crag to crag – boulder to boulder'. However, he admits 'other explanations' were prevalent, including, one suspects, his licentiousness.

The 9 December meeting of the War Cabinet that Keynes referred to was the first meeting of that body, newly formed after the fall of the Asquith coalition. Asquith, McKenna and most of the leading Liberals were excluded from office. Andrew Bonar Law became Chancellor of the Exchequer and Leader of the House of Commons. When Edwin Montagu refused the position of Financial Secretary and temporarily followed Asquith into the wilderness, Hardman Lever took the post. However, as Lever was without a seat in the House, Stanley Baldwin took on much of the day-to-day burden. Six months after Lever went to New York early in 1917 to be in daily contact with Morgans, Baldwin was named Joint Financial Secretary. Andrew McFadyean, who for a time acted as Baldwin's Private Secretary, recalled the Baldwin/Keynes relationship:

> I remember Keynes expatiating once on the obvious difficulty which Baldwin had in making up his mind for himself. Tiring of making it up for him, Keynes wrote a memo on a question of some importance which he suggested Ministers must decide. There were two courses between which a choice must be made; the pros and cons affecting each course were fully set out and by no hint did Keynes suggest which in his opinion was the better course. In due time the file reached Baldwin, and when he had read it he sent for Keynes. For half an hour the matter was discussed from every angle until, when Keynes had volunteered no opinion of his own Baldwin said, 'If you were in my place would you do A or B?' Keynes was not often defeated, but on that occasion he capitulated![11]

With the change of Government it fell to Lloyd George to approve the names for the next Honours List before they went forward to the King. Keynes's name was put forward for a CB (Companion of the Order of the Bath), but Lloyd George, in revenge for Keynes's past support for McKenna, struck it out. It took the strongest pressure from his Treasury colleagues to give Keynes his CB in the next List.

Bonar Law's move to the Treasury brought a further change. In January 1917, the First, or Finance, Division of the Treasury was split into two and a new body, 'A' Division, carved out of it to deal solely with external finance. Keynes, promoted to Temporary Principal Clerk, the position he would hold for the rest of his time in Whitehall, became its head. He reported directly to Sir Robert Chalmers and thence to Bonar Law.

Towards the end of the war Keynes's new Division would reach seventeen, excluding secretaries and typists. Many of its members – S. D. Waley,[c] Andrew McFadyean, Harry Siepmann, Ernest Rowe-Dutton – played important roles in later official policy-making, some up to 1946; while others –

c He changed his name from Schloss during the war.

Frank Nixon, Dudley Ward, Geoffrey Fry, Rupert Trouton and Oswald Falk – were associated with Keynes in various financial ventures after 1919. McFadyean remembered that

> I can claim for myself that I never before and never again worked so hard. . . . As juniors we were given during the war greatly enhanced power of initiative, responsibility, and freedom to make decisions . . . . We had very intensive training and grew up rapidly.[12]

Although the new year brought him new responsibilities, the second Coalition Government did not encourage Keynes. His letters took on a note of despair. Thus to Duncan he wrote:

> The Treasury depresses me just now. I am badly overworked, need a holiday and am filled with perpetual contempt and detestation of the new Gov*t* I should like to get away from it all. However McK[enna] who sees secret emissaries declares that peace must come soon; and all this note exchanging amounts after all to negotiation.[d] However, it's certain, I'm afraid, that Ll.G. will spin things out to let him taste a good draft of blood this spring. Did you read his last speech? 'The war is a road paved with gold and cemented with blood.' God curse him.[13]

In February 1917 the Federal Reserve Board lifted its effective ban on American banks investing in dollar-denominated British Government Treasury bills. The financial position eased somewhat, but the overwhelming scale of Britain's demands for dollars inevitably pressed against the limits of American finance. It was only America's entry into the war on 6 April 1917, the most important result of unrestricted German submarine warfare, that provided hope. As Keynes told his mother a bit later: 'If all happens as we wish, the Yanks ought to relieve me of some of the most troublesome of my work for the future'.[14]

The American declaration of war ruined Keynes's Easter weekend. He had gone down to Charleston on Thursday, hoping for peace and quiet. He was called back on Saturday, to prepare a long memorandum on inter-allied financial arrangements designed to brief the Governor of the Bank, who was about to go to America with the Foreign Secretary, A. J. Balfour.[15] The British hoped that the Americans would take over the financing of allied purchases in the United States while Britain would finance them in the rest of the world. The ensuing months of sorting out Anglo–American–Allied financial arrangements were far from

---

d In December 1916, the Germans made some proposals for a possible peace. These were followed by President Wilson's offer to mediate. There were then almost six weeks of notes until Germany announced the inauguration of unrestricted submarine warfare at the beginning of February 1917.

simple or stress-free, as two interrelated crises swept the Treasury and the Bank.

The two crises had different causes. The one concerning relations between the Treasury and Bank of England turned on personalities. The other, over American finance of the war effort and support of the sterling–dollar exchange rate, turned on American political conditions, personalities and misunderstandings.

The Treasury–Bank clash centred around the Governor, Lord Cunliffe, whose bluff, bullying manner had proved so successful in handling the 1914 financial crisis. While Lloyd George had been Chancellor, since he was fundamentally uninterested in finance and not prepared to take the trouble to learn, Cunliffe had a free hand and enjoyed the power this implied. When McKenna became Chancellor in May 1915, matters deteriorated. McKenna was both interested in and knowledgeable about finance, but lacked, for Cunliffe, Lloyd George's magnetism and willingness to let him get on with it. The Governor tried to bypass the Chancellor and to deal directly with the Prime Minister, with some success.[16] Throughout 1915 and 1916 there was friction. Beaverbrook went so far as to call it 'an armed truce', although it would seem that Cunliffe at the time was the more heavily armed, so completely had Asquith undermined the authority of his Chancellor in his dealings with the Bank.[17] Moreover, the number of occasions when the Governor and Chancellor might disagree increased as the financial pressures of the war grew.

When Law succeeded McKenna in December 1916, there was no nonsense as to the Governor's dealing with the Prime Minister: he must deal with the Chancellor – and his officials.[18] There was conflict early in 1917 over the terms of the massive new War Loan (the famous 5% War Loan 1929–47) and over the interest rates paid on foreign deposits in London. In both cases, the Chancellor's views prevailed over those of the Governor – and of the Chancellor's own advisers including Keynes.[19] As Keynes remarked at the end of the unsuccessful attempt to change the Chancellor's mind on the interest rate for the War Loan: 'No – we have had no effect, and quite frankly, his argument was beneath contempt, but I have a feeling that the old man is right.'[20] And he was. Moreover, with the creation of 'A' Division, with explicit responsibility for international finance on top of the older London Exchange Committee, the Governor was thrown into more and more contact with Chalmers and Keynes, neither of whom would be cyphers. Despite their early collaboration, Keynes had obviously fallen out with Cunliffe in 1915 or 1916, for the Governor later claimed that McKenna had verbally promised him that 'Mr Keynes should not meddle again in City matters'.[21] With the support of a vigorous Chancellor the outcome would be different. J. C. C. Davidson, Law's Private Secretary, described what could happen:

> Meetings took place frequently to deal with silver currency, on which Cunliffe, Keynes, and officials of the Colonial and India Office sat under the chairmanship of Sir Robert Chalmers. At one meeting Cunliffe, who was a curious character – he looked like a farmer, was definitely a bully and had withal a certain cunning – produced some figures that were out of date. Keynes, who never found it easy to suffer fools gladly, got tired of arguing with him and appealed to the chair. Chalmers, who had a high-pitched voice and looked like Buddha, remarked gently but acidly, 'Mr Governor, I fear that you are obsolete.'[22]

In 1917 the Bank was still a private company performing public functions. There was no established procedure for the ultimate resolution of any conflict as there would be after the nationalisation of the Bank in 1946. Moreover, under the Bank Act of 1844, the Bank had statutory responsibility for the gold standard. It might sensibly worry about the Government's overseas expenditure and its financing, especially as in a crisis the Treasury might, for example, use the gold forming the statutory cover for the Bank's note issue or directly mobilise the gold reserves of the joint stock banks or take a view on interest rates, changes in which were part of the normal Bank reaction to an external threat – and on which the Governor had been overruled in the spring of 1917. All of this lay in the background: it came to the foreground because Cunliffe was a member of the Balfour mission to the United States after the American declaration of war against Germany.

During the Governor's absence, from 18 April to 11 June, Keynes and Chalmers, the Chancellor's closest advisers, dominated the London Exchange Committee (charged with the day-to-day management of the foreign exchange position). Their position on the Committee was all the stronger because Cunliffe had kept so much in his own hands for so long. He had excluded his Deputy Governor from accompanying him on visits to the Treasury and failed to keep his Committee of Treasury (the top policy-making committee in the Bank) informed of his activities.

Anglo-American financial relationships in 1917 were complicated by several factors. William Gibbs McAdoo, the American Secretary of the Treasury, was insecure in his financial knowledge and concerned lest a false move should impair his personal political position. The Federal Reserve System, which had only opened for business in November 1914, was still trying to find its feet and lacked international experience, while the experienced New York bankers, who might have been of some help to the Wilson Administration, were politically at odds with the Democrats in power in Washington. This was particularly the case with J. P. Morgan & Co. Furthermore, any proposals for inter-allied finance had to go through Congress, which was not pro-British, pro-Wall-Street-banker or pro-Administration. It was a disagreeable but unavoidable requirement for Britain which, with its Irish problems heightened by the aftermath of the Easter Rising of 1916, its close Morgan connections and its commitments to finance its allies, was likely to be by far the largest borrower. Finally, as always, there were the underlying questions of financial power in the post-war world and its usefulness as a weapon to shape the peace to meet American interests.

On the American declaration of war, Sir Hardman Lever, the head of the British Treasury delegation in the United States, approached the Americans with a request for $500 million as quickly as possible and two later instalments of the same size five and six weeks later. The sums staggered the Americans, especially as Britain was not the only ally making requests. Although the American Treasury advanced $200 million to the British on 26 April and $100 million on 7 May pending Congressional approval, it also began to explore ways and means of reducing future demands. Eyes lit on the funds allocated by the British for maintaining the dollar–sterling exchange. Here there were doubts as to the compatibility of such support with Congressional intentions, which only allowed loans for war purposes, and as to the actual peg, $4.76⁷⁄₁₆, which the British had held since early 1916. It thus fell to the British Treasury to educate the Americans in the importance of the $4.76⁷⁄₁₆ régime while coping with fewer dollars from American borrowing than desired.

The tasks of education and day-to-day management largely fell to Keynes. They were complicated by American banks' withdrawing large sums from London to invest in Liberty Loans, more than $145 million between 14 April and 23 June,[23] and large British commitments for the purchase of American wheat. At the same time, the British Government found it harder to obtain short-term advances. On 29 June the British made a formal request for the reimbursement of Russian and Belgian expenses in the United States since 1 April 1917, for a settlement of the amount of assistance Britain would receive in July and August, and for US repayment of Britain's $400 million overdraft with Morgans out of the proceeds of the first Liberty Loan. Keynes drafted the request. The Americans in reply released the balance of the $185 million that they had promised for June.

At this stage Cunliffe returned from America, very pleased with himself. He thought that his journey had been a success, for he had established contacts with the American banking community, the Federal Reserve System and the Wilson administration. He had also, however, been a problem as far as the British Government and the Treasury were concerned. He had put American noses out of joint when he refused to visit the Federal Reserve Banks at Richmond and Philadelphia and went on a fishing expedition instead; he had repeatedly made attempts to force the Treasury to ship gold, which was the last thing it wished to do; and he 'seemed to lose few opportunities to undermine Treasury policy' by making statements contrary to undertakings that Lever had given McAdoo and by interfering with Lever's attempts to make a case for long-term American assistance.[24] The Treasury, of course, knew of this.

In London Cunliffe found Keynes and Chalmers firmly in control of exchange policy and, in the turmoil of the times, careless in providing the Bank and the London Exchange Committee with information they had promised. This smacked to him of *lèse-majesté*. On 3 July, after a verbal protest, he reminded the Prime Minister and the Chancellor of his predecessor's promise:

> In November 1915 . . . the late Chancellor . . . promised me verbally that Mr Keynes should not meddle again in City matters, which promise was, as far as I am aware, kept until Mr McKenna went out of office.
>
> . . . Yet the position today is that not only have all means of controlling the Exchange been taken out of our hands but all information is withheld from us even when we have the Chancellor's permission to obtain it, and requests for telegrams are not only refused but met with absolute incivility.
>
> The London Exchange Committee is therefore a mere cypher entirely superseded by Sir Robert Chalmers and Mr Keynes who in commercial circles are not considered to have any knowledge or experience in practical Exchange or business problems, and I am convinced that, short of a miracle, disaster must ensue.
>
> . . . I cannot remain a mere figurehead acting under men in whom I have no faith, unless the Cabinet after this warning is prepared to accept the entire responsibility.[25]

In verbal discussion, Cunliffe demanded Keynes's and Chalmers's dismissal. Bonar Law refused, saying that the two men were his officials acting on his responsibility and that if Cunliffe disliked the current state of affairs he should ask the Prime Minister to sack his Chancellor.

On the same day as Cunliffe's letters to the Prime Minister and the Chancellor, J. P. Morgan & Co. through a telegram to their London house, Morgan Grenfell, asked for the repayment of their $400 million overdraft in what was probably a mistaken attempt to strengthen Britain's hand in negotiating with the Americans. $85 million of the overdraft was in the Bank's name and part of the Bank's gold reserves held in Ottawa had been pledged as security. A further source of potential conflict was that Sir Hardman Lever had been authorised to instruct the Canadian Government as to the disposal of the gold. With co-ordination and consultation there might not be a problem, but Cunliffe was in no mood to co-ordinate, much less to consult.

On seeing Morgan's telegram, the Governor, without consulting his

Committee of Treasury or the Chancellor, immediately repaid the Bank's share of the overdraft in gold. On the following day, he noted that Lever was also using Bank gold to repay part of the remaining overdraft, thus affecting the amount of gold that would appear the next day in the Bank's published weekly return. On 5 July, again without consultation at the Bank or the Treasury, Cunliffe telegraphed the Canadian Government and instructed them to ignore any further instructions that Lever might give from New York.

That did it. Bonar Law went to Lloyd George and offered three choices: his ceasing to be Chancellor; Cunliffe's ceasing to be Governor; or an agreement that

> Lord Cunliffe should agree to work with me in reasonable spirit and with a full knowledge that the Chancellorship of the Exchequer is not in commission and that the views of the British Government as represented by me must be carried out.[26]

The following day, the Prime Minister called Cunliffe to 10 Downing Street. Strong words were exchanged: Cunliffe reported to his Committee of Treasury that Lloyd George threatened 'to take over the Bank'.[27] After over a month of drafting and redrafting of the appropriate apology that Cunliffe would make to the Chancellor and an agreement over the future role of the Bank in its wartime relations with the Treasury, a document emerged that did not go so far as put 'his resignation in the Chancellor's pocket',[28] but the incident effectively ended Cunliffe's tenure as Governor. On 6 November 1917 the Committee of Treasury, against Cunliffe's will, decided that in April 1918 Sir Brian Cokayne, then Deputy Governor, should become Governor and that Montagu Norman should become Deputy Governor. Cunliffe tried to reverse that decision without success through a City and press campaign that included *The Times* and *The Daily Telegraph*. Under the new team the wounds were quickly healed. But Cunliffe and Keynes would clash another day.

The Cunliffe quarrel was a passing incident in the midst of a hectic period, at least as far as the civil servants in charge of day-to-day policy were concerned. Keynes's letters did not mention the affair; nor did his father's increasingly cryptic diary. Rather his letters reflected the pressure of continuing external problems.

> I have been living in a continual crisis for the last two or three weeks, – the most serious since the war began.

> I have had a most fearful gruelling for the last five weeks, the worst on record, nine to thirteen hours a day of the harshest exertion.[29]

By the end of July he admitted that he was at 'the end of his tether' and escaped to Charleston, although only for three days, as he had to return to

London to deal with a visit by French and Italian ministers. At Charleston he managed a relaxing routine: breakfast in bed at 9:30; rising in time for lunch at 12:30; gardening, with an interval for tea and an hour's reading from 2 to 8 and bed at 10:30. He had even managed to do enough gardening that he reported 'I now aspire to higher duties'. According to Vanessa Bell, even at the end of another break at Charleston, he still looked exhausted and on 3 September he reported that his mind was 'in a state of confusion and fatigue'.[30] However, the sequence of Charleston visits over the spring and summer had resulted in a new intimacy between Maynard and Vanessa which showed in their letters until the early 1920s, when Lydia Lopokova would come between them.

Throughout the summer of 1917 the American exchange crisis continued, with Keynes bearing the brunt of the drafting and decision-making, meeting demands for information and demonstrating the heavier absolute burden borne by Britain even after America's entry into the war. Moreover, as he pointed out in a 'Note for Mr McAdoo' handed to the American Ambassador in London on 20 July:

> In short our resources available for payments in America are exhausted. Unless the United States Government can meet in full our expenses in America, including exchange, the whole financial fabric of the alliance will collapse. This conclusion will be a matter not of months but of days.
>
> ... If matters continue on the same basis as the last few weeks, a financial disaster of the first magnitude cannot be avoided in the course of August. The enemy will receive the encouragement of which he stands in so great need at the moment of the war at which he needs it most.[31]

At the end of the month another appeal from Keynes's pen went to America. The Treasury also decided to let the exchange go if necessary. Warning of the imminence of such a major change in policy was also passed verbally to Washington at the same time as the appeal and an associated warning of the sombre consequences of the proposed change in policy. This was successful in obtaining some American assistance – $50 million immediately and a promise of more over the coming months. That such action was planned and such warnings were even made indicate how much more serious the 1917 crisis was than the flurry eight months earlier. They also indicate that by the summer of 1917 financial dominance had passed from Britain to America. Despite Keynes's – and others' – efforts to reclaim it, it would remain with America for the rest of his life.

With the US promise of aid, the crisis subsided somewhat and Keynes got the already-mentioned week at Charleston. Soon, however, he was given a longer period of enforced idleness, for on 4 September 1917 he began his first journey to America as a member of a financial mission headed by Lord Reading, the Lord Chief Justice. The other members were Lady Reading and Colonel Ernest Swinton, Assistant Secretary to the War Cabinet. On departure, Keynes almost missed his boat train owing to his taxi not arriving on time. For his next mission, to avoid this risk, he booked the taxi for the previous evening and had it stand outside 46 Gordon Square all night![32]

The roots of the Reading Mission lay not only in the financial difficulties of the previous months, but also in the extremely confused state of Britain's financial relations with the United States at the time. Sir Hardman Lever had been in America since January, but his decision to base himself in the New York office of J. P. Morgan & Co., even after America's entry into the war which shifted the balance of decision-making to Washington, and Morgan's long-standing, open hostility to the Wilson Administration hardly helped to make him *persona grata* with McAdoo or Congress. On top of that there were problems with Sir Cecil Spring Rice, the Ambassador. Touchy over his status, he appeared to work actively against the Treasury's representative and his assistants, first Andrew McFadyean and then Basil Blackett, who also tended to be regarded as too junior by the Americans for high level negotiations in Washington, and to ensure that they were not accepted in Washington as the fully accredited representatives of the Treasury. Then there had been the confusion of the Balfour Mission in the spring. The Ambassador was uncooperative; the behaviour of the Governor of the Bank created uncertainties as to exactly what British policy was. By that stage, the Ambassador had lost his access to the President. By July, it was also the case that Lever was unacceptable to the Administration. In the interim, while deciding on a successor to Spring Rice, Lloyd George had sent Lord Northcliffe to co-ordinate the activities of the various British missions and in July named him the Treasury's representative. However, Northcliffe had been sent out largely because Lloyd George wanted to get rid of him from London. Although he was soon on good terms with McAdoo, Northcliffe knew nothing of finance and was still frustrated on occasion by the Ambassador. The Reading Mission had 'special plenary authority to deal with all financial questions without constant reference to His Majesty's Government', as well as instructions to act as the Government's representatives in other matters.

The Mission travelled to New York on the American liner *St Louis*. The work on the journey was not heavy, two hours a day, and Keynes was able to catch up on his reading and his sleep before arriving in New York on 12 September. The plan had been for Keynes to brief Reading on the journey to New York and then return to London, but on arrival Reading asked for his services for another 10 days. In the end Keynes stayed until 6 October, when he embarked on the *Aurania* in convoy from Halifax, Nova Scotia.

The Reading Mission, as Basil Blackett, perhaps optimistically, later put it, 'converted our relations with the US Treasury from those of an importune beggar to those of a fellow solvent creditor in the Alliance against

Germany'.[33] It made subsequent relations easier, although some misunderstandings inevitably remained. Lines of communication were regularised, with Lever left firmly in charge of finance and with Blackett as his Washington representative. Spring Rice remained a problem until he was replaced by Reading in December 1917. As Keynes commented in a confidential note to the Chancellor on his return:

[I]n his present nervous conditions Sir C. Spring Rice could not be regarded as entirely mentally responsible. It is obvious that his excitability, his nervousness, his frequent indiscretions, and also his absentmindedness render the proper conduct of business almost impossible.

At times, of course, he is perfectly normal and there was no sign of any diminution of his mental acuteness. But at other times he would act in a manner universally adjudged to be unworthy of his position. I formed the impression that two of the dominant impulses of his mind – namely dislike of the present US Administration and jealousy of whatever emissary HMG might send out from this country – also impelled him subconsciously in a manner of which his normal self was not properly and sanely aware. But whatever the explanation, the effects are a matter of universal comment throughout Washington.[34]

Keynes, who shared a house in Washington with the Readings, liked the Lord Chief Justice 'immensely', a feeling Reading reciprocated, parting with him with 'the greatest reluctance' and informing the Chancellor that 'I have talked to Keynes quite freely and mean that he shall be fully informed of my views, so that he may convey them to you, on all matters of finance and representation'.[35] Keynes made a less favourable impression on others. According to Basil Blackett, who was also reporting American reactions to dealing with the Treasury in London, 'Keynes is rude, dogmatic & disobliging (he made a terrible reputation for his rudeness out here)'.[36] Moreover, Keynes was not impressed by America. As he told Duncan Grant, 'The only sympathetic and original thing in America is the niggers, who are charming'.[37] Perhaps some of the problem came from the atmosphere. As he remarked to Edwin Cannan:

I have found America full of the utmost ferocity of war fever – far beyond what I could have expected or credited. There, at any rate, is a country where minorities get precious little quarter; and to my astonishment I find myself looking back to England again as a land of liberty![38]

In fact, he noted 'all prospects of peace seem now to be disappearing until Germany is *beaten*'.[39]

Keynes's return from Halifax on the *Aurania* was as part of a trooping convoy of seven liners with a cruiser and two destroyers as escorts. Again there were opportunities for relaxation – mornings in bed reading Lockhart's life of Sir Walter Scott, followed by lunch with the captain and a group of American colonels, 'innocent middle-aged gentlemen from the Mexican border', watching afternoon boxing matches put on by the troops, dinner and evenings of poker 'at moderate expense to my pocket'.e On 17 October, after passing to the north of Ireland and down through the Hebrides, the *Aurania* entered the Mersey. He was back in harness.

The spring and summer of 1917 brought Keynes a connection that he valued greatly in later years. That spring, H. S. Foxwell read a paper on inflation to the Institute of Actuaries. As a result of the discussion that followed, O. T. Falk, who later in the year would join 'A' Division, gave a dinner at the Café Royal on 19 June. His guests were Sir Charles Addis of the Hong Kong and Shanghai Bank; Foxwell; Keynes; A. W. Kiddy, a City editor; Geoffrey Marks, an actuary with the National Mutual Life Insurance Society; F. E. Steele; and Hartley Withers, a financial journalist. A month later Geoffrey Marks organised a second dinner. Addis, Keynes and Withers were unable to attend, but those who did included Sir Ernest Harvey, Chief Cashier of the Bank of England. At that second dinner the Tuesday Club was formed. It was to dine on the third Tuesday of every month at the Café Royal to discuss economic and financial matters. Its membership was always small and consisted of a mixture of City men, public servants, journalists and academics. Amongst those elected in the first few years were Sir John Anderson, Basil Blackett, R. H. Brand, Sir Josiah Stamp, Walter Layton, Dennis Robertson and Sir Henry Strakosch, all of whom had or would play significant roles in Keynes's life. While he was at the Treasury, he attended when he could and took part in the discussions, which were always off the record. He did not open a discussion until 24 July 1919 when he discussed 'Certain Aspects of the Treaty of Peace with Germany'. Most of the members were present that night, as well as Sir George Barstow of the Treasury and two veterans of 'A' Division, Dudley Ward and Harry Siepmann. Thenceforward he would regularly use the Club to try out ideas on a number of subjects.f The membership of the Club and its privacy meant that discussion was lively, informed and intelligent. The Controller of Finance at the Treasury or his successors were always members, as later were the senior economic advisers to the Government. Moreover, for particular

e His records show that he ended up in the end ahead £30.
f His subsequent openings of discussions, with their dates in brackets were: 'The Report of the Cunliffe Committee' (8 January 1920); 'The Government's Financial Policy' (8 July 1920); 'Devaluation' (10 November 1921); 'What Should be our Policy Towards France?' (14 March 1923); 'The Removal of the Gold Embargo' (14 January 1925); 'The Debt Redemption Proposals of the Colwyn Committee' (9 March 1927); 'The Balance of Trade' (12 October 1927); 'Are the Presuppositions of Free Trade Satisfied Today?' (9 April 1930); 'The Position in America' (4 July 1934); 'The British Industrial and Financial Outlook' (13 March 1935); 'The Psychology of Investment' (9 October 1935); 'Price Policy' (6 December 1939); and 'Our Prospective Economic and Financial Position in the Light of the Budget' (21 April 1942).

topics, there could always be guests with specific knowledge of the matter at hand – or no knowledge at all in the case of Duncan Grant on one occasion. For Keynes it was a way of being informed of opinion and of shaping it.

On his return from America Keynes was thrown again into the hurly burly of inter-allied finance. There were compensations, however, for 'A' Division was 'so well organised that it works nearly as well without me as with me'.[40] There was more travel – twice to Paris in December, once by special trains and destroyer, where Keynes noted with pride that he 'actually reached the point of talking French!' – this after almost three years of regular meetings where the convention was to talk 'own'. Treasury behaviour must have been galling to the French. There were also innumerable delegations in London. At one moment in November, the Romanians, French and Americans were all there at once, while on Christmas Eve he reported that with the French away there were only the Americans, Belgians and Greeks to plague him. He reported one particular week to his mother as follows:

> It has been rather a bad week with endless hours absolutely wasted in a newly established monkey house called the Inter-Ally Council for War Purchases and for Finance. I should imagine that the only possible analogy to Government by Inter-Ally Council is Government by Bolsheviks,[g] though judging by results the latter are more efficient. I cannot believe these things happen in Potsdam.
> Anyhow my day's work at the Treasury has begun as a result sometime between 6 and 8 p.m. and I have to keep rather bad hours. But perhaps my temper was spoiled by a bad cold which raged throughout. That at least is disappearing and to-morrow morning will be spent safely out of bed and out of hearing of any vain mendacious and interminable French or no less offensive and hateful Yank twang.[41]

In a letter to Duncan Grant on the same date, he added:

> What brutes and beasts they are. My temper has very seldom been worn so thin. I am coming to think that the Italians are on the whole my favourites.
> I work for a Government I despise for ends I think criminal.

This last sentence brings us to Keynes's increasing disillusionment with Lloyd George's Coalition Government – although he started with few illusions – and with the effects of the war on the social order. A few extracts from his letters over the next few months provide a flavour of his feelings – and later vision:

My Christmas thoughts are that a further prolongation of the war, with

g The Russian revolution had occurred in November 1917.

the turn things have now taken, probably means the disappearance of the social order we have known hitherto. With some regrets I think I am on the whole not sorry. The abolition of the rich will be rather a comfort and serve them right anyhow. What frightens me more is the prospect of *general* impoverishment. In another year we shall have forfeited the claim we had staked out in the New World and in exchange this country will be mortgaged to America.

Well, the only course open to me is to be buoyantly bolshevik; and as I lie in bed in the morning I reflect with a good deal of satisfaction that, because our rulers are as incompetent as they are mad and wicked, one particular era of a particular kind of civilisation is very nearly over.

I wonder how long your Cambridge queues are. If we put prices low enough and wages high enough, we could achieve the most magnificent queues even in peacetime. There never has been anything like enough caviar to go round. How soon do you expect piano queues?

$$\text{Length of queue} = \frac{\text{wages}}{\text{prices} \times \text{supplies}}$$

If w constantly increases while p and s diminish, q tends towards infinity. (24.12.17)

But the loss of control is mainly due to the certainty that the Cabinet is not behind us. What can an official do with a recalcitrant and extravagant Dep*t*. if he knows for certain that higher authority will let him down if he puts up a fight. (10.2.18)

The course of politics at the beginning of the week was deeply shocking. Bonar could have become Prime Minister if he had liked but funked it; and as no one else seemed inclined to take the job the Government struggled through, emerging, however, without many tail-feathers left. I have no idea what the military merits of the question may have been; but his [Lloyd George's] method of disposing of Robertson [the Chief of the Imperial General Staff] was an extraordinarily characteristic compound of humbug, chicaen [sic] and straightforward lying. (22.2.18)

Politics and war are just as depressing, or even more so, than they seem to be. If this Gov*t*. were to beat the Germans, I shall lose all faith for the future in the efficacy of intellectual processes; – but there doesn't seem much risk of it. Everything is always decided for some reason other than the real merits of the case, in the sphere where I have control. And I have no doubt that it is just the same with everything else.

Still and even more confidently I attribute all our misfortunes to [Lloyd] George. We are governed by a crook and the results are natural. In the meantime old Asquith who I believe might save us is more and more a student and lover of slack country life and less and less inclined for the turmoil. Here he is, extremely well in health and full of wisdom and fit for anything in the world – except controversy. He finds, therefore, in patriotism an easy excuse for his natural disinclination to attack the Gov*t*. People say that the politician would attack, but the patriot refrain. I believe the opposite is true. The patriot would attack but the politician (and the sluggard) refrain. (4.4.18)

During this period, Keynes's official activities were much the same as before. There was the new 'monkey house' of the Inter-Allied Council mentioned above. This had been set up to placate Congressional demands that American money be spent sensibly, but Keynes ended up believing that although it was 'a mere talking shop' that allowed its chairman Oscar Crosby, former Assistant Secretary of the American Treasury, to persuade 'himself that it is he who is really running the war', it tended 'to increase confidence all round and to convince the principal parties that all is above board and conducted with reasonable efficiency'. The existence of the Council also served a useful Treasury function, for members of the British American Board chaired by Austen Chamberlain, which supervised British purchases in America, could use the Council – and its chairman – as a means of restraining the purchasing departments.[42] Moreover, Chamberlain and Keynes got on well. As Edwin Montagu had remarked earlier,[43] 'Remember that he will accept his policy entirely from Bradbury and Keynes, who is a great friend of his'.

Keynes was also trying to reduce Britain's dependence on American loans by getting the Americans to take over directly the financing of the French and Italians and by obtaining dollar reimbursements for expenditures still made in support of her allies. According to Blackett, it took the Americans some time to see the implications of what Britain was requesting, but the matter finally came to a head over wheat. The United States had advanced dollar credits to Italy, France and Belgium for the purchase of wheat in North America. The British Wheat Export Company had bought the whole North American export crop, as well as the Indian and Argentine export crops. To minimise the use of scarce shipping space, the Company had used the North American wheat to supply Britain and the other grain to supply the allies. It had paid dollars for North American wheat and sterling elsewhere. It then asked for reimbursement in dollars. France complied, but there were US Treasury objections to spending dollars on non-dollar goods. The Inter-Allied Council set up a committee which supported Keynes's proposal for dollar reimbursement, but there was still the matter of obtaining American agreement, which implied that the United States would hold more French and Italian and less British debt.[44]

As Keynes was to find so often in the next war, the stumbling block was Congress:

The governing factor is the attitude of Congress to the US Treasury.

McAdoo is continually anticipating the same sort of political attack on his administration as has fallen on [others] .... McAdoo has been far too clever for his foes so far, and indeed he has been far too statesmanlike in his actions and has taken far too broad a line in his defence of his department to be seriously in danger. But he believes in being forewarned. That . . . is the point now. He does not want to be open to the particular accusation that he is lending money to France and Italy to spend outside the U.S., still less to spend it in Great Britain, and he is not at present prepared to regard the fact that Great Britain spends a corresponding amount in the U.S.A. as a sufficient defence. He is certainly not out of the wood as regards support of sterling exchange [rate] (but for which our position would be unassailable), and above all he is in continuous fear of being told that the British Treasury has out-manoeuvred him. It has to be remembered that Reading has the reputation here of a financial genius capable of out-generalling not merely McAdoo but the Germanest of Jews and the Jewest of Germans in this republic – and not altogether without reason.[45]

Other cases for reimbursement came up, and Crosby went to Washington to try to sort matters out. Eventually a scheme called the 'theory of constructive delivery and redelivery' was devised to solve the problem. If Italy bought wheat in a third country, it could be paid for indirectly with dollar credits by means of a convoluted exchange – the US sent American wheat to, say, Norway to be paid for by fish exported from Norway to Italy leaving Italy as the ultimate debtor to the United States.

Early in the spring of 1918, Keynes got himself more directly involved in reimbursement. In March, on one of his rare holidays from agricultural labour in Sussex, Duncan Grant picked up from Roger Fry's studio a copy of the catalogue for the forthcoming Paris sale of Dégas' collection. He was excited and the same evening tried to convince Keynes to persuade the Treasury to provide funds for purchasing some of the items for the nation. On 21 March, Keynes cabled Charleston that he had some money. The next day Vanessa wrote:

We are fearfully excited by your telegram & are longing to know more. This is a line to say do consult Roger before you go, as he'll know what to get hold of in Paris. Duncan says be as professional as possible in the buying & get at the right people. Otherwise some German or Scandinavian might trick you. Roger is either at 21 Fitzroy Sq. or 351 Guildford.

We have great hopes of you & consider your existence at the Treasury is at last justified.[46]

The same day Bunny Garnett added a note.

Nessa and Duncan say you must have professional advice & help in Paris about the pictures & advise you to consult Roger.

They are very proud of you & eager to know how you did it. You have been given complete absolution & future crimes also forgiven.

A day later, Keynes reported to Vanessa from 46 Gordon Square:

I've worked 23 hours in the last 35 and am worn out but must send you a line. I start for Paris to-morrow morning. My picture coup was a whirlwind affair, – carried through in a day and a half before anyone had time to reflect on what they were doing. I have secured 550,000 francs to play with; Holmes [Director of the National Gallery] is travelling out with us; and I hope we shall attend the sale together. . . .

Bonar Law was very much amused at my wanting to buy pictures and eventually let me have my way as a sort of joke.[47,h]

The sale was on 27 and 28 March. On his return to England, he went to Charleston, where Austen Chamberlain dropped him off with his personal prizes. He left them in the hedge by the lane while he carried his luggage and papers up to the house. There he wrote to his mother:

The Inter-Ally Council itself was largely a farce. But there were the contrasted interests of my Picture Sale and of propinquity to the great battle.[i] I bought myself four pictures and the nation upwards of twenty.[48]

Keynes's purchases – Ingres' 'Femme Nue', Delacroix's 'Cheval au Pâturage', a study by Delacroix for the Palais Bourbon,[j] and Cézanne's 'Pommes' – caused a stir in Bloomsbury. Virginia Woolf, who went with Roger Fry to 46 Gordon Square to see the Cézanne described his reaction to Vanessa:

Roger very nearly lost his senses. I've never seen such a sight of intoxication. He was like a bee on a sunflower.[49]

Later Mark Gertler made a pilgrimage to Gordon Square to see it. The National Gallery failed to spend all of its allocation, although it tried without success to retain the balance to spend when Degas' own pictures and studies went on sale on 6 and 8 May.

Life then became somewhat less hectic for Keynes. He managed ten uninterrupted days at Charleston between 17 and 27 May, a further five days in July and ten days in August. True, not being recalled to London cost

h Keynes later recalled, 'I asked Mr Bonar Law . . . to approve an allocation for this purpose, and he, remarking that this was the first occasion that he had even known me in favour of any expenditure whatever, agreed.' (KCKP, Box 13, JMK to Rowe-Dutton, 12 July 1943.)

i On 21 March the Germans had attacked on the Somme and in the next few days advanced over 40 miles splitting the British and French armies where they met. Paris was threatened.

j Keynes gave this to Duncan Grant.

him a daily bag of work from the Treasury, but each bag only took an hour or two. The weather remained fine; so he could spend a good part of each day outdoors. Another cost, if it was that, was to be a model for Vanessa, Duncan and Roger Fry, who were all painting his portrait. In fact, Keynes was frequently at Charleston now to break his London routine, even for the odd single day's weeding.

Despite the stresses of war, at the age of 35 he seemed in good health. In June 1918, for official statistical purposes, he had a medical examination. Not only was he passed Grade 1, but

> The result of the chest expansion was amusing. After measuring my capacity the doctor asked if my employment has always been sedentary. On my replying in the affirmative, he added 'Then I suppose you take very regular exercise', to which I answered, 'Since the war I have taken no exercise whatever', whereat he expressed astonishment.[50]

If we are to judge from his letters and papers, the summer of 1918 saw Keynes occupied much as before. He continued to try to maximise British independence under the new American-financed dispensation, to avoid possible post-war commitments, particularly French proposals for a continuation of wartime co-operation in the form of an inter-ally economic union, and to maintain the primacy of Treasury financial control over the departments.[51] He developed a close working relationship with the senior American officials in Europe, Oscar Crosby, Paul Cravath and Norman Davis, which proved useful at the time and would prove even more useful when it came to peace-making. For by now it was becoming clear that the war would soon be over. On the Western Front, allied armies had regained their losses of territory from the German spring offensive and were moving forward into areas they had not occupied since 1914. By the end of September they were through the Hindenburg Line and Germany had started the process that would lead to an armistice. On 13 October, he predicted to his mother 'six months from now expect me back at Cambridge'.

Keynes's social life also remained as before in many ways during the last months of the war. With the ready availability of sympathetic and relaxing Charleston, where the complexities of the triangular relationship between Bunny, Duncan and Vanessa had come very close to the surface in the first quarter of the year but were now resolving themselves, he was less likely than before to visit Garsington. For Vanessa, now pregnant by Duncan, Keynes was an important confidant. Vanessa would refer to the prospective infant as his 'god child'.[52] On the other hand, Keynes remained a regular visitor to the Asquiths and the McKennas, both in the country and in London. He became more closely involved with the Asquith children, although he still classed them as being among the frivolous.

You must come on Tuesday anyhow as I've arranged a dinner party for you on that day – you [Duncan], me, Virginia and E. Asquith. The object of the party is going to be to put E. A. in her place and make her feel she's aspiring to a society she's not fit for. So I am going to egg Virginia on to rag her to the top of her bent.[53]

Fortunately, perhaps, Elizabeth Asquith didn't come. Other names that appear in his appointments books after they begin again in mid-1918 or in letters are Lady Cunard, Lady Jekyll (McKenna's mother-in-law), Sir Thomas Beecham and Osbert Sitwell.

The main social event of the last days of the war was Diaghilev's return to London with new dancers and new productions. Lydia Lopokova was making her first London appearances. Keynes went on several occasions. On 23 September when he took Duncan, they ran into Ottoline and were introduced to Diaghilev afterwards and met Lydia. Duncan reported to Vanessa:

She was absolutely charming without any sort of sham feelings & perfect manners & very pretty & intelligent painted still with blue eyebrows. She has an old Italian husband who is a perfect darling.[54]

On 10 October, Keynes took Vanessa, Virginia Woolf, Roger Fry and Duncan Grant to the first performance of *Scheherezade* and then on to a party at the Sitwells at Carlyle Square, Chelsea. Lydia was also there. As Vanessa after a fall had been advised to take extreme care during the last months of her pregnancy, Keynes hired a brougham for the journey. Afterwards Vanessa thanked him:

Are you dining out every night & consoling yourself very easily for the loss of us? I suppose so. I think your god child's health and spirits will have been saved by my 10 days in London – thanks to good food & parties & the Barouche. It's very lively & though I was rather tired after our return journey I really feel I've got a new lease of life from having had such a complete rest from household worries.[55]

On 19 October he was back at the ballet again and he again went backstage to see Lydia 'who was as usual charming (making us pinch her legs to see how strong she was – which we did shyly. Clive should have been there)!'.[56] Also, according to some reports, Keynes met Lydia again at Montague Sherman's Armistice night party at his rooms in the Adelphi; although some memoirs mention his presence, others do not.[57] The problem is that he was supposedly in France, having gone on a week's tour through Belgium and Northern France on 7 November.[k]

We know that Keynes was in Belgium with Georges Theunis on 10

k KCKP, JMK to FAK, 6 November 1918. Keynes's appointments diary is of no help here. There are no entries for 7–13 November. However, even in the circumstances, it would hardly be likely to be a pick-up, spur-of-the-moment party.

November, when the two men tried to guess which one would be out of government service first.[58] He later provided a description of what he saw:

> A journey through the devastated areas of France is impressive to the eye and imagination beyond description. During the winter of 1918–19, before Nature had cast over the scene her ameliorating mantle, the horror and desolation of war was made visible to sight on an extraordinary scale of blasted grandeur. The completeness of the destruction was evident. For mile after mile nothing was left. No building was habitable and no field fit for the plough. The sameness was also striking. One devastated area was exactly like another – a heap of rubble, a morass of shellholes, a tangle of wire.
>
> To the British observer, one scene, however, stood out distinguished from the rest – the field of Ypres. In that desolate and ghostly spot, the natural colour and humours of the landscape and the climate seemed designed to express to the traveller the memories of the ground. A visitor to the salient early in November 1918, when a few German bodies still added a touch of realism and human error, and the great struggle was not yet certainly ended, could feel there, as nowhere else, the present outrage of war, and at the same time the tragic and sentimental purification to which the future will in some degree transform its harshness.[59]

NOTES

1 MLC, JNK Papers, Box 5, JMK to Foxwell, 27 February 1916.
2 KCKP, JMK to JNK, 5 June 1916.
3 *JMK*, XI, 187.
4 In 1939. *JMK*, XVI, 213.
5 *JMK*, XVI, 189–96.
6 Lloyd George 1938, 410, 612.
7 *JMK*, XVI, 197.
8 Ibid., 198–209.
9 Ibid., 215–22.
10 Ibid., 210–12.
11 McFadyean 1964, 63.
12 Ibid., 67.
13 BL, ADD.57931, JMK to D. Grant, 14 January 1917.
14 KCKP, JMK to FAK, 6 May 1917.
15 *JMK*, XVI, 226–38.
16 Beaverbrook 1956, 92–3; Boyle 1967, 109; above p. 251.
17 Beaverbrook 1956, 99.
18 Sayers 1976, I, 102–3.
19 Sayers 1976, I, 96–8.
20 James 1969, I, 58.
21 Below p. 273.
22 James 1969, 61.
23 *JMK*, XVI, 257.

24 Burk 1985, 129–30.
25 Beaverbrook Library, Lloyd George Papers, Cunliffe to Lloyd George, 3 July 1917; Blake 1955, 352.
26 Blake 1955, 353.
27 Sayers 1976, I, 105.
28 Ibid., 106 n. 2.
29 KCKP, JMK to FAK, 10 and 28 July 1917.
30 KCKP, JMK to FAK, 13 August 1917; KCCP, VBMK45, 31 August 1917; NUL, JMK to Vanessa Bell, 3 September 1917.
31 *JMK*, XVI, 250.
32 KCKP, JMK to FAK, 6 December 1917.
33 KCKP, L17, Blackett to JMK, 20 December 1917.
34 PRO, T172/446, 22 October 1917.
35 KCKP, JMK to FAK, 28 September 1917; PRO, T172/446, Reading to Law, 3 October 1917.
36 PRO, T172/446, Blackett to Hamilton, 1 January 1918.
37 BL, ADD.57931, JMK to DG, 17 October 1917.
38 BLPS, Cannan Papers, vol. 1023, JMK to Cannan, 13 October 1917.
39 BL, ADD.57930, JMK to DG, 10 October 1917.
40 KCKP, JMK to FAK, 6 December 1917; see also JMK to Blackett, 30 January 1918 in *JMK*, XVI, 270.
41 KCKP, JMK to FAK, 15 December 1917.
42 *JMK*, XVI, 268–9.
43 On 1 May 1917. Waley 1964, 121.
44 *JMK*, XVI, 274–85.
45 KCKP, T1, Blackett to JMK, 11 April 1918.
46 KCCP, VBMK41, 22 March 1918.
47 NUL, JMK to Vanessa Bell, 23 March 1918.
48 KCKP, JMK to FAK, 29 March 1918.
49 VWL, II, 230. See also VWD, I, 140–1.
50 KCKP, JMK to FAK, 26 June 1918.
51 For an excellent detailed study of Anglo-Allied financial diplomacy which does justice to Keynes's role, see Hemery 1988, esp. ch. 4.
52 For the complexities and problems, see Spalding 1983, 169–74; KCCP, VBMK47, 16 October 1918.
53 NUK, JMK to DG at the end of a letter to Vanessa Bell, 31 January 1918.
54 KCKP, DGVB38, [23 September 1918].
55 KCCP, VBMK47, 16 October 1918.
56 BL, ADD.57931, JMK to DG, 20 October 1918.
57 Sitwell 1949, 20; Garnett 1979, 94; Holroyd 1971, 749; Hill and Keynes (eds) 1989, 25.
58 *JMK*, XVII, 348.
59 *JMK*, II, 75–6.

12

NEGOTIATING THE PEACE

The Governor of the Bank came in yesterday and produced a dirty linen bag dated Sept. 28, 1872, and containing 1,000 sovereigns.

It was one of the original bags sent in payment of the original [French] indemnity, had lain in Spandau ever since, and had just been exported to us through Copenhagen.

(KCKP, T/16, JMK minute of 26 February 1915)

I am giving notice to the Treasury that, unless there is some quite unexpected turn in the negotiations with Germany, I must ask to be relieved of my duties as soon after June 1st as possible and anyhow not later than June 15th. I am utterly worn out mentally and nervously and deeply disgusted, depressed and dismayed at the unjust and unwise proposals we have made to Germany.

(KCKP, Box 3, JMK to W. H. Macaulay, 17 May, 1919)

As the war neared an end, attention turned to considering the problems of the peace and post-war reconstruction. This is not to say that there had been no consideration of such matters during the war – far from it: discussions had been proceeding in Whitehall since 1915. From March 1916 there was a series of official Reconstruction Committees and in July 1917 Christopher Addison became Minister of Reconstruction. On the domestic front there were substantial and sustained attempts to 'plan' a 'land fit for heroes' at the end of the war, although there were to be problems in implementing the plans. On the international side, post-war planning was much less organised. This reflected a number of points of conflict, within the Coalition Government and between Britain and her allies. For example, any discussion of post-war trade policy immediately raised the issue of protection, still far from dead in British politics. There were potential conflicts between European and Imperial interests, between Britain's interests as the world's largest international trading nation and proposals to restrict Germany's post-war international economic relations, and between European desires to limit German economic power as set out in the Paris Resolutions of June 1916 and American views on the openness of the

Plate 1 Cambridge from the south, July 1946 (Harvey Road is between the two church spires on the right): Department of Aerial Photography, Cambridge

Plate 2　JMK aged 10: Milo Keynes

Plate 3　Geoffrey Keynes, JMK and Margaret Keynes, 1895: Milo Keynes

Plate 4 JMK at Eton:
Milo Keynes

Plate 5 Neville
Keynes, 1905:
Milo Keynes

Plate 6   Florence Keynes, 1905: Milo Keynes

Plate 7 JMK in 1908
(pencil drawing by
Duncan Grant):
Milo Keynes
(© Duncan Grant
Estate)

Plate 8 JMK in 1911:
Milo Keynes

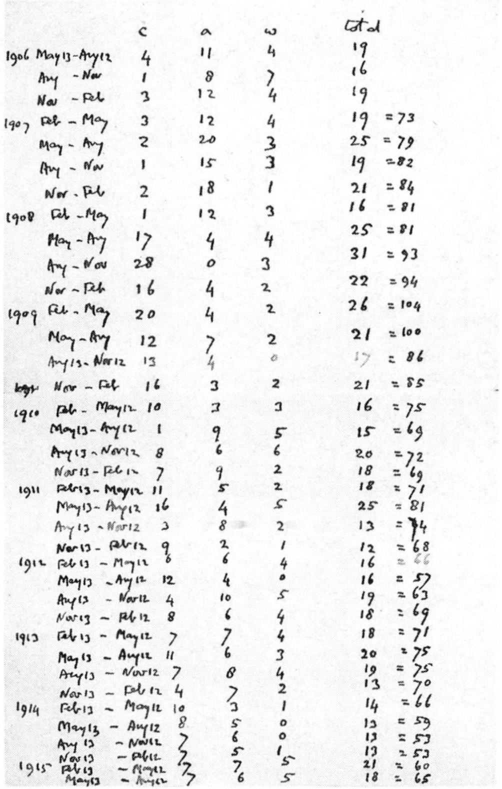

Plate 10 JMK's list of his sexual partners, 1915

Plate 9 JMK's tabulation of his sexual activity, 1915

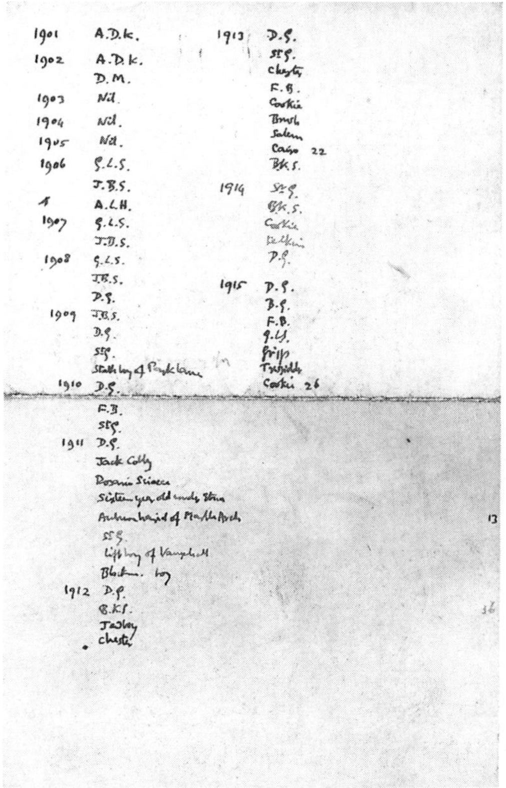

Plate 11 JMK amid the German delegation at Genoa, 1922: W.H. Haslam

Plate 12 JMK and Lydia outside the Registry Office after their wedding, August 1925: Milo Keynes

post-war world as set out in President Wilson's Fourteen Points and related speeches. International planning was also inhibited by uncertainty over the terms on which the war would end. As a result, although many issues had been raised, little had been decided. However, war-weary politicians were in a mood that might welcome easy ways out. Reparations appeared to be one such exit.

British discussions of reparations and indemnities during the war were inconclusive. Just before the war, British opinion had been considerably influenced by Norman Angell's *The Great Illusion* (1910). Angell had argued that the increasing commercial and financial interdependence of Europe made the idea that wars would in some sense 'pay' an illusion, for the disruption of international trade and finance would penalise the 'victor'. As part of his general argument, Angell tried to show that indemnities for war damages and costs were futile: large unilateral transfers would disrupt the exchanges, raise prices in the receiving country and thus reduce exports, and raise imports thereby reducing output in the receiving country. Angell saw proof of these contentions in the indemnity of £212,700,000 which France had paid Germany after the war of 1870–1 and which had been, in many eyes, the main cause of the German financial crisis, panic and depression of 1873.[1] Angell's views had been criticised, but they were still influential in many circles in 1916, most notably those associated with the journal *War and Peace* to which Keynes had contributed anonymously in April.[2] However, Angell's position did not command universal support and from the invasion of Belgium onwards voices were raised suggesting that a defeated Germany should make reparation for war damages or even pay the allies for their full costs of the war.

Keynes's substantive involvement in the issue first came in the form of a memorandum he wrote in collaboration with Professor W. J. Ashley at the request of the Board of Trade. This 'Memorandum on the Effect of an Indemnity' was completed early in January 1917.[a] The memorandum was a factual survey of previous experience with indemnities, of the forms in which wealth could be extracted from the Central Powers in current circumstances, and of the possible economic consequences of employing that wealth 'to make good damage in the territories over-run'. In its historical survey, the memorandum treated the French indemnity of 1871–3 as being 'the only

---

a *JMK*, XVI, 313–34. This memorandum was misdated in the *Collected Writings* as January 1916. As Sir Hubert Llewellyn Smith did not ask Keynes to undertake work on 'an important matter affecting "post-bellum" problems' until 4 June 1916 and as the first letter on the subject did not pass between Keynes and Ashley until 15 June 1916, the dating of the memorandum is an error, albeit one made on the original typescript. (See KCKP, Sir Hubert Llewellyn Smith to JMK, 4 June 1916; Ashley to JMK, 15 June 1916.) To judge from Ashley's papers in the British Library (BL, ADD.42246, ff. 12, 13, 78, 80–2 and 87) and Keynes's subsequent statement to R. H. Brand that it had been 'composed primarily by Professor W. J. Ashley, with whom . . . I collaborated' (Brand Papers, Box 11, JMK to R. H. Brand, 30 July 1918, quoted in Hemery 1988, 417 n. 2), it would seem that the drafting was primarily Ashley's.

precedent of any importance', and argued that the indemnity itself had little to do with the financial crisis of 1873, although the German Government's use of the funds did have some influence in hastening and intensifying the crisis. In its discussion of current circumstances, the memorandum examined the possibilities for once-for-all transfers of wealth at the end of the war in the form of ships, railways and public utilities in the ceded colonies; replacement railway rolling stock, machinery and livestock for that removed from territories occupied by Germany and Austria; and securities or cash; before turning to the question of a possible transfer of wealth through payments over a period of years. In this last case, the memorandum made clear that the size of future flows available would depend on how much immediately removable wealth the allies took, for such removals would affect the level of output in the territories of the Central Powers, as well as on allied tariff policies. Finally the authors turned to the effects of employing the proceeds on the restoration of territories overrun – i.e. to a situation where Britain received *no* indemnity payments whatsoever, and was merely spared the need to assist in the reconstruction of these areas. Throughout, the memorandum was a flat survey of possibilities. It did not even attach specific sums to many items. For this reason Lloyd George's later accusation that the Keynes-Ashley memorandum 'to the minds of City financiers and all burdened taxpayers . . . opened a vista of an expanding annual tribute which would ultimately cover the war taxes'[3] is utter nonsense, particularly as the document in question was never made public.

There, from Keynes's point of view, matters rested for a time. Further documents were circulated in Whitehall, such as an October 1916 Board of Trade memorandum 'Economic desiderata in the Terms of Peace', which did not exclude Britain as a possible indemnity recipient but was cautious in suggesting that the sums involved would do little more than repair physical damage, and an April 1917 Cabinet Committee report which took a similarly moderate line. Thereafter, there was little further thinking on the issues until the end of the war was imminent. However, as the costs of the war rose demands that 'the enemy pay' also rose, particularly from protectionists and imperialists. Then the sudden movement towards peace, coupled with American opposition to restrictive, anti-German post-war trade policies as suggested in the 1916 Paris Resolutions, put reparations and a possible indemnity at the centre of the stage.[b]

Matters first arose in the pre-Armistice negotiations at Versailles between 26 October and 3 November 1918. There the allies had to sort out amongst themselves the exact meaning of President Wilson's Fourteen Points and,

b In the discussion which follows, the terms 'reparation' and 'indemnity' will take on their accustomed meanings, even though there was some contemporary confusion: *reparation* comprises payment for repair or replacement of physical damage, while an *indemnity* is a cash payment to the victors analogous to the damages awarded to a successful claimant in a civil suit. See Hemery 1988, 414.

if necessary, make any reservations they had clear to all concerned, as the Armistice negotiations themselves were to be based on the American documents. The central matters were the third Point, which promised 'the removal, so far as possible, of all economic barriers and the establishment of an equality of trade conditions amongst all nations consenting to the peace' and the absence of any explicit reference to reparations in the original Points. In the discussions that followed, the allies effectively foreswore a trade war with Germany, although they agreed to tolerate some discrimination for the purpose of conserving materials needed for reconstruction. They also agreed on a reservation to Points seven, eight and eleven which defined the meaning of 'restored', and hence reparation, with reference to Belgium, France and Serbia: 'By it [restoration] they understand that compensation will be made by Germany for all the damage done to the civilian population of the Allies and their property by the aggression of Germany by land, by sea and from the air.' Such a reservation did not include an indemnity, only full reparation. Or at least that was what many people, especially in the Treasury and the Foreign Office, believed: it is less clear that this was Lloyd George's intention.[4]

During the Versailles discussions, Keynes made a series of 'Notes on an Indemnity' on 31 October which were flown over to the Chancellor. These 'Notes' made an attempt to estimate what Germany might be able to repay. Without crushing Germany, the Allies might expect to receive the equivalent of £1,000 million – half in the form of immediate transfers in kind, half in the form of cash payments over a series of years.[5] This total was unlikely to exceed the total physical damage incurred 'by land, by sea and from the air'. In the weeks that followed, this figure became something of a lower bound to estimates of the sums available. A contemporaneous estimate from the Foreign Office put the sum at £900–1,000 million, while the Board of Trade's estimates suggested that allied claims for reparation would amount under the Armistice terms to £2,000 million. The collection of this sum would probably require an army of occupation, so a smaller, clearly fixed sum for reparation would be all that would be possible. Any claim for an indemnity for war costs would be merely a bargaining ploy, for no other useful purpose would be served by such a sum.

In the period between the Armistice on 11 November and the opening of the Peace Conference on 18 January the departments of government prepared briefs in a relatively uncoordinated, independent way. The Treasury brief was entitled 'On the Indemnity Payable by the Enemy Powers for Reparation and other Claims'.[6] Again, Keynes was the author – and took sufficient pride in authorship to use its discussion of Germany's capacity to pay *verbatim* in *The Economic Consequences of the Peace*.[7] The memorandum was a long time in taking its final form: although its main conclusions may have been summarised by Bonar Law for the Cabinet on 26 November, the final version was not available until *after* the middle of December. By then a General Election had intervened and the Government had made certain unfortunate public commitments.[8]

The Treasury memorandum was divided into five sections. The first summarised the pronouncements of President Wilson and the allies: the Fourteen Points; subsequent relevant presidential statements; agreed allied understandings on or reservations to the meaning of these pronouncements; and the actual terms of the Armistice agreement. The second translated these terms into what individual countries might claim; while the third attempted to develop rough numerical estimates of the sums involved. There followed an estimate of Germany's capacity to pay and discussion of the likely effects of alternative forms of payment on the receiving countries before everything came together in the conclusion.

That was the form of the memorandum. What was its substance? The claim for reparation, it argued, had to be restricted to 'all damage done to the civilian population of the Allies and to their property by the aggression of Germany by land, by sea and from the air'. Taken with the fact that this phrase was designed to elucidate the word 'restoration', this ruled out any consideration of recovering the full cost of the war, which Keynes put at £25 billion. Moreover, the phrase covered was *direct* damage to civilians, not consequential losses (for instance, injuries to civilians knocked down during a blackout), but it would have to include damage done to civilians by the forces of both sides. Keynes's rough estimate of the amount of reparations required under these terms was £4,000 million, of which the British Empire accounted for 15 per cent, Belgium 15 per cent, France 62.5 per cent, Italy 2.5 per cent, and the rest of the allies 5 per cent. This estimate of 'requirements' turned out to be well above Keynes's estimate of Germany's 'capacity to pay'. Although the latter was higher than that made at the end of October, partly as a result of his having more time to get estimates of the value of particular items and partly as a result of his being more optimistic on such items as Germany's ability to run an export surplus over a period of years, it was still *below* the value of the likely claims based on a strict reading of the relevant documents. Germany's capacity to pay he estimated at (i) immediately transferable property of £800 million; (ii) raw materials transferred over a period of three years of £350 million; (iii) the value of property in ceded territory of £220 million; and (iv) tribute over 30 years of £1,900 million.[c] However, he emphasised that these estimates were *maximum* sums and that items (ii) and (iv), as well as (i) and (iv) were to some extent alternatives: if, for example, the allies stripped Germany of transferable property the possibilities of obtaining a flow of tribute would fall. The £3,000 million obtained by adding together items (i) to (iv) was thus in excess of what would be possible. If the allies could manage £2,000 million 'without evil indirect

c The comparable figures in October had been: (i) £600 million; (ii) not estimated; (iii) not estimated; and (iv) £2,000 million maximum.

consequences' that would be 'a very satisfactory achievement'.[9] However, even such a smaller sum would cause problems for Britain, as a stream of annual payments spread over a period of years would necessitate an expansion of German exports competitive with Britain's traditional staple industries – this at a time when Britain would be receiving a small proportion (15 per cent) of the total proceeds. The memorandum therefore suggested that the ideal strategy for Britain would be

> To obtain *all* the property which can be transferred immediately or over a period of three years, levying this contribution as ruthlessly and completely, so as to ruin entirely for many years to come Germany's overseas development and her international credit; but, having done this (which would yield more than £1,000 million, but less than £2,000 million), to ask only a small tribute over a term of years, and to leave Germany to do the best she can for the future with the internal resources remaining to her.[10]

By the time that Keynes's memorandum was ready for circulation, these terms, although harsher than those he had discussed earlier, were in the light of contemporaneous discussion mild in the extreme. The reasons for this change in circumstances are various. In Britain, the First World War had been accompanied by considerable Germanophobia.[11] Even the Treasury was not immune: it was during the war that S. D. Schloss changed his name to Waley and in July 1918 Keynes reported to his mother:

> I am losing a useful man (English name, English mother, natural born English subject, educated Rugby and Magdalen [College] Oxford, first in history, entirely unfit for any form of military service) because 58 years ago his father (who has been dead for years) came over as a lad from Bavaria. Could frenzy go further?[12]

The end of the war brought no reduction in such feelings, particularly as the propaganda machine of the Ministry of Information was just hitting its stride. Then on 10 October, seven days after the Germans had asked for an armistice, a submarine sank the mail packet *Leinster* in the Irish Sea with the loss of 451 lives, all civilian. Also, as the allied armies advanced into those parts of France and Belgium occupied by the Germans since 1914, there were reports of widespread destruction, some of it allegedly the result of deliberate German policy. Finally, with the closing stages of the war came the issue of German treatment of British prisoners of war. Most of these had performed forced labour in Germany or behind the lines, sometimes in considerable danger. With the German retreat and collapse they were being released pell mell without transport or provisions. All of these factors gave rise to considerable anti-German feeling, the notion of 'war crimes' and 'making Germany pay'.

Nor were matters helped by the General Election then in progress. On 14 November, the Government announced that Parliament would be dissolved on 25 November. The Coalition published its election programme on 18 November. Serious campaigning began almost immediately and lasted until polling day on 12 December. Although the Coalition's published programme dealt largely with established domestic issues – Home Rule for Ireland, social reform and the disestablishment of the Church of England in Wales – it was clear that the central appeal of the Coalition was its effectiveness in winning the war and its superior ability to win the peace. Soon there was talk of 'mandates' from the people and, as the election proceeded, words, perhaps inevitably, got wilder, especially those relating to the treatment of Germany.

The increasing incaution in the use of words on the hustings mirrored to some extent problems in Whitehall. These were centred around the personality and views of W. M. Hughes, the Prime Minister of Australia. Although he had been in England during the Armistice negotiations, a speaking tour in the North meant that he missed all of the Cabinet meetings that dealt with the actual Armistice terms, although he did receive Cabinet Conclusions. On his return to London, he proclaimed himself extremely unhappy with the terms agreed, especially the third of the Fourteen Points. He also attacked the Cabinet for having accepted such limited reparations. Moreover, in the course of November, as well as delivering a formal protest on behalf of the Australian Government over the Armistice terms, he began to speak out and to suggest that Germany should in the form of an indemnity be making some contribution to the overall costs of the war. His rhetoric, which suggested that the Armistice terms were likely to impair Imperial tariff autonomy and not compensate the overseas Empire for the blood and treasure expended during the war, not to mention relieve the British taxpayer of the burden of supporting the debt incurred in the course of the war, struck a responsive cord in conservative, imperialist and protectionist political circles and in the press, especially the Northcliffe press, and led to calls for a reconsideration of the issue of compensation from Germany – something that Lloyd George may have wanted on other grounds.

The upshot was that on 26 November the Imperial War Cabinet set up a committee to study how much Germany might pay without harmful side effects on the allies. Hughes was chairman of this Committee on Indemnity. Its other members were Walter Long, the Colonial Secretary; W. A. S. Hewins, a Conservative MP with decidedly protectionist views; Sir George Foster, the Canadian Minister of Trade and Commerce; Herbert Gibbs, a Conservative banker; and Lord Cunliffe, now the ex-Governor of the Bank of England. Keynes and Sir Hubert Llewellyn Smith were to serve the Committee as advisers. A. W. Flux from the Board of Trade was also available. The three had little to do. The Committee met four times between 27 November and 2 December, when it produced an interim report for the Inter-Allied Conference of 1–3 December. It then reconvened and held seven additional meetings before submitting its final report on 10 December. Keynes was present at three meetings of the Committee – 28 and 29 November and 2 December. He did not influence the outcome, for the Treasury estimates of what Germany could pay, outlined above, were not ready, even in a preliminary form, and were not circulated until after the event. In any case, they were far below those adopted by the Hughes Committee. It recommended that the allies submit a claim for the full cost of the war, £24,000 million – a figure which it had arrived at after one day – and which, amortised at 5 per cent, meant annual payments of £1,200 million – roughly what 'A' Division expected in total. Such sums flew in the face of the views of the officials present at the initial meetings: when the Committee reconvened after 3 December, those officials were not present. The Committee took evidence from witnesses after 3 December: Sir Charles Addis of the Hongkong and Shanghai Bank; Sir Eric Geddes, MP for Cambridge and First Lord of the Admiralty; and Hugo Hurst, the founder of the General Electric Company in Britain, but again they ignored any inconvenient evidence, such as Addis's estimate that Germany could pay no more than £60 million per annum (implying long-term reparations of £1,200 million at 5 per cent). Not surprisingly, the Committee's final report, rushed through to provide electoral ammunition, echoed its interim conclusions that the allies should claim for the full costs of the war and that annual payments of £1,200 million were possible in normal conditions with no serious adverse effects on the recipients. As its final act, the Committee nominated three of its members as the British Empire's reparations delegates to the forthcoming Peace Conference. Lloyd George eventually accepted two of them – Hughes and Cunliffe – adding as a third Lord Sumner, a distinguished Lord of Appeal who, although he had no direct experience of the matters he was to consider, at least had experience in adjudicating commercial cases where large sums of money and points of interpretation were at stake.

Between the completion of the Hughes Committee's work and its discussion by the Cabinet with the appointment of the British reparations delegates came the election. The Coalition had at first avoided fanning anti-German feelings or making much of the reparations/indemnity issue, focusing instead on reconstruction. This moderation did not last. Politicians could not fail to notice strong popular anti-German feelings, worries about high post-war taxation and interest in war crimes and German indemnities on the hustings, and moved to accommodate these, playing down reform in the process. Of course, some members of the Coalition, notably Bonar Law, remained cautious, but others were less restrained. In Cambridge, Sir Eric Geddes on 5 December stated that he favoured Germany paying the full cost of the war. On 10 December, he made his point more graphically:

We will get out of her all you can squeeze out of a lemon and a bit more . . . I will squeeze her until you can hear the pips squeak . . . I would strip Germany as she has stripped Belgium.d

The next evening in Bristol, after receiving the Hughes Committee's Report and working from a text prepared by Hughes, Lloyd George withdrew his earlier caution and set out his 'principles' of indemnity policy:

First, as far as justice is concerned, we have an absolute right to demand the whole cost of the War from Germany. The second point is that we propose to demand the whole cost of the War. The third point is that when you come to the exacting of it you must exact it in such a way that it does not do more harm to the country that received it than to the country which is paying it. The fourth point is that the Committee appointed by the British Cabinet believe it can be done.[13]

Lloyd George had doubtless been worried about the election results. He need not have been: 388 Coalition Unionists and 136 Coalition Liberals won seats; Independent Liberals lost their seats in droves; and Labour, with 59 members, became the Official Opposition. Of those Conservatives returned, 167 went to Westminster for the first time. It was of these that Baldwin remarked to Keynes early in the new session: 'They are a lot of hard-faced men who look as if they had done very well out of the war'.[14] Among them were a significant number, mostly Unionists, who believed that, despite the qualifications in speeches such as Geddes's and Lloyd George's, their election had been a result of their own anti-German campaigns and that the election results were a mandate for a punitive peace. The results depressed Keynes. He wrote of 'this dishonouring Coalition' and referred to the forthcoming Peace Conference as 'Paris-Litovsk' – an allusion to Germany's punitive peace treaty of Brest-Litovsk with revolutionary Russia in February–March 1918 whereby Russia lost Russian Poland, the Baltic States and the Ukraine and agreed to pay substantial reparations.[15] There was one consolation for him: he had managed to get the Treasury 'to accept that this Conference is the last work I do for them and that when it is over I am a free man'.[16]

Keynes spent most of late November and early December 1918 preparing for the Peace Conference. The major task was the Treasury indemnity memorandum. There was also a very preliminary scheme for the cancellation of inter-allied debts which he submitted to Sir John Bradbury on 29 November in the hope that it might form part of the brief for the British delegation at the Conference, but Bradbury could not win Bonar Law's support for

d The phrase 'squeeze her until you can hear the pips squeak' was only given currency through Keynes's *Economic Consequences of the Peace* (*JMK*, II, 90) and it appeared there because it had been said in Cambridge and the report of the speech had been clipped by Florence Keynes.

the scheme.[17] After Christmas at Charleston, Keynes returned to London to complete his preparations for Paris. He also prepared a scheme for the post-war stabilisation of sterling and its possible gradual return to pre-war parity with the dollar.[18]

During Keynes's long Christmas break at Charleston, at 2 a.m. on Christmas morning Vanessa was delivered of a daughter, later named Angelica. After the holiday, despite his Treasury cares, he found time to act as a friendly entertainer of Vanessa's sons, Julian and Quentin, taking them to the matinée of Diaghilev's *Children's Tales* at the Coliseum on 7 January. He reported to Vanessa:

> I fancy Julian thought the juggling the best turn; but Quentin was fascinated by the ballet and certainly preferred that. During the sentimental songs they carried on a loud conversation about the other persons.[19]

He also went with Duncan and Geoffrey Fry to the ballet and saw Lydia dance *The Good Humoured Ladies*. Afterwards, they visited Lydia 'who was charming & very bright in the head. She followed all the conversation in English about Finance & the Cabinet with the greatest esprit'.[20] On 10 January Keynes proceeded to Paris. The Peace Conference formally opened on 18 January.

> 'We are going into these negotiations with our mouths full of fine phrases and our brains seething with dark thoughts.'
> (Edwin Montagu to Lord Balfour, 20 December 1918,
> quoted in Lentin 1984, 30)

> 'This Peace Conf. would make the Congress of Vienna look like a prayer meeting.'
> (General Tasker Bliss, one of America's five commissioners at Paris,
> HUBL, Lamont Papers, 164–18, Lamont Diary, 11 March 1919)

The Paris to which Keynes came in January 1919 was for him, as for many of his contemporaries, a 'nightmare'. The Conference was not a small one: if all the delegations were added together their numbers would run into the thousands. The British delegation exceeded 200; the American 1,200. Hundreds of reporters combed Paris for scraps of news and fed each other rumours. Accommodation was at a premium, but through the efforts of Dudley Ward, his chief of staff, Keynes came relatively well out of the scramble, with a shared flat with Dudley Ward and Sydney Armitage-Smith, and a special sitting room for interviews at the Majestic, the British headquarters in the Avenue Kléber, as well as rooms at the Astoria. Although this assured him of space, it did not assure him of anything else. It was cold and the heating was either excessive or inadequate. The influenza pandemic of 1918–19 was raging. Food supplies were not always adequate: there was no fresh milk, butter or fresh vegetables to be had at the Majestic.[21]

Added to problems of physical existence was 'incessant overwork'.[22] For Keynes, this was particularly acute.[23] The day before he went to Paris, Lloyd George appointed a new Chancellor of the Exchequer, Austen Chamberlain who, despite his previous experience in the pre-war Treasury as Financial Secretary (1900–2) and Chancellor (1903–5), was less qualified for the job than Bonar Law. '[V]ery much as one might throw a bone to a dog', Lloyd George offered Chamberlain the post without the official residence at 11 Downing Street (which Law retained) or a seat in the War Cabinet (which he had hitherto held), but he successfully held out for the latter.[24] Lloyd George also saddled Chamberlain with a Cabinet Finance Committee made up of himself, Bonar Law and Lord Milner, which not only undermined his position but also made quick decision-making difficult. To provide officials such as Keynes with ready access to Cabinet authority in Paris, Edwin Montagu had the job of overseeing the financial negotiations. However, as Secretary of State for India he had other preoccupations. When he resigned as minister responsible for financial affairs at the beginning of April, it was over a fortnight before he was replaced by General Smuts, who, of course also had his own concerns as South African Minister of Defence. Thus, day-to-day responsibility fell heavily on Keynes's shoulders.

In carrying the burden he had little support. Initially he had a staff of four – Armitage-Smith, Ward, Falk and Fry – which the Lord Privy Seal asked him to consider cutting by 25 per cent on 16 January. Eventually his staff, including clerks and typists, rose to eighteen but its members were relatively junior and Keynes at 35 was the only one with significant experience of financial diplomacy. Despite his own abilities, which according to R. H. Brand meant 'by 10.30 a.m. he had done an amount of dictation that would occupy another man most of the day',[25] he was overworked. As he told his mother on 12 February after a bout of severe influenza:

> How I shall keep my health I do not know. The life here is about as unhealthy as possible – movement in draughty motor cars from one overheated room to another, excessive rich food and overwhelming work. Every day since I returned I've worked from 8.30 a.m. to midnight with intervals for meals only.[26]

To Vanessa Bell he commented:

> I've never known anything like the last three weeks, visits to Spa and to Brussels leaving me in a state of perpetual occupation whenever I am in Paris. I can't put my condition more strongly than by saying that for a whole week I hadn't leisure to read the *Times*. But it's all been very exciting and I'm absolutely absorbed in this extraordinary but miserable game. I wish I could tell you every evening the twists and turns of the day, for you'd really be amused by the amazing complications of psychology and personality and intrigue

which make such magnificent sport of the impending catastrophe of Europe.

. . . I am living for weeks together in a state of nervous excitement one would have thought only possible for hours. At the moment my health is perfect but I hope you'll take me in at Charleston when I finally relapse into insanity.[27]

He also reported to Bradbury that his staff, particularly Dudley Ward, was seriously overworked.[28]

Keynes's duties were enormously varied. Initially, he had little to do with the actual terms of the Peace Treaty itself. He continued to worry about inter-allied finance, at least until American support came to an end in March and the British ceased to cover allied overseas expenditures outside the United States. With the end of American support came the decision to let the exchange rate for sterling float. In this Keynes was an intermediary between the Chancellor and the Prime Minister, simply noting at the bottom of a note of a telephone conversation between Sir John Bradbury and Dudley Ward: 'I saw the Prime Minister tonight and obtained his agreement to the above. JMK 19.3.19'.[29] He was also involved with the Supreme Council of Supply and Relief. This later became the Supreme Economic Council into which were folded all inter-allied bodies concerned with finance, food, blockade control, shipping and raw materials. Except on the rare occasions when Austen Chamberlain was in Paris, Keynes was the British representative on the Council with full authority to speak and decide. Of course, he might consult a senior minister, Montagu or Smuts, but these consultations were not extensive.

In mid-March, as part of an appeal for more staff, he set out the range of Treasury responsibilities in Paris:

The following bodies of a more or less permanent character require Treasury representation and have to be staffed on the British side as regards the Secretariat &c out of Treasury section. Most of them meet very frequently.

Reparation Commission with three sub-Commissions (of which the third rarely sits)

Finance Commission with four sub-Commissions Supreme Economic Council

Finance Section of Supreme Economic Council

Left Bank of the Rhine Commission

In addition there are the Armistice negotiations with Germany [the Armistice was renewed monthly at this stage] and there is about to be set up a German Finance Commission at Versailles with three sub-Commissions on each of which we shall have to be represented.

There remains the usual Treasury business, so far as it is conducted in Paris, with the Americans, French, Roumanians, Greeks, &c.

The whole of the financial system of Europe, present and future, is (theoretically) in the hands of the above bodies.

The amount of work waiting to be done, persons to be received in interview and meetings to be attended, if the duties were performed properly, are of course quite beyond the capacity of the present staff. They, therefore, muddle along and opportunities are taken as they offer to enlarge the staff and improve the organisation.[30]

The initial set of responsibilities had been slightly smaller, but never small. And throughout he was a relatively junior official who when it came to the crunch could only call on the support of a lightweight Chancellor.

Almost immediately on his arrival in Paris, Keynes became involved in the negotiations for the renewal of the Armistice with Germany. On 11 January, he learned from Norman Davis of the American Treasury that the French were going to introduce new financial matters, including the disposition of the Reichsbank's gold and the control of the German note issue, into the negotiations. Another financial matter intruded because the original Armistice terms had included a provision for the allies to relax their naval blockade to allow food supplies through to Germany. Germany would have to pay for the food: the question was with what, particularly as any assets so used would not be available for later transfer to the allies in the form of reparations. Before the negotiations, the Supreme Council of Supply and Relief had agreed that food would be supplied on the condition that the Germans handed over their merchant marine. The Council was unable to agree on the matter of finance, but the Supreme War Council agreed that relief supplies should be a first charge on German assets, although the French, who had strenuously opposed the British and Americans on this point, retained the right to re-open the matter two months later.

Keynes and Dudley Ward attended the negotiations at Trier as the British Treasury representatives. The American, French and Italian treasuries were represented by Norman Davis, Comte de Lasteyrie and Professor Attalico.

The negotiations gave Keynes his first glimpse of Germany since 1912, as well as extensive opportunities for playing bridge. The morning after their arrival, they met the German financial delegation consisting of Dr Kaufmann, the President of the Reichsbank; three German Foreign Office representatives; Dr Ratjen, the German financial representative to the Armistice Commission and, lastly, a member of the Hamburg banking firm of Warburg. Keynes later described them:

A sad lot they were in these early days, with drawn, dejected faces and tired staring eyes, like men who had been hammered on the Stock Exchange. But from among them stepped forward into the middle place a very small man, very exquisitely clean, very well and neatly dressed, with a high stiff collar, which seemed cleaner and whiter than an ordinary collar, his round head covered with grizzled hair shaved so close as to be like in substance to the pile of a close-made carpet, the line when his hair ended bounding his face and forehead in a very sharply defined and rather noble curve, his eyes gleaming straight at us, with an extraordinary sorrow in them, yet like an honest animal at bay.[e]

This was Dr Carl Melchior, who acted as the German spokesman during the negotiations. By the time he first met Keynes at 47 he had already had several careers. He had been a lawyer before, in 1902, joining M. M. Warburg as counsel, where he gained a high reputation not only for his skills but also for his objectivity, his cultivated mind and his approachability. He fought in the war as a captain, but after a wound moved to the civilian front as director of the central food-purchasing agency until anti-Semitism led to his resignation in 1917, when he became the first non-family member to become a partner in Warburgs. With the post-Armistice Weimar Government he was the representative of the German Treasury on the delegation concerned with the Peace terms.[31]

The first meeting covered a number of issues of which the first was currency. The French, in light of violent Spartacist disturbances in Germany, were concerned with the safety of Germany's gold reserves and hoped to get them transferred to Frankfurt in the French occupation zone. The British and Americans suspected French motives and with German assurances that the reserves were widely dispersed but secure left matters as they were. The French also, having agreed to exchange marks for francs at pre-war par in Alsace Lorraine and contemplating similar policies for the areas they controlled on the left bank of the Rhine, worried about the depreciation of the mark and, therefore, control of the German note issue. Again, the Germans provided information as to the present position and matters remained as they were. The discussions moved to the matter of food supplies. As noted above, the allies had decided that they would offer food supplies as a means of gaining control of the German merchant marine, which they intended to take as a part of reparations and which would prove useful in the interim given the shortage of shipping. However, as representatives of the German shipping lines were not at Trier and as the Germans had no instructions on the issue, the discussion concerned payment for the foodstuffs with the Germans pleading for a credit which would be dealt with as a part of the final settlement at the Peace Conference (a variant on earlier French proposals) and the allies insisting on cash. The Germans eventually acknowledged that they might find a small sum for fats

---

e *JMK*, X, 395. This forms part of Keynes's Memoir Club paper 'Dr Melchior: A Defeated Enemy' first published in *Two Memoirs* (1949). In *Two Memoirs* this paper was dated as 'before January 1932, and probably in the summer of 1931'. It was actually read to the Club on 2 February 1921 (VWL, II, 456; VWD, II, 88–90).

and condensed milk. On the shipping issue, even after the arrival of the German shipping representatives, there was no progress. Both sides agreed to adjourn.

By the time the delegation returned to Paris, Keynes was feeling distinctly unwell. Two days later he took to his bed with influenza. Even though he was ill, as he told his mother, 'I have to attend to papers all through my illness on every day except when I turned my face to the wall and refused to see anything or anyone'.[32] And the illness was serious. As Clive Bell recorded:

> The accounts that were dripping through into Gordon Square were beginning to alarm me – and, as you know, I'm not easily alarmed for my friends – still you have such a habit of almost dying, my dear Maynard, that one of these days one fears you will do it.[33]

One of the accounts Clive had heard had been from a doctor at the French Legation who had said 'We have advices from Paris that Maynard is at death's door'. At the end of the month he was able to get ten days' leave; so he went to Simon Bussy's at Roquebonne near Menton. It was a good holiday, even if on trying the casino he lost all his francs and had to cash a cheque with his hostess to get back to Paris. While with the Bussys, he reflected on his experiences thus far:

> I don't feel that I have much to do with the Peace Conference or that it is any good trying to, and so far I've played no part whatever in it. A moment may come when it may seem worth while to try to intervene, but I greatly doubt it – all signs are to the contrary – and I should much like, in many ways though not I suppose in all, to be quit of the whole thing. I suppose they're doing quite as well as one could possibly hope, but I so dislike the morals and atmosphere of the whole.[34]

Keynes returned to Paris on 10 February, in response to a telegram from Dudley Ward, for another journey to Trier, another Armistice renewal, and another go at the ships and food issues. Beyond renewing the Armistice, the meeting accomplished next to nothing, for the Germans refused to surrender the ships without an arrangement over food; the French, despite the earlier decision of the Supreme War Council, refused to allow the Germans to use gold to pay for food; and the allies refused to provide credit for food.

March saw something of a breakthrough. The meeting between the allies and the Germans at Spa in Belgium had been preceded by concerted planning to provide for a shipment of substantial quantities of breadstuffs and pork products. The allies had prepared the ground by agreeing to some concessions to the Germans and assistance to them in getting the food from abroad. As yet, however, there was no agreement over finance and the whole offer was conditional on the Germans' surrendering their merchant marine. The meeting was deadlocked. Keynes then obtained permission to speak to

Melchior privately and explain to him informally how the ground lay in the hope that the Germans could get fresh instructions. In his memoir, Keynes set the interview out dramatically, stating that 'In a sort of way, I was in love with him' – a remark that has caused speculation as to the nature of their subsequent relationship.[f] The intervention failed: the allied delegation returned to Paris that evening.

The return to Paris brought the matter to a meeting of the Supreme War Council. The Anglo-American proposal before the Council was that the allies would inform the Germans that they were bound to deliver the ships; that the allies would undertake to deliver the food as soon as the ship transfers began; that Germany would be able to use her liquid assets, including gold, to pay for the food; and that Germany might, with a limited lifting of the naval blockade, export goods and purchase food in neutral countries. The debate was prolonged and dramatic, with a telegram delivered in the middle of it from General Plumer, head of the British occupying forces, asking for food without delay owing to civilian distress and possible unrest. It concluded with Lloyd George's humiliation of the French Finance Minister, Louis-Lucien Klotz, as he attempted to prevent the Germans from using their gold. In the end, the proposals went through with the rider that the Germans would have to give up their ships before they knew the allies' terms.

The final meeting in the sequence was at Brussels on 13–14 March. There Keynes, in the company of a Royal Navy captain, met Melchior again to tell him privately what the allies had decided. The proposals went through easily – although in the end little food actually moved, for difficulties continued over payments.[35] The business had taken two months.

After Brussels, Keynes remained in frequent contact with his German counterparts. It became closer when he succeeded in getting a German delegation, including Max Warburg, to the Château de Villette near Compiègne. His contacts with Melchior were to continue into the 1930s.

Food for Germany was not Keynes's only concern. He was deeply involved in the discussion of the non-reparations, financial clauses of the Treaty. He was involved in other relief discussions and policy with a £12.5 million Treasury grant to play with. In typical Treasury fashion, he still had £1–£1.5 million left as late as 22 May, despite 'large and incessant' demands.[36] He played a significant role in providing food for Austria.[37] Inter-allied financial problems continued. On 19 February he had formally to inform the French of the end of British financial assistance. Although the possibility had

f *JMK*, X, 415. On hearing the remark when the paper was first read, Virginia Woolf commented: 'I think he meant it seriously, though we laughed.' (VWD, II, 90). More recently, Stephen Schuker reviewing volumes XVII and XVIII of *The Collected Writings* in *The Journal of Economic Literature* for March 1980 (pp. 124–6) carried speculation further than Virginia Woolf had. From the available papers, there is no evidence that the relationship between the two men was ever physical, even if strong underlying feeling might have been there. One doubts if it affected Keynes's attitude towards Germany, which had been shaped years earlier.

been in the wind for some months, this produced a crisis which saw Keynes flying to London for a War Cabinet meeting on 25 February. The aircraft lost its way and landed in a ploughed field a hundred miles off course.[38] The outcome was an advance of £2 million, later expanded to £6 million, while the Chancellor went to Paris to discuss the issue with the French on 8–10 March. Chamberlain's discussions resulted in an agreement that the French would sell gold held on French account in the Bank of England under a 1916 agreement in return for a credit of £30 million. After two more months, all credits would end. This arrangement fell apart when the Bank of France refused to release the gold and with the end of allied support the French ceased to support their exchange rate, a week before the British, having run through their American credits, did likewise. Thus the wartime pattern of exchange rates broke down. Stability would not return for over seven years.

In the initial scheme of things, Keynes, as I have already noted, was to have very little to do with the reparations issue. Cunliffe, Hughes and Sumner were the British Empire representatives on the Commission on Reparation of Damage – Cunliffe and Sumner also serving as chairmen of its sub-Commissions on the size of the bill and on Germany's capacity to pay. Their instructions were the product of the Hughes Committee of November and December 1918 as confirmed by the War Cabinet on Christmas Eve 1918. 'A' Division in London provided them with financial data and Keynes's deputy in Paris, Dudley Ward, acted as the technical adviser to the three. None the less, as the senior Treasury official in Paris, Keynes was not uninformed of or uninvolved in the discussions.

His informal involvement would take several forms. There would be comments from his 'A' Division colleagues and papers passing over his desk which he might find time to read. There were also the close, productive relationships that he had developed in London during the closing stages of the war with his American counterparts, particularly Norman Davis, now the senior American Treasury representative in Paris. Such relationships became a way of passing information about intentions backwards and forwards. This could prove useful in the co-ordination of policy, as it had over the problems surrounding the renewal of the Armistice in January. If the information was misleading, however, it could produce problems, as it did over reparations. Keynes clearly knew American policy over the reparations/indemnity issue from Davis and Paul Cravath.[39] That policy, which strictly followed the pre-Armistice understandings, was congruent with his own views. Yet, rather than merely express his own views, he also intimated on occasion that they were also those of the British Government. At the end of November 1918 he told Norman Davis:

that the British have no intention of demanding any indemnities other than for the loss of the tonnage illegally destroyed by the enemy, and that it would be their desire to restrict the limitations regarding reparation and to limit as much as possible the various kinds of claims for indemnity that might be presented under the armistice terms, and that they are preparing data to substantiate any opposition to excessive demands for indemnity which might load Germany with a greater burden than could be carried or than would be advantageous to the associated governments.[40]

At the time, his Government had no policy: the Hughes Committee had just started meeting and Keynes had just started to prepare the Treasury memorandum, which did of course embody such as he told Davis. But by providing such misleading information, Keynes did not strengthen his own or his Government's position. It never reached the point of Virginia Woolf's comment: 'Maynard being behind the scenes is almost invariably wrong'.[41] Not that the Americans were not warned. On 28 February, before Keynes became actively involved in the negotiations, Thomas Lamont recorded in his diary a conversation with Sir William Wiseman on reparations:

Explained the whole Reparations situation. We were delaying partly because [we] thought there were 2 schools of English thought, and if we came up to [$] 40 billions then we might get thrown down by low party. W.W. said there was nothing to that. Only one man in the Govt. who was low and that was Keynes. He was fine in the Treasury, but in this Reparations matter his views did not count.[42]

Nor was the mis-estimation of future intentions always on one side: Keynes also would in the course of 1919 misjudge American intentions from the conversations of those with whom he worked.

The Commission on Reparation of Damage began work in the middle of January 1919. It did not make rapid progress. Both Britain and France, for differing reasons,[g] made attempts to include the entire cost of the war as a legitimate claim and the Americans resisted. No one except for the British had concrete demands for reparations or for the cost of the war ready for presentation. The result was deadlock. Combined with differences between the delegates to the Commission and the Treasury over the appropriate policy on German payments for food and raw materials this led to a

---

g It has been suggested recently that France was basically much more moderate than Britain but pressed a large claim for reparations and an indemnity for bargaining purposes (see Trachtenberg 1981, esp. ch. 2.). Such a position is a plausible one if the ends for which the high French opening bids were made were possible of attainment. It is clear, however, from Keynes's own papers that the link between France's reparations/indemnity bid and her ultimate objectives on trade policy and American financial assistance was not perceived by at least one reasonably well-informed observer. It seems also to have been missed by others. If this was the case, the strategy does not seem to have been well-designed or well-executed.

Treasury suggestion for the recall of Cunliffe, Hughes and Sumner and for a reconsideration of British policy. It was partially for this reason that, fully briefed by Norman Davis,[43] Keynes returned to London on 22 February.

A Cabinet meeting supported a change in tactics. There was to be an attempt to extract a sum as high as was consistent with Germany's capacity to pay and as much of that as possible while the Allies could enforce payment. Moreover, policy was to be conducted in concert with the Americans. Yet, for the moment, the Commission on Reparation of Damage was to be the forum for negotiations. There was no progress.

On 10 March, in an attempt to break the deadlock, and possibly to get the matter out of the hands of Cunliffe and company, Lloyd George agreed to attempt to resolve the problems through parallel negotiations between Edwin Montagu, Norman Davis and Louis Loucheur. These resulted in a recommendation through Norman Davis on 14 March of a figure of 120 billion gold marks or £6,000 million payable over 30 years – half in gold and half in German marks convertible into foreign exchange when conditions permitted. There was no agreement about the distribution of the proceeds. With Montagu absent from Paris after the death of his mother, this recommendation was undone on 17 March by recommendation from Cunliffe, Hughes and Sumner that Germany was capable of paying £1,000 million in the first two years and £600 million a year – half in gold, half in marks – for a probable period of fifty years. Lloyd George took this recommendation to a meeting of the Heads of State on 18 March, at which Keynes was present. There he proposed that all the experts should meet to settle Germany's capacity to pay. Thus Keynes, who had been watching from the sidelines, was brought into the discussions. He made it clear to Cunliffe and Sumner that he was not sympathetic to their figures, but agreed to be silent when he appeared with them in public.[44]

At the same time Lloyd George asked Keynes to prepare a scheme of reparations which would represent a capital sum having a present value of £5,000 million. With R. H. Brand, Keynes produced a scheme with annual payments rising from £50 million in the first two years to £400 million between 1951 and 1960. As the present value of such a stream was only £3,800 million, they added in a footnote a steeper graduation that would yield £4,800 million, but advised against this. Lloyd George held to a capital sum of £5,000 million if Sumner and Cunliffe would agree. They did not and there matters remained for the moment. As Keynes quoted Norman Davis on 25 March:

> If we can quiet down the Heavenly Twins [Cunliffe and Sumner] by agreeing to any fool report for the Three and then get rid of them by winding up the Commission [on Reparation of Damage] we could get around with some human beings and start afresh.[45]

He proposed as much to Lloyd George in the same letter, but the advice was ignored. Some regard this as a crucially missed opportunity, for at that stage

Keynes's 'fresh' basis would have included his 'Scheme for the Rehabilitation of European Credit' – a development and extension of his proposals of the previous November – which as it was would only see the light of day later in April.[46]

With agreement on a global figure for reparations looking remote, Keynes became involved in another attempt to secure Britain a reasonable level of receipts, an agreement to apportion any sums received. Sumner proposed a distribution between France and Britain in the ratio of 50:30. The French replied with 56:25. Lamont suggested a compromise to Keynes of 56:28. This compromise did not find favour with the French, who were unhappy with the 2:1 ratio of relative damage implied. Keynes suggested that the British accept 56:25 if the three percentage point difference went to the other allies.[47] Lloyd George declined the concession. In December 1919 the Anglo-French agreement on proportions would work out at 55:25 and at Spa in mid-1920 the figure became 52:22.

At this stage another element entered the picture. In the same 28 March memorandum to Lloyd George, Keynes mentioned pensions and separation allowances, about which there was clearly some doubt, even in the minds of the French, as to their admissibility under the Fourteen Points. These became the key to what followed. Lloyd George had reported to his delegation on 13 March, after discussions with Colonel House, that with suitable drafting it might be possible to get American agreement (or at least acquiescence) to the inclusion of pensions in the claim against Germany.[48]

General Smuts, who had been ill in England from mid-February, returned to Paris on 23 March. Over the next two days, he attempted to fill out his knowledge of what had occurred in his absence and on 26 March he wrote Lloyd George a powerful plea against peace terms that would destroy Germany, given the importance of a healthy, co-operative Germany to the economic and political future of Central Europe in the face of the threat of revolution. Three days later he suggested to Lloyd George a fresh approach to the issue of reparations which would divide the total into two categories: damage to persons and damage to property, a distinction also suggested by Keynes in a memorandum two weeks earlier.[49] No reparations total would be fixed, but Germany's obligation would be equal to the total of these categories of claim. The actual payments would be fixed by a permanent commission which would be free to vary Germany's obligations in the light of her capacity to pay. The proposal that the actual amount paid should depend on Germany's capacity as determined by an independent commission had also been made by others, including Keynes, while a proposal to omit a fixed total from the Treaty had been under discussion at the Council of Four on 26 and 28 March.[50] Coupled with Lord Sumner's argument for the inclusion of pensions and separation allowances, the Smuts proposal for a division of the bill provided Lloyd George with the basis for another approach. Keynes and Sumner drafted a memorandum along Smuts' lines, including the element of pensions and Lloyd George submitted it to the Council of Four on 30 March.[h]

The US President resisted the inclusion of pensions and separation allowances at the meeting of 30 March, but was won over by a memorandum from General Smuts the following day. Once Wilson had given way, the drafting was fairly straightforward, although it occupied several days. There was, however, one additional matter that seemed objectionable in principle, but harmless in practice in that it had no financial consequences. This was Article 231 of the Treaty, the infamous 'war guilt clause'. This required Germany to accept full responsibility for causing the war; allowed President Wilson to believe that the ensuing clauses were consistent with the engagements Germany had entered into in the Armistice; and gave a possible solution to Lloyd George's potential domestic political problems if the reparations total turned out to be too small.[51] The significant draftsmen of the clause were Keynes and John Foster Dulles.[52]

Keynes's attempts to keep the total of reparations down had included a revival of his November 1918 scheme for the cancellation of war debts. This scheme was a non-starter, for the American Treasury ruled out of court any discussion of rearrangement of the obligations of foreign governments to the United States. With the failure of this scheme, the absence of a total for reparations (which would make any near-term German international bond issue along the lines of France's borrowing for the 1871 indemnity unviable in the world's capital markets), and Smuts's report of the tragic conditions in Eastern Europe which he had seen in his early April visit to Austria and Hungary, Keynes made an attempt to monetise future reparations payments and allow the reconstruction and relief of Europe to proceed. He called it '*a grand scheme for the rehabilitation of Europe*'.[53] In sending it forward to Lloyd George, Austen Chamberlain noted:

> It is marked by all Mr. Keynes's characteristic ability and resource: it provides the stricken countries of Europe, whether allied or enemy, with a means of re-equipping themselves and restarting on a sound basis the trade and industry of the world; it provides equally for the new Nations which the Conference is calling into existence; and it offers hope to the enemy powers and provides them with the means by which, whilst accepting the arduous conditions of the peace which will be imposed upon them, they can restart their industrial life and put themselves into a position to meet their onerous obligations. . . .
>
> No other proposals of which I have heard offer comparable advantages. Indeed, there is no other comprehensive scheme in the field.[54]

h Hemery 1988, 227. There is some disagreement in the literature as to whether Lloyd George made this proposal in order to increase Britain's share of the proceeds or to increase the bill for reparations. Given the range of support for the proposal, it is probable that the motives were mixed. (Hancock 1962, 515; Elcock 1972, 174–5; Trachtenberg 1981, 70–1).

While Keynes was in England from 10 to 18 April, snatching a weekend at Charleston in his spare time, he was able to see his scheme presented to Cabinet.

The scheme was simple yet bold.[55] The ex-enemy states and the new states of Eastern Europe created by the Treaty would, with the ultimate guarantee of the principal allied and associated powers issue bonds with a present value of £1,445 million. The bonds would carry interest at 4 per cent and a sinking fund of 1 per cent. Of the sum thus raised £1,000 million would go to the recipients of reparations, thus providing funds to finance recovery in countries such as France and Belgium; £200 million would be used by the German Government for the purchase of food and raw materials; £76 million would discharge German debts to the European neutrals; and the remainder, £169 million, would find use for purchases of food and raw materials in Austria, Hungary and Bulgaria. No interest would be payable on the bonds until 1 January 1925.

Lloyd George passed the scheme to President Wilson, Clemenceau and Orlando. Keynes had some conversations with Herbert Hoover and Norman Davis which he interpreted as suggesting that there was at least some sympathy for the scheme in American circles in Paris. Sir William Wiseman's conversations with Colonel House were also encouraging.[56] American support was essential, for although the United States Government was only to be responsible for guaranteeing 20 per cent of the interest on the issue in case of the default of the enemy powers to meet their collective guarantee, US lenders were expected to take up most of the issue. Moreover, as the bonds would be acceptable 'in payment of indebtedness between any of the allied and associated governments' many might end up in the United States in payment of war debts. Of course, in the case of a general European default, the United States Government or private investors would be left holding the baby, but even in the conditions of 1919 this, although possible, was unlikely. However, Keynes was misled by his conversations. Not only was there 'immediate and violent opposition on the part of Washington', not to mention 'many thousand words of criticism and horror', but his American contacts in Paris were not sympathetic.[57] On 3 May, along with General Smuts, Keynes dined with Davis and Thomas Lamont to discuss American reactions. The Americans thought only in terms of helping the finances of the new European successor states. The Americans were not sympathetic to further loans to France or Belgium or to schemes that would merely help Germany pay reparations. He found the whole position 'disappointing and depressing'.[58] When formally asked for his reaction to the President's rejection of the scheme in a letter dated 5 May (which had incidentally been drafted by Lamont), Keynes minuted:

The President's letter, as it stands however, indicates a spirit far too harsh for the human situation facing us. In particular it is surely impossible for the Americans to disclaim responsibility for the Peace Treaty to which, wisely or not, they have put their name equally with other governments. The President, beginning with his Fourteen Points, has declared the necessity of reparations for the devastations of war. He cannot therefore dissociate himself from attempts to put this into execution.[59]

After the rejection of the scheme, Smuts recorded:

Poor Keynes often sits with me at night after a good dinner and we rail against the world and the coming flood. And I tell him that it is time for the Griqua prayer (the Lord to come himself and not to send his Son, as this is not a time for children).[i] And then we laugh, and behind the laughter is [Herbert] Hoover's terrible picture of 30 million people who must die unless there is some great intervention. But then again we think things are never as bad as that; and that something will turn up, and the worst will never be. And somehow all these phases of feeling are true and right in some sense.[60]

Although an allied committee came into being to discuss alternatives to Keynes's scheme and produced a report, the report was never discussed by the Three.

In early May, the Peace Treaty was nearing its final form before its presentation to the Germans. The experts who had been working in relative isolation on particular segments now saw things falling into place in a larger scheme, although the full Treaty was not complete until hours before its presentation to the Germans.[61] Keynes, who in his co-ordinating Treasury role had probably seen more fragments than many others at Paris and who had tried, through such devices as his financial rehabilitation scheme, to minimise its immediate impact, was far from enthusiastic about what he saw emerging, either in the terms of the Treaty or in the attitudes of the allies, particularly the Americans, whom the negotiation of the reparation chapter had left 'with the bitterest feelings towards their European associates' and whose sympathies were 'now much more with the enemy than with any of us'. He suggested that the Germans, who were now in better spirits than a few months before, would be unlikely to sign.[62] On 7 May the allies presented the draft Treaty for the Germans, who had fifteen days in which to reply. The Allies would then provide a riposte and set a final deadline for acceptance or rejection.

i The actual words are: 'Lord, save thy people. Lord, we are lost unless Thou savest us. Lord, this is no work for children. It is not enough this time to send Thy Son. Lord, Thou must come Thyself.' (Hancock 1962, 521).

The morning the Treaty was to be presented to the Germans, Herbert Hoover, who had received his copy at 4 a.m. on 7 May, went for a walk in the deserted streets of Paris:

> Within a few blocks I met General Smuts and John Maynard Keynes of the British delegation. We seemed to have come together by some sort of telepathy. It flashed into all our minds why each of us was walking about at that time of morning. Each of us was greatly disturbed. We agreed that the consequences of many parts of the proposed Treaty would ultimately bring destruction. We also agreed that we would do all we could among our nationals to point out the dangers.[63]

By that stage, Keynes had certainly started to consider his position.

Before we look at what he did, we must remember that before he went to Paris he expected that the Peace Conference would be his last piece of Treasury business. Also, the negotiations, apart from providing occasional emotional 'highs' over such matters as food for Germany and the presentation of his scheme for financial rehabilitation, had left him with a sense of foreboding that appeared regularly in his letters and memoranda.[64] On 12 April, while in England, he wrote to his mother from Charleston of his imminent return to Paris. He continued:

> This time, I hope for not more than about six weeks as I do not intend to go on after our affairs with Germany have come to a head one way or another. Perhaps not so long as at any moment the best plan may seem to be to chuck.
>
> The state of Europe is very desperate – the economic system jammed and the people without hope. But here in England everything seems very normal and everyone very comfortable and certainly very oblivious of what is going on the other side of the curtain.[65]

Just over a month later Keynes had made his decision to resign and *gradually* to disengage himself from the Conference. He first communicated his decision to his mother and Duncan Grant. The two letters were identical in many respects, but the one to Duncan was more informative as to his state of mind:[j]

> It's weeks since I've written a letter to anyone, – but I've been utterly worn out, partly by incessant work and partly by depression at the evil around me. I've been as miserable for the last two or three weeks as a

j BL, ADD.57931, JMK to DG, 14 May 1919. In his letter to his mother, he also mentioned that he had been invited to apply for the directorship of the London School of Economics, but he intended to decline it. Sir William Beveridge had also been asked; he accepted (Harris 1977, 249–50). A month later, Keynes would also be asked if he would accept the new Cassel Professorship of Banking and Currency at the School (Mackenzie (ed.) 1978, III, 120). He declined that as well. In 1938 the Chair would go briefly to Dennis Robertson (below p. 602).

fellow could be. The Peace is outrageous and impossible and can bring nothing but misfortune. To judge from the papers, no one in England yet has any conception of the iniquities in it. Certainly if I was in the Germans' place I'd rather die than sign such a Peace. Personally I don't think they will sign, though the general view is to the contrary. But if they do sign, that will be the worst thing that could happen, as they can't possibly keep some of the terms, and general disorder and unrest will result everywhere. Meanwhile there is no food or employment anywhere, and the French and Italians are pouring munitions into Central Europe to arm everyone against everyone else. I sit in my room hour after hour receiving delegations from the new nations, who ask not for food or raw materials, but primarily for instruments of murder against their neighbours. And with such a Peace as the basis I see no hope anywhere. Anarchy and Revolution is the best thing that can happen, and the sooner the better.

Thank God I shall soon be out of it and I suppose that it won't be many weeks before I've forgotten this nightmare. I'm writing to the Treasury to be relieved of my duties by June 1 if possible and not later than June 15 in any event.

One most bitter disappointment was the collapse of my Grand Scheme for putting everyone on their legs. After getting it successfully through the Chancellor of the Exchequer and the Prime Minister and seeing it formally handed to Wilson and Clemenceau, the American Treasury (of whom no more was asked than ours) turned it firmly down as a most immoral proposal which might cost them something and which Senators from Illinois wouldn't look at. They had a chance of taking a large, or at least human, view of the world and unhesitatingly refused it. Wilson, of whom I've seen a good deal more lately, is the greatest fraud on earth.

. . . Do write to me and remind me that there are still some decent people in the world. Here I could cry all day for rage and vexation. The world can't be quite as bad as it looks from the Majestic.

. . .

Do write to me.

His letter to his mother surprised her less than one might have expected, for she had seen Marjorie Bussy who had told her that Keynes had looked very worn down. Her reaction was typical:

How I wish I could run over to you & take you under my wing & protect you from the wicked world as I should do in a physical illness.[66]

Keynes's letter to Bradbury resigning his position does not appear to have survived, but it appears from the reply that he informed his superiors on 19

May. O. T. Falk resigned soon afterwards.[67] The Chancellor, recognising that Keynes had for some time wanted to get back into private life, appealed for him to stay until the situation became more clearly defined. In his reply Keynes stated that his reasons were not simply those of needing a rest and wanting to return to his own work: he had 'real and important' substantive grounds and therefore would stay only on certain conditions:

We have presented a draft Treaty to the Germans which contains in it much that is unjust and much more that is inexpedient. Until the last moment no one could appreciate its full bearing. It is now right and necessary to discuss it with the Germans and to be ready to make substantial concessions. If this policy is not pursued, the consequences will be disastrous in the extreme.

If, therefore, the decision is taken to discuss the Treaty with the Germans with a view to substantial changes and if our policy is such that it looks as if I can be of real use, I am ready to stay another two or three weeks. But if the decision is otherwise, I fear that I must resign immediately. I cannot express how strongly I feel as to the gravity of what is in front of us, and I must have my hands quite free. . . . The Prime Minister is leading us all into a morass of destruction. The settlement which he is proposing for Europe disrupts it economically and must depopulate it by millions of persons. The new states we are setting up cannot survive in such surroundings. Nor can the peace be kept or the League of Nations live. How can you expect me to assist in this tragic farce any longer, seeking to lay the foundations, as a Frenchman puts it, '*d'une guerre juste et durable*'?[68]

He enclosed a copy of a letter from General Smuts to the Prime Minister resigning from the Austrian Reparations Commission.

On 13 May Count Brockdorff-Rantzau provided a preliminary German assessment of the economic effects of the Treaty on Germany.[69] In words that Keynes would take over in his *Economic Consequences of the Peace*,[70] he outlined how over the two previous generations Germany had developed into an industrial state dependent on imported supplies of food and raw materials and suggested that after the deprivations of the war and the post-war blockade:

If the Conditions of Peace are put into force, it simply means that many millions of Germans will perish. This process would develop quickly since the health of the population has been broken during the war by the blockade and during the armistice by its increased severity.

No aid, important and of long duration as it might be, could bring to a halt this wholesale death. . . .

We do not know – and we doubt – whether the Delegates of the Allied and Associated Powers realise the consequences that would be inevitable if Germany, an industrial state with a dense population, tied to a world economy and dependent upon an enormous importation of raw materials and foodstuffs, finds itself all at once pushed back into a phase of development that would correspond to her economic position and population of half a century ago. Those who sign the Treaty will pass a sentence of death upon many millions of German men, women and children.

The publication of the draft Treaty and the initial German response to its iniquities produced a crumbling of support for Lloyd George. General Smuts on 14 May declared the Treaty unworkable and threatened not to sign it unless sensible concessions were made. Others in the Cabinet echoed this protest. Even Bonar Law urged concessions, including a fixed sum for reparations, a view still held by the Treasury, and urged on Lloyd George by Chamberlain and, on 2 June, by Keynes.[71] Lloyd George refused to be moved on the issue of a fixed sum, partially because in the absence of a tight agreement about proportions he risked being squeezed by French demands. The issue was discussed at the Council of Four on 3 and 9 June. By the latter date Keynes had left Paris.

The arrival of the German counter-proposals on 29 May produced a renewed British effort to change parts of the Treaty. Reparations were not the only issue at stake, but they were probably the most significant. With Lloyd George holding his ground on these and President Wilson holding his on other matters, there was little movement between the proposals of 7 May and the final terms submitted to the Germans on 16 June with seven days to reply. After a further German reply and an ultimatum, the Treaty with Germany was signed on 28 June 1919.

Keynes, who had continued his Treasury duties in the hope that there might be some changes in the Treaty, collapsed on 30 May. As he told Duncan:

> Partly out of misery and rage for all that's happening and partly from prolonged overwork, I gave way last Friday and took to my bed from sheer nervous exhaustion, where I have remained ever since. My first idea was to return to England immediately, but Smuts with whom I've been working intimately for changes in this damned Treaty declared that one can only leave the field *dead* and persuaded me to stay on and be available if necessary for the final discussion of these present days. So I dragged myself out of bed to make a final protest before the Reparation Commission against murdering Vienna, and did achieve some improvement. And I've been told the Cabinet met once again the truth about the German indemnity. However, the business will be determined in a day or two, and then I return to England, forever – bar certain very improbable changes in the possibilities of the case, – free at last from all responsibility and shame.[72]

Two days later he reported to Vanessa Bell that he was living alone in Sidney Peel's flat at 82 Boulevard Flandrin, spending most of his day in bed and only getting up for 'grand interviews' with Smuts, the Chancellor, the Prime Minister and the like.

> The result is that I'm already immensely better and nothing but my great prudence in matters of health keeps me still secluded. But I distinctly looked over the edge last week, and not liking the prospect, took to my bed immediately.[73]

Although he admitted that there was a chance of a real change in the Treaty, he thought 'it's too late and Fate must march to her conclusion'.

He was right. After saying farewell to the friends he had made in Paris and clearing up loose ends of official business, Keynes left Paris and Lloyd George on 7 June, leaving 'the twins to gloat over the devastation of Europe and to assess to taste what remains for the British taxpayer'.[74] He proceeded directly to King's – once more a free man. Coincidentally, but for the opposite reasons, Cunliffe left Paris on the same day.[75]

Although Keynes's failure to influence the whole financial settlement – reparations, relief and reconstruction – had been the result of allied intransigence, this was not the only reason. He had favoured a moderate settlement: yet he had been intimately involved in assisting in developing more onerous and objectionable schemes. Two American observers noted the contradiction in the positions of Keynes and others. Vance McCormick noted:

> It is amusing to hear criticism [of the terms] from Davis, Keynes and others who, when they had been talking with the Big Four, agree to everything they say and make no strong protest. I told them the time to fight is before they are committed.[76]

Then there was Thomas Lamont:

> It is all right to say that Cecil and Montagu and those people showed their dissent from Lloyd George's views, but why was not that dissent strong enough to force the British to line up with President Wilson.
>
> . . .
>
> Talk about liberal minded Englishmen? They all make me sick. If they had one-tenth the courage of their convictions they would have stood by the Americans and helped us get the sort of Peace we wanted. Instead of that, they threw us out at every turn.[77]

Even though Lamont admitted at the end of his letter, 'Perhaps I shan't be so mad tomorrow', he and McCormick had a point. But the specific names they mentioned other than Keynes's were also significant. Smuts, Cecil and Montagu, who might be called the supporters of Keynes's views, had limited influence with Lloyd George on this issue. They had other interests at stake that, except in Cecil's case, prevented resignation or, in Smuts's case, for a time contemplating refusing to sign the Treaty.[78] Moreover they could cling to the hope of working through Lloyd George, which meant with him, as the final outcome was still unclear. But Keynes's own minister, the Chancellor, was unwilling to go to the wall for him. And Keynes himself, with his energies drawn in many directions, had always been a relatively junior official. It was admitted by some that he was 'one of the most influential men behind the scenes', even if his perspective often seemed perhaps too narrowly financial.[79] Yet his range of contacts was limited largely to other officials at roughly his own level. Without strong ministerial support his case was lost. He would now look to another forum for his case – informed public opinion.

NOTES

1 Angell 1910, ch. VI.
2 *JMK*, XVI, 179–84.
3 *JMK*, XVI, 311.
4 On this issue, see Hemery 1988, 418–28; Lentin 1984, 12; Headlam-Morley, Bryant and Cienciala 1972, xxi, xxiii.
5 *JMK*, XVI, 342.
6 *JMK*, XVI, 344–83.
7 *JMK*, II, 106–31.
8 Below, p. 295–6; Bunselmeyer 1975, 85; Hemery 1988, 430.
9 *JMK*, XVI, 378.
10 Ibid., 382.
11 Bunselmeyer 1975, ch. 7.
12 KCKP, JMK to FAK, 21 July 1918.
13 Jones 1951, 162.
14 *JMK*, II, 91. For Baldwin's coining of the remark, see *JMK*, XVII, 15.
15 KCKP, JMK to FAK, 16 December 1918.
16 KCKP, JMK to FAK, 22 December 1918.
17 KCKP, T/14/2, 'Memorandum on the Treatment of Inter-Allied Debts arising out of the War', n.d. but submitted to Bradbury on 29 November. See also RT/1/1, JMK to Bradbury, 29 November 1918; Bradbury to Law, 30 November 1918; Law to JMK, 1 December 1918. Part of Keynes's memorandum is reprinted, but misleadingly dated in *JMK*, XVI, 418–19.
18 *JMK*, XVII, 168–71.
19 NUL, JMK to Vanessa Bell, 8 January 1919.
20 KCCP, DGVB91, no date but must be January 1919.
21 Headlam-Morley, Bryant & Cienciala 1972, xli–ii, 1.
22 Nicolson 1933, 45, 66.
23 Much of what follows leans heavily on Hemery 1988, ch. 6.
24 Dutton 1985, 155.
25 OBL, Brand Papers, File 198, R. H. Brand to Barbara Wootton, 20 November 1946.
26 KCKP, Box 35A, JMK to FAK, 12 February 1919.
27 NUL, JMK to Vanessa Bell, 16 March 1919.
28 KCKP, JMK to Sir John Bradbury, 11 February and 19 March 1919.
29 KCKP, PT/1, D. Ward to JMK, 19 March 1919 and JMK minute.

30 KCKP, PT/1, 'Treasury Section at Paris – Staff Arrangements' appended to JMK to Sir John Bradbury, 19 March 1919.
31 Rosenbaum and Sherman 1979, chs. 5 and 6.
32 KCKP, JMK to FAK, 30 January 1919.
33 KCKP, C. Bell to JMK, 2 February 1919.
34 BL, ADD.57931, JMK to DG, 9 February 1919.
35 See Keynes's minute to Bradbury of 9 May reprinted in *JMK*, XVI, 442–5.
36 As reported in a minute to Bradbury, *JMK*, XVI, 448.
37 *JMK*, XVI, 417.
38 KCKP, JMK to JNK, 22 February 1919.
39 See, for example, KCKP, Cravath to JMK, 12 December 1918 concerning Lloyd George's Bristol speech.
40 Burnett 1940, I, 425. For other notes of Keynes's views see ibid., 433–4, 435–6.
41 VWL, II, 313; see also II, 208.
42 HUBL, Lamont Papers, 164–18, Lamont Diary, 28 February 1919.
43 HUBL, Lamont Papers, 164–18, Lamont Diary, 20 February 1919.
44 Hemery 1988, 213.
45 KCKP, PT/1, JMK to P. Kerr, 25 March 1919.
46 Hemery 1988, 224.
47 *JMK*, XVI, 449–50.
48 Lentin 1984, 43.
49 SRO, Lothian Papers GD40/17/64, JMK, 'Reparation and Indemnity', 11 March 1919.
50 Burnett 1940, 60; Tillman 1961, 242.
51 Lentin 1984, 67, 74, 76.
52 Lentin 1984, 74.
53 KCKP, JMK to FAK, 17 April 1919.
54 *JMK*, XVI, 428.
55 The scheme is reprinted in *JMK*, XVI, 429–31.
56 KCKP, PT/1, Wiseman to JMK, 31.3.19.
57 *JMK*, XVI, 438; HUBL, Lamont Papers, 164–13, Davis and Lamont to Washington, 17 April 1919.
58 *JMK*, XVI, 438–40.
59 HUBL, Lamont Papers, 164–14, Wilson to Lloyd George, 5 May 1919; *JMK*, XVI, 441–2.
60 Hancock 1962, 521.
61 Hankey 1963, 134.
62 *JMK*, XVI, 450–6.
63 Hoover 1958, 234.
64 See above pp. 299, 302.
65 KCKP, Box 35, JMK to FAK, 12 April 1919.
66 KCKP, FAK to JMK, 16 May 1919.
67 Headlam-Morley, Bryant and Cienciala 1972, 142.
68 *JMK*, XVI, 459–60.
69 Burnett 1940, II, 7–9.
70 *JMK*, II, 144–6.
71 *JMK*, XVI, 467–9.
72 BL, ADD.57931, JMK to DG, 1 June 1919.
73 NUL, JMK to Vanessa Bell, 3 June 1919. See also his letter to his mother of the same date, reprinted in *JMK*, XVI, 470–1.
74 Ibid., 469.
75 F. Lloyd George 1967, 156.

76 HUBL, Lamont Papers, 164–19, Diary of Vance C. McCormick: excerpts, 22 May 1919.
77 Ibid., 165–25, T. W. Lamont to Florence Lamont, 7 June 1919.
78 Hancock 1962, 534–5. Montagu, of course had his Indian Reform Bill 'which is the main, if not the only, raison d'être for my existence in the Government' (Waley 1964, 204).
79 Vincent (ed.) 1984, 401 (entry for 9 April 1919).

13

ECONOMIC CONSEQUENCES OF THE PEACE

My mind has crossed a Rubicon. I have struck my tents and am on the march.

(KCKP, JMK to Norman Davis, 18 April 1920; *JMK*, XVII, 42)

After his return to England, Keynes did not remain long in Cambridge. On 12 June he went to London and the next day he proceeded, as he had long planned, to Charleston, which he was to use as his base for most of the summer.

By then he had started to receive suggestions that he write of his Paris experiences and his views on the Peace. On 10 June, General Smuts had written gently reproving him for leaving Paris. He continued:

I think it would be very advisable for you as soon as possible to set about writing a clear connected account of what the financial and economic clauses of the Treaty actually are and mean, and what their probable results will be. It should not be too long or technical, as we may want to appeal to the plain man more than the well informed or the specialist.[1]

Smuts was undecided about a campaign for a revision of the Versailles Treaty, although his letter to Keynes suggested that he had made up his mind in favour of one. The day that Keynes reached Charleston, Margot Asquith, inviting him to the Wharf in late July, also asked:

I want you to do me a great personal favour. Do it *now*. I want you to write and give me a description of the first Peace Conference meeting: of the room, time, day, date, 'personnel', temper and *nature* of the whole thing – describe the men simply and what the sum up in your own mind of the whole matter has been – I want it for my Diary.[2]

By mid-July, Smuts had changed his mind on the advisability of 'a regular attack on the Treaty', but Keynes was receiving encouragement from other quarters, for the British delegation at Paris had been 'smitten by *meaculpism'*.ᵃ Thus on 31 July, Lord Robert Cecil suggested that he should write 'a brilliant article . . . exposing from a strictly economic point of view the dangers of the Treaty'.ᵇ

By then Keynes did not need encouragement. He was already well into the manuscript. He had started it at Charleston on 23 June, although he thought he might 'not persevere with it'.³ But he did persevere. By 17 July, during a visit to Cambridge, he reported to Duncan:

> I am enjoying myself enormously, and find my rooms, books and solitude incredibly agreeable. . . . Most of the day I think about my book, and write it for about two hours, so I get on fairly well and am now nearly half way through the third chapter of eight. But writing is *very* difficult, and I feel more and more admiration for those who can bring it off successfully. I've finished to-day a sketch of the appearance and character of Clemenceau, and am starting tomorrow on Wilson. I think it's worth while to try, but it's really beyond my powers.⁴

On 26 July he offered the book, which he called *The Economic Consequences of the Peace*, to Macmillian, who accepted it two days later, although the terms changed over the ensuing weeks as Keynes was more optimistic than his publishers over the book's sales. Eventually, he retained the American rights and published the book in England on a commission basis. He was to pay all the costs involved in producing, distributing and advertising the book and to keep all the profits after paying Macmillan a royalty.⁵ He was to publish on this basis for the rest of his life. The title was one of many he considered. Others recorded in a notebook included 'The Character and Consequences of the Peace', 'The Consequences of the Peace' and 'Economic Aspects of the Peace', the first of which appeared in his agreement with Macmillan dated 21 September, before he reverted to his original intention.

At the beginning of August he settled down at Charleston with the book, after a whirlwind ten days in London, during which he opened a discussion at the Tuesday Club on the Peace terms; gave evidence to the Official Committee on Indian Exchange and Currency, which was picking up where the Chamberlain Committee had left off in the spring

a The phrase is Robert Vansittart's (Lentin 1984, 134). Another example of the same phenomenon was the foundation of what became the Royal Institute of International Affairs by some liberal members of the delegation at a meeting at the Majestic at the end of May, for the Institute's purposes themselves cast doubt on the effectiveness of the Treaty in keeping the European peace.

b There were also other groups preparing criticisms of the Treaty. For example, the Liberal 'Writers Group', which included Graham Wallas, J. A. Hobson, J. L. Hammond, L. T. Hobhouse, Gilbert Murray and G. L. Dickinson, commissioned 'a substantial pamphlet' criticising the Treaty and even considered asking Keynes to do the financial part (Clarke 1978, 199, 202–4).

of 1914 as well as examining the appropriate post-war exchange rate for the rupee;[6] addressed the Fight the Famine Council; went to the Diaghilev ballet season at the Alhambra twice (including the première of *The Three Cornered Hat*); and, with Clive Bell, threw an end-of-season ballet dinner party for thirty-three including a selection of Bloomsbury, members of the cast[c] plus Derain, the Picassos, Massine and Ernst Ansermet. He remained there, except for two overnight visits to London, until the beginning of October.

Keynes established a regular pattern of life at Charleston. He breakfasted at 8, worked on his book until lunch, read *The Times* and gardened until tea, when he turned to his correspondence.[7] Under such a régime he made rapid progress. By 17 August he reported to O. T. Falk that he was 'in the middle of Reparation'[8] and by 3 September he could report to his mother that he was writing 1,000 words a day fit for the printer and expected to have the book finished before the beginning of the Cambridge Michaelmas term. On 23 September he reported that he had completed and sent to the printer the first five chapters, leaving two to be written. He was running about ten days behind schedule. He reported of the remaining chapters:

> They weigh heavily on me, as I am getting rather stale and should like to take a month off from the arts of composition. But I suppose I must persevere.[9]

By the beginning of October he was in the last chapter. On 11 October he sent chapter 6 and the greater part of chapter 7 to Macmillans. The whole exercise had taken just over three months.

During composition and later during revision, Keynes was encouraged by comments and suggestions from his friends, many of whom heard him read sections, particularly his portrait of the Conference, aloud at Charleston. When he read this chapter, Leonard Woolf noted on 21 August:

> I think this is first rate & most amusing. I expect your psychological analysis of Wilson is absolutely correct. It explains everything. I hope you're doing Ll.G.[10]

He did 'do' Lloyd George during the summer, but he 'was not content with it' and felt 'a certain compunction' and did not send it to the printer. The Lloyd George fragment did not appear until 1933, when he included it in *Essays in Biography*.[11] One of the sources of advice against publishing the fragment was Asquith – or so Margot Asquith later remembered.[12]

One who read the chapter was Felix Frankfurter, a Harvard law professor

---

c He had hoped that Lydia Lopokova would come to the party. On 10 July, however, she disappeared from Diaghilev's company, according to press reports with a Russian officer. For the moment, she had not gone far – only to St John's Wood – but she missed the rest of that London season.

who had been in Paris representing the Zionist movement. Frankfurter had been involved since 1914 with the *New Republic*, an American liberal weekly financially supported by Willard and Dorothy Straight. Keynes had met Willard Straight, who worked for J. P. Morgan, in London in March 1915 and he had been a visitor to the offices of the magazine during his 1917 visit to Washington.[13] Frankfurter wrote:

> I'm full of exhilaration after reading your chapter, if the designation of a tragedy, however artistically and trenchantly done, can provide exhilaration. I agree with your own analysis from my own observations of him [Woodrow Wilson] and particularly his performance before he came to Paris. I feel more than ever that it might be a helpful stimulus to the circulation of your book in the States if you published a paper in the *New Republic* in advance of the publication.[14]

Frankfurter arranged publication of the book in the United States with the new firm Harcourt Brace and Howe with whom Walter Lippmann of the *New Republic* was also associated.[15]

By the time Keynes began circulating proofs for comment and read the chapter on the Conference to Carl Melchior and Paul Warburg in Amsterdam, it was October. On 26 September, while campaigning for Senate ratification of the Treaty, President Wilson had collapsed. He was rushed back to Washington where he suffered a massive stroke on 2 October. He never fully recovered his faculties. On 4 October, Lytton Strachey wrote:

> I seem to gather, from the scant remarks in the newspapers, that your friend the President has gone mad. It is possible that it should gradually have been borne upon him what an appalling failure he was, and that when at last he fully realised it his mind collapsed? Very dramatic, if so. But won't it make some of your remarks too cruel? Especially if he should go and die. Awkward! I pray for his recovery.
>
> As for madmen, it doesn't seem to be limited to Presidents of the United States. I suppose we must now 'definitively' make up our minds to spending the rest of our lives as visitors to a large lunatic asylum, who have unfortunately lost their way among the padded passages. – Or perhaps unpadded – for it's an asylum run on the cheap, & in need of repair.[16]

Others who saw the proofs or heard him read his portrait of the Conference suggested alterations. G. Lowes Dickinson in two undated letters asked him to tone down the chapter while retaining its bite, making a specific suggestion about Keynes's description of the President's legs. Paul Warburg also suggested restraint. As a result, some references to the President's physiognomy were removed and the references to his intellectual processes softened.[d] Arthur Salter, Secretary to the Reparation Commission, put the case for changes even more strongly in a letter dated 14 October. He thought that Keynes's picture of the Peace negotiations 'as essentially the outmanoeuvreing of a simple-minded "Presbyterian preacher" by two cunning diplomatists will have a disastrous effect', confirming long-standing American fears about diplomacy with clever Europeans. Keynes's personal criticism of the President might also affect American reactions to any revival of proposals for reconstruction loans to Europe similar to those Keynes had made the previous May. In his reply on 18 October, Keynes commented:

> I believe there is a good deal of force in what you say, and I am recasting my story to some extent. All the same, it will remain, I fear, rather extreme, as I feel that I personally, for better or worse, have no option but to go ahead on my own lines. The moderate people can do good and perhaps the extremist can also do good; but it is no use for a member of the latter class to pretend that he belongs to the former. Besides, it is such a hopeless business trying to calculate the psychological effects of one's actions; and I have come to feel that the best thing in all circumstances is to speak the truth as bluntly as one can. You will be glad to hear however that I am toning down the personal passages especially, though perhaps not enough to avoid

d The major changes in his discussion of the President's appearance occurred in lines 22–30 of page 25 in *JMK*, II. The original text ran:

> But his legs – a great surprise – were short and vulgar, causing his trousers to crease unpleasantly; and his hands, though capable and fairly strong, were creased and india rubbery, and absolutely wanting in any kind of taste, refinement or finesse. The first glance at the President disclosed in fact, that, whatever else he might be, he had little in him of the student or scholar; indeed that he was not even a man of taste and cultivation in the sense that Clemenceau and Mr. Balfour are exquisitely cultivated gentlemen of their class and generation.

In contrast, the final text ran (all changes appear in italics):

> But *like Odysseus, the President looked wiser when he was seated*; and his hands, though capable and fairly strong were wanting in taste *and* finesse. The first glance at the President disclosed in fact, that, whatever else he might be, *his temperament was not primarily that* of the student or scholar; *but he had not much even of that culture of the world which marks M.* Clemenceau and Mr. Balfour *as* exquisitely cultivated gentlemen of their class and generation.

For another example of substantive change see the alternative initial rendering of the passage cited on p. 327 below in footnote i.

altogether, in the minds of some people, such feelings of resentment as you fear.[17]

Over the next month, Keynes's preference for 'violent and ruthless truth telling – that will work *in the end*, even if slowly', as he told General Smuts on 27 November, strengthened. None the less, he kept the *New Republic* from publishing extracts from the book, especially chapter 3 on the Conference, until after the Senate had voted against unconditional ratification of the Treaty on 19 November 1919.[18] The first instalment of the *New Republic*'s serialisation which included the portrait of the President did not appear until Christmas 1919, *after* the book's publication in England.

The Economic Consequences of the Peace was several books in one: a trenchant political pamphlet attacking the morality of the Peace Treaty in the light of the understandings that had existed at the time of the Armistice; a technical discussion of the economic provisions of the Treaty; an illuminating, if nostalgic, discussion of relations between nations and classes before 1914; and a series of proposals for dealing with European problems as they existed in the second half of 1919. The various aspects of the book are, however, closely interwoven, and enlivened by vivid, mordant and arresting portraits of those involved.

The central message of the book was straightforward. Keynes stated it after outlining French aims at the Peace Conference, which he summarised as 'to set the clock back and undo what, since 1870, the progress of Germany had accomplished' (p. 22):[e]

> My purpose in this book is to show that the Carthaginian peace is not *practically* right or possible. Although the school of thought from which it springs is aware of the economic factor, it overlooks, nevertheless, the deeper economic tendencies which are to govern the future. The clock cannot be set back. You cannot restore Europe to 1870 without setting up such strains in the European structure and letting loose such human and spiritual forces as, pushing beyond frontiers and races, will overwhelm not only you and your 'guarantees', but your institutions, and the existing order of your society.
>
> (p. 23)

Underlying Keynes's analysis was his vision of Europe before 1914. Morality apart, this conditioned his view of the results of Paris. He suggested that the supposedly automatic and natural economic progress that Western Europe had experienced in the fifty years before 1914 had rested on four unstable bases. The first was the pre-war system of international

---

e All future references in the text to *Economic Consequences* will be to the text in *JMK*, II and will just give page references.

economic interdependence that had allowed the population of Central Europe, especially Germany, to expand with the labour force producing industrial exports to exchange for food and raw materials. The second was the minimal role that tariffs, different currency systems and political frontiers had played in impeding the economic life of Central Europe on which the economies of the rest of the Continent were heavily dependent. The third was the delicate psychology of pre-war European society which had arranged its affairs so as to favour the maximum accumulation of capital – the psychology of accepted inequality tempered by the understanding that those who received the bulk of the rewards deferred their consumption in favour of further saving – 'a bourgeois paradise lost':[19]

> Thus this remarkable system depended for its growth on a double bluff or deception. On the one hand the labouring classes accepted from ignorance or powerlessness, or were compelled, persuaded, or cajoled by custom, convention, authority and the established order of society into accepting a situation in which they could call their own very little of the cake that they and nature and the capitalists were co-operating to produce. And on the other hand the capitalist classes were allowed to call the best part of the cake theirs and were theoretically free to consume it, on the tacit underlying condition that they consumed very little of it in practice. The duty of 'saving' became nine-tenths of virtue and the growth of the cake the object of the true religion. There grew around the non-consumption of the cake all those instincts of puritanism which in other ages has withdrawn itself from the world and has neglected the arts of production as well as of enjoyment. And so the cake increased; but to what end was not clearly contemplated. Individuals would be exhorted not so much to abstain as to defer, and to cultivate to pleasures of security and anticipation. Saving was for old age or for your children; but this was only in theory – the virtue of the cake was that it was never to be consumed, neither by you nor by your children after you.
>
> (pp. 11–12)

The final element in the pre-war system had been the favourable terms on which industrial Europe had been able to exchange manufactured goods for food from the new areas of overseas settlement. The war, Keynes argued, had shattered in varying degrees all the bases of the pre-war economic order. European economic rehabilitation, as much as honouring pre-Armistice engagements and justice, should have been one of the major tasks of the Peace Conference.

Why reconstruction was not given such priority and why the Peace Treaty with Germany had taken the form it did required an explanation. In his third chapter, 'The Conference', Keynes provided much of the explanation in terms of the interaction of the three principals – Wilson, Clemenceau and

Lloyd George. He began on a note which echoed Lytton Strachey's *Eminent Victorians*[f]:

> I touch, inevitably, questions of motive, on which spectators are liable to error and are not entitled to take on themselves the responsibilities of final judgement. Yet, if I seem in this chapter to assume the liberties which are habitual to historians, but which, in spite of the greater knowledge with which we speak, we generally hesitate to assume towards contemporaries, let the reader excuse me when he remembers how greatly, if he is to understand its destiny, the world needs light, even if it is partial and uncertain, on the complex struggle of human will and purpose, not yet finished, which, concentrated in the persons of four individuals in a manner never paralleled made them in the first months of 1919 the microcosm of mankind.

> (p. 17)

Keynes proceeded to look at the protagonists, beginning with Clemenceau largely because he argued that the French normally opened with the most definite – and most extreme – proposals. With his 'impassive face of parchment' (p. 19) he 'was by far the most eminent member of the Council of Four . . . . One could not despise Clemenceau or dislike him, but only take a different view as to the nature of civilised man, or indulge, at least, a different hope.' (p. 18).

> He felt about France what Pericles felt of Athens, unique value in her, nothing else mattering; but his theory of politics was Bismarck's. He had one illusion – France; and one disillusion – mankind, including Frenchmen and his colleagues not least.[g] . . . His philosophy had . . . no place for 'sentimentality' in international relations. Nations are real things, of whom you love one and feel for the rest indifference – or hatred. The glory of the nation you love is a desirable end – but generally obtainable at your neighbour's expense. The politics of power are inevitable, and there is nothing new to learn about this war or the end it was fought for; England had destroyed, as in each preceding century, a trade rival; a mighty chapter had been closed in the secular struggle between Germany and France. Prudence required some measure of lip service to the 'ideals' of foolish Americans and hypocritical Englishmen; but it would be stupid to believe that there is much room in the world, as it really is, for such affairs as the League of Nations, or any sense in the principle of self-determination except

---

f 'For ignorance is the first requisite of the historian – ignorance which simplifies and clarifies, which selects and omits, with a placid perfection unattainable by the highest art.' (Strachey 1918, Penguin edn, 9).

g Thus he spoke of his Finance Minister Louis-Lucien Klotz as 'the only Jew I ever met who had no capacity whatever for finance' (Trachtenberg 1980, 41) and of Wilson, 'He exasperates me with his Fourteen Commandments when the good God had only ten!' (Elcock 1972, 33).

as an ingenious formula for rearranging the balance of power in one's own interests.

(pp. 20–1)

Against this old man, who viewed European history as 'a perpetual prize fight' (p. 22) in which France having won this round might postpone the next by temporarily crushing and containing Germany, were pitted Lloyd George and Wilson.[h] In the chapter itself, Keynes said little about the former, except to emphasise his 'unerring, almost medium-like sensibility to everyone immediately around him'. He continued:

> The British Prime Minister watching the company, with six or seven senses not available to ordinary men, judging character, motive, and subconscious impulse, perceiving what each was thinking and even what each was to say next, and compounding with telepathic instinct the argument or appeal best suited to the vanity, weakness, or self interest of his immediate auditor, was to realise that the poor President would be playing blind man's bluff in that party.

(p. 26)

He said little more, for he had excised the fragment he had written on the Prime Minister. In the original scheme it followed the portrait of Wilson.

Keynes emphasised the moral force of Wilson's pronouncements and the reality of the power that he held. Unfortunately,

> The President was not a hero or a prophet; he was not even a philosopher; but a generously intentioned man, with many of the weaknesses of other human beings, and lacking that dominating intellectual equipment which would have been necessary to cope with the subtle and dangerous spellbinders whom a tremendous clash of forces and personalities had brought to the top as triumphant masters in the swift game of give and take, face to face in council – a game of which he had no experience at all.

(pp. 24–5)[i]

According to Keynes, Wilson 'was not sensitive to his environment at all'

---

h Although Orlando, the Italian Prime Minister was one of the Four, he does not enter Keynes's portrait other than for the comment that he could not understand or speak English. Actually he understood it (M. Keynes (ed.) 1975, 23).

i The original version of this passage ran:

> The President was not a hero or a prophet; he was not even a philosopher; but a well-meaning and conscientious politician, under-equipped intellectually to cope with the subtle and dangerous spellbinders whom a tremendous clash of forces and personalities had brought to the top in the swift game of give and take, face to face in Council, – a game in which he had no experience at all.

(p. 26). He 'was like a non-conformist minister, perhaps a Presbyterian' (p. 26). His thought 'was essentially theological not intellectual' (p. 26). Although he had pronounced grand principles, he had no plans for filling them out. Moreover, although as ill-informed of European conditions as Lloyd George, 'his mind was slow and unadaptable' (p. 27).

> There can seldom have been a statesman of the first rank more incompetent than the President in the agilities of the council chamber. A moment often arrives when a substantial victory is yours if by some slight appearance of a concession you can save the face of the opposition or conciliate them by a restatement of your proposal helpful to them and not injurious to anything essential to yourself. The President was not equipped with this simple and usual artfulness. His mind was too slow and unresourceful to be ready with *any* alternatives. The President was capable of digging his toes in and refusing to budge. . . . But he had no other mode of defence, and it needed as a rule but a little manoeuvring by his opponents to prevent matters from coming to such a head until it was too late.
>
> (p. 27)

Moreover, Wilson could not make up for his own deficiencies through his advisers, for he would not use them effectively, nor, after the Council of Four replaced the Council of Ten, could he.[20] Thus over a period of months, according to Keynes, Wilson was manoeuvred towards the Treaty by both Clemenceau and Lloyd George. However, as he implied in the chapter – and made clear in the fragment – Clemenceau had emerged the victor, in part because Lloyd George enjoyed the process of wheeling and dealing as much as actually gaining concessions on substantive points.

In the fragment he published in 1933, Lloyd George received the status of a *femme fatale*.

> How can I convey to the reader, who does not know him, any just impression of this extraordinary figure of our time, this syren, this goat-footed bard, this half-human visitor to our age from the hag-ridden magic and enchanted woods of Celtic antiquity. One catches in his company that flavour of final purposelessness, inner irresponsibility, existence outside or away from our Saxon good and evil, mixed with cunning, remorselessness, love of power. . . .
>
> Lloyd George is rooted in nothing; he is void and without content; he lives and feeds on his immediate surroundings; he is an instrument and a player at the same time which plays on the company and is played on by them too; he is a prism, as I have heard him described, which collects light and distorts it and is most brilliant if the light comes from many quarters; a vampire and a medium in one.[21]

The 'old man' was too experienced and too cynical to fall for the *femme fatale*, but the non-conformist minister was hooked. 'No wonder', Keynes concluded, 'that in the eventual settlement the real victor was Clemenceau'.

> These were the personalities of Paris – I forbear to mention other nations or lesser men: Clemenceau, aesthetically the noblest; the President, morally the most admirable; Lloyd George intellectually the subtlest. Out of their disparities and weaknesses the Treaty was born, child of the least worthy attributes of its parents, without nobility, without morality, without intellect.[22]

In the next two chapters of *Economic Consequences* Keynes turned to the Treaty itself. He dealt first with the general economic aspects of the Treaty and then specifically with the reparations issue. He prefaced his discussion with his own interpretation of exactly what the Armistice agreement meant. He took it to mean that the terms of the peace were to be congruent with the addresses of the President with the two qualifications agreed by the allied governments concerning the freedom of the seas and the meaning of the restoration of the invaded territories. The latter was to include 'compensation ... for all damage done to the civilian population of the Allies and to their property by the aggression of Germany by land, by sea, and from the air' (p. 37). He allowed that the relevant statements of the President – the Fourteen Points of 8 January 1918 and the four speeches made on 11 February, 6 April, 4 July and 27 September 1918 – did leave the allies a free hand in some areas and were difficult to apply on a contractual basis in others. He was none the less prepared to argue that the terms submitted to the Germans on 5 November 1918

> had become part of a solemn contract to which all the Great Powers of the world had put their signature. But it was lost, nevertheless, in the morass of Paris – the spirit of it altogether, the letter in parts ignored and in other parts distorted.
>
> (p. 40)

He then turned to the product of Paris itself. The German economy before 1914 had depended on her overseas commerce, her exploitation of coal and iron and related industries, and her tariff and transport system. One effect of the Treaty, he argued, was 'systematically [to] destroy' (p. 41) the first two and to impair the third.

The destruction of Germany's overseas commerce had proceeded in a number of ways. Under the Treaty she had ceded to the allies the bulk of her merchant marine and undertook to build up to a million tons of new ships for the allies over the next five years. She ceded to the allies all overseas territories, as well as, without compensation for reparations purposes, all government public works such as harbours and railways in these territories. The property of private German individuals within the former colonies was subject to expropriation and the legal status of German nationals was left uncertain. The same sorts of provisions also applied to Alsace-Lorraine, which Germany ceded to France. Similar provisions also applied to German property rights in allied countries and these could extend to German interests in the territory of her neighbours and former allies, as well as Russia, China, Siam, Liberia, Morocco and Egypt. Finally, the provision that the Reparation Commission could demand payment up to £1,000 million in any manner it might fix before May 1921 put German assets in neutral countries at risk. The overall effect of the provisions was to remove the surplus that Germany had enjoyed on invisible trade in her pre-war balance of payments and shift it into deficit. As he was to point out later (p. 119), Germany's pre-war surplus on invisibles had been necessary to meet a visible trade deficit as well as to finance new investment overseas.

Keynes then turned to coal and iron. With the loss of the Saar coal mines to France and the possible loss of Upper Silesia,[j] he estimated that Germany would lose almost a third of her pre-war coal production. The loss of Alsace-Lorraine would cost her three-quarters of her pre-war iron output. Of course, all of these quantities would not be 'lost', as each area did consume some of its own output, but he was worried about the effects of the new political frontiers cutting across a previously highly integrated area. He argued that under a régime of free trade and free intercourse much of this might not matter, but in the mood of 1919 he was far from optimistic that the efficient pre-war economic organisation of these industries could continue. Moreover, the loss of Upper Silesian coal, when coupled with forced coal deliveries to the Allies, might cripple German industry.

Towards the end of his fourth chapter, Keynes turned to tariff policy and transportation. He did so because the provisions of the Treaty sharply diminished Germany's tariff autonomy *vis-à-vis* the allies and in the occupied area on the west bank of the Rhine. The Treaty's provisions affecting railway rates also allowed for substantial outside interference, as did international commissions for the Rhine, Danube, Elbe, Oder and Niemen rivers in which Germany's representatives would be in a minority. Germany's transport system would be further affected by the Treaty's provisions relating to the cession of railway rolling stock to the Allies, the provision of a full complement of such stock in ceded territories and the cession of up to 20 per cent of her inland navigation tonnage. As he concluded, 'the economic clauses of the Treaty are comprehensive, and little has been overlooked which might impoverish Germany now or obstruct her development in the future' (p. 70).

j As he acknowledged, the Upper Silesian position was uncertain, as its cession to Poland was subject to a plebiscite. In a footnote he allowed that the plebiscite would most probably leave it in German hands. Yet, for the purposes of his argument, he assumed in his main text that it would be lost to Germany. In the end, it was partitioned between Germany and Poland in a manner that basically reflected the national origins of those living in the area. As a result, Germany was not so badly off as Keynes's text implied.

This was not the end of the story, for Germany had still to bear the burden of the reparation clauses of the Treaty. Keynes turned his attention to that issue in chapter 5. His discussion was complicated by the need to render the economic magnitudes into a common currency at a time of high inflation and rapidly changing exchange rates. To these complications were added the inevitable uncertainties in 1919 as to the extent of the damage that had actually occurred – something that had plagued the discussions in Paris over both the total and its distribution. As a result, Keynes would have in later years to defend his admittedly rough estimates from critics who had the advantages of hindsight and more information.

Keynes began by estimating the sums due from Germany under a strict interpretation of the Armistice terms – *i.e.* for 'all damage done to the civilian population of the Allies and to their property by the aggression of Germany by land, by sea and from the air'. Before he attempted to put numbers on the items, he made use of his observations from his visit to the front just before the Armistice and his subsequent travels in France and Belgium that I have quoted in chapter 11.[23] When it came to the actual sums for which he thought Germany liable, allowing for considerable guesswork, he settled on a range of £1,600–3,000 million, with a most probable value of £2,000 million. Hence 'a wise and just act' would have been to ask the German Government for £2,000 million in the Treaty (p. 85).

This was not the figure implied by the decisions taken in Paris, although the Armistice conditions spoke in terms of direct damage, even if perhaps the French and the British expected more. Of course, in the period after the Armistice the Allies learned much more about Germany's weakness after four years of war – weakness heightened by the revolutionary turmoil accompanying the collapse of the German Empire and the establishment of the Weimar Republic. In Britain, as well, there was the General Election of December 1918, which, although it may not have affected Lloyd George's intentions, certainly affected his political position. In the second section of his reparations chapter, Keynes recounted the progress of the election campaign and the changes in the Coalition's public position on the reparations/ indemnity issue which moved it away from the terms of the Armistice agreement to implying that the allies had the right to demand the whole cost of the war from Germany and to encouraging the belief that it might possibly obtain such sums. He then described how the change in Britain's position and the financial difficulties of the European allies resulted in an inflation of the reparations demands, almost entirely in the form of pensions and separation allowances, as well as the Treaty provision that left the actual total of reparations to be decided by the Reparation Commission. In this discussion, he touched on Article 231 of the Treaty, the 'war guilt' clause, which he had drafted with Dulles, remarking on its draftsmanship and its expediency but playing down its long-term importance (pp. 93–4). Keynes then provided an estimate of what the sum demanded was likely to be:

£5,000 million for pensions and up to £3,000 million for direct damage. He followed this figure with the actual terms of payment set out in the Treaty, for these (with their inclusion of the expenses of occupation and refusal to remit interest) raised the sums involved to higher levels.

Such figures, however, meant little without an estimate of Germany's capacity to pay. For this purpose, he reworked the figures of his November/December 1918 Treasury memorandum to take into account subsequent events.[24] The resulting figures were: immediately transferable wealth £250–300 million; property in ceded territories or surrendered under the terms of the Armistice £100–200 million; and the present value of payments over a period of 30 years £1,700 million. As a safe maximum he took a figure of £2,000 million as his estimate of Germany's capacity to pay, although he allowed that if the allies nursed German trade and industry for a period of five or ten years, if there was substantial worldwide inflation, or if there were dramatic increases in productivity then higher nominal sums would become available. This figure of £2,000 million was a far cry from his estimate of Allied demands. He concluded the chapter with a pessimistic examination of the possible roles of the Reparation Commission and the German counter-proposals of May 1919, which he estimated as being worth £1,500 million. Finally,

> I cannot leave this subject as though its just treatment wholly depended either on our own pledges or on economic facts. The policy of reducing Germany to servitude for a generation, of degrading the lives of millions of human beings, and of depriving a whole nation of happiness should be abhorrent and detestable – abhorrent and detestable, even if it were possible, even if it enriched ourselves, even if it did not sow the decay of the whole civilised life of Europe. Some preach it in the name of justice. In the great events of man's history, in the unwinding of the complex fates of nations, justice is not so simple. And if it were, nations are not authorised, by religion or by natural morals, to visit on the children of their enemies the misdoings of parents or of rulers.
>
> (p. 142)

At this point, *Economic Consequences* left behind the details of the Peace Treaty to consider the present economic position of the Continent as a preliminary to Keynes's constructive proposals. The picture was painted in the darkest colours. Productivity levels in both industry and agriculture were far below pre-war levels. The transport system had broken down, impairing the exchange of what little was produced. The currency systems of the Continent were in disarray, further inhibiting exchange and the purchase of vitally needed supplies from overseas.

Keynes spent most of his space discussing inflation, *inventing* in the process a quotation that has passed into the currency of modern economic discourse:[25]

Lenin is said to have declared that the best way to destroy the capitalist system is to debauch the currency. . . . Lenin was certainly right. There is no subtler, no surer means of overturning the existing basis of society than to debauch the currency.

(pp. 148–9)

As Keynes's views on inflation were, along with his emphasis on the need for capital accumulation, to play an important role in his subsequent writings, it is worth spending a moment on them here. His basic argument was that the inflationary process undermines the capitalist system by arbitrarily redistributing wealth. Such arbitrary rearrangements produced disorder in the relations between debtors and creditors and reduced the process of wealth creation in whole or in part to a lottery. Moreover, the inflationary process, especially of the almost completely unanticipated variety experienced during and immediately after the First World War, when the experience of the previous century had been one of long-term price stability, created in the public estimation a class of 'profiteers' on whom governments sought to direct popular indignation:

These 'profiteers' are, broadly speaking, the entrepreneur class of capitalists, that is to say, the active and constructive element in the whole capitalist society, who in a period of rapidly rising prices cannot but get rich whether they wish or desire it or not. If prices are continually rising, every trader who has purchased for stock or owns property and plant inevitably makes profits. By directing hatred against this class, therefore, the European governments are carrying a step further the fatal process which the subtle mind of Lenin had consciously conceived. The profiteers are a consequence not a cause of rising prices. By combining a popular hatred of the class of entrepreneurs with the blow already given to social security by the violent and arbitrary disturbance of contract and of the established equilibrium of wealth which is the inevitable result of inflation, these governments are fast rendering impossible a continuance of the social and economic order of the nineteenth century.

(pp. 149–50)

Thus, as well as producing the currency fluctuations that impaired international trade and recovery, inflation was destroying the basis for capitalist accumulation itself.

But what were Keynes's remedies? As he admitted (p. 162) they were tentative and probably inadequate for the tasks at hand. They included a revision of the Treaty, a cancellation of inter-allied debts, an international reconstruction loan for Europe which would also assist currency stabilisations, and a change in the relations between Central Europe and Russia.

Keynes's proposals for Treaty revision centred on a marked reduction in Germany's obligations to the allies. He argued that the amount of the payments required from Germany, *including* the costs of the army of occupation (which under the Treaty was a charge prior and additional to that of reparations), should be limited to £2,000 million. To meet this sum, the immediate transfers of ships, property in ceded territory and the like should be reckoned at £500 million and the balance of £1,500 million should be paid without interest in 30 instalments of £50 million beginning in 1923. Germany would meet these instalments as she saw fit, any complaints about non-fulfilment being a matter for the League of Nations.[26] There would be no further expropriations of German private property except to meet private debts abroad.[27] As for coal, the Treaty revision would eliminate German deliveries to everyone bar France, where they would be limited and lapse if Germany lost Upper Silesia. The costs to Germany of the Saar arrangements would be substantially reduced. Finally, Germany, Poland and the successor states of the Austro-Hungarian and Turkish Empires would be required to join a free trade area for a decade. These measures would help to restore Germany's economic life and minimise the effects of the creation of new states and boundary changes on the economic life of Europe.

The revision of inter-allied indebtedness would see Britain renounce her share of reparations in favour of Belgium, France and Serbia and the complete cancellation of war-related, inter-governmental debts amongst the Allied and Associated countries, following Keynes's earlier Paris proposals.[28] Under such a scheme, the nominal losers would be Britain and the United States, the only creditors on such account, with the American loss running to £2,000 million and Britain's £900 million (of which £550 million represented loans to Russia), but as in earlier papers he 'justified' the result in terms of relative sacrifices incurred during the war itself.

Keynes prefaced his loan proposal with a weighty list of objections to it, given the existing policies of European governments.

> If I had influence at the United States Treasury, I would not lend a penny to a single one of the present governments of Europe. They are not to be trusted with resources.
>
> (p. 181)

Nevertheless, the United States should 'point the way and hold up the hands of the party of peace by having a plan and a condition on which she will give aid to the work of renewing life' (p. 181). He proposed a loan of £200 million for food and raw materials, plus a guarantee fund of a similar size to support currency stabilisation. The loan would be provided by the United States, Britain and the European neutrals, while the guarantee fund would be the responsibility of all the members of the League. The loan would carry the best security available and its repayment would rank ahead of all internal or international governmental debts or obligations of the recipients.

Keynes's proposals for Russia and Central Europe were in effect suggestions for restoring Germany's role as far as possible to its pre-war dimensions in the interests of stability. This meant an end to allied militaristic policies, particularly with regard to Poland ('an economic impossibility with no industry but Jew-baiting' (p. 185)), which served to weaken the existing German Government, itself under threat from both left and right. It also meant an end to the allied policies of intervention and blockade in Russia. The hope underlying these proposals was the restoration of Europe's trade with Russia which he believed essential for obtaining food supplies supplementary to those obtainable elsewhere and ensuring that the terms of exchange between foodstuffs and manufactures for Europe as a whole did not become too adverse.

Keynes ended his book by dedicating it 'to the formation of the general opinion of the future' (p. 189). The general view has been that he was in that extremely successful – too successful for many tastes. As Joseph Schumpeter remarked, the book 'met with a reception that makes the word *success* sound commonplace and insipid'.[29] In Britain and the United States the book sold 60,000 copies in the first two months and over 100,000 copies by the end of July 1920. Translations followed rapidly: German, French, Dutch, Danish, Swedish, Italian, Spanish, Romanian, Russian, Japanese and Chinese. Extracts and abbreviated versions were widely available. Keynes helped its influence along by sending copies to a wide range of people. Macmillan sent at least seventy-three from its London supplies to members of the Asquith and Lloyd George Governments, former Treasury colleagues, European bankers and financiers Keynes had met in connection with discussions of an international loan scheme in the autumn of 1919,[30] and to Bloomsbury friends and members of his family. He seems to have been almost as generous with copies in America, for as one scholar has noted, virtually every American collection of private papers she consulted during her work on the period 'contained evidence of Keynes having sent an inscribed copy of the book'.[31] Its role in the formation of opinion has been described by another historian as 'epoch-making'.[32]

Keynes summed up the initial reaction as follows:

> The book is being smothered ... in a deluge of approval; not a complaint, not a word of abuse, not a line of criticism; letters from Cabinet Ministers in every post saying that they agree with every word of it; etc. etc. I expect a chit from the PM at any moment telling me how profoundly the book represents his view and how beautifully it is put. Will it be my duty to refuse the Legion of Honour at the hands of Clemenceau. Well, I suppose this is their best and safest line.[33]

Most of the comments Keynes received raised issues that have been central to all subsequent discussions; so I might well consider them here as a preface to assessing the book from a longer-term perspective.

Much comment turned on his picture of the Conference in chapter 3, even though he had slightly softened the portraits of both Wilson and Clemenceau.[34] Lord Curzon, the Foreign Secretary, referred to his 'immortal picture', as well as noting that 'Wilson if he sees the book will never recover. It is wonderful Republican propaganda.'[35] Although some of his correspondents found his portraiture, especially of the President, too harsh, others, such as Paul Cravath, went the other way:

> I think you made a very correct diagnosis of Wilson's character. If anything, you are too charitable. You speak of him as the only man at Paris 'that really tried to be fair'. I think it would be more accurate if you referred to him as *'trying to appear to be fair'*.
>
> . . . I think Wilson was dominated by the less worthy ambition [than the national ambitions of Lloyd George and Clemenceau] of achieving a personal success – of getting the credit from the contemporary world and from posterity of having moulded the Peace Treaty in his own image. I believe that ambition dominated him from beginning to end and was the primary cause of his downfall.[36]

In the years that followed, Keynes devoted considerable space to the issue of his treatment of the President. His usual line – somewhat disingenuous given his opportunities for revision in the fall of 1919 – ran as this April 1920 comment to Norman Davis:

> I am sorry that you dislike so much what I had to say about the President. I wrote it last July before his illness. If I had been writing after his breakdown, I should have spoken more gently of a pitiful and tragic figure, for whom I feel a genuine sympathy and who in spite of everything was the one member of the Four who was *trying* to do right. I feel in retrospect that his breakdown really dated from April[k] and that up to then he had substantially maintained his position, and I am inclined, therefore, to attribute more of the blame to his impending illness. But that the President acted in Paris 'deliberately and wisely' – to quote your words – this I cannot allow. If 'deliberately', then surely he becomes one of the 'sinister diplomats', at any rate one of the greatest hypocrites in history; and as for 'wisely', surely no one can any longer maintain that. Could *worse* results have followed from any of the alternative courses open to him?. . .
>
> My account of what I deemed to be the President's psychology was

k Ferrell (1985, 159–61) reports that Wilson may have suffered two strokes before 1919. He also found it necessary to carefully husband his strength during his Presidency, working only three or four hours a day and spending his summers 'without much attention to public business'. The exception to this normal régime was the Peace Conference.

necessary for the purposes of my book, because it was essential to explain how it came about, in spite of the President's sincerity, that a perfidious peace was enacted. Melchior, for example, was disposed to the opinion that the Fourteen Points were a deliberate *ruse de guerre* on the President's part and that the whole thing was a put up job of the most scoundrelly description. Surely my view of the affair as the result of muddle, perplexity, and a want of clear sight helps to soften the position rather than exacerbate it. . . .

People much prefer to be thought wicked rather than stupid, and hence my account of the President is taken as much more hostile than it really is. The President, for me, was a fallen hero. I describe the others as very clever and very wicked; the President as sincere, well-intentioned and determined to do what was right, but perplexed, muddleheaded and a self-deceiver. *I* am, therefore, considered to be bitterly hostile to him. *You* claim the treaty as a piece of deliberate cleverness ('wisdom' is your word) on his part, and think you have defended him![37]

Even more comment, both then and since, related to the political wisdom of his publishing his portrait of the Conference, particularly given its likely effects in the United States, where ratification of the Treaty and the League of Nations depended on a two-thirds majority in the Republican-controlled Senate. Lord Reading questioned it, as to a lesser extent did Lord Robert Cecil and R. H. Brand. Others took the opposite line. Reginald McKenna, after repeating Reading's views, continued: 'Fudge! It will do nothing but good anywhere. Until we get back to the truth there is no hope for the world'.[38] This echoed Keynes's own preference for 'violent and ruthless truth-telling' and his belief, as he told Austen Chamberlain on 28 December:

The policy of humbugging with the Americans has been given a good trial and has not been a brilliant success. Who can say that the candid expression of views sincerely held may not open their eyes in the long run more effectively than oceans of semi-sincere platform sentiment.[39]

What one might call the Brand–Cecil–Reading view has remained the accepted view in many circles, and *Economic Consequences* has become the book that was an important cause of the Senate's rejection of the Treaty and the League of Nations.[40] One should, however, realise that as early as 4 March 1919 Senator Lodge had got thirty-nine Republican signatures (six more than necessary to defeat the Treaty) to a resolution disavowing the Covenant of the League of Nations as contrary to the Monroe Doctrine and American neutrality and that the Senate's first rejection of the Treaty occurred *before* the book appeared in either England or the United States.

Even though the book provided deadly ammunition to the Republicans, it would hardly be fair to say that the *Economic Consequences of the Peace* was of such crucial importance in a tangled web of events that lasted the better part of a year.[41]

Other suggestions of political *naïveté* came in other contexts, as critics sharpened their pens or defended their own positions on such matters as the size of the reparation demands, the cancellation of war debts or the exact nature of the Armistice contract. These suggestions frequently took the form that either political expediency or public opinion necessitated compromises with earlier statements and made sensible moves impossible or that Keynes – along with most Foreign Office and Treasury officials and many Americans, including President Wilson! – was naïve to take the Armistice agreement so literally. The repetition of these suggestions helped to push Keynes to formulate an explicit view of the relationships between politicians and officials and public opinion which was to colour his exercises in persuasion for the rest of his life.[42]

These suggestions also raised the question of the role of the professional economist as a policy adviser, for many of the suggestions of *naïveté* went hand in hand with the observation that Keynes was an economist.[43] There is the issue that Keynes, along with any adviser on technical matters of policy who is not a career civil servant, faced throughout his life. One of the standard – and one of the easiest – responses of politicians (or their civil servant advisers) to criticism or alternative proposals is to say that the alternatives are not politically feasible. This may, of course, be the case: professional politicians have to win elections and may in general be presumed to be more sensitive to and experienced in such matters than their professional economist advisers. It is also the case that the policy adviser cannot be too divorced from political realities. Repeatedly 'unrealistic' advice does not augur well for long-term influence. Nevertheless, as numerous discussions of the role of economists as government advisers have made clear, a policy adviser whose advice is too closely constrained by assessments of what is 'realistic' may also not prove useful over the longer term. As Professor Eric Lundberg remarked in a discussion of academic economists and their policy advice, there is a principle of 'optimum political naivety' in a successful adviser.[44] One has to know when not to give up; when not to bend. To be useful, Lundberg and others suggest, advisers must in the end remember that they are just advisers and are not responsible for the ultimate decisions. In such circumstances, reminding the emperor that he has no clothes may be a useful and important function. It would certainly be a habit of mind to cultivate.[45]

During most of his life after 1913, Keynes was active as an official policy adviser – and, if not an adviser, a critic. In giving advice, or for that matter criticism, he did not always expect to see his views accepted, although, of course, he hoped they would be. Frequently he saw the argument go against him either because politicians or senior civil servants found other professional advice more compelling in the circumstances or because of political considerations. That his advice was not always taken, that he probably lost more arguments than he won, did not diminish his usefulness. As John Williamson noted, on reviewing Keynes's Second World War contributions to post-war external economic policy discussions:

> On reflection (I admit I did not make notes as I read), I find it difficult to recall a single substantive decision that was decided in accordance with Keynes's wishes or because of his initiative. Can one really claim that this man helped to shape the post-war world in any significant way?
>
> ... I think that the judgement ... is unduly negative. ... Time after time in these volumes, one finds Keynes urging graceful concessions with a view to achieving agreement and maintaining the momentum towards co-operation, even when the sacrifice involved his own preferred proposals. ... The next leading economist with policy influence who chooses to use his authority to make concessions that succeed in achieving a second best will surely merit the sort of tributes that Keynes received.[46]

Yet even during 1940–6, as we shall see later, the older and wiser Keynes would lay himself open to charges of political *naïveté*. Not all critics accused him of this. There would also be those who came to believe that Keynes was a skilled political operator who subordinated the true to the possible – a view not unknown in Bloomsbury during 1915–18.[47]

Yet this does not dispose of the issue. Certainly it is the case that advisers should defer and bend. But should they do it forever? As Keynes put the issue to Norman Davis in April 1920, this is ultimately a personal decision:

> [T]here are two courses open to one at these crises, – to quit governmental circles and their inevitable shifts and compromises and to speak freely what you think the best course; or to stay on and make the best of bad circumstances by daily executive action. I chose one, you the other. You may well claim that for *immediate* purposes you may achieve more usefulness. I can only hope that in the long run I may help to make possible for you and Blackett and others what by action from within is now 'impossible', and to render avoidable what you now deem 'inevitable'.
>
> At any rate my views had become too far from those of the politicians for it to be possible for me to co-operate with them any longer on any terms; and I saw, and still see, no hope except a far-reaching revulsion of opinion on the part of the *general public*.[48]

Other criticisms of *Economic Consequences* fastened on details. Potentially the most damaging came from a member of the American delegation, C. H. Haskins, who stated that, according to Paul Mantoux, an interpreter for the Council, Keynes had never attended a regular session of the Council of Four. This charge cast doubt on his whole discussion of the Conference in chapter 3. When pressed, Haskins did not withdraw his accusation. Later, when, as a part of the investigations surrounding the possibility of awarding the 1923 Nobel Prize for Peace to Keynes, Mantoux was asked to confirm Haskins' report, he equivocated.[49] In his otherwise critical book, Mantoux's son, Etienne Mantoux, did not flatly support Haskin's statement.[50] However, the Council's own minutes – which were only kept for later meetings – record Keynes as present on at least eight occasions between 7 April and 4 June 1919. At one meeting, 29 April, Keynes replaced Sir Maurice Hankey and took the minutes.[1] This is not to claim that his description of the meetings of the Council was always accurate: there is the matter of Orlando's command of English. But mistaken or not, Keynes's account was at first hand.

There were also occasions where Keynes, as in his discussion of the possible outcome of the Upper Silesian plebiscite, took the worst – and for his argument the most favourable – outcome in the text and left that which he thought most probable, but was less favourable to a footnote. There were also mistakes, as when he suggested (p. 63) that Upper Silesia was dependent on Alsace-Lorraine for its iron ore.[51] Nor were his arguments free from inconsistency. Compare his criticism of the Treaty's terms for the Saar – 'an act of spoliation and insincerity' (p. 52) – with his own proposals (p. 167), which differ only in Germany receiving no credit for the mines against reparation and not having to pay for their return, which was not subject to plebiscite, in ten years rather than fifteen.

The bulk of the criticism related to his discussion of reparations. Critics have fastened on three aspects: the nature of the Armistice contract and hence the morality of the inclusion of the claim for pensions and separation allowances; the size of the claims for reparation; and Germany's capacity to pay. As to the first, I think it is clear that one is into the meanings of words, where reasonable men can and do differ. Even legal opinions varied: Lord Sumner provided a justification that satisfied Lloyd George; the American lawyers directly involved often supported Keynes's position. On the second, one must begin by noting that Keynes's 1919 estimate of Germany's liability for reparations was remarkably close to that of

---

1 He later re-worked his notes of that meeting for a student reading party at Hawse End near Keswick in 1925. The re-working appears in the Collected Writings in Essays in Biography (*JMK*, X, 27–32). The original notes from which he worked, with the title 'Council of Three, 29 April 1919, (*What actually happened*)', are in his papers. They also survived in Hankey's papers and appear in Roskill 1972, 85–7.

the Reparation Commission. In 1921 the Commission set Germany's liability at £6,600 million: Keynes's estimate was £6,400–8,800 million (p. 101, n. 4). Rather, the dispute has ranged over the size of particular items within the total, particularly the size of French claims, which Keynes believed indicated 'strict veracity inconsistent with the demands of patriotism' (p. 81).[m] The Reparation Commission award appeared as a global figure: it did not break it down under the particular heads under which it entertained claims. All we know is that the award represented less than 60 per cent of the sums claimed. Room remained for 'private' estimates and continued controversy. The various claims and counter-claims were also made during a period of rapidly changing prices and exchange rates. Estimates made at one date are not necessarily compatible with those made at another. The same would be true of expenditures actually incurred.[52]

In 1919 in his discussion of French war losses, Keynes used the pre-war exchange rate of 25 francs to the pound, implying that French inflation had been roughly the same as British, which was not the case. If he had adjusted for actual relative rates of inflation, a rate closer to 40 would have been appropriate. Even such an adjustment made to the claims of M. Dubois and M. Locheur would make them at least treble Keynes's 1919 maximum figure for physical and material damage. Adjusting the French claim of 1921 on a similar basis would make it just under five times his original estimate. The only defence offered in the modern literature for such figures is Mantoux's. He works from the French official figures for the costs of reconstruction, which came to FFrs 103 billion as compared with the claim of FFrs 127 billion. Since the French price level doubled between 1921 and 1926 and remained at about 75 per cent above the 1921 level until the slump when it returned to the 1921 level, it seems hard to accept the estimate of 103 milliard as being 'almost exactly the gold value of 127 milliard'.[53]

I come now to the most frequently discussed issue then and after – Germany's capacity to pay reparations and the economic consequences of such payments. Any discussion is complicated by several factors. The first arises from the fact that, at least in some sense, we know what happened. The second stems from the valuation of the deliveries of assets and transfers in kind that the Treaty required of Germany, not to mention the offsetting claims of the allies for occupation expenses.[54] The final complication arises from the transfer of any remaining sums to the allies.

For purposes of argument, let us take Mantoux's figures for a possible range of annual payments with a 5 per cent annuity and sinking fund. These are 7.3 to 8.6 billion marks (or £357 to £421 million at the pre-war

m He also thought other claims inflated, but controversy has centred on the French claims.

rate of exchange) – exclusive of any payments Germany might have to make for the costs of allied armies of occupation.[55] Such sums represent a significant proportion of Germany's 'normal' national income.[n] Taking 1925–9 as 'normal' and taking the highest average figure for national income in that period, such annual payments represent between 8.7 and 10.2 per cent of German national income.[56] Such a sum in context was hardly an impossible one for a government to raise in taxation. In the Second World War, for example, the British Government increased its tax receipts from £907 to £3,291 million.[57] The amounts involved in reparations were only useful to the allies if they received them not in marks but in their own currencies. It was this 'transfer problem' from marks to other currencies that would so exercise Keynes and his contemporaries.

One way of getting the figures into perspective is to look at historical examples. This was the procedure that Keynes and Ashley used late in 1916,[58] and it has found use by subsequent scholars. Their examples have ranged from Britain's subsidies to her allies during the Napoleonic Wars through French reparations after the defeat by Germany in 1870 and the rise in British overseas lending in the years immediately before 1914 to American foreign remittances in the post-1945 period. As a proportion of national income, the annual figures for these are as follows:

Britain 1793–1816	1–2.7 per cent
France 1871–5	7.5–12 per cent
Britain (change 1900–4 to 1911–13)	7 per cent
United States 1949–61	3.2 per cent[59]

The largest figures are for France while she paid the German indemnity of 1871, and the swing in Britain's overseas lending in response to normal economic incentives during the Edwardian boom. France's indemnity in 1871, of 5 billion francs, represented less than a quarter of a year's national income. The allies' post-1918 demands on Germany represented over one and a half times the highest estimates of Germany's national income in the second half of the 1920s.

Another possible approach compares the size of the annual transfers with the country's international transactions. It looks, for example, at the size of the relevant payments in relation to, say, export earnings, taking account not only of exports of goods but also of services where possible. The relevant figures here for the same examples are:

n Matters are bedevilled by the choice of a normal year. Keynes in 1919, with nothing else to go on, had to take a pre-war year. Others have taken a series of years: say, the late 1920s when Germany had recovered from the war. The choice of a particular year would make a difference for a growing economy. Further, the available estimates of national income have changed significantly over time. To give three examples, the figures used by Machlup, Mantoux and Trachtenberg for average income for 1925–9 have estimates ranging from 64 to 84 billion marks (Machlup 1964, 384; Mantoux 1946, 119; Trachtenberg 1980, 67).

Britain 1796–1805	4.9 per cent
Britain 1806–16	20.1 per cent
France 1872–5	30–40 per cent
Britain 1911–13	36 per cent (or 22 per cent of goods *and* services)
United States 1949–61	58 per cent (or 43 per cent of goods *and* services)

For Germany we do not have a strictly comparable figure, since all of the figures above are for the years in which the financial transfers actually occurred. In the German case, we have to compare the transfers demanded with the actual figures for either pre-war or post-war years. If we take the average for the years 1925–9, the 1921 annual demands range between 65 and 76 per cent of exports of goods – less if one allows for services.

The numbers 'prove' nothing. They establish only relative orders of magnitude. As such, they indicate that in terms of 'normal' national income and late 1920s average exports, the allies' demands for reparations from Germany were large relative to German demands on France in 1871 or to other historically large financial transfers. Moreover, it is worth noting that the German payments were to continue for a much longer period than those of, say, 1871. This ruled out the possibility of substantial recycling as had occurred in 1871, for when one talks of a stream of payments for several decades ahead, borrowing to service or anticipate a substantial portion of these payments is hardly feasible. Some borrowing might transfer some payments from earlier to later years when incomes and trade would be greater, but for payments the size of those demanded in 1919 a large proportion would have to come from current international earnings.

There is a further complication in that the reparations sum was set in nominal terms in foreign currency. A worldwide rise in prices would reduce the real resource costs of the transfer: a fall would increase it. In the nineteenth century, the trend of prices was flat, but fluctuations around that trend were significant and lengthy. To Keynes, a child of such a stable era, the risk of a significant fall in prices would make the effects of paying large nominal sums over a long period more worrying than it would to today's child of an inflationary world.

Most economists centred their interest on the ability of Germany to expand her exports and/or decrease her imports of goods and services to effect the transfer. Here the relevant issues relate to the time allowed for the changes in question, the magnitude of the changes, and the structure of the relevant markets.

On the question of time, Keynes admitted that if the allies nursed the German economy back to health over a period of five to ten years they could obtain larger streams of payments than otherwise. That much was common ground. There was room for disagreement as to the prospect of such time being allowed and the extent of 'nursing' involved. Keynes, looking at the Treaty and the financial policies of the allies, was pessimistic on both counts.

On the magnitudes involved, could Germany transform her international accounts so as to produce an export surplus of the relevant size even *if* the allies allowed? Was it possible by appropriate policy measures to reduce domestic consumption and raise Germany's net international receipts? To a modern economist, the answer would be 'yes *in theory*'. A mixture of tax, monetary and exchange-rate policies would reduce domestic consumption and raise the output of goods moving into international trade relative to those which did not. But in 1919 this was not a theoretical question. Keynes was arguing that the fat was not there on the consumption side and that, especially after the other allied depredations of the Treaty, the resources were not available and that they were not likely to be available in the foreseeable future. His opponents took a different view, often arguing that Keynes underestimated the recuperative power of the German economy *and* at the same time that the Treaty would in any case be modified to ease the burdens. Certainly, looking at the magnitudes involved, the figures above, though high, are not impossible for a more normal period. Whether the results would meet the needs or desires of the allies was another matter.

For any serious attempt by Germany to pay reparations would require a substantial net increase in her exports of coal and manufactured goods. Such an expansion would inevitably be at the expense of other producers. If those affected by such competition were the same countries who received the reparation payments and they received them in proportion to their demand for such goods, they could over time reallocate their labour and capital in other directions and enjoy a net rise in income and welfare. True, a problem would arise when the reparation payments came to an end 30 years later, but one can think of situations, as in the case of exporters of finite, non-renewable resources such as North Sea oil, where countries can plan for the ultimate rainy day. If, however, the distribution of reparation payments differed from the pattern of expanded German trade, after allowing for repercussions on incomes and demand in the recipient countries, problems might arise and countries might take steps to alleviate them which might affect Germany's ability to pay. Such problems would be more likely if Germany was a significant producer in any of the areas concerned and an expansion of German production affected relative prices. And Germany was significant: in 1913 her share of world production of manufactures (18.1 per cent) was second only to that of the United States and her share of world exports was, at 25.6 per cent, second only to the United Kingdom's.[60]

The question of whether Germany could 'pay' reparations on the scale demanded by the Treaty was never put to the test. In the late 1920s, German reparation payments averaged just over 1.5 billion marks – less than 2 per cent of national income or just over 13 per cent of exports.[61] The proportions rose with the 1929 slump, but it was only in those years that Germany's export surplus actually covered her reparations bill, for prior to 1929 German capital imports had more than offset her reparation payments. Thereafter the system collapsed. The general consensus amongst scholars is that she could have paid more than she did *if* there had been a willingness to pay in Germany, a willingness on the part of the allies to receive and a willingness to tackle associated problems. But whether she could have managed the figures of 1919 remains an open question.

In conclusion I should look briefly at a few minor details of Keynes's vision. It is clear that in 1919 he probably underestimated the recuperative power of capitalist economies after major wars. German recovery after 1918, as after 1945, was substantial. By the mid-1920s at the latest, output levels exceeded pre-war – as did real wages.[62] Her exports of manufactures did not return to pre-war levels, but the decline was not as severe as Britain's.[63] It is also the case that Keynes's long-standing worry about the secular tendency for the terms of trade between primary products (especially foodstuffs) and manufactures to turn automatically against the latter to the detriment of European standards of life was certainly misplaced, as well as theoretically incorrect,[o] although this long-standing Cambridge assumption was to last beyond his death. However, he was correct about the importance of frontiers, as the economic disintegration of the inter-war European economy was to demonstrate.[64] The psychological conditions surrounding nineteenth-century capitalist accumulation were fragile: as should be clear to a later generation with its repeated social conflicts over relativities, or the distribution of the cake, most frequently manifest in the process of wage inflation and the regular political outcries over 'rip-offs' and high profits, be they those of the banks, the oil companies and other visible 'beneficiaries' of the higher rates of inflation experienced in western economies in the 1970s, particularly if one remembers that the rates in question were far below those experienced immediately after the First World War.[65]

It is also interesting what Keynes missed. He certainly significantly underplayed French concerns about security from future German attack. He acknowledged that these had been an important part of Clemenceau's 'vision' of the world and had begged to differ about the wisdom of an attempt to ensure French security by weakening the German economy over the longer term. In disagreeing, he ignored the political dimension of such worries and as a result his success in Britain in making the moral and economic case against the Treaty left France feeling more isolated and more prone to use the reparations issue as the vehicle for prolonging conflict. If he had allowed for French concerns, he would have had to make clear that a softening of the

---

o What should really concern one in such cases are not the gross barter terms of trade considered in *Economic Consequences* and elsewhere but rather the single or double factoral terms of trade which relate to the actual resource costs involved.

Treaty's terms on reparations required other guarantees to France from her allies. It is also of interest how completely he missed the impact of the 'war guilt' clause. As much as French obsessions about security, that clause was to colour the next two decades of European politics with often disastrous consequences for all concerned. Much of this was to become clear in the ensuing two decades before Europe was engulfed in yet another war and Keynes involved in yet further discussions of post-war reparations from Germany.

NOTES

1 *JMK*, XVII, 3. The dating of this letter comes from Hancock 1962, 532.
2 Ibid. 4.
3 BL, ADD.57923, JMK to O. T. Falk, 25 June 1919.
4 BL, ADD.57931, JMK to DG, 17 July 1919.
5 The relevant correspondence and contract is on KCKP, EC1/4 and BL, ADD.55201.
6 For a discussion of this evidence see Chandavarkar 1990, 73–9.
7 KCKP, JMK to FAK, 6 August 1919.
8 BL, ADD.57923, JMK to O. T. Falk, 17 August 1919.
9 KCKP, JMK to FAK, 23 September 1919.
10 *JMK*, XVII, 4.
11 *JMK*, X, 20–6. The background to the fragment from which the quotations appear is in footnote 1 to page 20.
12 *JMK*, XVII, 5.
13 Swanberg 1980, 351; Mayer 1959, 337. *Pace* Swanberg, Keynes did not write for the magazine until after the war.
14 KCKP, Frankfurter to JMK, 18 August 1919. Keynes dined with Frankfurter and Louis Brandeis in London on 25 August.
15 KCKP, Frankfurter to JMK, 12 September 1919; Steel 1980, 173–4.
16 KCKP, GLS to JMK, 2 October 1919.
17 *JMK*, XVII, 6–7. Part of the Salter letter appears on pages 5–6.
18 KCKP, W. Lippmann to JMK, 23 October 1919.
19 Hynes 1990, 292.
20 For a picture of the disorganisation of the American delegation see Schwartz 1981, 115–23; Ferrell 1985, Ch. 9.
21 *JMK*, X, 23–4.
22 *JMK*, X, 26.
23 Above p. 286.
24 *JMK*, XVI, 359–79.
25 For the evidence on Keynes's 'invention' of Lenin's statement, see Fetter 1977.
26 The Reparation Commission would be dissolved or, if any duties remained for it, become an appendage of the League.
27 Austria would make no reparation payments.
28 Above p. 309.
29 Schumpeter 1946, 499.
30 Below p. 354.
31 Burk 1981, 1003. According to his papers Keynes sent copies to fifteen Americans: F. W. Taussig, Allyn Young, Herbert Hoover, O. Strauss, Colonel

House, Bernard Baruch, Norman Davis, Oscar Crosby, Paul Cravath, E. M. Bullitt, Walter Lippmann, Felix Frankfurter, Thomas Lamont, Paul Warburg, and Fred I. Kent.

32 Lentin 1984, 141.
33 KCKP, JMK to GLS, 23 December 1919.
34 Above, pp. 323, 327; KCKP, JMK to GLS, 16 December 1919.
35 KCKP, Curzon to JMK, 23 December 1919.
36 KCKP, Lord Robert Cecil to JMK, 31 December 1919; P. Cravath to JMK, 18 December 1919. See also *JMK*, XVII, for Austen Chamberlain's reaction.
37 *JMK*, XVII, 41–2; see also pp. 44–5, 48, 55–7.
38 KCKP, R. H. Brand to JMK, 23 December 1919; Reginald McKenna to JMK, 27 December 1919; Pamela McKenna to JMK, no date; Lord Robert Cecil to JMK, 31 December 1919 (*JMK*, XVII, 148).
39 *JMK*, XVII, 8, 13.
40 See, for example, Mantoux 1946, 8–11.
41 For a summary, see Ferrell 1985, Ch. 10.
42 The view is set out in *JMK*, III, chapter 1; see below p. 370.
43 Harrod 1951, 239–40; M. Keynes (ed.) 1975, 24–5.
44 F. Cairncross (ed.) 1981, 42.
45 Ibid.; Coats (ed.) 1981.
46 Williamson 1981, 541–2.
47 See Harry Johnson in Johnson and Johnson 1978, 211–12.
48 KCKP, JMK to N. Davis, 18 April 1920; *JMK*, XVII, 38.
49 *JMK*, XVII, 107–8.
50 Mantoux 1946.
51 Mantoux 1946, 77.
52 The franc–sterling exchange rate moved from 25.99 in January 1919 to 41.40 in December to 57.05 in December 1920. The rates for the next five Decembers were: 52.65, 63.95, 84.85, 87.45 and 129.875.
53 Mantoux 1946, 106; Harrod 1951, 227n.
54 The Allies valued these at 4.4 billion gold marks net; the Germans put the figure considerably higher (Schucker 1988, 106–7).
55 Mantoux 1946, 108.
56 If one took the 1913 national income figures for the post-war boundaries of Germany and adjusted them for the world-wide rise in prices during the war, the figure would come out higher.
57 Feinstein 1972, Table T31.
58 *JMK*, XVI, 314–22.
59 Machlup 1976, chap. XV; Trachtenberg 1980, 67–8.
60 Maizels 1964, 220.
61 Machlup 1964, 384, 392–3.
62 Phelps Brown and Browne 1967, Appendix 3.
63 Maizels 1964, 189.
64 Svennilson 1954.
65 Leijonhufvud 1981, especially 'Costs and Consequences of Inflation'.

14

ADJUSTMENTS TO A WAY OF LIFE

Keynes's resignation from the Treasury in 1919 was a milestone in more ways than one. Before his resignation he had talked of returning to academic life, but at 36 he was not going back on pre-war terms with a heavy load of teaching and supervision. To make this possible he had to find alternative sources of income to provide for his independence – and the more expensive style of life which had come with his relatively high Treasury salary. To this end, he plunged into the world of finance.

Before the war, as we have seen, Keynes had been an investor on a relatively small scale, initially for himself but later for friends such as Roger Fry. He had even indulged in a little speculation. After he left the Treasury he was to become more active – if not always more successful.

In his post-war financial dealings Keynes normally worked through the London brokers Buckmaster and Moore, often in collaboration with O. T. Falk, his former 'A' Division colleague. Falk had started his City career as an actuary with the National Mutual Life Assurance Society, of which he later became a director. Until 1932, when, after a disagreement with his partners, he left to form his own firm (O. T. Falk and Partners) he was a partner in Buckmaster and Moore.[1] Falk had a strong, often explosive, personality and firmly held views. He was a ruthless investor who brooked no interference from his clients. His relations with Keynes over the next two decades would often be stormy and, although the two remained friends to the end, marked divergences in their views developed after 1929 which, with their different operating styles, made collaboration difficult, if not impossible. By 1938 Keynes had severed all his business connections with Falk, with the exception of membership of the board of one firm where effective control lay in other hands.

Although he was also engaged in some share speculation at the time, in August 1919 Keynes's first large-scale speculative venture was on the foreign exchange market. By that time, the old régime of fixed exchange rates had disappeared and all major currencies were floating. His strategy was simple: in the forward market he sold short the currencies of France, Holland, Italy and, after March 1920, Germany, and bought US dollars, Norwegian and Danish krone and Indian rupees long. His speculations went well at first, and by 2 January 1920 his realised profits amounted to £6,154. Although he thought his exchange speculation would shock his father, Neville Keynes provided some collateral in the early stages of the speculation. In these early stages Maynard Keynes commented on his experience:

> Money is a funny thing – it seems impossible to believe that the present system will be allowed to continue much longer. As the fruit of a little extra knowledge and experience of a special kind, it simply (and undeservedly in any absolute sense) comes rolling in.[2]

His early success led him to embark on a more ambitious scheme with Falk – the Syndicate. In this the two would use their own capital and that of their friends for exchange speculation. The Syndicate had an initial capital of £30,000, half from Keynes and his friends. Keynes's group had three risk-taking principals: himself (using loans from his father, his brother-in-law A. V. Hill, his uncle Walter Langdon Brown and his sister-in-law Margaret Keynes), Geoffrey Keynes, and Duncan Grant (using his own funds as well as loans from his mother, Roger Fry, David Garnett, Vanessa Bell and Alix Sargant Florence).[a] The Syndicate began operations on 21 January 1920. At the end of March, the problem of dealing in large sums in very thin markets[b] led Falk to suggest that his group leave the Syndicate. The Syndicate was successful at first: by the end of April the Keynes group had realised profits of almost £9,000 and book profits of almost £8,000. Then came problems, as the currencies sold forward rose against sterling while the dollar and rupee fell; the denouement was rapid. By 14 May the Syndicate had realised profits of £10,408 and book losses of £3,146. On 19 May Falk warned Keynes that book losses exceeded realised profits, the available cover was less than 10 per cent of the outstanding commitments, and the Syndicate had either to increase its cover or to close out some positions. Keynes's separate personal speculative position was equally disastrous. He was wiped out. Aided by Buckmaster and Moore's not interpreting their cover rules as strictly as they might, he moved quickly to put matters in order. He closed out contracts, realised securities from his own portfolio, arranged with Macmillan for an advance payment on royalties due from *Economic Consequences* and borrowed £5,000 from Sir Ernest Cassel. When he closed out the Syndicate's positions, losses totalled £22,573; on his personal speculative account gains and losses (including dealing expenses) almost cancelled out (the deficit was £113 8s.0d.). The Syndicate had lost money in every currency it had dealt

---

a Grant's position in the scheme was ambiguous, as Keynes provided his brokers with a guarantee against his 'sustaining any loss' in respect of his funds.

b At the time, margin requirements were 10 per cent. Thus the Syndicate could take up forward positions up to an amount equal to ten times its capital and realised capital gains.

in, but the largest losses were in marks, francs and lire. Keynes had been right about the long-term trends in these currencies but could not survive the short run.[c]

On 1 August 1920, after Neville Keynes had written off £2,000 as a birthday present to his son, Maynard Keynes summarised the results of the whole affair:

Assets		Liabilities	
Securities	£19,000	Bank loan	£4,618
		Buckmaster	
		and Moore	£3,619
		Sir Ernest Cassel	£5,000
		J. N. Keynes	£3,000
		A. V. Hill	£2,400
		W. Langdon	
		Brown	£1,000
		M. E. Keynes	£1,200
	£19,000		£20,837

In addition, he believed that he had 'moral' debts of £6,750 to other participants in the Syndicate: Duncan Grant, £2,860; Geoffrey Keynes, £2,000; Basil Blackett, £400;[3] and Vanessa Bell £1,490.

Keynes does not appear to have been unduly perturbed by this setback. As he told Vanessa Bell in the midst of his 'slaughter of a large part of out holdings', 'It has been a beastly time, but I have kept fairly philosophical'.[4] If he was perturbed, he would never have been able, on 26 May, to open the approach to Sir Ernest Cassel that eventuated in the £5,000 loan as he did:

[M]y proposal is . . . as follows – that you authorise me to *sell* marks, francs and lire *forward* on your behalf and to close the transactions at my discretion, subject to your overruling instructions at any time. I would keep you informed daily as to the position. I am well accustomed to this business and know the ropes. I suggest as amounts[d]

Marks 5,000,000
Francs 5,000,000
Lire 3,000,000

or smaller or larger amounts as may commend itself [sic] to you. It would be necessary for you to put up (say) 20 per cent margin of the liability and to maintain 10 per cent intact.

The profits would be shared between us in such proportion as you

c On 26 May, the rates to the pound for these currencies were marks 127, francs 48, lire 63 as compared with the end of April figures of 220, 64.50 and 87. By the end of 1920 the figures were 260, 57.05 and 102.50.
d At the exchange rates he gave earlier in the letter, the sum involved was just over £190,000.

may deem fair. I anticipate very substantial profits with very good probability if you are prepared to stand the racket for perhaps a couple of months.

I must add . . . that I am not in any position to risk any capital myself, for the reason that I was a bear of these currencies at higher values than now current and have, at present prices, quite exhausted my resources. But the prospects for anyone who comes in at this present low shake-out level are very good. I am miserable at my own bad management in not being able to take advantage of the situation and hence apply to you at a moment when your aid would be of the greatest aid to me.[5]

Thus he was to restore his fortune as he had lost it – through speculation, primarily in currencies but also in commodities. By the end of 1920, he had repaid Cassel and Blackett. During 1922 he repaid the other Syndicate members, with the exception of Margaret Keynes, who left her £1,200 with him until 1936.[e] By 31 December 1922, Keynes had cleared off his debts and had become a substantial creditor with net assets of over £21,000.

Keynes's post-war financial activities extended beyond his own and his friends' investments. During the war he had remained in touch with College finances and made suggestions about investments – suggestions which, as we have seen, were not always gratefully received. With the end of the war and the prospect of his return to King's, W. H. Macaulay, the Vice Provost, wrote to him on 5 May 1919 to see if he would be willing to become involved in the financial side of the College.[6] Macaulay mentioned that John Clapham was extremely keen on the idea and John Sheppard also wrote encouragingly. Keynes, under the pressure of work in Paris, answered the letter on 17 May, after he had decided to leave the Treasury. His long letter set out the areas where he thought he might be useful. He did not think that the job would be onerous, nor did he believe his remuneration should be high.[7] The College's Estates Committee found his ideas congenial and invited the Annual Congregation 'to consider the advisability of creating a new annual office, with a view to utilising the services of Mr. Keynes in connection with the financial administration of the College'. The College made him Second Bursar at a stipend of £100 per annum in November 1919.[f] He became First Bursar in 1924 and retained the post until his death.

The first substantial result of his new position came in June 1920 when the College agreed to authorise an investment of £30,000 'in foreign government and other government non-trustee securities'. This was the origin of the Chest, whose investment remit was later broadened to include shares and even commodity speculation. This was a departure for Cambridge colleges,

e Most of the other former members of the Syndicate would leave their funds under Keynes's indirect control. They were to lose and regain their fortunes again after 1929.

f Second Bursar because Corbett, the former Second Bursar who had succeeded Grant as Bursar in 1919, was his senior.

whose investments of corporate as well as trustee funds were restricted by law to securities authorised by the Trustee Acts and to land. Some in Cambridge still believe that this King's decision to set up the Chest was illegal, and that for this reason Keynes consistently opposed King's having a law don. However, the King's statutes of 1882 and 1926 were loosely drawn and thus gave him the necessary authority. Other colleges could alter their powers of investment through changes in statutes – some, such as St John's, did not do so until the 1950s.[8] At the last audit of his bursarship, the Chest, which had received no net additions to its initial funds in the subsequent years, was worth over twelve times its original capital.

Nor was King's the only body which sought Keynes's financial advice. In June 1919 he was offered the chairmanship of the British Bank of Northern Commerce, a foreign-owned bank primarily concerned with the finance of trade with Scandinavia. A salary of £2,000, plus the claim that it would take only one morning a week, made it a tempting offer, but after consulting R. H. Brand and Sir Robert Kindersley of Lazards as well as Falk, he turned it down. In September he was asked to join the board of the National Mutual Life Assurance Society with the expectation of becoming its chairman – which he did in May 1921. He remained chairman until October 1938. Along with Falk, he also provided financial and foreign exchange advice to Sir Ernest Debenham between September 1920 and February 1924, and with Sir Henry Strakosch he advised on South African gold exports to the UK now that Britain was off the gold standard.

Keynes's growing City involvement marked another change in the balance of his life – one almost as large as his move from the India Office to Cambridge in 1908. Cambridge remained the focus for his intellectual – and much of his social – life, but it was no longer such a focus of his other activities as it had been before 1914. He reduced his regular Cambridge commitments in the years after 1919. The 1919–20 academic year was the last in which he gave more than eight lectures to the University. He resigned his Girdlers' Company lectureship in April 1920. Even the few lectures that he gave focused on his own intellectual concerns.

Table 2 Keynes's Lectures, 1920–30

1920–1	The Present Disorders of the World's Monetary System (Michaelmas)
1921–2	No Lectures
1922–3	Realistic Monetary Problems, Advanced (Michaelmas)
1923–4	Monetary Reform (Easter)
1924–5	The Theory of Credit Systems (Easter)
1925–6	The Theory of Credit Systems (Easter)
1926–7	The Theory of Money (Michaelmas)
1927–8	The Theory of Money (Michaelmas)
1928–9	The Theory of Money (Michaelmas)
1929–30	The Pure Theory of Money (Michaelmas)

In the autumn, or Michaelmas, term of 1919 his topic was 'Economic Aspects of the Peace'; in the winter, or Lent, term of 1920 it was 'Economic Aspects of the European Situation'. Both drew students from faculties other than economics. Austin Robinson from classics recalled 'the dense throng and the fight to find even standing room, for everyone was prepared to cut anything to hear Keynes'.[9] He also remembered the lecturer:

> I can still picture him there in the lecture room as a young man. His burning indignation with the world, with the Treaty as it was working out, his care for the world, the sense of importance of things that he was conveying to us – these stuck in my mind. Those few lectures made me decide that economics was my subject and not classics.[10]

Others were not so persuaded.[11]

Keynes also reduced his College teaching load. He still did some supervision, but far less than before the war and normally only for King's. In 1920 he became a supernumerary fellow and waived his claim to a dividend from King's. His Cambridge commitments thus became almost non-pecuniary, but no less strong or important. On the other hand he did not neglect Cambridge. He remained a member of the Economics Board and played an important role in University affairs as a member of the Council of the Senate, elected on the reform ticket, from 1920 to 1927.

The early 1920s were an important period for the Universities of Oxford and Cambridge and their Colleges. After requests for central government financial support, the Government in November 1919 appointed a Royal Commission under Asquith to inquire into the two ancient universities. The Royal Commission, its Report, the resulting Act of Parliament and the subsequent revisions of University and College statutes took six years. As Sidgwick had desired, the University gained much more responsibility for teaching and research, and the wherewithal to pay for it. Keynes made useful contributions to the discussions of pensions (the 1923 Act brought in a fixed retirement age), the organisation and finance of the Faculty system and the arrangements for taxing the Colleges to help finance the new responsibilities of the University. The major outstanding question remained the position of women. Keynes and his father had supported their full membership of the University, but all that came out of this round of reform was the admission of women to the expanded number of University teaching posts. Full membership would take another two decades.

Keynes was also active in the University at more informal levels. He revived his Monday evening Political Economy club and set it firmly on its feet along pre-war lines despite the occasional direct request from students to join.[12] The Society also needed much work. In 1919 there was only one active undergraduate Apostle left from the pre-war era, Peter Lucas. Keynes found himself heavily involved in vetting potential new members and in papers and discussions and helping to revive the traditions, concerns and conventions of a less troubled era. By 1921 he could report to the assembled brethren at The Dinner:

> Now the Society lives again, – not yet numerously but with a steady vitality. . . .
>
> After a light flicker towards interest in phenomenal events, the Society has now again, if anything more than ever, abstracted itself from the outside world and gazes inward. . . .
>
> We are back again in a Dark Age. . . . [T]he Society as a whole has withdrawn itself into a monastic seclusion, and, except that they talk too much about the herd instinct, are much more like what the Society always was, than the outside world is like what it used to be.[13]

In the following decade he was a faithful angel, frequently attending meetings and forming close friendships with new members.

Amongst his closest new friends was Sebastian Sprott, one of the first new post-war Apostles. The son of a country solicitor, Sprott was reading psychology at Clare when he joined the Society and became Keynes's lover. Close also to Lytton and Morgan Forster, Sprott later became a fringe member of Bloomsbury. Another of Keynes's serious young men was Gabriel Atkin, an artist, who appears to have been the only person other than Sebastian whom Keynes took down to Charleston. This relationship did not last after 1920. Otherwise, we know little. It would appear that the relationship with Sebastian was the closest one that he had: they toured North Africa together in the spring of 1921; Sebastian was invited several times to Charleston; and he joined Keynes for Christmas with Lytton at Tidmarsh in 1921. Sebastian was probably Keynes's last male lover.

In the autumn of 1919, as well as finishing *The Economic Consequences of the Peace* and re-establishing himself in King's, Keynes found himself involved in an attempt at international financial reconstruction. On 12 October, at the invitation of Dr G. Vissering, the Governor of the Netherlands Bank, and F. I. Kent, who had been in charge of wartime foreign exchange operations for the Federal Reserve, he went to Amsterdam. When he arrived, he found several other bankers, including C. E. ter Meulen of Hope & Co. and Paul Warburg. The group was expected to survey the financial position of Europe and suggest remedies. The resulting private discussions at Vissering's house ranged widely over such matters as the cancellation of war debts and an international currency scheme, but the main result was a proposal for an international loan which Keynes drafted with Warburg's assistance at Vissering's request. It was Keynes who suggested that the proposal should go to the first session of the League of Nations. The proposal itself was framed in very general terms and did not at this early stage contain possible sums. Rather it was designed to be the basis for discussion at an international financial conference. At a further meeting in Amsterdam on 2 and 3 November, the original group with the addition of R. H. Brand and representatives from the Swiss and Swedish financial communities discussed the Keynes/Warburg draft before leaving Keynes to prepare a final version. The participants intended to obtain further influential signatures before they presented it as a memorial to the League.

From this point complications intruded. The Peace Treaty and the League's covenant were still before the US Senate. Kent showed the draft memorial to the Wilson Administration, which proved unsympathetic; the Treasury refused to get involved in lending any more public money to Europe. This led Kent to withdraw his signature from the scheme and suggest a barter scheme as an alternative. Warburg suggested that instead of addressing the League, the signatories of each nation should approach their own governments or the Reparation Commission. He also recommended the deletion of the proposals for the remission of interest on or the cancellation of inter-allied war debts in an attempt to gain American support. This suggestion found favour, despite Keynes's objections, and the search for signatures began.

Brand was in charge of the search for signatories in England, as Keynes's disapproval of the change in the plan led him – rather oddly in my opinion as he was still prepared to sign the document and assist Brand – to refuse to take the initiative in a search.g More complications ensued when Lord Reading, who believed that the publication of *Economic Consequences* would do great harm in America and took the view that the book was a direct attack on the Government of which he was still a member, refused to sign the document if Keynes signed. Lord Reading's attitude was to Keynes 'absurd' and 'pure fudge',[14] but because others held Reading's view, Keynes, on Lord Robert Cecil's advice, did not sign the memorial he had largely drafted. Nor, in the end, did Lord Reading. The memorial was issued in all the countries represented at the second meeting in Amsterdam, except France (where there were too few signatories) on 16 January 1920. It had little immediate effect beyond helping to create a climate of opinion and in stimulating the American Secretary of the Treasury, Carter Glass, to state the Administration's opposition to any further government loans abroad. However, as part of a growing climate of opinion, it was one of the factors that led the Council of the League of Nations to call an international financial conference at Brussels in September 1920.

Keynes's visit to Amsterdam in October 1919 had one other result. It allowed him to meet Carl Melchior again. This time both were free of their official connections, for Melchior had resigned from the German delegation rather than

---

g Keynes also cited 'personal reasons' in his note of 13 December (*JMK*, XVII, 149), but it is hard to see what they were other than the effects of the publication of *Economic Consequences*. He could have foreseen these much earlier.

be a party to signing the Peace Treaty and, refusing appeals to be Minister of Finance, returned to banking in Hamburg. When he got to Amsterdam on 12 October, on an 'impulse' Keynes cabled Melchior that he would be there for a few days and would like to see him. On 15 October the two men met privately in Vissering's house. They had 'a long rambling gossip as two ordinary people'. Later they lunched together 'openly, like any other couple' with Paul Warburg, the brother of Melchior's Hamburg partner, and afterwards Keynes read them parts of Chapter 3 of *Economic Consequences*. Soon afterwards, he movingly described the day.[15] He had cemented a friendship. In the next few years it was to give him access to the highest circles within the German Government.

Keynes's meeting with Melchior, as well as with other neutral bankers in Amsterdam, also gave him information on German conditions which he passed back to his former Treasury colleagues.[16] His correspondence files and his appointments books show that he maintained contacts with many with whom he had formerly worked. This continued contact, along with reactions such as Lord Reading's to the draft Amsterdam memorial, raises the question of Keynes's position in official circles. The received view is that of Sir Roy Harrod, who suggested that as a result of *Economic Consequences* 'he remained an outlaw from British official circles for many years'.[17] It is hard to make sense of this statement. It is true that in the years after 1919 he was often in disagreement with the policies of the Government of the day, though on occasion he supported them. It is also true that he was not on good terms with certain senior Treasury officials, in particular Sir Otto Niemeyer, who enjoyed a meteoric rise to become Controller of Finance in May 1923 in succession to Basil Blackett, and F. W. Leith-Ross, who played an important role in international negotiations between the wars and became Niemeyer's deputy in October 1924. Neither Leith-Ross nor Niemeyer had been part of 'A' Division. It may also be the case that on occasion Keynes felt himself an outsider: one might read the opening pages of *A Revision of the Treaty* with its discussion of outside and inside opinion and limited circles as a coded way of saying that he felt himself not a part of the 'inside' opinion which *Revision* sought to influence.[18] But how can one call someone 'an outlaw from British official circles', who maintains regular contact with the Treasury's Controller of Finance before 1923, Basil Blackett;[h] who at their request advises three Chancellors of the Exchequer (Austen Chamberlain, Horne and Baldwin) and two Prime Ministers (Bonar Law and Baldwin); who turns up on lists of 'the great and the good' as vice-chairman of a Royal Commission on Indian tariff policy (from which he resigned) and a member of the Committee on Industry and Trade (which he declined); and who in 1927 becomes a member of the Other Club, a dining club founded in 1911

h The contact was so close, as we have seen above, that Keynes speculated on the foreign exchanges for Blackett. Later in the 1920s such speculation by a senior official would be grounds for at least a reprimand (O'Halpin 1989, 160–3).

by F. E. Smith and Winston Churchill.[i] One can go further and mention his well-maintained contacts with Lord Chalmers, Ralph Hawtrey, Arthur Salter, Andrew McFadyean, Lord Bradbury and Harry Siepmann. In these circumstances, we should suspend judgement on 'outlawry'.

One of Keynes's most interesting contacts with 'official circles' came almost immediately after the publication of *Economic Consequences*. It related to monetary policy. The background to his contact lay in the inflationary boom that swept across the international economy in the year after April 1919. In Britain, conditions at the end of the war were tailor-made for such a boom: there was a large Budget deficit; money, as a result of wartime financial policy, was cheap and plentiful; the war had created a backlog of replacement investment opportunities and shortages of consumer goods; and overseas markets were hungry for British exports. After a brief 'breathing space' during which the normal working week fell by 6½ per cent with no cut in weekly wage rates, the boom got under way in the spring of 1919. By the end of the year there was certainly full employment and industrial production and real output approached their pre-war levels. Prices were rising rapidly: in the last eight months of 1919 the cost of living rose 11 per cent and wholesale prices by 27 per cent, while money wages rose by 11 per cent and hours worked fell a further 6 per cent, again with no decline in weekly wages.[19]

At the end of the war, the Treasury rather than the Bank of England controlled interest rate policy. The source of the Treasury's control lay in its policy of borrowing from the market at short term by making Treasury bills available in unlimited quantities at a fixed price at a time when the Budget was (at least initially) in deficit and the amount of short-term debt requiring refinancing was large. In these circumstances, if the Bank of England attempted to raise Bank rate without an increase in Treasury bill rates, the public would reduce its purchases of such bills and the Bank, as banker to the Government, would be obliged to provide the necessary accommodation to the authorities and thus undo the tightening in monetary conditions intended by the rise in Bank rate. In the fall of 1919, the Bank and the Treasury brought the wartime and early post-war régime of cheap money to an end with a rise in Treasury bill rates from 3½ to 5 per cent. Bank rate, to which a large number of interest rates in the financial sector were linked, rose from 5 to 6 per cent. Soon afterwards, the Government accepted the 1918 recommendation of the Committee on Currency and Foreign Exchanges after the War, chaired by Lord Cunliffe, for limiting the fiduciary issue of wartime currency notes.[j] With this decision, under

i Members of the Other Club in 1927 included Churchill, Lloyd George and Lord Reading, all of whom by 1927 had had run-ins with Keynes and might have wished to exclude him.
j The Treasury had already been using the recommendation as a basis for its policy for several months before the Government made its announcement. See Howson 1974, and 1975, ch. 2.

the existing monetary arrangements, any increase in the demand for notes, either for transactions purposes or commercial bank reserves, caused by the continuing inflation and the rise in economic activity would result in a fall in the Bank of England's free gold reserves and a rise in interest rates.[k] The stage was set.

Keynes, who, according to his appointments diary, had seen Blackett privately on three evenings in December, formally entered the discussion of monetary policy on 28 December in the course of his reply to Austin Chamberlain's comments on *Economic Consequences*. After these, he continued:

> I was immensely glad to read of your decision about Currency Notes. *The Times* may sneer at it as an illusory step; but in fact it is, if anything, too drastic and will have far-reaching consequences. I believe that the Treasury Minute, if it is maintained, must logically end in a very high Bank rate and corresponding rates for Treasury bills. I was nearly moved to write to *The Times* in defence of the new policy; but had decided that it had better work its remedy in silence for the present.[20]

There matters stood for just over a month. By February 1920 the Chancellor was under pressure from the Bank, who wanted to raise rates further to restrain speculation, and from some of his colleagues, particularly Bonar Law and Lloyd George, who saw in cheaper money a way of facilitating a bond issue for housing construction, of reducing the cost of Government borrowing, and of allowing the banks to liquidate some of their portfolio of securities to facilitate an expansion of their lending. Chamberlain's reaction was to seek advice from the Bank and his officials. He also wrote to Keynes on 2 February:

> In a letter you wrote to me some time ago, you expressed your satisfaction at my having raised the Treasury bill rate, and, if my recollection serves me rightly, expressed the opinion that this policy was the beginning of wisdom and should be adhered to.... I am being strongly pressed to lower the rate again. Do you still adhere to your opinion? And, if so, what is the answer you would make to McKenna and others who argue that in the special circumstances of the time the raising of the Bank or Treasury bill rate has no effect upon borrowing or upon the [foreign] exchanges except to raise the price of money against Government itself?[21]

Keynes saw the Chancellor at 3.15 p.m. on 4 February. He supplemented the

---

k A limitation of the fiduciary issue of currency notes backed by Government securities meant that each additional issue of such notes had to be backed by an equivalent value of Bank of England notes. As the Bank Act of 1844 was still in effect, each additional Bank of England note had to be backed by an equivalent amount of gold.

interview with a memorandum on 15 February. In his record of the interview Chamberlain noted:

> K. would go for a financial crisis (does not believe it would lead to unemployment). Would go to whatever rate is necessary – perhaps 10% – and keep it at that for three years.[22]

'Three years' sounds uncharacteristic.

In his memorandum Keynes set out his reasoning. A rise in Bank rate was necessary, because now that wartime controls on borrowing and raw materials' allocations had ended, the only way to break the boom was to reduce the demand for savings. A sharp rise in interest rates would change businessmen's expectations of future prices and profits and reduce their demands for funds to finance inventories and fixed investment. This would not cause any serious rise in unemployment because industry's order books were so full that there was a wide margin of safety before industry found itself working far below full capacity. Unlike the Chancellor's other advisers – the Governor of the Bank, Blackett, O. E. Niemeyer, and R. G. Hawtrey – Keynes did not advocate dearer money to help Britain return to the gold standard. His argument was that of the author of *Economic Consequences*. As he concluded:

> [V]ery grave issues are at stake. A continuance of inflationism and high prices will not only depress the exchanges, but by their effect on prices strike at the whole basis of contract, of security, and of the capitalist system generally. The new state of affairs created by persistent inflation will only be tolerable under socialistic control, and that is where the present policy, if persisted in will necessarily lead us before probably we are really ripe for such a development.[23]

By the end of February, all of the Chancellor's advisers had 'joined in the chorus urging higher rates'.[24] Chamberlain, however, managed to hold off increasing interest rates until a decline in Treasury bill sales, rising Bank of England lending to the Government and falling Bank of England reserves forced a rise in Treasury bill rates on 13 April. Bank rate followed, rising to 7 per cent (a level it would not reach again until 1957) two days later. It remained there for almost a year. During the period before and after rates rose, Blackett kept Keynes informed about developments on this and other fronts, particularly European affairs. Keynes reciprocated.[25] They also met privately in May, November and December, as well as attending the Tuesday Club together in January, May, June and December. Thus Blackett would have heard Keynes proclaim that he was 'still a dear money man' on 8 July when he advocated an 8 per cent Bank rate and admitted that he would 'risk . . . a depression and possibly a [financial] crisis' to get rid of inflation.[26]

As a postscript to Keynes's preoccupation with inflation in 1920, it is worth recording that the Treasury papers and memoranda received by the Chancellor in February and March 1920 were discovered by S. D. Waley in 1942. Keynes arranged for their preservation as PRO T172/1384. He also provided a note, dated 7 January 1942, which opens the file and which states that in similar circumstances he would give 'exactly the same advice I gave then, namely a swift and severe dose of dear money'.[27]

Although those involved could not have known it, the rise in interest rates in April 1920 coincided with the onset of a sharp downturn in economic activity. Although retail prices and money wages continued to rise for some months, wholesale prices fell from April onwards and unemployment rose.[1] Sterling also started to rise against the dollar, precipitating in part Keynes's own financial crisis. The 1920 level of prices would not be reached again in Britain during his lifetime. It would take another world war to reduce unemployment in Britain to its 1920 level.

With the New Year of 1920 Keynes also took to the public platform. He gave speeches to the League of Nations Union and the University Liberal Club on 14 January and the Manchester School of Technology and the Manchester and District Bankers' Institute on 15 and 16 January. The first three speeches concerned the Peace Treaty, but the last dealt with the current state of the foreign exchanges. His addresses were circulated by the Fight the Famine Council with which he had become associated the previous summer. In the years to come he was to be in considerable demand as a public speaker.

In the Easter vacation Keynes took a long Italian holiday with Vanessa and Duncan. They left England on 17 March and did not return until the second week of May. When they passed through Paris on the way out, Keynes took the opportunity to see his French translator about *Economic Consequences* and to see Andrew McFadyean, then with the Reparation Commission. As the Syndicate was then doing well, it was a comfortable, even extravagant holiday. In Rome they stayed very comfortably at the Hotel de Russie in the Piazza del Popolo. Duncan and Vanessa hired a studio in the Via Marquetta, where Keynes also wrote. As well as a week in the Sabine Hills and dinner with a cardinal to meet the Pope's Secretary of State for Foreign Affairs, Keynes took the opportunity to do a considerable amount of shopping. He also encouraged Vanessa and Duncan to do likewise. By 16 April, he estimated to his father that by weight their purchases amounted to almost a ton. Keynes was buying furniture for Gordon Square and his rooms in Cambridge, while Vanessa and Duncan bought furniture, picture frames, clothing, pottery and pictures.[28] While in Rome Keynes re-established contact with an old Kingsman, W. H. Haslam, who was then Commercial Secretary at the British Embassy. Haslam was about to return to England

---

1 The cost of living index peaked in October 1920; money wage rates in January 1921.

where his family connections had resulted in a seat on the Board of the Provincial Insurance Company. He would later act as Keynes's secretary at the Genoa Conference in 1922 and bring him on to the Provincial Board as chairman of the investments committee.

The Italian holiday continued with a visit to the Berensons at I Tatti. Logan Pearsall Smith and Bob Trevelyan were also there. Originally, Duncan and Vanessa had planned to go to I Tatti for the last two days of Keynes's visit, but as Bernard Berenson was going away they changed their plans and came from the beginning.[29] Vanessa found Berenson a strain. As she told Roger Fry, 'If only he were honestly a stockbroker one would be quite at ease. . . . I'm sure that he has no more notion of what it is that's important in painting than a flea has'. Keynes was a 'huge success', although Vanessa recorded 'I think he is getting tired of it & it is certainly a lesson on the advantages of obscurity'.[30] Occasionally, however, even obscurity didn't help: at a party given for everyone at I Tatti by Charles Loeser Keynes ended up being shown the host's Cezannes while Duncan was closely questioned by the Governor of the Bank of Italy on the depreciation of the lira.[m] The two did nothing to rectify the mistake and when Berenson learned of this he was angry. It all became too much for Duncan and Vanessa, who left for Paris the day before Keynes. In Paris, the three saw Picasso and Braque, some of whose paintings Vanessa tried (without success, at least initially, owing to the collapse of the Syndicate) to persuade Keynes to buy after they returned to London.[n] Vanessa became ill in Paris; none the less she told Keynes, 'Oh it was nice in Italy with you two – in spite of all my ill behaviour I don't think I've ever enjoyed anything so much for a long time'.[31]

Keynes divided his summer between London and Charleston. Most of July was spent in London, where he met Colonel House at the McKennas and saw other old acquaintances such as Felix Frankfurter and Paul Cravath as they passed through. There was also the Russian Ballet, which had a London season from 10 June to 30 July. Keynes went twice with Sebastian Sprott. On the second occasion, he gave a small farewell supper party for the conductor Ernst Ansermet. Finally there were meetings of the Tuesday Club to attend, as well as the meetings of that post-war Bloomsbury institution, the Memoir Club. August and September found him primarily at Charleston. He had taken his manuscript of *Probability* down with him and by 13 September he had sent 200 pages off for a second proof. In addition to *Probability*, he had started on 'a History of Money since Solon' which, although he

m This confusion reminds one of Churchill's confusing Isaiah and Irving Berlin, inviting the latter to lunch at 10 Downing Street and conversing with him in the mistaken belief he was Isaiah Berlin (Colville 1987, II, 91).
n Keynes had bought a Picasso in 1919 and would buy another in 1937. He bought his first Braque in 1922–3 and a later one in 1937 (Scrase and Croft 1983).

would never publish it, would keep him occupied on and off for years.º
This was the summer that Keynes insisted that Charleston run on its own
time, 'Charleston time' or one hour in advance of British summer time (not
to be repeated, and then not at Keynes's behest, until the Second World
War), much to the inconvenience of visitors such as Virginia Woolf and
Lytton Strachey. In her diary Virginia recorded her impression of Keynes:

> Went to Charleston for the night, and had a vivid sight of Maynard by
> lamplight – like a gorged seal, double chin, ledge of red lip, little eyes,
> sensual, brutal, unimaginative: one of those visions that come from a
> chance attitude, lost so soon as he turned his head. I suppose though
> it illustrates something I feel about him. Then he's read neither of my
> booksP – In spite of this I enjoyed myself32

About the same time Lytton also observed:

> The Pozzo has reverted to Cambridge almost completely, & is in
> consequence more benign & less self-assertive than has lately been
> the case. His Object in Life remains ambiguous.33

Charleston was closed up for the season on the weekend of 9 October.

During the autumn of 1920, Keynes kept on with *Probability*. He
restricted his journalism almost entirely to defending *Economic Consequences* against his critics, who also occupied a considerable amount of
his correspondence. September saw the publication of a major article
'The Peace of Versailles' in the popular American monthly *Everybody's
Magazine*. Keynes had written the piece with its reconsideration of the role
of the President the previous May. He defended his basic position, but his
comments on President Wilson show the benefit of some distancing:

> Yet I, at any rate, though I have tried to express what I saw, and am not
> shaken in my opinions by subsequent passage of events, would shrink
> from controversy with critics on so doubtful and perplexed an issue as
> the feelings and motives of an individual. I have put on record in my
> analysis of the President the impression produced on a single observer
> and I claim no more for it. I wrote in a moment of disappointment but,
> to the best of my ability, in a spirit of greater historical objectivity than
> some of my critics have given me credit for. Events themselves have
> surely shown that he was not wise, and even that he was deluded. But
> I do not forget that he, alone amongst the statesmen of Paris, sought
> ideal aims and sincerely pursued, throughout the conference, the future
> peace of the world as his supreme and governing purpose. Even in the

---

o The surviving fragments of the manuscript, which grew almost to the scale of a fellowship
  dissertation, are gathered together in *JMK*, XXVIII, ch. 2. Keynes announced his beginning
  of the history to Lytton Strachey in August (KCKP, JMK to GLS, 12 August 1920).
p *The Voyage Out* and *Night and Day*.

futile stubbornness of the past few months, an element of nobility has been present.[34]

Later in the autumn, in a review of Bernard Baruch's *The Making of the Reparation and Economic Sections of the Treaty*, Keynes caught the spirit of Wilson's appeal and the sources of subsequent disappointment:

> [Baruch] counts too low the significance of words – of words which he believes will be empty and of professions which are disingenuous. It is dangerous to treat the living word as dead. Words live not less than acts and sometimes longer. The war, it may almost be said, was fought for words. Our victory raised the prestige of words, and the terms we promised enthroned them. But it was as though with the expiring breath of Germany the curse which had destroyed her was inhaled by those who stood over her. The realism which taught that words were the tools of emperors, not their masters, has won after all, and the spirit which invaded Belgium triumphed in Paris.

The publication of the article in *Everybody's* coincided with more controversy, partly because *Everybody's* published 'The Treaty and its Critic' by André Tardieu in November. Tardieu accused Keynes of having supported the policies he attacked in his book and of arguing from the German point of view rather than the French. With his mother's help in checking some sources, Keynes had no trouble briefly dispatching those charges.[35] At the same time as Keynes's article, *The Saturday Evening Post* on 18 and 25 September published two articles by Alonzo E. Taylor on European and American reactions to Keynes's arguments. These calm, quiet articles, which suggested that Keynes had weakened his case by placing so much of the burdens of his remedies on France and the United States rather than on Britain, caused him more problems in the correspondence that ensued. He could, as he did, re-emphasise the positive doctrine of his book: 'the economic unity of Europe; bad faith on our part in the reparation clauses; and demands which were economically and financially impossible' and deplore his American commentators focusing on secondary issues: 'whether I am a disappointed man; whether I left Paris in a bad temper; whether my conduct in Paris was consistent with my conduct since; and whether in writing as I do I am unduly influenced by the interests of my own country';[36] but to state that the answers to such questions 'cannot be a matter of public interest' was pushing the matter too far. Obviously, he had failed with some readers, although perhaps at the 'cost' of attracting others. At the end of the year he had similar difficulties in reviewing the Baruch memoir of the making of reparations at the Conference: conceding 'that the President being what he was, and the Allied leaders being what they were, then in the situation that Mr. Baruch describes the result could not have been otherwise', although, as I have noted above, Keynes put more emphasis on the symbolic importance of words.[37]

There was *Probability* to finish. He kept at it through the spring of 1921. The last chapter was 'still worrying me to death' in mid-May,[38] but he sent it to Dan Macmillan on 22 May. The index followed a month later and the book appeared on 2 August. Keynes had asked Macmillan to publish it on the same terms as *Economic Consequences* because it allowed him to set the price below the profit maximising level and it saved argument over the allocation of the heavy costs for corrections.[39] As he worked on it he realised that it would be his last foray into the field. He put it in an earlier draft preface: 'For I shall write no more philosophy having at the age of thirty-seven reached a time of life when the brain relents and easier subjects recommend themselves'.[40] Just before publication he wrote to John Venn, the author of the last systematic treatise on the logic of probability whose first edition had appeared 55 years earlier, saying that a copy of 'the latest link in the very continuous chain . . . of Cambridge thought' was coming.[41] As if to emphasise that continuity, Venn replied that Keynes's letter

> brought back recollections of the far past: – when Prof^r Fawcett told me that there was a promising young scholar at Pembroke, whom the authorities wanted to keep to Mathematics, but who had a real taste for the Moral Sciences: – could I look after him. As you know, the young scholar [J. N. Keynes] was one of my early encouragements in the work of starting lectures in a new department.

On its appearance the book was widely, and generally favourably, reviewed. Bertrand Russell, who had previewed some of Keynes's ideas as long ago as 1912 in his *The Problems of Philosophy* regarded it as 'one which it is impossible to praise too highly'.[42] C. D. Broad, who recalled reading proofs of it with Russell in the summer of 1914, regarded it as 'the best treatise on the logical foundations of the subject', while Harold Jeffreys recommended it to 'every student of science who aims at a real understanding of the subject'.[43] The criticisms ranged from the less serious, although irritating, of Keynes's almost Freudian failure to give Whitehead credit for Russell and Whitehead's *Principia Mathematica* to the more serious.[44] Keynes himself also discussed the book in correspondence with Broad, Jean Nicod and Léon Bachelier during 1922 and 1923.

In these discussions a new philosophical force appeared on the Cambridge scene, Frank Ramsey. At this stage he was a Trinity undergraduate, 'still an infant, aged about 18, and cannot remember before the war'. Keynes regarded this Apostle, 'mathematical friend' as 'certainly far and away the most brilliant undergraduate who has appeared for many years in the border-country between Philosophy and Economics'.[45] In 1924, aged 21, he would become a fellow of King's, where he remained until his tragic death in 1930. As Keynes told Broad,

Ramsey and the other young men at Cambridge are quite obdurate, and still believe that *either* Probability is a definitely measurable entity, precisely connected with Frequency, *or* is of merely psychological importance and is definitely non-logical. I recognise that they can raise some very damaging criticisms against me on these lines. But all the same, I feel great confidence that they are wrong. However, we shall never have the matter properly cleared up until a big advance has been made in the treatment of Probability in relation to the theory of Epistemology as a whole.[46]

Four years later, as he was arranging to see his German translator, F. M. Urban, in the course of a visit to Berlin, he continued in a similar vein.

Among those students in England for whose opinion I feel most respect I find a marked reluctance against abandoning some variant of the frequency theory. They admit that my criticisms hold good on the existing version, and they are not yet ready to prepare a version which can resist them. But they maintain all the same that they have a strong instinct that some kind of a frequency theory will be found in the end to be more fundamental to the whole conception of Probability than I have allowed. I shall not be surprised if they prove [to be] right. I suspect, however, that the first step forward will have to come through progress being made with the partly psychological subject of vague knowledge, and that further developments in a strictly logical field must await for a clear distinction between logical probability proper and the theory of what I have called vague knowledge.[47]

By then, Ramsey was close to the ideas of 'Truth and Probability' (1926) which criticised Keynes's theory of probability and laid down part of the foundations of the modern, subjectivist, theory which allowed probability to be treated in a frequentist manner. When that essay appeared posthumously in 1931,[48] Keynes reviewed the volume containing it for *The New Statesman and Nation*. In a brief, packed paragraph Keynes referred to Ramsey's criticism of his work.

[H]e was led to consider 'human logic' as distinguished from 'formal logic'. Formal logic is concerned with nothing but the rules of *consistent* thought. But in addition to this we have certain 'useful mental habits' for handling the material with which we are supplied by our perceptions and by our memory and perhaps in other ways, and so arriving at or towards truth; and the analysis of such habits of thought is also a sort of logic. The application of these ideas to the logic of probability is very fruitful. Ramsey argues, as against the view which I put forward, that probability is concerned not with objective relations between propositions but (in some sense) with degrees of belief, and he succeeds in showing that the calculus of probability simply amounts to a set of rules for ensuring that the system of degrees of belief which we hold shall be a *consistent* system. Thus the calculus of probabilities belongs to formal logic. But the basis of our degrees of belief – or the *a priori* probabilities, as they used to be called – is part of our human outfit, perhaps given us by natural selection, analogous to our perceptions and our memories rather than to formal logic. So far I yield to Ramsey – I think he is right. But in attempting to distinguish 'rational' degrees of belief from belief in general he was not yet, I think, quite successful. It is not getting to the bottom of the principle of induction merely to say it is a useful mental habit. Yet in attempting to distinguish 'human logic' from formal logic on the one hand and descriptive psychology on the other, Ramsey may have been pointing the way to the next field of study when formal logic has been put into good order and its highly limited scope properly defined.[49]

Whether these remarks represented Keynes's abandonment of the logical conception of probability so central to *Probability*, the traditional view, has been a subject of debate between B. W. Bateman and R. O'Donnell.[50] (Anna Carabelli, with her different conception of Keynes's early thought, is not a participant in this particular discussion.) As the evidence for both sides in this debate all derives from Keynes's writings of the 1930s, I shall return to it in Chapter 23.

NOTES

1 For an affectionate portrait of Falk, see Davenport 1974, 44–7.
2 KCKP, JMK to FAK, 3 and 23 September 1919.
3 Keynes had started speculating for Blackett early in 1920.
4 NWL, JMK to Vanessa Bell, 22 May, 1920.
5 *JMK*, XII, 6–8.
6 KCKP, Box 5a, Macaulay to JMK, 5 May 1919. For JMK's obituary notice of Macaulay see *JMK*, X, 351–7.
7 KCKP, Box 5a, JMK to Macaulay, 17 May 1919.
8 Wilkinson 1980a, 110, 174 n. 15; Boys Smith 1983, ch. 11.
9 Robinson 1947, 20.
10 Comment in Moggridge (ed.) 1974, 99–100.
11 Boys Smith 1983, 21.
12 Martin 1969a, 103.
13 KCKP, Address to The Dinner, 21 June 1921.
14 KCKP, JMK to R. H. Brand, 30 December 1919.
15 *JMK*, X, 428–9.
16 *JMK*, XVII, 130–6.
17 Harrod 1951, 254.
18 *JMK*, III, 2–4.
19 The best sources for the relevant statistics are Pigou 1947 and Dowie 1975.
20 *JMK*, XVII, 179.
21 On the replies, see Howson 1974, 1975. Chamberlain's letter appears in *JMK*, XVII, 180.

22 *JMK*, XVII, 181.
23 *JMK*, XVII, 183–4.
24 Howson 1974, 104.
25 KCKP, Blackett to JMK, 30 March, 1 and 9 September 1920; *JMK*, XVII, 189–93.
26 Ibid., 184–5.
27 Keynes's 1942 statement from (PRO T172/1384) appears in *JMK*, XVII, 185–6 and in Howson 1973. A similar statement to Richard Kahn appears in Moggridge and Howson 1974, 231.
28 KCKP, JMK to JNK, 15 April 1920; KCCP, VBRF 301, 11 April 1920.
29 KCCP, VBRF 303, 29 April, 1920. Compare Spalding 1983, 185, who suggests on the basis of VBRF 302 of 19 April that Vanessa and Duncan only went for the last two days.
30 KCCP, VBFR 303, 29 April 1920.
31 KCKP, JMK to VB, 17 May 1920; KCCP, VBMK29, 15 May 1920.
32 VWD, II, 69. For the Strachey comments on Charleston time see Holroyd 1971, 805.
33 BL, ADD.60712, GLS to James Strachey, 10 September 1920.
34 *JMK*, XVII, 56–7.
35 *JMK*, XVII, 79–80.
36 *JMK*, XVII, 88.
37 *JMK*, XVII, 97.
38 NUL, JMK to VB, 13 May 1921.
39 KCKP, TP1/2, JMK to Dan Macmillan, 19 March 1921.
40 KCKP, TP6/2. In the draft, the words 'at the age of thirty seven' are crossed out.
41 KCKP, TP1/2, JMK to J. Venn, 31 July 1921.
42 Russell 1922, 125.
43 Broad 1922, 72; Jeffreys 1922, 133.
44 A full collection of reviews is in KCKP, TP/3.
45 KCKP, TP1/1, JMK to C. D. Broad, 4 February 1922; 31 January 1922.
46 Ibid.
47 KCKP, TP1/2, JMK to F. M. Urban, 15 May 1926.
48 See Ramsey 1931 and Ramsey 1978.
49 *JMK*, X, 338–9.
50 See Bateman 1987, 1990; O'Donnell 1989, ch. 7; 1990. Others have taken views similar to O'Donnell's that Keynes did not abandon the approach of *Probability*, but his is the best documented.

15

REPARATIONS
AND JOURNALISM

In 1921 Keynes began a supplementary career which he would pursue until the mid-1930s, that of a journalist. The background to this career, which would become extremely lucrative, lay in the series of meetings between European premiers and their officials to sort out the unfinished business of the Peace treaties. Between 1920 and 1922 there were over twenty such meetings. As 1920 progressed, these meetings spent more and more time on the reparations issue, which the Treaty had left unclear in several ways. For example, the size of Germany's ultimate liability for reparations required a decision by the Reparation Commission. Also, although Germany had to provide a payment of £1,000 million in cash or kind before 1 May 1921, there were the problems of devising a scheme for the payment of Germany's remaining liabilities under the Treaty, of devising the means and channels whereby the payments might be made, and, given that Germany's payments would be less than her potential liabilities under the Treaty, of settling the distribution of payments. By the end of 1920, the premiers had agreed on the distribution of reparations and on a scheme for ensuring coal deliveries to France until the end of January 1921. A conference of experts meeting in Brussels in December 1920 had come up with a proposal for reparations payments over the ensuing five years which allowed for a considerable proportion of the sums involved to be paid in kind. The Brussels scheme also made suggestions about improving German finances and about enforcing payment in case of a German default.

These suggestions, along with the decisions taken at Boulogne in June 1920 as to the ultimate size of the German payments up to 1963, were the subject of further discussion in Paris at the end of January 1921. Once the results of the Paris Conference were known, C. P. Scott of the *Manchester Guardian*, which had become something of the liberal conscience on such matters, asked Keynes for a signed article. He responded within 24 hours on 30 January with a piece that 'delighted' Scott.[1] The article was extremely critical of the scheme whereby Germany would make a series of payments of £100 million a year in the first two years, rising to £300 million after 11 years, where they remained for another 31 years, *plus* the equivalent of 12 per cent of her export earnings. In case of default, the scheme allowed the Reparation Commission to intervene in the conduct of Germany's public finances.

Soon after this first experience of journalism, Keynes started to take the idea of further excursions more seriously. Just over a week later, in the course of negotiations for Lytton Strachey's move from the publishers Putnam to Harcourt Brace for his new book *Queen Victoria*,[a] he asked Alfred Harcourt about placing future articles in the American press. At this stage he was thinking of articles 'about questions arising from the peace treaty or reparation, about the foreign exchanges, or about such general financial and economic topics as the present industrial depression . . . of a type intended for the general reader'.[2] By the spring of 1921 he was placing most of his articles overseas as well as in Britain. The next year would see even more elaborate arrangements as his relationship with the *Manchester Guardian* developed.

In 1921 the occasions for Keynes's journalistic forays tended to be the successive stages in the reparations saga: Germany's counter-proposals to the Paris scheme made at the London Conference at the beginning of March; the subsequent Allied ultimatum; the French statement of intent over the occupation of the Ruhr; the Reparation Commission's decision as to Germany's liabilities under the Treaty; and the Allied reparation scheme presented as an ultimatum at the second London Conference in May. The highlight of his journalistic output in 1921 was a series of five widely syndicated articles for *The Sunday Times* which appeared between 21 August and 18 September under the title 'Europe's Economic Outlook'. Keynes had been asked to do the articles in May, but, despite the temptations of £600 for a week's work, he was determined to put them off until he was through with *Probability*.[3] The articles dealt with Germany's ability to pay the new, imposed, reparations settlement; the effects of the settlement on world trade; the causes of the current depression; the prospects for wages and the settlement of war debts. At the end of the year, Keynes was to use the reparations articles in his sequel to *Economic Consequences – A Revision of the Treaty*, which appeared in January 1922. I shall take the articles and the book together before turning to Keynes's views on the 1920–1 recession and the prospects for wages.

a The terms agreed with Harcourt Brace offered Strachey $10,000 for the American and Canadian rights, including serial rights. This compared with his 20 per cent royalty from Putnam for *Eminent Victorians*, which had amounted to £700 on immediate post-publication sales. Keynes advised acceptance on grounds of certainty. As *Queen Victoria* was very successful, this advice cost Strachey and his estate substantial sums. But this is with hindsight. At the current rate of exchange the new arrangement offered him before publication almost four times his early income from *Eminent Victorians*, and such a sum when invested would yield a substantial annual income. Anyway, as Keynes pointed out after the book had been a great success, 'Your best revenge will be to write a very bad book and sell it to him for $20,000.' (Holroyd 1967, 806–8; KCKP, JMK to GLS, 29 October, 3 and 9 November 1920, 28 August 1921; GLS to JMK, 20 October, 5 and 11 November and 27 December 1920 and subsequent correspondence.)

A Revision of the Treaty was a much less impassioned book than *Economic Consequences*. After eighteen months of controversy, it also contained a clearer statement of Keynes's views of the role of public opinion in politics. As he saw it, reform and change were the products of discussion through which public opinion was formed and guided. The political élite of senior politicians, civil servants and 'higher' journalists was open to two influences: rational persuasion and public opinion. It was privy to its own 'inner opinion' expressed 'upstairs, backstairs and behind-stairs' as to what was feasible and desirable.[4] In public speeches, newspaper articles and other forms of comment, however, the political leadership and 'higher' journalists formed an important part of what was taken as 'outer' or public opinion. Although in a democracy the élite was ultimately subject to public opinion, through its own links with that opinion it could significantly shape it. To Keynes, one of the duties of the élite was to prevent too wide a gap appearing between inner and outer opinion on any issue – if the gap became too wide, as it had over the treatment of Germany in 1918–19, the process of returning to sensible or feasible proposals could be lengthy and costly.

There was another complication. Outside public opinion was never as dogmatic or definite as it appeared in the press. For ordinary people there was always an element of doubt which left their views vulnerable to changing events. It also left them open to persuasion. With such a view of human behaviour – one not surprising for the author of *A Treatise on Probability* – Keynes saw persuasion as encouraging the articulation of outside opinion as well as altering the views of the élite. Thus his own exercises played a dual role: they removed and undermined old habits of thought or prejudices, highlighted likely trends and generally prepared the ground amongst the public at large; so that the élite, once persuaded, could successfully lead rather than follow.

In such a scheme of things, meetings with officials, ministers and MPs, public speeches, articles in the quality and popular press each had their role. In the early 1920s, Keynes was only beginning to learn how to use them to maximum advantage – although no one could deny that over the Peace Treaty he had not been successful. By the outbreak of the Second World War, he would be much more skilled – and perhaps more immediately successful. But the opening chapter of *A Revision of the Treaty* sets out his view of the process and of his perceptions of his role more clearly than his other published writings. Despite its consistency with *Probability*, most recent commentators on the book have not developed the point.[5]

Keynes's reparations journalism of 1921 and *Revision* shared several characteristics. First, he was even-handed in dealing with stupidity: silly German counterproposals, such as those in March 1921 in response to those of the Allies at Paris, were dealt with as sharply as those which came from the Allies. Second, he continued to maintain that the reparation proposals in place at the time, including those accepted by Germany in London in May

1921 (2 billion gold marks per annum, plus sums equivalent to 25 per cent of the value of her exports) were unrealistic for the near future and probably over the longer term. Here he used two main arguments: the difficulty of transferring the sums involved and the relationship between the annual payments and German per capita incomes.[b] (The third argument he used as Germany fell into hyperinflation: that the current German Budget could not cover reparation payments and Germany's attempt to pay reparations would therefore increase the existing budgetary disequilibrium and inflationary use of the printing press to cover government expenditures.) Finally, he continued to argue for the cancellation of war debts, partly because he did not believe that they would ever be paid and partly because he believed that removing them would provide a basis for lower reparations demands.

The articles and the book were both overly self-congratulatory. It was flattering to be proved right about such things as the size of Germany's liability under the Treaty, German production of hard coal in 1920, or the value of specific deliveries in kind from Germany, but on occasion Keynes was grasping at straws – providing marvellous ammunition for later critics such as Etienne Mantoux, who seized it with glee.

A Revision of the Treaty and the related journalism also show Keynes beginning to display a more vigorous and less mannered prose style. Thus:

> The thought of the two Prime Ministers in Paris, muddling over silly formulas, with M. Loucheur buzzing about between them – formulas which they all know to be silly – is, for anyone who realises what it is like, a thought of a gibbering nightmare.
>
> *(JMK, XVII, 212)*

Or:

> My complaint against M. Poincaré is that, without himself producing any fact or argument worthy of the name, he makes it a test of friendship to France that one should entertain on questions of fact beliefs which are now recognised to be erroneous in every country in the world outside of France.
>
> *(JMK, XVII, 288)*

Keynes had originally suggested to Harcourt Brace a second edition of *Economic Consequences*. Alfred Harcourt discouraged him, asking Keynes

---

b In making his estimate of German national income in both the *Sunday Times* and *A Revision of the Treaty* (*JMK*, XVII, 247–8; III, 55–8), Keynes managed to produce striking and absurd figures through an arithmetic slip. To convert national income in gold marks to paper marks he used a multiplier of 8; yet, when he was working out reparations in paper marks and converting post-reparations, post-tax income back into sterling he used a multiplier of 20. He thus ended up with German per capita income in sterling of £12 10s. per annum gross and £5 10s. net of taxes and reparations. His exercise was further flawed by double counting in his favour, as there is no need to deduct government spending from national income.

to 'give something near to prayerful consideration to making a new book' for he thought that Keynes would write a better book freed from the constraints of his earlier work and that a new book would be a greater commercial success. Keynes agreed and sent a draft table of contents for 'Essays Supplementary to *The Economic Consequences of the Peace*' on 3 August. Correspondence continued until 2 November, when Keynes sent Donald Brace, Alfred Harcourt's partner, a table of contents of *A Revision of the Treaty: Being a Sequel to Economic Consequences of the Peace* that follows the lines eventually published.

Putting the new book together was a rush. On Boxing Day 1921, from Tidmarsh where he had spent Christmas with Lytton and Sebastian and read parts of the book to the assembled company, he told his mother:

> In great haste I finished off the last chapter and despatched it to the printer before Christmas. I shall get the proof back tomorrow and so hope to have the whole thing printed off and the binders got to work by the New Year. But the last chapter is decidedly hurried and I should have much preferred to revise it at leisure. However at the present juncture prompt publication seems to me very important.[6]

Back in London six days later he continued:

> By Herculean efforts the book is finished and printed off, and the sheets were despatched to the binder on Saturday morning [31 December].*
> I had no opportunity to sleep over some parts of the last chapter, which is always dangerous, and the final correction had to be made by telegram. But on the whole I am rather satisfied with the last chapter . . . .
> * The book even has an index.

The book was not another *Economic Consequences*, but on the day he wrote the last words Keynes thought it 'honourable and workmanlike, but not sensational'.[7] The first English printing of 10,000 appeared in the bookshops on 10 January 1922. A reprint was ordered in February, but by July, when Keynes authorised the distribution of the type, sales had only amounted to 6,839 copies. Perhaps, as he suggested to Lytton in September, this was his equivalent of 'a very bad book'.[8]

Reparations and Treaty revision were not the only subjects Keynes addressed in his *Sunday Times* articles. In one of them, he turned to the causes of the depression which had started with the sharp rise in Bank rate in April 1920 and continued for over a year, bringing output, prices and money wages in England tumbling down from their early post-war peaks and pushing unemployment to a peak of 18 per cent in December 1921. In the other the subject was the earnings of labour. These were new subjects for Keynes.

Especially on the former, many of his views were to change considerably as his thinking developed.

Keynes's explanation of the 1919–21 boom and slump was straight-forward.[9] At the end of the war, when markets at home and overseas had been starved of supplies, dealers needed to rebuild stocks. At the time, Government finance was inflationary. There were severe shortages. In the circumstances, merchants and other middlemen, whose forecasts and consequent orders Keynes took as the mainsprings of the fluctuations of the credit cycle, were set a difficult problem. Not only had they to forecast the demands of consumers but they had also to forecast the level of prices. In 1919, owing to the exigencies of inflationary finance superimposed on the trade boom, this was difficult. The trend *seemed* upwards: wholesale prices in Britain were rising by an unprecedented 4 per cent per month. The level of final demand was also difficult to forecast: with low producer stocks and post-war shortages, many merchants were over-ordering in the hope of getting something like their normal requirements. They were entering into commitments well beyond the likely post-war level of consumption at prices which even the inflated post-war currencies of the world could not support if the goods came into existence. When Bank rate reached 7 per cent in the spring of 1920 and overseas markets collapsed, the whole process was reversed: previously optimistic merchants who had been badly burned by the collapse in orders now held off from further purchases and production fell far below the rate of current consumption.

Thus 'the psychology and miscalculations of traders' lay at the heart of Keynes's explanation. Such a story fitted in well with Marshall's. But its extreme emphasis on traders' decisions was more characteristic of the views of Keynes's former Treasury colleague, R. G. Hawtrey. Keynes had reviewed his *Currency and Credit* (1919) in the *Economic Journal* for September 1920, calling it 'one of the most original and profound treatises on the theory of money which has appeared for many years'.[10] Keynes's cure for the cycle was typically Marshallian with a twist of Hawtrey. The authorities, through the use of Bank rate, could 'damp down their [merchants'] ill-judged enthusiasm' on the upswing and provide 'the encouragement of which cheap money can give them' on the downswing as they alternatively overvalued and undervalued goods against money. Such a policy required the authorities to change rates early in the process of inflation or deflation. In 1919–20 rates had been raised far too late in the day and then kept too high for too long.

Keynes's discussion of the 'Earnings of Labour'[11] was less satisfactory. He did not have a well-developed theory of distribution. His explanation for the rise in real wages after 1918 to above pre-war levels for those in employment rested almost completely on *ad hoc* factors: the inflationary windfall profits of entrepreneurs, government policies to improve civilian 'morale' and a somewhat mysterious process whereby past savings were transformed into income. Dennis Robertson took him to task over this last, rightly perceiving a confusion between stocks and flows. Keynes also seemed to lack any sensitivity to working-class psychology, as he was told by Robertson and the left.[12] How else could one explain the following statement:

> It is worth while to add that in all countries the usual index numbers tend to exaggerate the increase in the cost of living (and consequently to understate the improvement in the labourer's real reward per unit of production), since they cannot make adequate allowance for the fact that, as prices do not all rise equally, every housewife can suffer less than the average increase by shifting her purchases from those articles of which the price has risen more than the average, to those of which it has risen less.[13]

To him the working class was much more of an abstraction than the capitalist or the rentier. There was, as well, an apparent belief that labour would just have to accept what trickled down to it from such growth as occurred. In part this reflected the view, first expressed in *Economic Consequences*, that capital accumulation was at the heart of economic progress and that, as post-war circumstances were less favourable towards saving, accumulation would be less rapid than it had been before the war. As population was still growing, and assuming that a larger labour force needed more capital equipment, one can understand Keynes's pessimism and even his Malthusianism. But the argument was not fully developed in the article. Robertson accurately characterised Keynes's 'summary of a "Liberal" economic policy as not only very *jejune* on its domestic side ... but almost as divorced from reality as (say) the constructions of Mr [G. D. H.] Cole'.[14]

In July 1921, at the instigation of Edwin Montagu, Secretary of State for India, Keynes was asked if he would be willing to serve as vice-chairman of a Royal Commission on Indian tariffs. At first, he was anxious to accept. He was attracted by the possibility that he might 'save India for modified Free Trade'. (The Viceroy, Lord Reading, was anxious to have him in that role.) But Keynes foresaw problems. First, he would have to be absent from England for an extended period and there would be a consequent loss of earnings which he conservatively estimated at £500 for three months. There was also the problem of arranging schedules so that he could match a three months' visit to India (the maximum he believed he could be away) with the proposed schedule of the Commission. However, he thought that he could manage three months from the middle of January 1922.[15] The India Office was accommodating: in addition to normal travelling expenses and subsistence allowance, they agreed to provide £500 in compensation for lost earnings. Thus his name was among those announced as commissioners, along with their terms of reference, on 7 October.[16]

Almost immediately a complication arose. C. P. Scott had been trying to get Keynes to do more for the *Manchester Guardian*. He had already proposed in September that Keynes go to Washington as special correspondent for the forthcoming disarmament conference. On 12 October the two met in London and Scott suggested that Keynes edit a substantial series of supplements to the *Manchester Guardian Commercial* surveying the economic and financial problems and prospects of post-war Europe. The supplements would be published in English, French, German, Italian and Spanish. The proposal looked extremely remunerative: Keynes's suggestion was an editorial fee of £200 per issue plus fees for individual articles he might write. After a further discussion with Scott in Manchester on 25 October, they came to terms. Keynes reported to Vanessa that these would give him 'an enormous income next year': he later estimated that combined with his other earnings it would be £8,000.[17] He gave some thought to the supplements while finishing off *Revision*, taking advantage of the December visit to London of the German Foreign Minister, Walther Rathenau to discuss the project, but the book took precedence until the end of the year. By year's end he was making his travel arrangements for India: he planned to leave for Paris on 27 or 28 January and to sail from Venice aboard the SS *Tevere* on 2 February 1922 – 'unless at the last moment there is some longed-for miracle by which I can slip out of the whole thing'.[18]

Once the book was out of the way, he approached Melchior in January for substantial assistance in organising German contributions to the *Manchester Guardian* Supplements. Melchior agreed and Keynes paid a flying visit to Amsterdam on 14 January to discuss details. In France his collaborator was Paul Franck, the translator of *Economic Consequences* and *Revision*, while for Russia Keynes worked closely with Arthur Ransome (now better known as the author of *Swallows and Amazons*), the *Guardian*'s Russian specialist, well-acquainted with the leaders of the revolution.

In the first three weeks of January Keynes's plans for the Supplements went forward on the assumption that he was off to India at the end of the month, even though he spoke of agreeing to go 'in a moment of imprudence'.[19] On 21 January, however, he saw Edwin Montagu and resigned from the Indian Fiscal Commission. He could have found better grounds for resigning if he had waited a day or two, for a telegram despatched from the Viceroy on 18 January had asked if Keynes would extend his stay in India until the end of May, as the Commission had changed its schedule. Keynes felt somewhat guilty over letting Montagu down.[20] It is unlikely that the pressures associated with combining the Indian commission with the *Manchester Guardian* Supplements were the main grounds for his resignation. Another complication had arisen, one most succinctly implied in a marginal note opposite 7 January 1922 in his appointments book: 'Lydia 10 weeks'.c

In 1922, without the prospect of the India visit and with Lydia Lopokova now an important factor in his life,d Keynes settled down to the *Manchester Guardian* Commercial Supplements. He was working towards bringing the first issue out in April and he had to have final copy three weeks before. Settling the production details, including the artwork, was a time-consuming business, as was organising the contributors. April was an attractive target date, for yet another international conference had been fixed for Genoa that month. The brainchild of Lloyd George, its subject was European economic reconstruction and the restoration of political harmony: the Peace Treaties and reparations were not on the agenda in the hope, ultimately fruitless, of gaining American participation. This gathering of representatives from thirty-nine nations, including for the first time since the revolution the USSR, raised hopes in many breasts. The Conference was to open on 10 April. The first Supplement eventually appeared on 20 April.

Preparing the Supplements for Genoa, Keynes decided to change their order to make the foreign exchanges the first subject instead of shipping. This meant that he had additional articles to write, for there were three contributions from his pen in that issue: 'The Stabilisation of the European Exchanges', 'The Theory of the Exchanges and Purchasing Power Parity', and 'The Forward Market in Foreign Exchanges'. The last two would appear, in a slightly reworked form, in his *Tract on Monetary Reform* (1923).[21] Meanwhile, contributions began to arrive and problems continued to arise, especially in France where the Supplements and their French contributors became a matter of domestic political controversy. None the less, he managed an impressive list of contributors including Asquith, Basil Blackett, Joseph Caillaux, Lord Robert Cecil, Paul Cravath, Benedetto Croce, O. T. Falk, Samuel Gompers, Maxim Gorki, Walter Lippmann, Carl Melchior, Francesco Nitti, Vittorio Emanuele Orlando, Piero Sraffa, and Dudley Ward, as well as the doyens of Continental professional economics – Andréadès, Cassel, Einaudi and Gide. The twelve Supplements, which made up a substantial volume, eventually included thirteen articles from Keynes's pen. Running through to January 1923, they were an immense critical success and, even if they fell short of the *Guardian*'s financial

c Chandavarkar (1990, 50) takes Harrod to task for suggesting that Keynes's resignation from the Fiscal Commission had something to do with his growing attachment to Lydia. He cannot see how Lydia's charm could have been allowed 'to override matters of state and to prevent acceptance of the singular intellectual challenge that the Vice-Presidency [*sic*] of the Indian Fiscal Commission represented'. Yet, if this was not the case, why did he resign *before* receiving the Viceroy's telegram, which, as the subsequent correspondence demonstrates, provided him with sufficient grounds for resignation, especially as his correspondence makes clear that he was looking for a suitable excuse?

d For the development of their relationship, see Chapter 16 below.

expectations, the editor C. P. Scott and his son were very pleased with the overall results.

Keynes's connection with the *Guardian* became even closer when he went to Genoa as the newspaper's special correspondent. He managed to syndicate his *Guardian* articles to the *Daily Express* of London, the New York *World* and its American syndicate, *L'Ère Nouvelle*, *Corriere della Sera* of Milan, *Berliner Tageblatt*, *Präger Presse*, *Neue Freie Press* of Vienna, *Algemeen Handelsblad* of Amsterdam, and *Dagens Nyheter* of Stockholm. Keynes was a very well connected correspondent: he had met almost all the financial experts at the Conference either in the course of his Treasury service or in Amsterdam in 1919 and his political connections were also extensive.

With the Supplements delayed until 20 April, the *Manchester Guardian* published Keynes's proposals for European exchange stabilisation in its regular columns on 6 April. Before publication he passed the article to Sir Robert Horne, the Chancellor of the Exchequer, who later received an advance copy of the first Supplement – with the result that Keynes was asked to attend several meetings of the British delegation at Genoa.[22] 'The Stabilisation of the European Exchanges: A Plan for Genoa'[23] proposed that the principal European currencies – sterling; the Swiss, French and Belgian francs; the Italian lira; the Swedish, Norwegian and Danish krone; the Dutch florin; the Spanish peseta and the Czech crown – stabilise against gold. Other countries could join the scheme at a later date. The rates suggested for stabilisation were related to current market rates rather than pre-war parities. Countries whose rates were at a discount from pre-war par could appreciate their exchange rates by half a per cent per month if they desired. In all cases, national gold reserves would not be available for internal circulation and would find use only for exchange support with the minimum quantity available being of the order of £50,000. To protect the gold reserves of the stabilising countries, Keynes suggested that the authorities widen the gap between the central bank buying and selling prices to 5 per cent.[e] This measure of exchange fluctuations would allow the central banks to bear the brunt of seasonal or other temporary fluctuations in confidence.[f] Finally, a further buttress for the scheme was Keynes's proposal that for a period of five years the Federal Reserve System stand ready to make temporary loans of gold to the participating countries, such loans to be guaranteed by the participating central banks. This was the first of many 'Keynes Plans' for the international monetary system: like many of its successors, it fell flat. Nevertheless, it showed where many of his later priorities would lie: a modicum of exchange stability to foster international trade and investment;

e The pre-1914 gap between the Bank of England's buying and selling prices had been ¹⁶/₁₀₀ of 1 per cent.

f It also meant that with the ½ per cent per month provision for appreciation that the proposal took on the characteristics of what in the 1960s would be reinvented as the crawling peg and band proposal.

avoidance of deflationary policies to improve exchange rates, given their implications for debtors and wage-earners; gold reserves for use not show. Finally, there was a preference for simplicity, for a minimum of machinery so as not to hinder immediate adoption by sensible policymakers.

Keynes left London for Paris on 8 April 1922. His party for Genoa consisted of himself, his secretary W. H. Haslam, who was also acting as correspondent for *The Economist*, and a stenographer. They set themselves up where the British Delegation was staying – at the Miramare Hotel in Santa Margherita Ligure about 20 miles south of Genoa. Soon after his arrival Keynes saw the Chancellor of the Exchequer and he met him and his officials to decide whether the stabilisation proposals should go before the full Conference. In the end, 'because of the weight of conservative opinion against Great Britain coming into any scheme', they decided no. Keynes saw this decision as 'intelligible but deplorable'.[24] He continued to join the British delegation in many of its unofficial financial discussions and joined another formal meeting with the Chancellor and his aides to discuss his own proposals for improving the operation of the foreign exchange market – proposals which made their way into the Conference's recommendations: the Genoa Resolutions on Currency.

From the notes kept by Haslam,[25] he also appears to have had easy access to other delegations: he saw Melchior on several occasions, alone as well as with Wilhelm Cuno, the head of the Hamburg-America Line and a future Premier of Germany; also Joseph Wirth, the German Chancellor; Carl Bergmann, the Finance Minister; Walther Rathenau, the Foreign Minister; and Rudolph Havenstein, the President of the Reichsbank on more than one occasion. He was, in fact, sufficiently close to the German delegation to be photographed with them. On 13 April he met Georgi Chicherin, the Soviet Foreign Minister, and, after the Soviet-German agreement at Rapallo on 16 April cancelling war debts and other claims and re-establishing diplomatic relations, Lloyd George called Keynes in to report on a further conversation with Chicherin on the day of the agreement.

In the three weeks that Keynes stayed at Genoa, he provided the *Manchester Guardian* with twelve articles.[26] These ranged from set pieces on the Conference and its Commissions, through reports on such developments as the German–Soviet Treaty of Rapallo and the progress of various proposals under discussion, to two articles on the Soviet financial system, where he utilised information gleaned from the Russian economist Evgeni Preobrazhensky. According to his reports to Lydia,[g] he was particularly proud of his first Soviet article 'The Financial System of the Bolsheviks',

g Although on Maynard's side a complete run has not survived, from Lydia's letters to Maynard it would appear that while Maynard was at Genoa the two began the practice that was to continue until Maynard's death 24 years later – a regular letter each day they were apart. Those that have survived are a gold mine for the biographer – as well as students of other subjects.

which he called 'the most interesting I have written so far'.[27] From the published articles, it is clear that he did not expect much from this 'international menagerie' with its 'spectacle of thirty nations, classified into their separate species of statesmen, experts and secretaries, assembled round green baize in polyglot multitude ... an epitome of the vanities and divisions of mankind'.[28] It lacked the necessary intellectual groundwork among a few important powers. Instead, he expected and the Conference delivered, when it could agree, a series of platitudes. He was particularly disappointed with the work of the Financial Commission, whose experts 'could hardly be surpassed in collective experience and intellectual power' but whose chief efforts 'in a bored and languid spirit ... have been devoted to getting through the business with a measure of intellectual self-respect and without appearing too obviously futile'. The result was 'academically respectable' but suggested that 'the time is not ripe to do anything in particular'.[29] As regards the Soviet Union, he recorded that 'never ... at any conference has the intellectual standard fallen so low'. Not surprisingly Keynes left Genoa on 4 May, at the end of his contracted three weeks for the *Guardian*.[30] The Conference continued for another fortnight.

After his return from Genoa, Keynes remained extremely active. He managed a brief holiday with Lydia late in June at Lindisfarne Castle, O. T. Falk's recently purchased country house in Northumberland, and a longer break in September with Lydia at Oare in Wiltshire where, the Charlestonians proving unwelcoming, he had taken a holiday house. But the continuing claim on his time was the remaining ten Reconstruction Supplements which he did not complete until late December 1922. These involved the usual organisation and editing, and another ten articles from his pen. He also became deeply involved in Germany and her problems, first as one of seven independent financial experts called in by the German Government to advise on the stabilisation of the mark, and later as an unofficial adviser to the British Government on war debts and reparations. By the end of the year, he could write to his mother 'I have been in rather close touch lately with him [Bonar Law] and the new Chancellor of the Exchequer [Stanley Baldwin] and have been talking with them almost as in old Treasury days'.[31] Finally, he started to become more involved than he had for several years in Liberal Party politics, notably in the Liberal Summer School movement.

The state of the German mark had provided one text for Keynes's sermon on inflation in *Economic Consequences*. In March 1921, he was predicting that the beginning of reparations payments would lead to a collapse of the mark and its supersession by a new currency unit, but for the rest of the year he made little comment – although he took some speculative profits as the mark lost two-thirds of its value.[32] By August 1922, when he travelled to Hamburg to address a World Economic Congress during Hamburg's Overseas Week, he could report that:

The prices in the shops change every hour. No one knows what his week's wages will be at the end of the week. The mark is at the same time valueless and scarce. On the one hand the shops do not want to receive marks, and some are unwilling to sell at any price at all. On the other hand, in Hamburg yesterday [27 August] the banks were so short of ready cash that the Reichsbank advised them to cash no cheques for more than 10,000 marks (about one pound sterling),[h] and some of the biggest institutions were unable to cash their customers' cheques for payment of weekly wages. The public is pessimistic and depressed and has lost all confidence.[33]

When he reached Berlin in November as a member of the Committee of Experts, the mark had fallen to over 26,000 to the pound. The other experts were Gustav Cassel, R. H. Brand, G. Vissering, Professor J. H. Jenks of Cornell University in upstate New York, Leopold Dubois, a Swiss banker, and B. Kamenka. Although the experts were unable to agree, the majority (Keynes, Brand, Cassel and Jenks) argued that stabilisation of the mark was possible under three conditions: a moratorium for at least two years in respect of Germany's Versailles obligations; some modest international support; and a balanced Budget. If these conditions were on their way to being met, stabilisation at 3,000–3,500 marks to the dollar (13,000–15,600 to the pound) was possible if Germany was willing to use her gold reserves to support the rate. It was here that they disagreed with the minority which emphasised the necessity of a large foreign loan organised by an international committee of bankers to support stabilisation.

Keynes's attitude to the problem of the mark had at its roots his theory of money and the exchanges, which was essentially Marshall's and Pigou's. The basis was the quantity theory of money, which he regarded as 'fundamental', stating that 'its correspondence with fact is not open to question'.[34] The demand for purchasing power by the public was in normal conditions a more or less stable function of their wealth and payments habits. Hence, there was normally a proportional relationship between the quantity of cash and the level of prices. As he put it, $n = pk$, where n is the cash in circulation, p is the price level of a consumption unit and k is the number of such units normally held by the public in the form of cash. The stability of k was crucial. If, for example, to finance a war, a government increased the supply of cash, this increase would push up prices but at the same time impose a tax on the holders of the original note issue. This idea of an inflation tax was one that Keynes had developed in Treasury memoranda as long ago as 1915.[35] Such a tax could be very productive, for the only way that the public could avoid it was to change its habits concerning the use of money. Keynes estimated that in the middle of 1922 the German Government was obtaining the equivalent of between £75 and £100 million per annum through an inflation tax.[36]

h Before 1914 a pound had been worth just over 20 marks.

Once the inflationary process got going, however, other factors entered in. First, a serious inflation on the German scale – between July and November 1922 prices rose tenfold – caused serious problems for government finance, since most taxes are collected in arrears and changes in the prices of public services – postal rates, railway rates, etc. – follow changes in costs with a lag. As the inflation proceeded, it became ever more difficult to balance the budget. Second, as inflation accelerated, the public became less willing to hold purchasing power in the form of currency. The government then needed a higher rate of inflation to gain command over the same volume of resources by increasing the note issue.

There was a further complication in the behaviour of the price of foreign currency – a more sensitive indicator of impending price changes than prices of goods in the domestic market. Also, with the deterioration in the usefulness of the domestic currency as a standard of value, individuals may begin to use foreign currencies. The exchange rate will decline further and there will be further upward pressure on the domestic price level as the prices of goods moving in international trade rise more rapidly than those of non-traded goods.[37]

This analysis could be applied to Germany or any other country experiencing very rapid inflation. Keynes applied it to Austria and Russia as well. What made the German case more complicated, and more interesting, was the role of reparations. Reparations payments increased the German Government's budgetary problem and, in so far as they were paid in cash, the immediate foreign exchange problem. Keynes appears to have also believed that Allied reparations demands probably discouraged Germany from getting her finances in hand, because the Government feared that if it achieved even a modicum of financial order Allied demands would rise.[38] Not that he believed that the German authorities were particularly sophisticated, much less able. As he told Carl Melchior on 17 November after his visit to Berlin, 'Their lack of psychological flair seemed to me to be only equalled by their lack of technical competence'.[39] As 1922 progressed Keynes began to tie together the issues of German financial reconstruction, a moratorium on reparations payments and a more moderate reparations settlement. If the latter two could be linked, he had come to believe that Germany could stabilise the exchanges quite easily, as long as she accompanied stabilisation with high interest rates and budgetary reform. The domestic currency supply had fallen so low in real terms that the prospect of price stability and high interest rates should lead to a large increase in the demand for money and an inflow of foreign resources which would more than cover any current account deficit in the balance of payments. Thus he looked to currency stabilisation as the first stage of solving the German problem. That accomplished, other matters would tend to look after themselves.

Keynes also supported the stabilisation of the less depreciated European currencies – the lira, the French and Belgian francs, the currencies of the former neutrals and the pound. As 1922 progressed, his arguments in favour of stabilising these took on more flesh. In his Genoa proposals, he had argued in favour of stabilisation because 'this would promote, as nothing else can, the revival not only of trade and of production but of international credit and the movement of capital to where it is needed most' and left it at that.[40] Later in the year, both in the Reconstruction Supplement for 7 December and in a lecture to the Institute of Bankers on 29 November, he added more flesh to the argument.[41] His basic point was that under the existing régime of flexible exchange rates there was not enough banking support available to finance seasonal imbalances so that exchange fluctuations were larger than they would otherwise be. Such large swings impeded trade and created sufficient market uncertainty that it was unlikely that exchange rates would stabilise by themselves in the foreseeable future. Before 1914, he argued, the existence of the gold standard had limited the possibilities of loss on short-term international movements of funds so that interest differentials brought about helpful uncovered movements of funds to finance the movement of crops. With floating rates, there was not the limit to losses implied by the gold points and what had been a bankers' business now became that of speculators'. Speculators needed larger prospects of profit to take uncovered positions, especially as both commercial and central banks disliked speculation and tried to discourage it. Seasonal swings in exchange rates were larger than necessary and the costs to traders were even higher than necessary, thus further discouraging trade. Exchange stabilisation would provide an important reference point for market participants.[i]

However, Keynes continued to argue against stabilisation at pre-war parities. In the case of Britain, his argument was if anything becoming stronger than before, although, because the balance of arguments was not clear cut, he was still prepared to allow that those who disagreed with him could have a plausible case. His argument against attempts to appreciate depreciated currencies rested as before on the effects of exchange appreciation, assuming that there was not a marked rise in world prices, on the burden of debts, especially war debts, on the community. Exchange appreciation implied a decline in the domestic price level which would favour those who owned titles to claims denominated in nominal terms. It would complicate public finance as governments would have to transfer a larger proportion of the real national income as debt service to rentiers. It would also discourage enterprise and industry. Although he mentioned in passing that it would also involve cuts in money wages, he did not make as much of this as he would in the years to come.[42] He could see no justice in appreciation – nor could he see justice in depreciation as an alternative to a capital levy for reducing the burden of large post-war national debts –

i The 1980s have provided some weak evidence against Keynes's proposition concerning seasonal swings. See Meltzer 1988, 31–2.

for the average age of contracts in existence was low and did not justify the costs of industrial depression.

As in 1918 and 1920, Keynes was emphasising the importance of price stability for the functioning of the capitalist system. Since changes in the value of money, upwards or downwards, affected different people or classes unequally through their effects on the distribution of income and wealth and on the level of output, a modicum of price stability was essential for both social stability and economic progress. He had not yet gone beyond his 1921 *Sunday Times* proposals for the use of central bank discount rates to maintain price stability, nor had he worked out the full implications of such a policy. These were to be tasks for 1923.j

Keynes's involvement with the Reconstruction Supplements had an interesting long-term spin off. At an early stage of planning the Supplements he had acquired the rights to the London School of Economics 'business barometer' and the Harvard 'business barometer', which he proceeded to publish in each issue along with similar statistical material from Western Europe. With the end of the Supplements in sight there arose the question of continuing to publish such material on a regular basis. The outcome was the London and Cambridge Economic Service, which was managed by an executive committee consisting of William Beveridge and A. L. Bowley from LSE and Keynes and Hubert Henderson from Cambridge.k Its first *Monthly Bulletin* appeared in January 1923. The purpose of the Service, in an era when most of the official statistical series that are now the bread and butter of financial journalists and working economists did not exist, was to help businessmen cope with the credit cycle by providing them with information. It did this by organising existing statistical material in a usable form; by developing such new indicators such as indices of share prices, money wages and industrial production; by providing in chart form series of what would now be called 'leading indicators' of economic activity with a brief commentary; and longer *Special Memoranda* on particular subjects. Keynes took an active part in the work of the Service until 1938. Before each issue he went to the meetings of the Editorial Committee which discussed the situation before A. L. Bowley prepared the commentary. During the first decade of the Service, he followed up his Reconstruction Supplement article 'Some Aspects of Commodity Markets' with seven *Special Memoranda* on 'Stocks of Staple Commodities' which were a by-product of his own commodity speculation.[43] The *Bulletins* and *Special Memoranda* seem to have been valuable to contemporaries, who paid £6 per annum (the equivalent

j His treatment of the position of labour also remained as unsatisfactory in the Reconstruction Supplements as it had in 1921. Compare *JMK*, XVII, 266–7 with IV, 27–8. Remedying this would take longer than would the working out of his views on the other issues.

k When Henderson left Cambridge to become editor of the *Nation and Athenaeum* a few months later, Dennis Robertson took his place.

of almost £150 at today's prices) for the service. They are now a boon to economic historians.[44]

At the end of 1922, the reparations problem was coming to a head. German inflation had been running above 50 per cent per month since July 1922 with all the expected consequences for the Government's financial position. Germany had made no cash payments on reparations account since 15 July and was falling behind on her promised deliveries in kind. The way was open for another round of negotiations, precipitated by a German note to the Reparation Commission on 14 November. This stated Germany could not stabilise the mark without a foreign loan and asked for a three- to four-year moratorium on all reparations payments except those for the devastated areas.

Bonar Law had succeeded Lloyd George as Prime Minister in mid-October. He invited the Belgian, French and Italian premiers to London for a preliminary discussion on 9 December before they met the Germans in Paris in January. They had before them a revised German proposal: Germany would try to stabilise the mark on her own and, during the moratorium, to raise an international loan, part of which would go towards reparations. The meeting got nowhere and adjourned on 11 December: Bonar Law spoke of an allied counter-proposal, while Poincaré, impatient of further delay, reiterated French demands for the occupation of the Ruhr. The Prime Ministers agreed only to ask the Germans to set out their proposals in more detail before the premiers met again on 2 January.

Keynes was involved in British planning for this meeting on two levels. First, he commented on the draft British proposals developed by Sir John Bradbury. He found them 'brilliant' and 'very ingenious' but so marred by 'intricacy and obscurity' that he had to read them three or four times to understand them.[45] He suggested adjustments to the scheme to make it more favourable to France and that a commission for inter-governmental debt replace the Reparation Commission to act as a clearing house and take responsibility for inter-allied debts and reparations. Bradbury adopted Keynes's second proposal, but not his first. Bradbury's proposal remained complicated: many members of the British delegation to Paris did not understand it, and Bergmann, the German representative in Paris quipped 'I would rather pay reparations than try to understand the Bonar Law Plan'.[46]

After seeing Bonar Law on 19 December, Keynes also produced his own plan for the Prime Minister on 23 December before departing to Tidmarsh with Lydia to spend Christmas with Lytton Strachey.[47] Like Bradbury's plan, it proposed a four-year moratorium on reparations payments and deliveries in kind beyond limited quantities of coal and coke and provided for a stabilisation of the mark under foreign supervision. When reparations payments resumed in 1927, Germany would pay 2 billion gold marks a year for 25 years. If she made additional payments, once these compounded at

6 per cent interest reached 5 billion gold marks, the occupation of the Rhineland would cease. Keynes's plan also involved British renunciation of her claims to allied debts in exchange for the scaling down of reparations. His plan saw Britain receiving a smaller share of reparations than did Bradbury's. It came to nought.

So did Bradbury's plan: the French refused to consider it in Paris in January because Britain refused to give up her share of reparations. Nor would the French accept a moratorium without more stringent guarantees. Poincaré called for the immediate seizure of 'productive pledges' or French control of some German production and revenues. The Conference was deadlocked.

Meanwhile, the French had succeeded on 26 December in getting the Reparation Commission to declare Germany in default on deliveries of timber. On 9 January 1923, with Britain again in a minority of one, the Commission declared Germany in default on coal deliveries. On 11 January, without waiting for Germany to default on cash payments due on 15 January, French and Belgian troops entered the Ruhr. The Germans in the occupied areas, with the financial support of the German Government (in other words further resort to the printing presses), adopted a policy of passive resistance.

After his visit to Germany as an expert in November 1922, Keynes remained in regular contact with Melchior, who on occasion passed his views on to Chancellor Cuno.[48] In the course of the spring this brought him closer involvement in the dispute.

The background was as follows. On 20 April 1923, Lord Curzon, the British Foreign Secretary, invited Germany to submit proposals for a settlement. She did so on 2 May, suggesting a moratorium until 1927, annual payments of £60 million after 1927 with additional annual payments of £15 million from 1929 to 1931 and £30 million after 1931 subject to the decision of 'an impartial international commission', and deliveries in kind as before but reckoned as part of the £60 million. All of this, with a suggestion of an international loan, was conditional on the evacuation of the Ruhr and the withdrawal of various restrictions on trade and credit. The proposals were rejected by France and Belgium on 6 May, while on 13 May Britain, expressing disappointment with the suggested sums and the lack of precise guarantees, suggested the Germans reconsider and elaborate their proposals.

In his correspondence with Melchior, very little of which survives, Keynes appears to have suggested that he come to Germany 'and lift the veil'.[49] Melchior supported the idea, but probably before he received Melchior's letter, Keynes took the initiative and wrote to Chancellor Cuno enclosing suggestions for a possible reply to the British Foreign Office. Continuing the discussion, with Melchior as an intermediary, Keynes emphasised the need to break new ground and to get away from the notion of a loan in favour of an annuity. He also stressed the need for German firmness rather than 'conciliations and moans' about 'how badly she is being treated'. He highlighted the absurdity of a loan of new money on German credit in an article in the *Nation and Athenaeum* of 26 May, a proof of which he sent to Melchior. The article emphasised the necessity of concentrating on the essential question of how much Germany could pay on a year-by-year basis.[50]

By this stage Keynes had decided to take things further by visiting Berlin over the weekend of 1–4 June. The day before he left London, he had an interview with Stanley Baldwin, who had succeeded the terminally ill Bonar Law on 22 May, and dined with Reginald McKenna, whom Baldwin intended to appoint Chancellor of the Exchequer after he recovered from paratyphoid fever and once a safe Parliamentary seat was available.[51] Keynes arrived in Berlin on the evening of 1 June. He spent the evening reviewing the situation and discussing the German draft reply to Lord Curzon's Note of 13 May.[l] Over the weekend, Keynes saw Cuno and the Foreign Minister von Rosenberg on three occasions as draft reply succeeded draft reply. He even undertook the task of translating the final version into English, perhaps to give him control of the tone of the version the Foreign Office would receive.[m] Those involved accepted his notion that the new note should contain no figures. Keynes returned to London on 4 June.

The German note delivered on 7 June was conciliatory. It repeated the idea of submitting her capacity to pay and the amount and method of her payments to an impartial international body. It raised the idea of an annuity rather than a large-scale loan and mentioned specific guarantees for the annuity. It also appealed for an end to the exchange of written notes and a session at the conference table in their place. Keynes commented favourably on the Note in the *Nation* of 16 June, as well as in a brief piece on the economic situation a week earlier.[52]

The German Note of 7 June remained unanswered for over a month. The French continued to insist on an end to German passive resistance in the Ruhr and strict adherence to the Treaty, while the British seriously questioned the legality of France's action. The occupation and the passive resistance continued – as did the German hyperinflation. In the seven months December 1922 to July 1923, the exchange value of the mark fell from 0.0136 cents to 0.00034 cents, while internal wholesale prices rose thirteenfold. By July wholesale prices were more than doubling weekly, as the German Government poured vast sums into supporting passive resistance in the Ruhr.

l Keynes was not the only Englishman consulted. Montagu Norman, the Governor of the Bank of England was also involved (Clay 1957, 208).

m This, plus his work on *Probability* and on the German press during the First World War says something about his working knowledge of German, even if he had to work slowly, and prompts one not to take too literally his self-deprecating remark about his command of the language in *A Treatise on Money* (*JMK*, V, 178 n. 1). See above pp. 172, 261n. 10.

In the *Nation*, both anonymously and above his own signature, and in other contributions to the press, Keynes tried to encourage Britain to end its policy of quasi-neutrality, to break with France publicly and to offer some encouragement to Germany. The British draft reply to Germany of 20 July was feebler than he had hoped: it called for an end to passive resistance in the Ruhr, its progressive evacuation, an impartial enquiry into Germany's capacity to pay and Allied discussions to reach a final settlement. The French and the Belgians were intransigent. They rejected any negotiations unless and until passive resistance ended, refused to withdraw from the Ruhr until they were paid and opposed an impartial inquiry. As a result of their intransigence, the final British Note of 11 August was equally uncompromising. It reaffirmed the need for an impartial enquiry, stigmatised French demands as a cover for the permanent occupation of the Ruhr, raised the issue of France's unpaid war debt to Britain, and suggested (as Andrew McFadyean had privately hinted to Keynes earlier)[53] that the occupation of the Ruhr was illegal under the Peace Treaty. The Cuno Government fell the same day. On 26 September, Germany abandoned passive resistance in the face of imminent financial ruin. Since the end of July prices had risen almost 215 times.

As the occupation continued, amidst reports of risings against the German Government from left and right and of a French-inspired declaration of a republic in the Rhineland, the British Government tried to find a solution. It revived the notion of an independent inquiry but linked it to a 1922 proposal from the American Secretary of State, C. E. Hughes, for American participation. The Americans reaffirmed their offer on 11 October. After testing the firmness of the American offer, Britain then suggested two possibilities: an independent inquiry or a committee of experts to advise the Reparation Commission. France opted for the latter but backtracked over the terms of reference. The Reparation Commission eventually saved the proposal by responding to a German request to investigate German resources and capacity to pay under Article 234 of the Treaty of Versailles and on 30 November appointed two Committees with terms of reference allowing for a wide-ranging inquiry. One was to look into balancing the Budget and stabilising the currency; the other into the flight of capital from Germany and its possible repatriation.

The Germans had now started to take firm control of their financial affairs. On 15 October the Government by decree set up the Rentenbank, endowed with a charge on the whole of German industry and agriculture, which would issue 'rentenmarks' with the value of one pre-war gold mark. The scheme went into effect on 15 November and on 20 November the paper mark was stabilised at 4.2 trillion to the US dollar or 1 trillion to the rentenmark. The Rentenbank took over the financing of the Government, within a fixed limit, until the Budget balanced. At the same time, the Reichsbank was forbidden to discount Treasury bills and made independent of the Government. Taxes were reformed, as were the finances of public enterprises.

When Keynes saw Bonar Law and Baldwin in December 1922, he probably discussed matters other than reparations. The other issue of the moment was Britain's war debt to America. During the war Britain had borrowed £1,030 million in the United States, most of it directly from the American Government. At the end of the war, Britain was required to give 5 per cent bonds for the credits she had received. The ultimate decision of the terms of repayment rested with Congress. By November 1922, Britain had paid only two instalments of interest on her debt.

On several occasions immediately after the war the British Government unsuccessfully sought solutions to the interrelated problems of Britain's debt to America, the European allies' debts to Britain and reparations. In February 1922 Congress passed the Debt Funding Act which created a Commission to negotiate with foreign debtors under the terms of the Act. The most important terms were that the principal of the debts was not to be reduced but that, through reductions in the rate of interest charged, the amount owing (principal + accrued interest) was and that repayment must be completed in 62 years. In April, the American Ambassador formally conveyed an invitation from the Debt Funding Commission to the British Government to open negotiations as soon as possible.

The Cabinet equivocated. Treasury ministers wished to meet the Commission. Others, worried by the implications of a possible settlement with America before the solution of the problems of reparations and inter-allied debts, urged delay. The Balfour Note of 1 August 1922 stating that Britain would restrict her claims for reparations and repayments by her creditors to the net amount required to meet her American obligations was the result. Meeting with a very hostile press in America, the Note served only to harden Congressional attitudes. Its effects in Europe were no better, for it complicated the reparations issue.

The Government did not adhere to the Balfour Note in the event. It planned to send a delegation to Washington in October 1922 for talks on the debt, but the collapse of the Lloyd George coalition, the accession of Bonar Law to power and the ensuing General Election meant that it was 27 December 1922 before the British delegation departed for Washington. Its members were Baldwin, Chancellor of the Exchequer, Norman, the Governor of the Bank of England, and two Treasury officials.

Keynes saw Baldwin on 18 December. Before he saw him, he sent him an extract concerning the American debt from a lecture he had given to the Institute of Bankers on 5 December.[54] He had there argued that the American debt proposals were beyond Britain's capacity to pay unless overseas lending in New York revived substantially or the level of American tariffs fell. He also pointed out that an immediate American debt settlement would make it difficult to stabilise sterling until economic fundamentals adjusted to the new situation. Presumably he said the same thing to Baldwin. He may have also touched on these matters when he saw Bonar Law the following evening on the reparations issue.

Baldwin went to America with Cabinet authorisation to settle as he saw fit, provided annual payments by Britain did not exceed £25 million, a sum later raised to £30 million ($146 million at the pre-war exchange rate). The Americans offered interest at 3½ per cent and amortisation over 61 years, which meant an annual payment of $187 million. Baldwin countered with 3 per cent and amortisation over 50 years. Discussions continued with Baldwin and Norman cast in the role that Keynes would himself play in 1945 – negotiating with the Americans in the hopes of a better offer and preparing the Cabinet in London for a settlement that was worse than the original instructions allowed. The 1923 delegation settled with the Americans on 3 per cent for the first ten years and 3½ per cent thereafter with a sinking fund throughout. Back interest was recalculated at 4½ per cent. The settlement meant payments of $161 million for 10 years and $184 million for 51 years. A press leak made public the details of the bargaining. Baldwin urged Bonar Law to accept, but the Cabinet favoured rejection and ended the negotiations. The delegation returned home to argue the matter in Cabinet on 30 January. When he landed in England, Baldwin informed waiting reporters of the terms and of his view that they were the best obtainable.

Keynes tried to influence events through J. C. C. Davidson, Bonar Law's Parliamentary Private Secretary and a close friend of Baldwin's. He recommended rejection of the terms 'in order to give them [the US Government] time to discover that they are just as completely at our mercy, as we are at France's and France at Germany's: it is the debtor who has the last word in these cases'. He also recommended that the matter be left for two years when circumstances might be less uncertain.[55] Bonar Law continued to oppose the settlement, but Baldwin convinced the Cabinet and when Reginald McKenna changed his position from opposing to supporting Baldwin, Law accepted the Cabinet view and did not resign. It took some months of further detailed negotiations to tie up the package. The terms of the agreement were published on 9 July 1923.

Keynes was remarkably restrained in his remarks on the agreement. Apart from a brief comment on a speech by the American Ambassador on the business-like character of the American loans which he cabled to the New York *World* in March, he said nothing until almost a month after the final terms were published. Then, in the *Nation*, he objected to the magnitude of the burden imposed on Britain, but found some hope in the fact that the arrangement was fixed in terms of gold, which he thought would depreciate over the longer term. In this respect, the nature of Britain's new American obligations fitted well into what was becoming his desired currency policy.[56]

The references to the *Nation and Athenaeum* reflect a new phase in Keynes's relations with the Liberal Party. This began in August 1922, when he had spoken at the Liberal Summer School on Reparations and War Debts.[57] The Liberal Summer Schools had grown out of discussions at Ernest Simon's farm in Herefordshire in the summer of 1920. Simon, a successful businessman who became Lord Mayor of Manchester in 1921, had asked E. T. Scott, son of the editor of the *Manchester Guardian*, Ramsay Muir, Professor of Modern History at Manchester, and the writer Phillip Guedella to this meeting. Their object was to devise for the Liberal Party, then still in contention with the Labour party to be the anti-Conservative party in the state, a modern and progressive policy. The first result was a preliminary Summer School at Grasmere in September 1921. The model for the schools was not the party conference with its pronouncements and resolutions but the British Association with its efforts at more popular discussion and education – from a liberal perspective. The method adopted was to decide on the issues and then get the best possible liberally oriented speakers.

Ninety-five attended the Grasmere sessions, which were addressed by the four founders as well as J. A. Hobson, Walter Layton and William Beveridge. The August 1922 Summer School at Oxford attracted 600. The following year there would be over 1,000 participants. Until 1939 the Summer Schools alternated between Oxford and Cambridge and became a major event in the Liberal year. Each made considerable efforts to attract young people: in 1924 and 1925 the *Weekly Westminster* offered essay prizes to cover the costs of residence and transportation. The joint directors of the Schools were Walter Layton and Ramsay Muir, who left Manchester University in 1921 to devote himself to independent thought and to the Liberal Party. In organisation and finance the Schools themselves remained independent of the Party.

Keynes became more involved in the autumn of 1922, probably as a result of a visit to Manchester, as a member of the committee co-ordinating work on future sessions. Now that Lloyd George's coalition had fallen, Keynes was again interested in the future of the Liberal Party, but he was not yet so involved as to support the party on the hustings in the November 1922 General Election. In the new year, his association became closer when he and a group associated with the Summer Schools acquired control of the *Nation and Athenaeum*.

The *Nation* had been edited since its founding by the Rowntree family in 1907 by the distinguished journalist H. W. Massingham. Although it had been important, it had never been financially successful and depended on Rowntree money. The paper had recently fallen on harder times. It had also adopted a rather negative, querulous tone in the face of the wickedness of the post-war world. Although it had not, as Leonard Woolf, a regular contributor, suggested become 'to all intents and purposes a Labour paper', it was not anti-Labour.[58] The paper's losses left it open to a takeover, for the Rowntrees were unwilling to put in additional funds without a change in editorial policy.[n] Massingham's decision to join the Labour Party and his resignation as editor in December 1922 opened the way for the Liberals. They had already attempted to merge the *Nation* with the *New Statesman*, which also had financial problems, but they failed when the *Statesman* found new backers. Keynes learned of the plans at a meeting with Walter Layton, his former Cambridge colleague, on 19 December 1922, but it was only in January 1923 that he became seriously involved in the discussions.

The original idea was that Ramsay Muir would be editor. If the paper was to be taken over by the Summer School group, Muir as a founder of the Schools was seen as essential, although he would be advised by an editorial committee including Keynes. Despite Muir's and, at least initially, Layton's hopes, this close link with the Summer Schools unravelled, partly as a result of Keynes's influence as a potential investor and prospective chairman.[o] The ostensible causes of the difficulties were the terms offered to Muir as editor: the salary, the amount the editor should write, the editor's discretion and the exact relationship with the Summer Schools. Keynes and Layton offered an editorial salary of £750 with additional payments to depend on increases in circulation; Muir held out for £1,000, which was the going rate for similar papers. Keynes held that the editor should confine himself to editing and write little beyond the 'Notes of the Week', while for Muir the attraction of the job was 'the opportunity of saying some things I want to say': he wanted to be 'the sole judge of how much I write'. Keynes thought that the editorial committee should be able to overrule the editor; Muir, while accepting his 'own inexperience & lack of knowledge of the writing world', held out for a purely advisory role. Unlike Keynes and Layton, he also had come to believe that the finances of the paper and thus an element of control should rest with Summer School investors if they took up shares.[59] Keynes could not see things Muir's way. He told Walter Layton:

> I should not be able to agree to the conditions he proposes. Apart from my growing doubts as to whether he is the right man for the job, what he suggests would make the relation between the editor and the editorial board very different from what we contemplated when it was first discussed. I should not think it worthwhile to give time and energy and risk money under the conditions that Muir would require for himself.[60]

If Layton was too committed to Muir, Keynes offered 'to drop out of the

n The Rowntrees offered Massingham an option to buy the paper, but he could not raise the funds.
o By 1931 directly and indirectly Keynes would have invested over £7,000 in the paper. The only larger contributions of £19,700 came from A. S. Rowntree and J. B. Morrell. The next largest contributors below Keynes were E. D. Simon and L. J. Cadbury with just over £4,000 each.

whole thing, bag and baggage'. Layton attempted to keep Muir on board. Muir himself was rather put out. As he asked Keynes:

> Is not your view on this question coloured by your view of me? You know, of course, nothing about me, & have probably never read a line I have written. But you naturally think of me as an inexperienced middle-aged provincial ex-professor, imposed upon the paper because of my half-accidental association with the Summer School people. You are honestly (& naturally) dubious about my capacity to do the work. And you weren't impressed by the results of our two talks: I watched you, with interest, at work upon the formation of a judgement.[61]

In the end, Keynes turned to his former student and current Cambridge colleague Hubert Henderson. Henderson agreed to be editor on 19 February. There were still attempts to keep Muir associated with the enterprise, which he (Muir) thought with Henderson, Layton and Keynes would too much represent the Cambridge school of economics.[p] One such attempt involved associating Phillip Guedella more closely with the editorial committee. These attempts came to nothing and Muir chose instead to run the *Weekly Westminster*, which failed a few years later.

There were also disputes about the rest of the editorial team, for example the literary editorship. Originally Naomi Royde-Smith, novelist and literary editor of the *Westminster Gazette*, was a strong candidate. Then, at the urging of Virginia Woolf, there was the suggestion that T. S. Eliot, still an employee of Lloyds Bank, should take the post, although Lytton did not think he was 'well-suited for that particular job'.[62] Keynes took the Eliot idea seriously and considered making Eliot literary editor with Miss Royde-Smith as Henderson's assistant editor.[63] While the negotiations went on, Keynes achieved 'Pretty complete victory. Ramsay Muir and Guedella have committed suicide and Miss Royde-Smith has been assassinated.'[64] Keynes saw Eliot on 27 February and 7 March to discuss terms, but Eliot's conditions were unacceptable to Keynes, as even Eliot expected when he referred to them as 'impossible'. Virginia Woolf, who it turned out also did not think Eliot 'the right person for the job' was 'relieved'.[q] Leonard Woolf took the job and became the only carry over from the Massingham régime. Although he was to find working with Henderson so difficult that he resigned several times, only to be persuaded by Keynes to stay, he remained literary editor until 1930.[65]

There were still 'endless hellish details to settle', including 'the scare that

---

p As Layton wrote to Keynes on 17 February, 'It is not our fault that all the best Liberals were trained in the Cambridge Economics School, but we must take some account of what the world thinks!' (KCKP, NS1/1).

q Eliot's conditions were a guarantee of two years' employment and that he give the bank three months' notice with a four months' leave of absence and that during those four months he do no work for the *Nation* (KCKP, NS1/1, T. S. Eliot to JMK, 21 March 1923; V. Woolf to JMK, Friday [23 February 1923]).

Massingham is going to die and make us bring out our first number with black ring', before the first issue of the new régime appeared on 5 May 1923.[66] This featured pieces from both Virginia Woolf and Lytton Strachey. Later issues drew heavily on Cambridge and Bloomsbury including Clive Bell, Morgan Forster, Lowes Dickinson, Frances Birrell, David Garnett, Simon Bussy, A. V. Hill and even A. C. Pigou, who, as well as later reviewing Keynes's *A Treatise on Money*, contributed an essay on 'Games'. Keynes himself was a substantial contributor, both under his own name and anonymously or pseudonymously as Siela.[r] As chairman, he generally did not interfere in the day-to-day affairs of the paper, although he and Henderson had a long talk each week on the significance of current developments. When Henderson was on holiday, Keynes often took over as editor with no marked change in the paper or its tone. This was not the relationship that developed after 1931, when the *Nation* merged with the *New Statesman* and Kingsley Martin took over as editor.

r Harrod (1951, 337) states that 'Keynes contributed nothing to the paper which was not signed or initialled, save for one note on Bonar Law'. This is untrue. The surviving marked copies of the paper in the Keynes papers indicate otherwise, and on 24 June 1923 he wrote his mother: 'I should like very much to have a new [scrapbook] volume of my *Nation* articles. But I shall have to mark a copy for you, since I write more than I sign.' (KCKP). The *Nation* scrapbooks, as they became, are in the Keynes Papers.

NOTES

1 *JMK*, XVII, 207.
2 *JMK*, XVII, 217.
3 NUL, JMK to VB, 13 May 1921.
4 *JMK*, III, 3. Chapter I of *Revision* contains Keynes's views on the issue.
5 It is not raised in Fitzgibbons 1988 and only touched on in Carabelli 1988, 163, 285 n. 11. However, see O'Donnell 1989, ch. 13.
6 *JMK*, XVII, 293.
7 NUL, JMK to DG, 21 December 1921.
8 KCKP, JMK to GLS, 28 August 1921.
9 *JMK*, XVII, 259–65.
10 *JMK*, XI, 411.
11 *JMK*, XVII, 265–71.
12 *JMK*, XVII, 278–9, 271.
13 *JMK*, XVII, 265–6.
14 *JMK*, XVII, 279.
15 *JMK*, XVII, 317–18, 319–20.
16 For further details see Chandavarkar 1990, 47–9.
17 NUL, JMK to VB, 26 October and 12 December 1921.
18 NUL, JMK to VB, 12 December 1921; 6 January 1922.
19 *JMK*, XVII, 326 to Melchior on 4 January.
20 *JMK*, XVII, 331–3.
21 *JMK*, IV, 70–80, 164–9 and 94–115.
22 *JMK*, XVII, 369; Howson 1985, 156.
23 *JMK*, XVII, 355–69.

24 *JMK*, XVII, 369.
25 A copy of these notes was given to the author by Mr Haslam.
26 They appear in *JMK*, XVII, ch. 16.
27 *JMK*, XVII, 403–8; KCKP, JMK to Lydia, 24 April 1922.
28 *JMK*, XVII, 372.
29 *JMK*, XVII, 410, 409, 408.
30 *JMK*, XVII, 422; KCKP, JMK to Lydia, 25 April 1922.
31 KCKP, JMK to FAK, 22 December 1922.
32 *JMK*, XVIII, 6–7.
33 *JMK*, XVIII, 29.
34 *JMK*, IV, 61.
35 *JMK*, XVI, 126–7.
36 *JMK*, IV, 50.
37 *JMK*, XIX, 21–3.
38 *JMK*, XVIII, 19, 35.
39 *JMK*, XVIII, 65; see also 87.
40 *JMK*, XVII, 360.
41 *JMK*, XVIII, 78–81; XIX, 52–7.
42 *JMK*, XVIII, 57; XIX, 58.
43 The Reconstruction Supplement article appears in *JMK*, XII, 255–65; the seven *Special Memoranda* in XII, 267–647; for Keynes's commodity speculation see XI, ch. 1.
44 Many of the series have been gathered together in Capie and Collins 1984. For a useful introduction to the Service see Robinson 1978.
45 *JMK*, XVIII, 93–4.
46 Middlemas (ed.) 1969, I, 224–5; Schuker 1976, 23.
47 *JMK*, XVIII, 97–9.
48 *JMK*, XVIII, 116. On these contacts see Bravo 1989.
49 *JMK*, XVIII, 141–3; the phrase is in Melchior's letter of 14 May 1923.
50 *JMK*, XVIII, 148; the *Nation* article follows on 150–6.
51 Middlemas and Barnes 1969, 180–1.
52 *JMK*, XVIII, 161–70.
53 *JMK*, XVIII, 200–1.
54 *JMK*, XVIII, 99–100; the relevant passages of the lecture are in XIX, 68–74.
55 *JMK*, XVIII, 103.
56 The March comment is in *JMK*, XVIII, 104, the *Nation* article on 193–7.
57 *JMK*, XVII, 12–17.
58 Woolf 1967, 96.
59 KCKP, NS1/1, Muir to JMK, 2 February 1923.
60 KCKP, NS1/1, JMK to W. Layton, 7 February 1923.
61 KCKP, NS1/1, R. Muir to JMK, 9 February 1923.
62 KCKP, NS1/1, GLS to JMK, 24 February 1923.
63 KCKP, JMK to GLS, 27 February 1923; NS1/1, JMK to P. Guedella, n.d.; P. Guedella to JMK, 26 February 1923.
64 KCKP, JMK to GLS, 9 March 1923.
65 Spotts (ed.) 1989, 275, 285.
66 KCKP, JMK to GLS, 6 April 1923.

16

LYDIA AND MAYNARD

I have long felt that marriage was the one thing left that could give a fresh stimulus to your brilliant career & develop your full powers by harmonising the big reserves of your emotional nature with your intellectual life.

(KCKP, Walter Layton to JMK, 19 August 1925)

Lydia Lopokova had disappeared from Diaghilev's company in July 1919. She spent most of the ensuing period in the United States. In March 1921 her manager telegraphed Diaghilev to see if she could rejoin the company. She returned in mid-April and reappeared in London in the company's season at the Prince's Theatre between 26 May and 31 July, dancing in twelve ballets. She then took a month's holiday before rehearsing for a production of *The Sleeping Princess*, which opened at the Alhambra Theatre (now the Odeon, Leicester Square) on 3 November. The ballet was a re-working of *The Sleeping Beauty* with additional music by Stravinsky. As an acquaintance of Clive Bell's, Lydia was occasionally at Gordon Square, but at the end of November Clive reported he had recently seen very little of her, adding that although he doubted it 'some say she has got an English flirt'. He also remarked in the same letter to Vanessa: 'She is a deep little thing for all her childish ways'.[1] Was Keynes the 'English flirt'? From the note in his diary quoted above,[2] it would seem he was. However, he had been in Cambridge more than usual for most of the autumn and there is no earlier sign of Lydia in his diary.[3]

On 7 December he went to London for the vacation. According to some reports, he went to the Alhambra frequently.[4] His engagement book is silent on that, but it is also silent on everything else he might have been doing during those December evenings. On 18 December, he had Lydia to lunch at 46 Gordon Square. He reported to Vanessa:

I again fell very much in love with her. She seemed to me perfect in every way. One of her new charms is the most knowing and judicious use of English words. I am going to the ballet tomorrow, and am asking her to sup with me afterwards at the Savoy.[5]

Clive reported to Vanessa three days later:

> I believe Maynard is really rather in love with Lydia – he took her to supper at the Savoy the other night – with Sebastian as a chaperone however.[6]

The next day, Keynes and Sprott went off to spend Christmas with Lytton Strachey at Tidmarsh.

Keynes was back in London on 28 December, when he reported to Vanessa:

> My other chief news is the progress of my affair with Loppy. I told you, I think, that she came to lunch here last Sunday week; last Friday I took her to supper at the Savoy after the ballet where we chatted until 1 a.m.; and now she has asked me to tea. What is to be done about it? I am getting terrified.[7]

He went to tea. The next week he went to the ballet once and saw Lydia on three other occasions, twice for lunch. Then came the entry opposite 7 January in his appointments diary.

Vanessa had taken Keynes's and Clive's earlier letters seriously. On 1 January 1922 she wrote from Paris 'very much excited about Loppi' and continued:

> As for Loppi *don't* marry her. Flight to India may save you. However charming she may be, she'd be a very expensive wife & would give up dancing & is altogether I'm sure much to be preferred as a mistress (dancing). But I think you're in great danger.[8]

Keynes, as we know, persisted. He also hoped that Vanessa would come back to London for a week or two and he offered to pay her fare.

> Not least because I'm in great need of much good advice from you. You needn't be afraid of marriage, but the affair is very serious and I don't in the least know what to do about it. I begin to think it's a good thing that I'm going to India. However, she's very adorable.[9]

The next day, he saw Lydia again and reported again to Vanessa:

> I'm in a terribly bad plight, almost beyond reason. Clive simply grins with delight at seeing me so humbled. However I long to have a good gossip with you.
>
> Douglas [Davidson] and Sebastian are here on Wednesday; but it doesn't interest me![10]

We do not know what passed between Keynes and Vanessa during her visit to London except from Duncan's reactions to Vanessa's reports:

> I'm rather distressed about Maynard. But I'm glad he's dead against

marriage because in 6 years time I think Loppy may be very difficult to deal with. An artist out of work is a terrible problem & very unsuited as a wife to one of Maynard's tastes. But I rather agree with Clive that they ought to make hay while the sun shines . . .[11]

But as Duncan noted to Vanessa ten days later, '[Y]ou once said that you thought it a want in him that there was no place for a female'.[12]

Duncan was rather more than distressed, as Vanessa reported once she had returned to France:

I have done my best to put him *au fait* with your affairs but he remains sphinx-like. He says he cannot write or say *anything* until he has seen for himself but will only remark academically that (as you ought to know) he disapproves of marriage. So you will have to wait until you see him. I think myself that he is a little suspicious of the whole affair & afraid of petticoats in the home, but all on general grounds. Also I think he finds it really almost impossible to visualise the situation – you have become almost a new character to him & he doesn't know you yet.[13]

Keynes continued to see Lydia regularly, spending, except for the occasional weekend, the whole term in London. He reported to Lytton on 27 January, 'Indeed I'm entangled – a dreadful business – and barely fit to speak to'. He threw a grand party for Lydia on 4 February, the night that the Diaghilev season ended. The next week, he reported to Vanessa:

I still love Lydia very much. We had a good deal of *éclairissement* on Sunday, which was painful for a moment, but seems to have made no real difference to us at all. Indeed we are extremely happy.

. . .

I suppose the Sphinx [Duncan] is right that he must see for himself. But at any rate now, I should feel very flat without her.[14]

At that point, Keynes was in bed for a week with influenza. Clive reported to Vanessa:

He ought to go away – with Lydia or not? I can't make out. She comes & sees him a great deal – often she lunches at his bedside & sometimes dines – every day she sees him – but she does not spend her days with him as one does at the beginning of a grand passion – not so much even as she did two or three weeks ago when she was far less free – is it wearing a little bit on her side?[15]

And Lytton reported to James Strachey:

Pozzo's Lopokova extravaganza is the only novelty. For a moment Vanessa feared the worst – viz. marriage; but I am told that is now considered hardly probable. *To what extent* the affair has gone cannot be discovered. I therefore suppose that it hasn't gone very far.[16]

By this stage, Keynes had taken over Lydia's domestic affairs. He moved her from the Waldorf Hotel in the Aldwych into Vanessa's rooms at 50 Gordon Square. Where then would she live once Vanessa returned from France? For a time she remained at No. 50, but in October 1922, on pressure from Vanessa, she moved down the east side of the square into the ground floor flat at 41 Gordon Square.

Lydia's arrival in Gordon Square and Keynes's growing attachment to her produced severe problems for Bloomsbury, especially for the Charlestonians. Keynes's earlier loves, such as Sebastian, fitted easily into Bloomsbury and Charleston. More often than not they were Cambridge; often they were Apostles. They could meet Bloomsbury on their own ground. Moreover, they did not really affect Keynes's flexible bachelor existence and they were not normally around when he was not in the Square. Lydia was definitely not Cambridge. Nor could she be described as 'apostolic'. When she was not on tour, she was around the Square – all the time. Inevitably the Bells bore the brunt of the disruption. In May, Clive commented:

> Lydia has quite destroyed all conversation at Gordon Square. When it is clever she can't follow; when it is *intime* she naturally doesn't know what we're talking about; we can't be much bawdy because she would be shocked. Her only topics are the Russian ballet, scraps of gossip about the Courtaulds[a] and obvious generalities. You've no notion how it bores me; and I'm not sure that you realise how utterly insipid & hideous it all is.[17]

Vanessa, when in London, bore the brunt of the changes. Lydia visited her regularly at 50 Gordon Square, even turning her earnings over to her for a time, which led Vanessa to implore Keynes to get Lydia to open a bank account.[18] Inevitably, she would drop in for gossips during the day and after the ballet. Vanessa burst out at one point to Roger Fry:

> I have been suffering rather from Lydia who has spent 3 solid hours sitting in my room gossiping. Duncan thinks it may be best for him to have a talk with Maynard & tell him that one must be able to have one's room to oneself if one is to lead this sort of communal life.[19]

She also raised the problem with Keynes:

> I don't think she does enough to work off her energies really. She does a good bit of dancing over Karin's head[b] after she gets back & has supper & she has to be restrained sometimes.[20]

A year later, she put it at length to Roger Fry:

> I don't see what can be done myself. The chief difficulties no doubt lie

a Samuel Courtauld, the head of the textile firm of the same name and a patron of the arts.
b Adrian and Karin Stephen lived below Lydia at 50 Gordon Square.

in my own character & hers. I suppose it's true, as you always tell me & as Maynard said, that it's almost impossible to know what I'm feeling. I don't show when I want Lydia to go & so she can't be expected to know. On the other hand *her* character is such that I feel if she had any suspicion she weren't wanted she'd probably never come near me at all which would be absurd. So between us I don't see how one is to make her see the truth which is that I want to see her in moderation & to feel that I can count on having a room to myself when I want to be alone or to see people like you or Virginia alone.[21]

Perhaps Vanessa summed it all up when, while discussing whether Lydia and Maynard would come to Charleston in the summer of 1922, she remarked to Clive:

I see that the introduction of *anyone* – especially female, for more than a week into such an intimate society as ours is bound to end in disaster.[22]

Clive and Vanessa both made their views known to Keynes on more than one occasion. He accommodated Vanessa with the move to No. 41. But he emphasised the importance to him of Lydia's being free to come to No. 46, where Clive had maintained a *pied-à-terre* after 1916.[23] The problem was only resolved when Lydia and Maynard married in August 1925 and took over all of No. 46 themselves. By then, the strains of the previous three and a half years had left their mark. Vanessa did resent the invasion of her privacy and the severing of her links with the No. 46, where she had lived with Virginia and her brothers after the death of Leslie Stephen; Clive resented the change in old styles of living, entertaining and conversation and Duncan was unhappy at breaking an important link with his past. As he put it in 1924, when much more had been settled:

Maynard's marriage is a grim fact to face. It will be more grim still, if Maynard sees it to be grim before embarking on it. Lord! Lord![24]

Other members of Bloomsbury, less immediately affected, were just amused. Virginia Woolf initially regarded it as 'endearing', but as the affair progressed she became worried about the possibility of marriage and began to echo the complaints of the others about Lydia's effects on conversation.[25]

If Lydia's reception, especially amongst the Charlestonians, caused Keynes difficulties, they do not seem to have caused him doubts after his initial expressions to Vanessa and Lytton. But he had lost these confidantes. Whether he had any doubts, although probable, is therefore unknown. Early in 1923 the recurrence in his diary of his pre-1915 symbolism for sexual acts on six occasions between 22 January and 9 March may suggest something but it is not clear what. (On most of the occasions he was in London with Lydia.)

As one might expect, once Lydia entered his life, he 'took care' of her – managing her finances and her career, and attempting to educate her – and, incidentally, Quentin Bell then aged 13. The education took several forms: expeditions in a hired Daimler, Quentin in tow, to Westminster Abbey, Hampton Court, the Tower of London, complete with lectures from Maynard; a programme of organised reading, particularly Shakespeare and Shaw; and the like.[26] The two kept up appearances, especially once they had decided to marry – and to undertake the proceedings for the annulment of Lydia's marriage to Randolfo Barouchi on grounds of bigamy.[c] There was also the matter of introducing Lydia to Harvey Road,[27] something Maynard accomplished in November 1923. Then there was the more general matter of Cambridge. Of course, several of Keynes's Cambridge friends knew what was going on – Sebastian, Dadie Rylands and Dennis Robertson. Dennis asked Lydia to dine with him in Cambridge in March 1924.[28] By May the gossip had reached A. C. Benson, the Master of Magdalene, but his circle overlapped considerably, at least as far as young men were concerned, with Keynes's.[29] Part of the problem was Lydia's occupation: the older generation equated ballerinas with chorus girls. But on her formal introduction to Cambridge on 31 July 1925, at a lunch supposedly in honour of Francesco Nitti, the former premier of Italy, she was a success. Mary Marshall, who had stayed with the couple in September 1924 at Tilton, the country house Keynes later acquired in Sussex, regarded Maynard's marrying Lydia as 'the best thing Maynard ever did'.[30] She was right.

Maynard's marriage to Lydia had to await the evidence to prove Barouchi's bigamy and then the progress of the resulting divorce case through the courts. The latter was a lengthy affair, because of a backlog of cases, and it was 15 January 1925 before Lydia obtained her decree *nisi*. In the following months, rumours of the impending marriage began to circulate in Cambridge: on 23 April the Vice-Provost asked Keynes if he could congratulate him; 'so I told him all about you', and by early May wedding presents started to arrive, the first from the Master of Trinity Hall. Lydia was amused:

> I giggled with laughter for the 'wedding present'. I don't want to be unkind but probably to the end of the year there shall be a good deal of trash accumulated.[31]

Plans proceeded.

27 July was Lydia's 'day of freedom'. She and Maynard arranged to marry with a minimum of delay. He went to St Pancras registry office the same afternoon.[32] They were married there on 4 August. Duncan Grant, 'against his will', and Vera Bowen, a friend of Lydia's, acted as witnesses.[33] In the

c He had not completed divorce proceedings from his first wife at the time of his marriage to Lydia. Kenneth Brown, Maynard's uncle, acted as Lydia's solicitor.

afternoon there was a wedding tea for the family at Gordon Square. The wedding was widely covered in the world's press: there were at least 20 cameras present on the steps of the registry office. It was more like an event in the film world and Lydia got top billing.[34] A more Bloomsbury celebration took place at Charleston on 19 August.

The same day, Frank Ramsey arrived for a visit with Maynard, Lydia and Wittgenstein at Oatlands, the house near Iford the Keyneses had taken for the summer. Ramsey provided a non-Bloomsbury glimpse of Lydia.

> I got here at tea time yesterday, and went for a long walk with Keynes and Wittgenstein and had a very good dinner. Lopokova I think is very nice but difficult because she is so unEnglish. (She even speaks English so badly.) I don't mean she's difficult to talk to, but difficult to see what her mind is really like. At first I put her mental age at 8, but now I see it's much greater. Keynes and Wittgenstein are awfully nice together, but I can't get a word in, they both talk such a lot.[35]

With marriage came the necessary re-arrangement of accommodation in Gordon Square. In January Keynes had announced that he wished to have all of 46 Gordon Square to himself. Vanessa and Duncan were 'in a high rage' over this: Vanessa had previously recorded the 'firm intention of keeping Lydia out of 46 as much as she possibly can', but soon the rage blew over – even if hurt feelings remained, exacerbated on occasion by disputes of what was whose.

> I must tell you my latest cause for quarrel with the Keynes'. Do you remember an abstract painting by Duncan – very long & with pieces of wood on it? He painted it in Fitzroy St., No. 22, long ago, then lent it to Maynard when he lived in Gower St., then it came to 46, & was in the dining room, then was moved up to M.'s room. Duncan gave it to me long ago, & when I moved I told M. it was mine. He denied it & said he'd had it so many years it was certainly his. Duncan agreed that it was mine. However M. then had it screwed to the wall – in their bathroom.
>
> So the other day I went in with a screwdriver & with the help of the sympathetic Mrs Uppington took it down and carried it off to No. 37! I am now waiting in some fear to see how angry Maynard will be when he discovers it.[36]

Maynard's reaction – he was on his way back from his first visit to the Soviet Union where he had met Lydia's relations and represented Cambridge at the 250th anniversary of the Soviet Academy of Sciences – has not survived.[d]

Firmly in possession of Gordon Square, Maynard and Lydia began

d This reconstruction differs from the one in which Vanessa had to invite Maynard to Charleston while she did the deed, as reported in Holroyd 1973, 903.

refurnishing and redecorating it. This involved removing traces of Clive's, Vanessa's and Duncan's occupancy – including their wall decorations. As Lydia put it: 'I like so much the passages in their new outlook, and that they have no frescoes [*sic*] – do not have them at Tilton, pictures are less dangerous'.[37] She repeated her determination to have none after seeing some of Carrington's decorations at James Strachey's. Doubtless the change to what Virginia Woolf called 'bright and tight and shiny' did not improve relations with Duncan and Vanessa.[38]

With marriage also came the question of a country retreat. Charleston, as I have recounted, was closed to them. During their 'courtship' they had taken houses at Studland near Marlborough and Tilton near Lewes. The summer of 1925 saw them at Oatlands at Iford just south of Lewes. Tilton had been a success from their point of view, but not from the Charlestonians who had at one stage contemplated moving away from Sussex to East Anglia – although a rent increase at Charleston was also a contributing cause.[39] Neither was Virginia Woolf pleased at the prospect of having the Keyneses so near.[40] Nevertheless, when Tilton became available in October 1925, Keynes jumped at it, took it on a long lease and made substantial improvements, including a library. Charleston put up with the *fait accompli*. The Keyneses were to give Bloomsbury endless sources of gossip. Even the children at Charleston dubbed Maynard 'the Squire'.[41]

The gossip became particularly biting when Keynes, on his mother's advice, gave up wine to try and ease a sore knee.

> The Keynes visit was lugubrious, somehow or other. For one thing the house [Oatlands at Iford] was so hideous. Then Lydia is a pathetic figure, to my mind – and so plain. Maynard is as engrossed as usual in his own concerns. He was very interesting on Russia & Wittgenstein; but there is a difficulty of some kind in one's intercourse with him – he seems so far off.
>
> ... Would you believe it? Not a drop of alcohol appeared. The Charlestonians declare that Il gran Pozzo is now immensely rich probably £10,000 a year;[e] I can believe it and water, water everywhere! Such is the result of wealth.[42]

Complete abstinence was not always the rule at the Keynes's. Duncan reported to Vanessa in April 1926, 'I had an enormous Sunday lunch with Maynard & Lydia to-day, rather good, *with* wine after some difficulty'.[43] But it was some years before relations became easier, especially with Vanessa, for the others thawed out earlier, even though they could always find something to mock – for example Virginia Woolf after she and Leonard had been to dinner:

---

e This was a gross overestimate, given the records summarised in *JMK*, XI, 2. Keynes's income in 1925–6 was just over £5,500.

Dined with Lydia & Maynard: two couples, elderly, childless, distinguished. He & she both urbane & admirable. Grey comes at Maynard's temples. He is finer looking now: not with us pompous or great: simple, with his mind working always, on Russia, Bolshevists, glands, genealogies; always proof of a remarkable mind when it flows thus vigorously into bypaths. . . . Lydia is composed & controlled. She says very sensible things.[44]

However, Lydia remained excluded from the Memoir Club until into the 1930s.[45]

With the reorganisation of Gordon Square and the acquisition of Tilton, Keynes's life settled into the pattern that would continue until his illness in 1937. This was a variant of the pattern he had established earlier in the decade. In term time he spent the middle of the week in London at company meetings, seeing friends and visitors and keeping up with affairs. He went up to Cambridge for a long working weekend which included bursaring – College meetings had been moved to Saturday mornings to suit him, though he spent much of them working through correspondence but ready to intervene at the appropriate moment if necessary – College teaching, the Society on Saturday evening, Sunday lunch at Harvey Road, and his Monday evening Political Economy Club. University vacations, although they included periods in London, were spent at Tilton, which became the location for the sustained periods of academic work on *A Treatise on Money* (1930) and *The General Theory* (1936). For part of at least one University vacation each year the Keyneses went abroad – over the next twelve years their destinations included the Soviet Union (three times), the United States (twice), Spain (twice), the South of France (twice) and Sicily – but Tilton became more and more the place to unwind, often with friends, and to create.

Tilton was unconventional, but enjoyable, when seen through non-Bloomsbury eyes, such as Samuel Courtauld's in 1932:

> They dressed like comedy boy scouts or beach minstrels – Geoffrey the first in shorts, open shirt & stockings of artistically contrasting colours – Maynard the second in brilliant horizontal striped jersey (chosen by Lydia) and too long grey trousers . . . also a good deal of nothing for sun bathing. . . . But it is a merry house, with owners, dogs & servants intermingled in constant good humour and laughter.[46]

The mention of Geoffrey Keynes also indicated a new note, for Maynard's marriage saw a change in his relationship with his brother. Previously the brothers had been relatively distant. But Geoffrey was a lover of ballet. This and Maynard's evolving shared interest in book collecting brought them closer together. Lydia encouraged Geoffrey's balletomania with the result that Geoffrey, inspired by his love of Blake, in collaboration with Gwen Raverat (his Darwin sister-in-law) and Ralph Vaughan Williams (a Darwin cousin) and Ninette de Valois eventually mounted *Job: A Masque for Dancing* under the auspices of the Camargo Society – one of Maynard's minor endeavours.[47]

Keynes's marriage – and occasional abstemiousness – did not prevent 46 Gordon Square from continuing to be a centre for large parties and high spirits. The guests may have been more varied than before, although it is hard to tell from, say, Virginia Woolf's description of a Twelfth Night party in 1923.[48] The format was the same – a few to dinner, a large number in afterwards, an entertainment, good talk and good fun. At their 1927 Christmas Party for instance, described by Frances Partridge,[49] the entertainment, with the programme printed by Lydia at the Hogarth Press, included Duncan as Caruso and Lydia and Maynard dancing the 'Keynes-Keynes'. Bunny Garnett regarded parties at 46 Gordon Square under the new régime as 'the grandest' parties in Bloomsbury, as well as the most elaborately conceived.[50]

Keynes's courtship of and marriage to Lydia meant that his circle of friends and his range of active interests widened. He had, of course, already started collecting pictures and supporting his artistic friends before and during the war. He had already developed a love for the theatre and the ballet. Now he became more actively involved in the performing arts. He had, from the beginning of their affair, interested himself in the details of Lydia's new productions, encouraging Duncan Grant to become involved as designer in a ballet, *Togo or the Noble Savage*, she danced in London and on tour with Massine in 1923 and *The Postman*, a divertissement with Rupert Doone in London in 1925.

Through Lydia, Keynes came into close contact with Samuel Courtauld, the chairman of the firm of the same name. Courtauld was then amassing the collection of impressionist paintings now housed in Somerset House, London. In 1925, together with Courtauld and James Hindley-Smith, Keynes founded the London Artists Association. The idea seems to have been Keynes's. He first talked to the artists in January, and on 8 February Lydia reported:

> Sam called me to say that he likes the idea very much of the Artists Cooperative Society, but he wants to speak to you to understand completely the scheme, and being Sam doubts the practicality of the idea, but he means well and desires to contribute.[51]

As the idea evolved, the Association became the agent of a group of artists, managing their business affairs and dealing in their works, while guaranteeing them a modest annual income to relieve them of pressing financial worries. Keynes successfully persuaded Courtauld on 10 February 1925 and the group took shape. The nucleus was of fairly well-established post-impressionists

– Vanessa, Duncan, Roger Fry, Bernard Adeney, Keith Baynes, Frederick Porter, Frank Dobson – but it expanded to include less established artists – William Coldstream, William Roberts and Paul Nash. It was to survive and thrive until the 1929 slump. Its last exhibition was held in 1934.

In these years as well, Keynes was approached to be a contributor to a possible centre for art, drama and music for Cambridge undergraduates. This idea evaporated quickly owing to a dearth of backers, but the idea of building a small theatre for the University seems to have survived, for in November 1924 he reported to Lydia that he had attended a meeting with Dennis Robertson on the subject.[52] Discussions continued into the new year. In April 1925, Keynes reported to Lydia that Alec Penrose had attempted to get him to commit himself to the scheme. He still approved of the idea, but with his existing financial commitments to the *Nation* and the London Artists Association, he reported, 'I can't run any more of these affairs'. He promised £250 if Penrose could raise the remaining £500 – which he doubted.[53] The scheme died, partially because of the revival of theatre in Cambridge the next year when Terence Gray took over the Festival Theatre. Only with the demise of the Festival in the 1930s would the project go forward: then Keynes would be the moving force and the prime source of finance.

The strength of Keynes's position in King's after his marriage was clearly demonstrated in the spring of 1926 when Walter Durnford, the Provost since 1918, died on 9 April and the College faced the choice of a successor. During Durnford's final illness, A. F. R. Wollaston put forward Keynes's name,[54] and by the beginning of the Easter term the College was deep in the politics of the succession.

The contest centred around John Clapham and Keynes, perhaps the most distinguished representatives of the two schools of thought amongst the fellows. Known as 'honest John', Clapham, a Yorkshireman of Wesleyan upbringing, was ten years older than Keynes, and a very distinguished, if conventional, scholar. He had been an efficient Tutor and a stern, but fair, disciplinarian. He took his religion seriously and represented much of the self-image of the more conventional seniors in King's and was certainly more akin to the University's conception of a Head of House. Former Provost, M. R. James, one of the conventional, wrote to a friend 'an anxious question whom they will elect – as long as it is not Maynard Keynes I think all will be well'.[55] Keynes, in contrast, was an agnostic and a known controversialist and had a past in which both Lydia and his homosexual adventures counted against him. He was also, at 42, perhaps a bit too young. He had given the College good service as Bursar. As a scholar, Keynes had, as yet, perhaps less distinction about him than Clapham, but he offered the younger fellows a more exciting, more interesting and challenging future.

Keynes was tempted by the notion of succeeding Durnford, but thought that the inclination to accept was 'a wrong inclination'.[56] As the discussions developed, it became clear that if Keynes did not stand he would have to persuade someone else to stand who would be likely both to win sufficient support to avoid a lasting split among the fellows and to persuade Clapham that he could safely stand down. At first, he tried the idea on Arthur Berry, who had been mathematical lecturer since 1889 and Keynes's director of studies.[57] There was also the possibility of A. E. Brooke, an uncle of Rupert Brooke and a former Dean who was now Ely Professor of Divinity. The matter became more pressing when James Gray reported to Keynes that the younger fellows had met and wanted to know if he would stand and, if not, his suggested next move.[58] From his papers it is clear that Keynes expected that he could win the election, but he hesitated:

> I'm still in a dreadful turmoil, swept now in one direction and now in another. I think I've heard by now all the advices which are any good and the answer must come out of my own *pupsik*. I shall give it a strong squeeze on Sunday. The alternatives are to stand or to throw all my influence for the election of Brooke. . . . Pray for me![59]

On the Sunday he discussed the issue with John Sheppard, who opposed his standing, and with his parents at Harvey Road, where his mother agreed with the decision he took later that day while his father 'would like me to be Provost and glow'.[60] He wrote later the same day to James Gray:

> Dear Gray,
>
> It is very difficult for me to answer your question decidedly, as I ought to do. After much painful thought, I am still in a state of indecision.
>
> In view of my actual and possible preoccupations in other directions, I hesitate about the idea of taking on so great a responsibility here. If I were elected to be Provost, I should of course put first the obligations of the office as I conceive them to be. But I would not willingly break off my various contacts outside Cambridge. I am very much afraid of finding some occasion where the course of action, which I should feel to be natural and proper and even obligatory on myself as a private person, might be deemed to be inconsistent with the position of being in part, as it were, a collective person. Perhaps I could put it another way by saying that the position of Provost may be in some ways unsuitable to a person of my activities and temperament.
>
> The reasons to the contrary, that is in favour of my standing, from my own feeling and affections are obvious and I needn't say anything about them.
>
> In finally making up my mind which I must do shortly, I am bound to be influenced by the general feeling, so far as I can ascertain it. I do not want to be supported by anyone who has not fully considered my reasons for hesitating, which I am sure are very real reasons. If hereafter

I were to feel the office a fetter, or if the College to think that I did not feel it sufficiently a fetter, it would be bad both for the College and for me.

I hope you will try to find out at the meeting you have called for Monday, whether the election of Brooke, if he were willing to stand, might not be received with more general consent by the College as a whole, than any other election is likely to be.

Yours sincerely,

J M Keynes

Keynes had hoped that this hesitant letter, which did not close the door on his election, would get Brooke elected. It took some time for matters to work out that way. By 14 May Clapham had not stood down and Brooke, despite overwhelming support, had not definitely agreed to stand. The next day, Keynes spoke to Clapham, who agreed to stand down in favour of Brooke.[61] That seems to have settled it: Keynes had chosen 'between the Provostry of King's and respectability and Gordon Square and scalliwags' and was '*not* lost to Bloomsbury' while the College avoided a split and possibly even a public scandal.[62] Brooke, 63 at the time of his election, performed his duties conscientiously for seven years. When he retired, the balance of College opinion had swung decisively away from conventional respectability and John Sheppard, who had become Vice-Provost in 1929, succeeded him as Provost.

The 1926 King's election was not Keynes's last opportunity for that type of office. He could have stood, but did not, in King's in 1933. In 1934, he was offered the Mastership of Christ's which he declined.[63] Indeed, from the mid-1920s he did nothing to change his position in Cambridge and when Pigou was about to retire as Professor of Political Economy in 1944, Keynes refused the offer of the chair – largely because he did not need it.[64]

As noted above,[65] by the end of 1922 Keynes had cleared off his debts to his Syndicate associates and had net assets in excess of £21,000. Leaving aside the substantial savings from his earnings from *Economic Consequences* and *A Revision of the Treaty* and his new career in journalism, over 70 per cent of the recovery had come through speculation, the bulk of it in currencies. Thus from the beginning of 1923 he was again a substantial investor on his own account.

Over the rest of the decade and into the next, his investment activities took several forms. There were his own affairs to manage. Then there was the College. In these, he was relatively free to follow his own inclinations, for he had by then almost complete discretion in College – subject only to the provisions of the law. Then there were his insurance companies. I have already mentioned the National Mutual of which he became chairman in May 1921. He also joined the board of the Provincial Insurance Company in December 1923 at the suggestion of W. H. Haslam with whom he had worked at Genoa and who had heard good reports of the advice that he had given Sir Ernest Debenham. Finally, there were three investment companies that he organised with O. T. Falk: the A.D. Investment Trust (July 1921), organised largely for former members of 'A' Division; the P.R. Finance Company (January 1923), an attempt to make the benefits of the A.D. more widely available; and the Independent Investment Company (January 1924). In all of them Falk was a co-director with as much, if not more, responsibility for day-to-day investment decisions, a ruthlessness in carrying them out and a tendency to resent interference. Throughout most of the decade, the team of Keynes and Falk worked well with no great marked divergence of views until 1929, although Keynes withdrew from the A.D. in November 1927, selling all his shares in the company.[f] Thus in the case of the companies' investment policies, especially as few records survive, it is hard to see Keynes's hand at work, except possibly in the operating principles of the Independent published in its prospectus.[66]

As an investor working on his own account, Keynes's experience in 1923–9 was mixed. In five of the seven years, his security investments did *worse* than the market as measured by the *Bankers' Magazine* index. If he had done as well as the market, he would have come out with capital gains of £10,800; instead he lost £14,800. He was more successful in currency and commodity speculation, although the return of most countries to the gold standard in the course of the decade meant there were few opportunities to speculate in currencies with substantial markets after 1925. His net gains were of the order of £10,000 in currencies and £17,000 in commodities, which covered stock market losses and provided the finance for his other activities when his expenditure exceeded his income. Commodity speculation was, however, his undoing at the end of the decade when his losses triggered such a marked deterioration in his financial position that he had little left to lose in the stock market crash of 1929 – his net worth falling from £44,000 at the end of 1927 to £7,815 at the end of 1929.

During this period, as later, Keynes was an active investor: within most years the value of his sales of securities exceeded the market value of his securities at the beginning of the year. After 1926 he also carried a large portion of his activities with borrowed money with outstanding loans amounting to more than half the value of his portfolio. More often than not, the securities of a few firms would dominate his portfolio: individual holdings well above 10 per cent of the total were common. This combination of concentrated individual holdings, large loans and considerable speculation, coupled with stubbornness in backing his own judgements in the face of adversity, could bring problems, as they did in 1928–31.

f His papers and his correspondence with Falk give no indication of his reasons for this decision.

In the 1920s, Keynes believed that he could use his knowledge of the determinants of the credit (or trade) cycle derived from his academic work to his financial advantage. Indeed, the founding of the Independent, which he had originally wanted to call the 'Credit Cycle Investment Company', makes this clear.[67] The prospectus of the company proclaimed:

> It is now known that the fluctuations in the values of long-dated and short-dated fixed interest securities and also of fixed interest securities generally and of ordinary share prices are all affected by a periodic credit cycle. Changes in the short period rate of interest affect the value of long-dated securities to a greater extent than should strictly be the case, with the result that considerable profits can be made from switching from one class to another at the appropriate phase of the credit cycle. Similar periodic changes also take place in the relative values of money on the one hand and of goods and real property on the other, which are reflected in the relative values of bonds and shares, representing as these do respectively money claims and property, so that here also the same principle of changing from one class to another at appropriate times can be applied.
>
> The result of accumulated experience on these matters is to make clear that the course of events is sufficiently regular for those who are in constant touch with the financial situation in certain instances to anticipate impending changes in the credit cycle.[68]

With such a strategy, assuming that the theory is correct, timing is everything. As an older and wiser Keynes told Richard Kahn in May 1938, '[I]t needs phenomenal skill to make much out of it'.[69]

Certainly, Keynes and Falk were not successful. Except for the Provincial, where the two had to contend with F. C. Scott, a man of speculative temperament and strong views of his own, all of the two men's companies ran into difficulties at the end of the decade. In part, this reflected the fact that Falk got everything badly wrong: in the course of 1928, he decided that markets had gone too high and that it was time to go liquid; in the summer of 1929 he decided that it was time to go into Wall Street on a substantial scale. In Keynes's case, there was a massive misjudgement in commodities (which also affected the P.R. to add to the woes precipitated by acting on Falk's views).

Keynes's misjudgement centred on rubber. At the end of 1927, with prices above 1s. 7d. per pound, Keynes owned seven forward purchase contracts for 177 tons of rubber maturing between April and December 1928, 12 tons maturing in 1929 and 12 tons maturing in 1930 – all entered into at prices ranging from 1s. 8¼ d. to 2s. 6d. per pound. The suspension, announced on 4 April 1928, of the Stevenson Rubber Restriction Scheme covering Ceylon, Malaya and the Straits Settlements reduced spot prices to 8½ d. to 9½ d. for the rest of 1928. Keynes's resulting losses brought a need for further finance at a time when he was heavily in debt to his brokers, who also asked for a higher margin, and forced him to make large sales of securities. Keynes's lack of cover for his loans brought further forced sales in 1929. Thus he had done most of his selling for other than 'credit cycle' reasons before markets collapsed, which was a blessing, particularly as the one major share remaining in his portfolio, the Austin Motor Company fell from 21s. to 12s. during 1928 and to 5s. in 1929.g All in all, the experience was not a heartening one and it brought the frightening fall in net worth recorded above.

In King's the experience was less disastrous both for the Chest and overall, because of greater caution on Keynes's part and because of legal restrictions which forced much of the portfolio into high quality, fixed-interest, Trustee securities. None the less, prospects were sufficiently gloomy for the College to defer its 1931 valuation for two months.h

Keynes's and Falk's company results were no more encouraging. The A.D., which Keynes had left in 1927, went under. The National Mutual, which had trumpeted the advantages of more aggressive investment policies, particularly in industrial shares, and moved to annual rather than quinquennial valuations to publicise the advantages of the policy, postponed its 1931 valuation and then changed to biennial ones. The P.R., whose shareholders included Keynes's Bloomsbury friends, his family and some of his former 'A' Division colleagues,i originally issued shares at £1. It did well through 1927, when unsuccessful speculation in commodities caught both it and Keynes. Heavy losses continued so that in the autumn of 1931 the break-up value of the firm was 2s. 11½d.j Finally, the Independent, which had an undistinguished career in the 1920s, was caught by the slump. Its difficulties were exacerbated by continued disagreements between Keynes and Falk and by Keynes's refusal, just before Britain left the gold standard in September 1931, to replace a large dollar overdraft with a sterling overdraft.70 In 1932 the company was reorganised. Keynes and Falk remained on the board but the management passed into more conventional hands. By the

g Its recovery to 35s. in April 1930 and 28s. 3d. by the end of the year gave him cause to recover his position (he sold 2,000 shares at 35s.) and led him to outperform substantially a dismal market in 1930.

h The College, largely as a result of Keynes's stubbornness, also began to farm on its own account land it had bought in Lincolnshire when the agricultural depression shattered its prospects of achieving rents commensurate with the cost of the land.

i Most members of the Syndicate ended up as shareholders in the P.R. when Keynes repaid them in 1922. A surviving list of shareholders for 15 October 1931 gives the following: Clive Bell (3,000); David Garnett (2,000); Roger Fry (2,000); Lytton Strachey (500); Walter Langdon Brown (2,000); Geoffrey Keynes (1,200); John Neville Keynes (2,500) and A. V. Hill (1,200). At the time Maynard Keynes held 2,000 shares.

j The outcome here was that Falk ended his connection with the firm. Keynes refused to sell out to Falk's former stockbroking partners at Buckmaster and Moore on the ground that he felt morally bound to restore his friends' capital for the second time. With Rupert Trouton as his co-director, he set out to restore the position. When they put the P.R., into voluntary liquidation in May 1935, each shareholder received £1 7s. 7.68d. per share. By this time, Keynes held over 14,000 shares.

time Keynes died in 1946, the funds underlying the ordinary shares had almost regained the issue price of January 1924.

No, Keynes's 1920s as an investor were not successful. Nevertheless in the middle years of the decade he retained a reputation for his financial acumen. To some extent this did reflect revealed skills. The mid-decade results were not all that unfavourable. If one compares the results of the results of the investments in shares for the Chest in King's with those for the Prudential Insurance Company (where Keynes was not involved), the Provincial and the National Mutual, one finds that the Chest weathered the slump most successfully and that there was little to choose between the Prudential and the Provincial (where Falk had left the board in 1926 and ceased to have any connection with the firm, even as a broker, in 1930), while the National Mutual did worst.[71] Certainly in the 1920s and later, his advice was sought by other Cambridge bursars: there were even pilgrimages from Oxford to obtain his views. When asked, Keynes's 'most emphatic advice to Colleges is to be *active*'.[k] That he certainly was.

k See the note by R. V. Lennard, a Fellow of Wadham College, Oxford, 26 November 1926. When he interviewed the officials of the Ministry of Agriculture a little later, he reported their views on Keynes's policies:

> King's has sold their isolated properties and concentrated their estates to secure economy of management. Mr French thinks Mr Keynes is too modest in attributing all the success of the policy adopted by King's to the agents. The great point about King's has been that when a good opportunity is pointed out to them, they 'go for it'. The swiftness of decision which marked their policy is due to Mr Keynes.
>
> (18 December 1926. Notes supplied by Lord Kahn)

NOTES

1 KCCP, CBVBamII 16, 29 November 1921.
2 Above p. 326.
3 NUL, JMK to VB, 30 November 1921.
4 M. Keynes (ed.) 1983, 9.
5 NUL, JMK to VB, 22 December 1921.
6 KCCP, CBVBamII 18, 25 December 1921.
7 NUL, JMK to VB, 28 December 1921.
8 KCCP, VBMK65, 1 January 1922.
9 NUL, JMK to VB, 6 January 1922.
10 NUL, JMK to VB, 9 January 1922.
11 KCCP, DGVB199, 15 January 1922.
12 KCCP, DGVB119, 25 January 1922.
13 KCCP, VBMK66, 4 February 1922.
14 NUL, JMK to VB, 9 February 1922.
15 KCCP, CBVBamII 23, 13 February 1922.
16 BL, ADD.60712, GLS to James Strachey, 15 February 1922.
17 KCCP, CBVBamII 25, 15 May 1922.

18 KCCP, VBMK71, 12 April 1922.
19 KCCP, VBRF312, Monday.
20 KCCP, VBMK71, 12 April 1922.
21 KCCP, VBRF311, 18 February 1923.
22 KCCP, VBCB138, 12 May [1922].
23 NUL, JMK to VB, 20 May 1922.
24 KCCP, DGVB194, 15 June 1924.
25 Nicolson 1975–9, II, 534, 594–5; III, 33, 115.
26 Q. Bell in Crabtree and Thirlwall (eds.) 1980; in M. Keynes (ed.) 1983; Lydia to JMK, 12 November 1922, 21 and 23 April 1923; 25 October 1923.
27 KCKP, Geoffrey Keynes to JMK, 16 February 1923.
28 KCKP, JMK to Lydia, 7 March 1924.
29 MCL, Benson Diaries, Vol. 174, 40–1, 11 May 1924; Newsome 1980, esp. ch. 12.
30 BL, ADD.55201, JMK to D. Macmillan, 5 September 1924; Harrod 1951, 365.
31 KCKP, JMK to Lydia, 23 April 1925; Lydia to JMK, 4 May 1925.
32 KCKP, JMK to FAK, 23 July 1925.
33 VWD II, 38.
34 KCKP, Polly Hill Letters, FAK to JNK, 4 August 1925.
35 KCC, Ramsey Papers, F. Ramsey to Lettice Baker, 20 August 1925.
36 BL, ADD.60714, James Strachey to GLS, 9 January and 1 January 1925; KCCP, VBRF363, 25 September 1925.
37 KCKP, Lydia to JMK, 14 October 1925. See also Lydia's letter of 5 March 1926 and VWL, III, 349.
38 VWL, III, 349.
39 KCCP, VBRF355, 21 September 1924; VBRF356, 6 October 1924; VWD, II, 318; VWL, III, 133, 137.
40 VWL, III, 213.
41 Stansky and Abrahams 1966, 26–7; Q. Bell in M. Keynes (ed.) 1983, 81–4.
42 BL, ADD.60721, GLS to Carrington, 29 September 1925.
43 KCCP, DGVB247, 18 April 1926. See also CBVBamII 59, 15 May [1927] and Nicolson 1978, III, 349, 376.
44 KCCP, VBRF378, 13 August [1926]; VWD, III, 181.
45 KCCP, VBRF378, 13 August [1926]; KCKP, M. MacCarthy to JMK, 26 May 1928; VWD, III, 181.
46 BL, ADD.52432, S. Courtauld to Lady Aberconway, 5 September 1932.
47 G. Keynes 1981, ch. 16; below pp. 578–9.
48 VWD, II, 222–4; see also L. Woolf 1968, 115–17; Rosenbaum (ed.) 1975, 23–4.
49 Partridge 1981, 137–8.
50 Garnett 1962, 63–5.
51 KCKP, JMK to Lydia, 26 January 1925; Lydia to JMK, 8 February 1925.
52 KCKP, JMK to Lydia, 6 and 18 June, 13 November 1924.
53 KCKP, JMK to Lydia, 24 April 1925.
54 KCKP, Box 5A, A. F. R. Wollaston to JMK, 9 March 1926 but posted 8 April.
55 Pfaff 1980, 214.
56 KCKP, JMK to Lydia, 23 April 1926.
57 KCKP, JMK to Lydia, 26 April 1926; Box 5A, A. F. R. Wollaston to JMK, 29 April 1926.
58 KCKP, Box 5A, J. Gray to JMK, 30 April 1926.

59 KCKP, Box 5A; JMK to Lydia, 30 April 1926; VWL, III, 259; VWD, III, 76.
60 KCKP, JMK to Lydia, 2 May 1926.
61 KCKP, JMK to Lydia, 14 and 15 May 1925. On the election see also Wilkinson 1980a, 78–80.
62 VWL, III, 259, 265.
63 KCKP, JMK to Lydia, 18 February 1934.
64 KCKP, UA1/1, JMK to Vice Chancellor, 28 January 1944.
65 Page 361.
66 *JMK*, XII, 33.
67 BL, ADD.57923, JMK to O. T. Falk, 3 September 1923.
68 *JMK*, XII, 33. This account of Maynard's investment activities leans heavily on the materials presented in Chapter 1 of volume XII.
69 *JMK*, XII, 100.
70 For his reasoning, which put the national interest above the interest of his shareholders, see *JMK*, XX, 611–12. See also below pp. 528–9.
71 *JMK*, XII, 96, 104.

17

THE RETURN TO GOLD

To debate monetary reform with a City editor . . . is like debating Darwinism with a bishop 60 years ago. But even bishops – so why not City editors? – move in the end.

(JMK in *The Times*, 28 March 1925, *JMK*, XIX, 348–9)

At the same time as he was becoming more involved in organised liberalism, Keynes became concerned with the large issues of British financial policy – unemployment and the choice of an exchange rate and a standard for sterling. At the end of the war, the Committee on Currency and Foreign Exchanges with Lord Cunliffe in the chair had recommended that the main goal of financial policy should be a return to the gold standard at the pre-war parity. In law this was defined in terms of the Bank of England's selling price for gold – 77s. 10½d. (£3.894) per troy ounce of 0.916 fineness. In most discussions, however, people worked on the basis of the dollar exchange rate when the United States was on the gold standard, as she was from 1919: $4.86656 to the pound.

The Government accepted the Cunliffe Committee's recommendation in the autumn of 1919. Sterling was then floating against the major currencies, after the authorities had ceased to support the wartime exchange rate of $4.76⁷/₁₆ in March 1919 and had by Order in Council prohibited the export of gold without official permission on 1 April 1919. With the formal end of hostilities and the ratification of the Peace Treaties, the legal basis for this Order disappeared. The Government took the power to regulate gold exports in the Gold and Silver (Export Control) Act of 1920. During its passage through the House of Commons, in response to a Liberal request, the Government agreed that the Act should expire on 31 December 1925. Thus, by chance, 1925 took on a certain significance.[1]

At the end of the war, as noted above,[2] Keynes had proposed a scheme where sterling would be pegged at 10 to 15 per cent below pre-war par through a tax on gold exports and left the possibility through Order in Council of reducing the tax to work sterling back towards pre-war par. The scheme came to nothing. At Genoa he advocated pegging sterling to gold at the existing exchange rate, $4.20, again leaving open the possibility of its appreciation to pre-war parity, this time over a period of at least 20 months. In December 1922 in a lecture to the Institute of Bankers, he still supported stabilisation at a devalued rate, this time between $4 and $4.50, but he was already less enthusiastic about taking sterling back to pre-war par.[3]

In the course of 1923 he thought out his position carefully in the course of expanding his Reconstruction in Europe articles on inflation, the exchanges and currency policy into A Tract on Monetary Reform which he published in December. In that book, he made a strong case for a policy that would aim at stabilising the domestic price level, largely on the ground that the contractual and social arrangements of contemporary capitalism worked best with stable prices. He believed that the Bank of England through its Bank rate policy and its ability to control the reserves of the banking system had the policy instruments available to ensure a modicum of price stability. If the Bank took domestic price stability as its goal, exchange rate policy needed rethinking, for if Britain returned to the gold standard international gold flows would lead her to inflate and deflate at the same rate as the rest of the world. One possible way of avoiding the problem might be an attempt to stabilise the international value of gold in terms of commodities. Such a proposal, largely the work of R. G. Hawtrey of the Treasury, had been part of the Genoa Resolutions on Currency.

Keynes found Hawtrey's proposal defective. With the existing distribution of the world's stocks of monetary gold, he argued that it would put the control of the British price level and the handling of the credit cycle in the hands of the Federal Reserve System in the United States. He did not believe that the Federal Reserve, which had opened for business in 1914, was experienced enough or sufficiently insulated from American sectional interests to manage the price level in the international interest. Moreover, he believed that there was a risk of gold falling in value as national monetary authorities restricted its unessential uses as hand-to-hand currency or commercial bank reserves and it became concentrated in central bank reserves. If this happened, pegging to gold permanently – and to contemporaries this is what a return to gold meant – would leave Britain running the risk of significant inflation.

Keynes thus believed that domestic price stability entailed flexibility in the exchange rate. After the experience of the previous few years, he did not come down in favour of freely floating exchange rates but suggested what might now be called a 'crawling peg'. The Bank of England would announce weekly, on Thursday when it announced Bank rate, its buying and selling prices for gold. It would change these prices only to prevent externally generated price disturbances from affecting Britain, while it would aim for domestic price stability through its use of Bank rate supported by open market operations to control the reserves of the banking system.

The whole package was set out in the Tract at the end of the year. Prior to that, however, bits and pieces of the argument appeared in various places. The argument for price stability had appeared in the Reconstruction Supplements. From the mid-July 1923 rise in Bank rate, he had become a regular and stern critic of attempts by the authorities to raise the value of sterling by reducing British prices and a strong proponent of the policy of price stability.[4] He began to speak repeatedly of the importance and the possibilities of conscious monetary management, especially to groups of Liberals.[5] He also began to speculate openly that the value of gold would fall. It was this prospect that gave him one of the few signs of hope after Britain settled her American war debts.[6]

In late 1923 and early 1924 the Bank of England and the Treasury, who both retained a return to gold at pre-war par as the ultimate goal of currency policy, were waiting upon events. At the turn of the year, sterling stood at $4.27½, below the level a year earlier but well above the low levels of February 1920 when it had touched $3.20. The Bank had regained control of domestic financial markets. Government income now exceeded expenditure and the authorities had managed to reduce the overhang of short-term debt. There were even hints of possible international economic stability: Britain's war debt to the United States had been settled; financial instability in central Europe had been reduced with a League of Nations stabilisation programme in Austria and the recent attempt at stabilisation in Germany; the reparations issue was back before the two committees established by the Reparation Commission at the end of November 1923. There were pressures from some of the overseas Dominions for a return to gold at pre-war par, but the Treasury and the Bank preferred to await further developments on the issues of reparations and inter-allied debts before proceeding.

The expert committees appointed by the Reparation Commission got down to work in January 1924. Both committees were strong ones: that on Germany's capacity to pay under the chairmanship of Charles Gates Dawes included Sir Robert Kindersley, Sir Josiah Stamp and Keynes's old Morgan acquaintance Thomas Lamont; that on Germany's export of capital was chaired by Reginald McKenna. Although Keynes wrote nothing about the work of the experts until their reports appeared in April 1924, he may have made his views known privately to Sir Josiah Stamp as he passed through Paris on his return from a holiday in Monte Carlo in January or at a meeting in London on 24 March.[7] Stamp provided him with an early copy of the Dawes Report, adding that 'Everyone in France is saying – "What will Keynes say?" So go easy on the vials of your wrath at present'.[8] Of the two reports, the Dawes Committee's was the more important, for the McKenna report on the export of capital, although technically interesting, rehashed past events and effectively demonstrated how bare the cupboard really was. The Dawes report attempted to settle reparations for the time being: it set up a schedule of payments, made provision for a foreign loan to Germany, established an acceptable control system and provided for adjustments in changed circumstances.

At first, as if following Stamp's injunction, Keynes gave the Dawes report an encouraging, although sceptical, welcome. He called it 'an honourable document', 'the finest contribution hitherto to this impossible problem'.

> It achieves an atmosphere of impartiality and exhibits scientific workmanship and sound learning. Though the language seems at times the language of a sane man who, finding himself in a madhouse, must accommodate himself to the inmates, it never loses its sanity. Though it compromises with the impossible and even contemplates the impossible, it never prescribes the impossible.[9]

He wondered however whether the scheme's one year moratorium on reparations gave Germany enough of a breathing space and whether the safeguards for her in the form of transfer protection limiting the amount remitted abroad to that consistent with currency stability would really work. He was none the less willing to give the scheme the benefit of the doubt. It was only as it moved towards reality at a Conference of Allied, American and German representatives in London between 16 July and 16 August and with the issue of the Dawes Loan on 15 October that he became critical. At first his criticism centred on details such as the problems of default and sanctions – hardly an irrelevant matter as French and Belgian troops remained in the Ruhr until August 1925. But as the Dawes Loan approached, he became more critical, calling the control system under the Agent General for Reparations 'not compatible with civilisation or human nature' and suggesting that as its reparations payments were above what Germany would voluntarily pay the scheme would fail.[10] With this view of the size of reparations, he remained critical of the scheme and its successor, the Young Plan of 1929.

While the Dawes Committee was sitting in the late winter of 1924, the British Government began the series of crabwise movements that would bring Britain back to gold at pre-war par on 28 April 1925. On 18 February, the new Labour Prime Minister, James Ramsay MacDonald, reaffirmed the Government's commitment to the recommendations of the Cunliffe Committee – a statement echoed by Philip Snowden, his new Chancellor, who a fortnight later mentioned the advantages of amalgamating the Bank of England note issue with the wartime issue of Treasury currency notes. The Bank of England did not ignore these statements. A week after the publication of the Dawes Report, its Committee of Treasury agreed to advise Snowden to appoint a Treasury Committee to consider the amalgamation of the two note issues. Such a committee would have to consider a return to gold, for the Cunliffe Committee had recommended that amalgamation await at least a year's experience back on the gold standard with a minimum gold reserve of £150 million. Agreed on the criteria for membership – known support for the Cunliffe recommendations and acceptability to the Governor of the Bank – the Treasury and Bank quickly settled the Committee on the Currency and Bank of England Note Issues. It comprised Austen Chamberlain (Chairman until he became Foreign Secretary after the Conservative election victory in November 1924), Sir John Bradbury (who succeeded Chamberlain as Chairman), Sir Otto Niemeyer, Professor Pigou and Gaspard Farrar. All except Chamberlain and Niemeyer had been members of the Cunliffe Committee. The members realised the terms of reference – 'to consider whether the time has now come to amalgamate the Treasury Note Issue with the Bank of England Note Issue, and, if so, on what terms and conditions the amalgamation should be carried out' – were a convenient cloak for a review of the problems of returning to gold: if they did not, the Chairman and the Governor of the Bank made it clear at the first meeting of the Committee on 27 June. When inviting witnesses, however, the Committee did nothing to make this implication clear, as official committees often do, with a set of questions. If Keynes's papers are any guide – and they seem consistent, given the testimony of other witnesses – the invitations to appear contained only the terms of reference and a copy of the Cunliffe Report.[11] It is surprising, however, that Keynes and other witnesses did not put 2 and 2 together. After giving evidence, both Keynes and Professor Cannan remarked on the unexpected shape of the Committee's Report.[12] If they had perceptively followed the trend of the questioning after their opening statements, something they could have done at leisure as they corrected the typescripts of their evidence, they could have gathered the Committee's intentions and even supplemented their evidence with material more germane to the issue. That Keynes did just this makes his subsequent 'complaint' seem rather forced.

Keynes appeared before the Committee on 11 July 1924.[13] He began with a discussion of the existing rules for the two note issues and possible measures of reform, saying that he did not want to raise the issue of Britain's ultimate currency policy unless he had to. He saw no particular reason for amalgamating the note issues. He had, however, strong reasons for altering the rules governing the issue of currency notes (which only provided for a decline in the issue) and a higher fiduciary limit for both issues. In his ideal world, he argued, he would prefer his long-advocated policy of concentrating Britain's gold reserves to meet a balance of payments deficit and of issuing notes domestically as the state of credit required without any fixed limit. When the Committee pushed him onto the larger issue of a return to gold, he advocated the official regulation of gold exports and imports in perpetuity. He did not favour an attempt to restore the pound to pre-war par through deflation: he believed that price stability in Britain would with American inflation see sterling rise above pre-war par. It was Keynes's expectation of long-term inflation which was his main reason at this time for not linking sterling to gold. Others held the opinion that American inflation – or as Keynes put it the assumption 'that the Federal Reserve is going to be overwhelmed [with gold] to precisely that degree which it pleases us should occur' or of 'a nice balance between skill and want of skill on the part of the Federal Reserve Board' – would ease Britain's return to gold. The expectation of American inflation was widely held.[14]

To make certain that his views on the gold standard were clearly understood by the Committee, he set them out in the next issue of the *Nation*, using as his stalking horse three recent statements by Sir Charles Addis and Sir Robert Kindersley (both directors of the Bank of England) and Walter Leaf (Chairman of the Westminster Bank) in favour of a deflationary policy to restore sterling to pre-war par. He pointed out the effects of deflation on the burden of the national debt, on money wages and unemployment and highlighted the advantages of price stability. He sent copies to Austen Chamberlain and Addis, as well as to McKenna and Baldwin. He continued to press the issue with Addis, concluding on a note that was to recur in future months and years:

> The more I spend my thoughts on these matters, the more alarmed do I become at seeing you and the others in authority attacking the problems of the changed post-war world with – I know you will excuse my saying so – pre-war views and ideas. To close the mind to the idea of revolutionary improvements in our control of money and credit is to sow the seeds of the downfall of individualistic capitalism. Do not be the Louis XVI of the monetary revolution. For surely it is certain that enormous changes will come in the next twenty years and they will be bad changes, unwisely and disastrously carried out, if those of us who are at least agreed in our ultimate objects and are aiming at the stability of society cannot agree in putting forth safe and sound reforms.
>
> . . . I seek to improve the machinery of society not to overturn it.[15]

Although the Chamberlain Committee continued its deliberations with a view to presenting a report to the Government in the autumn of 1924, public discussion of the return to gold abated. Keynes turned his attention to the related subjects of unemployment and foreign lending.

In the early issues of the *Nation* under its new management, Keynes, at first under his own name and subsequently anonymously, produced a weekly column 'Finance and Investment'. In many of these he provided investment advice. As 1923 progressed, the column focused more and more on issues of overseas securities, emphasising the risks for investors. Early in 1924, after a holiday at Monte Carlo with Lydia, under the guise of 'a French correspondent', he wrote an account of the devious means by which the pre-war Russian Government had influenced French comment on Russian affairs so as to increase French loans to that country – all of which had disappeared in the 1917 Revolution.[16] In the spring, he began to comment on the wisdom of Britain's lending overseas, particularly to the Empire.[17] This, plus his views on population growth and unemployment, lay in the background when on 12 April 1924 Lloyd George stated in the columns of the *Nation* that he viewed Britain's economic future with misgivings and argued that the most important immediate task was improving production. In the ensuing weeks, there were contributions on the subject from Sir William Beveridge, A. L. Bowley, Norman Angell, Walter Layton and Lord Weir before Keynes made his own on 24 May, asking 'Does Unemployment Need a Drastic Remedy?'.[18]

Naturally, his answer was, Yes. The settlement of Europe and a monetary policy aimed at price stability would not in themselves do the trick. Keynes agreed with Lloyd George and others 'that there is no time or place here for *laissez-faire*' and continued:

[W]e must look for succour to the principle that *prosperity is cumulative*. We have stuck in a rut. We need an impulse, a jolt, an acceleration.

What Britain needed, Keynes argued, was a substantial construction boom similar to the railway and building booms of the nineteenth century. Businessmen's expectations were depressed. A construction boom would lift their spirits and their investment and in the process pull unemployed labour away from the depressed industries. To initiate such an expansion, the Chancellor should cease using his sinking fund and budget surpluses to redeem the national debt and use the funds to promote domestic capital works – houses, roads, electricity generation.

To later commentators, such a programme with its notion of cumulative prosperity has looked suspiciously like the later Keynes programmes of *Can Lloyd George Do It?* (1929) and *The Means to Prosperity* (1933), or even the ideas associated with *The General Theory of Employment, Interest and Money* (1936). To them the key lies in words such as 'cumulative' and passages such as the following:

Current savings are already available on a sufficient scale – savings which from lack of an outlet at home, are now drifting abroad to destinations from which we as a society shall gain the least possible advantage. Private enterprise unaided cannot stop this flow. The policy of preventing public utilities from yielding more than a modest profit has gone so far that it is no longer worth the while of private enterprise to run a risk in a field where the gain is limited and the loss unlimited. We are in danger, therefore, of interfering with private initiative and yet substituting nothing for it. The advances under the Trade Facilities Act [of 1921], begun for a temporary emergency and on a small scale, point the way, perhaps, to a new method of administering an important part of the savings of the public. The next developments of politico-economic evolution may be found in the co-operation between private initiative and the public exchequer.

Sir Roy Harrod, for example, found the programme similar to those later associated with Keynes's name but argued that he had not yet developed a full rationale.[19] Peter Clarke took a similar view when he suggested the proposal 'relied heavily upon intuition' and continued:

> Mr Keynes the politician though, was not inhibited in backing his hunches by the failure of Professor Keynes the economist to provide adequate theoretical justification.[20]

This is misleading, for, although Keynes's rationale was not that of five years or a decade later, in the period surrounding the publication of this article he provided sufficient reasons for his proposals.

Keynes's case had two strands.

> I look, then, for the ultimate cure of unemployment, and for the stimulus which shall initiate a cumulative prosperity, to monetary reform – which will remove fear – and to the diversion of national savings from relatively barren foreign investment into state-encouraged productive enterprises at home – which will inspire confidence.

The case for credit control to achieve domestic price stability needs no elaboration at this point. It was the case developed in the *Tract*. The argument for capital development at home in part rested on the crucial role of accumulation in development stressed from *Economic Consequences* onwards and the rapid growth of the labour force with its need for co-operating capital equipment and housing.[21] The new elements in the justification were twofold: his view of the nature of the imperfections in Britain's capital markets and the current returns from home and foreign investment.

His view on capital markets was one which Keynes elaborated on several occasions in 1924. Investors, particularly those concerned with Trustee securities, had strong preferences for safe securities, in the case of Trustee issues heightened by law.[a] British national and local government and most imperial government securities had Trustee status. If the British Government, in the absence of buoyant conditions in other segments of the domestic securities market, used its sinking funds plus any budget surplus to repay debt, the individuals receiving the repayments would attempt to reinvest in similar classes of securities and, with no compensating increase in domestic issues of such securities, would put their funds into overseas equivalents – loans to Empire governments. The issue of these in London would be encouraged by the low interest rates payable on such safe securities resulting from Government policies and investors' preferences. Keynes argued that

a The Trustee Acts limited trustees' investments to particular securities unless otherwise specified in the original deed of trust.

the official policy of deflation, Government spending cuts and the industrial slump had actually reduced the supply of domestic Trustee securities and thus pushed funds into overseas issues. Policies that reduced debt repayments and stimulated domestic new issues would be more appropriate.

Of course, the contemporary critic could ask, what was wrong with new overseas lending? Would it not lead to orders in Britain and thus stimulate output and employment? Here Keynes deployed three arguments. The first and most straightforward was that, given the Trustee Acts and the Colonial Stock Act of 1900 which admitted Colonial and Dominion issues to Trustee status, lending to the Colonies and the Dominions was higher than it would otherwise be. Moreover, yields on such issues were too low, given the relative risks. As he said on more than one occasion:

> It is remarkable that Southern Rhodesia – a place in the middle of Africa with a few thousand white inhabitants and less than a million black ones – can place an unguaranteed loan on terms not very different from our own War Loan.[22]

Secondly there was a 'transfer problem', as in the payment of reparations.[23] Initially there would be a shift in claims on sterling between domestic and overseas residents.[b] Thereafter, the effect depended on the use made of these claims by the overseas residents. Making the most favourable assumptions that the claims were not transferred overseas until the borrower spent them on goods and services and that borrowing in Britain increased overseas demand for resources, the next step was to look at the effects of this rise in foreign expenditure. If it were spent in Britain on British-made goods with no import content in their manufacture, the transfer would be easily effected. If it were spent in third countries or used to finance domestic expenditure in the borrowing country, the process would be more roundabout. The exchange rate would initially be subject to downward pressures. If the world economy was subject to rigidities, it might be some time before the expansive effects of overseas expenditure affected employment in Britain. Even if they did, the depreciation in sterling, if allowed to occur, implied a fall in real wages in Britain.

Finally, Keynes argued that the relative risks of home and foreign investment to society were inadequately reflected in rates of return, even if one removed the distortions caused by the Colonial Stock Act. As he put it:

> Consider two investments, the one at home and the other abroad, with equal risks of repudiation or confiscation or legislation restricting profit. It is a matter of indifference to the individual investor which he selects. But the nation as a whole retains in the one case the object of

---

b The ultimate implications of the rise in foreign lending would also depend on the sources of the funds lent. In his discussion, Keynes ignored this matter by implicitly assuming that there was no change in the level of domestic savings and no shift in the usage of balances.

the investment and the fruits of it; whilst in the other case both are lost. If a loan to improve a South American capital is repudiated, we have nothing. If a Poplar housing loan is repudiated, we, as a nation, still have the houses. If the Grand Trunk Railway of Canada fails its shareholders by reason of legal restriction of the rates chargeable or for any other cause,[c] we have nothing. If the underground [railway] system of London fails its shareholders, Londoners still have their underground system.[24]

Over the next few months, Keynes's emphasis tended to centre more on the home versus foreign investment issue than on the capital works and unemployment issue.[25] Perhaps this reflected the fact that from the beginning of February 1924 he was thinking about a new book – a successor to the *Tract*.[26] This book was to be a more solid academic affair than the *Tract*. In November 1924, at an early stage in thinking about this new work, Keynes came to the conclusion that 'the expenditure, on the production of *fixed* capital, of public money raised by borrowing, can do nothing in itself to improve matters [in a slump] and it may do actual harm'[27] although he allowed tax-financed expenditures might be more effective. This represented reversal of many economists' views of the effects of loan-financed public works stretching back to before 1914. After a later change of mind on his part, and in a later campaign, Keynes would dub claims similar to his arguments of 1924 'the Treasury view'.

On 12 July 1924, Alfred Marshall, one of Keynes's links with the past, died. Keynes had last seen him eight weeks earlier, when he reported to Lydia:

> I have been touched this afternoon. I had news that my old master who made me into an economist (the one who had an 80th birthday two years ago – you will remember his photograph) could not live much longer; so I went to pay him a last visit. Lying in bed in his nightcap he looked like an old sage, which is what he is, – very Chinese. His voice was very weak but he told me how he first came to study economics, and how such study was a sort of religious work for the sake of the human race. He was still able to laugh, but he has no memory for what happens now and has probably forgotten my visit already. I held his hand and then went off to speak to his old wife who has given all her life to helping him do his work. She is calm and wise. He is now rather like a child and is often troublesome. He will do what the doctor tells him but not what she or the nurse says, and he calls out that, though he may be weak, he 'won't be bossed by women'.[28]

On Marshall's death, Keynes began composing a memoir of him for the

---

c The Grand Trunk had failed and become a part of Canadian National Railways. In 1923 an arbitrator declared the Grand Trunk's shares worthless.

Economic Journal. He used his own knowledge, materials from Mary Marshall and memories (and diaries) of Cambridge contemporaries such as his parents. He worked quickly at what he hoped might be 'a sort of history of Political Economy in England during the last part of the 19th century',[29] and completed his essay of over sixty pages in time for the September issue. Joseph Schumpeter in his 1946 obituary of Keynes called it 'the most brilliant life of a man of science I have ever read'.[d] It is a memoir which remains a classic and still features on undergraduate reading lists. A sympathetic, but critical, discussion of Marshall and his achievements, the memoir contained some sharp judgements on the nature of economics and economists, as well as a number of introspective judgements. Marshall 'was too little willing to cast his half-baked bread on the waters, to trust in the efficacy and co-operation of many minds and to let the world draw from him what sustenance it could'.[30] For Keynes,

> Economists must leave to Adam Smith alone the glory of the quarto, must pluck the day, fling pamphlets to the wind, write always *sub specie temporis*, and achieve immortality by accident, if at all.[31]

Again, on the nature of economics and economists:

> The study of economics does not seem to require any specialised gifts of an unusually high order. Is it not, intellectually regarded, a very easy subject compared with the higher branches of philosophy and pure science? Yet good, or even competent, economists are the rarest of birds. An easy subject at which very few excel! The paradox finds its explanation, perhaps, in that the master-economist must poses a rare *combination* of gifts. He must reach a high standard in several different directions and must combine talents not often found together. He must be mathematician, historian, statesman, philosopher – in some degree. He must understand symbols and speak in words. He must contemplate the particular in terms of the general, and touch abstract and concrete in the same flight of thought. He must study the present in the light of the past for the purposes of the future. No part of man's nature or his institutions must lie outside his ken. He must be purposeful and disinterested in a simultaneous mood; as aloof and incorruptible as an artist, yet sometimes as near the earth as a politician. Much, but not all, of this ideal many-sidedness Marshall possessed. But chiefly his mixed training and divided nature furnished him with the most essential and fundamental of the economist's necessary gifts – he was conspicuously historian and mathematician, a dealer in the particular and the general, the temporal and the eternal, at the same time.[32]

---

d Schumpeter admitted it was not perfect – that would have required another fortnight's work.

Much of this could be said of Keynes. Some of his later biographical sketches would be similarly introspective, and shared with this one echoes of his early paper 'science versus art'.

While Keynes's attention was diverted by the Marshall memoir, the implementation of the Dawes Report and the question of foreign investment, the Chamberlain Committee on the note issues continued its deliberations. The Committee's records show that Keynes's evidence, plus that of Reginald McKenna, had a considerable effect. Committee members in their correspondence and in early drafts of their report, while accepting the ultimate goal of a return to gold at pre-war par and realising that a deflationary monetary policy would achieve that goal, rejected a deflationary policy because they expected that American inflation might do the job instead. As a result they recommended that the Government maintain the current value of sterling, then well below $4.50, and restrain excessive overseas lending, while waiting for up to twelve months for American prices to rise.

The Governor of the Bank of England also did not rush matters. He did not raise Bank rate, but kept it at 4 per cent while the Federal Reserve Bank of New York reduced its discount rate from 4 to 3 per cent, partly to make Norman's position easier. Although he did not change Bank rate, Norman did push up other short-term rates in London towards Bank rate, thus making bill finance 1¼ per cent dearer in London than in New York, and began a policy of 'polite blackmail' to prevent new capital issues to countries outside the Empire.[33] From the available evidence, it would appear that he too, for the time being, was prepared to wait, for although he would have liked to see some changes in the Chamberlain Committee's draft report of September, they were not of the sort that would have precluded waiting for up to a year. It is therefore probable that if the Chamberlain Committee had reported in the autumn of 1924 it would have recommended that the authorities not take steps to force a return to gold at pre-war par.

Politics intervened before the Chamberlain Committee could finish its report or hold its final meeting with the Governor, scheduled for 13 October. On 8 October the first Labour Government was defeated in the House of Commons and the country was plunged into a general election. The result of 29 October was a substantial Conservative majority.

The election result markedly changed expectations. Sterling rose from below $4.50 to above $4.70 before the end of the year, partly as a result of a sharp rise in American capital exports and partly as a result of speculative anticipations that a return to gold was imminent. Unbeknownst to market participants, there had been a marked change in official views. In the midst of the campaign Governor Norman saw a return to gold as being as far away as 1927; on 4 November he started discussions with his Committee of Treasury of the possibility of obtaining credits in America to support sterling as it approached parity. Similar changes in view took place in the

Federal Reserve System. By mid-December Norman had discussed the issue with the new Chancellor of the Exchequer, Winston Churchill, and they had agreed to make serious preparations for a return to gold before the expiry of the 1920 Act, including a journey by Norman to New York to sound out American opinion and to make enquiries as to the possibility of an American credit to 'cushion' sterling over the transition to gold.

In New York, Norman found support for a return to gold, and a willingness to provide a credit of up to $500 million. There remained the task of persuasion in London, for Norman's colleagues at the Bank were uneasy and there was the need to obtain a firm Treasury commitment – not to mention a new report from the Committee on the Currency and Bank of England Note Issues now under Bradbury's chairmanship. It would take until 20 March 1925 for the authorities to come to a final decision and another five weeks before Churchill announced it in the House of Commons during his Budget speech on 28 April. Keynes was to react to these changes in circumstances and, although he was ultimately unsuccessful in influencing the direction of policy, his comments played an important role in the decision-making process.

In January 1925 discussion was restricted to the Bank of England and to the Bradbury Committee, which took evidence from Governor Norman and Sir Charles Addis on 28 January. Norman's evidence related to his visit to New York and his own views of how to proceed. Addis, representing the dissidents within the Bank's Committee of Treasury, did not share Norman's argument for urgency – a change of heart which Professor Sayers associates with his occasional contacts with Keynes and Sir Josiah Stamp.[34] Addis had been present on 14 January when Keynes had opened a discussion at the Tuesday Club on 'The Removal of the Gold Embargo'. Also present were Stamp, R. H. Brand, Dennis Robertson, R. G. Hawtrey, Hubert Henderson and Sir Henry Strakosch.[e]

In the Treasury, discussions did not begin in earnest until the Chancellor circulated what became known as 'Mr Churchill's Exercise' to the Governor, Bradbury, Hawtrey and Niemeyer at the end of January.[35] Bradbury remarked of the memorandum that 'The writer appears to have his spiritual home in the Keynes–McKenna sanctuary but some of the trimmings of his mantle have been furnished by the *Daily Express*.'[f] Churchill questioned the need to return to gold on a variety of grounds, worried about its effects on domestic industry and wondered why a return was such an urgent matter. As an attempt to probe his advisers' arguments it was brilliantly successful, drawing long, trenchant replies. By 6 February, Churchill had digested the

e No senior Bank or Treasury official who was a member of the Club was present. No record of Keynes's remarks survives.

f Moggridge (1972, 64). McKenna, the chairman of the Midland Bank had opposed an immediate return before the Chamberlain–Bradbury Committee; the proprietor of the *Daily Express* was Lord Beaverbrook.

replies and the draft report of the Bradbury Committee, but he still sought further answers on particular points as he mulled matters over in his own mind. As Niemeyer reported to his colleague F. W. Leith-Ross, who had gone to a League of Nations Financial Committee meeting in Geneva in his stead:

> Gold is excessively active and very troublesome. None of the witch-doctors sees eye to eye and Winston cannot make up his mind from day to day whether he is a gold bug or a pure inflationist.[36]

It was at this time that Keynes prepared what had become an annual survey for the *Nation* of the speeches of the chairmen of the London clearing banks to their shareholders. He began the article on 8 February and finished it a week later, taking great care over its tone.[37] It appeared on 21 February under the title 'The Return Towards Gold'.[38] He attempted to set the issue in a longer-term perspective by suggesting that monetary reformers such as himself faced a long period of argument before winning the day. He then turned to the matter at hand: 'whether it is prudent to hasten matters by a removal of the embargo on the export of gold'. His answer was, not in the present circumstances, given the uncertainties about American policy. Sterling had recently risen partly because the difference in interest rates between London and New York had led to a large short-term capital inflow to London, which he estimated at £100 million. If American interest rates rose in the near future as the Federal Reserve tried to damp down an incipient boom and if Britain was on the gold standard, she would face the need for dear money and severe deflation to maintain the exchange rate. If American interest rates did not rise while Britain returned to gold, Britain would have no need for deflation to attain parity and might even suffer some inflation with an inevitable subsequent reaction. As far as he was concerned, it was better to try to keep British prices stable, even if this required a higher Bank rate and restrictions on overseas lending (both of which he favoured), and to defer linking sterling to the dollar until American prices had settled at a higher level. He would not force sterling to pre-war par.

Keynes also touched eloquently on the reasons why he preferred a managed currency and why he saw grave dangers in linking sterling to the dollar.

> A gold standard means, in practice, nothing but to have the same price level and the same money rates (broadly speaking) as the United States. . . .
> The United States lives in a vast and unceasing crescendo. Wide fluctuations, which spell unemployment and misery for us, are swamped for them in the general upward movement. . . . Our rate of progress is slow at best, and faults in our economic structure, which we could afford to overlook while racing forward, are now fatal. . . . The United

States may suffer industrial and financial tempests in the years to come, and they will scarcely matter to her, but we, if we share them, may almost drown.

... Before the war we ... were the dominant partner in the gold standard alliance. But those who think that a return to the gold standard means a return to those conditions are fools and blind. We are now the debtors of the United States. Their foreign investments last year were double ours.... They hold six times as much gold as we do.... A movement of gold or of short credits, which is only a ripple for them, will be an Atlantic roller for us.... [I]t would be a mistake to believe that in the long run they will, or ought, to manage their affairs to suit our convenience.[39]

On reading this article, with its reference to 'the paradox of unemployment amidst dearth' in its final paragraph, together with a commentary by Niemeyer, who accepted Keynes as 'a serious critic of monetary policy', a troubled Churchill penned a powerful set of remarks about financial policy:

The Treasury have never, it seems to me, faced the profound significance of what Mr Keynes calls 'the paradox of unemployment amidst dearth'. The Governor shows himself perfectly happy in the spectacle of Britain possessing the finest credit in the world simultaneously with a million and a quarter unemployed.... The community lacks goods and a million and a quarter people lack work. It is certainly one of the highest functions of national finance and credit to bridge the gap between the two. This is the only country in the world where this condition exists. The Treasury and the Bank of England policy has been the only policy consistently pursued. It is a terrible responsibility for those who have shaped it, unless they can be sure that there is no connection between the unique British phenomenon of chronic unemployment and the long resolute consistency of a particular financial policy....

It may be of course you will argue that unemployment would have been much greater but for the financial policy pursued; that there is not sufficient demand for commodities either internally or externally to require the services of this million and a quarter people; that there is nothing for them but to hang like a millstone round the neck of industry and the public revenue until they become permanently demoralised. You may be right, but, if so, it is one of the most sombre conclusions ever reached. On the other hand I do not pretend to see even 'through a glass darkly' how the financial and credit policy of the country could be handled so as to bridge the gap between a dearth of goods and a surplus of labour; and well I know the dangers of experiments to that end. The seas of history are full of famous wrecks. Still, if I could see a way, I would rather follow it than any other. I would rather see Finance less proud and Industry more content.

You and the Governor have managed this affair. Taken together I expect you know more about it than anyone else in the world. At any rate, alone in the world you have had an opportunity over a definite period of years of seeing your policy carried out. That it has been a great policy, greatly pursued, I have no doubt. But the fact that this island with its enormous resources is unable to maintain its population is surely a cause for the greatest heartsearching.

Forgive me adding to your burdens by these Sunday morning reflections.[40]

In a powerful reply Niemeyer tried to allay the Chancellor's fears by arguing that, given its effects on world economic stability and the expansion of world trade, the return to gold was part of an employment policy. This may have assuaged Churchill's doubts, but either a dinner with Beaverbrook[g] or the rise in Bank rate from 4 to 5 per cent on 5 March in response to a rise in American rates raised new doubts.[h] The Chancellor therefore arranged for one more discussion of the issues on the evening of 17 March. There were present P. J. Grigg, his private secretary for 'the more mundane matters of finance and administration', Keynes, McKenna, Bradbury, and Niemeyer.[41] Until at least midnight Keynes and McKenna argued that at the pre-war parity sterling would be overvalued by 10 per cent and that the adjustment to the new rate would mean additional unemployment and industrial unrest over wage cuts, while Bradbury argued for the long-term advantages of a return to gold. After hearing both sides, Churchill asked McKenna:

But this isn't entirely an economic matter; it is a political decision, for it involves proclaiming we cannot, for the time being, complete the undertaking which we all acclaimed as necessary in 1918, and introducing legislation accordingly. You have been a politician; indeed you have been Chancellor of the Exchequer. Given the situation as it is, what decision would you take?

McKenna is said to have replied: 'There is no escape; you have to go back; but it will be hell'.[42]

On 19 March the Chancellor and the Governor met over lunch and agreed that a return to gold would be announced in the Budget. The next day a

---

g Martin Gilbert (1976, V, 99) suggests that 'towards the end of February' Churchill dined with Beaverbrook and the two men discussed the matter. A. J. P. Taylor (1972, 225–6) notes that the two men dined on 12 February but did not discuss the matter.

h Churchill was indignant at the rise in the rate, despite Leith-Ross's assurance that it was necessary for exchange support as Britain returned to gold (1968, 95). Keynes gave qualified support to the rise in Bank rate, although he was suspicious that it might presage a return to gold (*JMK*, XIX, 333–6).

meeting of the Governor, Chancellor, Prime Minister, Austen Chamberlain, Bradbury and Niemeyer confirmed the decision.

Keynes knew of neither meeting, but the evening discussion of 17 March certainly warned him of the trend of events. As a result, his opposition to a return to gold began to change its basis, first in remarks to the Commercial Committee of the House of Commons on 18 March[43] and then in articles and letters, most notably in the *Nation* in April. The shift was away from advocating a managed currency or even from delaying pegging sterling to gold to a straightforward argument that a return to gold in the present circumstances would leave sterling overvalued, not only against the dollar but also against Continental currencies, and necessitate a fall in British prices and money wages. He believed that the wisest course was to let the exchange rate adjust to the level of domestic prices rather than the other way around.

When the Chancellor announced the return on 28 April, Keynes rushed into print (in the *Nation*) with a comment that the authorities had returned to gold 'along the most prudent and far-sighted lines that were open to them'.[44] This reflected a misreading of the relevant legislation, which he mistakenly thought to allow the Bank to protect Britain against imported inflation by reducing the sterling price of gold. It weakened the force of the rest of the article which suggested that sterling was overvalued by 'not less than 5 per cent and probably 10 per cent'. The mistake, which Dennis Robertson also made, was pointed out to Keynes by a colleague and an undergraduate attending his lecture in Cambridge the following Friday.[45] But the words of praise were used by the Chancellor to advantage in the House of Commons. Once he had made the correction, and damned the Report of the Chamberlain-Bradbury Committee as 'somewhat trivial' and later as 'indolent and jejune', he concentrated on the overvaluation of sterling under the new régime.[46] He paid much more attention than previously to the relevant price statistics and to the distinction between goods which might be traded internationally and those which could not. Since competition tended to equalise the prices of tradeables in international markets, an international comparison of movements in their prices would understate the overvaluation of sterling; so he concentrated his attention on movements in domestic costs or the prices of non-traded goods. In doing so, he raised his estimate of the degree to which sterling was overvalued, eventually settling on a figure of *at least* 10 per cent.[47]

Meanwhile he prepared a more substantial discussion of the consequences of the return to gold which he offered to *The Times* at the beginning of July. Geoffrey Dawson, the editor, accepted it subject to seeing the final version. When he saw it, Dawson was 'rather embarrassed', for although he found it 'extraordinarily clever and very amusing', he thought it rather overdid the criticism.[48] He declined Keynes's article. Keynes then offered the piece to Beaverbrook for his *Evening Standard* under the general title 'Unemployment and Monetary Policy'. Beaverbrook accepted with alacrity.

It appeared as three articles on 22, 23 and 24 July. Keynes expanded the articles into a pamphlet which Virginia and Leonard Woolf's Hogarth Press, with no little turmoil, published in an edition of 10,000 copies less than a week later, under the title of *The Economic Consequences of Mr Churchill*.[49]

The Economic Consequences of Mr Churchill was concerned with three matters: the consequences of the return to gold; the reasons for the decision to return; and possible remedies. Working from the basis of the summer of 1924, when sterling was around $4.40, Keynes argued that the appreciation of sterling had been of the order of 10 per cent while money wages measured in sterling had risen slightly over 1924–5 and the cost of living had fallen slightly. The divergence between costs and the selling prices of producers of exports and import-competing goods, who had to meet competitors whose prices in foreign currency had changed little, meant increased unemployment. Nor had the 1924 position been ideal, for already Britain had an unemployment problem. The restoration of the competitive position of these producers would require a cut in money wages of 10 per cent.

But there was no mechanism to ensure such a reduction in money wages simultaneously across all industries, much less across all forms of money income. Rather there would be a series of separate struggles, beginning in the industries most exposed to foreign competition where those involved in any dispute would be asked to take a reduction in *real* wages. The main pressure for wage reductions would come from the primary unemployment caused by the fall in demand (or in profits) in the traded goods sector and by the policy of dear money and tight credit that the Bank of England would have to pursue to maintain the exchange rate in the face of rising imports and falling exports.

As his working example of the process at work, Keynes chose the coal industry where labour and management were currently in dispute. The industry, directly and indirectly through large consumers such as steel, had large export markets, few imported inputs and a wage bill which made up a large part of its total costs. Its management, Keynes estimated, would have to reduce sterling prices by almost 2s. per ton or about 10 per cent between 1924 and 1925 to remain competitive. The coal owners proposed to do so through reductions in wages and increases in hours worked. On grounds of social justice no case existed for such a reduction in wages or an increase in hours. Nor could Keynes see much ground for the owners to suffer. But the miners would bear the brunt of the adjustment.

> Like other victims of economic transition in past times, the miners are to be offered the choice between starvation and submission, the fruits of their submission to accrue to the benefit of other classes.
> . . . They are the victims of the economic juggernaut. They represent in the flesh the 'fundamental adjustments' engineered by the Treasury

and the Bank of England to satisfy the impatience of the City fathers to bridge the 'moderate gap' between $4.40 and $4.86. *They* (and others to follow) are the 'moderate sacrifice' still necessary to ensure the stability of the gold standard. The plight of the coal miners is the first, but not – unless we are very lucky – the last, of the economic consequences of Mr Churchill.

Why, Keynes asked, had Churchill made the decision?

[P]artly, perhaps, because he has no instinctive judgement to prevent him from making mistakes; partly because, lacking this instinctive judgement, he was defeated by the clamorous voices of conventional finance; and, most of all, because he was gravely misled by his experts.[50]

The experts' mistakes were the miscalculation of the extent of overvaluation caused by the appreciation of sterling and their underrating of the difficulty of reducing the level of money wages. Certainly, it would seem from the official record that the 'experts' *systematically* underestimated the maladjustment caused by the return to gold itself and, having done so, partially because they, like Keynes, expected inflation in the United States, paid little attention in detail as to how the British economy might have to adjust to sterling at $4.86.[51] As to Churchill's instinctive judgement, or lack of it, many observers have noticed that Churchill would often test his advisers' arguments favouring a given course of action by putting the opposite case very strongly or even making accusations of incompetence.[52] They have also noted that 'it was seldom, if ever, that he would reject the tested and sustained positions adopted by his technical advisers'.[53] If this was the case in 1925, 'Mr Churchill's Exercise', the 'Sunday morning reflections' of 22 February and the meeting of 17 March do not indicate, as some have suggested, that Churchill was opposed to a return to gold until his opposition 'was broken' by the weight of orthodox opinion.[i]

When it came to remedies, Keynes pulled his punches. Although he suggested that the only 'truly satisfactory' course of action was to reverse the

policy announced in the Budget and abandon the gold standard, he did not devote much attention to that alternative in 1925 – and even less afterwards.[54] He advocated other possible measures – a voluntary all-round reduction in money wages supplemented by an additional income tax on other forms of income, or, alternatively, an expansive monetary policy which might, through gold losses to the United States, lead to American inflation and reduce the need for a fall in British prices. As long as he was not prepared to advocate a departure from gold, his

---

i Robert Skidelsky in *The Times Business News* for 17 March 1969. Such is also the implicit view of Churchill's offical biographer, despite his recording of Churchill's 15 December 1924 note to Baldwin with its comment about the ease of returning to gold (Gilbert 1976, V, 99, 93).

positive proposals seemed half-hearted and he could advocate little else. In coming years he would devote considerable energy to devising other expedients.

The controversy, however, clearly exemplified Keynes's approach to the need for economic management: the need for forethought rather than instinctive reactions. He summed it up nicely just after he spoke of the miners as victims of the 'economic juggernaut':

> The truth is that we stand mid-way between two theories of economic society. The one theory maintains that wages should be fixed by reference to what is 'fair' and 'reasonable' as between classes. The other theory – the theory of the economic juggernaut – is that wages should be settled by economic pressure, otherwise called 'hard facts', and that our vast machine should crash along, with regard only to its equilibrium as a whole, and without attention to the chance consequences of the journey to individual groups.
>
> The gold standard, with its dependence on pure chance, its faith in 'automatic adjustments', and its general regardlessness of social detail, is an essential emblem and idol of those who sit in the top tier of the machine. I think that they are immensely rash in their regardlessness, in their vague optimism and comfortable belief that nothing serious ever happens. Nine times out of ten, nothing really serious does happen – merely a little distress to individuals or to groups. But we run a risk of the tenth time (and are stupid into the bargain), if we continue to apply the principles of an economics, which was worked out on the hypotheses of *laissez-faire* and free competition, to a society which is rapidly abandoning those hypotheses.[55]

Austin Robinson has pointed out that

> If Maynard Keynes had died in 1925 it would have been difficult for those who knew intimately the power and originality of his mind to have convinced those who had not known him.[56]

The early 1920s had certainly gained him a reputation as a passionate crusader. They had been relatively sparse in what is now regarded as one of the major activities of an academic – publishing for his professional colleagues. True, he had finally completed and published his *Treatise on Probability* but this reflected largely pre-war work and, for contemporaries if not recent scholars, hardly contributed to economics. In economics, although one could credit him with innovations such as the notion of inflationary finance as a form of taxation and the theory of interest parity in the market for forward exchange, he was not himself extending the frontiers of the subject. Within his chosen specialisation, monetary economics, in the Cambridge of the early 1920s A.C. Pigou, Frederick Lavington and Dennis Robertson were more active, if less popularly known.

433

Lavington, who had been Keynes's pupil before 1914 and his successor as Girdlers' Lecturer, published *The English Capital Market* in 1921 and *The Trade Cycle* in 1922. Both contained acknowledgements of assistance of Cambridge colleagues, but neither mentioned Keynes. The academic relations between the two seem to have been minimal. After the war Lavington was a sick man who rarely moved out of his college, Emmanuel. Doubtless they met to transact Faculty business, but there is only one letter between them surviving in Keynes's papers – from 1911 when Lavington had just taken his degree. Keynes's post-war appointments diaries record only one meeting on 30 April 1922 for dinner.

As for Robertson, he had published his Trinity fellowship dissertation as *A Study of Industrial Fluctuation* in 1915. In 1920 and 1921 he was preparing the first edition of *Money* (1922) for the Cambridge Economic Handbooks under Keynes's editorship. In his preface, Robertson acknowledged Keynes's assistance along with that of Pigou and Henderson.

As a monetary theorist Pigou was then best known for his article 'The Value of Money' in the *Quarterly Journal of Economics* in 1917. Along with Marshall's work this had formed the basis for Keynes's 1922 and 1923 expositions of the quantity theory. Pigou had also become the 'establishment's Cambridge monetary economist' with his memorandum on Currency and Exchange Fluctuations to the 1920 Brussels Conference and membership of both the Cunliffe and Chamberlain-Bradbury Committees. In 1927, he would publish his *Industrial Fluctuations*, a major contribution to the field.[j]

Keynes's contributions to monetary economics had come in his journalism and in his *Tract*, itself a reworking of his articles in the *Manchester Guardian* Commercial Reconstruction Supplements. The *Tract* was not a fully integrated performance: the discussion of the Cambridge cash balances approach to the quantity theory, which he added for the book, barely reflected the discussion of inflation as a tax on money balances. Indeed, one might argue that at the time of the book Keynes had not begun to analyse the major issues in his field of specialisation. He was living off his Marshallian inheritance, the intellectual capital of the past, for purposes of present controversy.

Only after publication of the *Tract* did Keynes turn to a substantial academic book on monetary theory. By then he was over 40 – an age when fundamental theoretical contributions to economics become rarer – and with a reputation as a publicist rather than a scientist – a balance of reputation that was to last for some time. Nevertheless, on 25 January 1924, he reported to Lydia: 'I wrote some pages about Theory of Money this morning'. A week later: 'I drew up a plan for a short new book which would be a successor to *Monetary Reform*'. The plan has not survived.[57] He did not get further

---

j When it appeared, Keynes found it 'rather miserable' and remarked, 'Perhaps Mrs Marshall is right that he should have married, his mind is dead, he just arranges in a logical order all the things we knew before.' (KCKP, JMK to Lydia, 21 February 1927).

that term or the next, although he reported thinking about the book a great deal while he prepared lectures for the Easter Term. He had enough other distractions, particularly journalism, which 'eats one up, leaves no energy for other matters'.[58] It was not until 14 July 1924 that he produced a draft table of contents which survives for the book, then entitled 'The Standard of Value'. At this stage it was divided into two parts: principles of thought and principles of action.

During that summer, despite interruptions, particularly for the composition of the memoir of Marshall which took much of July and most of August, Keynes seems to have spent a good deal of time thinking about his book. On 14 September Lydia wrote to Dennis Robertson:

> Maynard develops in his mind high and low bank rate but no one in this house has access to this particular mentality. I would feel very proud in your place.[59]

At the end of Lydia's letter was a note from Keynes inviting Robertson, then well advanced with his pathbreaking *Banking Policy and the Price Level* (1926), down to Tilton to discuss Keynes's partly formed ideas, which he said went 'half way to meet you'. We know nothing else of his progress until the end of the Long Vacation, when on 9 October 1924 he produced another draft table of contents – with 23 as compared to the earlier 14 chapters.

When term began a letter to Lydia on 12 October reported gossiping with Dennis Robertson about their work. Just over two weeks later came another report of lunch and an afternoon's discussion with Piero Sraffa, the son of the Rector of Bocconi University of Milan, whom Keynes had first met in 1921 through the good offices of Mary Berenson.[60] In 1921 Sraffa had been pursuing research in economics at the London School of Economics. Keynes took to him and persuaded him to write articles on Italian banking for both the *Economic Journal* and the *Manchester Guardian* Commercial Reconstruction Supplements. The latter got Sraffa into trouble with Mussolini and Keynes suggested that he return to London where he could probably find 'some congenial occupation' for him. When Sraffa tried to land at Dover at the end of January 1923 he was turned away by the British authorities and, despite Keynes's efforts with the Home Office, he did not return to England until the autumn of 1924. By then he was Keynes's chosen translator for the Italian edition of the *Tract*. Keynes reported to Lydia that they talked for three hours and that he had revealed his credit cycle theory and continued:

> He was enthusiastic; so I was satisfied. As usual, I thought him talented – no! not because he agreed, but because of the questions he asked. . . .
> The conversation . . . has made me very eager to begin writing my

new book. But I must put it off until I come back from Oxford[k] at the end of next week.

It was another month before he got back to the book. On 30 November, he reported to Lydia:

> I have begun my new book! – today, and have written one page. This is the first sentence: – 'I begin this book, not in the logical order, but so as to bring before the reader's mind, as soon as possible, what is most significant in what I have to say.' But I don't expect that it will survive into print. However, it is very well to have broken the ice which was beginning to freeze me in.[61]

He did not tell Lydia that on the same day he had drafted another table of contents for Part I of the book. The first chapter, entitled 'A Summary of the Author's Theory' and containing the sentence he quoted to Lydia, survives in manuscript.[62] By the end of the year he reported to Sraffa that he had made 'a good start' on the book and that 'I like my underlying theory quite as well when I begin to develop it as I did at the start'.[63]

In the new term Keynes got down to the book again and made 'quite good progress' and managed by the end of January 1925 to put 'the last touches on the first section of my book'. He then decided to apply his new theories to the quarter century before 1914: 'the figures fit the facts as well as could be expected'.[64] For three weeks writing 'The Return Towards Gold', College business and an attack of influenza kept him from his manuscript, but before the end of February he was back at it. He sent two draft chapters to Dennis Robertson for comment and appears to have done the same with Pigou.[65]

Keynes had so far centred his attention on the relationship between fluctuation in the stocks of goods in process (or working capital), changes in the volume of bank money and the demand for real balances (or cash balances adjusted for the expected rate of change of prices). From the surviving materials, which are very sparse, it is interesting to note that at this stage he was beginning to make the important analytical distinction between decisions to save and decisions to invest in physical capital and, as we have noted above, that he had come to rather pessimistic conclusions as to whether loan-financed public works could have beneficial effects in a slump.[66] Distinctions between the decisions to save and to invest were central to the book that Robertson was writing, while Keynes's conclusions about public works were at variance with Robertson's and with his own later views.

Keynes continued at his book, with interruptions, until early May. On 8 March he reported to Lydia:

> I wasted two more whole mornings on that same mathematical rubbish which I was doing on Thursday. Now at last this morning, after wasting

k Where he was to deliver his lecture 'The End of Laissez Faire'.

the better part of a week, I have satisfied myself that there is nothing whatever in it and have cheerfully torn it up.

Over Easter, he joined a reading party organised by Dennis Robertson and Austin Robinson in T. H. Marshall's house at Hawse End on Derwent Water.[l] From there, after a walk on Easter Sunday, he reported to Lydia:

> I explained and discussed and argued my new views about the Theory of Money (Yes! – $P = M/(wT + c)$) with Dennis and the other economists for about two and a half hours.[67]

From this period of work only two further draft tables of contents for the book, now called 'The Theory of Money', survive. Interruptions kept him from further work until the autumn.

For economic theory, the most important of the interruptions came from Dennis Robertson's *Banking Policy and the Price Level*. In May 1925 Keynes received the first proofs. He recorded his reactions in a series of letters to Robertson, as well as in his letters to Lydia.

> But I still don't like it – I can't help it – so I went round to tea in his room and criticised and bullied him; and I thought he seemed very sad. It would be better, I think, to let him print it as it is and say no more. (18 May)

> It won't do *at all* – I'm *sure* it's wrong; so afterwards I went round to bully him again and almost to say he ought to tear it up and withdraw it from publication. It's dreadful. When I've finished this letter, I shall write to him about it. (22 May)

> When I got back I found a long letter from Dennis pleading for his egg.[m] I think I shall tell him that, before he decides to publish he ought (1) to allow a little time to pass for reflection and (2) to get another opinion besides mine. (25 May)

> I worked again at Dennis's egg. I think I have discovered what is true in it and see how to express it correctly – it is very interesting and new and important, but wasn't right as he wrote it. Then I went round to talk with him about it and left him what I had written to think over.[n] (31 May)

> Dennis and I have at last come practically to agreement about what is right and tasty in the egg and what is not – which is a relief. (1 June)[68]

l This was the reading party at which he worked his old notes of a 1919 meeting of the Council of Three into the sketch discussed above (p. 340) and printed in *JMK*, X, 27–32.
m This appears in *JMK*, XIII, 30–3.
n This appears in *JKM*, XIII, 36–9.

Keynes provided Robertson with further comments on the revised version in September and then read the second set of proofs in November 1925 before giving the book his 'full benediction, approval and praises'. Their final discussion on the book was in the train to Cambridge after a meeting of the Tuesday Club in London on 11 November 1925.[69]

The major disputes had been over chapters V and VI, 'The Kinds of Saving' and 'Short Lacking and the Trade Cycle'. In his book Robertson remarked:

> I have had so many discussions with Mr J. M. Keynes on the subject-matter of Chapters V and VI, and have rewritten them so drastically at his suggestion, that I think that neither of us now knows how much of the ideas therein contained is his and how much is mine. I should like to, but cannot, find a form of words which would adequately express my debt without seeming to commit him to opinions which he does not hold. I have made a few specific acknowledgements in footnotes: happily there is less need for meticulous disentanglement as his own version of the Theory of Credit is to be published very soon.[70]

It would be four years before Keynes's book appeared.

In his *A Study of Industrial Fluctuation* (1915) Robertson had emphasised the real causes of industrial fluctuations. *Banking Policy and the Price Level* attempted

> to preserve and represent some part of the analytical framework of my *Study of Industrial Fluctuation* . . . and . . . to interweave with the mainly 'non-monetary' argument of that work a discussion of the relation between saving, credit creation and capital growth.[71]

In doing so Robertson made a sharp distinction between decisions to save and decisions to invest – a marked difference from the classical approach but one developing on the Continent in a literature of which he was then unaware.[72] Robertson's analysis of saving, with its several varieties of lacking, stinting, hoarding and splashing, proceeded in a language that did not catch on amongst economists. The distinction between this act and the acquisition of physical assets such as materials used in the production process and plant and equipment which economists call investment has passed into common usage. Having made the distinction because savings and investment decisions were normally made by different people and might have different determinants, Robertson examined the significance of divergences between the two in a pioneering exercise in macroeconomic dynamics. He concluded that the trade cycle was not primarily a monetary phenomenon and that 'the aim of monetary policy should surely be not to prevent all fluctuations in the price level'.[73] His conclusions ran counter to Keynes's line of argument in the *Tract* and in the fragments of his new book, as well as the arguments of R. G. Hawtrey, whose *Currency and Credit* (1919) was probably the most influential textbook on the subject in the 1920s. For Keynes, what was to matter was not Robertson's conclusions but the suggestiveness of the analysis. As he would say in 1936: 'I certainly date all my emancipation from the discussions between us which preceded your *Banking Policy and the Price Level*'.[74]

In the summer of 1925, by his own admission, Keynes 'led such a debauched vacation in controversy and travel that I haven't made any progress with my book'.[75] All he had to show were two more draft tables of contents in June and a signed contract with Harcourt Brace for a book entitled 'The Theory of Money and Credit'. Beyond 'some philosophical passages about Love of Money' written in November under the influence of the Collected Papers of Freud, then being translated by James Strachey for publication by the Hogarth Press, which ultimately found their way into Keynes's book, he did little more work on it until the spring of 1926.[76] The reason for the delay was at first '*too much to do*, no leisure, no peace, too much ... to think about'.[77] Another reason soon appeared – an attack of *mania numismatika*, a disease that had struck before.[78]

As noted earlier, Keynes had started working on ancient currencies in 1920.[79] His concerns were the origins of and relations between monetary standards. He appears to have put the work aside in 1921 and to have left it until January 1924, when he reported:

> I feel little better than a lunatic this evening. It is just like three years ago – the same thing has happened. Feeling rather leisurely, I returned to my old essay on Babylonian and Greek weights. It is purely absurd and quite useless. But just as before, I became absorbed in it to the point of frenzy. Last night I went on working at it up to 2 o'clock; and to-day I went on continuously from the time I got up until dinner time. Extraordinary! Anyone else would think the subject very dull. Some charm must have been cast on it by a Babylonian magician. The result is I feel quite mad and silly.[80]

The 1924 attack lasted just over 24 hours: a ride in the rain the next day with Dennis Robertson and Sebastian Sprott 'brushed the lunacy out of my head'.

The 1925 visitation was more serious. It started when

> This morning I had nothing to do! – so I took out the basket where my book lives and admired its table of contents. Then I read the first chapter. This needed a reference to my manuscript on ancient currencies. But once that was taken out, I was a lost man and spent the rest of the morning trying to remember my theories about Greek and Babylonian affairs. I feel drawn to waste a little more time over these things. ...

> Tonight my Political Economy Club comes – I would sooner think
> about ancient moneys.[81]

It took more than 'a little more time'. After the Political Economy Club he
worked until 2 a.m.; the following day until 1.30 a.m. and the next day for
five hours in the afternoon. Despite a vow on 6 December that he would
not give himself 'more than one more week's dissipation' before he 'put
it away for another year', he continued working on the subject for the
rest of the term. Despite Lydia's hope that 'Babylonia and her currency
will be deposited in Cambridge for a while', he brought the manuscript
to London for the vacation and worked for some days in the British
Museum. At the beginning of the new year, however, he seemed to have
little time for it, spending what leisure he had on three articles on the
French franc,[82] an appreciation of *Lombard Street* to mark the centenary
of Bagehot's birth,[83] an obituary for F. Y. Edgeworth, his fellow editor of
the *Economic Journal*,[84,o] written and oral evidence to the (Hilton Young)
Royal Commission on Indian Currency and Finance, and a major political
address in Manchester.[85] He did find time to discuss his results on ancient
currencies with Charles Seltman, a Cambridge currency historian and Frank
Adcock, a King's ancient historian.[86] Seltman encouraged him to publish his
results, but Keynes declined. Once free of pressing obligations, he was back
at the subject and it was not until towards the end of April that he would
report to Lydia

> Yesterday I finished going through so much of my book on Money as
> I have written. It is wonderful how I forget. There is more of it than
> I thought and I had the pleasure of reading it though as though it was
> someone else's. But I am appalled by the hard work which is still needed
> to finish it. I suppose I must begin seriously to-day, or soon.[87]

Thereafter, except for discussing them at dinner in October 1926 and at lunch
at Harvey Road in November 1927, Keynes dropped ancient currencies. The
diversion resulted in a few anonymous book reviews in the *Nation*, a few
generalisations in the *Treatise on Money* and the confidence to reject an article
for the *Economic History Supplement* to the *Economic Journal* on the grounds
that the 'subject used to be a speciality of mine on which I wrote something,
never published, almost on the scale of a fellowship dissertation'.[88] What
remains in his papers is of sufficient interest to modern specialists that they
urged publication and it appears in his *Collected Writings* as an example of
the working of a fine mind in an area well outside his range of expertise.[89]

We cannot tell from the surviving correspondence and draft tables of
contents how much he worked on his book during the rest of the Easter
term and the summer of 1926, but by the end of August calculations in the

---

o Edgeworth died on 13 February. Maynard's memoir appeared in the March *Economic
  Journal*.

margin of one draft table of contents, the first to be entitled 'A Treatise on Money', suggest that he had either written (or worked out in enough detail to guess the length) approximately 55,650 words of Book I, 'The Theory of Money'. He was also suggesting to Alfred Harcourt that the book would be published in the course of 1927. This was one of the many targets he would miss. The Michaelmas term, perhaps because Dennis Robertson was in India, was not productive: he reported 'a blue trance which must have lasted about half an hour whilst I had an inspiration about the next chapter but one of my book' on 18 October, demonstrating that 'my subconscious self (though not my conscious mind) is still thinking about that', but it was over three months before he returned to it on 21 January 1927.[90]

His renewed activity finished a chapter, but he put the book aside on 30 January, both because he had left the manuscript at Tilton and because he had to write his annual survey of the speeches of the Clearing Bank chairmen and another contribution to his series of London and Cambridge Economic Service *Special Memoranda* on 'Stocks of Staple Commodities'.[91] When he went to Tilton in February, he forgot to pick the material up and, perhaps as a result, he appears to have done nothing else that term. It was only in the vacation that he got back to it, in spite of the distractions of the Liberal Industrial Inquiry. Perhaps Dennis Robertson's return helped. May, June and September saw new draft tables of contents, of which the last was the most elaborate thus far. At the end of the summer, which had included visits to Tilton by Dennis Robertson, Roy Harrod and Piero Sraffa, Keynes told Dan Macmillan that he had spent a lot of time on the book, but was a long way from the end. There was 'a faint possibility, but a very faint one' that the book would be ready in the autumn of 1928, but the more likely date was now early 1929.[92]

As he worked on the book in 1927–8, Keynes seems to have made a number of decisions that fundamentally altered the shape of his *Treatise*. It is hard to document when the relevant changes took place. The second of only two draft tables of contents separated by a year[p] bears a much stronger family resemblance than the first to the book that finally appeared in October 1930. Keynes summarised the changes in later discussions with Robertson:

> When you were writing *Banking Policy and the Price Level* and we were discussing it, we both believed that inequalities between saving and investment – using these terms with the degree of vagueness with which we used them at that date – only arose as a result of what one might call an act of inflation or deflation on the part of the banking system. I worked on this basis for quite a time, but in the end came to the conclusion that it would not do. As a result of getting what were, in my opinion, more clear definitions of saving and investment,

p One was dated 23 September 1927; the other 6 October 1928 (*JMK*, XIII, 48–50; 78–82).

I found that the salient phenomena could come about without any overt act on the part of the banking system. My theory, as I have ultimately expressed it is the result of this change in view. . . . But I only reached my new view as a result of an attempt to handle the old view with complete thoroughness.[93]

In the tables of contents the emphasis shifted from the behaviour of the banks *per se* to a much more intensive examination of fluctuations in investment and their determinants. Such a shift is also evident in Keynes's related writings from the same period. In the surviving draft of Chapter 24 of the October 1928 table of contents, 'The Part Played by the Banking System', the emphasis (which is stronger after revisions in the spring of 1929 than in the first proof) is on the fact that price fluctuations can result from forces other than 'wanton or avoidable inflation brought on by the banking system itself'. Moreover, Keynes took explicit issue with Robertson.[94] In his September 1928 paper 'Is There Inflation in the United States?', an echo of a dispute about American market conditions then raging amongst members of the board of the National Mutual, he used the analysis he had developed to examine the emerging Wall Street boom and the need for deflationary measures by the Federal Reserve. The analysis may also lie behind his renewed advocacy of loan-financed public works expenditure.

In thinking through this change in view and incorporating it into his manuscript, Keynes seems to have worked fairly quickly. As was becoming usual, the demands of the Michaelmas term, particularly preparations for the annual King's audit, prevented him from doing much work before the Christmas vacation, although he lectured from the book on 10 October.[95] When he did get down to it again in Cambridge on 20 January 1928 (probably after some work during the vacation, for he reported 'getting a little stale at it') he had some of his previous work in proof. On 23 January, he reported to Lydia:

I still work hard at my book. Dennis came in last night and we had a long talk about the new theory. I think it will do and that it is very important. But it owes a great deal to him.

A week later:

This morning beautiful sunshine, and I worked speedily at my egg, finishing the first draft of 'The Pure Theory of the Credit Cycle' – 60 pages of Basildon; so I felt very cheerful and didn't care twopence one way or the other about the speculations [the beginnings of his rubber problems].[96]

By 5 February he had redrafted that chapter, now 82 pages long and ready to be typed for circulation. On 2 March he discussed it for two hours with Piero Sraffa, now, partly thanks to Keynes's efforts, a University Lecturer in Cambridge, and made corrections two days later. After an Easter journey to the Soviet Union with Lydia, he had another five chapters ready for the printers by 20 May. When he reported to Dan Macmillan at the end of June that he was getting on at a good pace, he still saw no chance of finishing in the autumn of 1928 and only just a chance of the spring of 1929.[97] He maintained his momentum over the summer, assisted by visits from Hubert Henderson and Frank Ramsey, who found the new quantity equation 'exciting'.[98] By the end of the vacation he could report to his publishers that, although the book had expanded into a much more substantial affair than he had originally envisaged, he had 'four-fifths of it . . . now completely finished' and could look forward to publication in May 1929. By the end of October two-thirds of the book had been set in type.[99]

There were to be further delays in finishing his *Treatise*. As they involved substantial changes in the text and were related to Keynes's practical policy controversies of 1929–30, I shall discuss them in Chapter 19.

NOTES

1 For details of the origins of the 1925 expiry date see Sayers 1976, III, Appendix 6.
2 Page 297.
3 *JMK*, XIX, 50–76.
4 *JMK*, XIX, 100–3 103–6, 107–9, 110–12.
5 *JMK*, XIX, 113–18.
6 See above p. 389.
7 Jones 1964, 210.
8 *JMK*, XVII, 235.
9 *JMK*, XVIII, 241; his doubts are on 237–40.
10 *JMK*, XVIII, 260–1.
11 *JMK*, XIX, 238–9.
12 *JMK*, XIX, 371; Cannan, 'Review of T. E. Gregory's *The Return to Gold*', *Economic Journal*, XXXV, December 1925, 615.
13 His evidence appears in *JMK*, XIX, 239–61.
14 Moggridge 1972, ch. 3 deals with the deliberations of the Committee and this expectation. For Keynes's ridicule of this view, see *JMK*, XIX, 213.
15 *JMK*, XIX, 271–2.
16 *JMK*, XIX, 168–72.
17 *JMK*, XIX, 200, 202–5.
18 *JMK*, XIX, 219–23.
19 Harrod 1951, 350.
20 Clarke 1988, 78.
21 *JMK*, XVII, 445; XIX, 123.
22 *JMK*, XIX, 205; see also 281–2.
23 For Keynes's discussion of the problem in 1924 see *JMK*, XVI, 227–8.
24 *JMK*, XIX, 282–3.
25 See, in particular, *JMK*, XIX, 275–84, 285–8, 328–32.
26 KCKP, JMK to Lydia, 1 February 1924. Further earlier material for this book is available in *JMK*, XIII.
27 *JMK*, XIII, 23.

28 KCKP, JMK to Lydia, 16 May 1924.
29 KCKP, JMK to FAK, 18 August 1924. In his letter to her of 15 August he mentions using JNK's diaries for the memoir.
30 *JMK*, X, 198.
31 *JMK*, X, 199.
32 *JMK*, X, 173–4.
33 Moggridge 1972, ch. 3. There were exceptions to the 'blackmail' for League of Nations' loans and the 'political' Dawes Loan. Few of the proceeds of the latter actually left London.
34 Sayers 1976, I, 142.
35 The 'Exercise' and the replies from its four recipients appear in Moggridge 1972, Appendix 1. They are also available on PRO T172/1499B.
36 Leith-Ross 1968, 91–2.
37 KCKP, JMK to Lydia, 8 and 15 February 1925.
38 *JMK*, IX, 192–200.
39 *JMK*, IX, 198–9.
40 PRO T172/1499B, Niemeyer to Churchill, 21 February 1925; Churchill to Niemeyer, 22 February 1925.
41 Grigg 1948, 174.
42 Ibid., 184. The whole evening's discussion is on 182–4.
43 *JMK*, XIX, 337–44.
44 *JMK*, XIX, 358.
45 KCKP, JMK to Lydia 1, 3, and 4 May 1925.
46 *JMK*, XIX, 363, 378.
47 *JMK*, XIX, 363–5.
48 *JMK*, XIX, 416.
49 VWL, III, 194, 195; Bell 1978, II, 38.
50 *JMK*, IX, 212.
51 Moggridge 1972, 84–94.
52 Grigg 1948, 175–6; Salter 1967, 248–50; Leith-Ross 1968; 118; Macmillan 1966, 204–5; Wheeler Bennett 1968, 27–8, 185–7, 191–2, 233.
53 Macmillan 1966, 205.
54 *JMK*, IX, 224, XIX, 425, 432.
55 *JMK*, IX, 223–4.
56 Robinson 1947, 25.
57 KCKP, JMK to Lydia, 1 February 1924. All subsequently mentioned draft tables of contents appear in *JMK*, XIII, ch. 2.
58 KCKP, JMK to Lydia, 2 and 4 May 1924.
59 *JMK*, XIII, 16.
60 What follows derives from material in KCKP, L/S, Mary Berenson to JMK, 15 July 1921; P. Sraffa to JMK, 25 December 1922, 6, 13, 22 and 26 January, 1923, 6 November 1924; JMK to J. C. C. Davidson, 29 January 1923.
61 KCKP, JMK to Lydia, 30 November 1924.
62 *JMK*, XIII, 19–22.
63 KCKP, JMK to Lydia, 1 and 5 December 1924; *JMK*, XII, 22.
64 KCKP, JMK to Lydia, 25 and 30 January and 1 February 1925.
65 *JMK*, XIII, 24–6, 28.
66 Above p. 403; *JMK*, XIII, 23.
67 KCKP, JMK to Lydia, 13 April 1925.
68 Both sides of the correspondence with Robertson, including the letters referred to on 25 and 31 May (but not the one contemplated on 22 May), are in *JMK*, XIII, 29–39. The letters to Lydia are in KCKP.

69 See, *JMK*, XII, 40–1; KCKP, JMK to Lydia, 12 November 1925.
70 Robertson 1926, 5. See also pp. 49 n. 1 and 76 n. 1, as well as Robertson's preface to the 1949 reprinting.
71 Robertson 1926, preface to 1949 edition vii.
72 Ibid., vii.
73 Robertson 1926, 39.
74 *JMK*, XIV, 94.
75 *JMK*, XIII, 40.
76 KCKP, JMK to Lydia, 9 November 1925; BL, ADD.60715, James Strachey to Alix Strachey, 9 June 1925; *JMK*, VI, 218–19.
77 KCKP, JMK to Lydia, 6 November, 1925.
78 *JMK*, XXVIII, 257n.
79 Above p. 362.
80 KCKP, JMK to Lydia, 18 January 1924.
81 KCKP, JMK to Lydia, 27 November 1925.
82 *JMK*, IX, 76–82; XIX, 455–65.
83 *JMK*, XIX, 465–71.
84 *JMK*, X, 251–66.
85 *JMK*, IX, 307–11.
86 He met Seltman for lunch on 14 February (KCKP, JMK to Lydia, 14 February 1926). His correspondence appears in *JMK*, XXVIII, 273–81.
87 KCKP, JMK to Lydia, 25 April 1926, reprinted in *JMK*, XXIX, 2.
88 *JMK*, XXVIII, 287–94; V, 10–12; VI, 134–5, 258; KCKP, JMK to Austin Robinson, 22 August 1941.
89 *JMK*, XXVIII, 223–73, 281–6.
90 KCKP, JMK to Lydia, 18 October 1926, 21 and 23 January 1927.
91 *JMK*, IX, 200–6; XII, 447–512.
92 BL, ADD.55202, JMK to D. Macmillan, 5 October 1927.
93 *JMK*, XIII, 273, a letter of 6 October 1931 which was not sent.
94 *JMK*, XIII, 89, 91.
95 KCKP, JMK to Lydia, 10 October 1927.
96 KCKP, JMK to Lydia, 20, 22 and 23 January 1928.
97 BL, ADD.55202, JMK to Dan Macmillan, 28 June 1928.
98 KCKP, Lydia to FAK, 30 July 1928; *JMK*, XIII, 78.
99 *JMK*, XIII, 51; BL, ADD.55202, JMK to Dan Macmillan, 25 October 1928.

18

INDUSTRY AND POLITICS

The test of a man's Liberalism today must not be his attitude towards the questions that were important a generation ago, but to those which are most important to the generation coming.

(JMK to the London Liberal Candidates' Association, 5 January 1927, *JMK*, XIX, 648)

As Keynes emphasised in *The Economic Consequences of Mr Churchill*, renewed difficulties in the coal industry were one of the first fruits of the return to gold. Before 1914 Britain had been the world's leading coal exporter. After 1919 the industry was subject to several forces which decreased demand (slower economic growth, increased use of substitutes and a general increase in fuel efficiency among consumers) as well as an expansion of potential supplies from new competitors. It faced problems of adjustment made more difficult by the sluggish growth of demand in the domestic market.

At first, these difficulties were hidden from British producers by a number of fortuitous events – the slow return to production of war-damaged Continental mines, the 1922 American coal strike and the 1923 occupation of the Ruhr – which kept demand for British coal to within a few percentage points of pre-war output. The end of these fortuitous stimuli coincided with the return towards gold. Profits declined and the owners began to put pressure on workers' hours and wages. The pressure was particularly acute as the wage agreement of May 1924 had occurred in the wake of Ruhr-induced prosperity and just before the final appreciation of sterling got underway. On 30 June 1925 the owners served notice that they would end the 1924 agreement within a month. Their new offer involved reduced money wages, an end to a national minimum addition to standard wages and a suggestion of longer hours. The miners rejected the offer and through the Trades Union Congress began to lay plans for concerted action.

In the interim, the Government appointed a Court of Inquiry under H. P. Macmillan, later chairman of the Macmillan Committee on Finance and Industry (1929–31) of which Keynes would be a member. Among the

Inquiry's members was Sir Josiah Stamp. It reported on 28 July and included an addendum, reluctantly written by Stamp,[1] that linked the industry's difficulties to the return to gold. Negotiations continued with the threat of a miners' strike until 31 July, when the Government, in exchange for agreeing to another inquiry into the industry and the provision of a temporary subsidy to wages, received an assurance from the owners that wages and hours would remain unchanged during the course of the inquiry. A Royal Commission chaired by Sir Herbert Samuel was appointed on 5 September. While the Commission sat, the Government pushed ahead with contingency plans against a general strike.

The Samuel Commission reported in March 1926. It rejected the employers' plea for longer hours, suggested a temporary reduction of minimum wage rates for higher paid workers combined with an extension of piece rates and profit sharing, accepted a further extension of nationally negotiated rates and an improvement in welfare and fringe benefits in the industry. It also reiterated the recommendation of the 1919 Sankey Royal Commission for the nationalisation of coal royalties and suggested various measures of industrial reorganisation under the present ownership.

With the publication of the Samuel Report, negotiations between the miners and the owners resumed. They did not get far: the owners talked of lower wages and district as opposed to national bargaining; the miners stuck to existing wages and hours and national bargaining and emphasised the potential gains from reorganisation. As before, the TUC and the Government were drawn into the negotiations. On 1 May, with no breakthrough in the negotiations and the end of the subsidy, the owners locked the miners out. The result was not only a mining dispute but a General Strike which lasted from 3 to 16 May.

Beyond his anti-gold-standard agitation, Keynes made only one contribution to public discussions before the Strike. In the *Nation* for 28 April he proposed that the 3s. per ton increase in net proceeds required for profitable operations come in equal shares from wages, the pooling of earnings from export sales and industrial reorganisation, spurred by a tapering Government subsidy per ton raised.[2]

During the General Strike he provided a brief comment for the *Chicago Daily News* and draft contributions to a 'symposium' in the *Nation* and the *New Republic* which failed to appear owing to the Strike, despite attempts to get the Woolfs' Hogarth Press to do the printing.[3] He blamed the General Strike on muddles. He did not see it as an attack on the constitution which required crushing, and argued that it was better to attempt to settle the dispute.[4] As he put it at the end of June in a seminar in Berlin, the General Strike was 'essentially senseless' for it had come about by 'a chapter of accidents'.[5]

Once it had collapsed and the miners were alone, he was again attempting to devise solutions that would lead to pressures to rationalise the coal industry. He emphasised the importance of national settlements as the goal with money wages at levels high enough to force the closure of less efficient pits and to encourage co-operation and cartellisation in international markets. He was still reacting to outside events and proposals. When the Government introduced legislation to increase the working day. Keynes regarded it as 'a balmy remedy' given existing overproduction and the inelastic demand for coal, but he was reacting as a critic not initiating proposals.[6]

The General Strike also produced discord in the recently reunited Liberal Party under Asquith, now Lord Oxford. During the Strike, the Liberal leadership agreed that a general strike went beyond the limits of legitimate constitutional action. There was, however, disagreement as to whether negotiations between the Government and the TUC should cease until the Strike ended with an unconditional surrender or whether they should continue. These differences in view led Lloyd George to miss a 'shadow cabinet' meeting on 10 May. Asquith did not at first take this seriously, but on further reflection and on the publication of Lloyd George's usual fortnightly American article which this time dealt with the Strike, he sent a letter to Lloyd George taking him to task for his absence and accusing him of disloyalty. Lloyd George's reply was conciliatory, but the damage was done: the leadership of the Liberal Party became a matter of public controversy which spilled over into the columns of the *Nation*. On 29 May it carried a leader entitled 'Lord Oxford's Blunder' and a note affirming that Lloyd George was in the right and that even if he was wrong this did not call for his ostracism from the councils of the Party. On the leader, Keynes commented to Lydia the day before publication:

> I like Hubert's leader this week very much. In the end it's just what I wanted. He cut out a paragraph to satisfy me. I shall now write to Margot [Asquith] much more shortly, saying that this leader just expresses my feelings.

Margot Asquith had been bombarding Keynes with letters defending her husband against Lloyd George, and he had tried to draft a letter telling her that he believed her husband's letter was 'a misfortune' and 'politically speaking a very bad business'.[7] He now received two letters from her, dated 31 May, concerning 'the savage and spiteful article' and cancelling an invitation to stay at the Wharf on 28 July. Relations deteriorated further when in a letter to the *Nation*, dated 12 June, Keynes attempted to stand back from the recent flurry of speeches and letters. He suggested that Lloyd George's past record – the coupon election of 1918, the Peace Treaty and the use of the Black and Tans in Ireland – were not the matters at issue, although Asquith's supporters made much of them. These had all been issues when the party had reunited two years earlier and Lloyd George's present critics had welcomed him back. Those who wished to expel Lloyd George from the Party could only make a case on the basis of his behaviour since reunification and here Lord Oxford had 'only half tried to make out a convincing or even coherent case'. Moreover, Lloyd George's radicalism appealed to Keynes and he thought that this radicalism joined with Lord Oxford's Whig tendencies would make the party stronger. If Lord Oxford could not collaborate with the Lloyd George view of the future, which included possible collaboration with Labour, then 'let us divide, amicably, but as soon as possible, into two separate groups', Whigs and Radicals.[8,a]

Keynes's letter brought a complete breach of relations with Lord Oxford: they never met again. Nor did Lord Oxford long remain leader of the Party. After recovering from a slight stroke he suffered on 12 June, he resigned his leadership in a letter published on 15 October 1926. He lived for another 16 months. After his death and Keynes's warm, personal obituary note in the *Nation*,[9] he and Margot Asquith were reconciled. They exchanged notes, gifts and visits until her death in 1945.

The coal dispute seems to have shifted Keynes's interests towards industrial problems. In 1926, combined with his long-standing interest in commodities, this involved him in the fortunes of one of Britain's largest industries, cotton. The cotton industry had grown up on the needs of consumers all over the world: in 1912, for example, it had exported over 85 per cent of its output. In the boom of 1919–20, there was a rash of amalgamation and recapitalisations which involved over 42 per cent of the spindles in the industry and reflected the high prices then ruling. This left firms overcapitalised and saddled with large debts and their bankers with poor loans. As the official historian of the Bank of England has put it:

> Two, if not three, of the smaller banks, and at least two of the Big Five were so deeply involved in Lancashire's financial mire that further deterioration and eventual exposure might have rocked the whole financial system.[10]

After the 1920–1 slump, although world demand for cotton goods revived, Britain's market share declined sharply from pre-war levels so that, although domestic demand held up, the industry had substantial, and growing, excess capacity. Believing that the decline in demand was temporary and encouraged by the unemployment insurance system, the industry went on to organised short-time working which continued into the second half of the decade. The body responsible for the management of organised short time was the Federation of Master Cotton Spinners.

On 24 October 1926 Keynes began to write an article on the Lancashire cotton trade for the 13 November issue of the *Nation*. He pointed out that world consumption of cotton was above pre-war, that Lancashire's falling

a He defined these terms two weeks later: 'A Whig is a perfectly sensible Conservative. A Radical is a perfectly sensible Labourite. A Liberal is anyone who is perfectly sensible.' (*JMK*, XIX, 542).

share of the market reflected Japanese competition and increased protection by former importing countries, and that almost all the loss in market share had occurred in the American and coarser sections of the industry, where trade was over 40 per cent down. The higher-quality Egyptian section had returned to full-time working. In the sections under pressure, he argued that short time aggravated the industry's problem by keeping weak firms and inefficient plants open. The overcapacity meant sales losses and higher overhead costs for efficient firms in addition to higher wage costs. On top of these difficulties came the return to gold. As a result, Lancashire's share of world supply was being eroded as fast as competitors could install new capacity. The solution lay in Lancashire's hands. It should face the facts and take steps to reduce capacity.

The industry's reaction to Keynes's article was immediate: the Manchester evening papers of 12 November, the day the *Nation* reached the streets in London, were full of critical comments. There was, however, also a positive response from the trade. The Short Time Committee of the Federation of Master Cotton Spinners invited Keynes to Manchester to discuss the issues he had raised in his article. Jumping at the chance he went to Manchester on 21 November to meet both the Short Time Committee and the General Committee of the Federation. After that meeting both sides issued a communiqué that made clear the changes Keynes had in mind. He favoured the abandonment of short-time working, the formation of a cartel or holding company with the assistance of the industry's bankers, and the concentration of production in the most efficient firms. In an article published in the *Nation* later in the week he repeated his recommendations.

At this time a committee existed to try to form a Cotton Yarn Association to reconstruct the spinning section dealing with American cotton. On 26 November the committee wrote to Keynes offering to come to London to discuss its aims and plans. Cambridge commitments and a meeting of an International Chamber of Commerce Committee on balance of payments statistics meant he could not meet the committee until 16 December, but in the interim he publicly endorsed the aims of the proposed Cotton Yarn Association.

By the time Keynes met the committee trying to form the Association, the Federation of Master Cotton Spinners had ended short time. Thus the way to reform was open. He threw himself behind the Association in a long article in the *Nation* of 24 December and he went back to Manchester on 4 January to address a meeting of spinners of American cotton and appeal for support for the Association on the grounds that: 'If you refuse to do anything now, you will just lose your money for a year or two more and then be driven to just the same thing in the end'.[11] He also appealed for support from the banks, 'those professional deaf-mutes' as he had called them in the *Nation*,[12] if only because widespread bankruptcies in the trade were not in their interests. Bankruptcies would not help banks' balance sheets; nor would they help the remaining firms in the trade unless the surplus capacity was scrapped. After the meeting he continued to give the Association support and advice, as well as encouraging individual manufacturers who wrote to him to join it. The Association was successfully launched on 18 February 1927. Its membership controlled about 75 per cent of the capacity of the American section.

The Association had a difficult time, although it had organised itself quickly and efficiently. After a brief spurt in demand in the spring of 1927 even more depressed conditions returned. Firms outside the Association with a quarter of the capacity were free to undercut Association prices, exceed the hours agreements, and thus take business away from the Association's members. This created considerable strain. Keynes highlighted the problem of these 'free riders' in an article in the *Nation* on 27 August 1927 and returned to Manchester on 6 September as the main speaker at a meeting in Manchester Town Hall which attempted to enlarge the membership. In a powerful speech putting the case for the expansion of the Association he also called for an unofficial cotton commission to investigate and pool knowledge concerning the industry. The meeting did not succeed and early in November the Association, by relieving its members of their obligations to observe a percentage of short time and a schedule of minimum selling prices, effectively ceased to exist.

The collapse of the Association disappointed Keynes. He realised that during the year Lancashire had come to recognise the long-term problem of surplus capacity, but he saw the atmosphere as 'discouraging – insensitive, stale, unadaptable – . . . towards any constructive effort'.[13] Events eventually produced a successor to the Association. With the collapse of the price and quota scheme of 1927, the Association began to work for a scheme of large-scale mergers of mills. Such a scheme needed a means of compelling formerly independent mills to enter; failing Government compulsion, this meant the active involvement of the banks. In July 1928, the leaders of the Cotton Yarn Association approached the Deputy Governor of the Bank of England. They received an 'encouraging negative', which became more encouraging and less negative once Governor Norman became involved, partly because of the links between the trade and the banking system. By October 1928 the Bank was fully committed to the policy of mergers and was working to overcome the opposition of the banks to writing off previous bad debts, of directors whose fees were at stake, of shareholders the unpaid-up balance of whose shares would be called, and of other interested trade participants.[14] In January 1929 the Lancashire Cotton Corporation was registered, with John Ryan of the Cotton Yarn Association as its managing director. Keynes enthusiastically welcomed the new Corporation in the *Nation* for 2 February 1929. He had played a part, albeit a secondary one, in a large industrial reorganisation which was to survive the 1929 slump with Bank of England assistance. The Lancashire Cotton Corporation may not have been the best solution to the long-term problems of the cotton textile industry which probably required integration across rather than within sectors.[15] But it was a successful palliative. Keynes's experience of Lancashire's problems did not increase his enthusiasm for or faith in the competitive solution to industrial problems.

The transfer of the *Nation* to the Keynes group and the rise of the Summer Schools movement to which Keynes made regular contributions during the 1920s were, as I have noted, both part of a process attempting to redefine the programme of the Liberal Party. The need for redefinition arose partly from the successes of the pre-1914 reform programme that had brought pensions, unemployment and health insurance, labour exchanges and the beginnings of progressive taxation but had left the party with few rallying cries for the post-war world beyond *laissez faire*, free trade, economy and the drink question. It was also a response to the rise in the fortunes of the Labour Party, which had become the official opposition in 1918, and the consequent jockeying among the parties for the role of the non-Conservative alternative. There was, finally, an element of rebuilding and reunion following the split in the Liberal Party after 1916. The attempt by the liberal reformers to capture the centre ground of British politics, although it was ultimately unsuccessful as the Labour Party under MacDonald became the non-Conservative alternative, had the effect of drawing to the Liberals many intellectuals and other professionals who after 1945 might have worked for the Labour Party or in the 1980s joined the Democrats in their various guises.

Keynes became one of the most important of the ideologues of the 1920s new liberalism. The position he took up had stronger links with the older Asquithian style – 'cool, intellectual and judicial, concerned with the establishment of a just and reasonable order of society as it appeared to cultivated and superior English minds' – than with the often non-rational populism of Lloyd George.[16] Throughout, he gave the appearance of a 'rationalist' whose writings represented a constant campaign, bristling with moral indignation, at the harm perpetrated by 'madmen in authority', 'lunatics' and others who acted according to rules of thumb or convention rather than thinking and arguing the relevant problems through. He always believed that 'a little clear thinking' or 'more lucidity' could provide grounds for reasonable decisions. As he put it to T. S. Eliot in 1945, when the two were discussing the possibilities of employment policy:

> It may turn out, I suppose, that vested interests and personal selfishness may stand in the way. But the main task is producing first the intellectual conviction and then intellectually to devise the means. Insufficiency of cleverness, not of goodness, is the main trouble. And even resistance to change as such may have many motives besides selfishness.[17]

Emphasising the need for clear thinking and lucidity that one would expect from the author of *Probability*, Keynes was an Asquithian élitist. As he remarked to the Liberal Summer School in August 1925 in words that did not appear in the published version of the speech:

> I believe that in the future, more than ever, questions about the economic framework of society will be far and away the most important of political issues. I believe that the right solution will involve intellectual and scientific elements which must be above the heads of the vast majority of more or less illiterate voters. Now, in a democracy, every party alike has to depend on this mass of ill-understanding voters, and no party will attain power unless it can win the confidence of those by persuading them in a general way that it intends to promote their interests or that it intends to gratify their passions. Nevertheless, there are differences between the several parties in the degree to which the party machine is democratised through and through and the preparation of the party programme is democratised in its details .... Traditionally the management of the Liberal Party was ... sufficiently autocratic. Recently there have been ill-advised[b] movements in the direction of democratising the details of the party programme. This has been a reaction against a weak and divided leadership, for which, in fact, there is no remedy except strong and united leadership. With strong leadership the techniques, as distinguished from the main principles of policy could still be dictated from above.[18]

Indeed, one of his main objections to the Labour Party was that the 'intellectual elements' would never 'exercise adequate control'. With the Asquithians, he also disliked Labour as a class party:

> If I am going to pursue sectional economic interests at all, I shall pursue my own. When it comes to the class struggle as such, my local and personal patriotism, like those of everyone else, except certain unpleasant zealous ones, are attached to my own surroundings. I can be influenced by what seems to me justice and good sense; but the *class* war will find me on the side of the educated *bourgeoisie*.[19]

Thus far, Keynes's views were not at odds with his pre-war predecessors. The notion of groups of professional politicians competing for votes has, despite its tinge of élitism, impeccable liberal credentials in modern political theory. In the 1920s he remained a firm adherent of free trade, although he came to be prepared to allow some of the post-1914 breaches of the principle – the McKenna and Safeguarding duties – to stand.[20] He was similarly at one with the old and new sections of the party in his view that there were in the circumstances of the 1920s few resources immediately available for

b This word is pencilled out in the manuscript.

expensive schemes of social improvement: the scope for economies in existing expenditure was limited to defence and overseas military commitments and the level of taxation was such that no large new sources of revenue were available, especially given the need for capital accumulation to employ a rapidly growing labour force.[21] This did not rule out substantial reforms in the future and it was not out of character for Keynes in the 1940s to become involved in two major sets of socially improving, redistributive schemes: those of his *How to Pay for the War* and the Beveridge proposals for social security. Where he broke new ground in the 1920s was in his view of the role of the state.

In this, Keynes has often been described as a 'neo' or 'new' liberal. Some have gone so far as to make him the 'founding father' of neo-liberalism,[22] although it is probably more fruitful to locate the origins of his views amongst the liberal reformers of the pre-war and inter-war years.[23] He set out his views in a series of articles, pamphlets and speeches, more often than not to Liberal Summer Schools, between the end of 1922 and the middle of 1927.[c] Although evolving somewhat in the last two decades of his life, they served him well right down to 1946.

Throughout, Keynes accepted the capitalist system. He agreed that it was in many ways morally objectionable, particularly in its overemphasis on the love of money. As he wrote in 1925:

> [The] moral problem of our age is concerned with the love of money, with the habitual appeal to the money motive in nine-tenths of the activities of life, with the universal striving after individual economic security as the prime object of endeavour, with the social approbation of money as the measure of constructive success, and with the social appeal to the hoarding instinct as the foundation of the necessary provision for the family and the future.[24]

None the less, it was probably more efficient for the attainment of economic ends than any alternative. He saw no advantage in revolution. The problem was to make capitalism 'as efficient as possible without offending our notions of a satisfactory way of life'.[25] He was not explicit as to what end this 'efficiency' was to be directed, although he strongly hinted that the objective was capital accumulation to reach a level of affluence where economic questions could take second place to moral ones.[26] It was only in 1928, in a paper to be published in 1930, 'Economic Possibilities for our Grandchildren',[27] that he set his view out in any detail.

c The relevant documents are: a speech to the 95 Club, 25 October 1922; the Editorial Foreword to the first issue of the Keynes/Henderson *Nation*, 5 May 1923; 'Currency Policy and Unemployment', 8 August 1923; 'The Liberal Party', 17 November 1923; 'Currency Policy and Social Reform', 13 December 1923; *The End of Laissez Faire*, November 1924 and June 1926; 'Am I a Liberal?', 1 August 1925; 'Liberalism and Labour', 9 February 1926; 'Liberalism and Industry', 5 January 1927; 'The Public and the Private Concern', 1 August 1927. All but the second, which is in volume XVIII, appear in *JMK*, IX and XIX.

When he faced the issue, he suggested that human needs fell into two classes:

> those needs which are absolute in the sense that we feel them whatever the situation of our fellow human beings may be, and those which are relative in the sense that we feel them only if their satisfaction lifts us above, makes us feel superior to, our fellows.[28]

This distinction between absolute needs and what economists have come to call positional needs is effectively one between needs capable of satiation and those which are not.[29] Keynes believed that capitalism, wisely managed, could, if there were no major wars and no important increases in population, be in such a position to satisfy absolute needs in less than a century and that society might then organise itself to devote its energies in other directions.

> I see us free, therefore, to return to some of the most sure and certain principles of religion and traditional virtue – that avarice is a vice, that the exaction of usury is a misdemeanour, and the love of money is detestable, that those walk most truly in the paths of virtue and sane wisdom who take least thought for the morrow. We shall once more value ends above means and prefer the good to the useful.[30]

How Keynes would handle the problem of the endless, largely futile, striving after positional goods, which some have argued lies at the heart of much discontent with post-1945 western affluence, he did not say – he could not have done so. He accepted that the demand for positional goods might be insatiable. But how would be wean society from their pursuit? One presumes it would have been a matter for persuasion. None the less, his was a vision of capitalism delivering certain goods in such abundance that the ordering of social arrangements simply to foster further accumulation would be unnecessary – a vision that has its parallels in John Stuart Mill and Marx. The link between economic growth and 'moral' improvement was also in Marshall.

Such was Keynes's end, the solution of the economic problem. The means lay in a *managed* capitalism. This involved a rejection of *laissez faire*: 'the conclusion that individuals acting independently for their own advantage will produce the greatest aggregate of wealth'.[31] He rejected it on several grounds ranging from the logical 'complications' posed by formal economic theory which limit the applicability of the economist's competitive model to the real world – complications which are, if anything, more strongly and elegantly formulated now than in 1924[32] – to the moral and the philosophical. As he summed up:

> Let us clear from the ground the metaphysical or general principles upon which, from time to time, *laissez faire* has been founded. It is *not* true that individuals possess a prescriptive 'natural liberty' in their economic activities. There is *no* 'compact' conferring perpetual rights

on those who Have or those who Acquire. The world is *not* so governed from above that private and social interest should always coincide. It is *not* so managed here below that in practice they do coincide. It is *not* a correct deduction from the principles of economics that enlightened self-interest always operates in the public interest. Nor is it true that self-interest generally *is* enlightened; more often individuals acting separately to promote their own ends are too ignorant or too weak to attain even these. Experience does *not* show that individuals, when they make up a social unit, are always less clear-sighted than when they act separately.[33]

As a result, he argued, one had to settle in detail, on a case-by-case basis, what, borrowing from Bentham, he called the Agenda and Non-Agenda of government – and to do so without presuppositions.[34] In his contributions to this subject, Keynes made a number of suggestions.

First, he made the distinction between matters which are technically *social* from those which are technically *individual*. The former, if they are not decided by or performed by the state would not be performed by anyone. His examples included the level and distribution of savings (including specifically the matter of home versus foreign investment discussed above (pp. 421–3)), population policy, the control of currency and credit and the provision of accurate information about general economic conditions.

Second, he concerned himself with broader issues of industrial organisation, for instance the appropriate organisation of public and semi-public corporations – their relations with Ministers, Parliament and local authorities. At this stage he did not advocate nationalisation: rather he was concerned with the efficient operation of what was already in the public sector, hoping to ensure that within appropriate guidelines such institutions should remain autonomous and professional.[d] Here there were questions of whether the Post Office or the telephone system should be run as a department of state under a Minister or as a public corporation, ultimately subject to Parliament but autonomous in its day-to-day operations. Similar considerations arose in connection with municipal enterprises. In all these cases, Keynes came down on the side of autonomy and professionalism, even at the cost of some centralisation, to provide varied, wide-ranging careers for the employees.

Under a related heading came the matter of the organisation of the private sector, where he observed a tendency towards large units of operation, the separation of ownership from control, cartels, trade agreements and

---

d He returned to this matter more concretely in 1944 in the context of electricity nationalisation. He argued that an industry should not be nationalised if it was to be run solely or primarily on commercial considerations. Where social considerations were important, nationalisation might be appropriate, but, even there, one needed what might call commercial considerations and efficiency to operate within generally broader guidelines (*JMK*, XXII, 454–77).

monopolies. Here Keynes put his faith in greater publicity in general and regulation in particular to protect investors and the general public. He was not averse to bigness in itself: in many cases he argued that it was inevitable. But he leaned towards solutions that would attempt to combine decentralised decision-taking with efficiency and the public interest.

Finally, in his speeches on the new liberalism, Keynes touched on more general questions of social reform. His major concerns were with what he deliberately and provocatively called sex and drug questions. Under sex questions, he referred to birth control, marriage laws, the treatment of sexual offences and abnormalities, and the economic position of women and the family. '[I]n all these matters', he remarked,

> the existing state of the law and of orthodoxy is still medieval – altogether out of touch with civilised opinion and civilised practice and with what individuals, educated and uneducated alike, say to one another in private.[35]

He accepted that these questions had their economic implications: the position of women and the family raised the whole question of how wages should be determined, a question which he simply mentioned in passing in 1925. Under drug questions, he put drink and gambling, as well as matters of 'permitted saturnalia, sanctified carnival' for a bored and suffering humanity. He gave away little of his own views as to the desirable direction of change. As in the case of the more strictly economic matters, which he characteristically, and perhaps conveniently, regarded as 'the largest of political questions',[36] he was at this stage throwing out questions for discussion. For some of them – and in more than just the regulation of currency and credit, his major professional concern – he later tried to present answers.

Keynes's substantive opportunity to refine and spell out his own ideas on economic policy beyond his traditional 'professional' concerns came in his speeches to Liberal Summer Schools. However, in July 1926, Lloyd George gave E. D. Simon and Ramsay Muir £10,000 to organise a Liberal Industrial Inquiry.[e] Lloyd George also made secretarial and office facilities available. As well as Keynes, Simon and Muir, the other members of the Inquiry's Executive Committee were Walter Layton (chair), Lloyd George, E. H. Gilpin, Hubert Henderson, Philip Kerr, C. F. G. Masterman, Major H. L. Nathan, B. S. Rowntree, Sir Herbert Samuel and Sir John Simon. Many of Keynes's friends served on the various committees of the Inquiry: R. H. Brand, Lawrence Cadbury, Sidney Russell Cooke, Dennis Robertson, and Sir Josiah Stamp. Keynes acted as chair of the committee on Industrial and Financial Organisation, working with Brand, Russell Cooke,

---

e An alternative usage would be Enquiry, but the acronym LIE seemed to be too much of a gift to Lloyd George's opponents, for it would 'provoke rude scoffing' (Reform Club, Eagar Papers, Box 12).

Henderson, Layton and Major Nathan. The work of research, discussion and drafting occupied the rest of 1926 and all of 1927 with Keynes and the others being whisked off to Churt, Lloyd George's country house, in hired Daimlers for working weekends as well as smaller meetings in London and Cambridge. The few surviving fragmentary records of the Inquiry suggest that the participants had considerable difficulties in transforming their views on general objectives into a workable programme.[37] It would appear that Keynes, whose views W. M. Eagar, the secretary to the Inquiry, thought 'constitute an admirable general objective but don't make an immediate programme', tried to push the Inquiry away from 'the impracticality, or uselessness, of inscribing pious ideas on a political banner of a kind which could not possibly be embodied in legislation'. To some degree Keynes succeeded, although when the report appeared on 2 February 1928 he found it

> Long winded, speaking when it has nothing to say, as well as when it has, droning at intervals 'Liberals, liberals all are we, gallant hearted liberals.' It would have been so much better at half the length speaking only what is new and important.[38]

Nevertheless, he considered the exercise valuable.

Keynes's contributions to the Inquiry's report *Britain's Industrial Future*, or the Yellow Book as it was and is known were substantial. He drafted most of Book II, 'The Organisation of Business' and chapters in Book V on 'Currency and Banking' and 'Reform of the National Accounts', inspired the proposals dealing with rural preservation and collaborated with others on chapters dealing with 'The Burden of Taxation', 'Rating Reform and the Rating System' and the final summary and conclusions. He was not involved directly in the sections on 'Industrial Relations' or 'National Development'. Some of his contributions fleshed out suggestions he had made during the previous few years. In some cases, the fleshing out was substantial, as in the case of company law and the control of monopoly. In the former case, he also provided a comment on the problems on investment that reflected his own experience.

> It is hardly an exaggeration to say that half the business of successful investment to-day in industrial shares consists of getting hold, in one way or another, of private information not available to the general body of shareholders and investors. The honest financier spends his time getting hold of true information to which he is not entitled, and the less honest in spreading false information for which, under the cover of general darkness, he can obtain credence. The actual proprietors of a concern are frequently at a serious disadvantage with 'outsiders' who can obtain access to 'inside' information. . . . At the same time, the knowledge by the public that there is such a thing as valuable 'inside'

information often puts them at the mercy of alleged 'inside' information which is only intended to deceive, or market tips which are part of a scheme of manipulation. The newspapers are full of a flood of gossip, advice and suggestion, in which items of real and of spurious 'inside' information are inextricably confused or intermingled.[39]

The remedy was a suggested reform of company accounts, severe restrictions on directors' trading in the shares of their own companies, plus publicity for such trading as occurred, and increased powers for auditors. In the case of monopolies, the main proposal was for greater publicity through regular Board of Trade inspection with the possibility of referral to a trust tribunal for further investigation, as well as the tighter regulation of trade associations.

When it came to public concerns, the proposals in Keynes's chapters were less developed, although Chapter II opened with a classic statement of the case for individualism.[40] His vagueness probably reflected the range of bodies considered – the Post Office, BBC, Central Electricity Board, docks and harbour boards, water boards, municipal enterprises and companies formed under private Acts of Parliament. The preferred form of organisation in the chapter was what we would now call public corporations (the report called them public boards) with substantial independence, staffed by professionals with good career prospects across the whole range of public enterprise. He hoped, where possible, that there would be a number of such concerns in each industry to allow the comparison of results, but the whole discussion did not even raise the problem of decision-making criteria. Although the chapter saw no immediate scope for the expansion of the public sector, it raised the possibility of public corporations controlling electricity, the railways and public transport in the London area.

In three areas Keynes worked up new proposals. The first was a proposal for an Economic General Staff, put forward by Sir William Beveridge in 1924, which proved influential in creating the climate of opinion that led the Labour Government in 1930 to the more limited experiment of an Economic Advisory Council. The second was a proposal for a Board of National Investment which would be responsible for all capital funds and expenditure of the central government, local authorities and *ad hoc* government boards and authorities, as well as the granting of Trustee status for new imperial capital issues, the regulation (in collaboration with the Bank of England) of new public issues for overseas governments and public authorities, and the administration of public support for private investment. In the next few years, Keynes would return to this proposal on a number of occasions. Finally, he began a campaign to reform the government's budgetary accounts – a campaign he was still waging, without much success, in June 1945 before the National Debt Inquiry.[41] The reforms he proposed would provide a clearer indication of the Government's activities than the existing cash accounts (which were subject, as Churchill demonstrated in the 1920s, to cosmetic alterations to suit the needs of the Chancellor of the Exchequer) and thus provide a better basis for economic analysis and intelligent discussion of budgetary policy.

Keynes's contributions to Liberal politics did not end with the *Nation*, the Summer Schools, or *Britain's Industrial Future*. He also played a role as a public speaker in the 1923, 1924 and 1929 elections. In 1923 he spoke for five candidates in the North West at Blackburn, Barrow-in-Furness and Blackpool, his audiences running to as many as 3,000, while the next year, despite a heavy cold, he managed to speak to the largest Liberal meeting in Cambridge for years. At the time he reflected on such meetings:

> They are always *exactly* the same – the same vamped up atmosphere and the same underlying boredom. It makes one feel a fool and a liar. No – I'm not cut out for politics. I do not enjoy it enough.[42]

Despite this activity, Keynes did not believe that the Liberal Party would again win an overall majority in Parliament. At best, he thought that it might win a third of the seats in any election.[43] Rather he believed that it would on many occasions hold a balancing position in Parliament – as often as every second election he suggested in 1924[44] – and could, in collaboration with the moderate sections of the other parties, most probably with Labour, get some of its ideas accepted. It was therefore for the sake of congenial ideas that he worked so hard for liberalism in the 1920s. As he told J. L. Garvin when discussing the Yellow Book:

> In fact, as things are at present, the Liberal Party, split and divided as it is and with uncertain aims, provides an almost perfect tabernacle for independent thought which shall at the same time be not too independent but in touch with the realities of politics and of political life.[45]

On 17 July 1928 Keynes wrote to Lord Beaverbrook to offer him an article for his *Evening Standard* which he claimed was in the same spirit as *The Economic Consequences of Mr Churchill*. The article, 'How to Organise a Wave of Prosperity', appeared on 31 July.[46] This concerned the recent rise in unemployment and the economic prospects, which with Government economy programmes and a prospective decline in local authority building were gloomy. Although prices had been falling for four years, money wages had scarcely changed. The deflation of costs implicit in the return to gold had not occurred and such a reduction in costs was necessary to stimulate employment. As Keynes saw it, there were three ways of getting a reduction: 'a general assault on money wages' such as had precipitated the 1926 coal strike; rationalisation, the contemporary term for an improvement in production methods; and working plant at a higher level of capacity. The first was politically impossible, especially as the Conservative Government under Baldwin had to face the electorate in 1929, and it would hit hardest those in the weakest bargaining position whose wages were already low. The second would raise unemployment in the short term. Although Keynes believed that businessmen should pursue rationalisation where possible, he thought there was a case for trying to operate the economy at a higher level of capacity. He advocated an expansion of public expenditure with a supportive, slightly expansionary, monetary policy. At this stage he did not present a developed rationale for his proposal.

> To have labour and cement and steel and machinery and transport lying by, and to say that you cannot *afford* to embark on harbour works or whatever it may be is the delirium of mental confusion.
>
> For several years past these policies have not lacked powerful advocates who have some claim to wisdom and experience – Mr McKenna, Lord Melchett, Sir Josiah Stamp, for example, amongst business authorities, Mr Lloyd George and Lord Beaverbrook amongst public men, and many economists and journalists.

Such a rationale waited on further thought and controversy.

The further thought came as Keynes worked his way towards the completion of his *Treatise* after the change in its direction during the early part of 1928. The controversy came with the general election that had to be called before the end of October 1929. The Liberal Industrial Inquiry's report on *Britain's Industrial Future* represented part of the Liberal Party's preparations for that election. During the winter of 1928–9 a special committee under the chairmanship of Seebohm Rowntree, attempted to distil the national development segments of the Yellow Book into an election programme. Keynes attended many of the meetings which ultimately produced a pamphlet *We Can Conquer Unemployment*, soon nicknamed the Orange Book because of the colour of its cover. The pamphlet provided the basis for Lloyd George's pledge to a meeting of Liberal MPs and candidates on 1 March 1929 that the Liberal Party, if elected, was ready

> with schemes of work which we can put immediately into operation, work of a kind which is not merely useful in itself but essential to the well-being of the nation. The work put in hand will reduce the terrible figures of the workless in the course of a single year to normal proportions.[f] . . . These plans will not add one penny to national or local taxation.

At the centre of the proposals was a large-scale programme of road building, house building, telephone service expansion, electrification, rail improvements, land drainage, and London transport improvements estimated to cost £100 million.

f Taken as the pre-war average level of unemployment of 4.7 per cent.

Keynes became one of the leading defenders of the proposals against Conservative opposition. As in 1923 and 1924, he was asked to stand for the Liberals in the Cambridge University seat, but again he declined the invitation, which then went to Hubert Henderson.[47] Although Keynes spoke in favour of the proposals,[g] the bulk of his support was literary – which provides a good source, along with related materials, for his ideas in the spring of 1929.

Keynes discussed possible and actual criticisms of the Liberal proposals when he welcomed them in the *Evening Standard* on 19 March; in a controversy with Sir Laming Worthington-Evans, the Secretary of State for War and a leading Conservative expansionist, in the *Evening Standard* between 19 April and 7 May; in a pamphlet written with Hubert Henderson, *Can Lloyd George Do It?*, which appeared on 10 May; and in a discussion of the Treasury's critical review of the Lloyd George scheme in a White Paper *Memoranda on Certain Proposals Relating to Unemployment* (Cmd. 3331), which appeared in the *Nation* on 18 May.[h] Leaving aside Keynes's attempt on 30 April to argue that he had supported such schemes for national development ever since he had realised the adverse effects of the return to gold on employment, which was untrue, his main concern in the controversy centred around two points: 'crowding out' and the ultimate effects of the programme on employment.

The argument that an expansion of public works financed by borrowing from the public would not increase total employment because they would displace, or 'crowd out', an equivalent amount of private sector investment lay at the heart of what became known as 'the Treasury view'. Winston Churchill as Chancellor of the Exchequer put the matter bluntly in his Budget speech of 15 April 1929:

It is the orthodox Treasury dogma, steadfastly held, that whatever

---

g He had intended to speak only once, in the City of London, but a deputation to Cambridge of two 'doughty bourgeois' from Leicester persuaded him to speak in that city on the eve of the poll (KCKP, JMK to Lydia, 26 May 1929).

h These appear in order in *JMK*, XIX, 804–8, 808–16; X, 86–125; XIX, 819–24. Peter Clarke (1988, 59 n. 33) also suggests that Keynes wrote a further, unsigned article of 23 February in the *Nation*, 'The Objections to Capital Expenditure'. His grounds for selecting this article as one by Keynes are that it is stylistically consistent with other Keynes material of the same period and that the Treasury took it as being by Keynes at a time when there was considerable contact between Keynes and Sir Richard Hopkins and Sir Frederick Leith-Ross of the Treasury. The problem with this attribution is that the article does not appear in his mother's collection of unsigned *Nation* articles which correspond with marked copies of that journal where they exist. Nor, although in the case of other pieces written when they were apart, did he mention it in his correspondence with Lydia. True, there are copies in the *Nation* files in the Keynes Papers with one cut up where it was incorporated into *Can Lloyd George Do It?* (*JMK*, IX, 115 para. 5, 117 para. 5, 119 3rd full para. 120 line 2), but this does not prove Keynes's rather than Henderson's authorship. For the attribution of anonymous Keynes articles see Moggridge 1988, 80–1.

might be the political and social advantages, very little additional employment and no permanent additional employment can in fact, and as a general rule, be created by State borrowing and State expenditure.[i]

This doctrine had crystallised within the Treasury in the course of the previous year in response to Keynes's 'How to Organise a Wave of Prosperity', discussions in the Cabinet of the possibility of a pre-election programme of public works, the Liberals' *We Can Conquer Unemployment* and subsequent discussions.[48] Its acknowledged intellectual origins lay in a 1925 article in *Economica* by Ralph Hawtrey, the Treasury's Director of Financial Enquiries, 'Public Expenditure and the Demand for Labour'. Hawtrey had argued that in normal circumstances, without an increase in bank lending, an expansion of loan-financed public works would raise interest rates and crowd out an equivalent amount of loan-financed private (or other public) investment. Crowding out would not occur if there were a sufficient increase in bank lending, because the rate of interest would not rise, so that the desired effect of public works could be achieved simply by an expansion in bank lending. Public works were 'merely a piece of ritual'.[49] But in early 1929, with sterling under severe pressure as a result of the Wall Street boom – Bank rate had risen to 5 ½ per cent on 7 February – monetary expansion, invariably labelled inflation within the Treasury, was not on the cards.[50]

I have already recounted how in the course of 1928 and early 1929 Keynes had been slowly and painfully reorientating his *Treatise* towards a savings-investment perspective.[51] That the reorientation was not complete is clear in his first journalistic support of the Lloyd George scheme, 'Mr Lloyd George's Pledge' in the *Evening Standard* of 19 March. There he mentioned that some of the savings necessary to support the domestic programme would come from a reduction in overseas lending, but the rest of the analysis was absent and he was reduced to ridiculing potential critics. The argument became more complex in his subsequent controversy with Sir Laming Worthington-Evans in the *Evening Standard*. By then Keynes had the advantage of Churchill's budget 'dogma' as a stalking horse. He stated flatly on 19 April that disequilibrium between saving and investment was 'at the root of many of our troubles'. Potential savings exceeded available domestic investment opportunities and the excess either went abroad or was used 'to enable other individuals to consume more than they produce' – to support the under- or *un*-employed. The excess savings would provide another source of finance for the Lloyd George schemes, along with the previously mentioned reduction in foreign lending. A final source would

i This is the version quoted by Keynes, which followed that in *The Times* (*JMK*, XIX, 809). The *Hansard* (Commons, CCXVII, col. 54) version referred to 'the orthodox Treasury doctrine which has steadfastly held'.

come from savings 'running to waste' owing to inadequate credit. Here the argument was that in existing circumstances the Bank of England could not increase the volume of credit because an expansion of credit would tend to reduce the rate of interest and lead to a rise in foreign lending with awkward consequences for the balance of payments. *Can Lloyd George Do It?* repeated these arguments more coherently in chapter IX. Its treatment of the effects of a reduction in foreign lending was still unclear. It argued again that the reduction in lending would not affect British exports; rather most of the reduction would come though a rise in imports of materials for the investment projects and for increased consumption, largely of food, of those previously unemployed. Why Keynes paid no attention to exports is unclear. Perhaps he simply assumed that the change would be too small to have a noticeable effect. Perhaps he just assumed exports depended mainly on the (real) exchange rate which was not going to change: since he believed British costs (hence the real exchange rate) were too high, additional foreign expenditure out of loans would probably go on *non-British* goods because they were cheaper. Finally, in passing in that pamphlet and more explicitly in his comment on the Treasury contribution to the White Paper in the *Nation* for 18 May 1929, he allowed for a further source of resources, the increase in national income resulting from the programme.[52]

Keynes divided the employment effects of the programme – assuming no (or at least minimal) crowding out – into three classes.[53] First, there was the employment provided directly to those working on the schemes. Second, there was the indirect increase in employment resulting from the increase in demand for other inputs for the schemes. He argued that the indirect, input-related employment was likely to be larger than the direct employment arising from the Liberal scheme. Third, there was 'the cumulative force of trade activity' coming from the increase in incomes and hence demand of those now employed and the effects on firms' expectations. In the summer of 1930, Richard Kahn would attempt to formalise the various direct and indirect employment effects (excluding those resulting from improved expectations) of an expansion of loan-financed expenditure on public works and to estimate the relevant 'multiplier', which later became an integral part of Keynes's thinking. At this stage, although in the rough and tumble of debate Keynes was continually revising and improving the defences for his position, his arguments were vague.

The debate surrounding the Liberal programme was lively. But it all fell somewhat flat. It certainly did little for the future of the Liberals, who came out of the election with only fifty-nine seats, more than in the previous Parliament but far below their hopes. The result left Keynes in 'a rather depressed state'.[54] It was the last election campaign in which he would take an active part for the Liberals or anyone else. Nor did he attend a Liberal Summer School again. The election also cost him some money: he won £10 from Winston Churchill on the result, but lost £160 betting on the Stock Exchange.

In the 1930s Keynes, while less involved in active party politics than in the 1920s, was reconsidering his position. For almost a decade he had worked hard to push the Liberal Party towards reform – with some success, especially in its 1929 election platform. The party's poor showing in that election and its subsequent reactions to the slump gave him cause to think again. In 1931 he withdrew his support from the National League of Young Liberals because life had gone out of the Party: it had become reactionary and come to concentrate on the ideas of the past.[55] By 1935 he was refusing to contribute to party funds, not only because he could not see the point of throwing money away but also because he was no longer convinced of the desirability of maintaining the separate identity of the party.[56] He was more inclined to support individual Labour candidates, such as Colin Clark who was running in South Norfolk, or to contribute to Labour in local London politics.[57] He did give £5 to support the Liberal candidate in Oxford in 1938, but he was prepared to give Stafford Cripps £50 – and to promise further contributions 'if what is happening seems to require and deserve it' – in order to support Cripps's attempt to organise a broad-based programme of reform and provide an alternative to the National Government, the Conservative dominated coalition in power since 1931.[58] With the outbreak of war, he moved back towards the Liberals. When he was raised to the peerage in 1942, he told the Liberal leader in the House of Lords, Viscount Samuel, that although he would like to sit as an independent he was 'in truth ... still a Liberal'. In 1945, he was inclined to refer to Liberal candidates such as Roy Harrod as 'funnies', but he gave the Party some financial support – a minimal £25.[59] Although surprised, he was not alarmed by Labour's overwhelming victory at the polls in an election in which as a peer he could not vote.

His disengagement from the Liberals in the 1930s did not mean that he eschewed politics. He remained chairman of the *New Statesman and Nation*, a journal definitely of the left, to the end of his life, though his correspondence with Kingsley Martin makes it clear that he was far from agreeing with much that appeared in that paper.[j] In the course of the 1930s he frequently commented on Labour policy proposals, more often than not sympathetically. Finally, I should note Keynes's relations with the left in another, more personal context, within the University, particularly the Apostles who included among their membership Anthony Blunt, Guy Burgess and Michael Straight.

The depression and the 1931 financial crisis had a traumatic effect on the left in Britain. The depression suggested that the crisis of capitalism had perhaps arrived. The financial crisis and the formation of the National Government in August 1931 left the organised Labour Party in disarray.

j The *Nation* had amalgamated with the *New Statesman* in 1931. See below p. 508.

The election of October 1931 returned the National Government under James Ramsay MacDonald with an overwhelming majority in the House of Commons: 52 Labour MPs, 4 Independent Liberals under Lloyd George and 6 Independents faced 471 Tories, 13 National Labour, 35 Liberal Nationalists, and 33 Liberals. Only one Labour member of MacDonald's 1929–31 Cabinet survived the electoral deluge. Labour had to regroup and rethink its policies at a time when groups further to the left could benefit both from the economic situation and from their independence from the Labour Government of 1929–31.

Keynes was unhappy with both the election campaign and its outcome. He thought, however, that for the Labour Party 'It will be good for them to go out into the wilderness for a time to find their soul again'.[60] He was also willing to give them a hand. On 13 December 1931 he addressed the Society for Socialist Inquiry and Propaganda, which had been founded by G. D. H. and Margaret Cole in June 1931, on 'The Dilemma of Modern Socialism'.

> I should like to define the socialist programme as aiming at political power, with a view to doing in the first instance what is economically sound, in order that, later on, the community may become rich enough to *afford* what is economically unsound.
>
> My goal is the ideal; my object is to put economic considerations into a back seat; but my method at this moment of economic and social evolution would be to advance towards the goal by concentrating on what is economically sound. . . . For it will have to be on the basis of increased resources, not on the basis of poverty, that the grand experiment of the ideal republic will have to be made.[61]

In thus reinterpreting his 'Economic Possibilities for Our Grandchildren' for a Labour audience, he was arguing that the economically sound – the central control of investment and the distribution of income to provide purchasing power for the output of modern industry – could take Britain towards the ideal society and that improvements in economic technique could make possible the solution of the problem of poverty. The Labour Party had to cease to be intellectually old-fashioned, or even anti-intellectual, to recognise that one of its major difficulties during the 1931 financial crisis had been its old-fashioned notions of economic soundness which 'made most of the Labour leaders agree with their opponents' and thus 'having a bad conscience . . . exceedingly ineffective for the practical purposes of government', and to realise that the party's present task was 'to discover, and then to do what was economically sound'.[62]

In this task Keynes did not intend a direct role for himself. His appointments diaries for the 1930s are singularly free of entries suggesting meetings with the emerging generation of senior Labour politicians. Yet it is also notable that many of the important figures in the groups that provided much of the basis for the programmes that emerged over the decade had close links with Keynes. The New Fabian Research Bureau, founded in 1931, drew heavily from the ranks of young 'Keynesians' – Colin Clark, James Meade and, to a lesser extent, Roy Harrod, Richard Kahn and Joan Robinson. The XYZ Club, started early in 1932 to inform the Party on finance and the City, had among its founders Nicholas Davenport, Keynes's colleague on the Board of the National Mutual and in the pages of the *Nation* and the *New Statesman*, and an early member was George Wansbrough, a former student.

When the first fruits of Labour's rethinking appeared as a policy report on currency, banking and finance, Keynes gave it a long and sympathetic two-part article in the *New Statesman* in September 1932. He naturally supported the proposal that sterling should be managed so as to maintain price rather than exchange rate stability. He welcomed the decision not to recommend nationalisation of the joint-stock banks, for 'as a piece of socialism it belongs to a late stage of socialisation and is not one of the indispensable first measures' – a point on which the Party Conference at Leicester disagreed when it reinstated the proposal in the Party programme.[63] He was sympathetic to the nationalisation of the Bank of England, although he thought that the suggestion for Parliamentary scrutiny of the details of policy was unhelpful, if understandable. He pointed out that

> With the personalities the same and knowledge no greater, it might not have made much difference if the machinery which the Labour Party desires had been in operation during the last ten years.[64]

However, it was a third resolution, to set up a National Investment Board, that drew most of his attention and the whole of his second article. He thought that the Party had not been ambitious enough because it had not realised the predominance of investment by public and semi-public bodies and the relative quantitative unimportance of private industrial investment and had therefore concentrated on controlling new capital issues.

> The task of a National Investment Board . . . is . . . first the mainte-nance of equilibrium between the total flow of investment on the one hand, and on the other hand the total resources available for investment at the price-level we are endeavouring to maintain . . .; and secondly a division of the aggregate of new lending between foreign and domestic borrowers which is appropriate to the foreign exchange level best suited to the stability of domestic prices.[65]

Although he would try to persuade Labour to do the economically sensible, in the 1930s and later another strand of thought became more prominent in Keynes's mind. It received its first extensive expression in 'National Self-Sufficiency'.

The nineteenth century carried to extravagant lengths the criterion of what one can call for short the financial results, as a test of the advisability of any course of action sponsored by private or by collective action. The whole conduct of life was made into a sort of parody of an accountant's nightmare. Instead of using their vastly increased material wealth and technical resources to build a wonder-city, they built slums; and they thought it right and advisable to build slums because slums on the test of private enterprise 'paid', whereas the wonder-city would, they thought, have been an act of foolish extravagance, which would in the imbecile idiom of the financial fashion have 'mortgaged the future'; though how the construction today of great and glorious works can impoverish the future no man can see until his mind is beset by false analogies from an irrelevant accountancy. . . .

But once we allow ourselves to be disobedient to the test of an accountant's profit, we have begun to change our civilisation. And we need to do so very warily, cautiously and self-consciously. For there is a wide field of human activity where we shall be wise to retain the usual pecuniary tests. It is the state, rather than the individual, which needs to change its criterion. It is the conception of the Chancellor of the Exchequer as the chairman of a sort of joint-stock company which has to be discarded.[66]

Many of these phrases reappeared just over three years later in 'Art and the State' where he referred to the 'utilitarian and economic – one might almost say financial ideal' as 'the most dreadful heresy, perhaps, which has ever gained the ear of a civilised people' and to Britain as being 'hag ridden by a perverted theory of the state'.[67] They also appeared in the General Theory.[68] Echoes survive in his wartime BBC broadcasts on the finance of post-war reconstruction and the founding of the Arts Council in 1945.[69] Such remarks represented a notable extension of Keynes's criteria of and agenda for state action. It was not one congenial to many on the left.

While sympathetic to Labour's attempts to develop new programmes, Keynes was less attracted by attempts by more conservative politicians and others to develop proposals for a 'middle way'. He found their investment proposals even less ambitious than some of Labour's. He also thought that the only sensible tack to take was to join in efforts to oust the present Government and its sympathisers.[70] Finally, as he worked towards his General Theory, he thought

first, that there is no room for a programme intermediate between that of Mr Baldwin and Sir Stafford Cripps, except on the basis of a new underlying economic theory and philosophy of the state; secondly, that such a new outlook is required if we are to avoid extremism during the next slump or two; and, thirdly, that the best way of occupying one's time is to busy oneself with forwarding a new understanding of the problem.[71]

Thus he did not sign the foreword to *The Next Five Years*, the product of a 1934–5 study group, even though he agreed that the practical proposals were 'nearly all excellent' and remarked that a government which adopted the programme of the volume would have his 'enthusiastic support'.[72] Perhaps he had more time for pushing Labour in a reformist direction because he believed that

> In this country henceforward power will normally reside with the Left. The Labour Party will always have a majority, except when something has happened to raise a doubt in the minds of reasonable and disinterested persons whether the Labour Party is in the right.[73]

Furthermore, as he put it in 1939,

> The question is whether we are prepared to move out of the nineteenth-century *laissez-faire* state into an era of liberal socialism, by which I mean a system where we can act as an organised community for common purposes and to promote economic and social justice, whilst respecting and protecting the individual – his freedom of choice, his faith, his mind and its expression, his enterprise and his property.[74]

His liberal-socialist vision, though not accepted in detail by many on the left, was to prove influential in segments of Labour Party thinking from the mid-1930s onwards.

Although Keynes had considerable sympathy for certain strands of Labour thought on social and economic policy, as I have noted, he had few points of contact with the new generation of Labour leaders. In part this reflected differences in age, in part differences in intellectual style. It was unlikely in the 1930s that he and Hugh Dalton would be on the same wavelength in a theoretical discussion, for Dalton's radicalism, although it had good Pigovian roots, did not extend much beyond distributional matters. The younger generation presented problems: Evan Durbin was a Hayekian in economic theory and Hugh Gaitskell was not much interested in macroeconomic theory at the time.[75] Beatrice Webb after lunching with him in June 1936 recorded in her diary that 'Keynes has an unmitigated contempt for the official Labour party (especially Morrison by the way)'.[76] He found many of them 'sectaries of an outworn creed mumbling moss-grown demi-semi-Fabian Marxism'.[77]

The reference to Marxism reveals another constraint on Keynes's possible sympathy for Labour: his continuing blind spot for Marx and his writings which dated from the 1920s. As he told Bernard Shaw in 1934:

> My feelings about *Das Kapital* are the same as my feelings about the *Koran*. I know that it is historically important and I know that

many people, not all of whom are idiots, find it a sort of Rock of Ages and continuing inspiration. Yet, when I look into it, it is to me inexplicable that it can have this effect. . . . I am sure that its contemporary *economic* value (apart from occasional but inconstructive and discontinuous flashes of insight) is *nil*. Will you promise to read it again, if I do?[78]

A month later he reported to Shaw:

But I've made another shot at old K.M. last week, reading the Marx–Engels correspondence just published, without making much progress. I prefer Engels of the two. I can see that they invented a certain method of carrying on and a vile manner of writing, both of which their successors have maintained with fidelity. But if you tell me that they discovered a clue to the economic riddle, still I am beaten – I can discover nothing but out-of-date controversialising.[79]

Almost a decade later he commented to Joan Robinson on the publication of her *Essay on Marxian Economics* (1942):

I found it most fascinating . . . . This is in spite of the fact that there is something intrinsically boring in an attempt to make sense out of what is in fact nonsense. However, you have got round it by making no undue attempt in this direction . . . .

I am left with the feeling, which I had before on less evidence, that he had a penetrating and original flair but was a very poor thinker indeed, – and his failure to publish his later volumes probably meant that he was not unaware of this himself.[80]

Elsewhere he referred to the notion of communism as a means of improving the economic situation as 'an insult to our intelligence'.[81] However he freely admitted that he was not 'a good Marxist scholar'.[82]

As well as being 'notoriously tone deaf' to Marx, he disliked Soviet Communism in the 1930s – more so than in the 1920s.[83] The economic experiment interested him, but it exhibited 'the worst example which the world, perhaps, has ever seen of administrative incompetence and the sacrifice of almost everything that makes life worth living to wooden heads'.[84] 'Stalin has eliminated every independent critical mind, even when it is sympathetic in general outlook . . . [and] produced an environment in which the processes of the mind are atrophied'.[85] He watched Stalin's purges and show trials with a horrified fascination.[86] When Kingsley Martin asked him to comment on Beatrice Webb's 80th birthday in 1936 'The only sentence which came spontaneously to my mind was "Mrs Webb, not being a Soviet politician, has managed to survive to the age of eighty"'.[87]

Despite his attitudes towards Marxism and the Soviet Union, Keynes maintained an ambivalent attitude towards some communists and some fellow-travelling organisations such as the Left Book Club. He described the Club as 'one of the finest and most living movements of our time'.[88] As he still saw Communism 'as a protest against the emptiness of economic welfare, an appeal to the ascetic in us' he was not surprised to see 'idealistic youth play with Communism because it is the only spiritual appeal which feels to them contemporary'.[89]

Then there was the Cambridge left and his dealings with undergraduates, which get raked over from time to time whenever British journalists get spies on their brains. It is a platitude to remark that Cambridge was more left-wing in the 1930s than in the 1920s, although one should note that one is talking of shifts in opinion in an institution where, for the most part, undergraduates and dons were overwhelmingly small 'c' conservatives or small 'l' liberals. Keynes came across members of the Cambridge left as colleagues, undergraduate members of his Political Economy Club, or Apostles. His public views are a matter of record, but in his personal relations, although he would certainly defend his own views and probably tease or attempt to goad others of differing persuasions, he was naturally concerned with the whole person rather than just politics. He could maintain his long-standing, affectionate and productive relationship with Piero Sraffa and respect Maurice Dobb, from whom he commissioned the Cambridge Economic Handbook *Wages* (1928). When some of the younger, left-wing generation became Apostles, he dealt with them as he dealt with others – as human beings, whose company he took advantage of if he enjoyed it. He appears to have enjoyed the company of Guy Burgess, his guest at a King's Feast on 24 February 1934 and whom, along with Morgan Forster, he invited to a party he arranged for Duncan Grant's visit to Cambridge for the same feast in 1935.[k] The same enjoyment marked his relations with Victor Rothschild, whom he saw frequently between 1933 and 1936. Rothschild, like Burgess, was an Apostle, but his political views were more orthodox.

Keynes had considerable respect for many young communists. As he put it in 1939:

> There is no one in politics today worth sixpence outside the ranks of liberals except the post-war generation of intellectual Communists under thirty-five. Them, too, I like and respect. Perhaps in their feelings and instincts they are the nearest we now have to the typical nervous non-conformist English gentleman who went to the Crusades, made the Reformation, fought the Great Rebellion, won us our civil and religious liberties and humanised the working classes last century.[90]

But he continued

---

k Burgess had been openly associated with the Communist Party until 1934, when he formally broke with it in what appeared to be mysterious circumstances, moved to London and worked for a right-wing MP with close ties to the Nazis. Actually Burgess remained a member of the Party throughout.

I sympathise with Mr Bevin in fighting shy of [Labour Party] contact with the professional Communists, regarding their body as a Trojan horse and their overtures in doubtful faith. But I should risk contact all the same, so as not to lose contact with the splendid material of amateur Communists. For with them in their ultimate maturity lies the future.

This leads to a related point. In his *The Climate of Treason*, Andrew Boyle alleges that 'the Society at Keynes's prompting officially suspended its proceedings'.[91] The origins of this statement are unclear. So too is the source for a similar statement in *Journey to the Frontier*, although Keynes is not brought into it.[92] Julian Bell's letters do mention the Society's being 'moribund, thanks to the party activities of the young' in December 1935 and that 'the bitterest thing about the communist hysteria at Cambridge has been the virtual death of the Society' in 1937.[93] Yet Michael Straight reports being invited to join the Society in the autumn of 1936, that the Society was then meeting in Keynes's rooms in King's and that Keynes gave him assistance in organising meetings, including one in February 1937 (recorded in Keynes's appointments diary) where one of the suggested guests was Anthony Blunt.[94] Straight's Communist politics were known to Keynes. His reports are hardly consistent with Boyle's suggestion. They are consistent with Keynes's trying to revive the institution and keep it going – not to protect it from Communist influence.[1]

1 They are also not consistent with Beatrice Webb's 1936 report of Keynes's 'unmitigated contempt . . . for the communist undergraduates' whom he thought were 'suffering from neurosis, due to the absence of any creed or code of conduct'. (BLPES, Passfield Papers, Beatrice Webb Diaries, vol. 50, p. 6185.)

NOTES

1 *JMK*, XIX, 400.
2 *JMK*, XIX, 525–9.
3 VWD, II, 77, 80, 82, 83; VWL, III, 260.
4 *JMK*, XIX, 530–4.
5 Ibid., 543.
6 Ibid., 534–7, 559.
7 KCKP, Margot Asquith to JMK, 22 and 28 May 1926; JMK to Margot Asquith [not sent], 26 May 1926.
8 *JMK*, XIX, 539, 541.
9 *JMK*, X, 37–40.
10 Sayers 1976, I, 320. The previous quotation is on page 319.
11 *JMK*, XIX, 605.
12 *JMK*, XIX, 601, 605.
13 *JMK*, XIX, 626.
14 Sayers 1976, 322–8; Clay 1957, 318–20.
15 Lazonick 1981.
16 Campbell 1977, 54.

17 *JMK*, XXVII, 384.
18 *JMK*, IX, 295–6.
19 *JMK*, IX, 297.
20 *JMK*, XIX, 150–1, 728–9.
21 *JMK*, XVIII, 126; XIX, 2–3, 3–4, 677. On the importance of the population issue to Keynes, see 'An Economist's View of Population' (August 1922) in XVII, 440–6.
22 Lambert 1963, 5.
23 Clarke 1978, 1988, esp. 78–83; Freeden 1986.
24 *JMK*, IX, 268–9.
25 *JMK*, IX, 294.
26 *JMK*, IX, 268.
27 *JMK*, IX, 321–32.
28 *JMK*, IX, 326.
29 Hirsch 1976, ch. 2.
30 *JMK*, IX, 330–1.
31 *JMK*, IX, 284.
32 *JMK*, IX, 284; Hahn 1982a.
33 *JMK*, IX, 287–8.
34 *JMK*, IX, 288.
35 *JMK*, IX, 302.
36 *JMK*, IX, 303.
37 Reform Club, Eagar Papers, Box 14, Eagar to Kerr, 27 August 1927; Kerr to Lloyd George, 2 September 1927; JMK to Kerr, 31 August 1927; Kerr to JMK, 2 September 1927.
38 *JMK*, XIX, 735.
39 *Britain's Industrial Future*, 85–6.
40 Ibid., 64–5.
41 *JMK*, XVIII, 403 ff.
42 KCKP, JMK to Lydia, 26 October 1924.
43 *JMK*, IX, 307.
44 *JMK*, XIX, 326.
45 *JMK*, XIX, 733.
46 *JMK*, XIX, 761–6.
47 KCKP, JMK to Lydia 16 October 1923 and 12 October 1924; *JMK*, XIX, 773–4.
48 For a brilliant reconstruction of Treasury thinking see Clarke 1988, ch. 3.
49 Hawtrey 1925, 43.
50 Sayers 1976, 224–6.
51 Above pp. 441–2.
52 *JMK*, IX, 120; XIX, 823.
53 *JMK*, IX, 102–7.
54 KCKP, JMK to Lydia, 5 June 1929.
55 *JMK*, XX, 527–8.
56 *JMK*, XXI, 373.
57 *JMK*, XXI, 373.
58 KCKP, JMK to Harrod, 20 October 1938; *JMK*, XXI, 502–3.
59 KCKP, JMK to Samuel, 24 June 1942; Harrod 1951, 593.
60 *JMK*, XXI, 10.
61 *JMK*, XXI, 34.
62 *JMK*, XXI, 36, 38.
63 *JMK*, XXI, 130.

64 *JMK*, XXI, 133.
65 *JMK*, XXI, 136.
66 *JMK*, XXI, 240–2.
67 *JMK*, XXVIII, 342–3.
68 *JMK*, VII, 131, 362.
69 *JMK*, XXVII, 270; XXVIII, 368.
70 See the June and September 1932 letters to Harold Macmillan reprinted in *JMK*, XXI, 109, 126.
71 See the July 1935 letter to Sir Arthur Salter reprinted in *JMK*, XXI, 355.
72 *JMK*, XXI, 354.
73 *JMK*, XXI, 36.
74 *JMK*, XXI, 500.
75 For Durbin's views see *JMK*, XXIX, 232–4. For an account of the evolution of Party thinking in Keynes's direction see Durbin 1985.
76 BLPES, Passfield Papers, Beatrice Webb Diaries, vol. 50, p. 6815.
77 *JMK*, XXI, 495.
78 *JMK*, XXVIII, 38.
79 *JMK*, XXVIII, 42.
80 King's College, Robinson Papers, JMK to Joan Robinson, 20 August 1942. I am indebted to Geoff Harcourt for reminding me of this letter.
81 *JMK*, XXVIII, 32.
82 *JMK*, IX, 91 n. 1.
83 Winch 1969, 348.
84 *JMK*, XXI, 92, 239, 233–4.
85 *JMK*, XXI, 246.
86 *JMK*, XXVIII, 17, 37–8, 72–3.
87 *JMK*, XXVIII, 95. See also ibid., 17–19, 57–8.
88 *JMK*, XXI, 496. On the politics of the Club see Pimlott 1977, 158–61; Edwards 1987, chs X–XIII.
89 *JMK*, XXVIII, 35.
90 *JMK*, XXI, 494–5.
91 Boyle 1979, 75.
92 Stansky and Abrahams 1966, 48.
93 Bell (ed.) 1938, 67; Stansky and Abrahams 1966, 49.
94 Straight 1983, 93–5.

19

THE EMERGENCE
OF THE *TREATISE*

Keynes on a committee is like yeast.
(KCKP, BE, J. H. Clapham to JMK, 18 September 1941
reporting a comment by Governor Norman)

While the 1929 British election campaign proceeded, there was yet another attempt to settle the reparations problem. Keynes had kept a watching brief on the progress of reparations and war debts in the years after the adoption of the Dawes scheme. On war debts, his comments had concerned the settlements that the other allies, France and Italy, made with Britain and the United States and their relationship to the flows of reparations under the Dawes plan. As he put it in 1926:

> Reparations and inter-Allied debts are being mainly settled in paper and not in goods. The United States lends money to Germany, Germany transfers its equivalent to the Allies, the Allies pay it back to the United States Government. Nothing real passes – no one is a penny the worse. The engravers' dies, the printers' formes are busier. But no one eats less, no one works more.[1]

In emphasising the link between reparations and war debts in the later 1920s, Keynes repeatedly highlighted the fragility of the arrangements. He wondered what would happen if lending to Germany ceased and reparations under the Dawes scheme or possible successors fell off. Then, he suggested, the existence of the long-term contractual payments between former allies would cause difficulties. He always took care to note the need for an American reconsideration of the war debt issue, especially if there was a change in the reparations settlement with Germany.

In discussing Germany's position as it was evolving after 1924, Keynes kept to the forefront the fact that she was not developing an export surplus. She continued to run trade and current account deficits in her balance of payments and was, in effect, using foreign loans to finance the deficits and to pay the rising reparations bills under the Dawes scheme. After

1925 Germany also experienced a period of rising prices and rising real wages.[a] Thus Germany was moving away from rather than towards the international economic position necessary for the long-term success of the Dawes scheme and, Keynes argued, breakdown or renegotiation of that scheme was inevitable.

Keynes was not, of course, the only person looking towards a renegotiation of the Dawes régime. In Germany there was pressure to replace the indefinite totals of the scheme – indefinite because they could be revised upwards and downwards according to a 'prosperity index'[b] and had no terminal date – with a definite, and lower, sum. There was also pressure to reduce the foreign controls on German economic policy that were an integral part of the scheme. Among the former allies there were fears as to the scale of German foreign borrowing, the increasing budget deficit and the possibility that the transfer of reparations or payments on Germany's overseas loans might be blocked. This mixture of fears and desires, which had been at least partly aroused by Keynes's journalism, plus a hope that perhaps there could be a final 'solution' of the problem, led to the appointment of another international committee in September 1928.[2] Chaired by Owen D. Young, the committee worked between 9 February and 7 June 1929 to produce new proposals. Among its members were Sir Josiah Stamp, Lord Revelstoke (replaced on his death by Sir Charles Addis), J. P. Morgan and Thomas Lamont. Carl Melchior found himself involved as an adviser to Hjalmar Schacht, the Governor of the Reichsbank and the German member of the committee.

During the deliberations of the committee, Keynes remained in touch with Stamp and Melchior.[3] In public he attempted to influence the committee's thinking and the course of events at two levels, the popular and the academic. The more significant was perhaps the latter, for it resulted in one of the classic controversies in the literature of international economics and gave Keynes further occasion to utilise, and to reconsider, the analysis that was to become his *Treatise*.

'The German Transfer Problem' appeared in the *Economic Journal* for March 1929.[4] Keynes sent a pre-publication copy to Stamp, who circulated it to the British, American and certain French members of the Young Committee, and to Melchior. Schacht read it after publication.[5]

The argument of the article started from the distinction made by the Dawes Committee between the budgetary problem of raising reparations

---

a According to later estimates, German industrial wage costs per unit of output rose by 12 per cent between 1925 and 1929, while those of her competitors fell substantially. Germany also had relatively unfavourable experience with her cost of living, export unit values and industrial profitability. See Phelps Brown and Browne 1967, appendix III.

b The index, devised by the Dawes Committee, depended on statistics for foreign trade, the budget, railway traffic, consumption of sugar, tobacco, beer and spirits, coal production and population. As the index rose above or fell below a predetermined level, payments to the Allies under the plan would be adjusted proportionately.

in marks from the German people and the transfer problem of converting these marks into foreign exchange. While in theory solving the budgetary problem might solve the transfer problem, in practice, Keynes suggested, the transfer problem was the more serious. He took as his basic premiss that German prices and unit wage costs had adjusted to a situation where, at a fixed exchange rate, domestic taxation covered the budgetary problem and overseas borrowing more than covered the transfer of reparations payments. If borrowing ceased, then, without a change in savings behaviour, Germany would have to shift resources from domestic capital investment to the production of exports or import-competing goods. German unit costs would have to fall substantially, since the volume of manufactured exports would have to rise by 40 per cent to cover reparations payments under the Dawes scheme as well as interest payments on previous borrowing. To achieve this there were only two alternatives: inflation in the rest of the world or deflation in Germany. In the existing situation, Keynes did not discuss the first alternative.[c] The only available course was deflation through the usual route of higher unemployment reducing money wages. He wondered whether such a reduction was politically or humanly feasible, especially as the resulting disorders might lead to withdrawals of short-term capital. Deflation would also adversely affect tax revenues and cause increased expenditures and thus increase the budgetary problem. He therefore hoped that Germany would retain the transfer protection of the Dawes scheme whereby she was not obliged to transfer reparations if in any one year she lacked the necessary balance of payments surplus. He also drew a parallel with the British situation:

> My own view is that at a given time the economic structure of a country, in relation to the economic structures of its neighbours, permits of a certain 'natural' level of exports, and that arbitrarily to effect a material alteration of this level by deliberate devices is extremely difficult. Historically, the volume of foreign investment has tended, I think, to adjust itself – at least to a certain extent – to the balance of trade, rather than the other way around, the former being the sensitive and the latter the insensitive factor. In the case of German reparations, on the other hand, we are trying to fix the volume of foreign remittance and compel the balance of trade to adjust itself thereto. Those who see no difficulty in this – like those who saw no difficulty in Great Britain's return to the gold standard – are applying the theory of liquids to what is, if not a solid, at least a sticky mass with strong inner resistances.[6]

The article resulted in extensive private correspondence and in comments and rejoinders published in the *Economic Journal*. The most important exchanges

---

c In his later rejoinder to Bertil Ohlin and in the *Treatise* he ruled it out on the grounds that Germany's foreign reserves were such a small proportion of world reserves that their use would have a negligible effect on prices elsewhere (*JMK*, XI, 479; V, 307).

were with the Swedish economist Bertil Ohlin, then at the University of Copenhagen. Ohlin accepted that some falls in German wages and prices would prove necessary,[7] but argued that Keynes's analysis was incomplete in that it ignored the role of income changes in the process of adjustment. Ohlin granted that less lending to Germany would lead to a fall in German investment and in German demands for imports, but he suggested that Keynes had left out of his story what would happen in the lending country, where the net effect would depend on the sources of funds for such lending and their alternative uses. As subsequent theorising by economists has indicated, what will happen eventually is uncertain, depending as it does on the magnitudes of several macroeconomic parameters and on official policy. In theory, Ohlin was right. As Keynes noted in his second reply to Ohlin:

> My original article . . . applied general principles to a particular case, without attempting to go deeply into the general principles themselves or even to enunciate them in a generalised form. As, however, the controversy . . . develops . . . the worst of it is that it moves, quite inevitably, from the particular to the general.[8]

Whether or not Keynes's 'particular piece of applied economics' had highlighted the crucial variables in the actual circumstances of 1929 is another matter. At the time he was writing the article, American long-term lending overseas had collapsed in the face of the Wall Street boom of 1928–9. He did not foresee the subsequent collapse in American and world incomes, despite which Germany contrived to achieve the balance of payments surplus necessary to transfer reparations – but at the cost of massive unemployment, social unrest and, in the end, Nazism.

The Young Committee's Report of 7 June 1929 recommended some reduction in reparation payments: under the Dawes scheme they ran at £125 million per annum adjusted by the 'prosperity index'; under the Young Plan they would start at £90 million, rising eventually to £125 million in 1965–6 before declining to £44 million in 1987–8. Deliveries in kind were to be carefully regulated and to disappear by 1939. French troops were to leave the Rhineland and foreign supervision of German finances through the Agent General for Reparations and foreign directors of the Reichsbank and the state railways was to cease. In return Germany accepted an obligation to pay reparations for a longer period than expected and she forswore transfer protection on a certain proportion of her annual payments and accepted less protection on the remainder. A new Bank for International Settlements was to monitor the operation of the scheme and assist the transfer process. A loan of £500 million (of which £100 million would go to Germany) was to start the scheme off. Finally, the members of the Committee linked German payments under the scheme to future American concessions to her allies on war debts.

Keynes was far from enthusiastic, even though, as he told Lydia on 3 June, 'I think it may be that Stamp has done good work for the world after all'. He was concerned about the reduced transfer protection and about the early demise of deliveries in kind.[9] He was, however, hopeful about the possibilities of the proposed Bank for International Settlements and pleased by the link forged between war debts and reparations. But as he told Andrew McFadyean:

> My own prophecy would be that the Young Plan will not prove practicable for even a short period unless the mark exchange is allowed to depart from its present parity, and I should not be at all surprised to see some sort of crisis in 1930.[10]

He was not far wrong in his forecast: there was a German crisis in 1930 and an even more serious crisis in 1931 which effectively meant an end to reparations.

With Easter term over, the 1929 general election and its associated controversy out of the way, and Keynes's comments on the Young Report in print, the way was now clear for a summer on the *Treatise*. Except for a week in Geneva at the end of July to deliver four lectures at the School of International Studies and a brief flurry of newspaper controversy on the 'Treasury view', where he made another attempt at setting out the sources of the resources for a scheme of Lloyd Georgian size,[11] he left the vacation free of other engagements. By the beginning of August, over 320 pages or nineteen of his thirty-two chapters of the book were in page proof; the rest was in draft or galley proof form. He was still working towards publication some time in October. In the course of August, however, with 400 pages in proof, he decided that he needed to re-write some chapters drastically and to rearrange the whole work into two volumes. He told Macmillans of this on 20 August. Within a month, he had almost finished the revisions to the first volume, 'The Pure Theory of Money', and was aiming to have it ready for press by the end of November with the second volume, 'The Applied Theory of Money', following a month later.[12] At the end of September, Richard Kahn, reading the proofs, remarked on the 'great courage' of Keynes's decision and, judging from its first fruits, 'how altogether right' he had been, particularly in his modification of the treatment of the Fundamental Equations.[13]

Richard Kahn had entered Keynes's intellectual life before this letter. In the August 1929 draft preface to the *Treatise*, Keynes thanked Hubert Henderson for his usefulness 'on the plan and architecture of an argument' and Kahn, Piero Sraffa and Frank Ramsey, 'but especially Mr Kahn', for their assistance in discovering 'innumerable mistakes and muddles'.

Kahn, the son of a Government Inspector of Schools, had come up to King's from St Paul's School in 1924. He took a second class degree in physics in June 1927 before turning to economics where, supervised by

Keynes and Gerald Shove, he obtained a first in Part II of the Tripos in June 1928. In the term before he took his Tripos, he began to appear in Keynes's correspondence with Lydia as his 'favourite pupil' writing 'one of the best answers I have ever had from a pupil'.[14] Once he had his first as well as a senior scholarship, he settled down to preparing a fellowship dissertation. At first, this was to be on British banking and related to the evolving *Treatise*, but the Midland Bank would not provide access to statistical material ('[L]et down again by McKenna!' was Keynes's comment). He turned to 'The Economics of the Short Period' with special reference to the cotton industry, where Keynes's earlier contacts gave him access to unpublished statistics and useful interviews.[15] The dissertation was submitted in December 1929. It was successful and he became a Fellow of King's in March 1930. An earlier essay for the University's Adam Smith Prize, which Pigou reported was certainly the best he had read since Keynes's 1909 essay on index numbers, and perhaps the best ever, was also successful.[16]

Before August 1929, not in January 1930 as Kahn has stated as if to dissociate himself from most of the creation of the *Treatise* and an earlier Keynes, he had become closely involved in Keynes's intellectual life.[17] He was to remain so until the war, eventually completely displacing Dennis Robertson. To Keynes's work, as well as to his own and others', especially that of Joan Robinson, Kahn brought a powerful mind with a flair for fruitful simplification and an emphasis on the bare bones of an argument.

The Michaelmas term of 1929, when time allowed, saw Keynes deep in revisions. He gave his lectures from proof sheets, concentrating on Book III, the theoretical core of the book, to an audience which on at least one occasion included Dennis Robertson. But he fell behind schedule with his revisions: it was mid-November before he passed his new proofs to Dennis Robertson and Pigou for comment. On the 24th he reported to Lydia that 'It looks as if my proof sheets will get through the criticism of Dennis and Pigou without serious damage'. But yet again things were to drag on much longer than expected.

The autumn of 1929 produced new distractions. The Wall Street crash on 24 October caused a brief relapse into 'a thoroughly financial and disgusting state of mind', not on his own account, for after the trials of the previous year he had little to lose, but for others, such as the P.R. When he provided a brief comment for the New York *Evening Post* on the crash, he pointed out that it had produced the prospect of lower interest rates in Britain, where the attractions of the New York market and the attempts of the Federal Reserve to damp down speculation had forced the authorities to push up Bank rate to 6½ per cent on 26 September. Although the dear money of the previous months would mean a bad winter of unemployment in Britain and Germany, the prospect of cheap money held out hope. 'If cheap money comes, I do not doubt its remedial efficiency.'[18] Little did he and his contemporaries foresee that the recession that Britain and the United States had been experiencing for some months would become known as the Great Depression.[d]

A further distraction came in November. The new Labour Government under James Ramsay MacDonald, which took office in June 1929, had been considering an inquiry into the British financial system.[19] As a result of Keynes's proposals in *Britain's Industrial Future*, as well as more general disquiet and demands for an inquiry stretching back over several years in places such as McKenna's speeches and articles in the pages of his *Midland Bank Review*, the deliberations of the Mond-Turner 'Conference on Industrial Reorganisation and Industrial Relations', and the House of Commons' discussion of the Currency and Bank Notes Act of 1928 (which carried through the amalgamation of the Bank and Treasury note issues), an inquiry was probably inevitable. Perhaps someone even recalled the Cunliffe Committee's recommendation that there might be a further inquiry to see how things had gone during the first post-war decade.[20] High interest rates in 1929 produced further criticism but probably only affected the inquiry's timing. With Lord Macmillan in the chair, a Committee on Finance and Industry that included Keynes was appointed in a Treasury Minute of 5 November 1929[e]

> to inquire into banking, finance and credit, paying particular regard to factors both internal and international which govern their operation, and to make recommendations calculated to enable these agencies to promote the development of trade and commerce and the employment of labour.

The Committee met for the first time on 21 November 1929.

Four days later, Keynes was invited to a luncheon with the Prime Minister. As he told Lydia: 'As you said, I am becoming more fashionable again, now I am on a Gov^t Com^{ee}'.[21] The meeting, and two further meetings on 9 and 16 December, were to discuss the current industrial situation and ways of improving the information and advice available to the Government. Keynes provided two papers for the meetings, which were also attended by officials, industrialists and academics. In one of the papers he revived the Yellow Book's proposal for an Economic General Staff.[22] On 24 January 1930 the Government announced an Economic Advisory Council, whose purpose was, according to the Treasury Minute of 27 January

d Before the 1930s the phrase 'Great Depression' had been attached to the period 1873–96.

e Other than Keynes its membership was as follows: Macmillan, a barrister specialising in public law, chairman; Lord Bradbury; Cecil Lubbock, a former Deputy Governor of the Bank; J. Frater Taylor, one of Norman's 'company doctors' from Armstrong Whitworth the armaments manufacturers; Lennox Lee, President of the Federation of British Industries; Sir Walter Raine, President of the Association of British Chambers of Commerce; A. G. Tulloch of the District Bank; Sir Thomas Allen of the Co-operative Wholesale Society; R. H. Brand; J. Walton Newbold, a former communist MP and editor of the *Social Democrat*; Ernest Bevin, General Secretary of the Transport and General Workers Union; Reginald McKenna; and Professor Theodore Gregory of the London School of Economics.

to advise His Majesty's Government in economic matters, to make continuous study of developments in trade and industry and in the use of national and imperial resources, of the effect of legislation and fiscal policy at home and abroad and of all aspects of national, imperial and international economy with a bearing on the prosperity of the country.

The Prime Minister was to chair the Council and the Chancellor of the Exchequer, the President of the Board of Trade, the Lord Privy Seal and the Minister of Agriculture were *ex officio* members. The non-ministerial members, chosen 'in virtue of their special knowledge of industry and economics', included Keynes.[f] The Council also had a small permanent staff. Hubert Henderson, partly at Keynes's urging, left the *Nation* and refused the offer of a chair at the London School of Economics to become the senior economist. The other members of the Secretariat were Thomas Jones and A. F. Hemming from the Council's predecessor, the Committee of Civil Research, and three economists H. V. Hodson, Colin Clark and Piers Debenham, the last unpaid. The Council had its first meeting on 17 February 1930.

It was, as Roy Harrod suggested,[23] a matter of luck for Keynes that the final stages of preparing the *Treatise* coincided with the Macmillan Committee – not to mention the Economic Advisory Council (EAC). After six years of thinking about monetary theory and practice, he had a chance to influence a major British monetary document – the report of the first full public inquiry in living memory into the financial system and the activities of the Bank of England – and to participate in the first institution created by the British Government to provide it with a regular source of economic advice. Yet this 'luck' had its costs. It meant that Keynes was very busy with official commitments: his appointments diary lists almost sixty-five formal meetings relating to the Macmillan Committee or the EAC between November 1929 and his final dispatch of the *Treatise* in September 1930. (There would be over a hundred meetings relating to the Macmillan Committee alone before he finished work on its *Report* in May 1931.) One result was that he had little time to consider comments on his academic work. In the case of Ralph Hawtrey, for example, Keynes sent him the first batch of proofs of the *Treatise* on 23 April 1930 and further batches up until the beginning of July. Hawtrey responded with instalments of a long commentary, which eventually appeared as Chapter VI of *The Art of*

---

f The other non-ministerial members were Sir Arthur Balfour, Managing Director of the steelmakers Arthur Balfour and Co.; Ernest Bevin; Sir John Cadman, Chairman of Anglo-Persian Oil and Iraq Petroleum; Walter Citrine, General Secretary of the Trades Union Congress; G. D. H. Cole; Ernest Debenham, a Director of Lloyd's Bank; Sir Andrew Duncan, Chairman of the Central Electricity Generating Board; Sir Alfred Lewis, Chief General Manager of the National Provincial Bank; Sir William McLintock, an accountant; Sir Josiah Stamp, Chairman of the London Midland and Scottish Railway; and R. H. Tawney, the economic historian.

Central Banking (1932). Apart from asking Hawtrey for amplification of a few definitions and picking up minor corrections, Keynes did not have time to consider Hawtrey's major points until 28 November 1930, almost a month *after* publication of the *Treatise*. Yet, in the end, he regarded Hawtrey's comments as 'tremendously useful'[24] and, as we shall see, they raised major problems with the analysis in the book. The busyness of the period also limited the time he had for discussions with Dennis Robertson, who was finding the book difficult to swallow, even though he thought that he approved of the book's main structure.[25,g] It is probable that Keynes was less obliged to defend his work against professional criticism during the final stages of creation than he was five years later.[h]

Keynes's work for the Macmillan Committee and the Economic Advisory Council coincided with the early stages and the intensification of the great depression. When he had been involved in the discussion of cures for Britain's economic problems in the spring of 1929, unemployment in Britain, although historically high, was lower than it had been earlier in the decade. True, Britain, as other countries, was labouring under the high interest rates resulting from boom on Wall Street. The related decline in American foreign lending, which had started in mid-1928, was, through its effects on debtor countries, many of whom were primary producers, beginning to affect the demand for British exports. Although some sectors of the economy had started to move into recession early in 1929, activity as a whole did not turn down until July, a month before the downturn in the United States, and observers such as Keynes could be fairly optimistic about the future in the autumn. It was not until early 1930 that Keynes started thinking of the *possibility* of an international recession, much less of 'a very severe international slump, a slump which will take its place in history amongst the worst ever experienced'.[26]

The slump added new difficulties to Britain's previous problems. It was one thing to suggest macroeconomic experiments during the sunshine of an international boom, but in an 'economic blizzard' as Ramsay MacDonald christened conditions in April 1930, when they were not as bad as they would become, many became cautious and inclined to inaction, emphasising the dangers of the situation and the risks of experiments. Most notable amongst those who would take this tack was Hubert Henderson. He became increasingly critical of Keynes's more adventurous and optimistic frame of mind.[27] But he was not alone. The change in economic circumstances and political mood was to complicate Keynes's exercises in persuasion. They were to make life hell for MacDonald's second Labour Government.

g Keynes's appointments books and his letters to Lydia record relatively little contact – fewer than half a dozen meetings.
h Richard Kahn was already acting as an intermediary between Keynes and others in Cambridge, as well as making his own comments. But in 1930 he was very young and one suspects less persistent and less recognised for his critical skills than he would be later.

Keynes's *Treatise* as it had evolved after 1924 was intended to be a definitive contribution to both pure and applied monetary theory. It covered extensive ground and to summarise the whole of the two volumes that appeared at the end of October 1930 would take me too far from my central concerns. Thus I shall concentrate on what Keynes regarded as the major themes and leave the interested reader to pursue the often stimulating discussions of subsidiary issues.[i]

At the centre of the *Treatise* as of the *Tract* lay the questions of price stability and of the control of the credit cycle. In the *Treatise*, however, Keynes began to explore the dynamic forces underlying changes in the price level, forces obscured in traditional formulations of the quantity theory such as the Cambridge cash balances approach with its single price level and its aggregative treatment of monetary influences. He produced a Janus-like book: it looked back to his Cambridge inheritance; it looked forward to some of the concerns of *The General Theory of Employment, Interest and Money* that would appear in February 1936.

The *Treatise* reflected earlier concerns in many of its basic premisses. It tended to assume that money was neutral – that changes in monetary variables could not affect the long-term equilibrium position of the economy's real variables. As he put it:

> Monetary theory, when all is said and done, is little more than a vast elaboration of the truth that 'it all comes out in the wash'.[28]

Despite this basic premiss, throughout the book Keynes provided examples of the forces that could produce contrary results.[j] The central theory of the book carried with it the implicit assumption, if not the logical necessity,[29] of a 'full employment' level of output with the adjustment to monetary influences occurring through changes in prices. Yet in the non-formal discussions of the book, he often concerned himself with movements of both output and prices: his favourite banana parable, which he also used in the Macmillan Committee, is a good example.[30] Even when he did so, however, he tended to assume (the banana parable is an exception) that there were forces in the economy tending to take the system to full employment, at least in a closed economy with no foreign trade.[k]

With these presuppositions and in light of his concern for the applicability of economic theory to policy, in the *Treatise* Keynes was in essence

---

i For instance, I shall not discuss his speculative aside relating the age of Shakespeare to the profit inflation induced by the dispersion of Spain's supplies of precious metals from the New World (*JMK*, VI, 137) which provided a peg for L. C. Knights' *Drama and Society in the Age of Jonson* (1937).

j See especially *JMK*, V, ch. 7 'The Diffusion of Price Levels'.

k In an open economy, he could conceive of a 'special case' where the adjustment mechanism could become 'jammed' at less than full employment. This 'special case' was relevant to Britain. See below p. 489.

elaborating the Marshallian cash balances quantity equation. For example, he took the total stock of money and the aggregate velocity of circulation and broke them down into constituent parts. Bank deposits were separated into income deposits, business deposits and savings deposits, each with its own velocity. In separating the different types of deposits and analysing their determinants, most notably in making a clearer distinction between income and wealth than had previously been made in Cambridge theory, Keynes recognised that it was often impossible to measure the new variables accurately. As a result, the *quantity* theory became what one might more properly call a *quality* theory, for, once the quantity of money ceased to bear any simple relation to the level of activity or prices, one could only at best use the theory for general qualitative analysis.[31] In attempting to flesh out the quantity theory for policy purposes, Keynes had to consider the different definitions of the price level relevant to the various real variables under consideration. This partially explains why he introduced into the book the long and intricate discussion (some of it a revision and rearrangement of his 1909 Adam Smith Prize essay) of price indices, standards of purchasing power and the diffusion of price levels. This discussion which occupied Book II prepared the way for his 'fundamental equations' – the heart of his theory.

Since 1930 social accounting – some of it inspired by the *Treatise*,[1] some by the *General Theory* and some by Keynes's *How to Pay for the War* (1940) – has developed in such a way that modern economists coming to the *Treatise* for the first time have to reorient their thinking, for many of Keynes's basic definitions differ from modern usage. Once over this hurdle, however, some have found in the fundamental equations a useful analytical framework which allows a more flexible analysis of sequences of events than in his other books. With their wider range of variables – several price and cost levels, alternative breakdowns of the level of output both anticipated and realised – the equations have a richness which, despite their flaws, makes them far more suggestive.[32]

The analysis crystallised in the Fundamental Equations rested on the distinction between saving and investment. Unlike most of his English predecessors other than Robertson, Keynes held that these activities were undertaken by different groups of people for different reasons and need not be equal. Inequality between them in the short period would result in a tendency towards inflation or deflation. Money incomes were earned by producers of both consumers' and capital goods but only the output of the former was available for current consumption. If those who earned money incomes spent them only in proportion to the share of consumers' goods

---

1 I am thinking here of the early work of Colin Clark, whose publication was supported by Keynes (Clark 1932; KCKP, Keynes to Daniel Macmillan, December 1931).

in total output, the system could remain in equilibrium. If, however, the proportion of income consumers desired to spend on consumption goods differed from their share in total output, producers would experience unexpected increments or decrements in profits from the level at which they would be happy to continue with the existing state of affairs. These unexpected profits or losses (windfalls as Keynes called them) would lead to changes in investment as businessmen attempted to alter the composition of output to meet the demands of the market.

In the *Treatise* the most important force for change was the level of investment. Keynes had emphasised since *Economic Consequences of the Peace* that capital accumulation was central to capitalism. 'If enterprise is afoot, wealth accumulates whatever may be happening to thrift; and if enterprise is asleep, wealth decays whatever thrift may be doing.' (VI, 132). The main determinant of investment was the rate of interest. Saving, on the other hand was a relatively stable function of the level of income and relatively insensitive to changes in the rate of interest (V, 180, 251). In these circumstances, a fall in the rate of interest would cause investment to increase – and, possibly, savings to decrease – thus generating a surplus of investment over savings, a rise in prices and windfall profits.

Following a line of argument associated with Knut Wicksell, Marshall's eminent Swedish contemporary, Keynes also distinguished between the *natural* and the *market* rates of interest. The natural rate was the rate at which savings would equal investment; the market rate was the rate actually ruling in the market. Divergences between the two were the primary causes of price changes and the primary task of monetary policy was to prevent their divergence and to provide price stability at full employment.

Thus far, I have given only the barest outline of the approach in the *Treatise*. At every turn Keynes added useful complications. His fundamental equations allowed for changes in prices caused by changes in the costs of production unrelated to monetary conditions such as a sharp upward shift in wage costs. In a way that looks modern to contemporary economists but looked odd to those working in the 1950s or 1960s, he adapted his equations to include a model of the external sector on both current and capital account. He also presented a well-developed model of the financial system with a strong emphasis on the several channels through which monetary changes operate. Added to all of this was a wealth of empirical information, for as he developed his analysis Keynes kept a sharp eye on its applicability to contemporary policy problems and provided empirical estimates of orders of magnitude where possible.

The shift to a savings–investment framework brought a changed view of the relative importance of long and short-term interest rates. Keynes's emphasis on long-term capital accumulation and his view that probably three-quarters of the fixed capital stock consisted of such long-lived instruments as buildings, railways and other infrastructure (VI, 88) implied that the *long*-term rate of interest was a main determinant of change. At the same time, Keynes had come to the opinion, perhaps because of his greater knowledge of the behaviour of commodity markets,[m] that changes in the *short*-term rate of interest were not important in determining working capital and stocks of goods (VI, ch. 29).

This shift in emphasis carried an important corollary. Given his contemporaries' and his own previous emphasis on the effects of changes in Bank rate and the fact that it remained one of the most readily available instruments of monetary management, Keynes had to develop a theory of the relationship between long and short rates – or, in the jargon of economists, the term structure of interest rates. Keynes's theory of the term structure implied that long rates were more stable than short-term rates, but that 'the long-term market rate of interest can be influenced to a certain extent in the desired direction by movements of the short-term rate' – that is by monetary policy (VI, 325).

This argument only took Keynes part of the way home, for while the theory of the term structure explained the relation between market rates of interest, for the context of the credit cycle it was the relation between the market rate and the natural rate that was crucial. Moreover, Keynes accepted that historically the long-term rate had moved sluggishly in response to changes in the natural rate. However he believed that more active policies by central banks, notably large-scale open market operations at the long-term end of the market could reduce this sluggishness.

Keynes's explanation of the determination of short-term rates – the interaction of the public's preferences concerning the form in which it would hold its wealth (cash, savings deposits or securities) and the policy of the banking system – also had important implications for the conduct of monetary policy. Shifts in asset preferences or in the demand for credit for particular uses (e.g. stock exchange speculation) could, with an unchanged stock of money, lead to changes in interest rates which would lead to changes in prices.

> Thus the total requirements of the monetary system are not associated in any stable or invariable manner either with the level of bank rate and its influence on the rate of investment or with the level of prices; so that we shall be misled if we lay much stress on the changes in the total quantity of money when we are trying to trace the causation and the stages of a transition.
>
> (V, 196–7)

Central banks could and should depend less on rules of thumb or simple

---

m It was his 'extremely wide acquaintance with commodity markets and their habits' that Keynes would use in arguing against Hawtrey's view of the importance of changes in the short-term rate of interest affecting stockholding behaviour in 1935 (*JMK*, XIII, 627–8).

reactions than they had in the past. Although on some occasions the process of diagnosis and effective action might be 'beyond the wits of man' (V, 227), monetary management was both possible and desirable.

In developing and analysing the distinctions between income and profit inflations (or deflations), Keynes came to consider a situation where the monetary mechanism was 'singularly ill-adapted' (VI, 245) – reducing the level of money wages. It was ill-adapted to this because it worked indirectly: to cause an income deflation it was necessary to increase the market rate above the natural rate to reduce investment and trust that the resulting unemployment would lead to a reduction in money wages. On the other hand, the monetary mechanism could deal with profit inflations and deflations, for it worked directly and involved the adjustment of the market rate to the natural rate.

One of the strengths of the *Treatise* was its careful integration of foreign trade and investment into the basic model. Coupled with Keynes's concern for policy issues, this led him to reconsider the desirability of an international standard of value – or what modern economists would call a system of fixed exchange rates. Taking considerable pains to elaborate the pros and cons of such a standard, he reversed his position of the *Tract* and came down in favour of an international standard, largely on the grounds of the utility of fixed exchange rates in encouraging foreign lending and foreign trade.[33] His support was not for the unregulated gold standard but for a standard similar to the sort advocated by Irving Fisher and Alfred Marshall, which would be stable in terms not of gold alone but of the prices of sixty internationally traded commodities. The scheme provided for some elements of national autonomy in monetary policy for example, through allowing a wider range of exchange rate fluctuations around their permanent parities than was usually the case under the gold standard.

He also reversed his earlier position on the gold exchange standard, which in *Indian Currency and Finance* he had seen as the wave of the future. He had become less enthusiastic after 1919 because he believed supplies of international liquidity were more likely to be excessive rather than deficient. This worry lay behind his reluctance to welcome the 1922 Genoa Conference proposals for an international convention based on the gold exchange standard to stabilise the purchasing power of gold,[34] and, together with the concentration of gold in the United States, behind his arguments against Britain's returning to gold in 1923–5. By 1928, however, Keynes had come to believe that a shortage of international liquidity was about to become a problem. The general return to gold had involved higher required gold reserves than pre-war and countries such as France were beginning to switch their foreign exchange reserves into gold.

He considered the gold exchange standard at both the theoretical and applied levels in the *Treatise*. At a theoretical level he noted the absence of reciprocal adjustment between reserve centres and other members of the system, which reduced the discipline the system imposed on the centres. Then there were the problems of shifts in the proportion of gold reserves to total reserves and of shifts in the composition of exchange reserves among currencies, which meant that reserve centres would have had to hold larger reserves than they otherwise would, thus reducing the gold-economising possibilities of the standard. As a result his 'maximalist' policy proposal in the *Treatise* was for an international central bank and an effective end to gold-exchange standard arrangements. The bank was to issue supranational bank money (SBM), into which all national currencies would be convertible, and which would rank equally with gold for reserve purposes. The bank would be able to increase world liquidity by lending to countries in balance of payments difficulties. Moreover, by conducting open market operations either in securities denominated in national currencies or in SBM it could maintain the value of SBM in terms of the prices of internationally traded commodities and avoid deviations between the natural and market rates of interest.[35] He also proposed a transitional 'minimalist' programme combining measures for gold economy and an international agreement on variations in statutory reserve ratios.

Any international standard with fixed exchange rates, and particularly one with perpetually fixed rates, will from time to time pose dilemmas for individual members of the system. The domestic circumstances of an individual country may require a monetary policy for internal balance which is different from that which adherence to the standard, or external balance, requires. It was for this reason that Keynes advocated wider fluctuations in exchange rates than under the gold standard and also allowed for controls on capital movements. The dilemma, according to Keynes, would be particularly acute for a country whose efficiency wages (Keynes's term for money wages adjusted for productivity changes) were too high to allow full employment at existing international interest rates, although these rates were appropriate for the system as a whole in that prices were stable. The monetary authorities could not then use monetary policy to increase employment, for lower domestic interest rates would result in capital outflows and a loss of reserves. The authorities would sooner or later be forced to reverse their interest rate policy if they wished to remain on the standard. Nor would monetary policy prove helpful in reducing money wages, as this was a long, slow and socially wasteful process. In these circumstances, rather than limp along with excessive unemployment resulting from the mixture of high efficiency wages and high interest rates, Keynes suggested that the authorities might have a 'reserve weapon'. Through loan-financed public works or capital development schemes, with an accommodating credit policy to allow for the expected needs for working capital, etc., the authorities could move investment up towards savings at the existing rate of interest, thus increasing employment. However, this was a *special case* only discussed briefly in the *Treatise* (VI, 337–8). In the general case, monetary policy was the appropriate instrument for the problem of maintaining full employment in an individual country.

The Macmillan Committee first met on 21 November 1930. A week later, it heard its first witness, Sir Ernest Harvey, the Deputy Governor of the Bank of England, substituting for an indisposed Governor Norman who had gone to the Mediterranean for a month's sea voyage. Initially Keynes asked very few questions – 16 on the first day, 30 on the second – but he soon came to play a dominant role in the Committee's proceedings. In part his role reflected his knowledge of institutional detail as befitted the author of 'The Applied Theory of Money'. The *Treatise* had also given him a conception of the role of the Bank of England and the financial system in the struggle for price stability which gave a coherence to his questioning and to his vision of the Committee's eventual report.

After it had heard eight City and Bank of England witnesses, Keynes tried to shape the Committee's approach to its task by taking the floor himself. He was, as the chairman put it, 'to discuss the general outlook of our inquiry'.[36] Keynes began with 'some account of the general character of the theory which influences my mind considering the practical issues which are before us',[37] commencing with the theory of Bank rate and working backwards and forwards over the relevant sections of his *Treatise*. The discussion was extremely lucid, its lucidity helped by the audience who asked for appropriate explanations and clarifications as he went along. On Bank rate he emphasised that in 1925

> We put a strain on Bank rate policy which had never been put on it during the 100 years or less that it had been the method in use. We never expected Bank rate to put wages down 10 per cent or anything of that order. One or two per cent if you estimated for the increase in efficiency was all that we asked it to do.[38]

After 1925 increasing productivity might have reduced the disparity between British and overseas costs but the fall in world prices and stabilisations abroad had more than compensated for this, leaving the gap even larger than it had been in 1925.[39] Britain had been left 'in a chronic position of spurious equilibrium' characterised by low profits. Bank rate policy could maintain external balance, but it had 'broken down as a practical method of restoring true equilibrium', that is, reducing British costs. The current policy tended 'to hamper without hitting, to injure without killing, and so to get the worst of both possible worlds': high unemployment and low profits.[40]

From his fairly straightforward discussion of Bank rate, Keynes moved to the theoretical meat of the *Treatise*, discussing, at a fairly high level, the transition between equilibrium positions. He told Lydia that his audience

> found my speech more perplexing as I thought they would. I think

that I did it all right. But it was unfamiliar and paradoxical, and whilst they couldn't confute me, they did not know whether or not to believe. However, it was progress, I think.[41]

Those present did have trouble with the basic definitions.[42] Keynes claimed a lot for his theory:

This has been read now by some of the principal economists of Cambridge, who did not start at all sympathetic to it, but they are now satisfied, I think, that it is accurate.[43]

He offered to provide members of the Committee with proofs, pointing out that the book would appear and receive outside criticism before the Committee reported.

In the last three days of his 'private evidence' Keynes discussed possible remedies for the current British situation, which the international recession was making ever more difficult. A change in the gold parity of the pound sterling was a last resort:

a remedy which in fact the powers that be would refuse to adopt except . . . under duress, and by that I mean only if all other remedies had failed us and in consequence of that the state of affairs had got very much worse than it is now.[44]

He turned to other remedies. In July 1925 he had proposed an all round reduction in money incomes through a national treaty, but the Committee's discussion, with Ernest Bevin present, showed up the difficulties of gaining trade union acceptance for that particular remedy. He passed briefly to bounties or subsidies for industry in general or for particular trades and to rationalisation – all ways of reducing British manufacturers' relative costs of production – before turning to other remedies designed to allow adjustment at the existing level of money wages. The first of these was protection. Keynes reported that he had 'not yet reached a clear-cut position as to where the balance of advantage [between protection and free trade] lies'.[45] He saw the long-term disadvantages of departing from free trade but he could see short-term advantages from increased protection. The ensuing discussion was extensive. He then moved away from remedies which would improve the foreign balance – *i.e.* raise foreign investment – to policies to increase domestic investment. (He saw no sense in reducing savings.) He raised the issue of the 'Treasury view' of public works on which he hoped that the Committee could arrive at 'a clear-cut opinion' after receiving advice from expert witnesses. This took the Committee back into the mire of savings, investment, business profits and losses – and brought another appeal from Keynes that he had already submitted his substantive treatment of the matter 'to some high academic authorities, who have accepted it as broadly correct',[46] before he passed on to the more mundane matter of methods. These were attempting through the banking system to drive a wedge between foreign and domestic interest rates, taxing foreign lending in a discriminatory manner, providing new institutions for long-term lending to small-scale borrowers, and public investment or public subsidisation of private investment. On his last day, 7 March, he touched on the possibilities of international co-operation to raise prices: a co-ordinated lowering of Bank rates and a reduction in legal reserve requirements or other measures, possibly through the Bank for International Settlements to economise on the use of gold.[n]

Keynes's 'private evidence' ran over five sittings of the Committee and occupied almost 10 hours.[47] Reginald McKenna also gave his own 'private' evidence' on 21 March. Then the Committee, which had devoted only four meetings to outsiders since Keynes had started his 'private evidence' on 20 February, returned to its task of hearing outsiders. It began with Governor Norman.

Norman's first appearance, on 26 March 1930, was not a success. According to Keynes, it left the Committee 'bewildered'. The Governor returned to the Bank 'thoroughly depressed'.[48] The chairman, who had been to the Bank for lunch to prepare the Governor for his appearance, tried to ease Norman's task. He led him on with questions that showed he had absorbed much of Keynes's practical evidence, including the proposition that the Bank rate mechanism was being set inappropriate tasks and the system becoming jammed (Q.3338 and 3339).[o] In brief answers Norman gave the impression that the 'financial machine' was working smoothly and that financial policy had little to do with Britain's current difficulties. Ernest Bevin intervened with some aggressive questioning on the return to gold and subsequent policy, but the chairman rescued Norman and tried to take him back to safer ground. Then Keynes, supported by McKenna, attempted to elucidate the operation of a restrictive monetary policy. The initial questioning led Norman into statements which nearly amounted to a repudiation of the orthodox theory of Bank rate (Q.3389) and forced him to reply 'I did not mean to repudiate it as I understood it.' (Ibid.). This prompted Keynes to try in a series of long statements, interspersed with almost monosyllabic

n In connection with the impending international shortage of gold, Keynes's long-standing fascination with alchemy reasserted itself. On 9 April, after a meeting of the Tuesday Club, McKenna revealed to Keynes that a 'new process' capable of producing gold in unlimited quantities at 1 shilling an ounce appeared to be commercially successful. McKenna gave Keynes the proceeds of 500 ordinary shares in the New Process Company Limited. Although sworn to secrecy by McKenna, Keynes did provide an account of the process and, more important, its implications for the international gold standard as managed by a Bank of England which had access to gold supplied by the process. See *JMK*, XX, 157–65. For other examples of his fascination with alchemy, including the results of his purchase of Newton's alchemical manuscripts, see *JMK*, I, 71; IV, 133; VI, 354; X, 369–70, 373–4, 377.

o Macmillan later confessed 'that [unlike in other inquiries] I never learned to move with ease in the realm of finance. Somehow my mind failed to grasp its principles and its technique baffled me.' Indeed, he suggested that his mind was 'incurably deficient in the power of understanding monetary problems'. (Macmillan 1952, 196–7).

replies from the Governor,[p] to take him along more congenial paths with the result that Norman reversed his initial position and agreed that there was some link between Bank rate policy and unemployment. Then McKenna, armed with a file of factual material, probably from his own bank's research department, tried to take the Governor over recent credit policy. This, too, was unilluminating, as the Governor did not appear to have the details clear in his mind. The remainder of the two-hour interview was equally unsuccessful, with the result that one author has suggested that the Governor's evidence was heavily edited and altered before publication. There appear to be no grounds for such an allegation.[49]

Keynes was also extremely sharp and close in his questioning of his professional colleagues, most notably Pigou, but his major confrontations during the sessions came with Sir Richard Hopkins, the Controller of Finance in the Treasury. The first took place on 16 May over the arrangements in the Currency and Bank Notes Act of 1928 for changes in the Bank of England's fiduciary issue and the tactics of the Treasury's management of the national debt. After the encounter, he remarked to Lydia:

> I had a rather exciting cross-examination at my Currency Com[ee] . . . Sir R. Hopkins . . . was the witness. He was very clever, but did not understand the technique of what we were discussing; – so the combination made good hunting. But it proved that the Treasury do not know any more than the Bank of England what it is all about – enough to make big tears roll out of the eyes of a patriot. But whilst the tears rolled, I enjoyed the hunting.[50]

That encounter, with more than 100 questions, was a mere preliminary. When Hopkins next appeared before the Committee, the subject became the 'Treasury view' of public works expenditure. Keynes's own discussion extended over almost ninety questions.[51] This was not a meeting between a quick-witted, lucid economist and an apparently unprepared and almost inarticulate central bank Governor. Keynes now had an extremely articulate and clever adversary, one who had clearly taken on board all the discussions in the year since Churchill's enunciation of the 'Treasury dogma'. In preparing for the confrontation, the Treasury had had the transcript of Keynes's private evidence, the record of Ralph Hawtrey's meetings with the Committee, plus regular briefings from F. W. Leith-Ross, the Treasury's watchdog on the Committee who attended all its sessions and received all its papers. With Hopkins's astute willingness to use the chair to protect him whenever the Committee tried to push him beyond his brief, this meant that the Keynes-Hopkins confrontation of 22 May was, according to the chairman, 'a drawn battle' (Q.5690).[52]

p Except for his opening statement, Norman's answers tended to run from one to a dozen words. On one occasion, he answered simply by tapping his nose three times (Sayers 1976, I, 329).

Part of the reason for the 'draw' was that, as Peter Clarke puts it, the 'Treasury view' had become a 'Whitehall view': a dogma had become a pragmatic proviso.[53] Thus, instead of trying to meet Keynes on the grounds of theory, Hopkins countered with the administrative difficulties of working through the existing planning and local authority structure, the problems of public opinion and the like. Many economic historians in the 1970s and 1980s, who had not had access to the materials surrounding the original formulation of the 'Treasury view' were led to suggest that the 'Treasury view' never existed, or existed only as the economists' straw man. They ignored the whole process of reformulation that had gone on for almost a year.[54]

As a result of Hopkins's reformulations, Keynes commented that the Treasury view 'bends so much that I find difficulty in getting hold of it' (Q.5625), but he concluded that Hopkins had convinced him that 'the Treasury view has been gravely misjudged' (Q.5690).

The same day as his duel with Hopkins, Keynes made a direct approach to the Bank to try and get his views across. He had sent the Governor a copy of his 10 May 1930 article in the *Nation*, 'The Industrial Crisis', in which he had commented on recent reductions in Bank rates in Europe and America and compared the seriousness of the economic situation with the limited measures so far taken.[55] Norman in his reply on 20 May had suggested the situation, especially in its international aspects, was 'more complicated' than Keynes realised.[56] Keynes took advantage of the Governor's reply to send him a fourteen-page letter summarising the position through the lenses of the *Treatise*. As he put it

> for reasons which are too long and complicated to explain here, *if* our total investment (home *plus* foreign) is *less* than the amount of our current savings (*i.e.* that part of their incomes which individuals do not spend on consumption), then – in my opinion – it is absolutely certain that business losses and unemployment *must* ensue. This, of course, is a difficult theoretical proposition. It is very important that a competent decision should be reached whether it is true or false. I can only say that I am ready to have my head chopped off it is false! At any rate the rest of the argument will assume that it is true.[57]

Keynes then set out the problem: with Britain's high costs of production, the rate of interest necessary to keep foreign lending within bounds was too high to permit total investment to equal total savings. His remedies followed the organisation of his 'private evidence' to the Macmillan Committee – increasing foreign investment, increasing home investment, decreasing saving – but he was more explicit about the magnitude of the problem and the difficulties of raising domestic investment in the absence of a large fall in world rates of interest. The Bank's response was a meeting on 23 June with the Governor and his advisers, the American economists O. M. W. Sprague and Walter

Stewart, both of whom subsequently received proofs of the *Treatise*.[58] For Keynes and Stewart, this was the beginning of a long friendship.[q] It was also the beginning of more frequent visits to the Bank, although until 1941 Keynes never had the easy access enjoyed by Dennis Robertson.

The Macmillan Committee continued to hear witnesses until the end of July 1930 before adjourning until mid-October. In the meantime Keynes was caught up in another substantial attempt to organise support for his views, this time through the Economic Advisory Council.

At its first meeting, 17 February 1930, Keynes suggested that the Council take a look at the fundamental economic problems facing the country, if only to prepare the way for plans in case the situation got worse. The Committee on Economic Outlook 1930 set up in response to Keynes's initiative was 'to supervise the preparation of a memorandum indicating the principal heads of the investigation (excluding those connected with currency) which should be embodied in a diagnosis of the underlying situation'.[59] Keynes was chairman: the other members were Sir Arthur Balfour, Sir John Cadman, Walter Citrine and G. D. H. Cole, with Hubert Henderson as secretary.[r]

The committee was slow to start work: but in its three meetings (on 21 March, 3 April and 1 May), it produced two reports and no little frustration. The first report, dated 3 April, consisted of a short note, signed by Keynes, Cadman and Cole, covering a memorandum by Henderson. Henderson saw no hope of a fall in unemployment, rather a serious risk of a rise. He was not optimistic about the prospect of increased efficiency in the export trades leading to a rise in exports and employment. Unless, therefore, one was simply to wait for some favourable external development, the only possibilities for improving the situation were 'tariffs, bounties, import control and the like, on the one hand, and a programme of home development on the other'. The recommendations for further inquiries followed on that basis.[60]

When this Report came to the Council at its third meeting on 10 April, Cadman dissociated himself from it, disagreeing with the Henderson memorandum and its suggestion that 'state aided development was a possible way of reducing unemployment'. At the same meeting, the Council received a note from Snowden, the Chancellor of the Exchequer, effectively barring any discussion of monetary policy or public works on the ground that these

q On his return to the United States in 1930 Stewart again became a member of Case Pomeroy and Co. Walter Case, the head of the firm, was a close friend of Keynes's until his death in 1937. Keynes was to consult Stewart during his wartime visits to America (*e.g. JMK*, XXIII, 82) and Stewart's position with the Rockefeller Foundation helped in the founding of the Department of Applied Economics in Cambridge at the end of the war.

r After a preliminary discussion between Keynes and Henderson, the exclusion of the currency issue (at least in so far as it referred to schemes of capital development) was removed at the instigation of R. H. Tawney during the second meeting of the EAC. Whether Tawney, who was high in the councils of the Labour Party and who was on the EAC for his political rather than his academic role, did this at the instigation of the Government is unknown.

were subjects for the Macmillan Committee. Keynes protested strongly at this overriding of a previous Council decision, especially as the Macmillan Committee was unlikely to report for a considerable time. He also urged the Council not to expect unanimity on controversial questions. The Council asked its committee to look at its report again in the hope of achieving some common ground. But Keynes and Cole resubmitted their earlier report, while Cadman and Balfour submitted their own report suggesting that state action was incapable of solving the problem and that the only effective remedy was wage and cost reductions. Ernest Bevin, who had replaced the indisposed Citrine on the committee, refused to sign either. The discussion at the May meeting of the Council was inconclusive.

There matters rested for two months. Then Keynes took advantage of a slight change in circumstances to press for a new type of enquiry. By the end of June 1930, several members of the EAC were unhappy with its working: agendas were overcrowded and it was difficult for such a large and varied body to provide advice on the main issues of policy. Keynes may have shared some of this dissatisfaction, but he was prepared to let the Council evolve naturally.[61] However, one by-product of the ensuing procedural discussions was a list of questions circulated by Prime Minister MacDonald, at Hubert Henderson's suggestion, at the July meeting of the Council. The hope was that the answers might enable the Council 'to concentrate on large questions of public policy'. The Prime Minister's questions asked for members' views on the causes of the present industrial difficulties; on the trade policy that the Government should adopt; on the possible means of increasing exports; and on the framework for imperial trade policy. Immediately after the meeting Keynes wrote to the Prime Minister with a suggestion of his own as to the best way of answering the first question.

> It is essentially a matter of economic diagnosis, the sort of thing for which economists, if they are any good at all, should be useful. It involves the sort of analysis that professional economists are constantly attempting, but with which most businessmen are unfamiliar. I think it would be worth trying to see if a small committee, composed of leading professional economists, could agree amongst themselves sufficiently to produce an answer. The answer, when produced, ought to be submitted to the criticism of businessmen. . . . There is no reason why the results should not be expressed in a manner intelligible to everyone. . . . It may be that economics is not enough of a science to be able to produce useful fruits. But I think it might be given a trial, and that we might assume for the moment, if only as a hypothesis, that it can be treated like any other science, and ask qualified scientists in the subject to say their say. I do not feel confident that the experiment would be successful. But I think it would be worth trying.[62]

He suggested possible members of such a committee: himself, Sir Josiah

Stamp, Hubert Henderson, Henry Clay (a Manchester University economist who had become industrial adviser to the Bank of England), Professor Lionel Robbins (recently appointed at the age of 31 as Professor of Economics at LSE), Pigou and Dennis Robertson. Such a body might be able to produce a diagnosis and a reasoned list of remedies by the end of October.

MacDonald had been taking a number of initiatives, including a Ministerial Panel on Unemployment, to deal with the growing unemployment problem in the summer of 1930. Perhaps on the principle that committees and conferences gave the impression of doing something, or in the hope that something useful might actually turn up, he was prepared to try out Keynes's idea. At the 24 July meeting of the EAC he announced the creation of a Committee of Economists which was

> to review the present economic condition of Great Britain, to examine the causes which are responsible for it and to indicate the conditions of recovery.

His announcement of the committee was a significant step in defining the grounds of future discussion of the short-term problems of British economic policy. It also marked the first time when an official body of professional economists received such a wide-ranging brief.

Keynes's committee did not include all the economists he had suggested: it excluded Clay and Robertson. Nonetheless, it was a strong one. Keynes was just finishing his *Treatise*; Pigou had recently published a new edition of his *Industrial Fluctuations* (1929); he and Stamp had recently given evidence to the Macmillan Committee; Robbins had worked with Sir William Beveridge on a revised edition of his *Unemployment: A Problem of Industry* (1930) and was well-versed in the European monetary literature of the period, particularly the work of Ludwig von Mises and Friedrich von Hayek, Austrian followers of Wicksell. One of the secretaries to the committee was Richard Kahn.

Most of the committee knew something about Keynes's *Treatise* position on economic policy in Britain. Kahn, Pigou and Henderson had all been involved in varying degrees in the evolution of the ideas of the book. Stamp had been exposed to it in conversation and at EAC meetings. Robbins was the outsider. As a guest of the Tuesday Club on 9 April 1930 he had heard Keynes's remarks on the question 'Are the presuppositions of Free Trade justified to-day?' and had doubtless gathered something of his views from his published writings and at meetings of the London and Cambridge Economic Service, but he only received proofs of the *Treatise* during the committee's sittings.

By this time, Keynes was putting the final touches to his book. He had continued to work at it during the winter and spring of 1930, in the interstices of his other commitments, dominated as they were by the

Macmillan Committee and the EAC. His reports to Lydia tell of his getting into the second volume in early February and, by late May, he was planning the last book – 'The Management of Money'.[63] There were also discussions with his colleagues. Robertson was 'full of resistances on certain points, – [though] not, I think, on the main structure' and unhappy, for Robertson had hoped 'now to be able to swallow it whole'.[64] Sometimes Robertson's reservations in detail were supported by Richard Kahn, sometimes not. These discussions appear to have lasted well into the summer, for on 18 July Keynes recorded that he was 'drastically re-writing the chapter which deals with the fundamental equations' in response to the 'obstinate misunderstandings' of Robertson and Pigou.[65] He did not have a revise of this chapter until well into August.[66] Then there were the comments of Ralph Hawtrey, who received proofs between the end of April and 5 July, but to whose comments Keynes did not reply substantively until after the book's publication. He finally saw the book off to the printer for the last time on 14 September, four days after the first meeting of the Committee of Economists.

Keynes hoped that his committee would do its job quickly: he had promised Macdonald a report by the end of October.[67,s] Some of his colleagues were sceptical: Pigou remarked that 'the members shall be genii if we get an agreed report out of terms of reference like them' and Robbins commented ominously, 'Ten days [between the first meeting and beginning to draft the report] is not a long time to cogitate about ultimate differences of principle – if any such exist'.[68] In the event, the committee just missed its deadline when it signed its report on 24 October, but it had taken more meetings than expected to get there: 10, 11, 26–8 September, 7, 8, 15, 16, 18–19, 22 and 23 October.

Before the first meeting, Keynes circulated various EAC memoranda, including some of the replies to the Prime Minister's questions; Pigou's heads of evidence to the Macmillan Committee;[t] a series of draft heads for discussion prepared by Richard Kahn; a note by Robbins on 'Possible Topics for Discussion' which he had sent Keynes on 31 August; and a 'semi-protectionist' letter written by Keynes to the *Manchester Guardian* on 14 August.[69] At this meeting, as well as asking for more papers – the Macmillan Committee evidence of Sir Josiah Stamp, Dennis Robertson, and Professor A. L. Bowley – the members of the committee agreed to defer a decision on Robbins's suggestion that they hear evidence from American and Continental economists on the causes of the slump and the British position

s Later the Prime Minister asked that the report be ready for consideration by the Government before Parliament reassembled on 28 October. This moved the deadline back to 20 October.
t Skidelsky in *Politicians and the Slump* (1967, 207) stated that at a meeting on 10 August Keynes asked Pigou to prepare a memorandum outlining the heads for subsequent discussion. There was no such meeting on 10 August and Pigou's paper was, as it clearly stated, the one he gave to the Macmillan Committee before he gave oral evidence to it on 29 May 1930.

until they had prepared a first draft of their report.ᵘ They spent the rest of that meeting and a brief meeting the next day discussing their approach to the terms of reference. At the end of the second meeting, they agreed that before their next meeting (scheduled for the weekend of 26–8 September at Stamp's home at Shortlands in Kent) each member would circulate his answers to a questionnaire that Keynes had drafted during that meeting. His questionnaire was brief:

I   In what ways would (a) British employment, (b) British prices, (c) British real wages be affected by (i) an increase of investment (a) in the world at large; (b) in Great Britain (ii) a tariff (iii) a reduction in British money wages (a) all round; (b) in the relatively highly paid industries?

II   How much too high (in order of magnitude) are (a) real wages (b) money wages at the existing level of world prices? What is your estimate of the increase (a) of real wages (b) of productivity per head since 1910–14? If your estimate of the excess of real wages is greater than your estimate of the increase in real wages per unit of productivity, how do you explain this?[70]

Keynes's own replies reflected two trends in his recent thinking, *as well as* the usual framework of the *Treatise* and the growing influence of Richard Kahn. These trends were apparent in his reply to the Prime Minister's questions, when he made two comments in passing:

When we come to the question of remedies for the local situation as distinct from the international, the peculiarity of my position lies, perhaps, in the fact that I am in favour of practically all the remedies which have been suggested in any quarter. Some of them are better than others. But nearly all of them seem to me to lead in the right direction. The unforgivable attitude is, therefore, the negative one, – the repelling of each of these remedies in turn. . . .

All the same, I am afraid of 'principle'. Ever since 1918 we, alone amongst the nations of the world, have been the slaves of 'sound' general principles regardless of particular circumstances. We have behaved as though the intermediate 'short periods' of the economist between one position of equilibrium and another really were short, whereas they can be long enough – and have been before now – to encompass the decline and downfall of nations. Nearly all our difficulties have been traceable to an unfaltering service to the principle of 'sound finance' which all our neighbours neglected. This 'long-run' policy is a grand thing in its way – unless, like the operators of systems at Monte Carlo, one has not the resources to last through the short run. Wasn't it Lord Melbourne who said that 'No statesman ever does anything really foolish except on principle'?[71]

ᵘ Robbins's suggested names were Jacob Viner, Wilhelm Röpke, Bertil Ohlin and Friedrich von Hayek.

Keynes had always been sceptical about arguments wrapped up in principles: one recalls his campaign against the return to gold, when they had been called 'hard facts', or the 'Treasury view'.[72] However, these 1930 remarks on 'principle' related to one case where his increased eclecticism showed up most strongly – protection. In his Macmillan 'evidence' he had raised the issue and had raised general arguments against free trade, but he had not reached a firm conclusion. By July 1930, he had 'become reluctantly convinced that some protectionist measures should be introduced'. By the time of his Committee of Economists, he could go even further and question the basic advantages of a high degree of specialisation in the manufacturing sector amongst countries.[73]

In setting down his replies to his own questions, Keynes re-cast his 'special case' of the *Treatise* in a strikingly effective way – one more effective than his previous schematic presentation for the Macmillan Committee which he had also used in his letter to the Governor of the Bank. He centred his analysis on two equilibria – 'equilibrium' real wages or those paid when all factors of production are fully employed and entrepreneurs are enjoying the Marshallian 'normal profits' necessary for them to persist in the same activities on the same scale, and 'equilibrium' terms of trade or the terms of trade that ensue when the level of domestic money wages relative to those abroad is such that the amount of foreign investment plus home investment equal the amount of saving at the world interest rate.[74] He argued that Britain's current problems mainly resulted from a deterioration in the equilibrium terms of trade uncompensated by an equivalent decline in money wages, for he could find no evidence that up to 1929 real wages had grown faster than output per head or that British industrial technology had suddenly become deficient. The effect of this analytical contrivance was advantageous: it centred on the important elements of the problem; whereas, for example, a concentration on real wage levels seemed to begin the analysis at the wrong end for policy purposes. He then examined the main determinants of changes in the equilibrium terms of trade: those affecting the current account of the balance of payments (foreign tariffs, declines in important foreign markets, changes in the exchange rate, and changes in relative efficiencies) and those affecting the incentives to lend overseas and hence the capital account (changes in borrowers' demands at home and abroad, and changes in supply conditions for home and foreign lending).

Organising his analysis in this way, Keynes then turned to a side issue, which he had not yet integrated into his story: Richard Kahn's preliminary investigations into the employment multiplier that he would soon present to the committee in outline form during the weekend at Shortlands. Kahn's 'multiplier' put a limit on the repercussions of a rise in home investment resulting from an increase in public works expenditures. The trick was to look at the repercussions in terms of the possible leakages from each round of expenditure that did not immediately return to the stream of incomes (taxes, savings, imports) and thus be able to estimate a *finite* geometric series. He could thus, if he knew the size of the various leakages, estimate the relationship between the initial expenditure and the final result, or the multiplier. At this stage, Keynes had picked up the estimate, which he took as 2, but he did not see the ultimately destructive implications of the concept for the pure theory of the *Treatise*.[75]

Having raised this side issue, which produced some controversy during the committee's proceedings but did not find its way into their report, Keynes returned to his questionnaire to put rough and ready estimates on the relevant items. He estimated abnormal unemployment at 1,500,000, of which one-ninth was a result of real wages running ahead of productivity by 2½ per cent, one-third was a result of the slump, and five-ninths the result of the deterioration in the equilibrium terms of trade. To solve the problem by reducing money wages would require reductions of the order of 40 per cent – it is hardly surprising that Keynes put so much emphasis on 'other expedients' to shift the equilibrium terms of trade in Britain's favour.

Other members of the committee took differing views on both sections of the questionnaire. The view most markedly opposed to Keynes's was that of Robbins. Deeply influenced by Hayek's and von Mises' development of Wicksell's ideas, he approached the problem in a dramatically different manner, although the terminology looked similar to Keynes's, given the common Wicksellian inheritance. For Robbins, the slump and its problems were the result of overinvestment in fixed capital during the previous boom which had resulted from the money rate of interest being below the natural rate. Viable remedies for the slump would have to take account of the peculiarities of that boom and the need to write off mistaken investments and to bring prices back towards more realistic, equilibrium levels. In such an analysis, any reduction in the rate of interest or increase in investment outside normal channels would merely exacerbate the difficulties caused by the initial overinvestment which had led to the collapse of the previous boom. What was required were measures that would decrease rigidities in the economic system and allow the necessary adjustments. Thus, whereas Keynes took the rigidity of money wages as almost a given and tried to adapt policy to this fact of economic life, Robbins took it as a source of so many of Britain's economic problems that the report should highlight this rigidity and the roles of unemployment insurance, monopolies and restrictive practices in creating it. With his emphasis on rigidities and his life-long, philosophical aversion to quantitative economics,[76] Robbins was unwilling to play the game of estimating aggregate figures for wages and productivity, especially as he believed the existing average figures reflected a less than optimal distribution.

The other members of the group were in varying degrees more prepared than Robbins to play the game according to Keynes's proposed rules. They were also more concerned to achieve some consensus and to minimise their theoretical differences – partly because of their longer experience in advisory committees and perhaps partly because some of them, notably Stamp and Henderson, did not have well-defined, clearly thought out theoretical positions. Pigou did have such a position, which as a result of long work in the field stretching from *Wealth and Welfare* (1912) to *Industrial Fluctuations* (1927 and 1929), had developed from the microeconomic theoretical relationship that saw the quantity of employment as a function of real wages and of the productivity of labour. From such a starting point – the reverse of Keynes's where real wages came in towards the end of the story – Pigou addressed himself primarily not to cyclical matters but to the longer-term question of the origins of the post-war increase in average unemployment in Britain over its pre-war level. To him, this was a reflection of labour immobility in the face of marked changes in the pattern of demand and the failure of the aggregate demand for labour to expand at the existing level of real wages. It was thus a problem of maldistribution at existing relative wages and of maladjustment between demand and price. Pigou could produce a long list of reasons for these problems in addition to the lack of labour mobility: the introduction of widespread unemployment insurance, greater resistance to wage cuts, and the uncompensated-for decline in prices relative to wages following the return to gold. Although his analysis focused on wages Pigou was not prepared, as a matter of practical policy as compared to theoretical possibility, to advocate selective or general money wage reductions. His approach thus left him dependent on improvements in efficiency and industrial organisation to raise the demand for labour in the longer term, and on various expedients to deal with unemployment in the short term until the longer-term improvements took effect.

By 1930, Henderson had a long record of collaboration with Keynes on campaigns to influence economic policy, if not of success in achieving that influence. From the time Henderson entered government service, however, a gap opened up between the two – one that grew as time passed and the economic situation worsened.[v] Their differences may have reflected a difference in their official positions, and hence sense of responsibility. They also reflected a difference in style and temperament. Henderson came to have less and less faith in formal economic analysis. He was also more inclined to see the blacker side of any situation than the more optimistic Keynes, who was, if anything, becoming more at home in the world of analysis, even if he always remained a critic of unnecessary formalism.

The first indication of the emerging gap between Keynes and Henderson had come in March 1930, when the latter expressed doubts as to the viability of the types of schemes they had both supported during the previous year's

v The gap continued to widen even after the end of the slump; in the Treasury during the Second World War they would be found almost invariably on opposite sides of any dispute.

election campaign. By the end of May Henderson had come to doubt the efficiency of expediting schemes of local works and to favour a scheme to promote industrial reconstruction financed by a 10 per cent tariff on manufactured imports.[77] The rationale for his change in view became clear in an exchange of letters he had with Keynes in late May and early June 1930.[78] He was 'scared by the Budget position' which he saw as 'extraordinarily dangerous' given the sharp rise in payments to the unemployed. In light of this, he put increasing weight on business psychology, moving towards the view that Britain's unemployment problem was of a long-term, structural nature. As a result, he became convinced of the need for either new sources of government revenue or reductions in unemployment benefits to protect the Budget and supportive of long-term programmes such as his own scheme for industrial reconstruction.

Keynes reacted to Henderson's changing views on two levels. On one level, he believed that Henderson's opinions were characterised by 'a lack of fundamental diagnosis' in that they concentrated on the by-products of the unemployment problem rather than the problem. If one concentrated on the problem and diagnosed its origins correctly in 'an inadequate level of total investment', then the core of Britain's difficulties could be seen to lie in high real wages and an excessively high market rate of interest. As he rejected the utility of an assault on the level of wages, particularly as he did not think that any *feasible* reduction would have much effect on the level of foreign investment, he wished to try to stimulate investment at the existing rates of interest and real wages and to 'twist and turn about trying to find some reasonable means of permitting investment of a fairly sensible kind in spite of its not yielding the current market rate of interest'.[79] At another level he also remained much more optimistic about business psychology and much more convinced of his powers of fundamental diagnosis – and of persuasion.

When it came to the Committee of Economists, Henderson's advice had become even more cautious. Prophesying that the current difficulties would become known as the 'Great Slump' and emphasising the dangerous aspects of the British position, he opposed 'anything in the nature of a gamble' when there was no guarantee of an improvement in the future. Henderson objected to raids on the sinking fund for reduction of the national debt to ease the budgetary position, and emphasised the needs for a reform of unemployment insurance, for protection and, if prices continued to fall, for lower money wages.[80]

The range of replies to Keynes's questionnaire revealed such significant divergences of view among the members of the Committee that drafting an agreed report was likely to prove a difficult business. So it did, especially when, in the course of the weekend discussions at Stamp's house, Keynes produced 'A Proposal for Tariffs Plus Bounties' recommending a 10 per cent tariff on all imports and a 10 per cent subsidy for all exports.[81] By this means,

Britain could gain some of the potential benefits to the trade balance of a 10 per cent devaluation of sterling without changing the foreign currency value of sterling-denominated obligations of foreigners. This proposal, although in sympathy with the positions of Henderson and Stamp, intensified the problems faced by Robbins, a passionate free-trader soon to be a leader in organising the group chaired by Sir William Beveridge which would produce *Tariffs: The Case Examined* in 1931.[82] The issue coloured the rest of the Committee's deliberations.

After almost 18 hours of discussion at Stamp's house, the committee adjourned until 7 October to give the chairman time to draft a report embodying the sense of their discussions. Keynes's draft[83] put as the major cause of Britain's (and other countries') current difficulties the recent collapse in world prices following on from their slightly declining trend between 1924 and 1929. In Britain's case, the difficulties were exacerbated by her return to gold at pre-war par, her high levels of taxation, her restrictive practices and barriers to labour mobility, which meant that she had 'no margin in hand to provide against a long process of falling prices unaccompanied by falling home wages'. Nor could he rule out the prospect of further price falls. The draft considered possible remedies, all of which required raising business returns to a more normal level. He classified them under four heads: those which increased businessmen's ability to pay existing money wages without a rise in the price level; those which raised the domestic price level relative to money wages; those which, although they might result in some rise in domestic prices, produced their main employment-creating effects through other means; and those which reduced money wages. He expressed a preference for any of the first three classes of remedy over the fourth. However, as he did not expect much relief from the first (the easing of restrictive practices, increased labour mobility – including that which might come from a reform of unemployment insurance – and increased technical efficiency), or from the second (a rise in the world price level),[w] most of his emphasis fell on the third class. These Britain could adopt on her own. All of these were ways of increasing investment either in Britain or abroad. They ranged from measures to raise business confidence through the *Treatise* menu of means of raising domestic investment at the existing internationally-determined rate of interest to an increase in foreign investment as a result of protection or his own tariff-bounty scheme.

The draft was incomplete: it did not discuss reductions in money wages in any detail; and, pending further discussion, it could not really reach any overall conclusions as to the near-term outlook nor include a summary of recommendations. When the committee met on 7 and 8 October to discuss Keynes's draft, they agreed on some verbal amendments and on asking

---

w Keynes's system logically included the devaluation of sterling at this point, but he rejected it by citing 'the obvious objections to this course' (*JMK*, XX, 437) without elaboration.

the draftsman for a revised version. They also agreed on 8 October that Professor Robbins, by this time in deep disagreement with Keynes and anticipating that his differences would carry through to the final report, should prepare a statement of his views for the next meetings in Cambridge during the weekend of 18–19 October.

By the time the committee arrived in Cambridge, the members had Keynes's revised draft, which he had discussed with Pigou,[84] and not only Robbins's passionate, wholesale rejection of Keynes's earlier draft but also another sharp reaction from Henderson. Given his theoretical position, Robbins was unable to adopt an expansionist approach. He was also unable to compromise over the tariff issue. Although Keynes tried to be accommodating, by recasting the report and incorporating a considerable amount of Robbins's statement on the causes of the depression, Robbins would hold out, especially on the tariff issue, and, after considerable wrangling and exchanges of high feelings with Keynes, submitted a separate report.

Henderson's reaction, although it might have been expected on the basis of his earlier discussions with Keynes, coming as it did at the same time as Robbins's revolt, produced considerable difficulties for the committee. In a powerfully argued memorandum, he stated

that the central argument of the Report is lacking in sense. It seems to me to run away, under cover of complex sophistication, from the plain moral of the situation it diagnoses; namely, that ... we have no alternative now but to face up to the disagreeable reactionary necessity of cutting costs (including wages) in industry and cutting expenditure in public affairs ....

That is the plain moral of the situation, as plain as a pikestaff. It is of course highly disagreeable in itself. Furthermore, it is the moral drawn by the ordinary, conservative, unintellectual businessman; and some may find it still more disagreeable that the ordinary businessman may be right. But, if we allow ourselves to be swayed by such distaste we run a danger of making applicable the Duke of Wellington's description of another controversy: 'All the clever fellows were on the one side, and all the damned fools were on the other; and, by God! all the damned fools were right.'

The Draft Report, as it seems to me, after half-recognising the truth of the foregoing, runs right away from it, and proceeds to twist and wriggle and turn in a desperate attempt to evade the logic of the situation. Its practical drift is that we may with luck be able to evade the necessity for reducing costs by adopting a series of expedients of the most different kinds, which are all labelled 'Remedies for Unemployment', but some of which, whether they deserve that description or not, are in no sense remedies for but aggravations of the fundamental maladjustment that has got to be put right. ...

[T]he ground on which this evasion is justified is nothing more or less than the expression of a hope that matters will right themselves in a few years in the ordinary course.[85]

Henderson argued that wage cuts and public retrenchment were necessary, that, given the state of the public finances, there was no room for anything but limited public works as a palliative, and that even if devaluation became necessary it would not succeed unless there was an earlier attempt to reduce costs. He accepted that his disagreement with Keynes was 'of a broad and almost temperamental nature' and that Keynes was more prepared to gamble on an early recovery of world prices even if he shared Henderson's estimate of the chances of success.[86]

Robbins's revolt and Henderson's declaration in favour of wage reductions meant that the Committee was, as Howson and Winch put it, 'in some disarray' during the preparation of its Report. Nevertheless the Report got written, largely thanks to Keynes's skilled chairmanship, and 'showed . . . few marks of the unresolved conflicts that lay beneath its surface'.[87] It lost the coherent elegance of Keynes's original draft, becoming an amalgam of his, Robbins's and Henderson's diagnoses, shorn of references to savings, investment or the rate of interest. Although there were occasional flashes of hope, it was more pessimistic than the original draft. The discussion of possible remedies lost its vigour and at several points there were marked disparities between the role of a factor in the diagnosis and its treatment of that factor in the remedies, particularly in the case of wage reductions. With the remarkably moderate discussion of wage reductions and Henderson's successful qualification of the argument for public works, the real centrepiece of the report became the discussion of tariffs. In an addition to a revenue tariff, Keynes, Stamp and Henderson came down mildly in favour of safeguarding duties on iron and steel, of a serious examination of the case for protecting pig and poultry products and of imperial preference. Furthermore, although only Stamp supported it, Keynes's tariff-bounty scheme went in almost word for word from his original proposal.[88]

The Committee of Economists had not fulfilled the hopes of Keynes's July letter to the Prime Minister. The members could not agree on the diagnosis; nor with Keynes's *Treatise* framework of analysis. Perhaps the experience encouraged Keynes just over five years later 'to bring to an issue the deep divergences of opinion between fellow economists which have for the present time almost destroyed the practical influence of economic theory and will, until they are resolved, continue to do so'.[89] None the less, the committee had produced a document which might have provided a basis for useful discussions within the EAC and the Government. Despite the disagreements, it did highlight the origins of Britain's difficulties and set out a number of possible remedies in a relatively clear and straightforward manner. Unfortunately, although the Report was on the agenda for the next five meetings of the EAC, the discussion did not come to much. MacDonald as chairman was not inclined to limit discussion to the main short-term remedies of the Report, rather than to raise red herrings or to let it drift on to other issues, while the contributions of the other Government members of the Council reflected their own deep disagreement on the central issue of protection. Yet, Keynes was to point out in March 1931, after the economic position had deteriorated further, protection had become almost essential if any of the bolder schemes to reduce unemployment such as public works were to succeed, given the further deterioration in the balance of payments and the Budget that they would cause.[90]

At Cabinet level, discussion of the Economists' Report was equally unsatisfactory. The deep split over protection, with Snowden, the Chancellor, resolute in his opposition, prevented any serious discussion of the issue. On 25 September, even before it received the Report, the Cabinet had already agreed that relief works had reached the limit of what was possible, that anomalies in the unemployment insurance scheme needed removal, and that there was little scope for other initiatives. Again the Prime Minister was probably partially to blame, for he was not prepared to push discussion of the issues in a divided Cabinet, and he became even more reluctant to do so in the face of apocalyptic economic warnings from his Chancellor and his officials early in 1931.[91] However, the issues raised in the Economists' Report did not go away: they continued to plague the Government, forcing it to react piecemeal, often temporising to buy time, until the 1931 financial crisis swept it from office.

With the Economists' Report out of the way, the Macmillan Committee once more became the major claim on Keynes's time. It resumed meeting on 16 October – normally on two afternoons a week – and started to discuss the shape of its report. Individual members often took the lead for a meeting or more. For example, J. Walton Newbold had the floor on 31 October and 7 November, R. H. Brand on 6 November, and Professor Gregory on 20 and 21 November. The wide-ranging discussions moved from the details of monetary policy to the relative merits of wage reductions, protection and devaluation as means of dealing with Britain's balance of payments problem. It was after almost six weeks of such discussions that Keynes took the lead for the discussions of 27 and 28 November and 5 December.[92]

Keynes did not retrace the arguments of the *Treatise* as he had done in February and March. His previous exposition was on the record and his book was in the bookshops. Nor did he spend time on the diagnosis of current problems. His main concern was now to make the case for detailed changes in existing monetary arrangements, in particular 'strengthening and supplementing the Bank of England's powers for evening out fluctuations in overseas capital transactions without upsetting the domestic situation'.[93] Keynes's proposals came under six heads: increasing the effective free reserves of the Bank by obliging the major British banks to hold a larger proportion of their reserves as deposits with the Bank of England rather than as notes; widening the gold points and making greater use of forward exchange operations to insulate the economy from international disturbances; developing more intimate relations between the Bank of England and the commercial banks so as to exploit their oligopolistic powers and thus provide another channel of influence (other than through changes in Bank rate) on the rate of interest in the discount market that was so important in influencing international flows of funds; regulating the flow of foreign lending; strengthening the balance sheet of the Bank of England; and increasing the statistical information available to the Bank and to the public. With the end of this second round of Keynes's 'private evidence', the Macmillan Committee turned to its report.

During the final drafting of the Macmillan Report, Keynes took his case for protection to the public. His public announcement of his support for a revenue tariff coincided with another important event. Throughout the years after 1923 the *Nation and Athenaeum* had not made money and had depended on financial help from its backers. With the slump and the departure of Henderson to the Economic Advisory Council, its position became more precarious. It continued publishing after Henderson's departure under a new, but temporary, editor, Harold Wright, another of the small band of pre-war Cambridge undergraduate economists, but the directors were finding the paper a burden. The editorship of the *New Statesman* then fell vacant. This weekly, founded as a Fabian paper in 1912, had been edited by Clifford Sharp who had finally broken down after years of heavy drinking. With the loss of editors for both papers, the idea of a merger, first contemplated in 1922, appeared feasible to both sides, especially as one possible editor, Kingsley Martin, a Cambridge graduate, former LSE lecturer and leader writer for the *Manchester Guardian*, was available and acceptable to both boards. The *New Statesman* board appointed him first, but made no public announcement while Keynes, acting for the board of the *Nation* entered into negotiations for amalgamation with the still profitable *New Statesman*. By January 1931 it was clear that the merger would come off and that Martin was acceptable to the *Nation* board: it was only a matter of terms. In this regard, John Roberts, the business manager of the *New Statesman* was a more tenacious negotiator than Keynes, perhaps because the paper was his life rather than a sideline. The negotiations dragged on for almost two months before final agreement. This saw the formation of a new publishing company whose shares went to the two predecessor companies. The *Statesman* group was in the majority and the *Nation* group put up £4,500 in cash to enhance the working capital of the new paper. Keynes became chairman of the combined board and held the post until his death.[94]

The first issue of the *New Statesman and Nation* appeared on 28 February

1931. Two days later, Keynes sent Kingsley Martin his 'Proposals for a Revenue Tariff'.[95] The article appeared on 7 March. Before publication, Keynes sent copies to the Prime Minister and the Chancellor of the Exchequer. MacDonald sent a limp reply, while Ethel Snowden refused to show it to her husband, who was ill, and returned it unread. As Maynard put it to Lydia when he sent on Mrs Snowden's letter, 'Evidently "we" have made up our mind'.[96]

The article caused a considerable stir. For weeks the columns of the *New Statesman and Nation* were full of criticism and defence of Keynes, the strongest criticism coming from Robbins, Sir William Beveridge, T. E. Gregory, Arnold Plant and G. L. Schwartz, who were engaged in preparing a free-trade counterblast *Tariffs: The Case Examined* (1931).[x] Keynes met his critics head on in both the *New Statesman* and *The Times*, as well as producing a more 'popular' version of his proposals for the *Daily Mail*.[97] In many respects, this was one of his more successful controversies, at least on scoring points, if only because he had brooded about the arguments for so long, but it left him depressed. He concluded his 'Economic Notes on Free Trade', his three-part reply to critics in the *New Statesman* on 11 April:

> Perhaps controversy with one's friends and colleagues is an essentially barren thing. But I come to the end of my attempt to deal with the controversy which I provoked . . . with an unusually arid flavour in my mouth. There is a great deal to be said on both sides about this tariff question. It is a difficult decision. But in this discussion we have not been reaching more than the fringe of what are for me the real problems. . . . [M]y critics have not taken any notice of, or shown the slightest interest in, the analysis of our present state, which occupied most of my original article and led up to my tariff proposal in my last paragraph. Is it the fault of the *odium theologicum* attaching to free trade? Is it that economics is a queer subject or in a queer state? Whatever may be the reason, new paths of thought have no appeal to the fundamentalists of free trade. They have been forcing me to chew over again a lot of stale mutton, dragging me along a route I have known all about as long as I have known anything, which cannot, as I have discovered by many attempts, lead one to a solution of our present difficulties – a peregrination of the catacombs with a guttering candle.[98]

Over the winter and spring of 1930–1, the drafting committee of Keynes, T. E. Gregory, Cecil Lubbock, R. H. Brand and the chairman was at work on the report of the Macmillan Committee. As one might expect, Keynes was the

---

x Dennis Robertson briefly sat in with the group, but avoided association with the final product. On the production of the book see Robbins 1971, 156–8 and Harris 1977, 316–19.

most active in shaping the result. But he did not have a free hand: Lubbock played the role of Bank of England watch-dog; Gregory the representative of the wider economics profession; and Brand the constructive, and far from compliant, interested and informed, City critic. Macmillan, probably losing interest and still thinking himself unable to grasp the complexities of the subject, remained in the background.

By 20 January 1931, Keynes had prepared a possible framework for the report. With its division between descriptive and historical matters on the one hand and conclusions and recommendations on the other, it survived into the published version. Between the middle of January and early April, when the drafting committee met relatively infrequently (nine times in all), he also provided drafts of a substantial proportion of the text. Then came the task of trying to win acceptance of his views in a crowded schedule of twenty-one meetings in the rest of April and May. Not unexpectedly, he met disagreement on basic matters: considerable resistance by some members towards his theory of the credit cycle and the analytical framework of the *Treatise* and, more importantly, a lack of agreement between the drafting committee and the full Committee on proposals for short-term domestic monetary action to mitigate the slump.[99] Strong words were exchanged. But over much of the ground covered by the Committee's terms of reference, agreement or disagreement with the analysis of the *Treatise* did not matter, and it was able to reach a high level of agreement on the diagnosis of the international situation and co-operative measures for its alleviation, as well as agreement on certain institutional reforms. But when it came to *domestic* measures to counter the slump, the whole Committee had in the end to agree 'to put into the report a few colourless sentences and then leave different groups of the Committee to deal with the less monetary aspects of the domestic situation in their own way'.[100] As a result, although all the members except Lord Bradbury signed the Report, there were in addition to Bradbury's 19-page Memorandum of Dissent no fewer than 71 pages of addenda and reservations contributed by all the other members of the Committee except the chairman.

The longest of these 'Proposals Relating to Domestic Monetary Policy to Meet the Present Emergency' began as Keynes's minority comments on the majority conclusions of the drafting committee. He worked it up into a more substantial document which he managed to get Sir Thomas Allen, Ernest Bevin, Reginald McKenna, J. Frater Taylor and A. G. Tulloch to sign.[y] The Addendum covered now familiar ground in stating that greater employment could come though increased exports, through the substitution of home-produced goods for imports, or through increased investment and

---

[y] He tried to persuade Sir Walter Raine and Lennox Lee also to sign the document. Before he signed it, Bevin managed to get Keynes to make some changes as well as reserving his and Sir Thomas Allen's position on some of the details of the proposed restrictions on imports.

continued to canvass the means to these ends. It rejected both money wage reductions and devaluation as possible remedies, but looked with favour on a back-door devaluation through a tariff-bounty scheme, on restrictions on imports and on schemes of capital development. In taking this line, the Addendum certainly went beyond the Macmillan Committee's terms of reference, as its authors admitted, but it did represent a forceful statement of a position supported by representatives of a wide range of backgrounds and opinions, namely two bankers, a trade union leader, a Bank of England 'company doctor' and a representative of the co-operative movement.[101] It was the product of almost two months' hard argument on Keynes's part.

Although the published Macmillan *Report* bears the date 23 June 1931, Keynes had signed it on 29 May before leaving for America the next day. Its immediate impact was reduced by the date chosen for its appearance, 13 July 1931 – the day that the first waves of the international financial crisis that was to sweep Britain off the gold standard reached London. The effects of its revelations of London's position as a short-term international debtor perhaps added fuel to the flames of distrust already sweeping over sterling.[102] But it was hardly a propitious atmosphere for calm consideration.

APPENDIX 3
KEYNES AND PROTECTION

As the discussions of the Macmillan Committee and the Committee of Economists show, in the course of 1930–1 Keynes's views about protection changed markedly. Before 1914 and after the war, he had been a fervent supporter of the classical liberal free-trade position. During the 1923 election in a powerful pair of articles in the *Nation* he had concluded that

> The proposal to cure the present unemployment by a tariff on manu-
> factured goods, which will also bring in a revenue of £25 millions, is
> a gigantic fraud, comparable in its intrinsic absurdity to the fraud of
> the 1918 Election about Germany paying for it all.[103]

Yet in March 1931 he was to propose a revenue tariff with duties of 15 per cent on all manufactured and semi-manufactured goods and 5 per cent on foodstuffs and certain raw materials with the aim of raising £40 million. What led to his change of mind?

The change had not come quickly. When Keynes first raised the prospect in his February and March 1930 'private evidence' to the Macmillan Committee, he did so largely on the grounds of logical completeness. As he put it on 6 March:

> I have not reached a clear-cut opinion as to where the balance of
> advantage lies. I am frightfully afraid of protection as a long-term
> policy; I am sure it is radically unsound, if you take a long enough
> view, but we cannot afford always to take long views, and I am almost

equally clear that there are certain short-term advantages in protection.
. . . It is very difficult for anyone of free trade origin, so to speak, at this
juncture to speak in a way that he himself believes to be quite truthful
and candid without laying himself open to misrepresentation and to
being supposed to advocate very much more than he really does. It is
very difficult . . . not to give a false impression.[104]

When Keynes raised the matter in opening the Tuesday Club discussion on
9 April 1930 on 'Are the Presuppositions of Free Trade Satisfied To-day?'
he may have appeared to have gone a bit further, but, as in the Committee
on Economic Outlook 1930, he was still turning the question over in his
own mind.[105] Even as he was putting the last touches on the *Treatise* and
discussing the circumstances of 1930, he was still tentative, although he was
'coming round to the view that there is also room for applying usefully
some method [such as a tariff] of establishing differential prices for home
and foreign goods'.[106] It was not until 21 July 1930 in his reply to the Prime
Minister's Questions that he declared 'I have, therefore, become reluctantly
convinced that some protectionist measures should be introduced'.[107]

Keynes's 1930–1 advocacy of protection rested on two foundations. First,
a devaluation of sterling was undesirable for a number of reasons relating to
Britain's international investment position. He seems to have feared that it
could be necessary in the event of a devaluation to compensate 'all *bona fide*
holders of short-term funds in London so that no one who trusted our credit
would be a loser' and that a devaluation would also result in losses to Britain
on her overseas investments which were denominated in sterling.[108] He also
thought devaluation would adversely affect London's position as a financial
centre and hence reduce Britain's invisible earnings.[z]

Tariffs were to Keynes more flexible than exchange rate changes. This
was an age when overnight devaluations along the lines that became
familiar after the Second World War were unknown. Changes in parities
by advanced countries, for instance France and Belgium, had occurred only
after substantial disruptions and even here the final decision had taken a
matter of years. As Keynes put it in November 1930:

> One need not sit down under the belief that tariffs are necessarily
> permanent; whereas devaluation is a thing you cannot be popping
> on and off. That is much more unthinkable than popping a tariff on
> and off.[109]

Keynes was aware of the risk that tariffs, once imposed, might never come

z Macmillan Committee, Notes of Discussions, 7 November 1930, 11. In the case of Britain's
foreign investments, it is true that there would be a loss in terms of the foreign currency
value of such investments, but it is not clear that most holders of such securities, who
were British, would feel worse off, or that they should be considered in the reckoning
any differently from any other British holder of sterling-denominated financial assets such
as bank deposits or government securities.

off, but he argued that this was a risk worth taking. After all, as he pointed out in March 1931 'all the chief protectionist measures of my time in this country – the Hicks-Beach duty on wheat, the McKenna Duties and the Safeguarding Duties – have been repealed, though one of them was reimposed'.[110] Perhaps he was overoptimistic, but there was some British historical evidence on his side.

Keynes's second argument for protection became more appealing as the Labour Government ran into increasing budgetary difficulties. The revenue from a revenue tariff or (given Britain's traditional trade deficit) a tariff-bounty scheme would ease the Budget position and reduce the need for other tax increases or expenditure cuts. A tariff to Keynes was probably 'the only form of taxation which will positively cheer people up'.[111]

With characteristic ingenuity, Keynes adduced several additional arguments in favour of his favoured course of action. For example, he argued that without a tariff, with its favourable effects on the Budget, on the balance of trade and on business confidence, 'a policy of expansion . . . is not safe or practicable to-day'.[112] He also took the view, to which he would revert in 1933, that the advantages of a high degree of international specialisation in the twentieth century were probably smaller than they had been in the nineteenth century, so that the efficiency losses from protection were also lower, especially as the flexible use of protection could reduce the output losses resulting from economic instability.[113]

Nonetheless, Keynes's advocacy of protection in 1930–1 was, as he emphasised, 'a question of a *choice* between alternatives, none of which are attractive in themselves' and 'a crude departure from *laissez faire*, which we have to adopt because we have no better weapon in our hands'.[114] Britain's return to gold in 1925 at an overvalued exchange rate had, without sufficient adjustment in her relative unit costs, meant that she entered the slump in a weakened competitive position and that her exports suffered more than those of her competitors in the downturn, while imports rose more strongly than elsewhere. Only a massive fall in the prices of raw materials had held the balance of trade deficit close to its previous level. In these circumstances, if one ruled out, as Keynes did, a deliberate devaluation or a wholesale attack on money wages, there were few palliatives left to shore up the position. Others, most notably Ernest Bevin in the Macmillan Committee and the Economic Advisory Council, made a different choice – for devaluation. Lord Bradbury, a traditionalist, took yet another position. He remarked in the course of one of several Macmillan Committee discussions of the subject:

> I am afraid of tampering with Free Trade. I am also afraid of tampering with the gold standard. If I had to choose between the gold standard as a remedy and Protection, I should be solid for tampering with the gold standard. I should much prefer it to protection.[115]

He did not believe, however, that his choices were that circumscribed and in his Memorandum of Dissent from the Macmillan *Report* argued in favour of measures, most of which lay outside the Committee's terms of reference, to restore the efficient working of the gold standard mechanism. Albeit for other reasons, Lionel Robbins made a similar choice.

It may be argued that Keynes was mistaken in espousing protection rather than devaluation. This would be the view of most economists. They would argue that protection, although a 'solution' to some of Britain's 1931 problems, was a second-best solution. A tariff-bounty scheme could produce an effect equivalent to devaluation on the trade balance, but it was probably (as Keynes recognised in his Macmillan Committee Addendum)[116] extremely difficult to implement under existing commercial treaties and likely to be countered by 'anti-dumping' legislation overseas. It would not, as Keynes failed to recognise, do anything like as much good as devaluation to improve Britain's invisible earnings. Protection, in itself, did nothing to remedy Britain's underlying competitive problem at $4.86 and even if recovery took world prices back to their 1929 level this disadvantage would remain, as would the problem of unemployment and the contemporary demands for protection to relieve it. In the interim, it would have stimulated retaliation elsewhere, thus further complicating the position of Britain's export industries.[aa] It is true that devaluation in the circumstances of 1930–1 might also have had extremely complicated side-effects on the international economy. At that time *every* possible 'solution' to Britain's economic problems had its messy aspects. By refusing openly to advocate devaluation and by lending his public support to protection, largely as a result of an understandably mistaken comparison of the costs and benefits of the two courses of action and of the possibility of sterling being pushed from gold in any case,[bb] Keynes helped to create the climate of opinion in which, after Britain left gold and did not need protection on Keynes's grounds, she got a highly protective tariff system anyway.

aa This should not be taken to imply that a devaluation of sterling would not provoke protectionist responses, as the 1931 depreciation did, only that the retaliation would be less than it would be with protection.

bb Throughout the discussions he recognised this possibility in private, but rated it as 'comparatively remote' and was, therefore, prepared to press for other measures first (*JMK*, XX, 486).

NOTES

1 *JMK*, XVIII, 281.
2 Kent 1989, 278–86.
3 *JMK*, XVIII, 305–11.
4 *JMK*, XI, 451–9. See also V, 296–308 where the original piece is converted into *Treatise* terms.
5 *JMK*, XVIII, 306, 311.
6 *JMK*, XIX, 457–8.
7 Ohlin 1929.
8 *JMK*, XI, 475.

9 *JMK*, XVIII, 329–36, 342–6.
10 *JMK*, XVIII, 347.
11 *JMK*, XIX, 828–34.
12 BL, ADD.55202, JMK to Dan Macmillan, 20 August and 25 September 1929; *JMK*, XIII, 117–18.
13 *JMK*, XXIX, 4.
14 KCKP, JMK to Lydia, 29 April 1928.
15 KCKP, JMK to Lydia, 11 October 1928. Kahn's dissertation appeared in print after his death in 1989. For the contacts and use of statistics see pp. viii, ix, xi.
16 KCKP, JMK to Lydia, 21 October 1929.
17 See Kahn's 1974 letter to Don Patinkin reprinted in Patinkin and Leith (eds) 1977, 148 and Kahn 1984, 174–5.
18 *JMK*, XX, 4.
19 Sayers 1976, 360–2; Clarke 1988, 103–4.
20 Committee on Currency and Foreign Exchanges after the War, *First Interim Report*, Cd. 9182, para 1.
21 KCKP, JMK to Lydia, 25 November 1929.
22 *JMK*, XX, 22–7.
23 Harrod 1951, 413.
24 *JMK*, XXIX, 10.
25 *JMK*, XIII, 122–3.
26 *JMK*, XX, 156, 319, 345. The last phrase was written in May 1930.
27 *JMK*, XX, 357–60, 362–4, 483–4.
28 *JMK*, VI, 366. For the rest of this discussion of the *Treatise*, references to volume and page will appear at the appropriate places in the text.
29 See Amadeo 1989, ch. 4.
30 *JMK*, V, 158–60; XX, 76–8.
31 Eshag 1963, 23.
32 For favourable views see Shackle 1967, ch. 13; Hicks 1967, ch. 11. For a contrary view see Patinkin 1976a.
33 For a detailed examination of the arguments see Moggridge 1986, 64–5.
34 *JMK*, XVII, 356, 382–3.
35 See Moggridge 1986, esp. 74–5.
36 *JMK*, XX, 38. Keynes's subsequent evidence appears on pages 38–157.
37 *JMK*, XX, 39.
38 *JMK*, XX, 57.
39 For modern confirmations of the situation see Redmond 1984 and Moggridge 1989, 278–81.
40 *JMK*, XX, 71.
41 KCKP, JMK to Lydia, 23 February 1930.
42 *JMK*, XX, 76–8, 80–1.
43 *JMK*, XX, 86, 87.
44 *JMK*, XX, 100.
45 *JMK*, XX, 120.
46 *JMK*, XX, 136.
47 After the meeting on 28 February, Keynes reported to Lydia (KCKP, 2 March 1930) that he had been speaking for 6½ hours. Pro-rating the complete evidence takes the total to 10 hours.
48 Sayers 1976, I, 336.
49 The suggestion comes in Boyle 1967, 258. The conclusive demonstration that this was not the case appears in Sayers 1976, I, 368–71.

50 KCKP, JMK to Lydia, 17 May 1930.
51 *JMK*, XX, 166–79.
52 On the detailed preparations for Hopkins's evidence, see Clarke 1988, ch. 7.
53 Clarke 1988, 152; the phrase 'Whitehall view' comes from Middleton 1985, 35–6.
54 See Middleton 1982, 1985; Peden, 1980, 1983, 1984, 1988; Booth 1983, 1989 and the very good discussion in Clarke 1988, ch. 4.
55 *JMK*, XX, 345–9.
56 Ibid., 349.
57 Ibid., 350–1. The whole letter appears on pages 350–6.
58 *JMK*, XIII, 173–5.
59 Howson and Winch 1977, 356. This classic study provides the basis for much of what follows.
60 *JMK*, XX, 329.
61 Howson and Winch 1977, 40.
62 *JMK*, XX, 368–9.
63 KCKP, JMK to Lydia, 3 February and 25 May 1930.
64 *JMK*, XII, 122–3.
65 *JMK*, XII, 135.
66 Ibid., 138.
67 *JMK*, XX, 416.
68 *JMK*, XX, 403.
69 *JMK*, XX, 385–7.
70 *JMK*, XX, 405.
71 *JMK*, XX, 375–6, 379.
72 Above pp. 431–2, 462–4.
73 *JMK*, XX, 378; XIII, 193.
74 *JMK*, XII, 179.
75 *JMK*, XIII, 187–9. See below pp. 534–5.
76 de Marchi 1988, 143–4; O'Brien 1988, 35–7.
77 Howson and Winch 1977, 66.
78 *JMK*, XX, 357–66.
79 *JMK*, XX, 362, 364, 365–6.
80 Howson and Winch 1977, 69.
81 *JMK*, XX, 416–19.
82 Robbins 1971, 155–8; Harris 1977, 317–18.
83 *JMK*, XX, 423–56.
84 KCKP, JMK to Lydia, 9 and 10 October 1930.
85 *JMK*, XX, 452–3. The whole memorandum appears on pages 452–6.
86 *JMK*, XX, 454.
87 Howson and Winch 1977, 71.
88 The whole report, including Robbins's dissent, is reprinted in Howson and Winch 1977, 180–242.
89 *JMK*, VII, xxi.
90 Howson and Winch 1977, 73–7 summarises the Council's discussions.
91 Marquand 1977, chs 23 and 24.
92 *JMK*, XX, 179–270.
93 *JMK*, XX, 183.
94 For details of the merger, see Hyams 1963, 115–23; *JMK*, XXVIII, 2–6.
95 *JMK*, XXVIII, 6–7.
96 Marquand 1977, 590; *JMK*, XX, 489; KCKP, JMK to Lydia, 8 March 1931. The article appears in *JMK*, IX, 231–8.

97 *JMK*, XX, 493–512.
98 *JMK*, XX, 505.
99 *JMK*, XX, 274–6, 277–80.
100 *JMK*, XX, 281.
101 The Addendum appears in *JMK*, XX, 283–309 and in Committee on Finance and Industry, *Report*, Cmd. 3897 (1931), Addendum I.
102 Sayers 1976, II, 389.
103 *JMK*, XIX, 156.
104 *JMK*, XX, 120.
105 *JMK*, XX, 329–30.
106 *JMK*, VI, 169.
107 *JMK*, XX, 378.
108 *JMK*, XX, 100.
109 Ibid., 29.
110 *JMK*, XX, 495.
111 *JMK*, XX, 379.
112 *JMK*, X, 236.
113 *JMK*, XIII, 193; XX, 380.
114 *JMK*, XX, 494, 495.
115 Macmillan Committee, Notes of Discussions, 7 November 1930, 29.
116 *JMK*, XX, 296.

20

CRISIS, CRITICISM AND NEW DIRECTIONS

Keynes set sail for New York with Lydia aboard the *Adriatic* on 30 May 1931. The purpose of the journey was to participate in the annual Harris Foundation lectures and seminars at the University of Chicago. The subject for 1931 was topical: 'Unemployment as a World Problem'. The programme required him to spend less than a fortnight in Chicago, 22 June to 2 July. He spent the rest of his visit in New York, Washington and Boston, renewing old contacts, making new ones and learning about American economic conditions. Those he saw were various: Walter Case, officials of the Federal Reserve Banks of New York and Chicago, Eugene Meyer, the Governor of the Federal Reserve Board, members of the staff of the *New Republic* (but not Walter Lippmann, who was in Europe), F. W. Taussig and Herbert Hoover. As well as his Harris Foundation lectures and seminars, he spoke to students at the New School for Social Research in New York and to members of the Chicago branch of the Council on Foreign Relations.

Of his Harris Foundation lectures, I need say little: his published analysis of the slump and the means to recovery followed the line of the *Treatise* and emphasised the predominant role of the rate of interest. In discussion he did mention the 'special case' in passing:

> I think the argument for public works in this country [the United States] is much weaker than in Great Britain. In Great Britain I have for a long time past agitated for a public works programme and my argument has been that we are such a centre of an international system that we cannot operate on the rate of interest, because, if we tried to force the rate of interest down, there is too much lending and we lose gold. . . .
>
> In this country you haven't a problem of that kind. Here you can function as though you were a closed system, and . . . for such a system I would use my first method operating on the long-term rate of interest.[1]

He allowed that public works might prove useful in circumstances other than the 'special case', but this allowance did not interfere with the general thrust of the presentations.[2] None the less, the depth of the depression in the United States left its mark and there are signs that the gloomy American prospects may have led him to contemplate the elliptical passage in the *Treatise* on the British slump of the mid-1890s in which money was continuously cheap:

> It may have been a case where nothing but strenuous measures on the part of the Government could have been successful. Borrowing by the Government and other public bodies to finance large programmes of work on public utilities and Government guarantees on the lines of the recent Trade Facilities and Export Credit Acts were probably the only ways of absorbing current savings and so averting the heavy unemployment of 1892–5.[3]

During the voyage home Keynes prepared a gloomy memorandum on 'Economic Conditions in the United States'.[4] In London, he sent the memorandum to the Prime Minister and other members of the EAC, senior directors of the Bank of England, Sir Walter Layton, editor of *The Economist*, and Francis Rodd of the Bank for International Settlements. In it he reported that senior Federal Reserve directors and officials were 'right-minded' on monetary policy and favourably inclined to 'trying the experiment of cheap money and abundant credit carried *à l'outrance*'. However, they faced the problem of carrying banking opinion with them, partly because of the views of the bankers and partly because of the views of their 'so-called "economists"' who thought that the way to restore equilibrium was for the prices of manufactures to fall to match the falls in raw material prices. He thought that the Federal Reserve might pursue an expansionist policy, but it might not carry it far enough. He did not expect 'magical results'. The reasons for his pessimism lay in the state of the American banking system, which would limit the beneficial effects of reduction in interest rates on the volume of bank lending, and in the state of the construction industries which would reduce the impact of any fall in interest rates that did occur.

At the heart of the banking problem was the banks' balance sheets. Keynes estimated that at least 10 per cent of the banking system (measured by assets) was already insolvent, and that the result of this, with the history of past failures and the prospect of 'more skeletons in their [the large New York banks'] cupboards than anyone yet knows for certain' was 'an absolute mania for liquidity'. Banks were inclined to hold large excess reserves, to reduce their lending and to unload lower-grade bonds whenever the market showed any signs of improvement. At the same time the public, distrusting the banks, had started to hoard currency on a large scale – his estimate was $400–500 million. In Chicago, where in the previous two months 50 small banks had suspended payments and 10 to 20 more were likely to follow suit, he found that safety deposit boxes were unobtainable and estimated that 'at least' $150 million in currency was now in such boxes. As a result of such processes, 'for many ordinary people in small towns up and down the country, it is a travesty of the case to suggest that credit is easy'. It would be some time before any large-scale open market operations could have any effect on long-term interest rates or on banks' willingness to lend.

Even if easier money percolated through the shattered banking system into lower rates and more available loans, the effects could be limited by obstacles to a rise in new investment. Keynes saw no need for new plant for leading manufacturing industries 'for a long time to come'; the railways had seen a fall in revenues which had 'broken their spirit and destroyed their credit'; the real estate market was characterised by excess capacity; and there was 'a marked absence of new inventions'; and many public authorities faced severe financial limitations on their ability to expand new construction. Nor did he see much prospect of a recovery in raw material prices, although he reported that 'Oil has been given away recently in Texas which must represent about bed-rock for prices.' He concluded:

> Before I went to the United States I was disposed to hold with some confidence that the first impulses to recovery in the rest of the world would have to come from America. I held this view so firmly that it was some time before I even questioned it. But eventually it was put to me point-blank in discussion that perhaps the opposite was true. And in the end I came to wonder whether this might not be the more probable opinion. We may have to drag along what seems an endless period until something happens to stir the dry bones elsewhere than in America.[5]

What later became known as the 1931 financial crisis had already started before Keynes left London in May with the failure of the Credit Anstalt bank in Vienna on 11 May. During the rest of May and early June, central banks and governments moved slowly to aid the Austrian authorities, who were experiencing large outflows of short-term funds. The slowness of reaction was a result of several factors: a lack of previous experience of such events; a lack of information on the magnitude of the potential trouble; and the fact that international co-operation was inhibited by political difficulties arising from Austria's relations with Germany, in particular a proposed customs union, and by other nations' attempts to use the crisis to achieve various other ends. Moreover, one of the means used to try to stem the crisis, standstill agreements under which foreign creditors agreed not to withdraw their outstanding claims, meant that the lenders caught by such agreements looked again at their remaining assets and tried to realise the most dubious. The crisis of confidence spread inevitably to Austria's neighbours, especially Germany, which was the world's largest short-term debtor. The Reichsbank began to lose reserves heavily from late May. On 19 June, when it appeared that the Reichsbank would be unable to meet its statutory requirements for covering the note issue in its next published balance sheet, there was an appeal for assistance from other central banks.

At the time the German situation came to the boil[6] – it had been simmering for quite some time – Keynes was in New York. Over the weekend of 13–14 June he saw Governor Meyer, who, as he reported to Hubert Henderson,

> was constantly on the telephone with the President, Morgans, etc. I was alone with him and he talked to me with astonishing freedom about all that was going on – so much so, that I can't but think he wanted me to pass something on. He was taking the line that he was opposed to the Federal Reserve System having anything to do with any patching up scheme or giving any assistance at the present stage. They would help nothing, he said, which was not on a permanent, sound economic basis. His public attitude was calculated to produce the impression that he was in favour of letting things rip. He then disclosed to me in private his own policy if he could persuade the President – to cut down all war debt payments by 50 per cent for a period of five years, the benefit to be passed on to Germany. He did not think it at all impossible that the President would be prepared to take this up at the right time. The President has at one time discussed on his own initiative the question of total remission (*not* suspension) for two years.[7]

The next day, Keynes reported to Henderson that fears of a German moratorium, plus the weakness of the American banking system, had resulted in continuing withdrawals from Germany. In this way officials and Ministers in London obtained additional background information to deal with the President's proposal of 20 June for a two-year moratorium on war debt and reparation payments.

While Keynes was in Chicago, the announcement of the Hoover moratorium and of a central bank credit on 24 June of $100 million for the Reichsbank temporarily calmed markets. On 22 June, however, in informal remarks before his first Harris Foundation lecture, he cast doubt on the Hoover proposal's chances of success since France would be asked to make very large sacrifices under it.[8] When these doubts became reality, the external run on Germany began again in earnest: this time after a large industrial failure triggered an internal run on the German banking system. An American–French agreement of 6 July on the Hoover proposal did not stem the outflow. As Keynes and Lydia left New York on 11 July, again aboard the *Adriatic*, no solution was in sight.

On 13 July, while Keynes and Lydia were still on the high seas, the German crisis took another turn with the failure of the Danat Bank and a Government decree proclaiming a two-day bank and stock exchange holiday, which turned out to be the beginning of exchange control and another standstill arrangement. In London the same day, the Macmillan *Report*, which revealed for the first time Britain's large short-term international indebtedness, became public; sterling, which had been close to parity with the franc and the dollar, dropped sharply on exchange markets. The British 1931 financial crisis had begun.

Sterling had been under some pressure throughout much of 1930 and by the year's end the Bank of England had needed support from the Bank of France and the Federal Reserve Bank of New York. The slump had arrived over the exchanges, resulting in a sharp fall in exports. The balance of trade had not at first deteriorated markedly because import prices had fallen substantially. However, the slump had started to affect Britain's invisible earnings from shipping and overseas investments – and would do so increasingly as time passed. Moreover, despite official controls on new overseas issues, the capital account had turned adverse as short-term balances were repatriated to the Continent, particularly to France. At the same time, although the Labour Government had launched a modest programme of public works early in its term of office, the slump began to play havoc with public finances, as payments to the unemployed rose and revenues fell off. By the beginning of 1931 there had been what Keynes called 'an extraordinary nervosity about in the London market' and 'a good deal of more or less open talk about the devaluation of sterling and the abandonment of [the] gold standard'. Keynes described this pessimism as 'complete moonshine as far as the near future is concerned', but he did not discount the possibilities of a crisis later.[9] In the event, the 'nervosity' dissipated as the Government appointed yet more committees to examine various aspects of the public finances, but the underlying situation remained potentially explosive.

In just over two months from the onset of the initial gold outflows on 13 July, the Bank of England lost over £200 million in owned and borrowed reserves in a desperate attempt to maintain sterling on the gold standard. During those two months, Keynes was usually on the edge of events, occasionally nearer the centre, trying to make up his mind as to the best course to follow – and to the most effective way to make his views known.

Keynes wrote nothing during the early stages of the crisis. Although he saw Walter Stewart on 21 July and Sir Josiah Stamp and Hubert Henderson (twice) at the end of the month, he did not otherwise make contact with anyone closely involved in policy-making. Initially, the Bank of England lost gold without raising Bank rate. It then moved it to 3½ per cent on 23 July. A week later, after arranging credits from the Bank of France and the Federal Reserve, and in the face of further reserve losses the Bank put Bank rate up to 4½ per cent. The next day, Parliament adjourned for the summer recess, a few hours before the *Report* of the May Committee appeared. This committee, chaired by Sir George May of the Prudential Insurance Company, had been set up in February 1931 to examine public expenditure and make proposals for economy. The *Report* painted a gloomier and more grossly exaggerated picture of the situation than anyone had expected – estimating a Budget deficit of £120 million by April 1932 and recommending increased taxation of £24 million and expenditure reductions of £96 million, the bulk of which would come from spending on unemployment, including a 20 per cent reduction in the rate of unemployment benefit. The Government published the *Report* without comment. It expected to consider its recommendations at leisure during the summer recess and make its own response to Parliament when it reassembled in October. For the moment, holidays had priority.

On 2 August, the Prime Minister, who had retired to his home at Lossiemouth on the north-east coast of Scotland, wrote to Keynes asking for anything he might write on the May *Report*.[10] Keynes replied from Tilton on 5 August,[11] saying that he did not expect to publish any comments on the *Report* because his views were 'not fit for publication; – they are not even fit for circulation to the EAC'. As he told MacDonald, he regarded the recommendations as 'a most gross perversion of social justice', although he could see them as part of a broader programme to bring incomes down to match the fall in prices. He did not recommend such a course, which would be 'both futile and disastrous'. His reasons were those he had used previously: economy measures would increase unemployment; the cut in money incomes to reach equilibrium 'would be more than those concerned would submit to' – at least 30 per cent and perhaps larger; and there was 'no practical means to secure [a reduction in rentier incomes] . . . or to secure even a modicum of social justice'. He now also had another, more important reason:

But above all – and this is the new fact within the last two months – it is now nearly *certain* that we shall go off the existing gold parity at no distant date. Whatever may have been the case some time ago, it is now too late to avoid this. We can put off the date for some time, if we are so foolish to borrow in terms of francs and dollars and so allow a proportion of what are sterling liabilities to be converted into franc and dollar liabilities, thus giving a preference to those of our creditors who are quickest to sell. But when doubts as to the prosperity of a currency, such as now exist about sterling, have come into existence, the game's up; for there is no object to foreigners keeping sterling balances if there is any appreciable doubt about their value. It is conceivable that we might have avoided this if we had been more clear-sighted. But we cannot avoid it now.

It will be difficult for the City to give clear guidance at the present time. The accepting houses, who constitute the major part of the Court of the Bank of England, are many of them more or less insolvent. The

Governor is probably near the end of his nervous resources.[a] It is now a problem for the Government rather than the City.

He proposed that the Government should 'try to convert disaster into success' by forming a new, sterling-centred, currency union based on a devaluation of at least 25 per cent. The union would include the Empire at first and later any other countries who wished to join. The currency unit for this union would not be fixed permanently in terms of gold, but would be managed, presumably along *Treatise* lines (for the letter did not spell out the details) to keep sterling prices stable.

As he warned the Prime Minister, Keynes did not make these views public. Instead, when he did comment on the May *Report* in the *New Statesman* for 15 August, he contented himself with an article which 'had little bearing on the immediate situation',[12] examining the effects of the implementation of the recommendations on unemployment and on the Budget. He estimated that economies of £100 million would increase unemployment by 250–400,000, improve the trade balance by £20 million and, allowing for repercussions, only reduce the Budget deficit by £50 million. He continued to temporise in public for several weeks.[13]

Events soon pushed the Government from its intention to consider the May *Report* at its leisure. The announcement of the central bank credits on 1 August failed to relieve pressure on sterling, for the state of the Budget still preyed on financial markets and there were some technical mistakes in the execution of policy which did not help.[b] In these circumstances, the Government had to appear to be doing something and the Bank advised the Chancellor that only a readjustment in the Budget position would do – and re-emphasised this repeatedly as it continued to support sterling, rapidly using up the July credits in the process and bringing nearer the day when the Government itself would have to borrow abroad to increase the reserves. On 11 August, summoned by the Chancellor, the Prime Minister returned to London. A Cabinet Economy Committee met four times in the next week before the full Cabinet met at 11 a.m. on 19 August to discuss the proposed Budget changes. The estimates before the Cabinet were even gloomier than those from the May Committee – the prospective Budget deficit was now

a Both of these last statements were accurate. Several accepting houses experienced difficulties as a result of the standstill agreements and Lazards, on the brink of closure in mid-July 1931, was supported by the Bank (Sayers 1976, II, esp. 530–1). The Governor had collapsed at a Committee of Treasury meeting on 29 July and was, with one exception on 5 August, out of the Bank until 28 September when the crisis was over. Sir Ernest Harvey, the Deputy Governor, and Sir Edward Peacock, a member of the Bank's Committee of Treasury, took over his burden.

b Notably the announcement of an increase in the fiduciary issue in order to release more gold for export, which was misinterpreted then – and still is (Cairncross and Eichengreen 1983, 65) – as increasing the money supply, and the decision not to support the exchanges on the first day of business after the announcement of the credits, which 'completely confused the market, caused chaos in the Continental exchanges, and administered an irreparable blow to confidence in the pound' (Sayers 1976, II, 395; see also ibid., 390–1, 394–5).

£170 million – and the Chancellor was proposing £89 million in tax increases and expenditure cuts of £78.5 million. Over the next few days the Cabinet met repeatedly to try to agree on a package that became even more difficult to accept as the leaders of the Conservative and the Liberal parties balked at the tax increases and insisted on more drastic economies, including a cut in unemployment benefit; the Cabinet decisively rejected a revenue tariff; and the leadership of the Trades Union Congress pushed for minimal expenditure cuts, a suspension of the sinking fund for reduction of the national debt, and a revenue tariff. The Government was trapped: it needed to borrow abroad to support sterling; to borrow it needed to produce a programme satisfactory to overseas financial markets (*i.e.* the City); yet it was unable to agree on a suitable programme. To surmount the crisis, on 24 August, MacDonald agreed to the King's request that he head a National Government made up of representatives of all three parties. This Government agreed to a programme of expenditure cuts and tax increases, including a 10 per cent cut in unemployment benefit and a partial suspension of the sinking fund, on 27 August. Two days later, the Government raised loans totalling £80 million in New York and Paris.

Keynes spent most of the crisis at Tilton, going up to London only for meetings in the middle of each week. He was, none the less, well-informed of the gravity of the situation. On 13 August he saw Hubert Henderson. On 19 August he had an interview at the Bank of England with H. A. Siepmann and O. M. W. Sprague, who at the request of the Bank's Committee of Treasury were 'to discuss the situation with the hope that the revelation of "the true facts" would convince him to change the tone of the articles he was writing on the financial crisis' – a classic piece of Bank overstatement, given he had only written one article.[14] Jay Crane, Deputy Governor of the Federal Reserve Bank of New York recorded the circumstances of the meeting:

> The feud between Sprague and Keynes continues. They are, of course, diametrically opposed and Keynes is, I think, doing a great disservice to his country. On the Continent, particularly the fear that England might deliberately abandon the gold standard, or at least go off temporarily to return at a lower level, has been widespread and can be charged to the influence of Keynes and his followers, who are many in England. Even at the Bank of England one hears men like Siepmann and Rodd admit quite frankly that the only way out is for England and most of the other European countries to go off the gold standard temporarily, leave France and the United States high and dry, and then return to gold at a lower level. Discussions along this line have undoubtedly been an important reason for the lack of confidence in sterling on the part of countries like Holland, Switzerland and Belgium, which were heavy sellers of pounds during the crisis. While I was at the

Bank of England, it was decided that some effort should be made to bring Keynes into camp and, if possible, keep him quiet. Sprague and Siepmann asked him to talk with them at the Bank, but I gather it was quite impossible to do anything with him.[15]

As Crane surmised, the Bank's effort was not successful. When Keynes came to discuss the National Government's programme in the *New Statesman* on 29 August, he linked it to the maintenance of the sterling parity, stated that it represented a point of view that was 'unacceptable' and suggested that in any case it would not do what it was designed to do.[16] In the ensuing weeks he became more open in his disagreement with the Government's decision to defend the parity, and suggested that it had not chosen efficient instruments, most notably a revenue tariff, to carry out its task.[17] As a stop-gap, he suggested that the Government call an international conference on the gold standard, and that in the meantime it restrict capital exports and exchange dealing and foreswear any further foreign borrowing. If the conference could not reach an agreement acceptable to Britain, she would leave the gold standard rather than deflate. This proposal was a mere cover, for he had become convinced of the inevitability of devaluation in the near future.[18]

He was extremely depressed. As he told Walter Case on 14 September:

> To read the newspapers just now is to see Bedlam let loose. Every person in the country of super asinine propensities, everyone who hates social progress and loves deflation, feels that his hour has come, and triumphantly announces how, by refraining from every form of economic activity we can become prosperous again.
>
> ... Sacrifice being the order of the day, everyone has agreed to sacrifice what he himself believes to be the only remedy for the situation.[19]

On 8 September the National Government met Parliament. On 10 September it brought in its taxation and economy measures – measures which Keynes regarded, in remarks to a meeting of Members of Parliament on 16 September, as 'the most wrong and foolish things which Parliament has deliberately perpetrated in my lifetime'.[20] Others were, perhaps, more impressed.[c]

However, the Bank continued to lose reserves, although there were days, such as those immediately after the formation of the new Government and after Snowden's Emergency Budget, when markets were firmer. Markets were generally nervous and skittish. Until 14 September, it might have been possible to believe that the corner would be turned, but then came a 'mutiny' aboard the warships of the Royal Navy at Invergordon in reaction to the

---

c Interestingly enough, but for different reasons, Montagu Norman agreed with Keynes (Federal Reserve Bank of New York, Harrison Collection, Conversation with Norman, 23 August 1931).

reductions in public service pay. This was ominous enough, especially to foreign opinion, but the Government's announced willingness to alleviate the hardships which had caused the disturbance unsettled markets even further. Continued talk of a general election did not help. Reserve losses mounted sharply; prices on the London Stock Exchange and Continental bourses fell sharply – and continued to fall; a banking crisis in Amsterdam added to London's difficulties. After the Bank lost £18¾ million on Friday, 18 September, a meeting between Sir Ernest Harvey, Sir Edward Peacock, the Prime Minister and the Chancellor decided to suspend gold convertibility after markets closed at noon on Saturday, when another £11 million went.

The day before the decision, the Treasury had begun to prepare for the eventuality by drafting a Gold Standard (Amendment) Bill. Keynes and Sir Josiah Stamp, who had been drafting a report for an Economic Advisory Council committee on the balance of payments, were brought into these discussions. According to Sir Frederick Leith-Ross this took place on 18 September,[d] when they discussed, among other things the adoption of exchange control. Keynes and Stamp supported controls; Leith-Ross and Sir Ernest Harvey opposed them. The latter carried the day, for there were only limited, temporary restrictions imposed on 21 September. On 20 September in a broadcast drafted by Hubert Henderson, Ramsay MacDonald told the nation of the suspension of convertibility and the Government rushed the necessary legislation through Parliament the next day, Monday 21 September 1931.

On Sunday Leonard and Virginia Woolf had been to Tilton: 'Maynard and Kahn talked like people in the war. We sat talking economics and politics'.[21] On Monday Keynes was exultant. Beatrice Webb, a guest at Tilton on 21 September with her husband and Walter Citrine, recorded in her diary:

> It so happened that on Monday (21) afternoon we were engaged to visit the Maynard Keynes; their car coming to take us the sixty miles to their country home – a ramshackle old farmhouse under Firle Beacon . . . a delightful setting. . . . Keynes accompanied by Citrine in the car of the GCTU joined us before dinner in a great state of inward satisfaction at the fulfilment of his policy of a measure of inflation. Apparently he either knows or expected the outcome of the crisis, for he said he assumed the announcement of going off the gold standard would come

---

d Keynes's appointments diaries do not record his being in London on that Friday. (Leith-Ross's chronology makes it Saturday 19 September, but this does not fit with the rest of the events he described, which took place on Friday.) They do record, however, Keynes's being at a meeting of the Economic Advisory Council's Committee on Economic Information on 21 September. As this meeting was held in the Treasury, Leith-Ross may have confused the dates. Keynes may not, of course, have recorded all his meetings in his appointments diary. Leith-Ross 1968, 140. The story is also in Boyce (1987, 365), who accepts Leith-Ross's dating.

over [the] wireless. . . . He had lunched with Winston [Churchill] who said that he (W.) had never been in favour of the return to the Gold Standard: he had resisted it in 1926 [*sic*] and had been overborne by the City backed up by Treasury officials. Keynes of course is enjoying a febrile self-complacency over the fulfilment of his prophecy in the *Economic Consequences of the War* or rather of the Peace. He was far too agitated and elated to care to be cross examined as I had hoped to cross examine him about his National Board of Investment, and he was very offhand and abstruse in his replies.[22]

Lydia reported the evening somewhat differently, but also noted:

We return soon next week, as being off 'gold Standard' changes the situation and the more exciting. M. is very pleased and says it is 'new chapter'.[23]

The rush to London amused the inhabitants of Charleston, who, other than Duncan Grant, had not seen Keynes during the crisis.[24] Later, they were surprised:

Duncan & I went to a cinema when we were in London last week & suddenly Maynard appeared on the screen enormously big, in a well-appointed library, blinking at the lights & speaking rather nervously, & told the world that everything was now going to be all right, England had been rescued by fate from an almost hopeless situation, the pound would not collapse, prices would not rise very much, trade would recover, no one need fear anything. In this weather one can almost believe it.[25]

It was not surprising that Keynes decided to leave Tilton and return to 'the hub' as Vanessa called it. During the week of 21 September there were three meetings of the Economic Advisory Council's Committee on Economic Information and a meeting of the Other Club. He remained in London until the weekend of 10 October. There were no more meetings of the EAC, but on 30 September he did record the Movietone newsreel that Vanessa and Duncan reported seeing,[e] and saw several people in the City and several connected with the *New Statesman*. As well, he unsuccessfully tried to dissuade the Prime Minister and Lloyd George from an election, both in letters and in visits to Chequers and Churt on Sunday 4 October.[26]

Despite his inside knowledge and his belief that there was a high probability that sterling would leave gold and depreciate, Keynes took no steps on his own account, or on behalf of institutions for whose financial affairs he was responsible, to take advantage of the exchange rate changes he believed probable. O. T. Falk had suggested that the Independent Investment

e This cinema film has survived. Part of it can be seen in Mark Blaug's 1988 video film for the Institute of Economic Affairs, *The Life, Ideas and Legacy of John Maynard Keynes*.

Trust, of which they were both directors, replace a dollar loan with a sterling loan, even though the company was in financial difficulties. Keynes replied on 18 September.

> What you suggest amounts in the present circumstances to a frank bear speculation against sterling. I admit that I am not clear that this would be against the national interest; for it may be better that the special credits [to the Bank of England and the Government] should be used up by Englishmen than by foreigners. All the same I am clear that an institution has no business to do such a thing at the present time. I should like to see exchange dealings controlled so as to take away the opportunity of choice. But meanwhile, one is not entitled to take matters into one's own hands. One has to fall in with the collective decision whether one agrees with it or not. I am confident that this would be the wish of our shareholders if we could consult them.[27]

The Independent did not switch its financing. The resulting loss exceeded £40,000.

Sterling's departure from gold also led Keynes to alter the thrust of his policy advice. Once the exchange rate was free to adjust to remove the disparity between British and overseas costs, the grounds for his tariff proposals of the previous year disappeared. In a letter to *The Times* on 28 September, he announced that 'the immediate question for attention is not a tariff but the currency question', for without the resolution of that question 'it is impossible to have a rational discussion about tariffs'.[28] In his own writings he thus put tariffs to one side.

The depreciation of sterling also meant that the 'special case' of the *Treatise* for public works was no longer relevant to the British situation. It was some time before he returned to the issue of loan-financed public works as a cure for unemployment, except vaguely along the lines of the 1892–5 argument mentioned above.[29] His emphasis switched to the need to reduce the rate of interest in Britain now that monetary policy was not constrained by the need to defend sterling's gold parity. This advice was consistent with the 'general' case of the *Treatise*.

As if to emphasise the disjunction caused by Britain's departure from the gold standard and the Hoover moratorium, Keynes almost immediately after 21 September decided to collect together an edited selection of his writings of the previous twelve years in a volume he provisionally called 'Essays in Prophecy'. He suggested the book to Macmillan on 3 October. Macmillan agreed two days later. On 16 October he delivered copy for the entire book, then called 'Essays in Prophecy and Persuasion'.[30] He soon changed the title to *Essays in Persuasion*. The book appeared in England on 27 November and two months later in America. It included his best writings on the Peace Treaty, inflation and deflation, the return to gold, the slump and politics, as well as 'Economic Possibilities for our Grandchildren'. It remains the best single-volume introduction to his ideas, even though some of them were to change markedly over the next four years. In introducing the book as 'the croakings of a Cassandra who could never influence the course of events in time', he echoed the peroration of his speech to members of the House of Commons on 16 September.[31] With Britain 'at a point of transition', 'in the pool between waterfalls', and 'having regained our freedom of choice', perhaps he hoped that both the future and his role in it would be different from the past.

Although 1930 and 1931 were dominated by the slump, the ensuing financial crisis and Keynes's attempts to shape events through the Macmillan Committee, the Economic Advisory Council and other private and public persuasion, they were also the years during which professional economists absorbed and reacted to *A Treatise on Money*. The reactions were such that on 1 November 1931, a week before he signed the Preface to *Essays in Persuasion*, he wrote to J. A. Hobson, the heretic economist whose books Keynes had regarded with orthodox disdain[f] in the years before 1914:

> In due course, I must be at pains to expound the whole matter again from the bottom upward in a manner better calculated to catch the attention of minds habituated to other channels of thought.[32]

A month later, he was even more explicit to Nicholas Kaldor, then a research student at LSE:

> Well, I must be more lucid next time. I am now endeavouring to express the whole thing over again more clearly *and from a different angle*; and in two years' time I may feel able to publish a revised and completer version. (Italics added)[33]

Over the ensuing months he would make similar statements to Japanese readers of the *Treatise* and to Ralph Hawtrey.[34] Keynes was remarkably quick in abandoning much of his *magnum opus*, the product of six years' work. Why had he done so?

When Keynes had finished the *Treatise* in September 1930, he had not been completely happy with it. As he told his mother: 'Artistically it is a

---

f Thus, Keynes had concluded his September 1913 *Economic Journal* review of Hobson's *Gold, Prices and Wages*:

> Belonging to no one race more than another, there lives an intellectually solitary race of beings who by some natural prompting of the soul think about monetary theory in certain specific, definite ways, superstitious or delusive, mystically, not materially, true, if true at all. All of these will find their natural instincts expressed here in forms more plausible-topical than they can usually shape themselves. Mr Hobson has given us a Mythology of Money, – intellectualised, brought up to journalistic date, most subtly interlarded (and this is how it differs from the rest) with temporary concessions to reason. (*JMK*, XI, 394).

failure – I have changed my mind too much in the course of it for it to be a proper unity'. He told his readers much the same thing:

> I could do it better and much shorter if I were to start again. I feel like someone who has been forcing his way through a confused jungle. Now that I have emerged from it, I see that I might have taken a more direct route.[35]

It was a large step, however, from saying that one might express the same ideas more straightforwardly, or even to say, as he did to Hobson, that he might take more account of his readers' preconceptions, than to say that he was working it out *'from a different angle'* that would take a matter of years to develop. That he had decided to do so reflected the reception of the *Treatise* by his professional colleagues.

As Keynes had finished the book, he had been so pre-occupied with his other activities that, as I have already remarked, he did not have time to consider the long comments that Ralph Hawtrey had provided on the proofs. It was almost a month *after* publication that he got down to considering and replying to Hawtrey's remarks, which might almost be regarded as the review they eventually became.[36] After publication, there were other academic reviews and discussions to consider.[37] The most important for what followed appeared in the autumn and winter of 1931–2: Dennis Robertson's 'Mr Keynes' Theory of Money' (*Economic Journal*, September 1931) and Friedrich von Hayek's 'Reflections on the Pure Theory of Money of Mr J. M. Keynes (*Economica*, August 1931 and February 1932). Both drew rejoinders from Keynes, as well as correspondence.[38] Finally, there were discussions in Cambridge, one set with Robertson and Pigou and another, not of course unrelated, involving certain younger members of the Cambridge Faculty, students and visitors to Cambridge.

The latter set of Cambridge discussions reflected the arrival in the late 1920s of a younger generation of economists who would have a major impact on the Faculty of Economics and on the economics profession over the next several decades. We have already met Piero Sraffa and Richard Kahn. The others included Austin Robinson, then a young fellow of Sidney Sussex recently returned from India, who would join Keynes on the *Economic Journal* in 1934; his wife Joan Robinson, about to commence a career of prolific publication; and James Meade, newly appointed a fellow of Hertford College, Oxford, who thanks to Dennis Robertson was spending the 1930–1 year in Cambridge in order to deepen his knowledge of economics. In the autumn of 1930, this group, the eldest of whom were in their early thirties, began to meet in Richard Kahn's rooms in King's to discuss the *Treatise*. Their discussions continued into the next term before they became a more formal 'seminar'. To this 'seminar', held in the Old Combination Room of Trinity College, came a larger group. Participation was by invitation, with undergraduates wishing to receive invitations having to satisfy an interviewing board of Richard Kahn, Austin Robinson and Piero Sraffa. The discussions in Kahn's rooms and the 'seminar' in Trinity took on the name of 'the Circus', presumably not because it was a travelling show of performing animals, acrobats and clowns but because it met the alternative dictionary definition of a scene of lively action and a group of people engaged in common activity – in this case trying to understand and, later, to criticise the *Treatise*. Keynes did not take part. Rather, Richard Kahn played in Margaret Meade's words, describing a later occasion, the role of the messenger angel 'who brought messages and problems from Keynes to the "Circus" and who went back to heaven with the results of our deliberations'.[39] The theological overtones seem to have been there from the beginning: in the autumn of 1930 Keynes began referring to Richard Kahn in his letters to Lydia as 'the little priest'.[40]

The comments and criticisms that Keynes received from these different sources varied. In many cases, however, they reinforced each other. However, if they came from outside, and they were taken up or echoed by members of the Circus or merely by Richard Kahn, who from this time forward was Keynes's intellectual confessor on economic-theoretical issues, they were more likely to strike home. Kahn's role in the process was critical, for he could as a fellow of King's nag Keynes constantly over the points at issue until the latter saw where the problem lay.[g] From Circus-induced dissatisfaction to the beginnings of creation, where Kahn played an important role, was but a short step.

To be effective, the comments had to create dissatisfaction with the theoretical sections of the *Treatise*. It was on those sections that Keynes's practical analysis of contemporary events had come to depend, as he had emphasised and reemphasised during 1930–1. Even before publication, in the comments that Keynes did not have time to consider fully, Ralph Hawtrey had pointed out that 'Mr Keynes' formula, the fundamental equations' was a tautology. Keynes could not use the equations to suggest that an excess of

---

g Schumpeter (1954, 1172) has suggested that Kahn's 'share in the historic achievement [that followed] cannot have fallen very far short of co-authorship'. In his Mattioli Lectures, particularly as delivered rather than as published, if one is to judge from the comments of Luigi Pasinetti, Kahn tried to deal with Schumpeter's point. He did so unsatisfactorily, if only because, as noted above (p. 480), he deliberately (and mistakenly) distanced himself too much from the *Treatise* and thus overly highlighted his own role in the new ideas that were later to emerge. It is clear in the surviving correspondence in *JMK* XIII, XIV and XXIX that, although Keynes was willing to change his mind, it was more often than not, especially after 1931, Keynes who was also setting the agenda for discussion. (Kahn 1984, 175, 177–8, 223–5, 240).
Keynes posed the problem neatly to Kahn on 13 August 1934:

But you *must not* get into the habit of never doing your own work but always someone else's for them. In the first place you will get subconsciously (or consciously) badly irked by it yourself; and in the second place you will end up by getting the credit for everything of any merit published by anyone during your lifetime!

investment over savings *caused* a rise in prices relative to costs, since he had defined savings and investment in such a way that the existence of such an excess meant that prices had risen.[41] Hawtrey also argued that the analysis of the *Treatise* assumed that changes in prices relative to costs occurred without any change in output.[42] Such a rigid assumption, which was challenged by the Circus with its discovery of the 'widow's cruse fallacy',[h] was well within the conventions of traditional monetary theory, but hardly seemed suitable for explaining the events of 1929–31. Keynes reflected the tradition as he took Hawtrey's point:

> The question of *how much* reduction of output is caused by a realised fall of price or an anticipated fall of price, is important, but not strictly a monetary problem.

> I repeat that I am not dealing with the complete set of causes which determine [the] volume of output. For this would have led me an endlessly long journey into the theory of short-period supply and a long way from monetary theory; – though I agree that it will probably be difficult in future to prevent monetary theory and the theory of short-period supply from running together. If I were to write the book again, I should probably attempt to probe further into the difficulties of the latter; but I have already probed far enough to know what a complicated affair it is.[43]

Hawtrey did not make all the running. Dennis Robertson, who was having growing difficulties with the book in 1931, also had an impact. It was he, along with Richard Kahn, who picked up the dependence of the divergence between the behaviour of the prices of investment goods and the prices of consumption goods on Keynes's assumption that profits were not consumed.[i] If that assumption went, then if investment rose, consumption would also rise, with markedly different results. Finally Hayek, as well as echoing definitional problems raised by Robertson and Pigou and the tautological issue raised by Hawtrey, pointed out that Keynes's book lacked a theory of capital and interest. Unlike Wicksell's classic *Interest and Prices* (1898) Keynes never explained the determination of the natural rate of interest on which so much rested. Hayek noted that Keynes had tried to remedy this defect *after* developing his basic theory, but had put it badly. As Hayek asked,

---

h The reference is to *JMK*, V, 125: 'Thus profits, as a source of capital increment for entrepreneurs, are a widow's cruse which remains undepleted however much of them may be devoted to riotous living'.

i Kahn pointed this out first (*JMK*, XIII, 203–7) and Robertson a few weeks later. Keynes did not at first take the point in – nor did he much like Robertson's comments, which he told Lydia 'doesn't come to so much as I expected, and honestly (I swear) it is not very good' (KCKP, JMK to Lydia, 3 May 1931) – but Kahn kept nagging (XIII, 219).

Would not Mr Keynes have made his task easier if he had not only accepted one of the descendants of Böhm-Bawerk's theory, but had also made himself acquainted with the substance of the theory itself?[44]

All of this criticism, and I have touched only on the most important points, was disappointing. In some cases, as with Hawtrey over output or with Hayek over capital theory, Keynes accepted the criticism.[45] On other points, however, he vigorously defended his position before giving way or before the discussion bogged down in terminological controversy as he and his critic talked past each other asking in a Moorite way 'Exactly what do you *mean* by *that*?'. On one occasion he unfairly counterattacked, turning his reply into a review of Hayek's recent book *Prices and Production* (1931)[j]:

> The reader will perceive that I have been drifting into a review of Dr Hayek's *Prices and Production*. And this being so, I should like, if the editor will allow me, to consider this book a little further. The book, as it stands, seems to me to be one of the most frightful muddles I have ever read, with scarcely a sound proposition in it beginning with page 45, and yet it remains a book of some interest which is likely to leave its mark on the mind of the reader. It is an extraordinary example of how, starting with a mistake, a remorseless logician can end up in Bedlam. Yet Dr Hayek has seen a vision, and though when he woke up he has made nonsense of his story by giving the wrong names to the objects which occur in it, his Kubla Khan is not without inspiration and must set the reader thinking with the germs of an idea in his head.[46]

Perhaps it was a reaction to Keynes's belief, noted on his copy of Hayek's review, that

> Hayek has not read my book with that measure of 'good will' which an author is entitled to expect of a reader. Until he can do so, he will not see what I mean or know whether I am right.[47]

This was no substitute for 'working it out all over again'. Keynes said as much when he concluded the subsequent correspondence with Hayek: 'I am trying to re-shape and improve my central position, and that is a better way to try and spend one's time than in controversy'.[48]

At the same time as these criticisms came hints of an alternative focus which would successfully take account of movements in output and prices. In August 1930, just before Keynes finished the *Treatise*, Richard Kahn, puzzled by Chapter 6 of *Can Lloyd George Do It?* which dealt with the amount of employment that would be provided by the Liberal proposals, developed a framework for analysing the ultimate impact on aggregate

---

j Hayek had to some extent asked for Keynes's response, for in his own review he referred his readers to *Prices and Production* (*Economica*, August 1931, 271).

employment of government expenditure on a public works project (now known as the employment multiplier). As noted above, he presented his early results to the Committee of Economists. In the months that followed, in conjunction with Colin Clark of the EAC and James Meade, Kahn worked out their implications more fully before publishing them in the *Economic Journal* for June 1931 under the title 'The Relation of Home Investment to Employment'. Kahn's article had two implications for Keynes's later work. Focusing on the supply curves for output as a whole, Kahn realised that the *Treatise*'s fundamental equations represented a limiting case: Keynes had assumed that output as a whole was inelastic to changes in demand. Relaxing that assumption would, as Hawtrey had also realised, markedly affect the analysis and be 'very much closer to the actual conditions that prevail today [1931]', although neither Hawtrey in 1930 nor Kahn in 1931 perceived how much that difference would be.[49] Kahn also, inspired by James Meade, provided in 'Mr Meade's Relation' an outline statement of the resources available for this additional investment when the supply of output was less than completely elastic to demand changes. The complete argument and its corollaries were not yet clear to Kahn – much less to Keynes – and would not be for some time.

Kahn was not the only one to discover the multiplier and not to understand its implications. Away from the discussions we are concerned with, L. F. Giblin, Ritchie Research Professor in the University of Melbourne, had sketched out the notion in his May 1930 inaugural lecture, *Australia 1930*, but neither he nor his colleagues appreciated the importance of his contribution. Closer to Cambridge, Ralph Hawtrey had stumbled on the multiplier in an unpublished discussion of the transfer problem that could have helped Keynes in his 1929 discussions with Ohlin.[50] In his comments on the proof sheets of the *Treatise* Hawtrey had provided a numerical example of the multiplier, with leakages into savings and income adjusting to equilibrate saving with a new level of investment. He elaborated his example in a January 1931 paper for the Macmillan Committee, but then removed crucial elements of the analysis in his published paper on the *Treatise* in *The Art of Central Banking* (1932). Yet whether Hawtrey's papers influenced Keynes, as Eric Davis has strongly claimed,[51] or even proved suggestive, is, as Peter Clarke argues, unascertainable. Hawtrey did, however, earn a place in the history of economics 'notably as the man who, having stumbled upon it [the multiplier], painstakingly suppressed news of its discovery in his subsequent publications', which were completely uninfluenced by the notion.[52]

Thus by the autumn of 1931 Keynes had started to work it out all over again. In the course of the visit to Tilton which ended on the weekend of sterling's departure from the gold standard, Keynes and Kahn had been discussing some of these issues. A note Keynes wrote on 20 September and Kahn's reply of 24 September indicate that both had a long way to go.[53] On 22 November, after the usual distractions of King's autumn audit were over,

Keynes reported to Lydia: 'I have begun again writing quietly in my chair about monetary theory'. He was still in that chair when immortalised in the often reprinted 1933 drawing by David Low.

In breaking sterling's pre-war parity with gold and, with the Hoover Moratorium, throwing the war debts and reparations issue back into the melting pot, the international financial crisis of 1931 provided, as Keynes pointed out in his Preface to *Essays in Persuasion*, the opportunity for a complete re-thinking of British economic policy. Keynes was fortunate in having an official forum for presenting his views. Coincidentally with the outbreak of the British phase of the 1931 financial crisis, Ramsay MacDonald had appointed a Committee on Economic Information of the Economic Advisory Council 'to supervise the preparation of monthly reports to the Economic Advisory Council on the economic situation and to advise as to the continuous study of economic development'.[54] It comprised Sir Josiah Stamp (chairman), Walter Citrine, G. D. H. Cole, Sir Alfred Lewis and Keynes, with Hubert Henderson and A. F. Hemming as secretaries.[k] The full Council did not survive the crisis: it met only once after April 1931, on 15 January 1932, when MacDonald noted that its discussions had been 'sometimes rather diffuse' and ineffective and proposed that it should meet less frequently and leave more of its work to committees. Although the EAC was not officially buried until 1938, the Committee on Economic Information (CEI) replaced the Council as far as economic policy advice was concerned. It was to produce twenty-seven reports between September 1931 and the outbreak of the Second World War.

It was the CEI and the meetings surrounding its first report on 'The Balance of International Payments', that brought Keynes into contact with policy-makers in the final stages of the financial crisis. That report, completed on 25 September,[55] gave an excellent account of the factors, largely the decline in invisible earnings, that had produced a deterioration of Britain's balance of payments during 1931 and, if the slump did not end, would make it even worse in 1932; a brief discussion of the effects of the depreciation of sterling and a recommendation that 'a decline in the gold value of sterling by 25 per cent would not be by any means excessive'.[56] It also emphasised the need for a comprehensive reconsideration of international economic policy, but did not go into details. Keynes at one stage would have had the report go further, for his draft conclusions of 21 September recommended the imposition of exchange controls and an international currency conference,[57] but his suggestions did not survive sterling's departure from gold. By that time,

k Citrine left the Committee in 1933. Henderson became a member when he left government service for Oxford in 1934. Other members added after 1932 were Sir Arthur Salter (1932–9); E. D. Simon (1932–6); Dennis Robertson (1936–9); Sir Sydney Chapman (February 1932); Sir Frederick Leith-Ross (1932–9) and Sir Frederick Phillips (1935–9). Piers Debenham became a secretary to the committee when Henderson left the civil service.

Britain's future international financial policy was the subject of an enquiry by another committee.

This committee, the Prime Minister's Advisory Committee on Financial Questions, was appointed on 19 September. It had no formal terms of reference, but MacDonald asked it in September to draw up 'an agenda of the financial problems from both the domestic and international standpoint that ought to be considered during the next few months with an elucidation of the issues raised' and in January 1932 to provide an 'opinion as to whether ... the time was approaching when a definite policy should be pursued in regard to sterling, and if so, as to what that policy should be ...'.[58] Keynes was not a charter member of this Committee, which consisted of MacDonald (chairman), R. H. Brand, W. T. Layton, Reginald McKenna, Lord Macmillan, Sir Josiah Stamp and Hubert Henderson (secretary). At the end of September, Sir Arthur Salter, recently returned from the League of Nations secretariat, joined the Committee. Keynes had yet to earn his way on.

He did so in the usual way – by making his views known. On 13 October he received a request from Sir Frederick Leith-Ross of the Treasury for his views on 'the practical measures which you consider that France and America and other countries should take, and have not taken, to operate the gold standard fairly'.[59] Keynes had not then completely made up his mind, but on 20 November he sent Leith-Ross a memorandum 'Notes on the Currency Question'.[1] Six days later he arrived at a meeting of the Prime Minster's Committee with the chairman, who had made him a member and circulated his 'Notes' to the Committee and to some members of Cabinet. The Committee did not discuss the memorandum at any length: its impact came in the Treasury, where it played an important role in crystallising official views on the future of sterling.[60]

In his 'Notes' Keynes argued, contrary to his August–September position, that the time was not ripe for an international currency conference, for 'it would merely be an occasion for France to exercise pressure to induce us to return to gold at too high a figure and at a premature date'.[61] He thought there was a case for an imperial currency conference, for all Empire countries except South Africa had left gold and many had linked themselves to sterling. They deserved consideration in any discussion of the future of sterling, and a successful, reformed sterling standard might serve as the nucleus for a new set of international monetary arrangements. If such a conference were to be held, Keynes argued, it could consider three alternative proposals: to continue as at present with a fluctuating exchange rate with no commitment to an ultimate range of rates; to return to gold at a new parity; or to manage sterling within not too narrow limits in terms of some price standard. Keynes argued strongly for the last course which involved an amalgam of proposals

1 *JMK*, XXI, 16–28. He also sent copies to Henderson and to the Governor of the Bank.

he had made in the *Tract* and *Treatise*. As in the *Tract* the Bank of England would announce prices at which it would be willing to buy and sell gold or gold-convertible exchange. It would, in prescribed circumstances, alter these prices slowly to take account of changes in the commodity value of gold.[m] As for the price index for stabilisation, Keynes took it straight from volume II of the *Treatise* where he had used the wholesale prices of sixty-two internationally traded commodities. Such an arrangement, he argued, would provide 'a good working compromise between the ideals of exchange stability and price stability', provide an anchor for sterling, maintain the traditional role of gold as the ultimate means of settling international imbalances, and leave open the questions of undertakings with gold standard countries and the ultimate exchange rate for sterling.[62] As for a base from which to begin this experiment, he considered the arguments for a whole range of exchange rates for sterling running from $4 to $3 (depreciations of 18 to 38 per cent from the old parity) before coming down in favour of a target rate of $3.40 to $3.60 (a depreciation of 30 per cent) as one which would not hurt Britain and provide primary producers adhering to a sterling standard with remunerative terms of trade.[n]

Keynes's target exchange rate fell at the lower end of the range under discussion in the Treasury and the Bank of England. His arguments supporting it influenced Frederick Phillips and Sir Richard Hopkins, both of whom had initially favoured a rate closer to $4, to move in his direction and away from the position of Hubert Henderson, who favoured $3.90. Although the officials did not like Keynes's price standard or his proposed imperial currency conference, by working out their reasoned reactions to Keynes's 'Notes' for a proposed Cabinet memorandum, they had to confront a number of basic issues relating to the future management of sterling. In this way Keynes's 'Notes' are part of the story behind the formation of the Exchange Equalisation Account (a fund to influence the value of sterling) announced in the Budget of 19 April 1932.

As well as influencing Treasury thinking, Keynes's case in favour of a low exchange rate for sterling prevailed in the 19 March 1932 report of the Prime Minister's Advisory Committee, 'Sterling Policy'. Although the Report did not specify a target rate, it expressed concern over the recent rise in sterling above $3.50 and recommended a reduction in interest rates from the crisis levels of 1931. (Bank rate rose to 6 per cent on 21 September, where it stayed until 18 February 1932.) Although the Report indicated the advantages in consolidating the sterling area and intra-imperial currency links, it followed

---

m These alterations should always be smaller than the gap between the gold points in order to minimise speculation. This refinement of his 1922–3 proposals, without acknowledgement of Keynes's previous suggestion, appeared again in the international monetary reform discussions of the 1960s under the rubric of a 'crawling peg with bands'.
n He repeated his general proposals, without discussing particular rates for sterling in the Prefaces to the German and Japanese editions of the *Treatise* (*JMK*, V, xxi–xxii).

the Treasury rather than Keynes in its attitude to an imperial currency conference, favouring quiet consultations amongst the financial authorities concerned rather than formal discussions and declarations. Here the Treasury and the Committee perhaps showed more practical wisdom than Keynes did, given the difficulties in dealing with the Dominions on such matters.[63]

The Prime Minister's Advisory Committee also received 'A Note on the German Riddle' from Keynes. In it reparations only entered the discussion because France had claimed that they had priority over private debts. Its concern was with the rehabilitation of German credit. Keynes included a scheme which allowed solvent German debtors to regularise their affairs with their foreign creditors. It came to nothing.[64]

In January 1932, Keynes made his first visit to Germany since he had passed through on his way to Russia in 1928. This time his destination was Hamburg, where he was to give a lecture on 8 January to the city's International Economic Society on 'The Economic Prospects, 1932'. Melchior acted as Keynes's host. Presumably it was Melchior who arranged an hour's meeting between Keynes and Chancellor Brüning in Berlin on 11 January. Keynes's timing was uncanny: on 9 January the Chancellor had announced that Germany could not resume reparations payments after the conclusion of the Hoover Moratorium in June. At the meeting, according to his memoirs, Brüning tried to convince Keynes that 'an "inflationary" programme would shake the foundations of any reasonable finance programme in Germany'.[65] This was probably Brüning's reaction to Keynes's suggestion in his Hamburg speech that Germany would leave the gold standard in the course of the year and end its policy of deflation.[66] We do not know Brüning's reaction to Keynes's suggestion, made in Hamburg and repeated in an article in the *New Statesman* after his return to England, that at this stage Germany and the Allies should finally settle reparations and war debts rather than face 'a general default in an atmosphere of international disgust'.[67]

The Hamburg visit was the last time Keynes saw Melchior, who died from a heart attack at the end of 1933. His speech there concluded with a tribute to his friend:

Hamburg for me will always be attached with the name and friendship of your great citizen Dr Melchior.

It is exactly thirteen years ago that we two first met – in a railway carriage in the station of Trier on the occasion of the negotiations between Foch and Erzberger for the second renewal of the Armistice. He and I were, I think, the first two civilians from the opposed camps to meet after the war in peaceful and honourable intercourse. When we two shook hands in that railway carriage on January 15 1919, there began the long and seemingly interminable series of financial negotiations of which we have not seen the end today. *I* have long

539

ago – thank God! – escaped from the toils of official service and have been a free individual man endeavouring no longer to mould directly the course of events, but to influence the opinion which in the long run determines things. But he has found it his duty for these long and terrible years to wear himself out, serving his country and serving the world too in the direct negotiations between governments, preserving under all provocations and difficulties the highest human standards of patience and truth.

I remember most vividly the impression which Dr Melchior made upon us members of the Supreme Economic Council of the Allies in those early days of suspicion and distrust at Trier and at the several conferences which succeeded it before the revictualling of starving Germany – which was our joint object – had been secured. In this man, we all felt, we met a true representative of the honour and uprightness of Germany. And that, as I know, has been the feeling of the many succeeding groups of representatives of the Allied Powers whom he has met. He had done his country and the world a great service.[68]

Keynes found the German economic situation and the prospective political situation very depressing. He published his 'broad reactions' in the *New Statesman*.

Germany today is in the grips of the most powerful deflation that any nation has experienced. A visitor to that country is offered an extraordinary example of what the effects of such a policy may be carried *à l'outrance*. . . . Nearly a third of the population is out of work. The standards of life of those still employed have been cruelly curtailed. There is scarcely a manufacturer or a merchant in that country who is not suffering pecuniary losses which must soon bring his business to a standstill. The export trades, until recently so flourishing, are rapidly losing their foreign orders. Parents see no careers or openings for their offspring. The growing generation is without the normal incentives of bourgeois security and comfort. Too many people in Germany have nothing to look forward to – nothing except a 'change', something wholly vague and wholly undefined, but a *change*. . . .°

Hamburg, living in a stupor, many miles of ships laid up silent in its harbour, with the elaborate traffic control of a great city but no traffic to be seen, is a symbol of Germany under the great deflation – a worse visitation, if it is to be continued, than even the great inflation was a few years ago. Germany today, still spick and span as ever, is like a beautiful machine

o To Walter Case, he put it more strongly: 'Today no one is making money; no one has an income which satisfies him; no one sees any chance of an improvement except as a result of drastic change.' (*JMK*, XXI, 48).

at a standstill, ready to spring to life at the press of a button, but meanwhile inanimate. But while the machine sleeps, its crew cannot sleep.[69]

January 1932 had originally been the date for an international conference on war debts and reparations at Lausanne. Renewed American isolationism and insistence on the absence of any link between war debts and reparations, plus an uncompromising German demand for a speedy political solution to the reparations problem, led to a delay until June. Keynes, whose thoughts turned increasingly towards 'an all-round cancellation of reparations and debts, leaving America fairly and squarely the responsibility for further difficulties on these wretched questions', tried as usual to influence the course of events through private suggestions and public persuasion.[70] His first proposal did not go so far as ultimate cancellation: it saw the European Allies agreeing to a substantial reduction in war debts and to Germany agreeing to make a token payment for reparations. In return, everyone would agree to let bygones be bygones. The Americans would then receive the scheme as a proposed basis for negotiation. If they rejected it out of hand, so be it: the air would be cleared. In any event, Keynes warned, in words with a prophetic ring for his own difficulties in Anglo-American negotiations a decade later:

> [T]here is no surer thing than never to take the advice of an American as to how to behave to Americans. They always recommend you fudge a little and adjust your speech to an alleged implacable and unalterable 'public opinion'. Yet if you follow this course there is nothing they dislike more. American 'public opinion' is an instance of the Emperor's clothes in Hans Andersen's story. It only needed the voice of a little child to discover to the whole city that in fact the emperor had nothing on. It may only need today the voice of a Europe speaking with the candour and directness of a little child to discover to the citizens of America that in fact they hold no such opinions as each is attributing to the others.[71]

On 9 July the Lausanne Conference agreed to end the Young Plan. Germany's reparations obligations were reduced to 3,000 million gold marks, delivered to the Bank for International Settlements in the form of 5 per cent redeemable bonds. The Bank was not to negotiate any of these for three years; it could not issue these bonds at less than 90 per cent of par; and it would cancel all bonds after 15 years. At the same time, Germany's creditors reached a gentlemen's agreement that this settlement depended on satisfactory settlements with their creditors. As Keynes put it, 'this is necessarily the end [of reparations] so far as Germany is concerned'.[72] The ball was firmly in the American court. Britain made only one more full and one token payment on her war debt to America, as did some other Allies. After June 1933 she made no further payments. Thus ended, fourteen years after Keynes's resignation from the Treasury, reparations and war debts.[p]

The management of sterling was not the only British economic problem that concerned Keynes and British politicians in the year after September 1931. There was Britain's decisive shift to protection, first in the Abnormal Importations (Customs Duties) Act of November 1931 and the more permanent Import Duties Act of February 1932. Keynes was not directly involved. He had withdrawn his support for protection immediately after sterling left gold and made his opposition to a general tariff clear to civil servants, indeed to anyone who could read.[q] None the less, his campaign for a revenue tariff the previous year was cited in favour of a measure of protection and it probably had some effect in preparing the climate of opinion. However its role was probably minimal, given Chamberlain's and Conservative commitments to such a course.[73]

The final strand of British policy on which Keynes expressed his views in the months after September 1931 was domestic macroeconomic policy, particularly monetary policy. Before September, he had repeatedly expressed the view that the rate of interest was too high, but, with the constraint of a fixed exchange rate for sterling, beyond emphasising the desirability of internationally co-ordinated reductions in interest rates, for Britain he could only advocate measures which would raise the level of investment in Britain at existing international rates of interest. Once sterling left gold, Britain could conduct domestic interest rate policy independently of rates in gold standard countries.

When Britain left gold, Bank rate rose to 6 per cent and the authorities in an attempt to raise foreign loans to defend sterling had just imposed large public expenditure cuts and tax increases and appealed for general economy in private expenditure. Before July 1931, however, the authorities had as a proclaimed subsidiary goal of monetary and debt management policy the creation of conditions which would allow them to convert much of the national debt to a lower rate of interest. At the centre of such a conversion

p Germany was still liable for payments of principal and interest on the Dawes and Young loans. Regular payments to some creditors continued until 1939. After the Second World War, these debts were taken over by the Federal Republic of Germany and were finally extinguished on 1 June 1980 (Bank for International Settlements, *Annual Reports*, 1975–6, 126–7; 1979–80, 168–9).

q Sir Herbert Samuel in his Memorandum of Dissent to the Cabinet's Committee on the Balance of Trade summed it up thus (Howson and Winch 1977, 70).

Mr Keynes is 'not now worrying about the Balance of Trade'. In his opinion, the Government need take no special action in regard to it. He had been in favour of an all-round tariff, but currency depreciation is doing what he wanted to do by that means, and better. Circumstances might, however, arise in the future which would change the situation and make some restriction advisable. If so, it would be better effected by a system of licences. And it is possible that budgetary or political conditions might be found to require a tariff for revenue.

was one large issue – the 5% War Loan issue of 1917 which was redeemable at the Government's option between 1929 and 1947. It represented over a quarter of the national debt and interest payments on this one issue represented one-eighth of budgetary expenditures. It was partly because of the possibility of converting this issue to a lower rate of interest that before the 1931 crisis, after the discrediting of the 'Treasury view' in the 1929 election, Treasury officials had put so much emphasis on confidence and budgetary orthodoxy. In the early months of 1931, Treasury officials began to make detailed preparations for a conversion scheme for this issue, drafting the necessary legislation to give the Government powers to act along the lines taken by Goschen in 1888 when converting £600 million of 3% Consols ultimately to a 2½ per cent basis and drafting the necessary prospectuses.[r] The financial crisis put paid to immediate action, but the Treasury had slipped into the 1931 crisis Budget measures the powers necessary if they were to follow Goschen's procedure.

There matters stood until the discussions of sterling policy in the Treasury and the Prime Minister's Advisory Committee. Both of these, as well as recommending a target value for sterling towards the bottom of the $3.40–$4.00 range, favoured cheaper money as a part of the package, although Keynes's more cautious approach to conversion probably succeeded in preventing the Advisory Committee from pressing for an early conversion.

Keynes's reason for caution was his fear that the authorities would not be patient enough and would convert as soon as interest rates began to fall significantly. In his 'Notes on the Currency Question' he stated that: 'The iron rule of the Treasury should be to issue no new loan, whether as a conversion issue or a new loan, unless it is repayable at the issue price, at their option, within ten years, unless it can be done on a 3 per cent basis'.[74] In January 1932, when writing 'Reflections on the Sterling Exchange', he also recommended caution. He later commended Neville Chamberlain's caution in not making conversion a part of his April Budget Statement.[75] By that stage, Bank rate had come down from 6 to 3½ per cent: it went to 3 per cent on the day after the Budget and to 2½ per cent on 12 May.

Matters had moved further than Keynes suspected. From the beginning of 1932, the Treasury and Bank had started to take further preliminary steps to be ready for conversion when the occasion presented itself. By 26 April Governor Norman's diary began to report meetings of a 'Hush hush Committee . . . at Treasury', which continued until 6 June 1932 when the Governor committed to his diary the figure of 3½ per cent. The next day, he told the Treasury that 3½ per cent was possible. Matters were carefully prepared. On 28 June, the Stock Exchange announced, without stating a

r The Goschen scheme required holders of the debt who dissented from the conversion to apply directly for cash. Those who did not so apply were deemed to have assented to the conversion.

reason, that it would be open on Saturday, 2 July. On 30 June, Bank rate was lowered to 2 per cent for the first time since 1897.[s] That evening, the Chancellor of the Exchequer, back in London from the Lausanne Conference expressly for this purpose, announced a conversion scheme to the House of Commons. The conversion was a success: 92 per cent of 5% War Loan 1929/47 was converted to a 3½ per cent basis.[76]

Keynes regarded 'the Conversion Scheme ... [as] a sound stroke of policy'.[77] He analysed it further in a memorandum for the CEI, 'A Note on the Conversion Scheme in Relation to the Long-term Rate of Interest', dated 18 July. This memorandum formed an appendix to its Fourth Report of two days later, before appearing in revised form in the *Economic Journal* for September 1932. In this longer discussion Keynes emphasised the importance of the 3½% War Loan as a first step towards long-term rates of interest lower than 3½ per cent and the various obstacles that the Government would have to overcome if the policy was to prove successful. In particular, the authorities would have to support the bond market 'with securities of different types and maturities in proportions in which it prefers them' and take particular care in avoiding an over-supply of long-dated issues which would react unfavourably on the long-term rate of interest.[78] Given the large disparity which the conversion had produced between longer-term bond yields in London and other financial centres, the authorities should also be prepared 'to sit quietly through a period of exchange weakness which may be calculated to make them nervous, without seeking to redress the situation by any deflationary measures whatever'.[79] Finally, the authorities had to make cheap money effective where it mattered – in the stimulation of new enterprise. This involved reductions in bank, building society and other institutional rates of interest, as well as a reopening of the London market to borrowers, initially for domestic purposes, as well as, perhaps, for a large imperial reconstruction loan. However he recommended continued controls on overseas issues.

By this stage Keynes had begun to doubt whether cheap money in itself would be enough to stimulate recovery. These doubts surfaced first in February 1932 when Keynes re-worked some of the material from his January Hamburg lecture for a lecture in a series sponsored by the Halley Stewart Trust with the title 'The World's Economic Crisis and the Way of Escape'. Before an audience of over 2,000, he set out his view of the causes of the world financial panic. He then outlined his grounds for hope, including the fact that the end of deflationary pressure might produce a strengthening tendency for sterling which would allow cheaper money. He continued:

> I am not confident, however, that on this occasion the cheap money phase will be sufficient by itself to bring about an adequate recovery of new investment. Cheap money means that the riskless, or supposedly

s It had stood at 2 per cent from 22 February 1894 to 10 September 1896 as well.

riskless, rate of interest will be low. But actual enterprise always involves some degree of risk. It may still be the case that the lender, with his confidence shattered by his experiences, will continue to ask for new enterprise rates of interest which the borrower cannot expect to earn. Indeed this was already the case in the moderately cheap money phase which preceded the financial crisis of last autumn.

If this proves to be so, there will be no means of escape from prolonged and perhaps interminable depression except by direct state intervention to promote and subsidise new investment. Formerly there was no expenditure out of the proceeds of borrowing, which it was thought proper for the state to incur, except war. In the past, therefore, we have not infrequently had to wait for a war to terminate a major depression. I hope that in the future we shall not adhere to this purist financial attitude and that we shall be ready to spend on the enterprises of peace what the financial maxims of the past would only allow us to spend on the devastations of war. At any rate I predict with an assured confidence that the only way out is for us to discover *some* object which is admitted even by the dead-heads to be a legitimate excuse for largely increasing the expenditure of someone on something![80]

From Keynes's point of view, this argument, although a variant of that put forward in *Can Lloyd George Do It?*, was a new proposal for state involvement in investment. Essentially, it was an argument for pump-priming – for promoting sufficient investment to raise the level of activity to the point where lenders' and borrowers' expectations changed sufficiently for cheap money to play its conventional role in promoting recovery. During the rest of 1932 it was this sort of argument that Keynes utilised for the encouragement of 'wise spending' – in particular the reversal of the local authority investment cuts of 1931 but also for more substantial state-aided schemes of investment.[81] Such encouragement soon took the form of joint letters to the press – to *The Times* on 5 July signed by forty-one academic economists and to *The Times* on 17 October over the signatures of Keynes, Pigou, Stamp, Arthur Salter, Walter Layton and D. H. MacGregor, Drummond Professor of Political Economy in Oxford. Both letters placed considerable emphasis on private investment and spending initiatives, as well as those by local authorities, but when challenged after the second letter by Professors Gregory, Hayek, Plant and Robbins of LSE on the ground of public spending, the authors of the letter of 17 October were immediately prepared to extend the argument in this direction as well.[82]

As one might suspect from three of the signatures on these letters, the case for the reversal of government expenditure policies had found another source of support, the Committee on Economic Information. By the autumn of 1932, the CEI had prepared four reports – one on the balance of payments (September 1931) and three surveying the economic situation (March, May and July 1932). It had also established a routine for discussing and preparing its reports which tells one something about the consensus reached on the Committee. For each report, the Committee would meet to discuss the topics it would raise and its general line of approach. Then Henderson (after May 1934 Piers Debenham) would prepare a draft for discussion at subsequent meetings. To minimise disagreement over inessentials, the Committee agreed that what each member was supporting in any particular report was not the exact form of words used but the general sense of the argument. Such a procedure and the absence of quibbles over detailed wording proved remarkably fruitful, for it enabled the Committee to avoid theoretical disagreements in almost every report and to maintain a remarkably consistent tone and viewpoint.[83] Such a method of proceeding probably heightened Keynes's influence on the Committee. It enabled him to avoid the problems of the Committee of Economists, where his roles of chairman, chief advocate and draftsman had dissipated his effectiveness and increased friction.

The CEI's first four reports had concentrated on international rather than domestic matters, although the May and July reports had both emphasised the potential role of cheap money. In October 1932 the economists' joint letter to *The Times* appeared the day before the CEI met to first consider the contents of its fifth report. The Committee decided to turn away from the international situation, where it did not expect any speedy improvement, to three aspects of the Government's domestic policies: the balanced Budget, the 1931 crisis curtailment of public works, and cuts in civil service pay and unemployment benefit. All three, it argued, had had deflationary implications for the economy; with the restoration of confidence in Britain's financial position and the successful conversion of War Loan, the time had come for a relaxation of budgetary policy. The Committee recommended an end to discouragement of local authority capital expenditures; reconsideration of the balanced budget; a suspension of the sinking fund and some borrowing to finance increased payments to the unemployed. In conclusion, the Committee mentioned the possibility of a national appeal for 'wise spending' on such things as home improvements and domestic equipment. It echoed these opinions when invited to discuss its report with the Prime Minister on 31 January 1933 and at his request turned its sixth report into a letter, 'Financial Policy, February 1933', elaborating the reasons for the adoption of such proposals at the present time. This 'letter' was discussed by Cabinet, but did not lead to any immediate change in policy.

There is one final piece to add to Keynes's 1932 advisory activities – the Keynes–Henderson Plan. This plan reflected less Keynes's changing ideas than his previous thinking and parallel work by another committee of the Economic Advisory Council. This plan had its origins in a paper

Hubert Henderson prepared in May 1932 with the title 'A Monetary Proposal for Lausanne'.[84] Keynes had lunch with Henderson, just before the paper was written, but his detailed influence on its contents is unknown. Henderson's paper suggested that the Bank for International Settlements issue gold equivalent notes for £1,000 million on an interest-free basis to countries on a formula related to some economic magnitude such as the pre-depression level of exports. In order to receive such notes, countries would have to adopt fixed exchange rates, remove exchange restrictions, and agree to repay the advances they had received as prices rose towards pre-depression levels. The countries could use their notes to repay debts and/or finance balance of payments deficits resulting from programmes of domestic expansion.

When Keynes saw Henderson's paper, he was enthusiastic. He wrote to the Prime Minister on 21 June that it was 'exactly what the situation required' and that a settlement of reparations combined with a scheme like Henderson's would lead him 'to begin to believe that our troubles are at an end'.[85] Although Treasury officials liked the plan, they did not think it was practical politics for the Lausanne Conference. Thus it did not surface in the summer of 1932. However, when the Lausanne Conference, as well as dealing with reparations, agreed to ask the League of Nations to call a world conference 'to decide upon the other economic and financial difficulties which are responsible for, and may prolong, the present world crisis', the Committee on Economic Information used part of its fourth report to put the scheme out on the table.[86]

The Prime Minister gave the proposal a slight push, for when he set up the Economic Advisory Council's Committee on International Economic Policy in August 1932 'to consider the programme of subjects to be discussed at the forthcoming International Monetary and Economic Conference and to advise him [the Prime Minister] personally as to points to which British policy should be specially directed', he included Keynes, Salter and Stamp from the CEI, along with Henderson and Francis Hemming as secretaries.[t] At the outset this Committee took up Henderson's proposal and in its own first report of 11 October 1932 presented a revision of the plan drafted by Henderson, Blackett and Keynes. This version was somewhat less ambitious than the original scheme, for the Bank for International Settlements loans would go only to central banks and governments needing help and would carry a gilt-edged rate of interest. As far as I can tell, Keynes was not enthusiastic about this more restrictive scheme, for when he finished an article on 'The World Economic Conference, 1933' late in November, his general scheme for the printing of international gold certificates was

---

t The other members of the Committee were Sir Charles Addis (chairman), Sir Basil Blackett (both, like Stamp, directors of the *Observer*), Walter Layton, Lord Astor (chairman of the *Observer*) and Lord Essendon (formerly Sir Frederick Lewis, a shipping company chairman).

less restrictive. He repeated it again on 17 February 1933 in the *Daily Mail*.[87] However, as a result of critical comments from the Treasury which suggested that the Committee had weakened the original Henderson plan, the Committee on International Economic Policy reverted to Henderson's original scheme when it presented its second report in April 1933. By then, Keynes had filled out the details of the Committee's proposal in his own way in *The Means to Prosperity*.

There is no record of any member of either of the EAC committees involved or of the Government objecting to Keynes's rather unusual procedure of publishing schemes similar to those being actively considered by the Government. Keynes did, however, give some of those involved a chance to object, as he sent his November article in draft to the Prime Minister and the draft of *The Means to Prosperity* to Henderson, as well as telling Viscount Astor of his plans.[88] It would seem that most welcomed the trial balloon. As well, of course, Henderson's proposals were a variant of Keynes's own proposals for a supernational central bank which could create credit that had appeared in the *Treatise* two years before.[89] Thus the way was prepared for another substantial public initiative.

By this time, Keynes had been 'working it out all over again' for over a year and had started to change his mind in rather fundamental ways. Before discussing the further evolution of his domestic policy advice in *The Means to Prosperity* in March 1933, let us see how his thoughts had evolved.

NOTES

1 Harris Foundation, *Reports of Round Tables: Unemployment as a World Problem*, 303. Keynes's published lectures appear in *JMK*, XIII, 343–67.
2 *JMK*, XIII, 364.
3 *JMK*, VI, 151–2
4 *JMK*, XX, 561–88.
5 *JMK*, XX, 589.
6 For a good summary of the position see Schuker 1988, ch. 3.
7 *JMK*, XVIII, 352–3.
8 *JMK*, XX, 554–5. He raised these doubts again on 1 July in a speech before the Chicago branch of the Council on Foreign Relations (ibid., 558–61).
9 *JMK*, XX, 485, 486.
10 *JMK*, XX, 589.
11 *JMK*, XX, 590–3.
12 *JMK*, XX, 594, a letter to Ramsay MacDonald, 12 August 1931. The article appears in *JMK*, IX, 141–5.
13 *JMK*, XX, 594–5.
14 Kunz 1987, 101, Sayers 1976, II, 397; JMK appointments diary.
15 Federal Reserve Bank of New York Archives, Jay E. Crane, Confidential Memorandum of European Visit, August–September 1931, 16 September 1931, 2.
16 *JMK*, XX, 596–8.
17 *JMK*, IX, 145–9, 240–2.

18 *JMK*, XX, 594, 595.
19 *JMK*, XX, 603–6.
20 *JMK*, XX, 608, 611.
21 VWD, IV, 45.
22 BLPES, Webb Diary, 5190, 23 September 1931.
23 KCKP, Lydia to FAK, 22 September 1931.
24 KCCP, VBCB237 and 238, 22 and 30 September 1931.
25 KCCP, VBCB201, 10 October [1931].
26 The letters are in *JMK*, XX, 617–21.
27 *JMK*, XX, 611–12.
28 *JMK*, IX, 243.
29 Above p. 519.
30 This title survived as an alternative in the preface (*JMK*, IX, xvii).
31 *JMK*, IX, xvii; XX, 611.
32 *JMK*, XIII, 336.
33 Ibid., 243.
34 *JMK*, V, xxvii; XIII, 172.
35 *JMK*, XIII, 176; V, xvii.
36 Hawtrey 1932, ch. VI.
37 For a survey of the reviews, see Dimand 1988, ch. 3.
38 *JMK*, XIII, 219–36, 243–56, respectively. There is also related correspondence in that volume on pages 211–14 and 257–66.
39 Lambert 1963, 250.
40 KCKP, JMK to Lydia, 26 October and 30 November 1930, 20 April and 10 May 1931.
41 *JMK*, XII, 132–3.
42 *JMK*, XIII, 152–3.
43 *JMK*, XIII, 145–6.
44 *Economica*, August 1931, 280.
45 *JMK*, XII, 145–6, 252–3. His easy acceptance of Hawtrey's criticisms raises doubts as to whether, even *if* later scholars can find a theory of output in the *Treatise*, Keynes believed he had such a theory (Amadeo 1989).
46 *JMK*, XII, 252.
47 *JMK*, XIII, 243.
48 *JMK*, XIII, 266.
49 Kahn 1972, 9–10 which reprints the 1931 article.
50 Above pp. 476–8
51 Davis 1980.
52 Clarke 1988, 242–3. For another, recent discussion of this 'multiple' discovery, see Dimand 1988, ch. 4. Clarke and Dimand both provide good guides to the previous literature.
53 *JMK*, XIII, Keynes's proposal 373–5 and Kahn's reply 375–6.
54 Howson and Winch 1977, 362.
55 Reprinted in Howson and Winch 1977, 243–54.
56 Howson and Winch 1977, 253.
57 *JMK*, XX, 613–15. See also, above p. 527.
58 Howson and Winch 1977, 369.
59 *JMK*, XXI, 1–2.
60 Howson 1975, 82–6, Appendix 4; Howson and Winch 1977, 103–4.
61 *JMK*, XXI, 16.
62 *JMK*, XX, 21.
63 Drummond 1981.

64 *JMK*, XVIII, 358–63.
65 *JMK*, XVIII, 364.
66 *JMK*, XXI, 43–4.
67 *JMK*, XVIII, 368–9; XX, 46.
68 *JMK*, XX, 47–8.
69 *JMK*, XXI, 48; XVIII, 366–7.
70 *JMK*, XVIII, 370.
71 *JMK*, XVIII, 376.
72 *JMK*, XXVII, 379.
73 The most accurate discussion of Keynes's direct role is in Howson and Winch 1977, 96–100. A more recent discussion by Barry Eichengreen (1981) covers the same ground less accurately. Eichengreen (ibid.) and Capie (1983, ch. V) both provide an indication of contemporary opinions.
74 *JMK*, XXI, 25.
75 *JMK*, XXI, 79–80, 106–7.
76 For details of the deliberations before the conversion, see Howson 1975, 1988 and Sayers 1976 on which this account is based. The quotation from the Governor's diary is in Sayers 1976, II, 437.
77 *JMK*, XXI, 112.
78 *JMK*, XXI, 115.
79 *JMK*, XXI, 120–1.
80 *JMK*, XXI, 60.
81 *JMK*, XXI, 109–10.
82 *JMK*, XXI, 138–9, 139–40.
83 The notable exception occurred in 1937 when an academic dispute between Keynes and Dennis Robertson over the theory of the rate of interest led to a note of dissent by the latter (below p. 605).
84 Henderson 1955, 103–6.
85 *JMK*, XVIII, 378. The best discussion of what followed Henderson's proposal is Howson and Winch 1977, 114–21.
86 The proposal is reprinted in Howson and Winch 1977, 275–81.
87 *JMK*, XXI, 215–16, 232.
88 KCKP, A/33, JMK to J. Ramsay MacDonald, 25 November 1932; *JMK*, XXI, 167.
89 *JMK*, VI, 358–61.

21

TOWARDS THE
GENERAL THEORY

The extent to which one sees one's destination before one discovers the route is the most obscure problem of all in the psychology of original work. In a sense, it is the destination which one sees first. But then a good many of the destinations so seen turn out to be mirages. Only a small proportion of one's initial intuitions survive the struggle of trying to find a route to them.

(BL, ADD.57923, JMK to O. T. Falk, 19 February 1936)

I *want*, so to speak, to raise a dust; because it is only out of the controversy that will arise that what I am saying will get understood.

(JMK to R. F. Harrod, 27 August 1935, *JMK*, XIII, 548)

Keynes's passage from his *Treatise on Money* to his *General Theory* has spawned a large literature. One of the matters this literature has not extensively considered is the way in which Keynes worked out his new ideas.

For all his books, the surviving papers suggest that at a very early stage *in every case* Keynes drew up a draft table of contents. He seems to have thought of the structure of his argument as a whole even before he put pen to paper on any details. This highlights something that many commentators, starting with Austin Robinson in 1947, have noticed: the important role of intuition in Keynes's thought processes.[1] From his 1909 paper to the Society on 'Science and Art' through his biographical sketches of his predecessors, both economists and scientists, he often commented on the same characteristic in others' work. Thus in the case of Marshall, he emphasised that 'those individuals who are endowed with a special genius for the subject [economics] and have a power-ful economic intuition' normally see 'their intuitions . . . in advance of their analysis and their terminology' and, therefore, 'great respect . . . is due to their general scheme of thought'. He also noted that Marshall lacked the power 'of continuous concentration . . . and . . . of continu-ous artistic sensibility to the whole' necessary for the complete suc-cess of a treatise.[2] He wrote similarly about the importance of intui-tion in his biographical sketch of Malthus and his obituary of Frank

Ramsey.[3] The strongest statement came in his biographical sketch of Newton:

> I believe that the clue to his mind is to be found in his unusual powers of continuous concentrated introspection. . . . His peculiar gift was the power of holding continuously in his mind a purely mental problem until he had seen straight through it. I fancy his pre-eminence is due to his muscles of intuition being the strongest and most enduring with which a man has ever been gifted. Anyone who has ever attempted pure scientific or philosophical thought knows how one can hold a problem momentarily in one's mind and apply all one's powers of concentration and piercing through it, and how it will dissolve and escape and you will find that what you are surveying is a blank. I believe that Newton could hold a problem in his mind for hours and days and weeks until it surrendered to him its secret. Then being the supreme mathematical technician he could dress it up, how you will, for purposes of exposition. . . .
>
> There is the story of how he informed Halley of one of his most fundamental discoveries of planetary motion. 'Yes,' replied Halley, 'but how do you know that? Have you proved it?' Newton was taken aback – 'Why, I've known it for years,' he replied. 'If you give me a few days, I'll certainly find you a proof of it' – as in due course he did.[4]

For Keynes, one can regard his tables of contents as sketch maps of how he intuitively thought of the route through the larger problem in book form. With his simpler publications – *Economic Consequences* and the *Tract* – one or two sketches usually sufficed. But for the complex major works – *Probability*, the *Treatise*, and the *General Theory* – the multiplicity of 'maps' illustrates his struggles to find the route and to keep the whole and the parts together.

Intuition was not present only on large-scale projects. It also appeared in his day-to-day work. Thus he might tell a potential contributor to the *Economic Journal*: 'You have not expressed it in a way on which I am able to bring my intuition to bear clearly'.[5] Similarly, in the development of particular ideas for the *General Theory* it is clear that he had intuitively grasped the essentials of many of them quite early. However, if there was little doubt in his mind about the truth, there was considerable trouble over the proof. Much of the scholarly disagreement over the exact dating of particular concepts has at its roots the criterion of discovery, truth or satisfactory proof. And even the 'proof' is sometimes unsatisfactory to modern theorists. Nevertheless, one of them writes:

> I consider that Keynes had no real grasp of formal economic theorising (and also disliked it), and that consequently left many gaping holes in

his theory. I none the less hold that his insights were several orders more profound and realistic than those of his recent critics.[6]

Believing that intuition ran ahead of analysis, Keynes acknowledged this facet of his own work and, as a result, expected much from his readers: 'Yet in writing economics one is not writing either a mathematical proof or a legal document. One is trying to appeal to the reader's intuitions'.[7] Here lay the basis of his fierce reaction to Hayek's criticism of the *Treatise* noted above.[8] Probably a similar reaction to what he believed to be unsympathetic criticism helped to mar his once pleasant and fruitful relationship with Dennis Robertson after 1931, although there were other forces at work.[9] Finally, even in his day-to-day applied economics, Keynes had a good intuitive grasp of statistical orders of magnitude, which he was prepared to pit against more formal, complete exercises – sometimes rather unscrupulously and sometimes unsuccessfully.[10]

Intuition was only part of the story. A second aspect of Keynes's theoretical work was its essentially practical motivation. Throughout his career he disliked theorising for its own sake and did not rate that aspect of professional activity that highly – or find appealing many theoretical pieces subsequently rated highly by his professional colleagues and successors. One need only think of his dismissive referee's 'report' on John Hicks' *Theory of Wages* (1932),[11] or his later comment on his *Value and Capital* (1939):

> I have now finished reading Hicks's book. I don't think I have ever read a book by an obviously clever man, so free from points open to specific criticisms, which was so utterly empty. I did not, at the end, feel a penny the wiser about anything. He seemed able to decant the most interesting subjects of all their contents, and to produce something so thin and innocuous as to be almost meaningless. Yet, in many ways, it is well written and clear, clever and intelligent, and without mistakes. But about nothing whatever. Simple things are made to appear very difficult and complicated, and the emptiest platitudes paraded as generalisations of vast import. A most queer book.[12]

Rather, Keynes was almost continuously absorbed in questions of policy. In attacking a policy problem, he would use traditional modes of thought until they broke down and then, and only then, would he fashion new tools to fill the gaps. It is not surprising that in his ideal world 'If economists could manage to get themselves thought of as humble, competent people, on a level with dentists, that would be splendid'.[13] Nor is it surprising that he believed that economists 'with their mixed subject matter, are, of all men, the least independent, as the history of their theory shows, of the surrounding atmosphere'.[14]

This intense practicality, which had its roots in *Probability*, coloured his working life as an economist. He defined the subject as 'a science of thinking in terms of models joined to the art of choosing models which are relevant to the practical world'.[15] Not that he put great faith in the simple-minded application of ideas from particular models: when asked in 1944 to comment on functional finance, a theoretical attempt to devise a general rule for counter-cyclical budgetary policy to maintain full employment, he remarked:

> I still say, however, that functional finance is an idea and not a policy; part of one's apparatus of thought but not, except highly diluted under a considerable clothing of qualification, an apparatus of action. Economists have to be very careful, I think, to distinguish the two.[16]

In connection with his own evolving ideas, he made the same point in 1935:

> [W]hat I am primarily interested in supplying is a sound and scientific way of thinking about our essential problems. Before this way of thinking can be translated into practice, it has to be mixed with politics and passions just like any other way of thinking, and the nature of the outcome is something which I cannot foresee in detail.[17]

Another characteristic of Keynes's thinking – not unexpected for the philosopher-author of *Probability* – was that he approached all problems with a desire to get to the fundamentals of an argument. As one Apostolic Treasury colleague of the Second World War, trained in economics, Frederic Harmer, put it:

> I would say that what dominated his approach to any matter was a philosophy – a habit of mind. He was always ready and eager to make the best possible synthesis of the available data, thence to carry this reasoning where it might lead him and to *offer* (I repeat offer) conclusions. But unlike many, he never forgot the fundamental importance of premises and the invalidity of good reasoning on incomplete premises (Propn.2.21 of [Russell and Whitehead's] *Principia Mathematica* refers). So while it was usually impossible to attack his reasoning, he was always ready and willing to revise his conclusions if his premises were attacked and could be shown to be wrong or imperfect. He could be pretty difficult in resisting attack, but if it succeeded – never mind whether from the office boy, or the office cat for that matter – he had a tremendous capacity of always being willing to start afresh and re-synthesise. . . . So the continuing value, as it seemed to me, of so much of his work in that time was provoking critical examination of the facts of the situation – the premises. I never felt that he regarded the conclusions he offered, in any given set of circumstances, as nearly so important as this.[18]

One can see clearly a commonality across his many contributions to public and professional discussions. In his *Economic Consequences of the Peace* he questioned the assumptions concerning the nature of the European economy implicit in the Peace Treaties. In his *Economic Consequences of Mr Churchill* and his later articles concerning the return to gold, he questioned the authorities' assumptions concerning the international economic position of Britain in 1925 and the mechanics of adjustment to an overvalued exchange rate. Again, in his discussions of the transfer problem in 1929 and of protection in 1930–1, he spent much of his time worrying about the assumptions underlying the traditional arguments. Perhaps one of Keynes's greatest sources of influence as a shaper of professional and public opinion comes from his laying bare with great clarity the implicit assumptions of others rather than quibbling over details.

Such an approach made for good journalism – and when he took the trouble Keynes was an extremely successful journalist. He may not have succeeded in moulding opinion in the short run – his campaigns of 1919–31 were *never* successful in the short run, as he recognised when he spoke of himself as a Cassandra – but he did have his long-term impact. His lack of short-term success may have reflected the fact that his time horizon was longer than that of the average working politician, who was (and still is) normally more concerned with what will happen next week or next month rather than two years hence and was used to muddling through and living from hand to mouth. It may also have reflected his passionate hatred of stupidity, which shines through his journalism – and doubtless hurt those he struck out at so tellingly. Yet his style may by its very long-term success have had damaging long-term results, for in his continued showing up of the shallowness of those who held orthodox opinions, he left his followers with a model for professional conduct which in less skilled, knowledgeable and flexible hands proved less successful and may have damaged British economics.[19]

This emphasis on assumptions or premises also provides a large part of the explanation of why he abandoned his *Treatise on Money* so quickly. His critics had succeeded in persuading him that many of *his* premises were wrong or imperfect. This same seriousness about premises would underlie much of the purpose of his *General Theory*. There, he would attack his 'classical' colleagues, not because they disagreed with him on policies to reduce the impact of the depression – he could hardly do that given their joint letters to *The Times* or their service together on committees displaying a fair degree of unanimity in their reports. Rather he had come to believe that their policy recommendations were inconsistent with the premises of their theories.[a] By the early 1930s Keynes, perhaps after the experience of the Committee of Economists, had come to believe

---

a See his remark in the *General Theory* congratulating Lionel Robbins because, in contrast to his contemporaries, 'his practical recommendations belong . . . to the same system as his theory' (*JMK*, VII, 20n). See also ibid., 182–5.

that this disjunction between theoretical premises and policy conclusions was a source of weakness in economists' attempts to influence economic policy. It often led to unnecessary and unhelpful public controversy and obscured the essential issues at stake. In 'thinking it out all over again', he was trying to get his professional colleagues to join him in a reconsideration of the foundations of their arguments.

By late February 1933 it was over fifteen months since he 'began again writing quietly in my chair about monetary theory'. By then, with *The Means to Prosperity* ready for publication in *The Times*, he had obviously moved a considerable way from his position during 1930–1. The question arises whether his renewed and vigorous advocacy of public works expenditures bore any relationship to his 'writing quietly' or whether it reflected other influences.

There is much more evidence for the preparation of what eventually became *The General Theory of Employment, Interest and Money* than for the *Treatise*. The evidence takes a variety of forms. There are draft tables of contents. Although these are fewer in number than for the *Treatise*, a greater number of the related draft chapters has survived from even the earliest stages. Fragments, often running over several chapters, exist for over half a dozen drafts of the book, and there are almost complete sets of proofs over which he corresponded with several other economists. Several sets of his students' lecture notes survive from his annual series of eight lectures which continued to be expositions of his current state of mind. These have been carefully collected, transcribed and collated by Professor T. K. Rymes in his *Keynes's Lectures, 1932–35: Notes of Students* (1987) and distilled into his *Keynes's Lectures, 1932–35: Notes of a Representative Student* (1989). Scholars might not normally put much weight on such notes, because if they were to compare their own students' notes with what they said or *intended* to say in class they might find large discrepancies.[b] They are in the hands of the reporters on such occasions and may have to decide, if they are fortunate, among several reporters' versions when the lecturer's own notes do not survive. In Keynes's case, there are eight sets of more or less independently taken notes, from good students, most of whom later became professional economists, which show high levels of agreement over what seems to have been said. On occasion, there are fragments of drafts from which Keynes seems to have been lecturing.[c] Much more correspondence also survives from this period than from the years of the *Treatise*, not only in the form

b In this connection, L. S. Pressnell recalls a remark attributed to Keynes that if one were too meticulous about making accurate lecture notes, one risked finishing up at university with – a good set of lecture notes.
c The surviving sets of lecture notes are R. B. Bryce, 1932–4; Alec Cairncross, 1932–3; D. G. Champernowne, 1934; M. Fallgatter, 1933; Bryan Hopkin, 1934 (with a few fragments of 1935); Lorie Tarshis, 1932–5; Walter Salant, 1933; Bryn Thring, 1933–4.

of Keynes's letters to Lydia but also in his correspondence with Richard Kahn, which is much more substantial than that with Dennis Robertson during the comparable *Treatise* period. Finally, there are Keynes's own publications, the publications of others involved in the process of creation, and subsequent memories and reconstructions of what went on. Although scholars will always hope for more, it is probably the case that with the *General Theory* they have the most voluminous record surrounding the creation of any classic work in economics, even excluding the continued post-publication material of elucidation, elaboration and defence.

To sort out how far on Keynes was towards what became the *General Theory* in February 1933, or at any other time up to his sending the book back to the printer for the last time at the end of 1935, we must have some notion of the distinctively 'new' elements of the final product. In doing so, I must remind the reader that the book is probably the least clear of Keynes's contributions to economics. If this were not the case, the extensive post-1936 discussions – which continue unabated – as to 'what Keynes really meant' would hardly continue to appeal to scholars or their readers. However I should note that, after some initial discussions of the 1930s and early 1940s, most of this interpretative literature, at least in book-length form, dates from *after* 1961. It followed a period of over twenty years of professional agreement as to what the *General Theory* was essentially about. Much of this seemingly endless subsequent discussion reflects attempts to look at Keynes's work in the light of more recent theories and preoccupations or to claim Keynesian paternity for one's own heterodox ideas. It also reflects the fact that the *General Theory*, unlike many classics in economics had *political* implications.[20] But it also reflects the richness and untidiness of a book that was breaking new ground. The untidiness and obscurity result from Keynes's own 'long struggle of escape'[21] from earlier forms of analysis. There are also reflections of his constant fretting – understandable after his experience with the *Treatise* – over matters of definition and presentation. Finally the room for divergent interpretations reflects strategic decisions Keynes took in the course of composing the book. The most important decision was reflected in a June 1935 note to J. R. Hicks:

> I deliberately refrain in my forthcoming book from pursuing anything very far, my object being to press home as forcefully as possible certain fundamental opinions – and no more.[22]

In these circumstances, it is not surprising that Keynes as a student of Marshall adopted a variant of what is now known as 'the Cambridge didactic style'.

> When faced by a subtle, yet complex, problem in the development of a concept, both pupil and master [Keynes and Marshall] would assault it

with all the resources at their command: logic, mathematics, statistics, intuition. Their intellects were too proud, resourceful, and thorough to go on with the thesis without firmly establishing the connections. Having satisfied themselves, however, they employed a curious device when it came to recording the results of their pursuits. Instead of leading the reader through the intricate analytical processes that their own minds had recently traversed, they would provide a short cut in the form of an assumption whose purpose was to eliminate consideration of the difficult problem they had faced and solved.[23]

If these Marshallian devices were not enough to confuse subsequent readers, Keynes also made mistakes, let his intuition rush beyond the limits of his current technical ability and his formal argument, and sometimes confused an issue by intruding as a social philosopher with a taste for the telling paradox. On each re-reading, nevertheless, one marvels at how much he managed to pack into a book of just under 400 pages. Undergraduates, well-trained by modern standards but fed from contemporary textbook distillations, are always amazed at how much *richer* the *General Theory* is.

After the publication of the book, in almost identical letters to Roy Harrod and Abba Lerner, Keynes set out the stages of his quest:

> You don't mention *effective demand* or, more precisely, the demand schedule of output as a whole, except in so far as it is implicit in the multiplier. To me, regarded historically, the most extraordinary thing is the complete disappearance of the theory of the demand and supply of output as a whole, i.e. the theory of employment, *after* it had been for a quarter of a century the most discussed thing in economics. One of the most important transitions for me, after my *Treatise on Money* had been published, was suddenly realising this. It only came after I had enunciated to myself the psychological law that, when income increases, the gap between income and consumption will increase, – a conclusion of vast importance to my own thinking but not apparently, expressed just like that, to anyone else's. Then, appreciably later, came the notion of interest being the measure of liquidity preference, which became quite clear in my mind the moment I thought of it. And last of all, after an immense lot of muddling and many drafts, the proper definition of the marginal efficiency of capital linked up one thing with another.[24]

This account of the stepping stones to the *General Theory* has four steps: (i) the enunciation of 'the psychological law' relating consumption to income; (ii) the theory of effective demand; (iii) 'the notion of interest being the measure of liquidity preference'; and (iv) the marginal efficiency of capital.

Scholarly accounts of the making of the *General Theory* have usually started from this list and sometimes added and subtracted elements. Peter

Clarke more or less sticks to the list, although his discussion implicitly adds another element – the notion that the whole might be more than the sum of its parts, which had been in Keynes's thought since his undergraduate contact with Moore and can thus hardly be 'new' to the *General Theory*, although Keynes may have recognised the greater significance of organicism in economics as he got older.[25] Don Patinkin, arguing that the notions of liquidity preference and the marginal efficiency of capital were both previously available, the former in the *Treatise* and the latter in the work of Irving Fisher, concentrates on the development of the theory of effective demand, most notably the equilibrating role of changes in income implicit in the multiplier.[26] Robert Dimand, in contrast, adds to the four elements the notions that the labour market may fail to clear because workers cannot adjust their real wages by bargaining for nominal wages, and the analysis of the effects of uncertain expectations on investment and the demand for money.[27]

The dating of the development of Keynes's thought may also be subject to scholarly disagreement for another reason – the nature of the evidence required to indicate that he had fully taken the relevant notion into his mode of thought. At one extreme one could take Patinkin's approach of *Anticipations of the General Theory? and Other Essays on Keynes* towards others' claims to have anticipated the *General Theory* – the exposition of the doctrine in a form intended for a professional readership – a criterion suitable for the question of accrediting a person with a scientific discovery. In his *Keynes' Monetary Thought*, when concerned with setting an upper limit to Keynes's own discovery of the central message of the *General Theory* he did not use publications but rather the evidence of lecture notes and other unpublished material.[28] At the other extreme is Peter Clarke's criterion of 'indications of developments in his thinking which represented his initial insights, even if they were disjointed flashes of illumination'.[29] Such a criterion will produce an earlier set of dates than either of Patinkin's criteria, but one still needs some additional evidence to ensure that these 'disjointed flashes' were more than just the potential 'mirages' that Keynes recollected in his letter to Falk quoted above.[30]

I believe that one should accept Keynes's retrospective account of how he came to his conclusions. In assessing how far he had got at any moment, however, I believe that we must go further than mere 'disjointed flashes' and seek out the evidence that, even if Keynes had not fully specified the route to his destination, he was reasonably certain that his 'flash' was not a 'mirage'.

The first evidence of Keynes's trying to reformulate his ideas comes from 1931. Just after Richard Kahn's September visit to Tilton Keynes toyed with the notion that when resources were less than fully employed changes in investment would lead to changes in output, but that if the share of profits[d]

---

d Profits in the *Treatise* sense of the returns to entrepreneurs above those which left them content with their existing scale of operations.

in output reached zero before output reached its maximum it was possible to have 'an equilibrium position short of full employment'.[31] However, it is clear that neither Keynes nor Kahn had taken in the implications of such an approach. Kahn was certainly at sea,[32] and it is far from clear that Keynes further pursued this line of thought at that time. The depreciation of sterling left him with other matters to worry about and these, plus the usual distractions of the Michaelmas term that had always slowed progress on the *Treatise*, meant that it was late November before he was 'working quietly in my chair'.

When he started again, it seems that he resumed the line of attack he was toying with in September. In a note to Ralph Hawtrey the following spring he was explicit:

> The main respect in which you may find the exposition easier [than in the *Treatise*] is that I now put less fundamental reliance on my conception of savings and substitute for it the conception of expenditure. Also generally speaking I do not have to deal with absolute amounts of expenditure, but with increments and decrements of expenditure. This is, so to speak, the inverse of saving, since saving is the excess of income or earnings over expenditure; but since there are two senses in which income can be used it is much preferable to use a term about which everyone agrees. The whole thing comes out just as conveniently in terms of expenditure. The main object of my treatment, however, will be to fill in the gap of which you complain that I do not follow up the actual genesis of change and am too content with a purely formal treatment of the first and final truisms.[33]

Keynes wrote this on 1 June 1932. He had by then given his first Cambridge lectures since the autumn of 1929 when he had lectured from the proofs of the *Treatise*.[e] Before delivering the lectures, which still carried their 1929 title, 'The Pure Theory of Money', he discussed them with Richard Kahn and Dennis Robertson.[34] When he lectured, Richard Kahn, Piero Sraffa, Joan and Austin Robinson were there 'to spy on me' and, afterwards, to argue.[35]

From this period there survives only a paper Keynes discussed with Robertson, 'Notes on the Definition of Saving', where output and the gross receipts of entrepreneurs are constant; a fragment of a subsequent 'chapter' where these were free to vary; and a resulting controversy with his younger Cambridge colleagues over the second fragment which appears to have formed part of a lecture.[36] Here we see Keynes using his *Treatise* definitions but trying to recast his analysis to allow for variations in output and the implications of movements of output and income in the same direction such that 'whenever there is a change in income there will be a change in

e He had not given any lectures during the 1930–1 academic year because of the Macmillan Committee's demands on his time.

expenditure the same in direction but less in amount'.[37,f] The exposition, which took changes in investment as the source of disturbances, did not have the formal elegance of the multiplier to link changes in investment tightly to changes in output. Nor did the joint comments from Kahn, the Robinsons and Sraffa, even though they did point out, in their criticism of Keynes's own attempt to bound the range of fluctuations, the condition that the marginal propensity to consume would have to be less than one for the equilibrium to be stable.[38] We do not know what passed in the 'nearly all day' of 'theoretical-dialetical' discussion with Richard Kahn and Joan Robinson, on Sunday 8 May 1932, which 'came to an amicable conclusion in the end'.[39] But it was all very preliminary, as Keynes recognised in his discussion of the younger group's 'manifesto' when he referred to his 'present half-forged weapons'.[40] How much of these he revealed to Bertil Ohlin, who 'even the stern Kahn and Joan admitted . . . could talk and argue like a rational being' when he visited Cambridge later in May, we do not know.[g]

During the summer of 1932 Keynes found more time to devote to economic theory than he had for several years. He was able to report to his mother on 18 September that he had written 'nearly a third of my book on monetary theory'. He was far enough on to give a signal of his changed mind and retitle his lectures 'The Monetary Theory of Production'.

Fragments of drafts of chapters, tables of contents, and students' lecture notes show that although Keynes was moving forward from the *Treatise* there were many loose ends. He had begun to make a distinction between a monetary economy and a real exchange (or real wage) economy where money was only a transitory link in the chain of transactions and where money wages were fluid. This attempt to make his break with traditional theory more explicit through a 'monetary theory of production' was to become more elaborate in his 1933 lectures until he dropped the whole notion as unable to do the job he wanted it to – to isolate the distinguishing characteristics of what he called classical economics.[41] He had developed the notion of liquidity preference which related the rate of interest to the relative desires to hold fixed-interest securities and money, going so far, according to Bryce's lecture notes for 31 October, as to state that 'in itself the rate of interest is *an expression of liquidity preference*'. He had had the glimmerings of the marginal efficiency of capital, as distinguished from the marginal productivity of capital. He had picked up the need for the attainment of equilibrium for changes in consumption to follow changes in earnings but by a lesser amount.[42] He had not yet extracted the formal elegance of the multiplier relationship and not clearly seen the equilibrating role played by changes in output. Rather, if there were a decrease in investment, in his 'model' output and employment

---

f Income was defined as the total earnings of all factors of production, including profits in the *Treatise* sense; expenditure as consumption plus capital investment.

g KCKP, JMK to Lydia, 22 May 1932; Ohlin (in Patinkin and Leith (eds) 1977, 162) remembered the visit, but not the subjects discussed.

fell until earnings became sufficiently small that the decline in expenditure *eventually* became less than the decline in earnings as 'sooner or later the most virtuous intentions will break down before the pressure of increasing poverty, so that savings will fall off'.[43] Then, and only then, did the equilibrating mechanism come into play. However, despite his failure to perceive the equilibrating role of changes in output before a certain point, he had captured the 'vision' of a society where the actual level of output could be in equilibrium at less than the 'optimum' output – 'at which, assuming an equilibrium distribution of incomes, every member of the community would prefer leisure to further opportunities to increase either consumption or saving'.[44] To reach such an optimum level would probably require a deliberate policy on the part of the authorities to stimulate the level of investment. At this stage, he still saw this policy as an interest rate policy.[45] Soon this would change.

Most of the pieces were coming on to the table. Now, if we take *strictly* Keynes's retrospective view of the development of his ideas in his letter to Roy Harrod quoted above, then, *if* he had developed a clear notion of liquidity preference, he must have developed the theory of effective demand. This is the position taken by Peter Clarke.[46] Yet, although there are traces of the multiplier relationship present in both students' lecture notes and in his own writings, it is not apparent the penny had dropped sufficiently clearly for Keynes that he could be considered to have successfully found a route for his intuition.

At this point any discussion of the chronology of the development of Keynes's ideas runs into problems. We have few firm dates for any fragments of manuscript until Keynes gave his next set of lectures to the University, again under the title 'The Monetary Theory of Production', in the autumn of 1933. By then it is certain that he had seen the equilibrating role of fluctuations in output that is associated with the theory of effective demand.[h] We are forced to rely on circumstantial evidence for a more precise dating.

Fortunately this evidence is not hard to find; so we can date Keynes's adoption of his output equilibrating model to late 1932 or early 1933 *at the latest*. This evidence takes several forms.

First there is the preparation of *Essays in Biography*. In the course of creating this volume, Keynes took up an old essay on T. R. Malthus. Parts of it dated as far back as a speech on population which he had given on

---

h Patinkin (1982, 18–19) acknowledges that *attached* to the material from which Keynes appears to have lectured on 14 November 1932 is a discussion which envisages output changes performing an equilibrating role, but he argues that we have no means of knowing whether it was included in the lecture of that date, given surviving students' notes. There are, however, stronger reasons for suggesting that it was not, for the language, most notably the use of the phrase 'propensity to spend' (*JMK*, XXIX, 56) would seem to be later. The relevant question is how much later. Given the similarity to his 1932 chapter 'The Parameters of a Monetary Economy', the language of which did appear in the 1932 lectures, it is highly probable that this draft was written soon after those lectures (compare *JMK*, XIII, 404–5 with XXIX, 56 and the Bryce and Tarshis lecture notes for 14 November 1932).

2 May 1914 to the Oxford Political Philosophy and Science Club. He had expanded it in 1922 for a paper to the London Political Economy Club and re-read it on various occasions in Cambridge. Keynes took advantage of Piero Sraffa's contemporary work on Ricardo, which included his correspondence with Malthus, to begin re-working the essay yet again. On 30 October 1932, he reported to Lydia.

> I have become completely absorbed in re-writing my life of Malthus, and sit by the hour at my desk copying bits out and composing sentences and wanting to do nothing else with a stack of papers around me. What a relief not to be writing arguments! What an easy and agreeable life fanciful writers must have!

He was still working on the essay on 20 November. Galley proofs were available in mid-December. It was 20 December before Piero Sraffa invited Keynes to quote what he liked from Malthus's letters. 'Only', he added' 'don't treat too ill my David'. On 9 January 1933, Keynes returned his galleys to Clarks for paging.[47] He finished the page proofs on 22 January and read the new Malthus essay to his Political Economy Club the next evening.[48]

This dating is important to our story, for among Keynes's revisions to his essay on Malthus were additions concerning the theory of 'effective demand' and Malthus's relations with Ricardo.[49] Was it a coincidence that these passages were added in October and November, or that the concluding passages concerning savings and investment and the rate of interest[50] were added in late December or early January? Peter Clarke certainly thinks not, although he is inclined to put more emphasis on the earlier rather than the later additions so that he can place the inception of the *General Theory* 'firmly in 1932'.[51] I am less certain, given the later addition.

Additional evidence favours 1933. On 4 January Keynes took part in a broadcast discussion with Josiah Stamp, the lines of which the two men had worked out together on 20 December and 3 January.[i] In the course of that discussion, the dialogue ran in terms of output reductions as the equilibrating means by which cuts in public spending normally financed by borrowing affected the economy.[52] The line was much clearer than it had been in Keynes's November lectures. It became clearer still over the next two months, first in an attack on the Ministry of Health's restrictions on local authority investment schemes. Using figures from the Building Industries National Council for the primary cut in expenditure involved and claiming that there was 'strong evidence' that there was an employment multiplier of 2, he argued the restrictions had put 250,000 men out of work.

---

i In the presence of a shorthand writer, they improvised a talk, corrected the results, blocked out the general lines of the broadcast with cue words, and then, within the agreed framework, allowed themselves some room for improvisation on the night. The result was a relaxed, natural exchange of views that reads extremely well. For the process, see KCKP, BR/2, JMK to Stamp, 12 December 1932; Stamp to JMK, 13 December 1932.

This brings me to the final piece of evidence, *The Means to Prosperity*. On 22 February Keynes offered a series of articles to *The Times* covering two topics: 'the question of evaluating the real advantage to the Budget of schemes of home expansion' and 'a programme of an international fiduciary gold currency' or the Keynes–Henderson proposals discussed above.[53] He completed the articles on 6 March. His domestic proposals centred on an expansionary Budget containing a mixture of increases in loan-financed capital expenditure of £60 million and cuts in taxation of £50 to £60 million, which would, he estimated using a very conservative multiplier, reduce unemployment by 750,000.[54] After publication between 13 and 16 March, which was delayed a week by the German elections and the Reichstag fire, he began to think of expanding the argument in three directions, the first being 'the train of reasoning by which I arrive at the multiplier relating secondary employment to primary employment'. This article, which he regarded as 'the dullest' of the two that eventually appeared, he placed in the *New Statesman* for 1 April 1933 under the title of 'The Multiplier'. He later incorporated it in the American version of the pamphlet combining his *Times* articles, *The Means to Prosperity*.[55] In 'The Multiplier' he argued that in an open economy with no foreign repercussions, allowing for changes in the marginal propensity to consume resulting from changes in the distribution of income and for less than perfectly elastic output with consequent opportunities for 'crowding out', the multiplier would probably be 2. He also set out the symmetrical mechanism for reductions in expenditure. It is clear that the penny had firmly dropped for the theory of effective demand by the time of this article. As a result, I think Don Patinkin goes too far in his dismissal of *The Means to Prosperity* as a source for dating the stages of the development of Keynes's ideas on the ground that it 'does not specify the broader theoretical framework that underlies his policy proposals'. The American version of *The Means*, which incorporates 'The Multiplier' does just that.[j]

Thus it would seem that by early 1933 *at the latest* the basic output-adjustment framework of the *General Theory* was in place, as were the

---

j Patinkin 1976a, 79. Patinkin (1982, 33–4) explicitly dismisses the American version of *The Means to Prosperity* as demonstrating that the penny had dropped by concentrating on the section 'The Raising of Prices', where there is, I agree, no discussion of the theory of effective demand with the equilibrating effect of changes in output. However, it would seem to me that the penultimate paragraph of the previous section, which did not appear in the English edition, makes the point clearly and explicitly (*JMK*, IX, 349):

> The argument applies, of course both ways equally. Just as the effect of increased primary expenditure on employment, on the national income and on the budget is multiplied in the manner described, so also is the effect of decreased primary expenditure. Indeed, if it were not so it would be difficult to explain the violence of the recession both here and in the United States. Just as an initial impulse of modest dimensions has been capable of producing such devastating repercussions, so also a modest impulse in the opposite direction will effect a surprising recovery. There is no magic here, no mystery; but a reliable scientific prediction.

theory of liquidity preference and the notion of the marginal efficiency of capital. Moreover, by this stage, even if it had not been the case in the lectures of the autumn of 1932, it was clear that Keynes had found a 'route' to his intuitions. This may partly explain the renewed vigour and confidence of his advocacy of loan-financed public works expenditures as compared with his 'wise spending' suggestions of the previous autumn. Certainly such a change in focus underlies the explicit appearance of 'The Propensity to Save' in the 1933 draft tables of contents – liquidity preference had already appeared in the second 1932 version.[56]

This does not mean that Keynes had fully worked out his ideas, much less found the form for expounding them to his professional colleagues. That would take another two years of hard work. It does mean that he had come a substantial part of the way.

Despite the distractions of *The Means to Prosperity* and the subsequent World Economic Conference,[57] Keynes seems to have made progress on his book during the remainder of the 1932–3 academic year[58] and in the following summer. On 17 July he reported to Joan Robinson that 'As a result of a pregnant conversation with Kahn, I've got on to a new technique of expression which looks very promising'.[59] A month later he told Dan Macmillan that he hoped that his book would appear in the first half of 1934. It appears from the surviving drafts of that summer that he also had settled on the title 'The General Theory of Employment'. Elements of tables of contents with that title appeared in students' lecture notes in the autumn even though he had used the title 'The Monetary Theory of Production' when the Economics Faculty had made up its lecture list in the late spring.[60]

Moreover, his students' lecture notes from that autumn show him much less tentative than he had been the previous year. He had, for example, enunciated the 'psychological law' underlying the propensity to consume and linked it firmly to the multiplier to get equilibrating movements in output. His theory of liquidity preference was now well-developed and his theory of investment was taking on the recognisable form which he would later call the marginal efficiency of capital. He appears to have coined the term by the end of the calendar year, although the phrase does not appear in students' notes.

The Michaelmas term's activities also included discussions of his summer's work with Richard Kahn, new drafting and, in December, Piero Sraffa making 'some exhausting difficulties' over the part of the book he had been asked to read.[61] Well might Sraffa make difficulties, for although Keynes had most of his 'big' concepts in place, the drafts and lecture notes make clear that he had still not settled on many appropriate definitions, nor the microeconomic skeleton on which he would hang the behaviour of his firms and workers. Finally, although he had started, with the help of Dennis Robertson, Gerald Shove, and Roy Harrod (who reviewed Pigou's book for the March 1934 issue of the *Economic Journal*), to examine critically Pigou's *Theory of Unemployment*, which had appeared in the autumn of 1933, he had not yet realised that it, and not the earlier, analytically unsatisfactory distinction between various types of economies,[62] would give him the appropriate example of the 'classical' theory from which he was dissenting.[63] Yet he had gone far enough to feel wryly detached from many of his theorist contemporaries. After a weekend visit from Ralph Hawtrey he reported to Lydia:

> Hawtrey has gone – very sweet to the last but quite mad. One can argue with him a long time on a perfectly sane and interesting basis and then, suddenly, one is in a madhouse. Are all the economists mad except Alexander[k] and me? It seems to me so, yet it can't be true. I have just been having a hopeless debate with Dennis. His mind, though frightfully ingenious, seems to me to be maliciously perverse. Again it is like arguing with a madman. But when I talk with Alexander, it is all so different.[64]

The reference to all other economists being mad was to recur later, in connection with Dennis Robertson.[l]

In 1934 Keynes made more rapid progress towards a complete version. Rather than the earlier series of fragmentary drafts, none of which, despite the length of tables of contents, came to much more than a hundred connected pages, large chunks of chapters began to survive into the proofs and final text more or less intact. As usual, 'stiff supervisions' from Kahn were invaluable. On 19 February he told Lydia 'Alexander has proved to me that "my important discovery" last week is all a mistake'. It is from this period that we find Kahn spending part of every vacation working with Keynes at Tilton. Keynes also began to expound his doctrines outside Cambridge lecture rooms, most notably to the American Political Economy Club in June.[65] There was still a lot of work ahead, particularly on the earlier chapters setting out the postulates of his classical predecessors and on the basic units in which he was prepared to work in the book.

By 13 September 1934 he had started sending chapters to the printers with instructions that they be ready in time for his Michaelmas term lectures, now called 'The General Theory of Employment', which would begin on 16 October. By the end of term, the fourteen chapters he had completed to date were in galley and ready for circulation. He was still searching for

k Lydia's nickname for Richard Kahn to distinguish him from Richard Braithwaite, also a fellow of King's.
l KCKP, JMK to Lydia, 4 April 1935. For a longer discussion of the relationship between Keynes and Robertson, see below pp. 497–603.

the best means of expressing himself. For example, on 5 November he told Lydia that he thought his lecture, which had dealt with the units used, the role of expectations, the definition of income and the marginal efficiency of capital was better articulated than the manuscript itself.

In the Christmas vacation Richard Kahn came down to Tilton on 21 December and stayed until after Christmas. After he left, Keynes continued working with growing enthusiasm. He began to speak frequently of revolutionising economics, even though he believed that it would be the end of the year before the book would be out.[66] By the time he was ready to return to Cambridge, he could report to Richard Kahn:

> I have done two more chapters for you, if you have time to look at them. Between them they cover the ground of the philosophical chapter ninety per cent rewritten. I rather want to know what you think of my latest concerning the fundamental characteristics of interest which has been considerably remodelled and is, I think, rather beautiful, if it is correct.[67]

Back in Cambridge on 16 January, Keynes decided to try his draft on Dennis Robertson. The result was more unsatisfactory than he expected. As he told Lydia on 19 February:

> I spent a most painful morning going through Dennis's comments on my book. It must, I think, be pathological. Whenever I write anything which is clearly incompatible with what he now believes, he simply reads different words for what are there.

It is clear from the surviving correspondence that Robertson did have severe difficulties with the book.[68] One of his problems centred around Keynes's presentation of his arguments as an attack on Marshall, whom Robertson went to great lengths to defend from some of the charges.[69] A related problem concerned Keynes's characterisation of the postulates of classical economics. A third concerned Keynes's definitions of effective demand, income, user cost and quasi-rent. Finally, he turned to what would be their main bone of contention for the rest of both their lives, the theory of the rate of interest. However, his real problem, as he put it to Keynes, was that 'a large part of your theoretical structure is still to me almost complete mumbo-jumbo!'.[70] Rather than attempting to resolve these difficulties, after one reply from Keynes which concluded, '*Everything* turns on the mumbo-jumbo and so long as it is obscure to you our minds have not really met', he suggested that he reserve judgement until he could read the finished book. He refused the offer of a set of page proofs in the autumn of 1935.[71] While it is clear that Keynes did make modifications as a result of Robertson's comments, knowing the latter's attitude he did not thank him in the preface to the published book.

In the next five months Keynes undertook considerable redrafting – so much so that he obtained a second galley proof of chapters 1, 3–9 and 11–17. By this time he was trying to keep his outside commitments to a minimum. For instance, he did not agree to go to an international monetary conference in Brussels until he could be certain that his going would not interfere with his progress.[72] He did agree, however, to give a paper on his new theory of interest in Oxford. The discussion was 'largely a duel' between himself and Hubert Henderson. He obviously talked about his work when, on 2 March 1935, Cambridge belatedly commemorated the centenary of Malthus's death, for this prompted correspondence, after 'some hours' of conversation, with Ralph Hawtrey to whom he agreed to send a set of proofs.[73] This set was ready at the beginning of June when Keynes dispatched copies to Hawtrey, Roy Harrod, Joan Robinson and, of course, Richard Kahn. Everything was now in galley bar the last chapters on the history of ideas and his concluding reflections.[74]

The correspondence with Hawtrey was voluminous. Although he remarked to Richard Kahn that 'Hawtrey's comments indicate that he hasn't the faintest idea what I'm driving at', Keynes continued the correspondence with some gusto for more than a year after the book was published. It is worth noting, however, that Keynes did not begin correspondence on Hawtrey's comments until he had finished responding to Roy Harrod's.[75] Although Hawtrey was out of sympathy with the book and as obsessively wedded to his own constructions as Dennis Robertson was to his, there was little of the tension that marked the Keynes/Robertson exchanges. As his obituarist remarked, Hawtrey combined 'great intellect and gentle character'.[76] Hawtrey himself remarked at the end of the correspondence:

> I have adhered consistently to my fundamental ideas since 1913, and in so far as they have developed and grown the process has continued since then. There has not been a departure followed by a relapse. I do not think this conservatism is a merit; indeed I should rather like to go in for something novel and extravagant if I could be convinced of it.[77]

Hawtrey's criticisms, many of which Keynes adopted on points of detail, covered several areas, including such matters as Keynes's treatment of expectations, especially the treatment of actual values as anticipated quantities. They centred on four topics – the marginal efficiency of capital, investment, the theory of the rate of interest, and the role of carrying costs versus the role of interest charges in decisions to hold stocks of goods or inventories. Much of the discussion reflected Hawtrey's own theory of the credit cycle, which emphasised the crucial role of changes in short-term rates of interest in producing changes in traders' inventories.

The correspondence with Roy Harrod was particularly fruitful in producing changes in the manuscript, even though some regard many of the resulting changes as harmful, probably because, although he echoed points made by others such as Dennis Robertson, Harrod did so from a more sympathetic position.[78] Harrod, too, disliked Keynes's treatment of the postulates of classical economics and he thought that the chapter on the mercantilists was, as Keynes reported to Joan Robinson, 'a tendentious attempt to glorify imbeciles'.[79] Most of his comments, however, concerned Keynes's treatment of the classical theory of the rate of interest, a matter which had also bothered Robertson and Hawtrey, and he pushed hard, and successfully, to get Keynes to make substantial changes. In the process he also drew out the rationale for Keynes's rather controversialist tone. At one point Keynes responded:

> But the general effect of your reaction, apart from making me realise that I must re-write all this drastically, if I am to make myself clear, is to make me feel that my assault on the classical school ought to be intensified rather than abated. My motive is, of course, not in order to get read. But it may be needed in order to get understood. I am frightfully afraid of the tendency, of which I see signs in you, to appear to accept my constructive part and to find some accommodation between this and deeply cherished views which would in fact be only possible if my constructive part had been partially misunderstood. That is to say, I expect a great deal of what I write to be water off a duck's back unless I am sufficiently strong in my criticism to force the classicists to make rejoinders. I *want*, so to speak, to raise a dust; because it is only out of the controversy that will arise that what I am saying will get understood.[80]

Harrod managed to convince Keynes that he had not misunderstood his theory and received 'absolution', as well as acknowledgement in the form of a diagram adapted from a December 1934 *Economic Journal* article of Dennis Robertson's, 'Industrial Fluctuation and the Natural Rate of Interest'.[81] Despite these adjustments, controversy over Keynes's 'liquidity preference' theory of the rate of interest – versus the 'loanable funds' theory associated with Robertson – would not abate for more than two decades.

As well as Harrod's comments – on paper and in a visit to Tilton at the end of September 1935 – there were, of course, contributions from Richard Kahn and Joan Robinson. Kahn was at Tilton in August and again in October. Both played a supportive role. Keynes would consult them on the comments of others, as he had been doing with Kahn since 1930–1. In Kahn's case, so little survives, except for the strong traces of his powerful analytical style, that, as noted above, Schumpeter was tempted to give him the status of 'almost co-authorship', just as Keynes was to warn him that the absence of his own publications would result in his 'getting the credit for everything of any merit published by anyone during your lifetime'.[82] Kahn certainly deserved Keynes's glowing acknowledgement in the preface to the *General Theory*. Yet the surviving materials show that Keynes was in control. He chose the destination and the main route. His colleagues and collaborators tried to keep him from unnecessary bogs and to improve his sketch map for his successors – but not always successfully.

By the end of the Long Vacation, Keynes had finished correcting the galleys again and by the end of October 1935 page proofs began to appear. By Christmas Eve he had done everything but correct the proofs of the Preface, dated 13 December 1935, and the index, which was prepared by David Bensusan Butt, an undergraduate King's economist. The book left his hands for the last time on 19 January 1936. It appeared in the bookshops on 4 February 1936. The rest is history.

NOTES

1 Robinson 1947, 44; see also Robinson 1971, 7–9.
2 *JMK*, X, 205n, 197.
3 *JMK*, X, 106–7; 335.
4 *JMK*, X, 364–5.
5 KCKP, EJ1/5, JMK to O. Lange, 10 April 1940.
6 Hahn 1982b, x–xi.
7 *JMK*, XXIX, 151; see also ibid., 35–7 and XIII, 469–70.
8 Page 534.
9 Below, pp. 597–603.
10 Patinkin 1976b, 1098–103.
11 *JMK*, XII, 861–2.
12 KCKP, JMK to R. F. Kahn, 11 April 1939.
13 *JMK*, IX, 332.
14 *JMK*, XX, 37.
15 *JMK*, XIV, 296.
16 KCKP, JMK to F. Machlup, 25 October 1944.
17 *JMK*, XXI, 348; see also XXVIII, 42.
18 Sir Frederic Harmer to E. A. G. Robinson, 8 February 1972 (reproduced with Sir Frederic Harmer's permission).
19 H. Johnson in Johnson and Johnson 1978, esp. 214–15.
20 For a detailed presentation of this argument see Patinkin 1989.
21 *JMK*, VII, xxiii.
22 Hicks 1977, 142.
23 Fouraker 1958/82, 276.
24 *JMK*, XIV, 85. The letter to Lerner, written two months earlier, appears in ibid., XXIX, 215.
25 Clarke 1988, 259–60, 269–72; O'Donnell 1989, 177–8.
26 Patinkin 1976a.
27 Dimand 1988, 128.
28 Patinkin 1982, esp. 11, 16, 85; 1976.
29 Clarke 1988, 258.
30 Page 551.
31 *JMK*, XIII, 371.
32 *JMK*, XIII, 375.
33 *JMK*, XIII, 173.
34 KCKP, JMK to Lydia, 15 February 1932; *JMK*, XIII, 294–301.
35 KCKP, JMK to Lydia, 25 April 1932.
36 *JMK*, XIII, 275–89; ibid., 289; XXIX, 39–42; ibid., 42–8; XIII, 376–80.

37 *JMK*, XXIX, 39.
38 *JMK*, XXIX, 43. For Keynes's attempt see ibid., 40.
39 KCKP, JMK to Lydia, 8 May 1932.
40 *JMK*, XIII, 378.
41 Barens 1990.
42 *JMK*, XIII, 386–7.
43 *JMK*, XIII, 386.
44 *JMK*, XIII, 389.
45 *JMK*, XXIX, 55; XIII, 406.
46 Clarke 1988, esp. 264.
47 BL, ADD.55203, JMK to D. Macmillan.
48 KCKP, JMK to Lydia, 23 January 1933.
49 *JMK*, X, 87–91, 94–100.
50 *JMK*, X, 101–3.
51 Clarke 1988, 267; the original exercise in dating the various additions in *JMK*, X, 71 was the work of Sir Austin Robinson.
52 *JMK*, XXI, 146. See also 148–53.
53 *JMK*, XXI, 163; above pp. 547–8.
54 *JMK*, XXI, 181–4.
55 *JMK*, XX, 168, 170, 171–8; IX, 341–6.
56 *JMK*, XXIX, 62–3 as compared with 49–50.
57 See below pp. 575–7.
58 KCKP, JMK to Lydia, 30 April, 19, 21 and 22 May 1933.
59 KCJRP, JMK to Joan Robinson, 17 July 1933.
60 Thus, for example, the lecture of 30 October 1933 follows the text of 'The Characteristics of an Entrepreneur Economy', while that of 13 November 1933 follows the notation and wording of 'Some Fundamental Equations'.
61 KCKP, JMK to Lydia, 4 December 1933.
62 Above p. 561.
63 Barens 1990.
64 KCKP, JMK to Lydia 30 October 1933.
65 Below p. 582.
66 *JMK*, XXVIII, 42; VWD, IV, 272; *JMK*, XXI, 344.
67 KCKP, 15 January 1935.
68 *JMK*, XIII, 493–523.
69 *JMK*, XIII, 504–6.
70 *JMK*, XIII, 506.
71 *JMK*, XIII, 520, 524.
72 *JMK*, XXI, 356.
73 KCKP, JMK to Lydia, 22 February and 4 March 1935; *JMK*, XIII, 565–6.
74 *JMK*, XIII, 526.
75 *JMK*, XIII, 634. The correspondence occupies ibid., 576–633; XIV, 3–54.
76 Black 1977, 369; see also 394.
77 *JMK*, XIV, 55.
78 Kahn 1984, 118; Milgate 1977; Young 1989, 57–62.
79 *JMK*, XIII, 426; Harrod's comment is in ibid., 555.
80 *JMK*, XIII, 548.
81 *JMK*, XIII, 557; VII, 180.
82 82 Above p. 532.

22

INTERNATIONAL AFFAIRS
AND THE ARTS

The Means to Prosperity had brought together two strands of Keynes's developing ideas. Not only did it contain proposals for a programme of internal expansion in Britain to raise incomes and business profits to such a level that private investment would revive under the influence of cheap money, but it also contained proposals to make such programmes possible elsewhere and suggested that the achievement of such programmes should 'be the central theme of the World Economic Conference' due to meet in London on 12 June.[1] Keynes laid great stress on the importance of simultaneity in such programmes as a means of reducing the adverse implications of such programmes for the balances of payments of individual countries. He also emphasised the need for cheap and abundant credit as an underpinning for the schemes.

This is where his version of the Keynes–Henderson Plan came in.[2] The plan, like Henderson's original proposal, envisaged an international authority issuing gold-convertible notes up to a limit of $5,000 million, although unlike Henderson he favoured using a new institution rather than the Bank for International Settlements. He also followed Henderson in stipulating that countries receiving the notes would agree to a fixed parity with gold. There was, however, to be a margin for exchange rate fluctuations of up to 2½ per cent on either side of parity. Moreover, Keynes continued,

> The *de facto* parity should be alterable, if necessary, from time to time if circumstances require, just like bank rate – though by small degrees one would hope. An unchangeable gold parity would be unwise until we know much more about the future course of international prices, and the success of the board of the new international authority in influencing it; and it would, moreover, be desirable to maintain permanently some power of gradual adjustment between national and international conditions.[3]

To make the note issue have a wider impact, Keynes's scheme saw for each country a maximum quota equal to its gold reserves at the end of 1928 or $450 million, whichever was smaller, rather than Henderson's less precise formula. In both plans the volume of the note issue should be varied to prevent prices rising above a certain level – in Henderson's that of 1928, in Keynes's 'some agreed norm between the present level and that of 1928'.

Keynes was pleased by the general reaction to *The Means to Prosperity*. On domestic policy, he told Richard Kahn, then in the United States, on 10 March

> It is hardly an exaggeration that there are no longer any serious obstacles to a reasonable policy, except Neville Chamberlain, Hilton Young and, perhaps, the Governor. But, of course, they hold the key positions.[4]

Six days later, Neville Chamberlain, the Chancellor of the Exchequer, invited him to discuss his *Times* articles. Before Keynes did so at the Treasury on 17 March, he noted to Richard Kahn, 'Could it be that the Walls of Jericho are flickering?'. He regarded the talk as 'very satisfactory'. The Chancellor 'seemed to be pretty virgin soil and to hear everything with an open mind and an apparently sympathetic spirit, but quite for the first time'.[5] The walls might be 'flickering', but, as Howson and Winch remark, 'not tumbling'. The Treasury was continuing to shift its ground on public works, but slowly.[6] As Keynes told Kahn on 7 April, 'But you mustn't suppose that all is beautiful in the garden. They will move a little in the right direction, but only a very little'. He was to call Chamberlain's Budget of 26 April 'A Budget that Marks Time' and to remark of the Chancellor:

> Mr Chamberlain boasted that he had made no attempt to *present* things as other than they are. He might also have added that he has done nothing to *make* them other than they are.[7]

On the Keynes–Henderson Plan there was more movement, in that the Treasury had a more modest version of it ready for presentation at the World Economic Conference.[8]

Keynes's involvement in issues facing the Conference went beyond the Keynes–Henderson Plan. Another subject to be discussed at the Conference was trade policy. In the months before the Conference Keynes turned once again to the issue of free trade versus protection.[a] He gave two major talks, both of which he published – an introduction, 'Pros and Cons of Tariffs' (published on 25 November 1932), to a series of BBC programmes and the first Finlay Lecture at University College, Dublin (19 April 1933) on 'National Self-Sufficiency'.[9] In both he accepted the basic logic of the free-trade position – the gains from specialisation and exchange.

> The free trader starts with an enormous presumption in his favour. Nine times out of ten he is speaking forth the words of wisdom and simple truth – of peace and good will also – against some little fellow who is trying by sophistry and sometimes by corruption to sneak an

a Harrod (1951, 446) suggested that changes in Keynes's views on trade policy were partly the result of 'revulsion from the futilities of the Conference'. This is hardly a tenable position, as Keynes had made them known *months before* the event. However, it is consistent with Harrod's general attempt to make Keynes's views conform to his own.

advantage for himself at the expense of his neighbours and his country. The free trader walks erect in the light of day, speaking all passers-by fair and friendly, while the protectionist is snarling in his corner. . . .

Nor does practical experience of tariffs in the least modify this general presumption. Quite the contrary. There is no important country with an old established tariff system which has not committed a hundred stupidities – stupidities difficult to reverse, once done, without doing a further injury – stupidities frankly confessed by all understanding people within the country itself.[10,b]

He was nevertheless prepared to allow exceptions, too many for some observers, to the general presumption in favour of free trade. The basis for these was that the world was embarking on a series of experiments to replace nineteenth-century *laissez faire*.

We each have our own fancy. Not believing that we are saved already, we each would like to have a try at working out our own salvation. We do not wish, therefore, to be at the mercy of world forces working out, or trying to work out, some uniform equilibrium according to the ideal principles, if they can be called such, of *laissez-faire* capitalism. . . . We wish – for the time at least and so long as the present transitional, experimental phase endures – to be our own masters, and to be as free as we can make ourselves from the interferences of the outside world.

Thus, regarded from this point of view, the policy of an increased national self-sufficiency is to be considered not as an ideal in itself but as directed to the creation of an environment in which other ideals can be safely and conveniently pursued.[11]

Keynes clearly recognised that such policies had their economic costs. He was unhappy about the nature of the experiments underway in Russia, Germany (where the Nazis, 'unchained irresponsibles', had come to power in January 1933) and Ireland.[12,c] However, the costs were probably lower than they had been in the nineteenth century because 'most modern mass production processes can be performed in most countries and climates with almost equal efficiency' and because in the developed countries at least, traded goods now formed a smaller proportion of consumption.[13] The combination of potentially lower costs and the higher incomes that had

b He then went on to look at the recently concluded Ottawa agreements between Britain and the Commonwealth as an example of what he meant. This caused some anxiety at the BBC, which, unsuccessfully, tried to get him to alter his remarks. (KCKP, JMK to Lydia, 25 November 1932).

c One supporter of the new German régime, Arthur Spiethoff, was extremely unhappy with 'National Self-Sufficiency'. When it appeared in *Schmollers Jahrbuch* in the summer of 1933 the final section of the article was badly mutilated in translation and anything vaguely critical of the new régime removed. Keynes disliked the changes, but allowed the article to appear on Spiethoff's responsibility. For the whole issue, see Borchardt 1988.

resulted from subsequent economic development probably made measures of national self-sufficiency an affordable luxury.

What is perhaps most interesting was the very limited range of examples where Keynes allowed that increased protection might prove useful in Britain in the context of 1932–3. Protection could raise employment in any individual country by shifting the burden abroad, but if adopted on a world scale such beggar-my-neighbour policies would increase unemployment in the world as a whole. His cases for protection were three: infant industries, such as the British motor industry,[d] old industries in the process of reconstruction or reorganisation such as iron and steel, and – in what would increasingly become something of a hobby horse for Keynes as he farmed the King's estates in Lincolnshire and, later, land at Tilton – agriculture. In the last case, his argument was one for diversity in national life and activities while allowing those involved a standard of living comparable to that in the towns.[14] Implicit in his more general argument for the freedom to experiment was his long-standing support for greater controls over long-term international capital movements, and, now, for controls over short-term flows. But when it came down to it, his plea for the freedom to experiment – and to protect such experiments – at least in the British context would have involved significantly *less* protection than existed at the time. Internationally, moreover, his hopes for the World Economic Conference were directed towards a reduction in barriers to trade. Those who have been inclined to cite Keynes in support of their protectionist views should do so with caution.

During late 1932 and early 1933 a preparatory commission of experts for the World Economic Conference met to draw up a draft Annotated Agenda, which mentioned, among other things the possibility of an International Credit Institute or Corporation. This suggestion, raised by the British, reflected the Treasury's current attachment to their alternative to the Keynes–Henderson Plan, the so-called Kisch Plan (named after the financial adviser to the India Office) for the lending of surplus gold reserves through the Bank for International Settlements, as well as proposals for a return to a reformed gold standard. The British also began a series of bilateral conversations, first with the French and, at the end of March, with the Americans. In the course of the latter, Keynes's *Means to Prosperity* proposals for an international note issue were raised by the Americans, only to be dismissed as impracticable, while the Kisch Plan was also rejected by the Americans.[15]

At this juncture, matters became more fluid. One of the earliest acts of the new Roosevelt Administration which took office in March 1933 had been to take the United States off the gold standard. First it had made gold exports by banks subject to government licence. In late March and

---

d It is not clear whether Keynes expected that protection in this industry would be necessary for much longer, for he referred to it as 'a triumphant vindication of the protection we gave to it' in the First World War (*JMK*, XXI, 208).

early April the US Government had issued some licences but not enough to remove uncertainties as to its future policy. During a news conference on 19 April the President made it clear that the Administration intended to let the dollar depreciate so as to raise domestic prices. On 20 April an Executive Order extended the restrictions from banks to all individuals. On the same day, Senator Thomas introduced an amendment to the Agricultural Adjustment Bill which would authorise the President to reduce the gold content of the dollar by up to 50 per cent of its former weight. The Bill, and the Thomas amendment, became law on 12 May. Until the autumn, when the Administration began active intervention to raise the dollar price of gold, the US dollar floated against those currencies which remained tied to gold or whose authorities did not intervene in the exchange markets to influence the course of exchange rates.

America's departure from gold occurred while a British mission headed by Prime Minister MacDonald was approaching New York by sea for further Anglo-American discussions on the forthcoming Conference. The depreciation of the dollar rendered much of the earlier work on an agenda obsolete and brought to the fore the issue of exchange stabilisation. Discussion of two aspects of this issue – short-term policy until the end of the Conference and the possibilities of a longer term arrangement – began in Washington in late April and continued in both London and Washington in May but without concrete result. On 10 June American, British and French central bank and Treasury representatives resumed discussions in London. After several days of meetings, they arrived at a temporary stabilisation agreement for the duration of the Conference. The agreement involved a dollar–sterling rate of $4. It included a technical arrangement among the three central banks to use specified amounts of gold to support the agreed exchange rates and provisions for reviewing the exchange rates if reserve losses exceeded specified levels. Although the agreement was extremely short-term and very flexible, it proved unacceptable to President Roosevelt. The matter was not completely closed, however: tripartite discussions continued alongside attempts to draft a more general long-term declaration for the Conference itself.

During the Conference, Keynes provided the *Daily Mail* with a series of articles recording the attempts of statesmen and their advisers to come to grips with the US departure from gold. He also joined Walter Lippmann, just before the Conference opened, for a transatlantic broadcast discussion of the issues facing the Conference. As in *The Means to Prosperity*, he was prepared to accept the risks of exchange rate stabilisation for Britain in the interests of general stability, a position which the Committee on Economic Information had also supported in its Seventh Report of 16 May.[16] Throughout the early stages of the Conference itself, Keynes was, as usual, fertile with schemes which could form the basis of an agreement with the Americans.[17] However, everything the Conference might or might not do depended on the American President, who in mid-Conference had decided to send a member of his Brains

Trust, Raymond Moley, to London. Until Moley arrived, hopefully with a better indication of what was on the President's mind, discussions stood in a state of suspended animation.

Moley arrived in London about midnight on 27 June. Keynes's appointments book records that he was to see Moley the next morning. Moley recorded that Roosevelt had agreed that he should consult Keynes on the tripartite stabilisation negotiations but did not mention meeting him until the following day when he had already seen a draft of a proposed Conference declaration on exchange stabilisation.[18] However, Herbert Feis records that Moley saw both Keynes and Lippmann on the morning of 28 June.[19] The Conference draft declared that gold should ultimately be re-established as the international standard but left the timing of stabilisation to individual countries and committed them in the interim only to take measures to limit exchange speculation. Moley guardedly recommended American acceptance of the draft to Roosevelt.

When the President's reply came, it was the famous 'bombshell'. Roosevelt flatly rejected the joint declaration and any attempt to reach a short-term stabilisation agreement. He justified his rejection in belligerent terms, referring to the 'old fetishes of so-called international bankers'. When the reply was released to the Conference on 3 July, it raised a storm. The next day, in the *Daily Mail*, Keynes supported the President's message as 'magnificently right' since it invited the Conference to avoid 'face-saving sentences' that 'trifle with the world's problems' and to get down to 'substantial business'.[20] He was one of Roosevelt's few supporters. Perhaps because of this, on the afternoon of 4 July, after he lunched with the Prime Minister at the Athenaeum and attended a meeting of the Committee on Economic Information, Keynes was to be found at the American Embassy working with Walter Lippmann, Herbert Swope and Raymond Moley on a statement which would justify the President's action, yet perhaps keep the Conference alive and rally the countries outside the European gold bloc. Sustained by sandwiches and whiskey, the four men had by 3 a.m. a draft for submission to the President.[21] According to Ramsay MacDonald, if this document had accompanied Roosevelt's rejection of the draft conference declaration, 'It would have saved the Conference'.[22] Now it could only keep the Conference going in a 'desultory and half hearted way'. The conference adjourned on 27 July until an unspecified date, never to meet again.[23]

The World Economic Conference also saw Keynes active in another capacity, as treasurer of the Camargo Society, which presented two gala performances of the first two acts of *Coppélia* and the second act of *Swan Lake* at Covent Garden for the assembled delegates. He subsequently defended the venue and the programme against critics in the *New Statesman*.[24] It was the last programme the Society presented.

From the early stages of his affair with Lydia, Keynes had been involved in her career. He was also peripherally involved in Cambridge theatre and he occasionally did unsigned reviews of the performing arts for the *Nation*.[25] At the time of their marriage, Lydia had expected that she would give up dancing, but this proved not to be so. She took part in Diaghilev's London seasons of November–December 1925 (dancing in *Petroushka*, *Boutique Fantastique*, and *Cimarosiana*); June–July 1926 (*Les Noces*); November 1926 (*Firebird*) and July 1927 (*Firebird*), as well as his Paris season of June 1926 (*Petroushka*, *Parade*). She was increasingly unhappy dancing, perhaps because she had grown plump, and it was only with some difficulty that Diaghilev, after failing to persuade her to dance for the last night of his 1927 London season, succeeded in getting her to dance in a gala for King Alfonso of Spain on 15 July 1927.[26]

Yet Lydia wanted to maintain her links with the ballet and the theatre. Keynes helped. In 1928 he was on the organising committee with Dennis Arundel, Edward Dent and Boris Ord for a Cambridge Amateur Dramatic Club production of Stravinsky's *Tale of a Soldier* and Shakespeare's *A Lover's Complaint*. Lydia danced the role of the Princess in the former and tackled her first English-speaking role in the latter, for which Duncan Grant designed the décor. Keynes provided an unsigned 'puff' in the *Nation* and was the financial backer for a brief London season.[27] Lydia also appeared in another ADC production, *Life's a Dream*, and in 1930, both in Cambridge and London, 'A Masque of Poetry, Music and Dancing' which included *Comus*, *A Lover's Complaint* and other pieces such as Frederick Ashton's *Dances on a Scotch Theme* and a Dowland pavane. There were the inevitable pieces for private parties in Cambridge and elsewhere.

After the deaths of Diaghilev and Pavlova in 1929, the future of ballet on a regular basis in England appeared bleak. The inevitable result was a meeting of possible supporters. Maynard and Lydia were invited. Arnold Haskell remembered:

> I talked with one guest in particular, who was more quiet and practical than the rest. We had an intense admiration for Trefilova. He seemed unusually well informed and I could not quite place him. Whenever I tried to nail him to a definite branch of art, he always escaped. Afterwards I found it was J. M. Keynes.[28]

At a second meeting a Committee was formed and Lydia, believing that it was a very serious step, 'like parting with one's virginity', with great reluctance joined as choreographic adviser. Afterwards, she would remark to Maynard, 'I see why it catches women, it [a committee] gives them an occupation'.[29] Camargo, named in honour of Marie-Anne de Cupis, La Camargo (1710–70) a courtesan and prima ballerina at the Paris Opera, was born. A dinner for backers at which Lydia proposed the toast to the guests and for which Bernard Shaw provided an appropriately debunking letter as a send-off was held on 16 February 1930. Then the planning began. Lydia's letters to Maynard carried regular reports as Camargo prepared for its first production at the Cambridge Theatre, London. Lydia did not dance, but made a speech from the stage proclaiming the birth of the British ballet.

1930 was hardly the ideal year to begin a major artistic venture, even one planning only four series of performances a year and paying nominal fees to its dancers, composers, choreographers and artist-designers. As Lydia put it to Maynard in January 1931:

> *Oh* Lank! Committee for ever and ever one could run 'Camargo' without a committee, only with cash, instead we all meet, and we are all different like Liberals.

Keynes became Camargo's treasurer as a result of the financial crisis. He ran the financial side of the organisation with parsimony: by the end of its first year the Society had produced eleven ballets for £2,500.

By the time the Society gave its last productions in 1933, it had provided six programmes for members, one season for the general public and the World Economic Conference galas. It was 'the fairy godmother for English ballet'.[30] It had provided Frederick Ashton, Antony Tudor and Ninette de Valois with opportunities for productions such as *Façade*, *Adam and Eve*, and *Job: A Masque for Dancing*. The last was an idea of Geoffrey Keynes's, designed by his sister-in-law Gwen Raverat with music by Ralph Vaughan Williams.[e] Lydia even managed to keep her foot in as a dancer – in the gala production of *Coppélia* and in *Cephalus and Procris* (1931), *Follow your Saint – The Passionate Pavane* (1931), *Façade* (1931), *Rio Grande* (1931) and *The Origin of Design* (1932), although she was now turning to other areas – the stage and radio. When Camargo ceased its own productions, it passed its assets, most importantly its sets and costumes, to the Vic-Wells Ballet, subsequently the Royal Ballet, where de Valois and Ashton were to create a national style and an international institution.

The end of the World Economic Conference marked the end of an era for Keynes. After his series of articles for the *Daily Mail*, he had 'given up writing for a living'.[31] Now at 50, he restricted his articles to *The Times* and the *New Statesman* and ceased his elaborate arrangements for syndication. Moreover, until the publication of the *General Theory* in February 1936, he wrote relatively little for these papers or for the profession.[f] Of course, he still did his other jobs for King's, his two insurance companies and the P.R., which he was nursing back to health, but he did not have the demands of

---

e Through Lydia Geoffrey Keynes had offered *Job* to Diaghilev in 1927, but he had declined it as 'too English and too old-fashioned'. It was first performed in July 1931 with financial backing from Geoffrey, Neville Keynes, Thomas Dunhill and Camargo and gave Ninette de Valois her first major success as a choreographer (G. Keynes 1980, 204).

f Between the end of July 1933 and the end of December 1935, Keynes published fewer than half as many pieces as he did in the period January 1929 to October 1930. Moreover the pieces were rather slighter in the later period. See also Patinkin 1987, 34.

a Macmillan Committee, while the Committee on Economic Information took far less time than the full EAC had done. He seemed to be reserving his energies for his book – and, as we shall see below, his project of building a new theatre in Cambridge.

Much of his published work in late 1933 and 1934, concerned the New Deal which had started with Roosevelt's inauguration on 4 March 1933. Initially, as we have seen, his concerns centred on the monetary policies of the new Administration as they related to the World Economic Conference, particularly America's departure from the gold standard. On that he commented to his mother:

> What an affair in the USA! I, at any rate, was taken completely by surprise. My little proposals [in *The Means to Prosperity*] are too modest and moderate for this hectic world. There seems to be nothing between a Government which does nothing whatever and one which goes right off the deep end![32]

After the Conference, his interests broadened to the whole range of New Deal policies, but it was the end of the year before he lighted on a means of commenting on them.

The device was an open letter to President Roosevelt. The idea seems to have come from Felix Frankfurter, whom Keynes had known since 1919 and who was spending the academic year as a visiting professor at Oxford. Frankfurter was Keynes's guest for King's Founder's Feast on 6 December 1933. Two days later, Frankfurter wrote to thank him for the occasion and continued:

> I do hope you'll find it convenient to write the kind of letter that we sketched in our talk for transmission to the President. For he is 'the trustee of experimentation' and I know that formulated directions from you may greatly help matters.

By 15 December, Keynes had more or less completed his letter. He passed it on to Frankfurter, who would get it to the President before it appeared in *The New York Times* and other American newspapers on 31 December. Keynes also offered a shorter version to English readers of *The Times*.[33]

Keynes opened his letter by echoing Frankfurter's phrase of 8 December and calling Roosevelt 'the trustee for those in every country who seek to meet the evils of our condition by reasoned experiment within the framework of the existing social system'. He argued that the Administration had a double task before it, recovery and reform, and that success in the former would make the latter possible, while immediate attempts at reform might impede recovery. It was largely because of their adverse effects on recovery that he was critical of the National Industrial Recovery Act and other restrictive, price-raising schemes. The Administration should instead concentrate on measures to raise the level of demand, particularly cheap money and loan-financed public works. Calling 'the recent gyrations of the dollar . . . more like the gold standard on the booze than the ideal managed currency of my dreams', he also urged the President to end his policy of raising the dollar price of gold by random daily amounts and to announce that the United States would buy and sell gold and foreign currencies at a fixed rate while reserving the right to change the rate to correct a serious payments imbalance or a change in relative prices. Although the advice may have been sensible, the tone of the letter was far from ideal. It sounded, as Herbert Stein put it, 'like the letter from a school teacher to the very rich father of a very dull pupil'.[34]

The effects of the letter are unclear. Walter Lippmann claimed that it was 'chiefly responsible for the policy which the Treasury is pursuing of purchasing long-term Government bonds with a view to making a strong bond market and to reducing the long-term rate of interest', but neither he nor his biographer provided any basis for this statement.[35] The general conclusion seems to be that it had little, if any effect.

Keynes continued to keep an eye on America. On 13 January he made a sympathetic BBC broadcast on 'Roosevelt's Economic Experiments', while in the *New Statesman* of 20 January he welcomed the President's 15 January request to Congress for power to fix the gold value of the dollar at between 50 and 60 per cent of its previous parity.[36] The legislation went through Congress quickly and, by a proclamation of 31 January 1934 under the Gold Reserve Act, Roosevelt fixed the value of the dollar at 59.06 per cent of its old parity, thus establishing a gold price of $35 per fine ounce that was to last until 1971.

Keynes soon had an opportunity to observe American affairs at first hand – 'to pay a visit of inquisitiveness to your side' as he told Walter Lippmann on 28 April. Columbia University had offered him an honorary degree. Working around the 5 June date of the Columbia convocation, he sailed to America aboard the *Olympic* on 9 May and arrived in New York, after the *Olympic* had struck and sunk the Nantucket Shoals lightship, on 15 May. Using Walter Case's New York investment firm, Case Pomeroy and Company as his base, he moved widely in New York circles, attending, for example, a dinner in his honour sponsored by the Council on Foreign Relations on 21 May,[g] a lunch on 22 May at the Federal Reserve Bank of New York with Carl Snyder and W. Randolph Burgess, and a dinner on 23 May with Raymond Moley.

He went on to Washington for a series of meetings that covered 25–30 May. He was very busy: on 25 May he saw Frances Perkins, the Secretary of Labor, Justice Brandeis, William Phillips, an Under-Secretary at the State Department, and Rexford Tugwell before an evening party thrown by Herbert Feis of the State Department; the next day he saw Kenneth Bewley of the British Embassy and Henry Morgenthau Jr., the Secretary of the Treasury before having dinner with Calvin Hoover, an economist from

---

g Among the guests were Walter Case, Allen and John Foster Dulles, William Langer, Russell C. Leffingwell, Ogden Mills, Wesley Mitchell, Walter Stewart and John Henry Williams.

Duke University who was then 'a minor brain truster' and whose book on Russia he had introduced to Macmillans. Sunday he had four appointments, including W. W. Rieffler of the Federal Reserve and Senator Costigan of Colorado, while Monday brought meetings at the Brookings Institution, then noted for its conservatively critical stance towards the New Deal, and with Joseph B. Eastman, the Federal Commissioner of Transportation, before he saw the President for an hour at 5.15 and dined with Thomas Corcoran of the Reconstruction Finance Corporation. The next day, he saw Louis Bean of the Agricultural Adjustment Administration, addressed a group of senators at lunch in the Senate on internal recovery policy and talked to a dinner meeting of National Recovery Administration organisers. No wonder he complained to Lydia of being tired and knowing 'much more than one small head can hold!'.[37]

On his meeting with the President, reports differ. Keynes found it 'fascinating' and 'made some Jenkins notes about his personal appearance', concentrating on his hands which he compared to Sir Edward Grey's.[38] He was surprised at the President's economic illiteracy, while the President thought 'He must be a mathematician rather than a political economist'.[39] Roosevelt reported to Felix Frankfurter, 'I had a grand talk and liked him immensely'.[40] However, to ask whether, on the basis of an hour's talk, Keynes influenced the future shape of the New Deal seems rather beside the point. Keynes probably learned more than the President.

Keynes spent the remaining days of his visit in and around New York. Over the weekend of 1–4 June, he spent some time at a National Industrial Conference Board meeting. On 5 June, his 51st birthday, he received his honorary degree at Columbia convocation. He gave a speech to the American Political Economy Club and attended a special farewell dinner at Case Pomeroy and Company before he and Lydia left New York on the *Olympic* on 8 June.

For the meeting of the American Political Economy Club, whose members included Wesley Mitchell, J. M. Clark, A. D. Gayer, James Angell, Joseph Schumpeter, Adolf Berle and Alvin Hansen, Keynes's paper was in three parts. The first was 'The Theory of Effective Demand', the second 'The Principle of the Multiplier' and the third attempted to address the contemporary American situation in the light of the theory he had outlined and the statistics he had been able to gather in Washington and New York.[41] Keynes presented the bare bones of his *General Theory* as it had evolved so far, including the propensities to consume and to invest and the theory of the multiplier with its leakages fully set out and with rough estimates of the lags involved that suggested that the effects of the multiplier did not reach their peak 'for at least a year'. He used the theory to analyse events over the past year and to suggest that, because of a flattening out of loan-financed expenditures by the Government the economy was probably in the middle of a mild recession. He argued that, 'as nothing is to be hoped for from business', official policy would be the key to recovery for some time to come.

The day before he met the American Political Economy Club, Keynes put his views in a more popular form, sending a copy to the White House on 5 June before they appeared as an 'Agenda for the President' in *The New York Times* on 10 June and *The Times* in London the next day. He put the issue as follows:

> I see the problem of recovery . . . in the following light. How soon will normal business enterprise come to the rescue? What measures can be taken to hasten the return of normal enterprise? On what scale, by which expedients and for how long is abnormal Government expenditure advisable?[42]

Arguing that business confidence was 'singularly lacking', in part because of the Administration's own policies, he suggested that for at least six months and probably a year recovery would depend mainly on the stimulus supplied by the authorities in the form of emergency expenditures. The authorities had started the year well, but recent declines in expenditure had been unfortunate. Expenditure of the order of $400 million a month (or what he thought was about 11 per cent of national income) was probably necessary for the next year. He suggested five ways in which the Administration could increase the effectiveness of its recovery policies: investment in housing and the railroads, re-opening the capital market after the turmoil following the recent securities and exchange legislation, reducing the long-term rate of interest to 2½ per cent (coupled with reductions in the maximum rate paid on savings deposits to 2½ per cent initially and 1 per cent eventually), and keeping exchange rate policy unchanged. Later he supplemented the article with a letter making corrections to his statistics.[43]

In the months that followed his American visit, Keynes made two further comments on the situation there. In November, he provided the Committee on Economic Information of the EAC with more detailed estimates of US Treasury emergency expenditures. In December he took the affirmative side of the reply to the question 'Can America Spend its Way into Recovery?' in *Redbook*. Harold Laski took the opposite view.[44]

So much for the extent and timing of Keynes's discussions of American conditions and policies in 1934, following his open letter to the President. Did they have any effect? I have already dealt with his interview with the President. There remains the more general, and nebulous question of influence. The question is complicated by the fact that, as in Britain, Keynes was not alone in advocating increased, loan-financed government expenditure as the key to recovery. Jacob Viner and a number of economists at the University of Chicago, for example, had been advocating the same policy in the United States for over a year, and there was a measure of agreement within the economics profession on the general lines of the argument, although also some opposition.[45] Most of this thinking had developed without contact with Keynes and his evolving new ideas – which is hardly surprising, since his own previous advocacy of public works in 1924 and 1928–31 needed no such stimulus.

The arguments of *Can Lloyd George Do It?* could easily be recast into the American context. Moreover the inclusion of the core of that pamphlet in *Essays in Persuasion*, which sold better in America than in Britain, made what had started life as a piece of campaign literature widely available.[46] His Halley Stewart Lecture on *The World's Economic Crisis and the Way of Escape* had appeared in *The Atlantic Monthly* for May 1932. This lecture had concluded with an advocacy of an expansion of loan-financed public expenditure, but one without any theoretical justification. That justification came in a more substantial way in *The Means to Prosperity*, the American edition of which differed substantially from the British version with its inclusion of 'The Multiplier'. Thus Keynes's ideas had received some American exposure before his open letter of 31 December 1933 or his arrival in New York on 15 May 1934.

It is hard to argue that Keynes was influential, *except* as one element in a very complex atmosphere. As of 1933–4 Keynes had not published the full, formal economic analysis underlying his views on fiscal policy. Yet his case for pump-priming expenditures was widely shared: Jacob Viner shared so much of the same ground that his not uncritical review of the *General Theory* let this whole matter pass without comment. Keynes's speech to the American Political Economy Club could not fill the analytical gap: it was impossible in a single paper to set out his own theory, then still in evolution, in full detail and apply it to American conditions. No, the distinctive analytical contribution would come later. In the interim all that Keynes could do was hint broadly where he was going and give heart to those who were advocating similar policies irrespective of their theoretical perspective. Keynes himself remarked after *The New York Times* pointed to the importance of his influence after his meeting with senators where he supported the National Housing Bill then before Congress, '[M]y alleged influence is no more than a dream of the journalists'.[47,h]

After the demise of Camargo, Lydia pursued a career as an actress. As Olivia in Tyrone Guthrie's production of *Twelfth Night* at the Old Vic between 18 September and 7 October 1933, she was not a success for the press or Bloomsbury. Virginia Woolf called her performance 'a dismal farce'.[48] In March 1934 as Nora in the Cosmopolitan Theatre's centenary production of *A Doll's House* she was 'a triumphant success', although Keynes had to meet £47 11s. of his £125 guarantee.[49] By this time, however, Keynes was planning on a larger scale.

h As for Keynes's influence on this particular piece of legislation, which became law on 28 June 1934, one can at most suggest that his intervention 'may have contributed to the turning point' in its passage (*JMK*, XXI, 321), but as he saw only nine senators one suspects that it was a small contribution.

When I last discussed Keynes's activities as in investor on his own account, I carried the story down to the slump, although I carried some particular details, such as the P.R. Finance Company, further. But as much of what follows depended on Keynes's personal financial resources, an examination of his financial position in the 1930s is necessary.

Whereas in the 1920s Keynes was generally less successful than the market, after 1929 his investments (treating Wall Street and London separately) outperformed the market on 21 of the 30 available accounting years and did so cumulatively by a large margin. Thus from a net worth of £7,815 on 31 December 1929, his net assets rose to a peak of £506,522 in 1936 before falling in the ensuing slump to around £200,000. They then recovered to £411,238 at the end of 1945.

More than in the early 1920s, a few securities dominated the portfolio: in 1929, 1937 and 1945 four or fewer securities accounted for half of his sterling portfolio, while in 1937 three securities accounted for more than half of his dollar-denominated holdings.[i] As he told Francis Scott of the Provincial in 1934:

> I get more and more convinced that the right method of investment is to put fairly large sums into enterprises which one thinks one knows something about and in the management of which one thoroughly believes. It is a mistake to think that one spreads one's risk by spreading too much between enterprises about which one knows little and has no reason for special confidence. Obviously this principle ought not to be carried too far. The real limitation, however, on its application in practice is in my experience the small number of enterprises about which at any given time one feels in this way. One's knowledge and experience are definitely limited and there are seldom more than two or three enterprises at any given time in which I personally feel myself entitled to put *full* confidence.[50]

Or, as he told the investment committee of the Provincial in 1938:

> To carry one's eggs in a great number of baskets, without having time or opportunity to discover how many have holes in the bottom, is the surest way to increasing risk and loss.[51]

Keynes's particularly successful baskets after 1929 included car company shares (Austin and Leyland), gold shares, American utilities and, later, aircraft firms.

In addition to large holdings, Keynes's investment policy became one of taking long views. He ceased trying to predict turning points in the credit cycle. Instead, as he put it, he concentrated on 'a careful selection of a few

---

i In May 1931, almost two-thirds of his portfolio was in two firms, both in the same industry.

investments (or a few types of investments) having regard to their cheapness in relation to their probable actual and potential *intrinsic* value . . . in relation to alternative investments at the time'.[52] Although he was an active investor, as ready as the next person to make small dealing gains from turns in the market, with his favourites, as with his speculations, Keynes was extremely stubborn during short-term market fluctuations. The story of his estimating the cubic capacity of King's Chapel for possible use as a grain store is true: on that occasion he did take delivery and eventually made money.[53] He even came to see a virtue in steadfastness and aiming primarily at long-term results, as readers of the largely autobiographical Chapter 12 of his *General Theory* were to learn. But the concentrated holdings, the stubbornness and the fact that a very large proportion of the portfolio was carried on borrowed money (at its peak at the end of 1936 his account books showed loans of £299,347) meant that Keynes always ran the risk of a repetition of the events of 1928–9 when his losses speculating on rubber had proved disastrous to his net worth. The combination of his heart attack and the slump of 1937–8 did just that, playing havoc with his net worth and his nerves.

Yet, despite the ups and downs, it is still the case that by 1934, with his net assets at almost £150,000, Keynes was a wealthy person. Now he was determined to use his wealth for a public purpose.

Keynes broached a possible scheme for a theatre to Lydia on 20 November 1933.

> I gave a rather good lecture this morning. Since then I've been amusing myself thinking out a plan to build a small, very smart, modern theatre for the College. Will you agree to appear in the first performance if it comes off? The argument is this. The ADC has been burnt down.[j] Our [King's] Peas Hill site, on which we intend to build soon, is of ideal size and position. Why should we not join with the ADC? – build a really good theatre to hold 400 to 500, give them Club rooms and certain rights over the theatre (say for four weeks in the year) and have the theatre to let as we choose for the rest of the year. The project fascinates me and I already begin to draw plans of my own for it.

The next Sunday he had a further report:

> I attended the Commee of the ADC on Friday and explained to the boys as well as I could how beautiful the new theatre would be. But I think they will refuse. The choice for them is between having their present affair as all their own and having something good which is not all their own; and they will probably prefer the first. However if the plan looks practical when we have gone into the details, I daresay we may go forward with it all the same as our own theatre.[54]

j It had lost its stage in a fire at the beginning of November.

The need for a theatre in Cambridge was all the more pressing because the town's two commercial theatres had also closed – the New Theatre to become a cinema and the Festival Theatre, famous beyond Cambridge for its productions of the late 1920s and early 1930s, because it had run out of wealthy backers. The site Keynes was thinking of was the interior of a piece of King's land bounded by Peas Hill, St Edward's Passage and Bene't Street where the College was talking of building an undergraduate hostel. The problem was how to bring the idea to fruition.

Despite his initial doubts, Keynes continued discussions with the ADC, who had a long and more encouraging meeting with him on 26 January 1934. The meeting was sufficiently encouraging for him to get authority on 17 February from the College's Estates Committee and Governing Body to continue discussions with the ADC, to draw up preliminary plans and to obtain estimates for both a theatre and a hostel. At this stage the plan was for King's to run the theatre. Keynes began planning with George Kennedy, the architect for the hostel who had already done some building for Keynes at Tilton, as well as for King's, and who had designed the Tavistock Theatre in London.

Matters moved slowly during the rest of the Lent and Easter terms. The ADC finally declined the proposal authorised by King's Governing Body in February, but this did not halt the planning. In fact, during the Easter term, Keynes approached Norman Higgins, who had founded the Cosmopolitan Cinema in Cambridge the previous year, and asked him if he would transfer his equipment to the proposed theatre and act as general manager. There was still the need for a College decision on the project. Keynes approached the Governing Body in July. He argued that he was convinced that there was no alternative to a theatre for the interior of the Peas Hill site; that the consequential loss of undergraduate rooms would be a necessary result of any other use made of the interior of the site, not just of a theatre; and that a theatre would be a good symbol of the interest in the theatre of his own Cambridge generation. He also revealed that, if the College was prepared to consider the theatre, as a fallback, he was prepared as a private individual to form a private company for the project. Despite the arguments of some younger enthusiasts, the College declined to get involved as a theatre owner, but it did agree to entertain a concrete proposal from Keynes in the Michaelmas term of 1934.

Keynes then moved to make his private scheme reality. He arranged a meeting of himself, Higgins, Miss J. M. Harvey (who had been Secretary of Camargo), Kennedy and George ('Dadie') Rylands (who had been involved in the theatre since his arrival in Cambridge in 1920 and in several theatrical ventures with Keynes) at Tilton over 15 and 16 September 1934. Plans were discussed, costs estimated and arrangements made to form a company for the purpose. On their way back to Cambridge on the Sunday, Higgins and Kennedy stopped at Glyndebourne to examine John Christie's new opera house, while Keynes, Lydia and Dadie went to Leonard and Virginia Woolf at Rodmell, where the atmosphere was subdued because of Roger Fry's death the previous Sunday.[55] The Tilton meeting had served its purpose: Keynes could develop his scheme for College approval. It went through the Estates Committee in October and Governing Body in November. The memorandum and articles of agreement for The Arts Theatre of Cambridge were registered on 14 December 1934. The company was to have a capital of £15,000, divided equally into ordinary £1 shares and £1 preference shares yielding 6 per cent.

Keynes expected to take up most of the ordinary shares and to dispose of the preference shares to Cambridge well-wishers. The response proved disappointing: only 2,350 preference shares were taken up. This, plus an increase in the company's capital and a loan to cover higher than expected costs, meant that by the time the theatre opened Keynes had taken up 12,500 ordinary shares and provided an interest-free loan of £17,450. As he put it to Lydia, when the initial offer of preference shares proved unsuccessful: 'The greatest comfort of all, I think, from having some money is that one doesn't need to badger other people for it!'.[56] Sean O'Casey, after receiving an invitation from David Garnett to meet him and Keynes in Cambridge for dinner on 31 October 1935,[k] noted

> I thank you for your kind invitation to meet yourself and Mr Keynes – though it sounds ominous to hear that he is building a repertory, or any other kind of a theatre, in Cambridge, or anywhere else. Is it out of his mind he is. He'll probably say I'm out of my mind when he hears my criticism of any idea to build any theatre here in England. Better by far to build a Convalescent Home for the English Dramatic Critics.[57]

During construction, Keynes took an all-embracing interest in the venture. This interest was to continue for the rest of his life. He took Lydia's advice and experience into account in ensuring the dressing rooms were as large and convenient as possible, concerned himself with the staffing of the proposed restaurant with direct access to the theatre and considered possible productions, particularly regular visits by the Vic-Wells ballet and opera companies whose needs set the standard for the orchestra pit. He also began looking for a house in St Edward's Passage that he could convert into a *pied-à-terre* for Lydia, little knowing how important it would eventually be for himself. The theatre opened on 3 February 1936, the eve of publication of the *General Theory*, with a gala programme danced by the Vic-Wells Ballet. Lydia was ecstatic, writing the next day, 'I am still delighted with the theatre. . . . It was more than nice of you to do it for me, your shank'.[58]

Keynes financed an opening season of four Ibsen plays – *A Doll's House, Hedda Gabler, Rosmersholm,* and *The Master Builder*, with Lydia in the

k Neville Keynes also attended (KCKP, JMK to Lydia, 28 October 1935).

female lead for the first and last. He provided an unsigned introduction to the programme for these plays he had come to love so many years before.[59] Nor was this Lydia's last performance in the theatre: in 1937 she played Célèmine in Molière's *The Misanthrope*, part of a programme which included a short ballet *Harlequin in the Street* with choreography by Ashton and costumes and setting by André Derain; in 1938 she took the female lead in Auden and Isherwood's *On the Frontier*. Keynes financed all the productions in which Lydia appeared: for *On the Frontier* he also acted as the producer. He also guaranteed the Vic-Wells' visits until 1938.

It took two years of careful, hard work to get the theatre on its financial feet. Keynes worked as hard as he could – and worked others hard, as Dadie Rylands noted when he and Keynes were discussing Higgins' exhaustion from overwork:

> But when, you ask, am I coming to the MORAL lecture? I come to it now. You must realise more than you do that you are known to be a hard taskmaster; Richard [Kahn] knows it, [Provost] Sheppard knows it, and I know it. You are very nearly as hard as the old Woolf.[1] Your fault is that you always drive a willing horse. Your excuse and defence are that work comes much more easily to you than to others; that you deal in general policy and large views and have forgotten the time and labour involved in the *detail* of execution . . . Then again you win the devotion of those who work for you as well as their admiration and that makes it impossible to complain; your position in the country and College is so important that we are ashamed to worry you with little things; you have too little use for those whose hearts are in the right place but have not the brains; e.g. Philbeam, Rylands, etc. (Grand exception Hugh Durnford.)
>
> Now Maynard, I am not pleased with you. . . . I cannot serve as a director if Victorian factory conditions are to be allowed.[60]

In this case, Keynes took the advice and mended his ways, at least for a time. He participated in all aspects of the enterprise, from running the box office, through the restaurant and the details of wine pricing, to reading plays in manuscript and seeing them through to production. On reading Auden and Isherwood's *The Ascent of the F6*, he reported himself 'much disappointed' as

> almost the greater part of it strikes me as puerile and perfunctory equally in theme, sentiment and diction. Since both the authors are as clever as monkeys, this return on their part to a sort of infantilism must be presumed to be deliberate. Yet I cannot but think that the play might strike the audience, as it strikes me, as being in the nature of a charade composed by exceedingly gifted boys of about 15 or 16 years of age.[61]

---

1 Leonard Woolf, for whom Rylands worked on the Hogarth Press.

Later he met Auden and was impressed, despite his fingernails. They talked of the play and Keynes took it in April 1937 for his theatre. When it was performed, he told T. S. Eliot that it was

> the best play of the year. But I remained exceedingly discontented with a good deal of it and angry that being so good it should not be better for the gifts in it seemed to be from God and the errors avoidable.[62]

And he took their next production. Before taking it, he invited the two of them to Tilton where they were the first visitors he had received in six months.[63]

Once the theatre was on its feet, he took the next step and in 1938 transformed The Arts Theatre, Cambridge, Limited into a trust. He arranged a mortgage from Barclays Bank for £12,000 to retire the remainder of his outstanding interest-free loan, gave the trustees his 12,500 shares, and agreed over the next seven years to give the trustees £5,000 so that they could take up the 5,000 unissued preference shares. The trustees were to be two representatives of the town, two from the University, plus the Provost of King's, Dadie Rylands and himself. He regarded the trust as a memorial to his parents' service to the town and the University over the previous half century.[64] Turning the theatre over to a trust incidentally had long-term advantages, for the deed of trust met the approval of the Customs and Excise. This meant that the theatre could apply for exemption from payment of entertainment duty for programmes of a partly educational character. This benefited the finances of the theatre so much that it had by 1946 repaid its mortgage and bought out the remaining preference shareholders. It also provided occasional humour:

> I am sure that you will like to know that the Customs have asked for a script or synopsis of 'The Wild Duck' to prove that the exhibition will contribute to the education of the audience.[65]

NOTES

1 *JMK*, IX, 355.
2 The Plan appears in *JMK*, IX, 357–64.
3 *JMK*, IX, 362.
4 KCKP, JMK to Richard Kahn, 10 March 1933.
5 *JMK*, XXI, 168.
6 Howson and Winch 1977, 128–31.
7 *JMK*, XXI, 194–7.
8 Howson and Winch 1977, 119–21.
9 *JMK*, XXI, 204–20, 233–46.
10 *JMK*, XXI, 205–6.
11 *JMK*, XXI, 239–40.
12 *JMK*, XXI, 239, 241, 243–4.
13 *JMK*, XXI, 237–8.
14 *JMK*, XXI, 209–10, 242.
15 Howson and Winch 1977, 117–20.
16 *JMK*, XXI, 251–9; Howson and Winch (1977, 122) discuss this report 'The American Situation and the World Economic Conference'.

17 *JMK*, XXI, 261–2, 266–7.
18 Moley 1971, 236–7.
19 Feis 1966, 211.
20 *JMK*, XXI, 273–4.
21 Moley 1971, 264–6; Feis 1966, 242–3; Steele 1979, 306–7.
22 Feis 1966, 245. The statement appears as appendix 6 of Moley 1971.
23 Hodson 1938, 196.
24 *JMK*, XXVIII, 320–2.
25 *JMK*, XXVIII, 312–16.
26 KCKP, Lydia to JMK, 15 November 1926, 30 May 1927; Buckle 1979, 476, 492.
27 *JMK*, XVIII, 317–18.
28 Haskell 1979, 167.
29 Ibid., 168; KCKP, Lydia to JMK, 30 January 1930.
30 Ninette de Valois in M. Keynes (ed.) 1983, 109.
31 *JMK*, XXVIII, 79.
32 KCKP, JMK to FAK, 23 April 1933.
33 The American version of the letter appears in *JMK*, XXI, 289–97; the English version follows on pp. 297–304.
34 Stein 1969, 150.
35 *JMK*, XXI, 305.
36 *JMK*, XXI, 305–9; 309–12.
37 KCKP, JMK to Lydia, 28 May 1934. This and the letter to Lydia referred to in the next note exist because Lydia did not accompany Maynard to Washington.
38 KCKP, JMK to Lydia, 29 May 1934; Harrod 1951, 20. The note from which Harrod quotes is now in the Harrod Papers at Chiba University in Japan.
39 Stein 1969, 150.
40 KCKP, Frankfurter to JMK, 23 June 1934.
41 The paper appears in *JMK*, XIII, 457–68.
42 *JMK*, XXI, 323.
43 *JMK*, XXI, 329–32.
44 *JMK*, XXI, 332–3, 334–8.
45 Davis 1971; Stein 1969.
46 KCKP, JMK to Lydia, 2 May 1932.
47 KCKP, JMK to A. L. Romnie, 5 June 1934.
48 VWL, V, 227; VWD, IV, 179; Dennis Arundel in M. Keynes (ed.) 1983.
49 See VWL, V, 282; VWD, IV, 205; KCKP, JMK to Lydia, 5 March 1934.
50 *JMK*, XII, 58.
51 *JMK*, XII, 99.
52 *JMK*, XII, 107.
53 *JMK*, XII, 10–12.
54 KCKP, JMK to Lydia, 26 November 1933.
55 VWD, IV, 244.
56 KCKP, JMK to Lydia, 26 May 1935.
57 KCKP, O'Casey to Garnett, 26 October 1935.
58 KCKP, Lydia to JMK, 4 February 1936.
59 *JMK*, XVIII, 326–8.
60 KCKP, G. Rylands to JMK, 20 December 1939.
61 KCKP, JMK to Maurice Brown, 29 July 1936.
62 KCKP, JMK to T. S. Eliot, 10 May 1937.
63 KCKP, JMK to W. H. Auden, 6 October, 1 and 14 November 1937.
64 *JMK*, XXVIII, 355.
65 KCKP, Mary Glasgow to JMK, 21 December 1943.

23

FERTILE OF MIND,
FRAIL OF BODY

I hope he won't get stronger *mentally* as his normal strength in the head is quite enough for me.
(Virginia Woolf to Lydia Keynes, 5 June 1937; VWL, VI, 134.)

The *General Theory* appeared in February 1936, priced at 5 shillings to make it readily available to students and, as it turned out, to ensure that Keynes made almost no money from it. Then began general discussion of Keynes's new views. The book was reviewed everywhere – in the daily press, the quality weeklies and monthlies, the professional journals. Keynes summed up the reaction to Roy Harrod in August 1936:

> [E]xperience seems to show that people are divided between the old ones whom nothing will shift ... and the young ones who have not been properly brought up and believe nothing in particular. . . .
> I have no companions it seems, in my own generation, either of earliest teachers or of earliest pupils.[1]

One can see this reaction from the older generation in the reviews from those Keynes cared most about, for Hubert Henderson, Dennis Robertson and A. C. Pigou were all unimpressed. Pigou was positively irritated. He found the discussion of Keynes's predecessors a 'macedoine of misrepresentations' and compared him unfavourably with Einstein:

> Einstein actually did for Physics what Mr Keynes believes himself to have done for Economics. He developed a far-reaching generalisation under which Newton's results can be subsumed as a special case. But he did not, in announcing his discovery, insinuate, through carefully barbed sentences, that Newton and those who had hitherto followed his lead were a gang of incompetent bunglers.[2]

Nor did he have much to say in favour of the positive doctrine which he found so obscurely presented that he could not be certain what Keynes intended to convey, for he found only minor improvements to existing doctrines. Robertson was critical of the awkward use of Marshall's comparative static method, but it was Keynes's liquidity preference theory of the rate of interest that naturally held centre-stage in his criticisms. Henderson, who had been growing more and more sceptical of economic theory in general since he had left Cambridge over a decade before, was also profoundly unsympathetic.

The same could be said of senior American economists. Frank Knight (born 1885) of the University of Chicago found that its chief value lay in the hard labour involved in reading it, 'for the direct contribution of the work seems . . . quite unsubstantial'.[3] He could see little in the book that would carry the profession further. Joseph Schumpeter (born 1883), who tore up his own work on monetary theory, *Das Wesen des Geldes*,[a] on the appearance of the *Treatise*,[a] was also extremely unsympathetic to the book's method and message. Keynes received a more sympathetic reception from Jacob Viner (born 1892) although he protested that the book 'will have more persuasive power than it deserves'. He was prepared to accept the outlines of Keynes's system, but he was doubtful as to its workings and empirical content. In particular, he was unhappy with the theory of liquidity preference, suggesting that one could treat the phenomena equally well in a quantity-theory framework and that 'Keynes had grossly exaggerated the extent to which liquidity preferences have operated in the past and are likely to operate in the future as a barrier to full employment', emphasising the 'widely present aversion to the waste of "dead" cash'. He believed that the best theory of the determination of the rate of interest was closer to the traditional view than Keynes's.[4] Finally Alvin Hansen (born 1887) reviewed the book twice. Although sympathetic in tone, his reviews concluded that the book was 'more a symptom of economic trends than a foundation stone on which a science can be built' and suggested that it would fare no better than the *Treatise on Money* given its defective theory of interest and 'its special notion of equilibrium at less than full employment'.[5] Ironically, Hansen, who moved from the University of Minnesota to Harvard within a year of the appearance of the first review, would become Keynes's major senior American disciple and interpreter.

On both sides of the Atlantic, it was young economists who took to the book, read it, analysed it and tried to develop it. Some of the enthusiasts had helped in the development of the theory – Joan Robinson, Richard Kahn, James Meade and Roy Harrod. Others had been Keynes's supervision pupils – Brian Reddaway, David Champernowne – or had heard the theory developed in lectures – Lorie Tarshis, Walter Salant, R. B. Bryce – or had been exposed to it at the London-Oxford-Cambridge research student seminars where Joan Robinson and Richard Kahn had tried to spread the word – Abba Lerner. Others came to the theory through the book, but had easily taken it from there – for instance, Paul Samuelson and J. R. Hicks.

a He did complete another version by 1935, but never published it. It appeared in German in 1970.

Bryce, Salant and Tarshis went from Cambridge, England to Cambridge, Massachusetts and helped to spread the word. In the course of 1936–7, often in fruitful collaboration and interaction, as at the September 1936 meetings of the Econometric Society at Oxford,[6] many of these younger economists discussed the book. There were reviews by Hicks, Reddaway and Lerner; and expositions by Robinson, Hicks, Meade and Harrod. Keynes read many of them and 'approved' of all where we know of no adverse comments, even though in later years one of these authors, John Hicks, would become less happy with the effects of his version on the economics profession. Many of these expositions attempted to formulate the model and did so on remarkably similar lines, as Oscar Lange, an early user of such models, pointed out in 1938.[7] All worked in terms of a simple three equation, two identity model that was to become the mainstay of undergraduate expositions of the theory – and still is. All, unlike Keynes, and I should here also exclude Joan Robinson, tended to play down the more exaggerated claims of the book and attempted to provide links with more traditional theory.

Keynes's reactions to the reviews are interesting. He replied to only Jacob Viner's at length in print, although, after some goading, he began a long controversy with Dennis Robertson over his theory of the rate of interest. In private, he expressed his views on some of the others, finding Pigou's review 'profoundly frivolous in substance' and being amused by what he took to be Knight's two main conclusions: 'namely, that my book caused him intense irritation, and that he had great difficulty in understanding it'.[8] Of the younger people's reviews and expositions he was tolerant, perhaps because he strongly believed that 'If the simple basic ideas can become familiar and acceptable, time, experience and the collaboration of a number of minds will discover the best way of expressing them'.[9]

Viner's review had been one of four in the November 1936 issue of the *Quarterly Journal of Economics* – the other three being by Wassily Leontief, Dennis Robertson and F. W. Taussig. Dismissing Leontief and Taussig in the first paragraph of his reply and using the second to deal gently with Robertson, since 'both he and I differ more fundamentally from our predecessors than his piety will allow', Keynes turned to Viner. Although he outlined all the components of his theory, he concentrated on Viner's discussion of hoarding and liquidity preference. The resulting article became famous in the subsequent literature, forming for many the basis of their post-1961 interpretations of the *General Theory*. The emphasis came down firmly on the importance of uncertainty in his thinking – a point he had already mentioned in private discussions with Hubert Henderson after their debate before the Marshall Society in May 1936[10] – especially as it concerned money and the liquidity preference theory of the rate of interest.

Money, it is well known, serves two principal purposes. By acting as a unit of account it facilitates exchanges without its being necessary that it should ever itself come into the picture as a substantive object. In this respect it is a convenience which is devoid of significance or real influence. In the second place, it is a store of wealth. So we are told, without a smile on the face. But in the world of the classical economy, what an insane use to which to put it! For it is one of the recognised characteristics of money as a store of wealth that it is barren; whereas practically every other form of storing wealth yields some interest or profit. Why should anyone outside a lunatic asylum wish to use money as a store of wealth?

Because, partly on reasonable and partly on instinctive grounds, our desire to hold money is a barometer of our distrust of our own calculations and conventions concerning the future.... The possession of money lulls our disquietude; and the premium which we require to make us part with money is the measure of the degree of our disquietude.[11]

Then he was off with an outline of his theory of the rate of interest, investment (where expectations concerning the future enter strongly), consumption and employment, but giving pride of place to his theory of the rate of interest as being central to his story. All in all, the article was a *tour de force* as an attempt to get away from narrow arguments about terminology and on to other ground. Whether it succeeded is another matter.[b]

The theory of the rate of interest was to prove Keynes's main ground for controversialising in 1936 and after. He devoted a paper to it in a *Festschrift* for Irving Fisher. He gave an early version of this paper as a lecture in Stockholm on his way to visit Lydia's relations in Leningrad at the end of September 1936. The paper and the surrounding discussion, and subsequent discussion in Cambridge where Bertil Ohlin gave the Economics Faculty's annual Marshall Lectures in November 1936, along with an earlier discussion of his ideas at an international monetary conference in Brussels in July 1935, provoked Bertil Ohlin to prepare a long, three-part article on developments in economic thinking in Sweden during the previous decade. In the end, Keynes

b Since Warren Young's *Interpreting Mr. Keynes: The IS-LM Enigma*, it has come into the literature that the *Quarterly Journal of Economics* paper 'was intended as a counterweight to the IS-LM approach as endorsed by Meade, Harrod and Hicks', as Peter Clarke (1988, 302) puts it, citing Young (1987, 9–10, 178). There are two problems with this line of argument. One is chronological. The *Quarterly Journal* paper appeared in February 1937. It was thus written before the end of 1936. Keynes did not 'catch up' on his reading and 'go through' Hicks's seminal paper, 'Mr. Keynes and the Classics', until late March 1937, although, of course, he may have browsed in it after Hicks sent it to him the previous October (*JMK*, XIV, 77, 79). The second is the praise Keynes bestowed on the three papers, going so far with Harrod to suggest that 'I should like to read your paper instead' of his own in Stockholm (*JMK*, XIV, 84). Given this praise, it would seem most unlikely, given his normal behaviour, that Keynes would, as Young suggests, turn and attack these views, especially without explicit attribution.

could only print the first two parts of Ohlin's article under the title 'Some Notes on the Stockholm Theory of Savings and Investment' in the *Economic Journal* for March and June 1937.[c]

Ohlin's articles were to have two important effects, only the second of which will concern me here. First, Ohlin told English-speaking readers of the results of recent Swedish theoretical thinking by members of what would become known as the Stockholm School. This bore similarities to Keynes's theory and raised the question of Swedish anticipations of the *General Theory* – a debate that continues.[12] Second, Keynes was provoked to write a paper, 'Alternative Theories of the Rate of Interest', in the June 1937 *Economic Journal*. This drew rejoinders from Ohlin, Hawtrey and Robertson in the next issue and a continuing series of exchanges with Robertson which did not conclude until September 1938.[13] As Keynes put it to Ohlin, he regarded the older theory of the rate of interest as established by the demand for and the supply of loanable funds or credit as 'fundamental heresy' and as incompatible with his liquidity preference theory.[14] In the course of the discussion, Keynes evolved, in what he hoped would be the interests of clarity, the notion of 'finance', the demand for accommodation by businessmen, arranged at the time of the decision to invest.[15] In equilibrium, he conceived of this as a revolving fund, but as the level of investment rose, this demand for finance in advance of any subsequent rise in incomes or savings could put upward pressure on the rate of interest by raising the demand for money. Keynes found this concept useful in analysis, as we shall see below, but his successors have taken varied views of it – as they have of the whole liquidity-preference/loanable-funds discussion, which at an important level was a case of two sides talking past each other, since the stock-orientated liquidity preference and the flow-oriented loanable funds concepts are formally different but equivalent ways of describing the same phenomena. Yet, at another level, when one gets beyond the comparative statics of formal analysis, the question remains more open, suggesting perhaps that Keynes's theory, augmented by 'finance', was one more example of the 'Cambridge didactic style'.[16]

Keynes's comment on Ohlin, his paper for the Fisher *Festschrift*, his reply to Viner and his correction to his use of the statistics of investment in the United States by Simon Kuznets in the *General Theory*, were all completed in the fifteen months following publication. During the same period, he also kept up an extensive correspondence with other readers and interpreters of the book. But defences of his book were not his only contributions to the scholarly journals during the period. On 21 April 1936, he delivered an Allocution on the life and work of William Stanley Jevons for the Royal

c The third part dealt less with Swedish developments and more with Ohlin's view of the *General Theory*. Parts of it appear in *JMK*, XIV, 191–200, along with Keynes's letter of reply (ibid., 187–91). The whole text appeared in *History of Political Economy* in the summer of 1981.

Statistical Society's celebration of the centenary of his birth. It is still one of the best introductions to the man and his work.[17] In October, the death of Herbert Somerton Foxwell, the Harvey Road neighbour of his youth, brought another long essay in biography, this time for the December *Economic Journal*.[18] Then, on 16 February 1937, he turned his eyes from the relatively short-term concerns of the *General Theory* to the longer-term problems of economic growth and development in his Galton Lecture to the Eugenics Society, 'Some Economic Consequences of a Declining Population'.[19] Added to these activities were his usual ones, plus watching over his theatre, and an important return to journalism. The pace took its toll.

The creation and subsequent discussion of the *General Theory* coincided with a sharp deterioration in Keynes's relationship with Dennis Robertson. As the reasons were complex, and the consequences were to affect Cambridge economics for decades after Keynes's death, I should spend some time on them.

To begin I should recapitulate the story down to about 1931. Robertson was seven years Keynes's junior. He came up to Trinity from Eton and turned to economics after obtaining a first in Part I of the Classical Tripos in 1910. He was Keynes's pupil until he took a first in Part II of the Economics Tripos in 1912. He stayed in Cambridge to write a dissertation that won him a fellowship at Trinity in 1914 and which appeared in 1915 as *A Study of Industrial Fluctuation*. While he was writing it, he stood in for Keynes in Cambridge when Keynes was ill with diphtheria in the Lent Term of 1914.[20] When war broke out, Robertson, a member of the Territorials, joined up. He was absent from Cambridge until 1919 when he returned to take up his Trinity fellowship.

In the following decade, the two men had been very close. Keynes respected Robertson's judgement and his ability. It was Robertson who was asked to review *Economic Consequences of the Peace* in the *Economic Journal*. It was Robertson, who in 1920 could hardly be regarded as an established monetary theorist, who was asked by Keynes to write the Cambridge Economic Handbook on *Money* (1922) (as well as *The Control of Industry* (1923)). Moreover, despite the fact that he had not been an Apostle as an undergraduate, he became a member of the Society when Keynes tried to rebuild it after the war. He also became a member of the Tuesday Club in November 1922, the only one of Keynes's younger Cambridge colleagues to do so until Richard Kahn joined nearly twenty years later in April 1941. As I have already described (Chapter 17 above), Keynes and Robertson were close intellectual collaborators in the early and middle stages of creation of the *Treatise*, with Robertson paying tributes to Keynes's influence and his forthcoming *Treatise* in both his *Banking Policy and the Price Level* (1926) and his major 1928 revision of *Money*. Robertson, like Keynes, had a deep love for the theatre but was also something of an actor; he was close to Lydia and was asked to write a play for Maynard and Lydia's party on 13 January 1926.[21] Keynes felt a strong sense of loss when Dennis was away in India in 1926–7 and reported the arrival of letters from Robertson, as well as his return, in letters to Lydia.[22]

The proofs of the *Treatise* did not reveal fundamental differences. Robertson was 'still full of resistances at certain points' of the first volume but 'not, I think, on the main structure'. He was sorry he could not 'swallow it whole'.[23] It was only in May 1931 that Robertson 'reluctantly' weighed in with more substantial criticisms, noting that the more he studied the book 'the more obstacles I find in the way of' subscribing to the 'fundamental analysis'.[24] Keynes was surprised, but only that the criticism was less than expected and 'not very good'.[25] At this same time, Robertson also disagreed with Keynes over protection and arranged to work with the group of LSE economists, organised by Lionel Robbins and Sir William Beveridge, who were developing *Tariffs: The Case Examined* (1931), the counterblast to Keynes's and other protectionists' proposals. Robertson withdrew from the project before publication. None of this, in itself, would have caused difficulties: Keynes could disagree with someone on matters of theory or policy and yet remain a friend – one needs only think of his relations with Hawtrey and Pigou. The correspondence may have become a bit more testy, but on technical matters the two had a history of being blunt, as in the exchanges on *Banking Policy and the Price Level* during 1925.[26] It is also clear from the correspondence, however, that Robertson was deeply troubled by disputes among economists:

> What a ghastly subject it is! Here are you saying that wage reductions are no good, and Pigou saying that they are a lot of good, and Walker saying that they are no good at the beginning of a slump but some good at the end, and now Isles saying that they are some good at the beginning but no good at the end! How I wish we could form a Cambridge front again![27]

This did not bode well for the future.

During the period up to 1931 Robertson had developed an international reputation as a scholar: according to Patrick Deutscher, in the 1920s he was the sixth most cited monetary economist in the profession (Pigou was third, Keynes was tenth) and in the 1930s he would be second (to Keynes).[28] He was a meticulous scholar, with a deep respect for the past and a determination to see all sides of any question. He also had doubts about his own originality, which went well beyond academic modesty.[29] He was the last person to lead a Keynes-like publicity campaign for his own views or their policy implications, for he was shy, somewhat withdrawn, vulnerable and easily hurt.[30] He had a melancholic streak and 'an almost unique capacity for self torture'. His strong feelings for young men also led to occasional difficulties.[31]

Difficulties between Keynes and Robertson, however, were the result of a coincidence of three events. First, Robertson's personal life, never easy, was thrown into turmoil by the death of his mother on 27 January 1935. As Keynes remarked to Lydia the next day, Robertson had 'never really separated from her'. Second, it was at this time that Keynes began sending Dennis the first proofs of the *General Theory*, sending them to him *before* he sent them to Hawtrey, Harrod or Joan Robinson. Discussions of them continued through January, February and early March 1935 until Robertson suggested that they break off.[32] Third, there was the problem of the emergence of the new, younger generation in Cambridge, and their beginning to seek their own places in the sun.

Most of this younger generation, especially its older members – Austin Robinson and Piero Sraffa – presented little problem. Nor was there a problem with Richard Kahn, although his rise as Keynes's theoretical confidant must have rankled with Robertson, especially as he was unsympathetic to Kahn's approach to theory.[33] But amongst the younger generation Joan Robinson caused the most severe problems.

Joan had returned from India with her husband, Austin, in 1929. She had become a part-time lecturer in 1931. As her published letters made clear, and as she admitted, she had 'rough manners in controversy'. As C. R. Fay put it: 'But it is an awful pity that she is so bloody rude'.[34] She also had definite views as to how economics should be taught – and she taught with flair.[35] As Pigou put it to Keynes in 1940 when they were discussing recent Tripos papers:

> My own guess – because there is no direct evidence – is that the parrot-like treatment of your stuff is due to the lectures and supervisions of the beautiful Mrs R. – a magpie breeding innumerable parrots! I gather that she propounds the Truth with an enormous T and with such Prussian efficiency that the wretched men become identical sausages without any minds of their own![36]

In the context of this biography, the 'truth' that mattered in the mid-1930s was Keynes's evolving system. One should emphasise the obvious: by that date Joan Robinson had developed her own considerable reputation as a scholar through her *Economics of Imperfect Competition* (1933) and several articles through which she would between 1936 and 1939 become the ninth most cited macroeconomist in Deutscher's tabulations.[37] It happened that in the late winter of 1935, just after she had failed to get a Cambridge lectureship (the post had gone to J. R. Hicks), she proposed a two-term course in money as a part of the second year lectures in economic theory. Claude Guillebaud of St John's had lectured previously, but he had moved to teach the first year; Robertson carried the main burden of the third year teaching in the area. Robertson had also just become chairman of the Faculty Board. Joan Robinson's proposal came to the Board on 1 March, when it agreed to offer the lectures. The next day, C. R. Fay wrote to Keynes suggesting that the matter be re-opened, as 'the provisional conclusion at which we arrived brought dismay to our Chairman'. Keynes reported to Lydia on 4 March:

> The trouble between Joan and Dennis (which I thought I had settled) may crop up again. He's getting dangerously near to trying to prevent her from lecturing; and if he were to succeed, the state of rift between the older people and the younger would be dreadful. I shall have to exert my full force, and it would end in Dennis being frightfully upset. Why are all economists mad?

Keynes put the matter very strongly to Fay that Cambridge was in danger of 'becoming a sort of London School of Economics, where differences of doctrinal opinion are capable of coming into the picture' and pointed out that the difficult situation arose in part because Joan Robinson was

> inferior in status in a way that does not entirely correspond to her attainments. If there were no University lecturers and we were appointing all over again, would she not have a superior claim to some of those who now have a superior status? I should think myself that there could be no doubt about it.[38]

That seemed to end matters for the moment.

They flared up again the next year – and the result clearly rankled with Robertson:

> (I) Yes, I accept the Cambridge lecture-list arrangement as the least bad in the circumstances. But of course I *don't* think it good that people coming over from other subjects [into Part II economics] should get their first introduction to this whole range of very controversial topics from someone who seems to think that everything that has been said and thought about it is 'moth-eaten' rubbish except one book – and that, whatever its merits, a very difficult one! And I *do* feel that over this business there is an atmosphere of dogmatism and proselytisation about into which our Socialists and Communist(s) have never landed us & which is new and un-Cambridge-y. However I realise it's no use at present our trying to see eye to eye about this: and also that the position is complicated by my inability, after years of effort for Austin's sake, to preserve personally cordial relations with Mrs. R.[39]

The rest of Robertson's letter concerned the *General Theory*. Yet relations were obviously strained with Robertson suggesting in a concluding paragraph, 'Will you give my love to Lydia? I think she regards me as a traitor and doesn't want to see me nowadays'. Despite the strain, Robertson's letter contained a request for help – advice on whom to consult professionally on his psychological problems. Keynes knew of no one, yet said, 'I am with you against full psychoanalysis.' He signed the letter 'Yours affectionately'.[40,d]

Relations between Robertson and Keynes did not get any easier over the next year or two: the correspondence was extensive and sharp (perhaps unnecessarily so on Keynes's part for someone in Robertson's somewhat fragile psychological state), with some of it finding its way into print on Robertson's side.[41] Keynes tried to minimise points of difference: Robertson to bring differences to a head and objecting to Keynes's tactic of pitching his argument against someone other than Robertson whenever possible.[42] Yet, with some attempts to keep the correspondence civil, it continued interminably, as readers of volumes XIV and XXIX of the *Collected Writings* can discover.

By this time, Robertson seriously began to consider leaving Cambridge. In the summer of 1937 he was offered the Price Professorship of International Economics, a research chair at the Royal Institute of International Affairs, and thought long and hard about it before declining it, a decision with which Keynes agreed.[43] Relations in the Faculty remained tense. There was a new lectureship to fill. It went to Joan Robinson. This was settled in February 1938. Although Kahn's notes on the result and Keynes's reaction make clear that there had been problems in the process, these were not created by Robertson.[44] Then there was reform of the Tripos, always a delicate issue as intellectual property is involved. Finally, when the Faculty discussed the attempt to begin an organised applied research programme in Cambridge, eventually the Department of Applied Economics, there were differences over organisation and personal. Keynes lamented to Pigou:

It is a great pity that everything becomes so political. What makes it all particularly morbid is that there is really no difference of opinion

d For Keynes's psychological advice I work from his pencilled draft found in the 1976 'Tilton laundry basket' find of Keynes papers that eventually formed Volume XXIX of *The Collected Writings* along with Robertson's original letter. In the version Robertson received, a copy of which was deposited in the Keynes Papers, the last paragraph was erased and the following note inserted:

I thought it right to keep this letter; but justifiable to erase a paragraph dealing, sympathetically and helpfully, with a very private and personal matter on which I had asked for his help and advice. DHR 1961

Robertson did take some professional advice during the summer of 1937 (KCKP, Robertson to JMK, 17 August 1937). He had had similar problems in the summer of 1933: 'I *think* the ghost-rabbit is in his hutch again, though God knows whether he ought to be.' See KCKP, Robertson to JMK, 22 October 1933; and also Robertson to JMK, 22 August 1936, which refers to his difficulties over 'the last three years'.

between myself and Dennis on major points. We are on the same side of the fence as against past doctrine and against many other economists, e.g. in America. But he seems to think it a duty to invent and magnify differences.[45]

Pigou took it more seriously, replying in a letter and a postcard the same day, 'I think all opportunities for removing his persecution complex ought to be taken' and 'Therefore add that for unrevealed reasons, this D. psychological business is much more important than it sounds and ought to be taken seriously'.[46]

Perhaps Pigou already knew what was likely to happen. T. E. Gregory had resigned his Cassel Professorship with special reference to currency and banking at the LSE. Robertson, one of the electors, offered himself as a candidate and got the job.[e] He broke the news to Keynes on 7 October 1938 (he was to start on 1 January 1939). To the news, Keynes responded to Robertson on 9 October:

> It's a great wrench and loss that you have decided to go away. I can understand the conflict of motives which went to your decision. But I think it may be a right one. The post is a good one and in many ways attractive. Here the state of struggle in the Faculty which has existed lately I have seen and hated. But it seemed to be too deeply rooted in feelings to be easily composed by reasonableness. It is all a great pity.
>
> ... Well, Dennis, I trust that time and some measure of absence, which will only be partial I hope, will obliterate the divisions of the last year or two.

This, for the moment ended the series of events, probably exacerbated by Robertson's psychological problems and, in the end, by Keynes's illness. Had Keynes been more robust – and in Cambridge – it might have gone differently, although one wonders. What is clear from the surviving correspondence is that the story is hardly Harry Johnson's. I have found no systematic evidence that 'Keynes had egged his young people on against him [Robertson]' a phrase he repeats twice, adding the word 'deliberately' on one occasion.[47] True, Keynes *once* spoke to Richard Kahn of 'perhaps forming a real organised party of reform' in the Faculty, but one swallow does not make a summer.[48] Nor was it the case, as Johnson suggests, that Robertson had been prevented from occupying the Cambridge professorship[49] by anyone other than Pigou, who had not retired – he was, after all, only 60 in 1938 when Robertson resigned to go to London and would thus hold the chair for some time

---

e According to one account, Robertson wrote his opinions on the various candidates, and then added words to the effect of 'If none of these will do, what about me?' The other electors, who had not thought of Robertson as a candidate, jumped at the chance.

even under the 1925 Statutes with their fixed retirement age of 65.[f] When he did retire, Keynes was offered the chair, but declined it, knowing full well who Pigou's successor would be – Robertson, who needed no persuading to return to Cambridge.[50]

Apart from what was becoming an important City event, Keynes's annual speech as Chairman of the National Mutual, which as usual dealt with the prospects for cheaper money, during 1935 he made only one contribution to public discussions of British economic policy – an article in *Lloyd's Bank Review* on 'The Future of the Foreign Exchanges'.[51] In 1936 there was not even an article. This did not mean that he was completely aloof from discussions, for he remained a member of the EAC's Committee on Economic Information. In 1935 and 1936 the Committee produced five surveys of the economic situation, a report on population statistics and a discussion of the economic outlook for the next few years. These reports and their preparation make it clear that one of the Committee's major preoccupations as the economy moved through its fourth year of recovery was the nature and timing of the next recession and the measures the state could take to minimise its impact. The consensus, both on the Committee and on its sub-committee on the Trend of Unemployment[g] was not very optimistic. The current recovery had started towards the end of 1932 and had been underpinned by a substantial rise in housebuilding in response to cheap money; the Committee feared it would at some stage face a slowdown in such building as the demand for housing approached saturation. Such a slowdown could lead to a serious recession which would be complicated by the fact that the one area of investment particularly sensitive to changes in the rate of interest, housebuilding, would now be dependent on the slowing rate of growth of population. The report on the Trend of Unemployment forecast the average unemployment rate over the next decade at 15½ to 16 per cent, rising to a peak of 20 per cent in 1940. Keynes, even more worried about the exhaustion of investment opportunities than his colleagues, was still less optimistic and saw the rate of unemployment as rising well above 20 per cent. Initially, the recession was expected to occur between 1936 and 1938, but the announcement in 1935 of a British five-year rearmament programme, the European devaluations in the context of the Tripartite Agreement of September 1936, and the spread of rising activity and prices throughout the world made prediction especially difficult.[52]

It was in these circumstances that Keynes, having decided 'that we are

f For those, like Pigou, appointed under the 1882 Statutes, there was no retiring age unless they elected to come under the new 1925 Statutes.
g The sub-committee had the task of advising Sir William Beveridge, the chairman of the Unemployment Statutory Committee, on probable future levels of unemployment so that he could set rates of contribution and benefit and avoid deficits in the Unemployment Insurance Fund.

now approaching the phase when it is more important to think about how to prevent the [next] slump than about how to stimulate the boom any further than it has already gone',[53] approached the editor of *The Times* through R. H. Brand with a proposal for a series of articles on that theme. *The Times* accepted the proposal and 'How to Avoid a Slump' appeared in three parts between 12 and 14 January 1937.

In these articles, Keynes argued that the economy was 'in more need of a rightly directed demand than of a greater aggregate demand' and that it was time to take measures to prevent investors' expectations overreaching themselves and producing an overreaction downwards in the next recession. The authorities should therefore concentrate any increases in demand on the depressed regions of the country. He also warned the authorities against using an increase in the rate of interest, as had occurred in previous booms, as a method of restraint. They must avoid it as they would 'hell-fire' for two reasons. First, he repeated the doctrine of the *General Theory*:

> A low enough long-term rate of interest cannot be achieved if we allow it to be believed that better terms will be obtainable from time to time by those who keep their resources liquid. The long-term rate of interest must be kept *continuously* as near as possible to what we believe to be the long-term optimum. It is not suitable to be used as a short-period weapon.[54]

Second, he argued that within weeks or months a low rate of interest would be necessary to stimulate investment; dearer money would merely intensify the slump. The authorities could instead limit new investment by controls on new Stock Exchange issues and could also hold back postponable public investment to provide ammunition against the slump. He suggested that the Chancellor should meet the costs of rearmament largely from taxation rather than borrowing and reduce barriers to imports, while beginning a process of long-term planning for public investment so that projects would be readily available for the recession.

Keynes returned to this theme of keeping the long-term rate of interest steady, if not lower, in his speech to the National Mutual on 24 February 1937. In another article in *The Times* of 11 March on the Chancellor's plans to borrow £80 million a year for five years for rearmament, he thought that the Chancellor might just get away with loan-financed defence expenditures on that scale with careful planning, if the authorities concentrated orders in the depressed areas, stood ready to control public sector investment and if, as was usual, the Service Departments found it difficult to spend up to their timetables. But the emphasis was on the need for long-term planning and for paying attention to the trade cycle. As in the January articles, there is no evidence to support Lord Kahn's suggestion that Keynes was supporting restraint when the level of unemployment stood at 12½ per cent so as to maintain 'a considerable reserve army of unemployment' to meet the needs of the more substantial rearmament programme that he desired and recognised as inevitable.[55]

The 11 March article was to be Keynes's last substantial contribution to discussions, beyond letters to the editor, for almost a year. During that time, however, developments elsewhere were providing evidence of the effectiveness of this and of his previous campaigns in shaping official attitudes.

Treasury officials were never insulated from Keynes's views and campaigns. Sir Frederick Leith-Ross, Chief Economic Adviser to the Government, attended meetings of the Committee on Economic Information from 1932 to 1939, while Sir Frederick Phillips joined the Committee in October 1935. Both took an active part in the Committee's deliberations.[56] Treasury officials also had to provide comments on the Committee's reports as they appeared and had to brief the Chancellor on the appropriate responses to make to matters under public and Parliamentary discussion, which inevitably included Keynes's evolving views. Thus from the Treasury's own files one can get a picture of official views on macroeconomic policy. In recent years, there have been several studies of these views.[57] These indicate that in the case of at least some senior Treasury officials, most notably Sir Frederick Phillips but not R. G. Hawtrey, there was a shift away from the classical 'Treasury view' of the 1920s that loan-financed public works merely crowded out private expenditure with little resulting effect on employment, but that there was no full-fledged conversion, especially as regards the details of monetary policy, where the Treasury's 'funding complex' was in fact undermining some of the effects of its policy of cheap money.

The Treasury's reaction to 'How to Avoid a Slump' is particularly revealing. Keynes's recommendations served as the basis for the Committee on Economic Information's 22nd Report of February 1937, 'Economic Policy and the Maintenance of Trade Activity' – although there was a note of dissent from Dennis Robertson to the recommendations concerning the rate of interest.[58] By this stage, Sir Frederick Phillips had independently come to see the need for a short-term policy that looked broadly like that of Keynes and the Committee on Economic Information, although he believed that dearer money might become necessary to keep the boom from getting out of hand. He used his skills to persuade ministers to act on the recommendations of the 22nd Report concerning public capital expenditure, tax policy and trade policy. The steps which followed involved full consideration of the recommendations in two interdepartmental committees – one on Trade Policy and one on Public Capital Expenditure. Delays in setting up the committees and the leisurely pace of their deliberations, partly the result of Leith-Ross's absences abroad, meant that by the time their reports appeared it was August 1937 and the economy was threatened by recession. But once the long-threatened recession did arrive, Phillips' Committee on Public Capital Expenditure prepared a revised report which, instead of the restraining measures of the previous version, recommended the preparation of additional public works schemes, and that, as private housebuilding showed signs of decline, the Ministry of Health should send out immediately a circular to local authorities requesting preparation of a building programme for the next five years. However, we should note that the changes were in many respects a triumph for the Ministry of Labour, whose representative, Humbert Wolfe, took the chair in Phillips' absence and played a major role in redrafting the Committee's conclusions to create a more positive document.[59] On 26 January 1938 the Cabinet approved in principle a Ministry of Health circular and the other recommendations. But the endorsement was only lukewarm: the circular did not go out until May 1938. The recession itself obviated any need for dearer money; this aspect of Keynes's programme came to pass as a result of external events, while in so far as Phillips' Committee followed any other monetary recommendations of Keynes's, it was 'because we cannot help it, not because it is right'.[60]

Thus, in a limited way, some of Keynes's ideas began to make their way into Whitehall. The emphasis should be on the word *limited*.

In April 1937, in a letter to *The Times*, Keynes attacked the perverse incentive effects of the Chancellor's proposed special tax on profits, the National Defence Contribution, which he thought 'a tax on enterprise, growth and youth as such'.[61] In June he wrote another letter on the 'gold scare' caused by rumours that Britain and the United States would reduce the price of gold. He did not return to the question of aggregate demand management until 22 December, when he wrote a letter attacking Sir Charles Mallet's view that public works were unlikely to mitigate the effects of a recession and calling again for the forward planning of such expenditure. He also renewed a plea, which he had raised at the beginning of the year and about which the authorities would do nothing until 1940, for improved official statistics for such forward planning and for ensuring that rearmament proceeded as efficiently as possible. However, even at the end of 1937, he did not believe that the recession which had started in the United States the previous summer had reached Britain.[62]

Keynes was wrong: the recession had arrived in Britain in September 1937 and lasted until September 1938.[63] On the American recession, which had followed a tightening of both monetary and fiscal policy, he wrote a letter to President Roosevelt on 1 February 1938 which advocated public works and publicly aided or guaranteed investments, particularly in housing, where he suggested that the Administration's policy had been 'really wicked', utilities, where he saw past official policies as inhibiting investment, and the railroads. He also suggested that the Administration adopt a different set of attitudes towards business on the following grounds:

Businessmen have a different set of delusions from politicians; and need, therefore, different handling. They are, however, much milder than politicians, at the same time allured and terrified by the glare of publicity, easily persuaded to be 'patriots', perplexed, bemused, indeed terrified, yet only too anxious to take a cheerful view, vain perhaps but very unsure of themselves, pathetically responsive to a kind word. You could do anything you liked with them, if you would treat them (even the big ones) not as wolves and tigers, but as domestic animals by nature, even though they have been badly brought up and not trained as you would wish. It is a mistake to think that they are more *immoral* than politicians. If you work them into the surly, obstinate, terrified mood, of which domestic animals, wrongly handled, are so capable, the nation's burdens will not get carried to market; and in the end public opinion will veer their way.[64]

The President handed the letter to his Secretary of the Treasury, Henry Morgenthau, perhaps the most unsympathetic member of the Administration to proposals such as Keynes's. He sent a bland reply. Keynes tried again on 25 March, suggesting that

further experience since I wrote seems to show that you are treading a very dangerous middle path. You must either give more encouragement to business or take over more of their functions yourself. If public opinion is not ready for the latter, then it is necessary to wait until public opinion is educated. Your present policies seem to presume that you possess more power than you actually have.[65]

This reply, like his original letter, seems to have had no effect on the Administration. The President's expansionary programme submitted to Congress on 14 April 1938 had its origins elsewhere.[66]

Keynes's relative inactivity during 1937–8 was due to illness. His problems began towards the end of the summer of 1936, when he began to complain of chest pains and breathlessness while taking exercise, which for him meant the occasional walk. In December the pains became worse and he found his movements even more restricted. During the vacation he felt a bit better, but at the beginning of January 1937 he had an attack of influenza. When he recovered from that he found that his chest pains and breathlessness were worse. By the end of January he was finding stairs a problem and he could only just manage the walk from King's to Harvey Road for Sunday lunch with his parents. The family doctor was called in and suggested rheumatism in the chest muscles and post-influenza problems as the cause. February brought another attack of influenza. The chest pains did not diminish. In an attempt to recover, Lydia and Maynard went off to Cannes for eight days on 13 March, but with little or no improvement he decided to consult his uncle, Sir Walter

Langdon Brown, who had been Regius Professor of Physic at Cambridge. Keynes saw his uncle on 31 March and reported 'nothing *prima facie* wrong' as regards heart, lungs, blood pressure, etc., although an electrocardiogram on 2 April probably should have caused some alarm.[67] Early in May there was a renewal of the problems followed by complete collapse in Cambridge. His uncle was now convinced that Keynes's heart had been damaged and that there was a need for a more complete investigation and a long rest. Over a month later, on 18 June, he was moved from Cambridge to Ruthin Castle in North Wales. He was to remain at Ruthin until 23 September.

Keynes did not go to Ruthin with overly high hopes. As he told Lydia on 24 June:

> Thank you so much for your tender and uncomplaining care all these weeks. But I hope I shall return from the garage a good second-hand machine in running order which can live and move with you a bit.

He seemed to have a combination of problems: septic tonsils, a damaged lung (probably a complication from his appendicitis and peritonitis in 1915) and a damaged heart. He told Richard Kahn on 25 June, 'I am in outrageously good *general* health apart from the details'. The recommended cure for the heart was a long period of motionlessness: there were even restrictions on his mental activities which were less successful. He wrote to Lydia on 27 June:

> I expect that the embargo on movements of the mind may be removed before the embargo on movements of the body. At least I hope so! For my mind is terribly active. They can take away drink from the patients who drink too much and food from those who eat too much. But they cannot take my thoughts away from me. When the Great White Chief comes round this afternoon, I shall have to confess that I have written a letter this morning to the Chancellor of the Exchequer.[68]

There was some relaxation on the movements of the mind and by 5 July he had prepared an article for the *New Statesman*. He called it 'a funny, perhaps silly sort of article' but it appears to have done him some good.[69] By 7 July he was 'now *encouraged* to do a modest amount of work every day' but found that he had no time![70] It was some time before more than his mind could move. It was the end of July before he was allowed to walk even briefly and to go on outings in the car in the surrounding countryside, and it was the end of August before he could sit at a desk and write letters.[71] By the time he left Ruthin it was clear that only a long rest would bring even partial recovery and that even then, as Lydia put it to Kahn, 'he could never work again as of old'. Keynes wrote in parentheses at this point, 'You wait and see'.[72] He was 54.

From Ruthin on 23 September, Keynes went to London and then, on 30 September to Tilton. At Tilton he rested, but walked increasing distances: he

Plate 13 JMK and Bertil Ohlin, Antwerp 1935

Plate 14 JMK and Richard Kahn at Tilton in the 1930s:
Austin Robinson

Plate 15 JMK and Lydia at Tilton, 1936: Milo Keynes

Plate 16   JMK and Lydia looking out over Gordon Square, February 1940:
The Hulton-Deutsch Collection

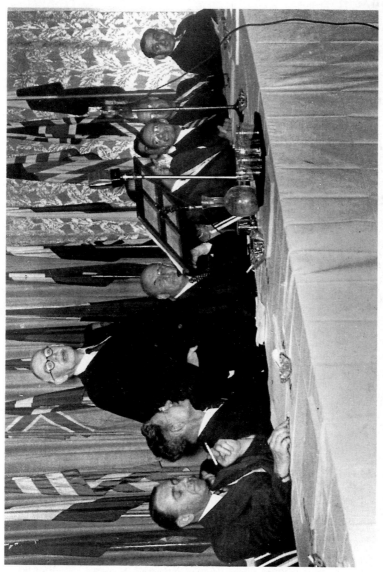

Plate 17 Addressing the Bretton Woods Conference, July 1944 (on JMK's right are Leslie Melville of Australia and Warren Kelchner of the US State Department; on his immediate right is Henry Morgenthau, the US Secretary of the Treasury; on his far left is Pierre Mendes-France of France): International Monetary Fund

Plate 18 JMK in his Treasury office the afternoon before his departure to negotiate the American Loan: Associated Press

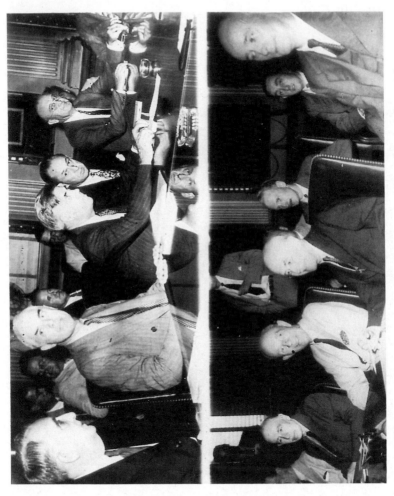

Plate 19 The opening of the American Loan negotiations (from left to right: top –
Frederick Vinson, William Clayton, Henry Wallace, Marriner Eccles and Thomas McCabe;
bottom – Edward Hall Patch, JMK, Lord Halifax, R. H. Brand and Sir Henry Self):
Associated Press

Plate 20   JMK and Lydia on the steps of 46 Gordon Square on his return from negotiating the American Loan: Associated Press

Plate 21 JMK and Lydia on their arrival in New York on the way to Savannah, March 1946: Associated Press

was up to two miles by early December. But there were setbacks and it is clear from Lydia's letters to her mother-in-law and from her diary that life could be a strain: she had continually to prevent Keynes from over-excitement, over-work or seeing visitors for too long. These cares and strains were to be her lot until April 1946.

Although the end of reparations in 1932 and 1933 removed Keynes's major foreign policy concern, events in 1933 had given him new worries. Hitler came to power; Germany had the Reichstag fire in February and her last elections in March 1933. At first, Keynes simply watched with horrified fascination, but as the Nazi régime began to move against the Jews he became more active. He recognised the irony of the situation, for like many of his class and generation there was a mild anti-semitism in his attitudes, which did not affect his dealings with individual Jews such as Richard Kahn, Carl Melchior, Piero Sraffa or Leonard Woolf. As he put it to Lydia on 23 April 1933, he 'made my usual conversation about the Jews in the Combination Room last night, and then immediately afterwards signed a petition for a great Mansion House Meeting to be called by the Lord Mayor in their favour!'.[h]

Soon he got beyond signing petitions. In 'National Self-Sufficiency' he had noted that 'Germany is at the mercy of unchained irresponsibles'.[73] He used even stronger words, when he wrote to Professor Arthur Spiethoff a second time about the 'curtailment' of his article to satisfy Nazi sympathies.

> Forgive my words about barbarism. But the word indicates the effect of recent events in Germany on all of us here. I would infer from your letter that you scarcely conceive the horror which some aspects of the present regime in Germany fill all people in this country. It is many generations in our judgement since such disgraceful events have occurred in any country pretending to call itself civilised. We only wish we knew how to make our protest more effective. For what I am saying is, you may feel assured, the virtually unanimous opinion of responsible circles in this country. If you tell me that these events have taken place, not by force, but as an expression of the general will of the country, that in our view would make some of the persecutions and outrages of which we hear, and of which we sometimes have fuller information than those living in Germany, ten times more horrible.[74]

Along with his Cambridge colleagues, Keynes was attempting to find assistance for academic refugees locally, as well as taking part in the meetings and activities of the newly formed Academic Assistance Council.

h For examples of his rather generalised anti-semitism, which had its parallels in that of Virginia Woolf, see *JMK*, X, 383–4; XXIII, 107; XXIV, 626; XXV, 364, 370. But see also XXVI, 193, which lightly carried over an earlier outburst from Keynes (below p. 727) and the warm concluding paragraphs of his memoir of Melchior (*JMK*, X, 428–9).

In the autumn, when at home the Germans sought 'escape in a return backwards to the modes and manners of the Middle Ages, if not Odin' and Germany withdrew from the Disarmament Conference and the League of Nations, Keynes commented to Lydia:

The news about Germany seems to me *frightfully* serious – I don't know what to conclude about it. Everyone must seem to be faced with the alternative of simply allowing Germany to re-arm as and when she likes, or of attacking her as soon as she begins to do so. Hideous![75]

His papers do not show how Keynes resolved his own dilemma in the short term, for he was silent in public about foreign affairs for almost two years. He gave a speech on 1 March 1935 to Gerald Shove's Lowes Dickinson Society which met weekly to discuss the means of preserving peace. He thought the speech 'wasn't much of a success', and 'I thought them dreadfully muddle-headed; but I suppose people who care about peace always are'.[76] He also wrote a short piece for the *New Statesman* that supported economic sanctions on Italy and providing arms and finance to Abyssinia in order to deter Italy from declaring war.[77] In the summer of 1936 he started commenting regularly. The initial impetus was the *New Statesman*'s support for the Labour Party's espousal of 'collective security' through the League of Nations while simultaneously opposing any increase in British armaments expenditure. Keynes had come to support rearmament and an agreement with France, an understanding with Russia and conversations with the Americans to begin to deter the German and Italian dictators.[78] His straightforward proposals produced a controversy which rumbled on in the *New Statesman*'s columns for some months. The controversy was complicated by the beginning of the Spanish Civil War. It became clear that although Keynes favoured rearmament, he was currently not in favour of risking war. He realised that this meant a painful period of uncertainty: 'No state of mind is more painful than a state of continuing doubt'.[79] This 'stance' implied support for a policy of non-intervention in Spain, largely, it would seem, because he did not see any alternative.[80]

Then came the most bewildering and most insensitive comment of all – his preface to the German translation of the *General Theory*, dated 7 September 1936. There is some uncertainty as to exactly which version of the preface Keynes passed for the press. The version that appears in the Royal Economic Society edition is the English version from his papers, but it differs from the version that actually appeared in the published German translation. The penultimate paragraph causes the problem. In the version of the preface in the Keynes papers, it began

Nevertheless the theory of output as a whole, which is what the following book purports to provide, is more easily adapted to the conditions of a totalitarian state, than is the theory of the production and distribution of a given output under conditions of free competition and a large measure of laissez-faire.[81]

The published German version, but not the draft in the Keynes papers, continued

> This is one of the reasons which justify calling my theory a *General* theory. Since it is based on less narrow assumptions than the orthodox theory, it is also more easily adapted to a large area of different circumstances. Although I have thus worked it out having the conditions in the Anglo-Saxon countries in view – where a great deal of laissez-faire still prevails – it yet remains applicable to situations in which national leadership is more pronounced.[82]

As Schefold notes, 'there remains a margin of doubt as to the responsibility for the text which finally appeared in German', particularly the three sentences quoted above.[83] However, even in writing what we know for certain he did, Keynes displayed remarkable insensitivity, indeed indifference, to a régime that put its political opponents into concentration camps and passed the anti-semitic Nuremburg laws. True, he had provided special German prefaces to his earlier German translations. But he did not need to provide one for the *General Theory*, and, if he felt he had to, why did he feel the need to go as far as he did even in the first quotation above? It is all shameful – and puzzling.

With enforced leisure at Ruthin, he turned again to foreign affairs. Again, the argument was that 'the claims of peace are paramount'.

> It is our duty to prolong peace, hour by hour, day by day, for as long as we can. We do not know what the future will bring, except that it will be quite different from anything we predict. I have said in another context that it is a disadvantage of 'the long run' that in the long run we are all dead. But I could have said equally well that it is a great advantage of 'the short run' that in the short run we are still alive. Life and history are made up of short runs. If we are at peace in the short run, that is something. The best we can do is put off disaster, if only in the hope, which is not necessarily a remote one, that something will turn up.[84]

The aim of British policy should be to avoid war, yet to make certain that, if war occurred, it happened in the most favourable circumstances. In this the 'brigand powers' were helping matters along by 'outraging every creed in turn' and 'spending a lot of money on an intensive propaganda to persuade the rest of the world that they are the enemies of the human race'.[85] Thus one waited, partially for public opinion to evolve, an argument he made clearer in an article he wrote but did not, on Lydia's advice, send to the *New Statesman*, three weeks after 'British Foreign Policy' from which I have just quoted.

This second article was stimulated in part by the death of Julian Bell, Clive and Vanessa's eldest son. He was killed on 18 July 1937 while driving an ambulance on the Republican side of the Brunete front outside Villanueva de la Cañada in Spain. He was 29 years old. It took a day or so for the news to reach England. When he heard it, Keynes wrote:

My dearest Nessa,

A line of sympathy and love from us both over the loss of your dear and beautiful boy with his pure and honourable feelings. It was fated that he should make his protest, as he was entitled to do, with his life, and one can say nothing.

With love and affection,
Maynard

Vanessa replied:

Dearest Maynard

I want to tell you that your words are almost the only ones I want to keep.

I tried to write to you the other day to thank you for what you wrote in the Nation [sic]ⁱ but I could not. I lost too much. I wanted Julian to read it. It is the message of our generation to the young.

Please get well. You are very dear to me & you must help us all.

Vanessa

Keynes had seen Julian only briefly on one occasion between his return from teaching in China on 12 March and his departure for Spain on 24 June. Before Julian had gone to China, he had edited a book of memoirs by First World War conscientious objectors, *We Did Not Fight*, providing a thoughtful but curious introduction which suggested that pacifism of the First World War variety was unlikely to be important in his generation. He concluded: 'I believe that the war resistance movement of my generation will in the end succeed by putting down war – by force if necessary'.[86] It was turning this notion over in his mind that had brought Keynes to draft his 'Further Thoughts on British Foreign Policy'. He wrote a rationale for his own earlier First World War views:

'Critic' [Kingsley Martin] wrote sympathetically last week of this country's running risks of war for Spanish democracy. Does there not underlie this a deep and disastrous confusion between the rights of personal protest and the criteria of national policy?

Many Englishmen are prone to feelings of profound indignation by happenings here and there in the world. It is an old-standing national propensity . . . . Such feelings give rise to a desire for some form of

i 'British Foreign Policy'.

active personal protest, which may range anywhere from writing a letter to *The Times*, getting up a fund, organising a meeting in the Albert Hall to laying down one's life as a true and devoted martyr. To such fanatics of the individual judgement as many of us are born to be, this right of personal protest is an essential and unsurrenderable privilege. No-one should, and as a rule no-one can, interfere with an individual's right to use it up to the limit. Julian Bell was entitled to make his protest with his life. His action was in no way inconsistent with the fact that in other circumstances he would probably have been a conscientious objector. On the contrary, it was deeply consistent, answering in both events to the indefeasible claims of private judgement and duty.

But the position of those who are not acting in an individual capacity, but are advising or representing the nation is entirely different. They have no similar rights of representative protest merely on the ground of their own individual feelings, but only if they are convinced that these feelings are also representative of the great majority.

... War resembles matters of faith and belief and differs from most other objects of public policy in that one may reasonably doubt whether even a large majority has a right to enforce it on the minority. But assuredly it is not a matter where the minority has a right to manoeuvre the majority into carrying out its will. Above all, ex-conscientious objectors[j] are not entitled to lead young Englishmen to death for a cause to defend which the average Englishman is in no wise led by his own impulses to honour.[87]

The resonances here with 'My Early Beliefs' and Keynes's own position over conscription in 1916 are clear. Keynes used a similar argument in private with Richard Kahn.[88]

Keynes maintained what had now become almost guerilla warfare in private with Kingsley Martin over the attitudes of the *New Statesman*. For instance, he attacked the *New Statesman*'s incitement of China 'to fight a war to a finish, so long as any Japanese soldier remains on Chinese soil' with no hope of effective outside assistance as unhelpful in moulding opinions against the dictators.[89] Apart from a September 1937 letter to *The Times* advocating the threat of economic sanctions against Japan unless she mended her ways,[90] Keynes's next public pronouncement on foreign affairs did not come until after Hitler entered Vienna on 13 March 1938 and incorporated Austria into the German Reich. In 'A Positive Peace Programme', he argued that the choice was now between resistance to the dictators and what he called 'positive pacifism'. If one opted for the latter, there should be a British initiative for a new European pact among Britain, France, Russia and any of the smaller states that wished to join. Its policy would be to end the Spanish

---

j Kingsley Martin had been a conscientious objector in the 1914–18 war. He had spent time in France with the Friends' Ambulance Unit.

War on a negotiated basis, with independence for Catalonia and the Basque provinces, to try to negotiate a settlement over the question of the Sudeten Germans in Czechoslovakia, and to attempt to provide collective security for Europe, as well as the nucleus for a European economic zone of free trade, investment and migration.[k] Such an initiative, he argued, might prevent war by re-acquiring for the democracies 'that capacity to appear formidable'.[91] The proposal caused something of a stir in anti-Chamberlain circles, but it was short-lived.

There matters rested until August–September 1938 – Munich. According to Lydia's notes about his health, Keynes was sufficiently worried about the international situation that it upset him on several occasions, despite his principle 'The inevitable never happens. It is the unexpected *always*'.[92,l] He did not foresee war. He favoured some Czechoslovakian frontier revisions, though not to the extent demanded by Hitler or conceded in the Munich settlement. He thought the Munich concessions, although not 'too great a price to pay for peace', were excessive, because 'with any sort of honest policy peace was never genuinely at risk'. He was very unhappy at how the settlement was achieved. He believed 'the whole nation *swindled* as never in its history'. His published article of 8 October, 'Mr Chamberlain's Foreign Policy', was far from approving, but still ambivalent.[93]

The final pre-war crisis over Poland in August 1939 caught him completely unprepared. He did not expect war when he went off on 14 August for a three weeks' cure at Royat. According to Lydia's notes, he was still optimistic on 30 August. This time he was wrong.

Beyond short articles or notes defending various details of his *General Theory* and an unsuccessful attempt to bring his debate with Pigou on the effects of flexible money wages to a head, Keynes's professional publications in the eighteen months after his illness were relatively few. This does not mean that he was inactive. I have just discussed his successive pieces on British foreign policy. He also began to make a limited return to public life. He made his annual speech to the National Mutual members on 23 February 1938. The next day he attended a meeting of the Council of the Royal Economic Society, held for his convenience at 46 Gordon Square. But these left him 'thoroughly exhausted' according to Lydia. In March he went up to King's for the fellowship elections. In May he managed a visit of over a fortnight to Cambridge during which he attended a College meeting, a Congregation and meetings in the Economics Faculty. However, he still tired easily and

---

k There could also be an offer to Germany of organised arrangements for 'all Austrian and German Jews who wish to migrate and be naturalised elsewhere'.

l On 11 September he remarked to Kingsley Martin: 'I believe in living from hand to mouth in international affairs because the successive links in the causal nexus are so completely unpredictable. One does well to evade *immediate* evils.' The echoes of *Probability* are strong (*JMK*, XXVIII, 120; VIII, 347–8).

Lydia kept his schedule manageable and her patient in line, although she could not control external events. Keynes would also get depressed about his own slow progress, which always seemed to be such that he would be told that it would be another six months. But there were good days. One of the best came on 11 September 1938. As Lydia reported it:

> I can hardly believe it, Maynard had a wonderful day. We had our memoir club 12 people, he read his paper at 5 o'clock for ¾ of an hour magnificently. At six o'clock I put him to bed, he was tired, but no pain, then had dinner with Desmond MacCarthy and David Garnett again a little tired but no worrying as in the past. It does seem wonderful to see his old self, his figure is a great success (that is my diet) and the friends say his face is of a much better shape.[94]

His memoir was 'My Early Beliefs' which had, as we have seen, its origins in an earlier Garnett memoir concerning D. H. Lawrence. The audience for the paper, as well as Lydia, comprised Clive, Vanessa, Quentin and Angelica Bell, Janie Bussy, Duncan Grant, David Garnett, Morgan Forster, Desmond and Molly MacCarthy, Leonard and Virginia Woolf. Yet for Quentin Bell and Janie Bussy this nostalgia for a long-dead world as Spain continued to fall to Franco and as the Munich crisis neared a climax seemed to make it clear that 'Bloomsbury belonged to the past'.[95]

Keynes's major professional publication of 1938 stemmed from the knowledge he had acquired over the years as a speculator and the author of a series of memoranda on 'Stocks of Staple Commodities' for the London and Cambridge Economic Service.[96] From this experience he had learned that commodity prices were remarkably unstable, even over short periods. One major reason for that instability was that stocks of primary commodities normally carned a negative rate of return, allowing for storage and interest costs, but subsidiary reasons included the fact that, because producers were unwilling or unable to hold stocks and because incentives were absent for manufacturers to purchase far in advance of needs, speculators knew that downward movements would be exaggerated and had no incentive to hold stocks unless prices were far below the normal future costs of production. Such commodity price instability had significant effects on general economic stability, and had in the past led to piecemeal stabilisation schemes for particular commodities. The abandonment of one of these, the Stevenson Rubber Scheme, had caused Keynes substantial capital losses in 1928–9.[97] As part of its preparations for a possible war, the Government in May 1938 had introduced an Essential Commodities Reserve Bill. This enabled the Board of Trade to obtain information about stocks of commodities essential in the event of war and to make provision for the maintenance of strategic stocks of such commodities. The bill became law in July 1938.

In his paper for the British Association for the Advancement of Science, 'The Policy of Government Storage of Foodstuffs and Raw Materials',[98]

Keynes made a number of proposals. There was a plea for the publication of more information, for he believed that here, as elsewhere information was essential for controlling the trade cycle. The major concern of his paper was with the powers that the Government had taken to purchase the commodities itself or to increase stocks physically stored in Britain but owned by others. Keynes wanted the authorities to use the latter power to induce traders and producers to hold larger stocks in Britain. Such arrangements might cost the authorities very little, facilitate the entrepôt and other commodity-related trades, and, most important, over the longer term provide the basis for a broader-based commodity price stabilisation scheme. He did little to develop such a scheme in this paper, but in 1941 this paper would be by his side when he turned to devising a scheme for post-war commodity price stabilisation.[m]

Keynes did not go to Cambridge to present his paper. Gerald Shove read it for him and he and Roy Harrod provided accounts of the discussion. Keynes sent copies to the Ministers concerned and to Henry Wallace, the American Secretary of Agriculture who was promoting the notion of 'an ever normal granary'. Keynes also corresponded with Sir Arthur Salter on the Essential Commodities Reserve Bill as it went through the Commons and on the paper itself. However, this was merely an idea: it was not the object of a co-ordinated Keynes campaign.

By the autumn of 1938 Keynes felt that he could be more active, as long as he reduced some regular commitments. In October he resigned the chairmanship of the National Mutual. This markedly reduced his London commitments, for it removed the need to attend the regular mid-week meeting around which he had organised his Cambridge life since 1920. It also ended the activity in which he had recently found least satisfaction, and the sense of responsibility for faults in the management of the Society.[99] This freedom allowed him to spend much of the autumn in Cambridge, working out of the flat in St Edward's Passage that he had organised for Lydia while building the Arts Theatre rather than in his old rooms in College. He was able to immerse himself in his theatre, bursaring and books without overstraining himself. He seemed to be making progress towards returning to normal, even if there were some setbacks.

His progress continued until he suffered a severe attack of influenza while in London at the end of February 1939. He could not consult his Cambridge physician and on the recommendation of friends he put himself into the hands of Dr Janos Plesch, a Hungarian who had been a Professor of Internal Medicine in Berlin with a fashionable practice and whose patients

m In January 1939 the Government gave serious attention to Keynes's paper when an interdepartmental committee was set up 'to consider exchange difficulties arising in relation to accumulation of stocks of essential materials. The papers for this committee are on PRO, BT 11/1037. For Keynes's later wartime scheme see below pp. 679–81.

had included Einstein. Plesch agreed with the Ruthin diagnosis of Keynes's malady but put more emphasis on the need to cure the infectious tonsils. Keynes soon came to call Plesch 'the Ogre' and his treatment 'a case of kill or cure'. The treatment – a saltless diet, injections, and three hours a day in ice – made Keynes feel dreadful. This treatment, which produced the sensations which 'most closely resemble those of a car being decarbonised', continued for most of March and it was not until the end of the month that he was allowed out from Gordon Square.[100]

Yet Keynes soon felt much better. By mid-April he was declaring Plesch 'the greatest genius that ever lived' and had developed a considerable affection for him. He started recommending Plesch to his friends. He would later declare of Plesch that 'it was he, and he alone, that brought me back into active life'.[101] He became completely at ease with him and over the ensuing years the surviving correspondence indicates that Keynes believed he could freely discuss his condition with him and expect results. Thus, in April 1939 he wrote to Plesch, who was in Monte Carlo and reporting he was doing badly at roulette:

> I suspect that you must have made a mistake about the relationship of arsenic and the date. I have reached the maximum to-day. If this is not the source of error, it must be that it is some less simple function of this number. Have you, for instance, tried multiplying the number of drops by 5 and subtracting your age? Some function will, I am sure, prove satisfactory, but one has to admit, of course, that roulette, like medicine, is still only an empirical science.[102]

He invited Plesch to Cambridge in June for the May Week performance of the Footlights Review and suggested that they go to King's Chapel for evensong the following day:

> You would hear English Church music in its most exquisite form and in the grandest possible environment. To my thinking, though exquisite, it is lifeless and even moribund and always falls on my emotions flatter than I expect. But if you have never been to one of these highly respectable, quasi-aesthetic Victorian performances where deathly moderation and pseudo-good taste have drowned all genuine emotion, you might find it an interesting experience.[103]

Keynes stood up well to the Easter term in Cambridge, including examining for the Tripos. By mid-July, back at Tilton, he reported to his father that he felt better than at any time since his illness. He was getting more exercise: on 13 August he walked to the top of Firle Beacon for the first time since his illness. With Lydia's close supervision, this improvement would continue for another year.

In late 1938 and early 1939 Keynes wrote one substantial article, 'Relative

Movements of Real Wages and Output', for the *Economic Journal*, where he responded to three empirical articles by John Dunlop and Lorie Tarshis which cast doubt on the 'stylised fact' that he had used in the *General Theory* that real and money wages moved inversely over the trade cycle. In the reply he put forward an embryonic statement of the hypothesis that firms' pricing decisions represent a mark-up on normal costs, a hypothesis that has proved popular with many post-Keynesian economists. In the next six months, Keynes produced two substantial review articles on League of Nations' publications for the *Journal*, as well as two substantial multi-part articles for *The Times* on rearmament finance. One of the former, his review of Jan Tinbergen's *Statistical Testing of Business Cycle Theories, I, A Method and its Application to Investment Activity*, is an important methodological statement which I shall deal with later. The latter two articles were particularly important for what followed, as the Treasury's views on borrowing policy were in a state of flux. Keynes's views also found their way into the 27th, and last, Report of the Committee on Economic Information, dated 20 July 1939.

Keynes had started attending meetings of the Committee on Economic Information again late in 1938 as the Committee prepared its December 1938 Report, 'Problems of Rearmament'. When this Report was being written, unemployment was still high and the Committee wanted to ensure that the Government did not, out of fear for the inflationary effects of its own programmes, take restrictive monetary and fiscal measures. The Committee concentrated on specific measures such as imposing priorities where conflicts arose or the discouragement of particular forms of consumption such as motor cars. As far as it could see, the most important contemporary problem was the deterioration in Britain's balance of payments position. Although it rejected devaluation, the Committee followed Keynes's lead in suggesting a number of ways of improving the capital account of the balance of payments through controls on certain types of transactions and a shift in borrowing from the sterling to the dollar areas. These were considered desirable alternatives to general credit restrictions and dear money.[104]

By the time Keynes returned to the problem in April 1939 in a two-part article in *The Times*, 'Crisis Finance: An Outline of Policy', circumstances had changed greatly. The Germans had marched into Prague and, with the beginning of staff conversations with the French, restraints on British rearmament expenditure were relaxed further. The implication, Keynes argued, was that the Chancellor would be wise to work on the assumption that the abnormal unemployment of the inter-war years would disappear during the current financial year. The problems of a war economy, if not war, were just around the corner.[105] The fundamental problem of the coming months would be the physical allocation of resources with labour and overseas resources proving to be the most serious bottlenecks.

If the Government watched the labour market and the balance of trade, it would, he argued, know when its programme plus private economic activity was pressing on available resources.[n] The Government should prepare for resource scarcities by setting up a co-ordinating authority inside the Treasury. This would maintain Treasury control once Britain entered the era when finance would no longer be the bottleneck.

But what of financial policy? Keynes did not believe that raising interest rates would have any role to play in restraining or co-ordinating demand and supply. As he put it:

> What object is there in offering an exceptionally high rate of interest? If private investment competes for limited resources, Government priorities and control of new issues are the appropriate remedy. On the other hand, the offer of a high rate of interest will overburden the Exchequer and disturb the national finances for a generation to come, and in the immediate present it will cause a ruinous depreciation to financial institutions.[106]

To avoid upward pressure on interest rates, Keynes recommended that the authorities raise loans *after* the expenditure had taken place so as not to aggravate the problem of 'finance' and to tap the savings from rising incomes as they became available. The Treasury, after setting a structure in interest rates from ½ to 2½ per cent, should also let the public decide how it wanted to balance its holdings of various maturities rather than force long-term debt on to the market.

In the next month, he broadcast on the BBC on the question 'Will Rearmament Cure Unemployment?'. He also answered critics of his article in *The Times* and as a result of the article made contact with Charles Madge. One of Cambridge's 'intellectual communists' of the earlier 1930s, Madge had, with Tom Harrison, founded Mass Observation and was investigating working-class savings behaviour. Their paths would soon cross again.[107] At the same time Keynes became convinced that he had not made the arguments in favour of the borrowing policy he advocated sufficiently clear; so he prepared a long memorandum, 'Government Loan Policy and the Rate of Interest', and sent it to the Chancellor of the Exchequer and the Governor of the Bank of England on 28 May. He also passed copies to R. H. Brand and Ian Macpherson, his stockbroker. Later he rearranged the memorandum for publication; it appeared in *The Times* of 24 and 25 July under the title 'Borrowing by the State'.[108] Publication led to further correspondence, in particular a series of exchanges with 'Lex' of the *Financial News*, who as 'Otto' Clarke would become a Treasury colleague late in the war.

---

n Given the lags involved, particularly in the labour market, it is surprising that Keynes put such faith in these indicators.

The memorandum went to the heart of the arguments on the issue. Keynes demonstrated that there was nothing that high interest rates could not do to restrain private expenditure competitive with the Government's programme that other measures could not do more effectively. He went on to argue that there was no necessity for the Government's borrowing programme to raise the rate of interest, as long as new issues followed the relevant expenditures and catered to the maturity preferences of the public, buttressing his case with relevant theoretical points and examples from American experience. He concluded the original memorandum, but not the published article, on a note for the future.

> The armament programme will bring abnormal unemployment to an end. Some day, and the sooner the better, we hope to stop the existing abomination and return to the ways of peace. Is that to mean a return to abnormal unemployment? It will go hard with the fabric of society if it does. To avoid this outcome, it will be necessary for productive investment, public and private, out of borrowed money to continue at a rate at least as high as this year's programme. How is this to be possible if we find ourselves saddled at the end of the armament period, as we were at the end of the late War, with a highish rate of interest?[109]

While Keynes was preparing his memorandum and articles, the Committee on Economic Information was preparing its last report, 'Defence Expenditure and the Economic and Financial Problems Concerned Therewith'. Keynes did not attend all the meetings – he attended those of 3 and 17 May and 6 June – but when he was unable to attend he provided the Committee with his views. He left his mark on the Report, particularly in the passages on interest rate policy where 'the main responsibility for the position eventually taken lies with Keynes' and in encouraging, yet restraining, the 'brave pioneering effort' of Piers Debenham to investigate statistically the excess of investment demand over capacity and the supply of voluntary savings likely to be available to finance new investment in 1939 in a non-inflationary manner.[110] The Report's expert rejection of the use of higher interest rates was, according to Professor Sayers,[111] an important influence in moving the Treasury to the view that it could finance rearmament and, in the event of war, at low interest rates, although it would still need the 'stiffening of nerve' that would come with Keynes's physical presence in the Treasury itself just over a year later.[112]

With this major exercise in persuasion on interest rates out of the way, Keynes turned to two long review articles of League of Nations' studies for the September 1939 *Economic Journal*. The one reviewing Tinbergen was still unwritten as late as 27 July. However, taking advantage of the fact that he had read Tinbergen's work in draft the previous year, he managed to finish his review by 4 August. When he submitted it, he thought it 'much too long and probably a waste of time'.[113] He said that

> It was frightfully difficult to run down all the points where, quite casually, he made all the necessary admissions. I was anxious not to accuse him too vehemently in the many cases where he had in fact, if one read carefully enough, pleaded guilty.[114]

Tinbergen's *Statistical Testing of Business-Cycle Theories*, vol. I, *A Method and its Application to Investment Activity* review dealt with the application of multiple correlation technique to the explanation of fluctuations in total investment, investment in residential building and investment in railway rolling stock. He was concerned with statistically testing some economists' theories of business cycles then available. For Tinbergen, the economist specified the theories and it was the job of the statistician to compute regression coefficients and thus determine the relative quantitative importance of the variables postulated *a priori*. However, as subsequent observers have pointed out, in Tinbergen's method 'judgement is allowed to play an important role in deciding whether an explanatory variable should be retained or discarded'. In this and other areas 'he does not offer any systematic methodology for dealing with . . . [such] problems'.[115]

Keynes's original comments on a draft of Tinbergen's study, his related correspondence with Roy Harrod, who had also read it for the League of Nations, and his published review all dealt with questions of methodology: 'the logic of applying the method of multiple correlation to unanalysed economic material, which we know to be non-homogeneous through time'.[116] His criticisms centred on six issues. The first five concerned the specification of the econometric equations, while the sixth concerned 'passing from statistical description to inductive generalisation' – something he remarked had concerned him 'thirty years ago'.[117] However, as Anna Carabelli has pointed out, all of the criticisms were cast in the language of *Probability*.[118]

Keynes's first five technical criticisms were well-taken.[119] He was concerned whether all relevant factors had been included in the equations, whether the factors were measurable, whether the factors were independent (thus avoiding spurious correlations, simultaneity and collinearity), whether the functional forms, in particular Tinbergen's assumption of linearity, were appropriate, and whether the treatment of time lags and trends was satisfactory. These problems have plagued econometrics since the beginning, although naturally practitioners have made many attempts to overcome them. In their discussion of the Keynes-Tinbergen issue, Pesaran and Smith re-estimate some of Tinbergen's work to show how sensitive its results were to some of the issues raised by Keynes.[120] They admit, as do most other econometricians, that, despite the occasional confusion, Keynes had a remarkable grasp of the technical issues.

The sixth topic Keynes dealt with was the matter of induction. Here he admitted 'I have not noticed any passage where Professor Tinbergen himself makes any inductive claims whatever'. However he saw the whole purpose of the exercise as inductive and remarked that 'Professor Tinbergen makes the least possible preparation for the inductive transition'.[121] He pointed out that Tinbergen had not practised the Lexis's procedure that he had praised in *Probability* – 'to break the period under examination into a series of sub-periods, with a view to discovering whether the results of applying our method to the various sub-periods taken separately are reasonably uniform'.[122] To econometricians this would be the equivalent to testing for structural stability: when done in a simple way for Tinbergen's work, the results are significant.[123] However, Keynes pushed the point further in his correspondence:

> The notion of testing the quantitative influence of factors suggested by a theory as being important is very useful and to the point. The question to be answered, however, is whether the complicated method here employed does not result in a false precision beyond what either the method or the statistics actually available can support. It may be that a more rough and ready method which preserves the data in a more recognisable form may be safer.[124]

Yet in his exchanges Keynes went even further – than most of his younger followers[125] and certainly most econometricians would go – in calling the whole econometric enterprise into question. In doing so he was echoing issues he had raised in *Probability* and in his earlier dispute with Karl Pearson.[126] As he put it to Roy Harrod:

> My point against Tinbergen is [this] . . . In chemistry and physics and other natural sciences the object of experiment is to fill in the actual value of various quantities and factors appearing in an equation or formula; and the work when done is once and for all. In economics this is not the case, and to convert a model into a quantitative formula is to destroy its usefulness as in instrument of thought. Tinbergen endeavours to work out the variable quantities in a particular case, or perhaps in the average of several particular cases, and he then suggests that the quantitative formula so obtained has general validity. Yet in fact, by filling in figures, which one can be sure will not apply the next time, so far from increasing the value of his instrument, he has destroyed it. All statisticians tend that way
> . . . The pseudo-analogy with the physical sciences leads directly counter to the habit of mind which it is most important for an economist proper to require.[127]

He went on to emphasise the moral scientific character of economics and the danger of treating material as constant and homogeneous through time. It is not surprising that he believed that rather than turning economics into a pseudo-natural science,

> *Progress* in economics consists almost entirely in a progressive improvement in the choice of models ... [for which] one does *not* fill in real values for the variable functions ... For as soon as this is done, the model loses its generality and its value as a mode of thought.[128]

As Pesaran and Smith note:

> From this perspective econometrics leads to two errors. First it regards the model as a testable representation of reality, confusing the tool with the object for which it is used. Second its premises (stable coefficients, measurable variables, etc.) exclude from consideration the interesting and important dimensions of economic problems. Thus there was a danger that mechanical procedures would displace insight and intuition and confine the scope of economics.[129]

Keynes's discussion of Tinbergen was the last time he explicitly referred to *Probability* in publications. In the literature, there has been a long-standing suggestion, alluded to above,[130] that by the 1930s Keynes had changed his view of probability from that espoused in his dissertation or in 1921. The suggestion takes a variety of forms, but the most influential suggests that, under the influence of criticism from Frank Ramsey, Keynes 'abandoned his logical theory of probability'.[131] The critical texts are normally his 'obituary' of Ramsey in *Essays in Biography* and 'My Early Beliefs' with its renunciation of the assumption of a bygone, youthful world. Under the influence of the work of Anna Carabelli, with its suggestion that the 'beliefs' concerned related to the period *before* substantive work on the fellowship dissertation, I have already discussed the latter point. Not surprisingly, she also runs a 'continuity thesis' when she argues that Keynes 'accepted none of the main points which are characteristic of the view of probability advanced by Ramsey in his 1926 article'.[132] This argument, which runs through Wittgenstein, plays down the earlier influences of Moore and Russell. An alternative 'continuity thesis' has been associated with Rod O'Donnell, who argues that 'Keynes's concession to Ramsey, whatever it amounts to, did not constitute a radical shift in the foundations of his thought'.[133] The basis of this argument, which has parallels in the work of others, has come under convincing fire from Bradley Batemen (1990), who convincingly argues that the evidence adduced in its support by O'Donnell does not exclude the more traditional interpretation. Doubtless the argument will continue, but for the purposes of my biography I find the Carabelli argument the more convincing.

After completing the Tinbergen review, Keynes and Lydia spent ten quiet days at Tilton before flying to Paris on their way to Royat. They intended to stay three weeks; they were back at Tilton on 29 August after two. Two days later, Hitler invaded Poland.

NOTES

1 *JMK*, XIV, 85.
2 Pigou 1936, 21, 18.
3 Knight 1936, 158, 141.
4 Viner 1936, 85, 89, 91.
5 Hansen 1936, 83.
6 Young 1987 provides a fascinating, detailed discussion of the interaction that occurred at Oxford.
7 Lange 1938, 187.
8 *JMK*, XIV, 87; XXIX, 217.
9 *JMK*, XIV, 111.
10 *JMK*, XXIX, 221–4, 226–9; see esp. 222.
11 *JMK*, XIV, 115–16.
12 Patinkin 1982.
13 All of Keynes's contributions appear in *JMK*, XIV, 201–15, 215–23, 229–33.
14 *JMK*, XIV, 185.
15 *JMK*, XIV, 208.
16 Shackle 1967, 114.
17 It appears in *JMK*, X, ch. 13.
18 Ibid., ch. 17.
19 *JMK*, XIV, 124–33.
20 KCKP, L/R, JMK to DHR, 8 April 1914.
21 KCKP, JMK to Lydia, 7 December 1925.
22 KCKP, JMK to Lydia, 5 October and 7 November 1926, 23 January, 2 February and 4 April 1927.
23 *JMK*, XIII, 122, 123.
24 *JMK*, XIII, 211.
25 KCKP, JMK to Lydia, 3 May 1931.
26 *JMK*, XIII, 29–41; above pp. 457–8.
27 *JMK*, XIII, 313–14.
28 Deutscher 1990, Tables 1 and 2.
29 See the 1948 Preface to the LSE reprint of *A Study of Industrial Fluctuation*.
30 On the last see Straight 1983, 58. But here the circumstances were particularly galling.
31 Robbins 1971, 221; Newsome 1980, 250, 364, 366; Annan 1990, 113.
32 *JMK*, XIII, 493–523, the request to break off is on 520.
33 *JMK*, XIII, 497.
34 *JMK*, XIII, 378; KCKP, C. R. Fay to JMK, 6 March 1935.
35 See also Turner 1989, 21–4.
36 KCKP, A. C. Pigou to JMK, [June 1940].
37 Deutscher 1990, Table 3.
38 KCKP, JMK to C. R. Fay, 5 March 1935.
39 KCKP, DHR to JMK, 28 September 1936. Part of the letter appears in *JMK*, XXIX, 163–4.
40 The body of Keynes's letter appears in *JMK*, XIV, 87–8.
41 See Robertson 1940, ix, 26 note 4. Compare with *JMK*, XIV, 94–5; XXIX, 166–7.
42 *JMK*, XXIX, 164.

43 KCKP, L/R, DHR to JMK, 17 August 1937; JMK to DHR, 31 August 1937.
44 KCKP, RFK to JMK, 14–18 February 1938; JMK to RFK, 19 February 1938.
45 KCKP, JMK to A. C. Pigou, 17 August 1938.
46 KCKP, A. C. Pigou to JMK, 20 August 1938.
47 Johnson and Johnson 1978, 136, 137.
48 KCKP, JMK to RFK, 19 February 1938.
49 Johnson and Johnson 1978, 139.
50 For the offer of the chair and Keynes's refusal, see KCKP, UA1/1, Hale to JMK, 22 January 1944, JMK to Hale, 26 January 1944, Hale to JMK, 1 February 1944.
51 *JMK*, XXI, 360–9.
52 For a detailed discussion of the Committee's discussions, see Howson and Winch 1977, 134–40.
53 *JMK*, XXI, 383.
54 *JMK*, XXI, 389.
55 Kahn 1974.
56 Howson and Winch 1977, 107.
57 Howson and Winch 1977; Peden 1980, 1984, 1988; Middleton 1982, 1985; Clarke 1988.
58 For this report, see Howson and Winch 1977, 140, 343–53.
59 Lowe 1986, 221–2.
60 Howson and Winch 1977, 145.
61 *JMK*, XXI, 413.
62 *JMK*, XXI, 427, 430, 444–5.
63 Howson 1975, 135, 138.
64 *JMK*, XXI, 436, 438.
65 *JMK*, XXI, 440.
66 Stein 1969, 108–13.
67 KCKP, JMK to FAK, 1 April 1937; see also his letter to his uncle on 25 March 1937 and his letters to Lydia of 22 and 24 January 1937.
68 The letter to the Chancellor appears in *JMK*, XXI, 416–17.
69 Below p. 611; KCKP, JMK to R. F. Kahn, 6 July 1937.
70 KCKP, JMK to R. F. Kahn, 7 July 1937.
71 KCKP, JMK to R. F. Kahn, 26 August 1937.
72 KCKP, Lydia to R. F. Kahn, 5 September 1937.
73 *JMK*, XXI, 244.
74 KCKP, JMK to A. Spiethoff, 25 August 1933.
75 *JMK*, XXI, 285; KCKP, JMK to Lydia, 15 October 1933. See also his comments to Kingsley Martin in *JMK*, XXVIII, 20–1.
76 KCKP, JMK to Lydia, 3 March 1935.
77 *JMK*, XXI, 370–2.
78 Ibid., 46–8.
79 Ibid., 49–50; see also 52.
80 Ibid., 55, 56.
81 *JMK*, VII, xxvi.
82 Schefold, 175.
83 Ibid., 1980, 176.
84 *JMK*, XXVIII, 62.
85 *JMK*, XXVIII, 62, 64.
86 *JMK*, X, 360.
87 *JMK*, XXVIII, 76–7. The whole piece occupies pages 73–8.
88 KCKP, JMK to R. F. Kahn, 12 and 24 July 1937.

89 *JMK*, XXVIII, 92–4.
90 *JMK*, XXVIII, 82.
91 *JMK*, XXVIII, 99–100, 102.
92 *JMK*, XXVIII, 117.
93 *JMK*, XXVIII, 117, 122, 124, 125–7.
94 KCKP, Lydia to FAK, 11 September 1938.
95 Q. Bell in Crabtree and Thirwall 1980, 86.
96 *JMK*, XII, 267–647; see above p. 383.
97 Above pp. 409-10.
98 *JMK*, XII, 456–70.
99 JMK, XII, 47; KCKP, JMK to RFK, 11 October 1938.
100 KCKP, JMK to RFK, 6, 14 and 25 March 1939.
101 VWL, VI, 306; KCKP, JMK to B. G. Catterns, 30 April 1942.
102 KCKP, JMK to Plesch, 18 April 1939.
103 KCKP, JMK to Plesch, 28 May 1939.
104 Howson and Winch 1977, 148–9.
105 *JMK*, XXI, 511.
106 *JMK*, XXI, 517.
107 Below p. 644.
108 *JMK*, XXI, 551–64.
109 *JMK*, XXI, 546.
110 Sayers 1956, 154; *JMK*, XXI, 579.
111 Sayers 1956, 155.
112 Ibid., 204.
113 KCKP, JMK to RFK, 27 July 1939; JMK to E.A.G. Robinson, 4 August 1939. Keynes's 1938 comments on Tinbergen's draft appear in *JMK*, XIV, 285–95.
114 KCKP, JMK to E. A. G. Robinson, 11 August 1939.
115 Pesaran and Smith 1985, 137. This discussion, as well as those of Carabelli 1988 and Morgan 1990, has good references to the earlier literature.
116 *JMK*, XIV, 285–6.
117 *JMK*, XIV, 315.
118 Carabelli 1988, ch. 10.
119 Patinkin 1976b, 1094–6.
120 Pesaran and Smith 1985, 140–4.
121 *JMK*, XIV, 315–16.
122 *JMK*, XIV, 316.
123 Pesaran and Smith 1985, 143–4.
124 *JMK*, XIV, 289; see also a similar suggestion to Tinbergen ibid., 294.
125 See, for example, Brown 1988.
126 Above pp. 162–3 and 205–7.
127 *JMK*, XIV, 299–300.
128 *JMK*, XIV, 296.
129 1985, 146.
130 Pp. 144 and 366.
131 Bateman 1990, 73. In this article and in Bateman 1987, he also provides references to the previous literature.
132 Carabelli 1988, 270.
133 O'Donnell 1990, 57.

24

HOW TO PAY FOR THE WAR

I spend my time trying to make them face up to the possible alternatives and choose wisely between them.

(KCKP, JMK to FAK, 25 December 1940)

On the outbreak of war, the Keyneses left Tilton for London and then Cambridge. Keynes did not see himself playing a major part in public affairs. He reiterated what he had told Richard Kahn when war threatened a year earlier, with adjustments for the fact that he was now far more fit: he would go up to Cambridge and by taking over more of the College bursaring and teaching in both the Faculty and College release those who could be more active for Government service. He also recommended Kahn to the Treasury. He told Josiah Stamp that he might be fit for committee work which involved a few meetings in London and quiet drafting on his own.[1]

Keynes began his quiet drafting without the committee work. On 14 September he produced a memorandum on the general principles of Government price policy which he sent to Stamp and Hubert Henderson (both already in Government service on the Survey of Economic and Financial Plans) and to the Treasury on 15 September.[2] This led to meetings with Sir Richard Hopkins and Sir Frederick Phillips and a request from the latter for his suggestions on exchange control. He complied on 24 September with his 'Notes on Exchange Control' which combined a brief memoir of his First World War experience in managing Britain's overseas position without controls with moderate suggestions for current controls. He pointed out:

It is well, therefore, to remember that we did get through after a fashion without blocking the exchanges; and this policy was not without considerable advantages of simplicity and efficiency.[3]

He did not now recommend complete control: he recommended controls over the most important transactions, leaving the less important to the free market, as long as recourse to this market did not cost the authorities too much foreign exchange net. He advised the Treasury 'to be cautious and cagey with its control system, and to cultivate turning a blind eye with the other one open'.⁴ Later in changed circumstances he was to change his mind on the extent of controls.

Late in September he found another outlet for his desire to become involved in a limited way, when he and a number of similarly aged administrators from the First World War – Walter Layton (formerly of the Ministry of Munitions), William Beveridge (formerly of the Ministries of Munitions and Food) and Arthur Salter (formerly Director of Ship Requisitioning) – who had not yet found the wartime niches that some, particularly Beveridge, desperately desired, began to meet at 46 Gordon Square to discuss and co-ordinate their attempts to influence the war effort.⁵ Lydia and Maynard called them 'the Old Dogs'. At first they met weekly: later less frequently. In the early period Keynes produced memoranda on the operation of the blockade and a series of notes on the war for President Roosevelt which included a proposal for the finance of post-war European reconstruction.⁶ Keynes also started to move more widely in London. On 12 October he went to the Other Club for the first time since his illness and tried without success to persuade Winston Churchill, then First Lord of the Admiralty, to remove wheat from the list of contraband goods, partly to influence German and world opinion and partly to dissipate Germany's foreign exchange reserves. On 6 December he went to the Tuesday Club for the first time since May 1937 to talk on 'Price Policy'. Among the new members he met that night was Hugh Gaitskell, then a temporary civil servant in the Ministry of Economic Warfare.

There were pressures for him to appear on a wider stage. The illness and death of Sir John Withers, one of the MPs for Cambridge University, meant that there would be a by-election. The Master of Magdalene, A. B. Ramsey, approached Keynes and told him that all three parties would sign his nomination papers, that he could sit as an independent and that in view of his health he would have lighter than normal duties. Keynes refused on health grounds, but the Master of Magdalene approached Plesch for an opinion. The result was unexpected, for as Keynes reported to Plesch:

> I had a visit from the Master of Magdalene yesterday, from which I gather you have let me down completely. So I would very much like to see you when I am up [in London] this week.⁷

After seeing Plesch and hearing his prognosis, Keynes had to find another excuse for declining the offer, which he did after discussions with Beveridge, Layton and Henderson.

> The active political life is not my right and true activity. I am indeed an extremely active publicist. And that is just the difficulty. I am on lines along which I can only operate usefully and have my full influence if I am aloof from the day to day influence of Westminster. I have become convinced that that would be actually destructive to my

present usefulness and would embroil me in the kind of controversy where my powers and my habitual line of approach would be at a disadvantage.[8]

Keynes wrote that letter on 24 November. By that time he was already embarked on what would be the most sophisticated and successful of his many campaigns as a publicist – *How to Pay for the War*.

In the first month of the war, Keynes's public comments on war finance were limited to two letters to *The Times*. He first commented on Sir John Simon's War Budget of 27 September, which among other measures raised the standard rate of income tax from 5s. 6d. to 7s. (and announced it would go to 7s. 6d. in the next Budget), increased surtax and introduced Excess Profits Tax (EPT) at 60 per cent. Keynes remarked on the 'utter futility of the old imposts' to solve the budgetary problems of war and described the Budget, except for EPT, as 'chicken-feed to the dragons of war'.[9] To emphasise his point and the need for low interest rates, he noted that the gains to the Chancellor from raising loans at 2½ rather than 3 per cent would be double the proceeds of all the tax increases announced in the Budget. His second letter replied to critics of the first, including J. R. Hicks. As he continued to correspond privately in early October with Hicks on the problems of war finance and inflation, Keynes made it clear that he had 'not quite made up my mind' on the exact balance between increased taxation and 'special measures of an unorthodox kind' to meet the budgetary problem.[10] Within a fortnight, he was on his way to a solution and, as important, to a method which would highlight the size of the problem and revolutionise subsequent budgetary practice.

On 20 October Keynes 'gave a brilliant lecture', according to Lydia's diary, to the Marshall Society in Cambridge under the title 'War Potential and War Finance'. He worked the material up for publication in *The Times* under the title 'The Limitation of Purchasing Power: High Prices, Taxation and Compulsory Savings' and sent copies of his draft to Sir John Simon, Clement Attlee, Lord Stamp, R. H. Brand and Hubert Henderson, as well as to the editor of the newspaper, who agreed to print it after Keynes had completed his initial discussions. He also spoke on the subject to a dinner meeting of officials, MPs and Ministers on 27 October and discussed it with Sir Richard Hopkins of the Treasury over lunch at 46 Gordon Square on 1 November.

With a 'reasonably encouraging' initial reaction, he refined his proposals into two articles, improving the balance, and altered some details, such as indexing compulsory savings on the advice of Henry Clay and others who believed it would divert discussion from his main proposal.[11] Owing to a leak through a neutral correspondent, his proposals appeared first in the *Frankfurter Allgemeine Zeitung* on 7 November. The articles appeared in *The Times* under the title of 'Paying for the War' on 14 and 15 November 1939.

To appreciate the issues that Keynes was dealing with, it is necessary to consider the principles of war finance. Any policy proposal during a total war, as Professor Sayers suggested,[12] must in some way satisfy one or more of four criteria: it must intensify the war effort of the nation by mobilising existing domestic resources for war as well as maintaining that mobilisation; it must increase the resources available by drawing on unused resources at home or on resources from abroad; it must make the burdens resulting from these transfers of resources from their peacetime uses as tolerable as possible; and it must minimise the post-war consequences of the war. What is possible or tolerable is, of course, a matter of opinion. Hence the crucial role of persuasion and of 'Paying for the War' and its successors in the story of Britain's Second World War mobilisation.

At the heart of 'Paying for the War' was the recognition that a long large-scale war not fought out of stocks accumulated before the start of hostilities (such as the Falklands episode of the 1980s) involves large shifts of resources away from their peacetime uses. In both world wars, although domestic output rose (by just under 25 per cent in the Second World War), the increase in Government expenditure on the war effort swamped the rise in output. The problem for the authorities, and for Keynes, was *how* to divert resources from peacetime uses to the needs of war – and, particularly in the Second World War, how to reduce consumption during a period of sharply rising real and money incomes.

As Keynes saw it, there were four possible ways in which the authorities could gain command of additional resources (as well as declines in investment, living off past stocks or allowing a deterioration in the current account of the balance of payments – all of which also occurred):

(1)   Individuals could voluntarily reduce their consumption expenditures and directly or indirectly make their savings available to the Government by taking up loans or increasing their cash balances.
(2)   Comprehensive rationing could reduce consumption by fiat.
(3)   Through inflationary policies, the authorities could initially bid the resources necessary for the war away from other uses and eventually place the command of these resources into the hands of those who would pass them on to the Government through taxation, voluntary savings or higher cash balances.
(4)   Increased taxation could reduce the resources available to the public for consumption and transfer them to the authorities.

Given the sums involved and the consequent need for very sharp rises in both average and marginal propensities to save, especially among groups that had not previously saved much, Keynes believed that voluntary savings would not provide the resources necessary for waging war without inflation. As for rationing, it would be inevitable for essential consumption articles in short supply, but unless it was comprehensive it would also divert demand to unrationed goods. Comprehensive rationing, on the other hand, would tie up substantial bureaucratic resources better used elsewhere for the war, and would be unnecessarily restrictive of consumers' choice and hence prove unpopular.[a] Inflation, which had borne the brunt of private demand restriction during the First World War, might prove effective in reducing consumption up to a point, but after this point it would, with a lag, lead to offsetting wage claims. Given the likely lags, prosecution of the war by this method would necessitate large *and continuous* price increases which would result in discontent, inequities and charges of profiteering, not to mention leaving the bulk of any post-war debt in the hands of the wealthy. Moreover, since workers were probably more 'index conscious' than previously, the inflation would be greater than that of the First World War, when prices had doubled in the course of the war. This left taxation, which would have to reach much further down the income scale than at present if it were to do the trick, as his preferred alternative. The need for a wider tax base pointed either to a general turnover tax, which had the disadvantage of requiring new bureaucratic machinery, or to an innovation within the existing machinery.

Keynes opted for innovation in the form of compulsory saving or deferred pay. A progressive percentage of all incomes above a stipulated minimum would be paid over to the Government. Part of this would be in the form of direct taxes; part in the form of compulsory savings credited to the accounts of individuals in the Post Office Savings Bank. These accounts would pay interest, but, except in certain circumstances, they would be blocked until the end of the war. They would then be released in instalments to meet the first post-war slump. The scheme had the advantage that it could operate through the existing arrangements for national insurance contributions.

Such were the bare bones of Keynes's scheme. To estimate its required scale, he faced a problem. In 1939 the British Government did not produce national income statistics. In collaboration with Erwin Rothbarth, an extremely able statistical assistant in the Cambridge Faculty of Economics whose pre-war research project had ended when David Champernowne entered government service, Keynes set about providing the necessary numbers, working from estimates previously published by Colin Clark. He published his estimates in the *Economic Journal* for December 1939, with supplementary notes in March and June 1940, as well as a privately printed 'Budget of National Resources' in March 1940.[13]

Reaction to the publication of *The Times* articles was immediate and substantial. The Beaverbrook press and the press of the left – the *Daily Worker, Daily Herald*, and *Tribune* – were hostile, as were Labour Party and trade union leaders – partly through misunderstandings.[14] Economists of all persuasions welcomed them, as was made clear by F. A. Hayek's sympathetic

a Keynes here probably underestimated the popularity of the notion of 'fair shares', although the revised proposals of *How to Pay for the War* certainly represented an attempt to meet the feeling that there should be fairness (below pp. 632–3).

exposition of them in the *Spectator* on 24 November. Keynes replied to the comments and criticisms in *The Times* on 28 November, where he noted that as yet 'the general public are not in favour of any plan' while some politicians seemed to prefer inflation:

> No one has to take responsibility for inflation, not even the Chancellor of the Exchequer. The adoption of my plan would require the approval of the Labour Party. But they will never be asked to agree to inflation. It will just happen. It is nature's remedy, ebbing up like the tides, silently and imperceptibly and inevitably. It engages in its support our *laissez-faire* traditions.[15]

Keynes soon began to receive suggestions that his *Times* articles appear as a pamphlet. A simple reprinting of the three articles and the statistical material from the *Economic Journal* would not fit well together. Instead, as he told Harold Macmillan on 27 November, he proposed to recast his material. This gained him the added advantage of being able to make further changes in the scheme to make it more acceptable, particularly to the left. He made extensive consultations, interspersed with letters to the press and one interview with Douglas Jay for the *Daily Herald* (which appeared only after Jay and Francis Williams protested against Lord Southwood's attempt to suppress publication).[16] His consultations included a meeting with Eleanor Rathbone and Eva Hubback, long-standing advocates of family allowances, on 17 January. He also met with various groups: the Labour Front Bench on 24 January, a committee of the General Council of the Trades Union Congress on 24 January, members of the House of Commons on 20 February and the Fabian Society on 21 February, when he was able to circulate proofs of the pamphlet.[17] He also corresponded extensively with, among others, F. W. Pethick-Lawrence, Sir Walter Citrine, Ernest Bevin, Harold Laski, G. D. H. Cole and Josiah Stamp.

The result was that his proposals in *How to Pay for the War: A Radical Plan for the Chancellor of the Exchequer* contained several alterations. The major changes affected those with lower incomes: he proposed a family allowance of 5s. per week per child up to age 15, the allowance to be paid directly to the mother, and a limited list of necessaries or 'iron ration' available at low fixed prices, even if this involved subsidies. These two changes would actually improve the position of the worst off as compared with before the war. But these concessions cost money; so Keynes had to make his scheme a more efficient generator of revenue in other ways. The first change was to recommend that children's allowances under the income tax system be reduced to zero. The second was to increase the progression of the combined rates of income tax and compulsory savings with the top rate reaching 85 per cent as compared with his previous 80 per cent.[18] He also widened the range of institutions with which deferred pay could be placed to include friendly societies, trade unions and other working-class savings institutions. Finally he proposed to repay the proceeds of the compulsory savings portion of the scheme in the first slump after the war through a means suggested by Hayek, a capital levy collected during the boom of the immediate post-war reconstruction period. Such a levy might be collected in instalments as a prelude to an annual wealth tax. Thus he had 'endeavoured to snatch from the exigency of war positive social improvements', including 'an advance towards economic equality greater than any which we have made in recent times'.[19] It was indeed a 'radical plan' – far more so than any later British post-war 'social contract' for wage restraint.

Before the publication of *How to Pay for the War* on 27 February 1940, Keynes sent almost 100 copies of the pamphlet to friends, colleagues and those he was trying to persuade, often accompanying them with requests for meetings. The day after publication, Lord Balfour arranged for a discussion in the House of Lords. On 6 March, with Ben Tillett in the chair, Keynes addressed members of the National Trade Union Club. The next day he saw the Chancellor of the Exchequer and a group of MPs, while on 8 March he saw the Governor of the Bank. Lydia's diary noted that he was 'on the whole standing interviews splendidly, came to the [Cambridge] train after seeing the Governor fresh as a button, in the evening went to the theatre'. On 11 March he held a BBC broadcast discussion of his ideas with Donald Tyerman.

Support for the new proposals was mixed. Although he was gaining ground on the left with some trade unionists and Labour Party advisers, he had made little progress with the Labour Front Bench and none with Ernest Bevin. In the City, he found support from the Governor of the Bank, 'with whom, after long estrangement, this scheme has brought a personal reconciliation', and several Bank of England directors, as well as his old supporters and friends, Samuel Courtauld, R. H. Brand and Reginald McKenna.[20] Yet there was opposition in the City from Lord Kindersley, the Chairman of the National Savings Movement, and those around him. Among economists and economist-administrators, there was very strong support. Dennis Robertson called it 'your best work since E.C.P.', while Professor Robbins joined Hayek in for once supporting a Keynes plan.[21,b] Keynes was making progress, except perhaps, as he had told Reginald McKenna at the end of January, with 'the bloody politicians whose bloody minds have not been prepared for anything unfamiliar to their ancestors', although here he suspected that it was a problem of leadership – and time.[22]

He kept up the pressure with letters to the press, often replying to questions or comments. In a letter to *The Times* of 12 March and in his privately printed 'Budget of National Resources' of 31 March he was also attempting to influence the shape of the Budget due on 23 April. He went to the House of Commons for the Chancellor's statement and came home 'excited' according to Lydia. Coming a fortnight after the

b There was some quibbling over family allowances from J. R. Hicks (*JMK* XXII, 107–10).

German invasions of Norway and Denmark, after a campaign in *The Economist* which had drawn unfavourable comparisons between British and German war expenditures, and after Keynes's own campaign but in the face of a lingering official horror of deficits, the Budget was according to the Chancellor himself 'voluntarism on trial'.[23] The major change in the Budget was the introduction of purchase tax, which along with increases in other indirect taxes and duties was expected to yield just over £100 million in a full year. The deficit was estimated at £1,500 million. Keynes's response was to take a new tack, not only to criticise the changes in the context of the Chancellor's spending commitments but also to criticise the scale of the commitments in comparison with their past growth and with Britain's economic capacity. He did this in a letter to *The Times* on 24 April, in the never-published preface to the French edition of *How to Pay for the War*, and in his advice to MPs. As he told Clement Davies on 3 May:

> At the present stage I believe there is a good deal to be said for concentrating on the inadequacy of the spending programme rather than the inadequacy of the fiscal programme. If we can get what we want done in the former respect, the inadequacy of the latter will be shown up.[24]

A week later events intervened. After a two-day debate on the British campaign in Norway which revealed a substantial erosion of support in his own party, Neville Chamberlain resigned on 10 May 1940 in favour of Winston Churchill, who proceeded to form a coalition for the duration. Earlier the same day Hitler had invaded Holland and Belgium.

From late February, in the intervals of his campaign for *How to Pay for the War*, Keynes started to turn his critical attention to other aspects of Government policy. The first stimulus came from his activities as an investor for himself, King's and the Provincial Insurance Company. A Treasury requisition order for a large block of American shares left him with over £1 million to re-invest and brought offers of a large block of shares of British American Tobacco from American sources. He took up this loophole in the exchange controls with Sir Frederick Phillips on 22 February, promising him on 4 March a memorandum on exchange control as soon as he was 'less preoccupied in other directions'. He began to collect information, often using Thomas Balogh (then preparing what became *Studies in Financial Organization* (1947) for the National Institute of Economic and Social Research) as a source, because, as he put it to Richard Kahn:

> I have learned to be cautious about public controversy unless I feel I know the other fellow's case beforehand better than he knows it himself.[25]

He also worried about the best means to attack this complex and technical issue, for it would not catch the interest of the general public and he might, in fact, increase foreign knowledge of the available loopholes.

Keynes began his new campaign in a tentative way with a speech to the Parliamentary Monetary Committee, who had invited him to talk on the rate of interest. Using the valid excuse that the success of wartime interest rate policy rested on the effectiveness of exchange control, he turned to the latter issue and argued that the existing controls were extremely unsatisfactory and costly to the war effort. After the meeting, he prompted P. C. Loftus and Robert Boothby to ask Parliamentary questions on the details of the existing controls and worked on his memorandum for Phillips. He finished a draft by 29 April and discussed it with Bank of England officials before revising it. His revisions took account of recent changes in the controls, such as the blocking of transactions in outstanding securities on 12 May, and the new turn in the war caused by the German offensive in the west. Further revisions followed more discussions with Bank of England controllers before he sent the final version to Phillips on 24 May. He met Phillips on 28 May and sent him further memoranda on 30 May, 4 and 11 June.[26]

These memoranda reflected the deteriorating military situation on the Continent: the Germans broke though at Sedan on 14 May; Holland capitulated on 15 May; the Germans reached the Channel at Abbéville on 20 May; Belgium capitulated on 28 May; and the evacuation of British and allied troops from Dunkirk took place from 27 May to 3 June. The memoranda were prepared amid meetings with Governor Norman, the new Chancellor of the Exchequer (Sir Kingsley Wood), the financial attaché at the French Embassy (Emmanuèl Monick), the Chairman of the Anglo-French Co-ordinating Committee (Jean Monnet) and interested MPs. The memoranda attempted to bolster French morale as well as to prepare the ground for an approach to the United States for the assistance necessary. The change in the war had badly upset the previous Anglo-French prospect of somehow operating on a war basis for three years before American assistance became absolutely necessary. The Anglo-French proposals came to nothing when the French sued for an armistice with the Germans on 17 June.

Britain's isolation after May 1940 brought Keynes another job. Each German success brought an increase in the number of enemy aliens subject to internment as the authorities successively tightened their regulations and as new countries such as Italy entered the war on the German side. The number involved was about 65,000. The Government proposed to intern them on the Isle of Man and then send them to the Dominions as shipping space became available. 'Valuable' aliens would, however, be allowed to remain in England with limited freedom of movement. Among those interned were a number of economists, notably Piero Sraffa, Erwin Rothbarth, Hans Singer and Edward Rosenbaum, on whose behalf Keynes intervened with all possible authorities from the Home Secretary downwards to obtain their release for normal teaching and research duties. In the end he was successful, but he worried about the 'thousands of more obscure people who cannot be dealt with in this way' and regarded the whole affair as 'the most disgraceful and humiliating thing which has happened for a long time'.[27]

Despite these calls on his energies, Keynes's health stood the strain. He was still subject to the rigid discipline of 'steady policy Gaspodina Lydia' which, despite Keynes's pleas, Plesch insisted must last until September.[28] He had occasional chest pains, but there were fewer bad days. When they did occur on 14 and 17 May Lydia was very upset, crying that she couldn't 'stand the strain of illness and war'. Keynes still spent long periods resting with his ice bag, but the reports from the Ogre ranged from 'not bad' on 5 June to 'good' on 19 June according to Lydia's diary. Keynes was still losing weight in August, but then his report from the Ogre was, according to Lydia 'wonderful'. By then he needed all his energy, for he was becoming more closely involved in the official war effort.

On 28 June, after a talk with the new Chancellor, Keynes was offered a further connection with the Treasury. The proposed link was membership of a Consultative Council which was to help and advise the Chancellor on special problems arising from war conditions. The Council was announced on 1 July and met for the first time a week later.

Keynes did not expect that his membership of the Council would involve much work, though it would improve his access to the Chancellor. To Pigou, he put the situation as follows:

> I have no idea whether my appointment, which you have probably seen, to a new super-dud Committee at the Treasury is going to be a complete washout or not. I have little confidence in it. The only advantage of it is that it gives me the chance of trying out my state of health rather gradually (that is to say if there is any work attached to it, which is not clear yet) . . .
>
> . . . All of this advisory business is a hopeless ploughing of the sands.

The first subject put before the Consultative Council was compensation for war damage – the possibility of such damage having become more real with the Germans on the other side of the Channel. This was something about which Keynes knew something: King's was a large property owner and the Bursar kept up with such matters. The problem was the scale of damage expected from air attack. As early as October 1936 the insurance industry had refused to accept war risks insurance: only the Government could handle risks on such a scale. In April 1937 the Cabinet had decided that insurance against damage from the air was impossible. An official committee considered whether any form of compensation was feasible. Its report, accepted by Cabinet, took as its general principle that in a major war the authorities could provide at most partial compensation after the end of hostilities. The Government announced in 1939 the vague commitment that, except for ships and their cargoes and for stocks of work in progress for which there were separate schemes, it would pay compensation on 'the highest scale compatible with the circumstances of the country' after the war. Keynes attacked this because it committed the Treasury to the maximum liability yet provided no security for individuals and, given the place of property in the portfolios of individuals and financial intermediaries such as insurance companies and building societies, it ran the risk of causing a collapse in credit and confidence if there were substantial damage. By the time he wrote his first memorandum on the subject on 9 July 1940 there had already been runs, and therefore moratoria, on withdrawals from building societies, and he argued that Stock Exchange prices had felt the effects of the uncertainty as individuals tried to value assets subject to the risks of bombing. Moreover, as individuals tended to overestimate 'unfamiliar, unpredictable and potentially catastrophic risks', the existing régime was bad for morale. He continued:

We cannot allow economic ruin (for people will regard the immediate deprivation of their income coupled with no clear understanding about the future as next door to ruin) to fall each night on a random collection of innocent persons. And what do we gain by thus spreading insecurity and panic? Nothing whatever in view of the promises the Treasury has already given, except in the event of a destruction of the national wealth so widespread that all commitments will have to be reconsidered. The notion that in such an event we can save the rest of the situation by bilking a large number of persons, who have no means of protecting themselves and are entirely without fault in the matter, of 10 to 25 per cent of their claims seems fanciful.

. . . The fundamental contradiction in the Government scheme lies in the fact that the safeguards provided, by which claims for war damage can be scaled down, will only take effect in circumstances, namely those of inordinately large damage, in which they will be quite unnecessary, because *all* the money commitments of the state will have to be scaled down.[29]

He argued for a change in the arrangements as soon as possible 'and not *after* the breakdown of credit and the destruction of morale have already occurred'. He was ready with estimates of the size of the problem and with a scheme that was 'Treasury minded' for insurance, assessment and compensation for movables and immovables. He provided further memoranda on details and, once the Blitz started, with statistics of the probability of damage drawn from the experience of branches of the Midland Bank supplied by Reginald McKenna. The outcome of this agitation was a

War Damage Bill introduced on 11 December 1940. It received Royal Assent on 26 March 1941. When it was introduced Lydia noted 'the war damages bill is well received, Jenkins is pleased although the Chancellor will get the thanks'. Keynes had made a start.

On 12 August 1940, Keynes took a further step into the Treasury: he received a room in the building and a share of a secretary, which he supplemented by bringing his own Mrs Stephens into the office. He had a bed near his room so he could rest in the building. As he told Provost Sheppard:

> I have no routine duties and no office hour . . . . But I have a sort of roving commission plus membership of various high up committees which allow me to but in in almost any direction where I think I have something to say. I am now allowed to know all the innermost secrets, which was not the case until this week, without the knowledge of which one cannot really advise to much purpose . . . .[30]

One committee he joined was the newly formed Exchange Control Conference made up of Treasury and Bank of England officials to keep exchange control under review, to deal with major administrative questions arising from the system of control, and to consider measures to control overseas expenditure. His appointment had followed a memorandum to the Consultative Council on 29 July on 'Foreign Exchange Control and Payments Agreements'. His memorandum also served as a basis for discussion for the first few meetings of the Conference.

Once Keynes was regularly physically inside the Treasury, he gained a marked increase in opportunities and potential influence. In addition to his network of friends, acquaintances, former students and colleagues, as noted above, he now had day-to-day access to official papers and to Treasury officials. He had no formal position in the hierarchy: 'he was just "Keynes", free to shoot at anybody – anybody, regardless of rank, was free to go to him with his troubles'.[31] As a result, he pops up in the departmental files on almost every subject where the Treasury was involved – and many where he thought it should be involved – and not only on the 'big' issues which will occupy the pages that follow. With his anomalous position, he did not need to respect formal lines of communication between departments. Richard Sayers, a former student then in the Ministry of Supply, found himself sent for in the winter of 1940–1 to discuss cotton margins. If Keynes was unsuccessful in getting his way through normal channels, he would go around them. For instance, having failed to obtain satisfaction in a dispute with the India Office, Keynes took his case, without informing the Chancellor, to Churchill, probably at a meeting of the Other Club. The result was an 'Action This Day' minute from the Prime Minister to the Chancellor which began 'Lord Keynes mentioned to me the other night' and went on to ask for the facts and a discussion in Cabinet.[32,c] As Lord Salter later remarked, 'He was the strangest civil servant Whitehall has ever seen, less the servant and more the master of those he served than any I have seen'.

In Keynes's forays outside his main fields of day-to-day interest, Dennis Proctor has described his method of operations:

> His instinctive attitude towards any new problem was, first, to assume that nobody was doing anything about it and, secondly, that, if they were, they were doing the wrong thing. He would let fly with a minute which would turn up in somebody's in-tray the next morning – or probably in several people's in-trays, since he liked to loose these missiles in a spray of carbon copies directed at several targets at once. One recognised the familiar typescript at a glance – a mixture of slight terror, some delight and immediate hostility. Then one read it – perhaps a page and a half in double spacing, written in that casual but unmistakable style which could never be disguised by the anonymity of official documents, polemic in tone, full of factual inaccuracies and ending with those strangely potent initials for which the single K [after he became Lord Keynes] never seemed quite a satisfactory substitute. Just as one feared: Maynard had got it all wrong, but this was going to cause a lot of trouble before it was finished with. The only thing to do was to arrange a meeting between him and those in the Treasury and other Departments who were handling the subject.[33]

At the receiving end in Washington in 1941, Edward Playfair would remark:

> We are getting quite adept at tracing Maynard's hand – are we right in thinking that he has recently become interested in Bolivian tin? Recent instructions to deliver a rather cock-eyed ultimatum on the subject to most of the American Cabinet, nine months late & based on false premises, we assume to be one of his wilder moments. Even Hermes nods.[34]

And so it went. In this role Keynes 'accepted a description of his functions as those of a pike put into Roman carp-ponds to chase the carp around to prevent them from getting lousy'.[35] But, more commonly, Keynes respected the views of those who knew their jobs and were doing them. He would accept correction from anyone, 'even the office cat' according to one of his Treasury colleagues.[36] One illustration comes from Sir Wilfrid Eady, who entered the Treasury in 1942 after a career in the Ministry of Labour, the Home Office and the Customs and Excise:

> As I sat one day in his room, attempting to argue with him, while

c Keynes became a peer in the 1942 Birthday Honours List.

he towered over me with his back to the fire, he said, with disarming gentleness, 'If I had taken you very young and had limitless patience, I might have taught you the elements of economics. As it is, I must assume that you understand your own art of administration.[37]

Some argue that by spreading himself so widely Keynes diminished his influence.[38] Yet as Otto Clarke noted in his diary on Keynes's death:

Appalling news of the death of Keynes. Felt bereft as at death of Roosevelt and Alekhine (the chess champion). He is the man whose career I would soonest match; I could never hope to match his all round genius, but I might hope to match his skill in forensic political economy. The extraordinary thing about him was his intellectual sex appeal and zing, always fresh and interesting and original and provocative . . . . His death leaves the Treasury in a terrible hole . . . . He has been the brains and the conscience. . . . It will be interesting to see whether the Treasury relapses into habitual slovenliness and complacency or whether some new man is found for providing stimulus.[39]

Working with Keynes could be amusing. Hugh Ellis-Rees wrote of one conversation:

The discussions [in 1944–5] of the possible treatment of the balances of European countries provided me with an opportunity of listening to an example of the remarkable versatility of Lord Keynes. Sir David Waley had been good enough to send him a note, on my behalf, pointing out that in my forthcoming negotiations in Lisbon for a Monetary Agreement, in which we were suggesting new credit margins of £5 million for both parties, the Portuguese might be expected to ask whether any sterling accumulated under this agreement would have the rights of convertibility. Sir David suggested that to give way to the Portuguese might be embarrassing in other cases, but at the same time, since we wanted the Agreement, it seemed hardly worthwhile to make a great case of it.

Lord Keynes was highly indignant at this suggestion, and we had a discussion with him during which he was critical and forthright. He condemned the idea that we might make any promises to countries like Portugal; he would much rather we had no Agreement at all, and that we should tell the Portuguese that unless they were prepared to lend us money on *our* terms, we would do without their goods; or insofar as we could not do without them, we would settle in gold for any deficit which would be insignificant.

After he had completely demolished the case, fearful of my reception in Lisbon, I ventured to make the remark that it seemed a pity to bring to an end the negotiations with a country that had treated us so well during the war, and I reminded Lord Keynes that we had been able to draw £80 m.-worth of escudos, when we were in great need, and had already obtained a very satisfactory funding agreement over 20 years.

Without any further comment and without turning a hair, Lord Keynes proceeded to argue the case in the contrary sense with unabated vigour. He noted that the amount in question was small, a mere £5m., that a well disposed country like Portugal would not necessarily exercise their rights of convertibility, and even supposing they did and other countries pointed to this precedent, we should be able to show that, of all the countries that were substantial holders of sterling balances, Portugal had been the only one to make a really satisfactory settlement.[40]

With his new room in the Treasury, Keynes began putting in more time at the office. By 24 August, he was up to five hours a day. Reports from the Ogre were good, but Lydia's discipline and the ice bags continued. He was now spending the week in London with long weekends at Tilton or, during term, in Cambridge. He found it easier to draft long memoranda on these weekends than in the office. With the beginning of the Blitz, life became more complicated. In London he was walking more than he had in years, not to mention 'perpetually running up and down the stairs to the deep Treasury basement' during daylight raids.[41] Then, on 18 September 1940, during a dinner of duck shared in the basement kitchen of 46 Gordon Square with his niece Polly Hill, his secretary Mrs Stephens and his driver from Tilton, a land mine burst at the opposite end of the Square.[d] The doors and windows of 46 were smashed but the closed shutters prevented any injuries. A time bomb in the Square made it impossible to make repairs for almost a fortnight; so he and Lydia removed themselves to Tilton. Lydia wished he would not go up to London but Maynard 'says he must do his duty'.[42] This meant long days, for often he had to go by road when train services were disrupted. He would breakfast at 7, leave Tilton by 8 and be back towards 8.30 p.m. Although, as he put it to his mother, 'life *is* a bit tiring', it was also the case that 'my state of health is truly magnificent. . . . This in spite of my having been subjected, one way and another, to far greater strain than I ever expected to meet again'. Plesch had been prescient when he had suggested both eighteen and six months previously that Keynes would feel his old self by September 1940.[43] In future months he would work even harder:

When we were at lunch the other day, you very properly reproached me for only working ten hours. Since then I have been raising it to 12 with the very best possible results to health, as you predicted.[44]

Keynes felt well enough to take on yet another job. At Eton the Masters'

d Gordon Square was blitzed again on 18 April 1941.

representative on the Governing Body was up for re-election at the end of 1940. Walter Hamilton and Richard Martineau, who shared the teaching of the Head Master's Division, considered that the incumbent had been less than assiduous in performing his duties. They went to Cambridge and under Lydia's watchful eye persuaded Keynes to stand. Thus from October 1940 he had another regular commitment which he carried out conscientiously, except when on official business in North America, for the rest of his life. Inevitably his interests turned to the College's finances and by the end of October he was advising the Bursar. He decided that the College's financial affairs had not been managed as well as they might have been since late in the nineteenth century and he devoted considerable time to them, joining the sub-committee to manage the College's estates, notably Chalcots in Hampstead and the investments sub-committee. His influence was beneficial, but limited, since he met his match in more conservative figures – Lord Quickswood, the Provost, and Jaspar Ridley, a banker. The Provost noted to Keynes in 1943:

> I find Governing Bodies' meeting usually very entertaining. I like to hear the naked covetousness with which you recommend Southern Preferred Stock, the most austere puritanism with which [Cecil] Lubbock meets such suggestions and the tergiversation of Ridley, who, agreeing with Lubbock, nevertheless votes with you because it is a poor heart that never rejoices and one must have a flutter sometimes.[45]

At this stage in his life, Keynes's affection for established institutions was deepening considerably.

Keynes's major preoccupation during his early period at the Treasury was of course the continuation of the campaign that he had started with 'Paying for the War'. With the transition to total war in May 1940, the pace of mobilisation had quickened. War expenditure in April had been running at £40 million a week; by July it stood at £57 million and was expected to rise further.[46] Registered unemployment, which was still 645,000 in June, was to drop quickly under the pressures of further expansion of the forces and the demands of essential industries.

Keynes's first attempt to shape budgetary policy from the 'inside' came, before he had his room, with the supplementary Budget of the new Chancellor, Kingsley Wood, on 23 July 1940. He wrote three 'Notes on the Budget' dated 11–14 July which tried to encourage the Treasury to utilise the available statistics so that it could get a better idea of the dimensions of the budgetary problem and the directions for a possible solution. As a rough guess, he put the needed new taxation at £200 million for the year from 1 July 1940 and suggested ways to close the gap through tax increases. Inside the Treasury, Keynes's calculations were subject to criticism by Dennis Robertson which caused some acid comments from officials on the usefulness of the estimates and, by implication, the proposed remedies. The calculations certainly do not appear to have influenced the outcome – a Budget that was the object of widespread criticism as being inadequate, a view accepted by the official historian of wartime financial policy, Professor Sayers.[47] Keynes thought the contemporary criticism too harsh: he put the Chancellor's shortfall from what was needed at £100–200 million per annum.[e] But in a letter to the Chancellor the day after the Budget, he continued:

> The real criticism of the Budget, to my mind, is not the magnitude of the immediate yield, but the fact that by depending so largely on existing taxes you have shot your last bolt and have done nothing to appeal to the imagination; whereas it would have been possible to lay new foundations which would prepare the way for important future developments if they are required at a later date.[48]

When he was settled into his Treasury room, Keynes began a major campaign to get his new colleagues to take a comprehensive view of the Budget problem and of possible solutions. Another series of 'Notes on the Budget', this time four in number, appeared between 21 September and 6 October. They opened with a general statement of his position:

> The importance of a war Budget is not because it will 'finance' the war. The goods ordered by the supply departments will be financed anyway. Its importance is *social*: to prevent the social evils of inflation now and later; to do this in a way which satisfies the popular sense of social justice; whilst maintaining adequate incentives to work and economy.[49]

He went on to predict that the next Budget, if it was to provide the revenue required to meet domestic expenditure without the aid of inflation[f] would see tax increases of the order of £400 million. This was not the end of the story, however. Although a failure to 'solve' the revenue problem would probably mean an initial rise in prices of at least 15 per cent, there were other upward pressures on prices, and hence wages, in the pipeline which would compound the problem. These included proposed rises in ocean freight rates, an attempt to limit Treasury food subsidies to the current level of £60 million and the recently announced purchase tax. To stabilise the cost of living might cost the Treasury another £50 million. But the corollary to increased subsidies could be more taxation and, perhaps, an understanding

---

e On 24 September, in an optimistic broadcast, 'British Finances after a Year of War', he went further to suggest that 'there has been no significant degree of budgetary inflation to date' (*JMK*, XXII, 244).

f Thus leaving to one side for purposes of discussion inflation arising from a rise in import prices or a spontaneous rise in money wages.

with the unions on wages. He argued that the government might get more mileage out of subsidies if it attempted to stabilise the official cost of living index and did so in a way which allowed the Ministry of Food to do a bit of 'profiteering' on non-staple and luxury foods outside the official index.g The task of stabilisation would also be helped by the removal of existing duties on sugar and tea and the introduction of standard lines of cloth at low prices (a precursor of the later 'utility' scheme). With these coherent rather than piecemeal price-stabilising measures in place, he proposed to close the revenue gap with changes in direct taxes, in particular a graduated war surcharge ranging from 25 to 50 per cent on individuals' net incomes after the deduction of existing direct taxes. Of this surcharge, £50 to £100 per taxpayer per annum would be treated as deferred pay.

This set of memoranda had a significant effect on Treasury opinion. On 21 October, Keynes joined Lord Catto (the Financial Adviser to the Chancellor), Sir Horace Wilson (the Permanent Secretary), Sir Richard Hopkins and Sir Frederick Phillips for a meeting with the Chancellor on Budget strategy. Keynes explained his method of estimating the budgetary gap and his proposals for meeting it, and provided a further explanation of a source of information he had started using to buttress his arguments – the surveys of wartime working-class spending and saving behaviour being carried out by Charles Madge under the auspices of the National Institute for Economic and social Research.h Catto agreed with Keynes's estimate of the gap, but had his own preferred proposal of a flat-rate war tax on gross income. The Chancellor asked for a rapid, but complete, examination of all the alternatives that would raise substantial sums, in particular the Keynes and Catto proposals, Lord Stamp'si proposal for an income tax equivalent to the Excess Profits Tax introduced in 1939, which had been raised to 100 per cent in the July 1940 Budget, and alterations to existing direct taxes. He also asked to be kept informed of the Madge surveys which Keynes was to discuss further with his Treasury colleagues. From this point onwards Keynes was a member of the Chancellor's top-secret Budget Committee.

In the ensuing months, the Keynes, Catto and Stamp tax proposals all fell

g The official cost of living index had not been revised since the First World War. Its weights were based on a household budget study of 1904. Although its coverage of foodstuffs was not too bad, representing about two-thirds of working-class food expenditure in 1937–8, its coverage of non-food items was very dated – for example, it excluded electricity. See *JMK*, XXII, 325 for a comparison of the index's weights with those resulting from the later survey of household expenditure.

h Keynes had provided a small sum for Madge to get started with his surveys, had supported his original proposal to the National Institute, suggested questions for use in the survey, and would publish the results as they appeared in the *Economic Journal*, as well as circulating them in the Treasury. His use of these materials represents the earliest use of social survey techniques in the formulation of fiscal policy in Britain. See *JMK*, XII, 810–29; XXII, 274–6.

i Stamp was Chairman of the Survey of Financial and Economic Plans (1939–41) and Chairman of the Official Committee on Economic Policy (1939–40).

by the wayside – either as a result of administrative problems or their looking 'too much like a rehash of income tax'.[50] The notion of working within the existing income tax structure thus took centre stage. However, the idea of deferred pay proved hardier and, in the form of post-war credits, it joined the changes in existing income tax rates and schedules as the centrepiece of the Budget planned for April 1941. Throughout, Keynes kept up a stream of memoranda – by 11 January 1941 he estimated that he was on his ninth major one[51] – to the Chancellor and his advisers, making objections, altering proposals and providing new information often from the Madge surveys and from another new source – official national income estimates.

At the time of 'Paying for the War', as noted above, the British Government did not publish estimates of the national income. Nor had they prepared any for their own internal use since an ill-fated exercise in 1929.[52] *How to Pay for the War* and Keynes's private attempts to estimate the national income led the successor to the Stamp Survey, the Central Economic Information Service of the Offices of the War Cabinet,[j] to attempt an estimate and through Austin Robinson to persuade the authorities that a more systematic exercise was essential. James Meade, then with the League of Nations in Geneva, was asked to take charge of the project. After returning across France during the German invasion, Meade began work in June 1940. By the end of July he had evolved the underlying accounting framework.[53] He was then joined by Richard Stone, a young Cambridge economics graduate then working in the Ministry of Economic Warfare, who became responsible for organising and perfecting the statistics. As Keynes settled into the Treasury, he took this project under his wing, easing it through obstacles and departmental jealousies, and persuading Sir Richard Hopkins to be a friendly supporter of the exercise. By early December 1940 the first results of Meade's and Stone's work were available. Soon after the turn of the year, Keynes submitted to the Budget Committee their paper 'National Income, Savings and Consumption', dated 6 January 1941, and in February used their estimates in his estimate of the budgetary 'gap'. He now put this at £500 million, well above his September 1940 guess of £400 million but closer to his December figure of 'appreciably greater than £400 million'.[54] £500 million was the figure the Chancellor presented to his Cabinet colleagues as the measure of the problem. That 'gap' had to be bridged by voluntary savings and/or tax increases if it were not to be 'automatically' closed as inflation pulled up nominal national income, savings and government revenues.

At this stage came the need for a 'Budget judgement' – how much of the gap to close by taxation on the assumption that voluntary savings would do the rest. The Chancellor settled on aiming at £250 million in new taxation,

---

j This was the direct successor to the Stamp Survey. In January 1941 the Service was split into the Economic Section of the War Cabinet Offices and the Central Statistical Office.

largely through changes in income taxes buttressed by post-war credits. He also decided to circulate after the Budget statement an additional document, a White Paper which would bear the title *An Analysis of the Sources of War Finance and an Estimate of the National Income and Expenditure in 1938 and 1940* (Cmd. 6261).

There remained a hectic six weeks until Budget day on 7 April. The Meade–Stone White Paper went through a series of proofs after 1 March and met the cautious, but constructive criticism of Dennis Robertson and the much less helpful attitude of Hubert Henderson. Final decisions had to be taken on the exact details of the taxation proposals and other aspects of the Budget and, of course, the Chancellor needed a Budget Speech. Keynes was involved in all these: he even tried his hand at a draft of the Budget Speech which included an exposition of the relevant White Paper figures and quotations from the Madge surveys.[55] On the day before the Budget he worked 13 hours straight. Although he was rather knocked out the next day, he reported to his mother: 'I went to the House of Commons for the Budget (I had never heard a Budget speech before) and thought the MPs in the mass a truly sub-human collection'.[56,k]

The Budget had a very simple structure. Excess Profits Tax was left at 100 per cent despite its perverse effects on efficiency powerfully pointed out by Keynes and others. There were a number of concessions, however, including a promised refund of 20 per cent of the tax paid at the end of the war for reconstruction purposes. The system of subsidies that had grown up piecemeal since the outbreak of war was brought together for a purpose – the Chancellor's commitment that he would endeavour to prevent any rise in the cost of living index number, apart from seasonal variations, above 125 to 130 per cent of the pre-war level, *i.e.* the level which it had already reached. Given the antiquity of the index number's coverage, he also extended his stabilisation commitment to some items such as electricity. He did not seek concessions from the trade unions, but he made it clear that his stabilisation commitment did not cover increases in the cost of living caused by rises in money wages. Finally the Budget brought sharp increases in income taxes: personal allowances fell, bringing 4 million new taxpayers into the net, earned income allowances fell and the standard rate of income tax went to 10 shillings in the pound (or 50 per cent) and the top rate of surtax to 19*s*. 6*d*. (or 97½ per cent). The increased tax payments resulting from the reductions in allowances were to be treated as forced savings. Each taxpayer would receive an annual statement of the taxes so paid. This would become a post-war credit which would be paid after the war in his favour in the

---

k This was not strictly true, for he had been in the House for Sir John Simon's April 1940 Budget statement (above p. 633).

Post Office Savings Bank. The global amount involved was estimated at £125 million per annum, a far cry from Keynes's original target of £550 million.[57] It was thus more of an experiment than the centrepiece of war finance.

Keynes was reasonably happy with the Budget as a whole. He told his mother:

> I am as well satisfied with the Budget as I could reasonably expect; and indeed got my way on a number of points as much as is good for me. The limited acceptance of deferred pay is most associated with me publicly. But the two points I attached most importance to and where I played a part were the stabilisation of prices, for which I had been fighting very hard, and the logical structure and method of a wartime Budget which, together with the new White Paper is really a revolution in public finance.[58]

Keynes was right: the logic and method of the 1941 Budget did represent a 'revolution', for it shifted the criteria for budgetary policy from the balance or lack of balance in the public accounts to the balance of the economy as a whole, while the logic of national income and expenditure accounting combined with the notion of the inflationary gap which would be closed by either taxation and voluntary savings at the existing price level or inflation, gave the authorities the means of coming to their Budget judgement. It was all rather crude, relying heavily on the judgemental skills of someone with Keynes's intuitive feel for orders of statistical magnitudes, but it was a beginning.

The stabilisation policy, the importance of Keynes's role in devising it which Harrod underrated,[59] also added coherence to the Government's anti-inflationary policy. The Budget did not solve the inflationary problem. But it contained it.[1] The official cost of living index stayed in its specified range: it was 127 in March 1941 and 132 in January 1945. A more complete index covering all items in consumers' expenditure in the national accounts kept drifting upwards, if much more slowly than before the 1941 Budget: it rose 17 per cent between 1941 and 1945.[60] Other signs of inflationary pressure continued to manifest themselves, notably shop queues and shortages, and money wage rates continued to rise, although there was a partial check to their rate of rise in the summer of 1941.[61] None the less, as Professor Sayers put it, 'at last Britain's leaders did have a financial policy', and to a large extent the fact that they had a policy and a means of systematically thinking

---

1 The policy bewildered foreign economists. After discussing the policy with officials of the US Bureau of the Budget, Lionel Robbins reported Arthur Smithies as remarking, 'Well, it's all very interesting. But I still don't see how you have done it' (Howson and Moggridge 1990b, 80).

about changes in it was the measure of Keynes's polemical and persuasive achievement.

NOTES

1 KCKP, JMK to RFK, 26 September 1938, 1 September 1939; JMK to Harrod, 7 September 1939; JMK to Stamp, 15 September 1939.
2 *JMK*, XXII, 4–9.
3 *JMK*, XXII, 12.
4 *JMK*, XXII, 13.
5 Harris 1977, 357; Salter 1967, 88.
6 *JMK*, XXII, 16–29.
7 KCKP, JMK to Plesch, 18 October 1939.
8 *JMK*, XXII, 38.
9 *JMK*, XXII, 30, 31.
10 *JMK*, XXII, 35.
11 KCKP, HP1/1, JMK to Hopkins, 16 November 1939; Clay to JMK, 9 November 1939.
12 Sayers 1956, 1.
13 *JMK*, XXII, 52–74, 124–32; XI, 235–7.
14 KCKP, Attlee to JMK, 30 October 1939; JMK to Attlee, 31 October 1939.
15 *JMK*, XXII, 74, 79.
16 Jay 1980, 82.
17 BLPES, Piercy Papers, 5/72, W. Piercy to H. V. Berry, 22 February 1940. I am indebted to Sue Howson for this reference.
18 *JMK*, IX, 400; compare ibid., 437 with XXII, 48.
19 *JMK*, IX, 368.
20 A good summary of reactions appears in his letter to Geoffrey Dawson of 11 March, reprinted in *JMK*, XXII, 101–4. A complete set of the relevant correspondence is in KCKP, HP1/1 and 1/2.
21 KCKP, HP1/2, Robertson to JMK, 6 March 1940; Hayek to JMK, 3 March 1940; Robbins to JMK, 29 March 1940.
22 KCKP, JMK to McKenna, 28 January 1940.
23 Sayers 1956, 35.
24 *JMK*, XXII, 132–5, 140, 143.
25 *JMK*, XXII, 156, 157.
26 *JMK*, XXII, 163–79.
27 *JMK*, XXII, 191.
28 KCKP, Plesch to JMK, 4 March 1940.
29 *JMK*, XXII, 435, 436–7.
30 KCKP, JMK to J. T. Sheppard, 14 August 1940.
31 Proctor in King's College 1949, 27. From January 1941, he was formally Economic Adviser to the Chancellor (Public Record Office 1972, 140).
32 *JMK*, XXIII, 331–2; Salter 1967, 88–9.
33 Proctor in King's College 1949, 26.
34 PRO, T175/121, Playfair to Waley, 3 April 1941.
35 Eady 1951, 920.
36 Sir Frederic Harmer, quoted above p. 554.
37 Eady 1951, 903.
38 Sayers 1956, 2.
39 Hubback 1988, 19; a slightly different version appears in Clarke 1982, 77.

40 PRO, T267/3, H. Ellis-Rees, 'The Convertibility Crisis', 1962, appendix to ch. 5.
41 KCKP, JMK to FAK, 15 September 1940.
42 KCKP, Lydia to FAK, 22 September 1940.
43 KCKP, JMK to FAK, 20 and 27 September 1940; JMK to Plesch, 29 September 1940.
44 KCKP, JMK to Plesch, 5 February 1941.
45 *JMK*, XII, 122–3.
46 Sayers 1956, 48.
47 Ibid., 56–7.
48 *JMK*, XXII, 214.
49 *JMK*, XXII, 218.
50 *JMK*, XXII, 255.
51 KCKP, JMK to FAK, 11 January 1941. The memorandum appears in *JMK*, XXII, 255–73.
52 Stone 1977; Patinkin 1982, 259–60.
53 Meade's exercise, 'Financial Aspects of War Economy', appears as chapter 7 of Howson (ed.) 1988.
54 *JMK*, XXII, 258.
55 *JMK*, XXII, 294–325.
56 KCKP, JMK to FAK, 14 April 1941.
57 *JMK*, IX, 398.
58 *JMK*, XXII, 353.
59 Harrod 1951, 493; Sayers 1956, 65.
60 Feinstein 1972, Table 61.
61 Sayers 1956, 92.

25

'SCRAPING THE BOTTOM OF THE BOX'[1]

During his first months in the Treasury not all of Keynes's energies were devoted to domestic financial affairs. Almost from the beginning he turned his eye to Britain's external financial position and to the shape of the post-war world. As the war progressed these two matters were to take more and more of his energies – and, in the end, his life.

Keynes arrived in the Treasury when Britain's overseas financial position had become particularly grave. At the outbreak of war, Britain's financial relations with the United States were constrained by the Neutrality Acts, which prevented Americans selling war matériel to the belligerents, and the Johnson Act of 1934, which prevented loans to countries, such as Britain, in default on their debts from the First World War. Congress eased the neutrality legislation in November 1939: Britain and other belligerents could buy arms so long as they paid cash and did not use American shipping – the 'cash and carry' principle. But this highlighted the other constraint – cash. In September 1939 the foreign assets of the Exchange Equalisation Account stood at £525 million and readily marketable securities held by British residents amounted to about another $1 billion (or £250 million at the current exchange rate of $4.03, which had just been pegged for the duration). The authorities assumed that they could somehow operate on a war basis for three years without American assistance: Treasury officials actually estimated that the foreign resources in hand would last two years when, like the 'old dogs', they hoped that changes in American policy would provide the resources to see the war through to victory. This three-year 'assumption' provided departments with the necessary guidelines for entering into overseas commitments which would affect the reserves.

The events of the spring of 1940 changed the basis for such calculations. With Britain now in a war which could be decided in the course of 1940, financial considerations could not stand in the way of defence. The pace of British defence expenditure in America came to depend solely on technical considerations, among them the capacity of the American defence industry and the competition between the British and American service departments for priority in access to the available output. In addition, with the fall of

France, the British Government took over existing French orders worth £125 million.

This scale of commitments was well beyond the resources the Government could see as forthcoming, even if the turn in the war had not produced a slump on Wall Street which slowed sales of British-owned dollar securities to a trickle. Now the authorities had to do more than rely on the hope of eventual American aid. They had to begin actively preparing the ground. With 1940 an American election year, it was unlikely that anything would happen until after November and then there would follow the usual delays for decisions and legislation. Until the end of July, it looked as if this strategy of working on the assumption that President Roosevelt would help after the election was a feasible one, for there seemed to be enough cash in prospect to last well into 1941. New calculations in August 1940 made this unlikely: new commitments, such as the programme for 3,000 aircraft a month, and American businessmen's worries over Britain's ability to pay which led to demands for larger cash advances implied that Britain's reserves could be exhausted soon after Christmas 1940. This would adversely affect the acceptability of the sterling debts with which Britain had been financing her war effort in most of the rest of the world.

Thus Keynes became involved in attempts to 'scrape the bottom of the box' to find more resources. He made a number of suggestions in August and September, including one which he had made to his friend Samuel Courtauld the previous April: that British firms with direct investments in the United States, such as Courtauld's subsidiary American Viscose, borrow dollars against these assets and turn the proceeds over to the Treasury for sterling.[2,a] Yet, as well as being ingenious in his suggestions for raising American dollars and being appropriately 'Treasury-minded' in blocking proposals that would bring little benefit, Keynes emphasised that the Treasury should impress on the Americans — as well as remember themselves — the disastrous consequences of stripping Britain of all her overseas dollar assets. In the short term, if Britain had no such assets when American assistance came, she would depend on the United States for dollars not only for her American commitments but also for her expenditures elsewhere in the world – a situation which he knew from his experience of 1917–19 'was a continuous source of friction between the Associated Powers' and which prejudiced the political status in both countries of much of the resulting debt.[3] In the long term, moreover, a Britain stripped of her dollar-earning international assets would require revolutionary changes in her post-war commercial policies if she were to balance her international payments in the face of the loss

---

a Although the Johnson Act prohibited lending to governments, it did not prevent lending to corporations. Other proposals from Keynes included selling stocks of ageing whisky to the Americans and trying to interest then in buying part of the large stock of wool Britain had purchased in Australia and New Zealand under her commitment at the beginning of the war to take the entire clip for the duration of the war and one year afterwards.

of that invisible income. This concern for the post-war consequences of current commitments also made him use his Other Club connections to try successfully to limit the long-term adverse financial consequences of British aid to Greece.[4]

Once Roosevelt had won the election on 5 November, the next question was what form American financial assistance would take. The answer came on 17 December, just three weeks after Lord Lothian, the British Ambassador in Washington, returning from a quick visit to London, told reporters that Britain was 'beginning to come to the end of her financial resources'. The name of the answer was Lend Lease – the provision of supplies to Britain not in exchange for money but acknowledged by some 'consideration' to be negotiated later.

The announcement of the policy did not mean immediate finance for supplies to Britain. It still left open the actual coverage of the principles embodied in the resulting legislation, the problem of 'interim finance' for orders placed between the announcement of the policy and the time the Bill became law, and the problem of paying for the 'old commitments' entered into but not delivered before the announcement. There was also, even after the announcement of Lend Lease, continued American pressure for Britain to liquidate some 'visible' overseas assets, partially to prove just how broke she was. Finally, British officials had to learn, or in Keynes's case relearn, the vagaries of the American political process.

Keynes's activities touched all of these areas, but, as he was also heavily involved in Budget-making, his participation grew more active in and after March 1941. He first provided a powerful case for Lord Halifax, Britain's new ambassador in Washington following Lord Lothian's sudden death in December, for Britain's retaining some of her liquid reserves.[5] Increasingly, however, his concern centred on the problems of paying for the old commitments and the financing of interim orders, which, although each went through Mr Morgenthau, the American Treasury Secretary, in advance, turned out to be excluded from Lend Lease. He began regular contacts with American officials in London, particularly the Ambassador, J. G. Winant, and his advisers Ben Cohen and E. F. Penrose. In conversation with Cohen he broached his proposal for borrowing dollars on the security of the assets of British firms in the United States. As compared with forced sales, such borrowing would preserve essential links between subsidiaries and their parents, not interfere with post-war exports and avoid the need for putting market valuations on assets that were often extremely hard to value independently of their connections with their British parent firms. Initially, nothing came from the suggestion, but the results of the 'show sale' of Courtauld's subsidiary American Viscose Corporation, which would probably have never happened if Samuel Courtauld had taken Keynes's suggestion of April 1940 seriously, made it look much more attractive to all concerned.[b] In June 1941 Britain obtained a $425 million dollar loan from the Reconstruction Finance Corporation against security of the shares of American subsidiaries of British insurance companies, listed and unlisted securities in American corporations not yet vested by the British Treasury for sale in the United States in which British ownership was substantial, and the earnings of American branches of forty-one insurance companies not incorporated in the United States. Keynes negotiated the arrangement.[c] But before this happened the problem of finance had become even more acute when, on 15 March in hearings before the House Appropriations Committee, the Director of the Bureau of the Budget[d] flatly stated that none of the proposed Lend-Lease appropriation of $7 billion could be used to pay for commitments under old UK contracts.

Lend-Lease matters were not the only Anglo-American issues in which Keynes was involved. He was also concerned with British war aims and British policy on surplus stocks of commodities.

War aims discussions had concerned Keynes as an 'old dog' back in the autumn of 1939. In 1940 his involvement was a result of the German Economics Minister's proposals for a German 'New Order' in Europe. This envisaged a post-war régime of free trade and multilateral clearing of current accounts at fixed exchange rates among all the countries of Europe. Relations with countries outside the 'New Order' area would be governed by barter arrangements and controls. The German propaganda machine soon came to proclaim that such a régime, which made gold superfluous within the area adhering to the 'New Order', would bring unprecedented prosperity to Western Europe in place of the chaos of the inter-war period.

b Under the initial agreement for the sale a group managed by Morgan Stanley and Company and Dillon Reed and Company paid $34,456,000 for 448,000 shares of AVC common stock. The group was to make its best efforts to sell AVC over the six months after 15 March 1941 at a price above the initial payment and their commission over and above 5 per cent of the initial payment would depend heavily on that price. On 3 June the group sold the reorganised company for $62,294,456. The Treasury received $54,445,514 for a company whose net assets in December 1940 were over $122 million and whose profits for 1940 were $11 million. In contrast a British arbitration tribunal awarded Courtaulds £27,125,000 ($109,313,750) in compensation, thus valuing the company at slightly more than twice the Treasury's proceeds from the forced sale. If Courtauld had taken Keynes's advice and obtained for AVC a dollar loan, it would have been so unattractive a purchase that a forced sale might have been averted, despite American hostility to the company which had been indicted for price fixing in 1932 and accused of evading American taxation. See Coleman 1969, ch. XV for details.

c In April 1941 the Reconstruction Finance Corporation also indirectly lent money to Britain when it provided $40 million for the American management of the Brown Williamson Tobacco Corporation so that it could buy out some of the interests of British American Tobacco.

d It is symptomatic of the lack of British understanding of American institutions and procedures at the time that members of the British Treasury assumed that he was a part of Mr Morgenthau's Treasury organisation rather than an independent official.

At the end of November 1940, Harold Nicolson, Parliamentary Secretary to the Minister of Information, approached Keynes to ask him if he would open a counter-campaign with a broadcast. He also sent Keynes a series of notes prepared for the purpose. Keynes was not impressed with the notes, which seemed to suggest that Britain would

> do well to pose as champions of the pre-war economic *status quo* and outbid Funk by offering good old 1920–21 or 1930–33, i.e. gold standard or international exchange *laissez faire* aggravated by heavy tariffs, unemployment, etc., etc.[6]

Certainly *he* was not the one to pose as the champion of the gold standard! He promised to give the matter some thought and perhaps draft a possible broadcast. Soon afterwards, Lord Halifax, then still Foreign Secretary, asked Keynes to draft a statement exposing the fallaciousness of the German promises. He did so and prepared a set of 'Proposals to Counter the German "New Order"' on 25 November, circulating them with a covering memorandum on 1 December.

Keynes's 'Proposals' are less important for their details than for their assumptions, many of which informed his subsequent thinking about the post-war world. He assumed that, although the post-war settlement would include punitive military and political measures concerning Germany, it would favour Germany's economic reconstruction and its central European economic leadership. Thus he echoed *Economic Consequences of the Peace*. Similarly there would not be the equivalent of the post-1918 starvation of Germany by the allies, and Britain and the United States would make surplus stocks of commodities available to Europe after the war. Finally Britain would offer a multilateral clearing system to post-war Europe, but one which would be more honest than the German proposal. Much of his text questioned German *bona fides* and disinterestedness, while offering a comprehensive programme appealing to 'the craving for social and personal *security*' after the war.[7] Keynes's 'Proposals' were subject to considerable interdepartmental discussion in Whitehall during November and December. He also discussed them with Harry Hopkins, Roosevelt's special assistant and confidant, when he was in London in connection with Lend Lease. A revised version of the 'Proposals' was circulated on 30 January, but it lay unused until May 1941. Then Anthony Eden, Halifax's successor as Foreign Secretary, decided to adopt it as the basis for a speech at the Mansion House on 29 May. By this time Keynes was in Washington, from where he made suggestions for changes and discussed it with President Roosevelt. As delivered the speech followed the lines of Keynes's draft 'well-wrapped in Foreign Office wool', as Brendan Bracken described it to Churchill on 20 May.[8]

Keynes's remaining major area of concern in the winter of 1940–1 was commodities. Britain had been accumulating stocks of surplus raw materials as a result of the disruption of pre-war channels of trade by the war and the blockading of enemy countries, and the desire to deny the enemy access to strategic materials. Australasian wool and Egyptian cotton provide good examples. With the stocks came questions of policy: what should be done with existing stocks? what should be done in future years? After a series of Whitehall committees, the Government decided to purchase, with or without American help, £200 million in surplus commodities and to tie these purchases with attempts to regulate future production. Sir Frederick Leith–Ross was appointed in November 1940 to co-ordinate and undertake the necessary negotiations. Keynes, with his long experience of commodity markets, was the Treasury representative on the committee of officials advising Leith-Ross.

Keynes had already touched on the surplus issue the previous July when he had suggested as a part of the Treasury's attempts to raise dollars that Britain buy commodities above her requirements from countries willing to accept sterling and sell them for dollars. Now he took an active part in advising Leith-Ross, maintaining a firm, 'Treasury-minded' attitude on prices to be paid, keeping a watching brief on official discussions of Anglo-American negotiations for agreements on particular commodities, and thinking about preliminary schemes linking current problems, post-war relief and possible longer-term arrangements for the stabilisation of primary product prices and outputs. By the late winter of 1940–1, discussions in London had reached the point where those involved needed to know more about American thinking on the same issues.

The stage was set for Keynes to visit the United States. Ambassador Winant and Ben Cohen, with whom Keynes had been discussing Lend Lease and direct investments, first broached the idea, but a visit would serve a number of other purposes. It would give British Treasury officials in Washington background information from London not easily communicated by letter or cable. It would also allow conversations with the Americans on several Treasury problems: Lend-Lease procedures, the 'old commitments', and the desirable future level of Britain's gold and foreign exchange reserves as they were rebuilt from their minuscule levels of 1940–1. And Keynes could plumb American thinking on primary products and war aims.[e]

In those disrupted wartime days, getting from London to Washington was less simple than before the war – or since. On this occasion, Maynard and

---

e Keynes had no instructions on, nor did he intend to take part in, the negotiations then proceeding in New York for the sale of AVC. He was, however, kept informed of developments and did communicate Whitehall's concerns over certain problems connected with the sale to those involved – Sir Edward Peacock of Morgan Grenfell and the Bank of England and T. Carlyle Gifford, who had been associated with the Independent Investment Company.

Lydia, accompanied by Lucius Thompson, a Kingsman then in the Bank of England, as secretary and the ever-present Mrs Stephens, left Poole by flying boat on 2 May. They arrived in Lisbon the same evening. They left Lisbon on 4 May for the Azores, where they stayed until the morning of 7 May, and then flew on to New York, where they arrived at 7 a.m. on 8 May. On arrival, Keynes met reporters before going on to meetings with those involved in the AVC sale. The party went to Washington the next evening, when Keynes and Thompson dined with Sir Frederick Phillips and Edward Playfair to bring them up to date on the purposes of the mission.[9]

Keynes was to be in the United States for much longer than he or anyone else expected: he did not leave New York until 29 July. He was extremely busy. On 28 June, he reported that in his first five weeks he had lunched or dined out forty-seven times, as well as carrying a heavy load of office work and meetings. According to Lydia, he often started dictating at 8 a.m. and came back to the hotel at 8 p.m. It was 'more dangerous than the blitz' and he noted 'I shouldn't have survived without Lydia – who provides constant rest, discipline and comfort'.[10]

Throughout the visit Keynes dealt primarily with Henry Morgenthau, Roosevelt's Secretary of the Treasury. Their relationship opened on the wrong foot. Morgenthau, always morbidly suspicious, believed that the purpose of Keynes's visit was to block the sale of AVC, a suspicion heightened by Keynes's regular contacts with Sir Edward Peacock and Carlyle Gifford. Morgenthau was also bewildered by the fact that Keynes had arrived without a letter of credentials from the Chancellor. Moreover, Keynes came with recommendations from Ambassador Winant and Ben Cohen whom Morgenthau thought were trying to operate behind his back. It took almost a fortnight to sort matters out. Even then matters were occasionally difficult when, for example, Morgenthau heard that Keynes had criticised the President at a party given by Felix Frankfurter or when he seemed to be overgenerous with advice outside his sphere of competence.[11]

On his side, Keynes found Morgie (or Morgy) – as the British called him – 'a difficult chap to deal with', indeed 'almost intolerably tiresome to deal with'. He found 'misunderstandings peep out of every corner' and agreed with others that Morgie was 'jealous, suspicious and subject to moods of depression and irritation'.[12] From the tone of his correspondence over the years that he was to have to deal with him, it is clear that Keynes did not think that Morgie was very bright and that he spent most of his time attempting to appease a public opinion that he didn't understand.[13] Yet, Maynard agreed with Lydia's observation: 'He is a good man and will do you no harm *on purpose*', even if he worried 'how easily he might without intending it!'.[14]

Keynes's difficulties in Washington may have also, at least initially, not been helped by a 'difference ... as regards approach'. As Edward Playfair put it:

> Maynard thinks we are a great & independent nation, which on the financial side is patently not true; & some months' experience here have shown us that the Americans don't see it in that light. I think he is inclined to ask as of right what they are only prepared to give us as a favour. It seems to me very important to keep moral indignation out of these discussions if we are to get anywhere. I find experience in credit negotiations with Spain, Roumania &c very useful. I recognise in ourselves the sentiments which we found so unreasonable in the Spaniards & in the Americans the sentiments which the Spaniards found so unreasonable in us.[15]

When Keynes saw Morgenthau on 13 and 14 May he

> expounded for an hour[.] Henry received him coldly & did not understand one word (he said as much himself). Next day F P[hillips] wrote it all down in words of one syllable & read it out to Henry, who understood it perfectly.

Keynes then set his proposals out in writing. He proposed a simple, clear-cut arrangement whereby Britain would keep certain supplies out of the Lend-Lease machinery, because they would cause either administrative complexities or political difficulties, and would be ready to pay cash for other items in the future, if political difficulties made it sensible to take them out of Lend Lease. In return, he asked the Americans to provide the necessary financial margin for such a scheme by taking over existing defence contracts and refunding advances already paid. The refund involved was $700 million; the takeover $1,300 million.[16]

The letter did not work. Although Playfair thought it 'a brilliant letter which moved me to tears & I thought would move Henry to tears', when Sir Frederick Phillips next saw Morgenthau 'Henry read passages out to FP in derisive tones (Maynard does *not* know this)'.[17] By the end of May, it was clear that the Americans might be able to stretch slightly the promise of $300–400 million relief on the old commitments which Morgenthau had given to Phillips before Keynes's arrival, and to take a few more items into Lend Lease. It remained to Britain to raise the funds to meet the rest. Here the 'Jesse Jones loan' (or the loan from Reconstruction Finance Corporation for which Jesse Jones was responsible) discussed above, came in – after Congress had increased the Corporation's resources and allowed it to lend to foreign governments on the collateral of American securities. By the time Keynes had left Washington, he thought that Morgenthau might take over an additional $100 million of the old commitments. Thus he thought that Britain could look forward to having free reserves of the order of $600 million by December 1942 – a far cry from the position of near default earlier in 1941.[18] But the concessions turned out to be still smaller – they totalled $200 million – and it took another year and American's entry into the war to obtain them.

While the financial discussions continued, Keynes and Phillips took part in a new Anglo-American Treasury committee to deal with day-to-day Lend-Lease problems – and, incidentally, succeeded in bringing more British needs inside the scheme – and Keynes attended to his other jobs in Washington. On 27 May he went to the State Department to discuss surplus policy with Dean Acheson, Leo Pasvolsky and Harry Hawkins. He outlined his own views of current and prospective problems, raising not only matters such as post-war relief already discussed in Leith-Ross's London Committee but also the idea of a comprehensive, international programme for stabilising world primary product prices.[19] The next day, he and the Ambassador met with the President over lunch for almost 2½ hours to discuss the draft of Mr Eden's Mansion House speech on the post-war economic settlement – a draft that had originated in Keynes's 'Proposals to Counter the German "New Order"' six months before.[20] From late May onwards he also embarked on a series of meetings with American economists. Although they sometimes spoke of general theoretical matters,[f] the major topic of conversation was the prospects for the American economy in the face of the growing defence programme. Keynes seems to have consistently disagreed with his American followers, who were much more optimistic than he as to the prospect of avoiding inflation in the near term.[21]

Keynes managed to get out of Washington for a few weekends: one in the Shenandoah Valley, another on the Skyline Drive, and one at Princeton. At Princeton, according to Lydia, 'he spoke so much to the economists that in the end he refused to see them and asked for the mathematicians'.[22] The object of his visit, as well as seeing Walter Stewart, who was advising

---

f See, for example, his letter to Mordecai Ezekiel on the latter's work on fluctuations in investment (KCKP, JMK to M. Ezekiel, 6 June 1941), which included the following statement of the role of the rate of interest:

> I am far from fully convinced by the recent thesis that interest rates play a small part in determining the volume of investment. It may be that other influences, such as an increase in demand, often dominate it in starting a movement. But I am quite unconvinced that low interest rates cannot play an enormous part in *sustaining* investment at a given figure, and when there is a movement from a higher rate to a lower rate in allowing a greater scale of investment to proceed over a very much longer period than would otherwise be possible. However, this is a topic which needs much fuller treatment than I gave it in my book, and I should much like to have the leisure to work it over again.

When Ezekiel published his two-part article 'Statistical Investigations of Saving, Consumption and Investment' in the *American Economic Review* for March and June 1942, he explicitly thanked Keynes in the initial acknowledgements to both parts. I am indebted to Don Patinkin for this information.

Morgenthau, was to discuss the financial arrangements being made with the Rockefeller Foundation for the founding of a Department of Applied Economics in Cambridge which had been interrupted by the war. That same weekend:

> I paid a call on Einstein. The old sage was in bed with his vast olive corrugated countenance crowned with a white shock of Struwelpeter hair, and a big toe protruding from under the counterpane. He was full of gusto and enthusiasm and urged above everything with all the emphasis he could command that if, when we are ready, we bomb Germany continuously and without remorse they most certainly will not stand it.[23]

This was the first time that they had met since October 1933, just prior to Einstein's departure for America. They never met again.

As Keynes's American visit progressed, a new issue came to dominate his discussions with American officials, the 'consideration' for Lend Lease. Section 3(b) of the Lend Lease Act of 1941 had set out the terms and conditions under which a country might receive such assistance. These were 'those which the President deems satisfactory and the benefit to the United States may be payment or repayment in kind or property or any other direct or indirect benefit which the President deems satisfactory'. Keynes first raised the matter with London on 25 May following a conversation with Dean Acheson.[24] From the outset, it appeared that the 'consideration' would take the form of a declaration of common post-war economic policy which would, since the State Department was involved, follow 'Mr Hull's ... well-known opinions concerning non-discrimination, in the presence of free trade bias, unrestricted access to raw materials and equal economic treatment of all countries'.[25] A formal proposal took some time in coming from the American side, partly owing to the need for interdepartmental discussions and partly because there had been no instructions from the top. In the interim there was rumour, kite flying, and informal discussion in which Keynes participated, on occasion making proposals off his own bat and without authority. He also tried to influence London opinion by trying his hand at a draft set of terms.[26] By the end of June nothing had as yet been passed over on paper.

At this point Keynes acted in a manner that was to cause future difficulties. As mentioned above, under Cordell Hull the State Department was strongly in favour of non-discrimination in trade restrictions and tariff reductions – so much so that R. H. Brand reported after a conversation with Eleanor Lansing Dulles a few years later:

> She told me it is absolutely necessary in the State Department to 'go to mass' and 'tell your beads' once a day in line with the

Hull principles. You cannot possibly write any memorandum, she said, without putting in two or three orthodox sentences on the above lines.[27]

It was with these entrenched attitudes that the State Department had been negotiating with the Board of Trade for alterations in the 1938 Anglo-American Trade Agreement. In the autumn of 1940, in their attempt to maximise their dollar earnings while discriminating against dollar area imports and letting goods from the sterling area in freely, the British had approached the Americans for modifications in the US tariff. The question of a *quid pro quo* or 'consideration' came up. Negotiations began for a supplementary trade agreement. The Americans had asked for British concessions in return, including an abatement of Imperial Preference and severe restrictions on Britain's use of exchange controls and quantitative restrictions on trade from the end of the war. Phillips, with Keynes's support, suggested to his London colleagues that it was far from clear that the State Department realised that, given her difficult balance of payments position after the war, Britain might have to continue to resort to import licensing and bilateral payments agreements. J. A. Stirling of the Board of Trade suggested that it might be useful if Keynes met Harry Hawkins of the State Department. On 25 June Keynes set out the problems of Britain's post-war balance of payments in gloomy terms. Shipping losses, sales of foreign assets, the fall in overseas earnings and the needs of reconstruction together suggested that Britain would have to increase her exports by 50 per cent over pre-war levels to achieve a semblance of 'equilibrium' in her balance of payments. She might be able to accomplish this only by resorting to discriminatory bilateral methods of relating imports from countries to the exports they took. Such forthright statements 'practically caused a deadlock' in the trade negotiations and so disturbed Hawkins that he hesitated to report them to Secretary Hull.[28] It also led to a major row between Keynes and Stirling. Keynes's realism may have been necessary, but he was unwise to inject it into the midst of the State Department's internal discussion of the 'consideration' for Lend Lease.

Keynes saw the President again on 7 July to discuss the 'consideration'. Roosevelt did not want a detailed agreement at this stage. He said that he favoured a preliminary, unpublished aide-memoire on the matter that would rule out a cash consideration, exchanges of territory or reverse lend lease on some future occasion. To Keynes's amusement, he was asked to convey the President's views to the State Department. He did so the same day. Dean Acheson was less amused.[29] After taking instructions from London, Keynes also presented an aide-memoire to Acheson on 15 July. After the deletions to his draft suggested by the Chancellor of the Exchequer and the Prime Minister, Keynes described the document as 'jejune'. This is not surprising since the only stated commitment, other than to return any Lend-Lease goods not destroyed or consumed, was:

The British Government will be happy to discuss with the United States Government in due course further measures of co-operation over a wider sphere.[30]

According to Keynes, 'Acheson thought it extremely unlikely that anything so one-sided would be agreed to'.[31] Keynes was not surprised at this reaction: his own draft had been much more ambitious.[32] He suggested that 'in truth it was for them to hand us a draft rather than the other way around', a view which Acheson shared.

Acheson handed the State Department's draft to Keynes on 28 July. The crucial section was Article VII, which suggested that the terms and conditions for aid and the benefits received by the United States

> shall be such as not to burden commerce between the two countries but to promote mutually advantageous economic relations between them and the betterment of world-wide economic relations; they shall provide against discrimination in either the United States of America or the United Kingdom against the importation of any produce originating in the other; and they shall provide for the formulation of measures for the achievement of these ends.

Keynes exploded:

> He said that he did not see how the British could make such a commitment in good faith ... that it saddled upon the future an ironclad formula from the nineteenth century ... that it contemplated the impossible and hopeless task of returning to a gold standard where international trade was controlled by mechanical monetary devices and which had proved completely futile.[33]

And there was much more in that vein. The next day, on reflection, Keynes wrote to Acheson

> My strong reaction against the word 'discrimination' is the result of my feeling so passionately that our hands must be free to make something new and better of the post-war world; not that I want to discriminate in the old bad sense of that word – on the contrary, quite the opposite.
>
> But the word calls up, and must call up – for that is what it means strictly interpreted – all the old lumber, most-favoured nation clause and the rest which was such a notorious failure and made such a hash of the old world. We know also that it won't work. It is the clutch of the dead, or at least the moribund, hand. If it was accepted it would be cover behind which all the unconstructive and purely reactionary people of both our countries would shelter. We must be free to work out new and better arrangements which will win in substance and not in shadow what the President and you and others really want. As I

know you don't dispute this, we shall be able to work something out. Meanwhile forgive my vehemence which has deep causes in my hopes for the future. This is my subject. I know, or partly know, what I want. I know, and clearly know, what I fear.[34]

On this note, Keynes left New York for London by air. In his almost three months in Washington he had made many contacts and friends, with some of whom he would become close in the years that followed. He had refreshed his memory of the vast differences between American and British political and administrative styles, many of which he had related with amusement in long letters to his colleagues in London. For example

The other main criticism . . . relates to the organs of government. To the outsider it looks almost incredibly inefficient. One wonders how decisions are ever reached at all. There is no clear hierarchy of authority. The different departments of the Government criticise one another in public and produce rival programmes. There is perpetual internecine warfare between prominent personalities. Individuals rise and fall in general esteem with bewildering rapidity. New groupings of administrative power and influence spring up every day. Members of the so-called Cabinet make public speeches containing urgent proposals which are not agreed as Government policy. In the higher ranges of government no work ever seems to be done on paper; no decisions are recorded on paper; no-one seems to read a document and no-one ever answers a communication in writing. Nothing is ever settled in principle. There is just endless debate and endless sitting around. . . . Suddenly some drastic, clear-cut decision is reached, by what process one cannot understand, and all the talk seems to have gone for nothing, being a fifth wheel to the coach, the ultimate decision appearing to be largely independent of the immense *parlez-vous*, responsible and irresponsible that had preceded it.

Nothing is secret, nothing confidential. The President laughed when I said his method of deceiving the enemy was apparently to publish so much vital information that they would not have the time to read it. . . . There is practically nothing you cannot get without asking for it.[35]

Yet for the young people in government in Washington, both economists and administrators, he had great praise and great hopes for the future.[36]

In many respects the Washington visit marked a watershed in Keynes's second Treasury career. During his first months, domestic financial concerns had been the centre of his interests, efforts and influence. From the summer of 1941, overseas issues would take up most of his time. This may have been deliberate Treasury policy – at least, according to Hugh Dalton, Keynes later thought it so.[37] It certainly reflected the fact that, after the 1941 Budget, domestic financial policy, although occasionally interesting in detail, had few grand principles left to settle – except when it came to planning the post-war world. On overseas issues, both wartime and post-war, there was much more. On these issues, Keynes soon became the dominant force in the Treasury, determining grand strategy and a high proportion of the tactics, spurring on the permanent officials with criticism and constructive help and leading the major negotiations. He remained the conscience and the optimist of the organisation, continually asking why? or why not? His position grew stronger over time because there was no strong counterweight in the office. Sir Frederick Phillips, who had played a major role in overseas financial matters in the late 1930s, was almost continuously in Washington from 1940, where, although he controlled the day-to-day tactics on most Anglo-American issues, he was isolated from London thinking on strategy. Phillips died suddenly in 1943. His former role in London was increasingly taken up by Sir Wilfrid Eady, a skilled negotiator, but one who lacked both Treasury background and experience and who did not have Phillips' ability to tackle Keynes on his own ground. More of the burden fell on the Permanent Secretary, from August 1942 Sir Richard Hopkins, Keynes's old Macmillan Committee antagonist, who, although he would play a formidable role, did not have the time or the energy to fill the gap on the external side. The same was true of his successor from March 1945, Sir Edward Bridges. Nor could Hopkins depend on the other outsiders for assistance: Hubert Henderson's health felt the strain of war and he left the Treasury in 1944,[g] as did Dennis Robertson, who on the international side was hardly a check on Keynes, except in his wilder enthusiasms. Thus there was a gradual shift in the balance of Keynes's influence, which probably reached its peak in 1945 over the American Loan negotiations when, as he put it afterwards, 'Cassandra cocks a snook' – he could be in a minority, not be believed (even inside the Treasury), and still get most of his own way.[38]

Just before Keynes went to Washington, on 16 April 1941 Lord Stamp was killed when a bomb fell on Shortlands, his country house in Kent. Not only did the nation lose a distinguished public servant but the Bank of England lost a director. It was some months before the Bank moved to replace him, but on 5 September Governor Norman, after consulting the Chancellor asked Keynes if he would take Stamp's place. His appointment was announced on 18 September.

The appointment was in many ways symbolic. At 58, the critic of the 1920s and the 1930s was now within the gates, not only of the Treasury but also at 'the other end of town'. Keynes saw it as such, remarking to his mother that he had better be careful or he would be a bishop next, and to

---

g Reading the wartime papers, one gets the impression that Henderson was even more 'minority minded' than Robertson could be, yet, not believing in the formidable organising power of economic analysis, he was less effective than Robertson in debate, even when he had the backing of senior career civil servants.

O. T. Falk that the 'old villain [Norman] loves his *institution* more than any doctrine'. But he did think 'The balance of sympathies and policies is widely reoriented'.[39]

Keynes was not a very active Bank Director: he was more than fully occupied at the Treasury. He did not, for example, take Stamp's place on the Bank's Committee of Treasury. Yet he did the normal new Director's stint on the Staff Committee, was full of suggestions for the fruitful use of the Houblon–Norman research fund established to mark the Bank's 250th Anniversary in 1944, and fond enough of the institution to mark the occasion with a birthday party in Ottawa.

> Eighteen of us – five each from the two [central] banks and the rest representing the British and Canadian Treasuries. I ventured a short discourse on the Bank's history suitably and acceptably indiscreet, Gordon and Clark replying in most flattering terms, the evening ending on a sentimental and friendly note. . . . [L]ast night was his evening and any Canadian who could not bring out some tale or reminiscence of Monty Norman felt badly out of it.[40]

Keynes was involved in the discussions that began in 1942 as to who would succeed Montagu Norman, who had been Governor since 1920. It would also appear that Keynes's own name came up as a candidate, but it does not appear to have received even the 'half-hearted' consideration that another in-house name, Otto Niemeyer's, received and certainly less than Keynes's own suggestion, Graham Towers, the Governor of the Bank of Canada, who was regarded as ' "too Keynesian" – no longer a term of abuse, but enough to send shivers down Threadneedle Street spines'. The post went to Lord Catto.[41]

On his return from Washington, the first thing that Keynes needed was a period of rest. Flying had aggravated the fatigue resulting from long, hot Washington days and evenings of contact-making and negotiating. In London he tried to put a few days in at the office between brief visits to Tilton, discussing his American trip with the Exchange Control Conference on 6 August and the Foreign Secretary on 12 August, but the strain proved too much: he called for the Ogre who recommended rest at Tilton.

Rest for Keynes was relative. He completed the arrangements for farming more land, taking over the Charleston farm and making Logan Thompson, the Tilton farm manager, his partner in the whole venture. He caught up on *Economic Journal* arrears. He began to think more intensively about post-war problems which were 'beginning to loom up – as not too hypothetical or too remote'.[42] On 21 August he reported to Richard Kahn that he had not yet put anything down on paper on the post-war monetary problem.[43] Two days later he managed a critical memorandum on a draft international wheat agreement which had just emerged from discussions in Washington.

Referring to it as 'chicanery', he was not impressed with the agreement and became even less so when he discussed it early the next month with Leith–Ross's Committee, especially against the background of the contemporaneous American proposals for Article VII.[44]

Article VII would occupy Keynes on and off for several months. Despite his outburst in his meeting with Dean Acheson before he left Washington, he had been optimistic about Britain committing herself to the President's 'spirit and purpose with which these post-war problems shall be approached'.[45] The problem was to find an appropriate form of words. The attempt was fraught with difficulties. Not only was discrimination in the form of Imperial Preference dear to the hearts of several Ministers and the basis of trading arrangements established with the Dominions, but the shape of the post-war world was sufficiently uncertain and frightening that bilateralism and discrimination in commercial policy might be inevitable, and perhaps desirable in itself, for a considerable period after the war. Complicating the position was the fact that many ministers were preoccupied with the present burdens of war and wanted to avoid the potentially divisive and time-consuming controversies that serious post-war planning would bring to the surface. On the other side were those concerned with reconstruction planning, who longed, if not for action, at least for guidance as to what assumptions they should make about the shape of the post-war world. There were also differences in the importance individuals accorded to the Anglo-American relationship and in the risks that they were prepared to run in holding out for a form of words radically different from the American draft.

At first, the pro-imperialists seemed to have the upper hand. Between 9 and 12 August Roosevelt and Churchill met off Newfoundland and drafted the set of war aims known as the Atlantic Charter. The fourth point in the Charter, which started as a British draft, ran

> Fourth, they will strive to bring about a free and equitable distribution
> of essential produce, not only within their territorial boundaries, but
> between the nations of the world.

The Americans tried unsuccessfully to add the words 'without discrimination and on equal terms'. This did not mean that the State Department had surrendered on Article VII – far from it. The British found this out when they attempted a redraft of Article VII in which the phrases 'working within the limits of their governing economic conditions' and 'balanced international economies' tried to leave some room for Imperial Preference and discrimination by not abandoning them in principle while still leaving the way free for change through negotiations. Keynes supported this redraft but hoped that there would be more emphasis on the need for not only a statement of principles but also early bilateral discussions. He emphasised the necessity for a serious response to the American draft.

There are enormous difficulties in the way of Anglo-American economic co-operation. No one can be more sensible of these than I am. . . . But it would be a great mistake to argue from these lurking difficulties that the members and officers of the Administration with whom we shall be dealing are either unfriendly or unreasonable. The truth is that they are enormously ignorant of our particular difficulties and problems. For this reason it is of the first importance that we develop our case in great detail and at great length, – on a scale which anyone over here except an academic economist would think very boring. Our only hope of getting a satisfactory agreed solution is by being extremely forthcoming with all relevant, and even irrelevant, information and extremely patient in endless discourse.[46]

His plea was unsuccessful. So too was the British attempt at a redraft of Article VII. Perhaps this was predictable given Mr Hull's anger about the Atlantic Charter and a recent speech by Sumner Wells which stressed American determination to eliminate trade restrictions and discrimination as part of her war aims.

Early in December 1941, the State Department presented a redraft of Article VII. This tried to meet some British worries in its reference to the expansion of employment and its reaffirmation of the Atlantic Charter. It also, in an additional paragraph, looked forward to conversations between the two countries with a view to meeting the objectives of the article 'in the light of governing economic conditions', thus taking over language from the British attempt at redrafting. Yet it still referred to discrimination – and in a broader context, as 'consideration' would 'include provisions for agreed action; to, amongst other things, 'the elimination of all forms of discriminatory treatment in international commerce and the reduction of tariffs and other trade barriers'.

In the new era of common effort which came the next week with the Japanese attack on Pearl Harbor, some in the Foreign Office urged acceptance of the new American redraft. Keynes was horrified at the suggestion that this would allow Britain to get her own way over the longer term.

The theory that 'to get our way in the long run' we must always yield in the short reminds me of the bombshell I threw into economic theory by the reminder that 'in the long run we are all dead'. If there was *no one* left to appease, the F. O. would feel out of a job altogether. . . . What will arouse suspicion will be our agreeing to unreasonable demands against our better judgement and then *inevitably* having to find some way of slipping out of our ill-advised words.[47]

'Then began two months of blind man's bluff' as Dean Acheson later put it.[48] Churchill deftly tried to avoid any commitment, given divisions at home;

others hoped that American entry into the war might put Anglo-American financial arrangements, including Lend Lease, on a new footing – a hope encouraged by America's short-lived suspension of Lend-Lease shipments on the outbreak of war against Japan. Despite the brief easing of pressure over the turn of the year while Churchill visited the United States, the State Department continued to press its draft, while the British pleaded for delay and hoped for clarifications that would imply that they were not simply trading Lend-Lease for Imperial Preference or a diminution of London's freedom to make her own economic policies in the difficult period after the war. In February, American pressure heightened. The hearings on the next year's Lend Lease appropriation loomed and American officials, who had told Congress earlier that they expected an early agreement with the British, faced the prospect of difficult questions. The Foreign Office again recommended acceptance while Keynes again warned of the dangers of 'appeasement *pur sang*'.[49] Yet, the Treasury was moving towards acceptance in principle and the beginning of discussions. Churchill was more forthright in his distaste for the whole process of bartering wartime economic aid between allies for policy concessions. It was of no avail in changing the draft. On 12 February, President Roosevelt, who had a week earlier warned Churchill that 'further delay . . . will be harmful to your interests and ours', cabled the Prime Minister to assure him that the document did not mean the trading of Imperial Preference for Lend Lease but rather that Britain and the United States would enter into 'a bold, forthright, and comprehensive discussion looking forward to the construction of what you so aptly call "a free, fertile economic policy for the post-war world" excluding nothing in advance'.[50] This assurance led Britain to drop her attempts to qualify or change the American draft and, after consulting the Dominions, she signed the agreement on 23 February. The mixture of a private Rooseveltian assurance and the publicly agreed wording of Article VII left much room for future misunderstanding.

Despite his comments about appeasement, Keynes was prepared to sign the agreement rather than risk a public breakdown in the negotiations, largely because he believed that the post-war financial implications of a breakdown would be disastrous. Such a breakdown would not directly interfere with wartime supplies, but the resulting frictions and delays might mean that Britain ended the war with exiguous reserves and with a harsh post-war Lend-Lease settlement which would reduce her authority and influence in other areas.[51] He did not think that signing would result in a new financial deal with the United States (for he was not certain that it would be possible to draft an arrangement that would satisfy Congress), but hoped for a more liberal interpretation of existing arrangements, including the taking over of the 'old commitments' – where the Keynes-Morgenthau arrangements of the previous summer had started slipping away almost as soon as Keynes had left Washington.[52] He was to be disappointed.

There was now a 'text' for negotiations about the shape of the post-war world. The relevant section of article VII ran:

> To that end [the promotion of mutually advantageous economic relations] between them and the betterment of worldwide economic relations they shall include provision for agreed action by the United States of America and the United Kingdom, open to participation by all other countries of like mind, directed to the expansion, by appropriate international and domestic measures, of production, employment, and the exchange and consumption of goods . . .; to the elimination of all forms of discriminatory treatment in international commerce, and the reduction of tariffs and other trade barriers.

One of Keynes's concerns about an early signing of Article VII had been a worry over possible misunderstandings about the meanings of words. He was thus a constant advocate of early face-to-face discussions about the principles of future policy prior to the signing of possibly ambiguous undertakings. His worry about the possible ill effects of the absence of discussions was heightened by reports that reached London of State Department views of what he actually believed.[53] Yet before Anglo-American negotiations could begin, there had to be something substantive to discuss. By February 1942 Keynes was well on the way to providing not only the items for an agenda but also a substantial portion of the subsequent working papers for discussion.

NOTES

1 The title of a minute from Keynes to Sir Richard Hopkins on 23 August 1940.
2 *JMK*, XXII, 182–3; XXIII, 10.
3 *JMK*, XXIII, 22.
4 *JMK*, XXIII, 29–40.
5 *JMK*, XXIII, 45–7.
6 *JMK*, XXV, 1.
7 *JMK*, XXV, 10.
8 *JMK*, XXV, 19.
9 For details of the early stages of the mission see the unsigned, undated series of notes presumably by Lucius Thompson on PRO, T247/113.
10 KCKP, JMK to FAK, 28 June 1941; Lydia to FAK, 21 May 1941.
11 Blum 1965, 246; *JMK*, XXIII, 97–9; PRO, T175/121, Playfair to Waley, 22 May 1941. For the background to the incident at Frankfurter's see *JMK*, XXIII, 95.
12 *JMK*, XXIII, 87–8, 91.
13 *JMK*, XXV, 369.
14 *JMK*, XXIII, 88, 91.
15 PRO, T175/121, Playfair to Waley, 16 May 1941.
16 *JMK*, XXIII, 73–8.
17 PRO, T175/121, Playfair to Waley, 22 May 1941.
18 *JMK*, XXIII, 155–61.
19 *JMK*, XXVII, 20–3.

20 Above pp. 653–4; *JMK*, XXIII, 108–12.
21 *JMK*, XXIII, ch. 5.
22 KCKP, Lydia to FAK, 2 June 1941. Notes from Keynes's lecture to the Princeton Economic Club on British budgetary policy survive in Federal Reserve Bank of New York, Pumphrey to Sproul and others, 2 June 1941. I thank Don Patinkin for a copy of this memorandum.
23 *JMK*, XXIII, 113.
24 *JMK*, XXIII, 94, 101–2.
25 *JMK*, XXIII, 102.
26 *JMK*, XXIII, 125, 137–40.
27 OBL, Brand Papers, Box 196, Brand to Eady, 26 February 1945.
28 PRO, T160/1200, Tel.3101, J. A. Stirling to Board of Trade, 4 July 1941.
29 *JMK*, XXIII, 154; Acheson 1970, 29.
30 *JMK*, XXIII, 162, 165.
31 *JMK*, XXIII, 162.
32 Maynard's draft appears in *JMK*, XXIII, 137–40.
33 *FRUS*, 1941, III, 11–13.
34 *JMK*, XXIII, 177–8.
35 *JMK*, XXIII, 105–6.
36 *JMK*, XXIII, 107, 192, 193.
37 BLPES, Dalton Diary, vol. 33, 3 August 1945.
38 The phrase comes from his notes for a talk to the Cambridge Political Economy Club on 2 February 1946 (KCKP).
39 KCKP, JMK to FAK, 6 September 1941; BE, JMK to Falk, 21 September 1941.
40 *JMK*, XXVI, 113.
41 KCKP, BE, J. Wedgwood to JMK, 6 October 1942; Fullerton, 1986, 192–4; Sayers 1976, 653–4.
42 KCKP, JMK to FAK, 18 August 1941.
43 *JMK*, XXV, 20; see below p. 670.
44 *JMK*, XXVII, 34, 37–40.
45 *JMK*, XXIII, 172.
46 *JMK*, XXIII, 205.
47 *JMK*, XXIII, 224–5.
48 Acheson 1970, 32.
49 PRO, T160/1105/F17660/02/3, Note of 5 February 1942.
50 Pressnell 1987, 387. Pressnell's discussion in chapter 3 has heavily influenced the shape of my discussion.
51 *JMK*, XXIII, 225–8.
52 *JMK*, XXIII, 219–23.
53 *JMK*, XXIII, 207–10; XXVI, 239–46.

26

THE CLEARING UNION

My Utopia

The right plan
(a) To prohibit tariffs altogether
(b) To have unqualified multilateral convertibility of currencies
(c) To make quantitative restrictions *compulsory* on any country having an adverse balance of *payments* so that it cannot outrun the constable.[1]

The 'Keynes Plan' is masterly. It combines the clarity of Mill, the ingenuity of Ricardo & the wisdom of Marshall.

(KCKP, G. Shove to JMK, 8 April 1943)

In mid-August 1941 Keynes did not see his way clearly enough to put pen to paper on the post-war currency problem. A little over two weeks later he was to do just that. On the evening of 3 September he retired to Tilton with Lydia 'to spend several days in peace writing a heavy memorandum on post-war currency plans'.[2] He did not succeed in working without interruption: he was called up to London for the day on 5 September, when he learned of the offer to become a director of the Bank of England. When he returned to the Treasury at mid-day on 8 September he had finished a document. Or, more accurately two documents: a long memorandum entitled 'Post-War Currency Policy' and a shorter 'Proposals for an International Currency Union'.[3] The former painted the background for all the subsequent drafts and discussions of the latter, as well as providing a masterful presentation of contemporary Treasury preoccupations.

Keynes divided his paper into four sections: the secular international problem, the contemporary British problem, an analysis of the problem, and the alternatives before Britain. As the second and fourth dealt with the contemporary British situation while the first and third were generalisations about the working of the international payments system in the past, I shall take the former first, leaving the latter to serve their originally intended purpose – providing the intellectual justification for the details of Keynes's substantive institutional proposals.

Britain would end the war in extreme international economic disequilibrium. Correcting this would require substantial changes in the pattern of international trade. The war interrupted Britain's ability to serve her export markets as she cut back exports to meet military demands. It also reduced her invisible exports as shipping losses and sales of overseas assets such as American Viscose took their toll. Yet her demand for imports of necessity remained large – indeed it might be abnormally large immediately after the war, given reconversion and reconstruction. She would also have to find the means of servicing (and protecting against withdrawal) the large overseas sterling balances that were already worrying policy-makers.[4] In these circumstances it might be necessary by bilateral bargaining to use the attractiveness of Britain as a market for food and raw materials as a lever for sales of British manufactures. This might be particularly the case because the American post-war policy proposals currently under discussion would be unlikely to help Britain. She was unlikely to be a recipient of liberal relief from the United States during reconstruction (and such relief would be only temporary); there was little prospect of American tariff cuts or restrictions on exports of American agricultural products (where the recent draft Wheat Agreement pointed in the opposite direction) to help Britain achieve the 50 to 100 per cent increase in the volume of exports necessary to balance her international accounts after the war; and, although (capital movements apart) the more or less continuous maintenance of a high level of employment in the USA would go a long way towards redressing the balance of payments problem, Britain could not lay her plans on this assumption.

Britain would end the war with comprehensive exchange controls and an extensive system of bilateral clearing and payments agreements. These, plus the leverage Britain could exert through a continuation of the wartime practice of Government-negotiated bulk purchases of food and raw materials, might allow her to restore her trade and balance it at a fairly high level of exports and even allow the relaxation of some objectionable features of such a régime. None the less, even though Keynes believed that such arrangements might be desirable in the *immediate* post-war period, he thought that in the long run a multilateral scheme would be preferable from her point of view – it would avoid previous trade wars and their political consequences and it would force the Americans to face squarely the important post-war issues.

In devising post-war arrangements, Keynes believed that policymakers should be alive to certain 'lessons from history'. The essential one was that the 'problem of maintaining equilibrium in the balance of payments between countries has never been solved since methods of barter gave way to the use of money and bills of exchange'.[5] In the previous 500 years the international monetary system had only 'worked' tolerably well for two 50-year periods: the Elizabethan age when the world was awash with silver from the Spanish Americas, and the Victorian age when Britain through her policies of free trade and heavy overseas lending kept the rest of the world adequately supplied with gold and sterling. Certainly

> to suppose that there exists some smoothly functioning automatic mechanism of adjustment which preserves equilibrium if only *we* trust to the methods of *laissez-faire* is a doctrinaire delusion which disregards the lessons of historical experience without having behind it the support of sound theory.[6]

The inter-war period, which had seen the breakdown of currency *laissez faire*, had provided tests which allowed Keynes to discard certain possible options. Floating exchange rates, competitive deflation, competitive exchange depreciation, trade restrictions and discrimination, and the automatic price-specie flow mechanism had not proved successful in restoring underlying long-term equilibrium. The only germ of a good idea had been the Schachtian one of getting rid of international currency altogether and reverting to international barter.

The reason why a freely convertible international metallic standard such as the gold standard had not worked to preserve equilibrium, except in isolated circumstances, was to Keynes quite straightforward: such a standard had a *deflationary* bias. First, for the deficit or debtor country the process of adjustment was compulsory; whereas for the creditor it was optional: the debtor could not let its reserves fall below zero and if it borrowed to augment its reserves such assistance would be subject to deflationary conditions. Second, the deficit country was always small in relation to the rest of the world: the deflationary effects of its reserve losses on its own economy would be much larger than the inflationary effects of the same reserve gains elsewhere. As the social strains of a downward adjustment in wages and prices were larger than those in an upward direction, this added another element of instability to the system, for measures taken to avoid downward adjustments might impair the beneficial properties of the system. In addition to its deflationary bias, the old system with its freedom of capital movements allowed not only the flow of productive resources from older to newer developing countries as before 1914 but also speculative or refugee capital flows that did not correspond to the productive international flow of resources and which in the inter-war period finally brought about the ruin of the old gold standard system.

Keynes concluded that a successful international monetary system should be guided by these 'lessons'.

> The object . . . must be to require the chief initiative [for adjustment] from the creditor countries, whilst maintaining enough discipline in the debtor countries to prevent them from exploiting the new ease allowed them in living profligately beyond their means.[7]

After the war:

> Social changes affecting the position of the wealth-owning class are
> likely to occur or (what is worse in the present conditions) to be
> threatened in many countries. The whereabouts of 'the better 'ole'
> will shift with the speed of the magic carpet. Loose funds may sweep
> round the world disorganising all steady business.
>
> Nothing is more certain than that movement of capital funds must
> be regulated; – which in itself will involve far-reaching departures from
> *laissez-faire* arrangements.[8]

Indeed it presupposed exchange controls covering all international transactions.

Keynes's positive proposals started from this last presumption, for, with
comprehensive exchange controls in place, the normal foreign exchange
market of many participating banks might be hard to regulate. He assumed
that all overseas transactions would pass through the hands of a country's
central bank. He then suggested that the transactions between central banks
be cleared through an international bank or Clearing Union. With individuals
dealing in national currencies through their central bank and with central
banks dealing with each other through the international clearing bank, it
would become possible to make the unit in which the international clearing
accounts were denominated the *numéraire* for the system as a whole, thus
giving rise to an international currency. In Keynes's scheme, each country
would denominate its national currency in terms of the international clearing
bank's unit of account, which itself would be expressed in terms of gold.
However, gold would only be convertible into international clearing bank
money in one direction: a central bank could increase the balance on its
account with the clearing bank by selling gold but it could not reverse
the process. This made the international clearing bank money the ultimate
reserve asset in the system.

Keynes had to devise a set of rules for the international bank which would
determine the world's access to supplies of international bank deposits and
achieve the principles of balance-of-payments adjustment which he believed
desirable. He gave each country a quota (equal to one half of the average
sum of the country's exports and imports over the previous five years) and
allowed countries overdrafts against this quota. Thus balance-of-payments
imbalances would be reflected in the international bank's accounts as
overdrafts for debtors and positive balances for creditors. Using the size
of these overdrafts and positive balances as a guide he could then devise a
set of rules which would encourage long-term international equilibrium for
the system.

For both debtor and creditor countries, in Keynes's September 1941 draft,
the quota set absolute limits to their positions with the international bank:
debtors could not owe more than their quota and surplus countries which

had credit balances larger than their quotas at the end of a year had to transfer the excess to the reserve fund of the international bank. However, long before it got to its quota limit, the size of a country's balance with the international bank would affect its balance of payments policies. For example, a deficit country could not overdraw its account by more than a quarter of its quota in any year. As the size of its overdraft rose, the rate of interest payable on that overdraft would rise. When its overdraft reached a quarter of its quota, the country would be allowed to change its exchange rate by up to 5 per cent within one year; once it reached half, it might be required to make such a change, to hand over any gold it held to reduce its overdraft, or prohibit outward capital transactions except with the permission of the governors of the international bank. It might be required to leave the system. For surplus countries there were similar provisions: a central bank in credit for more than a quarter of its quota might appreciate its exchange rate by up to 5 per cent within a year and it should allow foreigners to withdraw any balances or investments they held; a credit balance over half its quota would bring a required exchange rate appreciation of 5 per cent, an appreciation repeated in any year when its average credit balance increased by a further 10 per cent of its quota. Surplus countries would receive no interest on their credit balances: indeed they would *pay* interest at 5 per cent per annum on balances above a quarter of their quotas and 10 per cent per annum above a half, as well as having any excess above their quota confiscated.

Such were the bare bones of the scheme, which had its roots in many earlier 'Keynes schemes'.[9] Moreover, having found a way of creating command over resources by international agreement, Keynes realised that he had discovered a means of financing the activities of the international community such as an international police force, post-war relief and reconstruction, or the control of fluctuations in primary product prices through buffer stock schemes. Subsequent drafts would increase the number of examples – and Keynes would later try his hand at the detailed working out of a commodity stabilisation scheme within the context of his Clearing Union – but these were incidental to the basic vision. The heart of the matter was to encourage balance of payments adjustment.

At the time Keynes circulated his documents, they were but one set of several dealing with post-war matters that had come from various quarters. Within a few months they would be more than that, but in the interim there would be considerable discussion.

At first Keynes's proposals were commented on by very few, even within the Treasury. The main comments on the first draft came from Richard Kahn, then in the Board of Trade; James Meade of the Economic Section; Lucius Thompson and H. A. Siepmann of the Bank; and Ralph Hawtrey. The Bank officials, then as later, were less enthusiastic than anyone else. They were more inclined to let matters evolve naturally from the Schachtian use of controls and payments agreements that would characterise the post-war transition and the pre-war Tripartite Agreement of 1936, whose substantive restraints on the behaviour of its signatories were extremely limited. The reactions of Hawtrey, Kahn and Meade were much more positive and constructive. However, the tenor of the Bank's reaction, plus the tone of other Treasury memoranda then in circulation, particularly one by Hubert Henderson, on the shape of the post-war world, and the contemporaneous discussions surrounding Article VII prompted Keynes not only to redraft his detailed proposals but also to provide a longer justification for them.

The revised draft, dated 18 November was to open out the discussion into wider circles than its predecessor, and, as Lionel Robbins put it, to provide 'a real release of fresh air into this surcharged and stale atmosphere'. Dennis Robertson was even more enthusiastic:

> I sat up late last night reading your revised 'proposals' with great excitement, – and a growing hope that the spirit of Burke and Adam Smith is on earth again to prevent the affairs of a Great Empire from being settled by the little minds of a gang of bank-clerks who have tasted blood (yes, I know this is unfair!).
>
> And then also a growing hope that we shall choose the right things and not the wrong ones to have such rows with the Americans as we must have.[10]

Thus began the last great Keynes–Robertson collaboration, one that would stretch beyond the Bretton Woods Agreement of 1944. Although, as in their previous fruitful collaborations, there would be sharp words exchanged, the upshot for practical affairs was perhaps as important as its predecessors had been for economic analysis.

Keynes's revised draft was his most forthright in grasping several nettles relating to Article VII and the shape of the post-war world more generally. In it he made clear that he did not think that Britain would be able to ask the United States for direct financial assistance after the war:

> The US will consider that we have had our whack in the shape of lend lease and a generous settlement of 'consideration'. . . . We in particular, in a distressed and ruined continent, will not bear the guise of the most suitable candidate for the dole, however real and heavy our difficulties. The assistance for which we can hope must be *indirect* and a consequence of setting the world as a whole on its feet and of laying the foundations for a sounder political economy between all nations.[11]

Nor did he believe that 'a patched up contrivance' carried over from wartime experience – a clear reference to the Bank's view – which might work for the transition would provide the basis for a long-term solution. Thus he claimed that he aimed at a general solution which would benefit not only Britain but also other nations. This would have the advantage of minimising the influence of transitory political events and avoiding particular patterns of obligation, while providing, unlike the proposals of the Bank and its Treasury sympathisers, for means to restore international economic equilibrium.

Keynes also argued that his scheme, with creditor and debtor positions clearly registered in the accounts of the Clearing Union would allow for a limitation of the use of trade-disrupting protective measures. To this end, he proposed that, except for the three-to-five-year transition to the new régime and in defined cases of balance of payments deficit, there be a general agreement among members of the Clearing Union prohibiting tariffs or preferences above 25 per cent, direct or indirect export subsidies, import quotas or prohibitions, barter agreements and restrictions on the use of current trade receipts. In other words, the plan accepted a non-discriminatory system 'as the normal and desirable state of affairs', even though it allowed for regional customs unions or preferential areas.[12] In effect, he was making a case for a significant measure of 'disarmament' in the use of the weapons of international economic policy – one less hedged about with qualifications than many subsequent drafts.

The discussants of this draft included his Treasury colleagues Dennis Robertson, S. D. Waley and Lord Catto; Henry Clay of the Bank of England; the Board of Trade[a] and Roy Harrod, who over the next 18 months would be the most prolific of Keynes's corespondents. The Bank, ably supported by Hubert Henderson, continued to oppose a grand scheme, although after its comments on the second draft it decided to remain on the sidelines and 'allow J.M.K.'s stuff to percolate where it will' in subsequent discussion.[13] Perhaps it did not think it worthwhile to continue the critical struggle on a draft-by-draft basis. Its strategy of standing to one side, carefully preserving its options, was to cause difficulties later – and to create dangerous gaps in perceptions and understanding that affected subsequent policy.[b] From other directions, the comments were more constructive, centring on the issues of rules versus discretion (or whether the scheme went in S. D. Waley's words 'too far in reducing the gentle art of central banking to a science conducted by rule of thumb'),[14] the treatment of debtors and creditors, the role of exchange rate changes, Keynes's suggestions for commercial policy, and the role of controls on capital movements. The reaction was generally favourable. Keynes remarked, 'I have received more encouragement for this from all quarters in Whitehall than for anything I have ever suggested'.[15] Keynes's draft took on the status of the official Treasury proposal for post-war monetary arrangements. But, before it went the full round of

a Richard Kahn, who had gone to Cairo in October as economic adviser to Oliver Lyttleton, Minister of State in the Middle East, dropped out.
b Some of the problems surrounding the Bank's role in the discussions doubtless arose from the differing 'styles' of the hierarchical Bank and the much less structured Treasury, for the need to form a Bank 'view' limited the possibilities of give and take in discussion and, without strong leadership, encouraged conservatism.

interdepartmental committees and comment, Keynes was to redraft it again on 15 December.

In this third draft Keynes directly faced the central issue inherent in any such scheme – the matter of rules versus discretion. As he put it:

> Perhaps the most difficult question to determine is how much to decide by rule and how much by discretion. If rule prevails, the liabilities attaching to membership become clear and definite, whilst the responsibilities of the central management are reduced to a minimum. On the other hand, liabilities which would require the surrender by legislation of discretion normally inherent in a government, with the result that in certain circumstances sovereign rights would be infringed, will not be readily undertaken by ourselves or by the United States. If discretion prevails, we have to decide how far the ultimate decision can be left to the individual members and how much to the central management. If the individual members are too free, indiscipline may result and unwarranted liberties be taken. If it is to the central management that the discretions are given, too heavy a weight of responsibility may rest on it and it may be assuming the exercise of powers which it has not the strength to implement. If rule prevails, the scheme can be made more water-tight theoretically. If discretion prevails it may work better in practice.[16]

Keynes moved decisively towards discretion. In the case of surplus countries, the higher rates of interest charged on credit balances disappeared, as did any limit to such balances. Away went the requirement in some circumstances to appreciate the exchange rate. Instead such countries merely had to discuss matters with the Union when their credit balance exceeded one half of their quota for more than a year. With debtors the discretion rested more with the Union than the member in the form of conditional access to finance. Yet, tentatively in this draft and definitely in the next draft, the easing of the pressures towards balance of payments adjustment, particularly as regards creditors, went side by side with an increase in the amount of financing, and hence the time for adjustment, available.[c]

Other changes included an indefinite transitional period, slightly vaguer commitments over tariffs and no commitments at all over preferences, and the introduction of the possibility of state trading.

The ensuing round of discussion, the last before the proposal went to an interdepartmental committee and Cabinet, saw Keynes add further provisions concerning large debtors, a provision that for the first five years of the scheme exchange rates would be regarded as more provisional than subsequently, and

---

c In the first two drafts the formula for quotas gave Britain a quota of £624 million. In the third draft there was no explicit formula for quotas. In the fourth draft the revised formula gave Britain a quota of £1,475 million.

a provision for a general reconsideration of the scheme after five years. In these discussions, Keynes also set out clearly why he believed that exchange rate steps of 5 per cent were sufficient: the main long-term determinant of appropriate exchange rates were relative levels of unit wage costs, 'not as a rule anything that changes very suddenly'.[17] He also mistakenly believed that exchange rate changes of 5 per cent were sufficiently small in conditions of comprehensive exchange controls as not to lead to substantial speculation which could force the authorities' hands. At this stage, he added a provision which, by prohibiting further extension of gold exchange standard arrangements, ensured the dominance of the union's unit as the principal international reserve asset.[d]

Keynes's scheme went forward to Ministers as part of a larger document from the Treasury, which included an estimate of Britain's post-war balance of payments problem and discussions of the Clearing Union, of trade policies, of the American proposal by Hansen and Gulick for an International Economic Board and Development Corporation, and of Roy Harrod's international investment scheme. All in all, the 'Treasury sandwich' ran to 84 pages of which Keynes's proposals represented only 74 paragraphs.

Keynes completed his fourth draft over the weekend of 24–5 January 1942. The 'sandwich' went to the War Cabinet's Committee on Reconstruction Problems on 31 March and to the War Cabinet on 10 April. The major change in the scheme that resulted from the Cabinet discussions, other than a suggestion by Sir Stafford Cripps that the USSR be included as a founder member, was needed to meet an objection by Ernest Bevin, whose experience of deflation reinforced by dear money at the time of the return to gold in 1925 'drove him, against his inclinations, to support the General Strike' of 1926. This change made it clear that the measures the Clearing Union could ask a member to take to reduce its debit position

> do *not* include a deflationary policy enforced by dear money and similar measures, having the effect of causing unemployment; for this would amount to restoring, subject to insufficient safeguards, the evils of the old automatic gold standard.[18]

Between September 1941 and May 1942, the clearing union was not the only post-war iron that Keynes had in the fire. In the fall of 1941 he prepared and persuaded the Treasury to adopt as its proposed policy a scheme for financing post-war relief which was ready by the end of October. The scheme was cast in terms of European problems, for the war was still predominantly a European war even if it had spilled into the Middle East and North Africa. There were still some commodities in surplus and Britain, despite the strains of war, could see herself as being able to make a substantial commitment.

d Thus Keynes's 'ideal currency of the future' in *Indian Currency and Finance*, whose role he had restricted in the *Treatise*, died in 1942. For details, see Moggridge 1986, 73–7.

The Japanese attack on Pearl Harbor and her simultaneous swing south-wards through South East Asia transformed the situation. Instead of China being the only possible claimant for relief – and the British had always regarded her as America's concern – the exact limits of devastation became uncertain but would probably include Burma and Malaya, where Britain would have special responsibilities. The shift to global war also made it unlikely that the surplus commodities that Keynes had seen at the heart of Britain's contribution to relief would exist at the end of hostilities. The shift in the focus of the war towards the East, as well as developments in the Middle East in the course of 1941, meant that the growth of Britain's sterling area liabilities, which had worried Keynes, if few others, since as far back as 1940, now took an ominous upward spurt.[19] Finally, revisions in the official forecast of Britain's post-war balance of payments position as a part of the exercise surrounding the preparation of the 'Treasury sandwich' produced even more gloom. Britain looked more like needing post-war relief than being able to provide it. The change in position was reflected in the drafts of the Clearing Union where the assumption of no American post-war aid for Britain in the first draft had become one that Lend Lease would continue for up to two years after the war.[20] Any British relief contribution would have to come from somebody else's resources. It was Keynes in particular who pushed for the Treasury to inject these changed circumstances into the British discussions of post-war relief. He ended up as the final draftsman of the Treasury's May 1942 letter to Hugh Dalton, the minister responsible, to change the basis of past discussions.[21]

Keynes also tried his hand at a related problem which had been left to the official Committee on Post-war Economic Problems: international commodity policy. From the beginning he had allowed as one of the functions of his Clearing Union the possibility of financing an international buffer stock scheme to stabilise commodity prices.[22] Although the drafting of such a scheme might have fallen to other departments such as the Colonial Office or the Ministry of Economic Warfare (which was responsible for surpluses), the financial implications of the scheme, his expertise in the area, and his initiative meant that the drafting fell on Keynes in the Treasury. On 6 January 1942 he told Roy Harrod that he had gone so far as to dig out a copy of his 1938 article, 'The Policy of Government Storage of Foodstuffs and Raw Materials'.[23] By 20 January the first draft was complete. Further drafts followed in early February, late March and early April, before his fifth draft, dated 12 April, was ready for circulation to other departments as an official Treasury memorandum which would eventually go forward to the official Committee on Post-war Economic Problems and thence to Cabinet.[24]

The centrepiece of Keynes's commodity scheme was a series of buffer stocks for each of the main internationally traded commodities. The aim would be purchases and sales of each commodity in order to reduce short-term price fluctuations without disturbing longer-term price trends, while maintaining a roughly constant reserve – US Vice President Wallace's 'ever normal granary'. Each commodity would be managed by its own 'control' and there would be a central 'control' to ensure that the individual commodity schemes conformed to the general principles and to provide consistency in reactions to unforeseen problems.

So much for the basic principle. Turning principle into practice was a complex task. Some changes were cosmetic. For example, he added a section on a matter he had not considered in 1938 – the ability of such a scheme to stabilise world incomes. Others were matters of 'taste': for example Keynes's conception of using the Clearing Union to finance the accumulation of stocks met with disapproval from the Bank of England which understandably did not favour the intermingling of monetary and commodity plans. Other questions required analysis. What was the appropriate range of fluctuations between a control's buying and selling prices which would allow for the normal activities of merchants and yet avoid speculative swings? What should be a control's rule of thumb for prices when it began to accumulate or lose stocks chronically? Would a scheme to stabilise prices affect production decisions by leading to an expansion in output by high-cost producers? What basis should controls use to set prices? On such matters experts could come to considerable agreement. Others proved less tractable, particularly the question of regulating output by such methods as output restrictions, export quotas and subsidies. Related to these were differing views about the role or efficiency of the market – the Bank of England with its traditional dislike of 'speculation' found Keynes's proposals 'far too *laissez-faire*, inasmuch as they allow a place for private trading'[25] – and elements of disagreement as to whether the underlying purpose of the scheme was to stabilise prices which cleared markets or to stabilise producers' incomes at some remunerative level. The latter question of purpose highlighted the possible conflict between consumers' and producers' interests, something of which Keynes would learn more in the discussions that followed.

Although Keynes's commodity proposals had moved as quickly as those for the Clearing Union from first draft to interdepartmental discussion, it was to take almost a year more before they reached Cabinet on 8 April 1943. The major reason for the delay lay with Sir Frederick Leith-Ross of the Ministry of Economic Warfare and Sir Donald Fergusson, the Permanent Secretary of the Ministry of Agriculture. Both took exception to what they regarded as the inadequate treatment of output restriction schemes. Keynes tried – too hard in the view of Dennis Robertson and Roy Harrod – to meet them in subsequent drafts by allowing for output restrictions under international supervision while retaining the central role of the price system and relative costs of production. He could not satisfy his critics, especially Sir Donald Fergusson, who was resolutely against international arrangements in the spirit of Article VII and firmly convinced of the rightness of policies framed in the interests of his own Ministry's clients, British farmers.

Keynes's exasperation after almost a year of discussion began to show in his January 1943 reaction on Leith-Ross and Fergusson's comments on his latest draft.

> *Leith-Ross.* . . . [His] comments fall into two very distinct groups – according to whether the glosses are by an Elohistic commentator who is an extreme devotee of Free Trade or a Jahvistic scribe who is an equally extreme devotee of Restriction. I have more sympathy with the Elohistic authority, but if I met him all along the line the paper would receive the wrong emphasis . . . . Also it does not seem prudent tactics in a paper designed to protect the interests of primary producers generally to make its principal purpose appear to be the abolition of agriculture in the United States and most of Europe. . . .
>
> *Fergusson.* His contribution can only be described as barmy. One can try to meet, or compromise with, differences of opinion or criticisms of expression. But in this case every paragraph of his letter and several of his detailed comments show an almost lunatic misunderstanding of what the paper says or is driving at. It is a frightful nuisance. . . . But Fergusson is such a good fellow and so all-but aware of the above that I should not despair of persuading him to certify himself.[26]

Fergusson, and his Department, remained in a minority of one to the end. As a result, more so than with the Clearing Union, there remained a strong undercurrent of hostility to the commodity proposals which would resurface later in the war once the Anglo-American discussions on the post-war world had progressed further.

The preparation of the post-war schemes had been undertaken with the prospect of Anglo-American discussions. Such discussions had been envisaged as far back as the summer of 1941 when President Roosevelt suggested that 'three wise men' from each side sit down together to sort out the main lines of Anglo-American post-war policy.[27] They had also been advocated by Keynes after his return to London in August 1941 as necessary for clarity of thinking and meaning before, or at least soon after, Britain agreed to any form of words such as Article VII.[28] Article VII itself stated that such discussions were to take place 'at an early and convenient date'. But when?

The answer turned out to be almost never. The closest the two countries came to wide-ranging comprehensive discussions was to be in Washington in September–October 1943. Even these, 'the most important Anglo-American exchanges on economic issues not only during the war but for many years before and since', were informal, non-committal and exploratory.[29] Instead issues were tackled on a piecemeal, topic-by-topic basic. The reasons were to some extent political: for example, throughout much of 1942 the war was not going well and it hardly seemed the time for post-war discussions which might be carried on in a blaze of publicity in a year for Congressional elections. As well, 7 December 1941 had radically changed the situation. As Sir Frederick Phillips put it to Keynes in January 1943 after the latter had again raised the notion of an Anglo-American commission:

> The proposal may have had good points in 1941 but we are not in 1941. Very natural then for the main democratic belligerent and the main democratic non-belligerent to put their heads together on the future. But events, and Roosevelt with or ahead of them, have moved a very long way since. If there is to be publicity (and the good explanation to the public is the heart of the thing) never shall we see a joint Anglo-American Commission of this kind. There would have to be an official or semi-official Russian wise man, ditto Chinese wise man, with Canada squawking across the Border, and London insisting that Van Zeeland shall be on to represent Europe, and why should the I.L.O. and the League be ignored. By this time the idea has lost its attraction for me. The dilemma is that you must have a team from each country for no man can cover the ground. But it is hardly a workable idea to have a team from each of several countries to draft plans.[30]

Given the diffusion of power, decision-making and responsibility in the American political system as compared with the British, a concentration on limited, bilateral discussions seemed potentially more productive and less dangerous than multilateral, multi-issue talks.

But this was in the future. In the winter of 1941–2 the British expected that conversations would begin soon. Keynes was impatient: he made his impatience known to Ambassador Winant and his economic adviser E. F. Penrose, and Winant raised the possibility that he would return from his next visit to Washington with a small team of expert advisers who could open discussions. Winant made his suggestion to the State Department, only to be told that it was too early. And so it always seemed, despite several inquiries by Winant and Sir Frederick Phillips. In the meantime, the informal contacts among officials and advisers in London and Washington made it clear to both sides that both American and British plans for the post-war international monetary system were going forward. From discussions with Keynes, Nigel Ronald of the Foreign Office and James Meade, for example, Ambassador Winant was able to keep Washington informed of the broad evolution of British (and particularly Keynes's) thinking.

When communication of the plans began in July and August 1942 it was backstairs and roundabout. The Anglo-American conversations envisaged in Article VII were still some distance away and it was clear that when and if they came they would be in Washington rather than London. To try to push matters forward and to influence opinion before everyone's ideas crystallised, Sir Frederick Phillips cabled London on 8 July for permission to give the US Treasury an advance outline of the Clearing Union proposals. The same day he sent Sir Richard Hopkins a 'summary' of an American

Treasury draft paper on post-war financial arrangements with instructions that the British must not indicate that they knew of the document and that Keynes should be the only person to read it. The next day, Sir Frederick Leith-Ross sent London another copy of the scheme which, unknown to Phillips, he had received directly from Harry Dexter White. The American monetary cat was out of the bag. The British cat would remain concealed for a time, although Phillips did receive permission to give the Americans a verbal exposition of the Clearing Union.

The author of the American plan was Harry Dexter White, a man whose background and career were markedly different from Keynes's. White, the youngest son of a Jewish Lithuanian hardware dealer, was born in Boston in October 1892. He went into the family business after completing secondary school. He enlisted in the US Army six days after the United States declared war on Germany in April 1917. After service in France, he returned to the family business in 1919, but in February 1922 he enrolled at Columbia University as a student of government. He moved to Stanford and economics in the summer of 1923, taking his AB in October 1924 'with great distinction' and becoming a member of the national honours society Phi Beta Kappa. He received his AM from Stanford in June 1925.

White returned east for further graduate work at Harvard. His prize-winning dissertation for his Ph.D. was published as *The French International Accounts 1880–1913* (1933). One of a series of dissertations completed under F. W. Taussig, the doyen of American international economists of his generation, designed to test the then orthodox theory of balance-of-payments adjustment, it is, with Jacob Viner's *Canada's Balance of International Indebtedness 1900–1913* (1924) and John Henry Williams' *Argentina Under Inconvertible Paper 1880–1900* (1920), a classic in its field. In 1930 classic Ph.D. dissertations were not much use in a dismal job market: White hung on as an instructor at Harvard. In the fall of 1932, aged 40, he became Assistant Professor of Economics at Lawrence College in Appleton, Wisconsin, where he was promoted to full Professor a year later. This was far from the background or meteoric rise of Keynes, who had been a fellow of King's at 25 and editor of the *Economic Journal* and a member of a Royal Commission before he was 30.

White did not stay long in Wisconsin. In the summer of 1934, Jacob Viner, then advising Henry Morgenthau, recently appointed Secretary of the Treasury, asked White to help him in a survey of money and banking legislation and institutions. White's report, 'Selection of a Monetary Standard for the United States', submitted in September 1934, led to an appointment in the Treasury's Division of Research and Statistics from 1 November. It was in this capacity that he went to Europe in April and May 1935 to gather information on monetary conditions in Belgium and Holland and to investigate the possibilities of an exchange stabilisation agreement with

Britain. Keynes was one of the people he interviewed, but the interview did not make Keynes's appointments diary. The stabilisation agreement itself was not possible in 1935, but in September 1936 came the Tripartite Declarations of Britain, France and the United States.

White's rise in the Treasury was rapid, which is perhaps not surprising given his drive and ability. In October 1936 he became Assistant Director of his Division and by March 1938 he had his own empire carved out of the Division when he became Director of Monetary Research. This meant that he had responsibility for the American Stabilization Fund and hence for the Treasury's involvement in international affairs which grew as the world slid towards war. In April 1938 he became a member of Morgenthau's '9.30 Group' which met the Secretary every morning. Finally, in December 1941 he was given the status of an Assistant Secretary of the Treasury and formal responsibility for all Treasury matters with any bearing on foreign relations – most of which he had been attending to already.

By 1942, Keynes had already met White again during his 1941 Washington visit, when on at least one occasion the latter's intervention with Morgenthau had helped to foster the success of Keynes's mission.[31] Although he referred to White as a statistician, he recognised his influence with the Secretary from the outset.[32] He would almost certainly have regarded this rather short, stocky man with a moustache and rimless spectacles as one of 'the very gritty Jewish type' of younger American civil servants, for White did have an abrasive manner. An economist at the Federal Reserve Board once said, 'Of course, normally, Harry is the unpleasantest man in Washington'.[33] Later Keynes would appraise him as follows:

> Any reserves we may have about him are a pale reflection of what his colleagues feel. He is over-bearing, a bad colleague, always trying to bounce you, with harsh rasping voice, aesthetically oppressive in mind and manner; he has not the faintest conception of how to behave or observe the rules of civilised intercourse. At the same time, I have a very great respect and even liking for him. In many respects he is the best man here. A very able and devoted public servant, carrying an immense burden of responsibility and initiative, of high integrity and of clear sighted idealistic international purpose, genuinely intending to do his best for the world. Moreover, his over-powering will combined with the fact that he has constructive ideas mean that he does get things done, which few else here do. He is not open to flattery in any crude sense. The best way to reach him is to respect his purpose, arouse his intellectual interest (it is a great softener to intercourse that it is easy to arouse his genuine interest in the merits of any issue) and to tell him off frankly and firmly without any finesse when he has gone off the rails of relevant argument or appropriate behaviour.[34]

The exact origins of White's monetary plan are somewhat mysterious.

We know that on 14 December 1941 Morgenthau instructed him to prepare a memorandum on an inter-allied stabilisation fund which, among other things, would 'provide the basis for post-war monetary stabilisation arrangements: and . . . provide a post-war "international currency"'.[35] The speed with which White reacted suggests that he had already given thought to such a scheme, for the first surviving draft is dated 30 December. During the following months the draft was revised and expanded by White and his assistants, most notably E. M. Bernstein who had greater technical sophistication and powers of persuasion than his superior, and shown to a few outside the Treasury.[36] By early May an improved draft was ready for Morgenthau and then for the President and the Secretary of State. Full interdepartmental meetings started on 25 May and by July reached agreement to have informal bilateral discussions with the White Plan in the background but off the table. Soon after, the plan was 'leaked' to Keynes via Phillips and Leith-Ross.

White's plan envisaged two institutions, a Stabilisation Fund and a Bank for Reconstruction and Development. The Fund was to secure several purposes. Among the more important were to stabilise exchange rates, encourage productive capital flows, liberate blocked balances, correct gold maldistribution, shorten periods of international disequilibrium, reduce the necessity for exchange controls, eliminate multiple currency practices and promote sound credit policies.

The Fund to achieve these purposes was to be made up of contributions from members totalling at least $5 billion. Each member's share was to be a function of a complex formula whose components included gold holdings, gold production, national income, foreign trade, population, foreign investments and foreign debts. The initial quotas suggested by the formula were $3,196 million for the United States, $635 million for Britain and $138 million for Canada.[e] On accession members would pay 12½ per cent of their quota in gold, 12½ per cent in domestic currency and 25 per cent in interest-bearing securities whose interest and principal were payable in gold. The remaining 50 per cent was payable when called by the Fund's management. Membership would be open to any member of the United or Associated Nations who agreed within one year of joining or at the end of hostilities, whichever came later, to abandon all restrictions on exchange transactions with other members other than those approved by the Fund; to alter its exchange rate only with the consent of the Fund and to the extent and in the direction approved by the Fund; not to allow investment from any member without that member's permission and to make available to the government of a member all deposits, investments and securities of its nationals; not to enter into any bilateral clearing arrangements; not to adopt

e Each member would have 100 votes plus one vote for the equivalent of every million dollars subscribed in gold or currency.

any monetary or general price measure or policy which in the opinion of members with a four-fifths majority of the votes would sooner or later bring about serious balance of payments disequilibrium; to embark on a programme to reduce trade barriers; not to default on foreign obligations of the government or its agencies and not to subsidise the export of any good or service without the Fund's permission.

The Fund would fix the exchange rates among its members' currencies. Changes in these rates could only be made to correct 'fundamental disequilibrium' in the balance of payments and would require consent of four-fifths of the members' votes. This gave the US (and, acting as a unit, the British Empire and Commonwealth) an effective veto. To defend these fixed exchange rates, members could with their own currency purchase the currency of another member to meet their adverse balance of payments with that member, subject to the restriction that the Fund's holdings of the currency of the member making the purchase could not exceed its original contribution of gold, currency and notes. A member could exceed this limit with the approval of four-fifths of the members' votes if the Fund believed it could get rid of the excess within a reasonable period of time or if current and prospective gold holdings would be adequate to replace the excess or if the member agreed to carry out measures recommended by the Fund to correct its balance of payments disequilibrium.

In addition to these basic provisions, White's Fund proposal contained an ingenious scheme to free wartime blocked balances which could be helpful to Britain with her growing liabilities of sterling balances, a suggestion that members could borrow their own currencies from the Fund at low rates of interest and a provision whereby the Fund could supplement its own resources by borrowing from the members.

The proposal for a Bank for Reconstruction and Development was more ambitious. The Bank would have a capital of up to $10 billion divided among its members, who would also be members of the Fund, by a formula which made quotas equal to at least 2 per cent of national income with a ceiling of voting power of 25 per cent.ᶠ The Bank could also borrow on private capital markets. Its objectives were: to provide capital for reconstruction, to facilitate the transition to peace, to provide short-term capital to finance foreign trade, to redistribute world gold stocks, to eliminate the danger of worldwide financial crises and mitigate depressions, to help stabilise primary product prices and to raise standards of living. It could meet these objectives by lending directly from its own or borrowed resources, by guaranteeing loans by private investors or by issuing its own gold-convertible notes against 100 per cent of the obligations of a participating government (as long as it kept a gold reserve of 50 per cent against the notes it had issued).

f One share of $1 million gave one vote. Every country was to start out with fifty votes plus those it was entitled to by its shareholding. Members would pay one half of their shareholding on joining – half in gold and half in local currency.

The last provision was particularly interesting, for despite a long section in the White Plan which made fun of the notion of an international currency it provided just that, making the new unit, to which White did not give a name, equal to 50 cents US at the current gold price. Exactly how the scheme would have worked or exactly what effect it would have had on the Bank's lending capacity is unclear, for White did not spell matters out in detail.[37] Whether he would do so in the future was another question.

Such were the contents of the document 'leaked' to Keynes. He intended to look at it closely during the ten days' leave he planned to take at Tilton from 24 July. He did more than that. When he returned to the office on 3 August he wrote to both Phillips and Hopkins enclosing a memorandum discussing the White scheme and a redraft of his Clearing Union which he thought might go to the Americans.

Keynes's reaction to the White plan was mixed. 'It obviously won't work', he told Sir Richard Hopkins. To Phillips he went further:

Seldom have I been simultaneously so much bored and so much interested. . . . The general attitude of mind seems to me most helpful and also enlightening. But the actual technical solution strikes me as quite hopeless. He has not seen how to get around the gold standard difficulties and has forgotten all about the useful concept of bank money. But is there any reason why, when once the advantages of bank money have been pointed out to him, he should not collect and rearrange his other basic ideas around this technique?[38]

Although he saw the plan as 'in fact not much more than a version of the gold standard, which simply aims at multiplying the effective volume of the gold base' and as favouring the countries which had gold, he found several details of interest.[39] It was reassuring to see that the plan's objects were broadly the same as the British Treasury's, that the concessions of national sovereignty were 'the same or greater' than those in the Clearing Union, that the aid offered by the United States was 'far-reaching, though rather obscure' and that its attitude to *laissez faire* was not as extreme as the State Department's.[40] He fastened on the proposal concerning blocked balances which he quoted in full, since it suggested a possible development in American thinking, which the Treasury had been trying to instruct so as to reduce American pressure to keep Britain's gold reserves low. He also noted the positive attitude towards buffer stocks, which was the opposite of that attributed to the Americans by some opponents of his commodity proposals. Thus, although he was critical of the conception and the details of the Stabilisation Fund, he was more encouraged than disappointed by what he read – and he looked forward to discussions with the Americans.

Keynes's redraft of his own plan, which underwent a further revision before being ready for the Americans, contained several important changes from its predecessor approved by Cabinet. He included a new formula for quotas – the average of the sum of exports plus imports over the last three pre-war years. He also added a proposal that in the case of debtors seeking to increase their debit balances above one half of their quotas the governing board could 'recommend to the government of the member state any internal measures affecting its domestic economy which may appear to be appropriate to restore the equilibrium in its international balance' – surely something of a backtracking on the Bevin commitment of April.[41] He took a stronger line on the prohibition of subsidies and made a suggestion for dealing with wartime balances. He also tidied up the organisation and the exposition of the plan. The revised version went to the Americans on 28 August. Thus at least one set of international plans was on the table – or at least out from under it.

For the next several months, with one very important exception, such Anglo-American discussion as occurred centred on Keynes's plan. The exception was a meeting between Keynes and Harry White, who had come to England with Secretary Morgenthau to visit aircraft and munitions factories and inspect naval and military installations, to meet General Eisenhower's staff and, as the invasion of French North Africa was pending, to discuss the currency arrangements for the about-to-be-liberated territories which involved the preliminary fixing of a post-war exchange rate between the dollar, the franc and the pound. The plans for the expedition had not included a White–Keynes meeting on post-war currency, but Ambassador Winant thought it would be a good idea and Penrose managed to arrange it at short notice, even though it meant dragging Keynes out of another meeting. They discussed the size of the new institution, the principle of subscription as against that of created capital, the use of the Clearing Union for ancillary purposes, the role of White's Fund in exchange rate changes and the next steps in the negotiations. Although the meeting was entirely unofficial (the State Department had not given permission for the start of talks on post-war planning), it had its uses for each draftsman now knew more about the other's views.

The other discussions took place in Washington between Sir Frederick Phillips and a run of State Department officials under the chairmanship of A. A. Berle, then an Assistant Secretary of State. White attended only the first of these meetings, at which he admitted passing a copy of his plan to Keynes *via* Phillips. The meetings were largely devoted to exchanging documents. The State Department officials would submit questions on the Keynes Plan and Phillips would answer them on the spot or reserve them for an answer at the next meeting. Some questions covered technical points, but others underlined major American preoccupations: the total of quotas, the potential creditor liability of the United States, the prevention of debtors exhausting their quotas, and the possibility of reducing the total of credit available through the Clearing Union in inflationary conditions. Keynes characterised the sessions as 'a very harmless, almost too harmless an atmosphere. Nothing difficult or dangerous seems to arise there'. He wondered whether such 'desultory proceedings . . . with a few young men from the State Department' was the right way to proceed.[42]

To a large extent, the procedure was desultory because, despite Secretary Hull's November 1942 statement that the Americans were ready for consultations on Article VII, this was far from the case. The White Plan was redrafted seven times between November 1942 and January 1943 before it was officially transmitted to the British at the beginning of February.

Meanwhile the British had not been idle. At the end of October 1942 they discussed post-war planning with Dominion representatives. Keynes undertook to explain the Clearing Union and Phillips reported what he could of American reactions. These meetings also discussed the August 1942 version of Keynes's primary products paper and other schemes at much earlier stages of discussion. It was after these meetings with the Dominions and in the light of his own discussions with White that Keynes produced another draft of his Clearing Union for transmission to the Americans.

This draft reflected some of the concerns expressed in previous months. Quotas were smaller, only 75 per cent of the average exports in the last three pre-war years. There was provision for a generally agreed reduction in quotas if worldwide inflation threatened. The Union might require collateral on debit balances over 50 per cent of quotas. The Governing Board could remit charges on credit balances and reduce them on debit balances. There was also a new section on the obligations of creditors which emphasised that balance of payments surpluses were to some extent a matter of choice. In addition exchange rate changes became more difficult when '5 per cent' replaced '5 per cent within a year'.[43] Keynes was to have second thoughts on the wisdom of that alteration.

The question remained of what would happen next. The Americans proposed discussions with experts from a number of countries in the expectation that an agreed plan would emerge. This worried the British, who feared that the aim was to secure commitments to a rigid scheme in advance of Anglo-American talks on Article VII. The Treasury proposed that the Clearing Union be more widely circulated. The Americans countered by giving them the latest version of the Stabilisation Fund on 1 February 1943, when they made clear that it was being more widely circulated as a basis for discussion. The British asked them to hold off, which they did briefly. The British opened discussions with the European Allies on 26 February before passing copies of the Clearing Union to them in advance of a meeting of their finance ministers. They also sent copies to the Soviet Union and China with simplified summaries by Keynes. Soon after the Americans did the same thing, sending the Stabilisation Fund proposal to the finance ministers of thirty-seven countries with an invitation to join in discussions. With so many copies in so many hands leaks were inevitable. The Chancellor of the Exchequer therefore proposed to issue the Keynes Plan as a White Paper. When he told the Americans, President Roosevelt refused Morgenthau's suggestion that the Americans do likewise. However, the summary of the White Plan in the *Financial News* of 5 April 1943 – leaked to the journalist Paul Einzig by officials of one of the governments-in-exile – changed Roosevelt's mind. Both plans appeared publicly on 7 April 1943 – the Keynes scheme a further revision of his proposal of 9 November, the White Plan a slightly revised version of the version handed to the Allies.

The revisions of the Keynes Plan for publication were minor. The earlier notion of basic agreement among certain founder states (Britain and the United States) was redundant and disappeared. The discussion of trade restrictions was sharply curtailed, to be replaced with the suggestion that Clearing Union balances might be used as criteria for the use of such expedients. There was also explicit recognition that the resources of the Clearing Union were not to be used for medium-to-long-term loans.

The White Plan handed over to the British in February and published in a revised version in April was dramatically different from the one Keynes had seen the previous summer. The proposal for a Bank for Reconstruction and Development had disappeared. So too had the proposal for an international note issue – although a residue remained in the form of 'Unitas'. This came from a 3 December 1942 version of White's original proposal where the Bank could issue notes denominated in this new unit, which was equivalent to $10. These notes could be used for balance of payments purposes and were redeemable on demand only when presented to the Bank by the Stabilisation Fund.[44] Without the Bank, as Keynes put it 'Unitas seems to serve no purpose'. In the Fund it was a mere unit of account, in which the Fund would keep its accounts, quote exchange rates and (in the January and April 1943 versions) allow members to make deposits redeemable in terms of gold or the currency of any member. The existence of this relic of an earlier draft was to complicate subsequent thinking and discussions.

Other changes in the White Plan included a change in name from subscriptions to quotas (from 24 December 1942); a reduction in gold subscriptions for countries with low gold reserves; a liberalisation of the amounts that members could draw from the Fund, and the beginnings of an attempt to set out the borrowing country's repayment or repurchase obligations. There were also fewer peripheral matters: with the disappearance of the Bank, the commodity stabilisation and relief suggestions went, while the State Department's responsibility for trade negotiations meant that the discussion of trade barriers and subsidies disappeared.

The major new element in the scheme was the 'scarce currency clause' which appeared in the drafts at the same time as the relaxation of the limits on members' drawings. Initially this provision allowed the Fund to reinforce its holdings of a currency when they had dropped below 15 per cent of the member's quota, and then, when the Fund had purchased an amount of the currency equal to the initial gold and security contributions, to report to the country concerned analysing the causes of the reduction in the Fund's holdings, forecasting the balance of payments of the country and recommending steps to improve the situation. In the 16 December 1942 draft, an additional clause provided that when the Fund anticipated its holdings of a particular currency would be exhausted, the Board should propose an equitable method of distributing its holdings of the currency, attempt to increase its supply of the scarce currency by obtaining it from member countries and limit the right of members to purchase this currency by a rationing arrangement – *i.e.* to discriminate against the country's exports.

British reactions to the new clause were mixed. Roy Harrod, who first read the White Plan with this provision on a midnight train from London to Oxford was excited – so excited that on arriving home at 2 a.m. he wrote a long letter to Keynes emphasising that

> the Americans offer us in this what we could never have asked of them in negotiations especially after signing Article VII, namely that we (and other countries) should be allowed to discriminate against American goods if dollars are running short.
> It is definitely better than the C.U. proposal . . . .
> It is no discredit, if I may say so, to the author of the C.U. that he did not find this satisfactory solution. The Americans have happily played a card which according to the rules of the game we could not play.[45]

Keynes's reaction was cautious. Initially he commented that 'The proposals for rationing seem unworkable'. He found the proposal obscure, although he recognised that the workability of the clause was one of the three most important matters in the American scheme that needed clarification.[46] Taxed by Harrod, who, as usual, bombarded him with letters on the subject, Keynes remained uncertain.

> I agree that, read literally, the interpretation you give to this is the only one that makes any sense. Perhaps I ought to have attached

more importance to it. I interpreted it as a half-baked suggestion, not fully thought through, which was certain to be dropped as soon as its full consequences were appreciated. I cannot imagine that the State Department will put forward as their own solution the rationing of purchases from a scarce currency country. You must remember that the evidence as to the extent to which the State Department have accepted the document of Harry White's is somewhat flimsy. I should expect that the moment emphatic attention was drawn to this alternative it would be withdrawn.

I should hesitate, as at present advised, to make the assumption that this alternative is really open to us as the basis for our future policy.[47]

These exchanges occurred in March 1943. Keynes continued to be sceptical, perhaps not surprisingly in light of an initially hostile American reaction to a Canadian proposal for a scarce currency clause let-out in commercial treaties.[48] His comment in his House of Lords speech on 18 May was that the American proposal was 'somewhat obscure' on the matter, an opinion he still held in June.[49]

The 'scarce currency' provision of the White Plan was not the only aspect of the proposal to concern Keynes after March 1943. However, he turned increasingly to what would be the form of the ultimate compromise with the Americans. Although naturally attached to his own scheme, which he thought more fundamental and international than its American competitor, not to mention more elegant, he realised that 'the final results can be dressed up in terms of the language and set-up of either plan, according to taste'.[50] By mid-April, he told Phillips:

I have been quite conscious that we were in a sense propagating for the Harry White scheme by pressing the Clearing Union the way we have, but there was no harm in that. Indeed quite the contrary. After all, the Harry White Plan is not a firm offer. The real risk is that there will be no plan at all and that Congress will run away from their own proposal. No harm, therefore, at least it seems to me, if the Americans work up a certain amount of patriotic fervour for their own version. Much can be done in detail hereafter to improve it. The great thing at this stage is that they should get thoroughly committed to there being some plan; or, what is perhaps another way of putting the same thing, that their public should get thoroughly used to the idea that such a plan is inevitable.[51]

Less than a fortnight later, while still explicitly sceptical about the scarce currency clause, he told Roy Harrod that the compromise with the American scheme would involve accepting their form of drafting. By the end of June he had his own shot at a synthesis of the two schemes, a version christened the

'Whines Plan' by Dennis Robertson.[52] But before there could be compromise there had to be discussions.

NOTES

1 A note written by JMK when he sat next to James Meade during one of the prolonged Whitehall discussions of post-war international and commercial policy at which there was a debate between the Treasury and the Board of Trade/Cabinet Office on the terms on which quantitative restrictions might be imposed – the latter, as usual favouring strict, internationally agreed, rules. The note, which is in pencil and is undated, is in the possession of James Meade.
2 KCKP, JMK to FAK, 6 September 1941.
3 *JMK*, XXV, 21–40.
4 See above p. 652; below p. 757.
5 *JMK*, XXV, 21.
6 *JMK*, XXV, 21–2.
7 *JMK*, XXV, 30.
8 *JMK*, XXV, 31.
9 For a summary comparison of these with the Clearing Union in this and later versions see Moggridge 1986.
10 *JMK*, XXV, 66, 67.
11 *JMK*, XXV, 42–3.
12 *JMK*, XXV, 51, 55–7.
13 BoE, ADM 14/1, 801/3, Cobbold to Norman, 29 December 1941.
14 *JMK*, XXV, 67.
15 *JMK*, XXV, 100.
16 *JMK*, XXV, 73.
17 *JMK*, XXV, 105.
18 *JMK*, XXV, 142, 143.
19 See below p. 757.
20 *JMK*, XXV, 109, 136.
21 *JMK*, XXVII, 61–7.
22 *JMK*, XXV, 40–1.
23 *JMK*, XXI, 456–70; see above pp. 615–16.
24 *JMK*, XXVII, 112–34.
25 *JMK*, XXVII, 110. The Bank was to take a similar view, against Keynes's, on proposals to reopen the London Metal Exchange after the war.
26 *JMK*, XXVII, 166–7.
27 *JMK*, XXIII, 128, 140, 142, 195; PRO, T247.51, JMK to Stirling, 17 June 1941.
28 *JMK*, XXIII, 208, 204–5.
29 Pressnell 1987, 116.
30 *JMK*, XXV, 205.
31 *JMK*, XXIII, 150 n. 8.
32 *JMK*, XXIII, 157, 82.
33 *JMK*, XXIII, 101; Howson and Moggridge (eds.) 1990b, 72; see also 73 and 84.
34 *JMK*, XXV, 356.
35 van Dormael 1978, 40; Rees 1973, 137; Blum 1967, III, 228.
36 van Dormael 1978, 42; Horsefield 1969; I, 11–12; Oliver 1975, 111–12. A January 1942 inter-American meeting in Rio de Janeiro was induced to

recommend the calling of a special conference to consider the establishment of an international stabilisation fund.

37 Oliver 1975, 114–17.
38 *JMK*, XXV, 158, 159.
39 *JMK*, XXV, 160.
40 *JMK*, XXV, 161.
41 *JMK*, XXV, 174; below p. 678.
42 *JMK*, XXV, 197, 200.
43 *JMK*, XXV, 174, 454. It is far from clear whether this change was deliberate or merely a printing error. Nobody seems to have noticed it at the time.
44 Oliver 1975, 139–40.
45 *JMK*, XXV, 227; Harrod 1951, 544–6.
46 *JMK*, XXV, 219, 226.
47 *JMK*, XXV, 230.
48 *JMK*, XXV, 238–9, 242, 248–9, 256, 268, 332.
49 *JMK*, XXV, 279, 322.
50 *JMK*, XXV, 240, 266. See also his hint in his House of Lords speech in ibid., 278–9.
51 *JMK*, XXV, 242.
52 *JMK*, XXV, 268, 314.

27

DOMESTIC 'NEW JERUSALEMS'

Here I am back again in the Treasury like a recurring decimal – but with one great difference. In 1918 most people's only idea was to get back to pre-1914. *No-one* today feels like that about 1939. That will make an enormous difference when we get down to it.

(TCL, Pethick-Lawrence Papers,
JMK to Pethick-Lawrence, 21 June 1942)

Although after 1941 Keynes devoted most of his energies to the construction of the post-war international order and Britain's accession to it, he was inevitably involved in domestic issues. His involvement was limited, in part by other calls on his time and his state of health; in part by his absences in the United States and Canada for long periods in 1941, 1943, 1944 and 1945; and in part because he was probably deliberately excluded by the permanent Treasury officials from some of the key committees and discussions. That this last is a possibility is evident not only from James Meade's memory, but also from Keynes's own comment to Dalton in August 1945 noted above[1] and from his bemused remark to Meade in Washington in September 1943 when he found himself as chairman and Meade and Lionel Robbins as members of an Anglo-American committee on employment policies[a]:

it is amusing that we who in London are not allowed to know anything on this subject should be in charge of all international plans on the subject.[2]

The beginning of serious thinking about the post-war world on the home front dates from 1941. That year saw not only the appointment of Sir William Beveridge to an interdepartmental inquiry into the co-ordination of social insurance in June but also James Meade's first essay on the subject of employment policy, 'Internal Measures for the Prevention of General Unemployment' in July.[3] It also saw the setting up under Arthur

a Meade was also not a member of the official Steering Committee on Post-war Employment. Lionel Robbins, in his roles as Director and the diplomatic purveyor of the ideas of his colleagues, was the Economic Section representative (Robbins 1971, 188).

Greenwood, the Minister for Reconstruction, of a committee structure to receive post-war economic and social schemes. Keynes was not involved at that stage: he was out of the country for three months and after his return in August Lend Lease, Article VII and the origins of the Clearing Union kept him busy.

Keynes's first opportunity to shape the domestic post-war world came with what in Britain in the 1980s would be called a quango[b] for the arts. The outbreak of war had produced serious disruption for the arts. Theatres, cinemas and places of public assembly were closed for a few days, but they reopened. The BBC closed down its regional radio services. The call-up (and later in the course of 1940 internment) affected many arts organisations. At the same time, however, ENSA (the Entertainments National Service Association) was revived to provide entertainment for the troops. But no provision was made for civilian entertainment beyond the now-restricted normal channels.

All of this began to change when Lord De La Warr, the President of the Board of Education, approached the Pilgrim Trust on 14 December 1939 with an idea and an offer of £25,000 for a scheme for the encouragement of the arts. Meeting later the same day the Trust agreed to contribute £25,000 from its own funds. On 19 January 1940 the Committee for the Encouragement of Music and the Arts, generally known by its initials CEMA, was born. Its first chairman was Lord Macmillan of the Pilgrim Trust, the former chairman of the Committee on Finance and Industry. Among its members were Thomas Jones, secretary to the Trust, Kenneth Clark, Director of the National Gallery, and W. E. Williams, Secretary to the British Institute for Adult Education. Mary Glasgow was seconded from the Board of Education as secretary. CEMA took as its task the preservation of standards in music, drama and the visual arts, the provision of access to the arts for people cut off from them by wartime conditions, the encouragement of popular participation in music and drama and the assistance through these activities to artists who might otherwise be unemployed because of the war. In March 1940, the Committee became a Council when the Treasury announced its willingness to match private grants up to a maximum of £50,000 in the 1940–1 financial year. Although further funds expected from the Carnegie Trust were not forthcoming, CEMA was a going concern.

Implicit in the Council's purposes was the support of both amateur and professional artists. But that posed a larger question. Was it simply a 'social service' to entertain and occupy the populace for the duration of the war, or the beginning of something more substantial for established or upcoming professionals which would incidentally provide entertainment? Initially it was both, with the 'social service' element somewhat more dominant. Aid

b Quasi autonomous non-governmental organisation.

went to existing voluntary organisations, the British Institute for Adult Education expanded its 'Art for the People' programme of exhibitions of paintings, prints and industrial design, and travelling players went out under the sponsorship of the Royal Music Schools to 'make music'. At the same time, the London orchestras went on tour in smaller towns in the North, professional soloists went to factory canteens, churches, rest centres and the like, and both the Old Vic and Sadler's Wells Opera began a series of regional tours from the autumn of 1940.

The announcement of the Old Vic and Sadler's Wells tours under CEMA raised Keynes's hackles. In May 1940, at the suggestion of Norman Higgins, the manager of the Arts Theatre,[4] he had applied to CEMA on behalf of Donald Wolfit for a provincial tour and a possible Shakespeare season in London.[c] In the correspondence that followed he suggested that the Council was wasting its resources by sponsoring tours rather than guaranteeing companies against loss. He lost this round, but when CEMA announced its Old Vic tours he returned, suggesting that Wolfit receive a guarantee and offering to meet a quarter of it out of his own pocket. CEMA caved in and Wolfit received his guarantee.[5]

There, except for another guarantee scheme for the Pilgrim Players in 1941, matters rested for the rest of 1940 and 1941 as far as Keynes was concerned. At the end of 1941 the future of CEMA was under discussion. The Pilgrim Trust had put in £37,500 to get the scheme off the ground and thought that it should now move on to good works in other areas. The Treasury had contributed its initial £25,000, made a commitment for 1940–1 and an unconditional grant of £45,000 for nine months from June 1941. The end of the Pilgrim Trust's involvement implied a reorganisation of the Council, as Lord Macmillan and Thomas Jones sat as representatives of the Trust. On 17 December 1941, a month after Keynes felt 'as if the clutch of respectability was moving remorselessly on' when he became a Trustee of the National Gallery, R. A. Butler, President of the Board of Education, offered him the chairmanship. Butler also remarked in his letter that 'while the Council's work will still remain emergency war work, it does, I think, point the way to something that might occupy a more permanent place in our social organisation'.[6]

---

c Wolfit's association with the Arts Theatre had its brighter moments in the spring of 1940, when the company wanted to produce Ford's *Tis a Pity She's a Whore*. First, there was the matter of the audience: 'Nobody will come of course unless the title stimulates the curiosity of the RAF.' (KCKP, Box 11, JMK to D. Rylands, 7 April 1940).
Then there was the Lord Chamberlain:

> I am very much amused that the Lord Chamberlain washes his hands of the play, provided we produce it intact without the omission of a single word. Perhaps this could also form part of our publicity: – that the Lord Chamberlain insists on our making no concessions to modern squeamishness by the omission of a single expression and that his consent to its performance is conditional upon its being entirely unexpurgated. (KCKP, Box 11, JMK to D. Wolfit, 10 April 1940).

Keynes was tempted. He replied to Butler on Christmas Eve:

> Your suggestion that I should take on the chairmanship of C.E.M.A.
> is interesting and attractive – but I should like to talk to you before
> reaching a decision. . . .
>
> My reserves are – that my nature is such that, if I do take on such
> a thing, I shall spend a good deal of time on it, more perhaps than I
> can spare; – and that I have been in only limited sympathy with the
> principles on which it has been carried on hitherto.[7]

This last sentence was carefully marked by Butler's secretary.

Keynes met Butler at 4 p.m. on 6 January. Later that week he met Mary
Glasgow, with whom he had dealt over the Wolfit guarantee, and Ivor
Brown, CEMA's honorary Director of Professional Drama, and Kenneth
Clark.[8] These conversations, plus perhaps Norman Higgins' enthusiasm,
led him to accept Butler's offer on 14 January, when he reported:

> I was considerably consoled as regards the amount of work and
> responsibility likely to be involved in the near future by my talks
> with Miss Glasgow and Ivor Brown. It is evident that C.E.M.A. is a
> well organised, well run affair, moving on its own wheels, and I found
> very little I wanted to criticise or should feel moved to endeavour to
> change. Clearly it is after the war that the big opportunities will come.
> Meanwhile I feel that I can do what I suggest without involving myself
> in an amount of work to which I should be unable to do justice in view
> of my other preoccupations.[9]

Butler was 'very pleased' and noted 'I feel that the future of something
rather important depends on your influence and I could wish for no better'.[10]
Keynes's appointment, announced a month later, took effect from 1 April.
He would have a Treasury grant of £100,000 for his first year, plus a parting
gift of £12,500 from the Pilgrim Trust.

Keynes's arrival at CEMA brought changes. He had been worried 'lest
the welfare side was to be developed at the expense of the artistic side and of
standards generally', but he had been assured that Butler shared his views on
professionalism and 'that, with the disappearance of the Pilgrim Trust from
the management (combined with Miss Glasgow's bias in the right direction)
all ought to be well on this score'.[11] The emergency work did not cease:
Keynes's appointment coincided with the opening of regional offices to
handle much of the day-to-day detail. But from the beginning of his tenure
the amateurs' importance began to decline and the Council's commitment to
professionals increased. Arrangements similar to the 1940 one with Wolfit,
where commercial companies formed non-profit-distributing subsidiaries
operating under Council guarantee became common. One impetus was
the 1942 Budget which sharply increased Entertainments Duty, because
under an act of 1916, if a society presenting a live performance was not

conducted for profit and if the entertainment was partly educational, it could be exempted from duty. The first company to come under CEMA's wing was organised by the Tennent Group. Others followed when the Tennent experiment proved successful, provoking charges that under the amateur Keynes the commercial theatre was building up reserves at the taxpayers' expense. The Council's rules about non-profit-distributing companies were tightened in 1943.[12]

This intensive involvement with the commercial theatre meant considerable work for Keynes and CEMA. The non-profit companies had to satisfy the Customs and Excise for each production that the work in question was educational. To meet the rise in applications after the 1942 Budget, the Customs set up a plays committee to vet applications, but this led to long delays which frequently ended in refused exemptions. CEMA tried unsuccessfully to obtain automatic exemption for the productions it guaranteed. In the process, harsh words were exchanged. As Keynes put it to R. H. Carter of the Customs and Excise:

> Perhaps I should not have spoken of suggestions of illiteracy on the part of the [Plays] Committee; but one is always hearing of instances which do strike one as extremely odd. For example, they applied for a synopsis of Ibsen's 'Wild Duck'. I do not know what other inference you would draw from this application. When it was proposed to put on Gilbert Murray's translation of the 'Trojan Women' of Euripides, whilst of course exemption was ultimately granted, this alone, amongst a series of items, had to be deferred for further examination; presumably while they conducted an exploration into the question as to who Gilbert Murray might be, whether there was really a person with such a queer name as Euripides, and whether the Trojan Women were persons of good reputation![13]

The involvement with professionals also increased in other areas. In 1943 the Council took over the guarantee scheme for national symphony orchestras which had been run by the Carnegie Trust and extended it to string and chamber groups. The Sadler's Wells opera and ballet companies came fully under the Council. The Ballet Rambert was re-established to tour workers' hostels. The Ballets Jooss, which had been associated before the war with Dartington Hall, found itself stranded leaderless in America on the outbreak of war (Jooss himself was interned on the Isle of Man and was one of the aliens Keynes struggled to release in 1940) and was, at Keynes's instigation, brought back with its sets to work for CEMA as a non-profit-distributing company under Norman Higgins. It did not repeat its pre-war successes.

By July 1942 Keynes had begun to think about the future organisation of the Council. After two meetings with Butler on 17 and 22 September, the result was the organisation of panels for Music, Art and Drama. The idea was that Keynes would chair each panel and that panel decisions would have the force of Council decisions. The Council would meet less regularly – quarterly rather than monthly – and restrict itself to major questions of policy. The experiment failed. The panels had to meet more often than Keynes had time to attend; in the summer of 1943 they reverted to meeting under their vice-chairmen and the full Council had to confirm their financial and major policy decisions. The executive organisation of the Council remained a problem, and Keynes had to give CEMA far more time than he had bargained on.

By the time Keynes saw Butler in September 1942 CEMA had another iron in the fire. The Theatre Royal, Bristol, was the oldest building in England with a continuous history of dramatic performances. Closed down shortly after the outbreak of war, it had escaped destruction when Bristol was blitzed, only to be sold at auction. The new owners proposed to pull it down and build a warehouse. A local committee organised an appeal to save it. In late August 1942 Keynes seems to have heard of the situation from Sir Wilfrid Eady.[14] By 5 September, he was asking Miss Glasgow to put it on the agenda for the next meeting. Within a week Norman Higgins was asked to go to Bristol and report. By 21 September Keynes was suggesting a possible lease of twenty-one years with an option to break at three or five years. He asked Miss Glasgow, 'Is CEMA a body which is in a position to take a lease or do we have to invent some camouflage?'.[15] There was no need for camouflage. With Higgins' enthusiastic report on the building,[16] the Council leased the theatre, which reopened on 11 May 1943 with *She Stoops to Conquer* in which Dame Sybil Thorndike played Mrs Hardcastle. This play had been produced when the theatre first opened in 1766.

Keynes used the reopening of the Theatre Royal to provide *The Times* with an article, 'The Arts in Wartime'.[17] There he revelled at the anomalous situation which had led to the event:

> C.E.M.A . . . has, I am thankful to say, an undefined independence, an anomalous constitution and no fixed rules, and is, therefore, able to do by inadventure or indiscretion what obviously no one in his official senses would do on purpose. . . .
>
> Thus in an undisciplined moment we accidentally slipped into getting mixed up with a theatre building. Making the best of a bad job, we shall come clean to-night, without shirking publicity, in the hope of public absolution. And, the precedent having been created, it will, I hope, be officially improper not to repeat it.

The Times granted full 'absolution' in a fourth leader the same day.

Keynes used his *Times* article to discuss the evolving functions of CEMA. He paid tribute to the companies and groups performing 'national service for the enlargement of public contentment in time of war'. He emphasised that CEMA was seeking to aid 'all those who pursue the highest standards of original composition in all branches of the arts', thus making clear the gradual shift in policy that had been ocurring during his tenure. He suggested that if CEMA was preserved after the war, a fruitful line of development might lie in equipping 'the material frame for the arts of civilisation and delight'.

Keynes had been thinking about the future. In March 1943 he had told Butler 'some of my hopes and ... my perplexities about the post-war future'.[18] He saw questions such as: Should CEMA's purpose be to provide buildings for people or people for buildings? Should CEMA be a body like the University Grants Committee distributing grants to the arts? Or should CEMA be a more active operating body?[19] He was toying with the idea of calling a post-war successor to CEMA the Royal Council for the Arts.[20] When further meetings on the future of CEMA took place in June and November 1943, Keynes was ambitious. He told Sir Ernest Barker when the latter wrote to thank him for the 'lift' his *Times* article had provided:

> I have a grand scheme – and there is a chance of something coming of it[d] – to rebuild the Crystal Palace as a vast place of entertainment, where the British citizen of the future can spend a whole day, if he chooses, attending a cup tie, swimming in the bathing pools, lunching at the British Restaurant, hearing the Messiah or Grand Opera, attending a vast spectacle and winding up with fireworks. There is opportunity in that fine site for everything.[21]

It was well into 1944, however, before Keynes had much more time to worry about the future organisation of CEMA. In the interim, he had to deal with it as it was. On occasion this meant fending off the enthusiasms of Butler. In the first part of 1943 Butler pushed Keynes to appoint a Royal Academician to the Arts panel, only to be stonewalled with replies such as 'Is it wise to start so early in our life on the vicious practice of filling up with respectable deadheads?'.[22] The stonewalling failed when, owing to a misunderstanding, Butler appointed Thomas Monnington without consulting Keynes. The reaction was swift:

> As I have never heard of Monnington, I cannot reasonably object. It will, I think, be of some assistance to be able to tell members of my Panel that I was not consulted.[23]

It turned out that Butler had heard of Monnington from Kenneth Clark and had assumed that, as Clark was vice-chairman of the Arts panel, the rest of CEMA knew of the suggestion.

There were also the rows caused by the development and success of the non-profit-distributing companies, the running sore of dealing with the Customs and Excise over entertainment duty exemptions and worries over potential conflicts of interest as CEMA got more and more involved

d CEMA was at the time involved in negotiations for a redevelopment of the Crystal Palace site in South London. The Palace had been moved there after the 1851 Exhibition in Hyde Park.

in the artistic life of Britain. This last problem touched Keynes, given his chairmanship of CEMA and the Arts Theatre Trust and the fact that two CEMA-supported companies, the Ballets Jooss and the Norman Marshall group operated out of Cambridge with Norman Higgins having a hand in the management of them as well as the Arts Theatre. When confronted by the accusation of conflict of interest, Keynes replied:

> What can I reply to your crazy letter except that you would do better justice to yourself and be a worthier inhabitant of this planet if you would discover the facts before circulating such a document. . . .
>
> You ask me to circulate your concoction to the [drama] panel. But I am not inclined to do this until you have had the opportunity to tear it up.[24]

But the problems remained, if one is to judge by the surviving correspondence. By July 1943, Keynes was complaining, 'My work in connection with CEMA has lately got so heavy as to be incompatible with my other duties, which are not decreasing'.[25]

In March and April 1944, when his Treasury worries included the proposed International Monetary Fund and he had a bout of ill-health, Keynes even talked of resigning, He was only inhibited from doing so by Butler's entanglement in the passage of the 1944 Education Act.[26] Keynes noted to Miss Glasgow, 'I do not see how anyone can fulfil the proper functions of Chairman unless he gives something like a quarter of his time to it, rather than, as I do, about a twentieth'. By now he had come to the conclusion that the problems were organisational. He told Sam Courtauld:

> I do not think CEMA can safely expand, or even go on, as it is without the introduction of a far greater measure of internal discipline, and a little more consideration before someone leaps without telling anyone else. An added difficulty is that . . . there is no-one who has any clear conception as to where the line lies between the innumerable matters where the chap in charge must go ahead and those occasional commitments where no step can be made without higher authority. . . .
>
> I fancy, however, that further thought will not resolve the dilemma which at present presents itself to me, namely, on the one hand, that CEMA requires, if it is to reach harbour safely, a considerable internal re-organisation, and, on the other hand, that during the war the personnel necessary for such a re-organisation are simply not available.[27]

Of course, he could solve the problem with 'red tape' but freedom from the stuff had been one of CEMA's merits. There were suggested solutions from some quarters, including a Director General, but this required further thought about the post-war reorganisation of the Council which in the spring of 1944 Keynes did not have the time or energy to give.

His resigning mood passed, perhaps partly because in his absences in America CEMA was forced to run itself under the vice-chairmanship of Kenneth Clark, although there was a continuous flow of transatlantic suggestions and queries. One of these missives brought Keynes the chairmanship of a committee which would transform the Royal Opera House, Covent Garden into the home of resident ballet and opera companies.

The Royal Opera House, last rebuilt in 1858, confined its activities between the wars to *ad hoc* seasons of opera and ballet. It had passed into the hands of Covent Garden Properties Company Limited, a real estate company, which, on the outbreak of war, had leased the Opera House to Mecca Cafes as a dance hall. The lease to Mecca was to expire in December 1944. In July 1944 Leslie Boosey and Ralph Hawkes, the music publishers, announced that they had agreed to take a five year lease on the Opera House, making themselves responsible for the rent and the management. As they had no immediate prospect of tenants, they extended Mecca's dance hall tenure to September 1945, but they set about trying to make longer-term arrangements for opera and ballet. They approached CEMA. Keynes was away at Bretton Woods.[28] Kenneth Clark suggested that CEMA become much more extensively involved in making it the home of national opera and ballet companies. Keynes enthusiastically supported the idea by cable and accepted the chairmanship of the Covent Garden Committee to manage the transition. The stage was set for CEMA to reorganise itself for the long haul.

Between his return from Bretton Woods and his subsequent departure for the Stage II negotiations in Washington,[29] Keynes prepared a memorandum for Butler entitled 'Proposals for the Re-organisation of CEMA as a Permanent Peace-Time Body'. He discussed it with Butler on the evening of 19 September and found him 'generally favourable', willing to try and make some progress while Keynes was away.[30]

Keynes's proposal, which was outlined verbally to the Council on 28 September, was for a Royal Council of the Arts of eleven members, five of whom would form an Executive Committee. The committee, consisting of the President and Vice-President of the Council and three other members chosen for their special qualifications in music, drama or the representational arts would chair the advisory panels of outside experts. The principal executive officer of the Council would be the Director General, a full-time salaried official who, in Keynes's words, 'should come to be the premier office connected with the arts in Great Britain'. The Council would be financed by a fixed annual grant (Keynes's suggestion was £500,000) plus an annual grant-in-aid from the Ministry of Education.[e] When he took these proposals to CEMA in January 1945, Keynes suggested that while the legal

---

e The notion of the fixed annual grant was designed to allow the proposed body the means to enter into long-term commitments (PRO, T161/1189/S45851/03/1, Keynes to Barlow, 20 September 1944).

and financial arrangements might take some time to effect, the organisational changes could go ahead immediately.

CEMA was unhappy over the notion of a Royal Council – indeed the very phrase brought immediate murmurs of disapproval – with the result that the word Royal disappeared, making the transition to the Arts Council of Great Britain easy. However, Keynes obtained approval in principle to proceed further and approval for the administrative reorganisation involving the Executive Committee and the panels. The first meeting of the Executive Committee consisting of himself, Ifor Evans, Ivor Brown, Sir Kenneth Clark and Sir Stanley Marchant took place in Keynes's room in the Treasury on 14 February 1945.

The next step was to get the Government to accept the permanence of the organisation. Uncertainty as to CEMA's future was damaging the morale of the existing staff and making new appointments impossible. Keynes pressed for a quick announcement. As one bemused official in the Ministry of Education put it:

> Keynes pushes the Minister: the Minister pushes Wood, and Wood is, therefore, constrained to write this letter to you. In short, both Keynes and the Minister ask why, as in principle the continuance of C.E.M.A. seems agreed, we should not proceed with the business of incorporation with a Royal Charter. Cannot this be taken in hand without waiting for the settlement in detail of its future financial basis?
>
> . . . I should be very glad of your advice as to what I had better say to my Minister on the matter.[31]

The Coalition Government decided to continue CEMA in May 1945. On 12 June 1945, Sir John Anderson, the Chancellor of the Exchequer, announced that the Caretaker Government intended to incorporate CEMA in the name of the Arts Council of Great Britain. Afterwards, Keynes held a press conference and spoke on the BBC.[32]

Drafting the Charter took longer – it received approval on 10 July 1946 – although some aspects of the process went quickly. By the Chancellor's announcement it had been agreed that the Treasury rather than the Ministry of Education would be the sponsoring body.[f] In the interval there was the day-to-day running of CEMA, plus the arrangements over Covent Garden.

---

f Other issues took longer to resolve such as the question of Scotland and Wales or, as Keynes put it to Edward Hale in August 1945, 'the desire of the bag-pipers to be mentioned in the Charter'. Another problem was raised by Keynes, the amateur lawyer, who believed that with suitable wording of the Charter the Council could obtain exemption from local rates under the Scientific Societies Act of 1843 where exemptions might be claimed by 'any society instituted for Purposes of Science, Literature and Fine Arts exclusively . . . provided that such a Society be supported wholly or in part by annual voluntary contributions'. The point was accepted after some argument, but to no avail: Treasury grants did not fall under the heading of 'voluntary contributions'. Then there were the financial matters to clear up. (KCKP, Box 12, JMK to Hale, 9 August 1945; White 1975, 58).

At the first meeting of the, still unchartered, Arts Council on 31 July 1945, Keynes could announce the first Treasury subvention for Covent Garden of £25,000. By October it was clear that the Sadler's Wells Ballet would move to the Opera House. The Sadler's Wells Opera stayed out, leaving Covent Garden to form its own company. By the beginning of 1946 arrangements were well in hand for the first season which opened with a Royal Gala designed, in Keynes's words, to 'be a landmark in the restoration of English cultural life' and to 'symbolise the return of England's capital to its rightful place in a world of peace'.[33] The date was 20 February 1946, the production *The Sleeping Beauty* with its associations with Lydia. On the evening Keynes was slightly unwell and missed the formal presentations, but he did see a successful production. One of his last acts before his death would be to give £5,000 to the Royal Opera House Trust on 5 April 1946.

The activities of the Council and Covent Garden followed him wherever he went. At Bretton Woods he discussed the possibility of a visit to Covent Garden of the Russian ballet with M. S. Stepanov, the chief Russian delegate, taking the occasion to note 'I can almost boast that I am Commissar for Fine Arts in my country!'.[34] He failed on that occasion. In March 1946 he reported to Ninette de Valois that he had seen the Ballet Russe de Monte Carlo in New York and had seen Balanchine and Danilova, naturally with a view to a season at Covent Garden.[35] He did much of his council business by letter. Take, for example the last two items of a characteristically numbered letter from Tilton, dated 3 January 1946:

(4) Legal Advice: Yes, I suppose we ought to have a firm of solicitors. As I have been telling Webster, it ought to be illegal to employ solicitors! But if other people insist on going into all this nonsense, I suppose we have to also.
(5) Festival of Arts at Edinburgh: I will study this before the next Executive, though I fear I may find myself being rude to Rudi.[g]

When Keynes took over CEMA, its official grant was £100,000. When he died, it was £320,000 and a rise to £400,000 for the 1948–50 financial years had been agreed.[36] He had been successful in persuading the Exchequer that 'the support and encouragement of the civilising arts of life' were a part of its duties.[37]

On the domestic economic front, the first serious discussions of the post-war order in which Keynes was involved came in response to Sir William Beveridge's inquiry into Social Insurance and Allied Services. This had been envisaged as an interdepartmental examination of the social insurance system that had grown up piecemeal over several decades, with the aim of removing anomalies. Aside from Beveridge, its membership came entirely

g Webster was David Webster, the first administrator of Covent Garden under the new régime. Rudi was Rudolf Bing, the first director of the Edinburgh Festival.

from the civil service – a good indication of its limited initial purpose. Beveridge's ambitious interpretation of his terms of reference as a vehicle for major reform meant that in January 1942 his civil servant members of the Committee became assessors and advisers, thus leaving the Committee's eventual conclusions to Beveridge alone. (This also meant that Ministers and their officials would be free to treat the completed report without the apparent encumbrance of prior commitments.) By this stage, Beveridge had drafted two papers, 'Basic Problems of Social Security with Heads of a Scheme' (11 December 1941) and 'The Scale of Social Insurance Benefits and the Problem of Poverty' (16 January 1942), which outlined many of the proposals that would appear a year later in his report. When it became clear that there might be problems in financing his proposed scheme of a comprehensive system of insurance, family allowances and a universal health service, Beveridge approached Keynes for advice in March 1942.

Keynes could not make their first luncheon engagement on 9 March because of a minor infection, but when he suggested they meet on 23 March, he continued:

> I have read your Memoranda, which leave me in a state of wild enthusiasm for your general scheme. I think it a vast constructive reform of real importance and am relieved to find that it is so financially possible.[38]

His comments in this letter concerned possible changes in the values of contributions and benefits owing to changes in the price level during the war,[h] the possibility of financing pensions on a pay-as-you-go basis out of contributions to reduce the initial burden on the Budget, Beveridge's proposed tax on dismissals and his 'weak-kneed' attitude towards voluntary industrial assurance (working-class life insurance designed to pay burial expenses). Doubtless they discussed more when they met for lunch.

Official discussions of Beveridge's scheme were to merge with discussions of post-war employment policy. In part, this reflected Beveridge's basic assumption that 'full use' should be made of 'the powers of the State' to reduce unemployment to a minimum.[39] The level of employment and the national income after the war were also relevant to the question of whether Britain could 'afford' the scheme. In addition variations in social insurance contributions in responses to changes in the level of employment could in the eyes of some perform an important counter-cyclical role. James Meade was to make this proposal, which he discussed extensively with Keynes, to the Beveridge Committee.[i] Finally, at the same time that the

h He made it clear that he did not believe that benefits and contributions should be indexed, but should only be adjusted for 'major disturbances as, for example, between pre-war values and post-war values' (*JMK*, XXVII, 204).
i Keynes had suggested such a scheme when reviewing Meade's *Consumers' Credits and Unemployment* in 1938 (*JMK*, XI, 441–2). For Meade's proposals see Howson (ed.) 1988a, chapters 12 and 13.

Treasury became increasingly worried about the financial implications of the Beveridge proposals, it was attempting to deal with an Economic Section paper on employment policy for the official Committee on Post-War Internal Economic Problems.

The Treasury response to the Economic Section's document was deeply pessimistic about post-war prospects. It envisaged a repetition of pre-war experience, a brief inflationary post-war boom followed by a persistent tendency for aggregate supply to exceed demand. Its pessimism became even clearer when Keynes and Richard Stone prepared their first estimates of the level of national income in a typical post-war year, which they put at £6,500 million, plus or minus £200 million. They worked from a level of unemployment of 5 per cent, equivalent to 800,000 men out of work,

> chiefly on the ground that it seemed to us that this was about the highest level the public would stand without demanding that something very drastic be done about it, coupled with the fact that it did not seem to us impracticable to take drastic steps to bring it down to this total.[40]

Keynes himself regarded this estimate as 'rather on the pessimistic side', while his Treasury colleagues found it very optimistic. Hubert Henderson's estimate ran to 2 million unemployed.[41] Keynes's critics also believed that he was too optimistic about wartime gains in efficiency and hours worked. Their adjustments reduced the estimated post-war national income, in Henderson's case by over 10 per cent, implying, as Keynes noted, that the post-war level of consumption would be little better than that of 1941 with a bare minimum of investment. Keynes remarked

> I do not find it plausible to suppose that we shall put up with this in circumstances in which 2 million men are normally unemployed. It would cross someone's mind that it was not very sensible to suffer these severe privations with all that labour available to make something useful.[42]

With pessimism running at this flood, it was natural that the Treasury became alarmist about the potential cost of the Beveridge proposals. It was so alarmist by the end of June 1942 that Meade's scheme for varying social insurance contributions counter-cyclically was separated from Beveridge's inquiry to increase the scheme's chances of survival. Keynes, by now taking on the role of the inquiry's Treasury defender, was asking Beveridge for the latest version of his proposals so that he could deal more effectively with the critics. He also asked Beveridge to lunch with him on 1 July.[43] Before the lunch, Sir Richard Hopkins asked Beveridge if he could have a talk about the financial implications of the scheme before it went to the departments for comment. Keynes became the chosen intermediary. He saw Hopkins on 3 July and again had lunch with Beveridge on 6 and 7 July. Keynes reported to Hopkins that Beveridge would welcome an informal committee on what he calls the social security budget, with whom he could talk things over and discuss generally the methods of bringing the scheme as a whole within the financial possibilities, such committee to consist of representatives of the Treasury, the Economic Section and the Government Actuary with no-one else.[44]

Keynes also thought that Beveridge might be open to economies in his proposals for family allowances and pensions. The Treasury remained worried, despite these attempts to assuage doubts.[45]

At the end of July, the Treasury accepted the Keynes–Beveridge suggestion of a small committee. Consisting of Keynes, Lionel Robbins of the Economic Section and Sir George Epps, the Government Actuary, it met with Beveridge on 10, 21 and 24 August and 12 October. Keynes also dined with Beveridge on 12 August at the Gargoyle Club. He reported to the Treasury after each meeting.[46]

The proposals Keynes made to Beveridge centred on bringing in his scheme either by stages or at lower initial rates of benefit so as to

bring the initial stage within the range of financial possibility, pending the increase in the net national income to a figure which would allow a further margin for social services of one kind or another.[47]

Keynes's proposals emphasised changes that were 'politically possible and politically stable', *i.e.* those which had a measure of finality to them for the time being.[48] The bargaining, to judge from Keynes's reports, was hard, but amicable – presumably because it started from the premiss of favouring the scheme rather than simple Treasury-minded obstructionism. The upshot was a substantial potential saving to the Treasury – of the order of £300 million – and a firm ally for what followed, for as Keynes told Beveridge in the end, 'I feel confirmed in the feeling . . . that it is a grand document'.[49]

The Beveridge Report was published on 1 December 1942. The Government's attitude was ambivalent – so ambivalent that it only gave the document full publicity when it suddenly realised the propaganda value of doing so. Even then, the official publicity was ham-handedly half-hearted – an Army Bureau of Current Affairs pamphlet with a summary by Beveridge himself was withdrawn two days after publication. Despite the enthusiastic popular reception (the Report sold 650,000 copies),[50] the Government dragged its feet. The Treasury remained profoundly unhappy over the probable financial commitments involved, fearing that it would mean excessively high taxes and hinder post-war recovery, not to mention political controversy. Nor was the Conservative Party enthusiastic. The result was Cabinet agreement to accept the scheme in principle but to defer actual legislation until after the war. This satisfied no-one.

At 59, Keynes became Baron Keynes of Tilton in the birthday honours list of June 1942, another instalment of his growing 'respectability' following on Eton, the Bank, the National Gallery and CEMA. He first proposed to give his maiden speech in the House of Lords when it came to discuss the Beveridge Report. His theme was to be that he, too, was concerned about the post-war budgetary position, but that he welcomed the proposals because there was 'no cheaper scheme on the map', and it would be easy without it to slip piecemeal into arrangements that would be *more* expensive. There was nothing in the scheme 'which need frighten a mouse'.[51] He did not deliver this speech because of Treasury pressure and because of his fear that if he persevered his relations with his colleagues would be sufficiently soured so as to make him less effective on other fronts.[52] It was all very difficult and it did not bode well.

> [I]t is better to have got something, even if it is wrong in detail, because I believe the Civil Service has infinite power of making things work once it is clear that it intends to work it. My own feeling is that the first sentence [of the White Paper *Employment Policy*] is more valuable than the whole of the rest.(KCKP, JMK to E. A. G. Robinson, 5 June 1944)

Once the Beveridge Report was published, James Meade suggested to Keynes that there should be a similar report on post-war unemployment. Such a report would remove unease about post-war prospects, aid public understanding of the interconnections among the various post-war plans and probably 'ensure once and for all that a sensible policy in this field would in fact have to be adopted by any post-war Government'. He concluded:

> It may be that there are better methods of getting these ideas across, but it occurs to me, to be quite frank, that what we really need is a Keynes Report to follow up the Beveridge Report. People cannot be too enthusiastic about too many things at the same time. Personally I think the Keynes Report should have come before the Beveridge Report, but I do not want to see it postponed until a dozen other reports on matters of relative unimportance have anaesthetised the public.[53]

Keynes may have been flattered. (He might have been more flattered if he had known that Evan Durbin made the same suggestion to Clement Attlee, the Deputy Prime Minister, on more than one occasion.)[54] But he threw cold water on the idea. He thought that employment policy was essentially different from social insurance in that there was less need for a concrete plan and little need for legislation. Most of what was required was already under official consideration and it was 'much too soon to decide that those activities are not being quite well and fruitfully conducted'.[55] As a result, the position remained that the Economic Section continued to force the pace on employment policy, while the Treasury under Sir Richard Hopkins attempted to square the circle between reform and financial orthodoxy.

However there was pressure from another quarter, for Sir William Beveridge, who had actually been suggested by Oliver Lyttleton as a possible author of an official report on full employment only to be rejected on the somewhat odd ground that he was not an expert on the unemployment question, decided to pursue his own independent enquiry supported by a large team from outside government service.[56]

The next round in government discussions of employment policy centred around another Economic Section paper drafted by James Meade entitled 'Maintenance of Full Employment'.[57] As the paper went through various drafts, Keynes kept in touch with the Section, making suggestions as to both style and content. He also continued discussions with Meade on the finer points of stabilisation policy. He made clear his continuing preference for using changes in investment to stabilise demand with one exception, Meade's proposed counter-cyclical variations in social insurance contributions. His reasons were various: he still believed that the rapid attainment of capital saturation was desirable; he thought it would be easier to encourage investment rather than consumption in a slump; and he believed counter-cyclical tax changes would have little effect on consumption in the short run except for the working classes, who would be more efficiently affected by Meade's scheme.[58]

When the final version of Meade's paper was circulated in May, the Treasury was unhappy again. Hopkins found the paper typical of the Economic Section – 'academic, misleading and dangerous'.[59] Most unsympathetic was Hubert Henderson, who foresaw a very brief post-war boom followed by a long-term decline in the demand for capital goods against which official policy would be able to do little to prevent unemployment in the transition in the structure of demand towards higher levels of consumption.[60] Keynes replied on 25 May with a much more optimistic paper, 'The Long-Term Problem of Full Employment'.[61] He anticipated the post-war period would unfold in three stages: an initial period of excess demand lasting perhaps five years, a second period where demand was not excessive but broadly in line with supply given appropriate counter-cyclical policies lasting another five to ten years, and a third period 'when investment is so far saturated that it cannot be brought up to the indicated level of savings without embarking on wasteful and unnecessary enterprises'. Only in this third stage would it become necessary to encourage consumption and discourage savings. As this stage was only an academic possibility, as indeed was the second, Keynes argued that Ministers should worry only about the policies necessary for a careful, flexible handling of the difficulties of the immediate post-war period.

The reaction to Keynes's paper in the Treasury is perhaps best exemplified by Sir Wilfrid Eady's claim that it was 'a voyage into the stratosphere for most of us'. He warned that when the Treasury began considering measures for the period after the post-war transition, Keynes would 'find . . . [his]

official colleagues obtuse, bat-eyed and obstinate on much of this'. Keynes firmly, and probably tactlessly, replied:

> Very sorry, but it does seem to me quite essential that all of you should become accustomed to the stratosphere – if that is really what it is! For, if the argument which I have tried to bring into the open in my paper is not understood by those responsible, they are understanding nothing whatever. . . .
>
> And, after all, it is very easily understood! There is scarcely an undergraduate of the modern generation from whom these truths are hidden. And, once they have been digested and have entered into the apparatus of the mind, it is possible for most people to move fairly safely over a terrain otherwise most dangerous.[62]

Nor did Keynes's note satisfy Meade, who was for some years more pessimistic than Keynes over the length of the immediate post-war transition and determined on laying the groundwork now for achieving longer-term goals. When Meade's paper came before the Reconstruction Priorities Committee on 31 May, the Chancellor (Sir Kingsley Wood) argued that it went too far and that he wished to make a Treasury reply in due course.

At that meeting, the Committee asked the Lord President for proposals for future work on post-war problems such as the transitional period, the location of industry, the mobility of labour and public works. A new Steering Committee on Post-War Employment was set up in July 1943 under Sir Richard Hopkins. Its terms of reference leaned in Meade's direction, for it was to look at methods of controlling aggregate consumption and investment; the membership of the Committee – Hopkins, Eady and Gilbert from the Treasury and Robbins from the Economic Section, as well as representatives from the Board of Trade and Ministry of Labour – leaned in the opposite direction.

The extent of Keynes's relative optimism was even clearer in yet another exercise in estimating the post-war national income, this time for 1948. Keynes found himself in a minority of one in the view that the level of national income in 1948, even on a 'suitably conservative' and 'sufficiently' cautious view, would be well above £7,000 million as compared with his Treasury colleagues' estimate of £6,800 million, their difference largely reflecting disagreements over the post-war level of employment.[63] Keynes took the line that 'We cannot . . . regard the unemployment problem as substantially solved so long as the *average* figure is greater than 800,000, namely 5 per cent of the wage-earning population, or rest content without resort to drastic changes of policy so long as it exceeds 1 million'.[64] Yet his Treasury colleagues appeared to be thinking of average unemployment on the order of 2 million, as well as being pessimistic about the possible range of future fluctuations in national income.[65] This pessimism coloured many of the Treasury's subsequent submissions to the Steering Committee, for such high levels of unemployment would adversely affect government revenue and expenditure and increase the budgetary cost of a commitment to high employment.

Keynes's comments on Sir Wilfrid Eady's successive drafts of the Treasury reply to the Economic Section's paper concentrated partly on technical details but more importantly on the tone. He was prepared to let the Chancellor and his advisers be cautious and in some respects non-committal. Thus on the issue of deficit financing over and above that implied by Meade's social insurance contribution proposal, he wrote:

> About other forms of deficit financing I am inclined to lie low because I am sure that, if serious unemployment does develop, deficit financing is absolutely certain to happen, and I should like to keep free to object hereafter to the more objectionable forms of it. Assuredly the Chancellor of the Exchequer is entitled to take up at least as cagey a line as that. But I doubt if he needs to trail his coat by going into it in so much detail.
>
> Why not ride this all rather lightly? 'Deficit budgeting' the Chancellor might say 'may well turn out to be a last resort, from which some of my successors may not in practice escape. But a Chancellor of the Exchequer can scarcely be expected to bless it in advance as a general principle' – and let it go at that.[66]

Yet, although he disagreed 'fundamentally with the underlying theory' of Eady's draft paper – which was 'in the last analysis not much more than Neville Chamberlain disguised in a little modern fancy dress' – he spent less time trying to persuade Eady of what he regarded as the correct line than in keeping the Treasury out of 'academic and ideological controversies'.[67] He argued that the Treasury's pessimistic expectations might get the Chancellor into deep water with his Conservative colleagues, for it might lead them to suspect that he believed that free enterprise might not be able to prevent 'a chronic return to the sort of troubles we experienced before the war'. He also repeatedly emphasised to the Treasury draftsman the nature of his potential readership.

> More generally, I feel considerable doubt whether you will have succeeded in your aim of avoiding provocation, if you consider into whose hands this paper will go. It will be read by a number of advisory economists, more particularly by some of those who advise Labour Ministers. I feel quite sure that the document will be interpreted by them, and they will so inform their masters, that the Treasury is intending to stone-wall on everything to the last, and would much rather be drowned than learn to swim. This view would be reached, not so much as a result of anything positive that is said, but by the generally negative implications of the paper as a whole.
>
> I suggest, therefore, that something which at least looks much more constructive in intention would be safer.

And later,

> I wonder whether the Chancellor will wish to expose so much surface in an academic controversy. Rightly or wrongly this paper would provoke the deepest suspicions in nearly all the circles of the younger economists, and the Treasury would be regarded as past praying for.[68]

Keynes's comments may have had some effect in toning down the Treasury's document for the Steering Committee, but the result was still disappointing to the younger members of the Economic Section when it finally appeared in October 1943.[69]

At this time both Keynes and James Meade were in America. While they were away, Sir Richard Hopkins kept the Steering Committee hard at work and to its brief, which after all included the consideration of controlling the components of aggregate demand. That brief inevitably meant compromises. The Report circulated in January 1944 recommended stabilisation through changes in public investment, Meade's social insurance contributions proposal and tax credits to encourage consumption in a slump, even if there was little apparent agreement on their budgetary implications.

Keynes welcomed the Steering Committee's Report as 'an outstanding State Paper which, if one casts one's mind back ten years or so, represents a revolution in official opinion'. He was critical of details. Its recommendation, despite the Steering Committee's blessing in principle, that the Meade proposal should not find an early place in the statute book had 'too much of the air of fighting a rearguard action'. 'The Steering Committee', he continued, 'remind me of Lord Balfour who, when asked if he believed in progress, replied that of course he believed in progress but it should be as slow as possible'. He also attacked the section on Budgetary Considerations as having 'the air of having been written some years before the rest of the report' and offering potential critics 'so rich a feast' of 'budget humbug'.[70] But it was the Report's proposals for improved statistics in Appendix B that caught his imagination. As he concluded his comments,

> Theoretical economics has now reached a point where it is fit to be applied. Its application only awaits the collection of the detailed facts which the economist, unlike the scientist, cannot collect in a laboratory by private enterprise. . . . [A]ppendix B is the clue to the whole business. I should have almost made it (somewhat shortened up) the body of the Report, relegating the rest to appendices in small print which no-one would have been expected to read, for the excellent reason that, until appendix B has done its work, no-one can quantify his recommendations or say except in the most general terms what would to be done, and that, when appendix B has done its work, it will all be obvious and as clear as daylight with no room left for argument.[71]

By the time the Steering Committee reported, the Government was concerned that it might be upstaged by Sir William Beveridge's private full employment inquiry. In November 1943, the Treasury had issued instructions that temporary or permanent officials not give assistance even in private to Beveridge. The 'Beveridge ban' *may* have slightly slowed down the opposition, but it did not remove from the Government the need to do something positive. Thus began the process of turning the Steering Committee's Report into a White Paper. Keynes was only concerned peripherally: he was ill and away from the office during the period of the heaviest drafting and he was heavily involved in the final stages of getting the Anglo-American Joint Statement on the proposed International Monetary Fund ready for publication as a White Paper. He did comment on continuing disputes within the Treasury and attempts 'to whittle away any positive proposals which seemed likely to appear'.[72] His comments had little effect on the tone or details of the document as it passed through many hands before appearing as *Employment Policy* (Cmd. 6527) on 26 May 1944. For Keynes, its opening statement – 'This Government accepts as one of their primary aims and responsibilities the maintenance of a high and stable level of employment after the war' – was worth more than much of the detailed discussion that followed. Indeed, he could not make sense of the White Paper's discussion of monetary policy. To produce the White Paper, as he put it, was only 'to choose the pattern of our future policy'. Once Parliament had approved the policy there would come the time for 'the very extensive blueprints that will be needed to implement' it.[73]

Keynes wrote his last comments on the Employment Policy White Paper on 15 June 1944, the day before he left for the United Nations Monetary and Financial Conference at Bretton Woods. During the rest of 1944, he was only briefly in London; his comments on employment policy during the rest of the year largely concerned work by outsiders, notably Sir William Beveridge's *Full Employment in a Free Society* and the Oxford Institute of Statistics' collection *The Economics of Full Employment*, which Michal Kalecki sent him in December.[74]

During his absences progress continued in London. James Meade agreed to succeed Lionel Robbins as Director of the Economic Section at the end of the war. And the ground was laid for a discussion of post-war monetary policy. In July 1944, after a request from Mr Attlee, the Deputy Prime Minister and Lord President, for an Economic Section paper on a post-war capital levy, James Meade consulted Sir Richard Hopkins on the possibility of an inquiry into a post-war capital levy and what could be done to lighten the budgetary burden of debt interest. Hopkins, who had been in the Inland Revenue at the end of the previous war, knew all the pros and cons of a capital levy, but he believed, especially after consulting with Hubert Henderson, that in connection with the Government's employment policy commitments it might be useful to examine the whole issue of the goals and techniques of post-war monetary and debt management policy. He also knew 'Lord Keynes has promised to produce when he is able some far-reaching proposals in this sphere'. In August the Chancellor approved a joint Treasury–Economic Section–Inland Revenue committee on the national debt with the clear understanding that it would also consider cheap money and the measures to sustain it over a longer period. Keynes's prolonged absence in America meant that the committee, the National Debt Enquiry, was not set up until the third week of January 1945. Its members included Sir Richard Hopkins (chairman), Keynes, Sir Wilfrid Eady and Sir Herbert Brittain from the Treasury; Paul Chambers and Sir Cornelius Gregg from the Inland Revenue; and James Meade and Lionel Robbins from the Economic Section. As Hopkins was about to retire as Permanent Secretary of the Treasury and be succeeded by Sir Edward Bridges, the Inquiry did not meet, except for a preliminary, housekeeping meeting on 19 February, until 8 March when Bridges took over.[75,j]

After the preliminary meeting of the Inquiry, Keynes gave Meade and Robbins an indication of his views. As Meade recorded them on 26 February 1945:

> Keynes on the rate of interest showed himself in a typical mood: revolutionary in thought and very cautious in policy. He seemed to justify a 3 per cent rate of interest as being socially desirable in order to maintain pensions, etc., whereas in my mind the real social revolution is to be brought about by the most radical reduction of interest rates which is necessary to prevent general deflation.[76]

Meade also looked forward to the interaction among personnel of the Inquiry.

> It is going to be fun! Bridges very able and competent but without much technical knowledge of these subjects; Hoppy very wise and learned as the elder statesman making way for new blood; Maynard perverse, brilliant and wayward; Eady muddled and uncertain; and the Economic Section – can one hope – sane and scientific!

The first meetings of the Inquiry under Bridges were given over to an extended talk by Keynes, beginning with a summary of the bare bones of his *General Theory*. Meade remarked:

> It must have been very difficult for the layman and a terribly hard introduction for Bridges. Keynes still goes out of his way to give the maximum stress to the difference between his theory and old-fashioned orthodoxy. I felt definitely uncomfortable at his conclusions. He now

j However, Sir Richard Hopkins remained as an adviser to the Chancellor and an active member of the Inquiry.

holds the view that variations in the rate of interest (at any rate when it is as low as 3 per cent) have no effect upon investment. His conclusion is that the correct policy is to hold the rate at 3 per cent and not to let it rise in the short inflationary transition because any moderate rise will do little or nothing to restrain investment, and not to let it fall in the long run because a reduction will do little to promote investment and it is socially desirable that rentiers (i.e. universities, widows and orphans, etc.) should get some return on their capital.[77]

The emphasis on the fact that 'the euthanasia of the rentier should not take place just yet', although only touched on in Keynes's notes, was to be a major theme of his discussion if one is to judge from the minutes of the meetings and Meade's diary.[78] That, plus the belief that a move to lower rates of interest would be inappropriate 'when the opportunities for investment are exceptionally abundant and before conditions normal to the post-war epoch have been established', did not make him in favour of an early move to cheaper money.[79] After all, it had been a 3 per cent war.

Keynes's proposals for the Inquiry were relatively straightforward. He believed that since exchange controls removed the overseas constraint on interest rate policy and that physical controls, rationing, controls and taxation would bear the main anti-inflationary burden immediately after the war, monetary policy in the short term should meet official and social needs and yet leave the authorities the maximum freedom of action over the longer term. For these same long-term reasons he was averse to disturbing expectations by using monetary policy to curb inflation through tighter money. Rather the Treasury should leave long-term interest rates roughly where they were but leave open the option for lower rates later by altering the redemption terms of new issues. As for other interest rates, he suggested that the Treasury aim for a lower Bank rate, lower Treasury bill rates (partially in connection with his other proposals for the treatment of overseas sterling balances),[80] and slightly lower rates on five- to ten-year securities. In each major class of securities, the authorities should, as they had been doing during the war, simply set the rate and leave the market's liquidity preferences to determine the volume of tap securities it would take up at that rate. In current circumstances, the authorities should not attempt to impose their own 'counter-liquidity preference' by attempting to fund or lengthen the average maturity of the debt. Of course, if the prevailing long-term rate of interest became chronically too low and the rate of capital formation looked as if it would become chronically so high as to threaten inflation, he would change his mind about the level of long-term rates. But that was a matter for the future.[81]

Keynes's proposals for immediate policy were much more acceptable to many members of the Inquiry than were his reasons for them. Indeed, his extreme positions that 'productivity and thrift have got nothing to do with the rate of interest' and that 'the rate of interest should no longer be used to control inflation or deflation' drew a 'confession of faith' from Meade and Robbins, partly because they believed that such positions would be misleading for policy purposes.[82] According to Meade, despite the fact that the meeting had opened with Keynes being extremely and unnecessarily rude to Sir Herbert Brittain, he 'was quite calm and reasonable with Lionel and myself, thank goodness'.

After the discussions of 5 and 10 April, Keynes put his proposals in writing. They were subject to further discussion on 19 April before Sir Richard Hopkins was asked to prepare for submission to the Chancellor a draft on the future of cheap money on the lines of Keynes's proposals. In the course of preparing his draft, Hopkins read the *General Theory* (for the first time, according to Robbins) and Dennis Robertson's *Essays in Monetary Theory* twice. Robbins and Meade attempted in the course of drafting to persuade Hopkins to adopt their views. They found, not unnaturally,

> that he clearly has some sympathy for the point of view that we have been putting, – namely that although Keynes may be right in saying that one can fix the rate of interest where one likes it is not necessarily therefore wise to give up its conscious use as a means of controlling booms and slumps.[83]

The Inquiry's first report, replete with appropriate quotations from the *General Theory*, followed the lines of Keynes's proposals and went off to the Chancellor on 15 May 1945.[84]

Hopkins's report did not mark the end of the Inquiry, which met four more times in May and June 1945. When it discussed the relation between debt policy and employment policy on 18 May, Keynes was cautious, stating 'he was not sure how far new doctrines about the relation of budget deficits to employment policy would come to win acceptance before many years are past'.[85] At the last meeting on 28 June he made another attempt in his long campaign to reform the British budgetary accounts to allow for an annual capital budget. As before he was unsuccessful: he ran across the Treasury's attachment to its traditional forms and Meade's worry that

> it would encourage a very dangerous new financial orthodoxy . . . that in all circumstances the revenue budget should be balanced each year, and that employment policy would operate only by the variation of expenditure in the capital budget.[86]

The end of the National Debt Inquiry coincided[k] with the end of the Caretaker Government and the post-war general election of 5 July 1945. The results, announced on 26 July, brought the first majority Labour Government and a new Chancellor, Keynes's old student Hugh Dalton. Dalton asked Keynes to stay on in the Treasury and agreed he should have

k The minutes of the last meeting suggest that the members of the Inquiry expected to continue their deliberations after the election.

more part in the discussion of domestic problems.[87] Keynes would have very little opportunity to do so for some months owing to more pressing external problems.

NOTES

1 Page 662.
2 Booth 1983, 114 n. 6; Howson and Moggridge 1990b, 111.
3 Meade's paper is chapter 11 in Howson (ed.) 1988a.
4 KCKP, JMK to Higgins, 7 September 1940.
5 In the end Maynard paid £50 on the guarantee (KCKP, Box 11, D. Wolfit to JMK, 8 January 1941).
6 KCKP, Box 13, JMK to Courtauld, 6 November 1941. Keynes had been asked to be a Trustee by the Prime Minister on 29 October. His appointment was announced on 8 November. In March 1942 he declined to become a Trustee of the Tate Gallery (ibid., JMK to Lord Bearstead, 26 March 1942). The Butler letter is in KCKP, Box 12.
7 Arts Council, JMK to Butler, 24 December 1941.
8 Clark 1977, 26; see also KCKP, Box 12.
9 KCKP, Box 11, Higgins to JMK, 30 December 1941; Box 12, JMK to Butler, 14 January 1942.
10 KCKP, Butler to JMK, 17 January 1942.
11 KCKP, JMK to Ifor Evans, 28 January 1942.
12 Arts Council, JMK to Hale and Barlow, 'The Conditions for Tax Exemption', 5 July 1943; see also KCKP, Box 12.
13 Arts Council, JMK to Carter, 15 June 1944.
14 KCKP, Box 12, Eady to JMK, 21 August 1942.
15 Arts Council, JMK to Glasgow, 18 September 1942.
16 Higgins 1979, 47–8.
17 *JMK*, XXVIII, 359–62.
18 Arts Council, JMK to Glasgow, 30 March 1943.
19 KCKP, Box 12, JMK to Butler, 2 March 1943.
20 KCKP, Box 11, JMK to Butler, 15 February 1943.
21 KCKP, Box 12, JMK to E. Barker, 13 May 1943.
22 KCKP, Box 12, JMK to Butler, 2 March 1943.
23 KCKP, Box 12, JMK to Butler, 16 April 1943.
24 KCKP, Box 12, JMK to Ashley Dukes, 18 May 1943; see also Dukes to JMK, 6, 8, 12 and 19 May 1943.
25 KCKP, JMK to H. Farjeon, 2 July 1943.
26 Arts Council, JMK to Glasgow, 31 March 1944.
27 KCKP, Box 12, JMK to Courtauld, 20 April 1944.
28 See below p. 739–47.
29 Below pp. 775–80.
30 He also sent a copy of his memorandum to Sir Alan Barlow at the Treasury (PRO, T161/1189/S45851/03/1, JMK to Barlow, 20 September 1944).
31 PRO, T161/1189/S45851/03/1, Wood to Barlow, 14 February 1945.
32 The broadcast, 'The Arts Council: Its Policy and Hopes' appears in *JMK*, XXVIII, 367–72.
33 KCKP, Box 12, JMK to C. R. Attlee, 24 January 1946.

34 KCKP, Box 12, JMK to Stepanov, 18 July 1944.
35 KCKP, 5 March 1946.
36 KCKP, Box 12, Sir A. Barlow to JMK, 26 January 1946.
37 *JMK*, XXVIII, 368.
38 *JMK*, XXVII, 204.
39 Harris 1977, 390.
40 *JMK*, XXVII, 299.
41 *JMK*, XXVII, 303.
42 *JMK*, XXVII, 301–2.
43 *JMK*, XXVII, 219.
44 *JMK*, XXVII, 220.
45 Harris 1977, 410–11.
46 Ibid., 413; *JMK*, XXVII, 234–53.
47 *JMK*, XXVII, 229.
48 *JMK*, XXVII, 236, 237, 244. The main changes involved introducing the proposed subsistence level pensions in stages over a 16-year period, supplementing those actually paid in that interim with public assistance, and restricting child allowances, albeit at a higher level, to the second and later children.
49 *JMK*, XXVII, 255.
50 Addison 1975, 217.
51 *JMK*, XXVII, 261. For Keynes's notes for his speech see ibid., 225–61.
52 *JMK*, XXVII, 256.
53 *JMK*, XXVII, 214–15.
54 Howson 1992.
55 *JMK*, XXVII, 315.
56 Harris 1977, 434–5.
57 It appears in full in Howson (ed.) 1988a, chapter 14.
58 For Keynes's views, which suggest a strong sense of the role of 'permanent income' as the major determinant of consumption behaviour, see *JMK*, XXVII, 319–20.
59 PRO, T161/1168/S52908, Hopkins to Chancellor, 26 May 1943 quoted in Cairncross and Watts 1989, 79.
60 Henderson's paper, 'Note on the Problem of Maintaining Employment', appears in Henderson 1955.
61 *JMK*, XXVII, 320–5.
62 *JMK*, XXVII, 325–6.
63 *JMK*, XXVII, 343, 345.
64 *JMK*, XXVII, 335.
65 *JMK*, XXVII, 346.
66 *JMK*, XXVII, 353, 356–7.
67 *JMK*, XXVII, 358, 357.
68 *JMK*, XXVII, 355, 358.
69 Booth 1983, 113.
70 *JMK*, XXVII, 364, 365, 367.
71 *JMK*, XXVII, 371–2.
72 Cairncross and Watts 1989, 86.
73 *JMK*, XXVII, 377, 379.
74 *JMK*, XXVII, 380–3.
75 For the details surrounding the setting up of the Committee, see PRO, T230/94, T230/158 and T283/389. The quotation is from PRO, T273/389, Hopkins to Eady, 21 August 1944. See also Howson 1987, 438.
76 Howson and Moggridge (eds) 1990a, 46.
77 Ibid., 48.

78 *JMK*, XXVIII, 393; PRO, T230/94, National Debt Inquiry, 8 March 1945, 3; 22 March 1945, 2; 27 March 1945, 1.
79 *JMK*, XXVII, 400.
80 See below pp. 784–7.
81 For Keynes's notes for the Inquiry, as well as his interest rate proposals, see *JMK*, XXVII, 388–404.
82 Howson and Moggridge (eds) 1990a, 61. For Meade's agreement with the proposals see ibid., 59.
83 Ibid., 70; Robbins 1971, 187.
84 PRO, T233/158.
85 PRO, T230/95, National Debt Inquiry, 18 May 1945, 1.
86 Keynes's paper is in *JMK*, XXVII, 405–13. Earlier exercises in the same spirit appear in ibid., 277–80, 367–9. Meade's comment is in Howson and Moggridge (eds) 1990a, 95.
87 BLPES, Dalton Diary, vol. 33, 3 August 1945.

28

BRETTON WOODS

[T]his is one of the greatest triumphs of his life. Scrupulously obedient to his instructions, battling against fatigue and weakness, he has throughout dominated the Conference ... and I think he may well feel that with all the faults of the agreement which has emerged, something has been accomplished in the way of constructive internationalism which ... will not easily be brushed on one side.

(Lionel Robbins, 22 July 1944,
Howson and Moggridge (eds) 1990b, 193)

The proposals for the Clearing Union and the Stabilisation Fund were published in London and Washington on 7 April 1943. As might be expected, in both countries there was a tendency for subsequent discussants to play up the virtues of their particular national plans, if only because, to a considerable extent, each reflected national preconceptions. American reactions to *both* plans were probably the more hostile and more conservative. To some extent this reflected the general attitudes of business, banking circles and the press to the New Deal, but it probably also reflected the care the British took over publicity. Keynes, for example, met representatives of the leading national newspapers, MPs likely to take part in the subsequent parliamentary discussions of the schemes and even a group of clearing bank managers. In all of these he attempted to minimise hostility to the White Plan, which he thought 'more unpopular perhaps than it really deserves'. He emphasised the point again on 18 May when the House of Lords discussed both plans and finally gave Keynes an occasion suitable for his maiden speech.

Public opinion on the other side of the Atlantic is not, I fancy, as well prepared as it is here for bold proposals of this kind . . . . Most critics, in my judgement, have overstated the differences between the two plans which are born of the same climate of opinion and which have identical purpose. It may be said with justice that the United States Treasury has tried to pour its new wine into what looks like an old bottle, whereas our bottle and its label are as contemporary as the contents; but the new wine is there all the same.[1]

Keynes had already decided that the ultimate compromise would probably be along American lines.[2] Before any compromise was possible those involved had to be certain exactly what the plans meant and to establish where there was room for manoeuvre.

There was still the question of how those involved would ever reach a compromise. There had as yet been no serious Anglo-American discussions on Article VII. The discussions on the Clearing Union had been desultory. The American Administration had announced that the Treasury, not the State Department, was to 'carry the ball' in the ensuing monetary discussions. The Treasury had also planned bilateral discussions on the White Plan with the Canadians, the Australians and the European Allies, but said nothing about Anglo-American discussions. Eventually, the British did get involved, but only *after* the Americans seemed to have seen everyone else. They attended a general discussion along with representatives of other countries after the international conference on Food and Agriculture at Hot Springs in June 1943. These discussions 'accomplished precisely nothing beyond allowing for the release of a Babel of individual opinions'.[3] This conspicuous lack of success opened the way to bilateral Anglo-American discussions on 22 and 23 June 1943, but these were also a far cry from the discussions initially envisaged under Article VII. True, there were subsequent informal meetings between E. M. Bernstein and Dennis Robertson which attempted to elucidate what the White Plan really meant regarding the conditions under which members could use the Fund's facilities, but little more.

Sir Frederick Phillips and Dennis Robertson in Washington had kept Keynes well-informed of developments. There was a continual interchange of views, on the American proposals which were still subject to almost continuous revision, and on such things as the Canadian Plan for an International Exchange Union – dubbed 'off White' by Keynes – eventually tabled by the Minister of Finance in the Canadian House of Commons on 12 July 1943. Keynes, disappointed that the first international conference on the post-war world had concerned something as boring as food, was disappointed again by the Canadian Plan, whose publication he regarded as a tactical mistake, given the possible mediating role it might have played later.[4] However, in the course of these exchanges with his colleagues in Washington, Keynes's views as to the ultimate synthesis of the Clearing Union and the Stabilisation Fund began to take shape. He had come to the conclusion that Britain should accept the subscription principle of the White Plan, the concomitant limitation of a creditor's liability, the American formula for quotas and voting rights, the principle that no country should be compelled to change the gold value of its currency and an initial post-war dollar–sterling exchange rate of $4.[a] In return, Britain's essential conditions

a The official wartime peg for sterling was $4.03. The question of the post-war exchange rate arose as a result of the relations between the occupation currencies used by Allied forces in North Africa and later Italy where for convenience a cross rate of $4 found use. The effective existence of two rates was a nuisance and suggestions soon appeared that the simpler rate apply after the war. In the end, the $4.03 rate remained.

would be that the Fund would not deal in a mixed bag of national currencies but in the unit of account called Unitas still lurking in the White Plan after the original reason for its existence had disappeared; that the United States would revert to its original proposal of a gold subscription of 12½ per cent; and that the provisions for exchange rate changes would be more elastic and allow for greater national sovereignty.[5] Also, along with Sir Frederick Phillips, he began to push the Treasury to define its position on the White Plan's suggested provisions for abnormal war balances, a matter of some importance to Britain given the rapid growth of her overseas sterling liabilities.[6] The need for a definition of UK principles became urgent when the Americans agreed to 'informal and exploratory talks' at the end of July 1943. The time for crystallisation of opinion had arrived.

Britain assembled a strong team to send to Washington for the talks. It was led by Richard Law, then Parliamentary Under-Secretary of State at the Foreign Office, who had successfully led the British delegation at Hot Springs. The Treasury members were Keynes, Sir David Waley and Frank Lee, plus Lucius Thompson-McCausland, seconded from the Bank of England.[b] Lionel Robbins represented the Economic Section along with James Meade, who for this purpose as the author of the British proposals for an international commercial union represented the Board of Trade. The other Board of Trade representatives were Sir Percivale Liesching and R. J. Shackle. Nigel Ronald of the Foreign Office, C. L. M. Clauson of the Colonial Office and P. W. Martin of the Ministry of Food completed the team. In Washington they were joined by Dennis Robertson and Redvers Opie from the Embassy.[c]

The Delegation's instructions reflected the evolution of British views over several months with one or two recent additions. They could accept the American conception of a Fund made up of national contributions of currencies and gold, the insistence that voting arrangements bear some relation to quotas, a substantially smaller Fund than the Clearing Union with an American commitment limited to $2.3 billion, and an understanding on the exchange rates among the leading currencies. The aim would be an agreement with the Americans on a clear set of principles to go back to Ministers for consideration before they went to a drafting committee. The set principles should meet five minimum requirements:

b As Lucius Thompson, Thompson-McCausland had accompanied Keynes to Washington in 1941. His position in the delegation in 1943 was somewhat ambiguous: he had his own instructions from the Bank, was free to cable the Bank outside government channels if the delegation appeared to be compromising what the Bank regarded as essential principles, and was able to consult outside American opinion in the form of Walter Stewart, a former economic adviser to Governor Norman, if necessary. (BoE, ADM14/9 802/5, note by Thompson-McCausland, 31 August 1943).

c Sir Frederick Phillips would have been a member of the team had he not died suddenly in August 1943 while in London for consultations.

(i)   The Fund would be passive in exchange markets and not buy or sell national currencies. To achieve this, Unitas, the unit of account for the Fund, would be monetised.

(ii)   Initial subscriptions would involve a small proportion of gold (12½ per cent) with the remainder in the form of securities negotiable only in the event of default, withdrawal or liquidation.

(iii)   The Fund would be larger than the Americans had proposed (about $10 billion).

(iv)   Members would retain reasonable freedom to alter their exchange rates, although there might be some 'objective test' for guidance.

(v)   The scheme would not attempt to deal with abnormal war balances.

The last item was the result of very recent thinking on the British side. As late as 22 June 1943, Keynes was recommending that London 'tell Phillips that . . . we warmly welcome the proposal for dealing with the blocked balances'.[7] His suggestions sent 'a good many shudders' down Treasury and Bank of England spines: neither group wished to give any impression that sterling balances would be blocked in any way – a possibility Keynes had accepted 'a long time ago'.[8] It was unlikely that any scheme that emerged from the forthcoming negotiations would be large enough to handle the balances, even if one believed that a plan designed for current account transactions should become encumbered with such large capital sums. Finally, and most important, Britain had not as yet evolved a policy on the future treatment of sterling balances: it was thus hard to know what to do about the American proposal even if other doubts had not existed. The delegation was instructed to 'go slow' on the matter.

The Law Mission travelled to New York on the *Queen Mary*. Since the Americans were anxious to keep the talks informal and out of the public eye, members travelled in relays from New York to Washington. The attempt 'to slip into Washington unnoticed' were compromised when Keynes's party took the train:

> Keynes was in first-class form. . . . There was a flow of acid comment on the American countryside, their air-raid precautions, the lack of birds, the sterility of the land! He and Lydia and Ronald indulged in a tremendous discussion on modern painting; and the whole journey was rounded off by Lydia singing the Casse-Noisette music at the top of her voice and dancing it with her hands.[9]

The voyage had given the delegation a chance to prepare the ground for the discussions. In particular it gave them time to examine Harry White's 'Proposal for an International Bank for Reconstruction and Development' of 2 August which the delegation had received privately through Redvers

Opie. As noted above,[10] this scheme had originally been drafted at the same time as the Stabilisation Fund, but had been separated from it and shelved during 1942 as discussion concentrated on the Fund. In the summer of 1943 White revived the proposal. It was now much less ambitious, for the proposed Bank had lost the power to issue notes and was only to keep its accounts in terms of Unitas, but it still contained the original provisions for the financing of an International Essential Raw Material Development Corporation and an International Commodity Stabilisation Corporation. The Delegation agreed on the desirability of such an institution as the proposed Bank, but thought that this particular plan was not fit for publication 'since it would be heavily criticised and might bring contempt not only on the proposals in the document but also on the Stabilisation Fund'. The delegation could not indicate to the Americans that they had seen the proposal, but if the Americans put it on the table their chief criticisms would centre on the fact that international investment on the scale envisaged (up to $10 billion per annum) would not yield sufficient returns so that the sanctions on debtors would have to be weakened and on the need for making the relationship between the Bank and Fund clearer. If the Bank document did not appear, the delegation would press for a set of ground rules for international investment and for an International Development Corporation which would examine proposals and make recommendations on their timing.

Commercial policy, commodity policy, cartels, and employment policy were also on the agenda. Although Keynes had played a central role in developing the British proposals on commodity policy and had been peripherally, but occasionally strategically, involved in developing the British proposals on commercial policy as they evolved from Meade's original 'A Proposal for an International Commercial Union',[11] he was to be much less involved in these topics in Washington. On commercial policy, his remarks in 1941 meant that the State Department distrusted him. There were, however, also outstanding Lend-Lease and relief issues requiring discussion, and Keynes would also get involved in outlining British thinking on reparations to American officials formulating plans for them.[12]

On his arrival in Washington on 11 September, Keynes was caught up in a whirlwind of activity. As he told Sir Wilfrid Eady on 3 October,

> we are horribly over-worked and the pace is terrific. Several meetings every day and not nearly enough time to think out one's own policy or do one's home work; all of which is much aggravated by the fact that I am lunching or dining out at least ten times a week. Fortunately, as I found on the previous occasion, the climate of Washington, although not particularly agreeable in itself, does agree with my heart. I got over-exhausted one day and had to take a day off to recoup, but apart

from that I am remarkably well, in spite of talking and eating so much too much.[13]

Before the negotiations began, there were considerable doubts as to how Keynes would perform as a 'diplomat', especially after the problems of 1941. James Meade put it:

Keynes – who certainly has the imagination and the desire for a comprehensive sweep in these negotiations – yet remains an unknown figure in some ways. How far will his manner antagonise the Americans, as it has certainly done before? How far does he really believe in the commercial policy proposals?[14]

Initially, all went well. Lucius Thompson-McCausland reported to C. F. Cobbold at the Bank of England after two preliminary meetings at the US Treasury that Keynes 'has put our case with excellent clarity and good humour' and with a bias towards finding agreement rather than emphasising differences. When differences occurred, Keynes firmly presented the British position. Thompson-McCausland continued:

Yesterday we were discussing the American proposals for giving the Fund powers to check drawings if they seemed to be at an excessive rate. Keynes resisted. 'The trouble is', he said, 'that the Fund is there to be drawn on but you look on yourselves as never likely to draw on it. Neither will we draw on it.' An incredulous gasp from the Americans followed by Harry White with 'Do you mean that England will never draw on the Fund?' 'We should never let ourselves draw on terms like that.' This answer from Keynes drew appreciative smiles and applause from Pasvolsky and Berle, the two State Department representatives.[15]

Similarly on 21 September, after the first plenary session, James Meade recorded in his diary:

Keynes' speech was absolutely in the first rank of speechifying. I have never heard him better, – more brilliant, more persuasive, more witty or more moving in his appeal. His great appeal was that we should treat the whole economic problem as a unity and be prepared to present to the public a total solution which really did present a prospect of a radical solution of the problems of unemployment and of raising standards of living.[16]

Three days later Meade again reported a 'brilliant speech' favouring the monetisation of Unitas, limiting gold subscriptions and curbing the powers of the Fund.[17] Even Keynes seemed pleased with the early stages, reporting to Louis Rasminsky of the Canadian Foreign Exchange Control Board:

We are having most interesting and exciting discussions with Harry White and his associates in an atmosphere singularly free from unnecessary controversy or obstacle ... White has the immense merit that he takes a high intellectual interest in these questions and approaches them on that plane and not on official or bureaucratic lines.

... I think I can say for all concerned that the discussions are being thoroughly enjoyed.[18]

As the discussions developed and, perhaps, as the issues became more controversial and the participants more tired, things became more heated. By 4 October Meade was writing:

What absolute Bedlam these discussions are! Keynes and White sit next [to] each other, each flanked by a long row of his own supporters. Without any agenda or any prepared idea of what is going to be discussed they go for each other in a strident duet of discord which after a crescendo of abuse on either side leads up to a chaotic adjournment of the meeting in time for us to return to the Willard for a delegation meeting.[19]

Five days later,

Keynes has been storming and saying (when Bernstein in place of a short note of the Anglo-American interpretation to be placed on certain points of the directive produced yet another typically Bernstein document), 'This is intolerable. It is yet another Talmud. We had better simply break off negotiations.' Harry White has replied: We will try and produce something which Your Highness *can* understand.'

Negotiations were apparently broken off at lunchtime. No wonder Meade expostulated of Keynes 'That man is a menace in international negotiations' and thought that the monetary discussions had been 'seriously marred ... by Keynes' ill-manners'.[20]

Of course, as Meade implied, Keynes could be matched by Harry White, who earned the title 'that man' from Dean Acheson during the negotiations.[21] Others have also commented on White's 'truculence' and 'acerbity'.[22] However, Keynes knew that he had reacted 'rather violently' on 9 October and that the other members of the delegation thought that he 'had overdone it' – although he believed that it was on occasion important 'to react strenuously'. But Keynes did have something of 'a thing' about E. M. Bernstein:

Both the currency scheme and the investment scheme are, I think, largely the fruit of the brain not of Harry but of his little attaché, Bernstein. It is with him rather than Harry that the pride of authorship lies. And when we seduce Harry from the true faith, little Bernstein wins him back again in the course of the night. Bernstein is a regular little rabbi, a reader out of the Talmud, to Harry's grand political high rabbidom. He is very clever and rather sweet, but knows absolutely nothing outside the twists and turns of his own mind. There is, as I have expressed it, a very high degree of endogeny between his ideas. The chap knows every rat run in his little ghetto, but it is difficult to persuade him to come out for a walk with us on the high ways of the world.[23]

Yet, despite the dislike – and anti-semitism – of these comments, Keynes managed to develop a deep affection for Bernstein, who even managed to put Keynes's references to Talmudism to humorous good use.[24]

The Washington conversations lasted until 11 October, when Keynes went to New York for discussions with acquaintances on Wall Street, including representatives of the Federal Reserve Bank of New York, intended to explain the plans that were afoot and to seek to minimise future opposition to them. The monetary discussions themselves were quite fruitful: of points where there was an Anglo-American difference of view, six were solved, while another seven would be solved in the months that followed.

Perhaps the easiest British concession concerned the form of the ultimate statement, for Keynes had long accepted that the final draft provide for a Fund. Here the concession was graceful, for on 6 October Keynes offered to produce the relevant draft. He presented it the next day. There followed three American revisions, the last of which was 'yet another Talmud'. A fifth British draft emerged from the subsequent explosion. It included alternative paragraphs for the matters still in dispute.

Agreement was also quickly reached on the size of the Fund, which in the original White scheme was limited to $5 billion. Within the constraints of an American desire to keep its commitment to $2.3 billion, the negotiators readily agreed to an aggregate of $8.5 billion for members of the United and Associated Nations – equivalent to $10 billion for the world as a whole. They also agreed as to the working of the scarce currency clause which would allow all members of the Fund to discriminate against a currency declared scarce, the mechanism for altering the gold value of Unitas (a matter of little subsequent importance), the easing of the mechanics of withdrawal in cases where the Fund was in dispute with a member over the member's proposal to devalue its currency, and the currencies to be drawn from the Fund by a member in current account difficulties.

The matters which remained outstanding in the 'Anglo-American Draft Statement of Principles' were: the size of initial gold subscriptions to the Fund, the sterilisation of contributions, the roles of the Fund and of members in exchange rate changes, the exact supervision that the Fund might exercise over members' capital account transactions, the terms under which a member who had borrowed from the Fund might be required to repurchase its own currency (i.e. repay its borrowing), and the monetisation of Unitas. All would be resolved over the coming months, but some only after considerable controversy.

The final issue which would remain open even after Bretton Woods and Keynes's subsequent death related to the conditionality attached to drawings from the Fund. From the outset, both the American and British plans had contained stipulated quantitative limits as to the amounts a member might borrow. There was also agreement as to how the right to borrow would be modified in the scarce currency case. Disagreements arose over the role of the Fund within the quantitative limits and the extent to which access to resources might be conditional on the permission of the Governing Body of the Fund. The general view of the British, carried over from the Clearing Union, was that drawings should be unconditional, while the American view, carried over from the Stabilisation Fund, was that the Fund should police drawings from the outset. It was the first discussion on the matter that led Keynes to assert that Britain would never draw from the Fund under such conditions. Subsequent discussions did little to narrow the gap which became enshrined in Section 5 concerning the acceptability of members' currencies to the Fund. As Keynes put it to Jacob Viner:

> This is one of the matters on which we have not yet reached final accommodation. Our view has been very strongly that if countries are to be given sufficient confidence they must be able to rely in all normal circumstances on drawing a substantial portion of their quota without policing or facing unforeseen obstacles. Indeed, we have been inclined to think, on second thoughts, that the Clearing Union may have been too strict on this, though this was actually balanced under the Clearing Union by the much greater size of quotas. If the Clearing Union provisions were applied to the much lower quotas now contemplated, we gravely doubt whether those concerned, particularly the smaller countries, would feel adequate confidence. And I regard the increase of confidence as perhaps one of the major contributions that the plans can make to future stability. This, therefore, is a point about which, after further reflection, I cannot agree with you. No doubt it is a difficult issue. But I am sure it would be very unwise to try and make an untried institution too grandmotherly. When it has established traditions of action it might be easier. At the present stage it is confidence we want to confirm.[25]

Harry White's plan for an International Bank was also discussed in Washington. White's draft of 4 August had been considerably revised and redrafted three times by the Americans, in a series of meetings that began at the end of August. In the course of these it became clear that White 'was ready to abandon non-essential features of the Bank plan at the slightest hint of

opposition, particularly from Congress'.[26] By 24 September a draft was ready
for the British. In this draft the Bank's function as a long-term international
lending agency came to the fore, while the supplementary ideas, such as the
International Commodity Stabilisation Corporation, disappeared. The new
draft was passed to the British on 30 September, when White announced
to the meeting, from which Keynes was absent, that the scheme would
be presented to Congress on 3 October and subsequently published.
After British protests about the breach of previous understandings about
publication, White stepped back from his proposal, allowing that the scheme
would only be verbally presented to Congress in executive session and that it
would be circulated to other members of the United and Associated Nations
after a suitable time lag. But a discarded draft of the scheme was leaked, and
picked up by Paul Einzig of the *Financial News*. Secretary Morgenthau felt
obliged to publish a summary on 8 October.

On reading the Bank proposal, Keynes described his views to Sir
Wilfrid Eady:

> God knows what you will think of it when you see it, for it is an
> extremely odd document. In my opinion there are very genuine motives
> behind it. It is by no means what is wanted to do the trick, but it is
> capable in certain favourable circumstances of helping the situation.
>
> The trouble is that in order to meet alleged American feelings it
> has been wrapped up and camouflaged to look quite the opposite of
> its real intention. The result is, or so it seems to me, that an outside
> critic will regard it as the work of a lunatic, or as some sort of bad
> joke. . . .
>
> In my opinion, he [Harry White] is a perfect ass to approach the
> problem in this way. One cannot possibly attain useful results without
> facing the music, if there is music to face, and putting the scheme before
> the world for what it really is. You cannot humbug all the Continents
> simultaneously with a scheme intended to cover billions of dollars of
> trade. The thing must sail under its proper colours.
>
> Put shortly the camouflage adopted is the following. To all appear-
> ances the scheme makes no difference whatever between creditor
> and debtor countries. Debtor countries are called upon to play just
> as important a part in promoting overseas investment as creditor
> countries. There is no sort of linking up between the responsibility
> for overseas investment and the possession of a favourable balance of
> trade. Indeed, everything is done to dissociate these ideas as much as
> possible. Now clearly that is plain loony. Harry admits that without the
> least wish to dissent. Having put these lunatic robes on his Frankenstein
> he then proceeds at various stages to introduce jokers, which might
> actually cause the scheme to work out in practice in a way exactly the
> opposite of what it appears to be on the surface.

How an intelligent and wise man like him can believe that this is the right way to approach a great issue, heaven knows. . . .

It is rather a tragedy. For there are some very good ideas and immensely disinterested, fine international purpose in the scheme.[27]

Keynes and Sir David Waley had two unofficial talks with White about the proposal on 2 and 11 October. They were to have another on 16 October before Keynes and White had a private lunch, but this came to nothing when White left Washington early for a visit to Europe with Secretary Morgenthau. Keynes raised a number of matters of presentation and clarification, but he also made clear that the primary function of the Bank's capital should be to guarantee loans. There would then be less need for as large a capital as White proposed and no need for many of the odd provisions referring to debtors being responsible for international investment. But it was all very preliminary, for Keynes did not give the scheme his full attention for some months.

Keynes had intended to go on to London after his discussions with the New York bankers. He had, however, to return to Washington to deal with unfinished Lend-Lease business, in particular the attempt by the Americans to limit the rebuilding of Britain's gold and foreign exchange reserves in the face of the worrying rise in her overseas sterling liabilities and the related issues of changes in the coverage of Lend Lease and British Reciprocal Aid. These discussions had started in September but had been held up and complicated by a reorganisation of the relevant American agencies into the Foreign Economic Administration. He finally left Washington on 27 October and arrived back in London two days later. He had summed up the results of his discussions to his mother earlier in the month:

And we are very content indeed with what we have accomplished – greatly in excess of our best expectations. Everyone most kind, a great *will to agree*, and a remarkable comradeship growing up between the British and American civil servants with almost emotional scenes on parting. We all really are trying to make good economic bricks for the world after the war – however hopelessly difficult the political problems will be.[28]

The political problems were not long in coming. It took almost six months from the 'Joint Statement by Experts' that came from the Washington discussions to the 'Joint Statement by Experts on the Establishment of an International Monetary Fund' published in Washington and London on 22 April 1944. In other areas, further progress took even longer, for it was over a year before the commercial policy discussions resumed and over two years before any agreed document appeared.

Law's report of the Washington conversations was circulated to the War Cabinet on 17 December. On 21 December, the Cabinet asked

Law to prepare a further report focusing on the issues which required Ministerial decisions and asked Ministers to send Law the questions which they wished to raise. Discussions in Whitehall indicated that there was deep-seated opposition to many of the results of the Law Mission and some strange alliances developing. Opposition to the understandings on commercial and commodity policy came from the Ministry of Agriculture and its Conservative Minister, Robert Hudson, which vehemently opposed any limitations on its freedom to use quantitative import restrictions and subsidies. Leopold Amery, the Secretary of State for India, remained a determined supporter of tariffs and preferences and the expansion of intra-imperial trade. These two Ministers found an enthusiastic supporter in Lord Beaverbrook. Complicating matters further were Ernest Bevin's renewed worries that the proposed monetary arrangements would not prevent deflation and unemployment. Further complications came with the emergence of a significant undercurrent of Treasury opinion, centring around Sir Hubert Henderson and Sir Wilfrid Eady, in opposition to the monetary scheme – opposition heightened in its intensity and its effectiveness by the Bank of England's re-emergence as an opponent. The Bank had previously decided to let Keynes's 'stuff percolate where it will', presumably in the hope it would die a natural death. 'Since', as Keynes told Redvers Opie, 'it now seems possible that nature cannot be relied on to do its work, it is now felt, not to put it more strongly, that there is no need to keep alive any kind of an international scheme'.[29]

At the roots of the Treasury–Bank opposition were worries about the current account convertibility obligations of the monetary scheme which would carry with them the need to do something decisive about Britain's growing short-term sterling indebtedness, which was concentrated in India and Egypt, and bring forth the 'shudders' experienced by others earlier.[30] The Bank was also worried that the scheme would weaken the international position of sterling. Crucial to the developing alliances was the Bank's tendency to claim the Washington scheme was similar to the gold standard, raising all the hackles of people such as Amery, Beaverbrook and Bevin. Moreover the Bank was also coming to oppose the supplement to the monetary scheme that Keynes was coming to see as essential – large-scale post-war assistance from the United States so that Britain could smoothly manage the transition to peace. The opposition was all the more effective in that it quickly drew blood on commercial policy and then attempted to argue that, as the schemes were interconnected, progress should also cease on the monetary scheme.

Continued infighting within the Treasury and between the Treasury supporters of Article VII and the Bank served as the backcloth against which the British and Americans tried to narrow their remaining differences on the Fund. Between the end of the Washington talks and the publication of the Joint Statement, the 9 October draft went through seven redrafts, each marking a step towards agreement, By December Britain had accepted the American form of words concerning gold subscriptions, the sterilisation of contributions, the rules for changes in exchange rates and the right to make drawings subject to 'a wider and less specific definition of the criteria on which the Fund is entitled to act'.[31] In January came an agreed form of words concerning drawings for capital purposes, in February agreed repurchase provisions.

The 'monetisation of Unitas' took the longest to resolve. Although some members of the Law Mission believed that in fighting for the monetisation of Unitas Britain was pursuing shadow rather than substance,[32] Keynes remained attached to the idea. Back in London, the Bank argued that a monetised Unitas was essential, as did its Treasury supporters. By early December, while still preferring monetisation, Keynes had reached the position where 'I cannot persuade myself that the difference between the two schemes is really such as to make it a justifiable reason for an ultimate breach'.[33] By 26 January, he was prepared to argue in a Cabinet paper that 'all the members of the British Delegation to Washington concerned in these discussions, who have had the opportunity of appreciating, face to face, the great efforts made on the other side to reach agreement, are of the opinion that on this issue we should defer to the American view'.[34] Yet the issue remained unresolved. The Dominions discussions on Article VII which ran from late February until mid-March accepted this point of view, but the British still held off until mounting American pressure led the War Cabinet to agree in April 1944 that the non-Unitas version was acceptable.

The months of Anglo-American negotiations saw another issue come to the fore – the transition from war to peace. The October draft of the Joint Statement simply contained the words, 'Provisions shall be prepared to cover the transitional period and the definitive establishment of the Fund'. A British draft of 18 December provided the first substantive text. This was subject to further discussion before it went into the published Joint Statement. It made clear that the Fund was not to 'provide facilities for relief or reconstruction or to deal with international indebtedness arising out of the war'.[35] It also made clear that a member would not have to fulfil its obligations on exchange restrictions 'until it is satisfied as to the arrangements at its disposal to facilitate the balance of payments differences during the early post-war transition period do not unduly encumber its facilities with the Fund'. It maintained the importance of the ultimate goals of the Fund and the importance of these influencing the form that exchange restrictions took and the way they evolved. In particular, after three years from the inauguration of the Fund, a member would have to consult with the Fund on its current restrictions, although in dealing with members' proposals the Fund would 'give the member country the benefit of any reasonable doubt'.

That solved half of the problem. The other half was met by making clear to the Americans that Britain would not accede to the scheme until she had found a solution to her transitional balance of payments problem – a matter that Keynes was addressing in other memoranda.[36]

Keynes became increasingly concerned with the Bank's approach to the post-war monetary settlement. As he warned the Chancellor on 23 February:

> The Bank is not facing any of the realities. They do not allow for the fact that our post-war domestic policies are impossible without American assistance. They do not allow for the fact that the Americans are strong enough to offer inducements to many or most of our friends to walk out on us. They do not allow for the fact that vast debts and exiguous reserves are not, by themselves, the best qualification for renewing old-time international banking.
>
> Great misfortunes are not always avoided, even when there is no great difficulty in foreseeing them, as we have learnt from bitter experience. I feel great anxiety that, unless a decisive decision is taken to the contrary and we move with no uncertain steps along the other path, the Bank will contrive to lead us in new disguises, along much the same path as that which ended in 1931. That is to say, reckless gambling in the shape of assuming banking undertakings beyond what we have any means to support as soon as anything goes wrong, coupled with a policy, conceived in the interests of the old financial traditions, which pays no regard to the inescapable requirements of domestic policies. Ministers should realise that these things . . . are what the trouble is all about.[37]

He spoke to Lord Beaverbrook in even stronger terms less than a fortnight later:

> Twice in my life I have seen the Bank blindly advocating policies which I expected to lead to the greatest misfortunes and a frightful smash. Twice I have predicted it; twice I have been disbelieved; twice it has happened . . . My conviction is that here is a third occasion. The Bank is engaged in a desperate gamble in the interests of old arrangements and old-fashioned ideas, which there is no possibility of sustaining. Their plan, or rather their lack of plan, would, in my firm belief, lead us into yet another smash.
>
> . . . The whole thing is sheer rubbish from beginning to end. For God's sake have nothing to do with it![38]

There remained one other 'monetary' item for discussion, Harry White's proposed Bank for Reconstruction and Development, now in a version dated 24 November 1943. The Law Report had suggested that there were some advantages in the scheme and that as the Americans were likely to pursue the proposal the Treasury should explore it and report to Cabinet. There was some canvassing of opinion in the course of February: in the main it was critical but positive, although the Bank of England took up its now-customary negative stance. A problem was to get Keynes involved – and for him to find time and energy, for he was experiencing a bout of ill-health. The forthcoming talks with the Dominions provided a stimulus. On 21 February, he prepared a critical note, raising objections similar to those he had mentioned the previous autumn. However, he soon revised his memorandum for circulation to the Dominions' representatives, removing a typically damning concluding paragraph and replacing it with six extremely constructive ones which could provide the basis for further talks with the Americans. The revision began:

> We do not want to express our criticisms to the United States Treasury in a way that is non-co-operative or obstructive. We feel very strongly indeed that loans from creditor to debtor countries in the early post-war period are essential to avoid widespread economic chaos and much needless human suffering. Without them no International Monetary Plan can have a fair start and the reduction of barriers to trade will be frustrated by acute balance of payments difficulties.[39]

Keynes recommended that at this stage Britain should submit certain essential principles to the US Treasury rather than make drafting amendments or try to develop an alternative plan. These principles were that loans should not be tied to particular expenditures in particular countries, that no country should be required to subscribe to such loans unless its balance of payments position allowed and that the main functions of the Bank should be the expert evaluation of projects and the guaranteeing of the servicing of the loans. Finally he emphasised that the Bank should make loans for post-war reconstruction as well as for development.

The Dominions' representatives endorsed Keynes's paper and, at the same time that the British agreed the Joint Statement on the projected International Monetary Fund, the Chancellor communicated the results of the Dominions' discussions on the Bank. The American response was encouraging.

The publication of the Joint Statement on the Fund brought everything back into the public arena. There were extensive discussions in the press as well as debates in the Lords and the Commons. Keynes provided a preface to the White Paper containing the Joint Statement,[40] comparing the present document with the previously published Clearing Union. Following his 1943 practice and taking advantage of the fact that he was not formally a civil servant,[d] he undertook to see members of the press before publication and a number of Members of Parliament afterwards to answer questions and provide 'off the record' explanations. On 20 and 21 April he saw D. D. Braham of *The Times*, Ivor Brown of the *Observer*, Oscar Hobson

---

d As he put it 'I . . . live in a limbo (though it be, in all respects, nearer hell than heaven)' (*JMK*, XXV, 436).

of the *Financial Times*, and Paul Einzig of the *Financial News*. On 27 and 28 April he had two meetings with MPs, reporting to the Chancellor on the opinion he found.

At the time the White Paper appeared, Parliamentary opinion was not favourably inclined towards Anglo-American co-operation. A Parliamentary debate in April on Empire unity and imperial preference had revealed 'in nearly all quarters a strong gust of sentiment in favour of closer relations with the Empire, coupled with more than a suspicion of anti-American prejudice'.[41] When the same mood affected the House of Commons discussion of the Joint Statement on 10 May during which he spent 'seven hours in the cursed Gallery, lacerated in mind and body', Keynes explained the result to Leo Pasvolsky of the State Department as the result of a minority's support of extreme bilateralism and its successful efforts to move opinion against the scheme by taking advantage of the recent surge of imperial sentiment in the country and by presenting the proposals as 'tantamount to a return to the gold standard'.[42] He also saw another factor at work:

> The country is immensely exhausted and has made sacrifices, so far as encumbering the future goes, far beyond those of the other United Nations. The big public is just beginning to become acutely aware of our post-war troubles but does not see daylight any more than I do myself. Naturally, therefore, there is great anxiety that we should not be cutting ourselves off from conceivable expedients before we really know what expedients we are likely to need. On top of that, I think I ought frankly to add, is a somewhat irritated atmosphere, arising out of the naggings about lend-lease, and completely untruthful charges that we are trying to take improper advantages. There also appears to the general public to be a concentrated effort to prevent us doing anything at all to improve our export trade prospects after the war, which, whilst it is a luxury to you, is a matter of life and death to us. . . . Also, of course, everyone is frightfully wrought up and tense about the coming battle [the Allied landings in France]. The ordinary man's life is upset in many new ways. We are so near the scene of events that we all of us feel almost in the battle. Indeed a large part of the country is an armed camp and a training area. It is into this atmosphere that reports arrive that, so far as our relations with U.S. are concerned, everything has to be subordinated to a prospective election.[43]

Keynes wrote to Pasvolsky on 24 May. The previous afternoon, he had risen in the House of Lords to defend the Joint Statement. He did so enthusiastically despite the doubts and trials of the previous year. True, he regretted the loss of 'certain features of elegance, clarity and logic in the Clearing Union', but he regarded the new mongrel plan 'in some respects . . . a considerable improvement on either of its parents'. He saw advantages in the scheme's careful provisions for the transition, convertibility, additional reserves, scarce currencies and the creation of an international institution. Yet the arrangements allowed that 'the external value of sterling shall conform to its internal value as set by our own domestic policies and not the other way round', that Britain could retain control of the rate of interest untroubled by international capital movements, and that Britain would not need to 'accept deflation at the dictates of influences from outside'. To those who had argued that the plan had *not* preserved these safeguards, he replied

> I hope your Lordships will trust me not to have turned my back on all I have fought for. To establish these three principles which I have just stated has been my main task for the last twenty years. Sometimes alone, in popular articles in the press, in pamphlets, in dozens of letters to *The Times*, in text books, in enormous and obscure treatises, I have spent my strength to persuade my countrymen and the world at large to change their traditional doctrines and, by taking better thought, to remove the curse of unemployment. Was it not I, when many of to-day's iconoclasts were still worshippers of the Calf, who wrote that 'Gold is a barbarous relic'? Am I so faithless, so forgetful, so senile that, at the very moment of triumph of these ideas when, with gathering momentum, Governments, parliaments, banks, the press, the public, and even economists, have at last accepted these new doctrines, I go off to help forge new chains to hold us fast in the old dungeon? I trust, my Lords, that you will not believe it.[44]

The way was open for the next stage. The Americans had been pressing for almost a month to set a date for the ensuing conference. The British had held off until after the meetings with the Dominions early in May and the subsequent Parliamentary discussions. Immediately after the Commons debate, the Chancellor told Mr Morgenthau that Britain would respond to an American invitation to a conference at the earliest possible date and arrange for representatives of the European governments in exile to attend, but he warned that security arrangements surrounding the forthcoming Normandy invasion would be a constraint. The Americans were also constrained, for the conference could hardly overlap with the Republican National Convention at the end of June or the Democratic Convention which was to start on 19 July. Yet to make the new international economic order a part of the Democratic programme for the elections, the conference would have to precede their convention. Thus the US Treasury decided on a meeting early in July, with a drafting committee working for two or three weeks beforehand. On 26 May, after informing the British, Mr Morgenthau announced that the President had called a conference of representatives of forty-four governments to begin on 1 July to consider proposals for an International Monetary Fund and an International Bank for Reconstruction and Development. The site would be Bretton Woods,

New Hampshire, where the Mount Washington Hotel had good facilities and a suitable environment – Keynes had told Harry White that a July conference in Washington 'would surely be a most unfriendly act'.[45] Prior to the conference, a drafting committee would meet in Atlantic City, a site chosen out of consideration for Keynes's comfort.

This made for a tight timetable, given the restrictions on travel surrounding the invasion of France and the need for the party to travel by sea[e] – not to mention the fact that the Delegation had to receive its instructions. This last was no small matter, for new difficulties had arisen over the Fund and the Delegation's instructions on the Bank had to be worked up from the general principles of March to a detailed set of drafting instructions.

The problems concerning the Fund came from the Bank of England. The position had changed since the earlier Treasury–Bank discussions in that Lord Catto had moved from the Treasury in April to succeed Montagu Norman as Governor.[f] In the earlier discussions Catto had leaned towards the Bank view of the Joint Statement. He had worried about the exchange rate provisions of the scheme and suggested their amendment to emphasise the sovereign rights of members to fix and alter their exchange rates and to allow that where countries altered exchange rates without Fund agreement they would be suspended from the use of Fund facilities rather than being forced to withdraw. Now he added another difficulty, the obligation of convertibility. Here, even if arrangements were made to cover abnormal wartime sterling balances and those that accrued over the transition, overseas holdings of sterling would still be large since London acted as an international financial centre. These balances, Catto argued, would be convertible on demand under the Joint Statement beyond the needs of current account payments and he thought that the three-year transition period of the Joint Statement would be too short for Britain to acquire sufficient overseas assets as reserves to meet the contingency of possible withdrawals. He suggested that a much more restricted definition of convertibility and a much more gradual accession of Britain to the full obligations of Fund membership were desirable. He was even prepared to see Britain stay out for a period.

The Treasury rejected the Bank's restrictive approach to convertibility. But it did see the point of his convertibility worries for old sterling balances and instructed the Delegation to restrict the convertibility requirement to sterling needed for current transactions. It also accepted the so-called 'Catto clause' on exchange rates. Finally the Delegation was to press for a transition period of at least five years after the end of the European war, or, if

e Keynes's health, which was adversely affected by flying, was a factor here. However, his suggestion that the representatives of the European governments in exile travel with the British party meant that it could be a productive, working voyage.

f It had been expected that Catto would succeed Norman in April 1945. However Norman's health, which had not been good in 1943, collapsed completely in the second half of January 1944 and the changeover was moved forward a year at short notice.

necessary, three years after the Fund's inauguration, to make clear that the Chancellor's willingness to recommend the ensuing agreement to Parliament would be conditional on adequate transitional assistance for Britain outside the Fund and to make clear that all decisions were *ad referendum* and that the Government and Parliament could suggest amendments as a condition of adherence. Such instructions produced, as Keynes put it, 'a position of some difficulty' as the British had agreed that the Joint Statement could not be altered except by mutual agreement.

As for the Bank for Reconstruction and Development, Keynes tried his hand at outlining a possible compromise which would meet Britain's requirements. He conceded much to the American draft in form, but attempted to alter the substance that the bulk of the funds would come from creditors and most loans would be untied, the planning and co-ordinating functions of the Bank would receive more emphasis, the potential liabilities of the UK would be small and the management of the new institution would not be too dominated by the United States. After a meeting on 16 June, his proposals became the Delegation's instructions.

Later the same day, the Delegation left London. It sailed for the United States on the *Queen Mary*. Travelling with the party, which consisted of the Keyneses, Dennis Robertson, Lionel Robbins, Sir Wilfrid Eady and Nigel Ronald, with George Bolton and W. E. Beckett as secretaries,g were representatives of India, Belgium, China, Czechoslovakia, The Netherlands, Norway and Poland, as well as L. W. Casaday, the American Treasury attaché in London. During the voyage, which ended in New York early on 23 June, the Delegation got through an immense amount of work both on its own and with the other delegations aboard.

The results of the Delegation's efforts were two 'Boat Drafts'. The first dealt with the Fund. It raised the problems embodied in the Delegation's instructions – exchange clause, the meaning of gold convertible currencies (which research in the Bank suggested did not actually exist), the length of the transition and the nature of the convertibility obligation – as well as attempting to deal with the details of the management of the Fund. This was seen as 'largely automatic' and routine and would not require either 'a very high-powered Directorate permanently in residence' at the site of the Fund or 'a large and high-powered management'.[46] The second Boat Draft concerned the Bank, the subject of a day's discussions on board. It too followed the Delegation's instructions, but also allowed currency stabilisation loans and a more adventurous policy on lending for individual projects which allowed the Bank to make a small loss despite its obligation to break even overall.

From New York the Delegation proceeded directly to Atlantic City, where many of the other delegations had been in residence since 19 June. After settling in, Keynes met Harry White, who agreed that the

g R. H. Brand and Redvers Opie would join the team in New York.

forthcoming weekend would be spent in Anglo-American elucidations and British meetings with India and the Dominions. The first Anglo-American meeting concerned the Bank. Lionel Robbins recorded in his diary that

> This went very well indeed. Keynes was in his most lucid and persuasive mood; and the effect was irresistible. At such moments, I often find myself thinking that Keynes must be one of the most remarkable men that have ever lived – the quick logic, the birdlike swoop of intuition, the vivid fancy, the wide vision, above all the incomparable sense of the fitness of words, all combine to make something several degrees beyond the limit of ordinary human achievement .... He uses the classical style of our life and language, but it is shot through with something that is not traditional, a unique unearthly quality of which one can only say that it is pure genius. The Americans sat entranced as the God-like visitor sang and the golden light played round. When it was all over there was very little discussion. But so far as the Bank is concerned, I am clear that we are off to a flying start.[47]

A further discussion on the Bank at the end of the week among all the delegations also went well.

On the Fund, matters went less smoothly. On 30 June, after some initial discouragement, both from Louis Rasminsky and Harry White, Keynes reported that he believed that he had made substantial progress on the Catto clause on exchange rates, but there were always the lawyers:

> White and Bernstein have been brought over to our point of view, but they are having the usual trouble that always occurs in this country and is one of the causes of preventing anything sensible being done; that is that they have to consult their lawyers, who are proving difficult. In this lawyer-ridden country even more than elsewhere lawyers seem to be paid to discover ways of making it impossible to do what may prove sensible in future circumstances. However, we have every hope that something pretty good will result.[48]

Over the transitional period, there was not yet agreement, for the Americans had submitted a draft that was more restrictive than the Joint Statement, while the British, of course, wanted to move in the opposite direction. Keynes hoped that he would still get agreement on the British proposal. As to gold convertibility there seemed to be no problem, but on the general issue of convertibility the position was unclear. Keynes also reported that he expected difficulties over the management of the new institution and over quotas, where many smaller countries were unhappy over the size of their allocations, frequently because they believed that it reflected badly on their status relative to some similar power. Yet he thought 'all has really gone well indeed' and Lionel Robbins confided to his diary that 'most of the issues of principle that seemed to divide us have been resolved'.[49]

The Delegation travelled by overnight train from Atlantic City and arrived at Bretton Woods on the morning of 1 July. Everything was in confusion because the hotel's preparations for reopening after its wartime closure were incomplete. The manager in despair was rumoured to have locked himself in his office with a case of whisky. They settled in nevertheless. Keynes found himself directly above Mr Morgenthau, who was to be disturbed for the next three weeks by Lydia's dancing exercises.[50] Keynes took no part in the formal opening ceremonies.

That evening, he gave a small dinner party to celebrate the 500th anniversary of the concordat between King's and New College, Oxford. Those invited – Dean Acheson, Oscar Cox, H. H. Kung, Lionel Robbins, Dennis Robertson and Nigel Ronald – represented the Colleges or their sister foundations or Yale, where a more recent concordat existed. Keynes 'had been looking forward to the event for weeks as excitedly as a small boy'. He 'was at his most charming on the subject of the contribution of universities to civilisation'.[51]

The following day was one for making contacts and completing preparations. Keynes met those Dominions' delegates who had not been at Atlantic City, discussed sterling balances with the Indian representatives and met the Canadian Minister of Finance to discuss financial problems with the Anglo-Canadian Mutual Aid arrangements.

On 3 July the conference got down to business with opening sessions of the Commissions on the Fund and the Bank. As chairman of the latter Keynes opened the proceedings with a typically powerful speech setting forth an outline of the scheme they would be discussing. With these preliminaries out of the way, the serious business began. At the end of it all, Keynes would describe it to the Chancellor:

> The pressure of work has been quite unbelievable. It is as though, in the course of three or four weeks, one had to accomplish the preliminary work of many interdepartmental and Cabinet committees, the job of the Parliamentary draftsmen, and the passage through several Houses of Parliament of two intricate measures of major dimensions, all this carried on in committees or commissions, numbering anything up to 200 persons in rooms with bad acoustics, shouting through microphones, many of those present, often including the Chairman, with an imperfect knowledge of English, each wanting to get something on the record which would look well in the Press down at home, and one of the most important delegations, namely the Russian, only understanding what was afoot with the utmost difficulty and expense of time. On top of this the Press which is here in full force has had to be continually

fed and guided. And each of the Delegations expects some measure of social and personal consideration. . . . We have all of us worked every minute of our waking hours practically without intermission for what is now four weeks. . . . How people stood it at all is a miracle. At one moment Harry White told me that at last even he was all in, not having been in bed for more than five hours a night for four consecutive weeks. . . . But all of us . . . are all in.[52]

Although Lydia's 'iron rule' kept him to more sensible hours, and although he minimised it in public, Keynes felt the strain. Afterwards he reported to his mother that he was working 'up to the limit of capacity' and that 'I do not think I have ever worked so continuously in my life'.[53] And the effort told: he suffered one evening of prostration in Atlantic City after meetings from 9.30 a.m. to 7 p.m. without a break; two in the first week at Bretton Woods and three the second week.[54] Then on 19 July he suffered a mild heart attack after running upstairs to keep an engagement after a dinner with Mr Morgenthau. That incident got into the press when Lydia, a bit depressed by it all, talked to a lady friend she had encountered about the problems. The lady was the mother of a Reuters correspondent attached to the conference. Still, Lydia's letters to her mother-in-law suggest that Keynes bore the strains of the conference much better than she had expected, even if Lionel Robbins thought it was 'a race between the exhaustion of his powers and the termination of the Conference'.[55]

The pace of work and the organisation of the conference, with three Commissions and a multitude of committees and sub-committees, meant that participants could not be acquainted with everything that was going on. What they did know was largely the result of corridor gossip or delegation meetings. In the case of the British Delegation, this meant that most matters ultimately came to Keynes for approval, although on many concerning the Fund Dennis Robertson played an important co-ordinating role. As Keynes told Sir Richard Hopkins:

If anyone is picked out [for commendation] I think it would have to be Dennis, who has been absolutely indispensable. He alone had the intellectual subtlety and patience of mind and tenacity of character to grasp and hold on to all details and fight them through Bernstein (who adores Dennis), so that I, frequently occupied otherwise, could feel completely happy about the situation.[56]

Even this happy arrangement would leave problems behind, given the pace at which the proceedings went. At one point Keynes remarked that 'except for a fleeting five minutes in the lounge' he had not been able to get hold of his technicians for three days.[57] The Bretton Woods team was both understaffed and under-organised.

Relations with the American delegation were good. Keynes remarked particularly about his relations with Harry White, Secretary Morgenthau and Fred Vinson, deputy chief of the Office of Economic Stabilisation and vice-chairman of the American Delegation. As he said of Secretary Morgenthau soon after arriving at Bretton Woods:

> For the first time in my life I am really getting on with Morgy. In all the years I have known him there has never been a moment which was not sticky. Now all of that is changed. Why, I do not suppose he knows any more than I do. But there is no stickiness at all and we can chat together like cronies by the hour.[58]

Moreover, Keynes still held that view at the *end* of the conference.[59] At the start of the Atlantic City meetings, he also found a changed Harry White 'wreathed in smiles and amiability, hospitable, benevolent and complacent'. At Bretton Woods, White was still 'all smiles, kindness and geniality' and relations remained good throughout. The members of the two Treasuries were 'as if we were all members of a single office in Whitehall'.[60] The change in the tone of Morgenthau's relationship with Keynes seemed reciprocal: in one meeting with the American technicians he remarked:

> Now, I don't know what the experience of the rest of you has been with Keynes, but mine is, I feel that he has been absolutely sincere and wants this meeting to be a success.
> . . . Bernard Baruch has fed me full of this stuff that you can't believe Keynes, and Keynes double-crossed him at Versailles, and so forth and so on, and I have been looking for it, but have seen no evidence of it. I mean, Baruch even wrote it to me practically in so many words, 'Look out for this fellow, he is a double crosser,' and so forth. But I haven't seen any evidence of it.[61]

This does not mean that bargaining was not hard, but it meant that it was more civilised than previously.

As at Atlantic City, the Fund was the initial focus of discussion. After its opening meeting on July 3, Commission II dealing with the Bank did not meet again until 11 July. In many respects, the Fund discussions went well for the British. In spite of a strong warning from Louis Rasminsky that it was 'quite hopeless to expect them to accept' the substance of the Catto clause, as noted above the Americans had accepted it at Atlantic City. Although it was 8 July before everything was tidied up, the result was Article IV, sections 5 and 6, of the Articles of Agreement of the International Monetary Fund. Similarly the British concerns over the transitional period were dealt with, in spite of initial American attempts to tighten the Joint Statement. The implication of the Joint Statement that the transition would be quite limited disappeared. The Fund was to report on transitional payments restrictions after three years and members were to consult it after five. Moreover, the British, in spite (or perhaps because) of American attempts to move in the opposite direction were able to ensure that previous obligations, such as the Anglo-American Trade Agreement of 1938, did not interfere with the operation of the scarce currency clause. They also avoided a specific obligation to remove restrictions during the transition, while gaining an American commitment to deal with the 1938 Agreement through an exchange of notes.

On sterling balances the results were mixed. The British had hoped to avoid any public discussion of the ultimate fate of wartime overseas accumulations of sterling. They had hoped through private discussions to assuage known Indian worries and there to convey a pledge that there would be no repudiation. On board ship, however, it became clear that Keynes's persuasive private assurances would not work. At Bretton Woods the Indians presented a resolution asking that one of the objects of the Fund be the liquidation of abnormal wartime indebtedness. When the issue first arose in a committee, Lionel Robbins 'had to be uncompromising and declare explicity that H.M.G. did not regard these debts as appropriate for discussion by any part of the Conference'.[62] The issue came up again when the Egyptians put forward an even stronger resolution. The British stonewalled, but this meant that it would probably come up before Commission I, dealing with the Articles of Agreement of the Fund, where it would get full press coverage. When it did come up on 10 July in the form of a request for help over a period of years to ensure the convertibility of a portion of Indian balances, Keynes forcefully stated that Britain would settle her debts 'honourably', that she did not 'intend to ask assistance in this matter from the International Monetary Fund', and that the settlement of the debts 'was a matter between those directly concerned'.[63]

The drafting of the Fund's convertibility clauses to reach a compromise between the commitment to convertibility and the need to constrain the use of accumulated balances in the post-war world proved more troublesome. A draft was prepared before sailing, agreed on the boat and steered through both Atlantic City and Bretton Woods largely unchanged. Indeed, it went through so easily that the official historian of the Fund merely remarks that it went through smoothly.[64] Keynes also thought that both the language and the substance would meet the Chancellor's needs. There were rumblings in London about the result, but the Delegation seemed content until *after* the Conference.[65]

At the time the Delegation seemed to worry much more about issues such as the location of the offices of the Fund and the Fund's management. The Delegation had come hoping that the Fund would be located in Europe, while the Americans assumed that it would be in the United States. The British attempted to delay the decision until the first meeting of the new institution on the grounds that it was a 'political' matter for governments rather than 'technical' experts, and that it should wait until it was clear what other post-war institutions would exist. The Americans pressed for the United States in a form of words locating headquarters of the Fund in the country with the largest quota. Keynes put the British view to a meeting of the American Delegation where the Congressmen present made it clear 'that Congress will not accept [the] Fund unless it is located in the United States'.[66] The British withdrew their alternative, entering a reservation to allow them to reopen the matter later. As to management, the British worry concerned an American proposal that Executive Directors would have full-time duties and be permanently available at the Fund, since the British thought that the regular work of the Fund would not call for frequent policy decisions. Through a drafting compromise the matter was left over for the future.

The Bank discussions also went smoothly, although when Commission II began its serious work on 11 June there was some unhappiness with Keynes's chairmanship. As Dean Acheson reported to a meeting of the American Delegation:

> The first problem about the Bank is that the Commission meetings on the Bank, which are conducted by Keynes, are being rushed in a perfectly impossible and outrageous way. Now that comes from the fact that Keynes is under great pressure. He knows this thing inside out so that when anybody says Section 15-C he knows what that is. Nobody else in the room knows. So before you have an opportunity to turn to Section 15-C and see what he is talking about, he says, 'I hear no objection to that', and it is passed.
>
> Well everybody is trying to find Section 15-C. He then says, we are now talking about Section 20-D. Then they begin fiddling around with their papers, and, before you find that, it is passed.[67]

Morgenthau volunteered to tell Keynes to slow down – with some success.[68] The work of Commission II and its committees was, however, still hurried, given that the conference was scheduled to end on Wednesday 19 July. Although the conference was extended to the Saturday, those working on the Bank had little more than a week for all their deliberations. As with the Fund, there were arguments over quotas, especially after it was agreed that Fund and Bank quotas could differ. Since eligibility for Bank loans would bear no relation to a country's quota, there were strong incentives for nations to limit their contributions. There were also the competing claims of reconstruction and development. The Mexicans went so far as to press for them to be treated equally at all times, until they realised that this 'would, within no very distant period, reduce the claims of development to the zero which the claims for reconstruction would undoubtedly have become'.[69] They settled for equitable treatment. There were also the issues of stabilisation loans, of a lending policy based on other than normal commercial considerations, of the relationship between the Bank's capital and its guaranteed loans, and of loans for particular purposes. Conservative opinion – often to meet American banking views – prevailed on most issues. The whole exercise was complete except for the quotas by 20 July. On 21 July, Georges Theunis of Belgium reported the work of Commission II to an Executive Plenary Session and moved its acceptance. Keynes seconded the motion and added a memory.

> A quarter of a century ago at the end of October 1918, a few days before the Armistice, M. Theunis and I travelled together through Belgium behind the retreating German armies to form an immediate personal impression of the needs of reconstruction in his country after that war. No such Bank as that which we now hope to create was in prospect. To-day after a quarter of a century, M. Theunis and I find ourselves close together again and engaged in making better preparations for a similar event.[70]

He reckoned that he and Theunis were the only members of the conference who had been involved in the earlier exercise.

Then it was all over. On Saturday evening, 22 July, Keynes moved acceptance of the Final Act. He began by acknowledging the difficult tasks of the conference and paid tribute to both Morgenthau and Harry White, for he was certain 'that no similar conference within memory has achieved such a bulk of lucid, solid construction'. He was unaccustomedly generous to his *bêtes noires*:

> I should like to pay a particular tribute to our lawyers. All the more so because I have to confess that, generally speaking, I do not like lawyers. I have been known to complain that, to judge from results in this lawyer-ridden land, the *Mayflower*, when she sailed from Plymouth, must have been entirely filled with lawyers. When I first visited Mr. Morgenthau in Washington some three years ago accompanied only by my secretary, the boys in your Treasury enquired of him – where is your lawyer? When it was explained that I had none – 'Who then does your thinking for you?' was the rejoinder. That is not my idea of a lawyer. I want him to tell me how to do what *I* think sensible, and, above all, to devise means by which it will be lawful for me to go on being sensible in unforeseen conditions some years hence. Too often lawyers busy themselves to make common sense illegal. Too often lawyers are men who turn poetry into prose and prose into jargon. Not so our lawyers here at Bretton Woods. On the contrary they have turned our jargon into prose and prose into poetry. And only too often have they had to do our thinking for us.[71]

He went on to tell the delegates that they had now to sell the agreements to the world. He was encouraged by the 'critical, sceptical and even carping spirit' with which the conference had been watched and welcomed, for, as he put it, 'How much better that our projects should *begin* in disillusion than that they should *end* in it'. Then he concluded and moved acceptance of the Final Act. '[T]he delegates paid tribute by rising and applauding again and again'. As he left the room they rose and sang 'For He's a Jolly Good Fellow'.

The Keyneses left the next day for Ottawa. Malcolm MacDonald, the British High Commissioner, had sent his car, so that they could have a bit of a holiday by spending four days on the way. When they arrived, Keynes began, as at Bretton Woods, with a celebration, this time of the Bank of England's 250th anniversary.[72] But then it was back to the real world of Britain's continuing financial problems.

The work of Bretton Woods was accomplished under considerable pressure. At the time of the decision to extend the conference by three days, Keynes summed up the situation and the potential risks:

> [T]he technicians and draftsmen can handle the detail properly only when you have settled what it is all about, and I am afraid that they are dreadfully behindhand. It is not easy to keep track of it because none of us are seeing it as a whole, but in bits and pieces. And that is one of the troubles. . . .
>
> On the other hand, if we are hasty we shall find that there are a number of points which will be raised later, just logical errors and inconsistencies, and so forth, which will be very tiresome, and I think it will be dangerous to our project if there are too many opportunities for re-opening this at later stages.
>
> . . . There are, you see, certain final technical matters we haven't considered at all, what the lawyers call the final act, which embodies the results of this Conference. No attempt has yet been made to draft that, and it hasn't been considered by any body. It is a matter all Delegations will want to have at least half a day to look at. At present, no one has seen, as a continuous narrative, the work which has been done.[73]

The day of rest decreed for 17 July and the extension of the conference to 22 July were the result. The additional days did not solve the problem completely. As Keynes would recall later:

> We, all of us, had to sign of course, before we had a chance of reading through a clean and consecutive copy of the document. All we had seen of it was the dotted line. Our only excuse is the knowledge that our hosts had made final arrangements to throw us out of the hotel, unhousled, disappointed, unanealed, within a few hours.[74]

In many respects this might not have mattered. The Final Act of Bretton Woods was *ad referendum* to the governments involved, simply a record of what had taken place. However it would be difficult to alter the document. Proposed alterations were supposed to go to the conference secretariat, which had disappeared. The conference had authorised the US Government to publish the proceedings; hence changes involved the United States. The authorised depository of the Final Act, the US Government, could consider whether proposed amendments required another conference. But the US Treasury hoped 'to railroad both plans through [Congress] as an indivisible whole incapable of amendment'.[75] The Final Act was thus more final than Keynes had suggested. The only alternative to rejecting the whole agreement was to join the new institutions and seek an amendment or an interpretation from the Executive Directors, after the organisation came into operation, under Articles XVII and XVIII of the Fund Agreement.

Nor was all of this hypothetical, for difficulties of interpretation soon arose. One was raised by Paul Einzig who suggested that the emphasis on convertibility and exchange rate stability appeared to prevent possible intervention to prevent the emergence of black markets in members' currencies for such intervention would be contrary to the intentions of the Fund. This was easily solved when the Americans agreed to vote in favour of an interpretation which would avoid that difficulty.[76]

A more important difficulty was raised by Dennis Robertson on 31 July 1944 in a paper entitled 'A Note on the International Monetary Fund (An Essay in Rabbinics)', the subtitle echoing Keynes's (and presumably Robertson's) bemused attitude to the able Jewish officials in the American Treasury responsible for much of the drafting of the agreement. Robertson's paper concerned the obligations of a member to maintain convertibility. Discussion centred on two provisions of the Articles of Agreement – Article VIII, Section 2(a), 'Avoidance of Restrictions on Current Payments', and Article VIII, Section 4, 'Convertibility of Foreign Held Balances'. The first stated that members might 'impose restrictions on the making of payments and transfers for current international transactions' in three sets of circumstances: (a) during the transition, (b) if the scarce currency clause was invoked, and (c) with the approval of the Fund. The second dealt with the circumstances under which overseas balances would be convertible. These conditions, which excluded balances accumulated during the transition, stated that such balances would be convertible if they had been recently acquired as a result of current transactions or their conversion was 'needed for making payments for current transactions'. This raised a potential problem: would a member be able unilaterally to suspend convertibility if it was ineligible to obtain resources from the Fund either because it had exhausted its borrowing rights or because the withdrawal was regarded as a capital movement and the country was therefore ineligible for Fund assistance under Article VI, Section I? Robertson's initial elucidation, which was too narrow and did not raise the full extent of the difficulty that he had discovered, suggested that the obligation for conversion under Section 2(a) would exist even if a country could not use the Fund's resources for that purpose and even if it was not bound by the convertibility obligation under Section 4.[77]

Keynes, who was by then in Ottawa, welcomed Robertson's paper as 'an excuse for using a day . . . to divert the mind to something interesting away from the barren fields and waste lands of financial diplomacy' and replied with 'A Note on a Note on the I.M.F. (An Essay in Metarabbinics)'.[78] He denied that Section 2(a) created an obligation of convertibility. According to him, all that was involved was 'an obligation not to kill convertibility': there was 'no obligation "officiously to keep alive"'. If a non-resident holder of sterling earned in a current transaction wished to dispose of it within the appropriate margins around parity, he could not be forbidden to do so, but there was no obligation on the British authorities to provide him with foreign exchange. A member was required to provide foreign exchange for its currency, subject to the qualifications of Article VII Section 4, only to another central bank; so the foreign individual was completely at the mercy of its central bank. If this were not the case, Britain would lose the benefit of the qualification it had fought for in Section 4 according to which it was only obliged to convert under the section if it could use the Fund's resources for the purpose.

Keynes's distinction between the rights of individuals and of central banks went back to the presuppositions of the first draft of the Clearing Union. As he put it to Robertson on 14 August:

> I think the Americans were always rather confused as to whether they wanted central banks to support the private market in exchanges, or whether they wanted to concentrate transactions in the hands of the respective central banks. In my view the former is mere conservatism and cuts right across the philosophy of the Fund. With the other alternative, the general structure of the Fund begins to make sense.[79]

Robertson returned to the discussion on 29 August with some of the history of the drafting of the relevant clauses and a brief rebuttal of Keynes's position.[80] There matters rested between the two for the moment, but on 17 September 1944 Keynes raised the matter more generally, circulating a note within the Treasury and to the members of the Delegation to Bretton Woods.

At the beginning of this note, he emphasised the importance of the discussion:

> I have now carefully re-examined the text and am of the opinion that, on all the main points which have been raised as doubtful the strict interpretation is what I intended and thought it to be, and that, therefore, all is well. I am, however, disturbed that Professor Robertson takes a different view. If Professor Robertson's interpretation is correct, then, in my opinion, *the draft is not one which the Chancellor is justified in commending to the House of Commons.* (italics added)[81]

He proceeded to state his side of the argument as well as Robertson's and showed signs of annoyance that Robertson had not raised the matter with him until after the end of the conference. His annoyance was to grow in the following months.

Keynes's paper received a variety of replies, the only firm support coming from W. E. Beckett of the Foreign Office who had been legal adviser at Bretton Woods. As a result, Keynes asked the Chancellor for permission to raise the Robertson and Einzig points orally with Harry White while he was in Washington for the forthcoming Stage II negotiations and to take advantage of the provision that such 'drafting errors' could be corrected by the secretariat as envisaged at Bretton Woods. The Chancellor gave his permission.

The results of a conversation with Harry White, which was not very productive owing to White's preoccupation with his own proposals for the deindustrialisation of Germany, a subsequent letter to White and a discussion with White, Bernstein and Ansel Luxford, the legal adviser to the American Delegation at Bretton Woods, were mixed. The Einzig problem of interpretation was solved, as noted above, but the Robertson problem refused to go away. For Bernstein and Luxford 'knew all about ... and strongly supported, in substance, the interpretation sprung on us (or, at any rate, on me) after our return [sic] by Professor Robertson'. Although, according to Keynes, Harry White, once he grasped it, attached little importance to the point and intimated that he would have compromised if Keynes had raised it at Bretton Woods, he could not agree to Keynes's interpretation of the clause or see any procedure for altering it.[82] The ball was firmly back in the British court. Keynes had to decide whether or not the issue was of vital importance. He thought it was, since it restricted Britain's freedom to suspend convertibility unilaterally which he thought she would prefer to devaluation if she got into balance of payments difficulties. He was uncertain as to how this difficulty would be treated by the lawyers; so he proposed that the Chancellor write to Mr Morgenthau on the lines of Keynes's memorandum pointing out the problem and suggesting that he would inform Parliament that Britain's adherence to the Bretton Woods Agreements[h] was conditional on clarification through one of two possible redrafts. At a meeting with the Chancellor on 10 January 1945, Keynes was deputed to draft the letter.

The draft letter set out the preferred strategy:

[A]n attempt to secure an amendment here and now is, I agree, inadvisable, as well as difficult, since it would open the door to other amendments. It seems to me, therefore, that unless our two Governments can agree that this is a matter which must be put right in due course, so that no greater obligation is required than

h I use the plural because membership of the Bank was restricted to members of the Fund.

clearly appears, we must put ourselves on public record, not only with you but with all the other participants in the Conference, that in our opinion VIII 2(a) is faultily and inconsistently drafted unless it is read as implicitly qualified by VIII 4(b); and that we shall regard the satisfactory clearing up of this matter in the meanwhile as one of the essential conditions pre-requisite to our being in a position to accept eventual convertibility under Article XIV.

I still hope that we can, between us, find some way to avoid this. Do you not share my feeling that, in the case of a document prepared so hastily as the Final Act yet so difficult to amend, it would be a bad and dangerous precedent to seek by subtle interpretation to impose any obligation that did not appear, clearly and unambiguously, on the face of the document, or which had not been understood or accepted by those who signed it?[83]

The draft letter and Keynes's 29 December memorandum reopened discussion on a wider plane than just Whitehall because Keynes sent copies to Dennis Robertson, who had left the Treasury to return to Cambridge as Pigou's successor as Professor of Political Economy. The discussion cleared up matters in some ways, but left them muddied in others. The elucidation came in the recognition, pressed home by Robertson, that the text in the Final Act did not represent a drafting slip.[84] Rather, the clauses had been the object of intense discussion at Bretton Woods, where the initial British draft had put the section on balances first and the one on current transactions second. Along with the original phrasing this suggested that the former qualified the latter. The Americans and the Canadians had strongly disagreed with this and the United States had tried to add a sentence ruling out such an inference. Robertson resisted it. The British had then tried to get the qualification into the text; after a heated discussion with Louis Rasminsky of the Canadian Delegation to which Keynes had been summoned, this had ended in an impasse and even a possible breaking point in the negotiations. The compromise embodied in the Final Act then reversed the order of the clauses from the original British draft and ensured that the statement concerning current transactions was not dependent on that governing balances.

When the compromise was agreed, Robertson attempted to obtain Keynes's approval. According to recollections after the event, Robertson had not been able to see Keynes and had to depend on Sir Wilfrid Eady to clear matters. Eady recollected:

You, I think, were tied up at the time with some other anxiety. The crucial question is, when I gave you Dennis Robertson's note of 11th July, did you tell me that Dennis and the Americans and the Canadians could go to hell, or did you say 'Oh, all right then'. You think you said the former. Dennis thinks you said the latter. And I cut the inglorious figure of being completely blank, except that I do know that whatever you did say became a directive.[85]

After the event Robertson, who thought that he had received an affirmative answer via Eady, was sorry that he had not checked with Keynes to be certain that Keynes fully understood what he had agreed to.

Other participants' memories were of little more use. Lionel Robbins remembered hearing from Robertson that his difficulties with the Americans had been removed and that Eady had secured the necessary approvals. His diary merely gives the flavour of the period.

> [*11 July*] Nothing conspicuous has happened in connection with the Fund for the last two or three days, but it should not be thought that nothing is taking place. The draft document, which is gradually emerging on the basis of the agreed statement is a document of incredible complexity, and, as each paragraph of the statement is shaken out into the half dozen clauses it implies, the utmost vigilance is necessary to ensure that the differences between ourselves and the United States . . . do not once more become active. The main burden of this work has fallen on Dennis Robertson, who, next to Keynes, is the real hero of the conference so far as our delegation is concerned. If it were not for the friendly understanding between him and Bernstein, I do not know what would have happened to us by now. . . .
>
> [*12 July*] The debate on technicalities continues. We are experiencing much difficulty in reaching a satisfactory formulation of the clauses relating to capital transfer and multilateral clearing. . . .
>
> [*14 July*] Meanwhile the work on the Fund is going ahead very well. Last night, Bernstein and Robertson sat up until past three and reached substantial agreement on most of the technical questions still outstanding.[86]

Such was the position at the beginning of 1945. The question was what to do next. It did not seem possible, or wise, to hope that the difficulty might be eased by making appropriate changes in the commercial policy proposals then under discussion with the Americans so that Britain could offset through appropriate import controls what she had given away at Bretton Woods. The Chancellor could not stand up in the House of Commons and say that the problem was the result of an oversight by his agents at Bretton Woods. Nor could he stand up in the House and say, as Keynes put it,

> that he does not understand the meaning of clauses so fundamental as those which determine our obligation of convertibility, and that he is signing something ambiguous or meaningless, in the hope that at a later date, the meaning attached to it will be one which he will

752

find satisfactory. It is the extreme importance of the obligation of convertibility . . . which makes it difficult to fluff the point in a way which would be quite easy on something more trivial.[87]

Thus it seemed that a letter had to go to Secretary Morgenthau. It went on 1 February 1945. There followed a certain amount of black comedy: the United States refused to provide a written response and tried to suppress the existence of the letter or, successfully in the end, to get it redrafted so as not to suggest that the drafting of the Articles of Agreement was deficient through hurry and haste. There was also extensive and inconclusive discussion. By the time Secretary Morgenthau replied on 8 June to the redrafted letter, still dated 1 February, it was too late to do anything, as the Bretton Woods enabling legislation had passed the House of Representatives and any amendment would require new legislation. The letter reiterated the points made in previous discussions. The British could only hope for an interpretation from the Fund after it had been set up.[88] By this stage Keynes believed that, although the US Treasury's doctrine was 'unworkable', the arrangements would provide Britain with 'probably all the protection *we* could need' after the transition given that she could suspend the convertibility of balances, resort to import licensing and provide exchange for current transactions.[89] By then, as the commercial policy talks continued, recognition that exchange controls under the Fund allowed a measure of discrimination was becoming clearer. In reply to the Morgenthau letter, the Chancellor virtually closed the matter, leaving open the possibility of a future interpretation from the Fund but suggesting it was unlikely. The discussions had taken over ten months and the British Government's commitment to Bretton Woods had not gone before Parliament. This delay would cause difficulties later in the year.

Thus the matter ended without any change in the Final Act. The result beyond the future political difficulties already mentioned was the souring of Keynes's improved relations with Dennis Robertson. It is clear from the surviving papers that the fact that Robertson, rather than some outside critic, had originally raised the problem so soon after Bretton Woods did not help. Nor did subsequent misunderstandings as to who said what and when. Nor did Robertson's tendency in February 1945 to find benefits in his version, even if Keynes agreed with their importance in normal circumstances.[90] For in many ways this was Keynes's problem: he was worried about contingencies that *might* occur *after* the transitional period. It was a very unfortunate conclusion to a generation of often extremely fruitful collaboration. At least, as far as we can tell, Keynes did not tell his younger Cambridge colleagues of the affair, thus making Robertson's life as Professor even more difficult.[i]

i See Kahn in Thirlwall (ed.) 1976, 21–3. For a more malignant construction on the incident which would probably have been the more typical reaction of the younger generation see ibid., 59.

NOTES

1 *JMK*, XXV, 265, 278.
2 Above p. 692.
3 Howson and Moggridge (eds) 1990b, 74.
4 *JMK*, XXV, 298.
5 *JMK*, XXV, 308–9, 317.
6 See below p. 759.
7 *JMK*, XXV, 307.
8 *JMK*, XXV, 307.
9 Howson and Moggridge (eds) 1990b, 100.
10 P. 685.
11 It appears as chapter 3 of Howson (ed.) 1988b.
12 See below p. 776.
13 *JMK*, XXV, 353–4.
14 Howson and Moggridge (eds) 1990b, 95.
15 BoE, ADM 14/9 802/5, Thompson-McCausland to Cobbold, 18 September 1943.
16 Howson and Moggridge (eds) 1990b, 110.
17 Howson and Moggridge (eds) 1990b, 114.
18 *JMK*, XXV, 340.
19 Howson and Moggridge (eds) 1990b, 127.
20 Howson and Moggridge (eds) 1990b, 133, 135, 139.
21 *JMK*, XXV, 361.
22 Robbins 1971, 199n.
23 *JMK*, XXV, 373, 364.
24 *JMK*, XXVI, 193. For a similar Keynes–Bernstein story, this time about Bernstein's 'Cherokee' and Keynes's 'Good Christian English' see Horsefield 1969, I, 87.
25 *JMK*, XXV, 333.
26 Oliver 1975, 143.
27 *JMK*, XXV, 362–4.
28 *JMK*, XXV, 374.
29 *JMK*, XXV, 394.
30 Above p. 724.
31 *JMK*, XXV, 393.
32 Howson and Moggridge (eds) 1990b, 119.
33 *JMK*, XXV, 394.
34 *JMK*, XXV, 406.
35 Horsefield 1969, III, 135.
36 Below pp. 760–5.
37 *JMK*, XXV, 412.
38 *JMK*, XXV, 416–17.
39 *JMK*, XXV, 425.
40 *JMK*, XXV, 437–43.
41 *JMK*, XXV, 446.
42 *JMK*, XXVI, 3, 28. See also his letter to Harry White in ibid., 27.
43 *JMK*, XXVI, 29–30.
44 *JMK*, XXVI, 10, 16, 16–17.
45 *JMK*, XXVI, 27.
46 *JMK*, XXVI, 55.
47 Howson and Moggridge (eds) 1990b, 158.

48 *JMK*, XXVI, 68.
49 *JMK*, XXVI, 69, 67; Howson and Moggridge (eds) 1990b, 166.
50 Blum 1967, III, 258.
51 Howson and Moggridge (eds) 1990b, 169; Acheson 1970, 83.
52 *JMK*, XXVI, 106–7.
53 KCKP, JMK to FAK, 25 July 1944.
54 Howson and Moggridge (eds) 1990b, 6, 8 and 19 July 1944.
55 *JMK*, XXVI, 98; KCKP, Lydia to FAK, 6, 12 and 17 July 1944; Howson and Moggridge (eds) 1990b, 191.
56 *JMK*, XXVI, 109.
57 FDRL, Morgenthau Diaries, vol. 755, 87.
58 *JMK*, XXVI, 81.
59 *JMK*, XXVI, 106.
60 *JMK*, XXVI, 64, 81, 106.
61 FDRL, Morgenthau Diary, vol. 756, 54.
62 Howson and Moggridge (eds) 1990b, 171.
63 *JMK*, XXVI, 86–7.
64 Horsefield 1969, I, 83.
65 *JMK*, XXVI, 109; below pp. 748–53.
66 *JMK*, XXVI, 90; FDRL, Morgenthau diary, vol. 752, 33 ff.
67 FDRL, Morgenthau Diary, vol. 753, 143–4.
68 Blum (ed.) 1967, III, 274.
69 Howson and Moggridge (eds) 1990b, 180.
70 *JMK*, XXVI, 100.
71 *JMK*, XXVI, 102.
72 Above, p. 664.
73 FDRL, Morgenthau Diaries, vol. 755, 70–1.
74 *JMK*, XXVI, 149.
75 *JMK*, XXVI, 147.
76 *JMK*, XXVI, 137–8, 148. On the whole question of interpretation discussed here, see the illuminating and more detailed discussion in Pressnell 1987, 168–82.
77 Gold 1981, 2.
78 *JMK*, XXVI, 117; 118–22.
79 See above p. 673; *JMK*, XXVI, 123.
80 *JMK*, XXVI, 124–5, 126–7.
81 *JMK*, XXVI, 134.
82 *JMK*, XXVI, 148–9.
83 *JMK*, XXVI, 157–8.
84 *JMK*, XXVI, 160, 124–5, 170, 171–2.
85 *JMK*, XXVI, 170.
86 *JMK*, XXVI, 171–2; Howson and Moggridge (eds) 1990b, 180, 181, 184.
87 *JMK*, XXVI, 174.
88 Pressnell 1987, 177–82 and appendices 16a and 16b; van Dormael 1978, 236–9.
89 *JMK*, XXVI, 184.
90 *JMK*, XXVI, 164–6.

29

THE SHADOW OF DEBT

The old saying holds. Owe your banker £1,000 and you are at his mercy; owe him £1 million and the position is reversed.

(JMK, May 1945, JMK, XXIV, 258)

As the war passed through its fourth and fifth years, Keynes became increasingly concerned about the transition from wartime conditions to post-war normality. This reflected in part the fact that the new international institutions would not have the resources to provide transitional assistance: although such assistance had been a part of the early versions of both the Keynes and White Plans, by late 1943 it was clear that the new monetary institution would merely police exchange practices in the transition and leave the problem of assistance to other bodies. But this increased concern also reflected a growing realisation in Whitehall of Britain's deteriorating international economic position. This position was to form the backcloth for all the discussions that followed.

By the end of 1943, to an extent unprecedented among her non-Soviet allies, Britain had concentrated her economy on the task of winning the war. Over a fifth of her labour force was in the armed forces, while another third was directly employed in war production. The diversion of employment from serving the civilian home market and pre-war export markets was greater than elsewhere. The results showed up in the balance of payments; although shortages, taxation and rationing had reduced consumption to well below pre-war levels, helping, along with controls and a substantial expansion of domestic agriculture, to keep the volume of imports at below 80 per cent of pre-war levels, exports had been allowed to wither away to only 29 per cent of their pre-war volume. There had also been a deterioration in the terms of trade (import prices rose by more than export prices) and a decline in invisible earnings which had traditionally covered trade deficits. By the end of 1943 Britain had since the outbreak of war run a cumulative current account deficit of £5.9 billion. Lend Lease and Canadian Mutual Aid (net of British Reciprocal Aid) had financed less than half of this deficit. In financing the remainder her gold and foreign exchange reserves had initially played an important role, but, once they had reached a low of less than £60 million in the spring of 1941, there was no further hope from this source – indeed, larger reserves became essential. Britain had to depend on sales of overseas investments (£1 billion to the end of 1943) and incurring short-term liabilities, largely in sterling (£2.1 billion). This deterioration in the international investment position would make the post-war transition very difficult, for Britain would have to increase export earnings further to replace the lost investment income, as well as deal with these large short-term liabilities. And we must remember that in 1943 the war was far from over: it was probable that when peace came the position would be much worse.

Keynes had been aware of these growing difficulties and the problems they posed from early in the war.[a] From 1941 onwards he was particularly con-cerned with attempts to keep down Britain's growing sterling indebtedness in India and the Middle East, where the accumulating debts posed complex political and economic problems. In both, the war had created a seemingly 'permanent' balance of payments surplus. In part, this reflected a diminution of British exports to the areas as a result of production cutbacks and shipping shortages. In part, it reflected growing allied military expenditures and inadequate local arrangements for financing local defence expenditures. In the Middle East, the local governments were effectively bystanders and mounting allied military operations were reflected in rising sterling balances in London. In India, the outcome was the product of Anglo-Indian agreements in 1939–40 for reorganising and modernising the Indian army and for sharing the costs of Indian troops serving outside India, plus Britain's decision to use India as an arsenal for operations in the Middle East and, later, the war against Japan. In both areas costs were increased by substantial local inflations, aggravated during the war by harvest failures.[b] In London there was also concern, which subsequently proved unfounded in India on close investigation but was never subject to enquiries in the Middle East, that a lack of strict budgetary control for local purchases further inflated the cost of supplies for Britain.[1]

For the Middle East, Keynes's main contribution was to support an innovation which served both to reduce the rate of inflation and to slow down the build-up of sterling balances. The idea came to him in December 1941 via Richard Kahn, then Economic Adviser to Oliver Lyttleton, the Minister of State in the Middle East, from R. A. Harari, Chief Economic Adviser to GHQ Middle East. Harari's suggestion was that Britain sell gold, possibly obtained from the United States under Lend Lease, in local markets to remove surplus purchasing power and to reduce the hoarding of

a His concern about the post-war world had led him to oppose a proposed financial settlement with Greece at the end of 1940 and provoked his 1941 outbursts in Washington over post-war trade policy commitments (*JMK*, XXIII, 29–40; above pp. 652 and 660–1.

b In 1944 the wholesale price indices for Egypt and India stood at 311 and 302 as compared with 171 for Britain (January–June 1939 = 100) (Gardner 1956, 168 n. 2).

goods that was aggravating inflationary pressures in the wake of a recent harvest failure. Initially the proposal came to nothing: Britain did not have the gold, was worried about the precedent, and did not think it wise to put the proposal to the Americans when America's recent entry into the war offered the possibility of a more comprehensive 'new financial deal'. Those on the ground in Cairo, however, persisted in proposing gold sales, most notably at Anti-Inflation Conferences held in Cairo in September 1942 and in London in December. Events moved to favour such a programme: a payments agreement with Persia required Britain to settle a substantial part of her adverse balance of payments in gold at the official price at a time when the open market price stood at twice that level, while Britain's rising gold and foreign exchange reserves brought American threats to reduce them through cuts in Lend Lease or through demands for additional goods on Reciprocal Aid rather than as normal imports. Gold sales possessed several advantages: they would reduce inflation and hoarding, reduce the growth of sterling balances by an amount almost twice their cost to the reserves and help to protect Britain against further American attempts to reduce reserve growth.[2] At this stage in the winter and spring of 1943 the Middle-Eastern and Indian sterling balances' problems became merged into one for policy-makers.

Before 1944, India's growing sterling balances had been discussed much more than those of the Middle East. India had started the war as a substantial sterling debtor, owing about £360 million at long term. By early 1943, she had reduced this debt by over £300 million through repayments on maturity, open market purchases and Treasury vestings, yet her sterling balances had soared from their pre-war level of £40 million and were expected to reach over £600 million by the end of the year.[3] Although some members of the Treasury had been worried early in 1942 that India might end the war short of sterling,[4] these worries gave way to fears that India might make excessive demands on Britain's post-war export capacity and to a realisation that rising sterling balances were an irritant to Anglo-Indian relations. Attention shifted from attempts to revise the 1939–40 defence arrangements to a concern to moderate inflationary pressures, but behind every proposal lurked the desire to minimise post-war sterling balances.

Keynes, with his long experience with the London end of India's financial affairs, and Lord Catto, with his experience in both India and the City, played a prominent part in the ensuing discussions. Keynes's first suggestions were either a lump-sum contribution from India for the costs of the war, a revision of the terms of defence sharing, the vamping up of special claims, or something equivalent to Canadian Mutual Aid.[5] Treasury attempts to press them in March 1942 broke on the opposition of the India Office. Keynes attempted to move matters to a higher level. At a meeting of the Other Club on 16 July, he impressed the seriousness of Britain's growing indebtedness upon the Prime Minister, who then asked the Chancellor for the facts and a Cabinet discussion. Leopold Amery, the

Secretary of State for India, was annoyed.[6] In preparation for the discussion the Chancellor produced a memorandum which, starting from President Roosevelt's interpretation of Lend Lease and Reciprocal Aid 'that each of the United Nations should end up without a monetary war debt to any of its partners' repeated the Treasury's March proposals for a reallocation of expenditure responsibilities in Britain's favour. Amery rejected them and, after a half-hearted discussion, which showed that Kingsley Wood's heart was not in the scheme, the Cabinet agreed to defer a decision until the Prime Minister returned from a visit to Moscow and the Middle East.[7] Meanwhile, interdepartmental wrangling continued. Keynes at one point minuted that Amery was a 'dangerous lunatic' in believing that large Indian sterling balances were 'more likely to prove a blessing than a danger after the war' as they would help sales of British exports.[8]

When Cabinet discussed the matter again in September 1942, it agreed to send the Viceroy a telegram setting out arguments for new arrangements. Indian reaction was unfavourable. The Cabinet agreed to let matters be for the time being, on the understanding that the Chancellor retained the right to raise the subject at some later date. Keynes agreed, advising on 15 October 'that in view of the political situation in India, the whole matter should be deferred for the time being; the question of what India can properly be asked to pay for her own defence being put off until we have successfully defended her'. This decision, involving as it did the rejection of an Indian proposal for a partial contribution to offset British expenditures, cost £100 million in increased sterling balances by war's end.[9]

In the following months the various proposals to slow down the growth of Indian sterling balances began to overlap with longer-term suggestions, such as those in Harry White's Stabilisation Fund proposals, to tie up or fund a substantial portion of the balances after the war. Despite Keynes's brief enthusiasm for various schemes, the only action taken in 1943 was the implementation of the earlier proposal to sell gold on the open market, at first on an experimental basis in Persia and subsequently from June 1943 in the Middle East and India. This experiment, which 'may be claimed as one of the most successful in war finance',[10] owed much to the powerful and successful efforts of Keynes and Lord Catto to overcome Bank and Treasury objections. Gold sales of £11 million in the Middle East and £44 million in India had reduced sterling balances by £22 million and £77 million respectively. The cost of the sales may have been less than £55 million, as the use of the reserves for this purpose probably reduced American pressure on them from other directions. Moreover, the Americans were drawn into both schemes to keep down the costs of their local expenditures.

The gold-sales scheme was only a drop in the bucket in the face of the problem. Although it may have helped to moderate the inflation resulting from the Bengal famine, it did not prevent Indian balances from rising above £700 million by the end of 1943 and £1 billion a year later.

There was one more British assize on the problem, the Cabinet (and official) Committees on Indian Financial Questions which sat from the summer of 1943 into the summer of 1944 and again into 1945 with the Chancellor in the chair. Their origins again showed traces of Keynes's use of his contacts with the Prime Minister to shape events.[11] Keynes also tried to shape the Treasury's contribution to the proceedings and in December 1943 contributed a memorandum of his own. Although he resurrected earlier proposals, including the funding of Indian pension obligations in Britain, a post-war reconstruction fund, and even the weakening of the principle of the sterling area by transferring gold from Britain's to India's reserves (these last two were conceded in a small way in 1944 and 1945), he was becoming more and more enamoured of a *general* solution to the problem of the sterling balances as a part of the post-war clean up. His efforts to devise this general settlement were to affect the Committee's thinking more than the detailed proposals. As with so many wartime problems, the Indian one was allowed to drift. The result was that the ultimate settlement was more expensive for Britain than many of the wartime proposals: for example pensions were funded but at a higher interest rate than India originally proposed and the Treasury, under Keynes's influence, had rejected in 1943–4.[12]

By the time that Keynes turned to an explicit consideration of the post-war financial settlement, Britain had accepted that she, rather than some international body such as White's Stabilisation Fund, would have to deal with the sterling balances.[13] But a plan had eluded her. Thus the question of the treatment of the sterling balances was caught up in Keynes's general scheme.

Keynes's first substantial essay on the financial problems of the transition was written against the background of the continuing discussions of Indian sterling balances and of official and ministerial disagreements over the results of the Anglo-American conversations in Washington of September-October 1943.[14] He passed a first draft of his paper to Sir Richard Hopkins on 7 January 1944 and, after talking with Hopkins, he revised it for more general circulation on 11 January.

His 'Notes on External Finance in the Post-Japanese-Armistice Transitional Period' provided a rough, preliminary outline of views Keynes was to repeat in a series of powerful memoranda over the next two years.[15] He started from the most recent Economic Section estimates of the post-war balance of payments.[16] On this basis, he suggested that in the first two post-war years while Britain was moving towards balance in her international accounts, the combined worldwide deficits of Britain (£500–700 million) and the rest of the sterling area (£200–300 million) might amount to £1,000 million. The deficit of Britain and the sterling area with the dollar area of North and South America would be somewhat above that. In such circumstances reliance on the continuation of the wartime sterling arrangements – whereby members of the area had agreed to accumulate sterling, pool their accruing gold and dollar reserves in London, limit their imports of goods to essential needs through licensing, and operate similar systems of exchange control – would be dangerous. Members would want more freedom; they would be short of goods; they would be less constrained in their import demands by shipping shortages and wartime materials allocation arrangements; and the deterioration of a member's balance of payments position with the rest of the world would strain the central reserves. Nor would an extension of the area to Western Europe through payments agreements help. These countries were unlikely to be in surplus with the sterling area; they were likely to be dollar area debtors, adding to the strain on the central reserves; and if they were in the sterling area Britain's ability to tap into the gold and dollar resources these countries intended to use to finance reconstruction would be limited.

Keynes drew two conclusions. First, the wartime sterling area arrangements must be modified to limit the convertibility of accumulated sterling balances. He suggested members might take out of the central pool of gold and foreign exchange only as much as they currently put in, further drawings should be at the discretion of the London exchange control authorities, and after three years there should be a general scheme for the eventual release of the remaining wartime accumulations. Such an arrangement would make continued membership of the sterling area attractive, for it would produce access to hard currencies equivalent to current earnings and any additional releases agreed by London, instead of access only to the sterling area itself.

Second, these arrangements would require American aid to cover £500 million or about half of the transitional period deficit. Borrowing from Canada and South America, running down Britain's reserves and sterling area gold and dollar earnings from Europe would cover the rest. The form of the American aid should take the form of an interest-free, inter-governmental credit repayable over 50 years. With such a credit, Britain should be able to accede to the likely American conditions that there be no restrictions on current payments and no discrimination against American exports. Lest his readers think that such terms would be too harsh, Keynes warned that they might be far too easy and reduce the necessary pressures on Britain to restore equilibrium. As for 'the austere alternative' of taking no American aid that was being talked of in some circles opposed to the emerging Article VII settlement, he argued that it would involve such domestic austerity as to cause social and political difficulties, a reduction in Britain's overseas military and political commitments and further accumulations of blocked sterling balances which would increase the strain on the sterling-area arrangements.

This paper did not produce the sense of urgency Keynes intended.[17] Some Treasury and all Bank of England opinion remained uneasy about the

International Monetary Fund, agreement on which would be a prerequisite for American assistance, and the Bank was frankly opposed to Keynes's proposals for the sterling area and for a sizeable American loan. Although by April 1944 these views were not able to prevent the Fund proposal going forward, it was clear from the discussions in London that the full seriousness of Britain's post-war balance of payments position and the likely fragility of the wartime sterling area arrangements in peacetime conditions had not sunk in. Keynes therefore resumed his offensive in the middle of May with what Sir Wilfrid Eady called 'one of the most readable 10,000 official words of recent times'. After a series of meetings in the Treasury and discussions with R. H. Brand, Keynes revised the memorandum before it went to two meetings of Ministers and eventually to Cabinet.

'The Problem of Our External Finance in the Transition'[18] opened by pointing out that Britain's overseas financial position at the end of the war would be worse than it had been in 1919, not only because of the absolutely greater amount of overseas indebtedness, the more complete loss of foreign investments, and the larger adverse current balance, but also because her successful anti-inflationary policy had increased the real burden of the debt as compared with last time and her debts, instead of being largely to the United States, were more widely distributed. He highlighted the seriousness of what would follow:

> The Government's post-war domestic policy is based on the assumption that we shall be able to import all the raw materials and foodstuffs necessary to provide full employment and maintain (or improve) the standard of life. This assumption is, at present, an act of blind faith. No means of making it good has yet been found. There has never been a more distinguished example of 'It will all come right on the day'. This memorandum is an attempt to persuade those concerned to support faith with works. Otherwise, great disappointments and disillusions lie ahead.[19]

In an analysis bristling with barbs aimed at those Departments – the Ministries of Supply and Food, the Board of Trade, the Services – whose 'works' might have made his estimates more precise – but perhaps even more alarming – he set out his estimates of Britain's overseas deficit during the transition, which he put at three years. Instead of the £900–1,200 million for the gross deficit that he had used in January, he now put the deficit at £1,500–2,250 million, a sum which included an assumption that non-traditional holders of sterling would run down their sterling balances by as much as £500–750 million by taking exports or foreign currency. He also took account of the past and prospective contributions to the deficit of Britain as a 'Lady Bountiful' who was 'likely to continue her gracious activities until she feels the bailiff's clutch on her shoulder'.[20] Nor, having incurred this deficit, could Britain be assured that she would have then reached balance of payments equilibrium.

He then turned to possible solutions, casting his net more widely than he had done in January. He began with the sterling area as the place where, by restricting the repayment of sterling balances, the authorities could make the largest impact on the prospective deficit. He emphasised that this would require 'a material change in the present sterling area arrangements, about the practice of which there is a widespread and most dangerous misunderstanding'.[21] The sterling area was not, as many thought, an arrangement for blocking the transferability of balances; it was one for pooling exchange reserves, although wartime understandings and practices had prevented holders from freely using their balances. After the war, it would be 'an indispensable condition of our own situation that we should in practice convert the sterling area into the closed system which some people believe it to be already'.[22] In the immediate post-war period, individual members of the area would have access to the central reserves only to the extent of their current earnings, supplemented by any additional dollars Britain decided to make available. During this period, all abnormal sterling balances would be funded at a zero rate of interest except for necessary currency reserves which would receive the Treasury bill rate. If Britain avoided the payment of interest, she could probably discharge her abnormal liabilities over 40 years, although tied exports of capital goods might mean that some creditors were paid off earlier. Any contribution to the solution to the problem by outright gift or cancellation would be welcome, but he did not expect any significant alleviations from such sources.

The second means of ameliorating the problem was to start the transition with gold reserves that were as large as possible. This would involve persuading the United States to avoid further 'chiselling at Lend Lease' before the end of Stage II – the British term for the period between the defeat of Germany and the end of the Japanese war – and perhaps a reapportionment of shares of expenditure in India. America's taking over of responsibility for gold sales in the Middle East and India would also help, as would a renegotiation of the special account arrangements, often neglected in the dark days of 1940, which required Britain to settle bilateral payments imbalances in gold. But time was of the essence in such negotiations: Keynes estimated that each month's delay was costing the reserves £10–15 million.

The third possible source of alleviation, a changed attitude to incurring new overseas commitments, brought Keynes to a theme that would echo through a whole series of state papers right down to his death less than two years later. Here, he argued that contemporary British attitudes were composed of several unhelpful ingredients.

In the financial field we have never escaped from the consequences of the Dunkirk atmosphere when we fought alone: that it is *our* war; that if anyone helps it is nice of them, but we cannot, of course, expect that it should be otherwise than on their own terms; that so far as we, but not they, are concerned, the future must be sacrificed to the overwhelming needs of the present; and that if anyone wants a *douceur*, he must, in the interests of getting on with the war, have it. This is the ingredient of appeasement, right and inevitable once, not so clearly necessary now. Next there is our position as a Great Power, equal in authority and responsibility and therefore equal in the assumption of burdens. This is the ingredient of pride and prestige – equally understandable, but nevertheless shortsighted if pride and prestige are, in fact, to be preserved. And finally, the most sympathetic and natural of the ingredients, what we have called the gracious activities of Lady Bountiful, all-oblivious to the bailiff's clutch, the universal and unthinking benevolence of a family which has always felt rich and for whom charity has become not so much a sacrifice as a convention. How promptly and handsomely we should all subscribe to the Lord Mayor, if there were to be an earthquake in New York! It never occurs to Lady Bountiful that it may be her own dinner she is giving away. If she did, the gift would be worth a good deal more; but would she, in this case, give it?[23]

Keynes did not deny that Britain's largesse had won her many friends abroad, but he argued that in her present plight it was not sensible that she should, for example, provide external resources to countries which had large gold reserves available to finance reconstruction.

Finally, there was the assistance of the post-war export drive. This was likely to be inhibited by a slower pace of demobilisation than in the United States, by the lack of vigour in the current preparations, and by the limitations on British exports agreed with the Americans as part of the 1941 Lend-Lease arrangements – the so-called Export White Paper.[c] It was important, Keynes argued, that the last constraint be relaxed during Stage

c The Export White Paper (Cmd. 6311) of September 1941 grew out of Lend Lease. Once Britain began to receive help, American criticisms centred on the possibility of Lend-Lease goods being embodied in competitive British exports. The British Government unilaterally bound itself to a series of detailed restraints. Overall, the effect was to reaffirm that she was confining her exports to the minimum essential for supplying the vital needs of countries overseas, especially in the sterling area, or necessary for acquiring foreign exchange, especially in the Western Hemisphere. Although the White Paper was a general statement of principles, it came to be regarded, especially in the Lend-Lease Administration, as a legal code. This inevitably produced friction. As the prospect of peace became more real, Britain became more concerned with preparing the ground for the post-war expansion of exports and there were attempts to get American agreement to the modification or suppression of the White Paper. In 1943 and early 1944, these attempts had proved fruitless; so the matter was left over for the negotiations concerning the Lend-Lease arrangements for Stage II. See Sayers 1956, ch. XIII(iii).

II, without a diminution of Lend-Lease, if Britain was to make a beginning in coping with the fact that all Lend-Lease aid, except munitions, would cease with the end of the Japanese war.

However, even if Britain made progress on all four fronts during the remainder of the war, she would still need balance of payments assistance from the United States during the transition. There was no doubt, he suggested, that the Americans would provide what was needed – perhaps even too much. But Britain should concern herself with the terms and consequences of losing her financial independence and reduce her requirements to a minimum, say $2–3 billion. Such a sum would keep up the pressures for adjustment, be within her capacity to pay, and not carry any unacceptable terms, in particular any conversion of current sterling debt into dollar debt. As for suggested terms, his primary one was that any assistance should be interest-free, 'at any rate until we can see our way clearly to repay'.[24] He emphasised again in his conclusion that everything depended on minimising the need for assistance. Otherwise,

> the best alternative (and one which it is ill-mannered to mention, since it is so likely to be adopted) is to borrow all we can from the United States on any terms available, and in due course shuffle out.[25]

In the discussions of Keynes's memorandum there seemed to be greater awareness of the problems of the transition, but little consensus as to possible solutions. The Bank of England remained opposed to Keynes's preference for a clear-cut sterling balances scheme that involved substantial funding and others saw sufficient difficulties to lean towards a more piecemeal, case-by-case, approach – which may also have been their preferred solution. Yet circumstances required a public commitment such as that made by Keynes at Bretton Woods – a commitment which echoed the earlier note by Sir John Anderson, 'There is no question of repudiation. This can be stated'.[26] 'The Keynes pledge' at Bretton Woods plus the prospect of early talks seemed acceptable to the Indians and Egyptians. But there were no early talks: there were no discussions until *after* Britain committed herself to act under the terms of the December 1945 Anglo-American Loan Agreement.

Meanwhile, there was the problem of getting an acceptable settlement for Stage II. This had been in the background of Keynes's 1944 papers. The end of the war with Germany would mean a switch in the Allied war effort to the Far East, which under the existing arrangements would mean a sharp rise in expenditure which was liable to be reflected in a rise in sterling balances. There was also the need to renegotiate the basis of Lend-Lease allocations. With the end of the war in Europe, the fundamental principle of Lend Lease, 'the defense of the United States', could be interpreted in a manner to reduce the direct aid available to Britain. There was also the problem of the Export White Paper, for if Britain was to begin the necessary quintupling of the

1943–4 level of exports during the transition, she would have to start before V-J Day. Finally, there was the need to continue the education of American opinion as to Britain's post-war economic problems and prospects, for many of her Stage II proposals would be informed by the Stage III prospects. And all of this would have to come during a Congressional and Presidential election year, when the probabilities of trimming sails to meet the real or imagined fears and opinions of the American public would be at their greatest.

Keynes's statement of 'The Problem of Our External Finance in the Transition' was a part of the documentation that informed Cabinet discussions of the issues. The Cabinet authorised in July immediate steps on the export drive and early Stage II negotiations based on a full statement of Britain's needs. There was then a gap of several weeks before there was an opportunity to begin formal talks at the highest level. There were conversations between the Chancellor and Secretary Morgenthau during Morgenthau's European trip which lasted from 6 to 17 August. When the Chancellor 'put all the cards on the table face upwards',[27] his frankness made a considerable impression on Morgenthau, particularly with respect to the persistent American attempts to limit the growth of Britain's international reserves.[28] One result was a 9 September directive from President Roosevelt that existing Lend-Lease directives concerning Stage II be withdrawn. This cleared the way for the further discussions at the Octagon meetings in Quebec between 13 and 16 September 1944. There Mr Morgenthau's proposals for the deindustrialisation of Germany[d] meant that it was difficult to get Stage II on to the table, but on 14 September, after preliminary discussions between Morgenthau and Lord Cherwell, Churchill and Roosevelt agreed on guidelines for the discussions: global figures for munitions and non-munitions assistance to Britain of $3.5 and $3 billion respectively, a revision of the terms of the Export White Paper, and a joint negotiating committee with Secretary Morgenthau taking the lead for the Americans.

Although Bretton Woods had ended on 22 July, Keynes did not return to London until 24 August. He and Sir Wilfrid Eady had spent much of the month in Ottawa attempting to fill the gap between the Canadian Mutual Aid appropriation for 1944–5 of $450 million and the expected sterling area deficit with Canada of $1,475 million and to educate Canadian opinion on Britain's post-war plight. As part of the latter exercise, Keynes passed to the Canadians 'Statistics Bearing on the Dimensions of the United Kingdom Problem of External Finance in the Transition'. This was a reworking of his earlier Cabinet paper to cover Mutual Aid, the loss of British external assets

d One of Morgenthau's selling points for the proposals in discussions with the British was that it would give Britain better export opportunities.

and the wartime reductions in British standards of consumption. He put the potential deficit at £2,000 million and the underlying deficit, assuming various changes in policy, at £1,250 million. He suggested, without giving a figure, that Britain would have to borrow from both the USA and Canada. Keynes believed that his paper and his oral presentation of its substance 'produced a considerable effect ... put[ting] the Canadian civil servants and Ministers into a mood of wanting to find a way to meet us in so far as they can without involving themselves in political and parliamentary difficulties'.[29] The visit was certainly successful, as Canada agreed to find means of paying Britain $655 million, enough to cover the rest of the financial year and leave something over. Moreover, officials in Ottawa agreed that from a public relations point of view, the Keynes–Eady visit was as useful as any thus far during the war.

Despite his public responsibilities, the Ottawa visit gave Keynes the 'nearest thing I have had to a holiday for years'. He found Ottawa 'a place of peace and repose of mind' and saw Canada as a place where, if he had to, he might emigrate.[30] But there was more work ahead, for after he left Ottawa on 15 August, he had further visits to Washington and New York to talk not only of Bretton Woods and Stage II preparations but also of the post-war treatment of Germany.

Mention of the post-war treatment of Germany makes it necessary to discuss Keynes's involvement in this issue during the Second World War. Although he was not as intimately involved as in 1918-19, he played an important direct role – over and above his role in the creation of a climate of opinion through his writings between 1919 and 1932.

Keynes's first 'official' thoughts on the subject accompanied his 'Proposals to Counter the German "New Order"' of 1940.[31] In his covering note, dated 1 December, he had set out his reasoning.

(4) I have assumed that, this time, there will be no post-armistice starvation of Germany herself and that she will share, equally with her neighbours, in the surplus stocks; i.e. that *after the war is over* we shall not continue starvation and unemployment as an instrument for enforcing our political settlement. . . .

(5) In one passage I have gone further than this and have indicated that Germany under new auspices will be allowed to resume that measure of *economic* leadership in Central Europe which flows naturally from her qualifications and geographical position. I cannot see how the rest of Europe can expect effective economic reconstruction if Germany is excluded from it and remains a festering mass in their midst; and an economically reconstructed Germany will necessarily resume leadership. This conclusion is inescapable, unless it is our intention to hand the job over to Russia. To admit it is good European propaganda

in every quarter which attaches importance to social security. . . . I am assuming, in short, that our post-war policy towards Germany will favour economic reconstruction and will concentrate all our punitive and preventive measures in the military and political settlement.[32]

Such a statement seemed natural for the author of *The Economic Consequences of the Peace*. Keynes returned to the subject in September 1941 after a conversation with J. W. Beyen, the former President of the Bank for International Settlements who was Financial Adviser to the Dutch Government in exile. Beyen had told him the Dutch were concerned about reparations from Germany in connection with their post-war reconstruction. This prompted Keynes to suggest that it was time for the British to begin systematic thinking about the issue.[33]

To a series of informal discussions between Keynes, Hubert Henderson, S. D. Waley of the Treasury and Nigel Ronald and Sir William Malkin of the Foreign Office, Keynes contributed 'a catechism of questions requiring a decision', which included the warning 'The chief thing that matters is that Ministers should not suppose that the first thing that matters is to avoid the mistakes made last time'.[34] A resulting December 1941 Treasury memorandum, 'Compensation to be Required from the Enemy', raised the issues that Ministers might face, warning against statements impossible to fulfil and language that could provoke charges of bad faith from ex-enemy countries. It did not receive a wide circulation, largely because it was overtaken by the events of 7 December and also because of opposition from other departments.

The ensuing lull was broken by Hugh Dalton, President of the Board of Trade, who circulated a memorandum entitled 'Reparations' on 28 August 1942. Dalton held strong views on the treatment of Germany.[35] He thought that the time had come for a re-examination of the issues of reparations and economic security by an official committee. Although critical of the memorandum's contents, Keynes supported Dalton's proposal of an official committee. So did others. An interdepartmental Committee on Reparations and Economic Security under the chairmanship of Sir William Malkin was appointed.[e] This strong committee met thirty-three times between November 1942 and August 1943.

Keynes dominated the Committee's general discussions and wrote a substantial part of the report.[36] He prepared two papers for its discussions. One attempted to set out German responsibilities for reparation and restitution, the means by which she would make payments and the principles which would govern the distribution of the proceeds of reparations.[37] His emphasis was on payments in kind rather than the financial transfers characteristic of

---

e Keynes and Edward Playfair, the Treasury members, were joined by Lionel Robbins, James Meade, Nigel Ronald, Gladwyn Jebb, Percivale Liesching and Rear-Admiral R. M. Bellairs.

the 1919 Treaty.[38] The other paper moved on to newer ground, taking the line that a defeated and disarmed Germany would, after reconstruction was complete, have an advantage over the Allies in that she would not have to bear the costs of defence and would be able to use manpower and other resources in more productive ways. To ensure 'that the benefits of defeat and the burdens of victory should not be more financially disproportionate than is inevitable', Keynes suggested that a disarmed Germany (and Italy and Japan) should contribute to the resource costs of international peace-keeping, either by a new international body or a combination of Allies, through a levy on her export earnings.[39] His suggestion found its way into the Committee's report and, after his death, into Germany's initial financial contribution to the North Atlantic Treaty Organisation.

The Malkin Report of August 1943 assumed that, while there might be border adjustments Germany would remain 'a substantial unitary State', that there would be no attempt to deindustrialise Germany, and that there would be no measures to depress unduly the German standard of living or to impair peaceful employment opportunities. Because feelings and interests at the end of hostilities would be stronger than subsequently, it assumed that as much as possible of any claims come in once-for-all form and that any long-term provisions should not only appear just to the Allies but also appear sufficiently just to ensure the long-term co-operation of those who would be subject to them. It was this line of argument that made Keynes's peace-keeping suggestion so attractive to the committee.

The Committee first looked at the claims that the Allies could make at the end of the war – restitution of property, reparations, peace-keeping contributions, and pre-war private claims. It limited claims for restitution to identifiable property existing at the outbreak of hostilities which Germans had taken from Allied nationals. It believed that, as even limited claims for reparations would exceed Germany's capacity to pay, all that a detailed itemisation could do was affect notional shares. The question of shares would better be settled by 'a broad-bottomed bargain' amongst the governments concerned about percentages rather than absolute sums, using as a rough guideline losses of 'non-military property directly caused by the enemy in the course of military operations'. After the period of occupation and reparations, the Committee adopted Keynes's idea of a peace-keeping levy for as long as Germany remained disarmed and could not use conscription.[40]

When the Committee turned to Germany's capacity to pay, it argued that naming specific figures would be 'useless and unwise', given the uncertainties of the situation which might exist at the end of hostilities. It recommended instead 'an elastic formula which will be automatically adjusted to the facts of the future as they disclose themselves', by which, apart from the restitution of identifiable property, Germany would meet her reparations obligations out of existing assets and deliveries in kind or labour services over a period of three to five years as well as the peace-keeping levy on exports. The total reparations obligation would be determined by a Reconstruction Commission which should ensure that deliveries in kind were only for reconstruction purposes and that the deliveries and asset transfers would not unduly reduce the German standard of living, restrict essential imports, or impair disproportionately to their value German industrial capacity or ability to provide employment. Overall, the Committee expected that reparations payments might amount to $4 billion at 1938 prices or $6 billion at post-war prices, while the peace-keeping levy would be on a sliding scale rising from 10 per cent of export earnings under $1 billion to 25 per cent of earnings over $2 billion.[41]

As for long-term economic security, Germany would be prohibited from manufacturing armaments, civil aircraft, aero engines or their components. Existing plant in these industries would be removed or destroyed. There would also be restrictions on German stocks of imported strategic materials (manganese, chrome, tungsten, molybdenum, nickel and oil) and prohibition of the production of synthetic oil as long as Germany remained disarmed.

Soon after the report was signed, Keynes, Nigel Ronald, Lionel Robbins and James Meade left London for the Washington Article VII discussions.[42] It occurred to Keynes that it might be useful if he could discuss the Malkin Report with State Department officials working on similar questions. Richard Law cabled London on 16 September 1943 for permission for him to do so. Receiving no reply, Law presumed consent and Keynes spoke to a meeting on 28 September at the State Department attended by, among others, Dean Acheson, A. A. Berle, Averill Harriman and Leo Pasvolsky. Keynes heard later that the Americans 'were considerably interested, and even excited, in what was put before them' and hoped for further discussions.[43] But on 29 September, a meeting of Ministers in London bolted the door after the horse had fled, refusing Keynes permission for what he had already done – perhaps because of his previously published views on reparations.[44]

During the ensuing year the question of the post-war treatment of Germany was 'raised, though not fully discussed' at a meeting of the Foreign Ministers of the Big Four in Moscow in October 1943 and at the November 1943 Teheran Conference of Churchill, Roosevelt and Stalin.[45] At both meetings it was clear that there was a strong feeling in favour of dismemberment on the part of the Russians and Americans, but also that thinking had only reached a very preliminary stage. At the Moscow meetings Britain, the Soviet Union and the United States agreed to set up a European Advisory Commission in London to make recommendations to the Governments on questions surrounding the termination of hostilities. The Commission first met in January 1944. Both Britain and the United States set up national back-up bodies, the British ones being the Economic and Industrial Planning Staff (EIPS), an official interdepartmental committee on general armistice and post-war problems which advised a ministerial committee chaired by Clement Attlee. Although Keynes was undoubtedly aware of some of the ensuing discussions, for he had frequent contact with Playfair, the Treasury representative on EIPS, his next contribution would come through the Americans.

After the Bretton Woods Conference, Harry White and Secretary Morgenthau paid a visit to London and to the Normandy beachhead. On their flight to London, White gave the Secretary a copy of a report on reparations from the Executive Committee on Foreign Economic Policy, an American interdepartmental committee chaired by Dean Acheson. White, the normal Treasury representative on the Committee, had not attended recent meetings but had through his substitutes reserved the Treasury's position on the report which assumed that Germany would eventually be reintegrated into a multilateral world economy. Morgenthau, who had not previously been concerned with the post-war treatment of Germany, read the report 'first with interest, then with misgivings, finally with sharp disagreement'.[46] On his arrival in Britain, he was even more disturbed when he found the view of the Washington Committee reflected in a Supreme Headquarters Allied Expeditionary Forces (SHAEF) 'Handbook for Military Government in Germany' and in the papers of the European Advisory Commission. Both also assumed that the Allies should cause minimum disturbance to the German economy and that German industrial reconstruction was crucial for the post-war European recovery. Morgenthau, with his deep, long-standing Germanophobia and his horror at Nazi atrocities, set out to change the direction of policy towards Germany, with the full support of Harry White.

The centrepiece of Morgenthau's efforts was soon known as the Morgenthau Plan. At its heart was the belief that Germany should never again be in a position to wage an aggressive war. As there was little likelihood that American forces would remain in Germany for an extended period after the war to enforce sanctions, the sensible solution for Morgenthau was to destroy her economic capacity to wage war by dismembering the country and by crippling her industry. Such a programme would preclude substantial reparations. Before he left Britain, he made his views known to American officials in SHAEF and the European Advisory Commission. On his return to Washington on 17 August, he worked tirelessly to change the direction of Administration policy.

Keynes became peripherally involved when, in Washington for only a day on his way back to London, he asked Harry White to lunch on 20 August. Their conversation ranged widely – over the forthcoming Stage II negotiations, New York bankers' views of the Bretton Woods agreements, and British plans for Parliamentary action on Bretton Woods. They also touched upon reparations. As Harry White reported it:

We briefly discussed the reparations problem and he said that he was heartily in agreement with our view of the desirability of dismembering Germany and as to the relative unimportance of reparations. He explained, however, that in a report he submitted in Washington last year[f] he was specifically given terms of reference which did not include the assumption of the partition of Germany. He said that he had wanted to add a sentence at the end of his report (which, incidentally, was begun before the Teheran Conference) to the effect that he disagreed with the whole recommendation and preferred another solution, namely the partition of Germany. In short, Keynes seems to be in our corner.[47]

White put the matter even more strongly in conversation with Morgenthau.[48] Doubtless the notion that Keynes supported their position encouraged both White and Morgenthau. Whether he did is another matter. White's discussion of the Malkin Report was rather garbled. It is true that by the summer of 1944 Keynes had come to favour dismemberment, but his attitudes on other matters were not as simple as White believed.[49]

Morgenthau and White were remarkably effective in changing the thrust of American and British planning on Germany. By the end of August, Morgenthau had succeeded in getting the distribution of the SHAEF Military Handbook temporarily suspended. (It later went out with amendments to the relevant sections.) By 4 September, Morgenthau's staff had prepared a memorandum entitled 'Program to Prevent Germany from Starting World War III'. This memorandum, which was stronger than White and others of his staff desired, particularly in its proposals for the destruction of industry in the Ruhr, was the subject of considerable discussion as Roosevelt prepared for his meeting with Churchill at Quebec City. Roosevelt left Washington on 9 September with a copy of a slightly revised version of Morgenthau's plan, plus a run of briefing papers from the same mould.[50] The President was not committed to Morgenthau's views, but on 12 September, Morgenthau was summoned to Quebec City. He arrived the next day.

Before the Quebec meetings, the British had learned something of Morgenthau's thinking from their contacts in London and from a telegram from Lord Halifax in Washington. The Foreign Office reaction was that Mr Morgenthau's views were wrong – 'a starving and bankrupt Germany would not be in British or any European interests'[51] – and sent a telegram to that effect to Anthony Eden, the Foreign Secretary, for transmission to Churchill on 14 September. Before he received the telegram, Churchill had already heard the contents of the Morgenthau Plan from its author. He was not enthusiastic. As Morgenthau later remembered:

f Presumably his discussion of the Malkin Report in September 1943, reported above p. 770.

After I had finished my piece he turned on me the full flood of his rhetoric, sarcasm and violence. He looked on the Treasury plan, he said, as he would on chaining himself to a dead German.

He was slumped in his chair, his language biting, his flow incessant, his manner merciless. I have never had such a verbal lashing in my life.[52]

Morgenthau did not sleep well that night.

The next morning Morgenthau and White met Lord Cherwell and G. D. A. MacDougall. Morgenthau emphasised the connections between his proposals for a deindustrialised Germany and a strong post-war British export economy, a line he had taken earlier in Washington.[53] Cherwell was apparently more sympathetic and agreed to try the scheme, suitably dressed up by the Americans, on Churchill.[g] The attempt was successful: on 15 September Churchill and Roosevelt initialled a directive on Germany drafted by the former, which indicated that the metallurgical, chemical and electrical industries in the Ruhr and the Saar 'be put out of action and closed down' and looked 'forward to converting Germany into a country primarily agricultural and pastoral in character'.[54] This was over Eden's objections and without consulting the Foreign Office or Cabinet.[55] Whether Churchill's agreement was the price for the subsequent directive covering the Stage II negotiations is unclear, but it represented the high tide of the Morgenthau Plan.[56] Thereafter there was considerable backsliding in both Washington and London as the understanding on Germany met fierce opposition.

During that crucial month for the Morgenthau Plan, Keynes was in London. Except for two long weekends at Tilton, he was caught up in his usual London concerns – notably the *Journal* (although for almost the last time as he had determined to give it up)[h] and CEMA (now on its way to becoming the Arts Council). There were also the important loose ends concerning Bretton Woods.[57] At the same time there was yet another round of official discussions on commercial policy – made more urgent by American pressure to resume the talks in abeyance since the previous autumn, and made more difficult by concerns about Stages II and III, especially given Keynes's warnings on the balance of payments position. This round of discussions involved another Cabinet Committee, whose deliberations proved more complex than the Chancellor had anticipated.

g Cherwell's biographer asserts, without citing any evidence, that his subject did not support the Morgenthau proposals. However, he certainly succeeded in giving others the impression that he did (Birkenhead 1961, 267–8). Sir Donald MacDougall in his memoirs does not state Cherwell's position on the issue (MacDougall 1987, 47).

h RES, Council Minute Book, III, 17 May 1944 and 7 February 1945. In May 1944, Austin Robinson was appointed Joint Editor from 1 January 1945 and a committee was set up to consider future editorial arrangements. On 7 February 1945, Harrod was appointed Joint Editor.

Keynes provided Anderson with a memorandum which forcefully reminded his colleagues that Britain was committed to Article VII, that the 1938 Anglo-American Trade Agreement, unless denounced, limited Britain's freedom of action in any respect and that a break with the Americans now over commercial policy would be 'little less than crazy' given the transitional period safeguards of Bretton Woods and the need for post-war American assistance.[58] Then there were the final preparations for the Stage II negotiations, which Keynes was to lead. He was so busy that it was only at sea, after his departure for America on 21 September, that he found time to complete yet another memorandum on the post-war prospects.[59]

The tone of the memorandum, 'Decisions of Policy Affecting the Financial Position in Stages II and III', can best be judged from its peroration:

> We cannot police half the world at our own expense when we have already gone into pawn to the other half. We cannot run for long a great programme of social amelioration on money lent from overseas. Unless we are willing to put ourselves financially at the mercy of America and then borrow on her own terms and conditions sums which we cannot confidently hope to repay, what are we expecting? Are we looking forward to a spectacular bankruptcy (not, altogether, a bad idea) from which we shall rise next morning without a care in the world? Or are we following some star as yet invisible to me?
>
> Milton wrote: – 'War has made many great whom peace makes small. If after being released from the toils of war, you neglect the arts of peace, if your peace and your liberty be a state of warfare, if war be your only virtue, the summit of your praise, you will, believe me, soon find peace the most adverse to your interests.'[60]

Keynes's increased worry owed much to a Treasury forecast for the first year of Stage II of an overseas current account deficit of £1,581 million. Assuming that Stage II lasted a year, this would mean Britain's entering Stage III (when Lend Lease and Mutual Aid would end) with an overseas deficit running at about £1,500 million a year – even on the 'preposterously optimistic' assumption that exports doubled in value during Stage II. The optimism was 'preposterous' because it rested on the absence of any decisions to make it possible. The estimated deficit also depended on an assumed £550 million for war expenditure overseas, a figure that included nothing for expenditure in Europe and related only to India, the Middle East and Imperial lines of communication. Unless the figure was reduced to £300 million, '[W]e shall certainly start Stage III with an incapacitating handicap'. To conceive that military expenditure in Europe would be nil was unrealistic – Britain's current policy towards Germany seemed 'to be seeking the maximum rather than the minimum liability' and looked as if it would cost Britain more than it had after 1918. Similarly, the estimated deficit included no sums for the cost of relief, reconstruction or foreign credits. Yet, when it came down to it, as Keynes emphasised, the key to much of the Stage II (and Stage III) problem was the decision to maintain an overseas army of 1 million over and above the forces fighting Japan. Britain could not support such forces in Stage III and it would be a waste of resources to behave in Stage II as if she could. Thus his plea was for more prudence, more balance, more realism and more planning – and the paper was full of constructive suggestions as well as outraged criticism – at least until Britain could see her way more clearly into the post-war world. It was all very sensible advice from one who was about to set foot in America to beg for money.[61]

After leaving London, the Stage II party set sail from Glasgow on the *Ile de France*. Their destination was Halifax, Nova Scotia, from which they would proceed by train to Washington.[i] Keynes found the journey agreeable and restful. The weather was good; the accommodation was comfortable; and the workload was not too heavy. Keynes worked on his papers in the morning and relaxed in the afternoons and evenings, gossiping and reading *The Cloister and the Hearth*, *The Heart of Midlothian*, and *Barchester Towers*.

Even before he left London, Keynes had feared that his negotiations might be complicated by the Morgenthau Plan. Discussions with Lord Cherwell and others in Montreal confirmed these fears, as did his first impressions in Washington. First, Morgenthau and White 'were considerably more interested in their plan for deindustrialising Germany than in anything else' and were still trying to force its substance forward as post-war American policy over the determined opposition of the State and War Departments.[62] The bureaucratic infighting between the Treasury and other Washington agencies might jeopardise his own mission, particularly if Morgenthau lost or if he suspected Keynes, Brand and other senior members of the British missions in Washington of sympathising with his opponents. Second, partially as a result of their collaboration at Quebec City over the post-war treatment of Germany, Morgenthau and Cherwell had taken it upon themselves to organise the negotiations. Both had thought that the scheme for Stage II could go through without an elaborate committee structure, with the two of them acting as 'wise men' who would come to a decision with little consultation of others. Although Cherwell's view on procedure was that of a minority of one on the British side, it prevailed, for after Keynes met with Morgenthau he accepted the Secretary's preference for a small top-steering committee, although it was larger than two. Cherwell's belief that the British

---

i From Halifax to Montreal the party had the private car of the President of Canadian National Railways.

case should go forward in writing was not a minority view, and, although Keynes had intended to depend on an oral presentation of the case, on the advice of Sir Robert Sinclair he changed his mind. After a week's intensive work the mission's 'British Requirements for the First Year of Stage II' was ready for discussion. While drafting the 'book of words' as it came to be known, the party, in the light of a new pessimistic forecast of Britain's balance of payments position, increased Britain's case for assistance by reviving some old claims or 'half-dead cats' (as Keynes called them), largely in the hope that they would stir the Americans to provide some new assistance, or 'a new live dog' in the Delegation's language.[63]

While these preliminaries were being sorted out, there remained the problem of the Morgenthau Plan. Keynes reported his first meeting with Morgenthau and White to the Chancellor:

> Morgenthau started off on this before coming to our main business: said that he would like me to see their full proposal in the form which he had presented it to the President, provided I would regard this paper as something to be seen by no one except myself, though he agreed to my passing it on to you. He said that he would like [at] a later date to have a round table talk with me about it. All this was, of course, very embarrassing and I had to preserve an unwonted and uncomfortable reticence. I discovered that he by no means considers himself defeated on this issue, and is still on the warpath. . . . When Harry White broached the same subject I took the line that all plans relating to Germany which I had seen so far struck me as equally bad, and the only matter I was concerned with was that it should not be the British Treasury which had to pay reparations or support Germany. I gathered that the plan is not quite as crude as it appeared in the reports from Quebec. All the same it seems pretty mad, and I asked White how the inhabitants of the Ruhr were to be kept from starvation; he said that there would have to be bread lines but on a very low level of subsistence. When I asked if the British, as being responsible for that area, would also be responsible for the bread, he said that the U.S. Treasury would if necessary pay for the bread, provided always it was on a very low level of subsistence. So whilst the hills are being turned into a sheep run, the valleys will be filled for some years to come with a closely packed bread line on a very low level of subsistence at American expense. How am I to keep a straight face when it comes to a round table talk I cannot imagine. . . .
>
> Is it fair to send a poor official, whose cynicism about politicians is already more than it should be, into such a boiling?[64]

True to his word, Morgenthau sent Keynes a copy of the Plan on 5 October. Keynes saw that it was 'by no means as crude as the information first to hand might have suggested' and he even found himself in 'considerable sympathy' with parts of it, in particular its emphasis on the essentially German responsibility for the economy (at least after the initial period) and for the recommendation that the primary responsibility for the policing and civil administration in Germany after a brief occupation would fall on Germany's European neighbours. Yet there was still 'the absurd paragraph 4' which recommended that the Ruhr and its hinterland 'should not only be stripped of all presently existing industries but so weakened and controlled that it cannot in the foreseeable future become an industrial area'.[65]

Keynes seems to have avoided discussing the Morgenthau Plan with its author during the rest of his visit. He did meet President Roosevelt on 26 November, when he thought that the President's state of mind was much the same as it had been in Quebec City, but that overall his thoughts were 'obviously extremely fluid over the whole question'. Keynes thought that he had not made up his mind on even fundamental issues and did not intend to do so for some time. He certainly did not appear rushed.[66]

The alarms and diversions of the Morgenthau Plan deeply affected Keynes. E. F. Penrose of the American Embassy in London found him on his return 'not only unresponsive' but also 'perverse'.

> His attitude was defeatist, and while admitting that there was a muddle, he spoke as if it were a hopeless muddle, as if nothing could be done about it. The Morgenthau plan was wrong, of course, he said, but even the Morgenthau policy, if pursued consistently, might have been less harmful than the existing hodgepodge which was neither one thing nor the other but a confused blend of inconsistent ideas.[67]

Keynes himself told E. J. Passant of the Control Commission's Military Section, in reply to a paper on dismemberment, at the end of 1944:

> What frightens me most in the whole problem is that these issues are extremely likely to be settled by those (as I know by first-hand conversations), who have not given continuous or concentrated thought to it. The best consolation is that . . . you may be quite sure that no real decision whatever has been taken on the matters of main importance. This is a state of affairs which is necessarily a frightful nuisance to all those concerned with working out details and policies. Nevertheless, it may be the course of wisdom. That, in truth, is my own position at the moment. I am against reaching any important decisions whatever about the more distant future until events have provided us with more data.
>
> For, in fact, there is *no* good solution. *All* the solutions which are now being talked about are, not only bad, but very bad. This, however, is an added reason for suspending judgement in the hope that history

and the course of events will provide something better for us than we are capable of inventing for ourselves.[68]

In the interim, there were the Stage II negotiations where, Keynes reported, the decision to put everything in writing was a wise one.

> There was never at any time an opportunity for continuous or coherent oral exposition to the right audience. A Washington meeting has to be experienced to be believed. At the Main Committee any continuous argument or indeed more than a dozen sentences were always out of place. At the technical and other Sub-Committees there would be twenty-five or more persons present at any one time, but their composition would be continually changing as they floated in and out of the room to attend to telephone calls or other business, so we were seldom addressing the same audience for more than ten minutes together. One would suddenly discover that even the chairman had disappeared without explanation to return half an hour later, and the actual spokesman on the American side would break off his remarks at any moment to answer a call from without. Indeed in Washington the Ancient Mariner would have found it necessary to use a telephone to detain the wedding guest. For it is only on the telephone that one can obtain undivided attention. If you seek an interview, your American friend will spend half the time talking on the telephone to all quarters of the compass, until in despair you return to your own office and you yourself ring him up, when you can expect to secure his concentrated mind for as long as you like, while someone else wastes his time keeping a date with him in the chair you have so wisely vacated. No! Sir Robert Sinclair was right that a written document is best.[69]

As for the negotiations themselves, the military side went through 'with remarkable ease and celerity'. The Delegation asked for $3,000 million and came away with $2,838 million. The Delegation was not, however, able to get a formal and detailed document as a hedge against future political and administrative changes. It tried, but the proposal met with the 'great wrath' of the Navy and War Departments, so it decided not to press the matter and to be content with general covering letters and a public announcement committing the Americans to the principles.

On the non-munitions programme, the negotiations went more slowly. In the end the Delegation was almost as successful, getting $2,569 out of a requested $3,000 million with an American promise to find another $250–300 million on miscellaneous items – either by reviving some of the 'half-dead cats' or by making more liberal rulings about eligibility such as the one that occurred just after the negotiations in favour of pre-fabricated housing. The negotiations were slowed by a number of factors, heightened by the fact that the 1944 Presidential elections took place during the talks.

The first was shortages in the United States: although supplies of tobacco were adequate and the actual materials for Britain had been contracted for and set aside, a shortage of cigarettes in the United States made it impossible to agree to restore civilian tobacco supplies to Lend Lease. Similar problems arose with off-shore sugar, where again Lend Lease might have been interpreted as operating to the detriment of the American consumer. A claim for retrospective Lend Lease for certain oil and shipping expenses was impossible under the law according to Foreign Economic Administration lawyers, provoking Keynes into one of his characteristic outbursts.[j] Finally, the position was complicated by the fact that the Americans had not fully accepted the British case for some rebuilding of her international reserves during Stage II. Morgenthau accepted the case,[70] but it was never clearly accepted by the President or the Foreign Economic Administration. Keynes attributed this to the facts that the issue had not been agreed in principle at Quebec City, that the President was too preoccupied with the election to become convinced of the need for a change, and that, as far as the President was concerned, 'Mr Morgenthau has easier access to his presence than to his mind'.[71] It also seemed that the President was less sympathetic to British claims because he believed that there had been some British backing off from other commitments, intimately associated in his mind with the Lend-Lease agreements, made at Quebec City and because he worried about the domestic political consequences of its becoming known that Britain had stolen an edge on the United States in reconversion.[72] Even Keynes noted that the President had created an impression in the mind of Leo Crowley, and hence the whole Foreign Economic Administration, that there should be no change in the operation of Lend Lease, and that, as he noted Crowley's tendency to have 'his ear . . . so near the ground that he was out of range of persons speaking from an erect position', there may have been not only caution but also a change in policy.[73]

A change in view, or American caution, had its greatest impact on the Delegation's efforts to modify the terms of the 1941 Export White Paper so that Britain could begin the post-war export drive from 1 January 1945. The Administration had publicised V-E day as the date for the beginning of reconversion and a publicised earlier date for Britain would cause problems, especially as the War Production Board was having difficulty in restraining American industrialists from acting sooner.[74] A partial remedy was for Britain to pay dollars for most raw materials and manufactured goods and for the Foreign Economic Administration to promise that it would give the British maximum freedom under the terms of the White Paper

j 'Surely the plague of lawyers in Washington is a worse plague of Egypt than Pharaoh ever knew. It is only by a rare or lucky coincidence that what is administratively sensible is also lawful. . . . The place only carries on at all because of the wide reserve of discretionary power which becomes vested in the President in time of war, and what will happen when peace returns, with all its complications, heaven only knows.' (*JMK*, XXIV, 212).

until V-E day and after that date, although the White Paper would still be in place, to give complete freedom. This allowed the commencement of the export drive and, with the agreements that there should be enough supplies to allow some improvement of the civilian diet and that emergency houses could come under Lend Lease, did mark a significant easing of the programme.

Finally the discussions allowed the British to continue their attempts to increase American understanding of her plight. Here the 'book of words', which was widely circulated in the relevant departments played an important role. So did deliberate attempts at explanation by Keynes. On 31 October he gave a lecture on the operation of the sterling area and British thinking about the transitional arrangements to an audience made up not only of officials from the State Department and the Foreign Economic Administration but also senior British officials. He 'spoke with complete candour and lack of reserve' and without a text, which he realised would have taken months to get approved in London.[75] He also spoke to the Combined Chiefs of Staff on the financial burdens that Britain had assumed in the course of the war. He provided Morgenthau with a powerful statement of Britain's war expenses abroad – 'collectively a story of financial imprudence which has no parallel in history' – which might be useful if the latter had to go to Congress on Britain's behalf.[76]

As to Keynes's conduct of the negotiations, Frank Lee recorded that 'the news of his coming made all the difference to our spirits'. Lee continued

> Maynard's performance was truly wonderful. I think that occasionally he overplayed his hand and occasionally wore himself out in struggling for points that were not worth winning. But in general he was an inspiration to us all: it is no exaggeration to say that we felt like Lucifer's followers in Milton, 'Rejoicing in their matchless chief'. His industry was prodigious, his resilience and continuous optimism a constant wonder to those of us more inclined to pessimism, while I doubt whether he has ever written or spoken with more lucidity and charm. And, of course, the impression he makes on the Americans gives us an enormous advantage in any negotiations in which he participates. Take Harry White, for instance – that difficult nature unfolds like a flower when Maynard is there, and he is quite different to deal with when he is under the spell than he is in our normal day to day relations with him. I think that everyone on the United Kingdom side would agree that we could not have hoped to get anywhere near the results which have actually been achieved had it not been for Maynard's genius and inspired leadership.[77]

After the conclusion of his Washington negotiations, Keynes went to Ottawa on 28 November to discuss Canadian Mutual Aid supplies for Stage II.

Ottawa was in the throes of a conscription crisis.[k] Ministers were hardly in a fit state of mind to take extensive decisions on Keynes's Stage II proposals for Canadian aid.[78] None the less he managed extensive discussions with the relevant Ministers and their officials. He outlined the extent of Britain's needs, which went beyond the sums likely to come through Mutual Aid by about $1 billion; discussed ways of filling the gap, none of which seemed to suit both sides; and heard the first stirrings of Canadian alarm about possible post-war sterling area discrimination against Canadian as well as American exports. Although the discussions resulted in no decisions, they did allow for further education as to Britain's likely post-war problems. Keynes was even able to repeat his Washington lecture on the sterling area. Maynard and Lydia then proceeded to New York and London. They managed to return by sea on the SS *Nieuw Amsterdam*, then serving as a troopship, with thousands of 'seasick Americans' on board. During the voyage, Keynes wrote a Cabinet paper outlining the results of his mission.[79] The paper was full of warnings about the future.

On his return, Keynes spent a few days in the office tidying up the backlog of work. He wrote a letter to Sir William Beveridge on his *Full Employment in a Free Society*, dealt a telling blow at Lady Bountiful in a scathing minute on a Dominions Office proposal for aid to Newfoundland (which he calculated was the equivalent of an American grant to Britain of $15 billion), and prepared a note on a report by an official committee on public utility corporations.[80] On 22 December he retired to Tilton. The holiday, which lasted until the New Year, included a shoot for his friends and a vast Boxing Day party for his employees and their families. Lydia's prodigious feats of shopping in America now appeared as presents. The party ended with songs,

k Under the National Resources Mobilisation Act 1942, which was amended following a decisive 'yes' vote releasing the Government from an earlier pledge against introducing conscription, the authorities had the power by Order in Council to send overseas men conscripted for home defence under the Act. Heavier than expected casualties in Europe combined with a decline in voluntary enlistments had led to representations, accepted by the Minister of Defence, that the conscription of NRMA men for overseas service was the only means of getting establishments up to strength. The Minister had told the Prime Minister, Mackenzie King, this on 18 October. Day after day of Ministerial discussions ensued until 2 November, when the Minister of Defence resigned when King continued to believe that he could get the necessary reinforcements by voluntary means. When Ralston was replaced by General A. G. L. McNaughton, formerly Commander of the Canadian Army in Europe, there was no dramatic increase in voluntary enlistments. The Cabinet was constrained by the need to have a clear policy before Parliament met on 22 November. On the morning of the 22nd, McNaughton reported to King that the Chief of the General Staff had advised that voluntary recruiting would not meet the reinforcement problem. As McNaughton had joined the Ministry to give voluntarism a trial, this led King to believe that overseas conscription would be necessary. Persuading his Cabinet and caucus that it was necessary would be more difficult, although King managed it with only one more ministerial resignation on 26 November. However, debate on a motion of confidence in the Government continued until 7 December, when the Government won by a large majority despite substantial Quebec defections from its ranks.

recitations and a performance of *Little Red Riding Hood* by Duncan Grant and Clive Bell.

His holiday over, Keynes was back in harness. Although day-to-day concern with a multiplicity of Treasury matters continued – on 6 January another powerful memorandum on the criteria that should govern the operations of nationalised industries and the implications for the terms of compensation for former shareholders; the next day a devastating memorandum (which he supplemented later in the month) on capital issues controls[81] – he was spending more and more of his time preparing for the post-war world. This involved continued attempts to get the Articles of Agreement of the IMF drafted or interpreted correctly, keeping an occasionally amused eye on the resumption, at last, of Anglo-American talks on commercial policy, taking part in further British discussions on the post-war treatment of Germany before and after meetings of the Big Three at Yalta early in February, and leading the discussions of post-war monetary policy in the National Debt Enquiry.[82] Most of all, he directed his attention to the matter without which the Fund, the International Trade Organisation, domestic employment policy and even the Arts Council would probably not get off the ground – Britain's need for overseas finance in the transition, the terms on which it might be available, and the conditions which Britain would be wise to offer or accept.

In the early part of the year, except for a 'superb conversational' talk Keynes gave to the Exchange Requirements Committee on 9 January to impress upon Whitehall the seriousness of the foreign exchange situation after the war,[83] discussions of the financial needs of the transition were completely informal as suggestions emerged from various quarters in Washington and were transmitted back to Keynes by R. H. Brand or Frank Lee and as various Americans, most notably Samuel Rosenman, special counsel to President Roosevelt, and Laughlin Currie, administrative assistant to the President, passed through London. The discussions indicated that on the British side matters were still fluid: as Keynes and Eady put it to Rosenman 'the question was indeed in our minds, but we had not got our ideas clear about it, so that it was impossible at this stage to give even an official Treasury view – still less the views of His Majesty's Government'.[84] Yet, as Rosenman recorded Keynes as saying 'The only possible solution for Britain's problems today would be another brain-wave by your President Roosevelt – like Lend-Lease'.[85] But there were pressures on Britain, initially from Canada, to define her policy more concretely.

During the previous August and November Canadian officials had heard Keynes expound Britain's post-war problems and indicate that a long-term, ideally interest-free, loan would be necessary to ease the complications of the transition and sterling-area indebtedness. However, within a month of Keynes's second Ottawa visit in 1944, R. S. Hudson, the Minister of

Agriculture and a longstanding opponent of every aspect of Article VII, alarmed Canadian officials by saying that he and some of his colleagues had made it clear to Churchill that they would have none of the 'multilateral nonsense' and advocated controlled and preferential trade.[86] Keynes tried to defuse the issue on 16 January in a letter to Clifford Clark, the Canadian Deputy Minister of Finance.

> To judge from the reports in the papers here, our good Mr Hudson has caused some disturbance of mind in Ottawa. Since this is a private and personal letter, and since I am not a civil servant, I may make bold to say that you should not take him unduly seriously. Particularly if he gave any impression that any Cabinet decisions had been reached already along the lines he was taking, he was misleading you. On the other hand, I would also add rather emphatically that neither must you treat his point of view too lightly. He represents an attitude of mind which has some support in the Cabinet and a good deal of support both in Parliament and the press. It is an attitude very difficult to upset until we have something better to offer in concrete terms, which, with the help of you in Canada and our friends in Washington, we hope to be able to produce in due course. Meanwhile, we are in dead water. This has many disadvantages and allows too freely the unchecked growth of half-informed opinion, but I doubt if there is any effective remedy at this stage.[87]

Even while Keynes's letter was crossing the Atlantic, the Canadians were in the process of trying to help matters forward, for while Hudson had been making his remarks, Graham Towers, the Governor of the Bank of Canada, had been preparing a memorandum, 'Post-war Commercial Policy Aspect: A Proposal for Averting a Breakdown in International Trade Relationships'. In it he argued that Britain would be unable to move towards more liberal trading policies without massive foreign assistance. A liberal régime was in Canada's interests, given her dependence on British markets. Towers proposed that Canada should offer Britain a credit of $1,200 million at 2 per cent for the three years after the end of the Japanese war, repayment beginning after ten years with a waiver if repayments would threaten Britain's international reserves. He also recommended that Canada and the United States should take over some of Britain's sterling area indebtedness and that some of the remaining balances be scaled down. In return Britain would commit herself to non-discrimination against Canadian goods on balance-of-payments grounds.

Towers's proposals were the subject of a meeting of Ministers and officials, which also considered Canada's Mutual Aid proposals for Stage II, on 18 January 1945. The upshot was an agreement that Canada should send Britain a series of telegrams on both subjects. Drafting these telegrams took some time, but on 23 February three forthright telegrams, two for the Dominions

Secretary and one for the Prime Minister, went off from Ottawa. The first dealt with Stage II and agreed to continue Mutual Aid during that period on the scale suggested by Keynes the previous November. But it also suggested that with the end of the war in Europe discrimination against Canadian exports would be 'unnecessary and inappropriate' and might make it difficult for Canada to continue Mutual Aid. The second telegram aired Towers's credit proposal in general terms without disclosing detailed figures and asked for an early discussion on transitional finance. The third from Mackenzie King to Churchill emphasised the importance of the previous messages.

London as usual reacted cautiously, largely because of the uncertainty as to how far Britain could go independently of the United States in the direction the Canadians desired. After a month the British sent an almost encouraging interim reply, suggesting that the Stage II issues should be pursued in Ottawa, while inviting a Canadian delegation to London to discuss transition. These London conversations took place in the second half of May.

By mid-March, after ten days' rest in Cambridge, Keynes tried again to limit the drift towards an unprepared beginning of the peace with another powerful memorandum. After official and Ministerial discussions in March and April, this went to the War Cabinet on 15 May 1945 under the title 'Overseas Financial Policy in Stage III'. Supplemented and amended by later memoranda, it was to serve as the focus of all subsequent discussions preparing for the Anglo-American financial negotiations which opened in Washington in September 1945.

At the centre of the memorandum was a daring scheme which would make the problem of sterling more tractable and secure American assistance for the transition. This scheme involved making currently earned sterling convertible within a year from the end of the war – in the spirit of Bretton Woods, but without Britain giving up her transitional rights under that agreement. American assistance, essential to the scheme's success, would, Keynes argued, be attracted by just these same provisions.

Keynes suggested that there were three possibilities on which Britain could base her Stage III policy: Starvation Corner (Austerity in the first draft), Temptation and Justice. All would have to start from the current position. On admittedly optimistic assumptions, Britain at the end of the Japanese war would be running an overseas deficit of the order of £1,400 million per annum; with successful economies from his continuing bugbear of political and military expenditure overseas and an intense export drive Britain might get through the first year of Stage III with a deficit of £1,000 million; and over the transition to equilibrium as a whole Britain would have a cumulative deficit of £2,000 million. If the most extravagant hopes became reality, a deficit exceeding £1,000 million would still occur. Among the assumptions that underlay his forecast was that the existing sterling/dollar exchange rate was appropriate, an assumption that even his critics accepted as plausible,[88] although Keynes wondered aloud whether Britain's outdated export industries could cope:

> Even the celebrated inefficiency of British manufacturers can scarcely (one hopes) be capable of offsetting over wide ranges of industry the whole of this initial cost difference in their favour, though, admittedly, they have managed it in some cases. . . . The available statistics suggest that, provided that we have never made the product before, we have the rest of the world licked on cost. For a Mosquito, a Lancaster, Radar, we should have the business at our feet in conditions of free and fair competition. It is when it comes to making a shirt or a steel billet that we have to admit ourselves beaten by both the dear labour of America and by the cheap labour of Asia and Europe. Shipbuilding seems to be the only traditional industry where we fully hold our own. If by some sad geographical slip the American Air Force (it is too late now to hope for much from the enemy) were to destroy every factory on the North-East coast and in Lancashire (at an hour when the directors were sitting there and no one else), we should have nothing to fear. How else we are to regain the exuberant inexperience which is necessary, it seems, for success, I cannot surmise.[89]

Given the size of Britain's prospective balance of payments deficit, he remarked, 'This is not a well-chosen moment for a declaration of our financial independence from North America'. Yet such a declaration was implied by the advocates of economic isolationism and planned bilateralism. Starvation Corner, as he named this option, would require intensified rationing and controls and the national direction and planning of foreign trade, while overseas it would entail the postponement of Colonial development and Far Eastern reconstruction as well as 'a virtual abandonment of all overseas activities, whether military or diplomatic or by way of developing our trade, wealth and influence, which involved any considerable expenditure'. Or, as he put it in a later paragraph, Britain would have to retire from the world, 'as Russia did between the wars, to starve and reconstruct'. Above all, because Starvation Corner would run counter to the professed desires of the United States and Canada for the post-war world, Britain would not be able to expect these nations to acquiesce. She would have to expect strong and active opposition, which, because the policy would disrupt the traditional operation of the sterling area, would probably succeed in persuading some sterling area countries to leave, as well as limiting the possibilities of active support for the policy from Western Europe and South America.

> In short, the moment at which we have lost our financial strength and owe vast sums all round the world is scarcely the bright and brilliant occasion for asking all our creditors to join up with us against where financial power rests, not for the purpose of getting paid, but for the purpose of obliging us with a little more.[90]

Despite his strictures on the folly of deliberately choosing Starvation Corner, Keynes, stepping with great skill among the arguments for a 'sterling area solution' for the transition, still left it open as a disagreeable option of last resort, if, for example, Britain had tried for the better, internationalist solution and been rebuffed by a United States where isolationists had come to power.

Having thus dismissed the most disagreeable option, Keynes turned to the remaining two, both of which involved a mixture of internationalism and substantial North American assistance. He put the amount of aid necessary during the transition at between $5,000 and $8,000 million (£1,250–2,000 million). *Temptation* would arise when the Americans offered to lend Britain large sums on their terms, which he admitted would not be unreasonable from an American perspective. Such terms might include a low rate of interest, easy repayments starting in, say, ten years with a waiver of repayments in difficult circumstances, free multilateral convertibility of currently earned sterling area earnings from the outset, possibly a similar condition for pre-zero-hour sterling balances, an implementation of Article VII ideals on American lines, and a generous settlement of Lend Lease. He thought that such an arrangement would probably be easy to negotiate, but he argued that there were strong objections. It would substitute dollar debt for sterling debt. It would be 'wrong' to make economic policy concessions for the sake of financial aid. It would involve Britain agreeing to possibly intolerably large annual interest and amortisation payments with the resulting 'chronic condition of having to make humiliating and embarrassing pleas for mercy and postponement'. More fundamentally, it would be 'an outrageous crown and conclusion of all that has happened': Britain would be left in the same position as Germany with a debt burden of $20 billion and the same need to plead for mercy and deferment. None the less, if *Justice* proved impossible, some mitigated form of Temptation might serve as a fallback.[91]

Now, what was this 'sweet breath of Justice between partners, in what has been a great and magnanimous enterprise carried to overwhelming success'? It demanded substantial assistance from Canada, the United States and the sterling area. In addition to eliminating debts from Lend Lease and Canadian Mutual Aid, this assistance would total some £3,100 million (a sum raised to £3,230 million in the second draft). A proportion would come from the cancellation of outstanding British obligations, but £2,175 million would represent new money to permit early convertibility. The arguments for such assistance came in three parts. First Britain would ask the United States for a grant of $3,000 million in respect of her purchases there before Lend Lease came into operation. With this gesture in hand, Britain could then approach sterling creditors with a more detailed and severe proposal than he had previously put forward – one that became more severe in his later version. Debts owed to non-sterling area countries were largely covered by arrangements already made with the countries concerned. Of the not so covered amount of £169 million, £107 million owed to Argentina and Brazil could be settled by disposing of British investments there, while the remainder could be reckoned as normal working balances. As for the larger amount of sterling debt, that owed to countries in the sterling area, on the assumption that these would exceed £3,000 million by the end of the war, Keynes proposed a programme of cancellations, funding and freeing in the amounts £880 million (£750 million in the first draft), £1,500 million and £750 million respectively. Such a programme had as its justification the same one that occurred in the American case, a more equal redistribution of the costs of the common effort, but Keynes also believed that the sterling Dominions had been 'profiteering' from the war – enjoying the benefits of British war expenditures although not contributing as much to the war effort. In the case of South Africa, 'which has made so far a notoriously inadequate contribution compared with any other member of the Commonwealth', there should be a retrospective gold contribution of £50 million. Any country which declined to come into the settlement would have the whole of its sterling balances funded at an interest rate of ½ per cent per annum and the principal would become available at a rate of 1 per cent per year after five years but only for the purchase of British exports.[92,1]

There was still a third part of Justice – an American credit of $5,000 million, with $500 million from Canada. These credits would be available during the first ten years after the war and would carry a 1 per cent rate of interest and a sinking fund of 1 per cent beginning ten years after the war and rising to 2 per cent after a further ten years.

Justice would relieve Britain of a significant amount of her war debts, while on the remainder the interest and sinking fund commitments would be manageable and allow her to start the peace with sufficient reserves and the assurance of additional North American assistance if that proved necessary. As Keynes remarked

[W]ith such a settlement as the above we could face the economic future without any serious anxiety – except the perennial one of knocking some energy and enterprise into our third-generation export industries and of organising the new industries which our first generation is well-qualified to construct if the capital and the organisation can be arranged.[93]

Underneath Keynes's proposals was the question of timing. When should the Anglo-American talks on Stage III begin? Keynes argued that September 1945 was the earliest practicable date. By then not only would the German war have ended, but the founding conference for the United Nations would have completed its work and the US Congress would have dealt with both

---

1 Those accepting the settlement would receive 1 per cent per annum interest on their funded balances and after five years 2 per cent per annum of the principal would become available for purchases of British exports.

the Bretton Woods plans and another Lend-Lease appropriation. The death of President Roosevelt on 12 April 1945 and the need to let the Truman Administration find its feet also pointed to some delay. Pointing the other way was the fact that the negotiations might be lengthy: Keynes even suggested the possibility of a breakdown in their early stages. But before the British could approach the Americans, they had to agree on the terms of their proposals.

During April and May, Keynes carried on an extensive correspondence with R. H. Brand, largely, but not exclusively, on how the scheme would go down with the Americans and how best and when to approach them. Brand's assessment of American opinion was not optimistic: he began his comments on Justice with the words, 'But in a situation like this I feel that the saying of the nigger that "There ain't no justice nowhere" is amply justified'.[94] He questioned the wisdom of basing the claim for the gift on retrospective payments for Britain's pre-Lend-Lease expenditures because it implied that the United States should have come into the war in 1939. Any argument implying that the United States had not played a full part in the war would be disastrous. Brand also worried about the effects of the US Treasury's propaganda favouring the Bretton Woods proposals, for much of the argument presented seemed to assume that if the Bretton Woods legislation passed there would be no need for further American assistance.[95] As the spring progressed, Brand also became increasingly worried about what seemed to be a growing run of post-war claims on American resources.[96] The net effect of American events and the trend of American opinion was to make him seriously pessimistic – a view shared by Frank Lee, who in a meeting in the Treasury on 29 May, said that he strongly doubted the feasibility of Justice.

Keynes did receive some encouragement. Before his Stage III paper received general ministerial circulation, the Chancellor allowed him to send a copy to Lords Beaverbrook and Cherwell. At an evening meeting with Bernard Baruch, which both he and Beaverbrook attended, Keynes suggested that they 'have a long quiet conversation . . . to see whether, after all, there is much more common ground than appears on the surface'. Beaverbrook agreed to talk after he had a chance to read the paper. The meeting took place on 19 April. From Keynes's report to Brand and from Beaverbrook's letter to Keynes the next day, the crucial last sentence of which is not quoted by A. J. P. Taylor, Beaverbrook's latest biographer, it would appear that Beaverbrook would favour the bargain embodied in Justice, if Britain could get it, even though it would involve concessions on issues of importance to him.[97]

Keynes's other encouragement came from the Canadian delegation that came to Britain to discuss the telegrams of 23 February. The opening stages of these discussions were beautifully managed by Keynes. The party arrived in London on Thursday 16 May. On Friday morning, they attended the reopening of the National Gallery, 'a symbol of the peace'.[98] For the Whitsun weekend that followed he invited them to King's. The party travelled up to Cambridge on Friday afternoon and had a quiet dinner in Hall. Serious business started in the Audit Room on Saturday, Keynes emphasising that 'everything that was said [was] . . . highly unofficial – partly a personal, partly a Treasury view of the questions at issue' and presenting the substance of his Stage III paper which had gone to the War Cabinet two weeks before.[99] Douglas LePan, the secretary to the Canadian delegation, remembered,

> When Keynes opened the meeting, it seemed to me like a great conductor taking over. He had in front of him a Treasury print, which I saw later and which ran to more than 150 pages, containing not only his own crucial paper on the choices facing the United Kingdom but also much supporting material. That was his score for the meeting, but he very seldom consulted it – only occasionally for a stray figure or detail, but that was all. He would turn the pages, as a conductor would. But it was clear that everything he said was coming out of his head, out of his knowledge and mastery of the subject. . . . I have never listened to so fine a forensic performance. . . . Keynes's [argument], although it was necessarily heavily weighted with figures, often soared and fluttered and hovered, was bright with fancy, was variously inflected. It was more contrapuntal, had many more themes, was more orchestral. Yet it was conducted without Keynes ever raising his voice very far or his hands. Indeed they were often hidden.[100]

Keynes's exposition of his paper occupied all the time for business on the Saturday. Then came the Canadian comments. These were generally supportive, as both parties agreed on the ultimate goal of an internationalist solution. The Canadians thought that the mixture of a grant and loan might be difficult to get, unless the grant were linked to the highest political and economic objectives, possibly even territorial adjustments, since the Americans were 'shy of acting as a permanent Christmas tree'.[101] However, when Keynes, half playfully, suggested that the Canadians might prefer to accumulate sterling instead of lending dollars, he got courteous silence.

The rest of the weekend was spent on less grand, but still important, matters largely connected with the Mutual Aid arrangements for Stage II but also including the Canadian request that Britain should not discriminate against Canadian exports to the sterling area – a matter on which, after some hesitation, the British gave way a week after the Cambridge meetings.

It was not all work in Cambridge. Keynes had arranged that, as Monday was not a work day, both groups could remain in King's. On Saturday there was a formal lunch in King's which included the Provost of King's, the Master of Trinity and Mrs Trevelyan, the Master of John's and Mrs Benians and a sampling of Cambridge economists – Sir John Clapham, Dennis

Robertson, Joan and Austin Robinson. There was also time for visits to the Arts Theatre on Saturday evening for *Dombey and Son* and on Sunday for a Fauré centenary string quartet concert. The surroundings and the subject matter came together. After dinner one evening the party walked over the river to King's Fellows' Garden:

> It was a fine mild May evening and many of the bushes and trees were in bloom. I was amazed at the variety of colours and textures in the branches and at the variety of species – beeches, chestnuts, oaks, firs, cedars, limes – with islands cut in the lawn for shrubs and bushes. . . .
>
> As we walked about the garden paths, seemingly remote from the world, one of the Canadians, I think it was Bill Mackintosh, was moved to remark in admiration how beautiful it all was. Keynes, who was only a step or two behind, hesitated for only a moment and then said: 'Yes, it is beautiful, isn't it? And we want to keep it, you know. That is why you are here!'[102]

In spite of these encouragements, British preparations for Stage III did not get much closer to a decision, in part because of a forthcoming British General Election: Labour left the Coalition and on 23 May Churchill formed a Caretaker Government to hold office until the results of the election scheduled for 5 July were known. Much of the Anglo-American 'agreement' over Stage II seemed to be disappearing. In March 1945 Congress renewed the Lend-Lease Act, only with qualifications that funds under the programme should not be used for relief, rehabilitation or reconstruction and that the programme should end with the war. On V-E Day, when Stage II began, President Truman, accepting the advice of Leo Crowley and Joseph C. Grew, and without consulting the US Treasury, signed an order authorising the Foreign Economic Administration and the State Department 'to take joint action to cut back Lend Lease supplies'.[103] Crowley duly embargoed shipments to the Soviet Union and other European nations. There were protests. Some supplies were restored, but the Quebec understandings and the Morgenthau–Keynes settlement were dead: the level of Britain's external reserves had become a bargaining point again.[104] Military supplies under Lend Lease were restricted to the war against Japan: supplies for occupation forces in Europe were excluded. In June, the Continuation Act formally restricted Lend Lease to supplies needed directly against Japan. It was left to Churchill to raise the issue of the disparity between past promises and present performance with President Truman at Potsdam. Against this background the Treasury began its serious Stage III planning.

The Treasury discussions centred on the major issues: the overall approach to the immediate post-war problems; the type of American aid that would be acceptable; and the scope for convertibility with its implications for sterling balances and the sterling area. Some officials shared Keynes's frequently expressed view that too easy a flow of dollars might impair Britain's recovery by encouraging too relaxed an approach to her problems. The Bank of England was doubtful about Keynes's two-pronged approach for American assistance, suggesting instead an itemised claim for retrospective Lend Lease (about whose chances of success Keynes was not optimistic) and a secured credit, where the alternative to repayment would be the forfeit of collateral assets or the cession of territory such as West Indian islands (Jamaica being a favourite candidate).

As for the sterling area, the Bank of England continued to oppose any uniform solution for sterling balances largely on the grounds that the countries involved differed so much from each other. It also disagreed over the timing of the sterling area negotiations: did one give them priority and gamble on American aid or work in reverse order?

Within the Treasury Sir Wilfrid Eady collaborated with R. W. B. Clarke to produce what appeared to be a fallback 'Plan II' but what was in many respects a counterproposal reflecting the unease Eady felt about Keynes's proposals.[105] Plan II was an exploration of the implications of Starvation Corner. It was founded on greater pessimism than Keynes's as to the shape of the post-war world. Although Britain should open with a declaration that the British Government would co-operate with the establishment of an International Trade Organisation and recommend to Parliament adherence to the Bretton Woods institutions, their basic negotiating framework would be straightforwardly protective, contemplating an extended period of discriminatory trade and currency controls. The sterling area might be extended to include the French, Dutch and Belgian empires.

Keynes was not impressed with Plan II. He told its authors:

What these figures show, to express the substance of what in his #2 Sir W. Eady says in another way, is that, if a tidal wave were to overwhelm North and South America, our subsequent financial problems would not be too bad and nothing worse than starvation would supervene.

They do not help me with my essential difficulty which is as follows:

If, having failed to get financial assistance from U.S.A., our overall adverse balance of trade remains as before, from which countries can we expect to borrow what we have failed to obtain from U.S.A.? Deprived of the free use of their existing sterling resources, most of the countries suggested for the sterling group cannot expect to have an over-all favourable balance after the war out of which they can lend to us. Indeed, half the problem is that they also will have a large adverse balance with the Americans.

That is why I put the essence of the situation in the following form. If we have an overall adverse balance of trade, Plan II will not work. If we have not, any plan will work.

My next difficulty is that I see no prospect of the proposed members of the sterling group accepting membership of the club under Plan II conditions. They have everything to lose by doing so and nothing to gain. . . . What motive have they to rupture trade relations with U.S.A. in order to lend us money they have not got?[106]

Keynes's derisive queries did not by themselves result in Eady's retreating from Plan II. Rather, warnings from Brand that an extension of the sterling area might produce a strongly adverse reaction in the United States and reports from the Ministries of Supply and Food of the difficulties involved in Plan II seem to have done so. But the existence of Plan II, along with Eady's and Clarke's continuing affection for their creation, was to complicate later discussions.

During the summer, Keynes modified his own views in a series of memoranda.[107] First, he dropped the notion of trying to obtain $3,000 million in retrospective Lend Lease – largely, one suspects because he had become convinced that setting aside this sum in an explicit way would have unfavourable effects in the United States. He now aimed at a sum smaller than the original $8,000 million: on 23 July he dropped it to $4,000 million, but he later raised it to $5,000 million. He still thought in terms of a grant-in-aid, although by August 1945 he was prepared to entertain a credit whose terms were 'no more than a camouflage for what would be in effect a grant-in-aid'.[108] This to some extent reflected a lower estimated transitional deficit, but it also probably reflected his repeatedly expressed view that Britain could get along with sums smaller than those he had mentioned in the spring and his recurrent worry that Britain could not be trusted with too much money.[109]

With the smaller sum came a consequential redrafting of the sterling area arrangements. The amount of sterling that would be released dropped by two-thirds (from £750 million to £250 million and in September 1945 to £200 million). Further, the amount of sterling balances scheduled for cancellation rose to £1,000 million. Blocked balances would receive no interest, relieving the British balance of payments of £10–15 million per year. Once the balances were released, interest would be payable at the Treasury bill rate. Overall, the treatment of overseas holders of sterling promised to be more severe than earlier, perhaps reducing the incentives to enter the scheme, as the consequences of staying out remained the same as before.

Thirdly, there were changes in the convertibility option, perhaps because Keynes had become convinced that there would be adequate scope for trade and exchange controls under IMF rules.[110] At one point – in July – Keynes was prepared to go so far as to accept the convertibility obligations of the Fund (Article VIII) and renounce the transitional protection available under Article XIV. This suggestion disappeared under Bank of England prodding to become more restrictive: released sterling balances would merely be 'available' while new accruals would be convertible in the Bretton Woods sense.[111]

Meanwhile outside circumstances changed. The British General Election after the end of the European war did not return the Conservatives under Churchill. In the third Labour Government Hugh Dalton replaced Anderson at the Treasury, Ernest Bevin replaced Eden at the Foreign Office and Stafford Cripps replaced Lyttleton at the Board of Trade. The skeleton of the new administration was announced on 28 July before Attlee returned to the four-power Potsdam Conference on post-war political and economic arrangements with Ernest Bevin. On 6 August the Americans dropped an atomic bomb on Hiroshima. Five days later a second fell on Nagasaki. On 14 August the Japanese accepted the Allied terms of surrender. The opening of the new Parliament coincided with V-J Day, something that most of the Stage III planning had not anticipated for at least another year. On 17 August, on the advice of Crowley, President Truman decided that the law required that Lend Lease end. On 20 August, the decision was communicated to Britain and the next day it was made public. Stage III had begun.

NOTES

1 Sayers 1956, 254–5, 273–4.
2 *JMK*, XXIII, 265–76.
3 *JMK*, XXIII, 280.
4 Sayers 1956, 258.
5 *JMK*, XXIII, 328–31.
6 Barnes and Nicholson (eds) 1988, 822.
7 Ibid., 824.
8 *JMK*, XXIII, 330.
9 *JMK*, XXIII, 333; Sayers 1956, 261 n. 4.
10 Sayers 1956, 270.
11 Barnes and Nicholson (eds) 1988, 899.
12 Sayers 1956, 262.
13 Above p. 724.
14 Above pp. 731–4.
15 The memorandum appears in *JMK*, XXIV, 1–18.
16 For a discussion of these forecasts see Pressnell 1987, appendix 27.
17 Pressnell 1987, 227.
18 *JMK*, XXIV, 34–65.
19 *JMK*, XXIV, 34–5.
20 *JMK*, XXIV, 37.
21 *JMK*, XXIV, 42.
22 *JMK*, XXIV, 45.
23 *JMK*, XXIV, 55–6.
24 *JMK*, XXIV, 63.
25 *JMK*, XXIV, 65.
26 Pressnell 1987, 164; see above p. 744.
27 Sayers 1956, 469.
28 Blum 1967, III, 308–10; *JMK*, XXIV, 203.
29 Keynes's Canadian paper appears in *JMK*, XXIV, 76–97. His comment appears in ibid., 100.
30 KCKP, JMK to FAK, 7 and 14 August 1944; see also *JMK*, XXIV, 105–6.

31 Above pp. 653–4.
32 *JMK*, XXV, 9–10. Prior to this, in his November 1939 'Notes on the War for the President' he had touched on the matter of the peace terms in a very preliminary way (*JMK*, XXII, 27–8).
33 *JMK*, XXVII, 329–30.
34 *JMK*, XXVI, 334.
35 Pimlott (ed.) 1986, 490, 516.
36 Cairncross 1986, 20.
37 *JMK*, XXVI, 341–6.
38 For a wider summary of contemporary British discussions see Cairncross 1986.
39 The paper appears in *JMK*, XXVI, 337–41; the quoted phrase appears on page 339.
40 *JMK*, XXVI, 352, 355, 358.
41 *JMK*, XXVI, 360, 365–6.
42 Above pp. 723–31.
43 *JMK*, XXVI, 347.
44 Pimlott (ed.) 1986, 516. As well, the Malkin Report's crucial assumption that Germany would not be dismembered had not been discussed by ministers (Cairncross 1986, 33).
45 Woodward 1962, 449.
46 Blum, 1967 III, 534.
47 FDRL, Morgenthau Diaries, vol. 764, 90.
48 FDRL, Morgenthau Diaries, vol. 764, 554–5.
49 *JMK*, XXVI, 374.
50 Rees 1974, 253.
51 Woodward 1962, 475.
52 Blum 1967, III, 369.
53 Ibid., III, 350–1, 353, 354–5.
54 Woodward 1962, 476.
55 Ibid., 476; Blum 1967, III, 371.
56 Ibid., III, 373–4; Rees 1974, 272–3, 277–9; Woodward 1962, 477.
57 Above pp. 749–50.
58 *JMK*, XXVI, 314–17.
59 *JMK*, XXIV, 114–26.
60 *JMK*, XXIV, 125–6.
61 *JMK*, XXIV, 116, 122, 123.
62 *JMK*, XXIV, 133.
63 *JMK*, XXIV, 139.
64 *JMK*, XXIV, 133–4.
65 *JMK*, XXVI, 377. Keynes's comments are in ibid., 380–2.
66 *JMK*, XXIV, 183–4; *FRUS*, 1944, III, 79.
67 Penrose 1953, 275–6.
68 *JMK*, XXVI, 383.
69 *JMK*, XXIV, 195–6.
70 Blum 1967, III, 308 ff.
71 *JMK*, XXIV, 213.
72 Blum 1967, 319–21; Dallek 1979, 475, 477–8.
73 *JMK*, XXIV, 213, 204, 216–19.
74 *JMK*, XXIV, 219.
75 *JMK*, XXIV, 157–8. For the drift of the lecture, see ibid., 162–4.
76 *JMK*, XXIV, 167.

77 *JMK*, XXIV, 188.
78 For the crisis see Dawson 1961; Pickersgill and Forster (eds) 1968, II, chapters V–VII.
79 *JMK*, XXIV, 192–223. Parts of this paper have been quoted in my discussion of the negotiations.
80 *JMK*, XXVII, 380–1; XXIV, 225–7; XXII, 461–8.
81 *JMK*, XXII, 472–7; 421–31.
82 *JMK*, XXVI, 320–3; XXVII, 275–6; see above pp. 465, 715, 750–3.
83 Howson and Moggridge (eds) 1990a, 30; PRO, T231/156, Minutes of Meeting of 9 January 1945.
84 *JMK*, XXIV, 253.
85 Rosenman 1952, 241; see also *JMK*, XXIV, 255.
86 LePan 1979, 66–7.
87 *JMK*, XXIV, 232–3.
88 Clarke 1982, 52, 123.
89 *JMK*, XXIV, 262.
90 *JMK*, XXIV, 271, 275, 272.
91 *JMK*, XXIV, 276, 278, 277.
92 *JMK*, XXIV, 279, 268–9, 289.
93 *JMK*, XXIV, 289–90.
94 *JMK*, XXIV, 307.
95 *JMK*, XXIV, 309; Gardner 1956, 139–40.
96 *JMK*, XXIV, 322, 332–3.
97 *JMK*, XIV, 327, 328; Taylor 1972, 563.
98 PRO T236/31, JMK to F. Harmer, 14 May 1945. The Gallery's paintings had been stored during the war in a Welsh mine.
99 PRO T236/31, Notes of Discussions.
100 LePan 1979, 79.
101 Ibid., 93.
102 Ibid., 95–6.
103 Blum 1967, III, 447.
104 Ibid., III, 449.
105 See, for example, his interventions in the Cambridge discussions (LePan 1979, 92–3). For the Plan II memorandum see Clarke 1982, 126–35.
106 *JMK*, XXIV, 366.
107 Keynes's papers were 'The Present Overseas Financial Position of the U.K.', 20 July 1945 (revised 13 August) and 'Our Overseas Financial Prospects', 13 August 1945 (*JMK*, XXIV, 377–98, 398–411).
108 *JMK*, XXIV, 409.
109 *JMK*, XXIV, 344.
110 *JMK*, XXVI, 183–5.
111 *JMK*, XXIV, 392.

30

THE LOAN

How differently things appear in Washington than in London.
(Keynes to the House of Lords, 18 December 1945,
JMK, XXIV, 606)

As you may suppose, it was a very severe strain. For the first eight or nine weeks I was extremely well – provided I did not walk anywhere, scarcely conscious of physical deficiencies. . . . In the last few weeks, however, when I was conducting a war on two fronts and suffering the greatest responsibilities and irritations, I began to give way. Every two or three days, when there was something particularly annoying or tiring, symptoms would appear which made Lydia very cross. Whenever my emotions caused a discharge of adrenalin, it was more than the old heart could comfortably manage. So, in addition to the ice-bag, I took to spending as many hours out of twenty-four as practicable in a horizontal position.
(KCKP, JMK to J. Plesch, 5 January 1946)

The unexpected, swift end to the war and to Lend Lease meant that the new Labour Ministers and their officials had to make a number of decisions quickly. They had to decide what to do about supplies: the end of Lend Lease stopped loading, but what did one do about goods in transit or in stock, all of which would be included in the final Lend Lease settlement? The people still needed to be fed and the factories needed raw materials. Whitehall also had to decide what to do about payment for goods in the pipeline or in stock: the Foreign Economic Administration's suggested terms for these in August 1945 were payment over 30 years at $2\frac{3}{8}$ per cent.

Fortunately, unless one believes that his presence in Washington would have prevented or delayed Truman's decision, Will Clayton, the US Under-Secretary of State for Economic Affairs was in London for a meeting of UNRRA at the termination of Lend Lease. On representations from him and from the British Treasury Delegation in Washington, the termination terms were modified: Lend-Lease services for shipping would remain for a time; fresh civilian supply contracts could go through the Lend-Lease machinery for 60 days (later extended to the end of February 1946) on a cash reimbursement basis; pipeline goods and stocks would be financed 'on terms to be mutually agreed'.

Clayton's presence in London, along with that of Harry Hawkins of the State Department and Emilio Collado of the Treasury had also given British officials another chance to discuss informally post-war commercial policy and Stage III. It was clear from these discussions that the winding up of Lend Lease would necessarily involve formal commercial policy discussions, whereas the British wanted to concentrate on financial issues together with the Lend-Lease settlement.[1] It was also clear that the Americans were thinking in terms of a credit of at most $3,000 million. Now it was up to Ministers to make the decisions.

The critical meeting took place late in the evening of 23 August 1945. Present were the Prime Minister (Clement Attlee), the Chancellor (Hugh Dalton), the Foreign Secretary (Ernest Bevin), the President of the Board of Trade (Stafford Cripps), the Secretary of State for India (Lord Pethick-Lawrence), as well as the Ambassador to Washington (Lord Halifax) who was to head the mission with Keynes, R. H. Brand, five senior officials and Keynes.[2] Significantly, there were no Bank of England representatives or Board of Trade officials present. The Prime Minister asked Keynes to open the discussion. Keynes suggested that the negotiators be given no discretion and that the negotiations be *ad referendum*. His proposals followed the lines of recent discussions with one important change – that the negotiating team not be authorised to accept anything other than a grant-in-aid of $4 to 5 billion (including what was necessary to clear up Lend Lease). Keynes did not expect a grant, which was rather a benchmark: he had recognised a week earlier that the form of assistance was a matter of 'extreme difficulty', and at the evening meeting he admitted that the nature and terms of the financial assistance 'would constitute the greatest stumbling block'. Although he advised Ministers not to decide in favour of terms worse than a grant 'except after very long thought', he refused – on the grounds that 'he had been rather pushed off this in the course of discussion' – to support Sir Stafford Cripps's suggestion to go straight for a grant and to stand on that line.[3]

As a *quid pro quo* for a grant-in-aid and a satisfactory settlement for Lend Lease, Keynes proposed that Britain handle sterling balances along the lines contemplated earlier with general convertibility for released balances. The Government could safely advise Parliament to accept the Bretton Woods proposals 'provided that they were not coupled with dangerous concessions under the heading of commercial policy'. His expectations on commercial policy were also optimistic. He thought that Britain would not be asked to sign a detailed Treaty but only to join with an American invitation to an international conference in 1946, and that Britain might gain 'reasonable satisfaction' on the major outstanding issues – preferences, state trading, import programming, and American attempts to tighten up the provisions for exchange control in the Fund Articles of Agreement. Finally there was the possibility of a 'sweetener' in the form of cession of an island or islands in the West Indies.

After Brand, emphasising the danger of leaks, suggested Britain should not ask outright for a grant-in-aid but should develop her strong case for assistance and let the Americans propose terms, Ministers agreed with Keynes's recommendations. From the minutes of the meeting, it is hard to believe Dalton's later allegation that Keynes was 'almost starry eyed' or Harrod's suggestion that he painted too rosy a picture and ignored possible 'strings'.[4] To his friends he wrote 'This is the toughest mission yet, and I need your prayers' or 'I am off on the toughest mission yet with very moderate hopes indeed of sufficient success. But it is big game I shall be after'.[5]

Keynes left London on the morning of 27 August, accompanied by Lydia, and two members of the mission, Frederic Harmer of the Treasury, a former pupil of Keynes's in King's, and Edward Hall-Patch of the Foreign Office. At Southampton they boarded the *Pasteur*, which was carrying 4,000 homeward-bound Canadian troops, and were underway by 1.30. Off the Nab Light in the Channel the *Pasteur* passed HMS *Onslough* which signalled 'Best of luck to you and your distinguished passenger'. According to Harmer, 'M. purred'. The trip was enjoyable and restful. On 30 August, Harmer noted its effects on Keynes:

> M. is enjoying the trip and the rest and as a result is very – possibly over – confident. But he has an incredible capacity for quick adaptation. At present he is more than half persuaded that we shall find a pretty good atmosphere in Washington. I doubt it.[6]

The party landed at Quebec City on 1 September and flew on to Ottawa the next day.

In Ottawa, the team from London met with the High Commissioner and some of his officials as well as with Frank Lee and Ken Goschen, who had just come up from Washington. They discussed not only the Canadian position – which looked 'relatively plain sailing' – but also the Washington situation – which looked 'like being a very stormy passage'.

> Frank [Lee] commenting on Truman's handling of the whole L/L episode said the current cliché was that he shoots from the hip. M. said he preferred to describe it as dropping bricks from the hip.[7]

The next morning Keynes tried his Stage III ideas out on the Canadian Finance Minister and a group of senior officials – including W. A. Mackintosh, R. B. Bryce, Graham Towers, Louis Rasminsky, Norman Robertson and Hector McKinnon. In the afternoon, he talked commercial policy with

Norman Robertson and Hector McKinnon before joining the team for a dinner thrown by the Minister of Finance, J. L. Ilsley. The following days saw the same pattern of Delegation meetings and Anglo-Canadian discussions, with the British team throwing a return dinner for nineteen at the High Commissioner's residence on 4 September, before Keynes, Lydia and Hall-Patch left by train for Washington. Harmer followed by air the next morning.

In these Washington negotiations, Keynes would face a mixture of old and new faces. The chairman of the American team was Fred Vinson, the new Secretary of the Treasury. Keynes had met him at Bretton Woods. A conservative Democrat, he set high store on discovering the popular will and turning it into policy. With Morgenthau's departure from the Treasury, Harry White's star was waning, but he was still Vinson's most important adviser – and White was not as sympathetic to Britain's needs as, say, E. M. Bernstein and Ansel Luxford, both of whom he excluded from the technical committee to advise on Britain's financial position. The vice-chairman of the American team was Will Clayton, with whom the British had been dealing for some time. Clayton, a self-made man and passionate proponent of free enterprise and free trade, was determined to link financial aid to a reduction in trade and exchange restrictions. Yet like Dean Acheson, now Under-Secretary of State, he was sympathetic to Britain's plight. In the early stages of the negotiations Leo Crowley, head of the Foreign Economic Administration, was still active. '[O]ur Tammany Polonius' Keynes had called him the previous year.[8] Generally known as the Baboon by the British in Washington after Keynes remarked that his face reminded him of the 'buttocks of a baboon', Crowley inspired the code name for the major series of cables for the negotiations (BABOON from London to Washington, NABOB from Washington to London).[9] He was not known for his sympathy towards Britain's needs. Finally on the American side there was Marriner Eccles, the chairman of the Federal Reserve Board, who was broadly sympathetic to the case Britain would put, if somewhat unfriendly. All were working against a background of opinion that was indifferent to foreign affairs and anxious to return to normal at home, which meant an end to wartime restrictions and reductions in taxation.

On his arrival in Washington, Keynes was still optimistic. Indeed, he thought 'the atmosphere . . . rather too good', adding, without knowing how true it would be this time, 'One's experience in Washington has always been that when things look beastliest all will be glowing three months hence, and vice versa'.[10] His Ottawa talks had gone well – so well that, on the basis of a conversation with Graham Towers, he was moving to the view that the 'ideal plan' would be to go for his proposal of the previous spring, a grant of $3 billion and a credit of $5 billion. He also seemed to believe that Harry White was thinking along the lines of an interest-free 50-year credit of up to

$5 billion. Finally, he believed that Crowley's position in the Administration was deteriorating rapidly so that the Lend-Lease settlement could well be better than the 3(c) terms on which Crowley continued to insist.[11]

On 11 September the two Delegations had their first meeting to organise the negotiations. At the centre was a Top or Steering Committee. Below this there were a number of committees on the detailed subjects of the negotiations – finance, Lend Lease, commercial policy, military supplies, etc. In addition to servicing this committee structure, the British Delegation would have its hands full co-ordinating its activities and keeping London informed. On top of the formal committee and Delegation meetings, there were inevitably numerous private contacts and informal conversations.

On 12 September, the British held a press conference at the Embassy. After a short speech by the Ambassador, Keynes delivered 'brilliantly' a statement which had been prepared and vetted the same morning.

> He contrived to make it sound both dramatic and spontaneous and though he stuck strictly to his draft . . . it sounded amazingly spontaneous.[12]

He touched on Britain's war weariness, her post-war transitional balance of payments problem and the sterling balances. He then turned to the alternative possible approaches to the transition – the go it alone or the co-operative – and stated the British preference for working with the United States. Although he said little about the terms of co-operation, he emphasised the disadvantages of a loan on 'more or less commercial terms' and that Britain would prefer 'to do what we can to get on as best we can on any other lines which are open to us'. In answering reporters' questions, he went to great lengths to avoid alluding to any proposals which Britain might make. The whole business lasted 1¼ hours before the Ambassador brought things to a close and provided welcome drinks.

The next day, in the Board Room of the Federal Reserve, Keynes began to present the British case to the Anglo-American Top Committee. He started with Britain's general financial position, taking the line by now familiar to his colleagues and some of the Americans. His first session described the bleak balance of payments prospects with a cumulative deficit of the order of $6 billion, half of it in 1946. This took almost 2½ hours. The next afternoon, he continued his exposition for almost three hours, setting out Britain's war-weakened international balance sheet and emphasising the size of the sterling balances problem. Finally on 17 September, he concluded by stressing the post-war consequences of Britain's intensive concentration on the war effort and took advantage of information he had recently gained from Nicholas Kaldor – then a member of the Strategic Bombing Survey – who in the course of interviews with Albert Speer had found that the German concentration on the war effort and limitation of civilian consumption compared unfavourably with Britain's.

So far so good, although there was little American reaction to Keynes's statement of Britain's position beyond a comment by Clayton on the American perception of a difference between Lend Lease and the assistance given by the overseas sterling area countries – a hint that further American assistance might be linked to Britain's treatment of the balances – and a suggestion, again from Clayton, that some standards of living might have improved in Britain during the war.[13] Questioning became pointed when, on 19 and 20 September, Keynes began discussing the possible options open to Britain.

The first of these two meetings in 'a somewhat frigid atmosphere' did not go 'at all well', as Harmer reported, for Keynes, given his instructions that the British were not to make proposals, was 'skating very delicately and cautiously round the whole subject – rather overdoing it perhaps'.[14] Even Keynes was unhappy with the meeting, although he cheered up in the afternoon when Harry White told him that he did not think things were going badly.[a] The next day, in response to a request from Vinson to be more explicit as to the details and orders of magnitude involved in suggesting that Britain would cancel, fund and release wartime sterling balances, Keynes had to get down to brass tacks and reveal that he was thinking in terms of cancelling $4 billion, blocking $7,200 million (at no interest, with release in equal instalments over 50 years starting after 5 years) and releasing $800 million. Similar pressure brought out a statement of the amount of aid that Britain was seeking – $5 billion, exclusive of the Lend-Lease settlement. This sum would probably suffice, even given the risks in the commitments he had mentioned at the previous meeting – minimising import controls, ending the existing limitations on the convertibility of current sterling area overseas earnings and undertaking to bring into force for Britain the major part of the IMF Articles of Agreement and ceasing to take the protection of the transitional period arrangements under Article XIV.[15]

After five days of exposition before the Top and Finance Committees, Keynes had still received no important comments from the Americans except that they stressed the role a contribution by the sterling area could play in gaining American assistance. He thought that the Americans might even make assistance conditional on such a contribution. What had gone wrong?

To some extent it may have been the 'running in' period Keynes had suggested would be necessary. In any long, complex set of negotiations, it would take time for the participants to sort out negotiating positions, a process complicated in this case by the constant changes in the American team, especially on the Lend-Lease side, as post-war departures from government service took their toll. But ministers in London had also made a serious tactical mistake

a Two days earlier, White had warned Keynes 'that things will be pretty sticky for a bit and he mustn't lose his temper except at the right moments' (Harmer Diary, 17 September 1945, 24).

in not including commercial policy specialists in the original team, although they had attached a Board of Trade official to the team at the last moment. During his meetings in London in August Clayton had emphasised that it was 'essential that we discuss both finance and trade simultaneously' and that an understanding on trade would have to *precede* a request to Congress for financial aid.[16] Keynes saw trade and aid as being linked but thought that they could be kept separate in the initial stages of the financial talks. In Washington the Americans were 'in considerable distress' that senior commercial policy experts had not come. At the urgings of the President of the Board of Trade, the British asked for time to prepare for the negotiations, but to no avail.

At this point, James Meade, who had not seemed alarmed after the initial meeting of Ministers, commented in his diary:

> Keynes has really excelled himself. He got himself sent to Washington without the commercial policy boys ... on the grounds that the mission was solely a financial one. He has now got set up in Washington an Anglo-American committee to discuss commercial policy which he proposes to conduct himself, having at the last moment in England (while Liesching and Robbins were on leave) more or less sold to Ministers the crazy, lunatic, self-contradictory idea that we should join with America in a general convention to reduce trade obstacles all round but should maintain completely unfettered rights to programme (i.e. to restrict) our imports *ad infinitum* to any extent we desire.[17]

Robbins and Liesching were influential in reconciling London to the situation.[18] Keynes received instructions not to discuss commercial policy until a team arrived from London. He was 'very angry but took it well'.[19] The additions to the team, eight experts including Robbins and Liesching, were strong ones. They arrived in Washington on 27 September, quickly established good relations with Keynes and opened talks with the Americans on 1 October. However, the wait for people who should have been in Washington from the outset slowed the momentum of the negotiations.

The day after the commercial policy team arrived in Washington, Leo Crowley resigned. His resignation appears to have had nothing to do with the negotiations, but this additional change in personnel further complicated matters, as perhaps did the reaction of the British press to Crowley's departure, for they saw it largely in terms of the negotiations and the welcome disappearance of someone who was not a friend of Britain.[20]

By the time Liesching's team had arrived, Keynes's discussions with Clayton and Vinson had convinced him that 'a straight grant-in-aid of five billion is not on the map'. He had even started 'to be inclined to think it absurd to believe otherwise'. But, as Robbins, fresh from London continued:

> I perceive that we shall have great difficulty in dehypnotising London; and I think that Maynard will have to be told that, having himself made

the magic passes that now hold the King's Treasurers entranced in rapturous contemplation of ideal 'justice', it will be up to him, sooner or later, to use quite special arts to reverse the process and bring them back to considering soberly nice questions of more or less day-to-day convenience and expediency.

I am afraid it is going to be the monetisation of Unitas all over again, this time with perhaps even more incongruous consequences.[21]

Keynes had already started to persuade London to consider alternatives. In a letter and memorandum to the Chancellor on 26 September, he set out various possible schemes which would keep the costs of servicing an American obligation within tolerable limits. On 1 October he asked for permission to discuss these alternatives more freely and stated that, if ministers insisted on a grant-in-aid, they would have to face a possible breakdown in negotiations.[22] Nevertheless, he was still prepared to entertain the outside possibility that some part of the assistance might take the form of a grant-in-aid, thus probably encouraging London to persist in its efforts to obtain just that. The difficulties of persuading London were also exacerbated by the fact that, with Keynes away, the main burden of advising the Chancellor fell on Sir Wilfrid Eady, whose instinctive reactions were more restrictionist and anti-Article VII than Keynes's and who was considerably more scared than Keynes of the difficulties of servicing any American debt.[23,b]

Ministers were not prepared to give Keynes much freedom in initiating bargaining over terms. They would not accept a large loan at, say, 2 per cent. They would prefer to borrow for absolutely necessary imports and the Lend-Lease clean-up on Export–Import Bank 3(c) terms which were more expensive. They hankered for at least some grant-in-aid of, say, $2 billion and a line of credit of $3 to $4 billion at 1 per cent. If this failed, they would accept as a last resort interest and amortisation commitments of up to $100 million a year, subject to a waiver clause for balance of payments difficulties.

On this basis, Keynes continued his talks. His health, despite the heavy workload, remained fairly good. He had a slight heart attack on 6 October and Lydia was obviously worrying about him, but he had the resilience to recover quickly with rest. By 17 October, however, he was beginning to look 'very grey around the eyes'.[24] His relations with the Americans were under some strain, largely because he and Vinson found it hard to get along. On 8 October, Robbins reported that during a meeting on cartels,

We had one alarming incident when Maynard who was in a very benevolent mood released one of his ironical gibes about American lawyers and rubbed Vinson up the wrong way. For a moment it was like a bedroom scene in a Noel Coward play. Vinson, who is a very

b As Keynes put it on 26 September, a payment to the United States of $100 million would represent less than 2 per cent of Britain's prospective overseas earnings. 'Either we can manage this or we are sunk anyhow.' (*JMK*, XXIV, 505).

emotional creature, completely lost control of himself and shouted at the top of his voice. Fortunately it proved possible to cut in with a remark which turned the discussion into other channels. But it was very disquieting while it lasted.[25]

By 16 October, Harmer reported: 'M. was tired and rather irritable. He and Harry get on admirably, but V. evidently doesn't like him and one or two remarks went down badly'.

While the financial negotiations proceeded in a rather desultory way during the first half of October, the commercial policy talks made rapid progress. This reflected the desire on both sides to clear the path for the financial settlement; the fact that negotiations involved understandings, still with reservations, about broad principles subject to a future international conference rather than firm immediate commitments embodied in an international agreement; and Liesching's careful preparations and negotiating skills. Once the negotiators had agreed to leave the issue of Imperial Preference for a later British proposal, they quickly reached agreement on the approach to calling a trade conference, export taxes, state trading, subsidies and exchange controls, while views on cartels were coming together. Thus the way was clear for the financial negotiations.[26]

Early in October, there were still several proposals in the air, including a 'rather fascinating contraption' of Harry White's to deal with the funded portion of sterling balances. Sterling area countries could discount their funded London balances for dollars and Britain would owe the resulting interest-free sum to the United States, as well as the proceeds of a direct long-term credit.[27] After stirring up British interest for almost ten days, the White scheme proved to have been a non-starter. Moreover, it became clear that the $5 billion in assistance, which Keynes had assumed to be a central part of American thinking, was above the figure that they were contemplating, perhaps partly because Britain's emphasis on her inability to pay more than a small annual amount had led the Americans to think in terms of working from this amount to its capitalised sum on their 'semi-commercial' terms. When Halifax and Keynes met Vinson and Clayton on 18 October, the American proposal was for $3,500 million at 2 per cent and the Lend-Lease clean-up on 3(c) terms (i.e. 2⅜ per cent). Afterwards Keynes believed that there was 'nothing better . . . on the map' than $4 billion at 2 per cent with a waiver.[28]

Even before this proposal Keynes had decided to try and introduce a note of realism into London's assessment of the situation. His draft telegram of 16 October, discussed the following day and sent on the 18th – 'Very long, but a superb work. One of the best pieces of writing he has ever done. If anything can put the case to London, this surely will, according to Harmer'[29,c] –

c At the receiving end in London, James Meade called it 'superb' (Howson and Moggridge (eds) 1990a, 151).

summarised the way the negotiations had gone so far and the state of American opinion before concluding that 'we must think again, substituting prose for poetry'. 'Prose' involved accepting the American view that 'they must dress the thing up to look as ordinary as possible, to escape notice wearing a business suit'.[30] Keynes, thinking then that he might get his $5 billion at an annual servicing cost of $150 million beginning in five years, put forward possible grounds for a waiver of repayments – a breakdown in multilateral clearing, an international depression or dollar scarcity. He was prepared to outline other possible arrangements, although he thought their acceptance unlikely,[d] but he was now, even more strongly than before, emphasising to London the extreme gravity of the situation and the difficulties of the other alternatives if there were a breakdown in the negotiations.

> In conclusion we have naturally given some thought to the question whether there is a way out for us by obtaining a moderate amount here and now to meet our immediate necessities on commercial terms without making any commitments about Bretton Woods, commercial policy and the sterling area. . . . Those of us here who in recent weeks have been studying intensively our balance of trade prospects believe
>
> (a) That we cannot reduce our cumulative balance of trade deficit below 3 or 4 billion at the very lowest without great and almost insupportable sacrifices at home and abroad.
>
> (b) That it is an illusion to suppose that the sterling area can carry on as in time of war.
>
> (c) That we cannot hope, therefore, to get a net contribution on capital account exceeding, say, 1 billion dollars at the utmost from all other outside sources put together.
>
> (d) That our prospects are poor of even a small Government loan here without any commitment about Bretton Woods, commercial policy or the sterling area.
>
> (e) That we should soon have involved ourselves in as heavy a debt charge as what we are now boggling at.
>
> (f) That the measure of disruption of our economic life at home and of our external relations, which would be inevitable if a comprehensive settlement with America fails, can hardly be exaggerated.[31]

A breakdown would have such disastrous consequences that it could not be contemplated.

At this stage the team could only await London's instructions in the light of the telegram of 18 October and report their subsequent talk with Clayton and Vinson.

Opinion in London was confused and divided. Some wanted a last-ditch attempt to salvage an element of 'Justice' while in the Treasury and the Bank

---

d Three days later he told London to forget them.

there was an increasing animus towards Article VII and the idea of a waiver. James Meade thought he had seen 'the lowest point of Eady's and Cobbold's efforts'. Cobbold (now Deputy Governor of the Bank) seemed to relish the idea that Britain could 'show the Americans that we could be tough'. Meade continued:

> But it was not until I heard Cobbold on this occasion that I realised that he really delighted in a wrecking proposal of this kind. Clearly he does not want any general settlement on the lines contemplated with the Americans. He would like us to snap our fingers at the Americans and to develop the sterling area, – though God knows how we could get on in this way. He is a clever ass.[32]

The Ministerial instructions to the team were also divided. Plan A was an attempt to get a loan of $2½ billion at 1 per cent over 50 years ($2 billion for essential imports plus $½ billion for the Lend-Lease settlement) plus a further $2 billion on interest-free terms to deal with the sterling balances. With this assistance, Britain would support the American proposals for an International Trade Organisation and, subject to an interpretative declaration that 'fundamental disequilibrium' should include chronic or persistent unemployment, accept the Bretton Woods plans. Plan B envisaged a smaller total, $2.5 billion, with an additional $500 million Lend-Lease settlement, both on 'commercial terms' (2 per cent for 50 years) with no commitments for the post-war world.

These instructions arrived in a gloomy pair of telegrams on 27 October, one of which outlined the 'Plans' while the other attempted to justify them. On the first:

> M. took it reasonably calmly and we tried to comfort ourselves with the thought that it merely represented the conclusions of an inconclusive and muddled Cabinet meeting which had been sent out, more or less without comment, by Eady, knowing they would be demolished by the reply M. would send back.

But on the second, Harmer found 'M. white with rage and talking about resignation'. Overnight, however, while waiting for the Ambassador to return from New York, 'M. had thought it out very well and after writing and destroying one or two vitriolic drafts produced a very good one, good tempered but quite merciless in pointing out where London had gone wrong'.[33] Plan B, Keynes explained, was beyond the bounds of possibility: the Lend-Lease settlement would only come on 3(c) terms and the only other assistance available was in the form of Export–Import Bank loans at 3 per cent. Thus, if available, Plan B would cost $228 million per annum beginning in 1946. However, $2.5 billion was beyond the capacity of the Export–Import Bank and Keynes suggested that $500 million over and above the Lend-Lease settlement would be the maximum available *if* the Americans did their best. Since even mentioning Plan B might induce the Americans to let Britain stew in her own juice as financial pressures mounted, Keynes and Halifax had agreed to put only Plan A to the Americans while warning London to think of its next move. In the end the British team did not present even Plan A. They decided instead to take advantage of Cripps's request that Robbins return to London for discussions of the proposed commercial policy settlement to try to clear up the financial position, for even Plan A would only save $23 million a year as against Clayton's offer of $4 billion and lacked the generous waiver protection of the latter.[34]

When Robbins arrived in London, he carried with him a letter from Keynes to the Chancellor which noted that Plan B was 'so entirely out of touch with reality that we are left dazed' and suggested that 'dangerous and, indeed, demented advice is abroad'. Keynes's letter also warned against the apparent London view that 'a breakdown would be accepted with some complacency and even with a certain amount of relief': anyone who advised that route was leading the Chancellor 'into perils not less grave because their character and scope cannot be predicted beforehand with precision'. He even warned that the Labour Government was running the risk of its 1931 predecessor of being brought down by overseas financial difficulties.[35] These were strong words. But the sort of confusion that existed in London is mirrored in Dalton's memoirs where he reverses Plans A and B, making his commentary rather unhelpful.[36] Perhaps the confusion was the result of too much information. Douglas Jay remembered one of the almost daily informal, evening meetings of Attlee, Bevin, Cripps, Dalton and Morrison in the Cabinet room, with Bridges and Eady present:

> The plethora of telegrams did not always make for clarity. On one occasion quoting from one of them, Dalton said peremptorily to Bevin: 'Foreign Secretary, have you got the telegram?' 'I've got 'undreds', replied Bevin and Bridges trotted around the table to reshuffle the cards for him.[37]

Robbins's journey to London meant yet more delays in the negotiations. In the interim, the Delegation tried to make progress in relatively non-controversial areas, such as the Lend-Lease settlement. Keynes also tried to prepare a draft for the Americans on the liberalisation of the sterling area. He had promised it back in September. On 24 October he sent London a draft of what he proposed to pass over: a description of the area and an outline of the proposed settlement. On receiving it in London:

> Cobbold and Eady threw a fit saying that we could in effect give the Americans no assurances about getting our sterling creditors to scale down their balances or about the amount to which we could release sterling balances for conversion into dollars.[38]

The resulting cables to Washington gave hints of this attitude and led Keynes to explain that Britain was already committed to the substance of his draft from earlier conversations and his original instructions. After encouraging noises from London on 2 November, he passed his proposals in a slightly revised form to Harry White *before* they had received formal London approval.[39] Keynes, Brand and Harmer also met Harry White and a number of American technicians about the document on the afternoon of 5 November. By the time he had passed the draft to White, comments from London had caused Keynes to remove the proposed quantification of the cancellation, funding and release of the balances, as well as the notion that the negotiations on the balances would be completed before a certain date. What he had not revised was his discussion of how the area worked, which expressed the view that there had been deliberate discrimination in the operation of the sterling area dollar pool.

After Keynes had seen White, the Treasury provided its redraft on the working of the area which took the line that 'it is not the sterling area system that is discriminatory, but the wartime necessities of exchange control'. London had 'without exception provided foreign exchange for any expenditures authorised by any control in the sterling area'.[40] Keynes found London's redraft 'inaccurate, irrelevant or phoney'. It would appear to the Americans as 'an inept piece of special pleading'. As for the echo of the views of the Bank about the working of the exchange control system, he replied, 'Some fig leaves which may pass muster with old ladies in London wilt in a harsher climate'.[41] The team prepared a final draft for the Americans. However, the process of preparing it had weakened Eady's confidence in the handling of the Washington end of the negotiations – a source of potential trouble later.[42]

The sterling area draft was to provide another, unexpected complication that would dog the rest of the negotiations. On 5 November White expressed his disappointment that the proposals only covered the sterling area and raised the question of payments agreements with non-sterling area countries, where Keynes claimed that he had given no grounds for the Americans' belief that there was a commitment here and emphasised that Britain would retain her transitional rights under Bretton Woods.[43]

Robbins's and Hall-Patch's London visit concluded with a meeting of ministers which recommended a new set of instructions for the Delegation. The Cabinet approved them on 6 November. Plan B disappeared. As for Plan A, although ministers were reluctant to drop the original version, the negotiators could accept 2 per cent on the interest-bearing element of the $2 billion provided that this did not encourage the Americans to press for 3(c) terms for the Lend-Lease settlement. If necessary, the mission could go further and accept 2 per cent for as much as $4 billion repayable over 50 years with the first payments to begin in five years, with an option for a further $1 billion on the same terms. It was also allowed to discuss a waiver. Thus it appeared that the Government was prepared to consider terms *worse* than those at which it had so recently jibbed.[44]

Keynes took the new Plan A, and his further revised sterling area paper, to Vinson and Clayton on 6 November. They rejected Plan A at once, even with 2 per cent on the interest-bearing portion, and made clear their unwillingness explicitly to tie part of the aid to the sterling area solution. They also stressed that their offer of assistance had not yet gone beyond $3½ billion and that they were not definitely committed to bringing the Lend-Lease settlement on to the same terms as the main loan.[45]

From this point the negotiations became a nightmare. Keynes and Halifax spent long hours with Vinson and Clayton, yet nothing but further complications seemed to arise. The strain on Keynes began to tell. Frederic Harmer's diary gives an indication of Keynes's state.

[12 & 13 November] M. very nervy and difficult to deal with. He is quite exhausted and the effects are not easy for the rest of us. We had a great deal of trouble . . . and only a good deal of firmness and tact (with Lionel R. preeminent) got him to face it properly and not side step.

[15 November, 9.05 am] I went up and found M. in bed looking very shaken and white, and all he could say is that we had better pack up and go home.

[15 November, later] M. now very nervy and finding it difficult to control his feelings. . . . Harry [White] rang up just before lunch: and M. was appallingly rude to him on the telephone – just what we wanted to avoid.

. . . M. not at all in good form – far too worked up, and the whole atmosphere was very trying.

[16 November] Some very trying discussions ensued with M., almost uncontrollable. Very painful at times and it didn't do any good.

[17 November] We are all thoroughly worried by now. M's health cannot stand this strain and the consequent strain and difficulty for all of us is not inconsiderable. One of the first essentials must be to give him somehow or other a rest next week.

[19 November] M. was very good – much more himself – and though Eccles was again incredibly trying it all passed off fairly smoothly.

On 19 November Keynes told Robbins that he was exhausted.[46]

By 18 November, after these days of difficult discussions, Keynes and the team thought that the American proposals were now clear enough and firm enough to cable to London and outline their various difficulties. No further amounts had entered the discussions and the Delegation was still thinking in terms of $4 billion in new money and $500 million for the Lend-Lease settlement at 2 per cent over 50 years, repayment of principal and interest to begin after five years. The difficulties they reported in their cables were as follows:

(i) *The Waiver*: The Americans saw this becoming operative if Britain's net export earnings on current account (as defined by Article XIX of the IMF Articles of Agreement) over the previous five years were on average below the 1936–8 average adjusted for changes in prices and Britain's gold and foreign exchange reserves at the end of the previous year were less than 15 per cent of commodity imports averaged over the previous five years or less than a quarter of her demand or short-term liabilities at the end of the previous year. The waiver was thus clearly based on Britain's ability to pay rather than on the international criteria originally proposed by Keynes. The first part was no problem, for the Chancellor had accepted the ability-to-pay criterion. However, the reserve criterion was unacceptable to the mission which asked for suggestions for a formula more favourable to Britain to meet strongly held American worries over excessive reserve accumulation.

(ii) *Sterling balances*: The Americans' waiver proposals stated that the waiver would not be allowed unless annual releases or repayments of sterling balances released after 1950 or repayments on other loans arranged after 1945 were proportionately reduced. In addition, the American proposals made it impossible to accelerate the repayment of sterling balances without doing the same on the American debt. The mission tried to restrict the proportional repayment reduction to loans taken out in 1946 and to exclude colonial dependencies and some other specified repayments from the accelerated repayment restrictions.

(iii) *Convertibility*: Within the sterling area, except for military receipts up to 31 December 1948, all sterling receipts from current transactions within the sterling area would be freely available for current transactions in any currency without discrimination not later than 31 December 1946. Outside the sterling area, similar arrangements were also envisaged. The mission recommended rejection of these proposals outside the sterling area except in payments agreements where the freedom of both parties was not restricted.

(iv) *Discrimination*: The Americans proposed that British import controls should not discriminate among sources of supply, except in the cases of blocked balances or assistance in the recovery of devastated regions. The mission had reserved its position but recommended acceptance.

(v) *Accumulated sterling balances*: The American proposals related not only to the sterling area but also elsewhere and covered not only all balances accumulated during the war but also post-war military expenditures up to a certain date. They committed the British to early settlements that would divide balances into those to be released immediately, released in stages after 1950 or written off. The British proposals related only to wartime balances and post-war military expenditures in the sterling area, mentioned only early discussions and allowed the early release of balances in lieu of loans. Here the differences were not major, but under the surface lurked the issue of the proportions of the balances that would be funded, written off and released.

Keynes supplemented these cables with letters and telegrams asking for a quick reply and for sufficient room to negotiate and compromise. There was a need to reach agreement quickly, for he thought that the subject had 'gone stale', the situation was 'deteriorating' and 'delay weakens our position'.[47]

When the series of telegrams reached London, according to James Meade,

> The Treasury and the Bank had hysterics – instead of going calmly through the document and seeing what we could accept and what we couldn't they seemed prepared to put an end to the whole negotiations.[48]

However, after considerable discussion in Whitehall and a somewhat acrimonious meeting on 23 November at which the Lord President, suitably briefed by Meade, made a strong attack on the Treasury's handling of the negotiations, Ministers did manage to agree a set of instructions for the mission.[49] They were now prepared to accept a credit of not less than $4 billion (including the Lend-Lease settlement) at 2 per cent repayable over 50 years with repayments commencing after five years, the liberalisation of the sterling area along the lines of the earlier draft Keynes had passed to White, a commitment to recommend the Bretton Woods agreements to Parliament on the conclusion of the financial negotiations and to associate Britain with the already agreed commercial policy proposals. They were not prepared to complete the negotiations over the accumulated sterling balances before the end of 1946, to abrogate Britain's transitional rights under Bretton Woods to impose exchange controls on current transactions outside the sterling area, to give the American loan priority over other external obligations and to a reserve test for the waiver. Keynes and the Ambassador amplified these instructions in writing, excluding proposed amounts, in an attempt to bring the discussions back to the fundamental issues. They handed their document to Vinson and Clayton on 25 November.[50]

The document shocked the Americans. None the less, after Keynes was invited to an American technical meeting and found the attitude 'more conciliatory than at any meetings this delegation have attended since they came to Washington', he was optimistic about mutual accommodation.[51] But, the drafting suggestions that emerged from this technicians' meeting were soon caught up in a new crisis.

The immediate origins of the crisis lay in London's attempt to clarify the Keynes/Halifax note handed to the Americans on 25 November, although its roots lay much further back in the negotiations. On convertibility for sterling area countries the Chancellor declared 'We do not wish this formal and public promise to be made . . . [to] release all current earnings throughout the whole of the Sterling Area as from the end of 1946'.[52]

The Chancellor's clarification horrified the mission. They replied with a strongly worded cable providing the long history of the current earnings commitment from its approval by the August Meeting of Ministers before Keynes had left London, through the emphasis he had placed on it in his presentations in September and his discussion with White, to ministers' reaffirmation of the commitment to Robbins early in November. To adopt the Chancellor's clarification would affect the mission's *bona fides* and if it was pressed London could 'take it as assured that there will be no financial agreement'.[53] In addition to the horrified telegram from all the Delegation, angry words – 'sabotage', 'wreck', 'betrayal' – passed between Washington and London by various other means. Robbins, after recounting his own involvement in discussions on this issue, told Sir Edward Bridges.

> You know that I am not given to gestures. But I feel that I must say that if Keynes feels that as a result of this cutting away of the ground from under his feet he must tender his resignation, I should feel honour bound to go with him. I am too deeply implicated in conveying to him from Eady what I believed to be a true statement of the position.[54]

Dalton found this statement 'hysterical'.[55] Frederic Harmer privately recorded the atmosphere in Washington.

> M. was profoundly upset – not only because he thought it quite wrong on merits, but because he was committed, it was an integral part of the whole plan as he saw it, and he did not see how we could retract. Some very troubled days followed. M. at the point of extreme nervous tension and on the verge of physical collapse; Lydia in floods of tears at almost every occasion; and all of us in a pretty bad state of mental and nervous exhaustion. Telegrams passed to and fro: M's getting more and more desperate – he was more than once on the verge of resignation but was persuaded not to:[e] London is getting more and more curt, and completely uninformative.[56]

During this time of troubles, meetings continued with Vinson (Clayton having withdrawn on 25 November with a fever). Despite the antipathy between Keynes and Vinson, they managed to reach agreement on improved waiver provisions that removed the reserve criterion and they also discussed other areas of disagreement. Moreover, Keynes was able to report that the Lend-Lease settlement would now be within the terms of the loan agreement and that the sum involved would be $500 million. The sterling balances imbroglio prevented any more progress, particularly as London's resurrection of other issues previously thought settled increased the mission's difficulties.

e Robbins's notes indicate this as well: on 30 November he wrote 'Dramatic moment, Maynard threatens to resign.' (Howson and Moggridge (eds) 1990b, 241).

Relations between the mission and London were now at a low ebb. As Lord Halifax recorded a conversation with Sir Edward Bridges in his diary on 1 December,

> London was pretty fed up with the Americans and, unjustly, with Keynes. As he put it, they felt that they were negotiating with Keynes rather than with the Americans! He admitted that it had been difficult to get Dalton and other Ministers to read our telegrams.[57]

With the Bank of England and the senior Treasury officials in outright opposition to Keynes's ideas, London fell back on a suggestion that Keynes had made earlier, that at a late stage of the negotiations someone more senior than him from the Treasury might have to come out to wring the last possible concessions out of the Americans.[58] At Robbins's suggestion Sir Edward Bridges flew out to Washington accompanied by A. T. K. Grant. They arrived on 1 December at noon and were immediately embroiled in preparations for a meeting the next day with Vinson.

The vindication of Keynes's and the mission's position came quickly, as Bridges rapidly took in the situation and adjusted to the realities of Washington. The next day two meetings of the Finance Committee in Vinson's room discussed a new American draft plus Bridges' instructions. Vinson, suspecting London's dissatisfaction with Keynes and the mission 'went out of his way to build up the actions and effective negotiations by the older group'.[59] As Harmer recorded it: 'It entirely supported our view of what could be done, but it was not an enjoyable meeting'. The Delegation 'got quite a long way with . . . [Vinson] on various points, not all unimportant'.[60] But the amount of the loan was below expectations – $3,750 million,[f] plus $650 million for Lend Lease – and the British were not able to move the Americans on the issue of convertibility outside the sterling area – thus losing except in exceptional circumstances their transitional protection under Bretton Woods – or on the explicit commitment to come to an agreement with members of the sterling area on the release, funding and writing off of sterling balances. Indeed, the passages on trade discrimination were hardened. Lionel Robbins's note for the day perhaps expressed the mood – 'Exactly as expected humiliation'.[61]

This left the decisions to ministers. Bridges thought 'they will grumble but accept'.[62] Before they did accept there was a further crisis over the terms as ministers stuck on three points: the scope for discrimination through the specific retention of the scarce currency clause, the availability of transitional rights under the IMF and, a new issue, the apparent denial during the fifty-five years of the agreement of Britain's right to leave the

---

f President Truman had split the difference between the $3,500 million recommended by the Treasury and the $4,000 million recommended by the State Department.

International Monetary Fund. The Chancellor believed that to suspend negotiations over the limitation of Britain's rights under Bretton Woods would provide 'a clear and limited issue' favourable to Britain and he had even began to think out the lines of his speech to the House of Commons announcing the breakdown.[63]

Attlee, Cripps and Dalton cabled Washington to this effect and called the American Ambassador to 10 Downing Street telling him that these restrictions on Britain's freedom under Bretton Woods would make it impossible for the Government to recommend Bretton Woods to Parliament. Since Britain had to accede by the end of 1945 to make the Agreements operative, this would effectively kill the Fund and the Bank and also end the financial negotiations.[g]

The Americans yielded on the scarce currency clause and Britain's withdrawal from the Fund, but they would not yield on early general convertibility. If Britain pressed the point, negotiations would break down. The best the Americans would offer was a clause in which the two Governments after consultation could in exceptional circumstances agree to invoke the transitional period provisions.[64]

This sent the ball back to London, which made one final try – attempting to postpone convertibility until the end of 1948 and to elaborate the 'exceptional circumstances' clause. These proposals reached Washington late in the same evening (4 December) and the Delegation had to find Vinson, who was actively participating in a dance at the Willard, the Delegation's own hotel. He rejected the proposals. The Delegation made a last attempt to convince ministers to accept the package and, after a sputter from London trying to postpone convertibility until 31 December 1947 rather than one year after the effective date of the agreement, the two Delegations signed the agreement at 10.30 a.m. on 6 December 1945.

Later in the day, Keynes found time to prepare a comment for the Treasury on silver coinage, to send with Frederic Harmer a Founder's Day telegram to King's, and to write his old friend Calvin Hoover that 'only a change in [existing reparations] policy can prevent great misfortunes'. However, that last opinion was private: for the moment he intended to remain a 'demi-semi-official'. In the evening, Keynes gave a dinner at the Statler for the team and its supporting staff and 'made a brilliant speech'.[65]

On 7 December Brand, Bridges, Liesching, Shackle and Grant went to Ottawa for a weekend of preliminary discussions on a Canadian loan, while Keynes, after calling on President Truman, went to New York. He saw

g Countries with 65 per cent of the quotas under the agreement had to sign it and deposit instruments of ratification before 31 December 1945. Britain's quota of $1,300 million or 14.7 per cent of the total should not have been enough by itself to cause problems, but a number of countries were waiting on Britain before they signed. However, even if everyone other than Britain who acceded before 31 December had still done so, they would have represented only 64.53 per cent of the quotas (Horsefield 1969, I, 116–17).

private banking friends, talked to Federal Reserve officials on drawing the American loan when the time came, and collected a silver tankard bequeathed to the Bank of England by J. P. Morgan. The party reunited in New York on 11 December, embarked on the *Queen Elizabeth* and sailed at 10 p.m. that evening.[h] The ship docked at Southampton at 11 a.m. on 17 December.

While the *Queen Elizabeth* made its way quietly and uneventfully across the Atlantic, the Loan Agreement and the Bretton Woods Agreement began their way through Parliament, which did not have to approve the Commercial Policy proposals. The Commons debate commenced on 12 December. The package before the House had elements to displease almost everybody. Bretton Woods had had its critics from the beginning and it had not found new admirers in the sixteen months during which successive Governments had refused to take it before Parliament. Imperial Preference, which was a subject of the commercial policy understandings, had proved a rallying point for Conservative opponents of Article VII since 1941 and during the autumn of 1945, as James Meade put it, 'The Labour Ministers discovered the Empire'.[66,i] To both groups, the explicit commitment to end the wartime sterling area dollar pool was simply an added red flag to the bull. The vision of multilateralism in both the International Monetary Fund and the commercial policy proposals also had its critics from the left, for they seemed menaces to planning, full employment and the welfare state. Then, of course, there were the terms of the Loan itself, which attracted far more attention than the generous settlement of Lend Lease.

With the Loan there were several problems. To many, the linking of American financial assistance to Bretton Woods and the commercial policy proposals left a bad taste: it seemed then – and has seemed to many critics since – that Britain was forced to accept measures which may have been in America's long-term interest but were not in hers because of her dire financial straits. This was hardly helped in many eyes, including the Chancellor's, by the provisions of the Loan Agreement concerning convertibility and the consequent abrogation of transitional protection available under the IMF Articles of Agreement.

Only strong leadership could have carried the package through the Commons and left a positive impression in the House and in the country. The Government's defence was weak. It stressed Britain's need for the Loan and the importance of maintaining good Anglo-American relations, rather

h The master of the *Queen Elizabeth* was a relative, Charles Musgrave Ford, Keynes's grandmother's nephew.

i At the time Keynes commented:

> When I first knew D[alton] as an undergraduate at King's he was a passionate supporter of Joe Chamberlain and his room was plastered with placards about Imperial Preference, etc. Then one night when he was drunk he was converted to Fabianism by Rupert Brooke. Hence all our present troubles. (Harmer Diary, 7 November 1945, 55).

than the positive aspects of Fund and the commercial policy proposals. The Opposition's tactic was simply to abandon responsibility, although it had, of course, been associated with many of the agreements now coming to fruition, and to advise its members to abstain. With a three-line whip, the proposals passed by 343 to 100, with 169 abstentions. Twenty-three Labour backbenchers, including James Callaghan, Barbara Castle, Maurice Edelman, Michael Foot and Jennie Lee, defied the whip and voted against the Government.[67]

As he crossed the Atlantic Keynes heard reports of the discussions in the House. The House of Lords debate would begin the day he arrived in Southampton. He began to plan a speech to the Lords which would defend his efforts over the previous months and the resulting settlement. When he landed at Southampton his speech was not in its final form.

With just a brief stop at Gordon Square, Keynes went directly to the House of Lords. During the first day of debate, he remained silent except to provide Lord Simon with a piece of information. The debate made it clear that

> The ignorance was all-embracing. So far as the public was concerned, no-one had been at any pains to explain, far less defend, what had been done. And as for the insiders, so dense a fog screen had been created that such as the Chancellor and the Governor of the Bank had only the dimmest idea of what we had given away and what we had not.[68]

When he rose in the Lords to open the afternoon's proceedings on 18 December, Keynes was determined to dispel the fog. His speech was a powerful, frank description of the arrangements. He admitted disappointment with many of the terms: the amount of the Loan was 'cut somewhat too fine and does not allow a margin for unforeseen contingencies'; the charging of interest was 'out of tune with the underlying realities' ('I shall never so long as I live cease to regret that this is not an interest-free loan.'); the convertibility provisions could have given Britain more time and, like many other commitments, could have been less precise.[69] He was also frankly sympathetic in his exposition of the difficulties of the American negotiators.

> No one who has breathed that atmosphere for many troubled weeks will underestimate the difficulties of the American statesmen, who are striving to do their practical best for their own country and for the whole world, or the fatal consequences if the Administration were to offer us what Congress would reject.
>
> During the whole time that I was in Washington, there was not a single Administration measure of the first importance that Congress did not either reject, remodel, or put on one side.

That the Americans should be anxious not to allow too hot a pace to be set in this, their first major post-war operation of this kind is readily understandable. The total demands for overseas financial assistance crowding in on the United States Treasury while I was in Washington were estimated to amount to between four and five times our own maximum proposals. We naturally have our own requirements in view, but the United States Treasury cannot overlook the possible reaction of what they do for us on the expectations of others. Many members of Congress were seriously concerned about the cumulative consequences of being too easy-going towards a world unanimously clamouring for American aid, and often with too good reason.[70]

Keynes's speech was not only notable for its frankness. It also powerfully highlighted the futility of believing in the so-called sterling area alternative which would be

to build up a separate economic bloc which excludes Canada and consists of countries to which we already owe more than we can pay, on the basis of their agreeing to lend us money they have not got and only buy from us and one another goods that we are unable to supply.[71]

He also emphasised the generosity of the American terms as compared with those they were offering to the European Allies.[72] Finally, he repeatedly pointed to the future, not only by referring to the Loan itself in terms of British reconstruction and recovery but also by pointing to the long-term advantages of a successful recovery into a world where the currency and commercial policy proposals would be operative. In words that he would use frequently in the months to come, he continued:

[T]he outstanding characteristic of the plans is that they represent the first elaborate and comprehensive attempt to combine the advantages of freedom of commerce with safeguards against the disastrous consequences of a *laissez-faire* system which pays no direct regard to the preservation of equilibrium and merely relies on the eventual working out of blind forces.

Here is an attempt to use what we have learned from modern experience and modern analysis, not to defeat, but to implement the wisdom of Adam Smith. It is a unique accomplishment, I venture to say, in the field of international discussion to have proceeded so far by common agreement along a newly-trodden path, not yet pioneered, I agree, to a definite final destination, but a newly-trodden path, which points the right way. We are attempting a great step forwards towards the goal of international economic order amidst national diversities of policies. It is not easy to have patience with those who pretend that some of us, who were early in the field to attack and denounce the false premises and false conclusions of unrestricted *laissez faire* and its particular manifestations in the former gold standard and other currency and commercial doctrines which mistake private licence for public liberty, are now spending their later years in the service of the State to walk backwards and resurrect and re-erect the idols which they played some part in throwing out of the market place. Not so. Fresh tasks now invite. Opinions have been successfully changed. The work of destruction has been accomplished, and the site has been cleared for a new structure.[73]

His peroration recalled the advantages to Britain of a multilateral régime. After five hours of further debate, the Financial Agreement and related issues were carried.

Not only did the speech affect opinion. It also seemed to be a tonic to Keynes: 'He had shed all the traces of fatigue and was his indestructible self, radiant with triumph and friendship'.[74] He even found his position amusing:

I have regained my self-respect by finding myself once more in the minority, but this time actual events are being forced to follow the minority view, and Cassandra, though disbelieved, gets her way.[75]

Or as he would put it to his Cambridge Political Economy Club in February, 'Cassandra cocks a snook'.

But he was tired. At the dinner at the Savoy for the Delegation and others involved in the Loan negotiations he was to the distress of those around him 'forced to lie on a sofa and rest throughout most of the evening'.[76] After clearing up a few odds and ends at the Treasury, he went off to Tilton to rest. On Boxing Day he gave a party for his employees and the Charlestonians with the 'Washington booty' acquired by Lydia again providing presents. This time the guests performed their own version of Brains Trust with Duncan Grant taking the part of a bishop.[77] By this time Keynes had recovered. On 5 January he reported to Plesch that the rest had restored him to 'as good a state of health as I have been in a long time'. Lydia, however, was still very tired and had not recovered 'her bodily and nervous rhythm'. In the New Year she, too, would be under Plesch's care.

NOTES

1 *FRUS*, 1945, VI, 103–4; *JMK*, XXIV, 414–16.
2 The record of the meeting appears in *JMK*, XXIV, 420–5. By far the best documentary collection on the whole negotiations is Bullen and Pelly (eds) 1986. By far the most extensive discussion of the negotiations, on which I have leaned heavily, is Pressnell 1987, chapter 10.
3 *JMK*, XXIV, 417, 421, 423.
4 Dalton 1962, 73; Harrod 1951, 596–7.
5 NUL, JMK to Vanessa Bell, 26 August 1945; KCKP, JMK to Molly MacCarthy, 26 August 1945.

6 Harmer Diary, 2, 4.
7 Harmer Diary, 2 September 1945, 8.
8 *JMK*, XXIV, 218.
9 Roll 1985, 44.
10 *JMK*, XXIV, 453.
11 *JMK*, XXIV, 458, 457, 456, 454.
12 *JMK*, XXIV, 460–6; Harmer Diary, 12 September 1945, 19.
13 *JMK*, XXIV, 479, 483. See also Bullen and Pelly (eds) 1986, 137–8.
14 Harmer Diary, 19 September 1945, 25.
15 *JMK*, XXIV, 488. In going this far, Keynes almost certainly went beyond his instructions. The suggestions he dropped here may have helped to create problems later in the negotiations.
16 *FRUS*, 1945, VI, 104.
17 Howson and Moggridge (eds) 1990a, 132. For his earlier relative lack of concern, see ibid., 119–20.
18 Robbins 1971, 204–5.
19 Bullen and Pelly (eds) 1986, 132–3; Harmer Diary, 15 September 1945, 23.
20 *JMK*, XXIV, 511.
21 Bullen and Pelly (eds) 1986, 158; Howson and Moggridge (eds) 1990b, 224.
22 *JMK*, XXIV, 512, 514.
23 Howson and Moggridge (eds) 1990a, 127, 144; *JMK*, XXIV, 524–5.
24 Harmer Diary, 7 October 1945; KCKP, Lydia to FAK, 13 October 1945; Robbins to Meade, 17 October 1945.
25 Howson and Moggridge (eds) 1990b, 230.
26 For details of the commercial policy negotiations, see Pressnell 1987, 276–9.
27 *JMK*, XXIV, 531, 532–5, 540–1.
28 *JMK*, XXIV, 557, 562.
29 Harmer Diary, 17 October 1945, 42.
30 *JMK*, XXIV, 548, 549.
31 *JMK*, XXIV, 553–4.
32 Howson and Moggridge (eds) 1990a, 163–4.
33 Harmer Diary, 27 and 28 October 1945, 47, 48.
34 Bullen and Pelly (eds) 1986, 270–1, 273–5.
35 Dalton 1962, 77.
36 Ibid., 78.
37 Jay 1980, 137.
38 Howson and Moggridge (eds) 1990a, 164.
39 Harmer Diary, 2 November 1945, 51.
40 *JMK*, XXIV, 582, 588.
41 *JMK*, XXIV, 580, 584.
42 Pressnell 1987, 315.
43 Bullen and Pelly (eds) 1986, 309n.
44 Ibid., 289–91.
45 Ibid., 300–2.
46 Howson and Moggridge (eds) 1990b, 239.
47 The cables are in Bullen and Pelly (eds) 1986, 323–35. The emphasis on the need for speed and flexibility is in *JMK*, XXIV, 590–1, 592.
48 Howson and Moggridge (eds) 1990a, 177.
49 Ibid., 177; PRO, CAB78/37, GEN89/6th Meeting, 23 November 1945; Bullen and Pelly (eds) 1986, 354–6.
50 The text is in *JMK*, XXIV, 633–6.
51 Bullen and Pelly (eds) 1986, 368.

52 Ibid., 371. A telephone conversation between Wilfrid Eady and Frank Lee had warned the mission of what was to follow.
53 *JMK*, XXIV, 598.
54 PRO, AVIA38/1211, Robbins to Bridges, LETOD 388, 26 November 1945.
55 BLPES, Dalton Diary, 7 December 1945, 1.
56 Harmer Diary, 60–1.
57 Pelling 1984, 57
58 *JMK*, XXIV, 418.
59 *FRUS*, 1945, VI, 187.
60 Harmer Diary, 62, 61.
61 Howson and Moggridge (eds) 1990b, 241.
62 Birkenhead 1965, 555.
63 Dalton 1962, 84.
64 Bullen and Pelly (eds) 1986, 428, 430.
65 *JMK*, XXVII, 423–6; XVI, 400; Harmer Diary, 62.
66 The date of this discovery was the Ministerial meeting of 26 October which had discussed commercial policy and plans A and B. Above p. 806, Howson and Moggridge (eds) 1990a, 165.
67 Morgan 1984, 61.
68 *JMK*, XXIV, 626.
69 *JMK*, XXIV, 612, 613, 620.
70 *JMK*, XXIV, 614, 613.
71 *JMK*, XXIV, 620.
72 *JMK*, XXIV, 615–18.
73 *JMK*, XXIV, 611, 621–2.
74 Robbins 1971, 211.
75 *JMK*, XXIV, 625.
76 Jay 1980, 139.
77 KCKP, JMK to FAK, 28 December 1945; Spalding 1983, 331.

31

THE LAST MONTHS

I think the time has come for me to slip out of the Treasury. . . . Being of
a resigning temperament, I shall not last long in this *galère* in any case; so
I had better go when I go quiet and friendly.
                    (JMK to Lord Halifax, 1 January 1946, *JMK*, XXIV, 628)

Keynes remained at Tilton, resting and catching up on arrears of work, until
7 January 1946. He felt 'completely recuperated in health', probably, one
suspects, because for the first time in four months he had been 'free from
worry, and that is what really matters'. He had started to think of his future
relations with the Treasury: he told Bridges and Hopkins as well as Halifax
that he wanted to reduce his commitments.[1] He saw Bridges on 8 January
and Hopkins on the 16th. He did not resign; nor did he much reduce his
workload, although it is clear from his appointments diary for January
that he took several long weekends in a row, two of them in Cambridge.
On one of them, on 31 January, he received an honorary Sc.D. from the
University.

It is also clear from scattered comments in his correspondence that he was
not happy with policy as it was developing. He told R. H. Brand at the end
of January,

> Meanwhile the mixed chauvinism and universal benevolence of the
> F.O. and other departments and the weakness of the Chancellor in
> these matters are slopping away on everything and everybody in
> the world except the poor Englishman the fruits of our American
> loan. . . .
>
> It is not done on purpose. No one knows what is happening. . . .
> The Ministers, I am told, are reluctant to read their official papers and
> reach half the ramshackle decisions, particularly on overseas affairs, in
> the absence of anybody who really knows what it is all about. The
> Treasury, in the shape of Wilfrid, Sigi and the rest work hard in the
> right direction but with a singular lack of success. . . .
>
> Back of all this, England is sticky with self-pity and not prepared to
> accept peacefully and wisely the fact that her position and her resources
> are *not* what they once were. Psycho-analysis would, I think, show that

that was the real background to the reception of the American loan and the associated proposals.[2]

With this state of mind, it is not surprising that contemporaries such as James Meade believe that if he had lived longer, Keynes might have resigned from the Treasury and even written a stinging indictment of official policy.

Before he returned to London, Keynes decided to work up for publication in the *Economic Journal* a paper, 'Will the Dollar be Scarce?', which he had prepared with Frederic Harmer and David McCurrach in Washington in October for transmission to London.[3] He told Roy Harrod, who had succeeded him as editor of the *Journal* in April 1945, of his intention on 4 January. He completed a draft by 25 January. He received Treasury approval for the article on 2 February, but the same day Brand advised him that the article should not appear until the Loan was through Congress – that is, given the existing timetable, not before June 1946. Keynes agreed. This delay turned out to be fortunate, for it gave him an opportunity to get his material vetted in Washington during his forthcoming visit to the United States for the inaugural meetings of the International Monetary Fund and International Bank for Reconstruction and Development. He showed it to several people there, including Graham Towers and Harry White. The last letter he received from Harry White, dated 27 March, returned his proofs with the comment that 'Altogether the possibility of scarcity of dollars during the next five years seems to me, as it does to you, to be remote – barring, of course, untoward international political developments'.[4] After Keynes's death in April 1946 there was further official discussion as to whether the article should be published.[5] It appeared under the title 'The Balance of Payments of the United States' in June 1946, before the Loan was clear of Congress.[a] The views expressed in this paper are of considerable importance, since they underlay many of his comments on policy during the last months of his life, as well as the substance of his talk to the Cambridge Political Economy Club on 2 February.

The article opened with a statement of fact: if the IMF and other supporting bodies were to establish multilateral current account convertibility over a wide area, then the UK and US would reach bilateral external equilibrium if British exports to and American imports from the rest of the world reached the appropriate level. In other words, he was assuming that Britain's demand for imports would be determined exogenously, presumably by controls. On

a There are also suggestions in the literature that Keynes's executors had doubts about publication (Viner 1964, 265; Jacobsson 1972, 212). Yet it had already been submitted to and accepted by the *Economic Journal*, whose editor received the final version 'two days' after Keynes's death (Harrod 1951, 621). The letter from Keynes to Harrod was dated 20 April, but it could not have been sent until 25 April given the covering note. See also Kahn in Thirlwall (ed.) 1976, 9.

the demand for American exports he was more explicit. He built the core of his argument on past experience, plus certain assumptions about the post-war world. On the basis of statistics for the American current account balance for 1930–8, he was prepared to argue that the US surplus in the 1930s was not excessive. He went further and suggested that the balance of payments problem that the rest of the world had then had with the United States was due to large capital movements to the United States superimposed on this manageable surplus. The Bretton Woods régime with its controls on capital movements would provide a means of avoiding a repetition of that problem. Having looked at the current account as a whole, Keynes moved to a sub-problem: did imports into the United States fall by more than exports during depressions? Again, on the basis of evidence from the 1930s, he argued that this was not the case: imports, exports and American industrial production tended to move roughly in step. Finally he turned to the American international balance sheet position to suggest that, apart from gold holdings, the United States was a net debtor at the end of 1945. Moreover, foreigners' liquid claims on the United States had increased since 1938.

With respect to the prospective position in the near future Keynes assumed sufficient recovery abroad to satisfy America's demand for imports, present American export trends, existing relative prices and some international control of export subsidies. Making plausible assumptions about interest and amortisation on American post-war loans, he expected an American visible trade surplus of $2–3 billion after 1947 to be substantially offset by an invisibles deficit. Any remaining deficit would not result in unmanageable interest payments if met by borrowing. Moreover, foreigners' resources in the United States, gold reserves and current production could meet up to $1 billion of the overall deficit 'without suffering great embarrassment'. Therefore he concluded 'that the chances of the dollar becoming dangerously scarce in the next five to ten years are not very high'.[6]

Then, in a series of paragraphs which have caused much subsequent discussion, he suggested that 'In the long run much more fundamental forces may be at work, if all goes well, tending towards equilibrium, the significance of which may ultimately transcend ephemeral statistics'. He continued:

> I find myself moved, not for the first time, to remind contemporary economists that the classical teaching embodied some permanent truths of great significance, which we are liable to-day to overlook because we associate them with doctrines which we cannot now accept without much qualification. There are in these matters deep undercurrents at work, natural forces, one can call them, or even the invisible hand, which are operating towards equilibrium. If it were not so, we could not have got on even so well as we have for many decades past.[7]

The United States was becoming a high-cost country, a fact that would help restore equilibrium in normal circumstances. The recent United States' *Proposals for Consideration by an International Conference on Trade and Employment*, the document published simultaneously with the Loan Agreement, was designed to allow the classical medicine to do its work. 'It shows', he argued

> how much modernist stuff, gone wrong and turned sour and silly, is circulating in our system, also incongruously mixed, it seems, with age-old poisons, that we should have given so doubtful a welcome to this magnificent, objective approach which a few years ago we should have regarded as offering incredible promise of a better scheme of things.[8]

The Bretton Woods régime allowed countries to speed the operation of the classical medicine in less painful ways than previously. Between them the Bretton Woods Agreements and the Washington Proposals 'marry the use of the necessary expedients to the wholesome long-run doctrine' and were, as he had said in the House of Lords in December, 'an attempt to use what we have learned from modern experience and modern analysis, not to defeat, but to implement the wisdom of Adam Smith'.[9]

These references to 'natural forces', 'the invisible hand', 'the wisdom of Adam Smith' arouse strong feelings in economists and have led some to argue that Keynes had lapsed from the 'true faith', perhaps under American pressure. Yet the comments were mild compared to his private remarks to the Political Economy Club in Cambridge, where his notes ran:

> Assuming that the policy of deliberate economic isolationism should be rejected, have we nevertheless agreed to return to a version of 19th century *laissez faire* which is bound to break down?
>
> I consider this a grossly ignorant misunderstanding of what has happened.
>
> The classical doctrine
>
> Supplemented by exchange variations and overall import control. This seems to me the modern version of economic liberalism. My H of L speech. To that charge I would plead guilty. I can easily see that it is not acceptable to the totalitarians in our midst, but it seems to me soundly consonant with our national attitudes, instincts, principles of self-interest. A Totalitarian economy must be a large one. The British Empire for obvious reasons not a suitable unit for totalitarian experiments.
>
> Here is a genuine attempt at agreed rules and principles of action. My complaint would be that they do not go far enough in the liberal direction . . . But they go a long way. The opposite of the law of the jungle.[10]

Keynes's time-scale was wrong on a prospective dollar problem. The immediate post-war years were characterised by a dollar shortage which was not to be replaced by either rough equilibrium or a dollar glut for over a decade. Some of Keynes's assumptions about the details of the American and overseas balance of payments positions were incorrect. But Keynes's basic assumption of multilateral current account convertibility over a wide area did not occur. Objective circumstances may have made such convertibility impossible, but one must remember that the failure of Britain's attempt to meet the convertibility commitments of the 1945 Loan Agreement played a part in the outcome. And in the winter and spring of 1946 one of Keynes's major concerns was ensuring that Britain would do just that. His official successors were less assiduous.

Keynes's campaign was a continuation of one that stretched back through his 'Lady Bountiful' state papers of 1944 and 1945. It had two prongs: attempts to limit British overseas spending, particularly Government spending, to match her reduced means, and attempts to reach a settlement with the sterling area and other overseas holders of sterling balances compatible with the convertibility provisions of the Loan Agreement.

Keynes's contribution to the overseas spending issue was what James Meade at the time called 'a hair raising paper . . . on our overseas financial commitments'. It was sufficiently startling that he subsequently recorded:

> When I came into the office on Monday morning [11 February] . . ., I found an urgent message from the Lord President's secretary for a short brief on the paper by Keynes which the Chancellor has just submitted together with the import programmes for 1946 for discussion by the Cabinet that morning . . . . The Lord President who, like most Labour Ministers, cannot forget 1931 was in a great concern whether we were not in for another external financial crash, and also (shades of the May Report!) asked to know whether there should not be a similar general survey of our internal expenditure to see whether we were not overdoing things there as well.[11]

Keynes's paper, 'Political and Military Expenditure Overseas',[12] began by noting that the import programme was well in hand and that 'administrative methods for imposing austerity at home are in good working order', so much so that £1,030 million of the import programme of £1,075 million was classified as essential. In contrast

> the current and prospective demands upon us for political and military expenditure overseas have already gone beyond the figure which can, on any hypothesis, be sustained. . . . Ministers should not remain unwarned that they are going down the drain at a great pace, unless they can consider before it is too late whether a drastic and early change of policy may be preferable. It is *not* yet too late.

He argued that even before the Loan had passed Congress current gross political commitments plus prospective overseas military expenditures exceeded the entire American Loan, leaving nothing for domestic purposes. He emphasised that overseas resources were limited and that every use of them was an alternative to some other: an army of 100,000 Poles in Italy cost as much as the Ministry of Food's proposed easements for British diets. Ministers, he stated bluntly, had to choose and to act as if they were consciously doing so. He proceeded sometimes with biting irony to outline the commitments – £1,500 million gross and £1,000 million minimum net for 1946–8, as compared with the calculations of £600 million as the 'utmost' during the recent Loan negotiations. These commitments excluded funds for the Bretton Woods institutions, withdrawals of sterling balances by liberated territories or any release of sterling balances as a part of the sterling area settlement.

Keynes's solutions were inevitably drastic, most notably 'a virtual cessation of political loans', a reconsideration of Britain's economic policy towards Germany, and a halving of British forces outside Europe. His comments on the last two indicate the style:

> It seems monstrous that we should first de-industrialise and thus bankrupt the Ruhr to please Russia and then hand over the territory, or at any rate the industries, to an international body to please France, but that we alone should remain responsible for feeding the place. . . . Our present policy towards Germany, by which we have become involved in paying her large reparations, might rank as the craziest ever – if one did not remember last time. . . .

> We simply cannot afford to make our plans on the basis of being half and half-heartedly ready for war with Russia. Yet, what else does a great deal of our military expenditure mean? We are spending twice too much for solvency, and twice (or four times) too little for safety in conditions of hostility, and a war of nerves dispersed over two continents; thus making sure of the worst of both worlds.[13]

By 18 February, Dalton, who had circulated the paper deliberately to alarm his colleagues, thought that Keynes's piece 'has done good', but what good it did was probably to provoke anxiety rather than action.[14] Its short-term effects on expenditures were limited, although over time the German policy changed; troops were withdrawn from Greece; and the Polish army in Italy was disbanded. It was not to be the last of post-war defence reviews resulting from balance of payments pressures. They continued for more than a generation.

On sterling balances, Keynes and the Treasury were beginning to develop their position for the forthcoming negotiations under the terms of the

American Loan. In many respects Keynes's position remained unchanged: he continued in particular to distrust the Bank's preference for a more informal approach. As he put it on 5 February:

> If the Bank are right, as they may be in ordinary circumstances, that a substantial portion of the sterling balances is likely to stop here anyhow, that limits the inconvenience to the other party of turning a *de facto* into a *de jure* situation. But it is *not*, as I have already pointed out, a reason for our accepting *de jure* obligations which we shall be unable to fulfil, if the abnormal conditions arise (as, heaven knows, they are likely to in the world ahead of us), when we are called upon to do so. The bankers' 'ramp' of 1931 consisted not in what happened at the last moment, which was inevitable and indeed desirable, but in the reckless accumulation of liabilities in the immediately preceding years which we could not hope to meet when the tide turned. I think that we must ration ourselves this time in the extent to which we use the banker's bluff as a means of supporting (temporarily) the prestige of sterling.[15]

He continued to support the application of a general formula for the sterling area negotiations. Such formulae – which he continued to show great ingenuity in devising – might ultimately need 'cooking' to suit the circumstances of the particular case, but 'unless we *start out* with some general formula, we shall be at sea and will not be able to offer even the semblance of a justification for being fair'.[16] Finally, he continued to hope that by some means or other a proportion of the balances would be written off.

Where the Keynes of early 1946 differed from his earlier papers, at least in tone, was in his acceptance that the problem was extremely difficult politically. Nevertheless

> I plead that this is not a case where we can muddle through without a drastic solution, grasping no nettles and just hoping that it will be all right on the day.[17]

Because there was *no means* of avoiding political difficulties 'of a high order', the temptation of appeasement did not exist. This was an advantage. He was prepared to aggravate the political difficulties by tying the sterling area negotiations to the fact that many sterling area exchange rates were out of line with sterling and needed devaluation. In conversation he was prepared to use the negotiations to *force* exchange rate adjustments, if only because he believed that the area's exchange control arrangements could not withstand the maintenance of the disequilibria.[18] He was also prepared, at least briefly, to toy with the idea of only repaying, at least in the case of blocked balances, the local currency equivalent of the initial expenditure. Thus countries that devalued would see the local currency 'profits' resulting from the devaluation used to write down their sterling balances. On the other hand, if Britain devalued, the balances would be written up. But this proposal does not appear to have got outside the Treasury. By the time he died, the discussions had not got far, partially because everyone, including Keynes, was prepared to let matters drift, particularly as the Loan was not through Congress.[19] After he died, the drift continued, but for a different reason: the Treasury and the Bank seem to have decided on what James Meade called 'a super-bankers'-bluff' where very little of the balances would be cancelled and there would not be definite agreements about running them down – only gentlemen's agreements. As Meade remarked, 'Poor Keynes must have turned in his grave'.[20]

There were also domestic policy issues to consider. During Keynes's absence in the autumn of 1945 the new Government had made considerable progress in setting up machinery for the implementation of a full employment policy. The new Chancellor had also committed himself to cheaper money and had been presented with the recommendations of the National Debt Inquiry, which he started to implement with a cut in the Treasury bill rate from 1 per cent to ½ per cent on 23 October. He also accepted the Inquiry's recommendation and wartime practice of creating market expectations of lower rates so as gradually to improve the terms on which the Government could borrow by ceasing to issue 3% Savings Bonds 1965/75 on 15 December and offering to convert two maturing issues into 1¾% Exchequer Bonds in April 1946. On 17 January, Dalton met Keynes, Bridges, Hopkins, Eady and the Governors of the Bank to plan their next moves. They agreed to do nothing until they knew the results of the conversion offer, but in the course of the discussion it was clear that Keynes still held to the National Debt Inquiry view favouring a 3 per cent long-term bond with an early redemption date, although Dalton was worried that this would seem inconsistent with his desire to do better than 3 per cent and to make another cheaper money announcement in his forthcoming Budget. On his way to America in March and again after his return in April, Keynes suggested that the authorities be more aggressive in their new issue policy, going so far as to propose calling 3% Local Loans and offering in return a 2½ per cent issue either for 20 years or redeemable at Government option after 20 years. Nothing more happened before his death, but Keynes had certainly helped pave the way for Dalton's disastrous attempt to lower the long-term rate of interest to 2½ per cent at the end of October 1946.[21]

On the employment policy front, Keynes proved to be a helpful ally in James Meade's attempts to get his 1942 proposal for counter-cyclical variations in social insurance contributions embodied in the National Insurance Bill, although without the full automaticity both desired. He also kept a critical watching brief on the development of the Government's economic surveys, although, once Richard Stone had departed for Cambridge to be Director of the newly formed Department of Applied Economics, Keynes had less faith in the exercises. There were also Budget Committee meetings and, later after his return from America, contributions to drafting the Budget Speech. At least with Dalton, unlike John Anderson, it was not the case that 'The Chancellor proceeds *from* the pedestrian'.[22]

With the Parliamentary vote on the Loan Agreement, Britain acceded to the Bretton Woods institutions. By the end of 1945, 35 countries had taken at least the first steps towards joining and 30 were full members. The combined quotas exceeded the minimum necessary under the Bretton Woods Agreement; so it was time to get the new institutions staffed and operating. As part of this process, the United States was to organise the inaugural meeting of the Governors of the Fund and the Bank. On 28 January 1946, ten days after Keynes had learned of it informally from the American Treasury representative in London, the Americans issued invitations for a meeting beginning on 8 March at the General Oglethorpe Hotel, Wilmington Island, Savannah, Georgia.[23]

Keynes was naturally closely involved in the British planning for the meeting. As well as the general problem of staffing, there were two issues left over from Bretton Woods that the British thought important: the location of the Fund and the Bank and the details of the management of the new institutions, particularly the role of the Executive Directors. Both were to cause problems.

Keynes was appointed the British Governor of the two institutions on 19 February. At the time he looked forward to the meetings – at being present at the birth of the institutions on which he had lavished so much time and thought since 1941 and at having 'something of a holiday' in a warm climate. He did not expect that the work would be unduly strenuous. Both Lydia and Dr Plesch strongly favoured his making the journey.[24]

Maynard and Lydia sailed for New York on the *Queen Mary* on 24 February. The delegation consisted of Keynes and Ernest Rowe-Dutton of the Treasury and Roy Bridge and George Bolton from the Bank. R. H. Brand would join them in Washington. The ship was full of GI war brides and their babies. The crossing was rough, but he did not miss a meal.[25] He managed to prepare what has become known as 'the "Queen Mary" memorandum' for the Chancellor on the movement to cheaper money.[26] The party arrived in New York on 1 March.

In New York, Keynes spent time talking to Federal Reserve officials before travelling to Washington where he renewed acquaintance with old friends as well as discussed the passage of the Loan through Congress and the business of the forthcoming meetings with American officials. The omens were mixed. On 5 March he had heard rumours that the Fund and Bank were to be located in Washington – not New York as the British and others preferred. The next day, at the end of a meeting with Secretary Vinson, Keynes was officially informed 'somewhat shamefacedly'. He reacted 'very vehemently', only to be told that the decision was final.[27] On the management of the new institutions, he found the position more fluid. He had been taking the line that to attract good Executive Directors it would be essential that they be in close touch with officials at home. This, he thought, made it essential that they should not be continuously at the offices of the new institutions. It also fitted in well with his (and the British) long-standing view of the working of such institutions that the permanent officials, notably the Managing Director, have considerable day-to-day autonomy. As he put it to Brand, who supported the opposing view:

> Could any Managing Director be so gifted as to be capable of running with efficiency any institution with twelve polyglot directors with divergent interests, most of them interested in grinding their own axes rather than running the institution, who are in the office every day and on top of him and dictating his day-to-day policy?[28]

He thought he had some support for his views in the State Department, at least as regards the Fund, while Treasury Secretary Vinson, although non-committal showed 'considerable sympathy'. Thus Keynes believed that compromise was possible.[29]

One surprise was that the idea that Harry White would be Managing Director of the Fund, something that he and others had anticipated and hoped for, had suddenly been dropped. The official reason, according to Vinson, was that the Americans had decided that the President of the International Bank for Reconstruction and Development would have to be an American to maintain the confidence of the New York financial community and, as it would not be proper for both institutions to be headed by Americans, White's name had to go. The truth was more complex.

White had been under FBI surveillance since November 1945 after allegations that he had been involved in transmitting information to Soviet intelligence agents operating in the United States. On 23 January 1946, although he was still under surveillance, President Truman announced that he was nominating White as the American Executive Director of the Fund. At the time, he was also seriously considering White for the post of Managing Director. On 4 February the President received an FBI report, dated 1 February, on White. Truman sent a copy to Vinson and suggested that he, Vinson and Secretary of State Byrnes, who already had a copy, should meet and decide the next step. Before they met, the Senate confirmed White's nomination as Executive Director. The President decided to let White's appointment take its normal course, but White's chances of becoming Managing Director had vanished.[30]

On 8 March, Keynes travelled to Savannah. There he told the press that he and the British delegation 'eagerly anticipate[d] their brief sojourn in this gracious place'. Yet the next day, when he was the final speaker in the opening joint session of the meetings, he was ambivalent. When treating the affair as the christening of Master Fund and Miss Bank, whose names he thought should be reversed, he lightly called upon fairies to bring the new institutions the appropriate gifts before concluding:

> I hope that Mr Kelchner [the secretary] has not made any mistake and that there is no malicious fairy, no Carabosse, whom he has overlooked and forgotten to ask to the party. For if so the curses which the bad fairy will pronounce will, I feel sure, run as follows: – 'You two brats shall grow up politicians; your every thought and act shall have an *arrière-pensée*; everything you determine shall not be for its own sake or on its merits but because of something else.'
>
> If this should happen, then the best that could befall – and that is how it might turn out – would be for the children to fall into an eternal slumber, never to waken or be heard of again in the courts and markets of Mankind.
>
> Well, ladies and gentlemen, fairies or no fairies, this looks like being a very pleasant party and a happy christening and let the omens be good.[31]

Vinson was not amused. A lawyer and a politician, with a different conception of the new institutions, he took Keynes's remarks personally. One participant recalled him growling, 'I don't mind being called malicious, but I do mind being called a fairy!'[32]

Nor did the party turn out to be pleasant. As he told Richard Kahn:

> The Americans have no idea of how to make these institutions into operating international concerns and in almost every direction their ideas are bad. Yet they plainly intend to force their own conceptions through regardless of the rest of us. . . . At present I can only say I am pretty pessimistic. The Americans at the top seem to have no conception of international co-operation; since they are the biggest partners they think they have the right to call the tune on every point. If they knew the music that would not matter so much; but unfortunately they don't.[33]

His disappointment showed in his comments. He spoke of Mr Vinson's 'pathetic procession of stooges' who helped him in 'rail-roading' decisions through the meetings, of 'political and financial patronage . . . of the first order', of it being 'unlikely' that Mr Vinson had 'given ten minutes' thought to what he would like the institutions to be doing two years hence'.[34]

Much of the business was uncontroversial – the date of the institutions' financial year, minor mistakes in drafting the electoral rules for the Executive Directors, and interim financial arrangements. There was controversy when Vinson proposed an Executive Committee of twelve members with himself in the chair and Keynes as vice-chairman to which matters, particularly concerning procedure, could be referred. Initially Keynes thought that this committee would only exist for the period of the meetings, but he subsequently discovered from the press that Vinson intended it to continue in existence between meetings of the Governors thus making 'it possible for Mr Vinson . . . to butt in on the work of the Executive Directors whenever he felt inclined'. After strong objections from the British, French and Canadians this notion disappeared in favour of a procedures committee available for consultation about future business for the Governors and preparing agendas for future Board meetings.[35]

As expected, two matters were more controversial: the site of the head offices and the role of the Executive Directors. At Bretton Woods, it had been agreed, despite British objections, that the Fund and the Bank would be located in the country with the largest quota, i.e. the United States. Keynes had hoped that the two bodies would be in New York, close to the site of the United Nations Organisation and 'in the daily contacts which can be provided by a great centre of international finance . . . sufficiently removed from the politics of Congress and the nationalistic whispering gallery of the embassies and legations of Washington'. The Americans, as Keynes had learned in Washington, had decided otherwise and, despite support from France and India, Keynes could not reverse the American decision, which had widespread support elsewhere. He conceded defeat rather gracelessly in the end, referring to the 'unyielding attitude' of the American representative and noting that the arguments presented in favour of Washington had not persuaded him that a mistake was not being made.[36]

As for the duties of the Executive Directors, the Articles of Agreement required them to 'function in continuous session at the principal office of the Fund and . . . meet as often as the business of the Fund may require'. Each Executive Director would appoint an Alternate. The Americans believed that this meant that the Executive Directors and their Alternates should be full-time in Washington, while Keynes took it to mean that they were to be available to act whenever necessary. He could not see that there would be enough work for a group 'who could amount at the maximum to a mob of forty-eight'. He reported later that 'Mr Rasminsky of Canada had a nightmare of Directors and Alternates studying trends (which, we were told, might be one of their more chronic duties) *and voting on them*.' He feared that the presence of so many underemployed directors in Washington would limit the discretion of the Fund's permanent staff. Wondering whether there were sufficiently qualified people available, he worried that some countries might appoint less-qualified Directors. As he put it to Brand, 'Executive Directors will be retired Indian Civil Servants rather than Deputy Governors of central banks'. In the end, there was some compromise in that between them the Executive Director and his Alternate were to be continuously available.[37]

This compromise was, however, only partial, as became clear when it came to their salaries. Given the compromise, Keynes suggested that an

Executive Director should be paid a salary that would leave something over for his Alternate on the assumption that only one was in Washington at any time. The Americans who intended to appoint four full-time people to the two institutions resisted, suggesting $17,500 for a Director and $11,500 for an Alternate.[b] Even though these rates were maxima – part-timers would be paid on a *pro-rata* basis and Governors could appoint individuals on the assumption that they accepted less – when the issue came before the Governors, Keynes, on instructions from the Chancellor, voted against. It was the only negative vote of the meetings.

Thus the meetings were a disappointment for Keynes, although he admitted that they became mellower towards the end and that many American officials told him that many of his criticisms were justified. On the last evening, when Keynes left the dining room 'the whole company', according to Rowe-Dutton, 'rose to its feet to sing "For he's a jolly good fellow". For once the conference showed complete unanimity'.[38]

Keynes left the meetings for New York later by train the same evening. The next morning he had problems. He told Plesch:

> Unfortunately in the enormously long train in which we travelled back to New York, I walked too fast down the swaying carriages what seemed almost a quarter of a mile (and I think it must have been just about that distance) to the restaurant car. When I got there I was quite knocked out, and so remained for about an hour. This time I had no palpitations or heart symptoms at all, except that I felt exactly as though I was at the end of a long running race, but a certain measure of distress continued for much longer.[39,c]

After a night's rest in New York, he felt back to normal and spent his one free day in New York largely on Arts Council and Covent Garden business. He embarked on the *Queen Mary* on 22 March.

The voyage back was far from restful. Keynes himself left one report of it to Plesch:

> In common with about a quarter of the passengers, I got a stomach bug, like gastric flu, but not nearly so bad, on the boat. Painful, but only lasting a couple of days.[40]

As with his difficulties in the train to Washington, this was an understatement. Others reported that the part of the *Queen Mary* where Keynes had

b These salaries were net of tax in all countries. This made the salary for a British Executive Director the equivalent of £15,000, or four times that of the Permanent Secretary of the Treasury. For Americans, Keynes conceded, the salaries, although handsome, could be justified (*JMK*, XXVI, 223).

c Keynes's report understated the seriousness of his problem. Roy Bridge remembered helping to carry Keynes to the dining car, where he was laid out on a table. I am indebted to L. S. Pressnell for this information.

his cabin had been badly cleaned after crossing from England with returning GI brides and their babies and that those with cabins there suffered acute stomach disorders and diarrhoea. The crossing was also rough.

We know that on the voyage Keynes composed one document – a report on the Savannah Conference, which has served as the basis for much of what I have written above.[41] He also may have added some finishing touches to his *Economic Journal* article after gathering additional information in New York and Washington. Twenty-six years later, in an article in *The Banker*, Sir George Bolton suggested that he wrote something else as well.

> He spent the voyage writing an article for publication condemning American policy with extraordinary ferocity and passionately recommending H.M. Government to refuse to ratify the Fund and Bank agreement; such action would automatically have frustrated the U.S. and Canadian Loan Agreements. . . . [T]he publication in 1946 of such an explosive document as Keynes wrote would have had momentous political results; so Ernest Rowe-Dutton and I spent most of the voyage trying to dissuade Keynes from pursuing these proposals. Eventually, he agreed to destroy the paper.[42]

It would seem that Sir George Bolton's memory of the events of late March 1946 was misleading. On the matter of fact, Britain had already ratified the Fund and Bank agreements in December 1945; so Britain could not refuse to do so. It is hardly likely that Keynes would recommend withdrawal, even though he was obviously disappointed with the results of Savannah. Moreover, Keynes was drafting his Treasury report on board ship, which had many extremely sharp passages about American behaviour. Even Keynes on arriving in London felt it had 'the effect of giving greater emphasis of discontent than I really intend', noted that his 'own reactions to the Conference changed with further reflection', and proposed to 'rehash the document before it received wider circulation'.[43] On top of this was the *Economic Journal* article on which there already had been and would be later doubts about the wisdom of its publication in case it jeopardised the passage of the Loan through Congress. Indeed, as Brand reported to Eady on 1 May, Graham Towers who had seen it at Savannah was critical and by then Brand himself had recommended that the article not be published.[44] Since it is likely that Bolton would know of Towers's opinion – or knew of it later after Keynes's death when Sir Wilfrid Eady tried to decide what to do with the article – it seems likely that Bolton ran the draft Treasury report and the *Economic Journal* article together. For as the voyage lasted six days, during at least 'a couple' of which he was painfully ill, it seems unlikely that Keynes, who had also had the recent severe collapse on the train to New York, would have the physical energy to write a report of eighteen printed pages *and* an article which he subsequently destroyed – an article which Roy Bridge who acted as secretary to the Delegation does not mention.

Keynes was clearly exhausted on his return to London. Sir Wilfrid Eady later recalled:

> We were rather worried about Maynard when he came back from Savannah. He was not only very white, but he slumped in his chair, and very gentle as though he found it very difficult to revive interest in all the many daily things on which he guided us.[45]

He consulted Plesch immediately on his return and saw him again before he went down to Tilton on 12 April. The report was reassuring. During the week in the office before going down to Tilton 'he seemed much better' according to Eady's report to Brand.

In spite of his exhaustion, he was extremely busy in the fortnight between his return from Savannah and his going down to Tilton for Easter. He saw Camille Gutt, the Executive Director of the Fund for Belgium, Iceland and Luxembourg as well as a Minister of State and former Finance Minister of Belgium about his becoming the Managing Director of the Fund; took part in the series of meetings of Treasury and Bank officials on the Government's borrowing policy; drafted fragments of Dalton's Budget Speech for 9 April; joined in the discussion of his Savannah report and in a discussion of the forthcoming Economic Survey where faced with 'the whole battery of Keynes's wit, petulance, rudeness and quick unscrupulousness in argument' James Meade reported, 'I was actually reduced to tears'.[46] All of this was on top of his Arts Council, National Gallery and Provincial Insurance Company business. He had several evenings out, including a meeting of the Other Club. As well as his Treasury drafting, which included another report 'Random Reflections From a Visit to U.S.A.',[47] which went to the Prime Minister, Lord President, Lord Privy Seal and the Foreign, Dominion and Colonial Secretaries, he spent Sunday, 7 April drafting an article on 'Bernard Shaw and Isaac Newton', for a collection of essays in honour of Shaw's ninetieth birthday.[48] Apart from some final alterations to his *Economic Journal* article, this was the last thing he wrote for publication.

His 'holiday' at Tilton took the usual form. There was Treasury work to do, with a large bag of official papers requiring a couple of hours' work each morning. At the time of his death he was beginning a post-Budget memorandum for the Chancellor arguing that the wartime policy of cost-of-living stabilisation was now potentially unstable and that a gradual and controlled rise in prices and wages was desirable if the Chancellor was to avoid a sudden collapse of the policy. He also prophesied that in the future inflation was more likely to be caused by changes in costs than by excess demand. He offered no solution. There were also walks around the farm, consultations with Logan Thompson, and long periods of reading in the garden, sampling his latest acquisitions of rare books. On Thursday afternoon there was tea at Charleston with Vanessa and Clive Bell and Duncan Grant. There were also trips to the top of the Downs by car. On 20 April, his third ascent of the week, he decided to walk down from Firle Beacon with Lydia, leaving his mother to return by car. There were no problems with the journey. But next morning there was another attack. This time there was no recovery: in Lydia's presence, he died within three minutes. He was 63.

He was cremated in Brighton on 24 April. The mourners were Lydia, his sister Margaret, his mother and 'a number of tenants and farm workers' from Tilton.[49] His ashes were scattered on the Downs above Tilton where he and Lydia used to walk. Lydia's ashes were scattered beside them 35 years later.[d]

d Keynes's will stated that his ashes were to be deposited in the crypt at King's, but Geoffrey Keynes, 'not a very conscientious executor' according to his son Richard, forgot about that instruction and scattered them on the Downs. Thus when Richard Keynes, acting as Lydia's executor, had to deal with Lydia's ashes, he too could not follow the instructions in the will to put them beside Keynes's in King's and scattered them on the Downs.

NOTES

1 *JMK*, XXIV, 624; XXVII, 426–7, where the quotation also appears.
2 *JMK*, XXVII, 463–5.
3 It was originally sent on 25 October 1945 as NABOB SAVING 23.
4 Rees 1974, 371.
5 OBL, Brand Papers, Box 90, Brand to Eady, 1 May 1946.
6 *JMK*, XXVII, 444.
7 *JMK*, XXVII, 444.
8 *JMK*, XXVII, 445.
9 *JMK*, XXVII, 445; the original remarks are in *JMK*, XXIV, 621.
10 The notes are in KCKP, PS.
11 Howson and Moggridge (eds) 1990a, 216, 225.
12 *JMK*, XXVII, 465–81.
13 *JMK*, XXVII, 479, 480.
14 BLPES, Dalton Diary, vol. 34, 18 February 1946, 1.
15 *JMK*, XXVII, 462.
16 *JMK*, XXVII, 461.
17 *JMK*, XXVII, 463.
18 *JMK*, XXVII, 449, 455–6, 454–5; Howson and Moggridge (eds) 1990a, 226–7.
19 *JMK*, XXVII, 456–7, 486–7; XXVI, 210: Pressnell 1987, 362–3.
20 Howson and Moggridge (eds) 1990a, 290–1.
21 Howson 1987, 441–4.
22 Howson and Moggridge (eds) 1990a, 194, 200–1, 204, 213; *JMK*, XXII, 382.
23 Rees 1974, 367.
24 KCKP, JMK to FAK, 15 February 1946; *JMK*, XXVI, 209.
25 KCKP, JMK to G. L. Keynes, 5 March 1946.
26 Howson 1987, 444–5.
27 *JMK*, XXVI, 211.
28 *JMK*, XXVI, 208.
29 *JMK*, XXVI, 211.

30 Rees 1974, ch. 23.
31 *JMK*, XXVI, 214, 216–17.
32 Gardner 1956, 266 n. 4.
33 *JMK*, XXVI, 217.
34 *JMK*, XXVI, 217, 222, 225, 228.
35 *JMK*, XXVI, 226.
36 *JMK*, XXVI, 221; Horsefield 1969, I, 130.
37 *JMK*, XXVI, 225, 228, 208.
38 *JMK*, XXVI, 232 n. 51.
39 KCKP, JMK to Plesch, 20 March 1946.
40 KCKP, JMK to Plesch, 30 March 1946, a postscript to his letter of 20 March.
41 KCKP, L/B, JMK to R. H. Brand, 3 April 1946. The report appears in *JMK*, XXVI, 220–38.
42 Bolton 1972, 1387.
43 *JMK*, XXVI, 220. In the event Maynard did not substantially revise the document.
44 See above p. 822; OBL, Brand Papers, Box 197, Brand to Eady, 1 May 1946.
45 OBL, Brand Papers, Box 197, 23 April 1946.
46 Howson and Moggridge (eds) 1990a, 251.
47 *JMK*, XXVII, 482–7.
48 *JMK*, X, ch. 36.
49 *Cambridge Independent Press and Chronicle*, 26 April 1946.

ANNEX 1 – A KEY FOR THE PRURIENT: KEYNES'S LOVES, 1901–15

1901	ADK (Dillwyn Knox)
1902	ADK
	DM (Daniel Macmillan)
1903	nil
1904	nil
1905	nil
1906	GLS (Lytton Strachey)
	JBS (James Strachey)
	ALH (Arthur Hobhouse)
1907	GLS
	JBS
1908	GLS
	JBS
	DG (Duncan Grant)
1909	JBS
	DG
	StG (St George Nelson)
	Stable boy of Park Lane
1910	DG
	FB (Francis Birrell)
	StG
1911	DG
	Jack Colby
	Rosario Sciacca
	16-year-old under Etna
	Auburn haired of Marble Arch
	StG
	Lift boy of Vauxhall
	[undecipherable]
1912	DG
	BKS (B. K. Sarkar)
	Jew boy

Chester (Chester Purves)
1913 DG
StG
Chester
FB
Cookie (S. Russell Cooke)
Brush
Salem
Cairo
BKS
1914 StG
BKS
Cookie
Felkin (Elliott Felkin)
DG
1915 DG
BG (Bunny Garnett)
FB
GLS
Grip (unknown)
Tressider (J. T. Sheppard)
Cookie

BIBLIOGRAPHY

UNPUBLISHED PAPERS

Arts Council of Great Britain

Baker Library, Harvard Business School
   Lamont Papers

Bank of England
   Thompson-McCausland Papers

Bodleian Library, Oxford
   Brand Papers

British Library
   Ashley Papers
   Falk Papers
   Duncan Grant Papers
   Macmillan Archives
   Strachey Papers

British Library of Political and Economic Science
   Cannan Papers
   Dalton Diaries
   David Low Cartoon Collection
   Beatrice Webb Diaries

Cambridge University Library
   J. N. Keynes Papers
   J. N. Keynes Diaries
   G. E. Moore Papers
   University of Cambridge Archives

Federal Reserve Bank of New York
   Archives
   Harrison Collection

Sir Frederic Harmer
  Diary of the 1945 Anglo-American Loan Negotiations

Polly Hill
  Letters from J. M. Keynes to Margaret Keynes and A. V. Hill Letters from F. A.
  Keynes to J. N. Keynes

House of Lords
  Lloyd George Papers

India Office Library, London
  India Office Papers

Richard Keynes
  Letters from J. M. Keynes to Geoffrey Keynes

King's College, Cambridge
  Charleston Papers
  Joan Robinson Papers
  Keynes Papers
  Ramsey Papers

Magdalene College, Cambridge, Pepys Library
  A. C. Benson Diaries

Marshall Library, Cambridge
  J. N. Keynes Papers
  Marshall Papers

New York Public Library, Berg Collection
  Keynes–Strachey Correspondence

Northwestern University Library
  Keynes–Vanessa Bell Correspondence

Public Record Office, London
  Cabinet Papers
  Treasury Papers

Franklin Delano Roosevelt Library
  Morgenthau Diaries

Reform Club
  Eagar Papers

Royal Economic Society
  Minutebooks

Scottish Record Office
  Lothian Papers

Trinity College, Cambridge
  Montagu Papers
  Pethick-Lawrence Papers

The Collected Writings of John Maynard Keynes, Managing Editors Sir Austin
  Robinson and Donald Moggridge, London: Macmillan, 1971–1989.

I	*Indian Currency and Finance*
II	*Economic Consequences of the Peace*
III	*A Revision of the Treaty*
IV	*A Tract on Monetary Reform*
V	*A Treatise on Money, I The Pure Theory of Money*
VI	*A Treatise on Money, II The Applied Theory of Money*
VII	*The General Theory of Employment, Interest and Money*
VIII	*A Treatise on Probability*
IX	*Essays in Persuasion*
X	*Essays in Biography*
XI	*Economic Articles and Correspondence: Academic* (ed. D. Moggridge)
XII	*Economic Articles and Correspondence: Investment and Editorial* (ed. D. Moggridge)
XIII	*The General Theory and After: Part I, Preparation* (ed. D. Moggridge)
XIV	*The General Theory and After: Part II, Defence and Development* (ed. D. Moggridge)
XV	*Activities 1906–14: India and Cambridge* (ed. E. Johnson)
XVI	*Activities 1914–19: The Treasury and Versailles* (ed. E. Johnson)
XVII	*Activities 1920–2: Treaty Revision and Reconstruction* (ed. E. Johnson)
XVIII	*Activities 1922–32: The End of Reparations* (ed. E. Johnson)
XIX	*Activities 1922–9: The Return to Gold and Industrial Policy* (ed. D. Moggridge)
XX	*Activities 1929–31: Rethinking Employment and Unemployment Policies* (ed. D. Moggridge)
XXI	*Activities 1931–9: World Crises and Policies in Britain and America* (ed. D. Moggridge)
XXII	*Activities 1939–45: Internal War Finance* (ed. D. Moggridge)
XXIII	*Activities 1940–3: External War Finance* (ed. D. Moggridge)
XXIV	*Activities 1944–6: The Transition to Peace* (ed. D. Moggridge)
XXV	*Activities 1940–4: Shaping the Post-War World – The Clearing Union* (ed. D. Moggridge)
XXVI	*Activities 1944–6: Shaping the Post-War World – Bretton Woods and Reparations* (ed. D. Moggridge)
XXVII	*Activities 1940–6: Shaping the Post-War World – Employment and Commodities* (ed. D. Moggridge)
XXVIII	*Social, Political and Literary Writings* (ed. D. Moggridge)
XXIX	*The General Theory and After: A Supplement to Vols. XIII and XIV* (ed. D. Moggridge)
XXX	*Index and Bibliography* (ed. D. Moggridge)

ARTICLES, BOOKS AND DISSERTATIONS

Acheson, Dean 1970, *Present at the Creation*, London: Hamish Hamilton.
Addison, Paul 1975, *The Road to 1945: British Politics and the Second World War*,
  London: Cape.

Allen, Peter 1978, *The Cambridge Apostles: The Early Years*, Cambridge: Cambridge University Press.

Allen, Robert Loring 1991, *Opening Doors: The Life and Work of Joseph Schumpeter*, 2 vols, New Brunswick, N.J.: Transaction Publishers.

Amadeo, Edward J. 1989, *Keynes's Principle of Effective Demand*, Aldershot: Edward Elgar.

Angell, Norman 1910, *The Great Illusion: A Study of the Relation of Military Power in Nations to their Economic and Social Advantage*, London: Heinemann.

Annan, Noel 1951, 'A Man of Peerless Intellect', *The Listener*, 3 May.

——1979, 'A Spontaneous Liberality', *Times Literary Supplement*, 31 July.

——1984, 'Portrait of a Genius as a Young Man', *New York Review of Books*, 19 July.

——1990, *Our Age: Portrait of a Generation*, London: Weidenfeld & Nicolson.

Ashby, Eric 1958, *Technology and the Academics*, London: Macmillan.

Ashley, A. 1932, *William James Ashley: A Life*, London: King.

Asquith, Margot (Countess of Oxford and Asquith) 1943, *Off the Record*, London: Frederick Muller.

Austin-Leigh, R. C. 1981, *A Guide to Eton College* (rev. by R. C. Martineau & T. P. Connor), Eton: Eton College.

Ayer, A. J. 1977, *Part of My Life*, London: Collins.

Bagchi, A. K. 1989, *The Presidency Banks and the Indian Economy, 1876–1914*, Calcutta: Oxford University Press for the State Bank of India.

Barens, I. 1990, 'The Rise and Fall of the "Entrepreneur Economy": Some Remarks on Keynes's Taxonomy of Economies', in D. E. Moggridge (ed.) *Perspectives on the History of Economic Thought*, IV, Aldershot: Edward Elgar.

Barker, T. H. 1977, 'The Beginnings of the Economic History Society', *Economic History Review*, 2nd Ser., XXX (February).

Barnes, J. and Nicholson, D. (eds) 1988, *The Empire at Bay: The Leo Amery Diaries, 1929–1945*, London: Hutchinson.

Bateman, B. W. 1987, 'Keynes's Changing Conception of Probability', *Economics and Philosophy*, III (October).

——1988, 'G. E. Moore and J. M. Keynes: A Missing Chapter in the History of the Expected Utility Model', *American Economic Review*, LXXVIII (December).

——1990, 'The Elusive Logical Relation: An Essay on Change and Continuity in Keynes's Thought', in D. E. Moggridge (ed.) *Perspectives on the History of Economic Thought*, IV, Aldershot: Edward Elgar.

Beaverbrook, Lord 1956, *Men and Power 1917–1918*, London: Hutchinson.

Bell, Anne Olivier (ed.) 1977–84, *The Diary of Virginia Woolf*, 5 vols, London: Hogarth Press.

Bell, Clive 1956, *Old Friends: Personal Recollections*, London: Chatto & Windus.

Bell, Quentin (ed.) 1938, *Julian Bell: Essays, Papers and Letters*, London: Hogarth Press.

——1974, *Bloomsbury*, London: Omega Books.

Birkenhead, Earl of 1961, *The Prof in Two Worlds: The Official Life of Professor F. A. Lindemann, Viscount Cherwell*, London: Collins.

——1965, *Halifax: The Life of Lord Halifax*, London: Hamish Hamilton.

Black, R. D. Collison 1977, 'Ralph George Hawtrey, 1879–1975', *Proceedings of the British Academy*, LXIII.

——(ed.) 1972–81, *Papers and Correspondence of William Stanley Jevons*, 7 vols, London: Macmillan.

Blake, Robert 1955, *The Unknown Prime Minister: The Life and Times of Andrew Bonar Law, 1858–1923*, London: Eyre & Spottiswoode.

Blaug, Mark 1980, *The Methodology of Economics or How Economists Explain*, Cambridge: Cambridge University Press.

——1990, 'On the Historiography of Economics', *Journal of the History of Economic Thought*, XII (Spring).

Blum, J. M. (ed.) 1959, *From the Morgenthau Diaries*, vol. I, *Years of Crisis, 1928–1938*, Boston: Houghton Mifflin.

——1965, *From the Morgenthau Diaries*, vol. II, *Years of Urgency, 1938–1941*, Boston: Houghton Mifflin.

——1967, *From the Morgenthau Diaries*, vol. III, *Years of Achievement, 1941–1945*, Boston: Houghton Mifflin.

Bolton, Sir George 1972, 'Where the Critics are as Wrong as Keynes Was', *The Banker*, November.

Booth, A. 1983, 'The "Keynesian Revolution" in Economic Policy-Making', *Economic History Review*, 2nd Ser., XXXVI (February).

——1989, *British Economic Policy, 1931–49: Was There a Keynesian Revolution?*, Brighton: Harvester Wheatsheaf.

Borchardt, Knut 1988, 'Keynes' "Nationale Selbstgenugsamkeit" van 1933: Ein Fall von kooperativer Selbstzensur', *Zeitschrift für Wirtschaft und Sozialwissenschaften*, 108(2).

Bowley, A. H. n.d., *A Memoir of Professor Sir Arthur Bowley, 1869–1957*, privately printed.

Boyce, Robert W. D. 1987, *British Capitalism at the Crossroads, 1919–1932: A Study in Politics, Economics and International Relations*, Cambridge: Cambridge University Press.

Boyle, Andrew 1967, *Montagu Norman*, London: Collins.

——1979, *The Climate of Treason*, London: Hodder & Stoughton.

——1980, *The Climate of Treason*, 2nd edn, London: Cornet Books.

Boys Smith, J. S. 1983, *Memoirs of St John's College Cambridge 1919–1969*, Cambridge: St John's College.

Braithwaite, R. B. 1961, 'George Edward Moore 1873–1958', *Proceedings of the British Academy*, XLVII.

Bravo, G. F. 1989, '"In the Name of Our Mutual Friend . . .": The Keynes–Cuno Affair', *Journal of Contemporary History*, XXIV.

Broad, C. D. 1922, 'Critical Notes on J. M. Keynes's Treatise on Probability', *Mind*, XXXI.

——1950, 'John Neville Keynes', *Economic Journal*, LX (June).

Brock, M. and Brock E. (eds) 1982, *H. H. Asquith: Letters to Venetia Stanley*, Oxford: Oxford University Press.

Brown, A. J. 1988, 'A Worm's Eye View of the Keynesian Revolution', in J. Hilliard (ed.) *J. M. Keynes in Retrospect: The Legacy of the Keynesian Revolution*, Aldershot: Edward Elgar.

Brown, E. H. Phelps 1980, 'Sir Roy Harrod: A Biographical Memoir', *Economic Journal*, XC (March).

——1987, 'Lionel Charles Robbins, 1898–1984', *Proceedings of the British Academy*, LXXIII.

Brown, E. H. Phelps and Browne, M. H. 1967, *A Century of Pay*, London: Macmillan.

Brown, Neville 1988, *Dissenting Forebears: The Maternal Ancestors of J. M. Keynes*, Chichester: Phillimore.

Buckle, Richard 1979, *Diaghilev*, London: Weidenfeld & Nicolson.

Bullen, Roger and Pelly, M. E. (eds) 1986, *Documents on British Policy Overseas, Series I, Volume III, Britain and America: Negotiation of the United States Loan, 3 August – 7 December 1945*, London: Her Majesty's Stationery Office.

Bullock, Alan 1982, *Ernest Bevin Foreign Secretary*, Oxford: Oxford University Press.

Bunselmeyer, R. E. 1975, *The Cost of the War, 1914–1919: British Economic War Aims and the Origins of Reparation*, Hamden, Conn: Archon.

Burk, K. 1979, 'J. M. Keynes and the Exchange Rate Crisis of 1917', *Economic History Review*, 2nd Ser., XXXII (November).

——1981, 'Economic Diplomacy Between the Wars', *Historical Journal*, XXIV(4).

——1985, *Britain, America and the Sinews of War, 1914–1918*, London: Allen & Unwin.

Burnett, P. M. 1940, *Reparations at the Peace Conference from the Standpoint of the American Delegation*, New York: Columbia University Press.

Cairncross, A. 1986, *The Price of War: British Policy on German Reparations, 1941–1949*, Oxford: Blackwell.

Cairncross, A. and Eichengreen B. 1983, *Sterling in Decline: The Devaluations of 1931, 1949 and 1967*, Oxford: Blackwell.

Cairncross, A. and Watts, N. 1989, *The Economic Section, 1939–1961: A Study in Economic Advising*, London: Routledge.

Cairncross, F. (ed.) 1981, *Changing Perceptions of Economic Policy*, London: Methuen.

Campbell, J. 1977, *Lloyd George: The Goat in the Wilderness 1922–1931*, London: Cape.

Capie, F. 1983, *Depression and Protectionism: Britain between the Wars*, London: Allen & Unwin.

Capie, F. and Collins, M. 1984, *The Inter-War British Economy: A Statistical Abstract*, Manchester: Manchester University Press.

Carabelli, A. M. 1988, *On Keynes's Method*, London: Macmillan.

Ceadel, M. 1980, *Pacifism in Britain, 1914–1945: The Defending of a Faith*, Oxford: Clarendon Press.

Chandavarkar, A. 1990, *Keynes and India: A Study in Economics and Biography*, London: Macmillan.

Chasse, J. D. 1984, 'Marshall, the Human Agent and Economic Growth: Wants and Activities Revisited', *History of Political Economy*, XVI (Fall).

Clark, Colin 1932, *The National Income, 1924–1931*, London: Macmillan.

Clark, Kenneth 1977, *The Other Half: A Self Portrait*, London: John Murray.

Clarke, Peter 1978, *Liberals and Social Democrats*, Cambridge: Cambridge University Press.

——1988, *The Keynesian Revolution in the Making*, Oxford: Clarendon Press.

Clarke, Sir Richard 1982, *Anglo-American Economic Collaboration in War and Peace 1942–1949* (Sir Alec Cairncross ed.), Oxford: Clarendon Press.

Clarks 1935, *John Bates Clark: A Memorial Volume Prepared by His Children*, privately printed.

Clay, Sir Henry 1957, *Lord Norman*, London: Macmillan.

Coase, R. H. 1972, 'The Appointment of Pigou as Marshall's Successor: Comment', *Journal of Law and Economics*, XV (October).

——1975, 'Marshall on Method', *Journal of Law and Economics*, XVIII (April).

——1984, 'Alfred Marshall's Mother and Father', *History of Political Economy*, XVI (Winter).

Coats, A. W. 1968, 'Political Economy and the Tariff Reform Campaign of 1903', *Journal of Law and Economics*, XI (April).

Coats, A.W. 1972, 'The Appointment of Pigou as Marshall's Successor: Comment', *Journal of Law and Economics*, XV (October).

——(ed.) 1981, *Economists in Government: An International Comparative Study*, Durham, N.C.: Duke University Press.

Coats, A. W. and Coats, S. E. 1973, 'The Changing Composition of the Royal Economic Society, 1890–1960 and the Professionalisation of British Economics', *British Journal of Sociology*, XXIV.

Cole, M. 1971, *The Life of G. D. H. Cole*, London: Macmillan.

Coleman, D. C. 1969, *Courtaulds: An Economic and Social History*, Volume II, *Rayon*, Oxford: Clarendon Press.

Collini, S., Winch, D. and Burrow J. 1983, *That Noble Science of Politics: A Study in Nineteenth Century Intellectual History*, Cambridge: Cambridge University Press.

Colville, John 1987, *The Fringes of Power: Downing Street Diaries*, 2 vols, London: Sceptre.

Connolly, Cyril 1961, *Enemies of Promise*, Harmondsworth: Penguin.

Cornford, F. M. 1908, *Microcosmographia Academia: Being a Guide to the Young Academic Politician*, Cambridge: Bowes and Bowes.

Crabtree, D. and Thirlwall, A. P. (eds) 1980, *Keynes and the Bloomsbury Group*, London: Macmillan.

Creighton, D. 1957, *Harold Adams Innis: Portrait of a Scholar*, Toronto: University of Toronto Press.

Crick, B. 1980, *George Orwell: A Life*, London: Secker & Warburg.

Cunynghame, H. 1904, *A Geometrical Political Economy, Being an Elementary Treatise on Explaining some of the Theories of Pure Economic Science*, Oxford: Clarendon Press.

Dallek, Robert 1979, *Franklin D. Roosevelt and American Foreign Policy*, New York: Oxford University Press.

Dalton, Hugh 1962, *High Tide and After: Memoirs 1945–1960*, London: Frederick Muller.

Darroch, Sandra Jobson 1976, *Ottoline: The Life of Lady Ottoline Morrell*, London: Chatto & Windus.

Davenport, N. 1974, *Memoirs of a City Radical*, London: Weidenfeld & Nicolson.

Davis, Eric 1980, 'The Correspondence between R. G. Hawtrey and J. M. Keynes on the *Treatise*: The Genesis of Output Adjustment Models', *Canadian Journal of Economics*, 13 (November).

Davis, J. R. 1971, *The New Economics and the Old Economists*, Ames: Iowa State University Press.

Dawson, R. MacGregor 1961, *The Conscription Crisis of 1944*, Toronto: University of Toronto Press.

Dayer, Roberta Allbert 1988, *Finance and Empire: Sir Charles Addis, 1861–1945*, London: Macmillan.

Deacon, Richard 1985, *The Cambridge Apostles: A History of Cambridge University's Elite Intellectual Secret Society*, New York: Farrar, Strauss & Giroux.

Delany, Paul 1978, *D. H. Lawrence's Nightmare: The Writer and his Circle in the Years of the Great War*, New York: Basic Books.

——1988, *The Neo-Pagans: Friendship and Love in the Rupert Brooke Circle*, London: Macmillan.

de Marchi, N. 1988, 'Popper and the LSE Economists' in N. de Marchi (ed.), *The Popperian Legacy*, Cambridge: Cambridge University Press.

De Morgan, A. 1847, *Formal Logic: or The Calculus of Inference, Necessary and Probable*, London: Taylor & Walton.

Deutscher, P. 1990, *R. G. Hawtrey and the Development of Macroeconomics*, London: Macmillan.

Dimand, R. W. 1988, *The Origins of the Keynesian Revolution: The Development of Keynes's Theory of Output and Employment*, Aldershot: Edward Elgar.

Dowie, J. 1975, '1919–20 is in Need of Attention', *Economic History Review*, 2nd Ser., XXVIII (November).

Drummond, Ian M. 1981, *The Floating Pound and the Sterling Area, 1931–1939*, Cambridge: Cambridge University Press.

Durbin, Elizabeth 1985, *New Jerusalems: The Labour Party and the Economics of Democratic Socialism*, London: Routledge & Kegan Paul.

Dutton, David 1985, *Austen Chamberlain: Gentleman in Politics*, Bolton: Ross Anderson Publications.

Dyson, Freeman 1981, *Disturbing the Universe*, London: Pan.

Eady, Sir Wilfrid 1951, 'Maynard Keynes at the Treasury', *The Listener*, 7 June, 903 and 920.

Eatwell, J. and Milgate, M. (eds) 1983, *Keynes's Economics and the Theory of Value and Distribution*, London: Duckworth.

Edel, Leon 1987, *Writing Lives: Principia Biographica*, New York: Norton.

Edwards, Ruth Dudley 1987, *Victor Gollancz: A Biography*, London: Gollancz.

Eichengreen, Barry 1981, 'Sterling and the Tariff 1929–1932', *Princeton Studies in International Finance*, No. 48 (September).

Elcock, H. 1972, *Portrait of a Decision: The Council of Four and the Treaty of Versailles*, London: Eyre Methuen.

Eshag, E. 1963, *From Marshall to Keynes: An Essay on the Monetary Theory of the Cambridge School*, Oxford: Blackwell.

Feinstein, C. H. 1972, *National Income, Expenditure and Output of the United Kingdom 1855–1965*, Cambridge: Cambridge University Press.

Feis, H. 1966, *1933: Characters in Crisis*, Boston: Little Brown.

Feiwel, G. F. 1975, *The Intellectual Capital of Michal Kalecki*, Knoxville: University of Tennessee Press.

Ferrell, R. H. 1985, *Woodrow Wilson and World War I, 1917–1921*, New York: Harper & Row.

Fetter, F. W. 1977, 'Lenin, Keynes and Inflation', *Economica*, N.S., XLIV (February).

Fisher, I. N. 1956, *My Father Irving Fisher*, New York: Comet Press.

Fitzgerald, Penelope 1977, *The Knox Brothers*, London: Macmillan.

Fitzgibbons, A. 1988, *Keynes's Vision: A New Political Economy*, Oxford: Clarendon Press.

Fouraker, L. E. 1958/82, 'The Cambridge Didactic Style', *Journal of Political Economy*, LIVI (February), reprinted in Wood 1982.

Foxwell, H. S. 1887, 'The Economic Movement in England', *Quarterly Journal of Economics*, II (October).

Freeden, M. 1986, *Liberalism Divided: A Study in British Political Thought 1914–1939*, Oxford: Clarendon Press.

Fullerton, D. H. 1986, *Graham Towers and His Times: A Biography*, Toronto: McClelland and Stewart.

Furbank, P. N. 1977–8, *E. M. Forster: A Life*, 2 vols, London: Secker & Warburg.

Gardner, R. N. 1956, *Sterling–Dollar Diplomacy*, Oxford: Clarendon Press.

Gardlund, T. 1958, *The Life of Knut Wicksell*, Stockholm: Almquist & Wicksell.

Garnett, D. 1953, *The Golden Echo*, London: Chatto & Windus.

——1955, *The Flowers of the Forest*, London: Chatto & Windus.

——1962, *The Familiar Faces*, London: Chatto & Windus.

Garnett, D. 1979, *Great Friends: Portraits of Seventeen Writers*, London: Macmillan.
Garnett, Richard 1991, *Constance Garnett: A Heroic Life*, London: Sinclair-Stevenson.
Gathorne-Hardy, J. 1979, *The Public School Phenomenon*, Harmondsworth: Penguin.
Gathorne-Hardy, Robert (ed.) 1963, *The Early Memoirs of Lady Ottoline Morrell*, London: Faber.
——1974, *Ottoline at Garsington: Memoirs 1915–1918*, London: Faber.
Gilbert, M. 1976, *Winston S. Churchill*, vol. V, London: Heineman.
Goffman, Irving 1968, *Stigma: Notes on the Management of Spoiled Identity*, Harmondsworth: Penguin.
Gold, Joseph 1981a, *The Multilateral System of Payments: Keynes, Convertibility and the International Monetary Fund's Articles of Agreement*, Washington: International Monetary Fund, August.
——1981b, 'Keynes on Legal Problems of International Organization', *Connecticut Law Review*, 14 (Fall).
Grieves, Keith 1988, *The Politics of Manpower, 1914–1918*, Manchester: Manchester University Press.
Grigg, P. J. 1948, *Prejudice and Judgment*, London: Cape.
Hacking, Ian 1987, 'Was There a Probabilistic Revolution 1800–1930?', in L. Kruger, L. J. Daston and M. Heidelberger (eds), *The Probabilistic Revolution: Ideas in History*, Cambridge Mass.: MIT Press.
Hahn, F. H. 1982a, 'Reflections on the Invisible Hand', *Lloyds Bank Review*, March.
——1982b, *Money and Inflation*, Oxford: Blackwell.
Hall, Peter A. (ed.) 1989, *The Political Power of Economic Ideas: Keynesianism across Nations*, Princeton: Princeton University Press.
Hamouda, O. F. and Smithin, J. N. (eds) 1988, *Keynes and Public Policy After Fifty Years*, Volume I, *Economics and Policy*, Aldershot: Edward Elgar.
Hancock, W. K. 1962–8, *Smuts*, 2 vols, Cambridge: Cambridge University Press.
Hansen, A. H. 1936, 'Mr Keynes on Unemployment Equilibrium', *Journal of Political Economy*, XLIV (October).
Hankey, Lord 1963, *The Supreme Command at the Paris Peace Conference 1919: A Commentary*, London: Allen & Unwin.
Harris, J. 1972, *Unemployment and Politics: A Study in English Social Policy, 1886–1914*, Oxford: Clarendon Press.
——1977, *William Beveridge: A Biography*, Oxford: Clarendon Press.
Harris, S. E. 1955, *John Maynard Keynes*, New York: Scribner.
Harrison, R. 1963, 'Two Early Articles by Alfred Marshall', *Economic Journal*, LXXIII (September).
Harrod, R. F. 1937, 'Mr Keynes and Traditional Theory', *Econometrica*, V (January)
——1951, *The Life of John Maynard Keynes*, London: Macmillan.
——1957, 'Clive Bell on Keynes', *Economic Journal*, LXVII (December).
——1960, 'A Comment', *Economic Journal*, LXX (March).
Haskell, Arnold 1979, *Balletomania*, Harmondsworth: Penguin.
Hawtrey, R. G. 1925, 'Public Expenditure and the Demand for Labour', *Economica*, V (March).
——1932, *The Art of Central Banking*, London: Longmans.
Headlam-Morley, A., Bryant R., and Cienciala, A. (eds) 1972: *Sir James Headlam-Morley: A Memoir of the Paris Peace Conference 1919*, London: Methuen.
Heclo, H. and Wildavsky, A. 1974, *The Private Government of Public Money: Community and Policy inside British Politics*, London: Macmillan.

848

Hemery, J. A. 1988, *The Emergence of Treasury Influence in British Foreign Policy 1914–1921*, unpublished Cambridge University Ph.D. dissertation.

Henderson, Sir Hubert 1955, *The Inter-war Years and Other Essays*, (ed. Sir Henry Clay), Oxford: Clarendon Press.

Hession, C. H. 1983, *John Maynard Keynes: A Personal Biography of the Man Who Revolutionized Capitalism and the Way We Live*, New York: Macmillan.

Hey, J. D. and Winch, D. (eds) 1990, *A Century of Economics: 100 Years of the Royal Economic Society and the Economic Journal*, Oxford: Blackwell.

Hicks, J. R. 1936, 'Mr Keynes' Theory of Employment', *Economic Journal*, XLVI (June).

——1937, 'Mr Keynes' and the Classics: A Suggested Interpretation', *Econometrica*, V (April).

——1964, 'Dennis Holme Robertson, 1890–1963', *Proceedings of the British Academy*, L.

——1967, *Critical Essays in Monetary Theory*, Oxford: Clarendon Press.

——1977, *Economic Perspectives: Further Essays on Money and Growth*, Oxford: Clarendon Press.

Higgins, Norman 1979, *The Cambridge Arts Theatre, 1936–1968: A Personal Record*, Cambridge: privately printed.

Hill, P. and Keynes, R. (eds) 1989, *Lydia and Maynard: Letters between Lydia Lopokova and John Maynard Keynes*, London: Andre Deutsch.

Himmelfarb, G. 1968, *Victorian Minds*, New York: Knopf.

Hirsch, F. 1976, *The Social Limits to Growth*, Cambridge: Harvard University Press.

Hodson, H. V. 1938, *Slump and Recovery, 1929–1937*, London: Oxford University Press.

Hollis, C. 1960, *Eton: A History*, London: Hollis & Carter.

Holroyd, Michael 1971, *Lytton Strachey: A Biography*, Harmondsworth: Penguin.

Homberger, Eric and Charmley, John (eds) 1987, *The Troubled Face of Biography*, London: Macmillan.

Hoover, Herbert 1958, *The Ordeal of Woodrow Wilson*, London: Museum Press.

Horsefield, J. K. 1969, *The International Monetary Fund 1946–1965*, 3 vols, Washington: International Monetary Fund.

Houghton, W. E. 1957, *The Victorian Frame of Mind, 1830–1870*, New Haven: Yale University Press.

Howson, S. 1973, '"A Dear Money Man"?: Keynes on Monetary Policy, 1920', *Economic Journal*, LXXXIII (June).

——1974, 'The Origins of Dear Money, 1919–20', *Economic History Review*, 2nd Ser., XXVI (February).

——1975, *Domestic Monetary Management in Britain 1919–38*, Cambridge: Cambridge University Press.

——1985, 'Hawtrey and the Real World' in C. G. Harcourt (ed.), *Keynes and His Contemporaries*, London: Macmillan.

——1987, 'The Origins of Cheaper Money, 1945–7', *Economic History Review*, XL (November).

——1988, 'Cheap Money and Debt Management in Britain 1932–51' in P. L. Cottrell and D. E. Moggridge (eds) *Money and Power: Essays in Honour of L. S. Pressnell*, London: Macmillan.

——1992, *The Monetary Policies of the 1945–51 Labour Governments*, Oxford: Clarendon Press.

——(ed.) 1988a, *The Collected Papers of James Meade, I, Employment and Inflation*, London: Unwin Hyman.

Howson, S. (ed.) 1988b, *The Collected Papers of James Meade, III, International Economics*, London: Unwin Hyman.

Howson S. and Moggridge, D. E. (eds) 1990a, *The Collected Papers of James Meade, IV, The Cabinet Office Diary, 1944–1946*, London: Unwin Hyman.

——1990b, *The Wartime Diaries of Lionel Robbins and James Meade, 1943–45*, London: Macmillan.

Howson, S. and Winch, D. 1977, *The Economic Advisory Council 1930–1939: A Study of Economic Advice During Depression and Recovery*, Cambridge: Cambridge University Press.

Hubback, D. 1985, *No Ordinary Press Baron: A Life of Walter Layton*, London: Weidenfeld & Nicolson.

——1988, 'Sir Richard Clarke – 1910–1975: A Most Unusual Civil Servant', *Public Policy and Administration*, III (Spring).

Hyams, E. 1963, *The New Statesman: The History of the First Fifty Years*, London: Longmans.

Hynes, S. 1968, *The Edwardian Turn of Mind*, Princeton: Princeton University Press.

——1990, *A War Imagined: The First World War and English Culture*, London: Bodley Head.

Jacobsson, Erin E. 1979, *A Life for Sound Money: Per Jacobsson – His Biography*, Oxford: Clarendon Press.

Jaffé, W. 1965, 'Biography and Economic Analysis', *Western Economic Journal*, III (Summer).

——(ed.) 1965, *Correspondence of Leon Walras and Related Papers*, 3 vols, Amsterdam: North Holland.

James, P. 1979, *Population Malthus: His Life and Times*, London: Routledge & Kegan Paul.

James, Robert Rhodes 1969, *Memoirs of a Conservative: J. C. C. Davidson's Memoirs and Papers, 1910–1937*, London: Weidenfeld & Nicolson.

Jay, Douglas 1980, *Change and Fortune: A Political Record*, London: Hutchinson.

Jeffreys, H. 1922, Review of Keynes's *Treatise on Probability*, *Nature*, CIX, 2 February.

Jenkins, Roy 1964, *Asquith*, London: Collins.

Jevons, H. A. 1886, *Letters and Journal of W. Stanley Jevons*, London: Macmillan.

Johnson, Elizabeth 1960, 'Keynes' Attitude to Compulsory Military Service', *Economic Journal*, LXX (March), 160–5.

Johnson, Elizabeth and Johnson, H. G. 1978, *The Shadow of Keynes*, Chicago: University of Chicago Press.

Jones, J. H. 1964, *Josiah Stamp, Public Servant: The Life of the First Baron Stamp of Shortlands*, London: Pitman.

Jones, Thomas 1951, *Lloyd George*, London: Oxford University Press.

——1954, *A Diary with Letters*, London: Oxford University Press.

Jones. T. W. 1978, 'The Appointment of Pigou as Marshall's Successor: The Other Side of the Coin', *Journal of Law and Economics*, XXI (April).

Jonung, L. 1981, 'Ricardo on Machinery and the Present Unemployment: An Unpublished Manuscript by Knut Wicksell', *Economic Journal*, 91, 195–205.

Kadish, A. 1982, *The Oxford Economists in the Late Nineteenth Century*, Oxford: Clarendon Press.

——1989, *Historians, Economists, and Economic History*, London: Routledge.

Kahn, Richard 1972, *Selected Essays on Employment and Growth*, Cambridge: Cambridge University Press.

——1974, 'What Keynes Really Said', *Sunday Telegraph*, 24 September.

Kahn, Richard 1984, *The Making of Keynes' General Theory*, Cambridge: Cambridge University Press.

——1989, *The Economics of the Short Period*, London: Macmillan.

Kaminsky, A. P. 1986, *The India Office, 1880–1910*, London: Mansell.

Kent, Bruce 1989, *The Spoils of War: The Politics, Economics, and Diplomacy of Reparations 1918–1932*, Oxford: Clarendon Press.

Keynes, F. A. 1950, *Gathering up the Threads: A Study in Family Biography*, Cambridge: Heffer.

Keynes, G. L. 1981, *The Gates of Memory*, Oxford: Clarendon Press.

Keynes, J. M. (ed.) 1926, *Official Papers by Alfred Marshall*, London: Macmillan.

Keynes, M. (ed.) 1975, *Essays on John Maynard Keynes*, Cambridge: Cambridge University Press.

——1983, *Lydia Lopokova*, London: Weidenfeld & Nicolson.

King's College 1949, *John Maynard Keynes, 1883–1946: Fellow and Bursar*, Cambridge: King's College.

Knight, F. H. 1936, 'Unemployment and Mr Keynes' Revolution in Economic Theory', *Canadian Journal of Economics and Political Science*, III (February).

Koot, G. M. 1987, *English Historical Economics, 1870–1926: The Rise of Economic History and Neomercantilism*, Cambridge: Cambridge University Press.

Kunz, Diane B. 1987, *The Battle for Britain's Gold Standard in 1931*, London: Croom Helm.

Laidler, David 1991, *The Golden Age of the Quantity Theory: Aspects of the Development of Monetary Economics during the Period 1870–1914*, London: Philip Allen.

Lambert, R. 1963 (with S. Milham), *The Hothouse Society: An Exploration of Boarding-School Life through Boys' and Girls' Own Writings*, London: Weidenfeld & Nicolson.

——1975 (in collaboration with R. Bullock and S. Milham), *The Chance of a Lifetime: A Study of Boys and Coeducational Boarding Schools in England and Wales*, London: Weidenfeld & Nicolson.

Lange, Oscar 1938, 'The Rate of Interest and the Optimum Propensity to Consume', *Economica*, V (February).

Lawson, Tony and Pesaran, Hashem (eds) 1985, *Keynes's Economics: Methodological Issues*, London: Croom Helm.

Layton, Walter 1961, *Dorothy*, London: Chatto & Windus.

Lazonick, W. 1981, 'Competition, Specialisation and Industrial Decline', *Journal of Economic History*, XLI (March).

Leavis, F. R. 1953, *The Common Pursuit*, London: Chatto & Windus.

——1968, *A Selection from Scrutiny*, 2 vols, Cambridge: Cambridge University Press.

Leijonhufvud, A. 1981, *Information and Coordination*, New York: Oxford University Press.

Leith-Ross, Sir Frederick 1968, *Money Talks: Fifty Years of International Finance*, London: Hutchinson

Lentin, A. 1984, *Lloyd George, Woodrow Wilson and the Guilt of Germany: An Essay in the Pre-History of Appeasement*, Leicester: Leicester University Press.

Leontief, W. W. 1936, 'The Fundamental Assumption of Mr Keynes's Monetary Theory of Unemployment', *Quarterly Journal of Economics*, LI (November).

LePan, D. 1979, *Bright Glass of Memory: A Set of Four Memoirs*, Toronto: McGraw Hill-Ryerson.

Lerner, A. P. 1936, 'Mr Keynes' General Theory of Employment, Interest and Money', *International Labour Review*, XXXIV (October).

Levy, P. 1979, *Moore: G. E. Moore and the Cambridge Apostles*, London: Weidenfeld & Nicolson.

Lively, Penelope 1988, *According to Mark*, London: Penguin.

Lloyd George, F. 1967, *The Years that are Past*, London: Hutchinson.

Lloyd George, David 1938, *War Memoirs of David Lloyd George*, 2 vols, London: Oldhams.

Lowe, R. 1986, *Adjusting to Democracy: The Role of the Ministry of Labour in British Politics, 1916–1939*, Oxford: Clarendon Press.

McCormmach, R. 1983, *Night Thoughts of a Classical Physicist*, New York: Avon Books.

MacDougall, Donald 1987, *Don and Mandarin: Memoirs of an Economist*, London: John Murray.

McFadyean, Sir Andrew 1964, *Recollected in Tranquillity*, London: Pall Mall Press.

McGuinness, B. 1988, *Wittgenstein: A Life*, I, *Young Ludwig (1889–1921)*, London: Duckworth.

Machlup, F. 1964, *International Payments, Debts and Gold*, New York: Scribner.

Mackenzie, Norman (ed.) 1978, *The Letters of Sidney and Beatrice Webb*, volume III, Cambridge: Cambridge University Press.

Macmillan, Harold 1966, *Winds of Change, 1914–1939*, London: Macmillan.

Macmillan, Lord 1952, *A Man of Law's Tale*, London: Macmillan.

McWilliams-Tullberg, R. 1975a, *Women at Cambridge: A Men's University – Though of a Different Type*, London: Gollancz.

——1975b, 'Marshall's "Tendency to Socialism"', *History of Political Economy*, VII (Spring).

Maizels, A. 1964, *Industrial Growth and World Trade*, Cambridge: Cambridge University Press.

Maloney, John 1985, *Marshall, Orthodoxy and the Professionalisation of Economics*, Cambridge: Cambridge University Press.

Mantoux, E. 1946, *The Carthaginian Peace or The Economic Consequences of Mr. Keynes*, London: Oxford University Press.

Marquand, David 1977, *Ramsay MacDonald*, London: Cape.

Marshall, A. 1961, *Principles of Economics*, 9th variorum edition, ed. by C. W. Guillebaud, 2 vols, London: Macmillan.

Martin, B. K. 1969a, *Father Figures*, Harmondsworth: Penguin.

——1969b, *Editor*, Harmondsworth: Penguin.

Mayer, A. J. 1959, *Political Origins of the New Diplomacy 1917–18*, New Haven: Yale University Press.

Meade, J. E. 1936–7, 'A Simplified Model of Mr Keynes' System', *Review of Economic Studies*, IV.

Meltzer, A. H. 1988, *Keynes's Monetary Theory: A Different Interpretation*, Cambridge: Cambridge University Press.

Meyers, G. 1977, *Homosexuality and English Literature, 1890–1930*, London: Macmillan.

Middlemas, K. (ed.) 1969, *Thomas Jones' Whitehall Diary*, Volumes I and II, London: Oxford University Press.

Middlemas K. and Barnes, J. 1969, *Baldwin*, London: Weidenfeld & Nicolson.

Middleton, R. 1982, 'The Treasury in the 1930s: Political and Administrative Constraints to the Acceptance of the "New" Economics', *Oxford Economic Papers*, N.S., XXXIV (March).

——1985, *Towards the Managed Economy: Keynes, the Treasury and the Fiscal Policy Debate of the 1930s*, London: Methuen.

Milgate, M. 1977, 'Keynes and the Classical Theory of Interest', *Cambridge Journal of Economics*, I (June) reprinted in Eatwell and Milgate (eds) 1983.

Mill, J. S. 1863, *Utilitarianism and Representative Government* (A. D. Lindsay ed.), Toronto: Dent, 1910.

Moggridge, D. E. 1972, *British Monetary Policy 1924–1931: The Norman Conquest of $4.86*, Cambridge: Cambridge University Press.

——1980, *Keynes*, 2nd edn, London: Macmillan.

——1986, 'Keynes and the International Monetary System, 1909–46' in J. S. Cohen and G. C. Harcourt (eds) *International Monetary Problems and Supply-Side Economics: Essays in Honour of Lorie Tarshis*, London: Macmillan.

——1988, 'On Editing Keynes' in D. E. Moggridge (ed.), *Editing Modern Economists*, New York: AMS Press.

——1989, 'The Gold Standard and National Economic Policies 1919–1939' in P. Mathias and S. Pollard (eds) *The Cambridge Economic History of Europe*, vol. VIII, Cambridge: Cambridge University Press.

——1991, 'Keynes on the 1914 Financial Crisis: A Note with Documents', *Research in the History of Economic Thought and Methodology, Archival Supplement*, II.

——(ed.) 1974, *Keynes: Aspects of the Man and his Work*, London: Macmillan.

Moggridge, D. E. and Howson, S. 1974, 'Keynes on Monetary Policy 1910–1946', *Oxford Economic Papers*, NS, XXVI (July).

Moley, Raymond 1971, *After Seven Years: A Political Analysis of the New Deal*, Lincoln: University of Nebraska Press.

Moore, G. E. 1903, *Principia Ethica*, Cambridge: Cambridge University Press.

——1922, *Philosophical Studies*, London: Routledge & Kegan Paul.

——1959, *Philosophical Papers*, London: Allen & Unwin.

Morgan, K. O. 1984, *Labour in Power, 1945–1951*, Oxford: Clarendon Press.

Morgan, Mary S. 1990, *The History of Econometric Ideas*, Cambridge: Cambridge University Press.

Murphy, A. E. 1986, *Richard Cantillon: Entrepreneur and Economist*, Oxford: Clarendon Press.

Myint, H. 1948, *Theories of Welfare Economics*, London: Bell.

Nadel, Ira Bruce 1984, *Biography: Fiction, Fact or Form*, London: Macmillan.

Newsome, D. 1980, *On the Edge of Paradise: A. C. Benson: The Diarist*, London: John Murray.

Nicolson, H. 1933, *Peacemaking 1919*, London: Constable.

Nicolson, N. and Trautman J. (eds) 1975–80, *The Letters of Virginia Woolf*, 6 vols, London: Hogarth Press.

O'Brien, D. P. 1988, *Lionel Robbins*, London: Macmillan.

O'Donnell, R. M. 1982, *Keynes: Philosophy and Economics – An Approach to Rationality and Uncertainty*, Cambridge University Ph. D. dissertation.

——1989, *Keynes: Philosophy, Economics and Politics: The Philosophical Foundations of Keynes's Thought and their Influence on his Economics and Politics*, London: Macmillan.

——1990, 'Continuity in Keynes's Conception of Probability', in D. E. Moggridge (ed.), *Perspectives on the History of Economic Thought*, IV, Aldershot: Edward Elgar.

O'Halpin, E. 1989, *Head of the Civil Service: A Study of Sir Warren Fisher*, London: Routledge.

Ohlin, B. 1929, 'Transfer Difficulties Real and Imagined', *Economic Journal*, XXXIX (June).

Oliver, R. W. 1975, *International Economic Co-operation and the World Bank*, London: Macmillan.

Ollard, R. 1982, *An English Education: A Perspective of Eton*, London: Collins.

Parsons, T. 1931, 'Wants and Activities in Marshall', *Quarterly Journal of Economics*, XLVI (November).

——1932, 'Economics and Sociology: Marshall in Relation to the Thought of His Time', *Quarterly Journal of Economics*, XLVI (February).

Partridge, F. 1981, *Memories*, London: Gollancz.

Passmore, J. 1968, *A Hundred Years of Philosophy*, Harmondsworth: Penguin.

Patinkin, D. 1976a, *Keynes's Monetary Thought: A Study of its Development*, Durham, N.C.: Duke University Press.

——1976b, 'Keynes and Econometrics: On the Interaction between the Macroeconomic Revolutions of the Interwar Period', *Econometrica*, XLIV (reprinted in Patinkin 1982).

——1982, *Anticipations of the General Theory? and Other Essays on Keynes*, Chicago: University of Chicago Press.

——1987, 'John Maynard Keynes' in volume 3 of J. Eatwell, M. Milgate and P. Newman (eds), *The New Palgrave: A Dictionary of Economics*, London: Macmillan.

——1989, 'On Differing Interpretations of the *General Theory*', *Proceedings of the British Academy*, LXXV.

Patinkin, D. and Leith, J. C. (eds) 1977, *Keynes, Cambridge and The General Theory*, London and Toronto: Macmillan and University of Toronto Press.

Pearson, K. 1897, *The Chances of Death and Other Essays*, 2 vols, London: Edward Arnold.

Peden, G. C. 1980, 'Keynes, the Treasury and Unemployment in the Later 1930s', *Oxford Economic Papers*, XXXII (1).

——1983, 'Sir Richard Hopkins and the "Keynesian Revolution" in Employment Policy, 1929–1945', *Economic History Review*, 2nd Ser., XXXVI (May).

——1984, 'The "Treasury View" on Public Works and Unemployment in the Interwar Period', *Economic History Review*, 2nd Ser., XXVII (May).

——1988, *Keynes, the Treasury and British Economic Policy*, London: Macmillan.

Penrose, E. F. 1953, *Economic Planning for the Peace*, Princeton: Princeton University Press.

Pelling, Henry 1984, *The Labour Governments 1945–51*, London: Macmillan.

Pesaran, H. and Smith, R. 1985, 'Keynes on Econometrics' in Lawson, Tony and Pesaran, Hashem (eds) *Keynes's Economics: Methodological Issues*, London: Croom Helm.

Petrides, A. 1973, 'Alfred Marshall's Attitude to and Economic Analysis of Trade Unions: A Case of Anomalies in a Competitive System', *History of Political Economy*, V (Spring).

Pfaff, R. W. 1980, *Montagu Rhodes James*, London: Scolar Press.

Phelps Brown, E. H. and Browne, M. 1967 *A Century of Pay*, London: Macmillan.

Pickersgill, J. W. and Forster, D. F. (eds) 1968, *The Mackenzie King Record*, vol. II, *1944–1945*, Toronto: University of Toronto Press.

Pigou, A. C. 1905, *Principles and Methods of Industrial Peace*, London: Macmillan.

——1936, 'Mr J. M. Keynes's *General Theory of Employment, Interest and Money*', *Economica*, III (May).

——1947, *Aspects of British Economic History 1918–1925*, London: Macmillan.

——(ed.) 1925, *Memorials of Alfred Marshall*, London: Macmillan.

Pimlott, B. 1977, *Labour and the Left in the 1930s*, Cambridge: Cambridge University Press.

Pimlott, B. 1985, *Hugh Dalton*, London: Cape.

——(ed.) 1986, *The Second World War Diary of Hugh Dalton 1940–45*, London: Cape.

Plumptre, A. F. W. 1947, 'Keynes in Cambridge', *Canadian Journal of Economics and Political Science*, XIII (August).

Political Economy Club 1921, *Minutes of Proceedings, 1899–1920, Roll of Members and Questions Discussed, 1821–1920*, Volume VI, London: Macmillan.

Pressnell, L. S. 1987, *External Economic Policy Since the War*, Volume I. *The Post-War Financial Settlement*, London: Her Majesty's Stationery Office.

Price-Jones, D. 1983, *Cyril Connolly: Journal and Memoir*, London: Collins.

Public Record Office 1972, *The Second World War: A Guide to Documents in the Public Record Office*, London: Her Majesty's Stationery Office.

Ramsey, F. P. 1931, *The Foundations of Mathematics and Other Logical Essays*, London: Routledge & Kegan Paul.

——1978, *Foundations: Essays in Philosophy, Logic, Mathematics and Economics*, London: Routledge & Kegan Paul.

Reddaway, W. B. 1936, 'The General Theory of Employment, Interest and Money', *Economic Record*, XII (June).

Redmond, John 1984, 'The Sterling Overvaluation of 1925', *Economic History Review*, XXXVII (November).

Rees, David 1973, *Harry Dexter White: A Study in Paradox*, London: Macmillan.

Regan, Tom 1986, *Bloomsbury's Prophet: G. E. Moore and the Development of His Moral Philosophy*, Philadelphia: Temple University Press.

Riesman, David 1990, *Alfred Marshall's Mission*, London: Macmillan.

Roach, J. P. C. (ed.) 1959, *A History of the County of Cambridge and the Isle of Ely*, Volume III, *The City and University of Cambridge*, London: Oxford University Press.

Robbins, (Lord) Lionel 1971, *Autobiography of an Economist*, London: Macmillan.

——1973, Review of *Essays in Biography*, *Economic Journal*, LXXXIII (June)

Robertson, D. H. 1926, *Banking Policy and the Price Level: An Essay in the Theory of the Trade Cycle*, London: P. S. King.

——1936, 'Some Notes on Mr Keynes' General Theory of Employment', *Quarterly Journal of Economics*, LI (November).

——1940, *Essays in Monetary Theory*, London: Staples.

——1951, *Utility and All That*, London: Staples.

Robinson, E. A. G. 1947, 'John Maynard Keynes 1883–1946', *Economic Journal*, LXVII (March).

——1971, *John Maynard Keynes: Economist, Author, Statesman*, London: British Academy.

——1978, 'The London and Cambridge Economic Service: An Historical Outline', *Kraus Bibliographical Bulletin*, 26 (June).

Roll, Eric 1985, *Crowded Hours*, London: Faber & Faber.

Rosenbaum, E. and Sherman, A. J. 1979, *M. M. Warburg & Co. 1798–1938: Merchant Bankers of Hamburg*, London: C. Hurst.

Rosenbaum, S. P. (ed.) 1975, *The Bloomsbury Group: A Collection of Memoirs, Commentary and Criticism*, Toronto: University of Toronto Press.

——1982, 'Keynes, Lawrence and Cambridge Revisited', *Cambridge Quarterly*, II (Autumn).

——1987, *Victorian Bloomsbury: The Early Literary History of the Bloomsbury Group*, Volume I, London: Macmillan.

Rosenman, Samuel 1952, *Working with Roosevelt*, London: Rupert Hart-Davis.

Roskill, S. *Hankey: Man of Secrets*, vol. II, *1919–31*, London: Collins.

Rothblatt, S. 1968, *The Revolution of the Dons: Cambridge and Society in Victorian England*, New York: Basic Books.

Russell, B. 1922 Review of Keynes's *A Treatise on Probability*, *Mathematical Gazette*, XI (July)

——1978, *The Autobiography of Bertrand Russell*, 1 Volume ed., London: Allen & Unwin.

Salter, A. 1967, *Slave of the Lamp: A Public Servant's Notebook*, London: Weidenfeld & Nicolson.

Sayers, R. S. 1956, *Financial Policy 1939–45*, London: Her Majesty's Stationery Office.

——1976, *The Bank of England, 1891–1944*, 3 vols, Cambridge: Cambridge University Press.

Schefold, B. 1980, 'The General Theory for a Totalitarian State?: A Note on Keynes's Preface to the German Edition of 1936', *Cambridge Journal of Economics*, IV (June).

Schneewind, J. B. 1977, *Sidgwick's Ethics and Victorian Moral Philosophy*, Oxford: Clarendon Press.

Schuker, S. A. 1976, *The End of French Predominance in Europe: The Financial Crisis of 1924 and the Adoption of the Dawes Plan*, Chapel Hill: University of North Carolina Press.

——1980, 'Review of Volumes XVII and XVIII of *The Collected Writings of John Maynard Keynes*', *Journal of Economic Literature*, XVIII (March), 124–6.

——1988, 'American "Reparations" to Germany, 1919–1933: Implications for the Third World Debt Crisis', *Princeton Studies in International Finance*, 61 (July).

Schulkind, J. 1985, *Virginia Woolf: Moments of Being*, 2nd edn, London: Hogarth Press.

Schumpeter, J. A. 1936, 'The General Theory of Employment, Interest and Money', *Journal of the American Statistical Association*, XXI (December).

——1946, 'John Maynard Keynes 1883–1946', *American Economic Review*, XXXVI (September).

——1952, *Ten Great Economists: From Marx to Keynes*, London: Allen & Unwin.

——1954, *A History of Economic Analysis*, New York: Oxford University Press.

Schwartz, J. A. 1981, *The Speculator: Bernard M. Baruch in Washington, 1917–1965*, Chapel Hill: University of North Carolina Press.

Scrase, David and Croft, Peter 1983, *Maynard Keynes: Collector of Pictures, Books and Manuscripts*, Cambridge: King's College and Fitzwilliam Museum.

Shackle, G. L. S. 1967, *The Years of High Theory: Invention and Tradition in Economic Thought 1926–1939*, Cambridge: Cambridge University Press.

——1972, *Epistemics and Economics*, Cambridge: Cambridge University Press.

——1974, *Keynesian Kaleidics*, Edinburgh: Edinburgh University Press.

Shone, Richard 1976, *Bloomsbury Portraits*, Oxford: Phaidon.

Sidgwick, A. and Sidgwick E. M. 1906, *Henry Sidgwick: A Memoir*, London: Macmillan.

Sidgwick, H. 1874, *The Methods of Ethics*, London: Macmillan.

Sitwell, O. 1949, *Laughter in the Next Room*, London: Macmillan.

Skidelsky, Robert 1967, *Politicians and the Slump: The Labour Government of 1929–1931*, London: Macmillan.

——1985, *John Maynard Keynes*, Volume I, *Hopes Betrayed, 1883–1920*, New York: Viking.

——1988, 'Keynes's Political Legacy' in Hamouda, O. F. and Smithin, J. N. (eds) *Keynes and Public Policy After Fifty Years*, Volume I, *Economics and Policy*, Aldershot: Edward Elgar.

Spalding, Frances 1983, *Vanessa Bell*, London: Weidenfeld & Nicolson.

Spotts, Frederic (ed.) 1989, *The Letters of Leonard Woolf*, New York: Harcourt Brace Jovanovich.

Stansky, P. and Abrahams, W. 1966, *Journey to the Frontier: Julian Bell and John Cornford, Their Lives and the 1930s*, London: Constable.

Steel, R. 1980, *Walter Lippmann and the American Century*, London: Bodley Head.

Stein, H. 1969, *The Fiscal Revolution in America*, Chicago: University of Chicago Press.

Stephen, Leslie 1885, *Henry Fawcett*, London: Smith Elder.

Stigler, George J. 1976/82, 'The Scientific Uses of Scientific Biography with Special Reference to J. S. Mill' reprinted in Stigler, *The Economist as Preacher*, Oxford: Blackwell.

——1988, *Memoirs of an Unregulated Economist*, New York: Basic Books.

Stigler, Stephen M. 1986, *The History of Statistics: The Measurement of Uncertainty before 1900*, Cambridge, Mass.: Harvard University Press.

Stone, J. R. N. 1977, *Inland Revenue Report on National Income, 1929*, Cambridge: University of Cambridge, Department of Applied Economics.

Strachey, Barbara 1981, *Remarkable Relations*, London: Gollancz.

Strachey, Barbara and Samuels, Jayne (eds) 1983, *Mary Berenson: A Self–Portrait from her Letters and Diaries*, London: Gollancz.

Strachey, Lytton 1918, *Eminent Victorians*, London: Chatto & Windus (Penguin edn).

Straight, Michael 1983, *After Long Silence*, London: Collins.

Svennilson, I. 1954, *Growth and Stagnation in the European Economy*, Geneva: United Nations.

Swanberg, W. A. 1980, *Whitney Father, Whitney Heiress*, New York: Scribners.

Taussig, F. W. 1936, 'Employment and the National Dividend', *Quarterly Journal of Economics*, LI (November).

Taylor, A. J. P. 1972, *Beaverbrook*, London: Hamish Hamilton.

Thirlwall, A. P. 1987, *Nicholas Kaldor*, Brighton: Wheatsheaf.

——(ed.) 1976, *Keynes and International Monetary Relations*, London: Macmillan.

Tillman, S. P. 1961, *Anglo-American Relations at the Paris Peace Conference*, Princeton: Princeton University Press.

Trachtenberg, M. 1980, *Reparations in World Politics: France and European Economic Diplomacy, 1916–1923*, New York: Columbia University Press.

Trend (Lord), Burke 1982, 'Policy and the Public Purse', *Times Literary Supplement*, 16 July, 755–7.

Turner, Marjorie S. 1989, *Joan Robinson and the Americans*, Armonk, N.Y.: M. E. Sharpe.

Ullmann, S. O. A. (ed.) 1965, *Men, Books and Mountains: Essays by Leslie Stephen*, London: Hogarth Press.

van Dormael, A. 1978, *Bretton Woods: Birth of a Monetary System*, London: Macmillan.

Vincent, J. (ed.) 1984, *The Crawford Papers: The Journals of David Lindsay twenty-seventh Earl of Crawford and tenth Earl of Balcarres 1871–1940 during the years 1892–1940*, Manchester: Manchester University Press.

Viner, J. 1936, 'Mr Keynes and the Causes of Unemployment', *Quarterly Journal of Economics*, LI (November).

——1964, 'Comment on My 1936 Review' in R. Lekachman (ed.) *Keynes' General Theory: Reports of Three Decades*, New York: St Martin's Press.

Waley, S. D. 1964, *Edwin Montagu: A Memoir and an Account of his Visits to India*, London: Asia Publishing House.

Walker, D. A. 1983, 'Biography and the Study of the History of Economic Thought', *Research on the History of Economic Thought and Methodology*, I.

Weatherall, D. 1976, *David Ricardo: A Biography*, The Hague: Martinus Nijhoff.

Wheeler-Bennett, Sir John (ed.) 1968, *Action this Day: Working with Churchill*, London: Macmillan.

Whitaker, J. K. 1977, 'Some Neglected Aspects of Marshall's Economic and Social Thought', *History of Political Economy*, IX (Summer).

——(ed.) 1975, *The Early Economic Writings of Alfred Marshall*, London: Macmillan.

——(ed.) 1990, *Centenary Essays on Alfred Marshall*, Cambridge: Cambridge University Press.

White, E. W. 1975, *The Arts Council of Great Britain*, London: Davis Poynter.

Wilkinson, L. P. 1980a, *A Century of King's, 1873–1972*, Cambridge: King's College.

——1980b, *Kingsmen of a Century, 1873–1972*, Cambridge: King's College.

Williams, Bernard 1982, 'The Point of View of the Universe: Sidgwick and the Ambitions of Ethics', *The Cambridge Review*, 7 May.

Williams, P. M. 1977, *Hugh Gaitskell: A Political Biography*, London: Jonathan Cape.

Williamson, J. 1981, 'Review of Volumes XXV and XXVI of *The Collected Writings of John Maynard Keynes*', *Economic Journal*, XCI (June), 541–4.

Wilson, Trevor 1986, *The Myriad Faces of War: Britain and the Great War 1914–1918*, Cambridge: Polity Press.

Winch, Donald 1969, *Economics and Policy: A Historical Study*, London: Hodder & Stoughton.

Winstanley, D. A. 1947, *Later Victorian Cambridge*, Cambridge: Cambridge University Press.

Wood, J. C. (ed.) 1982, *Alfred Marshall: Critical Assessments*, 4 vols, London: Croom Helm.

——1983, *John Maynard Keynes: Critical Assessments*, 4 vols, London: Croom Helm.

Woodward, Sir Llewellyn 1962, *British Foreign Policy in the Second World War*, London: Her Majesty's Stationery Office.

Woolf, L. 1960, *Sowing*, London: Hogarth Press.

——1964, *Beginning Again*, London: Hogarth Press.

Wortham, H. E. 1927, *Oscar Browning*, London: Constable.

Young, Warren 1987, *Interpreting Mr Keynes: The IS–LM Enigma*, Cambridge: Polity Press.

——1989, *Harrod and His Trade Cycle Group: The Origins and Development of the Growth Research Program*, New York: New York University Press.

Zytaruk, G. J. and Boulton, J. T. 1981, *The Letters of D. H. Lawrence*, Volume II, *June 1913–October 1916*, Cambridge: Cambridge University Press.

DRAMATIS PERSONAE

ABRAHAMS, Lionel (later Sir Lionel) (1869–1919), civil servant; educated City of London School and Balliol College, Oxford; entered India Office, 1893; Financial Secretary, 1902–11; Assistant Under-Secretary of State, 1911–17.

ACHESON, Dean Goodenham (1893–1973), public servant; US Assistant Secretary of State, 1941; Under-Secretary of State, 1945–7; Secretary of State, 1949–53.

ADCOCK, Frank Ezra (later Sir Frank) (1888–1968), historian; educated Leicester and King's College, Cambridge; Fellow, King's College, 1911–68; Professor of Ancient History, Cambridge, 1925–51.

ADDIS, Sir Charles Stewart (1861–1945), banker; educated Edinburgh Academy; with Hong Kong and Shanghai Bank in China, 1883–1903; London Manager, 1905–21; Chairman, London Committee, 1921–33; Director, Bank of England, 1921–32; member, Young Committee, 1929.

ADENEY, Bernard (d. 1966), painter; educated Royal Academy, Slade School; Founder Member of London Group, 1913; Member, London Artists Association, 1925.

AINSWORTH, Alfred Richard (1879–1959), civil servant; educated Dulwich College and King's College, Cambridge; Apostle; Lecturer in Latin, Manchester University, 1902; Edinburgh, 1903–7; Inspector, Board of Education, 1908; Assistant Secretary, 1931–9; Deputy Secretary, 1939–40.

ALLEN, Reginald Clifford (later Lord Allen) (1889–1939), Labour politician; educated Berkhamstead, Bristol and Peterhouse, Cambridge; *Daily Citizen*, 1911–15; imprisoned three times as conscientious objector; Chairman, Independent Labour Party, 1922–6; Director, *Daily Herald*, 1925–30.

ALLEN, Sir Thomas (1864–1943), businessman; Chairman, Co-operative Wholesale Society; member, Committee on Finance and Industry, 1929–31.

AMERY, Leopold Charles Maurice Stennett (1873–1955), politician; educated Harrow and Balliol College, Oxford; Conservative MP, 1911–45; First Lord of the Admiralty, 1922–4; Secretary of State for the Colonies, 1924–9; for Dominion Affairs, 1925–9; for India and Burma, 1940–5.

ANDERSON, Sir John (later Viscount Waverley) (1882–1958), public servant; educated Universities of Edinburgh and Leipzig; entered Colonial Office, 1905; Chairman, Board of Inland Revenue, 1919–22; Permanent Under-Secretary of State, Home Office, 1922–32; Governor of Bengal, 1932–7; MP for Scottish Universities,

1938–50; Lord Privy Seal, 1938–9; Home Secretary, 1939–40; Lord President of the Council, 1940–3; Chancellor of the Exchequer, 1943–5.

ANDREADAS, Andreas (1876–1935), economist; Lecturer in Economics, University of Athens, 1902; Professor, 1906.

ANGELL, James Waterhouse (1898–1985), economist; member of faculty, Columbia University, 1924–66; Professor, 1931–66; Office of Civilian Requirements, War Planning Board, 1941–3; Foreign Economic Administration, 1943–5; US Representative, Allied Commission on Reparations, Germany, 1945–6; Technical Adviser, US delegation to Bretton Woods, 1944.

ANGELL, Ralph Norman (later Sir Norman) (1872–1967), publicist; Labour MP, 1929–31; Nobel Peace Prize, 1933; best known for *The Great Illusion* (1910) with its theme that armed aggression did not pay.

ANSERMET, Ernst (1883–1969), conductor; toured with Diaghilev Ballet from 1915; founded Orchestre de la Suisse-Romande, 1918.

ARMITAGE-SMITH, Sir Sydney Armitage (1876–1932), civil servant; educated University College School and Merton College, Oxford; entered Treasury, 1902; Assistant Secretary, 1913; Secretary General, Reparation Commission, 1924–30.

ARUNDEL, Dennis (1898–1988), actor and opera producer; educated Tonbridge and St John's College, Cambridge; a leading figure in Cambridge theatre in the 1920s.

ASHLEY, William James (later Sir William) (1860–1927), economic historian; educated Balliol College, Oxford; Fellow of Lincoln College, 1885–8; Professor of Political Economy, University of Toronto, 1888–92; Professor of Economic History, Harvard University, 1892–1901; Professor of Commerce, University of Birmingham, 1901–25.

ASHTON, Frederick William Mellandaine (later Sir Frederick) (1904–88), choreographer; Founder Choreographer, Sadler's Wells (later Royal) Ballet; Principal Choreographer, 1933–70; Director, 1963–79.

ASQUITH, Cyril (later Lord Asquith) (1890–1954), barrister, judge; educated Winchester and Balliol College, Oxford; Fellow, Magdalen College, Oxford, 1913; Lord Justice of Appeal, 1946; Chairman, Royal Commission on Equal Pay, 1944–6.

ASQUITH, Elizabeth see BIBESCO, Princess Elizabeth.

ASQUITH, Emma Alice Margaret (Margot) (née Tennent) (1862–1945), married H. H. Asquith, 1894.

ASQUITH, Herbert Henry (first Earl of Oxford and Asquith) (1852–1928), politician; educated City of London School and Balliol College, Oxford; Liberal MP, 1886–1918, 1920–4; Home Secretary, 1892–5; Chancellor of the Exchequer, 1905–8; Prime Minister, 1908–16.

ASQUITH, Violet see BONHAM CARTER, Violet.

ASTOR, Waldorf (second Viscount Astor) (1879–1952), public servant; educated Eton and New College, Oxford; Unionist MP, 1910–19; controlled *The Observer*, 1911.

ATTLEE, Clement Richard (later Lord Attlee) (1883–1967), statesman; educated Haileybury and University College, Oxford; Labour MP, 1922–55; Leader of the Opposition, 1935–40, 1951–5; Lord Privy Seal, 1940–2; Secretary of State for

Dominion Affairs, 1942–3; Lord President of the Council, 1943–5; Deputy Prime Minister, 1942–5; Prime Minister, 1945–51.

ATTOLICO, Bernardo (1880–1942), Italian and international public servant.

AUDEN, Wystan Hugh (1907–73), poet; educated Gresham's School and Christ Church, Oxford.

BACHELIER, Louis, French mathematician. His *Calcul des probabilités* (1912) and *Le Jeu, la chance, et le hasard* (1914) were referred to by JMK in his *Treatise on Probability*. In the 1930s he was a Professor at the University of Besançon.

BAGENAL, Barbara (1891–1984) (née Hiles), student at Slade School, 1913–14; attached to David Garnett, 1916; apprentice at Hogarth Press, 1917; married Nicholas Bagenal, 1918.

BAGENAL, Faith see HENDERSON, Faith Marion Jane.

BAKER, Philip Noel see NOEL-BAKER, Philip.

BAKST, Léon (1866–1924), Russian painter and ballet designer; designed *Schéhérazade* (1910), *Jeux* (1913), *Sleeping Princess* (1923) for Diaghilev.

BALANCHINE, George (1904–83), choreographer; associated with Diaghilev Ballet in later 1920s; helped organise Ballets Russes de Monte Carlo, 1932; Founder, New York City Ballet, 1946.

BALDWIN, Stanley (first Earl Baldwin of Bewdley) (1867–1947), statesman; educated Harrow and Trinity College, Cambridge; Conservative MP, 1908–37; Joint Financial Secretary to the Treasury, 1917–21; President, Board of Trade, 1921–2; Chancellor of the Exchequer, 1922–3; Prime Minister, 1923–4, 1925–9, 1935–7; Lord President of the Council, 1931–5.

BALFOUR, Arthur (later Lord Riverdale) (1873–1957), industrialist; Chairman, Committee on Industry and Trade, 1924–9; member, Economic Advisory Council, 1930–1.

BALFOUR, Authur James (later Earl of Balfour) (1848–1930), statesman; educated Eton and Trinity College, Cambridge; Conservative MP, 1874–1922; President, Local Government Board, 1885–6; Secretary for Scotland, 1886–7; Chief Secretary for Ireland, 1887–91; Leader of the House of Commons, 1891–2, 1895–1902; Prime Minister, 1902–5; Leader of the Opposition, 1906–11; First Lord of the Admiralty, 1915–16; Foreign Secretary, 1916–19; Lord President of the Council, 1919–22, 1925–9.

BALOGH, Thomas (later Lord Balogh) (1905–85), economist; in the City of London, 1931–9; National Institute of Economic and Social Research, 1938–47; Institute of Economics and Statistics, Oxford, 1940–55; Fellow of Balliol College, Oxford, 1945–73; Reader in Economics, Oxford University, 1960–73.

BALSTON, Thomas (1883–1967), writer; educated Eton and New College, Oxford; Duckworth & Co., 1921–34; Partner, 1923; Director, 1924.

BARGER, George (1878–1939), chemist; educated University College, London and King's College, Cambridge; Fellow of King's, 1904–10; Head of Chemistry Department, Goldsmiths' College, London, 1909–13; Staff, Medical Research Committee, 1914–19; Professor of Chemistry, Royal Holloway College, 1913–14; Edinburgh, 1919–37; Glasgow, 1938–9.

BARKER, Sir Ernest (1874–1960), scholar; educated Manchester Grammar School and Balliol College, Oxford; Fellow of Merton College, 1898–1905; of St John's College, 1909–13; of New College, 1913–20; Principal, King's College London, 1920–8; Professor of Political Science, Cambridge and Fellow of Peterhouse, 1928–39.

BARLOW, James Alan Noel (1881–1968), civil servant; educated Malborough and Corpus Christi College, Oxford; Clerk, House of Commons, 1906; Board of Education, 1907–15; Ministry of Munitions, 1915–18; Ministry of Labour 1919–33; Private Secretary to the Prime Minister, 1933–4; Under-Secretary, Treasury, 1934–8; Joint Second Secretary, 1938–48.

BAROUCHI, Randolfo, first husband of Lydia Lopokova, 1916–25; Diaghilev's business manager.

BARSTOW, Sir George Lewis (1874–1966), civil servant and company chairman; educated Clifton and Emmanuel College, Cambridge; entered Local Government Board, 1896; Treasury, 1898; Assistant Secretary, 1919–27; Director, Anglo-Persian Oil Company, 1927–47; Director, Prudential Insurance Company, 1928; Chairman, 1941–53.

BARUCH, Bernard Mannes (1867–1975), businessman; Chairman, War Industries Board, 1918–19; member, Supreme Economic Council, 1919; American Delegate on Economic and Reparations Clauses of the Treaty of Versailles, 1919.

BAYNES, Keith Stuart (1887–1977), artist; educated Harrow, Trinity College, Cambridge and the Slade School.

BEAN, Louis Hyman (b. 1896), economist; joined Department of Agriculture, 1923; Economic Adviser, Agricultural Adjustment Administration, 1933–9; Chief, Bureau of Agricultural Economics, 1939–41; Assistant to Director, Board of Economic Warfare, 1942; Bureau of the Budget, 1943–7.

BEAVERBROOK, Lord (William Maxwell Aitken) (1879–1964), newspaper proprietor (*Daily Express* 1916; *Evening Standard*, 1923); Minister of Information, 1918; Minister for Aircraft Production, 1940–1; Minister of State, 1941; Minister of Supply, 1941–2; Lord Privy Seal, 1943–5.

BECKETT, W. E. (later Sir Eric) (1896–1966), lawyer; educated Wadham College, Oxford; Fellow of All Souls College, Oxford, 1921–8; Second Legal Adviser, Foreign Office, 1928–45; Legal Adviser, 1945–53.

BEECHAM, Sir Thomas (1879–1961), conductor; educated Rossall School and Wadham College, Oxford; founded New Symphony Orchestra, 1906; presented Diaghilev's Russian ballet, 1911; founded London Philharmonic Orchestra, 1931; founded Royal Philharmonic Orchestra, 1946.

BÉKÁSSY, Ferenc (1889–1915), poet; educated Bedales and King's College, Cambridge; Apostle.

BELL, Angelica (b. 1918), daughter of Vanessa Bell and Duncan Grant; married David Garnett, 1942.

BELL, Arthur Clive Heward (1881–1964), art critic; educated Marlborough and Trinity College, Cambridge; married Vanessa Bell, 1907; publications include *Art* (1913); *Civilisation: An Essay* (1928); *Old Friends* (1956).

BELL, Julian Heward (1908–37), poet; elder son of Clive and Vanessa Bell; educated King's College, Cambridge, 1927–31; Apostle; killed while driving an ambulance for Spanish Medical Aid in battle of Brunette, July 1937.

BELL, Quentin Claudian (b. 1910), writer, art historian; second son of Clive and Vanessa Bell.

BELL, Vanessa (1879–1961) (née Stephen), painter; elder daughter of Leslie and Julia Stephen, moved with her sister and brothers to 46 Gordon Square on death of her father, 1904; married Clive Bell, 1907; affair with Roger Fry, 1911–12; relationship with Duncan Grant from 1914; moved to Wissett Lodge, 1916; moved to Charleston, 1916.

BELLAIRS, Rear-Admiral Roger Mowbray (1884–1959), entered Royal Navy, 1900; retired list, 1932; Representative on League of Nations Permanent Advisory Commission, 1932–9; Admiralty, 1939–46.

BELLOC, Joseph Hilaire Pierre René (1870–1953), poet and author; educated Oratory School, Birmingham and Balliol College, Oxford; Liberal MP, 1906–10.

BENSON, Arthur Christopher (1862–1925), man of letters; educated Eton and King's College, Cambridge; Eton master, 1885–1903; Fellow of Magdalene College, Cambridge, 1904; Master 1915–25.

BENSON, Edward White (1829–96), educated King Edward School, Birmingham and Trinity College, Cambridge; master at Rugby, 1852–9; first master, Wellington College, 1859–72; Bishop of Truro, 1877; Archbishop of Canterbury 1882–96.

BERENSON, Bernard (1865–1959), connoisseur and art dealer; educated Harvard University; married Mary Costelloe, 1900.

BERENSON, Mary (1864–1945) (née Pearsall Smith), married Frank Costelloe, 1885; two daughters Rachel and Karin; lived with Bernard Berenson, 1891–1900; married Berenson, 1900.

BERGMANN, Carl, German representative at the Brussels and Genoa Conferences.

BERLE, Adolf Augustus Jr. (1895–1971), Professor of Law, Columbia University, 1927–64; Assistant Secretary of State, 1938–44; US Ambassador to Brazil, 1945–6.

BERNSTEIN, Edward Morris (b. 1904), economist; Assistant Director of Monetary Research, US Treasury, 1941–6; Assistant to Secretary of the Treasury, 1946; Director of Research, IMF, 1946–58.

BERRY, Arthur (1862–1929), mathematician and economist; educated King's College, Cambridge; Fellow of King's, 1886–1929.

BEVERIDGE, Sir William (later Lord Beveridge) (1879–1963), economist and social reformer; educated Charterhouse and Balliol College, Oxford; Director of Labour Exchanges, 1909–16; Director, LSE, 1919–37; Master of University College, Oxford, 1937–45; Liberal MP, 1944–5.

BEVIN, Ernest (1881–1951), trade unionist and statesman; General Secretary of Transport and General Workers Union, 1921–40; Minister of Labour and National Service, 1940–5; Foreign Secretary, 1945–51; Labour MP, 1940–51.

BEWLEY, Thomas Kenneth (1890–1943), civil servant; educated Winchester and New College, Oxford; entered Treasury, 1913; Financial Adviser, HM Embassy, Washington, 1933–9; Principal Assistant Secretary, 1939–43.

BEYEN, Dr Johan Willem (1897–1976), Treasury of The Netherlands, 1919–23; Alternate President of Bank for International Settlements, Basle, 1935–7; President

1937–40; Director, Lever Bros and Unilever Ltd 1940–6; Executive Director, IMF, 1948–52.

BIBESCO, Princess Elizabeth (1897–1945), only daughter of H. H. Asquith; married the Romanian diplomat Prince Antoine Bibesco in 1919.

BING, Rudolf Franz Joseph (later Sir Rudolf) (b. 1902), impresario; General Manager, Glyndebourne Opera, 1925–49; Artistic Director, Edinburgh Festival, 1947–9; General Manager, Metropolitan Opera, New York, 1950–72.

BIRRELL, Augustine (1850–1933), author and statesman; educated Amersham Hall and Trinity Hall, Cambridge; Quain Professor of Law, London, 1896–9; Liberal MP, 1889–1900, 1906–18; President, Board of Education, 1905–7; Chief Secretary for Ireland, 1907–16.

BIRRELL, Francis Frederick Locker (1899–1935), journalist, critic and bookseller; educated King's College, Cambridge, 1909–12; Apostle.

BLACKETT, Basil Philpott (later Sir Basil) (1882–1935), public servant; educated Marlborough and University College, Oxford; entered Treasury, 1904; Treasury representative, Washington, 1917–19; Controller of Finance, Treasury, 1919–22; Finance Member, Viceroy's Council, 1922–8; Director, Bank of England, 1929–35.

BLACKETT, Patrick Maynard Stuart (later Lord Blackett) (1897–1974), scientist and adviser to governments; Fellow of King's College, Cambridge, 1923–33; Professor of Physics, Birkbeck College, London, 1933–7; Langworthy Professor of Physics, University of Manchester, 1937–53; Professor of Physics, Imperial College, London, 1953–65; Nobel Prize for Physics, 1948.

BLANCHE, Jacques-Emile (1862–1942), French painter and critic; Duncan Grant was among his pupils.

BLISS, Tasker Howard (1853–1930), army officer; Chief of Staff, US Army, 1917–18; US Permanent Military Representative, Inter-Allied Supreme War Council, 1918–19; Commissioner, American Commission to Negotiate Peace, Paris, 1919.

BLUNT, Anthony Frederick (later Sir Anthony) (1907–83), art historian and spy; educated Marlborough and Trinity College, Cambridge; Apostle; Fellow of Trinity, 1932–6; Reader in the History of Art, University of London, 1939–47; Professor, 1947–74; Deputy Director, Courtauld Institute, 1939–47; Director, 1947–74; Keeper of the King's Pictures, 1945–52; of the Queen's Pictures, 1952–72.

BOLTON, George Lewis French (later Sir George) (1900–82), banker; Bank of England, 1933; Adviser, 1941–8; Executive Director, 1948–57; Director, 1957–68; Chairman, Bank of London and South America, 1957–70.

BOND, Henry John Hales (1801–83), physician; educated Corpus Christi College, Cambridge; Regius Professor of Physic, Cambridge, 1851–72.

BONHAM CARTER, Helen Violet (née Asquith) (later Baroness Asquith) (1887–1969), married Maurice Bonham Carter, 1915; lifelong Liberal activist and internationalist.

BOOSEY, Leslie Arthur (1887–1978), President, Boosey & Hawkes Ltd, music publishers.

BOOTHBY, Robert John Graham (later Lord Boothby) (1900–86), politician; Conservative MP, 1924–58; PPS to Chancellor of Exchequer (Churchill), 1926–29; Parliamentary Secretary, Ministry of Food, 1940–1.

BOWEN, Vera (1889–1967), ballet and theatrical producer; close friend of Lydia Lopokova.

BOWLEY, Arthur Lyon (later Sir Arthur) (1869–1957), statistician; educated Christ's Hospital and Trinity College, Cambridge; taught statistics, LSE, 1898; Reader, 1908–19; Professor, 1919–36; Director, Oxford Institute of Statistics, 1940–4.

BRACE, Donald Clifford (1881–1955), publisher; with Henry Holt & Co., 1904–19; founded Harcourt Brace & Co., 1919; President, 1942–8; Chairman, 1948–9.

BRACKEN, Brendan Rendall (later Viscount Bracken) (1901–58), publisher and politician; director of Eyre & Spottiswoode, 1925; acquired *Financial News, Investors' Chronicle*, and joint ownership with Sir Henry Strakosch of *The Economist*; Conservative MP, 1929–51; Minister of Information, 1941–5; First Lord of the Admiralty, 1945.

BRADBURY, John Swanwick (later Lord Bradbury) (1872–1950), civil servant; educated Manchester Grammar School and Brasenose College, Oxford; Joint Permanent Secretary, Treasury, 1913–19; British Delegate, Reparation Commission, 1919–25.

BRADSHAW, Henry (1831–1886), scholar, antiquary and librarian; educated Eton and King's College, Cambridge; Fellow of King's, 1858–68; University Librarian, 1867–86.

BRAHAM, Dudley Disraeli (1875–1951), journalist; educated New College, Oxford; joined Berlin office of *The Times*, 1901; remained with the newspaper to 1914; editor of various Australian newspapers, 1914–30; rejoined *The Times*, 1931–45.

BRAITHWAITE, Richard (1900–90), philosopher; educated King's College, Cambridge; Apostle; Fellow of King's, 1924–90; University Lecturer in Moral Science, 1928–34; Sidgwick Lecturer, 1934–53; Knightbridge Professor, 1953–67.

BRAND, Robert Henry (later Lord Brand) (1878–1963), banker and public servant; educated Marlborough and New College, Oxford; Fellow, All Souls, 1901–63; served in South Africa under Lord Milner, 1902–9; Lazard Brothers, merchant bankers, 1909–60; Imperial Munitions Board, Canada, 1915–18; Head of British Food Mission, Washington, 1941–4; Treasury Representative in Washington, 1944–6; Chairman, British Supply Council in North America, 1942, 1945–6; UK delegate to Bretton Woods, 1944.

BRANDEIS, Louis Dembitz (1856–1941), jurist; Justice, US Supreme Court, 1916–39.

BRAQUE, Georges (1882–1963), painter, sculptor and engraver.

BRETT, Dorothy (b. 1883), studied at the Slade, 1910–16, a close friend of Carrington and resident at Garsington in 1917.

BRIDGE, Roy Arthur Odell (1911–78), banker; educated Dulwich College; Bank of England, 1929–69; Deputy Chief Cashier, 1959–63; Adviser to the Governors, 1963–5; Assistant to the Governors, 1965–9.

BRIDGES, Edward Ettindene (later Lord Bridges) (1892–1969), public servant; educated Eton and Magdalen College, Oxford; Fellow, All Souls, 1920–7; Treasury, 1919–38; Secretary to the Cabinet, 1938–45; Permanent Secretary, Treasury, 1945–56.

BRITTAIN, Sir Herbert (1894–1961), civil servant; entered Treasury, 1919; Third Secretary, 1942–53; Second Secretary, 1953–7.

BROAD, Charlie Dunbar (1887–1971), philosopher; educated Dulwich College and Trinity College, Cambridge; Fellow of Trinity, 1911, 1923–71; Lecturer in Philosophy, University of St Andrews, 1911–20; Professor of Philosophy, University of Bristol, 1920–3; Sidgwick Lecturer in Moral Science, 1931–3; Knightbridge Professor of Philosophy, Cambridge, 1933–53.

BROCKDORFF-RANTZAU, Count Ulrich Karl Christian Graf von (1869–1920), German Foreign Minister, 1919; Head of the German Delegation to Versailles, 1919.

BROOKE, Alan England (1863–1939), biblical scholar; educated Eton and King's College, Cambridge; Fellow of King's, 1889–1939; Provost, 1926–33; Ely Professor of Divinity, 1916–26.

BROOKE, Justin (1885–1963), farmer; educated Bedales and Emmanuel College, Cambridge; founder of Marlowe Society, 1907.

BROOKE, Rupert Chawner (1887–1915), poet; educated Rugby and King's College, Cambridge; Apostle; Fellow of King's College, 1912; died of blood poisoning while sailing to the Dardanelles.

BROWN, Ada Haydon (1837–1929), grandmother of JMK.

BROWN, Edward Kenneth (1879–1958), uncle of JMK; solicitor.

BROWN, Ivor John Carnegie (1891–1974), author and journalist; Drama Critic for *The Observer*, 1929–54; Editor, 1942–8; Associate Editor and Hon. Director, 1948–54; Director of Drama, CEMA, 1940–2.

BROWN, John (1830–1932), grandfather of JMK; pastor of Bunyan Meeting, Bedford, 1864–1903.

BROWN, Sir Walter Langdon (1870–1946), physician; educated St John's College, Cambridge and St Bartholomew's Hospital; Regius Professor of Physic, Cambridge, 1932–45.

BROWNING, Oscar (1837–1923), historian; educated Eton and King's College, Cambridge; Apostle; Fellow of King's, 1859–1923; Eton master, 1860–80; University Lecturer in History, 1883–1908.

BRÜNING, Heinrich (1885–1970), politician and political scientist; Member of the Reichstag, 1924–33; Reich Chancellor, 1930–2; Lecturer on Government, Harvard University, 1937–9; Professor, 1939–52.

BRYCE, James (later Viscount Bryce) (1838–1922), jurist, historian and statesman; educated Belfast Academy, Glasgow University and Trinity College, Cambridge; Fellow, Oriel College, Oxford, 1862–89; Regius Professor of Civil Law, Oxford, 1870–93; Liberal MP, 1885–1906; Chancellor of the Duchy of Lancaster, 1892–4; President, Board of Trade, 1894; Chief Secretary for Ireland, 1905–6; Ambassador to the United States, 1907–13.

BRYCE, Robert Broughton (b. 1910), public servant; educated University of Toronto, St John's College, Cambridge, and Harvard University; Department of Finance, Canada, 1938–45; Executive Director, IBRD, 1946–7; Secretary to the Treasury Board, 1947–53; Secretary to the Cabinet, 1954–63; Deputy Minister of Finance, 1963–70.

BURGESS, Guy Francis de Moncy (1911–64), spy; educated Eton and Trinity College, Cambridge; Apostle; BBC, 1936–8, 1941–4; Foreign Office, 1944–51.

BURGESS, Warren Randolph (1889–1978), banker; with Federal Reserve Bank of New York in 1920s; Deputy Governor, 1930–6; Vice Chairman, 1936–8; National City Bank, 1938–52; Under-Secretary, US Treasury, 1955–7.

BUSSY, Dorothy (1865–1960) (née Strachey); married Simon Bussy, 1903; settled at Roquebrune in the South of France.

BUSSY, Jane Simone (1906–60), painter; only child of Simon and Dorothy Bussy.

BUSSY, Simon Albert (1869–1954), painter; married Dorothy Strachey in 1903.

BUTLER, Harold Beresford (later Sir Harold) (1883–1951), civil servant; educated Eton and Balliol College, Oxford; Fellow of All Souls, 1905; entered civil service, 1907; Deputy Director, ILO, 1920–32; Director, 1932–8; Minister at HM Embassy, Washington, 1942–6; Warden, Nuffield College, Oxford, 1939–43.

BUTLER, Richard Austen (later Lord Butler) (1902–82), politician; educated Marlborough and Pembroke College, Cambridge; Conservative MP, 1929–65; Minister of Education, 1941–5; of Labour, 1945; Chancellor of the Exchequer, 1951–5; Leader of the House, 1955–61; Home Secretary, 1957–62; Foreign Secretary, 1963–4.

BUTT, David Bensusan (b. 1914), economist; educated King's College, Cambridge; civil servant, 1938–62; Economic Section, 1946–52; Assistant Secretary, Treasury, 1952–62; Australian National University, 1962–76.

BYRNES, James Francis (1879–1972), US politician; Congressman, 1911–25; Senator, 1931–41; Justice, US Supreme Court, 1941–2; Director of Economic Stabilization, 1942–3; Director of War Mobilization, 1943–5; Secretary of State, 1945–7.

CABLE, Sir Ernest (later Baron Cable) (1859–1927), businessman; senior partner Bird & Co., Calcutta and London; F. W. Heilgers & Co., Calcutta and London; member, Royal Commission on Indian Currency and Finance, 1913–14.

CADBURY, Lawrence John (1889–1982), chocolate manufacturer; educated Leighton Park and Trinity College, Cambridge; Managing Director, Cadbury Brothers, 1919; Director, Daily News Ltd, 1922–50; Director, Bank of England, 1936–8, 1941–61.

CADMAN, John (later Lord Cadman) (1877–1941), scientist and public servant; educated Durham University; Professor of Mining, Birmingham University, 1908–20; technical adviser (1921), Director (1931) and later Chairman, Anglo-Persian Oil Company.

CAILLAUX, Joseph (d. 1944), French politician; Minister of Finance, 1899–1902, 1906–9, 1911, 1913–14, 1925–6, 1935; Minister of the Interior, 1911–12; President of the Council, 1911–12.

CAIRNCROSS, Alexander Kirkland (later Sir Alec) (b. 1911), economist; educated Glasgow University and Trinity College, Cambridge; civil servant 1939–46; Economic Adviser, Board of Trade, 1946–9; Professor of Applied Economics, Glasgow University, 1951–61; Economic Adviser, HM Government, 1961–4; Head, Government Economic Service, 1964–9; Master, St Peter's College, Oxford, 1969–78.

CAIRNES, John Eliot (1823–75), economist; Professor of Political Economy, Trinity College, Dublin, 1856–61; Queen's College, Galway, 1856–70; University College, London, 1866–72.

CALLAGHAN, James Leonard (later Lord Callaghan) (b. 1912), politician; Labour MP, 1945–87; Chancellor of the Exchequer, 1964–7; Home Secretary, 1967–70; Foreign Secretary, 1974–6; Prime Minister, 1976–9.

CANNAN, Edwin (1861–1935), economist; educated Clifton and Balliol College, Oxford; joined LSE, 1895; Professor of Economics, 1907–26.

CANNAN, Gilbert (1884–1945), novelist; part of Lady Ottoline Morrell's circle.

CAPRON, John W. (d. 1958), churchman; educated Eton and King's College, Cambridge; ordained 1910.

CARRINGTON, Dora (1893–1932), painter; educated Slade School; introduced into Bloomsbury by Lady Ottoline Morrell; met Lytton Strachey, 1915; lived with Lytton Strachey at Tidmarsh and Ham Spray, 1917–32; married Ralph Partridge, 1921; committed suicide after death of Lytton Strachey.

CARSON, Edward Henry (later Lord Carson) (1854–1935), Ulster leader; educated Portarlington School and Trinity College, Dublin; MP, Dublin University, 1892–1918; Solicitor General for England, 1900–5; Attorney General, 1915–16; First Lord of the Admiralty, 1916–18; MP, Belfast, 1818–21; Lord of Appeal, 1921–9.

CARTER, Sir (Richard Henry) Archibald (1887–1958), civil servant; educated Eton and Trinity College, Cambridge; India Office, 1924–36; Permanent Secretary, Admiralty, 1936–40; Chairman, Eastern Group Supply Council, New Delhi, 1941–2; Chairman, Board of Customs and Excise, 1942–7; Permanent Under-Secretary of State for India, 1947; Joint Permanent Secretary for Commonwealth Relations, 1948; Chairman, Monopolies Commission, 1949–53.

CASE, Walter Summerhayes (1885–1937), investment banker; founded Case, Pomeroy & Co., a private investment company emphasising specialised research, 1916.

CASSEL, Sir Ernest Joseph (1852–1921), financier and philanthropist.

CASSEL, Gustav (1864–1944), economist; Professor of Economics, University of Stockholm, 1904–33.

CASADAY, Lauren Wilde (1905–69), economist; US Treasury Attaché in London, 1943–5.

CASTLE, Barbara (née Betts) (b. 1910), politician; educated St Hugh's College, Oxford; Labour MP, 1945–79; Minister of Overseas Development, 1964–5; of Transport, 1965–8; Employment, 1968–70; Social Services, 1974–6.

CATTO, Thomas Sivewright (later Lord Catto) (1879–1959), banker; Chairman of Andrew Yule & Co., 1919–40; in Calcutta, 1919–28; Director, Yule, Catto & Co., London, 1919–40; Managing Director, Morgan Grenfell, 1928–40; Director, Bank of England, 1940; Financial Adviser to Treasury, 1940–4; Governor, Bank of England, 1944–9.

CECIL, Edgar Algernon Robert Gascoyne (later Viscount Cecil) (1864–1958), educated Eton and University College, Oxford; Conservative MP, 1906–10; Independent MP, 1911–23; Minister of Blockade, 1916–18; Assistant Secretary of State for Foreign Affairs, 1918–19; Lord Privy Seal, 1923; Chancellor of the Duchy of Lancaster, 1923–7.

CHALMERS, Robert (later Lord Chalmers) (1858–1938), civil servant; educated City of London School and Oriel College, Oxford; entered Treasury, 1882;

Chairman, Board of Inland Revenue, 1907–11; Permanent Secretary, Treasury, 1911–13; Governor of Ceylon, 1913–16; Under-Secretary of State for Ireland, 1916; Joint Permanent Secretary, Treasury, 1916–19; Master of Peterhouse, 1924–31.

CHAMBERLAIN, Arthur Neville (1869–1940), politician; educated Rugby and Mason College, Birmingham; Conservative MP, 1917–40; Postmaster-General, 1922; Chancellor of the Exchequer 1923–4, 1931–7; Minister of Health, 1923, 1924–9; Prime Minister, 1937–40.

CHAMBERLAIN, Joseph Austen (1863–1937), politician; educated Rugby and Trinity College, Cambridge; Unionist MP, 1892–1937; Postmaster-General, 1902–3; Chancellor of the Exchequer, 1903–5, 1919–21; Secretary of State for India, 1915–17; Foreign Secretary, 1924–9; First Lord of the Admiralty, 1931.

CHAMBERS, Stanley Paul (later Sir Paul) (1904–81), civil servant and businessman; educated City of London School and LSE; Income Tax Adviser to Government of India, 1937–40; Assistant Secretary and Director of Statistics and Intelligence, Board of Inland Revenue, 1942–5; Commissioner of Inland Revenue, 1942–7; Director, Imperial Chemical Industries, 1947–68, Chairman 1960–8; President, National Institute of Economic and Social Research, 1955–62.

CHAMPERNOWNE, David Gawen (b. 1913), economist; educated Winchester and King's College, Cambridge; Apostle; Fellow of King's, 1937–48; Director, Oxford University Institute of Statistics, 1945–8; Professor of Statistics, 1948–59; Fellow of Nuffield College, 1945–59; Reader in Economics, Cambridge, 1959–79; Professor, 1970–8; Fellow of Trinity since 1959.

CHAPMAN, Sydney John (1871–1953), economist and civil servant; educated Manchester Grammar School, Owens College, Manchester and Trinity College, Cambridge; Stanley Jevons Professor of Political Economy, Manchester, 1901–18; Board of Trade, 1915; Permanent Secretary, 1919–27; Chief Economic Adviser to HM Government, 1927–32.

CHERWELL, Lord (Frederick Alexander Lindemann) (1886–1957), scientist and public servant; Professor of Experimental Philosophy, Oxford, 1919–56; Personal Assistant to Winston Churchill as Prime Minister, 1940–5; Paymaster-General, 1942–5.

CHICHERIN, Georgi Vasilevich (1872–1936), Soviet Foreign Minister in 1920s.

CHRISTIE, John (1882–1962), educated Eton and Trinity College, Cambridge; founded Glyndebourne Opera, 1934.

CHURCHILL, Winston Leonard Spencer (later Sir Winston) (1874–1965), statesman; educated Harrow and Sandhurst; MP (Unionist) 1900–4; (Liberal) 1904–22; (Conservative) 1924–64; President, Board of Trade, 1908–10; Home Secretary, 1910–11; First Lord of the Admiralty, 1911–15, 1939–40; Minister of Munitions, 1917–18; Secretary for War, 1918–21; Colonial Secretary, 1921–2; Chancellor of the Exchequer, 1924–9; Prime Minister, 1940–5, 1951–5; Leader of the Opposition, 1945–51.

CITRINE, Walter McLennan (later Lord Citrine) (1887–1983), trade unionist; General Secretary, Trades Union Congress, 1924–46; Director, National Coal Board, 1946; Chairman, British Electricity Board, 1957–9.

CLAPHAM, John Harold (1873–1946), economic historian; educated Leys School and King's College, Cambridge; Fellow of King's, 1898–1904, 1908–46; Professor of Economics, Leeds, 1904–8; Professor of Economic History, Cambridge, 1928–38.

CLARK, Colin (1905–89), economist; educated Oxford and LSE; staff, Economic Advisory Council, 1930–1; University Lecturer in Statistics, Cambridge, 1931–7; Under-Secretary of State for Labour and Industry, Queensland, Australia, 1938–52; Director, Institute for Research in Agricultural Economics, University of Oxford, 1953–69.

CLARK, John Maurice (1884–1963), economist; Professor of Economics, Columbia University, 1926–52.

CLARK, Kenneth Mackenzie (later Lord Clark) (1903–83), author and arts administrator; educated Winchester and Trinity College, Oxford; Director, National Gallery, 1934–45.

CLARK, William Clifford (1889–1952), economist and public servant; Professor of Economics, Queen's University, Canada, 1915–23; Professor of Commerce, 1931–2; investment banker in New York and Chicago, 1923–31; Deputy Minister of Finance, Canada, 1932–52.

CLARKE, Richard William Barnes ('Otto') (later Sir Richard) (1910–75), public servant; educated Clare College, Cambridge; served in Ministries of Information, Economic Warfare, Supply and Production, 1939–45; Assistant Secretary, Treasury, 1945; Under-Secretary, 1947; Third Secretary, 1955; Second Secretary, 1962; Permanent Secretary, Ministry of Aviation, 1966, Ministry of Technology, 1966–70.

CLAUSON, Sir Gerard Leslie Makins (1871–1974), civil servant; entered Inland Revenue, 1914; Colonial Office, 1919; Principal, 1920; Assistant Secretary, 1934; Assistant Under-Secretary of State, 1940–51.

CLAY, Sir Henry (1883–1954), economist; educated Bradford Grammar School and University College, Oxford; Stanley Jevons Professor of Political Economy, Manchester, 1922–7; Professor of Social Economics, 1927–30; Economic Adviser, Bank of England, 1930–44; Warden, Nuffield College, Oxford, 1944–9.

CLAYTON, William Lockhart (1880–1966), US Federal Loan Administration and Vice-President, Export-Import Bank, 1940–2; Assistant Secretary of State, 1944–5; Under-Secretary of State for Economic Affairs, 1945–7.

CLEMENCEAU, Georges (1841–1929), Prime Minister of France, 1906–9, 1917–20.

CLOUGH, Anne Jemimah (1820–92), first Principal of Newnham College, Cambridge.

COBBOLD, Cameron Fromanteel (later Lord Cobbold) (1904–87), banker; educated Eton and King's College, Cambridge; entered Bank of England as Adviser, 1933; Executive Director, 1938–45; Deputy Governor, 1945–9; Governor, 1949–61.

COHEN, Benjamin Victor (1894–1963), lawyer; Adviser to US Ambassador in London, 1941; Assistant to Director, Office of Economic Stabilization, 1942–3; General Counsel, Office of War Mobilization, 1943–5; Counsellor, Department of State, 1945–7; Legal Adviser to the American Delegation at Bretton Woods.

COKAYNE, Sir Brian (later Lord Cullen) (1864–1932), banker; educated Charterhouse; entered Antony Gibbs & Co., 1883; partner, 1901; Director, Bank of England, 1902–15, 1920–32; Deputy Governor, 1915–18; Governor, 1918–20.

COLDSTREAM, William Menzies (later Sir William) (1908–87), artist; educated Slade School and University College, London; Member, London Artists Association.

COLE, George Douglas Howard (1889–1959), economist and publicist; educated St Paul's and Balliol College, Oxford; Fellow of Magdalen College, 1912; Fellow of University College, Oxford, 1925–44; Reader in Economics, 1925–44; Chichele Professor of Social and Political Theory, 1944–57.

COLE, Horace (1881–1936), hoaxer and art connoisseur; educated Eton and Trinity College, Cambridge; friend of Adrian Stephen; took part in the *Dreadnought* hoax, 1910.

COLE, Margaret Isobel (later Dame Margaret) (née Postgate) (1892–1980), socialist activist and author; educated Roedean and Girton College, Cambridge; married G. D. H. Cole, 1918.

COLEFAX, Lady Sybil (*c*.1875–1950), society hostess; cultivated members of Bloomsbury from 1922.

COLLADO, Emilio Gabriel (b. 1910), US Treasury Department, 1934–8; State Department, 1938–48; Associate Economic Adviser, Special Assistant to Under-secretary, Director of Office of Financial and Development Policy, Deputy on Financial Affairs, 1939–45; US Executive Director, IBRD, 1946–7; Standard Oil Co., 1947–75.

COOKE, Sidney Russell (1895–1930), stockbroker; educated Cheltenham and King's College, Cambridge; partner, Rowe & Pitman; Director National Mutual Life Assurance Society to 1930.

CORBETT, William John (1866–1925), educated Eton and King's College, Cambridge; Fellow of King's 1892–1925; First Bursar, 1917–25.

CORCORAN, Thomas Gardiner (1900–81), lawyer; Adviser to the Secretary of the US Treasury, 1933; Counsel, Reconstruction Finance Corporation, 1932, 1934–41; involved in drafting many important New Deal Acts.

CORNFORD, Frances Crofts (née Darwin) (1886–1960), poet; married Francis Macdonald Cornford, 1908.

COSTELLOE, Karin see STEPHEN, Karin.

COSTELLOE, Ray see STRACHEY, Ray.

COSTIGAN, Edward Prentiss (1874–1939), lawyer; member, US Tariff Commission, 1917–28; Democratic Senator for Colorado, 1931–7.

COURTAULD, Samuel (1876–1947), industrialist and art patron; educated at Rugby; Director of Courtaulds, 1915; Chairman, 1921–40; endowed Courtauld Institute of Art, University of London.

COX, Katherine ('Ka') (1887–1938), educated Newnham College, Cambridge, 1906–10; member of Neo-Pagans; close friend of Virginia Woolf.

COX, Oscar Sydney (1905–66), lawyer; Assistant to General Counsel, US Treasury, 1938–41; General Counsel, Lend-Lease Administration, 1941–3; Assistant Solicitor General, 1942–3; General Counsel, Foreign Economic Administration, 1943–5.

CRANE, Jay Everett (1891–1973), various jobs at Federal Reserve Bank of New York to 1935; Vice-President and Director, Standard Oil, 1935–57.

CRAVATH, Paul Drennan (1861–1940), lawyer; US Treasury representative on House Mission to Inter-Allied War Conference, 1917; Counsel of American Mission to Inter-Allied Council on War Purchases and Finance, 1918.

CRIPPS, Sir (Richard) Stafford (1889–1952), statesman; educated Winchester and University College, London; Solicitor-General, 1930–1; Labour MP, 1931–50; Ambassador to USSR, 1940–2; Lord Privy Seal and Leader of House of Commons, 1942; Minister of Aircraft Production, 1942–5; President of Board of Trade, 1945–7; Chancellor of the Exchequer, 1947–50.

CROCE, Benedetto (1866–1952), idealist philosopher and historian.

CROSBY, Oscar Terry (1861–1947), Assistant Secretary, US Treasury, 1917–18; President, Inter-Allied Council on War Purchases and Finance, 1917–19; Special Commission of Finance in Europe, 1918–19; Financial Adviser, US Peace Commission, 1919.

CROWLEY, Leo T. (d. 1972), member, President Roosevelt's Cabinet, 1942–3; Head, Office of Economic Warfare, 1943; Foreign Economic Administration, 1943–5; Chairman of a railway company, 1945–63.

CUNARD, Maud, later Emerald (1872–1948), society hostess; married to Sir Bache Cunard, heir to the shipping fortune.

CUNLIFFE, Walter (later Lord Cunliffe) (1855–1920), banker; educated Harrow and Trinity College, Cambridge; launched Cunliffe Brothers, merchant bankers, 1890; Director, Bank of England, 1895–1911, 1918–20; Deputy Governor, 1911–13; Governor, 1913–18.

CUNNINGHAM, William (1849–1919), economic historian; educated Trinity College, Cambridge; Professor of Economics, King's College, London, 1891–7; Fellow of Trinity, 1891; Archdeacon of Ely, 1907–19.

CUNO, Wilhelm (1876–1933), Reich Chancellor 1922–3.

CUNYNGHAME, Henry Hardinge (1848–1935), civil servant and amateur economist; educated St John's College, Cambridge; fell under Marshall's influence; author of *Geometrical Political Economy* (1904).

CURRIE, Lauchlin (b. 1902), economist; Assistant Director of Research and Statistics, Federal Reserve Board, 1934–9; Administrative Assistant to the President, 1939–45; Deputy Administrator, Foreign Economic Administration, 1943–5; Director of first World Bank country mission, to Colombia, 1949–50; resident in Colombia since 1950.

CURZON, George Nathaniel (later Marquess Curzon) (1859–1925), educated Eton and Balliol College, Oxford; Fellow of All Souls, 1883; MP, 1886–92; Viceroy of India, 1899–1905; Chancellor, University of Oxford, 1907; Lord Privy Seal, 1915–16; President, Air Board, 1916; Lord President of the Council, 1916–19, 1924–5; Foreign Secretary, 1919–24.

DAKYNS, Henry Graham, educated Rugby and Cambridge; a classics master at Clifton College, Bristol; a friend of Sidgwick and J. A. Symonds, whom Marshall met while teaching at Clifton.

DALTON, Edward Hugh John (later Lord Dalton) (1887–1962), economist and politician; educated Eton, King's College, Cambridge and LSE; Lecturer in Economics, LSE, 1919–25; Cassel Reader in Commerce, 1920–35; Labour MP 1924–9, 1935–59; Parliamentary Under-Secretary, Foreign Office, 1929–31; Minister of Economic Warfare, 1940–2; President of Board of Trade, 1942–5; Chancellor of the Exchequer, 1945–7.

DANILOVA, Alexandra, ballerina and choreographer; member, Mariinsky Theatre ballet; 1922–4; with Diaghilev, 1925–9; Ballets Russes, 1933–8; Ballets Russes de Monte Carlo, 1938–51; went to the US in 1934.

DARWIN, Sir George Howard (1845–1912), mathematician and astronomer; educated Trinity College, Cambridge; Fellow of Trinity, 1868–78; Plumian Professor of Astronomy and Experimental Philosophy, Cambridge, 1883–1912.

DARWIN, Gwen see RAVERAT, Gwen.

DARWIN, Margaret see KEYNES, Margaret.

DAVENPORT, Nicholas (d. 1979), stockbroker, journalist and author; educated Cheltenham and Queen's College, Oxford; financial correspondent for the *Nation and Athenaeum*, 1923–30; the *New Statesman and Nation*, from 1930; director, National Mutual Life Assurance Society, 1931–69; Deputy Chairman, 1960–9.

DAVIDSON, Douglas, a painter and friend of Lytton Strachey and Duncan Grant.

DAVIDSON, John Colin Campbell (later Viscount Davidson) (1889–1970), politician; educated Westminister and Pembroke College, Cambridge; Private Secretary to Bonar Law, 1910–20; Conservative MP, 1920–3, 1924–37; Chancellor of the Duchy of Lancaster, 1922–3, 1931; Chairman, Conservative Party, 1926–30.

DAVIES, Clement Edward (1884–1962), lawyer and politician; Liberal MP, 1929–62; Leader of the Liberal Party, 1945–56.

DAVIES, Sarah Emily (1830–1921), organiser of a College for Women opened at Hitchin, 1869; transferred to Cambridge (Girton College), 1873; Mistress of Girton, 1873–5.

DAVIES, Theodore Llewellyn (1870–1905), educated Marlborough and Trinity College, Cambridge; Apostle; Fellow of Trinity, 1894–1900.

DAVIS, Norman Hezekiah (1878–1944), businessman and banker; Assistant Secretary, US Treasury, 1919–20, Under-Secretary of State, 1920–1.

DAWES, Charles Gates (1865–1951), businessman and banker; US Comptroller of the Currency, 1897–1901; Director, Bureau of the Budget, 1921–2; Vice President, 1925–9; Ambassador to Great Britain, 1929–32; Nobel Peace Prize, 1925.

DAWSON, George Geoffrey (1874–1944), born Robinson and assumed name of Dawson in 1917; educated Eton and Magdalen College, Oxford; Fellow of All Souls, 1898–1944; editor of *The Times*, 1912–19, 1923–41.

DEBENHAM, Ernest Ridley (later Sir Ernest) (1865–1952), businessman; Director, Lloyds Bank and Royal Exchange Assurance Company; Director, Debenham & Freebody, before 1930; member, Economic Advisory Council.

DEBENHAM, Piers Kenrick (1904–64), staff, Economic Advisory Council, 1930–9; Cabinet Office, Economic Section and predecessor organisations, 1939–41.

De La WARR, 9th Earl of (Herbrand Edward Dundonald Sackville) (1900–76), educated Eton and Magdalen College, Oxford; Lord Privy Seal, 1937–8; President, Board of Education, 1938–40; Postmaster-General, 1951–5.

DENT, Edward Joseph (1876–1967), musical scholar; educated Eton and King's College, Cambridge; Fellow of King's, 1902–8; Professor of Music, Cambridge, 1926–41.

DERAIN, André (1880–1954), artist; appreciated by Clive Bell and Roger Fry; designed decor for Massine's *La Boutique Fantasque* (1919).

DIAGHILEV, Serge Pavlovich (1872–1929), Russian impresario; brought Russian opera and ballet to Paris, 1909–10; Ballets Russes, 1911–29; first London season, June 1911; entertained by Lady Ottoline Morrell.

DICKINSON, Arthur Lowes (later Sir Arthur) (1859–1935), innovative accountant; educated Charterhouse and King's College, Cambridge; head of Price Waterhouse in the United States, 1910–11; partner of Price Waterhouse, London, 1913–23.

DICKINSON, Goldsworthy Lowes (1862–1932), political philosopher; educated Charterhouse and King's College, Cambridge; Apostle; Fellow of King's, 1887–1932; champion of League of Nations.

DOBB, Maurice Herbert (1900–76), economist; educated Charterhouse, Pembroke College, Cambridge, and LSE: Lecturer in Economics, Cambridge, 1924–59; Reader in Economics, 1959–65.

DOBBS, Archibald Edward, classicist; Fellow of King's, 1908–14.

DOBSON, Frank Owen (1888–1963), sculptor.

DULLES, Allen Welsh (1893–1969), lawyer and diplomat; US Department of State, 1916–26; American Peace Delegation, Paris, 1919; Chief, Division of Near Eastern Affairs, 1922–6; Office of Strategic Services in Europe, 1942–5; Deputy Director, Central Intelligence Agency, 1951–3; Director, 1953–61.

DULLES, Eleanor Lansing (b. 1895), economist and civil servant; educated Bryn Mawr, LSE and Harvard; taught at Simmons College and Bryn Mawr; Social Security Board, 1936; Bureau of Economic Warfare, 1942; Department of State, 1942–62.

DULLES, John Foster (1888–1959), lawyer; member, US Delegation to Paris Peace Conference, 1919; US Secretary of State, 1953–9.

DUNCAN, Sir Andrew Rae (1884–1952), public servant; Secretary to Government Shipbuilding Committees, 1916–18; Coal Controller, 1919–21; Chairman, Central Electricity Generating Board, 1927–35; British Iron and Steel Federation, 1935–40, 1945–52; Director, Bank of England, 1929–40; Conservative MP, 1940–50; President, Board of Trade, 1940, 1941–2; Minister of Supply, 1940–1, 1942–5.

DUNDAS, Robert Hamilton ('Robin') (1884–1960), classicist; educated Eton and New College, Oxford; Lecturer, University of Liverpool, 1906–9; Lecturer, Christ Church, Oxford, 1909; Student of Christ Church, 1910–57.

DURBIN, Evan Frank Mottram (1906–48), economist and politician; educated New College, Oxford; Lecturer in Economics, LSE, 1930–40; Economic Section, 1940–2; Personal Assistant to Deputy Prime Minister, 1942–5; Labour MP, 1945–48; Parliamentary Secretary, Ministry of Works, 1947–8.

DURNFORD, Walter (1847–1926), classicist; educated Eton and King's College, Cambridge; Fellow of King's 1869–1926; Eton master, 1870–99; Provost of King's 1918–26.

EADY, Craufurd Wilfrid Griffin (later Sir Wilfrid) (1880–1962), civil servant; educated Clifton and Jesus College, Cambridge; entered civil service, 1913; Ministry of Labour, 1917–38; Deputy Under-Secretary, Home Office, 1938–40; Deputy Chairman, Board of Customs and Excise, 1940–1; Chairman, 1941–2; Joint Second Secretary, Treasury, 1942–52.

EAGAR, Waldo McGillycuddy (1884–1966), Secretary, Liberal Land Enquiry, 1923–7; Liberal Industrial Inquiry, 1926–8.

EASTMAN, Joseph Bartlett (1882–1944), Federal Co-ordinator of Transportation, 1933–6; Director, Office of Defense Transportation, 1941–4.

ECCLES, Marriner Stoddard (1890–1977), Governor, US Federal Reserve Board, 1934–51; Chairman, 1936–48; member, US delegation to Bretton Woods, 1944.

EDELMAN, Maurice (1911–75), author and politician; educated Trinity College, Cambridge; Labour MP, 1945–75.

EDEN, Anthony (later Earl of Avon) (1897–1977), politician; educated Eton and Christ Church, Oxford; Conservative MP, 1923–57; Foreign Secretary, 1935–8, 1940–5, 1951–5; Secretary of State for the Dominions, 1939–40; Secretary of War, 1940; Prime Minister, 1955–7.

EDGEWORTH, Francis Ysidro (1845–1926), economist; educated Balliol College, Oxford; Professor of Political Economy, King's College, London, 1888; Tooke Professor of Economic Science and Statistics, 1890; Drummond Professor of Political Economy, Oxford, 1891–1922; Fellow of All Souls, 1891.

EINAUDI, Luigi (1884–1961), economist and statesman; Professor of Public Finance, University of Turin, 1902–49, 1955; Bocconi University of Milan, 1904–26; Member, Italian Senate, 1919–45; Governor, Bank of Italy, 1945–8; President of the Italian Republic, 1948–55.

EINSTEIN, Albert (1879–1955), physicist; Professor of Physics, Prague, 1911; Aurich, 1912; Leyden, 1912–28; Berlin, 1914–33; Institute for Advanced Study, Princeton, 1933–55.

EINZIG, Paul (1897–1973), journalist and author; *Financial News*, 1921–45; *Financial Times*, 1945–56.

EISENHOWER, Dwight David (1890–1969), public servant; Supreme Commander, Allied Forces in Europe, 1943–5; President of the United States, 1953–61.

ELIOT, Thomas Stearns (1888–1965), poet, critic, dramatist; educated Harvard University; introduced to Bloomsbury by Lady Ottoline Morrell.

ELLIS-REES, Hugh (later Sir Hugh) (1900–74), public servant; educated University of London; Inland Revenue, 1919–38; Assistant Controller, Clearing Office, 1938–9; Treasury, 1940–8; Financial Adviser, HM Embassy, Madrid, 1940–4.

ELMHIRST, Dorothy Whitney (1887–1968), active in social and educational work; married Willard Straight, 1911; Leonard Elmhirst, 1925; co-founder of Dartington Hall.

EPPS, Sir George Selby Washington (1885–1951), actuary; educated Highgate School and Emmanuel College, Cambridge; Deputy Government Actuary, 1926–36; Government Actuary, 1936–44.

ERZBERGER, Mattias (1875–1921), German politician; Minister of Finance, 1919–20.

ESSENDON, Lord see LEWIS, Frederick William.

ETCHELLS, Frederick (1886–1973), artist; friend of Roger Fry, Duncan Grant and Adrian Stephen.

EVANS, Ifor Leslie (1897–1952), educated St John's College, Cambridge; Fellow, 1923–34; Principal, University College, Aberystwyth, 1934–52.

EZEKIEL, Mordecai Joseph Brill (1899–1974), economist; Economic Adviser to US Secretary of Agriculture, 1933–44; economist, FAO, 1947–50; Deputy Director, Economic Division, 1951–8; Head, Economic Department, 1959–60; Assistant Director-General, 1961–2.

FALK, Oswald Toynbee (1879–1972), financier; educated Rugby and Balliol College, Oxford; Treasury, 1917–19; partner, Buckmaster & Moore, 1919–32; Falk and Partners, 1932–72.

FARRER, Gaspard, banker; member of Barings; member, Cunliffe and Chamberlain-Bradbury Committees.

FAWCETT, Henry (1833–84); economist; educated King's College School, London, and Peterhouse, Cambridge; Fellow of Trinity Hall, Cambridge, 1856; Professor of Political Economy, Cambridge, 1863–84; Liberal MP, 1865–84; Postmaster-General, 1880–4.

FAY, Charles Ryle (1884–1961), economic historian; educated King's College, Cambridge and LSE; Fellow, Christ's College, Cambridge, 1908–22; Professor of Economic History, University of Toronto, 1921–30; Reader in Economic History, University of Cambridge, from 1930.

FEIS, Herbert (1893–1972), economist and historian; Economic Adviser, Department of State, 1931–7, Adviser on International Economic Affairs, 1937–43; Special Consultant to Secretary of War, 1944–6.

FELKIN, Arthur Elliott (1892–1968), educated King's College, Cambridge; Secretariat, Reparations Commission, 1919–23; League of Nations and United Nations, 1923–55.

FERGUSSON, John Donald Balfour (later Sir Donald) (1891–1963), civil servant; educated Berkhamstead and Magdalen College, Oxford; entered Treasury, 1919; Assistant Secretary, 1934; Permanent Secretary, Ministry of Agriculture and Fisheries, 1936–45, Ministry of Fuel and Power, 1945–52.

FISHER, Irving Norton (1867–1947); Professor of Economics, Yale University, 1900–35.

FLORENCE, Alix Sargant see STRACHEY, Alix.

FLORENCE, Philip Sargant (1890–1982), economist; educated Rugby and Gonville and Caius College, Cambridge; University Lecturer in Economics, Cambridge, 1921–9; Professor of Commerce, University of Birmingham, 1929–55; Dean of the Faculty of Commerce and Social Science, 1947–50.

FLUX, Alfred William (later Sir Alfred) (1867–1942), economist; educated St John's College, Cambridge; Fellow of St John's, 1889; Lecturer in Political Economy, Owens College, Manchester, 1893; Professor, 1898; Professor of Economics, McGill University, 1901–8; Statistical Adviser, Board of Trade, 1908–32.

FOCH, Ferdinand (1851–1929), soldier; Marshall of France; Supreme Allied Commander, 1918; Chairman of the Armistice Commission, 1919.

FOOT, Michael (b. 1913), politician; Labour MP, 1945–55, since 1960; Employment Secretary, 1974–6; Lord President of the Council and Deputy Prime Minister, 1976–9; Leader of the Opposition 1980–3.

876

FORSTER, Edward Morgan (1879–1970), writer; educated Tonbridge and King's College, Cambridge; Apostle; first novel, *Where Angles Fear to Tread* (1905).

FOSTER, Sir George Eulas (1847–1931), Canadian politician; Conservative MP, 1882–1900, 1904–21; Senator 1921–31; Minister of Finance, 1888–96; Minister of Trade and Commerce, 1911–21.

FOXWELL, Herbert Somerton (1849–1936), economist; educated University of London and St John's College, Cambridge; Fellow of St John's, 1874; Professor of Political Economy, University College, London, 1881–1927.

FRANCK, Paul, JMK's French translator for *Economic Consequences of the Peace* and *Revision of the Treaty*.

FRANKFURTER, Felix (1882–1965), lawyer; Professor, Harvard Law School, 1914–39; Justice, US Supreme Court, 1939–62.

FRY, Geoffrey Storrs (1888–1960), public servant; educated Harrow and King's College, Cambridge; Home Office, 1913–17; Treasury, 1917–19; Private Secretary to Bonar Law, 1919–21, 1922–3; to Baldwin, 1923–39.

FRY, Roger (1866–1934), painter and critic; educated Clifton and King's College, Cambridge; Apostle; Metropolitan Museum, New York, 1906–10; organised Post-Impressionist exhibitions in London 1910, 1912; Omega Workshops, 1913–19; *Vision and Design* (1919); Slade Professor of Art, Cambridge, 1933.

FURNESS, Robert Allason ('Robin') (later Sir Robert) (1883–1954), public servant; educated Rugby and King's College, Cambridge; Egyptian Civil Service, 1906–23; staff of High Commissioner, 1919; Oriental Secretary to the High Commissioner, 1923–6; Deputy Director General, Egyptian State Broadcasting, 1933–4; Professor of English, Faud I University, 1936–44; British Council Representative in Egypt, 1945–50.

GAITSKELL, Hugh Todd Naylor (1906–63), economist and politician; educated Winchester and New College, Oxford; Lecturer in Political Economy, University College, London, 1928–38; Reader, 1938–45; Principal Private Secretary to Minister of Economic Warfare, 1940–2; Principal Assistant Secretary, Board of Trade, 1942–5; Labour MP, 1945–63; Parliamentary Secretary, Ministry of Fuel and Power, 1946–7; Minister of Fuel and Power, 1947–50; Minister of State for Economic Affairs, 1950; Chancellor of the Exchequer, 1950–1; Leader of Labour Party, 1955–63.

GALTON, Sir Francis (1822–1911), statistician; educated Trinity College, Cambridge; founded Eugenics Laboratory, University College, London, 1904; founded *Biometrica*, 1901.

GARNETT, David ('Bunny') (1892–1981), author; educated Royal College of Science (now Imperial College); entered Bloomsbury through friendships with the Olivier sisters, Rupert Brooke, Geoffrey Keynes and Adrian Stephen; became friendly with Duncan Grant, 1914; with Duncan and Vanessa at Wissett and Charleston, 1916–18; married Rachel Marshall, 1921; married Angelica Bell, 1942; member of Memoir Club, 1933.

GARVIN, James Louis (1868–1947), journalist; editor of *The Observer*, 1908–42.

GAYER, Alfred David (1903–51), economist; educated St Paul's School and Lincoln College, Oxford; taught at Columbia University, 1931–40; Queens College, City University of New York, 1940–51.

GEDDES, Sir Eric Campbell (1875–1937), politician; Unionist MP, 1917–22; First Lord of the Admiralty, 1917–18; Minister of Transport, 1919–21; chairman of 'Geddes Axe' Committee on National Economy, 1921–2.

GERTLER, Mark (1891/2–1939) artist; educated Slade School; resident at Garsington, 1915; drifted away from Bloomsbury after 1918.

GIBBS, Herbert Cokayne (later Lord Hunsdon) (1854–1935), merchant banker; educated Winchester and Trinity College, Cambridge; joined Antony Gibbs & Sons, 1879; partner, 1882.

GIBLIN, Lyndhurst Falkiner (1872–1951), economist; educated University of Tasmania and King's College, Cambridge; Government Statistician, Tasmania, 1919–28; Ritchie Professor of Economics, University of Melbourne, 1929–40.

GIDE, Charles (1847–1932), economist; Professor at the College de France, 1919–32.

GIFFIN, Sir Robert (1837–1910), economist and statistician; Assistant Editor, *The Economist*, 1868–76; Chief, Statistical Department, Board of Trade, 1875–97.

GIFFORD, Thomas Johnston Carlyle, Treasury representative in the United States concerned with the sale of British-owned dollar securities, 1939–41.

GILPIN, Edmund Henry (later Sir Harry) (1876–1950), businessman and Liberal politician.

GLASGOW, Mary Cecilia (1905–83), civil servant; educated Lady Margaret Hall, Oxford; Inspector of Schools, 1933–9; Secretary General, CEMA and Arts Council, 1939–51.

GLASS, Carter (1858–1946), politician; US Congressman, 1902–18; Secretary of the Treasury, 1918–20; Senator for Virginia, 1920–46.

GODLEY, Sir John Arthur (later Lord Kilbracken) (1847–1932), civil servant; educated Rugby and Balliol College, Oxford; Assistant (1872–4) and Principal (1880–2) Private Secretary to Gladstone; Fellow, Hertford College, Oxford, 1874–80; Permanent Under-Secretary of State for India, 1883–1909.

GOMPERS, Samuel (1850–1924), trade unionist; one of the founders of the American Federation of Labour, 1886; President, 1886–94, 1895–1924.

GORDON, Donald (1901–69), public servant and businessman; Bank of Canada, 1935–49; Secretary, 1935; Deputy Governor, 1938–9; Alternative Chairman, Foreign Exchange Control Board, 1939–49; Chairman, Wartime Prices and Trade Board, 1941–4; President, Canadian National Railways, 1950–66.

GORKI, Maxim (1868–1936), Russian novelist.

GOSCHEN, George Joachim (later Viscount Goschen) (1831–1907), statesman; educated Rugby and Oriel College, Oxford; Liberal MP, 1863–85; Liberal Unionist MP, 1887–1900; Chancellor of the Exchequer, 1886–92; converted national debt from 3 per cent to 2½ per cent basis, 1888.

GOSCHEN, Kenneth (1907–89), member administrative staff, British Treasury Delegation in Washington, 1945.

GRANT, Alexander Thomas Kingdom (1906–88), economist and civil servant; educated University College, Oxford; Lecturer in Political Economy, University

College, London, 1938–9; Treasury, 1939, Under-Secretary, 1956; Under-Secretary, Export Credits Guarantee Department, 1958–66; Fellow, Pembroke College, Cambridge, 1966–73.

GRANT, Alister Campbell, educated Christ's College School, Christchurch, New Zealand; a student at King's College, Cambridge, 1900–April 1903 before returning to New Zealand.

GRANT, Charles Eustace, educated Eton and King's College, Cambridge; Fellow of King's, 1875; Third Bursar, 1880–7; Second Bursar, 1887–92; First Bursar, 1892–1917.

GRANT, Duncan James Corrower (1885–1978), painter; cousin of Lytton Strachey; educated St Paul's and Westminster School of Art; studied in Paris under Jacques-Emile Blanche, 1906–7; affair with JMK, 1908; began exhibiting 1909; co-director of Omega Workshops 1913; lived with Vanessa Bell from 1915; member, London Artists Association, 1925–31.

GRAY, James (later Sir James) (1891–1975), zoologist; educated Merchant Taylors' and King's College, Cambridge; Fellow of King's, 1914–75; Professor of Zoology, 1937–59.

GREENWOOD, Leonard Hugh (1880–1965), classicist; educated King's College, Cambridge; Apostle; Fellow of King's, 1904–6; Fellow of Emmanuel College, Cambridge, 1906–65.

GREGG, Sir Cornelius (Joseph) (d. 1959), Chairman, Board of Inland Revenue, 1942–8.

GREGORY, Sir Theodore (1890–1970), economist; educated LSE; Assistant Lecturer, LSE, 1910–19; Cassel Reader, 1919–27; Cassel Professor, 1927–37; Economic Adviser to Government of India, 1938–46; member, Indian delegation to Bretton Woods, 1944.

GRENFELL, Edward Charles (later Lord St Just) (1870–1941), banker and politician; educated Harrow and Trinity College, Cambridge; partner J. S. Morgan & Co. (from 1909 Morgan Grenfell), 1904–41; Director, Bank of England, 1905–40; Conservative MP, 1922–35.

GREW, Joseph Clark (1880–1965), diplomat; joined US Foreign Service, 1904; Under-Secretary of State, 1924–7, 1944–5; Ambassador to Turkey, 1927–32; to Japan, 1931–41.

GREY, Sir Edward (later Viscount Grey) (1862–1933), statesman; educated Winchester and Balliol College, Oxford; Liberal MP, 1885–1916; Foreign Secretary, 1905–16.

GRIGG, (Percy) James (later Sir James) (1890–1964), public servant; educated Bournemouth Secondary School and St John's College, Cambridge; entered Treasury, 1913; Private Secretary to the Chancellor of the Exchequer, 1921–30; Chairman, Board of Customs and Excise, 1930, Board of Inland Revenue, 1930–4; Finance Member, Viceroy's Executive Council, 1934–9; Permanent Under-Secretary of State for War, 1939–42; Secretary of State for War, 1942–5; Nationalist MP, 1942–5.

GUEDELLA, Phillip (1889–1944), historian and essayist; educated Rugby and Balliol College, Oxford; five times unsuccessful Liberal candidate 1922–31.

GUEST, Frederick Edward (1875–1937), politician; educated Winchester; Liberal MP, 1910–22, 1923–9; Conservative MP, 1931–7; Secretary of State for Air, 1921–2.

GUILLEBAUD, Claude William (1890–1971), economist; educated St John's College, Cambridge; Fellow of St John's, 1915–71; Girdlers' Lecturer, Cambridge University, 1942–56, Reader 1956–7.

GULICK, Luther Halsey (b. 1892), economist; Consultant on post-defense planning, National Resources Planning Board, 1941–3; Special Assistant, US Treasury, 1941–3; Director, Office of Organizational Planning, War Production Board, 1942–4; Chief of Program and Requirements Division, Office of Foreign Relief and Rehabilitation Operations, State Department, 1943; Secretariat of UNRRA, Atlantic City, 1943, acting Chief, 1944; member, US Reparations Missions, 1945–6.

GUTHRIE, William Tyrone (1900–71), actor and theatre director; educated Wellington and St John's College, Oxford; Administrator, Old Vic and Sadler's Wells, 1939–45; Director, Old Vic, 1951–2.

GUTT, Camille Adolphe (1884–1971), Belgian journalist and statesman; member, Young Committee, 1929; Minister of Finance, 1934–5, 1939–45; of Economic Affairs, 1940–5; Managing Director, IMF, 1946–51.

HALDANE, John Burdon Sanderson (1892–1964), geneticist; educated Eton and New College, Oxford; Fellow, New College, 1919; Reader in Biochemistry, University of Cambridge; dismissed owing to divorce case, 1925, reinstated, 1926; Fullerian Professor of Physiology, Royal Institution, 1930–2; Professor of Genetics (then of Biometry), University College, London, 1933–57.

HALIFAX, Lord (Edward Frederick Lindley Wood) (1881–1959), public servant; educated Eton and Christ Church, Oxford; Conservative MP, 1910–25; President, Board of Education, 1922–4, 1932–5; Viceroy of India, 1925–31; Secretary of State for War, 1935; Lord Privy Seal, 1935–7; Lord President of the Council, 1937–8, 1940; Secretary of State for Foreign Affairs, 1938–41; HM Ambassador at Washington, 1941–6.

HALL-PATCH, Edmund Leo (later Sir Edmund) (1896–1975), public servant; Assistant Secretary, Treasury, 1935–44; Financial Commissioner in Far East, 1940; Assistant Under-Secretary of State, Foreign Office, 1944, Deputy Under-Secretary of State, 1946–8; Head of British Delegation, OEEC, 1948–52.

HANKEY, Maurice Pascal Alers (later Lord Hankey) (1877–1963), public servant; educated Rugby; joined Royal Marines; Secretary, Committee of Imperial Defence 1912; Chief, War Cabinet Secretariat, 1916; Secretary to the Cabinet, 1923–38; Minister without Portfolio, 1939–40; Chancellor of the Duchy of Lancaster and Paymaster-General, 1940–2.

HANSEN, Alvin H. (1887–1975), economist; University of Minnesota, 1921–37; Chief Economic Analyst, Department of State, 1934–5; Special Economic Adviser, Federal Reserve Board, 1940–5; Littauer Professor of Political Economy, Harvard University, 1937–56.

HARARI, Ralph Andrew (1892–1969), merchant banker; educated Pembroke College, Cambridge; Chief Economic Adviser, GHQ Middle East during the Second World War.

HARCOURT, Alfred (1881–1954), publisher; began with Henry Holt & Co., 1904–19; founder and until 1942 President of Harcourt Brace & Co.

HARDMAN, Frederick McMahon (1895–1914), educated Eton and King's College, Cambridge; took Part II of the Economics Tripos, 1913; killed in action 25–27 October, 1914.

HARDY, Geoffrey Harold (1877–1947), mathematician; educated Winchester and Trinity College, Cambridge; Fellow of Trinity, 1900; Cayley Lecturer in Mathematics, Cambridge, 1914; Savilian Professor of Geometry, Oxford, 1920; Sadlerian Professor of Pure Mathematics, Cambridge, 1931–42.

HARMER, Frederic (later Sir Frederic) (b. 1908), civil servant; educated King's College, Cambridge; Apostle; entered Treasury, 1939; temporary Assistant Secretary, 1943–5; served in Washington, 1944, 1945, for economic and financial negotiations; resigned December 1945; subsequently government director of British Petroleum Co. and Chairman of P&O Steamship Co.

HARRIMAN, Averill (1891–1986), businessman and public servant; Chairman, Union Pacific Railroad, 1932–42; partner, Brown Brothers Harriman & Co., 1931–46; Limited Partner, 1946–86; Special Representative of the President to the United Kingdom, 1941; to the USSR, 1943; London representative on the Combined Shipping Board, 1942; on the Combined Production and Resources Board, 1943; US Ambassador to the USSR, 1943–6; to the United Kingdom, 1946; Secretary of Commerce, 1946–8.

HARRISON, Tom (1911–76), biologist, anthropologist and pioneer of social surveys; educated Harrow and Pembroke College, Cambridge; founder (with Charles Madge) of Mass Observation.

HARROD, Roy Forbes (later Sir Roy) (1900–78), economist; educated Westminster and New College, Oxford; Student of Christ Church, Oxford, 1923–67; University Lecturer in Economics, 1929–37, 1946–52; PM's Statistical Branch, 1940, PM's Office 1940–2; Statistical Adviser to Admiralty, 1943–5; Fellow, Nuffield College, Oxford, 1938–47, 1954–8; Nuffield Reader in Economics, 1952–67.

HARVEY, Sir Ernest Musgrave (1867–1955), banker; educated Marlborough; entered Bank of England, 1885; Comptroller, 1925–8; Director, 1928–9; Deputy Governor, 1929–36.

HARVEY, Josephine Mary, Secretary to the Camargo Society and the Arts Theatre, Cambridge.

HASKINS, Charles Homer (1870–1937), historian; taught at Johns Hopkins, 1890–2; Professor of History, University of Wisconsin, 1892–1902; Harvard, 1902–31.

HASLAM, William Heywood (1889–1981), businessman; educated King's College, Cambridge, 1908–11; Army and Admiralty Intelligence, 1915–18; Commercial Secretary, British Embassy, Rome, 1918–20; member of board of Provincial Insurance Company, 1922–57.

HAVENSTEIN, Rudolph (d. 1923), President of the Reichsbank, 1908–23.

HAWKES, Ralph (1898–1950), director of Boosey & Hawkes Ltd, music publishers.

HAWKINS, Harry Calvin (b. 1894), Department of State, 1931–5, Assistant Chief, Division of Trade Agreements, 1935–6, Chief, 1936–40; Chief, Division of Commercial Treaties and Agreements, 1940–1; Chief, Division of Commercial Policy and Agreements, Director, Office of Economic Affairs, 1944; Economic Counsellor, US Embassy, London, 1944–8; Professor of International Economic Relations, Tufts College, from 1948.

HAWTREY, Ralph George (later Sir Ralph) (1879–1975) economist; educated

Eton and Trinity College, Cambridge; Apostle; entered Treasury, 1904, Director of Financial Enquiries, 1919–45.

von HAYEK, Friedrich August (b. 1899), economist; Director, Austrian Institute for Economic Research, 1927–31; Lecturer in Economics, University of Vienna, 1929–31; Tooke Professor of Economic Science and Statistics, LSE, 1931–50.

HEATH, Sir Thomas Little (1861–1940) civil servant; educated Clifton and Trinity College, Cambridge; entered civil service, 1884; Joint Permanent Secretary, Treasury, 1913–19; Comptroller-General, National Debt Office, 1919–26.

HECKSCHER, Eli Filip (1879–1952), economist; Professor of Economics and Statistics, Stockholm University College of Commerce, 1909–29; Research Professor 1929–45.

HEMMING, Arthur Francis (1893–1964), Secretary, Economic Advisory Council, 1930–9; Principal Assistant Secretary, War Cabinet Offices, 1939–41; Administrative Head, Central Economic Information Service, 1940, and Central Statistical Office, 1941; Principal Assistant Secretary, Ministry of Home Security, 1941–4; Ministry of Fuel and Power, 1944, Under-Secretary, 1946–53.

HENDERSON, Faith Marion Jane (née Bagenal) (1889–1979), educated Bedales and Newnham College, Cambridge; married Hubert Henderson, 1915.

HENDERSON, Hubert Douglas (later Sir Hubert) (1890–1952), economist; educated Rugby and Emmanuel College, Cambridge; Fellow of Clare College, Cambridge, 1919–23; University Lecturer in Economics, 1919–23; Editor, *The Nation and Athenaeum*, 1923–30; Joint Secretary, Economic Advisory Council, 1930–4; Fellow, All Souls College, Oxford 1934–52; Economic Adviser, Treasury, 1939–44; Drummond Professor of Political Economy, University of Oxford, 1945–51; Warden, All Souls College, 1951–2.

HEWINS, William Albert Samuel (1865–1931), political economist and politician; educated Pembroke College, Oxford; first Director of LSE, 1895–1903; Secretary, Tariff Commission, 1903–17; Chairman, 1920–2; Conservative MP, 1912–18.

HICKS, John Richard (later Sir John) (1904–89), economist; educated Clifton and Balliol College, Oxford; Lecturer in Economics, LSE, 1926–35; Cambridge, 1935–8; Professor of Political Economy, Manchester, 1938–46; Official Fellow, Nuffield College, Oxford, 1946–52; Drummond Professor of Political Economy, Oxford, 1952–65; Fellow of All Souls, 1952–65.

HIGGINS, Norman (1898–1974), first General Manager (later Managing Director) of the Arts Theatre, Cambridge, 1935–69.

HILFERDING, Rudolf (1879–1941), Marxist politician economist; German Minister of Finance, 1923, 1928–9.

HILL, Archibald Vivian (1886–1977), physiologist; educated Trinity College, Cambridge; Fellow of Trinity, 1910–16; of King's 1916–25; Nobel Prize for Physiology and Medicine, 1922; Professor of Physiology, University of Manchester, 1920–3; at University College, London, 1923–5; Fullerton Research Professor, Royal Society, 1926–51.

HILL, Margaret Elizabeth (Polly) (b. 1914), educated Newnham College, Cambridge; temporary civil servant, Treasury and Board of Trade, 1940–1951; journalist, West Africa, 1951–3; Senior Research Fellow, University of Ghana, 1954–65; Fellow,

Clare Hall, Cambridge, since 1965; Smuts Reader in Commonwealth Studies, Cambridge, 1973–79.

HILL, Margaret Neville (née Keynes) (1885–1970), sister of JMK; educated Wycombe Abbey; assists Eglantyne Jebb in running Juvenile Employment Exchange founded by Florence Keynes, 1907; married A. V. Hill, 1913; founded Hornsey Housing Trust, 1933; established Hill Homes Ltd for the elderly, 1944.

HINDLEY-SMITH, James Dury (1894–1974), art collector; founder, London Artists' Association, 1925.

HITLER, Adolf (1889–1945), Chancellor of the German Reich, 1933–45; Head of the German State, 1934–45.

HOBHOUSE, Arthur Lawrence (Later Sir Arthur) (1886–1965), educated Eton, University of St Andrew's and Trinity College, Cambridge; Apostle; farmed in Sussex and Somerset after 1919; Liberal MP, 1923–4; contested elections of 1922, 1924 and 1929.

HOBHOUSE, Leonard Trelawny (1864–1929), philosopher and journalist; educated Corpus Christi College, Oxford; Fellow of Corpus, 1894; leader writer, *Manchester Guardian*, 1897–1902; Professor of Sociology, LSE, 1907–29.

HOBSON, Ernest William (1856–1933), mathematician; brother of J. A. Hobson; educated Derby School, Imperial College and Christ's College, Cambridge; Fellow of Christ's, 1878; University Lecturer in Mathematics, 1883–1903; Stokes Lecturer, 1903; Sadlerian Professor of Mathematics, 1910–31.

HOBSON, John Atkinson (1858–1940), economist and publicist; educated Derby School and Lincoln College, Oxford; noted for *The Physiology of Industry* (with A. F. Mummery) (1889); *Imperialism* (1902).

HOBSON, Oscar Rudolf (later Sir Oscar) (1886–1961), journalist; educated Aldenham and King's College, Cambridge; Financial Editor, *Manchester Guardian*, 1920–9; Editor-in-Chief, *Financial News*, 1929–34; City Editor, *News Chronicle*, 1935–59.

HODSON, Henry Vincent (b. 1906), educated Greshams School and Balliol College, Oxford; staff of Economic Advisory Council, 1930–1; Editor, *The Round Table*, 1934–9; Assistant Editor, *Sunday Times*, 1946–50; Editor, 1950–61.

HOLDEN, Sir Edward Hopkinson (1848–1919), clearing banker; entered banking, 1866; joined Birmingham and Midland Bank, 1881; General Manager, 1890; became London and Midland Bank, 1891; Managing Director; 1898; Chairman, 1908–19; Liberal MP, 1906–10.

HOLDERNESS, Sir Thomas William (1849–1924), civil servant; passed into Indian Civil Service, 1870; served in India, 1872–1901; Secretary, Revenue, Statistics and Commerce Department, India Office, 1901–12; Permanent Under-Secretary of State, 1912–19.

HOLMES, Charles John (1868–1936), painter and critic; educated Eton and Brasenose College, Oxford; co-editor *Burlington Magazine*, 1903–9; Director of the National Portrait Gallery, 1909–16; National Gallery, 1916–1928.

HOOVER, Calvin Bryce (1899–1974), economist; taught at Duke University, 1924–74; Professor, 1927–74; Chief, Economic Intelligence and Economic Adviser to US Group, Control Commission for Germany, 1945.

HOOVER, Herbert Clark (1874–1964), mining and metallurgical engineer, 1895–1914; War Relief Administrator, 1914–19; US Food Administrator, 1917–19; Secretary of Commerce, 1921–9; President, 1929–33.

HOPE-JONES, William, educated Eton and King's College, Cambridge; Assistant Master at Eton from 1907.

HOPKINS, Harry L. (1890–1946), US Secretary of Commerce 1938–40; Adviser to President Roosevelt, 1940–5.

HOPKINS, Sir Richard Valentine Nind (1880–1955), civil servant; educated King Edward's School, Birmingham and Emmanuel College, Cambridge; entered Inland Revenue, 1902; Chairman, Board of Inland Revenue, 1922–7; Controller of Finance and Supply Services, Treasury, 1927–32; Second Secretary, 1932–42; Permanent Secretary, 1942–5.

HORNE, Sir Robert Stevenson (later Viscount Horne) (1871–1940), politician and businessman; Unionist MP, 1918–37; Minister of Labour, 1919–20; President, Board of Trade, 1920–1; Chancellor of the Exchequer, 1921–2.

HOUSE, Edward Mandell (1858–1938), businessman; political adviser to Woodrow Wilson; member, American Commission to Negotiate Peace, 1918–19.

HUBBACK, Eva M. (née Spielman) (1886–1949), educator and proponent of family allowances.

HUDSON, Robert Spear (later Viscount Hudson) (1886–1957), politician; educated Eton and Magdalen College, Oxford; Conservative MP, 1924–9, 1931–52; Minister of Agriculture, 1940–5.

HUGHES, Charles Evans (1862–1948), US Secretary of State, 1921–5.

HUGHES, William Morris (1862–1952), Australian trade unionist and politician; Member, New South Wales Parliament, 1894–1901; Member, Federal House of Representatives, 1901–52; Labour leader and Prime Minister, 1915–17; Nationalist leader and Prime Minister, 1917–23.

HULL, Cordell (1871–1955), US Secretary of State, 1933–44.

HUNTER, William Bernard (later Sir William) (1868–1924), Secretary and Treasurer, Madras Presidency Bank; Managing Governor, Imperial Bank of India.

HURST, Hugo (later Lord Hurst) (1863–1943), co-founder of General Electric Company, 1889; Chairman, 1910.

ILSLEY, James Lorimer (1894–1967), Minister of National Revenue, Canada, 1935; Minister of Finance, 1940–5; Minister of Justice, 1946–8; Chief Justice of Nova Scotia, 1950–67; Chairman, Canadian Delegation to Bretton Woods, 1944.

ISHERWOOD, Christopher William Bradshaw (1904–86), novelist; educated Repton and Corpus Christi College, Cambridge; early novels published by Hogarth Press; early plays with W. H. Auden produced at Arts Theatre, Cambridge.

ISLES, Keith Sydney (1902–77), economist; educated Universities of Tasmania, Adelaide and Cambridge; Lecturer in Political Economy, University of Edinburgh, 1931–7; Professor of Economics, University College, Swansea, 1937–9; Adelaide, 1939–45; Belfast, 1945–57; Vice Chancellor, University of Tasmania, 1957–67.

JACKSON, Henry (1839–1921), classicist; educated Trinity College, Cambridge; Apostle; Fellow of Trinity, 1864–1921; Reguis Professor of Greek, 1906–21.

JAMES, Montagu Rhodes (1862–1936), biblical scholar and antiquary; educated Eton and King's College, Cambridge; Fellow of King's, 1887; Director, Fitzwilliam Museum, 1893–1908; Provost of King's 1905–18; Provost of Eton, 1918–36.

JAY, Douglas Patrick Thomas (later Lord Jay) (b. 1907), journalist and politician; educated Winchester and New College, Oxford; Fellow, All Souls College, 1930–7, 1968–; financial journalist on *The Times*, 1929–33, and *The Economist*, 1933–37; City Editor, *Daily Herald*, 1937–41; Assistant Secretary, Ministry of Supply, 1941–3; Principal Assistant Secretary, Board of Trade, 1943–5; Personal Assistant to the Prime Minister, 1945–6; Labour MP, 1946–83; Economic Secretary, Treasury, 1947–50, Financial Secretary, 1950–1; President of Board of Trade, 1964–7.

JEBB, Hubert Miles Gladwyn (later Lord Gladwyn) (b. 1900), diplomat; educated Eton and Magdalen College, Oxford; Private Secretary to Permanent Secretary, Foreign Office, 1937–40; Ministry of Economic Warfare, 1940; Acting Counsellor, Foreign Office, 1941; Head of Reconstruction Department, 1942; Counsellor, 1943; Assistant Under-Secretary of State, 1949; Permanent UK Representative to UN, 1950–4; HM Ambassador to France, 1954–60.

JEBB, Sir Richard Claverhouse (1841–1905), classicist; educated Charterhouse and Trinity College, Cambridge; Apostle; Fellow of Trinity, 1863; Regius Professor of Greek, Cambridge, 1889–1905; Conservative MP for the University, 1891–1905.

JEFFREYS, Harold (1891–1989), theorist of probability and geophysicist; educated St John's College, Cambridge; Fellow of St John's, 1914–89; Plumian Professor of Astronomy and Experimental Philosophy, 1946–58.

JENKS, Jeremiah Whipple (d. 1929), political economist; Professor, University of Indiana, 1889–91; Cornell University, 1891–1929.

JEVONS, William Stanley (1835–82), economist; educated University College, London; Tutor, Owens College, Manchester, 1863; Professor of Logic, Political Economy and Philosophy, 1866–9; Professor of Political Economy, University College, London, 1876–81.

JOHNSON, William Ernest (1858–1931), logician; educated Perse School and King's College, Cambridge; University Lecturer in Moral Science 1896–1901; Sidgwick University Lecturer in Moral Science and Fellow of King's, 1902–31.

JONES, Jesse Holman (1874–1956), Chairman, Executive Committee, Export-Import Bank, 1936–43; Administrator, Federal Loan Agency, 1939–45; US Secretary of Commerce, 1940–5.

JONES, Thomas (1870–1955), civil servant and administrator; Deputy Secretary to the Cabinet, 1916–30; Secretary, Pilgrim Trust, 1930–45

JOOSS, Kurt, choreographer who became famous after the success of his ballet *The Green Table*, a savage comment on the injustices of the Treaty of Versailles, first performed in London in 1933. Subsequently associated with Dartington Hall and the Arts Theatre, Cambridge.

KAHN, Richard Ferdinand (later Lord Kahn) (1905–89), economist; educated St Paul's and King's College, Cambridge; Fellow, King's College, Cambridge, 1930–89; temporary civil servant in various government departments, 1939–46; Professor of Economics, University of Cambridge, 1951–72.

KALDOR, Nicholas (later Lord Kaldor) (1908–86), economist; educated LSE; Lecturer and Reader in Economics, LSE, 1932–47; National Institute of Economic and

Social Research, 1943–5; Chief of Economic Planning Staff, US Strategic Bombing Survey, 1945; Director, Research and Planning Division, UN Economic Commission for Europe, Geneva, 1947–9; Fellow, King's College, Cambridge, 1949–86; Reader in Economics, 1952–65, Professor 1965–75; Special Adviser to Chancellor of the Exchequer, 1964–8 and 1974–6.

KALECKI, Michal (1899–1970), economist; Institute for Research on Business Cycles and Prices, Warsaw, 1929–36; Oxford University Institute of Economics and Statistics, 1940–5; United Nations Secretariat, 1946–54; Polish Academy of Sciences, 1955–61; Central School of Planning and Statistics, Poland, 1961–70.

KEELING, Frederic Hillersdon ('Ben') (1886–1916), educated Winchester and Trinity College, Cambridge; refounded Fabian Society in Cambridge; killed on the Somme.

KENT, Fred I. (1869–1954), banker; Deputy Governor, Federal Reserve Bank of New York, 1917–18; Director, Division of Foreign Exchange, Federal Reserve Board, 1918; US representative on Organising Committee for the Reparation Commission, Paris, 1919–20.

KERR, Philip Henry (later Marquess of Lothian) (1882–1940), journalist and statesman; educated Oratory School and New College, Oxford; member of Milner's 'kindergarten'; founder and first editor of *The Round Table*, 1910–16; Private Secretary to Lloyd George, 1916–21; Chancellor of the Duchy of Lancaster, 1931; HM Ambassador to the United States, 1939–40.

KEYNES, Florence Ada (née Brown) (1861–1958), married John Neville Keynes 1882; active in local politics and community affairs in Cambridge; mother of J. M. Keynes.

KEYNES, Geoffrey Langdon (1887–1982), surgeon and bibliophile; educated Rugby, Pembroke College, Cambridge and St Bartholomew's Hospital; RAMC, 1914–18; married Margaret Darwin, 1917; Senior Consultant Surgeon in RAF, 1939–45.

KEYNES, John Neville (1852–1949), philosopher and economist; educated Amersham Hall, University College, London and Pembroke College, Cambridge; Fellow of Pembroke, 1876–82; University Lecturer in Moral Science, Cambridge, 1884–1911; University Registrary, Cambridge, 1910–25.

KEYNES, Lydia (Lady Keynes) (née Lopokova) (1892–1981), ballerina; married J. M. Keynes 1925.

KEYNES, Margaret Elizabeth (née Darwin) (1890–1974), sister of Gwen Raverat and wife of Geoffrey Keynes.

KEYNES, Margaret Neville see HILL, Margaret Neville.

KIDDY, Arthur William (1868–1950), financial journalist; City Editor, *Daily News*, 1891–9; *Standard*, 1899–1915; *Morning Post*, 1915–37; Associate City Editor, *Daily Telegraph and Morning Post*, 1937–46; Editor, *Bankers' Magazine*, 1895–1945.

KINDERSLEY, Sir Robert Molesworth (later Lord Kindersley) (1871–1954), merchant banker; partner, Lazard Brothers, 1906; Chairman, 1919; Director, Bank of England, 1914–46; Chairman, War Savings Committee, 1916; National Savings Committee, 1920–46.

KING, William Lyon Mackenzie (1874–1950), Prime Minister of Canada, 1921–26, 1926–30, 1935–48; Secretary of State for External Affairs, 1921–30, 1935–46.

KISCH, Sir Cecil Herman (1884–1961), civil servant; educated Trinity College, Oxford; entered Post Office, 1907; India Office, 1908; Secretary, Financial Department, 1921–33; Assistant Secretary of State, 1933–43; Deputy Under-Secretary of State, 1943–6.

KITCHENER, Horatio Herbert (later first Earl Kitchener of Khartoum) (1850–1916), soldier; educated Royal Military Academy Woolwich; first commissioned, 1871; involved in military affairs in Egypt and the Sudan, 1882–98; Governor General of the Sudan, 1898; Commander-in-Chief in South Africa, 1900–2; in India, 1902–9; Secretary of State for War, 1914–16.

KLOTZ, Louis-Lucien (1868–1930), French politician; Minister of Finance, 1910, 1911, 1917–20.

KNIGHT, Frank Hyneman (1885–1962), economist; Professor of Economics, University of Chicago, 1927–58.

KNOX, Alfred Dillwyn (1883–1943), classicist and cryptographer; educated Eton and King's College, Cambridge; Fellow of King's, 1909; joined Naval Intelligence (Room 40), 1915; Foreign Office, 1920–43.

KUNG, H. H. (1881–1957), businessman and politician; Governor, Bank of China and Minister of Finance from 1933.

KUZNETS, Simon (1901–85), economist; National Bureau of Economic Research, 1927–61; Professor of Economics, University of Pennsylvania, 1930–54; Johns Hopkins University, 1954–60; Harvard University, 1960–71.

LAMB, Henry Taylor (1883–1960), painter; pursued (unsuccessfully) by Lytton Strachey; a good friend of many in Bloomsbury.

LAMONT, Thomas William (1870–1948), banker; partner, J. P. Morgan & Co., 1911–48; Adviser, American Commission to Negotiate Peace, 1919.

LANGE, Oscar Ryszard (1904–65), economist; taught at University of Chicago, 1938–45 and Warsaw, 1948–65.

LANGER, William (1896–1977); historian; taught at Harvard University, 1927–64; Professor, 1936–64.

LASKI, Harold (1893–1950), political theorist; educated Manchester Grammar School and New College, Oxford; Professor of Political Science, LSE, 1926–50; Labour Party National Executive Committee, 1936–49, Chairman, 1945–6.

LASTEYRIE, Charles Comte de (1879–1935), French civil servant and politician; represented French Treasury at Trèves, Spa and Paris Conferences, 1919; Minister of Finance, 1923–4.

LAVINGTON, Frederick (1881–1927), educated Emmanuel College, Cambridge; Board of Trade, 1911–18; Lecturer in Economics, Cambridge, 1918–21; Girdlers' Lecturer, 1921–7.

LAW, Andrew Bonar (1858–1923), statesman; Unionist MP, 1900–6, 1906–10, 1911–23; Leader of the Opposition, 1911; Secretary of State for the Colonies, 1915–16; Chancellor of the Exchequer, 1916–18; Lord Privy Seal, 1918–21; Prime Minister, 1922–3.

LAW, Richard Kidston (later Lord Coleraine) (1901–1980), statesman; educated Shrewsbury and St John's College, Oxford; journalist; Conservative MP, 1931–54;

Financial Secretary, War Office, 1940–1; Parliamentary Under-Secretary, Foreign Office, 1941–3; Minister of State, 1943–5; Minister of Education, 1945.

LAWRENCE, David Herbert (1885–1930), novelist; introduced to Ottoline Morrell by David Garnett and thus met many from Bloomsbury.

LAYTON, Sir Walter Thomas (later Lord Layton) (1884–1966), economist; educated University College, London and Trinity College, Cambridge; Fellow of Gonville and Caius College, 1909; Lecturer in Economics, Cambridge, 1908–19 (University Lecturer from 1912); Ministry of Munitions, 1916–18; Editor, *The Economist*, 1922–8; Director-General of Programmes, Ministry of Supply, 1940–2; Chief Adviser, Programmes and Planning, Ministry of Production, 1942–3; Head of Joint War Production Staff, 1942–3.

LEAF, Walter (1852–1927), classical scholar and banker; educated Harrow and Trinity College, Cambridge; Apostle; Fellow of Trinity, 1875; Director, London and Westminster Bank, 1891; Chairman, 1919.

LEE, Frank Godbould (later Sir Frank) (1903–71), public servant; educated Downing College, Cambridge; Colonial Office, 1926–40; transferred to Treasury, 1940; Treasury Delegation, Washington, 1944–6; Ministry of Supply, 1946; Deputy Secretary, 1947; Permanent Secretary, Board of Trade, 1951–9; Ministry of Food, 1959–61; Joint Permanent Secretary, Treasury, 1960–2; Master, Corpus Christi College, Cambridge, 1962–71.

LEE, Janet ('Jennie') (later Baroness Lee) (1904–88), politician; Labour MP, 1929–31, 1945–70; married Aneurin Bevan, 1934; Minister of State for the Arts, 1967–70.

LEE, Lennox Bertram (1864–1949), calico printer; educated Eton; entered the family calico printing firm, 1889; initiator of Calico Printers Association, 1899; Chairman, 1908–47; President, Federation of British Industries, 1929–30.

LEFFINGWELL, Russell Cornell (1870–1960), lawyer, banker and Treasury official; Assistant Secretary, US Treasury, 1917–20; partner, J. P. Morgan & Co., 1923–40; Director, J. P. Morgan & Co. Inc., 1940–59.

LEITH-ROSS, Frederick William (later Sir Frederick) (1887–1968), civil servant and banker; educated Merchant Taylors' and Balliol College, Oxford; entered Treasury, 1909; Private Secretary to Asquith, 1911–13; Deputy Controller of Finance, 1925–32; Chief Economic Adviser to HMG, 1932–46; Governor, National Bank of Egypt, 1946–51.

LePAN, Douglas (b. 1914), author, academic and diplomat; educated University of Toronto and Oxford; taught at University of Toronto, 1937–8; at Harvard, 1938–41; joined Department of External Affairs, 1945; Assistant Under-Secretary of State, 1958–9; Professor of English, Queen's University, 1959–64; Principal, University College, University of Toronto, 1964–70; University Professor, 1970–9.

LERNER, Abba Ptacha (1903–82), economist; Assistant Lecturer, LSE, 1935–7; later positions at various American universities; Professor of Economics, University of California, Berkeley, 1965–71.

LEVER, Sir Samuel Hardman (1869–1947), chartered accountant; Financial Secretary to the Treasury, 1916; Joint Financial Secretary, 1917–19; Treasury representative in the United States, 1917–19.

LEWIS, Sir Alfred Edward (1868–1940), Director, National Provincial Bank; member, Economic Advisory Council.

LEWIS, Frederick William (later Lord Essendon) (1870–1944), industrialist and shipowner; joined Furness & Co., 1883; Director, Furness Withy & Co., 1899; Deputy Chairman, 1914.

LIESCHING, Sir Percivale (1895–1974), civil servant; educated Brasenose College, Oxford; entered Colonial Office, 1920; Dominions Office, 1925, Assistant Under-Secretary, 1939–42; Second Secretary, Board of Trade, 1942–6; Permanent Secretary, Ministry of Food, 1946–8; Commonwealth Relations Office, 1949–55.

LIPPMANN, Walter (1889–1974), US journalist and author; specialist writer for *Herald Tribune*, 1931–62; for *Washington Post* and other newspapers, 1963–74.

LLOYD GEORGE, David (1863–1945), statesman; Liberal MP, 1890–1945; President of Board of Trade, 1905–8; Chancellor of the Exchequer, 1908–15; Minister of Munitions, 1915–16; Secretary of State for War, 1916; Prime Minister, 1916–22.

LOFTUS, Pierre Creagh (1877–1956), associated with Adnams & Co., Brewers, 1912; Conservative MP, 1934–45.

LONG, Walter Hume (later Viscount Long) (1858–1924), statesman; educated Harrow and Christ Church, Oxford; Conservative MP, 1880–1921; President, Local Government Board, 1900–5, 1915–16; Chief Secretary for Ireland, 1905; Secretary of State for the Colonies, 1916–18; First Lord of the Admiralty, 1919–21.

LOPOKOVA, Lydia see KEYNES, Lydia.

LOUCHEUR, Louis Albert Joseph (1872–1931), engineer and French politician; Minister for Armaments, 1917–18; Minister for Industrial Reconstruction, 1918–20; Minister for the Liberated Regions, 1921; Minister of Labour, 1928–30.

LUBBOCK, Cecil (1872–1956), banker; educated Eton and Trinity College, Oxford; Director, Bank of England, 1909–23, 1925–7, 1929–42; Deputy Governor, 1923–5, 1927–9.

LUBBOCK, Samuel Gurney (d. 1958), schoolmaster; educated Eton and King's College, Cambridge; Assistant Master, Eton, 1897–1934.

LUCE, Gordon Hannington (1889–1979), educated Emmanuel College, Cambridge; Apostle; Professor of English, University of Rangoon.

LUXFORD, Ansel Frank (1911–71), lawyer; Counsel's Office, US Treasury, 1935–9; specialist on foreign funds and economic warfare, 1940–2; Assistant Counsel for Foreign Funds Control, 1942–3; Assistant General Counsel, 1944; Chief Legal Adviser to the US Delegation at Bretton Woods.

LYTTLETON, Oliver (later Lord Chandos) (1893–1972), Conservative MP, 1940–54; President of Board of Trade, 1940–1; Minister of State in Middle East and Member of War Cabinet, 1941–2; Minister of Production and Member of War Cabinet, 1942–5; President of Board of Trade and Minister of Production, 1945; Secretary of State for the Colonies, 1951–4.

McADOO, William Gibbs (1863–1941), businessman; Secretary, US Treasury, 1913–18.

MACAULAY, William Herrick (d. 1936), mathematician; educated Winchester and King's College, Cambridge; Apostle; Fellow of King's, 1879–1936; Second Bursar, 1887–1902; Vice-Provost, 1918–33.

MacCARTHY (Charles Otto), Desmond (1877–1952), literary journalist; educated

Eton and Trinity College, Cambridge; Apostle; married Mary Ware-Cornish, 1906; Secretary for First Impressionist Exhibition; Literary Editor, *New Statesman*, 1920–7; senior literary critic, *Sunday Times* from 1928.

MacCARTHY, Mary Josefa (Molly) (née Ware-Cornish) (1882–1953), writer; daughter of an Eton master, later Vice-Provost; married Desmond MacCarthy, 1906.

MacCOLL, Dugald Sutherland (1859–1948), painter and critic; educated University College, London and Lincoln College, Oxford; Keeper, Tate Gallery, 1906–11; Wallace Collection, 1911–24.

McCORMICK, Vance Criswell (1872–1946), industrialist; Chairman, War Trade Board, 1917–19; Economic Adviser to the President, American Commission to Negotiate Peace, Paris, 1919.

McCURRACH, David F., economist; wartime government service in Washington; subsequently University of St Andrews.

MacDONALD, James Ramsay (1866–1937), statesman; Labour MP, 1906–18, 1922–35; Prime Minister, 1924, 1929–35; Lord President of the Council, 1935.

MACDOUGALL, George Donald Alistair (later Sir Donald) (b. 1912), economist; educated Shrewsbury and Balliol College, Oxford; Lecturer, University of Leeds, 1936–9; First Lord of Admiralty's Statistical Branch, 1939–40; PM's Statistical Branch, 1940–5, 1951–3; Economic Director, OEEC, Paris, 1948–9; Official Fellow, Nuffield College, Oxford, 1952–64; Head, Government Economic Service and Chief Economic Adviser to the Treasury, 1969–73.

McFADYEAN, Andrew (1887–1974), public servant; educated Oxford University; entered Treasury, 1910; Secretary, Reparation Commission, 1922–4; Secretary, Dawes Commission, 1924; Commissioner of Controlled Revenues, 1924–30.

MACGREGOR, David Hutchison (1877–1953), economist; educated University of Edinburgh and Trinity College, Cambridge; Fellow of Trinity, 1904; Drummond Professor of Political Economy, Oxford, 1926–45; Assistant Editor, *Economic Journal*, 1926–34.

McKENNA, Pamela (née Jekyll), wife of Reginald McKenna.

McKENNA, Reginald (1863–1943), statesman and banker; educated Trinity Hall, Cambridge; Liberal MP, 1895–1918; First Lord of the Admiralty, 1908–11; Home Secretary, 1911–15; Chancellor of the Exchequer, 1915–16; Chairman, Midland Bank, 1919–43.

McKINNON, Hector (1890–1973), public servant; Secretary of Advisory Board on Tariff and Taxation, Department of Finance, Canada, 1926–30, Commissioner of Tariff, 1930–40; Chairman of Tariff Board, 1940–59; Chairman, Wartime Prices and Trade Board, 1940–1; President, Commodity Prices Stabilization Corporation, 1941–6.

MACKINTOSH, William Archibald (1895–1970), economist; National Employment Commission, Canada, 1936–8; Research Adviser, Royal Commission on Dominion-Provincial Relations, 1938–9; served in Departments of Finance and Reconstruction and Supply, Ottawa, 1939–46; Professor of Economics, Queen's University, Canada, 1927–61; Principal, 1951–61.

McLINTOCK, Sir William (1873–1947), chartered accountant; senior partner Thomson McLintock & Co.

MACMILLAN, Daniel (1886–1965), publisher; educated Eton and Balliol College, Oxford; Director, Macmillan & Co., 1911; Chairman and Managing Director, 1936–63; Chairman, Macmillan Holdings, 1964–5.

MACMILLAN, Harold (later Lord Macmillan) (1894–1986), publisher and politician; educated Eton and Balliol College, Oxford; Conservative MP, 1924–9, 1931–64; Minister of State in North Africa, 1942–5; Minister for Air, 1945; Minister of Housing and Local Government, 1951–4; of Defence, 1954–5; Foreign Secretary, 1955; Chancellor of the Exchequer, 1955–7; Prime Minister, 1957–63.

MACMILLAN, Hugo Pattison (Lord Macmillan) (1873–1952), judge; educated Glasgow and Edinburgh Universities; Lord of Appeal in Ordinary, 1931–9, 1941–7; Minister of Information, 1939–41; Chairman, Committee on Finance and Industry, 1929–31; Pilgrim Trust, 1935–52.

McNAUGHTON, General Andrew George Latta (1887–1966), soldier and public servant; Chief, Canadian General Staff, 1919–35; commanded Canadian troops in Britain, 1940–3; Minister of Defence, 1944–5.

McTAGGART, John Ellis (1866–1925), philosopher; educated Trinity College, Cambridge; Apostle; Fellow of Trinity, 1891–1925.

MADGE, Charles Henry (b. 1912), social scientist; educated Winchester and Magdalene College, Cambridge; founded (with Tom Harrison) Mass Observation, 1937; Professor of Sociology, University of Birmingham, 1950–70.

MAINE, Sir Henry James Sumner (1822–88), jurist; educated Christ's Hospital and Pembroke College, Cambridge; Apostle; Fellow of Trinity Hall, 1845; Regius Professor of Civil Law, 1847–54; Corpus Professor of Jurisprudence, Oxford, 1869–77; Master of Trinity Hall, 1877–88.

MALKIN, Sir William (1883–1945), lawyer; educated Charterhouse and Trinity College, Cambridge; entered Foreign Office, 1911; Assistant Legal Adviser, 1914–25; Second Legal Adviser, 1925–9; Legal Adviser, 1929–45.

MALLET, Sir Charles (1862–1947), public servant; educated Harrow and Balliol College, Oxford; contested seats for the Liberals, 1900, 1917, 1922, 1929; Liberal MP, 1906–10; Financial Secretary, War Office, 1910–11; Secretary for Indian Students, India Office, 1912–16.

MALLORY, George Leigh (1887–1924), mountaineer; educated Winchester and Magdalene College, Cambridge; master at Charterhouse, 1911–16, 1919–23; Assistant Secretary, Board of Extra Mural Studies, Cambridge, 1923; died on Mount Everest, 1924.

MANSFIELD, Katherine (pseudonym of Kathleen Murry) (1888–1923), writer; born in New Zealand but partly educated in England; returned to England, 1908; introduced to Bloomsbury, 1914; lived at 3 Gower Street after JMK left for 46 Gordon Square; married Middleton Murry, with whom she had had a long-standing affair, 1918.

MANTOUX, Paul (1877–1956), economic historian; interpreter, Supreme War Council and Paris Peace Conference, 1919.

MARCHANT, Sir Stanley (1883–1949), organist; Professor, Royal Academy of Music, 1913–36; Principal, 1936–49; Professor of Music, University of London, 1937–48.

MARKS, Geoffrey (1864–1938), Actuary and Manager, National Mutual Life Assurance Society, 1893–1933; Director, 1926–35

MARSHALL, Alfred (1842–1924), economist; educated Merchant Taylors' School and St John's College, Cambridge; Fellow of St John's, 1865–77, 1885–1908; Principal, University College, Bristol, 1877–81; Professor of Political Economy, University College, Bristol, 1877–83; Fellow, Balliol College, Oxford, 1883–4; Professor of Political Economy, Cambridge, 1884–1908.

MARSHALL, Mary Paley (1850–1944), economist; educated Newnham Hall, Cambridge; taught economics at Newnham, 1875–7, 1885 onwards; married Alfred Marshall, 1877; founded Marshall Library of Economics, Cambridge, 1925; Honorary Assistant Librarian, 1925–44.

MARSHALL, Thomas Humphrey (1893–1981), sociologist; educated Rugby and Trinity College, Cambridge; Fellow of Trinity, 1919–25; Lecturer in Sociology, LSE, 1925; Reader, 1930; Professor, 1954–6; Head of German Section, Research Department, Foreign Office, 1939–44.

MARTEN, Sir Clarence Henry Kennett (1872–1948), teacher; educated Eton and Balliol College, Oxford; Eton history master, 1895–1929; Vice-Provost, 1929; Provost, 1945–8.

MARTIN, Basil Kingsley (1897–1969), editor; educated Mill Hill School and Magdalene College, Cambridge; Bye-Fellow of Magdalene, 1920–4; Assistant Lecturer in Politics, LSE, 1924–7; Editor, the *New Statesman and Nation*, 1931–60.

MARTIN, Percival William (1883–1972), international civil servant; educated Haberdashers' Aske's and Columbia University; attached to International Labour Organisation between the wars; Head of Division, Ministry of Food, 1943–5; Social Sciences Division, UNESCO, 1945–52.

MASSINE, Leonide Fedorovich (1896–1979), dancer; joined Diaghilev's Ballets Russes in 1914; choreographer of *The Good Humoured Ladies* for Lopokova; broke with Diagilev, 1921–5; returned 1925–8.

MASSINGHAM, Henry William, (1860–1924), journalist; joined *Eastern Daily Press*, 1877; went to London, 1883; editor of the *Nation*, 1907–23.

MASTERMAN, Charles Frederick Gurney (1874–1927), politician and author; educated Christ's College, Cambridge; Liberal MP, 1906–18, 1923–4; Chancellor, Duchy of Lancaster, 1914–15.

MAURICE, Frederick Dennison (1805–72), divine; educated Trinity College and Trinity Hall, Cambridge; Apostle; Professor of English Literature and History, King's College, London, 1840–53; Professor of Moral Philosophy, Cambridge, 1866–72.

MAY, Sir George Ernest (later Lord May) (1871–1946), entered Prudential Insurance Company, 1887; Secretary, 1915–31; Chairman, Committee on National Expenditure, 1931.

MAYOR, Fiona Macdonald (1872–1932), novelist; educated Newnham College, Cambridge; first book *Mrs Hammond's Children* (1902); first novel, *The Third Miss Symons* (1913).

MAYOR, John Eyton Bickseth (1825–1910), classical scholar and divine; educated Christ's Hospital, Shrewsbury and St John's College, Cambridge; Fellow of St John's,

1849–1910; master at Marlborough, 1849–53; University Librarian, Cambridge, 1854–7; Professor of Latin, 1872–1910.

MAYOR, Robert John Grote ('Robin') (1869–1947), civil servant; educated Eton and King's College, Cambridge; Apostle; entered Education Department, 1896; Assistant Secretary, Board of Education, 1907–19; Principal Assistant Secretary, 1919–26.

MEADE, James Edward (b. 1907), economist; educated Malvern College and Oriel College, Oxford; Fellow, Hertford College, Oxford, 1931–7; Economic Section, League of Nations, 1937–40; Economic Section of the War Cabinet, 1940–7; Director, 1946–7; Professor of Commerce with Special Reference to International Trade, LSE, 1947–57; Professor of Political Economy, Cambridge, 1957–67; Senior Research Fellow, Christ's College, Cambridge, 1967–74.

MELCHETT, Lord (Alfred Moritz MOND) (1868–1930), industrialist; educated Cheltenham, Cambridge and Edinburgh; managing director of his father's chemical business; incorporated Imperial Chemical Industries, 1926; Liberal MP, 1906–28; Minister of Health, 1921–2.

MELCHIOR, Carl (1871–1933), lawyer and banker; Counsel, M. M. Warburg & Co., Hamburg, 1902; partner, 1917; Member, German Delegation to Paris Peace Conference, 1919; German Representative on the Young Committee, 1929.

MENGER, Carl (1840–1921), economist; Extraordinary Professor, University of Vienna, 1873; Professor of Political Economy, 1879–1903.

MEREDITH, Hugh Owen (1878–1964), economist; educated Shrewsbury and King's College, Cambridge; Fellow of King's, 1903–8; Lecturer in History, University of Manchester, 1905–8; Girdlers' Lecturer in Economics, Cambridge, 1908–11; Professor of Economics, Queen's University, Belfast, 1911–53.

MEYER, Eugene (1875–1959), newspaper executive; Federal Farm Loan Commissioner, 1927–9; Governor, Federal Reserve Board, 1930–3; Chairman, Reconstruction Finance Corporation, 1932; Publisher, *Washington Post*, 1933–46; Editor, 1940–6; Chairman, 1947–59.

MILLS, Ogden L. (1884–1937), lawyer; US Congressman, 1921–7; Under-Secretary of the Treasury, 1927; Secretary of the Treasury, 1932–3.

MILNER, Alfred (later Viscount Milner) (1854–1925), statesman; educated Tübingen, King's College, London and Balliol College, Oxford; Fellow, New College, Oxford, 1876; private secretary to G. J. Goschen, 1884, 1887–9; Chairman, Board of Inland Revenue, 1892–7; High Commissioner for South Africa, 1897–1905; member of War Cabinet, 1916–18; Secretary of State for the Colonies, 1918–21.

MISES, Ludwig von (1881–1973), economist; educated University of Vienna; Vienna Chamber of Commerce, 1909–34; Professor, Graduate Institute of International Studies, Geneva, 1934–40; New York University, 1948–69.

MITCHELL, Wesley Clair (1874–1948), economist; Professor of Economics, Columbia University, 1913–19, 1922–44; Director of Research, National Bureau of Economic Research, 1920–45.

MOLEY, Raymond (1886–1975), lawyer and journalist; Professor of Law, Columbia University, 1928–54; US Assistant Secretary of State, 1933.

MONICK, Emmanuel Georges Michel (b. 1893), Inspector General of Finance,

France, 1920–45; Financial Attaché in Washington, 1930–4; in London, 1934–40; Governor of the Bank of France, 1945–9.

MONNET, Jean Omer Marie Gabriel (1888–1979), public servant; Deputy Secretary General, League of Nations, 1919–23; member, British Supply Council, 1940; Director, Commissariat du Plan, France, 1946–50; President, Action Committee for the United States of Europe, 1955–75.

MONNINGTON, Walter Thomas (later Sir Thomas) (1902–76), painter; President, Royal Academy, 1966–76.

MONTAGU, Beatrice Venetia (née Stanley) (1887–1948), correspondent of Asquith, 1912–15; married Edwin Montagu, 1915.

MONTAGU, Edwin Samuel (1879–1923), statesman; educated Trinity College, Cambridge; Liberal MP, 1906–22; Parliamentary Under-Secretary of State for India, 1910–14; Financial Secretary to the Treasury, 1914–16; Chancellor of the Duchy of Lancaster, 1915; Minister of Munitions, 1916; Secretary of State for India, 1917–22.

MOORE, George Edward (1873–1958), philosopher; educated Dulwich College and Trinity College, Cambridge; Apostle; Prize Fellow, Trinity College, Cambridge, 1898–1904; University Lecturer in Moral Science, Cambridge, 1911–25; Professor of Philosophy, Cambridge, 1925–39.

MOREL, Edmund Dene (1873–1924), publicist and social reformer; co-founded the Congo Reform Association, 1904; Honorary Secretary, 1904–14; Honorary Secretary, Union of Democratic Control, 1914–24; Labour MP, 1922–4.

MORGAN, John Pierpoint (1837–1913), financier; founder of J. P. Morgan & Co.

MORGENTHAU, Henry Jr. (1891–1967), Under-Secretary and Acting Secretary, US Treasury, 1933–4; Secretary, 1935–45.

MORRELL, Ottoline Violet Anne (1873–1938), hostess; married Phillip Morrell, 1902; lived at 44 Bedford Square, 1906–15; Garsington Manor 1915–27; 10 Gower Street, 1927–38.

MORRELL, Philip Edward (1870–1943), lawyer; educated Eton and Balliol College, Oxford; married Lady Ottoline Cavendish-Bentinck, 1902; Liberal MP, 1906–18.

MORRISON, Herbert Stanley (later Lord Morrison) (1888–1965), politician; Labour MP, 1923–4, 1929–31, 1935–9; Minister of Transport, 1929–31; Minister of Supply, 1940; Home Secretary and Minister of Home Security, 1940–5; Member of War Cabinet, 1942–5; Lord President of the Council and Deputy Prime Minister, 1945–51; Secretary of State for Foreign Affairs, 1951.

MOZLEY, John Rickards (1840–1931), a schools inspector; Professor of Pure Mathematics at Owens College, Manchester, 1865–85.

MUIR, John Ramsey Bryce (1872–1941), historian and politician; educated University College, Liverpool and Balliol College, Oxford; Lecturer in History, Liverpool, 1899; Professor of Modern History, Liverpool, 1906–13; Manchester, 1914–21; Director, Liberal Summer School from 1921; Liberal MP, 1923–4.

MURRY, John Middleton (1889–1957), journalist and critic; educated Christ's Hospital and Brasenose College, Oxford; married Katherine Mansfield, 1918; founder editor of *Rhythm* 1911–13; editor, the *Athenaeum*, 1919–21; founder editor of the *Adelphi*, 1923–30.

NASH, Paul (1889–1946), artist; educated St Paul's School and Slade School; official war artist in both World Wars.

NATHAN, Harry Louis (later Lord Nathan) (1889–1963), lawyer and public servant; Liberal MP, 1929–34; Labour MP, 1934–5, 1937–40; Minister of Civil Aviation, 1946–8.

NEWBOLD, John Turner Walton (1888–1943), politician; educated Manchester University; Fabian, 1908; member, Independent Labour Party, 1910–21; member, Communist Party, 1921–4; Communist MP, 1922–3; member, Labour Party, 1924–31.

NICHOLSON, Joseph Shield (1850–1927), economist; educated King's College, London and Trinity College, Cambridge; Professor of Political Economy, Edinburgh, 1880–1925.

NICOD, Jean (1892–1924), French philosopher; educated at the Sorbonne and Cambridge, where he spent the War and came under Russell's influence; taught at lycées in Toulon, Cahors and Laon, 1918–21; League of Nations, Bureau of Labour, 1921–4; his *Geometry in the Sensible World* and *The Logical Problems of Induction* were published posthumously with the first English translations of 1930 financed by Russell and an anonymous donor.

NICOLSON, Harold George (1886–1968), diplomat and author; educated Wellington and Balliol College, Oxford; diplomatic service, 1909–29; National Labour MP, 1935–45.

NIEMEYER, Otto Ernst (later Sir Otto) (1883–1972), public servant; educated Balliol College, Oxford; entered Treasury 1906; Controller of Finance and Supply Services, Treasury, 1922–7; Bank of England, 1927, Director, 1938–52.

NIJINSKY, Vaslav (1889–1950), dancer; danced with Diaghilev 1909, 1911–13, 1916–17; mental breakdown 1917.

NITTI, Francesco (1868–1923), Premier of Italy, 1919–20.

NIXON, Frank Horsfall (later Sir Frank) (1890–1956), public servant; educated Pembroke College, Cambridge; entered Treasury, 1912; Director, Economic and Financial Section, League of Nations, 1920–8; Comptroller General, Export Credits Guarantee Department, 1926–44; Joint Managing Director, UK Commercial Corporation, 1940–6.

NOEL-BAKER, Philip John (later Lord Noel-Baker) (1889–1982), educated King's College, Cambridge; Labour MP, 1929–31, 1936–70; PPS to Secretary of State for Foreign Affairs, 1929–31; Joint Parliamentary Secretary, Ministry of War Transport, 1942–5; Minister of State, Foreign Office, 1945–6; Secretary of State for Air, 1946–7, for Commonwealth Relations, 1947–50; Minister of Fuel and Power, 1950–51; Nobel Peace Prize, 1959.

NORMAN, Montagu Collet (Lord Norman) (1871–1950), educated Eton and King's College, Cambridge; Deputy Governor, Bank of England, 1918–20; Governor, 1920–44.

NORTHCLIFFE, Viscount (Alfred Charles HARMSWORTH) (1865–1922), journalist and newspaper proprietor; founded *Daily Mail*, 1896; *Daily Mirror*, 1903; chief proprietor of *The Times*, 1908.

NORTON, Henry Tertius James (1886–1937), mathematician; educated Eton and Trinity College, Cambridge; Apostle; Fellow, Trinity College, from 1910.

O'CASEY, Sean (1880–1964), dramatist and author; *Juno and the Paycock* (1924).

OHLIN, Bertil Gothard (1899–1979), economist; Professor of Economics, University of Copenhagen, 1924–30; Stockholm School of Business Adminstration, 1930–65; Liberal Member of Swedish Parliament, 1938–70.

OLIVIER, Brynhild (1887–1935), married Arthur Popham, Keeper of the Print Room, British Museum; mother of Anne Olivier (b. 1916), wife of Quentin Bell.

OLIVIER, Daphne (1889–1950), sister of Brynhild and Noel; educated Bedales and Newnham College, Cambridge.

OLIVIER, Noel (1892–1969), doctor; educated Bedales and London School of Medicine for Women; Neo-Pagan; long-standing affair with James Strachey.

OPIE, Redvers (1900–84) economist; educated Oxford and Harvard Universities; Fellow of Magdalen College, Oxford, 1931–45; Counsellor and Economic Adviser, British Embassy, Washington, 1939–46; Senior Staff Member, Brookings Institution, 1947–53; Economic Counsellor, American Chamber of Commerce, Mexico City, 1966–78.

ORD, Bernhard Boris (1897–1961), musician; educated Royal College of Music and Corpus Christi College, Cambridge; Fellow of King's College, 1923–61; Organist, 1929–57; Choirmaster, 1936–58; University Lecturer in Music, 1936–58.

ORLANDO, Vittorio Emmanuele (1860–1952), Italian politician; Prime Minister of Italy, 1917–19.

PAGE, William Morton (1883–1950), mathematician; educated King's College, Cambridge; Fellow of King's, 1908; HM Inspector of Schools, 1908–28; Director of Education Services, Air Ministry, 1929–44.

PAISH, Sir George (1867–1957), economist; Assistant Editor, *The Statist*, 1884–1900; Joint Editor, 1900–16; Adviser to the Chancellor of the Exchequer, 1914–16.

PALGRAVE, Robert Harry Inglis (1827–1919), banker and economist; editor *Dictionary of Political Economy* (1894–99); author of *Bank Rate and the Money Market* (1903).

PARTRIDGE, Frances Catherine (née Marshall) (b. 1900), writer; educated Bedales and Newnham College, Cambridge; married Ralph Partridge, 1933.

PASSANT, Ernest James (1890–1959), historian; educated Downing College, Cambridge; Fellow of Sidney Sussex College, Cambridge, 1919–46; University Lecturer in History, 1926–46; Foreign Office, 1939–41; Naval Intelligence, 1941–5; Foreign Office, 1945–6; Director of Research, Librarian and Keeper of the Papers, 1946–55.

PASVOLSKY, Leo (1893–1953), economist; Special Assistant to US Secretary of State, 1936–8, 1939–46; Chief, Division of Special Research, Department of State, 1941–2, Supervisor, Division of Political and Economic Studies, 1943; Executive Director, Committee on Post-War Programmes, 1944.

PEACOCK, Sir Edward Robert (1871–1962), merchant banker; educated Queen's University, Canada; Director, Bank of England, 1921–4, 1929–46; partner, Baring Brothers, 1924–54.

PEARSON, Revd J. B., divine; Lecturer in Moral Sciences, St John's College, Cambridge in the late nineteenth century.

PEARSON, Karl (1857–1936), mathematician and biologist; educated University College School and King's College, Cambridge; Goldsmid Professor of Applied Mathematics and Mechanics, University College, London, 1884–1911; Galton Professor of Eugenics, 1911–33.

PEEL, Sidney Cornwallis (later Sir Sidney) (1870–1938), civil servant; educated Eton and New College, Oxford; Financial Adviser to the Foreign Office, 1918; member, British Delegation, Paris Peace Conference, 1919.

PENROSE, Alec Peckover Doyle (1896–1950), educated Leighton Park School and King's College, Cambridge; Apostle; Fellow of King's, 1925; Supernumerary Fellow, 1928.

PENROSE, Edward F. (1895–1984), economist; International Labour Organisation, 1938–41; Special Assistant to US Ambassador, London, 1941–4; US Delegation, UN, 1946–7.

PERKINS, Frances (d. 1965), US Secretary of Labor, 1933–45.

PETHICK-LAWRENCE, Frederick William (later Lord Pethick-Lawrence) (1871–1961), politician; educated Eton and Trinity College, Cambridge; Fellow of Trinity, 1897–1903; Labour MP, 1922–31, 1935–45; Financial Secretary, Treasury, 1929–31; Secretary of State for India and Burma, 1945–7; joint editor, *Votes for Women*, 1907–14.

PHILLIPS, Sir Frederick (1884–1943), civil servant; educated Emmanuel College, Cambridge; entered Treasury 1908, Under-Secretary, 1932; represented Treasury in USA, 1940–3.

PHILLIPS, William (1878–1968), diplomat; Assistant Secretary of State, 1917–20; US Minister to The Netherlands, 1920–2; to Canada, 1927–9; Under-Secretary of State, 1922–4, 1933–6; Ambassador to Belgium, 1922–4; to Italy, 1936–41.

PICASSO, Pablo (1881–1973), artist.

PIGOU, Arthur Cecil (1877–1959), economist; educated Harrow and King's College, Cambridge; Fellow of King's, 1902–59; Girdlers' Lecturer in Economics, 1904–8; Professor of Political Economy, 1908–43.

PLANT, Arnold (later Sir Arnold) (1898–1978), economist; Professor of Commerce, LSE, 1930–65; Adviser, Production Council, 1940, Production Executive, 1941, Ministry of Production, 1942–5, Cabinet Office, 1945–6; member, Monopolies Commission, 1953–6.

PLAYFAIR, Edward Wilder (later Sir Edward) (b. 1909), educated Eton and King's College, Cambridge; Inland Revenue 1931–4; Treasury, 1934–56; Control Office for Germany and Austria, 1946–7; Permanent Under-Secretary of State for War, 1956–9; Permanent Secretary, Ministry of Defence, 1960–1.

PLESCH, Dr Janos, JMK's physician after 1939.

PLUMER, Herbert Charles Onslow (later Viscount Plumer) (1857–1932), soldier; educated Eton; commanded II Corps in France, 1914–15; Second Army, 1915–18; Commander in Occupied Territory, 1918–19; Field Marshall, 1919.

PLUMPTRE, Arthur Fitzwalter Wynne (1907–77), economist and public servant; educated University of Toronto and King's College, Cambridge; member, Department of Political Economy, University of Toronto, 1931–41; Financial Attaché,

Canadian Embassy, Washington, 1942–45; Wartime Prices and Trade Board, 1942–7; Head, Economic Division, Department of External Affairs, 1949–52; Deputy Permanent Representative of Canada to North Atlantic Council and OEEC, 1952–4; Director, International Economic Relations, Department of Finance, 1954–5; Assistant Deputy Minister, Department of Finance, 1955–65; Principal, Scarborough College, University of Toronto, 1965–1972.

POINCARÉ, Raymond (1860–1934), statesman; Prime Minister of France, 1911–13, 1922–4, 1926–9; President, 1913–20; Minister of Foreign Affairs, 1922–4; Minister of Finance, 1926–8.

PORTER, Frederick (1871–1949), artist; member of London Artists' Association.

PREOBRAZHENSKY, Evgweni Alexeyevich (1886–1937), Marxist theoretician and economist.

PRICE, Langford Lovell Frederick Rice (1862–1950), economist and economic historian; educated Dulwich College and Trinity College, Oxford; first lecturer under Toynbee Trust; Fellow of Oriel College, Oxford, 1888–1928; Reader in Economic History, 1909–21.

PROBY, Grenville (Hamilton) (1883–1947), barrister; educated Eton and Trinity College, Oxford; Clerk of the House of Lords, 1907–44.

PROCTOR, Philip Dennis (later Sir Dennis) (1905–83), educated King's College, Cambridge; Apostle; entered Ministry of Health, 1929; Treasury, 1930, Third Secretary, 1948–50; Deputy Secretary, Ministry of Transport and Civil Aviation, 1953–8; Permanent Secretary, Ministry of Power, 1958–65.

PURVES, Patrick John Chester (1890–1967), international civil servant; educated Fettes and King's College, Cambridge; served with League of Nations and United Nations.

QUICKSWOOD, Lord (Hugh Richard Heathcote Gasgoyne CECIL) (1869–1956), politician; educated Eton and University College, Oxford; Conservative MP, 1895–1937; Provost of Eton, 1936–44.

RAINE, Sir Walter (1874–1938), coal exporter; member, Committee on Finance and Industry, 1929–31.

RALSTON, James Layton (1881–1948), statesman and soldier; Minister of National Defence, Canada, 1926–30, 1940–4; of Finance, 1939–40.

RAMSAY, Allen Beville (1872–1955), educated Eton and King's College, Cambridge; Assistant Master, Eton, 1895–1925; Master of Magdalene College, Cambridge, 1925–47.

RAMSAY, Malcolm Graham (later Sir Malcolm) (1871–1946), civil servant; educated Winchester and New College, Oxford; entered Treasury, 1897; Private Secretary to the Prime Minister, 1902–5; Principal Clerk, 1905–14; Assistant Secretary, 1914–19; Controller of Establishments, 1919–21; Comptroller and Auditor-General, 1921–31.

RAMSEY, Frank Plumpton (1903–30), philosopher; educated Winchester and Trinity College, Cambridge; Apostle; Fellow of King's, 1924; University Lecturer in Mathematics, 1924–30.

RANSOME, Arthur Mitchell (1884–1967), journalist and author; in Russia as a correspondent for various newspapers, including *Manchester Guardian*, 1913–19; remained with *Manchester Guardian* until 1926; published *Swallows and Amazons* (1930).

RASMINSKY, Louis (b. 1908), educated University of Toronto and LSE; Economic Section, League of Nations, 1930–40; joined Bank of Canada 1940; Foreign Exchange Control Board, Canada, 1940–3; Deputy Governor, Bank of Canada, 1955–61, Governor 1961–73.

RATHBONE, Eleanor Florence (1872–1946), social reformer; Independent MP, 1929–46; advocate of family allowances.

RATHENAU, Walther (1867–1922), German Minister of Reconstruction, 1921; Foreign Minister, 1922.

RAVERAT, Gwendolen Mary (née Darwin) (1885–1957), painter and wood engraver; educated Slade School; married Jacques Raverat, 1911; published *Period Piece*, a memoir of her childhood, 1952.

RAVERAT, Jacques Pierre (1885–1925), painter; educated Bedales, the Sorbonne and Emmanuel College, Cambridge; Neo-Pagan; married Gwen Darwin, 1911.

READING, Lord (Rufus Daniel ISAACS) (1860–1935), Liberal MP, 1904–13; Lord Chief Justice, 1913–21; HM Ambassador to the United States, 1918–19; Viceroy of India, 1921–6; Foreign Secretary, 1931.

REDDAWAY, William Brian (b. 1913), economist; educated King's College, Cambridge; Fellow, Clare College, Cambridge, since 1938; Lecturer in Economics, Cambridge, 1939–55; Director, Department of Applied Economics, 1955–69; Reader in Economics, 1957–65; Professor of Political Economy, 1969–80; Statistics Division, Board of Trade, 1940–7.

REDDAWAY, William Fiddian (1872–1949), historian; educated Leys School and King's College, Cambridge; Fellow of King's 1907–49.

REVELSTOKE, Lord (John Baring) (1863–1929), banker; partner, Baring Brothers; Director, Bank of England, 1898–1929.

RICHMOND, Herbert William (1863–1948), mathematician; educated Merchant Taylors' School and King's College, Cambridge; Fellow of King's, 1892–1948.

RIDLEY, Sir Jaspar Nicholas (1887–1951), banker; educated Eton and Balliol College, Oxford; Chairman, Coutts & Co. and National Provincial Bank.

RIEFLER, Winfield William (1897–1959), economist and central banker, joined Federal Reserve Board, 1923; Director of Research and Statistics, 1923–32; Chairman, Central Statistical Board, 1933–5; Professor, Institute for Advanced Study, Princeton, 1935–48; Assistant to the Chairman, Board of Governors of the Federal Reserve System, 1948–59; Secretary, Federal Open Market Committee, 1952–9.

ROBBINS, Lionel Charles (later Lord Robbins) (1898–1984), economist; educated LSE; Lecturer in Economics, LSE, 1925–7; Fellow and Lecturer, New College, Oxford, 1927–9; Professor of Economics, University of London, 1929–61; Economic Section of the War Cabinet Offices and predecessor organisations, 1940–1; Director, 1941–5.

ROBERTS, John (d. 1967); Assistant Manager, the *New Statesman*, 1914–19; Advertising Manager, 1919–20; Business Manager, 1920–47; Managing Director, 1947–67.

ROBERTS, William (1895–1980), artist; educated St Martin's School of Art and Slade School; Omega Workshops, 1913–14; official war artist in both World Wars.

ROBERTSON, Dennis Holme (later Sir Dennis) (1890–1963), economist; educated Eton and Trinity College, Cambridge; Fellow, Trinity College, Cambridge, 1914–38, 1944–63; University Lecturer in Economics, 1924–8; Girdlers' Lecturer, 1928–30; Reader, 1930–8; Cassel Professor of Economics, LSE, 1938–44; Adviser, Treasury, 1939–44; Professor of Political Economy, Cambridge, 1944–57.

ROBERTSON, Norman Alexander (1904–68), Under-Secretary of State for External Affairs, Canada, 1941–6.

ROBERTSON, Sir William Robert (1860–1933), soldier; enlisted 1877; Chief of General Staff, 1914–15; Chief of Imperial General Staff, 1915–18; Commander-in-Chief, Army on the Rhine, 1919–20.

ROBINSON, Edward Austin Gossage (later Sir Austin) (b. 1897), economist; educated Marlborough and Christ's College, Cambridge; Fellow of Corpus Christi College, 1923–6; Fellow of Sidney Sussex College since 1929; Lecturer in Economics, Cambridge, 1929–50; Assistant Editor, *Economic Journal*, 1934; Joint Editor, 1944–70; Economic Section, 1939–42; Ministry of Production, 1942–5; member, British Reparations Commission, Moscow and Berlin, 1945; Economic Adviser to Board of Trade, 1945–6; Professor of Economics, Cambridge, 1950–65.

ROBINSON, Joan (née Maurice) (1903–83), economist; educated St Paul's School and Girton College, Cambridge; married E. A. G. Robinson, 1926; Assistant Lecturer in Economics, Cambridge, 1931–7; Lecturer, 1937–49; Reader, 1949–65; Professor of Economics, 1965–71.

RODD, Francis (later 2nd Baron Rennell of Rodd) (1895–1978), banker and company director; Bank of England, 1929–32; Manager, Bank for International Settlements, 1930–1; served in the Army 1939–44.

RONALD, Nigel Bruce (1894–1973), diplomat; educated Winchester and Magdalen College, Oxford; Assistant Private Secretary to Foreign Secretary, 1929–34; First Secretary, Foreign Office, 1930; Counsellor, 1939; Assistant Under-Secretary, 1942; HM Ambassador to Portugal, 1947–54.

ROOSEVELT, Franklin Delano (1882–1945), President of United States 1932–45.

RÖPKE, Wilhelm (1899–1966), economist and social philosopher; Professor of Economics, Jena, 1924; Graz, 1928; Marburg, 1929; Istanbul, 1933–7; Graduate Institute for International Studies, Geneva, 1937–66.

ROSE, Charles Archibald Walker (1879–1961), businessman; educated King's College, London; served in Consular Service in China, 1898–1911; Advanced Student, King's College, Cambridge, 1911–12; Commercial Attaché, Shanghai, 1915; Peking, 1917; later Director of British American Tobacco Company and Chartered Bank.

ROSENBAUM, Eduard (1887–1979), librarian; Director, Commerzbibliothek, Hamburg Chamber of Commerce, 1919–33; Secretary, Economics Section, German Delegation, Paris Peace Conference, 1919; acquisitions librarian, LSE, 1935–52.

ROSENBERG, Frederick Hans von, German Foreign Minister, 1922–3.

ROSENMAN, Samuel Irving (1896–1973), lawyer; Counsel to Governor Roosevelt, 1928–32; Justice, New York Supreme Court, 1932–42; Special Counsel to President Roosevelt, 1943–5; to President Truman, 1945–6.

ROTHBARTH, Erwin (1913–44), economist; educated LSE; Assistant in Statistical Research, Cambridge, 1938–40; lectured in Cambridge 1940–4.

ROTHSCHILD, Nathaniel Mayer Victor (later 3rd Baron Rothschild) (1910–90), scientist; educated Harrow and Trinity College, Cambridge; Apostle; Fellow of Trinity, 1935–9; Director, BOAC, 1946–58; Chairman, Agricultural Research Council, 1948–58; Assistant Director of Research in Zoology, Cambridge, 1950–70; various directorships in the Royal Dutch Shell Group, 1961–70.

ROUTH, Edward John (1831–1907), mathematician; educated University of London and Peterhouse, Cambridge; Fellow of Peterhouse, 1855; Hon. Fellow, 1883; successful coach of 28 Senior Wranglers.

ROWE-DUTTON, Sir Ernest (1891–1965), entered Inland Revenue, 1914; Treasury, 1919; Financial Adviser, HM Embassy, Berlin, 1928–32, Paris, 1934–9; Third Secretary, Treasury, 1947–9.

ROWNTREE, Arnold Stephenson (1872–1951), Director, Westminster Press and Associated Newspapers; Liberal MP, 1910–18.

ROWNTREE, Benjamin Seebohm (1871–1954); joined family firm, 1889; Chairman, 1925–41; published surveys of poverty in York, 1898 and 1936.

ROYDE-SMITH, Naomi Gwiadys (d. 1964), writer; Literary Editor, *Westminster Gazette*, 1912–22.

RUNCIMAN, Walter (later Viscount Runciman) (1847–1937), shipowner; founded Moor Line, 1889; Liberal MP, 1914–18.

RUSSELL, Alys (née Pearsall Smith) (1867–1961), married Bertrand Russell, 1894; separated, 1911; divorced 1921.

RUSSELL, Bertrand Arthur William (1872–1970), philosopher; educated Trinity College, Cambridge; Apostle; Fellow, Trinity College, 1895–1901, 1944–70; Lecturer, 1910–15; married Alys Pearsall Smith, 1894; Dora Black, 1921; Patricia Spence, 1936; Edith Finch, 1952.

RYLANDS, George Humphrey Wolferstan ('Dadie') (b. 1902), don; educated Eton and King's College, Cambridge; Apostle; Fellow of King's College since 1927; a Bursar, 1939–47.

SALANT, Walter (b. 1911), economist; educated Harvard and Cambridge Universities, 1929–38; Head, Research Division, Office of Price Administration and predecessor agencies, 1940–6; Council of Economic Advisers, 1946–52; Senior Fellow, Brooking Institution, 1954–76.

SALTER, Sir (James) Arthur (later Lord Salter) (1881–1975), public servant; educated Brasenose College, Oxford; Director, Economic and Finance Section, League of Nations, 1922–31; Gladstone Professor of Political Theory and Institutions, Oxford University, 1934–44; MP (Independent) for Oxford University, 1937–53; Head, British Merchant Shipping Mission, Washington, 1941–3; Senior Deputy Director-General, UNRRA, 1944; Chancellor of Duchy of Lancaster, 1945; Minister of State for Economic Affairs, 1951–2; Minister of Materials, 1952–3.

SAMUEL, Sir Herbert (Louis) (later Viscount Samuel) (1870–1963), politician; educated University College, London and Balliol College, Oxford; Liberal MP, 1902–18, 1919–35; Chancellor of the Duchy of Lancaster, 1909–10, 1915–16; Postmaster-General, 1910–14, 1915; President, Local Government Board, 1914–15;

Home Secretary, 1916, 1931–2; High Commissioner for Palestine, 1920–5; Chairman, Royal Commission on the Coal Mining Industry, 1925–6.

SAMUEL, Stuart Montagu (later Sir Stuart) (1856–1926), Liberal MP, 1900–16; member of Samuel Montagu & Co.

SAMUELSON, Paul Anthony (b. 1915), economist; educated Universities of Chicago and Harvard; Massachusetts Institute of Technology since 1940.

SANGER, Charles Percy (1871–1930), barrister; educated Winchester and Trinity College, Cambridge; Apostle.

SCHACHT, Hjalmar Horace Greely (1877–1970), President of Reischsbank, 1926–30, 1935–9; Reichsminister of Economics, 1934–7.

SCHMOLLER, Gustav von (1838–1917), economist; Professor of Economics, Halle, 1864; Strasbourg, 1872; Berlin, 1882–1913; leader of the historical school and the leading economist of Imperial Germany.

SCHUMPETER, Joseph Alois (1883–1950), economist; Professor of Economics, Graz, 1911–21; Bonn, 1925–32; Harvard, 1932–50; State Secretary of Finance in Austria, 1919.

SCHUSTER, Sir Felix Otto (1854–1936), banker; Governor, Union Bank of London, 1895–1918.

SCHWARTZ, George Leopold (b. 1891), financial journalist; Secretary, London and Cambridge Economic Service, 1923; Lecturer in Economics, LSE, 1929–44; Deputy City Editor, the *Sunday Times*, 1944–71; Editor, *Bankers' Magazine*, 1945–54.

SCOTT, Charles Prestwich (1846–1932), journalist; educated Corpus Christi College, Oxford; Editor, *Manchester Guardian* 1872–1929, which he purchased in 1905; Liberal MP, 1895–1905.

SCOTT, Edward Taylor (1883–1932), journalist; educated Rugby, Corpus Christi College, Oxford, and LSE; financial journalist, 1909–11; joined *Manchester Guardian*, 1911; Editor, 1929–32.

SCOTT, Francis Clayton (1881–1979), educated Bedales and Oriel College, Oxford; Chairman, Provincial Insurance Company.

SCOTT, Geoffrey (1884–1929), architectural historian; educated New College, Oxford; friend of Mary Berenson.

SEELEY, Sir John Robert (1834–95), historian; educated City of London School and Christ's College, Cambridge; Professor of Latin, University College, London, 1863–9; Professor of Modern History, Cambridge, 1869–95; Fellow of Gonville and Caius College, 1882–95.

SELTMAN, Charles Theodore (1886–1957), archaeologist and numismatist; educated Queens' College, Cambridge; Fellow of Queens', 1933; University Lecturer in Classics.

SHACKLE, George Lennox Sharman (b. 1903), economist; educated LSE and Oxford; Statistical Branch, Prime Minister's Office, 1940–5; Economic Section, 1945–9; Reader in Economics, University of Leeds, 1950; Brunner Professor of Economic Science, University of Liverpool, 1951–69.

SHACKLE, Robert Jones (1895–1950), Assistant Principal, Board of Trade, 1920; Principal, 1929; Assistant Secretary, 1935; Principal Assistant Secretary, 1942–7; Under-Secretary, 1947.

SHAW, George Bernard (1856–1950), playwright and critic.

SHEPPARD, John Tressider (1881–1968), classicist; educated Dulwich College and King's College, Cambridge; Apostle; Fellow of King's College, 1908–68; Provost, 1933–54.

SHOVE, Gerald Frank (1887–1947), economist; educated Uppingham and King's College, Cambridge; Apostle; Lecturer in Economics, Cambridge 1923–45; Reader, 1945–7; Fellow of King's College, 1926–47.

SIDGWICK, Henry (1838–1900), philosopher; educated Rugby and Trinity College, Cambridge; Apostle; Fellow of Trinity, 1859–69, 1885–1900; Hon. Fellow 1881; Knightbridge Professor of Philosophy, 1883–1900.

SIEPMANN, Harry Arthur (1889–1963), public servant; educated Rugby and New College, Oxford; Treasury, 1912–19; Adviser to Governors, Bank of England, 1926, Executive Director, 1945–54.

SIMON, Ernest Emil Darwin (later Lord Simon) (1879–1960), industrialist and public servant; educated Rugby and Pembroke College, Cambridge; Lord Mayor, Manchester, 1921; Liberal MP, 1923–4, 1929–31.

SIMON, Sir John Allsebrook (later Viscount Simon) (1873–1954), statesman; educated Fettes and Wadham College, Oxford; Fellow of All Souls, 1897; Liberal MP, 1906–18, 1922–40; Secretary of State for Foreign Affairs, 1931–5; Home Secretary 1935–7; Chancellor of the Exchequer, 1937–40; Lord Chancellor, 1940–5.

SINCLAIR, Sir Robert (later Lord Sinclair) (1893–1979), businessman; Chairman, Imperial Tobacco Ltd; Prime Minister's Panel of Industrialists, 1939; Deputy of Minister of Production, Washington, 1942–3; Chief Executive, Ministry of Production, 1943–5.

SINGER, Hans (b. 1910), economist; educated Universities of Bonn and Cambridge; taught at Manchester, 1938–44; Glasgow, 1946–7; Sussex, 1969–75; United Nations, 1947–69.

SITWELL, Francis Osbert (1892–1969), man of letters.

SMITH, Frederick Edwin (later Earl of Birkenhead) (1872–1930); educated Wadham College, Oxford; Fellow, Merton College, Oxford, 1896; Conservative MP, 1906–19; Solicitor-General, 1915; Attorney-General, 1915–19; Lord Chancellor, 1919–22; Secretary of State for India, 1924–9.

SMITH, Sir Hubert Llewellyn (1864–1945), civil servant; educated Corpus Christi College, Oxford; Permanent Secretary, Board of Trade, 1907–19; Chief Economic Adviser to the Government, 1919–27.

SMITH, Logan Pearsall (1865–1936), essayist; educated Harvard and Balliol College, Oxford.

SMITHIES, Arthur (1907–81), economist; Treasury Department, Commonwealth of Australia, 1935–8; Assistant and Associate Professor of Economics, University of Michigan, 1938–43; Economist and Chief of Economic Bureau, US Bureau of the Budget, 1943–8; Director, Fiscal and Trade Policy Division, Economic Cooperation Administration, 1948–9; Professor of Economics, Harvard University, 1948–81.

SMUTS, Jan Christian (1870–1950), statesman; educated Stellenbosch University and Christ's College, Cambridge; Minister of Defence, South Africa, 1910–19; Prime Minister, 1919–24, 1939–48.

SMYTH, Austen Edward Arthur Watt (1877–1949), classicist; educated Winchester and Trinity College, Cambridge; Apostle; Fellow of Trinity, 1902–8; Clerk, House of Commons, 1900; Assistant Librarian, 1905; Librarian, 1908–47.

SNOWDEN, Ethel (née Annakin) (1881–1951), suffragette and temperance activist; married Philip Snowden, 1905.

SNOWDEN, Philip (later Viscount Snowden) (1864–1937), politician; Labour MP, 1906–18, 1922–31; Chancellor of the Exchequer, 1924, 1929–31; Lord Privy Seal, 1931.

SNYDER, Carl (1869–1946), economist and statistician; Federal Reserve Bank of New York, 1920–35.

SORLEY, William Ritchie (1855–1935), philosopher; educated Edinburgh and Cambridge; Professor of Logic and Philosophy, Cardiff, 1888–94; Moral Philosophy, Aberdeen, 1894–1900; Cambridge, 1900–33.

SOUTHWOOD, Viscount (Julius Salter ELIAS) (1873–1946), newspaper proprietor; entered Oldhams Brothers, 1894; Managing Director, 1920; Chairman, 1934; acquired *The People*, 1925; control of *Daily Herald*, 1929.

SPEER, Albert (1905–81), Reich Minister for Armaments and War Production, 1942–4.

SPIETHOFF, Arthur August Kaspar (1873–1957), economist; Professor of Political Economy, Pargue, 1908; Bonn, 1918–39.

SPRAGUE, Oliver Mitchell Wentworth (1873–1953), economist; Assistant Professor, Harvard, 1908–13; Professor of Banking and Finance, 1913–31; Economic and Statistical Adviser to the Bank of England, 1930–3.

SPRING-RICE, Sir Cecil Arthur (1859–1918), diplomat; educated Eton and Balliol College, Oxford; entered Foreign Office, 1882; HM Ambassador to the United States, 1913–18.

SPROTT, Walter John Herbert ('Sebastian') (1897–1971), psychologist; educated Felsted School and Clare College, Cambridge; Apostle; Demonstrator in Psychology, Cambridge, 1922–5; Lecturer in Psychology, Nottingham, 1925–8; Reader, 1928–48; Professor, 1960–4; Professor of Philosophy, 1948–60.

SRAFFA, Piero (1898–1983), economist; educated Turin and LSE; Professor of Political Economy, University of Cagliari, 1925–83; University Lecturer in Economics, Cambridge, 1927–31; Assistant Director of Research in Economics, 1935–63; Reader in Economics, 1963–5; Fellow of Trinity College, Cambridge, 1934–83.

STALIN, Joseph (1879–1953), Leader, USSR and Communist Party, 1924–53.

STAMP, Sir Josiah Charles (later Lord Stamp) (1880–1941), public servant; entered Inland Revenue as clerk 1896; B.Sc., London, 1912; Assistant Secretary, Board of Inland Revenue, 1916–19; Secretary and Director, Nobel Industries, 1919–26; President, London, Midland and Scottish Railway, 1926–41; Director, Bank of England, 1928–41; member, Economic Advisory Council, 1930–9.

STANLEY, Venetia see MONTAGU, Venetia.

STEPANOV, M. S., Deputy People's Commissar of Foreign Trade, USSR, in 1940s; Chairman of Soviet Delegation to Bretton Woods, 1944.

STEPHEN, Adrian Leslie (1883–1948), psychiatrist; educated Westminster and

Trinity College, Cambridge; called to bar, 1907; married Karin Costelloe, 1914; qualified as a doctor, 1926.

STEPHEN, Karin (née Costelloe) (1889–1953), psychologist; educated Bryn Mar and Newnham College, Cambridge; married Adrian Stephen, 1914; qualified as a doctor, 1925.

STEPHEN, Sir Leslie (1832–1904), man of letters; educated Eton, King's College, London and Trinity Hall, Cambridge; Fellow of Trinity Hall, 1854–67; editor *Cornhill Magazine*, 1871–82; first editor, *Dictionary of National Biography*, 1882–91.

STEPHEN, (Julian) Thoby (1880–1906), educated Clifton and Trinity College, Cambridge; called to the bar 1904.

STEPHEN, Vanessa see BELL, Vanessa.

STEPHEN, Virginia see WOOLF, Virginia.

STEWART, Walter W. (1885–1958), economist; Professor of Economics, Amherst College, 1916–22; Director, Division of Research and Statistics, Federal Reserve Board, 1922–5; Vice President, Case, Pomeroy & Co., 1926–7; Chairman, 1930–9; Economic Adviser to the Bank of England, 1928–30, 1931; Professor, Institute for Advanced Study, Princeton, 1933; involved with the Rockefeller Foundation, 1931–50.

STIRLING, John Ashwell (1891–1965), civil servant; educated Rugby; Department of Overseas Trade, 1917–27; Export Credits Guarantee Department, 1927–35; Commercial Relations and Exports Department, Board of Trade, 1935; Assistant Secretary, Board of Trade, 1944.

STONE, John Richard Nicholas (later Sir Richard) (b. 1913), economist; educated Westminster School and Gonville and Caius College, Cambridge; C. E. Heath & Co., Lloyd's Brokers, 1936–9; Ministry of Economic Warfare, 1939–40; Central Economic Information Service, 1940; Central Statistical Office, 1940–5; Director, Department of Applied Economics, Cambridge, 1944–55; P. D. Leake Professor of Finance and Accounting, Cambridge, 1955–80; Fellow, King's College, Cambridge, since 1945.

STRACHEY, Alix (née Sargant Florence) (1892–1973), psychologist; educated Bedales, Slade School and Newnham College, Cambridge; married James Strachey, 1920.

STRACHEY, Dorothy see BUSSY, Dorothy.

STRACHEY, James Beaumont (1887–1967), psychologist; educated St Paul's and Trinity College, Cambridge; Apostle; married Alix Sargant Florence, 1920; qualified as an analyst, 1922; embarked on complete edition of Freud's works, completed in 23 volumes in 1966.

STRACHEY, (Giles) Lytton (1880–1932), biographer and essayist; educated University College, Liverpool and Trinity College, Cambridge; Apostle; embarked on a career of journalism, 1905; first book, *Landmarks of French Literature* (1912); *Eminent Victorians* (1918); resided Mill House, Tidmarsh, 1917; Ham Spray House, Hungerford, 1923.

STRACHEY, Marjorie Colville (1882–1964), teacher and writer; educated Allenswood School, Royal Holloway College and Somerville College, Oxford.

STRACHEY, Philippa ('Pippa') (1872–1968), Secretary, London Society for Women's Suffrage and organiser of the 'Mud March' of February 1907.

STRACHEY, Ray (née Rachel Costelloe) (1887–1940), writer and suffragist; educated Kensington School and Newnham College, Cambridge; married Oliver Strachey, 1911; active in various women's suffrage organisations.

STRAIGHT, Dorothy see ELMHIRST Dorothy.

STRAIGHT, Michael (b. 1916), educated Dartington Hall, LSE and Trinity College, Cambridge; Apostle; Editor of the *New Republic* 1945–56.

STRAIGHT, Willard Dickerman (1880–1918), Imperial Maritime Customs Service, Peking, 1902–4; Reuters, 1904–5; State Department, 1905–9; represented US banking group in China, 1909–11; J. P. Morgan & Co., 1911–15; married Dorothy Whitney, 1911; founded the *New Republic*, 1914.

STRAKOSCH, Sir Henry (1871–1943), financier; Managing Director, Union Corporation, 1902–24; Chairman, 1924–43; member, Financial Committee, League of Nations, 1920–37; Chairman, Economist Newspaper Ltd., 1929–43.

STUART, James (1843–1913), engineer; educated Universities of St Andrews and Cambridge; Fellow of Trinity, 1867–1913; Professor of Mechanism, 1875–89; founder of the system of University Extension in Cambridge; Liberal MP, 1884, 1885–1900, 1906–10.

SUMNER, Viscount (John Andrew HAMILTON) (1859–1934), judge; educated Manchester Grammar School and Balliol College, Oxford; Fellow of Magdalen College, Oxford, 1882–9; Judge, King's Bench Division, 1909–12; Court of Appeal, 1912–13; Lord of Appeal in Ordinary, 1913–30.

SWINTON, Ernest Dunlop (1868–1951), commissioned Royal Engineers, 1888; Assistant Secretary, Committee of Imperial Defence, 1913; Controller of Information, Civil Aviation Department, Air Ministry, 1919–21; Chichele Professor of Military History, Oxford, 1925–39.

SWITHINBANK, Bernard Winthrop (1884–1958), civil servant; educated Eton and Balliol College, Oxford; entered Indian Civil Service (Burma), 1909; Commissioner, 1933–42; Adviser to the Secretary of State for Burma, 1942.

SWOPE, Herbert Bayard (d. 1958), journalist; war correspondent for the New York *World* and the St Louis *Post Dispatch* on the German side, 1914–16; Assistant to B. M. Baruch at War Industries Board, 1917–18; Chief correspondent for *The World* at the Paris Peace Conference, 1919; Executive Editor, *The World*, 1920–9.

TARDIEU, André Pierre Gabriel Amedée (1876–1945), French politician; Member of Chamber of Deputies, 1914–36; Minster of Liberated regions, 1919–20; Prime Minister, 1929–30, 1930, 1932.

TARSHIS, Lorie (b. 1911), economist; educated University of Toronto and Trinity College, Cambridge; taught at Tufts University, 1936–9, 1942–6; Professor of Economics, Stanford University, 1946–71; University of Toronto, 1971–7.

TAUSSIG, Frank William (1859–1940), economist; educated Harvard University and University of Berlin; on Harvard Faculty, 1885–1935.

TAWNEY, Richard Henry (1880–1962), historian; educated Rugby and Balliol College, Oxford; Fellow of Balliol, 1918–21; Lecturer in Economic History, LSE, 1917, 1920–3; Reader, 1923–31; Professor, 1931–49.

TAYLOR, Cecil Francis (1886–1955), schoolmaster; educated Emmanuel College, Cambridge; Apostle; taught at Clifton from 1912.

TAYLOR, J. Frater (1873–1960), 'company doctor'; worked in Canada, largely on behalf of the Bank of Montreal, 1914–25; involved in Armstrong, Whitworth & Co. for Bank of England and Barings, 1925–9; Managing Director, Securities Management Trust, 1929.

TEMPERLEY, Harold William Vazeille (1879–1939), historian; educated Sherborne and King's College, Cambridge; Fellow of Peterhouse, 1905–39; Master, 1938–9; Reader in Modern History, 1919–31; Professor, 1931–9.

TER MEULEN, Jacob (1884–1962), Librarian, Economic Academy, Rotterdam, 1921–3; Peace Palace, The Hague, 1923–52.

THEUNIS, Georges (1873–1966), Head of Belgian Commission for War Supplies, London, 1914–18; Belgian Delegate at Reparations Commission, 1919; Belgian Ambassador-at-large in USA, 1939–44; Governor, Banque Nationale de Belgique, and delegate to Bretton Woods, 1944.

THOMPSON, Logan, JMK's farm manager and later partner in farming Tilton.

THOMPSON-McCAUSLAND, Lucius Perronet (1904–84), educated King's College, Cambridge; *Financial News*, 1929–34; Moody's Economic Service, 1929–39; Bank of England, 1939–65; Adviser to the Governor, 1949–65.

THORNDIKE, Dame Sybil (1882–1976), actress.

TILLETT, Ben (1860–1943), labour leader; founded Dockers' Union, 1887; Secretary until amalgamation with the Transport and General Workers Union, 1922; Labour MP, 1917–24, 1929–31.

TINBERGEN, Jan (b. 1903), economist; Central Bureau of Statistics, The Hague, 1929–36, 1938–45; League of Nations, Geneva, 1936–8; Director, Central Planning Bureau, The Hague, 1945–55; Professor of Development Planning, University of Rotterdam, 1933–73; Leiden, 1973–5.

TOWERS, Graham Ford (1897–1975), banker; Assistant General Manager, Royal Bank of Canada, Montreal, 1933–4; Governor, Bank of Canada, 1934–54.

TOYNBEE, Arnold (1852–83), economic historian; educated Pembroke College and Balliol College, Oxford; Fellow of Balliol, 1878.

TREVELYAN, George Macauley (1876–1962), historian; educated Harrow and Trinity College, Cambridge; Apostle; Fellow of Trinity, 1898; Master, 1940–51; Regius Professor of Modern History, Cambridge, 1927.

TREVELYAN, Robert Calverly (1872–1951), poet; educated Harrow and Trinity College, Cambridge; Apostle.

TROUTON, Rupert (1897–1965), businessman; educated Winchester; Treasury, 1916–19; King's College, Cambridge, 1919–21; stockbroker, 1921–45; Director, Hector Whaling, 1928–61; an occasional business associate of JMK's in the City of London.

TRUMAN, Harry S. (1884–1972), Vice-President of USA, 1945; President, 1945–53.

TUDOR, Antony William Cook (1908–87), choreographer; pupil of Marie Rambert; first ballet, 1931; Ballet Rambert, 1930–8; Sadler's Wells, 1931–6; American Ballet Theatre, 1939–80.

TUGWELL, Rexford Guy (1891–1979), economist and public servant; taught at Columbia University, 1920–37; Professor of Economics, 1931–7; Assistant Secretary, US Department of Agriculture, 1933; Under-Secretary, 1934–6.

TULLOCH, Angus Alexander Gregorie (1867–1932), banker; educated Dover College and Pembroke College, Cambridge; Managing Director and Deputy Chairman, District Bank; member, Committee on Finance and Industry.

TURNER, Saxon Sydney (1880–1962), civil servant; educated Westminster and Trinity College, Cambridge; Apostle; entered civil service 1904; Treasury, 1913.

VALOIS, Ninette de (b. 1898), dancer and choreographer; with Diaghilev, 1923–5; founder of the Royal Ballet.

VANSITTART, Robert Gilbert (later Lord Vansittart) (1881–1957), diplomatist; educated at Eton; entered diplomatic service, 1903; transferred to Foreign Office, 1920; Private Secretary to the Secretary of State, 1920–4; Private Secretary to the Prime Minister, 1928–30; Permanent Under-Secretary of State, Foreign Office, 1930–8; 'kicked upstairs' as Diplomatic Adviser, 1938–41.

VAUGHAN WILLIAMS, Ralph (1872–1958), composer; educated Charterhouse, Trinity College, Cambridge and Royal College of Music.

VENN, John (1834–1923), logician; educated Gonville and Caius College, Cambridge; Fellow of Caius, 1857–1923.

VERRALL, Arthur Woolgar (1851–1912), classical scholar; educated Trinity College, Cambridge; Apostle; Fellow of Trinity, 1874–1912; first King Edward VII Professor of English Literature, 1911–12.

VINER, Jacob (1892–1970), economist; University of Chicago, 1916–17, 1919–46; Princeton, 1946–60; Special Assistant to Secretary of US Treasury 1934–9; Consultant to Department of State, 1943–52.

VINSON, Frederic Moore (1890–1953), Director, US Office of Economic Stabilization, 1943–5; Federal Loan Administrator, 1945; Director, Office of War Mobilization and Reconversion, 1945; Secretary of Treasury, 1945; Chief Justice, 1946.

VISSERING, Gerard, Governor, Netherlands Bank in the 1920s.

WALEY, Arthur David (born Schloss) (1889–1966), translator and poet; educated Rugby and King's College, Cambridge; Assistant Keeper of Prints and Oriental Drawings, British Museum, 1913–29; Honorary Fellow, King's College, Cambridge, 1945; Companion of Honour, 1956.

WALEY, Sir (Sigismund) David ('Sigi') (born Schloss) (1887–1962), civil servant; educated Rugby and Balliol College, Oxford; entered Treasury, 1910; Assistant Secretary, 1924–31; Principal Assistant Secretary, 1931–46; Third Secretary, 1946–7; European Recovery Department, Foreign Office, 1948.

WALLACE, Henry Agard (1888–1965), US Secretary of Agriculture, 1933–40; Vice-President of USA, 1941–5; Secretary of Commerce, 1945–6.

WALKER, Edward Ronald (1907–88), economist and diplomat; Lecturer in Economics, University of Sydney, 1927–31; student in Cambridge, 1931–3; Professor of Economics, University of Tasmania, 1939–46; entered Australian diplomatic service, 1946.

WALRAS, Léon (1834–1910), economist; a journalist in the 1850s and 1860s he applied unsuccessfully to obtain an academic appointment in France; Professor of Economics, Lausanne, 1870–92.

WANSBROUGH, Arthur George (b. 1904), businessman; educated Eton and King's College, Cambridge; Labour candidate, 1935; Director, Bank of England, 1947–9.

WARBURG, Max Moritz (1867–1946), banker; partner, M. M. Warburg & Co., 1893; business partner in Hamburg of Carl Melchior.

WARBURG, James Paul (1896–1969), banker; Monetary Adviser, American Delegation, World Economic Conference, 1933.

WARD, Dudley (1885–1957), public servant; educated St John's College, Cambridge; Assistant Editor, *The Economist*, 1910–12; Treasury, 1914–19; Treasury Representative, Brussels Conference, 1920.

WARD, James (1843–1925), philosopher and psychologist; educated Spring Hill College and Trinity College, Cambridge; Apostle; Fellow of Trinity, 1875–1925; Professor of Mental Philosophy and Logic, 1897–1925.

WATERLOW, Sidney Philip Perigal (1878–1944), diplomat; educated Eton and Trinity College, Cambridge; entered diplomatic service 1900; resigned 1905 but rejoined 1914; acting First Secretary at Paris Peace Conference, 1919.

WEBB, Beatrice (née Potter) (1858–1943), social reformer; met Sidney Webb in the course of her co-operative studies and married him in 1892, thus beginning a partnership of publication and public service; member, Royal Commission on the Poor Laws, 1905–9.

WEBB, Montagu de Pomeroy (1869–1938), businessman and publicist; *Who's Who* recreation 'monetary reform'.

WEBB, Sidney James (later Lord Passfield) (1859–1947), social reformer; educated Birkbeck Institute and City of London College; civil servant, 1878–91; launched LSE, 1895; founded *New Statesman*, 1913; Labour MP, 1922–9; President, Board of Trade, 1924; Secretary for the Dominions and the Colonies, 1929–30; for the Colonies, 1930–1.

WEBSTER, David Lumsden (later Sir David) (1903–71), Administrator, Covent Garden Preliminary Committee, 1944–6; General Administrator, Royal Opera House, Covent Garden, 1946–70.

WEDD, Nathaniel (1864–1940), classicist; educated King's College, Cambridge; Apostle; Fellow of King's, 1888–1940.

WEIR, Andrew (first Baron Inverforth), shipowner; Surveyor-General of Supply, 1917; Minister of Munitions, 1919–21.

WESTCOTT, Brooke Foss (1825–1901), divine; educated Trinity College, Cambridge; Fellow of Trinity, 1849–82; Regius Professor of Divinity, 1870–90; Fellow of King's College, Cambridge, 1882–90; Bishop of Durham, 1890–1901.

WHITE, Harry Dexter (1892–1948), economist; Assistant Director of Research, US Treasury, 1934; Director of Monetary Research, 1942; US Executive Director, International Monetary Fund, 1946–7.

WHITEHEAD, Alfred North (1861–1947), mathematician and philosopher; educated Sherborne and Trinity College, Cambridge; Apostle; Fellow of Trinity,

1884–1947; Professor of Applied Mathematics, Imperial College, 1914–24; of Philosophy, Harvard, 1924–37.

WICKSELL, Johan Gustav Knut (1851–1926), economist; educated Uppsala University and later London, Paris and Berlin; Professor at Lund, 1900–16.

WICKSTEED, Philip Henry (1844–1927), economist and man of letters; educated University College School and University College, London; Unitarian minister, 1867–97; extension lecturer 1897–1918.

WILDE, Oscar Fingal O'Flahertie Wills (1854–1900), poet and playwright; imprisoned for homosexual offence, 1895.

WILLIAMS, Francis (later Lord Williams) (1903–1970), journalist; Editor, *Daily Herald*, 1936–40; Controller of News and Censorship, Ministry of Information, 1941–5; Adviser on Public Relations to Prime Minister, 1945–7.

WILLIAMS, John Henry (1887–1980), economist; Professor of Economics, Harvard University, 1929–33; Dean, Graduate School of Public Administration, 1937–47; Nathanial Ropes Professor of Political Economy, 1933–57; W. L. Clayton Professor of International Economic Affairs, Tufts University, 1957–63; Vice-President, Federal Reserve Bank of New York, 1936–47; economic adviser, 1933–52; economic consultant, 1952–64.

WILLIAMS, Orlando Cyprian ('Orlo') (1883–1967), educated Eton and Balliol College, Oxford; Clerk, House of Commons, 1907–48.

WILLIAMS, William Emrys (later Sir William) (1896–1977), educationalist; educated Manchester University; Secretary, British Institute of Adult Education, 1934–40; Director, Army Bureau of Current Affairs, 1941–5; Director, Bureau of Current Affairs, 1946–51.

WILSON, Sir Horace (1882–1972), civil servant; educated LSE; entered civil service, 1900; Permanent Secretary, Ministry of Labour, 1921–30; Chief Industrial Adviser to HM Government, 1930–9; Permanent Secretary, Treasury, 1939–42.

WILSON, Thomas Woodrow (1856–1924), President of USA, 1912–21.

WINANT, John Gilbert (1889–1947), Governor of New Hampshire, 1925–7, 1931–5; Assistant Director, International Labour Organisation, 1935, 1937; Director, 1938–41; US Ambassador to Great Britain, 1941–6.

WIRTH, Karl Joseph (1879–1956), German politician; Reich Chancellor, 1921–2.

WISEMAN, Sir William George Eden (1885–1962), banker and diplomatist; educated Winchester and Jesus College, Cambridge; Chief Adviser on American Affairs, British Delegation, Paris, 1919; member of Kuhn, Loeb & Co., New York, afterwards.

WITHERS, Hartley (1867–1950), financial editor and author; City Editor of *The Times*, 1905–10; Editor of *The Economist*, 1916–21.

WITHERS, Sir John (1863–1939), lawyer; educated Eton and King's College, Cambridge; founded Withers & Co., 1896; Conservative MP, Cambridge University, 1926–39; Fellow of St Catharine's College, Cambridge, 1920–39.

WITTGENSTEIN, Ludwig Josef Johann (1889–1951), philosopher; educated Linz, Berlin, Manchester and Trinity College, Cambridge; Apostle; Fellow of Trinity, 1930–6; Professor of Philosophy, 1939–47.

WOLFE, Humbert (1886–1940) civil servant; educated Bradford Grammar School and Wadham College, Oxford; entered civil service, 1908; initially concerned with unemployment insurance and labour exchanges; Head, Employment and Training, Ministry of Labour, 1934–8; Assistant Secretary, 1938–40.

WOLFIT, Sir Donald (1902–68), actor manager.

WOLLASTON, Alexander Frederick Richmond (1875–1930), naturalist and explorer; educated King's College, Cambridge; Fellow of King's, 1920–30.

WOOD, Sir Howard Kingsley (1881–1943), politician; Conservative MP, 1918–43; Postmaster-General, 1931–5; Minister of Health, 1935–8; Secretary of State for Air, 1938–40; Lord Privy Seal, 1940; Chancellor of the Exchequer, 1940–3.

WOOLF, Leonard (1880–1969), author; educated St Paul's and Trinity College, Cambridge; Apostle; Ceylon Civil Service, 1904–12; married Virginia Stephen, 1912; founded Hogarth Press, 1917; literary editor, *Nation and Athenaeum*, 1923–30; joint founder and editor, *Political Quarterly*, 1931–59.

WOOLF, Adeline Virginia (née Stephen) (1882–1941), novelist and critic; married Leonard Woolf, 1912; began reviewing for *Times Literary Supplement*, 1905; first novel, *The Voyage Out* (1915); founded Hogarth Press, 1917.

WORTHINGTON-EVANS, Sir Laming (1868–1931), politician; Conservative MP, 1910–29; Secretary of State for War, 1921–2; 1924–9; Postmaster-General, 1923–4.

WRIGHT, Harold, educated Emmanuel College, Cambridge; Editor of the *Nation and Athenaeum*, 1930–1.

YOUNG, Edward Hilton (later Lord Kennett) (1879–1960), politician; educated Marlborough, Eton, University College, London and Trinity College, Cambridge; Assistant Editor, *The Economist*, 1908–10; City Editor, *Morning Post*, 1910–14; Royal Naval Volunteer Reserve, 1914–18; MP (Liberal), Norwich, 1915–29; joined Conservatives 1926; MP (Conservative), Sevenoaks, 1929–35; Minister of Health, 1931–5.

YOUNG, Gerrard Mackworth (1884–1965), civil servant; educated Eton and King's College, Cambridge; entered Indian Civil Service, 1907.

YOUNG, Geoffrey Winthrop (1876–1958), mountaineer; educated Marlborough and Trinity College, Cambridge; Assistant Master, Eton, 1900–5; Inspector of Secondary Schools, 1905–13; Reader in Comparative Education, University of London, 1932–41.

YOUNG, Owen D. (1874–1962), businessman; Vice-President, General Electric, 1913–22; Chairman, 1922–39; Chairman, Radio Corporation of America, 1919–33; Chairman, Expert Committee on Reparations, 1929.

YULE, George Udny (1871–1951), statistician; educated Winchester and University College, London; Newmarch Lecturer in Statistics, University College, 1902–9; University Lecturer in Statistics, Cambridge, 1912–31; Fellow of St John's College, Cambridge, 1922–35.

ZEELAND, Paul van (1893–1973), academic and statesman; Vice-Governor, National Bank of Belgium, 1934–5; Prime Minister, 1935–7; Foreign Minister, 1935–6, 1949–54.

INDEX

Page numbers in heavy type indicate biographical details